Social Problems

A Down-to-Earth Approach

ELEVENTH EDITION

James M. Henslin

Southern Illinois University, Edwardsville

PEARSON

Boston Columbus Indianapolis New York San Francisco Upper Saddle River
Amsterdam Cape Town Dubai London Madrid Milan Munich Paris Montréal Toronto
Delhi Mexico City São Paulo Sydney Hong Kong Seoul Singapore Taipei Tokyo

Editor-in-Chief: Dickson Musslewhite
Publisher: Charlyce Jones-Owen
Editorial Program Manager: Beverly Fong
Editorial Assistant: Maureen Diana
Director of Marketing: Brandy Dawson
Executive Marketing Manager: Maureen Prado Roberts
Marketing Assistant: Karen Tanico
Senior Managing Editor: Ann Marie McCarthy
Senior Project Manager: Cheryl Keenan
Procurement Manager: Mary Fischer
Procurement Specialist: Diane Peirano
Associate Director of Design: Blair Brown
Art Director: Anne Bonanno Nieglos
Cover and Interior Design: Ilze Lemesis
Cover Art: Mihalis A./Fotolia
Director of Media & Assessment: Brian Hyland
Digital Media Editor: Alison Lorber
Senior Media Project Manager: Nikhil Bramhavar
Project Manager, Supplements: Emsal Hasan
Editorial Development: Dusty Friedman
Composition and Full-Service Project Management:
Lindsay Bethoney/PreMedia Global
Printer/Binder: Courier/Kendallville
Cover Printer: Lehigh-Phoenix Color
Text Font: 11/12 Adobe Garamond Pro

Credits and acknowledgments borrowed from other sources and reproduced, with permission, in this textbook appear on appropriate page within text or on pages 541–542.

Library of Congress Cataloging-in-Publication Data

Henslin, James M.
Social problems: a down-to-earth approach / James M. Henslin, Southern Illinois University, Edwardsville. — Eleventh Edition.
pages cm
Includes bibliographical references and index.
ISBN 978-0-205-96512-0
1. Social problems. 2. Deviant behavior. 3. Equality. 4. Social change. 5. Symbolic interactionism. 6. Functionalism (Social sciences) 7. United States—Social conditions—1980- I. Title.
HM585.H45 2013
361.1—dc23
2013019238

10 9 8 7 6 5 4 3 2 1

Combined Volume: ISBN-10: 0-205-96512-1
ISBN-13: 978-0-205-96512-0
Instructor Review Copy: ISBN-10: 0-205-96708-6
ISBN-13: 978-0-205-96708-7
A la Carte ISBN-10: 0-205-91559-0
ISBN-13: 978-0-20591559-0

PEARSON

Part III Problems of Social Inequality

A Global Glimpse

Issues in Social Problems

Technology and Social Problems

Thinking Critically About Social Problems

Spotlight on Social Research

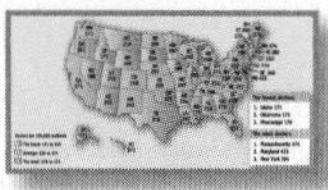

Social Maps illustrate the old Chinese saying, "A picture is worth ten thousand words." They allow you to see at a glance how social characteristics are distributed among the fifty U.S. states or among the nations of the world. The U.S. Social Maps are a concise way of illustrating how our states compare on such factors as divorce, voting, poverty, or women in the work force. The global Social Maps show how the world's nations compare on such characteristics as income, the percentage of the elderly, and the number of large cities.

These Social Maps are unique to this text. I have produced them for you from original data. At a glance, you can see how your state compares with your region and the other states—or you can see how the United States compares with other countries. If you have suggestions for other Social Maps that you would like to see in the next edition, please let me know.

Jim Henslin

henslin@aol.com

The Exciting Potential of Social Problems

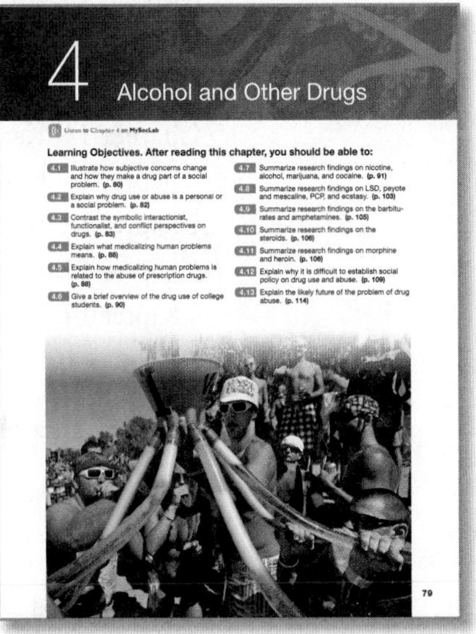

4 Alcohol and Other Drugs

Listen to Chapter 4 on MySocLab

Learning Objectives. After reading this chapter, you should be able to:

4.1 Illustrate how subjective concerns change and how they make a drug part of a social problem. **(p. 80)**

4.2 Explain why drug use or abuse is a personal or a social problem. **(p. 82)**

4.3 Contrast the symbolic interactionist, functionalist, and conflict perspectives on drugs. **(p. 83)**

4.4 Explain what medicalizing human problems means. **(p. 88)**

4.5 Explain how medicalizing human problems is related to the abuse of prescription drugs. **(p. 88)**

4.6 Give a brief overview of the drug use of college students. **(p. 90)**

4.7 Summarize research findings on nicotine, alcohol, marijuana, and cocaine. **(p. 91)**

4.8 Summarize research findings on LSD, peyote and mescaline, PCP, and ecstasy. **(p. 103)**

4.9 Summarize research findings on the barbiturates and amphetamines. **(p. 105)**

4.10 Summarize research findings on the steroids. **(p. 106)**

4.11 Summarize research findings on morphine and heroin. **(p. 106)**

4.12 Explain why it is difficult to establish social policy on drug use and abuse. **(p. 109)**

4.13 Explain the likely future of the problem of drug abuse. **(p. 114)**

79

Social Problems is perhaps the most exciting, enticing course in the sociological curriculum. In this course, you will be focusing on events of life that rivet your students' attention. You will be touching on matters that elicit not only fears, but also the hope for constructing a better society. The scope of the problems reviewed in this text is equally as broad, focusing on such intensely individual topics as abortion and rape, as well as on such global problems as poverty and war. You can expect emotional reactions, probing questions about causation, and discussions on how we can change our current situation. This text is designed to stimulate critical thinking and to guide students in evaluating current social problems and their potential solutions.

The goal of this book is to make the study of social problems down-to-earth, that is, to present the analysis of social problems clearly and to show how social problems relate to the student's own life. Instructors and students alike have responded positively to this approach. Instructors have commented on how the clear presentation of the sociological perspective helps their teaching, and students have written saying that this text stimulates their thinking and learning. A primary reason for this positive response is that I have personalized social problems. This orientation, which enhances learning, continues in this pleasant milestone of the eleventh edition.

You can expect that this text will enliven your classroom, that it will be a source of provocative discussions about the major issues facing our society. The potential is that from the ideas presented in the fascinating topics of this text, your students will learn a perspective from which they can view social life and their place in it.

Let's review some of the major features of this text.

Spotlight on Social Research

This edition expands the popular and unique feature called *Spotlight on Social Research,* in which sociologists share their personal research experiences with students. Writing specifically for *Social Problems: A Down-to-Earth Approach,* these researchers explain how they became interested in a particular social problem and how they collected their data. They take students "into the field" with them, offering an over-the-shoulder look as they recount how they confronted and solved difficulties in doing their real-world study of social problems.

The authors who share their research experiences with us in this feature are

Chapter 2: Phyllis Moen: Discovering that the elderly are "young people who got old"

Chapter 3: Edward Laumann: Studying human sexuality—and the stigma that comes from doing this research

Chapter 4: James Inciardi: Exploring prescription drug abuse in Miami's club culture

Chapter 5: Ruth Horowitz: Getting an insider's perspective on Chicano gangs

Chapter 5: Jim Henslin: Doing research on a serial killer

Spotlight on Social Research

The Miami Club Culture: Prescription Drug Abuse Among Ecstasy Users

Until his death in 2009, **JAMES A. INCIARDI** *was director of the Center for Drug and Alcohol Studies at the University of Delaware. He was also a member of the International Advisory Committee of the White House Office of National Drug Control Policy. His research focused on substance abuse, criminal justice, and public policy. Here is what he wrote for you.*

Miami, Florida, historically a major tourist destination, is also a major player in the U.S. club drug scene. With the restoration of Miami's art deco districts and the popularity of the South Beach area, Miami has become an international destination for partying, sexual tourism, and club drug use. To "get high," about 80 percent of ecstasy users in the Miami club culture appear to be using prescription narcotics (OxyContin, Vicodin, Percocet, and morphine), "downers" (Xanax and Valium), and stimulants (Ritalin and Adderall) (Kurtz et al. 2005).

To investigate this abuse of prescription drugs, we conducted focus groups with scores of young adults from a wide variety of racial–ethnic backgrounds. To achieve a "better high," prescription drugs are also used in *combination* with club drugs. Popular combinations include marijuana, Ritalin, and alcohol; prescription narcotics with methamphetamine and ecstasy; and hydrocodone with cocaine. Some participants described the practice of "colon rolling," also known as "booty bumping"—dissolving prescription and other drugs and then taking the solution rectally with an eye dropper or turkey baster. Some preferred this anal route of administration because it made the drugs' effects slower and more even. Of particular note in this regard was the "Royal Flush"—a dangerous combination of methamphetamine, ecstasy, and Viagra.

The focus group participants reported extremely diverse sources for obtaining the prescription drugs they abused. These included drug dealers, on the street and in nightclubs; HIV-positive patients, who have access to prescription medications through their physicians; parents and other relatives; pharmacy employees; online pharmacies; under-the-door apartment flyers advertising telephone numbers to call; Medicaid and Medicare fraud; doctor shopping; leftover supplies following an illness or injury; visits to Mexico, South America, and the Caribbean; prescriptions intended for treatment of drug dependence or mental illness; theft from pharmacies and hospitals; friends and acquaintances; and "stealing from grandma's medicine cabinet." All participants said they had no difficulty in obtaining prescription medications, although they were often happy to take what was available without seeking a specific drug or brand name.

Most participants described the "high" from prescription drugs as less exciting and less euphoric than that from illicit drugs, but they perceived prescription drugs to be purer, safer, more respectable, and more legal, as well as producing fewer withdrawal symptoms.

Chapter 6: William Chambliss: A personal journey into the study of crime

Chapter 7: Herbert Gans: Doing research on the exploitation of people in poverty

Chapter 8: Nazli Kibria: Studying identity problems of Asian Americans

Chapter 8: Rafael Ezekiel: How a Jew entered the world of Neo-Nazis and Klans

Chapter 9: Kirsten Dellinger: Discovering how the meaning of sexual harassment changes with work settings

Chapter 9: Donna Eder: Sitting in on adolescent conversations

Chapter 10: William Cockerham: Solving the medical mystery of unexpected deaths in Russia

Chapter 11: Kathleen Ferraro: Gaining an unwelcome insider's view of intimate violence

Chapter 11: Cynthia and Robert Reed: Choosing not to have children

Chapter 12: Jack Goldstone: Why population changes make a difference for your life

Chapter 13: Robert Gottlieb: Discovering changing meanings of the environment

Chapter 14: Morten Ender: An "embedded" sociologist in the military

Scope and Coverage of the Eleventh Edition

Social Problems is a pleasure to teach. The fascinating and often controversial matters you will review with your students range from prostitution and pornography to inequalities of social class, race-ethnicity, and gender. Part of the pleasure of teaching this course is to experience with your students the broad range of vision that these social problems encompass. At times, your students will be focusing on the comparative safety or danger of their own neighborhoods, while at other times their eyes will be on the changing relationships of power among the nation-states of the world. All of the problems are significant, whether they are as intensely personal as suicide and victimization or as broad as global stratification and capitalism.

In this text, your students will explore the vital social issues that face our nation and the world, events and conditions that influence their present and their future. Not only will your students gain a sociological understanding of these problems, but they also will be able to explore—and evaluate—their own ideas and opinions about specific social problems. As the course progresses, they will attain greater awareness of the social forces that shape not only their orientations to social problems but also their perspectives on social life. The ideas in this book, then, can penetrate students' thinking, giving shape to a lasting sociological perspective, one they will take out of the classroom and into their everyday lives.

The Sociological Task: The Goal of Objectivity

This process of insight and self-discovery—so essential to sociology and good teaching—is one of the most rewarding aspects of teaching Social Problems. But teaching a class in social problems presents a special challenge, for it requires objectivity in the midst of deep controversy, objectivity while examining emotion-producing topics, some of which may challenge your own values. In this text, I attempt to present both sides of controversial topics objectively. I know, of course, that it is impossible to achieve total objectivity, no matter how ardently we may desire or pursue it, but objectivity should be the hallmark of Social Problems. I have tried to attain it in this text.

When you turn to Chapter 1, you will immediately see this purposeful attempt to bring objectivity to the text. In this opening chapter, I use abortion as a substantive issue to illustrate basic sociological principles. Beginning the text with this topic helps jump-start your course, as it places your students squarely in the midst of one of the most debated and heated issues in the United States. This topic also brings deep-seated attitudes to the surface. Used creatively, this approach allows us to illustrate the social origin of ideas, which is essential to the objective understanding of social problems.

To determine whether I had achieved objectivity on this sensitive issue, I sent the first chapter to national officers of both pro-choice and right to life organizations for review. I was elated when *both sides* responded with practically the same words--that their side was represented accurately, but that the text seemed "too fair" to the other side.

Within this framework of objectivity, the goal of this text is to present the major research findings on social problems, to explain their theoretical interpretations, and to describe clearly the underlying assumptions and implications of competing points of view. In endeavoring to reach this goal, I strive to present the most recent research on the sociology of social problems and to introduce competing views fairly. If I have been successful, your students not only should find themselves content when they read about views with which they are in agreement but also they should attain a clear understanding of views with which they are in disagreement. This should hold true for students of all persuasions, whether "radical," "liberal," "conservative," or anywhere in between. This orientation helps the text to serve as a strong foundation for an exciting class.

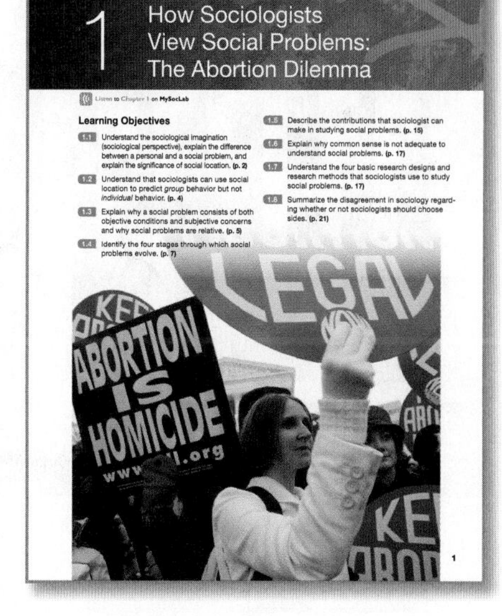

1 How Sociologists View Social Problems: The Abortion Dilemma

Listen to Chapter 1 on MySocLab

Learning Objectives

1.1 Understand the sociological imagination (sociological perspective), explain the difference between a personal and a social problem, and explain the significance of social location. **(p. 2)**

1.2 Understand that sociologists can use social location to predict *group* behavior but not *individual* behavior. **(p. 4)**

1.3 Explain why a social problem consists of both objective conditions and subjective concerns and why social problems are relative. **(p. 5)**

1.4 Identify the four stages through which social problems evolve. **(p. 7)**

1.5 Describe the contributions that sociologist can make in studying social problems. **(p. 15)**

1.6 Explain why common sense is not adequate to understand social problems. **(p. 17)**

1.7 Understand the four basic research designs and research methods that sociologists use to study social problems. **(p. 17)**

1.8 Summarize the disagreement in sociology regarding whether or not sociologists should choose sides. **(p. 21)**

Incorporating Theory into Your Teaching

Students often find the word *theory* to be frightening. Many expect to land squarely in the midst of vague, abstract ideas, where they wander blindly in a foggy marsh. But theories don't have to be like this. Students can find theories clear and easy to understand—even enjoyable—*if* they are presented creatively. I have been pleased with how students and instructors alike have reacted favorably to the ways in which sociological theories are presented in this text. One of the main reasons for this favorable reaction is that I embed the theories in clarifying contexts. For example, when I first introduce the theories in Chapter 2—symbolic interaction theory, functional theory, conflict theory, and feminist theory—I make them concrete. The topical focus of this chapter is aging, so I apply each theory to problems that the elderly confront. This makes the theories much easier to understand.

In the following chapters, I consistently apply most of the theories to *each* social problem. This approach helps give students a cohesive understanding of what otherwise might appear to be a disparate collection of problematic events and issues. The effect is cumulative, for each new chapter allows students to broaden their understanding of these perspectives. As one reviewer said, some texts in social problems mention theory in an initial chapter and then dispense with it thereafter, but this text follows through with the "theoretical promise" of its introductory chapters.

Chapter Organization and Features

To further help your students do well in this course, I use a consistent structure within the chapters. This gives your students a "road map" to guide them through each social problem, letting them know what to expect as they read the chapters. Except for the first two introductory chapters that orient the student to social problems and the sociological perspective, I use the following framework to analyze each social problem:

Opening Vignette This brief opening story, which presents essential elements of the social problem, arouses student interest in the social problem, stimulating the desire to read more about it.

The Problem in Sociological Perspective This broad sociological background sets the stage for understanding the particular social problem.

The Scope of the Problem The basic data on the extent or severity of the problem allow students to grasp the problem's wider ramifications.

Looking at the Problem Theoretically These theoretical analyses of the problem or some major aspect of it generally

11.1

Nancy and Antoine were pleased. Their 4-year-old daughter, Janelle, had been accepted at Rainbow Gardens Preschool in Manhattan Beach, California, a prosperous suburb of Los Angeles. The preschool came highly recommended by their close friends, whose son was attending the school. With Nancy's promotion and Antoine's new job, schedules had become more difficult, and Rainbow Gardens was able to handle their need for flexible hours.

She had begun to have nightmares.

At first, Janelle loved preschool. She would happily leave whichever parent drove her to school for the pleasures of her little friends and the gentle care of loving teachers. Then, gradually, almost imperceptibly, a change came over her. At first, Janelle became reluctant to leave her parents. Then she began to whimper in the mornings when they were getting her ready for school. And lately she had begun to have nightmares. She was waking up crying and screaming several times a week, something she had never done before. They took Janelle to a counselor. She said it was nothing to worry about, that all kids go through things like this from time to time. This was just a "developmental adjustment" and a "separation anxiety." Their daughter would be just fine in a little while.

When allegations of sexual abuse of 3-, 4-, and 5-year-olds at Rainbow Gardens made headlines, parents around the nation were devastated. The unthinkable had become real. "Was it happening at our preschool, too? Could it be happening with our child?" they wondered. But for Nancy and Antoine, it was more than a nagging question. Overnight, Janelle's nightmares, her crying, and her bed-wetting took on new meaning. Those gentle teachers, so affectionate with the children, child molesters? Janelle undressed, photographed, forced to commit sexual acts with adults, and threatened with the death of her puppy if she told?

Nancy and Antoine don't know. It is either this or simply a "developmental adjustment," maybe just a normal "separation anxiety." Now it is Nancy's and Antoine's turn for nightmares.

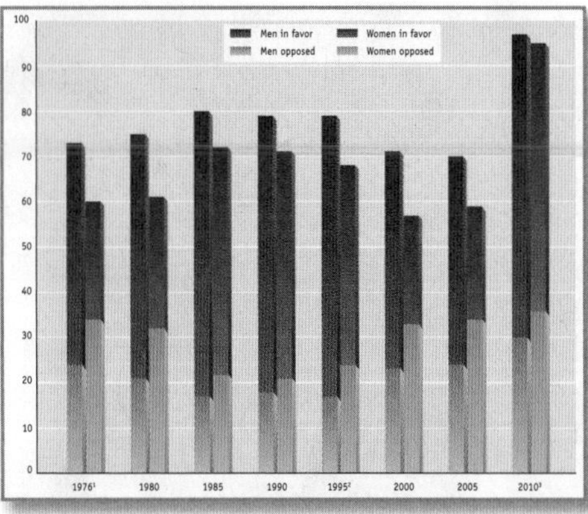

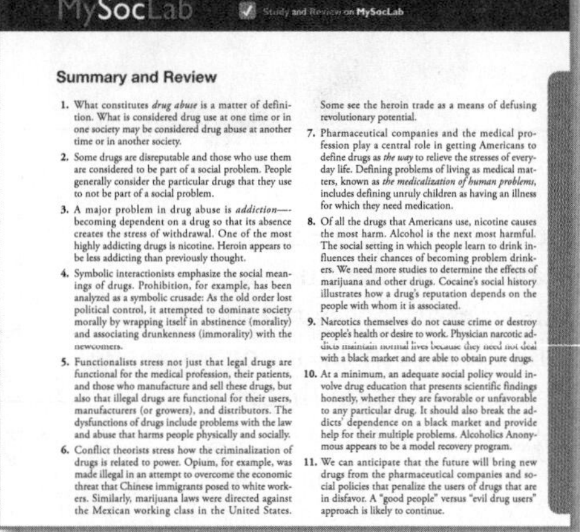

Summary and Review

1. What constitutes *drug abuse* is a matter of definition. What is considered drug use at one time or in one society may be considered drug abuse at another time or in another society.
2. Some drugs are disreputable and those who use them are considered to be part of a social problem. People generally consider the particular drugs that they use to not be part of a social problem.
3. A major problem in drug abuse is *addiction*—becoming dependent on a drug so that its absence creates the stress of withdrawal. One of the most highly addicting drugs is nicotine. Heroin appears to be less addicting than previously thought.
4. Symbolic interactionists emphasize the social meanings of drugs. Prohibition, for example, has been analyzed as a symbolic crusade: As the old order lost political control, it attempted to dominate society morally by wrapping itself in abstinence (morality) and associating drunkenness (immorality) with the newcomers.
5. Functionalists stress not just that legal drugs are functional for the medical profession, their patients, and those who manufacture and sell these drugs, but also that illegal drugs are functional for their users, manufacturers (or growers), and distributors. The dysfunctions of drugs include problems with the law and abuse that harms people physically and socially.
6. Conflict theorists stress how the criminalization of drugs is related to power. Opium, for example, was made illegal in an attempt to overcome the economic threat that Chinese immigrants posed to white workers. Similarly, marijuana laws were directed against the Mexican working class in the United States. Some see the heroin trade as a means of defusing revolutionary potential.
7. Pharmaceutical companies and the medical profession play a central role in getting Americans to define drugs as *the way* to relieve the stresses of everyday life. Defining problems of living as medical matters, known as *the medicalization of human problems*, includes defining unruly children as having an illness for which they need medication.
8. Of all the drugs that Americans use, nicotine causes the most harm. Alcohol is the next most harmful. The social setting in which people learn to drink influences their chances of becoming problem drinkers. We need more studies to determine the effects of marijuana and other drugs. Cocaine's social history illustrates how a drug's reputation depends on the people with whom it is associated.
9. Narcotics themselves do not cause crime or destroy people's health or desire to work. Physician narcotic addicts maintain normal lives because they need not deal with a black market and are able to obtain pure drugs.
10. At a minimum, an adequate social policy would involve drug education that presents scientific findings honestly, whether they are favorable or unfavorable to any particular drug. It should also break the addicts' dependence on a black market and provide help for their multiple problems. Alcoholics Anonymous appears to be a model recovery program.
11. We can anticipate that the future will bring new drugs from the pharmaceutical companies and social policies that penalize the users of drugs that are in disfavor. A "good people" versus "evil drug users" approach is likely to continue.

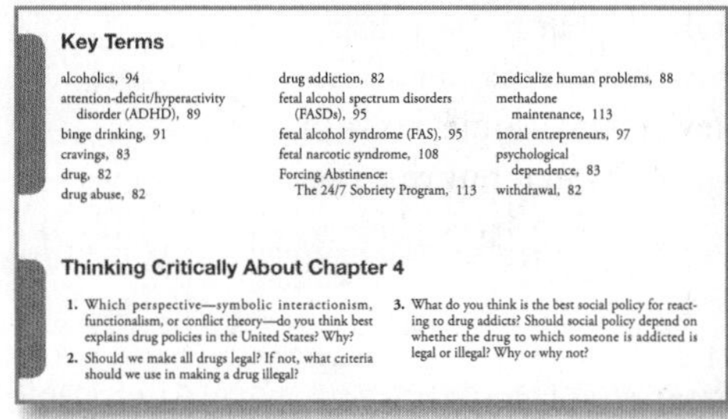

Key Terms

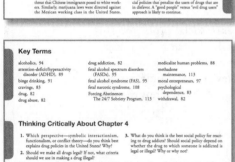

alcoholics, 94
attention-deficit/hyperactivity disorder (ADHD), 89
binge drinking, 91
cravings, 83
drug, 82
drug abuse, 82
drug addiction, 82
fetal alcohol spectrum disorders (FASDs), 95
fetal alcohol syndrome (FAS), 95
fetal narcotic syndrome, 108
Forcing Abstinence: The 24/7 Sobriety Program, 113
medicalize human problems, 88
methadone maintenance, 113
moral entrepreneurs, 97
psychological dependence, 83
withdrawal, 82

Thinking Critically About Chapter 4

1. Which perspective—symbolic interactionism, functionalism, or conflict theory—do you think best explains drug policies in the United States? Why?
2. Should we make all drugs legal? If not, what criteria should we use in making a drug illegal?
3. What do you think is the best social policy for reacting to drug addicts? Should social policy depend on whether the drug to which someone is addicted is legal or illegal? Why or why not?

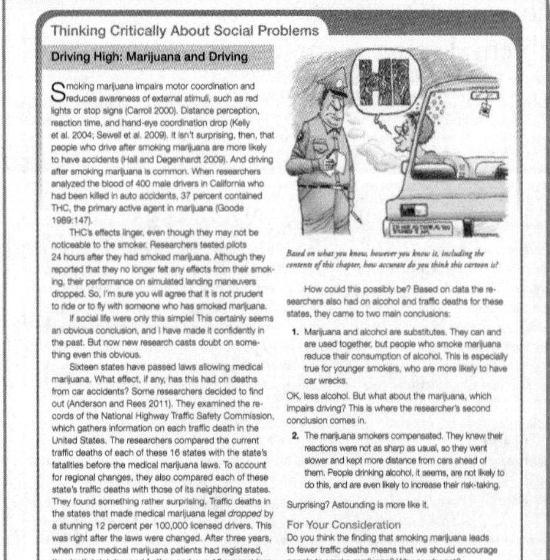

Thinking Critically About Social Problems

Driving High: Marijuana and Driving

Smoking marijuana impairs motor coordination and reduces awareness of external stimuli, such as red lights or stop signs (Carroll 2000). Distance perception, reaction time, and hand-eye coordination drop (Kelly et al. 2004; Sewell et al. 2009). It isn't surprising, then, that people who drive after smoking marijuana are more likely to have accidents (Hall and Degenhardt 2009). And driving after smoking marijuana is common. When researchers analyzed the blood of 400 male drivers in California who had been killed in auto accidents, 37 percent contained THC, the primary active agent in marijuana (Goode 1989:147).

THC's effects linger, even though they may not be noticeable to the smoker. Researchers tested pilots 24 hours after they had smoked marijuana. Although they reported that they no longer felt any effects from their smoking, their performance on simulated landing maneuvers dropped. So, I'm sure you will agree that it is not prudent to ride or to fly with someone who has smoked marijuana.

If social life were only this simple! This certainly seems an obvious conclusion, and I have made it confidently in the past. But now new research casts doubt on something even this obvious.

Sixteen states have passed laws allowing medical marijuana. What effect, if any, has this had on deaths from car accidents? Some researchers decided to find out (Anderson and Rees 2011). They examined the records of the National Highway Traffic Safety Commission, which gathers information on each traffic death in the United States. The researchers compared the current traffic deaths of each of these 16 states with the state's fatalities before the medical marijuana laws. To account for regional changes, they also compared each of these state's traffic deaths with those of its neighboring states. They found something rather surprising. Traffic deaths in the states that made medical marijuana legal *dropped* by a stunning 12 percent per 100,000 licensed drivers. This was right after the laws were changed. After three years, when more medical marijuana patients had registered, the death total dropped further, and was 15 percent less.

Based on what you know, however you know it, including the contents of this chapter, how accurate do you think this cartoon is?

How could this possibly be? Based on data the researchers also had on alcohol and traffic deaths for these states, they came to two main conclusions:

1. Marijuana and alcohol are substitutes. They can and are used together, but people who smoke marijuana reduce their consumption of alcohol. This is especially true for younger smokers, who are more likely to have car wrecks.

OK, less alcohol. But what about the marijuana, which impairs driving? This is where the researcher's second conclusion comes in.

2. The marijuana smokers compensated. They knew their reactions were not as sharp as usual, so they went slower and kept more distance from cars ahead of them. People drinking alcohol, it seems, are not likely to do this, and are even likely to increase their risk-taking.

Surprising? Astounding is more like it.

For Your Consideration
Do you think the finding that smoking marijuana leads to fewer traffic deaths means that we should encourage people to smoke marijuana? Why or why not?

begin on the more personal level, with symbolic interaction theory, moving from there to functional theory and concluding with conflict theory.

Research Findings The current and classic sociological research presented in this section, supplemented by studies from other academic disciplines, introduce students to primary research. In addition, the feature written by researchers themselves, *Spotlight on Research,* helps students understand how a researcher's personal background leads to interest in a social problem and how research on social problems is actually done.

Social Policy This focus on actions that have been taken or could be taken to try to solve the social problem highlights the assumptions on which social policies are based and the dilemmas that social policies create.

The Future of the Problem As we look at the direction a social problem is likely to take, given what we know about the problem's dimensions and trends, students are given a glimpse into what likely lies ahead and its possible effects on their lives.

Summary and Review This succinct point-by-point summary of the main ideas in the chapter reinforces what the students are learning. Your students may find this summary helpful for review purposes, especially for refreshing their memory before a test. Some students also find it useful as a preview of the chapter, reading the summary *before* they read the chapter.

Key Terms When a term first appears in the text, it is set in bold and is defined in context. The key terms are also listed at the end of each chapter.

Thinking Critically About the Chapter At the end of each chapter are several questions designed to help students evaluate what they have read. Many of these questions lend themselves to stimulating class discussions.

New in This Edition

Writing about social problems is challenging because social problems are ever-changing. To get an idea of how current this edition is, note that I have written ten new boxes. These boxed inserts take your students to the cutting edge of social problems, providing a source of provocative ideas and stimulating in-class discussions.

You can assume that I have updated the topics, figures, and tables from the previous edition, so I won't list these numerous updates. Instead, I will list just the *new* tables and the many *new* topics.

Chapter 1 Abortion as a medical condition covered by the Health Reform law • Table 1.3 The Four Stages of Social Problems • Table 1.5 Bias and Objectivity in Research Questions

Chapter 3 Thinking Critically about Social Problems: Just What Is Pornography? And What Makes It a Social Problem? • Table 3.1 Pornography's Effects • Wall Street firm hired prostitutes for a Super Bowl weekend • Sex robots • New research on effects of pornography on men who are hostile to women • Feminist porn

Chapter 4 Thinking Critically about Social Problems: Smoking Marijuana and Driving • Thinking Critically about Social Problems: Watch Out What You Step on in Dubai! • Using Ritalin and Adderall as "good-grade" drugs • Drunk driving among women as an emerging new femininity that incorporates more traditionally masculine behaviors • Colorado and Washington allow the possession of up to 1 ounce of marijuana • The federal Drug Enforcement Administration is closing medical marijuana dispensaries • Portable meth labs: Meth being made in vans and cars (also in motel rooms) • In Mexico's drug war, bodies hung from overpasses or sent to city hall;

reporters and bloggers are being beheaded • The *24/7 Sobriety Program* • Roger Clemens found not guilty of perjury for denying he used steroids

Chapter 5 Thinking Critically about Social Problems: Why So Few Pakistani Women Are Raped—Or Why We have to Be Cautious about Crime Statistics • Participant observation by Victor Rios of youth gangs in Oakland, California, confirms earlier research on how ideas of masculinity encourage violence • Seven of ten rapes are committed by a "friend," relative, or intimate partner • Young men between the ages of 17 and 29, 11 percent of the U.S. population, make up *57 percent* of the killers • U.S. murder rate plunged by half (51 percent) from 1991 to 2010

Chapter 6 R. Allen Stanford sentenced to 110 years in prison for a $7 billion Ponzi scheme • Public defenders so overworked they are refusing cases • In the economic crisis, courts add "user fees" for those arrested, hurting the poor

Chapter 7 Countrywide Financial was fined $335 million for discriminating against Latino and African American borrowers • With welfare reform, one in five low-income single mothers has no earnings and no cash government assistance

Chapter 8 Executive Order allowing young unauthorized immigrants to get work permits and stay in the United States • U.S. Supreme Court upholds the states' right to check the immigration status of people the police stop or arrest • Susana Martinez of New Mexico, the first Latina to become a state governor

Chapter 9 Thinking Critically about Social Problems: Affirmative Action for Men? • Spotlight on Social Research (by Donna Eder): Sitting in On Adolescent Conversations • An incipient social movement to end male circumcision • The math scores of U.S. girls relative to those of boys are not improving • The first Asian American woman, Mazie Hirono, was elected senator from Hawaii • Both males and females who are given a single dose of testosterone seek higher status and show less regard for the feelings of others • Dominance behavior, such as winning a game, produces higher levels of testosterone • Of the movies nominated as best pictures for the Academy Awards, men are about twice as likely as women to have speaking parts • The emergence of prison rape as a social problem

Chapter 10 Issues in Social Problems: Doctors, Please Wash Your Hands! • Technology and Social Problems: "Need a New Body Part? Grab Your Printer" • Generic versions of the antiretroviral drugs have lowered the cost to treat an AIDS patient from $12,000 to $335 a year • Researchers have begun to match specific genes with mental illnesses • Nevada sent discharged mental patients on one-way bus trips to 47 states

Chapter 11 During our economic crisis, more wives went to work, and husbands did more housework and childcare • Most incest occurs between brothers and sisters • The *widowhood effect,* higher death rates among those whose spouse dies

Chapter 12 Spotlight on Social Research (by Jack Goldstone): Where the People Are • Globally, 51 percent of the world's people live in cities • A 5,500-year old city was discovered in Norway buried under sand • About 5 *billion* bushels of corn go into a year's production of ethanol • Sandy Hook shooting deaths of 20 kindergartners • South Dakota has made it legal for teachers to carry guns

Chapter 13 Thinking Critically about Social Problems: From the Toilet to the Tap: Overcoming the Yuck Factor • Technology and Social Problems: The BioStove: The Technological Fix • Kiribati, an island nation facing flooding due to global warming, is making plans to move its population of 106,000 to Fiji, 1,500 miles away • The Fukushima nuclear disaster • Fracking is producing such abundant supplies of natural gas that the United States could become a net exporter of energy • The BioStove that reduces smoke from wood by 94 percent and also produces electricity

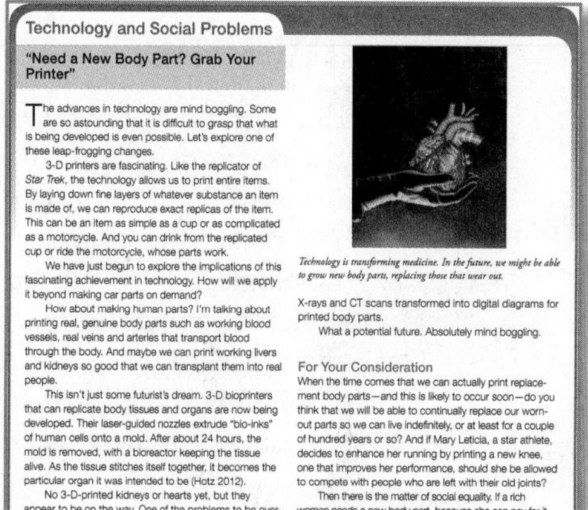

Technology and Social Problems

"Need a New Body Part? Grab Your Printer"

The advances in technology are mind boggling. Some are so astounding that it is difficult to grasp that what is being developed is even possible. Let's explore one of these leap-frogging changes.

3-D printers are fascinating. Like the replicator of *Star Trek*, the technology allows us to print entire items. By laying down fine layers of whatever substance an item is made of, we can reproduce exact replicas of the item. This can be an item as simple as a cup or as complicated as a motorcycle. And you can drink from the replicated cup or ride the motorcycle, whose parts work.

We have just begun to explore the implications of this fascinating achievement in technology. How will we apply it beyond making car parts on demand?

How about making human parts? I'm talking about printing real, genuine body parts such as working blood vessels, real veins and arteries that transport blood through the body. And maybe we can print working livers and kidneys so good that we can transplant them into real people.

This isn't just some futurist's dream. 3-D bioprinters that can replicate body tissues and organs are now being developed. Their laser-guided nozzles extrude "bio-inks" of human cells onto a mold. After about 24 hours, the mold is removed, with a bioreactor keeping the tissue alive. As the tissue stitches itself together, it becomes the particular organ it was intended to be (Hotz 2012).

No 3-D-printed kidneys or hearts yet, but they appear to be on the way. One of the problems to be overcome is developing a capillary system to feed the developing tissue. But if you look carefully at the gleams in the bioengineers' eyes, you will see the reflection of patients' X-rays and CT scans transformed into digital diagrams for printed body parts.

Technology is transforming medicine. In the future, we might be able to grow new body parts, replacing those that wear out.

What a potential future. Absolutely mind boggling.

For Your Consideration

When the time comes that we can actually print replacement body parts—and this is likely to occur soon—do you think that we will be able to continually replace our worn-out parts so we can live indefinitely, or at least for a couple of hundred years or so? And if Mary Leticia, a star athlete, decides to enhance her running by printing a new knee, one that improves her performance, should she be allowed to compete with people who are left with their old joints?

Then there is the matter of social equality. If a rich woman needs a new body part, because she can pay for it should she be given precedence over a poor woman? How about a prisoner convicted of rape and murder? Should he be given the same consideration as your sociology instructor?

Spotlight on Social Research

Where the People Are

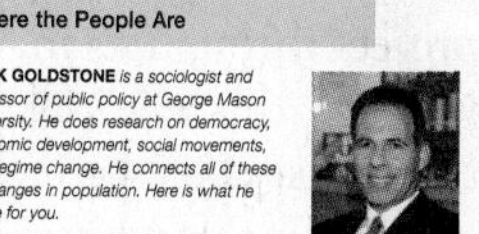

JACK GOLDSTONE *is a sociologist and professor of public policy at George Mason University. He does research on democracy, economic development, social movements, and regime change. He connects all of these to changes in population. Here is what he wrote for you.*

Like most people, I never thought much about population. Countries grow over time, of course, and I always assumed that was a good thing. People had one, two, or three children, they grew up and had children, and so society continued from one generation to the next. I didn't think there was much else to it.

There were worries in the 1960s that global population growth was going too far too fast. Paul Ehrlich and others revived the concerns of Thomas Malthus—a nineteenth-century English parson that you read about in this text—that population growth was going to crowd the planet and use up all our food, land, and water. It was true that population growth reached alarming levels in the late 1900s, as world population surged to five, then six billion people. Yet despite that growth, the global economy grew and food production more than kept up. More and more people in India and China were lifted out of poverty. The rate of population growth slowed down. And the air and water got cleaner in Los Angeles, Tokyo, and New York.

While these events reassured most people, I noticed something odd about this picture. Growth was not slowing down evenly around the world. Instead, the Most Industrialized Nations were experiencing a drastic decline in the number of children, to less than two children per woman, even as life expectancy increased. The result was that these rich countries had more and more older people relative to the number of younger workers. Meanwhile, in many of the Least Industrialized Nations, especially in Africa, the Middle East, and central Asia, population growth was continuing at very high rates. In these countries, women continued to bear large numbers of children, and more and more of them were surviving to have children themselves. Africa, which in 1950 had far fewer people than Europe, was on its way to having as many people as China and India *combined*. More importantly, the world was dividing into two different groups of countries—rich countries that were getting older and had shrinking or stagnant populations, and poorer countries that were very young (some with half their population under 15!) and growing very fast.

What will happen in this unbalanced world? As we saw with the Arab Revolts of 2011, the Least Industrialized Nations that don't satisfy the demands of their surging young populations for jobs are likely to see youth movements and regime change. Then there are the middle-income countries—like Brazil, Turkey, Mexico, and India—that have lowered their population growth rate to a moderate level, but that are still providing solid growth in the labor force of young workers. In these countries, we can expect to see strong economic growth in the years ahead.

In a class by themselves are the Most Industrialized Nations that face shrinking numbers of young workers combined with rising numbers of retirees who need pensions and vast amounts of expensive health care. Major worries of these nations are budget deficits, sluggish economies, and a reduced ability to fund both social and military spending.

This imbalance of population growth is driving a vast global migration. To find jobs, young people and families are moving from poor countries with fast-growing populations to the richer countries with slow-growing populations. In countries like the United States, Canada, and Australia, the recent immigrants are contributing to changes in domestic politics. The minorities are becoming important groups of voters, and they are demanding change.

As you can see, population *does* matter. It is not just some abstract concept. Our current unevenness in global population growth is changing what is happening within countries and between countries. A whole new field of *political demography* is emerging. The focus in this emerging area of study is on how population changes can reshape politics. These days, I find myself explaining these patterns to government officials, who are worried about spending and security; to business executives, who are concerned about where their future workers and markets will be found; and to seniors and youth organizations, who are trying to figure out their place in this fast-changing world. I consider myself fortunate to be able to teach others how national and global processes of population change can help us understand some of the major events that are taking place in our world, and in some instances upsetting the political order.

Chapter 14 Thinking Critically about Social Problems: Cyber War and Cyber Defense • China is claiming sovereignty over disputed islands in the East China Sea • The United States is developing PGS, Prompt Global Strike, allowing it to quickly strike targets anywhere on earth with conventional weapons • Russia has banned Americans from adopting Russian children • The United States is cleaning up Agent Orange from one of its former bases in Vietnam • Boston Marathon bombings

Suggestions for Using This Text

An author of a social problems text, as well as those who teach this course, must decide whether to begin with a more "micro" or "macro" approach to social problems. Each approach has much to commend it. The choice in this text is to introduce the micro level and go from there to the macro level. I begin by focusing on problems of personal concern to students—issues about which they are already curious and have questions they want answered. In my teaching experience, this approach provides a compelling context for helping students become familiar with the sociological perspective and sociological theory. From there, we examine broader social problems, those whose more apparent connections to global events often make them seem more remote to students.

This is nothing more than a preference, and it is equally as logical to begin with problems that involve large-scale social change and then to wrap up the course with a focus on more individualistic problems. Instructors who wish to begin with the more macro problems can simply move Part II of this text to the end of their course. Nothing else will be affected.

Invitation for You to Respond

This text flows from years of teaching Social Problems, with students from diverse backgrounds. The reactions of students to my teaching have been a powerful factor in writing this text. Similarly formative has been the feedback that instructors have graciously shared. I have designed this text to help make your course more successful—so it would both challenge students' thinking and make the sociological perspective clear and readily understandable. What matters, of course, is how this text works in *your* classroom. I would appreciate your feedback—whether positive or negative—as this is one of the ways I continue to be a lifelong student of social problems and develop more effective ways of teaching students. If you would, please let me know about your classroom experience with this text. You can reach me at *henslin@aol.com*

Acknowledgments

A successful textbook depends not only on an author having the right background and skills, but also on a team of people who have the right background and skills—and who wholeheartedly support the project through its many phases. I want to acknowledge the contributions of the people I have worked with on this edition. Thanks go to Charlyce Jones-Owen for coordinating the many related items that must coalesce if a text is to appear; to Dusty Friedman for working so closely with me for such a long time as we struggled with a seemingly infinite number of details; to Jenn Albanese for providing background research and for responding to my ongoing stream of e-mails; to Kristin Ruscetta for copyediting; and to Kate Cebik for again looking for just the "right" photos.

I am also grateful to the many instructors who have offered valuable comments during the development of *Social Problems: A Down-to-Earth Approach*. I would like to acknowledge these reviewers, too.

Reviewers

Sharon Arnold, *Lebanon Valley College*

Gary Burbridge, *Grand Rapids Community College*

Allison Camelot, *Saddleback College*

Carole A. Campbell, *California State University–Long Beach*

Cheryl Childers, *Washburn University*

Susan Claxton, *Floyd College*

Shawna Cleary, *University of Central Oklahoma*

Al Cook, *Trinity Valley Community College*

Sandra Emory, *Pensacola Junior College*

David Fasenfest, *Wayne State University*

Wayne Flake, *Eastern Arizona University*

Michael W. Flota, *Daytona Beach Community College*
David O. Friedrichs, *University of Scranton*
Michele Gigliotti, *Broward Community College*
Rosalind Gottfried, *San Joaquin Delta College*
Charles Hall, *Purdue University*
Daniel Hall, *South Puget Sound Community College*
Carl M. Hand, *Valdosta State University*
Rosa Haritos, *University of North Carolina at Chapel Hill*
Rachel Ivie, *South Plains College*
Sharon Jackson, *Fontbonne University*
Cardell Jacobson, *Brigham Young University*
Joseph F. Jones, *Portland State University*
Victor M. Kogan, *Saint Martin's College*
Rosalind Kopfstein, *Western Connecticut State University*
Wilbrod Madzura, *Normandale Community College*
Paul Magee, *North Lake College*
Marguerite Marin, *Gonzaga University*
Daniel Martorella, *Quinnipiac College*
Stephanie Medley-Rath, Lake Land College
Amanda Miller, *University of Central Oklahoma*
Mark Miller, *East Texas Baptist University*
John Mitrano, *Central Connecticut State University*
Sharon Erickson Nepstad, *University of Colorado–Boulder*
Kevin R. Ousley, *East Carolina University*
Lesli Overstreet, *Bridgewater State College*
Dennis L. Peck, *The University of Alabama*
Carla Pfeffer, *Purdue University*
Bonni Raab, *Dominican College*
Adrian Rapp, *Lonestar College*
Richard P. Rettig, *University of Central Oklahoma*
Barbara L. Richardson, *Eastern Michigan University*
Daniel M. Roddick, *Rio Hondo College*
Edwin Rosenberg, *Appalachian State University*
Annette M. Schwabe, *Florida State University*
James P. Sikora, *Illinois Wesleyan University*
Sheryl Skaggs, *University of Texas, Dallas*
Stephen Soreff, *Boston University*
K. S. Thompson, *Northern Michigan University*
Melodie Toby, *Kean University*
Richard T. Vick, *Idaho State University*
Brian Ward, *University of Maryland*
Linda Whitman, *Johnson County Community College*
Gary Wyatt, *Emporia State University*

Authors of Supplements

I want to also thank those who have written the text's supplements, which help incorporate other components into the teaching experience. Thanks go to Myriam Levy, LA Mission College; Josh Packard, University of Northern Colorado; Joyce D. Meyer, Licensed Clinical Social Worker; Jacqueline D. Smith, Syracuse University; Alecea Standlee, Concord University; and Megan Vertucci, Marion Technical College.

I hope that this text provides understanding and insight into the major problems facing our country, many of which have global ramifications—and all of which have an impact on our own lives.

James M. Henslin, Professor Emeritus
Department of Sociology
Southern Illinois University, Edwardsville

Anita Henslin

The author at work—sometimes getting a little too close to "the action."

I was born in a rented room in a little town on the bitterly cold Canadian border in Minnesota. My mother hadn't completed high school, and my father hadn't even made it beyond the 7th grade. Our home, a converted garage, didn't have indoor plumbing. One of my colder memories goes back to age 10 or 11 when I froze my nose while delivering newspapers in my little northern village. I was elated at age 16 when my parents packed up the car and moved to sunny California, where I graduated from high school and junior college. During the summer following high school graduation, while working as a laborer on construction projects, I took a correspondence course in Greek from the University of California at Berkeley. Indiana was where I graduated from college. I was awarded scholarships at Washington University in St. Louis, Missouri, where I earned my master's and doctorate in sociology. After winning a competitive postdoctoral fellowship from the National Institute of Mental Health, I spent a year studying how people adjust to the suicide of a family member.

My primary interests in sociology are the sociology of everyday life, deviance, and international relations. One of my main goals in sociology is to make sociological concepts and research findings down to earth. Among my books are *Sociology: A Down-to-Earth Approach* (Allyn and Bacon), in its 12th edition; *Essentials of Sociology: A Down-to-Earth Approach* (Allyn and Bacon), in its 10th edition; and *Down to Earth Sociology: Introductory Readings* (Free Press), going into its fifteenth edition. There is also *Mastering Sociology* (Allyn and Bacon), in its first edition. I have published widely in sociology journals, including *Social Problems* and *American Journal of Sociology*. The topics range from the esoteric ethnomethodological locationalities to the everyday nitty-gritty of cabdrivers shooting midnight craps in St. Louis alleys.

While a graduate student, I taught at the University of Missouri at St. Louis. After completing my doctorate, I joined the faculty at Southern Illinois University, Edwardsville, where I am Professor Emeritus of Sociology. With its fascinating variety and its focus on the major issues facing the nation, Social Problems has always been a joy to teach. What a pleasure to introduce students to the sociological context of issues that have such far-reaching effects on both their current lives and their future!

I enjoy reading (obviously), but also fishing, kayaking, and a little weight lifting. My two favorite activities are writing and traveling. I especially enjoy visiting other cultures, even living in them. This brings me face to face with behaviors and ways of thinking that challenge my perspectives, begging me to explore why they and I view the world so differently. These cultural excursions take me beyond the standard research and make sociological principles come alive. They provide a more global context for interpreting social problems, which I am able to share with you in this text.

I am grateful to be able to live in such exciting social, technological, and geopolitical times—and to have access to portable broadband Internet while I pursue my sociological imagination.

Instructor's Manual

For each chapter in the text, the Instructor's Manual provides chapter summaries and outlines, learning objectives, classroom activities, discussion topics, recommended films, Web sites, and additional references. The Instructor's Manual is available to adopters for download at Pearson's Instructor's Resource Center, www.pearsonhighered.com/irc

Test Bank

The Test Bank contains approximately 1,100 questions, including multiple choice, short answer, and essay formats. All questions are labeled and scaled according to Bloom's Taxonomy. The Test Bank is available to adopters to download at Pearson's Instructor's Resource Center, www.pearsonhighered.com/irc

MyTest

The MyTest software allows instructors to create their own personalized exams, to edit any or all of the existing test questions, and to add new questions. Other special features of this program include random generation of test questions, creation of alternative versions of the same test, the ability to scramble question sequence, and test preview before printing. For easy access, this software is available within the instructor's section of MySocLab for *Social Problems: A Down-to-Earth Approach,* Eleventh Edition, or at www.pearsonhighered.com

Powerpoint™ Presentation

The online PowerPoint presentations for *Social Problems: A Down-to-Earth Approach,* Eleventh Edition, offer a robust suite of supplementary lecture materials. Professors have the option of choosing from Lecture and Line Art. Additionally, all of the PowerPoints are uniquely designed to present concepts in a clear and succinct way. They are available to adopters for download at Pearson's Instructor Resource Center, www.pearsonhighered.com/irc

Seeing the Social Context: Readings to Accompany Social Problems

(ISBN: 0-205-56875-0)
edited by James M. Henslin
This brief reader contains fifteen readings, chosen and introduced by Jim Henslin.

MySocLab™

MySocLab is a state-of-the-art interactive and instructive solution for the Social Problems course, designed to be used as a supplement to a traditional lecture course, or to completely administer an online course. MySocLab provides access to a wealth of resources all geared to meet the individual teaching and learning needs of every instructor and every student. Highlights of MySocLab include:

- MySocLab for *Social Problems* provides all the tools you need to engage every student before, during, and after class. An assignment calendar and gradebook allow you to assign specific activities with due dates and to measure your students' progress throughout the semester.

- The **Pearson Etext** lets students access their textbook anytime, anywhere, and anyway they want, including *listening online.* The eText for *Social Problems* features integrated videos, Social Explorer activities, additional readings, and interactive self-quizzes.
- A **Personalized Study Plan** for each student, based on Bloom's Taxonomy, arranges activities from those that require less complex thinking—like remembering and understanding—to more complex critical thinking—like applying and analyzing. This layered approach promotes better critical thinking skills, helping students succeed in the course and beyond.

New Features of MySocLab

Two exciting new features of MySocLab are Social Explorer and MySocLibrary.

- **Social Explorer** activities connect with topics from the text, engaging students with data visualizations, comparisons of change over time, and data localized to their own communities.
- **MySocLibrary** available in the Pearson eText 200 classic and contemporary articles that enable students to explore the discipline more deeply. Multiple choice questions for each reading help students review what they've learned—and allow instructors to monitor their performance.

MySocLab and Social Problems, Eleventh Edition

New to this edition are correlations to the many resources in MySocLab with topics within each chapter. Icons are now included in the margins that connect resources and content, making the integration of MySocLab even more flexible and useful to instructors for making assignments and for engaging students by giving them the opportunity to explore important sociological concepts, and enhance their performance in this course.

1 How Sociologists View Social Problems: The Abortion Dilemma

Listen to Chapter 1 on MySocLab

Learning Objectives. After reading this chapter, you should be able to:

1.1 Understand the sociological imagination (sociological perspective), explain the difference between a personal and a social problem, and explain the significance of social location. **(p. 2)**

1.2 Understand that sociologists can use social location to predict *group* behavior but not *individual* behavior. **(p. 4)**

1.3 Explain why a social problem consists of both objective conditions and subjective concerns and why social problems are relative. **(p. 5)**

1.4 Identify the four stages through which social problems evolve. **(p. 7)**

1.5 Describe the contributions that sociologist can make in studying social problems. **(p. 15)**

1.6 Explain why common sense is not adequate to understand social problems. **(p. 17)**

1.7 Understand the four basic research designs and research methods that sociologists use to study social problems. **(p. 17)**

1.8 Summarize the disagreement in sociology regarding whether or not sociologists should choose sides. **(p. 21)**

Lisa felt desperate. The argument with her grandmother seemed to have gone on forever, and they both were now at their wits' end.

"You don't know what you're doing, Lisa. You're taking the life of an innocent baby!" her grandmother said once again.

"You're wrong! There's only one life involved here—mine!" said Lisa. "I told you. It's my body and my life. I've worked too hard for that manager's job to let a pregnancy ruin everything."

"But you don't understand! It's not a baby!"

"But Lisa, you have a new responsibility—to the baby."

"But you don't understand! It's not a baby!"

"Of course, you're carrying a baby! What do you think it is, a puppy?"

"You're being ridiculous! You're trying to judge my life by your standards. You never wanted a career. All you ever wanted was to raise a family."

"That's not the point," her grandmother pressed. "You're carrying a baby, and now you want to kill it."

"How can you talk like that? This is just a medical procedure—like when you had your appendix taken out."

"I can't believe my own granddaughter is saying that butchering a baby is like taking out an appendix!"

Lisa and her grandmother look at each other, knowing they are worlds apart. They both begin to cry inside.

The Sociological Imagination

1.1 Understand the sociological imagination (sociological perspective), explain the difference between a personal and a social problem, and explain the significance of social location.

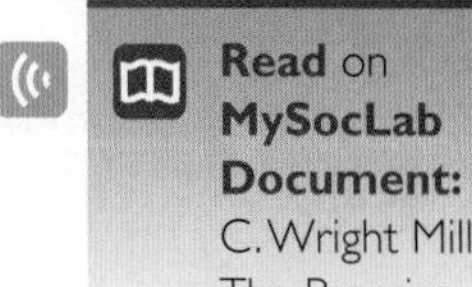

Read on
MySocLab
Document:
C. Wright Mills,
The Promise

Like Lisa and her grandmother, when we are confronted with problems, we usually view them in highly personal—and often emotional—terms. Our perspective is usually limited to our immediate surroundings. With our eyes focused on the things that are close to us, the larger social forces recede from view. Yet it is these broader social patterns that shape the particular problems we experience. In this text, you will learn how to connect your personal life with the larger social context. You will also understand how social problems develop and how we might be able to solve them.

What is the Sociological Imagination?

One of the goals of this text is to help you develop your **sociological imagination**. This term, coined by sociologist C. Wright Mills, refers to looking at people's actions and attitudes in the context of the social forces that shape them. As Mills (1959b) said, to understand our experiences in life, we must understand our historical period and the social forces that are sweeping the time in which we live.

Another way of saying this is that we want to understand how our **personal troubles** (the problems we experience) are connected to the broader conditions of our society. As with Lisa and her grandmother, for example, attitudes toward abortion don't "come out of nowhere." These attitudes are related to conditions in society: in this case, technology (birth control and surgical techniques), gender relations (women's rights), and the law (abortion being legal or illegal). Change these, and ideas about abortion will change. As we apply the sociological imagination in this text, you will discover how forces greater than yourself set the stage for the personal troubles that you experience.

Watch on **MySocLab** **Video:** Applying the Sociological Perspective

Applying the Sociological Imagination to Personal Troubles. To better understand the connection between personal troubles and historical change, let's apply the sociological imagination to Lisa and her grandmother. This means that we want to examine the larger context that shaped their views about abortion. When Lisa's grandmother was growing up, marriage and motherhood were considered a woman's destiny, her purpose in life. Without them, a woman was incomplete. At this time, careers for women were an interlude between completing education and marriage. Abortion was illegal, and almost everyone agreed that abortion was murder. Some women who had abortions were taken to their destination blindfolded in a taxi. They endured unsanitary surgery with a high risk of postoperative infection and death.

Lisa grew up in a different society. To be sure, it was the same society geographically, but not socially. Lisa learned different ideas about herself and her place in life. The women's movement had transformed ideas about women's education, career, marriage, and motherhood. It had also transformed women's ideas about the choices they could make about their bodies, including the right to terminate a pregnancy. Some say that a woman's right in this area is absolute: She can choose to have an abortion at any point in her pregnancy, even if she is 9 months along. If married, she does not even have to let her husband know about it.

In our opening vignette, neither Lisa nor her grandmother saw this finely woven net that had been cast over them, one that now turned their lives upside down, making them confront one another like opponents instead of the close friends they are. Like Lisa and her grandmother, social change also hits us on a personal level: We feel its impact in our own intimate and everyday lives. As with Lisa and her grandmother, the winds of social change affect what we think and feel and what we do—and how we relate to one another.

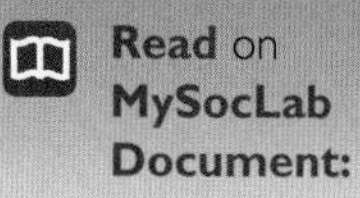

The sociological imagination (also called the **sociological perspective**) helps us to see how larger social forces influence our personal lives. We tend to see events in our lives from a close-up perspective—the immediate things that are impinging on us. In contrast, the sociological imagination invites us to place our focus on the social context, to see how it shapes or influences our ideas, attitudes, behaviors, and even our emotions. The social context occurs on three levels: broad, narrow, and intimate. The *broad* social context includes historical events such as war and peace, economic booms and busts, depression and prosperity. The *narrow* social context includes gender, race–ethnicity, religion, and social class. The *personal* social context refers to the relationships we share with family, friends, or co-workers. These are not just abstract ideas, things irrelevant to your life. Rather, these levels come together to make up the social context that shapes the way you look at life.

The Significance of Social Location. The term **social location** refers to where you are located in society. It includes not only physical places, such as your neighborhood and city, but also personal characteristics, such as your education, sex, race–ethnicity, age, health, and marital status. Our social location is central to our relationships with other people. As sociologist Peter Berger (1963:40) said,

> *To be located in society means to be at the intersection point of specific social forces. Commonly one ignores these forces . . . one also knows that there is not an awful lot that one can do about this.*

Few of us know how significant our social location really is. We all are aware that our social location has an impact on our lives, but our awareness is foggy. We are so caught up in the immediate present—the demands on our attention to get through everyday life—that few of us perceive the impact of our social location. Yet in their many studies, sociologists have documented how our social location influences almost all aspects of our lives. For example, if you are a woman, social location even influences whether or not you will have an abortion.

You might think that I am exaggerating to make a sociological point, but I'm not. Look at Table 1.1 on the next page, and you will see the differences made by age, race–ethnicity, marital status, and length of pregnancy. Look at age: Women in their early 20s are the most likely to have abortions. You can see how much lower the rate of abortion is before the early 20s and how it drops sharply after this age. Now look at the influence of race–ethnicity. As you can see, African American women are the most likely to have abortions. Their rate is more than four times that of white women. Another striking difference—one that cuts across both age and race–ethnicity—is marital status:

TABLE 1.1 ▸ Who Has Abortions?

Abortions	Number of Abortions	Percentage of All Abortions	Abortion Rate per 1,000 Women[1]
Age			
Under 15	6,000	1%	3
15–19	192,000	16%	18
20–24	397,000	33%	38
25–29	298,000	25%	29
30–34	177,000	15%	18
35–39	106,000	9%	10
40 and over	37,000	3%	3
Race–Ethnicity			
African Americans	458,000	37%	48
Whites	411,000	34%	11
Latinas	267,000	24%	24
Others[2]	90,000	7%	18
Marital Status			
Married	188,000	16%	7
Unmarried	1,024,000	84%	31
Length of Gestation			
Less than 9 weeks	747,000	62%	NA[3]
9 to 10 weeks	207,000	17%	NA
11 to 12 weeks	119,000	10%	NA
13 or more weeks	139,000	12%	NA
Number of Prior Abortions			
None	646,000	53%	NA
1	322,000	27%	NA
2 or more	245,000	20%	NA

[1]Based on the number of U.S. women in the category. These data are for 2008, the latest year available.

[2]The source uses this general category to include everyone other than African Americans, Latinas, and whites.

[3]Not Available or Not Applicable.

Source: By the author. Based on *Statistical Abstract of the United States* 2013:Tables 104, 105.

Unmarried women are more than four times as likely as married women to have abortions. You can also see that four of five abortions take place before the 11th week of pregnancy, and close to half of the women who have an abortion have had one before.

Suppose, then, that on your campus some women in their early 20s are pregnant. Can you see how much more likely they are to have an abortion if they are single than if they are married? During the first two months of pregnancy than after this?

Social Location

1.2 Understand that sociologists can use social location to predict *group* behavior but not *individual* behavior.

The Group, Not the Individual. It is important to emphasize that social location does *not* determine our actions. Rather, it means that people in each corner of life are surrounded by particular ideas, beliefs, and expectations. As each of us grows up in a particular location, we are exposed to those specific influences, and they help shape our actions. For example, you are of a certain race–ethnicity and age. You are also either married or single. But this does not mean that you will do some particular thing, such as, if you are a woman, having or not having an abortion. Social location makes a profound difference in our attitudes and behaviors, but in any individual case, it is impossible to know in advance the consequences of those influences. We can't say that any particular woman will have an abortion. But—and this is important—as Table 1.1 makes apparent, sociologists can make predictions about *groups*, because groups do follow well-traveled social avenues.

In Sum ▸ Sociologists stress the need to use the sociological imagination to understand how personal troubles are related to changes in society. The sociological perspective helps make us aware of how the social context—from our historical era to our smaller social locations—influences our ideas, behaviors, and personal troubles.

The social context also shapes our views of what is or is not a social problem and of what should be done about it. Let's look more closely at how this shaping takes place.

What Is a Social Problem?

1.3 Explain why a social problem consists of both objective conditions and subjective concerns and why social problems are relative.

Because **social problems**—aspects of society that a large number of people are concerned about and would like changed—are the focus of this text, it is important to understand clearly what social problems are. We might think that social problems are natural things, much like hurricanes or earthquakes. But they are not. Social problems are *socially constructed.* This simply means that people decide if some condition of society is or is not a social problem. This will become clearer as we examine this process.

The Characteristics of Social Problems

Explore on **MySocLab** **Activity:** Why Do Sociologists Study Social Problems?

Social Problems: Objective Conditions and Subjective Concerns. Social problems have two essential components. The first is an **objective condition**, a condition of society that can be measured or experienced. With abortion, this objective condition includes whether abortions are legal, who obtains them, and under what circumstances. The second essential component is **subjective concern**, the concern that a significant number of people (or a number of significant people) have about the objective condition. For abortion, subjective concern goes in two directions: Some people are concerned that some women give birth to unwanted children, while others are concerned that some women terminate their pregnancies. To see how subjective concerns about abortion differ in another part of the world, see the Global Glimpse box on the next page.

Social Problems Are Dynamic. To say that social problems are dynamic is to say that as society changes, so do social problems. Until 1973, abortion was illegal, and any doctor who performed an abortion could be arrested and put in prison. In that year, the U.S. Supreme Court transformed the social problem of abortion when it made a landmark ruling in a case known as *Roe v. Wade.*

Consider how the Court's ruling affected the two essential elements of this social problem—its objective conditions and subjective concerns. Before 1973, its *objective conditions* were based on abortion being illegal, especially the dangerous conditions in which most abortions took place. And the *subjective concerns?* People were upset about two main things—that women who wanted abortions could not get them and that women faced dangers from botched, underground abortions.

As growing numbers of people became concerned that women could not have legal abortions, they worked to change the law. Their success transformed the problem: After *Roe v. Wade,* large numbers of people became upset that abortion had become legal. Convinced that abortion is murder, these people began their own campaigns to change the law. For their part, those who favor legal abortion oppose each step these people take. We'll look more closely at this process in a moment, but at this point I simply want you to see how social problems are dynamic, *how they take shape as groups react to one another.*

A Global Glimpse

Only Females Eligible: Sex-Selection Abortion in India—and the United States

"May you be the mother of a hundred sons" is the toast made to brides in India, where the birth of a son brings shouts of rejoicing, but the birth of a daughter brings tears of sadness.

Why? A son continues the family name, keeps wealth and property within the family, takes care of aged parents (the elderly have no social security), and performs the parents' funeral rites. Hinduism even teaches that a man without a son cannot achieve salvation.

A daughter, in contrast, is a liability. Men want to marry only virgins, and the parents of a daughter bear the burden of having to be on guard constantly to protect her virginity. For their daughter to marry, the parents must also pay a dowry to her husband. A common saying in India reflects the female's low status: "To bring up a daughter is like watering a neighbor's plant."

This cultural context sets the stage for female infanticide, the killing of newborn girl babies, a practice that has been common in India for thousands of years. Using diagnostic techniques (amniocentesis and ultrasound) to reveal the sex of the fetus, many Indians have now replaced female infanticide with sex-selective abortion. If prenatal tests reveal that the fetus is female, they abort it. Some clinics even put up billboards that proclaim "Invest Rs. 500 now, save Rs. 50,000 later." This means that by paying Rs. 500 (500 Indian rupees) to abort a female, a family can save a future dowry of 50,000 rupees.

Not all women who are pregnant with a female fetus go along with this idea. Some resist, even though their husbands and other relatives urge them to have an abortion. With profits in mind, medical personnel also try to sell reluctant women on the abortion. One clinic has hit on an ingenious technique: Nurses reach under the counter where they keep the preserved fetuses of twin girls. When a woman sees these bottled fetuses, the horror of double vigilance and two dowries is often sufficient to convince her to have an abortion.

National newspapers headlined the events in one clinic: A *male* fetus had been unintentionally aborted. This news sparked protests, and the Indian legislature passed

A social movement whose goals are to stop female feticide (aborting fetuses because they are female) and to improve the status of women is in its initial stages in India.

a law forbidding doctors to tell would-be parents the sex of their fetuses. Physicians who violate the law can be sent to prison and banned from their profession.

Seldom enforced, however, this law is ignored. An eminent physician has even stated publicly: "The need for a male child is an economic need in our society, and our feminists who are raising such hue and cry about female feticide should realize that it is better to get rid of an unwanted child than to make it suffer all its life."

Here is one way to measure the assault on females in India: Sex-selection abortion and female infanticide are so common that India has 10 to 15 million fewer girls and women than it would have if these practices didn't exist.

In an interesting twist, sex-selection abortion is coming to the United States. As U.S. demographers have pored over their data, they have found that Indian immigrants have fewer female children than they would by chance.

Based on Kusum 1993; Holman 1994; Roberts 2009; Wheeler 2009; Jha 2011.

For Your Consideration

Granted the cultural situation that Indians face, do you think that Indians in poverty should practice sex-selection abortion? Why or why not? Do you think that the U.S. Congress should pass a law against sex-selection abortion for Americans?

Social Problems Are Relative. *What some view as a social problem, others see as a solution.* As you can see from how people line up on either side of the abortion issue, what people consider to be a social problem depends on their values. A **value** may be defined as a belief about whether something is good or bad. People's values contrast so sharply that some view the *Roe v. Wade* decision of 1973 as a victory, while others see it as a disaster. It is the same with other social problems. Mugging, for example, is not a social problem for muggers. Nor do Boeing and other corporations that profit from arming the world consider the billions of dollars spent on weapons to be a social problem. In the same way, nuclear power is not a social problem for the corporations that use it to generate electricity. The Issues in Social Problems box on the next page explores this further.

Let's apply this principle to the subjective concerns about abortion. Look at Table 1.2 below. You can see that whether people view abortion as favorable or unfavorable colors the way they view everything connected with abortion. Subjective concerns about social problems, then, can sort people into such contrasting worlds that, like Lisa and her grandmother, it becomes difficult for people to communicate with one another.

View on MySocLab **Figure:** The Debate over Values in Sociological Research

TABLE 1.2 ▸ How People's Definitions of Abortion Affect Their Views

	The Views (Definitions) of		
	People Who Favor Abortion	**People Who Oppose Abortion**	**People Who Do Abortions**
What Is Abortion?	A woman's right	Murder	Part of my work
What Is Aborted?	A fetus	A baby	A fetus
Who Is the Woman?	An individual exercising her rights	A mother	A client
What Is the Act of Abortion?	A service to women	Killing a baby	A medical procedure
Who Is the One Who Does the Abortion?	A skilled technician	A killer	A professional

Source: By the author. Modified from *Roe* 1989.

Competing Views. As you know, our pluralistic society is filled with competing, contrasting, and conflicting groups. This variety certainly makes life interesting, as it means that we are exposed to competing, contrasting, and conflicting views of life. But in such a dynamic world with groups fiercely promoting their particular ideas, whose definition of a social problem wins? The answer centers on **power**, the ability to get your way despite resistance. After abortion became legal, most observers assumed that because the opponents of abortion had lost, they would quietly fade away. As you know, this assumption was naive. Feelings were so strong that groups that had been hostile to one another for centuries, such as Roman Catholics and Baptists, began to work together to try to stop abortion. Shocked at what they considered the killing of babies, they took to the streets and to the courts, fighting battle after battle over this issue.

These, then, are central characteristics of social problems: objective conditions, subjective concerns, dynamism, relativity, and competing views. Let's see how these fascinating characteristics of social problems apply to the development of abortion as a social problem.

The Natural History of Social Problems: Four Stages

1.4 Identify the four stages through which social problems evolve.

Social problems go through four stages, called *the natural history of social problems.* To illustrate this process, we will look at abortion in the United States. To do so, we need to stress again that abortion used to be illegal in all fifty states. Abortion was

Issues in Social Problems

A Problem for Some Is a Solution for Others: The Relativity of Social Problems

Here is a basic sociological principle: As we interact with others—from our family and friends to people at school and work—their perspectives tend to become part of how we view life. Among these perspectives are ways to view social problems.

Our views are not written in stone. Many of us think that the subjective concerns we have about some social problem are the only right and reasonable way of viewing some objective condition. But from where did our views originate except from our experiences with particular groups and our exposure to certain ideas? Just as our social locations are the source of our subjective concerns, so our views can change if our journey in life takes us in a different direction. If it does, we travel to other social locations. There, as we experience new groups, we encounter different ideas and information. You might have already felt this tugging and pulling in your college experience, as you associate with new groups of people and are exposed to competing ideas and values. In short, our views, or subjective concerns, are related to our experiences.

This relativity of subjective concerns is central to the social problem of abortion. How do you define the status of the unborn? Is the fetus a human being, as some believe, or only a potential human, as others believe?

Let's look at the two main opposing views.

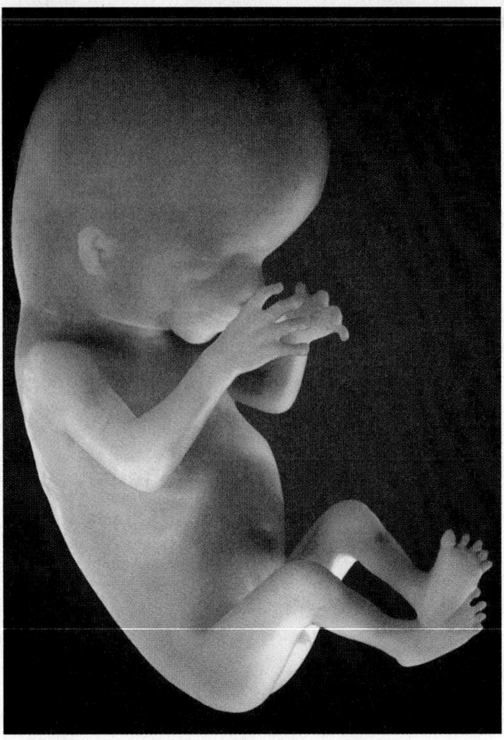

How people define the unborn is the essence of their position on abortion. That which is pictured here is about eleven weeks' gestation. To describe it, those on one side of the abortion controversy use terms such as fetus and "product of conception," while those on the other side call it a baby.

The Fetus Is *Not* a Human Being

This is the position of most people who believe that abortion is a woman's right. "The fetus is a potential person that looks increasingly human as it develops" (NARAL Pro-Choice America). It follows, then, that abortion is not killing, but, rather, a medical procedure that removes a potential person, with the emphasis on *potential*. Women should have the right to have abortion for *any* reason. The reason might include health problems or financial pressures, but it might also be to attain goals, to limit family size, to finish school, or simply to win a promotion at work. The reason should be solely up to the woman. The state has no business limiting women's rights and should permit abortion on demand.

WHAT DO YOU THINK?

The Fetus *Is* a Human Being

This is the position of most people who oppose abortion. It follows, then, that abortion is murder, the killing of unborn babies, the most defenseless of all humans. How can anyone justify murdering a baby? We need to protect and nourish babies, not kill them. To say that women have a right to abortion is the equivalent of saying that women have the right to murder their children. It is not just the woman's body that is involved in a pregnancy: There are two bodies, and the other one is a baby. The exception to this concept of abortion occurs when another human life, the mother's, lies in the balance. The state has no business legalizing murder, and abortion should be illegal.

WHAT DO YOU THINK?

allowed only under special circumstances, such as when pregnancy endangered the mother's life.

To see how this changed, we need to go back to the outbreak of German measles that hit Hawaii in 1964 and 1965. During this time, many obstetricians aborted fetuses to prevent them from being born with deformities. This was a turning point for

Hawaiian physicians, who began to change their views on abortion. The rate of abortion in Hawaii never fell back to its pre-1964 level, and in 1970, Hawaii changed its law, making abortion a private, noncriminal act.

Now that we've set this brief background, we can trace the natural history of abortion as a social problem in the United States. As we do so, we'll pick up events in Hawaii, and go from there. This will let you see the four social stages of social problems. For a summary, look at Table 1.3.

TABLE 1.3 ▸ The Four Stages of Social Problems

1. The Beginning: Pressures for Change Defining the problem Emergence of leaders Initial organization
2. The Official Response Reactions to the growing pressure Reprisal, condemnation, accommodation, cooptation
3. Reacting to the Official Response Taking sides Acts of approval and disapproval Further divisions of dissident elements
4. Alternative Strategies Continuing controversy New strategies to overcome the opposition

Note: Our society is marked by continuous unrest and agitation about numerous matters. Very few of these issues turn into social problems. Most remain diffuse matters of discontent.

Around some social problems, a social movement develops. The trigger that sometimes launches a social movement is a dramatic event that captures the imagination, desires, or discontent of large numbers of people, often accompanied by organizing of some sort that transforms those emotions into an organized force for change. The variety is fascinating. It can be sudden and violent, acts of rage built on decades of discontent that soon dissipate, as with the Arab Spring of 2012. Or it can be slow and deliberate, simmering for decades, as with abortion in the United States.

Source: By the author.

The First Stage: Defining the Problem, the Emergence of Leaders, and Beginning to Organize

Defining the Problem. As you have just seen, for a social problem to come into being, people have to become upset about some objective condition in society. This concern involves a shift in outlook, a questioning of something that people had taken for granted. This change in perspective often comes about when values change, making an old, established pattern no longer look the same. This is what happened with abortion. The 1960s were a period of turmoil that brought wrenching social change to the United States. Young people—primarily teenagers and those in their 20s—began to challenge long-established values. The women's movement was especially significant, encouraging women to speak out and demand equality. Within this agitational and supportive context, many women decided that they should not have to break the law to terminate a pregnancy, that they had the right to safe, legal abortions.

The Emergence of Leaders. As people discussed their concerns about abortion being illegal, leaders emerged who helped to crystallize the issues. In Hawaii, Vincent Yano, a Roman Catholic state senator and the father of 10, took the public stage. He argued that if abortion were a sin, it would be better to have no abortion law than to have one that allowed it under certain circumstances (Steinhoff and Diamond 1977).

This reasoning allowed Yano to maintain his religious opposition to abortion while favoring the repeal of Hawaii's law against abortion.

Organizing around the Issue. Another leader emerged, Joan Hayes, a former Washington lobbyist. She went even further, arguing that the major issue was the right of pregnant women to choose whether or not to have a baby. Hayes used the media effectively. Concentrating on influential people, she organized leaders in medicine, business, labor, politics, religion, education, and the media. Focusing on women's choice, she aroused public support for her position.

The Second Stage: Crafting an Official Response

It is important to stress that the stages of a social problem don't have neat boundaries. The edges are blurry, and the stages overlap. In the years before Hawaii changed its law, legislators had introduced several bills to soften the state's abortion law. These bills were not passed, but since their purpose was to broaden the circumstances under which abortion would be permitted, they were attempts to redefine abortion. You can see that the first stage of defining the social problem and the second stage of developing an official response to it were intertwined.

The turning point in Hawaii came when Senator Yano announced that he would support the repeal of the abortion law. This stimulated other official responses from organizations such as the Chamber of Commerce and the Roman Catholic Church. Public forums and legislative hearings were then held, which generated huge amounts of publicity. This publicity served as a vital bridge between the passive public at large and the leaders who were advocating repeal of Hawaii's abortion law. As Hawaiians became keenly aware of the abortion issue, polls showed that most favored repealing the law. In 1970, Hawaii did just that.

The Third Stage: Reacting to the Official Response

An official response to a social problem certainly does not mean the end of a social problem. Some will even see the official response as part of the problem, fueling the continuation of their struggle. This is just what happened with abortion in 1973. In that year, the U.S. Supreme Court concurred with the Hawaiian legislation and struck down all state laws that prohibited abortion. Incensed by what they saw as legalized murder, antiabortion groups held protests, trying to swing public opinion to their side.

Besides inspiring new opposition, an official response can also stimulate efforts at bringing about even more change. In this case, those who had fought to strike down the abortion laws were also dissatisfied: Their Supreme Court victory fell short of what they wanted. It was still difficult for women to obtain abortions as most U.S. counties did not have facilities to perform them. To solve this, proabortion groups began to promote the development of abortion clinics around the country.

Figure 1.1 on the next page shows the success of these efforts. In 1973, the first year of legal abortion, 745,000 abortions were performed. This number climbed quickly to one million, then to a million and a half, where it reached a plateau. In 1995, the total began to drop, and it now is 1.2 million a year, the lowest number it has been in decades. Figure 1.2 on the next page presents another overview of abortion. From this figure, you can see that the number of abortions per live births climbed sharply after abortion was legalized. After plateauing for about 10 years, it then began to drop. Today, for every 100 live births there are 28 or 29 abortions. This is the lowest ratio since 1975.

A Note on Terms. Before we look at the fourth stage of social problems, we need to pause and consider terminology. Terms are always significant, especially so when we deal with sensitive matters. You probably noticed that I just used the term *proabortion* to refer to those who favor the legal right to abortion and *antiabortion* to refer to those who oppose this legal right. (The longer terms would be *pro-legal-abortion* and *anti-legal-abortion.*) I am trying to avoid the terms *pro-choice* and *pro-life,* which are used by advocates on each side of this social problem. Pro-choice and pro-life represent

FIGURE 1.1 ▸ Number of Abortions and Live Births

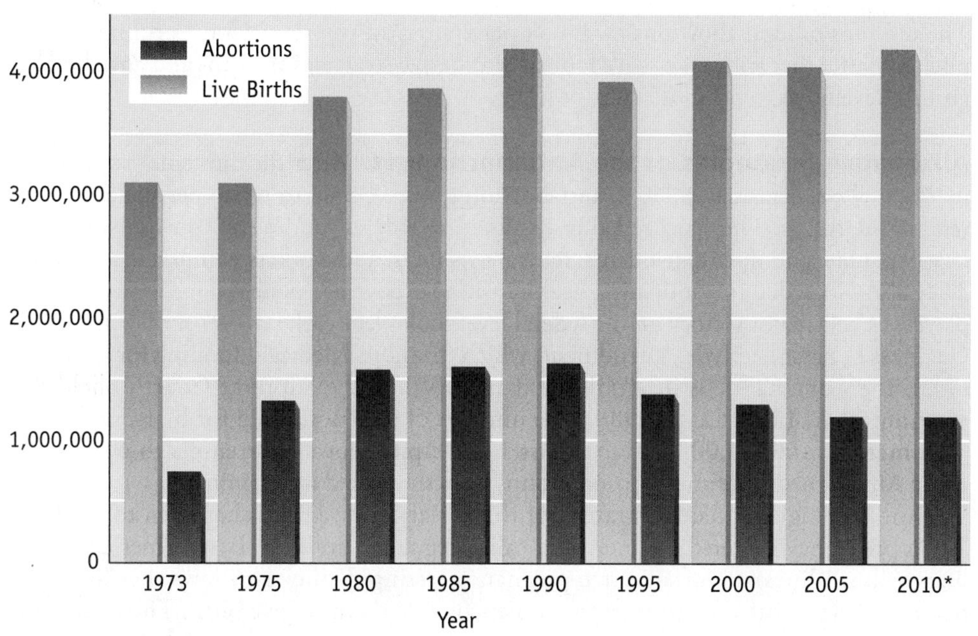

*Author's estimate

Source: By the author. Based on *Statistical Abstract of the United States* 2003:Tables 83, 95, 104; 2013:Tables 96, 104.

FIGURE 1.2 ▸ Number of Abortions per 100 Live Births

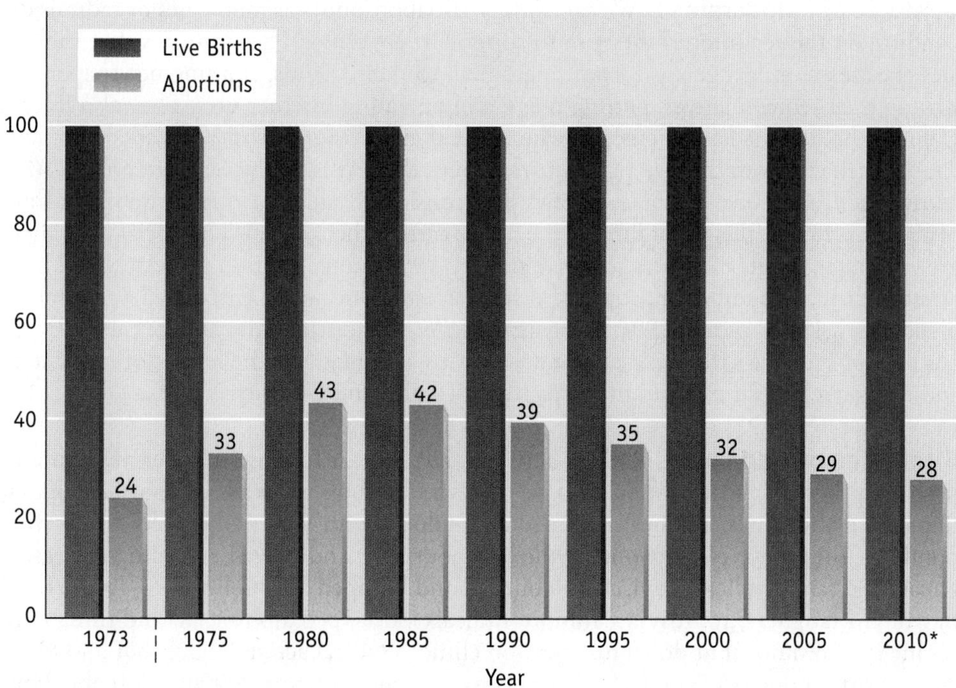

*Author's estimate

Source: By the author. Based on *Statistical Abstract of the United States* 1988:Tables 81, 103; 2013:Tables 96, 104.

one-sided, hardened attitudes and positions. (As discussed in the Preface, neither side involved in the abortion issue prefers the terms I have chosen. For detailed background, see the Preface, pages xxi–xxvii.) If I have succeeded in my intentions, even if you do not like the terms I have chosen, whether you favor the legal right to abortion or oppose it, you will feel that I have provided a balanced presentation of your view.

The Fourth Stage: Developing Alternative Strategies

The millions of legal abortions that took place after the Supreme Court's ruling led to a pitched battle that still rages. Let's look at alternative strategies the pro- and antiabortion groups developed to promote their positions.

Alternative Strategies of the Antiabortionists. After the Supreme Court made its *Roe v. Wade* decision in 1973, antiabortion groups began to try to persuade states to restrict the ruling. They succeeded in eliminating federal funding of abortions for military personnel and their dependents, federal prisoners, and workers with the Peace Corps. They also succeeded in eliminating health insurance coverage of abortions for federal employees. Their major victory on the federal level took place early: In 1976, they persuaded Congress to pass the Hyde Amendment, which prohibits Medicaid funding for abortions unless the woman's life is in imminent danger. When the Supreme Court upheld this amendment in 1980 (Lewis 1988), the number of abortions paid for by federal funds plummeted from 300,000 a year to just 17. Despite repeated attempts to change the Hyde Amendment, the antiabortion groups have succeeded in retaining it.

Another highly effective strategy of the antiabortion groups has been to establish "crisis pregnancy centers." Women who call "pregnancy hotlines" (sometimes called life lines or birth lines) are offered free pregnancy testing. If the test shows they are pregnant, they are directed to counselors who encourage them to give birth. The counselors inform women about fetal development and talk to them about financial aid and social support available to them during pregnancy. They also advise women about how to find adoptive parents or how to obtain financial support after the birth. Some activists also operate maternity homes and provide adoption services.

Strategies of Moderates ▸ We can classify antiabortionists as moderates or radicals depending on the techniques they use to support their views. The strategies that moderates choose are mild, such as forwarding e-mail to their friends, running newspaper ads, writing their representatives, posting blogs, and operating Internet sites. They also feature women who have had abortions, but who regret their decisions, as speakers at conferences. Taking their cue from the civil rights movement of the 1950s, in the years after *Roe v. Wade* many practiced passive resistance to laws they considered unjust. Lying immobile in front of abortion clinics, they went limp as the police carried them to jail. This social movement grew so large and its members so active that by 1990 more abortion protesters had been arrested than the number of people who were arrested during the entire civil rights movement (Allen 1988; Lacayo 1991; Kirkpatrick 1992). Since then, the U.S. Supreme Court has upheld state laws that restrict demonstrations at clinics and the homes of clinic staff, and this tactic has shrunk into the background (Walsh and Goldstein 2000).

Strategies of Radicals ▸ Radical activists, in contrast, choose more extreme methods to try to stop abortions. Some have thrown blood on the walls of abortion clinics, unplugged abortion machinery, jammed clinic doors with Super Glue, and set off stink bombs. Others have called women who had abortions and played recordings of babies screaming. Some radical activists have burned and bombed abortion clinics. In the town in which I taught, Edwardsville, Illinois, radicals kidnapped a physician and threatened his life if he did not shut down his abortion clinics. Radical activists have shot and killed eight abortion doctors. These extreme acts have been condemned by both proabortionists and antiabortionists alike.

Alternative Strategies of the Proabortionists. Proabortion groups have also developed alternative strategies. Their counterattack typically takes three primary forms: campaigning, lobbying lawmakers, and publicizing their position. At the center of their position is the belief that abortion is a woman's private decision in which government should not be involved. They stress that "without the right to choose abortion, any other guarantees of liberty have little meaning for women" (Michelman 1988). One alternative strategy is to recruit women who had abortions when it was back-alley business. They use their stories to warn the public about what it would be like if the right to abortion is taken away. Their ultimate message is that thousands of women will die from underground abortions if it does not remain legal.

Central to the efforts of the proabortionists is protecting *Roe v. Wade* and preventing attempts by the antiabortionists to chip away at or overturn the ruling. They have been successful in getting California and five other states to codify *Roe,* that is, to guarantee abortion rights in their states if *Roe* is overturned (Solomon 2006).

Making Mutual Accusations. As a key strategy, each side points a finger at the other. As it promotes its own point of view, each side paints the other as grotesque, uncaring, and evil. Proabortionists accuse antiabortionists of being concerned about fetuses but not about pregnant women. They also point to the killing of physicians as evidence of hypocrisy—people who say they stand for life kill others. For their part, antiabortionists accuse proabortionists of suppressing information about the health risks of abortion—and of murdering innocent, unborn children.

The Controversy Continues: The Supreme Court after *Roe v. Wade.* ▸ In the abortion debate, the U.S. Supreme Court remains the final arbiter. If either side on this issue succeeds in getting a law passed, the Supreme Court decides whether that law is constitutional. Consequently, a primary alternative strategy of both proabortionists and antiabortionists is to try to influence the president's choice of Supreme Court nominees and how the Senate votes on them. For the past three decades, U.S. presidents have taken strong positions on abortion and have proposed nominees for the Supreme Court that reflect their position. We can expect this stacking of the Court to continue.

Four Supreme Court rulings since the 1973 *Roe v. Wade* decision are especially significant. The first is *Webster v. Reproductive Services* (1989). In this ruling, the Court concluded that the states have no obligation to finance abortion. Individual states can ban abortions at state hospitals and refuse to fund counseling services for women who

Like Lisa and her grandmother in the chapter's opening vignette, why might this grandmother and granddaugher have different opinions about abortion? Both were born and raised in the United States. What does it mean to say they grew up in different societies?

are considering abortion. The second significant decision is *Casey v. Planned Parenthood* (1992). In this ruling, hailed as a victory by the antiabortionists, the Supreme Court ruled that to get an abortion, women under the age of 18 must first obtain the consent of at least one parent. This ruling also requires a waiting period of 24 hours before an abortion can be performed. During this waiting period, the woman must be given materials on fetal development, as well as a list of adoption agencies in the area. In a nod to the proabortionists, the Court ruled in this same decision that a wife has no obligation to inform her husband before she has an abortion.

The third significant decision, hailed as a victory by proabortionists, occurred in 1994 when the Supreme Court upheld FACE, the Freedom of Access to Clinic Entrances Act. This law requires demonstrators to remain 300 feet away from the entrances to abortion clinics. If not, they face up to 3 years in prison. The Court ruled that this law does not violate freedom of speech.

The fourth major Supreme Court decision came in 2007. In *Gonzales v. Carhart,* the Court upheld the Partial-Birth Abortion Ban that Congress had passed in 2003. This law bans a procedure in which the doctor dilates the woman's cervix, then pulls the fetus through the birth canal feet first until only the head remains inside. Using scissors or another sharp instrument, the doctor then punctures the head and compresses the skull, so it, too, can fit through the dilated cervix (Rovner 2006).

This ruling highlights the significance of terms. The proabortionists call this procedure intact dilation and extraction, a dry-sounding medical term, while the antiabortionists call it partial birth abortion, an emotionally evocative term. That Congress called its law the Partial-Birth Abortion Ban indicates the success that the antiabortion groups had in formulating this law and in this Supreme Court ruling.

The Controversy Continues: Coming Supreme Court Decisions. As you have seen, in developing alternative strategies both sides have been successful in getting laws passed that favor their position. The proabortionists managed a stunning victory when they succeeded in getting abortion listed as a medical condition covered by the health reform law. This aspect of the law has aroused intense opposition from Roman Catholics, as it violates their religious beliefs and conscience. Roman Catholic hospitals and colleges, including Notre Dame, have sued the federal government, an issue that will be decided by the Supreme Court (Radnofsky 2012). Other issues the Supreme Court is likely to face include state laws that require women who want an abortion to view sonograms of their fetus, outlaw abortions after a heartbeat has been detected, and require abortion clinics to meet hospital standards and have hallways five feet wide (Bassett 2011; Eng 2012; Eckholm 2013).

No Middle Ground. The alternative strategies pursued by the proabortionists and the antiabortionists are merely skirmishes in a drawn-out war. Each side is seeking total victory, and neither is satisfied with strategies that bring anything less. What the antiabortionists want is a *Federal Right to Life Law,* a constitutional amendment that would assert that human life begins at conception. Abortion would then be officially classified as a type of murder. For their part, what the proabortionists want is a *Federal Freedom of Choice Law* that would remove all state and federal restrictions on abortion. You can see how incompatible the views and goals of abortion activists are.

The final results of this struggle for and against legal abortion are still unclear. On *each* side of this issue are highly motivated people who consider their view the only "right" way of looking at the world. Each views the other as misinformed and unreasonable. Each is rationally and emotionally dedicated to its own view of morality: One argues that the only moral course of action is to outlaw abortion because it kills babies. The other argues that the only moral course of action is to keep abortion legal because it is part of women's freedom to make decisions about their own bodies. With no middle ground to bridge this chasm, there is no end in sight to this bitter, determined struggle, and the groups are likely to continue to tensely confront one another for some time.

The Role of Sociology in Social Problems

As you have seen with the example of abortion, social problems are filled with conflicting emotions, views, and values. In the midst of such turmoil, how can sociology help?

1.5 Describe the contributions that sociologist can make in studying social problems.

A basic human characteristic is to think of our world in personal and moral terms. In the chapter's opening vignette, for example, Lisa may think that her grandmother is narrow-minded, and her grandmother may wonder how Lisa acquired such casual morals. Most of us are convinced that our views on moral issues are right, that people who hold contrary views are ignorant, short-sighted, and wrong. Our defenses go up when anyone questions our moral positions.

It is difficult to penetrate such self-protective attitudes and defenses, especially since they go beyond the rational and are clad in emotions. Let's see how **sociology**, the systematic and objective study of human groups, can help us see past the emotions that surround social problems.

Sociology as a Tool for Gaining an Objective Understanding of Social Problems

If we want an objective understanding of social problems, sociology can help. Here are five contributions that sociologists can make:

Watch on **MySocLab**
Video: Qualitative Methods in Research

1. *Sociologists can measure objective conditions.* In the case of abortion, sociologists can gather information on the number of abortions performed in clinics and hospitals, trends in the number of abortions and who has them, and how the states differ on making abortion accessible. They also can determine how women make their decisions to have or to not have an abortion, how they adjust to their decision, and how their decisions affect their relationships with their husbands or boyfriends.
2. *Sociologists can measure subjective concerns.* Sociologists can also determine people's attitudes and views about social problems (Becker 1966). Such information is useful in evaluating potential social policies. Establishing sound social policy involves more than measuring public opinion, of course, but accurate measurements can guide policy makers. Table 1.4 on the next page, which summarizes Americans' attitudes about the legality of abortion, provides an example of how sociologists measure subjective concerns. Note again how significant *social location* is, how people's attitudes are related to their sex, race–ethnicity, age, education, income, politics, and place of residence.
3. *Sociologists can apply the sociological imagination.* They can place social problems into their broad social context. For example, abortion is related to people's ideas about individual freedom and privacy, sexuality and sex roles, and when life begins. It is also related to ideas about standards of living and parenting, what is and is not moral, and the role of religious institutions in a pluralistic society (Lerner et al. 1990).
4. *Sociologists can identify possible social policies.* To address a social problem, sociologists can suggest potential courses of action for public and private agencies, educational programs, public awareness campaigns, and legal changes.
5. *Sociologists can evaluate likely consequences of social policies* (Becker 1966). Sociologists can estimate the social effects of a proposed social policy. On abortion, for example, they can estimate how a policy might affect the birthrate, population growth, crime rate, and expenditures for welfare and education.

That sociologists can do objective research does not mean that sociology has all the answers. Far from it. Sociologists can suggest which consequences are likely

TABLE 1.4 ▸ Should Abortion Be Legal or Illegal?

This question was asked of a representative sample of Americans: *"Do you think abortions should be legal under any circumstances, legal only under certain circumstances, or illegal in all circumstances?"*

	Always Legal	Legal Under Certain Circumstances	Never Legal
Overall Average	27%	50%	22%
Sex			
Male	24%	55%	19%
Female	29%	45%	24%
Race–Ethnicity			
White	29%	48%	21%
Nonwhite1	22%	54%	22%
Black	30%	47%	20%
Age			
18–29 years	32%	45%	23%
30–49 years	29%	49%	21%
50–64 years	26%	53%	19%
65 years and older	18%	52%	25%
Education			
High school or less	21%	48%	29%
Some college	32%	50%	17%
College graduate	24%	58%	16%
College postgraduate	35%	49%	15%
Income			
Under $20,000	23%	46%	29%
$20,000–$29,999	16%	53%	30%
$30,000–$49,999	25%	45%	27%
$50,000–$74,999	33%	52%	15%
$75,000 and over	33%	56%	10%
Politics			
Republican	13%	52%	34%
Democrat	38%	47%	14%
Independent	29%	52%	18%
Region			
East	27%	50%	22%
Midwest	24%	46%	28%
South	22%	51%	25%
West	37%	51%	11%

[1]As used in the source, "nonwhite" refers to anyone who did not self-identify as white or black.

Note: Because the "no opinion" category is not included in the source, the rows do not always add to 100.

Source: Sourcebook of Criminal Justice Statistics 2012:Table 2.101.

to result if some particular social policy is followed, but they have no expertise for determining which social policy *should* be followed. Social policy is based on values, on the outcomes that people want to see. *Because sociology cannot dictate that one set of values is superior to another, it provides no basis for making value decisions.* We'll come back to this in a moment, but first let's consider using common sense to solve social problems.

Sociology and Common Sense

1.6 Explain why common sense is not adequate to understand social problems.

Do we really need sociological research? Why don't we just follow common sense? We all have experiences that "tell" us that some things are true and others are not. We use **common sense**, the ideas common to our society (or to some group within our society), to get through daily life, so why don't we just use common sense to solve social problems?

The short answer for why common sense is not adequate is that some of our ideas are built on faulty assumptions. For example, a commonsense idea is that abortion is a last resort. For some women, it is, of course, but this is not always the case. Soviet Russia provides a remarkable example. In the Soviet Union, abortion was a major means of birth control, and the *average* Russian woman used to have six abortions in her lifetime (Yablonsky 1981; Eberstadt 1988). The abortion rate dropped after the collapse of the Soviet Union, but abortion became part of the culture, and there are still more abortions than births in Russia (Regushevskaya 2009; Kishkovsky 2011).

Another commonsense idea is that women who don't want to get pregnant use birth control. Sociologist Kristin Luker (1975), who studied an abortion clinic in California, found that many women had not used contraceptives. It wasn't that they were ignorant. Rather, some felt that contraceptives interfered with intimacy, others that they caused side effects, and still others that they cost too much. Some women didn't use them because their boyfriends didn't want them to. Some even avoided contraceptives to protect their self-image: If they used contraceptives, they might think of themselves as "available" or sexually promiscuous. In short, for a variety of reasons some women take chances—and when they get pregnant some have abortions.

Another commonsense idea is that women who have abortions did not intend to get pregnant. Sociologists have found that this, too, isn't necessarily true. Leon Dash (1990), who studied pregnancy among teens in Washington, D.C., found that many poor, young, unmarried girls get pregnant on purpose. Some want children so that, as they said, "I can have something to hold onto, that I can call my own." Some boyfriends also urge their girlfriends to get pregnant, so that they will "feel like a man." And, as Luker discovered, some women get pregnant to test their boyfriend's commitment. When they learn that their relationship isn't going to work out, they decide that they don't want to bear a child after all, and they choose abortion as a way out of their dilemmas.

Since it is easy for commonsense ideas to be wrong, we need solid, objective research. To see how sociologists produce these kinds of findings, let's turn to how they do their research.

Methods for Studying Social Problems

1.7 Understand the four basic research designs and research methods that sociologists use to study social problems.

When sociologists study social problems, they choose from several **methods** (ways of doing research). Which method they select depends on three factors. The first is the question they want to investigate. Suppose, for example, that you want to find out how people form their ideas about abortion. To answer this question, you would use a different method of research than if you want to compare the abortion rates of high school dropouts and college-educated women. A second factor is the matter of practicality. You might want to do face-to-face interviews with people across the country, but you can't because you have neither enough money nor time. A third factor is ethics. Some methods that might yield good data are unethical. They might cause emotional harm or violate people's privacy.

Watch on **MySocLab** **Video:** Research Methodology

Let's look at the methods that sociologists use to study social problems. We shall first distinguish how sociologists design their studies, then describe how they gather their data.

View on **MySocLab** **Figure:** Steps in the Research Process

Four Basic Research Designs. Most research falls into one of four **research designs**: case studies, surveys, experiments, and field studies. Let's look at each.

Case Studies ▸ The **case study** is used to gather in-depth information on a specific situation. As the name implies, the researcher focuses on one case—an individual, an event, or even an organization such as an abortion clinic or a crisis pregnancy center. Let's suppose that you want in-depth information about how women experience abortion. You might want to learn how the women wrestle with the decision to give birth or to have an abortion, whom they talk to about it, even how they feel during the abortion and how they adjust afterward. A case study could provide this type of depth of understanding.

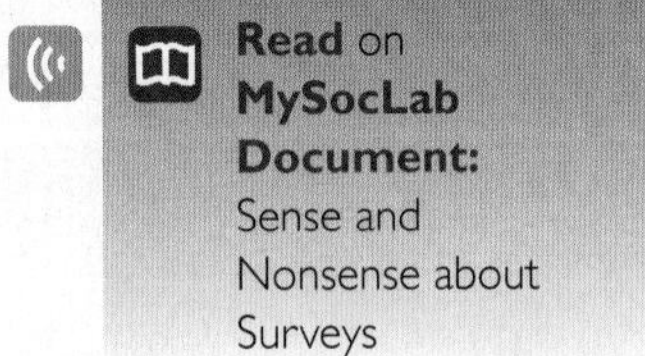

Read on MySocLab Document: Sense and Nonsense about Surveys

Surveys ▸ While case studies provide rich detail, you cannot generalize from them. They can provide remarkable insight, but if you focus on just one woman, how can you know whether her experiences are similar to those of other women? To overcome this limitation, sociologists use **surveys**. In a survey, you focus on a **sample** of the group you want to study. (Sociologists use the term **population** to refer to the target group.) Samples are intended to represent the entire group that you are studying. Done correctly, surveys allow you to **generalize** what you find—that is, you are able to apply your findings to people who belong to the group but who are not in your sample.

The best sample is a **random sample**. This is a sample in which everyone in your population has an equal chance of being included in your research. When researchers do national surveys, whether on attitudes toward abortion or anything else, they need to get information from only about 2,000 people. Yet, random samples are so powerful that these surveys can accurately represent the opinions of 300 million Americans.

Experiments ▸ Another research method is the **experiment**. If you were to use this method, you would randomly divide people who have certain characteristics (such as women between the ages of 18 and 21 who have had an abortion) into two groups. You would expose half of them to some experience (such as a video of a woman giving birth). These people are called the **experimental group**. You would do this to see how something you measure, such as their attitude toward abortion, differs from that of the **control group**, those who do not view the video. Differences in the experimental group are thought to be generalizable to people who share their characteristics (in this case, young women who have had an abortion).

Experiments are rare in the study of social problems, partly because ethics do not allow us to create problems for people. (Having a woman who has recently had an abortion watch a video of a birth is likely to cause stress.) However, you can use experiments in more limited ways. For example, you could measure attitudes toward abortion before and after listening to a lecture on abortion.

Field Studies ▸ In **field studies** (or **participant observation**), researchers go into a setting that they want to learn more about. (This is called "going into the field.") For example, Magda Denes (1934–1996) who was on the proabortionist side of this issue, wanted to know what an abortion clinic was like—for the women and the staff (1976). She obtained permission to be present in an abortion clinic and observe what took place. The result was a moving book, *In Necessity and Sorrow.* Denes reported her findings objectively. She tells us that the emotional experience was much more intense than she expected. She describes picking up fetuses from the trash barrel, their little arms broken, cut, and bleeding. Her book highlights conversations she had with doctors about how the fetus stops moving about half an hour after they inject saline solution into the placenta. No other research method could obtain information like this.

Four Methods for Gathering Information. After selecting a research design, sociologists decide how to gather their information. They choose from four basic techniques: interviews, questionnaires, documents, and observations.

Interviews ▸ If you use an **interview**, you ask people questions on the topics that you want to explore. You can choose from two types of interviews. If you use a **structured interview**, you ask everyone the same questions (for example, "What is your relationship

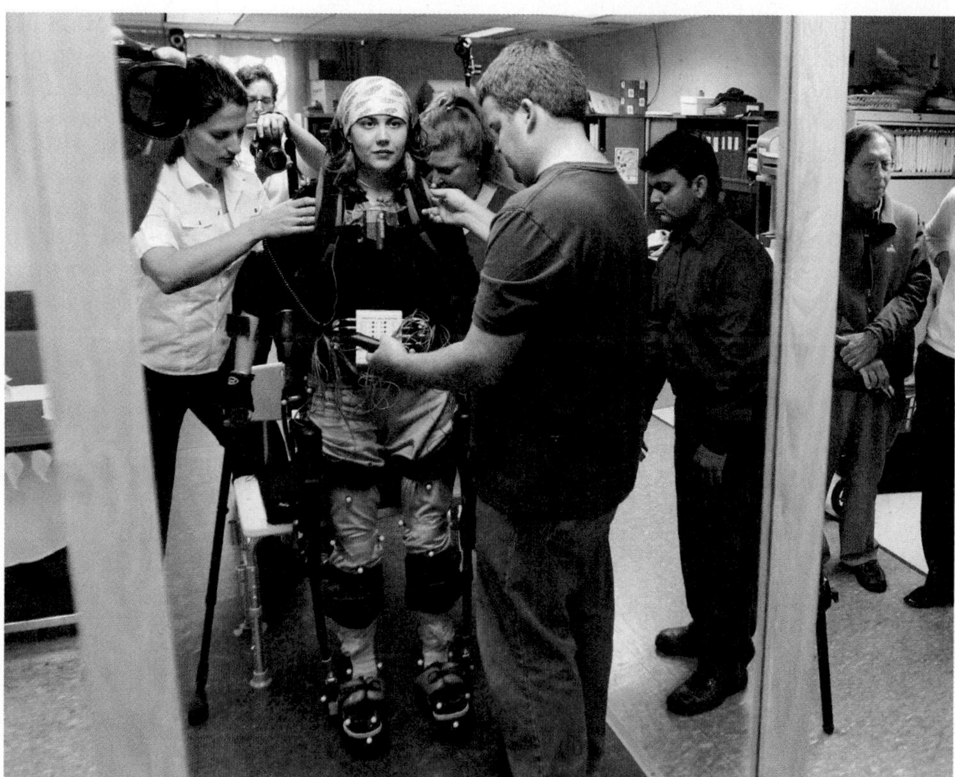

This woman, paralyzed four months ago, is taking her first steps with bionic legs. To study what you see in this photo, sociologists would record what the workers and the woman are saying and doing. They would also analyze how this technology is affecting her life.

to the man who made you pregnant?"). If you use an **unstructured interview**, you let people talk in depth about their experiences; however, you must make certain that everyone covers certain topics (such as contraceptive history, family relations, and the reasons for the abortion).

Questionnaires ▸ If you use the second technique, **questionnaires**, you ask people to answer written questions. These can be in paper/pencil form or they can be questions on a computer program. Your questions could be either *open ended* (people answer in their own words) or *closed ended* (people choose from a list of prepared answers). An open-ended question might be "What is your relationship to the man who made you pregnant?" The woman would put the relationship in her own words. A closed-ended form of this question would ask the woman to check an item on a list, such as husband, boyfriend, casual acquaintance, other. It is easier to compare answers to closed-ended questions, but open-ended questions tap a richer world, eliciting comments, attitudes, and even topics that you might not anticipate.

Documents ▸ Written sources or records, called **documents**, can also provide valuable data about social problems. You might examine official records like census data or hospital records. Kristin Luker, for example, analyzed the records of 500 women who came to the abortion clinic that she studied. Or you might look at more informal records, such as journals, blogs, e-mail, and Internet discussion groups. These documents can reveal people's behaviors and provide insight into how they cope with troubles.

Observation ▸ The fourth technique, **observation**, is just what the term implies: To use it, you observe what is occurring in some setting. You watch and listen to what is taking place and record or take field notes on people's actions or what they say. You might use an audio or video recorder, but if recording will interfere with what people are doing or saying, you take notes instead, either while something occurs or afterward. If you use *overt observation,* you will identify yourself as a researcher, but if you use *covert observation,* the people in the setting will not be aware that you are studying them.

Combining Methods ▸ Sociologists often combine research methods. For example, to do research on the abortion clinic, Luker used three of these methods: observation, interviews, and documents. Not only did she observe women and abortion providers in the clinic, but she also interviewed women who were having abortions and examined the clinic's records on its patients.

Striving for Accuracy and Objectivity. When doing research, it is essential to remain objective. Look at Table 1.5 below, in which we compare biased and neutral questions. The bias of the questions on the left should be obvious to you. But what is biased about number two on the antiabortion side? The bias is just a tad less apparent. To make it more obvious, think about the terms father and baby. They make assumptions that bias the question in an antiabortion direction.

Few of us would try to slant our research in some direction, but like everyone else, those of us who are sociologists get our ideas and opinions from the groups with which we associate and the ideas to which we are exposed. No matter how we dislike it, this means that we have biases. Fortunately, we have a safeguard that helps us overcome our biases. Before they are published, reports on our research are sent to fellow sociologists who critique them. Each article submitted for publication includes details on the methods that were used. As the referees analyze a report, they look for flaws of any sort, including biases. They then recommend or do not recommend its publication.

To help you better understand how sociologists do their research, I asked several researchers to share their experiences with you. The result is a feature in this text called *Spotlight on Social Research*. For an overview of this feature, see the box on the next page.

TABLE 1.5 ▸ Bias and Objectivity in Research Questions

One way to evaluate the results of survey research is to examine the questions that the researchers asked. You would not expect any researcher to use questions as biased as the examples in this table. Extremes are used to help you to see how questions can shape answers.

Bias in social research is usually subtle, not easy to detect. The bias sometimes slips in because the researcher lives within a particular social world in which his or her views are taken for granted, and the researcher does not recognize the bias. Regardless of their source, biased questions produce biased results.

Biased Questions	Neutral Questions
The Antiabortion Bias	
1. What is your opinion about killing babies by abortion?	1. What is your opinion about abortion?
2. What is your opinion about women not having to inform the father of the baby before they have an abortion?	2. If a husband or boyfriend gets a woman pregnant, do you think he should be informed before the woman has an abortion?
The Proabortion Bias	
1. What is your opinion about forcing a woman to have a baby when she wants an abortion?	1. What is your opinion about abortion?
2. Why do you think that any man who gets a woman pregnant should have a say in the woman's choice of what to do with her own body?	2. If a husband or boyfriend gets a woman pregnant, do you think he should be informed before the woman has an abortion?

Source: By the author.

Spotlight on Social Research

An Overview of This Feature

Sociologists do a lot of research on social problems. In fact, this is one of their favorite areas of study. As we review social problems in this text, you will be introduced to both classic research and the most recent research findings.

To acquaint you with researchers in social problems, 10 chapters have a boxed feature titled *Spotlight on Social Research.* Each box features a researcher who has studied a particular social problem. These boxes are unique, for the researchers themselves have written them.

The research that you will read about in *Spotlight on Social Research* is incredibly varied. With these researchers, you will visit a youth gang in Chicago, a bar in Chicago's inner city where gangsters hang out, and neo-Nazis in Detroit. You'll even be present at a Klan rally. In a study of workers at two magazines, you will learn how views of sexual harassment differ from one work setting to another. You will also learn how one sociologist became so interested in military matters that he went to Iraq. One researcher recounts how his picking beans in the fields of Washington led to a lifetime of doing research on crime. Another researcher shares how her own abuse at the hands of her husband while she was yet a student motivated her to do research on intimate violence.

As these researchers reflect on their studies, they pull back the curtains to let you look behind the scenes to see how research is conducted. To help provide a broader context for appreciating their research, I open each box by sharing a little about the researcher's background and how the researcher became interested in a particular social problem.

I think that you'll enjoy *Spotlight on Social Research*. The "inside" information that these researchers share gives a unique flavor to this text. From these reports, you will learn things about research that are not available anywhere else. I am grateful to these researchers for taking time out of their research and teaching to share their experiences with me. It was a pleasure corresponding with them and gaining insight into their work.

"That's the worst set of opinions I've heard in my entire life."

To attain their goal of objectivity and accuracy in their research, sociologists must put away their personal opinions or biases.

Should Sociologists Take Sides?

The Problem of Determining Morality. Let's go back to the issue I mentioned earlier (pp. 15–16) that sociologists can do objective research but that sociology does not provide a basis for making value judgments. Our four research methods allow us to gather objective information on social problems, but they do not reveal what attitude or social policy is "correct." Abortion, for example, is interwoven with thorny philosophical and religious issues concerning the "great questions" of life, death, morality, freedom, responsibility, and ultimate existence. Sociologists can study people's ideas about such topics, but sociology has no basis to judge whether someone's ideas are right or wrong, much less determine the ultimate meaning that may underlie such issues.

To take a position on a social problem is to take sides—and because sociology does not equip us to make judgments about values and morality, sociology cannot tell us which side to take. Even so, the question of taking sides on social problems is debated hotly among sociologists, for, like other thoughtful people, sociologists have their own subjective concerns about social problems. Let's look at this debate.

1.8 Summarize the disagreement in sociology regarding whether or not sociologists should choose sides.

Watch on **MySocLab**
Video: Objectivity: Fact or Fiction

1.8

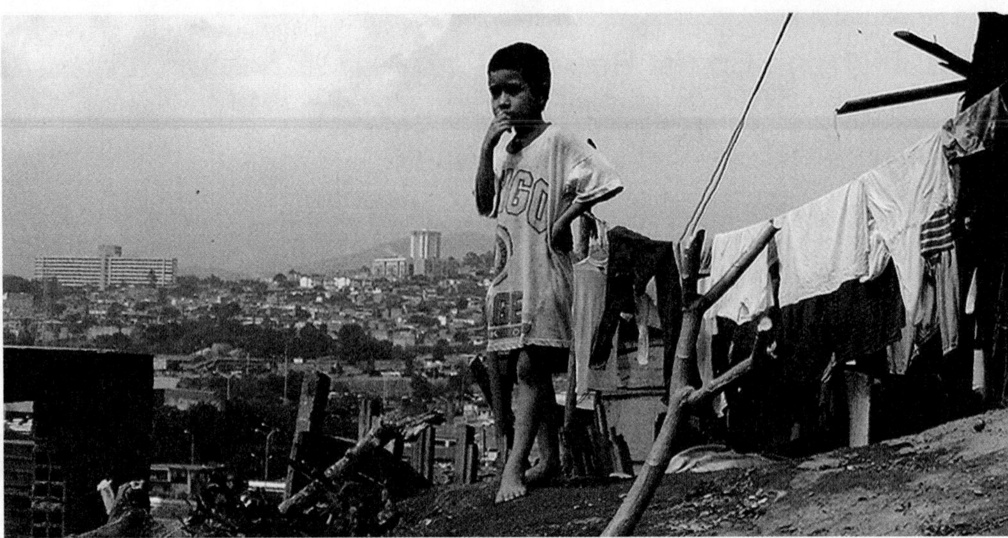

A problem sociologists grapple with when they analyze social problems is objectivity (dispassionate analysis) versus partisanship (taking sides). When it comes to poverty, as in this photo I took in Medellin, Colombia, taking sides wins hands down.

Taking the Side of the Oppressed. Many sociologists are convinced that they have a moral obligation to take a stand on social issues. "If sociology is not useful for helping to reform society," they ask, "of what value is it?" They stress that although sociology does not provide a basis for making moral choices, it does provide sociologists the ability to relate the surface manifestations of a social problem (such as poverty) to deeper social causes (such as the control of a country's resources by the wealthy and powerful). They say that sociologists have the obligation to do their research objectively—but that they should side with those who are being hurt and exploited. Some go farther than this and say that sociologists have a moral obligation to make the oppressed aware of their condition and to organize them to do battle against those who oppress them.

This view that we should take the side of the oppressed—a popular view running through sociology since its origins—does not give us a direction for taking sides in the abortion dilemma. Those who take the proabortion view would argue that they are siding with women who are hurt and exploited. But those who take the antiabortion view would argue that they are siding with the hurt and exploited unborn. We end up full circle to where we started. Again, sociology cannot provide the basis for choosing values.

Uncovering Values. To better bring these views into focus, let's assume that some sociologists have studied unmarried pregnant teenagers. After analyzing the problems that these young women confront and the consequences for their children, they conclude that unmarried pregnant teenagers should have abortions. Arguments can be made for and against this position, of course, but the question is: Should sociologists promote such a point of view?

To make this issue clearer, let's consider an even more extreme case. Suppose that sociologists analyze the soaring costs of Social Security and Medicare. They become convinced that these programs are bankrupting the nation and that the solution is to euthanize the physically and mentally handicapped. Let's also assume that one of their conclusions is that all people, after celebrating their 80th birthday, should be "put to sleep" by means of painless drugs? Arguments can be made for and against this position, of course, but the question is: Should sociologists promote such a point of view?

I doubt that any sociologist would ever support any of these proposals, but I think you get the point. Whenever someone takes any position on a social problem, values of some sort underlie that person's views. We sociologists, who develop our values just as everyone else does, are no exception to this principle.

Taking Sides: Divisions and Agreement. Besides taking sides as individuals, sociologists sometimes take sides as professionals. This has created divisions within sociology—especially during the Vietnam War and again with the Iraq War. The debate centers on whether or not our professional groups—such as the Society for the Study of Social Problems and the American Sociological Association—should take a public stand against a war. Although wars come and go and issues change, this broad cleavage among sociologists remains. As mentioned, the most popular view among sociologists is that we should work toward changing society in order to help the less powerful. Some, however, are convinced that sociology's proper role is only to investigate and to report research findings objectively. They say that if sociologists want to take sides on any issue, they should do so as private citizens, not as sociologists.

This ongoing debate keeps sociologists sensitive to the boundaries between objectivity and partisanship. Although there is little room for middle ground, most sociologists attempt to resolve this dilemma by separating research findings from their own values and opinions. What they observe and measure, they attempt to report dispassionately and to analyze as accurately as possible.

Despite their disagreements about taking sides on social problems, sociologists agree that they are in a unique position to study social problems and that they should produce thorough and objective studies. Sociologists possess the tools to do such research, and their studies can be valuable for both the public and policy makers.

A Personal Note. I sincerely hope that the coming chapters help you to acquire a sociological imagination that will allow you to work toward creative solutions for the pressing social problems we face. We sociologists can provide facts on objective conditions, sensitize you to the broader context that nourishes social problems, and suggest the likely consequences of any particular intervention. Your decisions about what should be done, however, will have to be made according to *your* values.

MySocLab  Study and Review on MySocLab

Summary and Review

1. Sociologists use what is called the *sociological imagination* (or perspective) to view the social problems that affect people's lives. This means that they look at how *social locations* shape people's behavior and attitudes.
2. A *social problem* is some aspect of society that large numbers of people are concerned about and would like changed. It consists of *objective conditions* (things that are measurable) and *subjective concerns* (the ideas, feelings, and attitudes that people have about those conditions). Social problems are relative—one group's solution may be another group's problem.
3. Social problems go through a natural history of four stages that often overlap: defining the problem, crafting an official response, reacting to the official response, and pursuing alternative strategies.
4. The sociological understanding of a social problem differs from a commonsense understanding because the sociological perspective (or imagination) is not based on emotions or personal values. Instead, sociologists examine how social problems affect people, view the causes of social problems as located in society rather than in individuals, and use objective methods to gather information about social problems.
5. Sociologists are able to make five contributions to the study of social problems: They can help determine the extent of a social problem, clarify people's attitudes toward social problems, apply the sociological imagination to social problems, identify potential social policies for dealing with social problems, and evaluate likely consequences of those policies.

6. To study social problems, sociologists use four major research designs: *surveys, case studies, experiments,* and *field studies.* Sociologists gather information in four basic ways: *interviews, questionnaires, documents,* and *observation.* These methods are often used in combination.

7. Because social problems can be viewed from many vantage points, sociologists disagree on whether they should choose sides as professionals. They do agree, however, that sociological studies must provide objective, accurate, and verifiable data.

Key Terms

case study, 18
common sense, 17
control group, 18
documents, 19
experiment, 18
experimental group, 18
field studies, 18
generalize, 18
interview, 18
methods, 17
objective condition, 5
observation, 19
participant observation, 18
personal troubles, 2
population, 18
power, 7
questionnaires, 19
random sample, 18
research designs, 17
sample, 18
social location, 3
social problems, 5
sociological imagination, 2
sociological perspective, 3
sociology, 15
structured interview, 18
subjective concern, 5
surveys, 18
unstructured interview, 19
value, 7

Thinking Critically About Chapter 1

1. What are the differences between personal problems and social problems? Apply this distinction to abortion; to robbery.
2. If you were a sociologist and you wanted to study abortion, which research design would you use? Why?
3. Do you agree with the author's statement that science, including sociology, cannot answer questions of morality? Why or why not?
4. Do you think that sociologists have a responsibility to take sides on social problems? Why or why not?

2 Interpreting Social Problems: Aging

Listen to Chapter 2 on MySocLab

Learning Objectives. After reading this chapter, you should be able to:

2.1 Identify the three major theoretical frameworks that sociologists use to interpret social problems. **(p. 27)**

2.2 Explain functionalism and apply it to social problems. **(p. 28)**

2.3 Explain conflict theory and apply it to social problems. **(p. 33)**

2.4 Explain feminist theory and apply it to social problems. **(p. 36)**

2.5 Explain symbolic interactionism and apply it to social problems. **(p. 38)**

2.6 Discuss the possible generational struggle regarding the elderly. **(p. 44)**

In 1928, Charles Hart, an anthropologist working on his Ph.D., did fieldwork among the Tiwi, a preliterate people living on an island off the northern coast of Australia. Every Tiwi belongs to a clan, and to help Hart fit in they assigned him to the bird (Jabijabui) clan and gave him an adoptive mother. Hart described his "mother" as "toothless, almost blind, withered," adding that she was "physically quite revolting and mentally rather senile." He then described this remarkable event:

> How seriously they took my presence in their kinship system is something I never will be sure about.... However, toward the end of my time on the islands an incident occurred that surprised me because it suggested that some of them had been taking my presence in the kinship system much more seriously than I had thought. I was approached by a group of about eight or nine senior men.... They were the senior members of the Jabijabui clan and they had decided among themselves that the time had come to get rid of the decrepit old woman who had first called me son and whom I now called mother.... As I knew, they said, it was Tiwi custom, when an old woman became too feeble to look after herself, to "cover her up." This could only be done by her sons and her brothers and all of them had to agree beforehand, since once it was done they did not want any dissension among the brothers or clansmen, as that might lead to a feud. My "mother" was now completely blind, she was constantly falling over logs or into fires, and they, her senior clansmen, were in agreement that she would be better out of the way. Did I agree?
>
> I already knew about "covering up." The Tiwi, like many other hunting and gathering peoples, sometimes got rid of their ancient and decrepit females. The method was to dig a hole in the ground in some lonely place, put the old woman in the hole and fill it in with earth until only her head was showing. Everybody went away for a day or two and then went back to the hole to discover to their great surprise, that the old woman was dead, having been too feeble to raise her arms from the earth. Nobody had "killed" her; her death in Tiwi eyes was a natural one. She had been alive when her relatives last saw her. I had never seen it done, though I knew it was the custom, so I asked my brothers if it was necessary for me to attend the "covering up."
>
> They said no and they would do it, but only after they had my agreement. Of course I agreed, and a week or two later we heard in our camp that my "mother" was dead, and we all wailed and put on the trimmings of mourning.
>
> —Charles Hart in Hart and Pilling 1979:125–126.

The method was to ... put the old woman in the hole and fill it in with earth until only her head was showing

I don't know about you, but I was shocked when I read Hart say that he did not hesitate to agree that the old woman should be "covered up." His only concern was whether he would have to watch the woman die. In our society, too, we have people who would like to find ways to "cover up" the elderly who seem to have outlived their social usefulness. "Why spend precious resources (all that money) on people who have only a few years—or just a few months—more to live?" goes their reasoning. "Wouldn't we be better off ushering them off the stage of life—with dignity, of course?"

This kind of thinking sends chills down the spine of most of us. But let's suppose that programs of euthanasia were put into effect. Who would decide which old people were "socially valuable," and which were not? Would the frail elderly turn out to be just the first targets? Might others follow, those whom some officials decide are "useless"—or at least of "less value"—and for the good of the general society need to be "covered up"?

Suggesting that something like this is even possible might sound ridiculous. But, then, we must recall that the Nazis under *der Führer* developed such programs. Few human groups choose "covering up" as their solution, but every society must deal with the problem of people who grow old and frail. If you read closely, you may have noted that the Tiwi "covered up" only old women. This is an extreme example of the discrimination against females that is common throughout the world. We will return to this topic in Chapter 9. In this present chapter, we want to consider how theories help us to understand social life. As we do this, we will explore the social problem of the elderly.

Sociological Theories and Social Problems

As sociologists do research on social problems, they uncover a lot of "facts." If you have just a jumble of "facts," however, how can you understand anything? To make sense of those "facts," you have to put them in some order, so you can see how they are related to one another. To do this, sociologists use theories. A **theory** explains how two or more concepts (or "facts"), such as age and suicide, are related. A *theory*, then, gives us a framework for organizing "facts." As it does so, it provides a way of interpreting those "facts" of social life.

In this chapter, we shall look at three main theories that sociologists use—functionalism, conflict theory, and symbolic interactionism. Before we begin, you may want to look at an overview of these theories, which are summarized in Table 2.1. Because each theory focuses on some particular "slice" of a social problem, each provides a different perspective on the problem. As you study these theories, keep in mind that each theory is like a spotlight shining into a dark room: It illuminates only a particular part of that room. Taken together, these theories throw more light on a social problem than does any one by itself.

2.1 Identify the three major theoretical frameworks that sociologists use to interpret social problems.

Explore on **MySocLab** **Activity:** Sociological Theories

Watch on **MySocLab** **Video:** Importance of Sociological Theory

TABLE 2.1 ▸ A Summary of Sociological Theories

	Functionalism	Conflict Theory	Symbolic Interactionism
What is society?	A social system composed of parts that work together to benefit the whole	Groups competing with one another within the same social system	People's patterns of behavior; always changing
What are the key terms?	Structure Function System Equilibrium Goals	Competition Conflict Special interests Power Exploitation	Symbols Interaction Communication Meanings Definitions
What is a social problem?	The failure of some part to fulfill its function, which interferes with the smooth functioning of the system	The inevitable outcome of interest groups competing for limited resources	Whatever a group decides is a social problem for that group
How does something become a social problem?	Some part of the system fails, usually because of rapid social change	Authority and power are used by the powerful to exploit weaker groups	One set of definitions becomes accepted; competing views are rejected

Source: By the author.

Functionalism and Social Problems

Introducing Functionalism

2.2 Explain functionalism and apply it to social problems.

A major theory that sociologists use to interpret social problems is **functionalism** (or *functional analysis*). Functionalists compare society to a self-adjusting machine. Each part of the machine has a **function**. When a part is working properly, it fulfills that function, and the machine hums along. Some functionalists use the analogy of the human body: A human has many organs, and when an organ is working properly, it contributes to the well-being of the person. Like the parts of a machine or the organs of a human body, society's parts also have functions. When a part is working properly, it contributes to the well-being (stability or equilibrium) of the other parts.

To see why functionalists stress that the parts of society contribute to the well-being of one another, consider health care and Social Security. Of the vast sums spent on health care for the elderly, some goes into medical research. The discoveries of medical researchers help not only the elderly but also children and adults of all ages. In the same way, Social Security brings benefits not only to the 44 million retired and disabled workers who get monthly checks, but also to the 70,000 people who work for this federal agency (*Statistical Abstract* 2013:Tables 507, 535). Their families also benefit. So do businesses across the nation, as the billions of dollars paid by Social Security work their way through the economy.

As you know, the parts of society don't always work properly. Functionalists call these failures **dysfunctions**. Dysfunctions can be minor, and soon resolved. But if dysfunctions linger, they can create problems for other parts of society. *And this is what a social problem is from the functionalist perspective—the failure of some part of society, which then interferes with society's smooth functioning.* Many dysfunctions show up when we examine the agencies that serve the elderly. Among these is "red tape," a term that refers to the strict regulations that make it difficult for an agency to accomplish its purposes. For example, an agency's rules can delay the benefits that people need or prevent elderly people with medical problems from receiving health care.

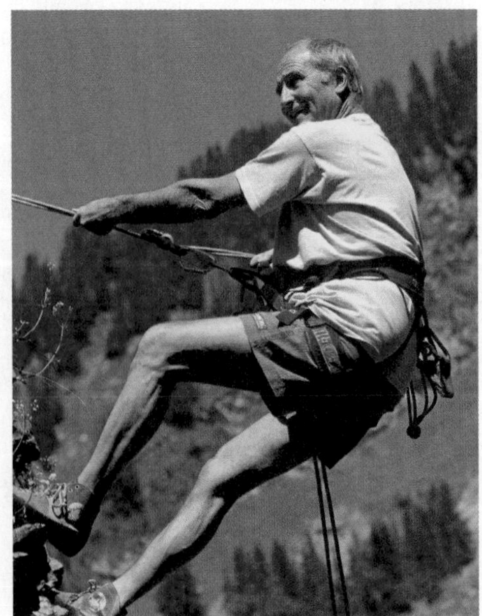

No stereotype does justice to the variety of the elderly. The two lifestyles represented here are likely a reflection of lifestyles followed in earlier stages of the life course. These choices also have a major impact on health, as we discuss in Chapter 10.

The Development of Functionalism

Auguste Comte: Organs Working Together. Functionalism has its roots in the origins of sociology (Turner 1978). Auguste Comte (1798–1857), who is called the founder of sociology because he coined the term, regarded society as being similar to an animal: Just as an animal has tissues and organs that are interrelated and function together, so does society. For a society to function smoothly, its parts must be in balance.

Emile Durkheim: Normal and Abnormal States. Sociologist Emile Durkheim (1858–1917) built on this idea that a society is composed of parts that perform functions. When society's parts perform the functions they are supposed to, he said, a society is in a "normal" state. When society's parts fail to perform their functions, society is in an "abnormal" or "pathological" state. To understand society, Durkheim stressed that we must look not only at function—how each part contributes to society—but also at **structure**—how the parts of a society are related to one another.

Robert Merton: Functions and Dysfunctions. In the 20th century, sociologist Robert Merton (1910–2003) dropped the idea that society is like an animal but refined functionalism's concepts. He defined functions as the beneficial consequences of people's actions. Functions can be either manifest or latent. A **manifest function** is an action that is *intended* to help some part of the system. For example, Social Security is intended to make life better for the elderly. Improving the quality of life of the elderly, then, is a *manifest* function of Social Security. As Merton emphasized, our actions can also have **latent functions**, consequences that help some part of the social system but were not intended for that purpose. For example, the salaries paid to the 70,000 employees of the Social Security Administration help to stabilize our economy. Because this beneficial consequence of Social Security was not intended, however, it is a *latent* function.

Merton (1968) stressed that human actions also have dysfunctions. These are consequences that disrupt a system's stability, making it more difficult to survive. If a part fails to meet its functions, it contributes to society's maladjustment and is part of a social problem.

Because the consequences of people's actions that disrupt a system's equilibrium usually are unintended, Merton called them **latent dysfunctions**. For example, the Social Security Administration has thousands of rules, written in incredible detail, designed to anticipate every potential situation. If the 70,000 employees of this agency were to follow each procedure exactly, the resulting red tape would interfere with their ability to serve the elderly. Because these rules are not intended to have this effect, they are latent dysfunctions.

In Sum ▸ Functionalists sensitize us to think in terms of systems. Instead of seeing something in isolation, we need to see how it is related to other parts of the same system. As we do so, we look for both functions and dysfunctions. Let's apply functionalism to the social problem of aging.

Applying Functionalism to Social Problems

From the functionalist perspective, *society* is a social system composed of interconnected parts that function together. Each of those parts, if it is working well, contributes to the equilibrium of society. *Equilibrium* simply means that society's parts are balanced, that they are adjusted to one another. A *social problem,* then, is a condition in which some part of a society is not working well.

To explore functions and dysfunctions of our growing numbers of elderly, let's look at nursing homes.

A common fear is that old age will bring dementia, frailty, dependence, even the lack of control over bodily functions. In nursing homes, the elderly are sometimes treated as though they were little children.

Functions of Nursing Homes. With all the negative news and views about nursing homes, it might surprise you that we are going to look at their *functions.* Let's consider how these homes have helped society adjust to social change. Care of the elderly used to fall primarily upon women's shoulders. Because women worked at home and there were few organized settings for the elderly, daughters, sisters, and aunts cared for the elderly at home. Then came the social change that upset this arrangement among these "parts" of society: More women began to work outside the home, and life expectancy increased. As a result, there were more frail elderly who needed care, but fewer women available to care for them. To replace these former caretakers, nursing homes were developed.

Today, at any one time, 3.1 percent of Americans age 65 and over live in nursing homes (Feng et al. 2011; *Statistical Abstract* 2013:Tables 16, 198). This is the total at any one time. Over the years, 37 percent of all people who reach age 65 or over enter nursing homes (Kemper et al. 2006). Most of the elderly in nursing homes are not typical of older people: Most are ill and have no family, and close to half are age 85 and older. As you can see, nursing homes are a way that society adjusted to social change.

Read on **MySocLab Document:** Care Options for Older Mexican Americans: Issues Affecting Health and Long-Term Care Service Needs

Nursing homes also have *latent* functions. Many adult children find that providing care and shelter for their elderly parents strains their relationship. Some find that after they place a parent in a nursing home, the love that had been obscured by duty gradually recovers. As one 57-year-old daughter reported to sociologists, "My mother demanded rather than earned respect and love. We had a poor past relationship—a love/hate relationship. Now I can do for her because I want to. I can finally love her because I want to" (Smith and Bengtson 1979:441). Because the restored love was not an intended purpose of the nursing home, it is a latent function.

Dysfunctions of Nursing Homes. As you know, nursing homes also have dysfunctions. Few nursing homes are pleasant places. Some analysts refer to them as "houses of death" or "human junkyards." Every time I have visited a nursing home, I have found it to be a depressing experience. Some stink of urine, and it is sad to see lonely people clustered together, most of them waiting to die. After being admitted to a nursing home, most elderly people decline physically and mentally. One reason is the dehumanized way they are treated: segregated from the outside world, denied privacy, and placed under rigid controls.

A common dysfunction of nursing homes is neglect—ignoring patients or not giving them their medications on time (Zhang et al. 2011). Some neglect comes from conscientious workers who are assigned so many responsibilities that they can't keep up with them all. Other neglect comes from workers who don't care about their patients. Here is an example of atrocious neglect:

> *A nursing home patient was sent to the hospital for the treatment of a bedsore. The hospital staff treated the condition and gave the nursing home instructions on how to keep the wound clean and dressed. Several days later, family members noticed an odor and seepage from the wound and asked that the patient be returned to the hospital. The hospital staff looked at the bandage and saw that it had not been changed as they instructed. When the bandage was removed, insects crawled and flew out of the wound. (Harris and Benson 2006:87)*

Another dysfunction is the use of "chemical straitjackets." To control unruly patients, nursing home personnel used to tie patients to chairs or to beds, where they would stay restrained all day. After investigations revealed this abuse, there was a public outcry, and nursing homes turned to drugs such as Thorazine and Prozac to restrain patients. These "chemical straitjackets" keep elderly patients quiet, but they also can reduce people to empty shells of their former selves—or kill them (Levinson 2011). Here is a case that startled investigators:

In a California nursing home nestled in an idyllic setting, the director didn't like disruptions. She found life much more pleasant when everyone was quiet and didn't bother her. Drugging the elderly brought about the peace and quiet she enjoyed—even if her staff had to hold people down and force the drugs down their throats. Three patients died from overdoses. (Hendren 2010)

It is estimated that chemical restraints kill about 15,000 elderly nursing home patients a year (Hendren 2010). If this estimate is anywhere near accurate, do you think that using "chemical restraints" might be a modern form of the "covering up" that the Tiwi used to practice?

Research on nursing homes shows that abuse is common (Harris and Benson 2006). Sociologists Karl Pillemer and David Moore (1989) surveyed nursing homes in New Hampshire. Thirty-one percent of the staff reported that during the past year they had seen physical abuse—patients being pushed, grabbed, shoved, pinched, kicked, or slapped. Eighty-one percent said they had seen psychological abuse—patients being cursed, insulted, yelled at, or threatened. When asked if they themselves had abused patients, 10 percent admitted that they had physically abused them, and 40 percent admitted to psychological abuse. The most abusive staff members were those who were thinking about quitting their jobs and those who thought of patients as being childlike.

With the public painfully aware of abuse in nursing homes, the decision to place an elderly family member in a nursing home can be agonizing. Even though an aged parent is too sick to be cared for at home, to place the parent in a nursing home is viewed by many as a callous denial of love and duty. Nursing homes don't have to be abusive places, however. To see how two major units of society, the government and the family, can work together to provide high-quality care for the elderly, see the Global Glimpse box on the next page.

Functionalism and Social Problems: A Summary

In Sum ▸ Table 2.3 on page 33 presents an overview of functionalism. As you look at this table, begin with the column marked *Action.* This column refers to actions that have taken place in the social system. The examples in this table refer to business, government, medicine, and the family, but we could include other social institutions. The column titled *Manifest Function* refers to a beneficial consequence that was intended by the action. The column titled *Latent Function* refers to a beneficial consequence of the action that was not intended. The last column, *Latent Dysfunction,* refers to an unintended harmful consequence of the action.

Remember that functionalists assume that society is like a well-oiled, self-adjusting machine. They examine how the parts of that machine (society, or some social system) are interrelated, adjusting to one another. As society undergoes change, a social problem arises when some part or parts of society do not adjust to the change and are not functioning properly.

A Global Glimpse

The Coming Tidal Wave: Japan's Elderly

With one of the world's lowest birthrates, Japan's population is aging faster than that of any other nation. In 1950, only 66 Japanese turned 100. Now, it's 1,700 a year. To see how rapidly Japan's population of elderly is growing, look at Table 2.3. Currently, 23 percent of the Japanese are age 65 and over (*Statistical Abstract* 2013: Table1350). In another generation, 2 of every 5 will be elderly. Both Japan's current and projected totals of elderly are unprecedented in the history of the world.

TABLE 2.2 ▸ Japan's Population Age 65 and Older

1950	1975	2000	2025	2050
5%	8%	17%	30%	40%

Think about the implications of such a large percentage of elderly. What will happen to Japan's health care services? About half of the Japanese elderly will be age 75 and over. More than 1 million of them are expected to be bedridden. Another million are likely to be senile. Japan's medical bill will soar. How will Japan be able to meet the health needs of this coming tidal wave of elderly?

We need to place this question in the context of Japanese culture, specifically, the obligations of one generation to another. The Japanese believe that because parents took care of their children, the children are obligated to care for their parents. Unlike in the United States, most aged Japanese live with their adult children. As the number of elderly mushrooms, will the Japanese be able to carry on their traditional caregiving and protective roles?

Because Europe faces similar problems, but not on such an immense scale, Japanese leaders decided that they could learn from the Europeans. But when Japanese observers saw Europe's lower work ethic, higher taxes, and lower savings—all leading to a declining ability to compete in global markets—the Japanese decided to work out their own plan. One goal is to reduce inequality among the aged. With this goal in mind, the government has begun to unify the country's pension systems and has increased spending for social security. To care for the elderly who have no families and those who are the sickest, the government is building thousands of nursing homes.

To improve the quality of life for the healthy elderly, the government is financing 10,000 day service centers. These day service centers will be available to the poor and rich alike. The government will also provide transportation to physiotherapy centers and offer free testing for the early detection of cancer and heart disease. The government has also created a new position called "home helper." After passing a government examination, 100,000 specialists will help the elderly at home.

Japan's low birthrate amidst a surging older population has led to a search for alternative workers to care for the elderly. The Japanese do not want a lot of immigrants, and in an Orwellian twist, Japanese companies are coming up with an unusual answer: Humanoids. One is able to carry patients. Another robot, called Hello Kitty Robo, is able to speak messages and display images. To keep residents of nursing homes mentally active, robots will ask riddles and quiz residents on math problems. They will also chat with residents and ask about their health.

These services and facilities are not intended to replace family care for the elderly but, rather, to supplement it. They are meant to strengthen the family, not crowd it out. Gnawing at these ambitious plans, however, is a disturbing economic reality. For over two decades, Japan has been in the midst of a depression that won't let loose. Japan's federal deficits are huge, and, as with the United States, a financial reckoning looms on the horizon. It seems inevitable that some of Japan's plans for the elderly will have to be shelved. Regardless of economic conditions, however, the tidal wave of elderly is on its way. It will arrive on schedule—whether Japan is ready or not.

Based on Freed 1994; Nishio 1994; Otten 1995; Mackellar and Horlacher 2000; "Hello Kitty Robot ..." 2006; *Statistical Handbook of Japan 2009*; Mori and Scearce 2010.

For Your Consideration

Do you think that the Japanese model of care for the elderly would work in the United States? Why or why not?

TABLE 2.3 ▸ Old Age: A Functionalist Overview

Related Parts of the Social System[1]	Action	Manifest Function	Latent Function	Latent Dysfunction
Economic (business)	Pension and retirement benefits	Provide income and leisure time for the aged	Jobs for younger workers	Displacement of the elderly; loss of self-esteem; loss of purpose
Political (government)	Social Security payments	Stable income for the aged; dignity in old age	Employment for 70,000 people by the Social Security Administration	Inadequate income; many recipients live on the edge of poverty
Medical	Technological developments; gerontological specialties	Longer and healthier lives for the population	The elderly become more independent	The Social Security system becomes costly
	Medicare and Medicaid	Provide good health care for the elderly	Financing bonanza for the medical profession	High cost; "Rip-off" nursing homes
Family	Adult children live apart from their parents	Independence of both younger and older generations	Institutionalized care for the elderly; greater mobility of younger workers	Isolation of elderly parents; loneliness and despair

[1]As used here, "parts" of the social system are social institutions.

Source: By the author.

Conflict Theory and Social Problems

Introducing Conflict Theory

2.3 Explain conflict theory and apply it to social problems.

"We couldn't disagree more," reply conflict theorists to the functionalist position. The parts of society do not work together harmoniously. If you look below the surface, you will see that society's parts are competing with one another for limited resources. There are only so many resources to go around, and the competition for them is so severe that conflict is barely kept in check. Whether they recognize it or not, the elderly are competing with younger people for money and health care. If the competition heats up, open conflict between the younger and the elderly could erupt, throwing society into turmoil. In short, the guiding principle of social life is disequilibrium and conflict, not equilibrium and harmony, as the functionalists say.

From the conflict perspective, social problems are the natural and inevitable outcome of struggle over limited resources. No matter what a social problem may look like on its surface, at its essence is conflict between groups. As the more powerful exploit society's resources, they oppress the less powerful, creating such social problems as poverty, discrimination, and war. As those who are exploited react to their oppression, other social problems emerge: street crime, escapist drug abuse, suicide, homicide, riots, revolution, and terrorism. To study social problems, we need to penetrate their surfaces and expose their basic, underlying conflict.

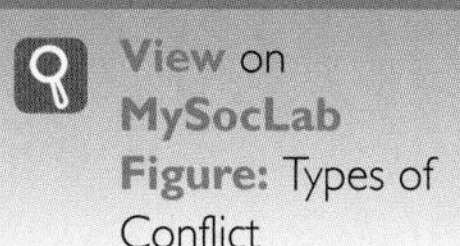

The Development of Conflict Theory

View on MySocLab Figure: Karl Marx's Model of Society

Karl Marx: Capitalism and Conflict. Karl Marx (1818–1883), the founder of **conflict theory**, witnessed the Industrial Revolution that transformed Europe. Dirty, crowded cities grew even dirtier and more crowded as farmers and laborers in poverty fled rural areas to seek work in factories. With men hungry for work, competing for the few jobs available, the new factory owners were able to pay near-starvation wages. Poverty and exploitation grew, political unrest followed, and upheaval swept across Europe.

Shocked by the suffering and inhumanity that he saw, Marx concluded that the hallmark of history is a struggle for power. In this struggle, some group always gains the top position, and, inevitably, that group oppresses the groups beneath it. Marx also concluded that a major turning point in this historical struggle occurred when **capitalism** became dominant in the Western world—that is, when a small group of people gained control over the means of production and made profit their goal. As machinery replaced workers' tools, the **capitalists** (owners of the capital, factories, and equipment) gained the power to exploit workers.

Because tens of thousands of families from farms and villages had crowded into the cities in a desperate search for work, the capitalists, who owned the means of production, were able to impose miserable working conditions. They paid workers little—sometimes only enough to buy a loaf of bread for 12 hours work—and fired them at will. Through their money, the capitalists also controlled politicians. When workers rebelled, the capitalists could count on the police to use violence to bring the workers under control. "This misery," said Marx, "is going to lead to a bloody day of reckoning when the workers overthrow their oppressors. The workers will establish a classless society in which the goal will be not profits for the few but, rather, the good of the many."

In Marx's time, workers were at the mercy of their bosses. They lacked what some workers today take for granted—a minimum wage, 8-hour workdays, 5-day workweeks, coffee breaks, paid vacations, medical benefits, sick leave, unemployment compensation, pensions, social security, even the right to strike. Conflict theorists remind us that the workers who enjoy such benefits today have them not because of the generous hearts of the rich but because workers at an earlier period fought for them—sometimes to the death.

Georg Simmel: Subordinates and Superordinates. Some sociologists have extended conflict theory well beyond the relations between workers and capitalists. Sociologist Georg Simmel (1858–1918), for example, compared the relationships of superordinates (people who occupy higher positions) with subordinates (those who are in lower positions). Simmel noted that a main concern of superordinates is to protect their positions of privilege. Because subordinates possess some power, however, the more powerful must take them into consideration as they make their decisions (Coser 1977). Consequently, superordinate–subordinate relationships are marked not by one-way naked power but by exchange. If employers want to lower the benefits of a pension plan, for example, they must get unions to agree. In return, the workers will insist on a trade-off, such as increased job security.

Simmel argued that conflict also has benefits. For example, when the members of a group confront an external threat, they tend to pull together (Giddens 1969; Turner 1978). In times of war, for instance, antagonistic groups often shelve their differences in order to work together for the good of the nation. Workers might give up their right to strike, as U.S. workers did during World War II. During this war, the U.S. Justice Department even asked Lucky Luciano, head of the Mafia at that time, to spy on dock workers. When the Russians invaded Afghanistan in 1979, clans that hated each other worked together for 10 years to repel them. The same thing happened during the United States' experience in that country.

Lewis Coser: Conflict in Social Networks. Sociologist Lewis Coser (1913–2003) analyzed why conflict is especially likely to develop among people who have close relationships with one another. He pointed out that whether we refer to husbands and wives or to bosses and workers, each is part of a system in which the parties have worked out expectations about their relative power, responsibilities, and rewards. These expectations, however, are easily upset. Actions by either party, such as making decisions to adjust to changing times, can offend the other and lead to conflict.

Applying Conflict Theory to Social Problems

Social Conflict and Social Security. As we apply the conflict perspective to the elderly, let's see how Social Security came about. In this drama, the three major players are elderly workers, younger workers, and employers. A fourth, Congress, also appears. From this perspective, Congress represents the interests of the employers.

Let's start with the historical background. Because of their experience, older workers used to be prized. Before production by machine, work took a lot of skill, and it took years to develop these skills. Then came the Industrial Revolution, which turned things upside down. To make things by machinery rather than by hand didn't take much experience or skill. With young workers learning to run the machines quickly—and willing to work for less—the owners fired many of the elderly. This pushed the elderly into poverty, because in those days there was neither unemployment compensation nor Social Security. By the 1920s, *two-thirds* of all Americans over 65 could not support themselves (Holtzman 1963; Hudson 1978). In short, industrialization transformed the elderly from a productive and respected group to a deprived and humiliated group.

Then the Great Depression struck, bringing even more suffering to millions of elderly. In 1930, in the midst of national despair, Francis Everett Townsend, a physician, spearheaded a social movement to rally the elderly into a political force. He soon had one-third of all Americans over 60 enrolled in his Townsend Clubs. From this base of power, the elderly demanded "old-age pensions" (Holtzman 1963). Townsend's ultimate goal was for the federal government to levy a national sales tax of 2 percent to provide $200 a month for every person over 60. This is the equivalent of about $2,600 a month today. Townsend argued that the elderly's increased spending would lift the nation out of the Depression.

By 1934, the Townsend Clubs had gathered hundreds of thousands of signatures on petitions, and the Townsend Plan went before Congress. This was an election year, and Congress felt vulnerable to a grassroots revolt by older people. But Congress was caught in a bind: About 25 percent of workers were unemployed, and the country was

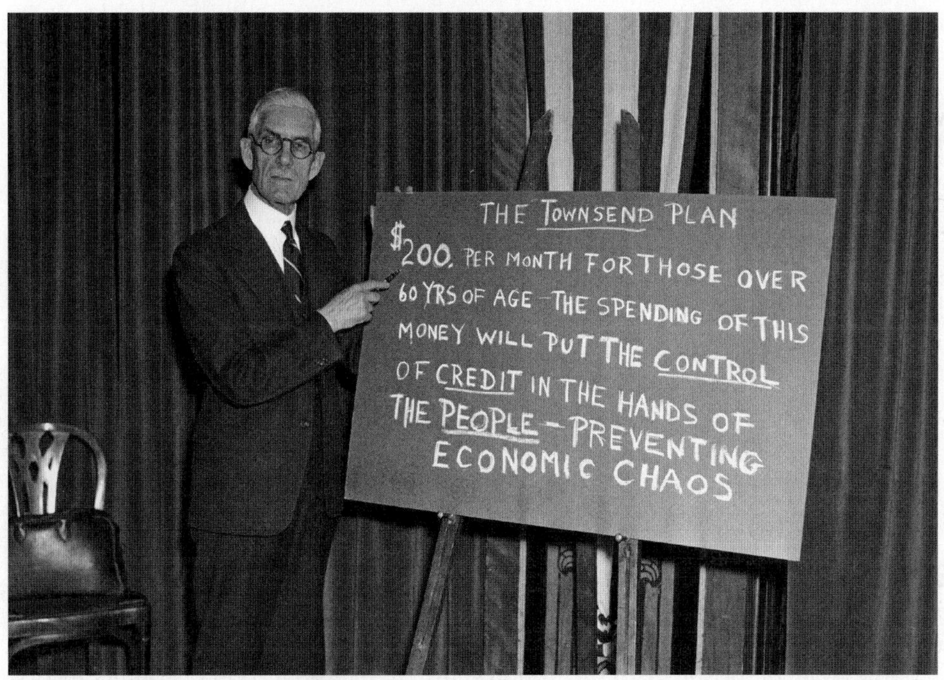

The U.S. elderly are a potent political force today. They were not considered so until Dr. Francis Everett Townsend (pictured here) organized them as a political force in the 1930s. Townsend proposed a radical $200 per month pension plan for the elderly in the midst of the Great Depression. His plan and campaign against Congress frightened politicians.

strapped for money. Many also feared that if younger people knew that the government was going to give them pensions when they were old, it would sap their incentive to work and save (Schottland 1963). Congress looked for a way out. But how could they reject the Townsend Plan without angering the clamoring crowds of elderly? Seizing the opportunity to take center stage, President Franklin Roosevelt announced his own, more modest Social Security plan in June 1934—with the first payment starting 8 years later. Relieved at this way out of its bind, Congress embraced Roosevelt's proposal.

Although the Townsend Clubs did not get their plan passed, they did force Congress to pass Social Security. The clubs then turned to the goal of improving Social Security. Benefits were not scheduled to begin until 1942, which would leave millions of workers without support. As the Great Depression lingered, dragging even more old people into poverty, the clubs stepped up their pressure. As a result, Congress voted to begin paying Social Security benefits in 1940 and to increase the amounts paid to the destitute elderly (called old-age assistance grants).

In Sum ▸ When conflict theorists analyze a social problem, they look for how interest groups compete for scarce resources. In this example, they emphasize that today's Social Security benefits did not come from generous hearts in Congress, but from the political power of the elderly, who had banded together to push their own interests. To appease the elderly and avoid a political crisis, Congress gave in, but granted as little as it thought it could get by with. Only when the elderly stepped up the pressure did Congress increase benefits—and that reluctantly. The elderly, however, paid dearly for their benefits: They were removed from the workforce when Congress set a mandatory retirement age of 65 (which was revoked in 1978). This, in turn, gave employers the goal they wanted: a younger, less costly workforce.

Conflict Theory and Social Problems: A Summary

Conflict and Social Problems. At the root of each social problem lies competition over the distribution of power and privilege. This means that social problems are inevitable, for power and privilege are limited and groups are competing for them. Most conflict is limited to political struggle, not a battle to the death. Retired Americans, for example, have not fought bloody battles in the streets, but they have formed political lobbies to compete for resources with other groups. Understanding that power and privilege lie at the root of social problems helps analysts to penetrate the surface and pinpoint what any particular social problem is all about.

Two Types of Social Problems. From the conflict perspective, social problems come in two forms. One is the trouble experienced by people who are exploited by the powerful. The other is the trouble experienced by the powerful when the exploited resist, rebel, or even appeal to higher values. Although their resources are limited, the exploited do find ways to resist. Some go on hunger strikes or campaign for political office. Others take up arms against those in power. As we saw with the Townsend movement, the elderly—a group weak in and of itself—were able to unite and seize the initiative during a troubled period, forcing a change to improve their circumstances.

Introducing Feminist Theory

2.4 Explain feminist theory and apply it to social problems.

In the 1970s, sociologists started to apply the conflict perspective to the relationships of women and men. From their analyses came **feminist theory**, which examines male–female relationships from the perspective of the powerful oppressing the powerless and the reactions to that oppression. Feminists go beyond studying these relationships: They also want to change them and, in so doing, to transform society. They argue, as Marx did, that the first step in bringing about fundamental change is for the oppressed to become aware of the source of their oppression. In this application of conflict theory, women must become aware of how their oppression is rooted in their relationships with men.

Just as Marx took a broad historical view as he examined the relationship of workers and employers and the control of resources, so feminist theorists have taken a broad historical view. As they examine historical relationships between women and men, they place their analytical lens on **patriarchy**, the dominance of men-as-a-group over women-as-a-group. They stress that throughout history men have had greater power than women in both public and private spheres and that men have exercised this power to control women. Feminist theorists analyze how men maintain and create boundaries and obstacles to prevent women from gaining or exercising power.

The Development of Feminist Theory

In the 1970s, *feminist theory* was an umbrella term used to describe the application of conflict theory to the relationships of women and men, with an emphasis on the oppression of women and the need to bring about fundamental change. In the 1980s and in later years, feminist theorists split into several branches. Here are five of the main ones. As you can see, each makes its own application of feminist theory (Code 2000).

- **Radical feminism** The central thesis of radical feminists is that we must dismantle society in order to get rid of patriarchy. The goal of radical feminists is to free both men and women of rigid gender roles by waging war against patriarchy. This type of feminism attracts much negative publicity, and many people assume that this is the only kind of feminism there is.
- **Liberal feminism** The central argument of liberal feminists is that all people are created equal and deserve access to equal rights. Liberal feminists argue that patriarchy and oppression exist because our institutions socialize men and women into believing oppressive ideology.
- **Socialist feminism** Socialist feminists, the closest kin to Marx, stress that there is a direct link between capitalism and the oppression of women. The main rewards go to those who perform in the workplace, not in the home. Women's traditional work in the home is not respected because it often produces nothing tangible.
- **Cultural feminism** Cultural feminists argue that we need to appreciate the biological differences between men and women. They claim that women are inherently kinder and gentler than men. If women ruled the world, patriarchy, oppression, and capitalism would not exist, and the world would be a better place.
- **Ecofeminism** Ecofeminists stress that patriarchy is oppressive not only for women but also for the environment. They point out that men want to dominate not only women but also nature. Women need to free themselves from the dominance of men and take the lead in protecting the natural environment.

I don't want you to get the idea from this list that there are just five branches of feminist theory. These are simply five of its many divisions. One variety after another has evolved, and today there are such branches as indiginest feminism, postcolonial feminism, spiritual feminism, radical-cultural feminism, eco-socialist feminism, and even anarchist and cyborg feminism (Code 2000). Regardless of the particular branching, the central point that unites them is their focus on unequal power relations between men and women. Let's take a quick look at how feminist theory applies to social problems.

Applying Feminist Theory to Social Problems: Focusing on Gender

To apply feminist theory to social problems, we examine relations between women and men. To continue with our example of the elderly, we can begin by focusing on *the gender division of labor,* how men and women are sorted into different types of work.

"Work" in this context refers not only to jobs but also to types of activities. Caring for elderly parents, for example, is usually defined as "women's work." This places the burden for the care of the elderly mainly on daughters, not sons. Ideas about paid work also come into play, especially the common assumption that a husband's wages are more vital than his wife's. This encourages men to focus more on their work and less on family relations, including the care of elderly parents.

The number of elderly has been increasing over the past century and will continue to do so in the foreseeable future. Who will take care of the growing numbers of frail elderly? Will we simply multiply our nursing homes, those places perceived by the elderly as vile places to go to die? This isn't what the elderly want, and here is where the gender issue I just mentioned comes into play. Sociologist Barbara Mascio (2007) found that elderly parents still expect their daughters to take care of them, regardless of whether their daughters have the money or the time to do so.

This is just one aspect of the social problem of the elderly that we could look at through the lens of feminist theory. The point to remember is that feminist theory views the root of social problems as conflict that originates in patriarchy. From this perspective, social problems are seen as the result of a struggle over power and privilege among men and women.

Symbolic Interactionism and Social Problems

Introducing Symbolic Interactionism

2.5 Explain symbolic interactionism and apply it to social problems.

The Significance of Symbols in Social Life. The sociological theory that focuses on how we make sense out of life is called **symbolic interactionism**. The essence of this perspective is that we see the world through **symbols**, things to which we attach meaning and that we use to communicate with one another. Symbolic interactionists study how symbols, such as the terms we use to classify people, give us our view of the world. As we use the symbols that our culture provides to communicate with one another, we share and reinforce the ways we look at life. The images on television, movies, and videos, the printed and spoken word, our gestures, tone of voice, clothing, even hairstyles—all are symbols by which we communicate ideas, even views of life. And our views include what we consider to be social problems.

This might seem vague, so let's go back to our example of the elderly. What does "old age" mean? When we first see a person who is advanced in years, we tend to classify him or her as an "old person." As we look at this person, we tend to see the characteristics that our culture packs into the symbol "old." In our culture, this symbol often includes being weak, unattractive, unstylish, and over the hill. Because everyone internalizes the symbols that dominate their culture, many elderly also see themselves in such terms. "Old person," however, doesn't mean the same thing in all cultures. In some cultures, old age brings images of wisdom or power or privilege. Someone from such a culture, then, tends to perceive an old person in a different way—and so does that elderly person.

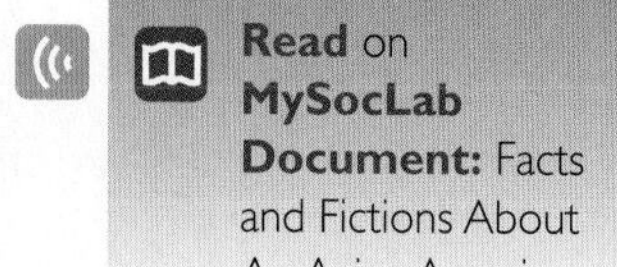
Read on **MySocLab** **Document:** Facts and Fictions About An Aging America

Changing Symbols, Changing Perception. Biologically, old age creeps up on us all. As the years pass, we feel our bodies gradually age. Sociologically, however, old age comes suddenly—perhaps at retirement, with the first Social Security check, or upon admittance to a nursing home. Our images of old age are largely negative. We use phrases such as old and sick, old and crabby, old and dependent, old and useless. Take your pick. None is pleasant.

During an earlier period of the United States, though, "old" summoned positive images. Back then—and strange to our ears—"old" was associated with wisdom, ability, generosity, even graciousness and beauty. Why did earlier generations have ideas of old age so startlingly different from ours? To find out, Andrew Achenbaum (1978) traced the history of aging in the United States. He found that 200 years ago people placed a high value on the elderly because most people died young. With so few people reaching old age, those who did were admired for their accomplishment. The younger also perceived the elderly as having accumulated valuable knowledge during their lives. At this time, people also placed a higher value on being actively involved in work, and to quit working simply because of age was considered foolish. Because the elderly were more skilled at their jobs—this was before machinery displaced individual skills—younger workers looked up to them.

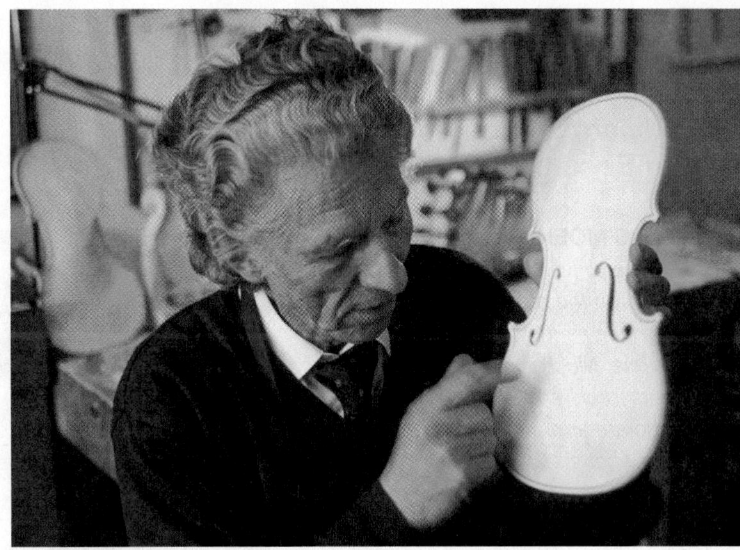

Prior to machine production, the elderly were given high respect because of their skills. Respect for the elderly dropped as machines replaced human skills. Exceptions remain, such as this artisan in Cremona, Italy.

How did such a fundamental shift occur in the meaning of old age? Achenbaum traces this change back to the late 1800s, an era that saw major advances in public health, especially improvements in sanitation. As a result, many people reached old age, and no longer was being elderly a distinction. During this time, ideas about work were changing, too. With machinery and mass production, work was becoming "deskilled." No longer did it take years of apprenticeship under highly skilled workers to learn how to do a job. The new machines were social levelers; they made the younger workers just as knowledgeable and productive as the older workers. As the elderly lost the uniqueness that had brought them respect, the meaning of "old person" began to change. Old age began to suggest uselessness rather than usefulness, foolishness rather than wisdom.

Don't miss this central aspect of symbolic interactionism and social problems: *Because symbols change, so do the matters considered to be social problems.* Earlier in our history, when most people died young, some people survived the odds and reached old age. At that time, if they had problems because of their age, those problems were matters for them or their family to handle. They were no one else's responsibility. Old age was a *personal* problem, not a *social* problem. Today, in contrast, with so many people reaching old age, we think of elderly people as a group. We tend to lump them together, and we consider social action (laws and policies) to be appropriate for solving their problems. A major transition has occurred: *What was once a personal problem has become a social problem.*

In Sum ▸ From our brief review of what it meant to be elderly during an earlier period in the United States, we can see that as society changes, so do its symbols. Because the term *social problem* is also a symbol, what people consider to be a social problem also changes from one historical period to another. What we now take for granted, we may later see as a problem, and what we now see as a problem, we may later take for granted. *From the perspective of symbolic interactionism, then, social problems are whatever people in a society define as social problems.*

For more on how changing symbols produce changed perception and how different social locations lead to different views of the social problem of old age, read the *Spotlight on Social Research* box on the next page.

The Development of Symbolic Interactionism

Symbols are so essential for what we become that we could call them the element that separates us from the rest of life on this planet. Symbols allow us to think about other people and objects, even when they are not present. We also symbolize our own self, that is, we think about our self in certain ways, such as young, attractive, and personable.

How we symbolize our self is vital for the choices we make. For example, as we saw in Chapter 1, some women risk unwanted pregnancies because the use of contraceptives would conflict with their self-image. To match our self-image, we choose the clothing we wear and

Spotlight on Social Research

Studying Young People Who Became Old

PHYLLIS MOEN, *professor of sociology at the University of Minnesota, does research on the problems and challenges people face as they advance through the life course. Much of her research focuses on the careers and working lives of people who are approaching retirement age. Here is what she wrote for your text.*

Gerontologists are scholars who study older people. I became a gerontologist by the back door. I started out (and continue to be) a life-course sociologist, interested in people's pathways through work and family roles and relationships, and how our pathways are shaped by gender and social policy.

When I was a young professor at Cornell University, I found out that one of my colleagues (Robin M. Williams, Jr.) had, many years previously (in the 1950s), interviewed a random sample of young women in Elmira, New York. This is the only project he had never completed, and Robin regretted over the years never having followed through on it. One of my graduate students, Donna Dempster-McClain, and I got together to study his 1950s data and were fascinated by the differences in women's lives then from our own. Donna and I got the bright idea of reinterviewing these women 30 years later, and reinterviewing their (now adult) daughters as well. We thought this a wonderful opportunity to document the ways tremendous social changes in gender roles touched women's lives across the generations. With the help of graduate students, other committed researchers, and a grant from the National Institute on Aging, we found almost all of these women and reinterviewed them and their daughters, capturing their remarkable life histories from the 1950s through the 1980s. What we knew cognitively but hadn't counted on emotionally was that these young mothers in the 1950s had, three decades later, aged. And that is how I got into studying older people!

Because my focus has been on lives and not any one age group, my perspective is not on people as being "old." I always encourage students to capture the life histories of older people, to see the remarkable ways they have come to be the people they are today. Students who do so often find that interviewing earlier cohorts (and especially their own grandparents, great grandparents, aunts and uncles) offers a window on history and time. If you ask them, you may find that these people born in a different time and into a different world have defined social problems very differently when they were in their teens and twenties. They certainly have had distinctive experiences, opportunities, and challenges, and as a consequence, continue to have distinctive viewpoints about contemporary social issues.

Asking about the timing of people's trajectories and transitions in education, paid work, and family life helps to reveal the "person" behind the stereotypes and myths about older people. The interviewees may be in their 60s, 70s, or 80s, but still see themselves as the same person they were years ago—the kid attending school, the employee starting a job, part of a couple buying the first house and raising a family—in what seems to them like only yesterday. I continue to study differences in life pathways by cohort and gender, especially as people move from their career jobs to what are traditionally thought of as the retirement years.

My research breaks the myths and stereotypes about retirement as the gateway to being "old." I find that most older workers and retirees in their 60s and early 70s want to work—whether for pay or as a volunteer, but not full-time! Boomers can look forward to unparalleled health and longevity as they age, along with potential "second acts": opportunities for flexible new careers, whether as paid employees or as unpaid volunteers. The large baby boom cohort confronts this transition in a climate of uncertainty and ambiguity, where career jobs and pensions often disappear in the face of globalization, mergers, and downsizing.

And, for the first time in history, women are also retiring in unprecedented numbers. Couples often face two retirements: his and hers. My research shows that couples may live together longer "retired" than they did prior to retirement. But they seldom plan for retirement, beyond thinking about the age or date they will retire. It is the same way many young people plan for the wedding but not the years of married life. And yet the retirees I interview typically say they should have planned for life in retirement: how they will spend the 10, 20, or 30 years of healthy, "youthful" living they can now look forward to.

the type of car we drive, as well as the music we listen to, the type of career we aspire to, and for some, even the shampoo we use. Symbols are central to our lives and relationships.

Let's look at two of the theorists who developed symbolic interactionism.

Mead and Taking the Role of the Other. George Herbert Mead (1863–1931) taught at the University of Chicago, where symbolic interactionism flourished. At one point, from the 1920s to the 1940s, this department of sociology and this perspective were so intertwined that the term **Chicago School of Sociology** was used to refer to both.

Read on **MySocLab Document:** George Herbert Mead, Self and Society

Mead focused on the role of symbols in social life. Symbols are so important, he said, that without them we couldn't even have social life. What he meant is that symbols allow us to have goals, to plan, to evaluate, even to know what love is. Mead concluded that even our self-concept, which evolves during childhood, is based on symbols. One of the major means by which we develop our self-concept is learning to **take the role of the other**. That is, as children we gradually become capable of putting ourselves in someone else's shoes, able to understand how that person feels and thinks and to anticipate how he or she will act. After learning to understand the perspective of a few individuals, we learn to take the role of people in general—which Mead called the **generalized other**.

One of Mead's favorite examples was baseball. Let's use it.

Suppose that you are a high school senior. After an exhausting, but exhilarating, season, your team has made it to the playoffs for the state championship. Now, in the final game of the series, it is the bottom of the ninth inning. The score is tied, there are two outs, and the bases are loaded. You are at bat. Everything depends on you. You can imagine the intense pressure you would feel, unlike anything you've experienced before. This could be your moment of glory—or of bitter defeat and humiliation. In a moment, you will either be carried on the shoulders of shouting teammates or walking dejectedly, head down, to the dugout.

At this climactic moment, you probably would sense a heightened awareness of what Mead called the *generalized other*. In this instance, the term would refer to your teammates, your coach, the opposing team, your family, and the fans. You sense how they will feel if you strike out or get a hit.

Cooley and the Looking-Glass Self. Charles Horton Cooley (1864–1929), who taught at the University of Michigan, was also a central figure in the development of symbolic interactionism. He analyzed how the self develops through interaction with others. He said that *people come to view themselves as they think others perceive them.*

Read on **MySocLab Document:** Charles Horton Cooley, The Looking-Glass Self

Cooley said that our interactions with others create a **looking-glass self**, which he summarized in the following couplet

Each to each a looking-glass
Reflects the other that doth pass.

By *looking-glass self*, Cooley meant that our self has three elements: (1) how we imagine we appear to others, (2) how we think others feel about what they perceive, and (3) how we feel about this reflected image. An essential aspect of our looking-glass self is that it produces the way we feel about our self. We can apply this principle to the elderly: If a society reflects negative images to its old people, the elderly tend to think of themselves negatively.

Berger and Luckmann and the Social Construction of Reality. Sociologists Peter Berger (1929–) and Thomas Luckmann (1927–) are key figures in the development of one of symbolic interactionism's major concepts, the **social construction of reality**. Let's take a brief look at this strange-sounding term and see if we can bring it down to earth.

The idea is simple enough. Things happen to you, and when they do you have to figure out what they mean. For example, if a stranger makes an unexpected contact with you, you have to decide whether it is a "shove," an "accidental touch," or even a "groping." These three are significantly different, and you can see how your reaction will depend on how you interpret the contact. As you go through life, then, you continuously make sense out of what happens to you. A more formal way of saying this is that you are involved in the social construction of reality.

Applying the Social Construction of Reality: When Does Old Age Begin? ▸ The concept is simple, but its implications are profound. It means that reality does not come with built-in meanings, but, rather, you construct your realities as you apply symbols to your experiences in life. Let's apply this idea to the question of when "old age" begins.

Did you know that "old age" is rooted more in social experiences than in biology? Certainly, there is nothing magical about turning 65—or any other age—that automatically makes someone "old." Yet the 65th birthday has become a standard marker of old age. Why? Strangely, it is rooted in 19th-century German politics. At that time, Otto von Bismarck (1815–1898), the architect of the German empire, was fighting a political movement known as socialism. In order to weaken the appeal of socialism to Germans, Bismarck pioneered the idea of social security payments to older people. But at what age should such payments begin? To force some of his generals out of power, Bismarck chose 65 as the mandatory retirement age. Bismarck's arbitrary decision stuck, becoming a symbol that significantly affects how we perceive age today.

Applying the Social Construction of Reality: What Does Suicide Mean? ▸ Not all cultures have the same symbols, so the social construction of reality changes from culture to culture. This yields remarkably different views of life. Consider the family of a Japanese military officer who has purposely fallen on his sword after losing a battle. To understand why he took his life, their culture provides the symbols of honor and duty, and Japanese interpret the individual's death in those terms. Now think about Americans who have just learned that their sister has committed suicide: They don't have symbols like this to help them figure out why she took her life. Their symbols include the responsibility of friends and family in preventing suicide, which leads them to such questions as "Am I to blame for not picking up on hints of suicide?" "Should I feel guilty?" "What could I have done differently?"

Although the answers that the Japanese and the Americans get regarding the suicide are different, the principle is the same. Both the Japanese and the Americans are using the symbols their culture provides to socially construct reality. They come up with different answers because they use a different set of symbols. To catch a glimpse of Americans as they work out answers to the "why" of suicide, see the Thinking Critically box on the next page.

In Sum ▸ The social construction of reality is part of everyday life. We all try to make sense of what happens to us—whether this means figuring out why we received an A or an F on a test, why we were promoted or fired at work, or even why we like or dislike a television program or video game. In short, the events of life do not come with built-in meanings, and we all use the symbols provided by our culture to make sense out of life. Symbolic interactionists call this process *the social construction of reality.*

Applying Symbolic Interactionism to Social Problems

The Social Construction of Social Problems. What does it mean to say that social problems are socially constructed? This means that social problems don't have an independent existence. They are not like grapefruit that you pick out at the grocery store. Social problems don't exist until some condition of society is called a social problem. Until then, that condition is simply a characteristic of society, like any other.

To make this point clearer, let's go back to the elderly. That there are old people in a society does not mean that there is a social problem in that society. The status of the elderly depends on how the elderly are viewed or labeled. We saw how the elderly were once admired and respected in the United States and how their status dropped sharply with the Industrial Revolution. At this point in our history, when few of the elderly are poor, their status is improving. If this continues, we might come to the point where more positive features of social life are associated with old age and the elderly receive greater respect. In short, because social problems are socially constructed, what is considered a social problem changes over time.

Thinking Critically About Social Problems

Making Sense of Suicide: Socially Constructing Reality

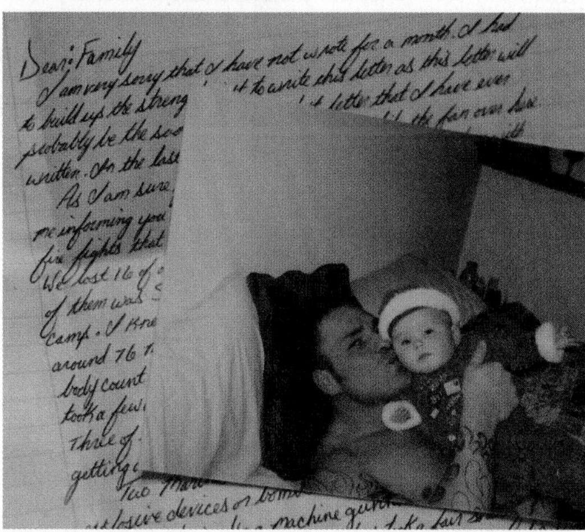

When this man took his life, his family and friends went through a process called the social construction of reality.

Some of the most difficult research I have done was to interview the friends and family of people who had committed suicide. Their wrenching emotional turmoil created similar feelings within me. The interviews yielded rich data, however, and here are some things I found concerning suicide and the social construction of reality.

After someone commits suicide, people who were close to that person try to make sense out of what happened. As their shock wears off, they mentally relive events associated with the dead person. They begin to interpret these events in light of the suicide. As they do so, the events take on new meaning. Survivors ask why the individual took his or her life. As they explore this "why," some confront the horrifying possibility that they themselves could have been part of the reason. They then face this burning issue: "If I had done something different, maybe he (she) would still be alive."

This search for meaning and for cause leads survivors to reconstruct the past, which can be a tortured process. Listen to this father of a 25-year-old who shot himself with a handgun. You can hear the questions that plague him as he reconstructs events in his search for answers regarding his son's death:

> I've wondered where it began if it was suicide. Was it in grade school? Or college? Or was it all this girl? Could I have done something different? Or wouldn't it have helped? Wondering which is right and which is wrong… . I think this thing or that thing could have been done to change the course of events. But you just don't know. I even thought, "If we hadn't moved from St. Louis to Crestview years ago."

As a part of our everyday life, we all use the symbols our culture provides to interpret what happens to us, that is, to socially construct our reality. When it comes to death by suicide, however, our culture does not offer satisfactory symbols. This leaves people confused as they search for meaning. Consider how different it is when someone dies from a disease. That person's family members don't face this type of challenge to the self. Seldom does the symbol *disease* trigger the question "Could I have done something different?" Instead, the symbol of disease points to causes beyond us—to germs and chances in life and other factors usually beyond a person's control. The symbol *suicide,* in contrast, denies us this more comfortable interpretation of causation.

Our culture offers many symbols to help people adjust to the death of loved ones. Among them is "God's will." This symbol, if it can be used, moves causation clearly beyond the survivors of the deceased, allowing easier acceptance of the event. If God called the individual home, the survivors certainly bear no responsibility for the death. The family members of a suicide, however, are denied this category. Listen to this woman as she struggles with the meaning of her husband's death:

> Well, I would have felt in my own mind that God had called him from the earth and that he had a reason for calling him, and that we could have accepted it as Christians that it was the will of God, and that we could feel in our hearts that God, in his tenderness, had taken him up with him. I can't feel that this was the will of God.

In Sum

From these examples, you can see that culture provides symbols (labels, categories, concepts, words, and terms) that people use to interpret the events of their lives. By looking at how the survivors of suicide search for meaning, we can observe the social construction of reality as it occurs. We can see that the usual symbols offered by our culture are denied these people, plunging them into uncertainty, a search for meaning that often ends in despair. These examples can make us more aware of how we use our culture's symbols to provide meaning for our experiences. You can see that if our culture provided different symbols, we would interpret our experiences differently. The social construction of reality, a concept sometimes difficult to understand, is an ordinary part of our everyday lives.

For Your Consideration

Why do the suicides of a Japanese general after a failed battle and the suicide of a lonely U.S. woman in her 80s have different meanings? Where do those meanings come from? What is meant by *the social construction of reality* and how is suicide an example of it?

Symbolic Interactionism and Social Problems: A Summary

Symbolic interactionists stress that social problems are socially constructed. This means that a social problem is an objective condition of society that people have labeled a "social problem." If they don't place this label on that objective condition, it is not a social problem. If they do, it is. To understand a social problem, then, we need to understand how some objective condition was turned into a social problem. We must also take into account what that problem means to the people involved in it.

In the coming chapters, we will apply these theoretical perspectives to the social problems that we analyze. To conclude this chapter, let's look at the probable future of "old age" as a social problem.

The Future of the Problem: The Pendulum Swings

Changing Objective Conditions and Subjective Concerns

2.6 Discuss the possible generational struggle regarding the elderly.

Images of poor, ill, neglected grandparents have been used to promote social programs for elderly Americans. Such images are misleading. Economic growth and the expansion of state and federal programs have greatly reduced the poverty rate of the aged. Consider this: In 1970, 25 percent of the elderly were poor, but now just 9 percent are (*Statistical Abstract* 1990:Table 746; 2013:Table 725). This means that the elderly's rate of poverty today is considerably *less* than the 15 percent overall rate of poverty in the United States.

Will the poverty rate of the elderly remain low? To try to move the United States out of its current economic crisis, Congress passed a series of spending bills that total an amount that none of us can grasp. The total runs perhaps $3 trillion or more, a bill that future generations are going to have to pay. If the nation tightens its belt as the bills come due, the elderly might be asked to tighten theirs, too. Reduction of federal programs for the elderly would mean an increase in their poverty rate. With the political clout of today's elderly accompanied by the ardent desire of our elected officials to remain in office, however, any serious reductions are unlikely.

A major concern of the public and of politicians is the costs of health care for the elderly. Look at Figure 2.1 on the next page. You can see how the costs of Medicare and Medicaid have soared. These costs have exceeded the wildest projections of earlier years. As you know, the cost of Social Security is also a growing concern. In 1950, Social Security payments ran $784 million, but today they run $725 billion. Analysts are alarmed when they see that today's payout is 925 times larger than the amount paid in 1950 (*Statistical Abstract* 1997:Table 518; 2013:Table 555).

These increases cannot continue indefinitely. If we project the escalating costs of Social Security, Medicare, and Medicaid into the indefinite future, they eventually would be larger than the entire production (gross domestic product) of the United States. This is impossible. So when and how will this change? No one has the answer, but you can see that a crisis is in the making. Could this crisis even pit the young against the elderly? Let's turn to this possibility.

The Emerging Struggle

First, look at another reason that the objective condition of this social problem is likely to get worse. Today, about one of seven or eight Americans is age 65 or over, but from Figure 2.2 on page 46, you can see that in about 20 years or so, this total will jump to one of five. As discussed in the Issues in Social Problems box on p. 47, one of the fastest growing groups of the elderly is those who are age 100 or more. The rapid increase of the elderly means that the costs of Social Security and health care will increase even faster than they are now.

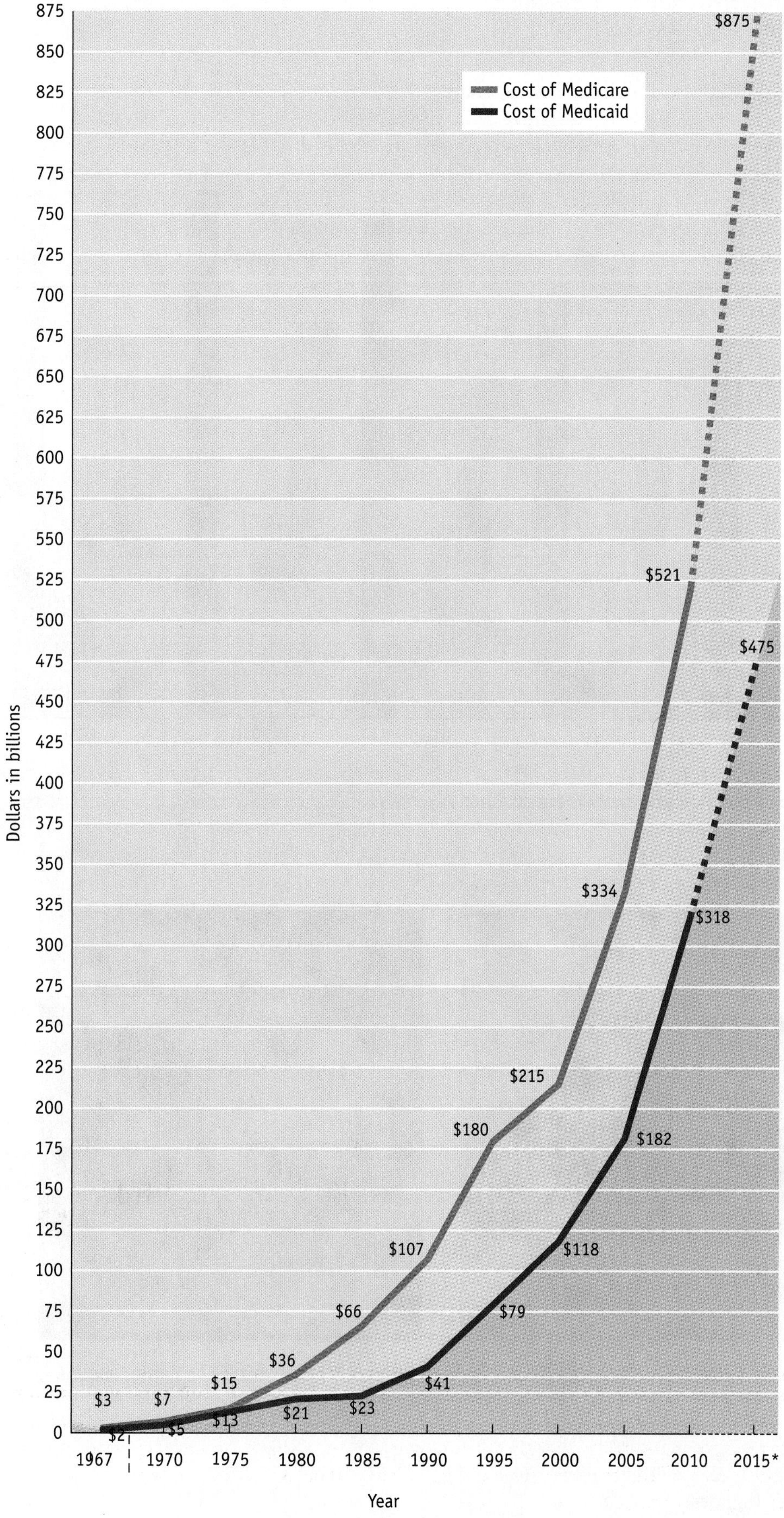

FIGURE 2.1 ▸ Health Care Costs for the Elderly and Disabled

Note: Medicare is intended for the elderly and disabled, Medicaid for the poor. About 20 percent of Medicaid payments ($63 billion) go to the elderly. (*Statistical Abstract* 2013:Table 154).

Source: By the author. Based on *Statistical Abstract of the United States*, various years and 2013:Tables 147, 155.

Explore on MySocLab Activity: The Graying of America

FIGURE 2.2 ▸ The Graying of America

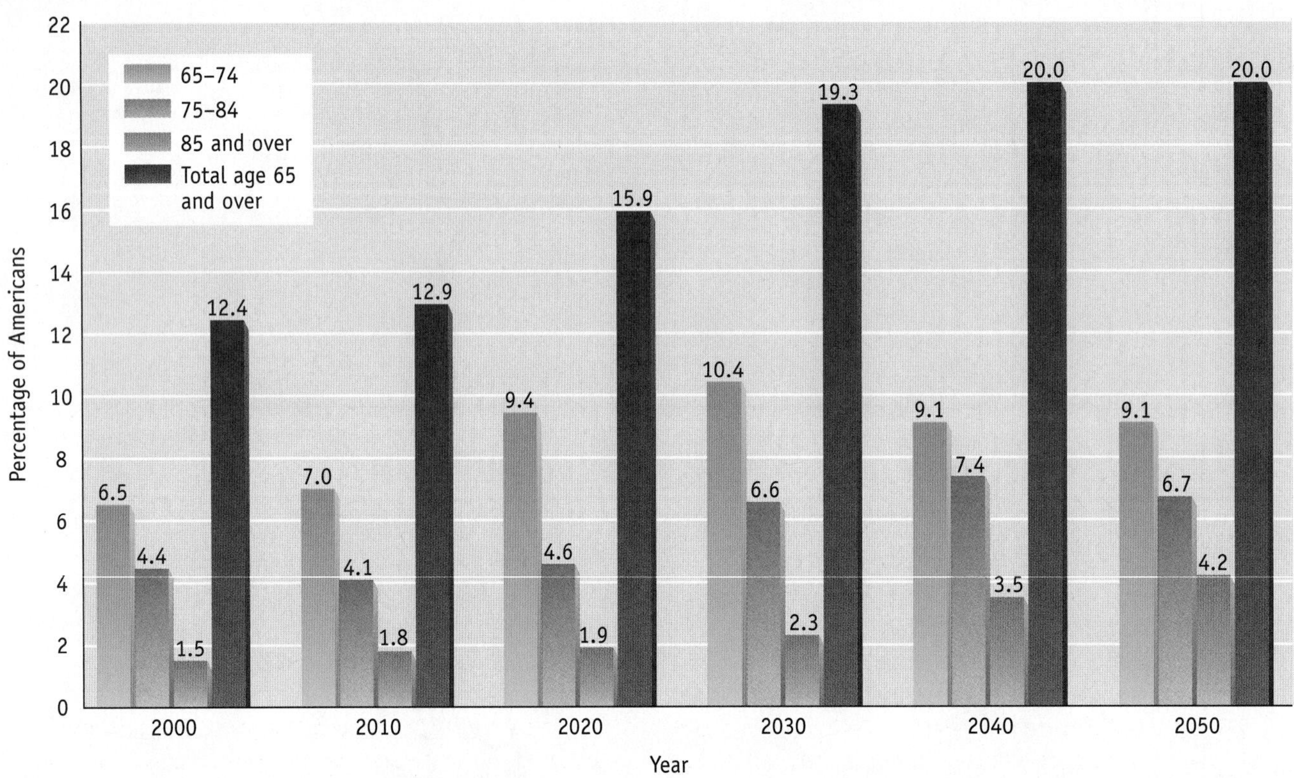

Source: By the author. Based on *Statistical Abstract of the United States* 2002:Table 12; 2013:Tables 7, 9.

Poverty of the aged is a global problem. I took the photo of the woman searching through garbage in Riga, Latvia, and the photo of the man begging on the street corner in Rome, Italy. In all societies, people who have more money have fewer physical and mental health problems and an easier time adjusting to old age.

Issues in Social Problems

The New Centenarians

The oxymoron *new* centenarians may seem strange, since the word *centenarians* refers to someone who has reached age 100 or more. Apparently, though, centenarians are new to the world. Some population experts think that before 1900 only one person a century made it to age 100 or beyond (Himes 2001).

While reaching 100 isn't exactly common today, it is frequent. About 60,000 Americans report that they are age 100 or more (Juncosa 2008). Census officials think that people fudge a bit about their age when they get to be very old. They become proud about making it that far, and they tend to tack on a few years. Even if we lop off 10,000 people, this still leaves us with about 50,000 folks who have managed to reach age 100 or more.

The increasing number of people reaching 100 years of age is new to the world scene. Shown here is a 104-year old man in Syracuse, New York, dancing with one of the guests at his birthday party.

As you probably would expect, more women than men reach 100. In fact, women centenarians outnumber men centenarians *four to one.* (The men have quite a choice of mates, but little interest.) Because the average woman outlives the average man, about 25 percent of men centenarians are married, but only about 4 percent of the women. Then there is this surprising statistic: About 20 percent of centenarians report no disabilities (Himes 2001). They are still healthy and feeling good.

No one knows exactly why the "new" centenarians have appeared at this point in world history, but our improved public health, modern medicines, and ample food supply certainly play a part. On the individual level—why Dick and Jane make it to 100 while Bill and Mary do not—there appear to be three main reasons: genetics, lifestyle, and just plain luck. With regard to genetics, some people inherit physical problems that bring an earlier death. For lifestyle, some people take better care of their bodies, while some like to ride motorcycles and jump out of airplanes. Then there is the matter of luck—or the lack of it. You can simply be in the wrong place at the wrong time, such as visiting the World Trade Center on September 11, 2001. Or be driving on an interstate highway when a boat unhooks from a trailer in the oncoming lane and smashes into your car, taking your head with it, as happened to two friends of mine.

This continuing trend toward longer life has brought with it a new term, the *supercentenarians,* those who have made it to 110 or beyond. There are about 75 or 80 supercentenarians in the United States.

Our centenarians and supercentenarians have arrived on the world scene because of natural causes. Those causes are being put under a microscope. If the genetics researchers learn how to manipulate our genes, we may one day be talking about the new centenarians and a half, or even the double centenarians.

For Your Consideration

Centenarians are one of the fastest growing segments of our population. While still relatively rare today, they are destined to become more common. What do you think the consequences will be for society?

Here is how the battle is shaping up. To protect their gains, older Americans have organized a powerful political lobby. This group, AARP (formerly called the American Association of Retired Persons), boasts 40 million members, a staff of 1,800, and 160,000 volunteers. Politicians, whose foremost goal appears to be to get reelected, find it difficult to ignore such numbers. If they try to reduce benefits for the elderly, they are flooded with letters, e-mail, and telephone calls. They are accused of being stingy and threatened with being voted out of office. Look at the Issues in Social Problems box on next page.

Issues in Social Problems

The Gray Panthers

Who We Are

We are a group of people—old and young—drawn together by deeply felt common concerns for human liberation and social change. The old and young live outside the mainstream of society.

Ageism—discrimination against persons on the basis of chronological age—deprives both groups of power and influence. Besides being a movement of older and younger persons, as Gray Panthers we consider ourselves distinctive in the following ways:

We are against ageism that forces any group to live roles that are defined purely on the basis of age. We view aging as a total life process in which the individual develops from birth to death. Therefore, we are concerned about the needs of all age groups and ageism directed at any age group.

We have a strong sense of militancy. Our concern is not only for education and services, but also for effective nonviolent action with an awareness of timing and urgency.

We advocate a radical approach to social change by attacking those forces that corrupt our institutions, attitudes, and values, such as materialism, racism, sexism, paternalism, militarism, and extreme nationalism.

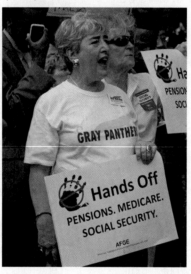

The elderly have become a powerful political force. It is perilous for politicians to ignore their demands.

What We Want

1. To develop a new and positive self-awareness in our culture that can regard the total life span as a continuing process in maturity and fulfillment.
2. To strive for new options for lifestyles for older and younger people that will challenge the present paternalism in our institutions and culture, and to help eliminate the poverty and powerlessness in which most older and younger people are forced to live, and to change society's destructive attitudes about aging.
3. To make responsible use of our freedom to bring about social change, to develop a list of priorities among social issues, and to struggle nonviolently for social change that will bring greater human freedom, justice, dignity, and peace.
4. To build a new power base in our society uniting presently disenfranchised and oppressed groups, realizing the common qualities and concerns of age and youth working in coalition with other movements with similar goals and principles.
5. To reinforce and support each other in our quest for liberation and to celebrate our shared humanity.

Reprinted by permission of The Gray Panthers

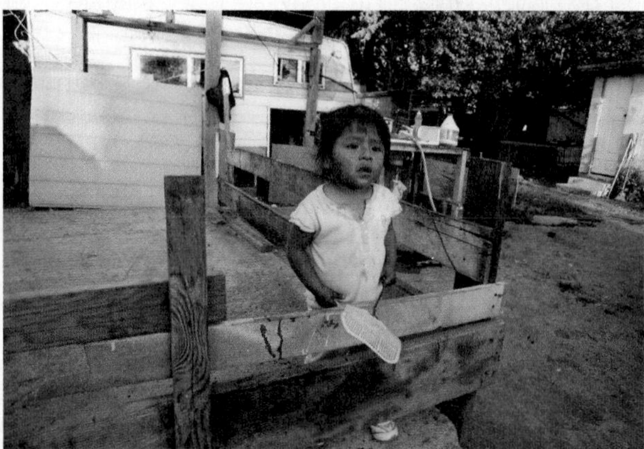

In the United States, a land of wealth and bountiful resources, we can ask why millions of children continue to live in poverty.

The interests of the younger and older groups are running on a collision course. Consider Social Security again. The money a worker pays to Social Security is not put into that worker's own account. Instead, money that is collected from current workers is given to retired workers—a sort of chain-letter arrangement by which the younger support the older. The number of people collecting Social Security benefits is growing faster than the number of people entering the workforce. This represents a major shift in the **dependency ratio**, the number of workers compared with the number of people who receive Social Security. Presently, the ratio is about 4 to 1: Four workers pay Social Security taxes to support each person who is collecting Social Security. In about a generation, this ratio will drop to about 3 to 1 (Melloan 1994; *Statistical Abstract* 2013:Tables 554, 555).

Another indicator of the potential coming conflict is this: The U.S. government has collected over $2 trillion more in Social Security taxes than it has paid to retirees (*Statistical Abstract* 2013:Table 557). Supposedly, officials have placed this huge excess in a trust fund, reserved for future generations. The "fund," however, does not exist. In a fraud perpetrated on the elderly, this money has disappeared. Just as fast as the excess money has come in, the federal government has "borrowed" it, spending it on whatever it desires (Henslin 2013). The Social Security Trust Fund is supposed to prevent an intergenerational showdown, but as some have pointed out, there is no fund, and you can't trust it. A day of reckoning between generations can't be far off.

MySocLab  Study and Review on **MySocLab**

Summary and Review

1. The frameworks that sociologists use to interpret their research findings are called *theories.* To interpret social problems, sociologists use three major theories: *functionalism, conflict theory,* and *symbolic interactionism.* In this chapter, we look at *feminist theory* as part of conflict theory. Each theory provides a different interpretation of society and of social problems. No theory is *the* right one. Rather, taken together, these perspectives give us a more complete picture of the whole.
2. *Functionalists* see society as a self-correcting, orderly system, much like a well-oiled machine. Its parts work in harmony to bring the whole into equilibrium. Each part performs a *function* (hence, the term *functional analysis*) that contributes to the system's well-being. When a part is functioning inadequately, however, it creates problems for the system. Those *dysfunctions* are called social problems.
3. *Conflict theorists* view social problems as an outcome of unequal power. Those in power try to preserve the social order and their own privileged position within it. They take the needs of other groups into consideration only when it is in their own interest to do so. As they exploit others, the powerful create social problems, such as poverty, discrimination, and war. Other social problems, such as revolution, crime, suicide, and drug abuse, represent reactions of the oppressed to their exploitation. *Feminist theorists* also focus on the exploitation of the powerless by the powerful, looking at *patriarchy* or male dominance as the primary cause.
4. *Symbolic interactionists* view social problems not as objective conditions but as broadly held views that some matter is a social problem; that is, if people view something as a social problem, it is a social problem. If they do not, it is not. As people's views (or definitions or symbols) change, so do their ideas about social problems.
5. The future will bring both a larger number and a larger percentage of elderly. This will put further strain on Social Security and the medical systems. A struggle for resources between the younger and elderly is likely to develop.

Key Terms

ageism, 48
capitalism, 34
capitalists, 34
Chicago School of Sociology, 41
conflict theory, 34
cultural feminism, 37
dependency ratio, 48
dysfunctions, 28
ecofeminism, 37
feminist theory, 36
function, 28
functionalism, 28
generalized other, 41
latent dysfunctions, 29
latent functions, 29
liberal feminism, 37
looking-glass self, 41
manifest function, 29
patriarchy, 37
radical feminism, 37
social construction of reality, 41
socialist feminism, 37
structure, 29
symbolic interactionism, 38
symbols, 38
take the role of the other, 41
theory, 27

Thinking Critically About Chapter 2

1. Of the three theories identified in this chapter, which one do you think does the best job of explaining social problems? Why?
2. Select a social problem other than aging:
   - How would functionalists explain the problem?
   - How would conflict theorists explain the problem?
   - How would symbolic interactionists explain the problem?
3. What do you think are the main problems that we are likely to face in coming years regarding the "graying of America" (the aging of the U.S. population)? Propose solutions to these problems.
   - Why do you think that your solutions might work?
   - What might prevent your solutions from working?

3 Social Problems Related to Sexual Behavior

Listen to Chapter 3 on MySocLab

Learning Objectives. After reading this chapter, you should be able to:

3.1 Explain the role of sociology in determining morality and studying social problems. **(p. 52)**

3.2 Contrast various attitudes toward prostitution. **(p. 54)**

3.3 Explain the functionalist perspective on prostitution. **(p. 56)**

3.4 Explain the conflict/feminist perspective on prostitution. **(p. 58)**

3.5 Summarize the research findings on types of prostitutes, becoming a prostitute, pimps, and male prostitutes. **(p. 58)**

3.6 Explain changes in pornography in the U.S. **(p. 65)**

3.7 Explain the symbolic interactionist perspective on pornography. **(p. 66)**

3.8 Explain the controversy over pornography and understand the major research findings on pornography. **(p. 70)**

3.9 Discuss the issue of making consensual behavior illegal—and its alternatives. **(p. 74)**

3.10 Explain the likely future of prostitution and pornography. **(p. 76)**

Jack Helmer (a pseudonym) has been attracted to little girls since he can't remember when. Even as a little boy, he liked to spend time with them. Now at 45, Jack still enjoys their imaginations and finds their conversations delightful. It used to be that whenever he had the opportunity, he would babysit for them.

Every cab driver knew where the kiddie brothels were located

The problem is that Jack's interest in little girls is also sexual.

Fifteen years ago, Jack was arrested for molesting a minor and put on probation for 3 years. During his probation, he was charged with molesting his girlfriend's 10-year-old daughter. For this offense, he served 5 years in prison.

Jack was especially displeased when his name, address, and photo appeared on an Internet sexual offenders' website. Knowing that both the police and the neighbors were watching him, Jack kept away from children. One day he read about an area in Phnom Penh, the capital of Cambodia, with brothels that feature children. Jack decided to travel to Cambodia, far from the prying eyes of the police and neighbors.

It took Jack quite a while to save the money for the trip, but by cutting down expenses, he managed to put together what he needed for the flight and hotel. When he arrived in Phnom Penh, Jack found that what he had read was correct. Children were available for sexual purposes, and the fees were low. Every cab driver knew where the kiddie brothels were located.

Jack should have read a little more closely. What he missed was that the United States had passed laws to prosecute predatory crimes against children outside the U.S. borders.

When Jack returned from Cambodia, federal officials were waiting at the airport. Jack is now serving a 20-year prison sentence.

On Sex, Morality, and Sociology

3.1 Explain the role of sociology in determining morality and studying social problems.

You will recall from our discussion in Chapter 1 that objective conditions alone are not adequate to make something a social problem. Also essential are subjective concerns: A lot of people must dislike or be upset about an objective condition and want to see it changed. The events in our opening vignette easily meet this definition of social problems.

We will come back to discuss the sexual abuse of children, but before we move into the topics of this chapter, it is important to lay a little groundwork. First, what do we mean by sex? Let's define **sex** in a fairly standard way as those activities associated with arousal, intercourse, and reproduction. Second, it is important to stress a sociological principle that is fundamental to this chapter: As much as we may prefer it to be otherwise, *sex is never only a personal matter*. All societies control or channel human sexual behavior, primarily through the social institution of marriage and family. We learn our first ideas of morality, including sexual morality, in the family, and we don't take challenges to our opinions of what is right and wrong about sexual behavior lightly.

Because many people view the topics of this chapter in moral terms, it is also important to stress another point made in the first chapter: *Sociology does not make moral judgments*. Sociologists take positions on social issues, of course, because they are members of society and share many of the ideas common in their society. I don't know of a single sociologist, for example, who would defend the prostitution of children or their use in pornography. When it comes to adult prostitution and pornography, however, there is a wide variety of opinion among sociologists, just as there is among the general public.

As stressed in Chapter 1, although sociology has no basis for taking a moral stand on human behavior, even though sociologists do, sociology is well-equipped to study the two essential conditions of social problems, its objective conditions and its subjective concerns, the controversies that make contemporary life so exciting. To learn more about studying sex in America, you might want to look at the *Spotlight on Social Research* box below.

Spotlight on Social Research

Studying Sex in America

EDWARD LAUMANN, *dean of the Social Science Division at the University of Chicago, has done research on health, politics, power, status, and sex. Although he has a long history of theoretical work in how people form, maintain, and dissolve relationships, it is his research on sex that has received the most attention. Here is what he wrote for your text.*

In the 1980s, when we were in the midst of an AIDS epidemic so vicious that the number of people with this disease was doubling every 10 months, I organized a workshop on AIDS and Society. As I listened to the presentations, I became convinced that there would be no magic bullet to stop this epidemic through immunization. To contain the spread of AIDS, people would have to change their behavior. Robert Michael, an economic demographer, and I concluded that we needed a national sex survey to document the sex practices of Americans. With this information, we could design ways to persuade people to take defensive measures.

Research into human sexual behavior is often considered "illegitimate," even by many social scientists. Despite this disapproval, we wanted the University of Chicago to pool its strengths in survey and sample design to conduct this national survey. John Gagnon, a sexologist, joined our research team. When the National Institutes of Health announced a search for research proposals to combat AIDS, we submitted our design for a national sex survey. We won that competition.

When *Science* magazine reported that our proposal was under review at the White House's Office of Management and the Budget, the *Washington Times* picked the story up with screaming headlines. Within a few days, a White Paper was circulating to every member of the House and Senate. One objection was that sex reports normalize immoral sexual behavior, such as masturbation and anal and oral sex. Another was that the government has no business invading people's private lives, even if it is for reasons of the public's health. Michael and I were accused of being fronts for a cabal of homophiles who were attempting to legitimize gay sex.

Although the Senate Appropriations Committee recommended that our survey be funded, the House Appropriations Committee disagreed. For two years, we lobbied congressional staffers, senators, and representatives for their support in funding the research, but with few results. Then Senator Jesse Helms submitted an amendment to an appropriations bill that transferred the funding that had been intended for our sex survey to a "say no to sex" campaign. The Senate voted 66 to 34 in favor of the amendment, giving me the dubious distinction of having Congress trying to stop my research.

With government funding cut off, we turned to private foundations. The Robert Wood Johnson, Henry Kaiser, Rockefeller, and MacArthur foundations agreed to fund our research. To share the results of our survey with the scientific community, we wrote *The Social Organization of Sexuality.* This is a technical book, and as some have noted, it took the University of Chicago to take the fun out of sex.

We felt strongly that the public needed to know what we had discovered, and we wanted to have a hand in framing the public's understanding, not leave it to others. To do this, we arranged for Gina Kolata, a *New York Times* reporter who specializes in science and health news, to write a companion volume, *Sex in America.*

Prostitution is sometimes called the "oldest profession" because it goes so far back in history. This 1890 painting of a Parisian prostitute seeking clients is by Pierre Andre French.

Let's begin, then, with an overview of prostitution, one of the areas of human behavior that upsets a lot of people.

Prostitution

Background: Getting the Larger Picture

3.2 Contrast various attitudes toward prostitution.

It is no accident that **prostitution**, the renting of one's body for sexual purposes, has been called "the world's oldest profession." Accounts of prostitution by both females and males reach back to the beginning of recorded history, and prostitution exists in one form or another almost everywhere. Let's take quick look at how attitudes about prostitution differ.

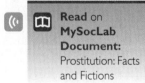

Read on **MySocLab Document:** Prostitution: Facts and Fictions

Attitudes Toward Prostitution. You might be surprised to learn that prostitution used to be part of some religions. Some early inhabitants of the Mediterranean area, Asia Minor, and West Africa viewed prostitution as a service to their gods (Henriques 1966). Some groups there practiced **temple prostitution**, requiring every woman to perform an act of prostitution before she was allowed to marry. Some women were dedicated to the gods as *sacred prostitutes*—either for a specific time or for life. On a visit to India, I was surprised to find that in some villages temple prostitution still exists.

In ancient Greece, the portraits and statues of high-class prostitutes, called ***hetaerae,*** were placed "in the temples and other public buildings by the side of meritorious generals and statesmen" (Henriques 1966:64).

In some countries, prostitution is viewed as a necessary evil—something for which there is a demand that will be satisfied whether the activity is legal or illegal. In New Zealand, for example, prostitutes, called sex workers, are licensed to work in brothels. They are required to follow safe sex practices, and like other workers they have legal labor rights. "Offensive" signs are banned (Weitzer 2009).

In the United States, attitudes toward legalizing prostitution vary greatly. Although illegal in all parts of the United States, except in most of Nevada, prostitution flourishes. Let's look at this aspect of prostitution.

Prostitution Today

Eliot Spitzer, Governor of New York, arranged for a 22-year-old prostitute to take a train from New York and meet him at a Washington, D.C. hotel, where he paid her $5,500. What he didn't know was that the police were recording his telephone call. During an outburst of national publicity and indignation, Spitzer resigned.

Although attitudes toward prostitution are mixed, few will tolerate a governor with a wife and three children who visits prostitutes—especially a governor who had taken a public stance for "family values," a crusading former prosecutor who had his eye on the White House (Bone 2008).

Prostitution flourishes in the United States, most of it underground. As in this instance, only occasionally does prostitution come to the attention of the public. If it flourishes, you might wonder how many prostitutes there are in the United States. Using sampling techniques, researchers estimate that there are 23 prostitutes per 100,000 Americans, a total of 69,000 prostitutes (Pottêrat et al. 1990; Brewer et al. 2000). They also estimate that the average prostitute has 694 customers a year. This average comes from a huge range—from just one or two a week for prostitutes like the one who visited Eliot Spitzer to perhaps 5,000 a year for those who work in crack houses.

The only place in the United States where prostitution is legal is Nevada. But women are not licensed to sell sex in Reno, Las Vegas, and Lake Tahoe. Officials in these counties have banned prostitution for fear that it would drive out family vacationers. From the photo on this page, however, you can see that prostitution, although illegal, is practiced almost openly in Las Vegas.

Prostitutes try to keep up with the times. Massage parlors, escort services, corporate prostitution, and sex tourism have replaced the "whorehouses" of yesterday. Under cover of a legitimate service, "massage parlors" offer sex for sale. Escort services use the Internet to arrange dates for a fee, which is not illegal, and the client privately negotiates the inclusion of sexual services. Prostitutes, both men and women, advertise on Craigslist and Eros.

Some corporations offer prostitutes as sexual perks for their employees or customers. A Wall Street firm paid $250,000 to rent a Miami mansion for a Super Bowl weekend, its executives lounging around the pool with rent-a-dates (Pulliam and Bray 2011). A New York telephone company held what it called a "pervert" convention, a raucous week during which prostitutes provided sex for the company's suppliers (Carnevale 1990). Top salesmen, especially valued, are sometimes rewarded with prostitutes (Holm and Dauer 2011).

Our opening vignette is about **sex tourism**, where people visit a foreign country with the goal of having sex with prostitutes. Some use Internet-based advertisements to choose specific prostitutes ahead of time. Some travel agencies specialize in sex tourism, booking the flight, reserving the hotel room, and arranging for the prostitutes. We explore sex tourism further in the Global Glimpse box on the next page.

With this brief overview, let's use the functionalist lens to look at prostitution.

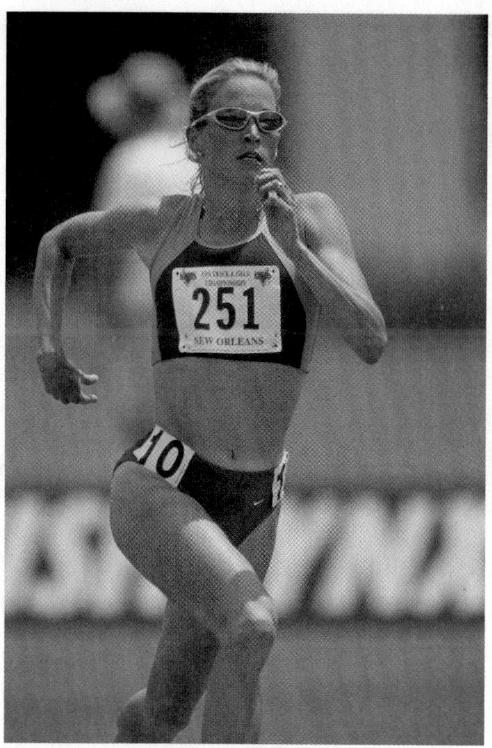

Prostitution scandals occasionally show up in unexpected places. Suzy Favor Hamilton, who competed in the Olympics three times as a middle distance runner, later became a $600-an-hour prostitute in Las Vegas.

From this photo that I shot in Las Vegas, would you know that prostitution is illegal in this city?

A Global Glimpse

Sex Tourism and the Patriotic Prostitute

A new wrinkle in the history of prostitution is the "patriotic prostitute." Patriotic prostitutes are young women who are encouraged by their government to prostitute themselves to help the country's economy. Patriotic prostitution is part of *global stratification,* the division of the world's countries into "have" and "have-not" nations. Some have-nots, or Least Industrialized Nations, view some of their women as a cash crop, encouraging prostitution as a way to accumulate capital for investment or to help pay interest on their national debt. A notorious example is Thailand, where in a country of 30 million females, between a half million and a million are prostitutes. About 20,000 are under the age of 15.

In some countries, government officials encourage prostitution by telling young women that they are performing a service for their country. In South Korea, officials issue identification cards to prostitutes, which serve as hotel passes. In orientation sessions, they tell these young women, "Your carnal conversations with foreign tourists do not prostitute either yourself or the nation, but express your heroic patriotism."

With such official blessings, "sex tourism" has become a global growth industry. Travel agencies in Germany advertise "trips to Thailand with erotic pleasures included in the price." Japan Airlines hands out brochures that advertise the "charming attractions" of Kisaeng girls. If men fly JAL, they can look forward to "a night spent with a consummate Kisaeng girl dressed in a gorgeous Korean blouse and skirt."

The advertising is attractive, showing beautiful young women with "come hither" smiles. What the ads fail to mention is the miserable sex slavery that underlies sex tourism. Some of the prostitutes were sold as children. Others are held in bondage while they pay off their families' debts. Some are even locked up to keep them from running away.

A large part of Thailand's economy depends on prostitution. This photo was taken in Bangkok, Thailand's capital.

There apparently is no end to customers who seek such sex. Occasionally, law enforcement even nets a prominent individual, such as a U.S. senator who allegedly paid to have sex with underage girls in the Dominican Republic.

The enticing ads also leave out AIDS. In Nairobi, where about 10,000 prostitutes serve this thriving industry, perhaps half are infected with AIDS. Nor is the destruction of children mentioned. Although customers pay more for young girls and boys, especially for those who are advertised as virgins or "clean," the children are vulnerable to infection from lesions and injuries during intercourse. When they become too sick to service clients—or their disease becomes too noticeable—the children are thrown into the streets like so much rubbish.

Based on Gay 1985; Shaw 1987; Hornblower 1993; Beddoe et al. 2001; Leuchtag 2004; Adams 2013.

For Your Consideration

What is your opinion about sex tourism? Do you think that American Airlines and the other airlines should get into the competition and start advertising sex tourism? Why or why not?

Prostitution Viewed Theoretically: Applying Functionalism

3.3 Explain the functionalist perspective on prostitution.

The Social Functions of Prostitution. On the most obvious level, prostitution flourishes because it satisfies sexual needs that are not met elsewhere. This, of course, is precisely why prostitution will never be eliminated. In a classic article that goes back about 75 years or so, sociologist Kingsley Davis (1937, 1966) concluded that prostitutes provide a sexual outlet for men who

1. have difficulty establishing sexual relationships (such as disfigured or shy men or those with handicaps)

2. cannot find long-term partners (such as travelers and sailors)
3. have a broken relationship (such as the separated or divorced)
4. want sexual gratification that they can't get from their wives or girlfriends.

Other researchers (Freund et al. 1991; Gemme 1993; Monto 2004; Weitzer 2009) note that prostitutes also provide a sexual outlet for men who

5. want quick sex without attachment
6. are sexually dissatisfied in marriage
7. want to have sex with someone who has a specific body type, age, or race–ethnicity.

Another function has been explored by sociologists (Bernstein 2001; Huff 2011). For some men, prostitution is not a fleeting, detached arrangement. They visit the same prostitute repeatedly, or have her come to his place, and they develop emotional connections with her. They share personal feelings and intimate thoughts that they aren't comfortable sharing elsewhere. Some are even convinced that the woman from whom they are buying sex has special feelings for them. Some escort services specialize in meeting this need, offering for higher fees women who specialize in what they call "the girlfriend experience."

The Functionalist Conclusion: Prostitution as a Way of Controlling Sexual Behavior. Most of these findings may seem obvious, but from them functionalists draw a surprising conclusion. Prostitution, they say, is *a way of controlling men's sexual behavior*. By this, they mean that by meeting such needs as those I just described, prostitution channels men's sexual desires away from unwilling women to women who, for a price, are willing to satisfy the men. For example, some people (whom prostitutes call "kinkies," "weirdos," and "freaks") achieve sexual gratification by inflicting pain on others (**sadists**) or by having others inflict pain on them (**masochists**). Some customers receive sexual satisfaction from humiliating women (Pilot 2008). Others enjoy being humiliated, being told by the prostitute that they are "no good" and having her spank them or urinate on them. Others combine the sex act with fantasy role playing; they may wear costumes or ask the prostitute to do so. Some wear diapers; others have sex in coffins (Hall 1972; Millett 1973; Prus and Irini 1988). Few men who have such desires can satisfy them in traditional relationships. Prostitution redirects these men to a willing outlet, where prostitutes satisfy them for a fee and the clients then go back to their regular lives.

Read on **MySocLab Document:** Human Rights, Sex Trafficking, and Prostitution

Men like these, however, are not the typical customers of prostitutes. Most customers (called "johns") are "regular" married, middle-aged men (Monto 2004; Sawyer and Metz 2009). Why do married men patronize prostitutes? There appear to be two main reasons: Some find their wives sexually unreceptive, while others desire sexual variety that their wives are unwilling to provide—especially fellatio (oral sex), apparently the act most requested of prostitutes (Melody 1969; Heyl 1979; Gemme 1993).

Functionalists stress that when people demand a service that is not supplied by legitimate sources, a hidden, or "subterranean," source will develop to meet the need. The underground channeling of illegitimate services to clients, called a **black market**, is built on **symbiosis** (a mutually beneficial relationship). Those who purchase a service, those who provide it, and those who suppress it all benefit from the illegal activity. The clients of prostitutes purchase the sex they want; prostitutes work with a minimum of legal hassles (even calling their occasional fines the price of "licensing"); pimps and criminal organizations earn untaxed income; and for a price, police who are "on the take" look the other way.

In Sum ▸ Functionalists view prostitution as a means of controlling or channeling sexual behavior. Prostitutes meet the needs of the sexually unattached and of those who want sexual acts that are not readily available to them. Prostitutes provide access to sexual variety in an unattached and fleeting relationship. Also important, prostitutes do not threaten the male ego—it is unlikely that a john will be "turned down."

The Conflict/Feminist Perspective

3.4 Explain the conflict/feminist perspective on prostitution.

The feminist perspective contrasts sharply with that of the functionalists. Taking this approach, feminists diverge into two points of view. In the first, where the exchange of sex for money is between willing, consenting adults, they view prostitution as a form of female empowerment. The women, called *sex workers,* choose to sell sex: This is their business, and no men should make laws to tell them what they can or cannot do with their bodies. The sex workers should organize, unionize, and demand higher wages and good working conditions.

In the second point of view, feminists see prostitution as one more indication of the imbalance of power and resources between men and women. For these feminists, who call prostitution "sexual slavery" and "paid rape," prostitution is simply another of the many ways that men exploit and degrade women. They point out that some men exploit prostitutes for their own pleasure, while other men (pimps and police "on the take") exploit prostitutes for profit.

Research on Prostitution

3.5 Summarize the research findings on types of prostitutes, becoming a prostitute, pimps, and male prostitutes.

Types of Prostitutes. Besides escort and corporate prostitutes that I already mentioned, what are other kinds of prostitutes? Let's do a quick overview.

Call girls, the elite of the prostitutes, can be selective in choosing their customers. Building a steady, repeat business, they usually meet their customers at their own places or at the clients' (Weitzer 2009). To keep up with appointments, they use cell phones, pagers, tablets, and e-mail. To keep up with their clients' demand for variety, some call girls fly from city to city, where new customers await them (Campo-Flores 2002).

Convention prostitutes, as the name implies, are women who specialize in conventions. Posing as secretaries or sales agents, they roam hotel lobbies, display rooms, and cocktail parties. Some organizers of conventions make arrangements for prostitutes to be available.

Apartment prostitutes rent apartments outside of their own homes and set up businesses at which they work set hours. Some apartment prostitutes are married women who match their apartment hours with the husbands' working hours. Some husbands are ignorant of the wife's activities and think that she has a regular job.

Hotel prostitutes work out of a hotel and share their fees with the bell captain, desk clerk, or bellboys who steer johns to them (Reichert and Frey 1985; Prus and Irini 1988). Because this "added service" attracts male guests, some hotels provide the prostitutes a free or discounted room.

House prostitutes work in a brothel or "whorehouse." During the 1800s and early 1900s, almost all large U.S. cities and many small ones had brothels, which were located in an area known as the "red light district." A red bulb shining from a window or house informed outsiders of what went on behind those closed doors.

Brothels are now an unusual form of prostitution in the United States, but some still exist. Barbara Heyl (1979) studied house prostitutes and reported on the selection process that occurs once a john enters the whorehouse. Typically the women gather in the living room while the john looks them over and makes his selection. The manager of the house (the "madam") keeps 50 to 60 percent of the prostitutes' earnings.

Bar girls, also known as "B-girls," wait in bars for customers. Some pay or "tip" the bartender for using the bar. Others hustle drinks (get johns to buy overpriced drinks), receiving a fee for each drink they sell.

Streetwalkers, who have the lowest status among prostitutes, are the most frequently arrested. They are visible to the public, as they "work the street" in view of police and customers. In some U.S. cities, streetwalkers are aggressive, hailing passing cars and opening the doors of cars that have stopped at traffic lights. Many are drug addicts involved in other criminal behaviors.

Parking lot lizards frequent truck stops, moving from one truck to another in search of clients.

As you can see, prostitutes are often classified by the place where they work, a list that could be extended. For a different form of prostitution, see the box on Technology and Social Problems on the next page.

Technology and Social Problems

"Female College Student Available: Wants Sugar Daddy"

> *I AM CURRENTLY ATTENDING COLLEGE. MY GOAL IS TO BECOME A CORRECTIONAL COUNCLER AND EVENTUALLY A LAWYER SO I CAN FIGHT THE DOJ (Department Of Justice) TO CHANGE THE WAY THE CORRECTIONAL SYSTEM IS RUN.*
>
> And I am very playful. Am I what you're looking for?

I found this Internet ad (with the caps and misspelling) especially amusing because of its unusual juxtaposition of the serious (change the DOJ) and the kittenish feminine (playful). The image of a sexually playful lawyer whose goal is to reform the Department of Justice and make society a better place is almost mind boggling.

"Will you be my Sugar Daddy? I want to be your Sugar Baby."

This ad reminds me of the young women who, paraded on stage in swimsuits, their bodies ogled as they are judged by officials on a 1 to 10 ranking, are asked to show their "talents." After twirling flaming batons, when asked about their goals in life, they recite something about ending war, eliminating global poverty, and changing the world.

There is something ludicrous about it all.

But let's get back to this form of prostitution, women who are offering their bodies for sale on the Internet.

Here is one who wants $5,000 to $10,000 a month to be "made happy":

> I'm a petite 18-year old from France. I'm looking for a mentor who can provide me with the finer things in life and make me happy.

Some women let their potential sugar daddies know that they are sincere sugar babies. This woman is looking for a real emotional connection with a man she can trust:

> I'm just a young model still trying to decide which direction i want to take in this crazy world. I know i want to start a business one day. But haven't quite decided on anything. I'd love to meet an older wiser man that lets me pick his brain and feel like i can look up to him. Someone that will help me choose the right path for me and truly does care about my well-being. I want someone who makes me feel like a woman and treats me like a lady should be treated!

But just so the man doesn't start thinking that such a relationship will be without cost, she adds:

> People always ask "well How do we get started?" A good way to get started is start the allowance ! *hint* If you're a real SD, i wont have to worry about any of my own expenses and i shouldn't have to bring up an allowance.

Sugar Daddies advertise, too.

Some are actually Sugar Granddaddies. A 73-year-old heads his ad: "Play with Daddy in his Paradise"

This man is looking for a woman who is "funny, lazy, whose idea of the 'good life' is playing with her Silver haired Papi at Pepes Hideaway, my popular boutique hotel, in tropical Mexico."

Unfortunately, if you read Pepe's ad all the way through, you will find that Viagra hasn't been able to work its magic on him. At least he's up front about this.

Maybe a younger sugar daddy is preferable, one in his 40s who doesn't need Viagra. This one, who describes himself as Generous Gentleman, says he is athletic and a sports fan. He likes volleyball, basketball, and football.

Or if you are looking for someone a little more intellectual who likes to travel, this sugar daddy says he is "Well read and avid film buff. Love to cook and dine at the finest restaurants. I have traveled the world on business and there are dozens of places i would like to revisit for pure pleasure."

Each potential sugar daddy lists his budget. Hardly any offers to spend less than $5,000 a month on the "ONE sweet, outgoing, young girl who wants to have a great time and enjoy life to the fullest," the one they "want to spoil me and I will spoil you in return."

The sugar daddy/sugar baby relationship has been around as long as older men have had the money to buy themselves young women—and that point is lost in history. What is new is this technological twist—the Internet allowing the interested parties to discuss their arrangements frankly before they get involved.

This form of prostitution comes so close to the boyfriend-helping-his-girlfriend that neither party is likely to feel like a prostitute or john. It is also so close to the girlfriend/boyfriend relationship that the participants are not likely to be touched by the law.

For Your Consideration

Do you think sugar babies are prostitutes and sugar daddies are johns? Other than the frankness about their intentions, what is the difference between these individuals and a woman whose boyfriend helps pay her rent—or her college tuition?

Becoming a Prostitute. Researchers typically study streetwalkers, as they are visible and easily accessible. This means that most of the research on prostitution comes from poor women who have been arrested. Other prostitutes are less accessible to the police—and to sociologists. Keep this biased sampling in mind as we examine how women become prostitutes.

Why does someone become a prostitute? The simplest reason is money—to make as much of it as easily as possible. This is an oversimplification, however, for running through the accounts that prostitutes give of their early home life are themes of poverty, emotional deprivation, and sexual abuse (James and Meyerding 1977; Davis 1978; Hodgson 1997; Farley et al. 2011). For streetwalkers, this conclusion does seem to apply: Abused as children, most often by men, these women become locked into a way of life in which they continue to be victimized by men—by pimps who exploit their bodies for profit and by johns who exploit them for sexual pleasure.

But bad childhoods certainly do not apply to all prostitutes. In the Issues in Social Problems box below, a call girl who was in a course I was teaching gives us the other side.

Issues in Social Problems

Me, a Prostitute?

Many women learn to be prostitutes gradually, going through a process similar to the one recounted here. This account, written by one of my students, who wishes to remain anonymous, has been reproduced as it was originally written (including typos and misspellings). To keep the impact of what she wrote, I have adjusted the dollar totals to account for inflation.

I am a average looking blond with blue eyes. I am a female of twenty years of age. My mother is a elementary school teacher with a doctorit degree. My father is the head of instramentation for a large oil company. He write books, makes movies and teaches around the world. I have one sibbling. She is 10 years old. My parents are very old fashioned. they are strickt with both my sister and I. We are Hard-Shell-Baptist, and attend church no-matter-what. They've instilled wonderful values in me. We live in the country on a farm (pleasure, we don't grow things). Our home is large and because both of my parents work we have a maid that comes three days a week to clean. I've always had to work around the house. Cooking meals, cleaning and doing farm chores such as, feeding the horses and cows, have always been a part of my dayly routine. Yet, there's never been anything I've ever done without. Anything that could be bought was automatically mine, just for the asking. Our entire family is close. We visit one another frequently and have get-togethers regularly.

There was nothing about the looks of the student who wrote this box to set her apart from other students.

I am from a family with an average annual income of over $100,000.00. My parents have never neglected me. No one has ever abused me. I've caused my share of trouble, but it was all jouvenile, never anything against the law of the state. I've never been a misfit. I was one of the "cool" kids. I was in with the "popular" crowd. I was in Student Government and Peer Leadership in High School. I was elected Snow Queen my junior year. I never had any problems with guys. There was always plenty around my house. I just could never get attached to guys my age, they came and they went . . . no big deal! I had a taste for older men even then.

When I was seventeen, I met a guy who was twenty-two. He was exciting and fun. He was my first love. He was also the first guy I'd ever had sex with. Kinky wouldn't even begin to explain him. We went out for about a year and a half. Through him I met Jesse. A gorgeous Spaniard, queer as a three dollar bill, but one of the nicest people you'll ever meet. Jesse is a "BIG" record promoter for a famous record corporation. We've been friends since the day we met. We call each other all the time and "dish" on guys.

I called Jesse up one day and asked if he'd get me tickets to go to a concert I wanted to see. He said sure as he had a million times before. Only this time he too had a request. He said, "I'm in a bit of a bind. I need someone to pick up a client and show him around town Friday!" "Cool!" I said. Jesse went

(continued from previous page)

on to explain, "You'll be given $400.00 to buy him dinner, go dancing, or whatever else he may want to do . . . what's left is yours to keep." "Wow, thats great," I exclaimed! I thought to myself, what could be better, a date in which we can do anything, the sky's the limit . . . you get payed for playing!!! What could possibly be better than that?

I made about $140. I had a wonderful time and so did the client. I told Jesse I loved being a escort and to fix me up as often as he liked. I was assigned many men after that. I'd say a good 75 percent wanted to finish off their evenings with sex. Some even would get quite insistent. I asked Jesse what to do. Jesse said do what you want to do, guys will offer you their own money (as a write off to their own company as entertainment). To sleep with me, I thought. He said, "Do what you want to do, if you want the money, go for it! If you don't keep standing firm!" I told Jesse I couldn't do it. So, he began to filter my dates more so and more so. He was always careful not to set me up with the weirdo's or the real wild party hardy guys. I mostly got the married with three kids and a dog type from then on.

I worked at the pace of picking up $40–$200 per date, for about three months; about 60 guys total. Then I met with a client from Europe for the second time. He was a very attractive man of 40. His black hair was salted with a whitened silver. He was a family man. Though, as was the story with many of the men I escorted, he was having alot of problems with his wife. While sitting at a bar he whispered in my ear, "Would you splease consider being with me tonight?" Knowing I'd turned him down the last time he was in town, he reached into his pocket for inspiration. $1,000.00 in crisp $100.00 bills he waved out like a fan and placed on the table. I looked at him and shook my head "No" I said. He put his hand on my arm and said, "How much do I have to offer you, $1,200, $1,400?" At this point I was getting pissed! In order to control my temper I flew off to the restroom in a rage. I remember standing at the sink, looking into the mirror, and thinking who in the hell does this man think he is!! I don't need his money! But still that much money, for sex?! . . . how could it be? I went back to the table with thousands of thoughts running through my mind. He looked at me and said, "I'm sorry if I upset you, but, I'm willing to give you all the money I have with me, $2,000 dollars. Hows that sound?" My initial thought was to slap the crap out of him, however, the things I could do with $2,000 cash. I agreed and it wasn't hard. No commitments, no future to worry about, and no love to get in the way of habitions. I went home that night with 20 crisp $100 dollar bills and four $20's left over from the date, in my coat pocket. There's nothing to it. I can spend $200 on myself and stick the rest in a savings account. It's no biggy!

I told Jesse about it. I told him I couldn't believe how easy or how much money I made. He laughed and asked me if I had plans of ever doing this again. I said sure, it's no problem. I made over $20,000 in the 4 months to follow. Enough to buy me a new car. I never have made $2,000 in a evening again but, it became a game to me. How high can you raise the bid? How much will it take to make this man make an offer straight up? How much teasing can you get buy with, without having him drop his attention?

I've worked more than 2 yrs. I've totally mellowed out of the games. If it looks good to me, and if I find the man attractive I'll do it. I've become very secure financially. I have multiple CD's, bonds and ect. I have three savings accounts and alot of money tied up in the stock market. My only regrets are I have to keep it a complete secret from everyone. My parents, who mean more to me than the world, my family, and even my dearest friends. I miss out on the average everyday social life of a college student. I have to lie to practically everyone I meet. But, nowhere will I find a job in which I can save as much money for my future. Or for that matter when I get out of college and get a respectable job in advertising, make that kind of money. But, my life will be back to a "normal" one. One in which I can be proud of, one which I can share with my friends and family, one in which I can make a "honest" living.

When we turn our focus on more privileged prostitutes, then, the themes of abuse and emotional deprivation are less likely to appear. Call girls often become prostitutes much like anyone chooses any occupation (Lucas 2005; Pilot 2008; Weitzer 2009). Some take pride in their work and have high self-esteem. In a study of call girls in Australia, seven out of ten said they would "choose this work" if they had it to do over again (Weitzer 2007).

For young prostitutes (ages 10 to 15), the motivation is different. Sociologist James Hodgson (1997) found that the primary reason they became prostitutes was neither money nor abuse. Instead, they had "fallen in love" with a pimp, who, after seducing them, insisted they "turn tricks" to help out.

Three Stages in Becoming a Prostitute. As you saw in the box "Me, a Prostitute?" becoming a prostitute is often a gradual process. Nanette Davis (1978), a symbolic interactionist who interviewed prostitutes in three correctional institutions in Minnesota, identified three stages.

1. In the first stage, women *drift* from casual sex to their first act of prostitution. During this "drift," they face a series of forks in the road. The choices they make channel them toward or away from prostitution. Circumstances that lead to drifting toward prostitution include broken homes, dropping out of school, pregnancy, drug use, a juvenile record, and having sex at a young age. On average, these women first had sexual intercourse at age 13 (the youngest was age 7, the oldest 18). The girls engaged in casual sex for an average of 4 years before they drifted into prostitution. One prostitute described it this way:

   > *I was going to school and I wanted to go to this dance the night after. I needed new clothes. I went out at ten o'clock and home at twelve. I had three tricks the first time, and fifteen dollars (about $50 in today's money) for every trick. (Davis 1978:206)*

2. Davis calls the second stage *transitional deviance*. During this stage, (which lasts an average of 6 months), girls experience **role ambivalence**—that is, they are not sure they want to be prostitutes. They feel both attracted to and repulsed by prostitution. To help overcome their ambivalence, many girls tell themselves that what they are doing is normal. As one girl said,

   > *I'm a person who likes to walk. There's nothing wrong with picking somebody up while you're walking. I always like walking around at night, and girls will be tempted. Girls like the offer. They like to see what a guy is going to say. (Davis 1978:203–209)*

3. Davis calls the third stage *professionalization*. During this stage, the girls identify themselves as prostitutes. They begin to build their lives around this identity and defend the selling of sex. Some sound as though they have read the functionalist perspective—they claim they reduce marital tension by giving unsatisfied men a sexual outlet. Others say that prostitution helps prevent rape.

TABLE 3.1 ▸ Arrests for Prostitution and Commercialized Sex, by Age

Age	Percent	Number
Under 18	1.7%	804
Under 10	—	1
10–12	—	5
13–14	0.2%	85
15–17	1.5%	713
Over 18	98.3%	47,477
18–24	27.4%	13,209
25–34	28.9%	13,953
35–44	23.5%	11,344
45–54	14.6%	7,035
55–64	3.1%	1,512
65 and older	0.9%	424
Total arrested:		48,281

Note: The source does not list prostitution separately, but includes it in a category called prostitution and commercialized vice. Consequently, the totals include a large proportion (31 percent) of males (Table 39 of the *UCR*).

Source: By the author. Based on *FBI Uniform Crime Reports* 2011:Table 38.

Age of Prostitutes. Look at Table 3.1 to see how young and how old some prostitutes are. The involvement of children in the sex industry angers most people. We shall return to this topic in the section on child pornography.

The Pimp and the Prostitute. Why would a woman rent her body, knowing she might be hurt by sadists, risk death by AIDS, and then turn the money she makes over to a man? Let's use the sociological perspectives to explain this.

Functionalists would emphasize the services that pimps provide: They locate customers, screen out sadistic johns, and bail prostitutes out of jail. Some pimps do these things, but researchers have found that pimps are more likely to make the girls they control find their own customers, remain unconcerned if they are beaten up, and be unavailable when they are arrested (Hodgson 1997; Weitzer 2009). For this reason, we have to move beyond functionalism for an explanation.

Conflict–feminist theorists would claim that the answer lies in the pimp's power. They, not the prostitutes, rule the streets.

To control women, the pimps use their greater physical strength, and they are ruthless in using it. Consider what a former prostitute said:

I saw a girl walk into a bar and hand the pimp a $100 bill. He took it and burned it in her face and turned around and knocked her down on the floor and kicked her and said, "I told you, bitch, $200. I want $200, not $100." Now she's gotta go out again and make not another hundred, but two hundred. (Millett 1973:134)

Symbolic interactionists would stress that there is more to the story than services or power. They look for an answer in what pimps mean to prostitutes. Take the background of a typical young street prostitute. She is likely to have run away from an intolerable home life. Pimps play on her insecurities and fears. Even older girls remain emotionally dependent. Many pimps offer a sense of belonging, affection, and tenderness. Some hold out the hope of marriage, children, even a home in the suburbs after they save enough money from the girl's earnings. Pimps, however, are exploiters, and they may be making the same promises to several women. They tell each that she is the special woman in their lives, cautioning her not to tell the others so the two of them can use the earnings of the other women to fulfill their plans.

Pimps are unconcerned about the welfare of their women, except as it affects their earnings. To them, the women are money machines, and they use and abuse their human ATMs at will. The pimp's real interest is making sure that the women "work the streets" whether they are sick or not and that they aren't poached by other pimps (Weitzer 2009). Another interest of pimps is to gain and maintain prestige from other street men. The pimp's street status depends on the number of women he controls in his "stable"; on how aloof he remains from these women while making them bend to his will; and on his personal grooming, jewelry, cars, leisure, and free-spending ways (Milner and Milner 1972; Williamson and Cluse-Tolar 2002).

Symbolic interactionists stress that to understand people we need to grasp what things mean to them. In this case, we need to understand what the pimp means to the prostitute. For some, he becomes the whole world, representing the little bit of security she has. When we take an insider's view into a subculture, the world looks like a different place—and it is. This is precisely the point: to see from within in order to understand human behavior. This is often difficult to do with oppositional subcultures—those that contradict the standards and experiences of mainstream society.

Male Prostitutes. Male prostitutes can be classified by whether their customers are men or women. Let's look at each type.

Men who sell sex to women are sometimes known as "gigolos." In 1980, sociologist Ed Sagarin concluded that this is "an infrequent behavior, for which there is little demand and probably more folklore than reality." Since then, sexual norms have changed, and it is apparent from the "beach boys" of Bali to the "rent boys" of the Internet that it is now more common for women to pay men for sex (Lee-Gonyea et al. 2009; Dumas 2012). Some Internet sites even have a customer satisfaction section. One woman wrote:

Now I'm not the type of lady to kiss and tell so I'll just leave it up to the reader's imagination, but this I will say: he's no amateur when it comes to romance and taking good care of a woman's needs. I will definitely call upon this fine gentleman's services again in the near future (Lee-Gonyea et al. 2009:339-340).

Heidi Fleiss, who was arrested for running a call girl operation in Hollywood, decided to open "The Stud Farm," a brothel in Nevada where women customers could hire male prostitutes (Friess 2005). Nevada authorities refused to give Fleiss a license on the basis that she is a convicted felon, but they were also against the idea of a brothel *for* women. The owners of a legal brothel in Nevada liked the idea, and after long, bureaucratic wrangling, they were able to get approval to hire "shady men" for their "Shady Lady Ranch." Apparently, this was the first time in world history that men have been licensed to sell sex (Powers 2010). With few women wanting "prostidudes," the endeavor

Male prostitutes soliciting customers outside a gay bar in Pattaya, Thailand.

was short-lived. The Shady Lady's Website now says that it features "shady ladies" for the working man.

More commonly, men sell sex to other men, with the prostitutes gathering in areas known as "meat racks," public settings such as parks or certain street corners. Sociologist David Luckenbill (1986) found that male prostitutes have a hierarchy that parallels that of female prostitutes: At the bottom are street hustlers, in the middle are bar hustlers, and at the top are escort prostitutes who work for dating agencies. At each level, the charge per trick increases and the prestige goes up.

Although rare, houses of male prostitution also exist. Sociologist David Pittman (1971) studied a brothel in St. Louis that was exclusively for male clients. To recruit prostitutes, the "madam" (a man) advertised for male models. When young men applied, he explained why he really wanted to hire them. Customers selected a prostitute by viewing a catalog of nude photographs. The prostitutes' short career followed this pattern: high popularity when first hired, intense pressure to keep up sexual performance, the abuse of drugs and alcohol, a decline in sexual performance, loss of customers, and being fired.

Back in the 1960s, sociologist Albert Reiss, Jr. (1961) did research on teenaged prostitutes that became classic. Reiss found that the boys he studied, although paid by older men to receive oral sex, had a heterosexual identity. This piqued his curiosity, so he pursued it. Reiss found that to keep identifying themselves as heterosexuals the boys (1) allowed no emotional attachment to the men, (2) made money their only motivator, (3) tolerated nothing other than receiving oral sex, (4) never associated with a homosexual in public, (5) reserved sexual gratification for girlfriends, and (6) made sure they were seen with a girlfriend in public.

Prostitution among boys has become more open since Reiss studied it (Cates and Markley 1992; Beddoe et al. 2001). Many see the apparent increase in boy prostitution as a social problem in and of itself. As with heterosexual prostitution, a related problem is sexually transmitted diseases.

Prostitution as a Social Problem: Subjective Concerns. Why does prostitution arouse so much subjective concern? Here are major points of view that I have culled from the extensive literature on prostitution:

1. Morality: Prostitution involves sexual relations among people who are not married to one another.

2. Morality: Sex is bought and sold, not freely given in a loving relationship.
3. Exploitation: Prostitution exploits women's bodies, degrades their spirits, and subjugates them to men.
4. Property: Prostitution ruins "good" neighborhoods. It depresses property values by bringing in unsavory characters and illegal activities such as drug dealing.
5. Crime: Victimless or not, prostitution is illegal.
6. Corruption: Profits from prostitution corrupt police and judges, uniting these "enforcers of morality" with pimps, madams, and organized criminals.
7. Disease: Prostitutes spread AIDS and other sexually transmitted diseases.
8. Aesthetics: People feel disgusted when they see used condoms and tissues discarded in public places, including schoolyards.

Let's turn to pornography, another sexual behavior that arouses subjective concerns.

Pornography

3.6 Explain changes in pornography in the U.S.

Originally, *pornography* referred to erotic writings by prostitutes or to descriptions of the life of prostitutes. (*Porna* is Greek for "prostitute.") There are always problems with definitions, but for our purposes we can define **pornography** as writings, pictures, or objects of a sexual nature that people object to as being filthy or immoral.

As discussed in the Issues in Social Problems box on the next page, what is or is not pornography is not decided easily.

Background: Getting the Larger Picture

From the box you just read, you can see that deciding that something is pornographic is like deciding what beauty is. The decision lies in the eye of the beholder. Some people think that nude statues are pornographic, but for others, those same statues are works of art. Are movies that show sexual intercourse pornographic? More would probably say they are. How about movies or photos that depict oral sex? A larger number would probably say yes. How about those that depict anal intercourse? The number would probably increase. How about movies that show sex between humans and animals? Or those that show adults having sex with children? At this point, the rate of agreement that these are pornographic would jump.

The Pornifying of America. From its beginnings as an underground cottage industry, pornography has grown into an open and aggressive multibillion-dollar-a-year business. Behind today's pornography lies an extensive network of people who profit from it: writers, publishers, actors, and filmmakers; owners of bookstores, video stores, theaters, and Internet sites; corner newsstands and supermarket chains; and banks and financiers. HBO and Time Warner profit from selling pornographic movies, as do Holiday Inn, Marriott, Hyatt, Hilton, Sheraton, and other hotels that offer pay-per-view pornography. The proliferation of XXX programs makes sure that Internet service providers and cable and telephone companies get their share. Like politics, pornography makes strange bedfellows.

Much of pornography has moved from back alley ventures to the mainstream. Shown here is Jenna Jameson, who stars in porn movies, attending an Oscar party in Beverly Hills, California.

Pornography has become so common that we can say that the United States has become *pornified.* Sexual norms eased just as new forms of technology allowed pornography to proliferate. Previously, people would risk their reputations if they were seen visiting a porn shop, which likely was in a seedy part of town. The Internet allows people to pursue pornography in private. About one in three Internet users visits adult Web sites each month. They average eight visits a month, with their average visit lasting 12 minutes (Edelman 2009). Although

Thinking Critically About Social Problems

Just What Is Pornography? And What Makes It a Social Problem?

Materials intended to cause sexual excitement have existed since early history. Pornography abounded in the Roman Empire, as shown by excavations of the Mediterranean resort city of Pompeii, which was destroyed by an eruption of Mount Vesuvius in 79 A.D. There, archaeologists uncovered brothels decorated with mosaic murals of men and women engaging in a variety of sexual acts. The *Kama Sutra,* an Indian religious book that goes back 1,300 years, describes sexual acts in explicit detail. It includes not only illustrations of sexual positions but also instructions on how prostitutes can please their customers (Henriques 1966). Our own society is filled with representations of almost every sort intended to cause sexual excitement—from movies and videos to comic books and novels. We even license stores that specialize in selling objects whose purpose is sexual arousal.

But what makes representations designed to arouse people sexually a social problem? Remember that we need both objective conditions and subjective concerns. The wall decorations of Pompeii were intended to arouse people sexually, but it is most unlikely that either prostitutes or clients objected to them. Similarly the illustrations of the *Kama Sutra* did not arouse concern by the priests, their followers, or the prostitutes of the time. These objects were *not* part of a social problem.

As time passes, ideas of life change, including what is good and bad, the stuff that goes into morality. So it is today, and many object to the sexual illustrations of Pompeii and the *Kama Sutra*—and similar depictions of sexual acts wherever they may occur—whether in movies, writing, or objects. This is the subjective concern that we need in order to have a social problem. And we have it in abundance.

Globally, the Internet has become the primary source of pornography. Shown here is a digital porn performer signing photos of herself for fans at the Adult Entertainment Expo in Las Vegas.

Not everyone has these objections or concerns, of course, which takes us to the heart of the relativity of social problems.

For Your Consideration

In your eyes, what makes something pornographic? Do you think pornography is a social problem? Why or why not?

some Internet sites target women, the vast majority of sites are directed to men—action packed, with men dominant, bending both resisting or nonresisting women to their will (Tsatsou 2012).

Pornography Viewed Theoretically: Applying Symbolic Interactionism

3.7 Explain the symbolic interactionist perspective on pornography.

Many Americans are concerned about pornography and its possible effects on people's morality and relationships. But what should be done about pornography has also been a matter of controversy. Even to determine what is and is not pornography has bedeviled legislators, the police, and the courts. Let's apply symbolic interactionism as we look at some major Supreme Court decisions.

Trying to Determine Meanings: Roth v. United States ▸ The problem of defining pornography has plagued the courts since the 1950s. In 1957, the U.S. Supreme Court took upon itself the job of defining pornography for the nation. It failed miserably. In *Roth v. United States,* the Court ruled that materials are pornographic or obscene when

1. "Taken as a whole," the "dominant theme" appeals to "prurient interest" in sex.
2. The material affronts "contemporary community standards."
3. The material is "utterly without redeeming social value."

Our technological revolution is changing some people's lives in surprising ways. Shown here is Roxxxy, the world's first sex robot. She has artificial intelligence and skin and can talk. Speech is not likely to be her primary appeal.

You can see why the *Roth* decision didn't settle anything. Look at its major terms, which I have placed in quotes above. *Prurient,* for example, means "lewd or impure." But this word solves nothing—it simply takes us back to the initial question of what pornography is. What is lewd or impure to me might be humorous or delightful to you. The Court's supposed guidelines, instead of clearing up matters, only muddied them further. It is doubtful that the terms were even clear to the Court.

As symbolic interactionists emphasize, until people attach meaning to something, words are merely sounds and human acts merely behavior. If two people look at the same photo or watch the same movie, video, or stage play, one might see sexual intercourse as an expression of beauty, art, and love, while the other perceives the filth and depravity of pornography. What, then, does the Court's phrase *redeeming social value* mean? Where does it leave us if I decide that the sexual content of a book or movie has "redeeming social value," but you do not?

And so the search for agreement on meaning marches on. Where some claim that certain materials violate *contemporary community standards,* others say that those same materials reflect community standards. Still others say there are no community standards! The Internet, developed after the *Roth* decision, has muddied the waters even further. Does "community" refer to the place where the materials were produced, or to where they were downloaded? Or do the people who exchange sexually explicit photos on the Internet form a "community"? If so, should it be their values by which we judge something as pornographic or not? What a wild decision that would be!

California v. Miller ▸ As you can see, the *Roth* decision didn't clarify a thing—and its ambiguities made it difficult for prosecutors to obtain convictions for pornography. In 1973, in *California v. Miller,* the Court tried to remove these ambiguities. It kept the dominant "prurient" theme, and said that "contemporary community standards" meant the local community. The Court simply gave up on trying to figure out what it had ever meant by "redeeming social value" and dropped the term (Lewis and Peoples 1978:1071).

What is or is not pornographic remained in the eye of the beholder, and cities split on how to handle the matter. Some cities banned the sale of images of sexual acts, while others restricted them to designated areas. Some cities took a permissive route, not only allowing the sale of images of sexual acts but also allowing live performances of sexual acts. With such glaring inconsistencies, pornography again landed in the lap of the Supreme Court. This time the Court gave up on the fruitless task of trying to define anything. It just took a middle ground and ruled in 1976 (*Young v. American Mini*

Theaters) and 1986 (*Renton v. Playtime Theatres*) that it is constitutional to restrict the location of adult movie theaters.

A Matter of "Taste." If you or I view sexual images, our backgrounds of experience come into play. A significant part of our backgrounds is our social class, one of several factors that helps to determine if we perceive images and acts as pornographic or not. The significance of social class became evident in a later Court ruling that some nudity, such as that in theater productions and art, is permissible because it is "tasteful." In contrast, forms of nudity such as striptease dancing are not "tasteful." They are "low-art," if "art" at all, and can be made illegal and their participants arrested (Heins 1991).

"Tasteful"? The question of what is or is not "tasteful" merely takes us full circle. We end up back at the original question of what pornography is. Whose "tastes" are we talking about? As conflict theorists would point out, the Supreme Court justices followed the usual dominance by the ruling class: They decided that their own class-based preferences for nudity (the "theatre," not some scudsy, back-alley striptease joint that they wouldn't be caught dead in) are "artistic," "tasteful," not pornographic. In contrast, the nudity that the lower classes enjoy are "not artistic," "not tasteful," but pornographic—and the police can prosecute that type to their hearts' content.

Child Pornography. Hardly anyone says that "redeeming social value" or "community standards" are an adequate defense for producing images of children in sex acts with adults or with other children. Yet in the 1970s, child pornography was not illegal and used to be sold fairly openly. Adult bookstores featured children in magazines that bore such titles as *Lollitots* and *Moppets* (Dubar 1980). Some of the children were as young as 3 or 4, but most buyers of these magazines seemed to prefer prepubescents between the ages of 8 and 10.

As states passed laws against child pornography and judges began to send offenders to prison for possessing these materials, magazines and movies featuring children practically disappeared. Child pornography, however, did not disappear. It just went underground, resurfacing on the Internet. There, people who are stimulated by sex with children "meet" in chat rooms, where they share stories of their exploits, real or imagined. Some buy, sell, or swap files of children who have been bribed, tricked, or forced into sex acts. The photos, movies, and streaming videos are illegal, but the use of passwords and encryption, as well as locating Internet sites in countries whose laws are weak and where officials could care less, make it difficult for law enforcement agents to track down those responsible for child pornography. Sting operations occasionally net dozens of offenders (Soens 2012)

Who is aroused sexually by watching children in sex acts? You might think it is the scum of the earth, but the facts are quite different. While we have no random samples of viewers of child pornography, the viewer is likely to be your neighbor. What do I mean by this? Simply that many ordinary, "good" people regularly view child pornography. This is a logical conclusion to draw from those who are caught in sting operations, who offer to swap files, or who are found to have images of child porn on their computers: Teachers, doctors, police, and FBI agents are among them ("Former FBI Agent . . ." 2012; Lamberti 2012).

Child pornography is marked by inconsistent and contradictory rulings. In 2002, in *Ashcroft v. Free Speech Coalition*, the U.S. Supreme Court ruled that it is legal to possess virtual child pornography—that is, computer-generated images of children in sex acts. Because no real child is involved, the Court concluded, there is no victim. In reaction, the next year Congress passed the PROTECT Act, specifying that it is illegal to produce, distribute, or possess "a visual depiction of any kind of a minor engaging in sexually explicit conduct." This includes drawings, cartoons, sculptures, and paintings—unless Congress added, it has "serious literary, artistic, political, or scientific value."

This, of course, once again takes us back to the original problem of determining "value" and "merit."

Although the Court has not explicitly overthrown its 2002 *Free Speech* decision, computer-generated images of children having sex seem to be illegal. This seems to also apply to drawings and paintings, perhaps even to four-fingered comic characters on the Internet. "These are just lines on paper," claim those who think the law preposterous. It will take more decisions by the Court to clarify what is legal and illegal. In the midst of such confusing rulings, people are being arrested for possession of cartoons that some officials view as obscene or pornographic (Kravets 2009).

As you can see, these are thorny issues. With no easy answers, they must be sorted out by lawmakers, lawyers, and judges—and all within an inconsistent, changing society whose ideas of morality are continuously evolving. The topic of the Thinking Critically box below examines another issue that is being sorted out.

Thinking Critically About Social Problems

Restitution for Child Pornography?

> "It is hard to describe what it feels like to know that at any moment, anywhere, someone is looking at pictures of me as a little girl being abused by my uncle and is getting some kind of sick enjoyment from it. It's like I am being abused over and over again." Amy

Amy was just a little girl when her uncle (now in prison) began to molest her—and take pictures of himself having sex with her. He also made videos of his abuse. And he posted the photographs and videos on the Internet, where they have been circulating for over 10 years. Over those same years, the images of Amy have been showing up in the pornographic collections of men who have been arrested for possessing child pornography.

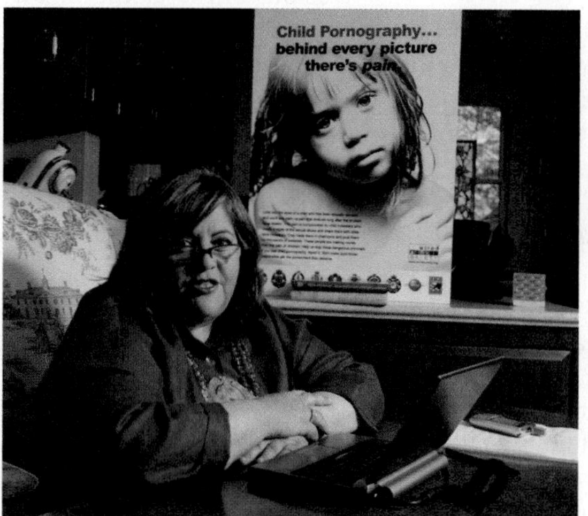

Shown here is Parry Aftab, head of an Internet safety group whose purpose is to protect children from pornographic exploitation.

Now an adult, Amy gets notices from the courts whenever prosecutors identify her images in these collections. She has received more than 800 notices.

Amy decided to fight back: "Those men who are looking at my pictures and watching those videos aren't innocent. They are guilty of exploiting me, just like my uncle did."

Amy went to an attorney, who agreed with her. He said that these men should have to pay restitution for the harm that was done to her. Amy and her attorney decided that she was owed $3.5 million for damages.

Amy is suing any individual caught with images of her being abused. So far, she has collected $245,000. Amy and her lawyer plan to keep these lawsuits going until Amy receives the full $3.5 million.

Some judges assess huge fines, but not all judges agree with the law, and a little judicial rebellion has appeared. Some judges order payment of just $100. Others are refusing to order any restitution. They say, in legal language, that "the link between possession and the harm done is too tenuous to reach the level of proximate harm." In plain terms, this means that those who made and distributed the images have harmed Amy, but not those who possess or view the images.

Despite the confusion and conflicting decisions, the U.S. Supreme Court has refused to hear the case.

Based on Forliti 2010; Schwartz 2010; Richey 2011.

For Your Consideration

Do you think that someone who views photos of a child being abused sexually owes restitution to the child? How has that person harmed the child?

Controversy and Research on Pornography

3.8 Explain the controversy over pornography and understand the major research findings on pornography.

Like other social problems, pornography is not only about controversy, but also about emotions. Fear is one of those emotions. A common fear concerning pornography is that it destroys people's morals, perverts their sense of sexuality, and even encourages men to rape. Does it? While we can't measure whether pornography corrupts morals or perverts sexuality, as these are personal judgments—people's sense of right and wrong—we can report on the relationship of pornography and rape.

The National Commission on Obscenity and Pornography. In the 1960s, pornography bothered Americans more than it does now. It was seen as such as serious issue that the president of the United States (Johnson) appointed a National Commission on Obscenity and Pornography. In 1970, the commission concluded that pornography affects some people more than others. Unlike Kinsey et al. (1953), who reported that erotic materials arouse males considerably more than females, the commission found that women and men are about equally aroused by watching pornography (Schmidt and Sigusch 1970). Table 3.2 gives a nutshell summary of what they found.

TABLE 3.2 ▸ Pornography's Effects

More Sexual Stimulation	Less Sexual Stimulation
Younger	Older
More educated	Less educated
Not actively involved in a religion	Actively involved in a religion
More sexual experience	Less sexual experience

Note that these conclusions center on sexual arousal, not on social harm. As pornography proliferated, so did subjective concerns that pornography is harmful. Keep in mind that pornography was in its infancy at that time. This was before the Internet.

The Meese Commission. Dissatisfied with the mild conclusions of the Commission on Obscenity and Pornography, in the 1980s President Reagan asked the attorney general to appoint another commission to study the effects of pornography. This group, the Meese Commission (1986:39), concluded that pornography poses a threat to women—that "there is a causal relationship between exposure to sexually violent materials and an increase in aggressive behavior directed towards women." Pornography makes rape seem "legitimate," said the Commission, and an increase in pornography "will cause an increase in the level of sexual violence directed at women."

Cause, Effect, and Concerns About Morality. You might be wondering how the National Commission on Obscenity and Pornography and the Meese Commission could have come to such different conclusions. One concluded that pornography causes no harm, while the other claimed that it causes rape. People at the time wondered, too.

Here is a clue to solving this puzzle: The Meese Commission (1986:39) said that "common sense" makes it evident that violent pornography causes rape. You might recall that in Chapter 1 I stressed that "common sense" can be quite wrong. If all we need is common sense, we wouldn't need science, and science requires verifiable evidence. Critics said that the Meese Commission was predisposed to see pornography as evil and as the cause of crime. This colored the commission's views, leading it to misinterpret the evidence and ignore studies that contradicted the ideas it already had before it began its review (Baron 1987; Brannigan 1987; Linz et al. 1987).

It turns out that the Meese Commission confused **correlation** (two or more things occurring together) with **causation** (one thing producing an effect in something else). In particular, the Meese Commission jumped from its finding that rapists had viewed substantial amounts of pornography (a *correlation*) to the conclusion that the pornography *caused* their rapes.

Even though the Meese Commission confused correlation with causation, its conclusion could still have been right. Maybe pornography does cause rape, but the Meese Commission just didn't have the evidence. Many people have this fear about pornography that shows violence against women.

If the Meese Commission would have been able to make pornography increase in society, we could have seen if rape increased. This would still be a correlation, but it would be in the right direction, suggesting that the Meese Commission was right. On the other hand, if the unthinkable happened—the Meese Commission increased pornography and rape dropped—we would know that the Meese Commission was wrong.

Neither the Meese Commission nor anyone else could perform such a social experiment, of course, so we might still be left wondering about the relationship of pornography to rape. But then a surprising thing happened, and history changed a bit. After the Commission finished its report, the United States and other countries did their own *natural experiment,* and we were able to measure the results.

Pornography laws loosened, and the Internet was invented. As the use of personal computers began, a few sites on the Internet appeared that featured explicit sex. Then as computers became common, such sites multiplied, becoming popular with both men and women, the young and the old. From being an under-the-counter, back room, furtive purchase, pornography moved into the mainstream. It grew immensely, with Americans spending billions of dollars a year on pornography. Pornographers now hold their own annual trade show in Las Vegas.

In addition to more than a *million* free sites, the Internet offers thousands of pay sites, each charging a fee for access to photographs and streaming movies and videos. Some sites feature professional actors, others highlight amateurs. Sites are indexed, from A to Z, anal to zoo. Viewers can choose teenagers and grannies; whites, blacks, Asian, Hispanic; skinny, heavy; little breasts, big breasts; heterosexual, homosexual; and, of course, a variety of types of sexual activity. If someone likes to watch people having sex with animals, that is available, too. The list goes on and on, expanding to satisfy what seems to be everyone's taste. If there is a market for sexual preference, some Internet entrepreneur somewhere is more than eager to meet it.

So what was the result of this natural experiment? Did rape increase, as the Meese Commission stressed would be the commonsense result? Look at Figure 3.1. You can see that rape increased a little, then decreased a lot. The U.S. rape rate (the number of rapes per 100,000 people) was 37 in 1980. The rate increased to 43 in 1992 and then began a long drop. At 28, the rape rate is now much lower than it was before pornography began to flourish.

What can we conclude? First, the results do not support the commonsense idea that pornography causes rape. Second, the evidence goes against common sense and

FIGURE 3.1 ▸ Forcible Rape in the United States

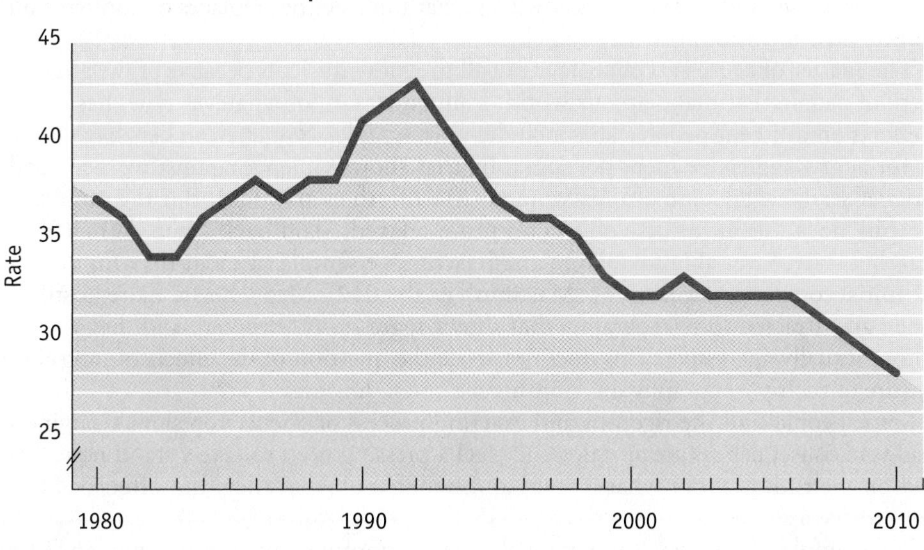

Source: By the author. Based on *Statistical Abstract of the United States* 1990:Table 283; 2013:Table 312.

points in the other direction, that pornography *reduces* sex crimes. The members of the Meese Commission would roll over in their graves at such a suggestion, but we need to look at evidence with open minds, not try to confirm our commonsense ideas.

Listen on **MySocLab Audio:** NPR: Tracking the Child Sex Trade in Southeast Asia

This is still a correlation, not causation, but this unexpected finding also shows up in other countries In 1965, Denmark made hard-core pornography legal. When it did, that country's sex crimes against children dropped (Kutchinsky 1973). The same thing happened in the 1980s when Japan allowed the sale of hard-core pornography. And 20 years later when the Czech Republic decriminalized the possession of child pornography, what do you think happened? Common sense might predict that offenses against children would increase. But they didn't. Instead, sexual abuse against children dropped there, too (Diamond 2009).

How can this possibly be? These results fly in the face of what so many people would expect. The answer is probably this: Some men who would like to have sex with children find it more appealing to masturbate to pornographic images than to face the threat of shame and prison if they indulge their fantasies with real children. Some who molest children may not even prefer children: They take children as substitutes because they are unable to relate sexually to adults. For these people, too, pornographic images may provide a substitute.

One thing is clear: As pornography in the United States—including that depicting violence against women—has become more common, rape has become less common. It is difficult to determine cause and effect in human behavior, but one thing seems certain: If an increase in pornography were accompanied by an *increase* in sexual attacks, there would be an outcry to get rid of it. The evidence, though, goes in the direction of pornography *reducing* sexual attacks. Listen carefully: To protect women, do you hear an outcry to increase pornography?

In the three countries that legalized child pornography, sex crimes against children dropped. As outrageous as it might seem to common sense, it is possible that child pornography might be a way to *protect* children. But if so, can you imagine any group demanding that child pornography be legalized "for the sake of the children"?

Science Versus Social Action. This is science at work. When research is published, it enters what we might call the "courtroom of science," where it is judged by a jury of critical scientific peers. When researchers report their findings, other researchers meticulously examine their research. They challenge the research and repeat the study or reanalyze the original data to publish their own conclusions. This critical process exposes researchers' biases and errors. The knowledge that builds either replaces or confirms our commonsense ideas about social problems.

The matter of cause and effect is made all the more difficult because of the amazing variety of people that make up our world. Human action, of whatever type, has different effects on different people. This includes pornography. Some researchers have found that for angry, aggressive men, pornography that shows violence against women tends to trigger sexual aggression against women (Malamuth et al. 2000). But the same pornography does not have these effects on more relaxed, "laid back" men. When these researchers were later able to analyze a representative sample of men, they found that their initial conclusions were right (Malamuth et al. 2012). Men who are more hostile to women are attracted to pornography that shows aggression to women, and they tend to be more sexually aggressive. This does not settle the question of the effects of long-term exposure to such pornography on "non-hostile" men, however.

Some people find the rigorous and exacting process of science too slow. Convinced that severe consequences are at stake, they feel a pressing need to take a stand now. And based on their ideas about what is right and wrong and what they find offensive, they often do take a stand.

For example, many people are upset about how pornography portrays women. They are convinced that pornography teaches men to view women as "pieces of meat" and that it teaches women to devalue their own bodies. Whether pornography causes sex crimes is not the point, they insist. Even if it does not, the degrading portrayal of women in pornography is another way that men debase and victimize women. This is reason enough to ban pornography—at least the type that shows violence against females. As discussed in the Thinking Critically about Social Problems box below, though resistance to pornography is strongly rooted, it has lost to the porn industry.

Thinking Critically About Social Problems

The Pornifying of America: Crushing Resistance and Co-Opting Feminists

Pornography has become big business, but to have a market for the many magazines, millions of photographs, and tens of thousands of pornographic videos and movies required a change in attitude. In the United States, pornography met deep resistance. Almost everyone considered pornography immoral. How did porn manage to prosper in the midst of attitudes that would destroy it?

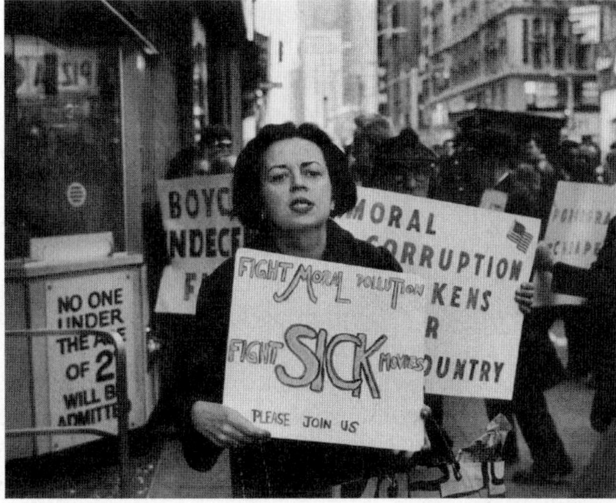

I chose this photo to illustrate the extensive change that has occurred regarding pornography. In the 1960s/1970s, opposition to pornography was based on morality. Today's opposition, what little remains, concerns the exploitation of children and young women.

Religious conservatives view pornography as a moral issue, a matter of sin. They see the growing pornography industry as a sign of the growing depravity of U.S. culture. Conservatives continue to put up stiff resistance, but as pornography becomes more common, further resistance has come to be viewed as labor wasted on a lost cause. Occasionally, a religious leader will bemoan pornography, but he or she is preaching to the choir—and some in this choir view pornography at home (Diamond 2009).

Feminists split on this issue. Some find pornography to be morally objectionable, but they don't want to be seen as aligned with those they consider religious fanatics. Their position is not that pornography is sinful, but that it degrades and exploits women. Not only are women shown as a bunch of body parts to be used for the pleasure of men, but also many women who work in the porn industry suffer sexual and emotional abuse. These feminists find themselves opposed by feminists who say that pornography liberates women sexually, freeing them from the prudishness that had entrapped them. For them, pornography becomes a means to encourage women to explore and express their full sexuality. They support better working conditions and health standards for women who work in pornography. As you can imagine, the porn industry has been delighted by this division among feminists, who, united as vocal opponents, could have influenced antipornography legislation. Resistance here, too, is quiet.

The victory of the porn industry has been so far-reaching that criticizing pornography has become "uncool, unsexy, and reactionary" (Paul 2005). To argue that pornography is part of women's freedom, not their oppression, makes it difficult to take a stand against it.

How great is the victory of the porn industry? Women's magazines now discuss pornography from the perspective of equal opportunity for women—how women can introduce pornography into their sex lives and how it gives women the chance to get "in touch" with their sexuality (Paul 2005).

Some feminists have gone beyond this and are producing what they call "feminist porn." Their goal is to get more women involved in producing pornography so it no longer reflects solely the "men's view," which, they say, directs men's sexual desires to just certain types of women, primarily skinny ones with big breasts. They want their feminist porn to expand men's sexual appetites to include fat women, women with cellulite, and so on.

Now this is quite a change.

For Your Consideration

Do you think the United States has been "pornified"? Why or why not? What effects do you think pornography is having on society?

Social Policy

3.9 Discuss the issue of making consensual behavior illegal—and its alternatives.

I made the point earlier in this chapter that sex is not merely a personal matter, that the social group with a stake in our sexuality sets up ways to channel or control it. Even consensual acts behind closed doors can be public issues. For example, purchasing a prostitute's services or watching child pornography in one's own home can lead to criminal charges. Running through a great deal of the controversy that surrounds human sexual behavior as a social problem are the issues of consent and legality. Let's look at these central issues.

The Question of Making Consensual Behavior Illegal

Sociologists use the term **victimless crime** to refer to illegal acts between consenting adults. The crime has no victim because the people agree to do something with, to, or for one another. Someone pays someone else for sex, for example. The transaction may be illegal, but it occurs with the consent of the people involved.

In most crimes, someone acts against another person. There is a victim and a perpetrator (a "perp," as the cops say). When a victim reports a crime, the police know where and when it happened and who the victim is. Without a victim, however, the police end up spending precious public resources attempting to determine that a crime occurred, and then prosecutors have difficulty in obtaining convictions because the people involved consented to what took place. Unless there is a public outcry, both the public and the police prefer that law enforcement agents pursue criminals who have victims—thieves, muggers, rapists, and murderers.

Not all prostitution and pornography involve victimless crimes, however. There can be force, threats, drugging, deception, or less than informed consent. If there is force, it is rape, a different matter entirely. If there is less than informed consent, there is also a victim. Cameras surreptitiously slipped under women's skirts in public, for example, does not involve consent. Neither is child pornography a victimless crime. The children are not of age to give their consent, and child pornography often involves the abuse of adult authority. To deal adequately with social policy, we must separate such instances from those that involve full consent.

Alternatives to Making Consensual Behavior Illegal

Legalizing Prostitution. Because prostitution is a commercial transaction—a business—some argue that it should be legal. We license and tax businesses, so why not prostitution? Those who favor legalization point out that prostitution is not going away, no matter what anyone thinks, and they suggest it is time for the state to regulate it. We discuss this in the Thinking Critically box on the next page.

The Matter of Privacy. Central to deciding social policy is the issue of privacy. The argument is that if adults want to have sex in private, why should it concern the state? It may be a sin to some, but should those people's attitudes make it a crime?

There is yet another side to the privacy argument—the right of *privacy from* people who are involved in sexual acts. Those who find such behavior repugnant should not have to see it. Even if these behaviors become legal, the law should prohibit street solicitation by prostitutes, sex in public places, and nudity and or sexual acts on the covers of magazines in supermarkets.

To allow people to pay for sex *and* ensure that others don't have to see it if they don't want to, some suggest *segregation*—limiting these activities to specified areas. This is the solution chosen in Nevada, where counties decide whether or not to license houses of prostitution, determine how many brothels will be allowed, and where they will be located. Segregating prostitution to a certain area of the city helps the *freedom from* issue. To this end, blatant advertising can be banned even in those areas. Prostitutes could advertise for customers in newspapers, on the Internet, or even by a red light in an apartment window, but they could not solicit on the streets. Nor could pornographic sites show sexually explicit marquees or posters. This would allow the patrons of prostitutes

Thinking Critically About Social Problems

Should We Legalize Prostitution?

YES

1. Prostitutes perform a service for society. They provide sex for people who can't find other sexual partners. They even help marriages by providing an outlet for sexual desires that the marriage partner doesn't want to be involved with.
2. To keep prostitution illegal stigmatizes and marginalizes women who want to work as prostitutes. It also corrupts police officers, who accept bribes to allow prostitutes to work. Pimps control some prostitutes by force, and some prostitution is run by organized crime, with women held in bondage. Legalizing prostitution will eliminate these problems.
3. If prostitution is a legal occupation, the government can regulate it. Prostitutes will be licensed and taxed. The *taxes* will bring in revenue sorely needed in these perilous economic times. The *licensing* will ensure that prostitutes have regular medical checkups. The prostitutes will be required to display a dated and signed medical certificate confirming that they are free of sexually transmitted diseases.

NO

1. Prostitution is immoral, and we should not legalize immoral activities. The foundation of society is the family, and we should take steps to strengthen the family, not tear it apart by approving sex as a commercial transaction outside the family.
2. Prostitution degrades and exploits women. To legalize prostitution is to give the state's approval to women's degradation. Legalization would also affirm class oppression: Most prostitutes come from the working class and serve as objects to satisfy the sexual desires of men from the more privileged classes.
3. The legalization of prostitution will not stop prostitutes from infecting their clients with sexually transmitted diseases (STDs). A prostitute can receive and transmit the HIV virus and other STDs before the disease shows up in blood tests. Even though prostitutes are licensed, they will spread STDs during this interval.

For Your Consideration

Do you think we should legalize prostitution? Why or why not? What are the sources of your particular attitudes?

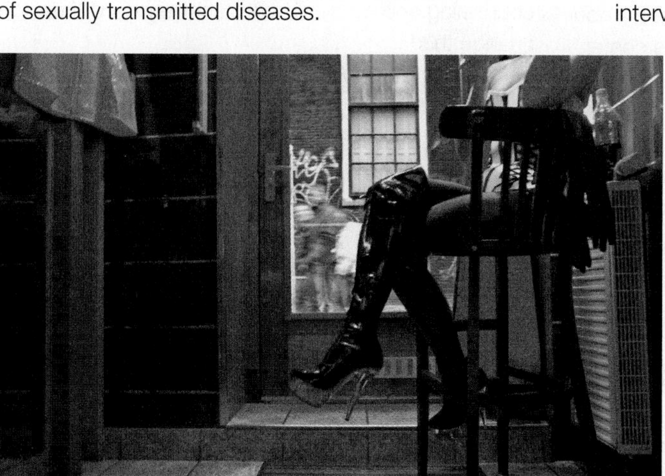

This photo shows a prostitute in the red light district of Amsterdam, Holland. Shoppers do window shopping as they stroll along the canal side streets.

and the consumers of pornography to carry out their consensual activities in private, while respecting the rights of others to avoid seeing their activities.

The Matter of Children. The use of children in prostitution and pornography is an entirely different matter. Almost everyone agrees that children should be protected from sexual exploitation. Their position is: If the purpose of the law is not to protect the defenseless of our society, then what is its purpose? As the Issues in Social Problems box on the next page shows, private citizens can help to protect children from sexual victimization.

Issues in Social Problems

Applying Sociology: Taking Back Children from the Night

Lois Lee isn't afraid to apply her sociological training to social problems. Lee did her master's thesis on the pimp–prostitute relationship and her doctoral dissertation on the social world of the prostitute. After receiving her Ph.D. in sociology from United States International University in 1981, Lee began to work with adult prostitutes. They told her, "You know, it's too late for you to help us, Lois. You've got to do something about these kids. We made a choice to be out here . . . a conscious decision. But these kids don't stand a chance."

A 17-year-old who was arrested for prostitution in an intervention program in Dallas, Texas.

Lee began by taking those kids, the teenagers who were prostituting themselves, into her home. In three years, she brought 250 to her home, where she lived with her husband and baby son. Lee then founded "Children of the Night," which reaches the kids by means of "a 24-hour hotline, a street outreach program, a walk-in crisis center, crisis intervention for medical or life-threatening situations, family counseling, job placement, and foster home or group placement." By providing alternatives to prostitution and petty crime, Children of the Night has helped thousands of young runaways and prostitutes to get off the streets.

Lee's work has brought her national publicity and an award from the president of the United States. She credits her success to her sociological training, especially the sensitivities it gave her "to understand and move safely through intersecting deviant worlds, to relate positively to police and caretaking agencies while retaining a critical perspective, to know which game to play in which situation."

As Lee said during a CBS interview, "I know what the street rules are, I know what the pimp game is, I know what the con games are, and it's up to me to play that game correctly. . . . It's all sociology. That's why when people call me a social worker I always correct them."

Lee is now battling for a change in the way underage prostitutes are treated after they are rescued from the streets. Currently, they remain in juvenile custody, are sent to foster care, or are even returned to the dysfunctional home where the abuse began. The girls do not get the counseling and medical treatment they need. Lee wants to change this.

Based on Buff 1987; Markman 2009; Rosenthal 2012.

For Your Consideration

Do you think teen prostitution is a different kind of problem than that of women and men in their 20s who rent their bodies? Why? How would you solve this problem?

The Future of the Problem

3.10 Explain the likely future of prostitution and pornography.

With the rapid social change that engulfs us, it is difficult to peer far into the future. Assuming that the United States does not devolve into a dictatorship, which could drive prostitution and pornography underground, I foresee the following.

Prostitution and the Future

Perhaps the easiest forecast in the entire book is this one: The demand for the services of prostitutes will continue. There will always be sexually deprived, frustrated, or adventuresome people who want to patronize prostitutes, as well as those who want to pay for specialized sexual services.

Although prostitution will continue to flourish, it will remain illegal in almost all areas of the United States. The police will overlook all but the most blatant acts, both because they feel that they have better things to do and because many of them are convinced that sexual acts between consenting adults should be legal. The prostitution of those under the age of consent is another matter. We are likely to see an increased emphasis on these children as victims, rather than as lawbreakers. If so, more concern will be placed on their treatment, rather than on locking them up in juvenile facilities.

Just as technology influences almost all aspects of our lives, so it will affect prostitution. Perhaps the most intriguing potential is the sex robots that entrepreneurs are developing (Yeoman and Mars 2010). The early models of these robots look like scantily dressed women. When these robots are launched, I assume they will come in a variety of forms to match the varied tastes of customers: younger and older, smaller and larger, different skin colors, and so on. I also assume that male homosexuals and women won't be left out—that there will be sex robots equipped with male appendages.

Pornography and the Future

Changes in pornography are likely to be driven by two forces: technology and profits. As each new communication technology appears, pornography will be adapted to fit it. With the ease of producing and viewing moving images, with video cameras and DVDs, for example, more people will produce pornography. Because pornography is so profitable, it is likely that the mainstream media will embrace it even more. Cable television is likely to offer more explicit programs than its current XXX options, perhaps at some point broadcasting live sex programs. The line between pornography and art will continue to blur, making it difficult to distinguish between pornography and regular films. See the Technology and Social Problems box on electronic pornography below.

Some continuing clash between the pro- and antipornography forces seems inevitable, for the values of these groups are contrary, and each desires to control the media. But pornography is now so entrenched in our society that it is likely that those who oppose it will limit themselves to an occasional statement decrying the fall of American values and then retreat into enclaves of people who agree with their views.

Technology and Social Problems

Pornography on the Internet

What is the problem? Why can't people electronically exchange nude photos with one another if they want to? If this were the issue, there would be no problem. The real issue, however, is quite different. What disturbs many people are the photos that show bondage, torture, rape, and bestiality (humans having sex with animals). Judging from the number of such sites on the Internet, apparently many people derive sexual excitement from such photos and videos.

The Internet has transformed the way people view pornography—and the way people make sexual contact.

The Internet abounds with "chat rooms." No one is bothered about the chat rooms that center on Roman architecture or rap music or turtle racing. But chat rooms where the focus is on how to torture women are another matter. So are those where the participants talk about seducing grade school children—or that extol the delights of having sex with four-year-olds.

Any call for censorship raises the hackles of civil libertarians, who see all censorship as an attack on basic freedoms. Censorship, they say, is just the first step toward a totalitarian society. If we let the government censor the Internet just an inch, it will stretch that inch into a mile and censor other things it doesn't like—such as criticisms of government officials. Taking this approach, some defend the right to display and exchange photos of children who are being sexually abused. Most civil libertarians appear to draw the line at child pornography, but only reluctantly; and they don't want the line drawn any further.

Based on O'Connell 1998; Locy and Biskupic 2003; Foley 2008; Boden 2012.

For Your Consideration

Do you think it should be legal to exchange photos of women being abused sexually or tortured? Should it be legal to discuss ways to seduce children? If not, on what basis should these activities be banned? If we make them illegal, then what other communications should we prohibit? On what basis?

MySocLab ✓ Study and Review on MySocLab

Summary and Review

1. All societies attempt to channel sexual behavior in ways they consider acceptable. When the violation of sexual norms is felt to be a threat to society, especially to the family, it is considered a social problem.
2. Through the lens of functionalism, we saw that *prostitution* persists because it serves social functions. From a functionalist perspective, as prostitutes service customers who are sexually dissatisfied or whose sexual desires are deviant, they relieve pressures that otherwise might be placed on people who are unwilling to participate. The three stages in becoming a prostitute are drift (drifting from casual sex into selling sex), ambivalence, and professionalization. Some young men who sell sex to men manipulate symbols to maintain heterosexual identities.
3. Deciding what is and is not pornographic has confused many, including the U.S. Supreme Court. In the tradition of symbolic interactionism, the Court has ruled that what a community decides is pornographic is pornographic—for them. The Court has also made rulings on pornography based on social class preferences.
4. Social scientists have been unable to determine the social effects of pornography; but where hard core pornography has become legal, violent sex crimes have decreased. Feminists are split on the issue of pornography, from those who say it dehumanizes women and encourages men to see women as sexual objects to those who say that pornography liberates women and produce what they call "feminist porn." Social activists take action on the basis of their convictions, not on the basis of proof about causation.
5. *Victimless crimes* are illegal acts to which the participants consent. Prostitution and pornography are classified as victimless crimes by sociologists when adults are involved, but not when children participate, since children cannot give full consent. The suggestion that the government legalize prostitution runs into huge opposition.
6. The interests of people who approve and disapprove of prostitution and pornography are likely to continue to clash, but those who disapprove of them are likely to be fighting rearguard actions.

Key Terms

Thinking Critically About Chapter 3

1. This chapter began by stating that all societies control human sexual behavior. Why do you think this is true? What is it about sex that makes us inclined to control the sexual behavior of others? Be sure to base your answer on group aspects of society, not on personality or individuals.
2. What is your opinion about pornography? Do you think pornography triggers sex crimes or serves as a safety valve that protects people from them? On what do you base your opinion?
3. What is your opinion of the following? Child pornography is illegal, and people are arrested and put in prison for possessing it. Pictures of tortured and sexually abused women are legal.

4 Alcohol and Other Drugs

Listen to Chapter 4 on MySocLab

Learning Objectives. After reading this chapter, you should be able to:

"Debbie! What's this?"

Seeing the familiar plastic bag, Debbie felt her face redden. Why hadn't she put it away as she always did? She swallowed, then burst out defiantly:

"My purse! You've got no business snooping in my purse!"

Mom, it's you who's hooked.

"I was just looking for a match—but I found a lot more! I never expected a daughter of mine to be a drug addict."

"Drug addict, huh? That's funny! Just because someone smokes grass doesn't mean she's a drug addict."

"Everybody knows marijuana is the first step to the hard stuff, like heroin."

At this, Debbie shook her head in disbelief at her mother's thinking. Then she said, "Mom, it's you who's hooked. The first thing you do in the morning is light up a cigarette and have a cup of coffee. And after that you start popping Prozac."

"Don't you compare my medicine to your drugs. My doctor prescribes Prozac for my nerves."

"Okay, then what do you call your martinis? And I know why you dug in my purse for a match—it's because you're hooked on cigarettes."

"Don't you talk back to me, young lady. Ever since you started college, you think you know it all. Just wait 'til your Dad gets home."

"Yeah, sure. Then you'll do the same thing you do every night—talk about it over a drink."

The Problem in Sociological Perspective

4.1 Illustrate how subjective concerns change and how they make a drug part of a social problem.

Just as Debbie's mother was shocked to discover that her daughter smokes marijuana, hundreds of thousands of other parents have had similar rude awakenings. The use of marijuana has become so common that it shows up among presidential candidates. Bill Clinton and Barack Obama have smoked marijuana, although Clinton said, "But I didn't inhale." Everyone needs a good laugh now and then. Barack Obama was more open as he discussed his use of marijuana as a young man.

A Quick Historical Background

Marijuana and Cocaine. Some people think that smoking marijuana is something new. Far from it. Over 4,000 years ago, a Chinese emperor recommended marijuana for medical use: "female weakness," rheumatism, malaria, constipation, and absent-mindedness (Hart and Ksir 2011). And about 600 years ago, the Spanish conquistadors found that the natives of Peru chewed coca leaves for the stimulating effects of cocaine (Hart and Ksir 2011).

Tobacco. When Christopher Columbus landed in North America, he found that Native Americans smoked tobacco. This plant wasn't native to Europe, and he took some back with him. Europeans tried it, liked it, and smoking tobacco became common. King James I of England was sure that smoking would cause health problems, and in 1604 he wrote a pamphlet warning his subjects that tobacco was "harmful to the brain and dangerous to the lungs" (Hart and Ksir 2011). Other rulers went somewhat beyond issuing warnings. In 1634, the czar of Russia ordered officials to slit the noses of tobacco smokers. The rulers of China went further—they had smokers' heads cut off. Turkish rulers also ordered smokers to be put to death (Goode 1989). All of these anti-tobacco campaigns failed.

Caffeine. After coffee was introduced to the Arab world during the 1500s, Islamic religious leaders became upset when people drank coffee to help them stay awake during long vigils. Stating that coffee was intoxicating and prohibited by the Koran, religious leaders ordered coffee dealers to be beaten across the soles of their feet (Brecher et al. 1972). A century later, in 1674, a group of English women wrote a pamphlet titled "The Women's Petition Against Coffee." They complained that their men were leaving "good old ale" in order to drink "base, black, thick, nasty, bitter, stinking, nauseous" coffee. Even worse, the coffee, they said, was making their men less sexually active (Meyer 1954).

Opium in the United States. How attitudes toward drugs change. Today coffee is fine, and Starbucks dot the landscape. Office workers take approved "coffee breaks." It is the opposite with opium. In the 1800s, you could buy opium across the United States—in drugstores, grocery stores, and general stores. You could even order opium by mail. Opium was advertised as a cure for diarrhea, colds, fever, teething, pelvic disorders, and even athlete's foot and baldness (Inciardi 1986). Opium was so popular that each year U.S. mothers fed their babies about 750,000 bottles of opium-laced syrup. To smoke cigarettes or drink alcohol was more offensive than to use opium (Isbell 1969; Duster 1970; Brecher et al. 1972).

If you want to protect your throat, smoke Lucky Strikes! Ideas about cigarette smoking have changed just a tad since the publication of this ad in 1937.

Why This Brief History of Drugs? Can you see how people at different times define the same drug as good and as bad? Before we get farther into this chapter, it is important for you to grasp this essential point: *No drug is good or bad in and of itself* (Szasz 1975). You are familiar with today's dominant view of tobacco—and the health warnings on cigarette packages. But contrast today's views with that of the 1940s and 1950s. As you can see from the ad for Lucky Strikes, doctors actually used to recommend cigarettes as *good* for people's health.

This drives home the point that I made in Chapter 1 about objective conditions and subjective concerns. It is *not the objective conditions*—such as some particular drug being harmful—that makes its use a social problem. Rather, it is *subjective concerns that make a drug part of a social problem.* As you saw with opium and tobacco, what once was considered drug use at a later date can be viewed as drug abuse. And from the history of coffee, you can see that what once was considered drug abuse at a later time may be viewed as normal drug use. As with abortion and prostitution, which we discussed in earlier chapters, people acquire different views of drugs and line up on opposing sides of the issue.

In Sum ▸ Whether a drug is considered good or bad, and therefore acceptable or unacceptable, does not depend on the drug's objective conditions. Rather, this depends on people's subjective concerns, which change over time. Subjective concerns are the central principle that determines whether the use of a drug is approved or is considered drug abuse. I shall stress this principle over and over in this chapter.

The Scope of the Problem

A Personal Problem or a Social Problem?

4.2 Explain why drug use or abuse is a personal or a social problem.

Explore on **MySocLab** **Activity:** The Downward Spiral: Drug Use and Socioeconomic Status

Debbie, in our opening vignette, is like the 6 million other 18- to 25-year-old Americans who smoked marijuana during the past month (*Statistical Abstract* 2013:Tables 11, 209). To her, marijuana is no big deal. It makes her feel good, and she likes to smoke with her friends. Debbie's mother is also like a lot of other Americans—she drinks coffee, alcohol, and sodas, smokes cigarettes, and ingests a variety of substances that *she* has a hard time thinking of as drugs.

Marijuana, alcohol, nicotine, and caffeine are all drugs. Drugs are not just substances that are sold in alleys or exchanged furtively for money in an SUV someplace. A **drug** is a substance that people take to produce a change in their thinking, consciousness, emotions, bodily functions, or behavior. We can define **drug abuse** as using drugs in such a way that they harm one's health, impair one's physical or mental functioning, or interfere with one's social life. Once again—the reason that a drug is part of a social problem is not because the drug is harmful but *because the substance is socially disapproved.* From this come clashing perspectives, such as those of Debbie and her mother.

We live in a pro-drug society, surrounded by drug use. We are born with the aid of drugs, and drugs help ease our departure from this life. In between, we use drugs for sickness and for pleasure, to relieve anxiety, queasy stomachs, headaches, and all sorts of other pains and discomforts. As with alcohol, we take drugs to help us be sociable. As with coffee, tea, and colas, we take drugs routinely, unthinkingly, and habitually. You know that cigarettes are addictive, but so are coffee, tea, Coke, and Pepsi. Some people "just can't get going" in the morning without their "fixes" of caffeine.

Most of us take the use of drugs for granted, but when drug use interferes with someone's health or how that person gets along in life, we begin to question it. This we consider a *personal* problem. But if large numbers of people become upset about a drug and want to see something done about it, then that drug becomes part of a *social* problem.

Addiction to Drugs

A serious problem with some drug use is **drug addiction**, or *drug dependence.* Someone who is addicted comes to depend on the regular consumption of a drug to make it through the day. When people think of drug addiction, they are likely to think of addicts huddled in slum doorways, the dregs of society who steal to support their habits. Let's look at drug addiction a little more closely.

> *A guest speaker came into sociologist Lori Fowler's class. As he stood at the front of the class, he reached into a pocket and pulled out a vibrating voice machine. He lowered the high collar covering his tracheotomy and set the vibrating machine onto his throat. He talked through the machine and told the students how, even after losing his voice, he still smoked cigarettes through his tracheotomy hole.*

This man was certainly addicted, but it gets worse. Here is what can happen with Buerger's disease:

> *In this disease the blood vessels become so constricted that circulation is impaired whenever nicotine enters the bloodstream. When gangrene sets in, at first a toe or two may have to be amputated. If the person continues to smoke, the foot may have to be amputated at the ankle, then the leg at the knee, and ultimately at the hip. Somewhere along this gruesome progression gangrene may also attack the other leg. Patients are told that if they will just stop smoking, this horrible march of gangrene in their legs will stop. Yet surgeons report that some patients vigorously puff away in their hospital beds following even a second or third amputation. (Brecher et al. 1972:216)*

Whether the addiction is to nicotine or to heroin, why don't drug addicts just quit—especially when they know it is ruining their lives or hurting their loved ones? The reason is to avoid **withdrawal**, the intense distress—nausea, vomiting, aches and pains, nervousness, anxiety, and depression—they feel when they abstain from the drug. Withdrawal creates **cravings**, intense desires for the missed drug. Even after someone has kicked the habit, the craving can last for years. And even after the craving is over, people may still experience an occasional desire for the drug. This is referred to as **psychological dependence**.

On a personal note, I used to be a drug addict, although I never thought of myself as one. I began smoking at age 13 and quit 26 years later. The physical withdrawal was severe for 6 weeks, and then tapered off. The psychological dependence continued much longer. Even 3 years after quitting, I would dream that I was smoking cigarettes. These dreams were so vivid and disturbing that I would awaken abruptly—feeling guilty for having fallen back into the habit.

Looking at the Problem Theoretically

It is legal to use drugs as lethal as alcohol and nicotine, and yet people are sent to prison for using milder drugs. Why? Remember that subjective concerns outweigh objective conditions. To understand the *social* significance of drugs, let's look at drugs through our three theoretical lenses.

4.3 Contrast the symbolic interactionist, functionalist, and conflict perspectives on drugs.

Symbolic Interactionism

What Does a Drug Mean? The Temperance Movement. From previous chapters, you know that symbolic interactionists stress that objects and events have no meaning by themselves, that objects and events take on whatever meanings people give them. Let's look at how this principle applies to alcohol. This drug has been a part of U.S. culture since the arrival of the Pilgrims, who brought beer with them (Lender and Martin 1982). Yet in 1919, alcohol was prohibited from being produced, sold, or consumed, beginning a 14-year period of our history known as Prohibition.

Sociologist Joseph Gusfield (1963) analyzed how Prohibition came about. He noted that Anglo-Saxon Protestants had settled in New England, and their customs and religion dominated the region. Then in the 1820s, uneducated, poor immigrants poured into this area from Italy, Germany, and Ireland. The educated and well-to-do New Englanders were offended by the drinking of the new immigrants and by their Roman Catholic religion. The established Protestants viewed them as ignorant, Catholic drunkards.

This photo from the late 1920s or early 1930s shows one response to the endless attempt to eradicate alcohol from American life.

Bootlegged (illegal) alcohol was one response to Prohibition, leading to organized crime. Shown here is Al Capone, on vacation in Florida. Capone controlled the alcohol that supplied the "speakeasies" of Chicago during Prohibition. Capone was ruthless. At his orders, men were executed.

As new immigrants continued to pour in, the members of the establishment gradually lost political power. They then began a campaign (called Temperance) to turn the new immigrants into clean, sober, and godly people whose customs would reflect the traditional Anglo-Saxon moral leadership of New England. Abstinence came to symbolize hard-working people with good reputations. Drinking, in contrast, was associated with unreliable drifters, uneducated immigrants of questionable background. To abstain from alcohol became a requirement for anyone who strove for higher social standing.

As the United States grew more urban and secular, Protestants saw their power and values slipping even further. Intensifying their efforts to uphold Temperance, they rejoiced in 1919 when the Eighteenth Amendment to the Constitution was passed. Overnight, it became illegal for Americans to buy even a glass of beer. Prohibition, Gusfield says, marked the victory of middle-class, Protestant, rural values over working-class, Roman Catholic, urban values. Prohibition, of course, did not stop people from making and drinking alcohol, and gradually the forces behind Temperance weakened. Fourteen years later, in 1933, this grand experiment in drug control was repealed, and again Americans could drink alcohol legally.

It may be difficult for us today to understand how any adult could have been arrested for possessing a bottle of beer, but from the Temperance movement you can see how the meanings of *alcohol* can change. It is the same with other drugs. You've already seen this with coffee and tobacco, and shortly we'll consider the changing meanings of the word *marijuana*.

Making a drug illegal—or keeping one legal—can certainly differ from common sense. Let's consider this in the Issues in Social Problems box.

Issues in Social Problems

Sociology and Common Sense: Legal and Illegal Drugs

Common Sense	Sociology
1. Illegal drugs are harmful, and legal drugs are not harmful.	**1.** The harm that a drug causes is not the reason that it becomes illegal. Making a drug illegal is a political process. If a drug is classified as illegal, some interest groups have managed to get their views translated into law.
2. If a legal drug is discovered to be addictive and is abused, it will be made illegal.	**2.** Some addictive drugs are backed by well-financed interest groups (alcohol, nicotine, Prozac, Valium, and OxyContin) and remain legal.
3. If a non-narcotic drug has been classified mistakenly in the law as a narcotic, it will be reclassified.	**3.** Marijuana was classified incorrectly as a narcotic in the 1937 Marijuana Tax Act. Although knowledge of this error is common, no interest group has been powerful enough to get this misclassification corrected.

For Your Consideration

Why do you think sociological findings sometimes, as here, differ so greatly from common sense?

Functionalism

The Social Functions and Dysfunctions of Drugs. When functionalists study drug use, whether it is legal or illegal, they examine its functions and dysfunctions. While *functions* are the intended positive effects of the drug use, *dysfunctions* are its unintended negative effects. A function of recreational drug use is to "loosen" people up, or otherwise help remove tensions that interfere with sociability. These drugs are also functional for those who make money from growing, processing, distributing, and selling them. These same drugs are dysfunctional for those who abuse them and for their family members.

The use of prescription drugs is functional both for the medical profession and for the patients they serve. A striking example is the use of prescription drugs to treat mental health patients. In the 1950s, more than 500,000 Americans were locked up in mental hospitals. Today, the total number of beds in psychiatric hospitals has dropped 85 percent, to just 76,000 (*Statistical Abstract* 2013:Table 175). This decline is due in large part to the discovery of mood-altering drugs, the psychopharmaceuticals. These drugs allow several hundred thousand people to remain at their jobs and with their families.

Prescription drugs also have dysfunctions. Some drugs are not adequately tested before they are approved. They turn out to have severe side effects, some causing disabilities and deaths. Others bring harm when doctors prescribe them for purposes for which they were not intended. As mentioned in Chapter 2, some doctors use prescription drugs as "pharmacological straitjackets." Instead of trying to find out what is wrong with a patient or with a patient's social environment, the physician takes the easier route and prescribes mood-altering drugs. "Doped-up" patients become befuddled and lethargic, and some suffer permanent neurological damage. As sociologist Donald Light (2011) says, the harmful side effects of prescription drugs are an overlooked epidemic, leading to over a million hospitalizations a year.

The dysfunctions of drugs—not just prescription drugs but also nicotine, alcohol, heroin, and others—extend far beyond the individual. They include crimes that are committed to support addiction, the spread of AIDS among addicts who share needles, the deaths and injuries from automobile accidents, and the loss to society of a reservoir of human potential. The *Personal Account* on the next page illustrates how drug addiction is devastating not only for the addict but also for that individual's family.

Conflict Theory

Let's turn to the conflict perspective, which has an entirely different focus.

Drug Laws as Political Tools. As conflict theorists point out, drug laws are sometimes used as political tools. In general, it works like this: If a particular drug (such as crack cocaine) is common among some group, to make that drug illegal allows authorities to unleash the police against this group. In contrast, by keeping a drug legal (such as a prescription drug), the state can protect favored groups that profit from that drug (physicians, pharmacies, and pharmaceutical companies).

U.S. history is littered with examples of how drug laws have been used as political tools. You might be surprised to learn that drug laws once targeted Chinese immigrants. In the 1800s, the transcontinental railroad was being built to connect the east and west coasts of the United States. Short of labor to complete this gigantic project, the railroads recruited thousands of men in China. When the railroad was completed, these men began to compete for jobs with whites. Soon after this came the financial panic and depression of 1873. With severe competition for jobs and the Chinese willing to work for lower wages than the whites, tensions ran high. In some areas, the whites rioted, beating and killing the Chinese. Many of these Chinese men smoked opium, a legal drug at the time, and to target men who threatened the jobs of whites, in 1875 San Francisco and other West Coast cities passed laws that made smoking opium illegal. The target was not the opium, but the Chinese (Morgan 1978). Even the U.S. Congress got involved. In 1887, it passed a law that prohibited the importation of opium *by the Chinese* but not by white Americans (Szasz 1975).

Conflict theorists point out how politicians use drug laws to control the poor, sometimes called "the dangerous class," those whose members are likely to rebel. As a result, many poor people are in prison for drug violations. Some conflict theorists take this a step further and suggest that the devastation of the ghetto by heroin and cocaine is intentional, a way to keep people from rebelling. With drugs becoming the addicts' passion, the goal around which their life revolves, they can't become involved in social change. As conflict theorist Andrew Karmen (1980:174) said, heroin users become "too passive when nodding and

Personal Account

Addiction: Not the Individual Alone

While I was working on this chapter, Jenn, who was helping with research, mentioned that her brother had died a few months before, "after a long struggle with an addiction to alcohol and OxyContin." She stressed how addiction is not just a "street" experience and what devastating effects addiction has on families. I asked if she would share her experience with us. This is what she wrote.

Hi Jim,

I am writing to tell you about my brother, Matt. He died this summer while receiving treatment for alcohol and OxyContin addiction. Matt was 37 and left a wife and four young children behind.

Alcohol was always an issue with Matt. He belonged to a partying crowd in high school and had occasional run-ins with the police for underage drinking. As he moved into adulthood, the partying continued, but he became a union carpenter and worked 50–60 hours a week. So, we worried, but assured ourselves that if he never missed a day of work because of drinking, then he had it under control. He didn't, though, and a DUI arrest initiated what would be a 10-year on-and-off participation in Alcoholics Anonymous, with on-and-off success.

Matt married, and this seemed to help. Then two months after his first child was born, she died of SIDS. I can't possibly describe what this was like; it was beyond words. Around the same time, Matt had hernia surgery for a work injury and received his first prescription for Percocet. This chain of events was his undoing, and his addiction to alcohol made it increasingly difficult to resist using pills. It was not a quick decline; it was a multi-year pattern of 6 months of sobriety and hard work until union work would dry up, and his alcohol and pill use would increase, followed by a week in rehab. What always shocked me about rehab was the hours he would have to spend on the phone trying to find a rehab with an open bed, and the ridiculous requirement that he arrive intoxicated. So, we would take turns waiting for a clear-headed and determined Matt to make his calls; then we would buy a bunch of nips so he could drink them on the way.

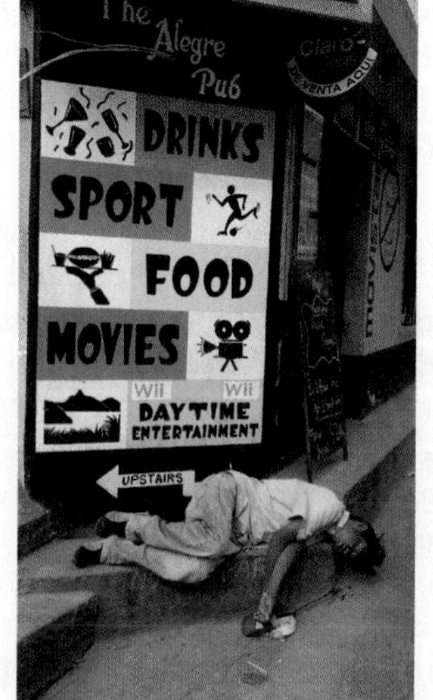

Drug abuse can ravage the individual's body, employment, and social standing. As this box stresses, the individual's family also suffers.

He would clear his body of toxins, and after 5–6 days of rehab would be making calls to find work. He never stayed very long, always anxious to return to work and to not incur charges after his insurance was used up. He and his wife had gone on to have four more children, and he had a lot of demands on his income and time. Things grew worse. His sober periods became shorter and shorter, he lived through one overdose, he lost his driver's license for 8 years, his marriage became strained, and he lived more and more at my parents' house so they could drive him to work.

A year and a half ago, Matt called me for what I had started to call a "rehab drive." This time he was determined to do a long rehab stint. He ended up doing six months in a sober house in Nantucket and was able to work construction there. We felt glimmers of hope. But he missed his children terribly and came home for Christmas. Once home, he underwent a quick decline. He was drinking and using pills. He was starting to have big memory gaps. So much of his personality disappeared. It didn't seem like there was much of "him" left in him. My parents were afraid to go away for the weekend and leave him alone. I am ashamed that I avoided some of his calls because he was asking me for money.

Last summer, he was back in the hospital, so we felt like we could go on vacation while he was in a safe place. We took his kids and went up to Maine with my parents. We felt sad on Father's Day because his kids were without their father. We were right to feel that way because he died in the hospital on Father's Day morning. He was on "dry out" medication, but he obtained alcohol inside the hospital and died from a toxic reaction of the alcohol and anti-anxiety medication. Nurses checked on him as he slept, and he was alive at 7:30 A.M. but was dead by 10:30. Two days later, his wife received a letter from him saying how dedicated he was to getting better and returning to his family.

Addiction consumes all the energy in a family. Could I have done more for Matt? Probably, but taking care of his kids, taking care of my kids, being a bright spot for my parents, supporting my younger brother, reacting to emergencies, all felt like a lot.

Thanks for the opportunity to tell this story,

Jenn

For Your Consideration

From this case, what costs of drug addiction do you see to the individual? To the family? To society? What changes do you think might improve the way we deal with drug addiction?

too self-absorbed when they aren't high to fight for community control over the schools, to organize tenants for a rent strike, or to march on City Hall to demand decent jobs."

Our history provides numerous examples of how those in power use drugs to consolidate sentiment against disfavored groups. During the 1800s, evil Chinese men were said to be lurking in opium dens to seduce innocent white women. During World War I, German pharmaceutical firms and anarchists were supposedly smuggling heroin into this country. With the outbreak of World War II, Japan was identified as the force behind the narcotics trade. Then during the Cold War of the 1950s, the Soviet secret police were fingered as the sinister heroin supplier. During the Korean War, China became the culprit. During the Vietnam War, North Vietnam was named as the mastermind of the narcotics trade (Karmen 1980). With our War on Terror, the Taliban and al Qaeda were fingered as the new evil suppliers (Perl 2001). We'll see what new enemies pop up to seduce innocent Americans to evil drugs.

In Sum ▸ Each theory contributes to the understanding of drugs as a social problem. Symbolic interactionists stress how drugs become powerful symbols that affect social life, as was the case with alcohol and the great drug experiment known as Prohibition. Functionalists examine the functions and dysfunctions of drug use—how, for example, some psychiatric patients benefit from legal mood-altering drugs, while those same drugs impair the physical or social functioning of other patients. Conflict theorists analyze how drug laws are used to control groups that pose a threat to current power arrangements.

Research Findings: The Use and Abuse of Drugs

Let's examine the medicalization of human problems, the use of drugs by students, and why people have different experiences with the same drug.

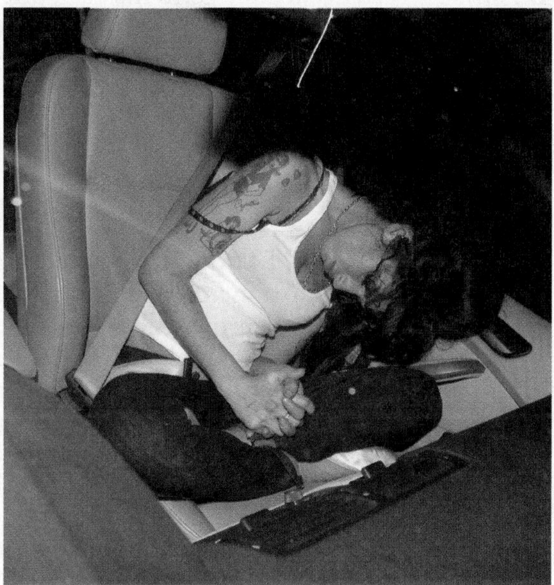

Among the many stars who have died from drug abuse are Michael Jackson and Amy Winehouse. Winehouse was photographed passed out in her car after a night of partying. A couple of years later, she died from alcohol poisoning.

Medicalizing Human Problems

4.4 Explain what medicalizing human problems means.

Heath Ledger, promising actor (Brokeback Mountain, The Dark Night) *was found dead at age 28. The coroner ruled that Ledger died from an accidental overdose of oxycodone, hydrocodone, diazepam, temazepam, alprazolam, and doxylamine (Barron 2008).*

Though extreme, celebrity deaths like those of Heath Ledger, Elvis Presley, and Michael Jackson pinpoint one of today's major drug problems: the abuse of legal prescription drugs. Let's get a quick overview of what has led up to this type of abuse.

Expanding the Medical Model. Physicians have always taken care of people's bodies, and, often, of their personal problems as well. However, until the 1930s, they lacked tools to treat personal problems. At that time, the pharmaceutical industry began to produce psychoactive drugs. Swept up in the ensuing drug revolution, physicians began to **medicalize human problems**. They prescribed antidepressants and antianxiety drugs for conditions that people used to assume were a normal part of life that they had to cope with. Anxiety, distress, irritability, inability to concentrate, feeling "down," even feelings of not "fitting in"—all became "medical conditions" for physicians to treat. This was an amazing transition: from ordinary personal problems of everyday life to medical conditions, from personal coping to the need to see a doctor for prescription drugs.

More recently the same thing has happened again, this time with kids who give their parents and teachers a hard time. For a one-sided presentation that is likely to either make you smile or make you angry, read the Thinking Critically box on the next page.

Profits provide a strong motivation to expand the medical model to every possible problem of life. The drug companies flood television and magazines with ads for medications that you *cannot* buy over the counter. People see the ads and imagine themselves living happy, carefree lives—running across sunny fields of wild flowers—if only they could just get their hands on Xanax, Prozac, or some other drug. They tell their doctors what they want, and the doctors (who make money from writing prescriptions) comply. Pharmacists joyfully go to the bank after counting the little pills and putting them in little plastic tubes. And the drug companies make huge amounts marketing these drugs. Pristiq and Cymbalta each rake in over $1 billion a year (Kalayjian 2010; Pierson 2012).

4.5 Explain how medicalizing human problems is related to the abuse of prescription drugs.

Abusing Prescription Drugs

View on **MySocLab**
Figure: Age 12 and Older Reporting Nonmedical Use of Prescription-Type Psychotherapeutic Drugs, by Type of Drug

Listen on **MySocLab**
Audio: NPR: Texas Considers 'Conscience Clause' for Pharmacists

The "Good-Grade" Drugs. High school students have discovered a way to turn Adderall and Ritalin to a use that was never intended by the pharmaceutical companies. They have found that these drugs produce a laser-like focus, allowing them to concentrate as they study and take tests. The drugs also allow them to stay up most of the night studying and to still be alert in school the next day. To get what the students refer to as the "good-grade" drugs, many fake symptoms of ADHD to psychologists, saying that they have a hard time concentrating and are easily distracted, even looking out the window while talking to the psychologist. The misuse of these drugs is more common among "good" students from "good" high schools who are tying to get into "good" colleges. The use of the "good-grade" drugs continues in college. Unfortunately, in the process of obtaining these "good" goals, some users get addicted (Schwarz 2012).

The "Getting High" Drugs. Some prescription drugs produce a "high," which makes them desirable as recreational drugs. Among the favorites are Xanax, Valium, and OxyContin. To enhance the drugs' effects, many drink alcohol while taking the pills.

Thinking Critically About Social Problems

Doping Problem Kids: ADHD and the Ritalin Riddle

Children have always driven parents and teachers wild. All kids "act up" sometimes, and some seem to do it all the time. From kids who won't sit quietly at their desks to kids who talk back or hit other kids, there is no end to the problems.

If only you could just give these kids a drug to settle them down, like the drugs they give to all those unruly old folks in the nursing homes, which you read about in Chapter 2. And this is exactly what has happened. Parents and teachers kept complaining about problem kids. The doctors listened—and they came up with a special kid medicine. Give that problem kid some Ritalin, and smooth out your life.

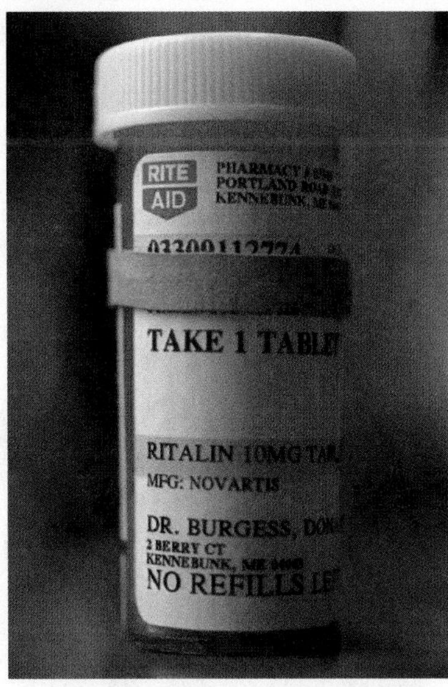

Although there is increasing awareness of the burden that Ritalin places on schoolchildren, the problem continues.

Of course, you can't dope kids because they are rambunctious. You have to have an illness to justify giving kids drugs to settle them down. Illnesses require names, and the medical profession needed one to turn those problem behaviors into an illness. At first, all they could come up with was hyperactivity, which simply means that a kid is highly active. Not too good. The limitations of that name are obvious. The doctors needed something better, something more frightening and official-sounding. Their new name did the trick, **attention deficit/hyperactivity disorder (ADHD)**. Now any kid who has *that* must really be sick.

No one knows what these terms mean—although you can get a list of symptoms: The child is forgetful, the child doesn't pay attention, the child daydreams, and on and on. Sounds like they might be future poets. If you apply the term ADHD to the child, though, you know the child has a real illness. And an illness, as everyone in our medicalized society knows, calls for medicine. Evidently, an epidemic of ADHD has swept though our schools, for 3 million U.S. schoolchildren receive ADHD drugs, including Ritalin and Adderall (Sroufe 2012).

If you think I'm being unduly severe in my cynicism, listen to child psychiatrist Carl Kline. He phrases this even stronger. Ritalin, he says, is "nothing more than a street drug being administered to cover the fact that we don't know what's going on with these children" (Livingston 1997). Child psychologist Alan Sroufe (2012) adds, "No study has found any long-term benefit of attention-deficit medication on academic performance, peer relationships or behavior problems, the very things we would most want to improve."

It is so handy to medicalize human problems. If something we don't like is a medical matter—a "sickness"—then the problem can be solved by drugs. We used to say that children who disrupted the classroom were *unruly* and in need of discipline by parents and school. Now we label these kids *sick*—as having an illness that medicine can cure (Shorter 2010).

If you've got a good thing going, why not expand it? Incredibly—at least to me—doctors now prescribe drugs for toddlers who are going through their "terrible twos" (Kalb 2000). No special name here—not yet, but I'm sure one is on the way. I suggest that these little ones probably have "two terribulus."

There are times when I think that with so much Ritalin being shoved into our kids, there has to be a good reason for it. Then I read something, such as a standard medical report, that convinces me otherwise. In a prestigious psychiatric journal, I read a report innocuously titled "3-Year Follow-up of the NIMH MTA Study." In this report, the twenty-one M.D. and Ph.D. authors (Jensen et al. 2007) mention the treatment of children (ages 7–10) for ODD. No, I didn't make that term up. It is their acronym for Oppositional Defiant Disorder. And of courses there are kids who are defiant. They give us trouble, so let's label them and shove drugs down their throats. At least someone has a sense of humor in calling the kids ODD. But isn't it time to say that the emperor has no clothes?

Ritalin and the other drugs do work. Hundreds of thousands of foggy, drugged kids now sit much more quietly in their classrooms. Unfortunately, some get hallucinations, most commonly seeing or feeling snakes and worms. Others get tics, lethargy, depression, brain damage, even cancer (Harris 2006). The drugs also stunt growth (Sroufe 2012).

For Your Consideration

I warned you that this presentation would be one-sided. Go ahead and refute it.

Some call OxyContin "hillbilly heroin" because its effects are similar to those of heroin or opium, but it is much cheaper. OxyContin's sensations last up to 12 hours, and unlike heroin, OxyContin can be chewed in pill form, eliminating the need for injections (Cahoun et al. 2008). Using prescription drugs to get "high" is the topic of the Spotlight on Social Research box below.

Drug Use by College Students

4.6 Give a brief overview of the drug use of college students.

For an overview of the drug use of college students, look at Table 4.1. The sample on which the research on this table is based is so good that we can generalize these findings to *all* college students across the nation. Don't try to generalize these findings to all colleges, however. They apply to college students in general, but not to specific colleges. For example, at some colleges hardly anyone binge drinks, while at others four out of five do (Wechsler and Nelson 2008). Colleges differ in their cultures, and for good reason some are known nationally as party schools, while others have higher academic reputations.

Spotlight on Social Research

The Miami Club Culture: Prescription Drug Abuse Among Ecstasy Users

Until his death in 2009, **JAMES A. INCIARDI** *was director of the Center for Drug and Alcohol Studies at the University of Delaware. He was also a member of the International Advisory Committee of the White House Office of National Drug Control Policy. His research focused on substance abuse, criminal justice, and public policy. Here is what he wrote for you.*

Miami, Florida, historically a major tourist destination, is also a major player in the U.S. club drug scene. With the restoration of Miami's art deco districts and the popularity of the South Beach area, Miami has become an international destination for partying, sexual tourism, and club drug use. To "get high," about 80 percent of ecstasy users in the Miami club culture appear to be using prescription narcotics (OxyContin, Vicodin, Percocet, and morphine), "downers" (Xanax and Valium), and stimulants (Ritalin and Adderall) (Kurtz et al. 2005).

To investigate this abuse of prescription drugs, we conducted focus groups with scores of young adults from a wide variety of racial–ethnic backgrounds. To achieve a "better high," prescription drugs are also used in *combination* with club drugs. Popular combinations include marijuana, Ritalin, and alcohol; prescription narcotics with methamphetamine and ecstasy; and hydrocodone with cocaine. Some participants described the practice of "colon rolling," also known as "booty bumping"—dissolving prescription and other drugs and then taking the solution rectally with an eye dropper or turkey baster. Some preferred this anal route of administration because it made the drugs' effects slower and more even. Of particular note in this regard was the "Royal Flush"—a dangerous combination of methamphetamine, ecstasy, and Viagra.

The focus group participants reported extremely diverse sources for obtaining the prescription drugs they abused. These included drug dealers, on the street and in nightclubs; HIV-positive patients, who have access to prescription medications through their physicians; parents and other relatives; pharmacy employees; online pharmacies; under-the-door apartment flyers advertising telephone numbers to call; Medicaid and Medicare fraud; doctor shopping; leftover supplies following an illness or injury; visits to Mexico, South America, and the Caribbean; prescriptions intended for treatment of drug dependence or mental illness; theft from pharmacies and hospitals; friends and acquaintances; and "stealing from grandma's medicine cabinet." All participants said they had no difficulty in obtaining prescription medications, although they were often happy to take what was available without seeking a specific drug or brand name.

Most participants described the "high" from prescription drugs as less exciting and less euphoric than that from illicit drugs, but they perceived prescription drugs to be purer, safer, more respectable, and more legal, as well as producing fewer withdrawal symptoms.

As you can see, alcohol is by far college students' favorite drug, followed by marijuana and nicotine. All other drugs shrink in comparison with these three. For the first ten editions of this book, nicotine in the form of cigarettes was the second most popular drug. But over the past 20 years, cigarette smoking dropped each year while marijuana smoking stayed about the same, going up or down a little each year. The result is that marijuana has now nudged out nicotine as male college students' second most popular drug, and comes close to this for female college students.

As you can see from this table, men use more drugs than women. The two exceptions are the use of barbiturates and LSD. The difference in LSD usage is slight.

A major concern of college officials is **binge drinking**, five or more drinks in a row for men, or four or more drinks for women, on a single occasion. From this table, you can see why binge drinking is a concern. During just the past two weeks, more than two of five male college students and a third of the women binge drank. To say the least, that's a lot of hangovers. But there is more. Students who binge drink are more likely to experience a wide range of problems, from academic difficulties to risky sexual behavior (Wechsler and Nelson 2008). A life-threatening consequence of binge drinking is alcohol poisoning. Too much alcohol interferes with the body's involuntary reflexes—including the gag reflex. If someone's gag reflex isn't working properly, that person can choke to death on vomit. (On a personal note, one of my former students was tried for manslaughter when his one-night stand suffocated from swallowing her vomit. It certainly was not a pretty death, and it made for sensational headlines in our local newspaper.)

TABLE 4.1 ▸ What Drugs Do Full-Time College Students Use?

	Men	Women
In the Last 30 Days		
Alcohol	67.8%	63.1%
Been Drunk	47.1%	41.4%
Marijuana	24.1%	13.2%
Cigarettes	19.8%	14.2%
Amphetamines	5.2%	3.4%
Tranquilizers	1.6%	1.2%
Ecstasy	1.6%	0.6%
Cocaine	1.6%	0.5%
LSD	0.6%	0.7%
Barbiturates	0.3%	0.7%
Heroin	0.0%*	0.0%*
Daily Use		
Cigarettes	8.7%	6.9%
Alcohol	5.6%	2.3%
Marijuana	6.7%	2.8%
Alcohol Binge[1]	44.3%	32.2%

[1]Five or more drinks in a row in the last 2 weeks

*A few, but so few the total is less than 0.05%.

Source: By the author. Based on Johnston et al. 2011:Tables 8-3, 8-4.

Research Findings: The Recreational Mood Elevators

Nicotine

4.7 Summarize research findings on nicotine, alcohol, marijuana, and cocaine.

Nicotine as a Social Problem.

Let's suppose that you are on your way to the airport, leaving for a long-awaited vacation. You are listening to the radio and anticipating your arrival in sunny Hawaii. Suddenly, an announcer breaks into your reverie with a flash bulletin: Terrorists have hidden bombs aboard five U.S. jumbo jets scheduled for takeoff today. On each jet will be 220 passengers and crew.

The announcer pauses, then adds: "The authorities have not been able to locate the bombs. Because no one knows which flights will crash, all flights will depart on schedule."

In your mind's eye you can see the planes plummeting from the skies, leaving a trail of agonizing screams as the passengers and crew meet their pitiful destiny. One of these planes might be yours.

What would you do? My guess is that you would turn your car around and go home. Adios to Hawaii's beaches, and hello to your own backyard.

If five fully loaded U.S. jets, each carrying 220 passengers and crew members, crashed each and every day, what would the death toll be in a year? If you answered about 400,000, you would be right. And each year, more than 400,000 Americans die from cigarette smoking (Centers for Disease Control and Prevention 2013a). It is mind numbing, but these "crashes" continue without letup, day after day, year after year. The passengers *know* that one of the "jets" will crash that day; yet they climb aboard anyway, hoping that it won't be *their* jet that crashes.

Obviously no one would get on a jet if they crashed like this. Who in their right mind would take the risk that *their* planes would not be among the five that crashed that day? Yet smokers do. They know that nicotine is lethal. They also know that smoking-related deaths are lingering and painful, a burden to both the victims and their families. Although smoking cuts the average smoker's life by 13 or 14 years, one of five (19 percent) of Americans over the age of 17 continue to smoke (*Statistical Abstract* 2013:Table 206). They put this deadly poison to their lips, hoping that it won't be their plane that goes down.

You might be surprised to learn how common smoking used to be. Professors and students even smoked in class. I used to smoke cigars as I lectured, and students would put their cigarettes out by squishing them underfoot. Look at Table 4.2. You can see that at the height of addiction, *most* men smoked. So did one of three women. Men's cigarette smoking has been more than cut in half, and close to this for women. Today one of five men and one of five or six women smoke.

What happened? The answer is a social movement, one that followed the pattern described in Chapter 1 (pages 7–14). As awareness grew of how smoking ravishes the body, leaders emerged, officials responded, and smokers and nonsmokers confronted one another. One battled to limit smoking, the other to preserve the right to smoke anywhere. One fought under the banner of freedom from harm, the other under freedom of choice. The nonsmokers, as you know, won the battle. Legislation outlawed smoking on commercial flights, in airports, workplaces, and public buildings. Even bars became "smoke free." Smokers are forced to smoke outside, even in the cold of winter, where others stare at them as some sort of outcast.

Figure 4.1 on the next page gives you a picture of this sharp decline. This drop in smoking represents the prevention of hundreds of thousands of premature deaths, as well as the avoidance of untold suffering. It also shows what citizens can accomplish when they unite for a cause—even when they face well-financed campaigns from big business to prevent their success.

TABLE 4.2 ▸ Cigarette Smoking by Sex and Age

	1965	1975	1985	1995	2005	2010*
By Sex						
Male	52%	43%	33%	27%	23%	21%
Female	34%	32%	28%	23%	18%	18%
By Sex and Age						
Males						
18–24 years	54%	42%	28%	28%	28%	23%
25–34 years	61%	51%	38%	30%	28%	26%
35–44 years	58%	51%	38%	32%	26%	23%
45–64 years	52%	43%	33%	27%	25%	23%
65 and over	29%	25%	20%	15%	9%	10%
Females						
18–24 years	38%	34%	30%	22%	21%	17%
25–34 years	44%	39%	32%	26%	22%	21%
35–44 years	44%	40%	32%	27%	21%	19%
45–64 years	32%	33%	30%	24%	19%	19%
65 and over	10%	12%	14%	12%	8%	9%

*Latest year available

Sources: By the author. Based on *Statistical Abstract of the United States* 1994:Table 212; 1997:Table 221; 1998:Table 238; 2013:Table 206.

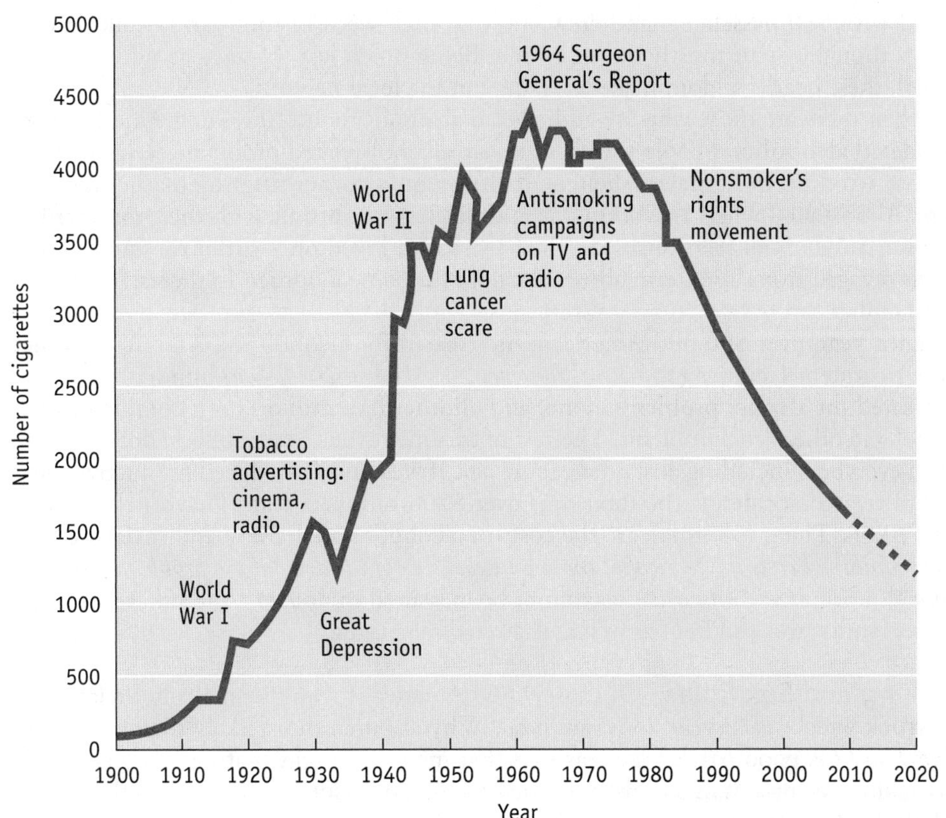

FIGURE 4.1 ▸ Number of Cigarettes That Americans Age 18 and Older Smoke Each Year

Sources: By the author. Based on Economic Research Service, U.S. Department of Agriculture, *Statistical Abstract of the United States* 2009:Table 981. Projections are by the author.

Facing a shrinking market, the tobacco industry strives to recruit new smokers, spending $13 billion a year to promote cigarettes and chewing tobacco. Ad campaigns are designed to convince young people that smoking is sexy and adultlike (Cokkinides et al. 2010). To recruit new smokers where there are no antismoking laws or where such laws are less severe, tobacco companies have turned to the Least Industrialized Nations. Many men in these countries already smoke, so the companies are targeting young women as their new smokers ("Las tabacaleras . . ." 2010). The global death toll from what is called the *brown plague* is 5 million deaths a year (Jha 2009). The industry's seductive advertising is bound to entice more women in these nations to smoke, with the result that women will increase share their of the globe's tobacco deaths.

Because the health care costs of tobacco victims fall largely on the government in the form of higher Medicaid bills, the individual states sued the tobacco companies. In exchange for dropping their suits, each state was awarded $209 billion from cigarette manufacturers. This huge settlement, to be paid over 25 years, did not put a single cigarette company out of business. To cover their huge fine, the cigarette manufacturers merely raised prices of the cigarettes they sell their addicts. How have the billions paid in fines helped the health of cigarette smokers? This may not come as a surprise, but the states simply grabbed the money and used it for whatever they wanted. They are spending just 2 percent on programs to prevent or reduce smoking. The other 98 percent goes to whatever they decide to spend it on ("Broken Promise . . ." 2009).

Alcohol

Alcohol as a Social Problem. Alcohol is more dangerous than its broad social acceptance would imply. Alcohol-related motor vehicle accidents kill 9,400 Americans each year. That's about 26 each and every day (*Statistical Abstract* 2013:Table 1109). To go back to the analogy I used for nicotine, this is the equivalent of a passenger plane

Watch on **MySocLab Video:** Housing Alcoholics

loaded with 180 passengers and crew crashing each week of the year. Drunk-driving deaths, though, occur mostly one at a time. Being much less spectacular, although just as final, these deaths seldom make anything but the local news.

Then there are those who are addicted to alcohol. About 10 million Americans are considered **alcoholics**, people who have severe alcohol-related problems. Relatively few of them wind up in homeless shelters or sitting on a corner uttering blathering nonsense. Almost all—whether working or middle class—continue with their routines but have impaired social relationships. Their work and loved ones suffer the most. Their organs ravaged from long-term abuse, alcoholics become a burden to themselves and to their families.

Each year, over 800,000 Americans are treated for alcohol problems at substance abuse treatment facilities (*Statistical Abstract* 2013:Table 207). Two hundred thousand are treated for alcohol problems alone, and another half million for a combination of alcohol and other drug problems. The cost of treatment runs several billion dollars a year, which everyone, including abstainers, must pay. If we consider reduced productivity and alcohol-related accidents, the total runs over $200 billion a year (Thavorncharoensap et al. 2009). Then, too, there are the costs of alcohol-related crime and social welfare. *These combined costs make alcohol the most expensive of all drug abuse problems*. Alcohol abuse also brings with it costs that cannot be measured in dollars—the sufferings of the spouse, family, and children, as well as shattered marriages.

Drinking and Sex Roles. Of those 9,400 Americans who die in alcohol-related car and truck wrecks each year, most are men. Why are men more likely than women to drive drunk? A good part of the reason is that men are taught that drinking is *macho.* Risk-taking behavior is one of the ways that young (and older) men prove to themselves and others that they are *real* men. Driving after drinking too much is often a symbol of male potency (Snow and Cunningham 1985; Peele, 1987). ("Did you see what John did last night? He was so smashed he could barely see, and he drove through the rain and made it to the dorm. Look where he parked!" [Car is sitting next to the main entrance, hanging over the curb, half on the street and half on the sidewalk.] "What a guy!")

I've been through this stuff myself. And so have my friends. And, frankly, not all of us made it alive through this period of proving our budding masculinities.

Perhaps. But too much, and you won't hear a thing.

Gender Transitions. We are in the midst of fundamental gender change. As you know, women have entered occupations and taken on roles (such as positions of authority at work) that were traditionally reserved for males. One consequence of this invasion of traditionally masculine turf is that women are also adopting many masculine behaviors. As a result, "feminine" is being redefined in more traditionally masculine terms. Getting publically drunk and blowing off steam used to be part of a masculine role. Now more women are adopting this behavior. One indication is an increase in the arrest of women for drunkenness and disorderly conduct (Henslin 2013:Table 6.2). You saw another indication with the frequency of women's drinking and binging shown on Table 4.1 (page 91). Women college students in England report that they feel pressure to keep up with the men in their drinking. They also report riskier driving and sex when they do (Carpenter et al. 2008).

Health Consequences of Alcohol. To understand any social problem, we need solid research—whether the findings match anyone's preconceived notions or not. Research on alcohol, for example, shows both positive and negative consequences for health. Let's continue with the negative consequences.

Because binge drinking is prevalent among college students, as you saw on Table 4.1, and most readers of this text are college students, I want to stress this significant finding: Heavy drinking is bad for health. Heavy drinkers are more likely to die from strokes and heart attacks (Rehm et al. 2003; Beck 2011). They are also more likely to have problems with their endocrine, metabolic, immune, and reproductive systems and to be diagnosed with diabetes, epilepsy, and depression. Heavy drinking also brings several types of cancer—from lung cancer to cancers of the tongue, mouth, liver, esophagus, larynx, stomach, colon, and rectum. For women, heavy drinking brings more breast cancer and other breast diseases (*Seventh Special Report* 1990; Rehm et al. 2003; Kruk and Aboul-Enein 2006; Berkey et al. 2010; Centers for Disease Control and Prevention 2013b).

Now let's look at the health *benefits* that come from light-to-moderate drinking of alcoholic beverages. Light-to-moderate is defined as one to two drinks a day, 5 or 6 days a week. This type of drinking brings better health. It relaxes people, reducing their anxieties, but it does more than this. Compared to people who don't drink alcohol, light-to-moderate drinkers have only one-third as many heart attacks (Rehm et al. 2003). Red wine is especially good for the heart, but it seems to make no difference whether someone drinks red wine, white wine, beer, whiskey, or vodka. Whatever its source, alcohol apparently stimulates production of HDL—the "good" cholesterol.

Would You Give a Baby a Beer or a Whiskey? Alcohol, Pregnancy, and Childbirth. Embedded within this social problem is another problem: Pregnant women who drink. When a pregnant woman drinks alcohol, the alcohol enters not just her circulatory system but also that of her fetus. (*"If she drinks, the baby drinks."*) Unlike the woman, the fetus cannot metabolize alcohol. The alcohol becomes concentrated in the fetus's blood, raising its blood alcohol level higher than that of the woman's ("Effects of Alcohol" 2007).

The consequences of drinking while pregnant are anything but pleasant. Each year about 5,000 babies are born in the United States with a cluster of problems called **fetal alcohol spectrum disorders (FASD)**. The most serious is **fetal alcohol syndrome (FAS)**, which causes mental deficiencies and birth defects. Born addicted to alcohol, these children suffer painful withdrawal for a week to 6 months. They are irritable, their little hearts beat irregularly, and some go into convulsions. Some suffer brain damage, making learning, memory, speech, and coordination difficult. As you might expect, groups that have higher rates of alcoholism also have higher rates of fetal alcohol syndrome. FAS is most common among Native Americans, whose rate is several times the national average ("Fetal Alcohol Spectrum . . . " 2007; Centers for Disease Control and Prevention 2013c).

Significance of How People Learn to Drink. *How* one learns to drink can set the stage for having or not having alcohol-related problems (Velleman 2009). Studies of groups with low rates of alcoholism indicate five behaviors and attitudes that are key to low-problem drinking (Hanson 1995):

- Drinking is a regular part of life.
- Drinking alcohol is neutral—neither bad nor good.
- Drinking alcohol is not a sign of adulthood or virility.
- Abusive drinking is not tolerated.
- Drinking alcohol starts early in the home, with the parents providing examples of moderate drinking.

Apparently, people who learn to drink in these contexts are much less likely to have problems related to alcohol. To appreciate why, reverse these five points. Perhaps you can see why these conditions would lead to alcohol-related problems:

- Drinking alcohol is considered something special.
- Alcohol is viewed as either sinful or as a substance that makes the world more pleasant.
- Drinking is considered a sign of adulthood.
- Getting drunk is tolerated, even approved, perhaps found to be humorous.
- Learning to drink is a sneaky and secretive activity, taking place outside the home.

Now look at Figure 4.2. About one of every seven tenth-graders and one of four high school students have been drunk in just the past month. A large number of teenagers are learning to drink in ways that maximize problems with alcohol, not minimize them.

Marijuana

Tobacco and alcohol ravage the body and kill their users. Marijuana does not. If you are above a certain age, it is legal in all states to possess cigarettes and alcoholic beverages. Throughout the country, in contrast, no matter what your age, and despite the state laws of Colorado and Washington, the possession of marijuana violates federal laws. Why did marijuana become illegal? You might enjoy the Issues in Social Problems box on the next page.

FIGURE 4.2 High School Students and Alcohol

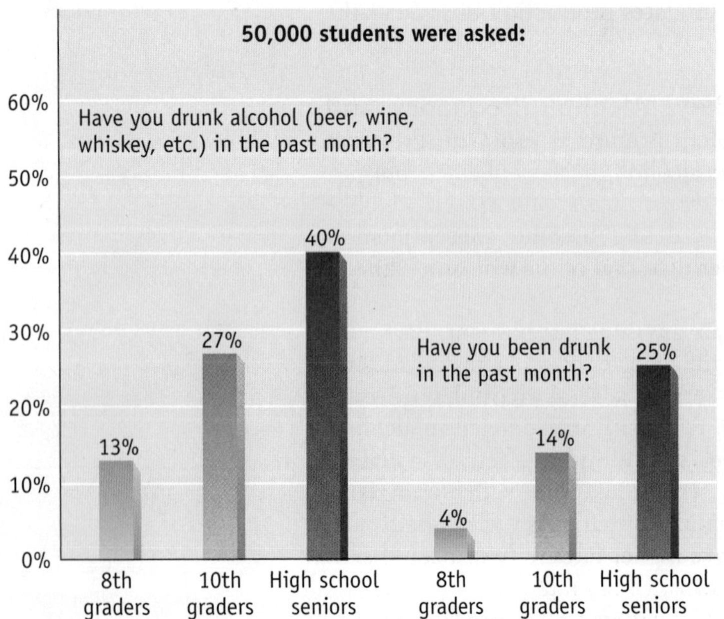

Source: By the author. Based on Johnston et al. 2012:Table 7.

Marijuana was not a popular drug, and as long as it was confined to "bohemian" or marginal groups, it posed no cultural threat to mainstream society. Then came the norm-bending 1960s, and with them the rebellious youth who embraced marijuana. Government officials panicked, thinking that the country was going to hell in a handbasket. Confused, but knowing that "we have to do something," Nevada made the possession of even a single joint punishable by up to 6 years in prison, while Alaska legalized the possession of marijuana for personal use (Goode 1989). Then both states decided they had made a mistake. Alaskans revoked their law, and Nevadans made the possession of up to 1 ounce of marijuana punishable only by fines, with no jail time. As you know, the controversy continues. Although

Issues in Social Problems

The Crusade Against Marijuana: Assassin of Youth

Moral entrepreneurs are crusading reformers who battle to enforce their ideas of morality. It was their impact that led to the Marijuana Tax Act of 1937, the federal law that made marijuana illegal. The primary moral entrepreneur who crusaded against marijuana was Harry Anslinger, the head of the Treasury Department's new Bureau of Narcotics. With the country in the midst of the Great Depression, Congress had cut his budget, and Anslinger saw marijuana as an opportunity to strengthen his faltering organization (Dickson 1968). Anslinger chose wisely, for marijuana was not popular with mainstream Americans but was associated with Mexican immigrants who were seen as taking jobs away from citizens (Helmer 1975; Galliher and Walker 1977). And he had strong allies: Fearing that marijuana might compete with alcohol, the liquor industry backed Anslinger (Rockwell, 1972).

In his relentless campaign to make marijuana illegal, Anslinger told little stories to frighten people to support him. Here is one he published in a popular magazine:

> There was this young girl. . . . Her story is typical . . . a friend produced a few cigarettes of the loosely rolled "homemade" type. They were passed from one to another of the young people, each taking a few puffs.
>
> The results were weird. Some of the party went into paroxysms of laughter; every remark, no matter how silly, seemed excruciatingly funny. Others of mediocre musical ability became almost expert. . . . The girl danced without fatigue, and the night of unexplainable exhilaration seemed to stretch out as though it were a year long. . . . With every puff of the smoke the feeling of despondency lessened. Everything was going to be all right—at last. The girl was "floating" now, a term given to marijuana intoxication. Suddenly, in the midst of laughter and dancing, she thought of her school problems. Instantly they were solved. Without hesitancy, she walked to a window and leaped to her death. (Reasons 1974)

Here's another of Anslinger's stories:

> An entire family was murdered by a youthful addict in Florida. When officers arrived at the home they found the youth staggering about in a human slaughterhouse. With an ax he had killed his father, his mother, two brothers, and a sister. . . . He had no recollection of having committed the multiple crime. The officers knew him ordinarily as a sane, rather quiet young man; now he was pitifully crazed. They sought the reason. The boy said he had been in the habit of smoking something which youthful friends called "muggles," a childish name for marijuana. (Anslinger and Cooper, 1937)

With Anslinger traveling the country, swearing that this killer weed drove girls to suicide and transformed boys into killers, it is little wonder that his campaign frightened Congress into making marijuana illegal.

For Your Consideration

What reasons are presented here to explain why marijuana was made illegal? Why do you think that the federal law that made marijuana illegal has not been changed since 1937?

smoking marijuana violates federal law, some states allow the medical use of marijuana. Colorado and Washington have made it legal for people 21 and over to possess up to an ounce of marijuana (Tarm 2013).

By 1979, one of three Americans ages 18 to 25 smoked marijuana at least once a month. Since then, the popularity of marijuana has dropped by half, and today one of five or six (18 percent) of this age group smokes marijuana this often (*Statistical Abstract* 1998:Table 237; 2013:Table 209). To say that the popularity of marijuana has dropped is relative, of course. Eighteen percent of today's 18–25-year-olds means that 6 million people of this age smoke marijuana at least once a month. *Half* (53 percent) of Americans ages 18 to 34 have smoked marijuana at some point in their lives (*Statistical Abstract* 2013:Table 209). (Of course, some, like Clinton, "didn't inhale.")

Figure 4.3 on the next page summarizes marijuana use among high school and college students.

FIGURE 4.3 ▸ Who Smokes Marijuana?

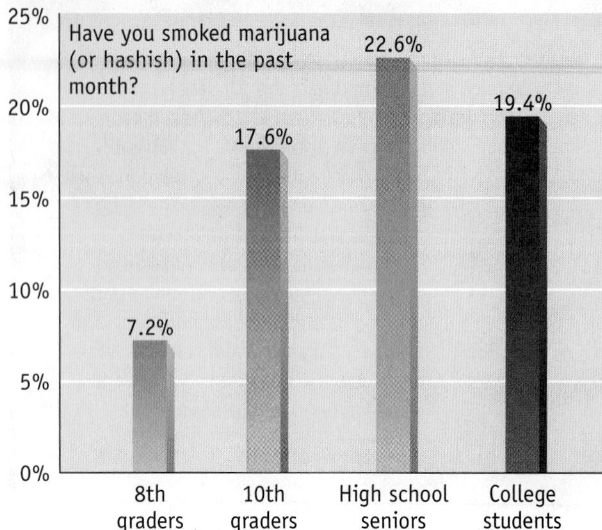

Source: By the author. Based on Johnston et al. 2012:Table 2-3.

Health Consequences of Smoking Marijuana. How does marijuana affect its users' health? Let's take a look at the research.

As with cigarettes, smoking marijuana damages the respiratory system. Compared with nonsmokers, marijuana smokers have more bronchitis, and they cough and wheeze more (Moore et al. 2004). Marijuana presents a special risk for men, as smokers are more likely to get testicular cancer. The risk is highest among those who start smoking before the age of 18 and those who smoke marijuana more than once a week (Daling et al. 2009). Smoking marijuana also reduces a man's sperm count and his sperm's motility; that is, the sperm become lazy swimmers. Marijuana doesn't let women off the hook either. It also affects their reproduction by reducing estrogen, suppressing ovulation, and increasing the risk of miscarriage (Lee et al. 2006; Wang et al. 2006).

Researchers have also found positive aspects of marijuana. Marijuana relieves symptoms of glaucoma and migraine headaches. Some of the chemicals in marijuana reduce swelling in stroke victims, helping them regain their neurological functions (Zhang et al. 2009). Others reduce muscle spasticity and help the immune system of people stricken with multiple sclerosis (Chiplock 2009; Grant et al. 2010). Marijuana also relieves asthma, epilepsy, and pain, and alleviates withdrawal from alcohol and narcotics (Carroll 2000). A matched sample of people with HIV/AIDS who smoke and do not smoke marijuana indicates that marijuana relieves anxiety, depression, fatigue, nausea, and vomiting. These patients also report what the researchers call "pleasant" side effects (Corless et al. 2009).

A surprising health effect of marijuana is featured in the Thinking Critically box on the next page.

Addiction and Marijuana. When marijuana smoking reached the height of its popularity a generation ago, alarmed parents and officials warned youth that it was addictive. Marijuana smokers scoffed, saying that they could quit at any time. And they were right—or at least most of them were.

But there is more to the picture than this. Recent research shows that about 2–3 percent of marijuana smokers do become addicted to cannabis, or THC. They become preoccupied with making certain that they are able to smoke every day, and they suffer symptoms of withdrawal when they try to stop smoking (Roffman and Stephens 2006). We need more research in this area to see if these findings hold up.

Social Consequences of Smoking Marijuana. Researchers have found that high school students who smoke marijuana tend to receive poorer grades than those who don't smoke marijuana. They are also more likely to drop out of school (Kleinman et al. 1987; Fergusson et al. 2003) and by midlife to have attained less education than nonsmokers (Ryan 2010). Can we then say that smoking marijuana causes low grades, dropping out of school, and attaining less education?

These are "facts," but as we reviewed in Chapter 1 all "facts" have to be interpreted, and this is one possible interpretation. But if we probe deeper, we find that compared with their classmates, heavy marijuana smokers are more likely to come from broken homes, to drink more alcohol, to commit more delinquent acts, and to be involved in a subculture that places less value on academic achievement. In other words, despite these facts, we don't know that smoking marijuana leads to doing poorly in school. Marijuana is just "one element in a complex picture of interrelated problems and behaviors" (Kleinman et al. 1987; White 1991). Again, we need more research.

Thinking Critically About Social Problems

Driving High: Marijuana and Driving

Smoking marijuana impairs motor coordination and reduces awareness of external stimuli, such as red lights or stop signs (Carroll 2000). Distance perception, reaction time, and hand-eye coordination drop (Kelly et al. 2004; Sewell et al. 2009). It isn't surprising, then, that people who drive after smoking marijuana are more likely to have accidents (Hall and Degenhardt 2009). And driving after smoking marijuana is common. When researchers analyzed the blood of 400 male drivers in California who had been killed in auto accidents, 37 percent contained THC, the primary active agent in marijuana (Goode 1989:147).

THC's effects linger, even though they may not be noticeable to the smoker. Researchers tested pilots 24 hours after they had smoked marijuana. Although they reported that they no longer felt any effects from their smoking, their performance on simulated landing maneuvers dropped. So, I'm sure you will agree that it is not prudent to ride or to fly with someone who has smoked marijuana.

If social life were only this simple! This certainly seems an obvious conclusion, and I have made it confidently in the past. But now new research casts doubt on something even this obvious.

Sixteen states have passed laws allowing medical marijuana. What effect, if any, has this had on deaths from car accidents? Some researchers decided to find out (Anderson and Rees 2011). They examined the records of the National Highway Traffic Safety Commission, which gathers information on each traffic death in the United States. The researchers compared the current traffic deaths of each of these 16 states with the state's fatalities before the medical marijuana laws. To account for regional changes, they also compared each of these state's traffic deaths with those of its neighboring states. They found something rather surprising. Traffic deaths in the states that made medical marijuana legal *dropped* by a stunning 12 percent per 100,000 licensed drivers. This was right after the laws were changed. After three years, when more medical marijuana patients had registered, the death total dropped further, and was 15 percent less.

Based on what you know, however you know it, including the contents of this chapter, how accurate do you think this cartoon is?

How could this possibly be? Based on data the researchers also had on alcohol and traffic deaths for these states, they came to two main conclusions:

1. Marijuana and alcohol are substitutes. They can and are used together, but people who smoke marijuana reduce their consumption of alcohol. This is especially true for younger smokers, who are more likely to have car wrecks.

OK, less alcohol. But what about the marijuana, which impairs driving? This is where the researcher's second conclusion comes in.

2. The marijuana smokers compensated. They knew their reactions were not as sharp as usual, so they went slower and kept more distance from cars ahead of them. People drinking alcohol, it seems, are not likely to do this, and are even likely to increase their risk-taking.

Surprising? Astounding is more like it.

For Your Consideration

Do you think the finding that smoking marijuana leads to fewer traffic deaths means that we should encourage people to smoke marijuana? Why or why not?

Subjective Concerns. Marijuana is an excellent example of the subjective nature of social problems. Reactions range from perceiving marijuana as a threat to society to viewing it as a treatment for medical problems. Until 1937 when the Marijuana Tax Act was passed, marijuana was an ingredient in about thirty medicines that physicians prescribed for their patients (Carroll 2000). The change was sudden and startling, from marijuana being legal for anyone in any state to the federal government punishing anyone of any age for possessing it. But the punishment was nothing like what you find in Dubai, the topic of the Thinking Critically box on the next page.

Thinking Critically About Social Problems

Watch Out What You Step on in Dubai!

If you get the chance to do some international traveling, take it. It is wonderful for broadening your perspective on life. You will get to experience customs remarkably different from the ones you are used to.

Always, of course, be careful. Stay away from dark alleys—those sorts of things. But you already know all that.

But here is something you might not know. In Dubai, the capital of United Arab Emirates, you can end up in prison for doing something that is taken lightly in the United States. Or you can be guilty of *nothing* and still end up in prison.

Here's an actual case:

Keith Brown, from England, a youth counselor and a father of three, was stopped as he walked through Dubai's main airport. Customs officials found *a speck of marijuana on the tread of his shoe*. The speck weighed less than a grain of sugar. Brown was arrested and sentenced to four years in prison (Hale 2008).

Could Brown have stepped on the marijuana someplace? Of course. Maybe in the taxi on the way to the airport. Or maybe even on the floor of the airport itself. Unlike in the United States (where he wouldn't have been arrested at all), the happenstance possibilities of how the fleck got on Brown's shoe made no difference to the customs officials, the Dubai police, or the judge.

Be careful in Dubai—or stay away from it.

Terminal 3 at the airport at Dubai

Before you rush off to judgment, though, we need to look back at our own history. To gain a little broader perspective, consider this: A judge in Alabama once sentenced a man *to death* for selling marijuana ("First Death Sentence" 1991).

For Your Consideration

The United Arab Emirates (as you probably have figured out) has a zero tolerance drug policy. Do you think the United States would be better off if we put such a policy into effect? Why or why not?

Despite the legal risks, 17 million Americans pay tens of thousands of illegal distributors to sell them marijuana. At the same time, thousands of enforcement agents make tens of thousands of arrests and seize *4 million pounds* of marijuana each year (*Statistical Abstract* 2013:Tables 11, 209, 335).

As you have seen with alcohol, as subjective concerns change, a drug's social reputation can change. A drug can be vilified and then rehabilitated. The movement to legalize marijuana, discussed in the Issues in Social Problems box on the next page, involves such changing subjective concerns.

Cocaine

The Social History of Cocaine. Cocaine, too, has an interesting social history. As mentioned, in the 1500s the Spaniards reported that the people of Peru chewed coca leaves. The Spaniards attributed the drug's effects to the devil and said that cocaine was evil.

That didn't stop the Spaniards from bringing the cocaine plant back home with them, though. By the 1800s, in Europe cocaine was being used in medicines. Cocaine also became a popular recreational drug—and far beyond Spain. By the late 1800s, Sigmund Freud, the founder of psychoanalysis, and Sir Arthur Conan Doyle, the creator of Sherlock Holmes, swore that cocaine got their creative juices going. When Angelo Mariani, a French chemist, introduced a wine that contained the coca leaf extract, the pope enjoyed the wine so much that he presented Mariani with a medal (Hart and Ksir 2011). By this time, hundreds of thousands of Americans were sipping cocaine

Issues in Social Problems

Medical Marijuana Dispensaries and Legalizing Marijuana

For over 50 years, arguments have been made for and against the legalization of marijuana. The bases of the arguments for its legalization have ranged from the medicinal benefits of marijuana to its misclassification in federal law as a narcotic. Some have presented a simple argument—Marijuana is fun, and its use or nonuse should be a matter of individual choice. Their message, repeated over and over, is that the government has no business dictating to a free people what they can and cannot smoke.

The contrary argument is also simple: Marijuana is evil, and people need to be protected from it.

To repeat, whether or not a drug is legal does not depend on the harm that the drug causes but, rather, on its social reputation. Marijuana has had a lot of negative associations—from people who "steal the jobs of good Americans" to rebels, school dropouts, the poor, and a criminal underworld. As tens of millions of Americans smoked marijuana over the past 40 to 50 years, subjective concerns surrounding marijuana have eased.

If this process continues, the next generation will wonder what the fuss was all about, why their predecessors would have put anyone in jail for smoking this plant—sort of like this generation looks in bewilderment that anyone would ever have been jailed for drinking beer and cocktails.

The national legalization of marijuana could be on its way. In violation of federal law, medical dispensaries of marijuana first appeared in San Francisco, tentatively and with a bit of fear. When the federal government hesitated to make them an issue, more opened in other parts of California. The city councils of San Francisco, Los Angeles and other cities now regulate the dispensaries, determining how many can operate where (Wingfield and Scheck 2010).

The green light was turned on when the Obama administration declared that it would not pursue medical marijuana dispensaries for violating federal law (Anderson and Rees 2011). Where these dispensaries are available and state law is lenient, the medical reasons for being able to purchase marijuana have expanded. No longer does one have to be in chemotherapy or suffering horrible pain during one's last days on earth. Rather, the "patient" can have a back ache, trouble going to sleep, or even just feel a little anxious. (Maybe anxious that the dispensary might close?)

The social movement to legalize marijuana, going back decades, has gained momentum recently. This photo is a reminder of how closely this movement is related to the social movements surrounding alcohol of earlier generations.

It is possible that we have taken the first steps to making marijuana legal.

If so, when will the final steps follow? Making marijuana legal will require the neutralization of many who are opposed to marijuana. The final argument that will bring about legalization will likely assert that

1. Laws haven't stopped people who want to smoke marijuana from smoking it.
2. Enforcing anti-marijuana laws is expensive, and we can use those resources to enforce laws against serious offenses.

And the assertion that is likely to drive the nail in the coffin of the anti-marijuana laws:

3. We can tax marijuana and raise billions of dollars to (Pick one): create jobs, reduce the federal deficit, help the poor, improve schools, patrol our borders, or hire more police and make society safer.

But will such arguments win the day? The push to legalize marijuana is being met by a strong reaction against its legalization, even against its use for any reason. The federal Drug Enforcement Administration has stepped in, closing dispensaries and sending letters to the landlords of others, threatening to confiscate their assets (Onishi 2012). The head of the Drug Enforcement Agency is eager to stop Colorado and Washington from allowing the sale and possession of marijuana (Tarm 2013).

For Your Consideration

Do you think that marijuana will be legalized? Are you for or against its legalization? Why?

as a "pick-me-up," for cocaine had become an ingredient in *Coca*-Cola, a drink that is named after the coca leaf.

Yet by 1910, cocaine's reputation had changed profoundly. It had been transformed from a medicine and a "pick-me-up" into a dangerous drug, much as Dr. Jekyll became Mr. Hyde—a story, by the way, that Robert Louis Stevenson wrote in three days while he was high on cocaine (Ashley 1975). What led to such an abrupt change and the drug's social downfall?

In the late 1800s, reporters began to link cocaine with poverty and crime. They reported that gunmen used cocaine to get up their nerve to commit robberies (Ashley 1975). These news stories led to a public outcry, and in 1903 the Coca-Cola Company found it prudent to eliminate cocaine from its drink. Even today, however, Coca-Cola contains an extract from the coca leaf (Miller 1994). In the early 1900s, it was still legal to use cocaine in products, as long as the cocaine was listed as an ingredient. Although cocaine is a stimulant, in 1914 the Harrison Act mistakenly classified cocaine as a narcotic, making it illegal to sell or purchase the drug.

The Black Market in Cocaine. The Harrison Act paved the way for a black market in cocaine, a market that still exists today. Over 100 *tons* of cocaine are seized by federal agents as it is being transported to the United States. Some cocaine is even delivered by submarines (Schmidt and Shanker 2012). About 15 percent of Americans age 12 and over—about 38 million people—have used cocaine. Close to 2 million use this drug at least once a month (*Statistical Abstract* 2013:Tables 11, 209). As we saw in Table 4.1 on page 91, in just the past month about 1.2 percent of full-time college students used cocaine. This comes to about 160,000 students (*Statistical Abstract* 2013:Table 277). Though snorting is the preferred method of use, smoking cocaine base, called *freebasing,* is also popular.

Uses of Cocaine. Cocaine has a distinctive medical use. Surgeons apply cocaine as a local anesthetic and as a vasoconstrictor (a substance that reduces blood flow to the area to which it is applied). The drug is so effective that cocaine is the medical profession's anesthetic of choice for surgery involving the nose, throat, larynx, and lower respiratory passages. The most common use of cocaine, however, is to obtain a high—feelings of well-being, optimism, confidence, competence, and energy. Cocaine also has a reputation as an aphrodisiac; it is thought to create or heighten sexual desires, to increase sexual endurance, and to overcome frigidity and impotence (Inciardi 1986:78–79).

From the coca plant comes an abundance of legal products: soap, shampoo, toothpaste, flour, tea, calcium and iron supplements, even a substance to grow hair (Forero 2006). Before he became president of Bolivia, Evo Morales was a farmer who used to grow coca. Morales argues that farmers should be able to grow coca and that its legal products should be accepted internationally. U.S. officials disagree and want all coca plants eradicated.

Can cocaine be addicting? This man in Wales was so addicted, snorting so much cocaine, that his nose collapsed. His heart was also damaged.

Dysfunctions of Cocaine. Whether from the powder or crystal ("crack") form, cocaine's "high" is intense. Those who become addicted to cocaine report a craving so strong that "they will give up many of the things they value—money, possessions, relationships, jobs, and careers—in order to continue taking the drug" (Goode 1989:198–199). Some women rent their bodies for crack, giving us the term "crack whore."

In the 1980s, there was a national panic about "crack babies," children with severe health problems born to women who used cocaine. The initial reports were scary, but much to the surprise of everyone the damage turned out to be much less severe than originally feared. Problems include slight developmental delay and, in school, problems with attention and self-control ("Prenatal Substance Exposure" 2008; Rose-Jacobs et al. 2009; Ackerman et al 2010).

Racial injustice is part of crack cocaine's social history. In 1986, Congress made possessing or selling crack a federal offense, with penalties more severe than those for powder cocaine. Because powder cocaine is more likely to be used by whites and crack cocaine by African Americans, African Americans were sentenced to longer terms than whites (Riley 1998; Moore 2009). After charges of racial discrimination, the U.S. District Court in Georgia declared in 1994 that crack cocaine and powder cocaine are one and the same drug. Despite this, the disparity in sentencing continued. In 2010, Congress passed a law that narrows the penalty for crack and powder cocaine violations.

Principles Underlying a Drug's Social Reputation. From this brief social history of cocaine, we can see the principles that help to determine a drug's social reputation and its acceptability:

1. A drug's reputation is not based on objective conditions. It does not, for instance, derive from tests showing that one drug causes more physical or psychological harm than another. If such a scientific approach characterized a drug's social history, alcohol would be banned and marijuana would be available in grocery stores (Ashley 1975).
2. Like humans, drugs gain their reputation and acceptance through the people and events with which they are associated.
3. Drugs associated with higher-status (or "respectable") people are likely to be defined as good and desirable, while drugs associated with lower-status (disrespected, poor) people are likely to be defined as bad and undesirable.
4. The reputation or social acceptability of drugs changes over time.

Research Findings: The Hallucinogens

LSD

4.8 Summarize research findings on LSD, peyote and mescaline, PCP, and ecstasy.

Perhaps the most famous of the hallucinogens is LSD (lysergic acid diethylamide). This drug was first synthesized in 1938 by Albert Hoffman, a Swiss chemist. Hoffman discovered that LSD was psychoactive when he accidentally inhaled a minute dose of the drug. Here is what he says happened to him:

> *Last Friday, April 16, 1943, I was forced to stop my work in the laboratory in the middle of the afternoon and to go home, as I was seized by a peculiar restlessness associated with a sensation of mild dizziness. Having reached home, I lay down and sank in a kind of drunkenness which was not unpleasant and which was characterized by extreme activity of imagination. As I lay in a dazed condition with my eyes closed (I experienced daylight as disagreeably bright) there surged upon me an uninterrupted stream of fantastic images of extraordinary plasticity and vividness and accompanied by an intense, kaleidoscope-like play of colors. This condition gradually passed off after about two hours. (Hoffman 1968:184–185)*

It takes so little of this tasteless, odorless substance to experience its intense, mind-altering effects that an ounce contains 300,000 doses. When people first started experimenting with LSD, psychotic reactions and suicides made headlines across the nation. Sociologist Howard S. Becker (1967) studied the drug culture and found that people who took LSD in its early days thought it might create panic—and they were likely to experience panic. Gradually, however, a subculture grew around LSD. As it did, people's expectations changed—and so did their experiences. When people who had already experienced LSD introduced the drug to their friends, they told them what to expect. When a novice saw strange colors, walls breathing, or felt a unity with plants, their "trip guides" assured them that this was normal, that it was temporary, and that they should relax and enjoy the sensations. As negative LSD experiences were replaced with positive ones, the panics and suicides disappeared from the news.

LSD reached its height of media attention in the mid-1960s with the hippie culture (Goode 1989:178–179). Since then, the popularity of this drug has dropped, and it has practically disappeared from the media. But with 13 million full-time college students, the 0.7 percent who took LSD in the past month translates to about 90,000 students (*Statistical Abstract* 2013:Table 277).

Peyote and Mescaline

Peyote, a small cactus that produces hallucinatory experiences, was being used by some Native Americans when the Spanish arrived in North America. Mescaline, which is synthesized from peyote, produces similar visual effects. Both peyote and mescaline have had famous proponents: Havelock Ellis (1897, 1902) was enthusiastic about peyote and Aldous Huxley (1954) sang the praises of mescaline. In the 1960s and 1970s, anthropologist Carlos Castaneda (1968, 1971, 1974) popularized the use of peyote among a cultlike following. Members of the Native American Church, who use peyote for religious purposes, claim constitutional protection under freedom of religion. The U.S. Supreme Court ruled, however, that Oregon could arrest these users (Hart and Ksir 2011).

Psilocybin

In the 1500s, the Spanish also found that Native Americans in Mexico were using a mushroom (*Psilocybe mexicana*) for its hallucinatory experiences. Because the mushrooms were associated with pagan rituals, the Roman Catholic Spanish launched campaigns against them, and their use seemed to disappear. Then in the 1930s it was discovered that natives of southern Mexico were still using the mushrooms. Their active ingredient is psilocybin, which was isolated by Albert Hoffman in 1958 and later synthesized. As with peyote, reports about the effects of this drug often contain a spiritual or religious emphasis (Hart and Ksir 2011).

PCP

PCP (phencyclidine hydrochloride), often called *angel dust,* was synthesized in 1957 by Parke-Davis and sold as a painkiller. As people soon discovered, this drug produces hallucinations. Because PCP requires little equipment to manufacture, it is often made in home laboratories. PCP affects the central nervous system, making it difficult to speak. Users report altered body images, feelings of unreality, euphoria, and a sense of power, loneliness, or isolation. Others experience numbness and even feelings of dying (which is why some users refer to PCP as "embalming fluid"). Higher dosages can result in loss of inhibition, disorientation, rage, convulsions, or coma (Crider 1986; Hart and Ksir 2011).

Ecstasy

Ecstasy (MDMA, methylenedioxyamphetamine) is a popular party drug that produces an euphoric rush like that of cocaine combined with some of the mind-altering effects of the psychedelics. Its users say that Ecstasy, sometimes called "the love drug," relaxes them and increases empathy and feelings of intimacy. They also report that it enhances sensual experiences, making touching and other physical contact more pleasurable. Negative side effects for some users are mental confusion and anxiety. The main concern about this drug, though, is that it may cause brain damage (Carroll 2000; Hart and Ksir 2011).

Research Findings: The Barbiturates and the Amphetamines

Barbiturates

4.9 Summarize research findings on the barbiturates and amphetamines.

In 1862, Dr. A. Bayer (the Bayer of aspirin fame from Munich, Germany), combined urea with malonic acid and made a new compound, barbituric acid. Of the 2,500 drugs that have been derived from barbituric acid, the best known are phenobarbital (Luminal), amobarbital (Amytal), pentobarbital (Nembutal), and secobarbital (Seconal). Physicians use the barbiturates as anesthetics and treat anxiety, insomnia, and epilepsy. The barbiturates provide an experience similar to that of alcohol. Regular barbiturate use leads to physical dependence. Withdrawal causes nausea, anxiety, sweating, dizziness, trembling, muscular twitching, and sometimes convulsions, coma, and death. Because the risk of death is higher for those who stop "cold turkey" (abruptly), physicians usually substitute a long-lasting barbiturate and then withdraw it slowly (Hart and Ksir 2011).

Amphetamines

Amphetamines—Benzedrine, Dexedrine, Methedrine, Desoxyn, Biphetamine, and Dexamyl—are referred to as "uppers," "pep pills," "bennies," "dexies," "speed," "meth," "crystal," and "ice" (Carroll 2000). Discovered in 1887, Benzedrine became popular in the 1920s in over-the-counter inhalers intended to dilate the bronchial tubes. Later Benzedrine was available by prescription in tablet form for hyperkinesis and, in 1939, as an appetite suppressant. During World War II, the military gave amphetamines to soldiers to help them stay awake. At this time, people began to soak the amphetamines from Benzedrine inhalers, and amphetamine abuse began.

"Speed" (methamphetamine dissolved in liquid) is used by "speed freaks," who inject the drug, sometimes every 2 or 3 hours, for "runs" of 3 or 4 days. Each injection of this kind produces a "rush" or "flash," a sudden feeling of intense pleasure, followed by moderate feelings of euphoria. Some users hallucinate, while others develop feelings of paranoia, or become hostile and aggressive—symptoms that have been called

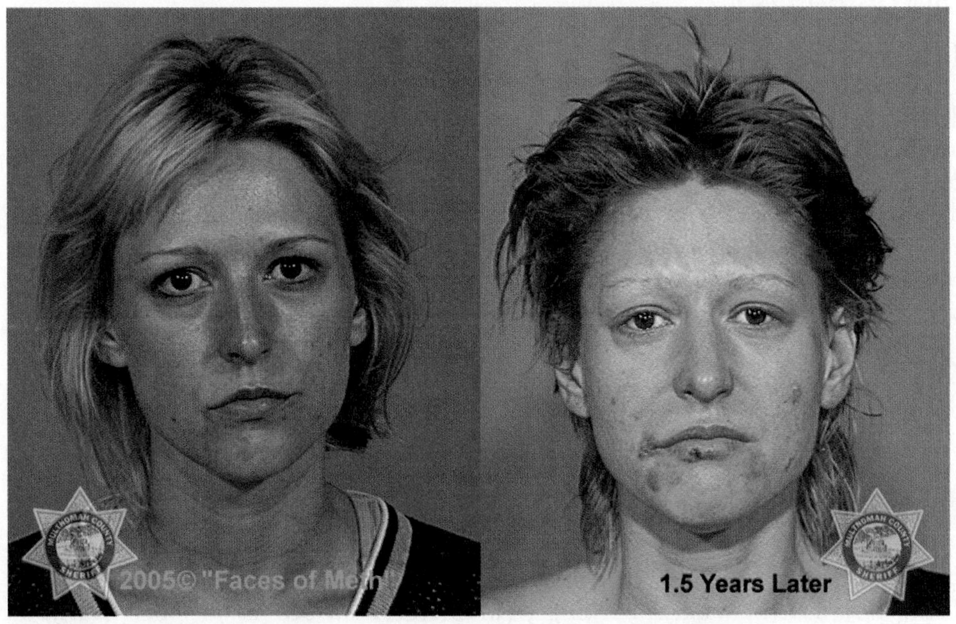

These two photos are of the same person—before and after meth addiction. For some, it takes but a couple of years or less for this type of transition to occur.

the *amphetamine psychosis* (Ray and Ksir 2004). Heavy amphetamine use is sometimes accompanied by behavioral fixations, such as counting the corn flakes in a box of cereal over and over again or repeatedly cleaning the same room. Amphetamine withdrawal can bring with it outbursts of aggression, feelings of terror, and thoughts of suicide or homicide (Carroll 2000; Julien 2001).

Methamphetamine ("meth") addiction has become a widespread problem. Because meth can be made easily at home, "meth labs" have sprung up all over the country. Some make meth in motel rooms, while others turn vans and cars into portable meth labs (Saulny 2010; Crum 2012). These home manufacturers use pseudoephedrine, which is found in some cold and sinus medicines. Because of this abuse, several states have made these medicines, such as Sudafed, available only by prescription (Garrison 2010). Meth's side effects include high blood pressure and high fevers (Zernike 2006). The photos on the previous page give a small indication of why officials are concerned about meth addiction and meth manufacturing.

Research Findings: Steroids

4.10 Summarize research findings on the steroids.

The anabolic steroids have solid medical uses, including the treatment of breast cancer and building muscle in people whose bodies are wasting away with AIDS (Westreich 2008). Soviet trainers used to use steroids to "bulk up" their athletes for the Olympics. They succeeded in building muscle, but they also discovered that steroids can create a dependence that causes depression when the drug is withdrawn and that heavy usage can bring heart disease and strokes that can strike athletes in the prime of life. Steroids' side effects also include liver cysts and shrinking testes. Not surprisingly, men want to avoid steroids' feminizing side effects: When they use steroids they also often take antiestrogen agents.

It is not the side effects of steroids, however, that have caught the attention of the public. It is the illegal use of steroids by athletes to build body mass and muscle that has raised concerns, the topic of the Thinking Critically box on the next page.

Research Findings: The Narcotics—Morphine and Heroin

4.11 Summarize research findings on morphine and heroin.

Watch on **MySocLab** **Video:** Opium Addiction

Morphine

To understand the narcotics, it is necessary to start with a little flower, the opium poppy. On Figure 4.4 on page 108, you can see the process by which morphine and heroin are derived from this flower. Morphine is a painkiller, so potent that doctors use it on the battlefield to give wounded soldiers immediate relief from their wounds (Holbrook et al. 2010). An unfortunate aspect of morphine is that it is highly addicting. Because of this, the government controls morphine, making it available only for limited medical use.

The narcotic of most interest is heroin, which also comes from the opium poppy and is equally as addicting. Let's focus on it.

Heroin

> *Junk [heroin] yields a basic formula of . . . total need. . . . Beyond a certain frequency need knows absolutely no limit or control. In the words of total need: "Wouldn't you?" Yes you would. You would lie, cheat, inform on your friends, steal, do anything to satisfy total need. Because you would be in a state of total sickness, total possession, and not in a position to act in any other way. . . . A rabid dog can't choose but bite.*

This is how novelist William Burroughs (1975:135) described his addiction to heroin. His description matches the common view that heroin is so addictive and its withdrawal pains so severe that addicts will do anything to avoid withdrawal. Is it true?

Thinking Critically About Social Problems

Steroids and Athletes

Anabolic steroids are so common at gyms that body builders call them "gym candy." No one seems to be much bothered that these muscular hulks, in competition with one another for the largest this or that, use steroids to "beef up." The attitude seems to be, "So what? How else can they look like *that* in bodybuilding competition?"

Arnold Schwarzenegger and Lou Ferrigno, you can pose proudly. No one really cares how you got to look like that, just that you did. What hulks!

But when it comes to athletes using steroids in competitive sports, it is a different matter. The concern is that steroids enhance performance, giving athletes who use them an unfair advantage.

Marion Jones was a star athlete who became a role model for girls. She even won a gold medal at the Olympics. She denied under oath that she had used steroids. She was stripped of her medal and put in prison for perjury.

Lance Armstrong—who won the prestigious Tour de France cycling race seven consecutive times—now disgraced and stripped of his medals and lucrative product endorsements for using drugs.

Roger Clemens, one of baseball's best pitchers, also denied that he used steroids. After denying under oath that he had used steroids, he was tried for perjury and found not guilty.

Barry Bonds, who broke the all-time home run record, left the San Francisco Giants amidst accusations of steroid use. After an investigation of eight years and a lengthy trial for perjury, Bonds was found guilty of one count of obstruction of justice and given a $4,000 fine and sentenced to a month-long house arrest at his 50,000 square foot home in Beverly Hills ("Barry Bonds . . ." 2011).

Mark McGwire broke Roger Maris' record for the most home runs in a season. Maris' record of 61 had stood since 1961. In the year that McGwire broke what had become almost a mythical record, it was apparent that McGwire was beefing up. Fans were even commenting on his chest and biceps, wondering whether he was using steroids.

As concerns about athletes using steroids grew, in 2005 Congress held an investigation. Called to testify, McGwire refused to say whether he had used steroids. Finally, to the dismay of his fans, in 2010 McGwire admitted steroid use in the 1990s (Kepner 2010). He said that he was sorry he had taken steroids, but in a backhanded justification for doing so, he also said that he had taken them only to overcome sports injuries. He added that he was certain that he would have beaten Maris' home run record even without steroids. Then, to cover all bases, McGwire called Maris' widow and told her he was sorry. Apparently, this was adequate as the St. Louis Cardinals hired McGwire as a hitting coach (Dodd 2011).

For Your Consideration

Why shouldn't athletes be allowed to take steroids if they are willing to take the health risks? Let's assume that medical doctors can control the health risks associated with steroid use. Why shouldn't physicians be allowed to prescribe steroids to athletes?

Do you think that athletes should be required to undergo drug testing? All athletes, including those in high school and college? Why or why not?

When a team of sociologists headed by Bruce Johnson (Johnson et al. 1985) explored heroin addiction, they found something different. They rented a storefront in a Harlem neighborhood that had "the highest number of street-level heroin abusers in the country." For two years, a research staff of former heroin users built rapport with 201 current users. From the day-to-day reports they collected, the researchers found that many heroin users are *not* physically addicted. They use heroin once or twice a day for a period of time, and then—without suffering withdrawal symptoms—they go for several days without the drug. Other researchers have noted that some people

FIGURE 4.4 How Opium Is Converted Into Heroin

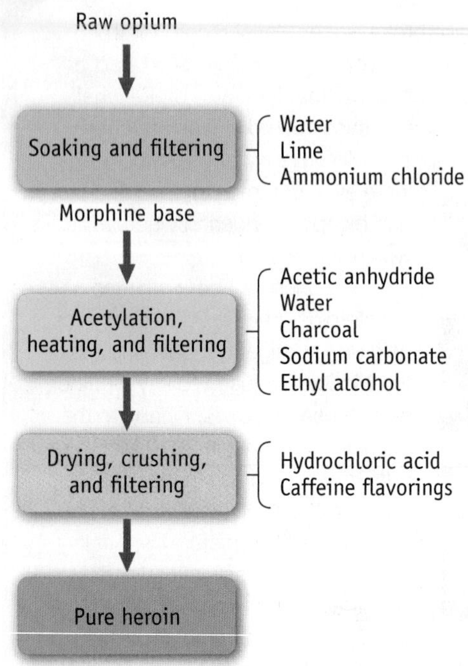

Source: By the author. Based on *Newsday* 1974 and Drug Enforcement Agency 2001.

use heroin on an occasional basis, such as at weekend parties, without becoming addicted (Spunt 2003).

Researchers found something similar among U.S. soldiers who returned from Vietnam. About 14 percent had used heroin in Vietnam, a heroin far stronger than any available back home. After the soldiers came home, were reunited with family and friends, and went back to work, most stopped using heroin. Few had any physical problems. As the assistant secretary of defense for health and environment said, "Everything that I learned in medical school—that anyone who ever tried heroin was instantly, totally, and perpetually hooked—failed to prepare me for dealing with this situation" (Peele 1987:211).

These findings so contradict reports of William Burroughs and other addicts that it can make your head swim. Certainly Burroughs did not make up his description of his own addiction to heroin. Nor did Johnson and his associates make up their findings. How, then, can we reconcile such contradictory reports? The simplest explanation seems to be that heroin is addicting to some people, but not to others. Some users of heroin do become addicts and match the stereotypical profile. Others are able to use heroin on a recreational basis.

Again, we need more research. Who, under what circumstances, become addicted? What are the social reasons? Are there also biological factors?

Fetal Narcotic Syndrome. As with alcohol and cocaine, pregnant women who use narcotics deliver babies who are addicted. Suffering from **fetal narcotic syndrome**, these newborns have tremors, and they can't sleep. In distress, they frantically suck their tiny fists. They also are more likely to be born prematurely and to be underweight (Hamdan 2010).

Heroin, Crime, and the Law

Heroin causes crime, destroys people's incentive to work, and devastates its users' health.

Read on **MySocLab Document:** Association is Not Causation: Alcohol and Other Drugs Do Not Cause Violence

Everyone knows that this statement is true. But is it? Once again, let's compare sociology and commonsense assumptions about social life.

Researchers studied physicians who had become addicted to narcotics. Did these doctors get high and hold up cabbies? No. Did they mug pedestrians, burgle houses, or become prostitutes? Not a one. Did they stop working? No. Did their health deteriorate? Again, no. (Winick 1961)

Why not? The answer lies in their social position. Like street-corner addicts, the physicians also need narcotics to avoid withdrawal pains. But unlike poor street addicts, the physician addicts had no need to prey on others. By diverting (stealing) the narcotics from legal, medical sources, they had access to a cheap supply. From this research, it is also apparent that the narcotics don't make people stop working. These doctors continued to work as doctors. And their health was fine. They had access to pure drugs, as well as to well balanced, nutritious food. The common stereotypes about narcotics causing crime and destroying health and the incentive to work are simply not true.

Here is how Jerome Jaffe (1965:292), a physician who studied physician addicts, put it:

> *The addict who is able to obtain an adequate supply of the drug through legitimate channels and has adequate funds, usually dresses properly, maintains his nutrition, and is able to discharge his social and occupational obligations with reasonable efficiency. He usually remains in good health, suffers little inconvenience, and is, in general, difficult to distinguish from other persons.*

This research on doctors is supported by observations of middle-class weekend users of heroin. They, too, find no need to prey on others. They pay for their heroin from their earnings at work (Spunt 2003).

Narcotics, then, do *not* cause the things we commonly associate with them: robbery, burglary, prostitution, unemployment, and poor health. Yet these things are common to narcotic addicts—that is, to *poor* street addicts. *Life circumstances make the difference, not addiction to narcotics.*

Social Policy

The Dilemmas of Social Policy

4.12 Explain why it is difficult to establish social policy on drug use and abuse.

Like abortion, the drug problem is surrounded by irreconcilable differences of strong opinion, emotions, stereotypes, and prejudices. Complicating social policy even further are contrasting moralities, subcultural values, and conflicting laws. Consider this: The health findings on alcohol suggest that we should encourage light to moderate drinking, but discourage heavy drinking. Which of our high schools and colleges—or our churches and state governments—would promote such a policy? ("Okay, class, this is why you should drink a beer or two almost every day.")

Watch on **MySocLab** **Video:** Drug Test in Russian Schools

Even trying to analyze the health consequences of drugs poses a dilemma. As Oakley Ray (1998) put it,

> *From a medical point of view no drug is safe. With some doses, modes of administration, and frequency of use, all drugs cause toxic effects and even death. It is equally true that at some doses, modes of administration, and frequency of use all drugs are safe. The concern here is whether a drug, used the way most people use it today, is physically harmful. From this position, alcohol and marijuana are relatively safe drugs the way most people use them. Nicotine, in contrast, is a very harmful drug, since the usual amount of cigarette smoking does increase the mortality rate.*

Theory and Social Policy. From a medical standpoint, then, no drug is safe, and all drugs are safe. Rational social policy should be built around the dimension of *social harm*. Why prohibit drugs, for example, that don't cause social harm? But as *symbolic interactionists* would want to know, From whose point of view do we define social harm? As you know, the middle class would define harm differently than would inner-city residents. And why should we force the perspective of one group on the other? For *functionalists*, the question would be, When do drugs interfere with people reaching their goals or when do they interfere with the welfare of society? And how do we determine this? *Conflict sociologists* might suggest something entirely different—that social policy is made with the approval of the ruling class and is ultimately a form of social control, especially of groups that might upset the balance of power.

The "Get Tough" Approach. Currently, a *get-tough* approach is the dominant sentiment in the United States—passing strict laws and putting teeth in them. What is wrong with a get-tough policy? Recall again that in some societies officials used to beat people's feet for drinking coffee and slit noses and cut off heads for smoking cigarettes. Even draconian measures don't work when people crave drugs.

In the 1980s, President George H. W. Bush declared a "war on drugs." He ordered the Coast Guard, the Customs Service, the Border Patrol, the Immigration and Naturalization Service, and the Drug Enforcement Agency to stop illegal drugs from coming into the United States. The Pentagon even attempted to build a "fence" of radar-equipped balloons at the Mexican border (Fialka 1988). The result? Even more drugs flowed into the United States, so much so that the price of heroin dropped, and its purity increased. So much for that war.

Some just shake their heads and say that if we can't stop the drugs from coming in, at least we can lock up the dealers and users. *This is impossible*. As we have reviewed, millions of Americans use illegal drugs. During just the past month, about 16 million Americans smoked marijuana. How many dealers does it take to supply just the marijuana smokers? If each dealer has twenty-five customers, there are over 600,000 dealers. We simply don't have enough jails and prisons to lock all of these people up.

Lurking in back of a "lock-'em-up" approach is the assumption that to jail a dealer is to eliminate that dealer's drug deals. Such an assumption is absolutely false. The arrest of a dealer is a business opportunity for eager wanna-be dealers who are waiting to take over vacated territory. Get rid of one dealer, and two more jostle to take that person's place.

Get-tough policies fuel black markets. They produce fountains of profits for those who are willing to take the risk. This harsh reality surfaced with Prohibition, when the United States made selling and drinking alcohol a criminal act. An underground network immediately sprang up to keep that drug supply going—as it will for any drug that we make illegal. It is even worse for addicting drugs: To get the money to purchase them, poor addicts prey on others. The latent dysfunctions of criminalizing drugs—the bankrolling of organized crime and an increase in muggings, burglaries, thefts, prostitution, and premature deaths—are they not worse than the original problem that the laws address?

The profits in the black market for drugs are so huge that they can finance armies and threaten to topple governments. Look at what is happening in Mexico, the topic of the Global Glimpse box on the next page. Then contrast this with the Global Glimpse box on Uruguay on page 112.

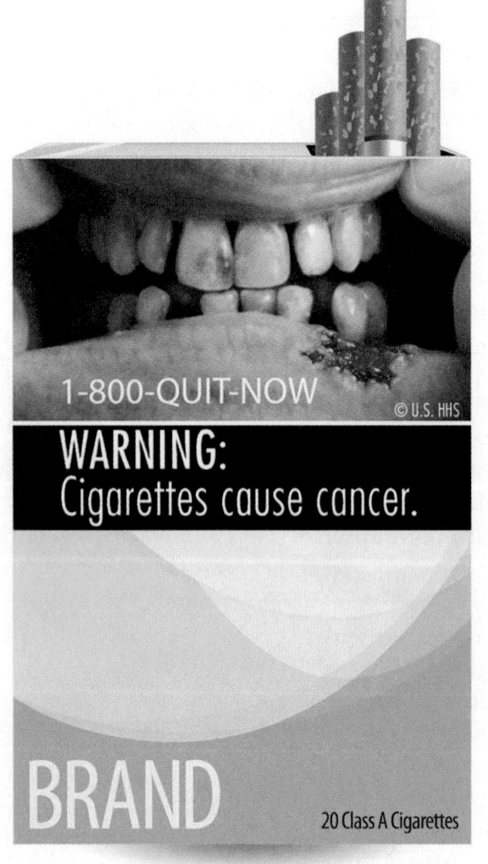

For the health of the public, state and federal governments have battled cigarette advertising. This proposed packaging for cigarettes was struck down by federal courts.

Deciding Social Policy

Within this morass of emotions, dilemmas, and contradictions, let's try to suggest social policy that has a rational basis and might have a chance of accomplishing something.

Banning Advertising. An adequate social policy can begin by banning *all* advertising for drugs known to be harmful. Nicotine is certainly a case in point. As it now stands, when young people open magazines and newspapers, smiling, happy, healthy young people beckon them to join their carefree lifestyle of pleasurable smoking. To ban all advertising for cigarettes and tobacco products would remove this source of enticement.

Drug Education. Many programs of drug education have been tried, but researchers do not agree that any work. Some programs even seem to backfire. Students who are given information about drugs use drugs in greater moderation, but the information they receive piques their curiosity and more of them use drugs (Blum et al. 1976; Levine 1986). This isn't what is intended, of course. DARE, Drug Abuse Resistance Education, was a popular program. It worked fine in experimental situations, but when applied in real-life large-scale settings, it was not effective (Clayton et al. 1996; Weiss et al. 2008). When other researchers reviewed the same data, they concluded that the program does work (Gorman and Huber 2009). With researchers bogged down in disagreements about methods and analyses, we cannot conclude that any program yet developed reduces drug use among students. Perhaps in coming years effective drug education programs will be developed.

A Global Glimpse

Mexico's Drug War

It was a typical night at *El Sol y Sombra* in Uruapan, a little town in Michoacán, Mexico. Some couples were dancing to Norteño, while others were flirting. As the drinks took effect, the problems of life receded.

The reverie was broken abruptly when several men burst into the nightclub, waving machine guns and shooting into the air. The music stopped, and the revelers, their alcohol-induced escape suddenly cut short and fearing that their time had come, huddled against the walls. Instead of more shooting, the men threw a garbage bag onto the middle of the emptied dance floor.

Five human heads rolled out, the eyes staring ghastly into space, the blood still dripping from the freshly severed necks.

"Now that's something you don't see every day," said a bartender when reporters talked to him later. "Very ugly."

That's an understatement, even in Michoacán where drug-related violence is an almost daily occurrence. The drug dealers have killed judges and prosecutors. They have even raided police stations with machine guns, grenades, and bazookas. In one town, after receiving death threats, eighteen of the thirty-two policemen resigned (McKinley 2006a, 2006b).

Putting severed heads on display sends an impressive message.

Since some people—although hard to imagine—might not get the message, the dealers are leaving notes alongside the heads. At *El Sol y Sombra*, the note said, "The family does not kill for money. It does not kill women. It does not kill innocents. It kills only those who deserve to die. Everyone should know, this is divine justice."

"The family" ("*la familia*) is the term this group has given itself.

At another location, this note accompanied other severed heads: "See. Hear. Shut Up. If you want to stay alive."

Not surprisingly, the police are finding it difficult to locate anyone who has seen or heard anything.

If the drug dealers have their way, they will take over Mexico. They likely will not succeed in doing so, but their influence has grown. Drug money is powerful, and throughout Mexico it has corrupted the police and politicians. No one knows whom to trust any longer. Even the head of Mexico's drug enforcement had to resign. Apparently, even he was on the drug payroll.

In 2006, Felipe Calderón, Mexico's president, declared war on the drug cartels. He sent soldiers into troubled cities, practically taking over some. Although the army patrols the cities and attacks the drug gangs, the rival cartels, still battling for control of the lucrative drug trade, continue to slaughter one another.

Tens of thousands of people have been killed in Mexico's war against drugs. From this photo taken in Saltillo, Mexico, you can see that the drug police wear masks. If not, drug lords will know who they are and order their kidnapping, torture, and execution.

One group dumped 49 headless, mutilated bodies along a busy highway that leads from Monterrey to the United States. Another 41 were dumped alongside the highway near Reynosa, Mexico ("49 Bodies . . ." 2012). The gangs hunt down people who dare to criticize them, torturing and beheading journalists and even bloggers who report on their activities ("Mexican Drug Gang . . ." 2011). Sometimes the gangs brazenly hang the bodies from highly-traveled overpasses and deliver others to city hall ("Horror as Nine . . ." 2012). The bodies are intended as a warning to rival gangs, but they also serve as a warning to police not to get involved, and to regular citizens to see nothing and stay out of the way. The death toll comes to about 60,000 (Cordoba 2012).

As Mexico's drug violence has spiraled out of control, it is spilling into U.S. border cities. U.S. officials fear that these cities will become battlegrounds. For now, the problem continues without solution, with the drugs heading north and the guns and cash heading south.

For Your Consideration

What do you think can be done to solve this problem? The drug violence is fueled by a war over drug profits. Some suggest that we strike the problem at its root: If drugs were made legal, the profits would disappear overnight. What social problems do you think legalization would produce?

A Global Glimpse

Uruguay's Proposed Solution to Marijuana

"The problem with the laws against marijuana is their consequences. The demand is still there, the profits are high, and this leads to violence among the dealers," said one official in Uruguay.

"Yes, of course. We all know this," replied another official. "And we know there isn't much we can do about it."

"Yes, there is," said the first official. We can legalize marijuana. The United States has been bullying us with its drug policies for years. They think that whatever they want is right. They've got most of the users, and the money flows down from them and creates violence in South America."

"Right. But what do you mean by legalize? Doesn't marijuana need controls?"

"Sure it does. And it can be a source of profit, too, which can go to the government instead of the criminals. What I propose is that we license the farms where marijuana will be grown, the factories to manufacture marijuana cigarettes, and we sell the packages of cigarettes. Only those 18 and over can buy them."

"Sort of like we do with tobacco cigarettes?"

"Exactly," said the first official. "You've got the idea."

"Then we solve the crime problem and get more taxes. This could even reduce our police budgets."

"Right."

"I'm on board. Let's get busy and convince the others."

"And," said the first official, "our grass is going to be the best. It will be legal, reasonable in price, and quality. We'll drive the illegal drug dealers out of business."

This idea, quite bold, perhaps somewhat radical, was proposed in this little South American country of less than 4 million people. The lawmakers are deciding the issue as I write this.

Based on Moffett and Kaplan 2012.

For Your Consideration

What do you think about the Uruguayan proposal? Do you think this approach would work in the United States? Would you vote for it?

It seems that drug education should be based on scientific studies, not on someone's ideas of what drugs are "good" and "bad." Such a program would require that we determine *both* the beneficial and the harmful effects of drugs—and that we communicate these findings, even if they go against our biases. For example, if scientific evidence shows that marijuana is safer than tobacco, which appears to be the case, then, like it or not, we need to communicate that information. We cannot shy away from communicating either the good or the bad effects of marijuana or any drug just because we have a bias for or against a drug.

View on **MySocLab Figure:** the Past Month Use of Selected Illicit Drugs among Youths Ages 12

Drug Addiction. We need an adequate social policy to deal with drug addiction. Jailing addicted people does not address addiction. Upon release, most of them go back to their drugs. A successful program cannot focus on addiction as though addicts live in a social vacuum. It must take into account the background of an addict's life. Addiction is often part of subcultural orientations and deprivations—often poverty, unemployment, dropping out of school, hopelessness, despair, and a bleak future. To be successful, drug programs must reflect the life realities of drug abusers.

People who become drug dependent are strongly motivated to continue their drug use. With cigarettes available legally, nicotine addicts have no difficulty obtaining their drug. Cigarettes are available in any community, and tobacco crops are even subsidized by the Department of Agriculture. With the average cost of supporting a nicotine habit running close to $2,000 a year, cigarette addicts do not mug, steal, or kill to obtain their drug. In contrast, the black market that supplies heroin and cocaine drives up the price of these drugs, and many of their users are involved in crime to support their addiction.

A successful drug addiction program, then, might include free or inexpensive drugs. For example, heroin addicts could be prescribed heroin by physicians who would treat them as patients. As Arnold Trebach (1987:369) put it back in the 1980s,

> *The availability of prescribed heroin would mean that multitudes of addicts would be able to function as decent law-abiding citizens for the first time in years. Their health should be much improved because their drugs would be clean and measured in labeled dosages. The number of crimes they commit should drop dramatically. By implication, addicts to other narcotics, such as morphine and codeine, would also reap the same benefits. They would be eligible to receive maintenance doses of the drugs on which they are dependent. Hordes of potential crime victims would, accordingly, be denied the pleasure.*

Such a policy would break the addicts' dependence on the black market, removing a major source of profit for organized crime. It would also eliminate the need for addicts to prey on others. If the program provided only such benefits, it would be a night-and-day improvement over our present situation. But for success we would still need a three-pronged attack: counseling for personal problems, practical help in seeking and maintaining employment, and clinical services for those who want to end their addiction.

Methadone maintenance illustrates how the labels *illegal* and *legal* play a key role in developing social policy. Methadone, a synthetic narcotic, was developed by the Germans during World War II as a painkiller for wounded soldiers (Wren 1998). Although methadone is addicting, it is given orally in clinics to help break addiction to heroin. This transfers addiction from an illegal drug, heroin, to a legal drug, methadone.

Why transfer someone's addiction from one narcotic to another? The major reason is that this frees the addicts from the black market, removing the need to commit crime to support their drug habit. But if we are going to supply drugs to addicts, why not simply give them the drug to which they already are addicted? The answer goes back to the labels attached to drugs, their social reputation: The narcotic heroin is evil; the narcotic methadone is good.

Methadone maintenance programs were supposed to include counseling for patients and job training. For budgetary reasons, these programs were cut, leaving only the "bare bones" of the original plan—giving methadone to addicts. This failing alerts us to a danger of social policy: Politicians who fund a program may not see it in the same way as do the professionals who designed it. If politicians and bureaucrats cut costs, they dismantle the original program in all but name.

Forcing Abstinence: The 24/7 Sobriety Program. A judge in South Dakota originated the *24/7 Sobriety Program.* To stay out of jail, anyone convicted of an alcohol-related crime—from drunk driving to minor crimes—has to show up twice a day for a breathalyzer test. If they fail to appear or if the test shows they have been drinking, they go directly to jail for a day. They can choose to go to alcohol treatment courses if they want to, but they cannot choose not to take the test twice a day. Apparently, 99 percent show up twice a day sober (Kleiman et al. 2012).

Alcoholics Anonymous. Alcoholics Anonymous (AA) is a successful drug program whose principles have been applied to other addiction treatment programs, such as Cocaine Anonymous. Started in 1935 in Akron, Ohio, by two alcoholics, AA has grown into a worldwide organization of 116,000 local groups with more than 2 million members ("AA Fact File" 2012). Central to AA's success is that it is directed and staffed by people who have experienced alcohol addiction themselves—and have overcome it. They know firsthand what the addicts go through. Intimately familiar with the addicts' orientations, they can talk their language on a "gut level."

The essentials of Alcoholics Anonymous are summarized in what this group calls the Twelve Steps of Alcoholics Anonymous. To overcome addiction to alcohol, the AA has their members affirm the following

1. We admitted we were powerless over alcohol—that our lives had become unmanageable.
2. Came to believe that a Power greater than ourselves could restore us to sanity.
3. Made a decision to turn our will and our lives over to the care of God *as we understood Him.*
4. Made a searching and fearless moral inventory of ourselves.
5. Admitted to God, to ourselves, and to another human being the exact nature of our wrongs.
6. Were entirely ready to have God remove all these defects of character.
7. Humbly asked Him to remove our shortcomings.
8. Made a list of all persons we had harmed, and became willing to make amends to them all.
9. Made direct amends to such people wherever possible, except when to do so would injure them or others.
10. Continued to take personal inventory and when we were wrong promptly admitted it.
11. Sought through prayer and meditation to improve our conscious contact with God, *as we understood Him,* praying only for knowledge of His will for us and the power to carry that out.
12. Having had a spiritual awakening as the result of these Steps, we tried to carry this message to alcoholics, and to practice these principles in all our affairs.

To put these steps into practice, members meet weekly with others who have overcome alcohol addiction or who are struggling to overcome it. From their fellow members, they draw encouragement to continue their abstinence. They also carry the telephone number of a sponsor, "someone who has been through it." They can call this person at any hour for personal support, learning to handle crises without turning to alcohol.

Principles of Successful Social Policy. To be effective, a social policy must match the culture of its target group. A policy must be geared to the group members' age, race–ethnicity, gender, and social class, as well as to the members' values, lifestyle, and problems. This means that programs for different groups must have different emphases. For example, a program that is successful with middle-class youth will fail if it is transferred without modification to inner-city youth.

To be effective, drug programs should offer an alternative lifestyle and reward conventional behavior (Faupel and Klockars 1987). This means that drug abusers need to be integrated into a community of people where "straight" values are dominant, including social networks that value employment and nonexploitative relationships. Without job training and placement, poor addicts are left where they started, with little way out.

Finally, if drug education is to be successful, it is essential that it be related to *the realities of the users.* Nonusers' ideas about morality and the risks of using drugs are not the same as those of users. To try to impose some outside reality onto drug users is a recipe for failure.

The Future of the Problem

The social reputations and acceptability of drugs will continue to influence people's lives profoundly. Some drugs will remain in disrepute, their users disgraced and stigmatized, while other drugs will maintain their social approval. Advertised in glossy magazines and on television, they will continue to be an accepted part of social life.

With advances in chemistry, a new generation of drugs will appear. Designed to work only on particular receptors of the brain, these drugs will be more precise in their effects.

The market for these drugs will be high, matching the desires of many to take drugs to help them cope with the problems of life. This targeted market will stimulate the demand for new, high-tech drugs, putting even greater pressure on "physician drug dealers."

If the "good" people continue to view those addicted to drugs as "bad" people, they will continue to turn a blind eye to what happens to these "bad" people. The devastating consequences of anti-drug laws will be written off as things these "bad" people deserve. Lurking in the shadows of social policy, this perspective of "us" and "them" needs to be brought into the light where it can be examined thoroughly.

4.13 Explain the likely future of the problem of drug abuse.

MySocLab

 Study and Review on MySocLab

Summary and Review

1. What constitutes *drug abuse* is a matter of definition. What is considered drug use at one time or in one society may be considered drug abuse at another time or in another society.
2. Some drugs are disreputable and those who use them are considered to be part of a social problem. People generally consider the particular drugs that they use to not be part of a social problem.
3. A major problem in drug abuse is *addiction*—-becoming dependent on a drug so that its absence creates the stress of withdrawal. One of the most highly addicting drugs is nicotine. Heroin appears to be less addicting than previously thought.
4. Symbolic interactionists emphasize the social meanings of drugs. Prohibition, for example, has been analyzed as a symbolic crusade: As the old order lost political control, it attempted to dominate society morally by wrapping itself in abstinence (morality) and associating drunkenness (immorality) with the newcomers.
5. Functionalists stress not just that legal drugs are functional for the medical profession, their patients, and those who manufacture and sell these drugs, but also that illegal drugs are functional for their users, manufacturers (or growers), and distributors. The dysfunctions of drugs include problems with the law and abuse that harms people physically and socially.
6. Conflict theorists stress how the criminalization of drugs is related to power. Marijuana laws were directed against the Mexican working class in the United States. Some see the heroin trade as a means of defusing revolutionary potential.
7. Pharmaceutical companies and the medical profession play a central role in getting Americans to define drugs as *the way* to relieve the stresses of everyday life. Defining problems of living as medical matters, known as *the medicalization of human problems*, includes defining unruly children as having an illness for which they need medication.
8. Of all the drugs that Americans use, nicotine causes the most harm. Alcohol is the next most harmful. The social setting in which people learn to drink influences their chances of becoming problem drinkers. We need more studies to determine the effects of marijuana and other drugs. Cocaine's social history illustrates how a drug's reputation depends on the people with whom it is associated.
9. Narcotics themselves do not cause crime or destroy people's health or desire to work. Physician narcotic addicts maintain normal lives because they need not deal with a black market and are able to obtain pure drugs.
10. At a minimum, an adequate social policy would involve drug education that presents scientific findings honestly, whether they are favorable or unfavorable to any particular drug. It should also break the addicts' dependence on a black market and provide help for their multiple problems. Alcoholics Anonymous appears to be a model recovery program.
11. We can anticipate that the future will bring new drugs from the pharmaceutical companies and social policies that penalize the users of drugs that are in disfavor. A "good people" versus "evil drug users" approach is likely to continue.

Key Terms

alcoholics, 94
attention-deficit/hyperactivity disorder (ADHD), 89
binge drinking, 91
cravings, 83
drug, 82
drug abuse, 82
drug addiction, 82
fetal alcohol spectrum disorders (FASDs), 95
fetal alcohol syndrome (FAS), 95
fetal narcotic syndrome, 108
medicalizing human problems, 88
methadone maintenance, 113
moral entrepreneurs, 97
psychological dependence, 83
withdrawal, 82

Thinking Critically About Chapter 4

1. Which perspective—symbolic interactionism, functionalism, or conflict theory—do you think best explains drug policies in the United States? Why?
2. Should we make all drugs legal? If not, what criteria should we use in making a drug illegal?
3. What do you think is the best social policy for reacting to drug addicts? Should social policy depend on whether the drug to which someone is addicted is legal or illegal? Why or why not?

5 Violence in Society: Rape and Murder

Listen to Chapter 5 on MySocLab

Learning Objectives. After reading this chapter, you should be able to:

- **5.1** Explain the sociological perspective on violence. **(p. 118)**
- **5.2** Explain why violence is a social problem—its subjective and objective dimensions. **(p. 119)**
- **5.3** Compare the biological, learning, and sociological explanations of violence. **(p. 122)**
- **5.4** Explain the symbolic interactionist perspective on violence. **(p. 125)**
- **5.5** Explain the functionalist perspective on violence. **(p. 128)**
- **5.6** Explain the conflict perspective on violence. **(p. 129)**
- **5.7** Explain how rape was transformed from a personal problem to a social problem. **(p. 130)**
- **5.8** Be familiar with the main social patterns of rape. **(p. 132)**
- **5.9** Be familiar with the types of rapists. **(p. 135)**
- **5.10** Summarize the reactions to rape. **(p. 136)**
- **5.11** Summarize the social patterns of murder. **(p. 139)**
- **5.12** Explain the social patterns of murder. **(p. 142)**
- **5.13** Discuss the findings on mass murder and serial murder. **(p. 144)**
- **5.14** Identify social policies that can reduce or prevent violence. **(p. 146)**
- **5.15** Discuss the likely future of violence. **(p. 148)**

Most faculty meetings are rather dull. The tedium is occasionally interrupted by a colleague who is upset about something and says a few choice words. Even this seldom happens, and when it does it's usually nothing more than a little venting about something the dean or some other administrator has done. Faculty meetings like this are typical, including those at the University of Alabama at Huntsville.

This one, though, was different, destined to go down in the history books.

> She took the usual pen and notebook to the faculty meeting. She also took a loaded handgun.

Amy Bishop, assistant professor in the Department of Biological Sciences, took the usual pen and notebook to the faculty meeting. She also took a loaded handgun. As she sat in the meeting, she fumed that these imbeciles, so beneath her, had the temerity to reject her. None of them had invented an automatic cell incubator, as she had. They were so jealous that they had denied her tenure, and now she would have to look for a faculty position elsewhere. With four children and a husband tied to his job in Huntsville, this wouldn't be easy.

Amy's anger grew as she listened to Gopi Podila, chair of the department, drone on and on about trivial matters. And here she was, facing this momentous event in her life that *he* had caused. And these other morons, just sitting there and nodding like chickens as he talked, *they,* too, were the cause of her problem. She couldn't stand it any longer. She had an answer for these idiots.

Amy had been fingering the pistol in her purse, quietly wondering whether she should go through with her plan, but the more she thought about what these people were doing to her, the more she knew they deserved it. She silently took the gun from her purse, and aiming it at Gopi, pulled the trigger. Then she turned the gun on the others who were still sitting there staring at her in disbelief. Amy continued to fire as they began to scramble away, killing three and wounding three more.

Amy walked calmly out of the room, as though she had just attended a regular faculty meeting. She called her husband, told him the meeting was over, and asked if he could pick her up.

What the Huntsville administrators didn't know when they hired Amy was that in addition to getting her Ph.D. in microbiology from Harvard, she also had been a suspect there. Amy had an argument with a professor, and someone mailed him a pipe bomb. Fortunately for him, it had not gone off.

The university also didn't know that Amy had hit a woman on the head at IHOP because the woman had taken the last booster seat. Amy wanted that seat for her child.

There was one other little incident that the university didn't know about either. When Amy was 19, she shot her brother with a shotgun. He died on the kitchen floor, bleeding from massive chest injuries. The killing had been ruled an accident.

Amy's lawyer says that Amy doesn't recall the faculty meeting.

Based on Dewan and Zezima 2010; Dewan et al. 2010; Sweet et al. 2010.

The Problem in Sociological Perspective

5.1 Explain the sociological perspective on violence.

Violence grabs our attention, whether we see it on the street or on television. Audiences watch enraptured as television recounts the sordid details of the latest rape or murder. The more gruesome the violence—or the more unusual it is, as with Amy Bishop—the greater the attention. In this chapter, we will examine violence from many angles. Let's begin by using the sociological perspective to better understand violence.

The Sociological Perspective on Violence

Violence, the use of force to injure people or to destroy their property, goes far beyond individuals or what some term "violent personalities." Sociologists note that some societies encourage violence, while others discourage it. As a result, some societies have high rates of violence, and others have low rates. The sociological question is, *What is it about a society that increases or decreases the likelihood of violence?* Throughout this chapter, we shall grapple with this central question.

The Scope of the Problem

Let's see how extensive rape and murder are. In this brief overview, we will compare the rates of rape and murder in the United States with rates in other parts of the world. First, let's distinguish between violence as a personal problem and violence as a social problem.

What Makes Violence a Social Problem?

5.2 Explain why violence is a social problem—its subjective and objective dimensions.

If two people get into a fight and end up in the hospital, this is their *personal* problem. The same is true if a woman, enraged at discovering her husband with a lover, shoots them. And the same is true if a man rapes a woman. Although these examples involve severe, bitter violence, they portray only objective conditions. To be a *social* problem, violence must also arouse widespread subjective concerns. A large number of people must be upset and want something done about it.

The Subjective Dimension of Violence. *Subjective concerns* of violence are widespread. Parents worry about their kids walking to school. Women feel vulnerable as they get on elevators or as they walk alone at night from their classrooms to their cars. They feel relief when they get inside their cars—after they've shut and locked their car doors.

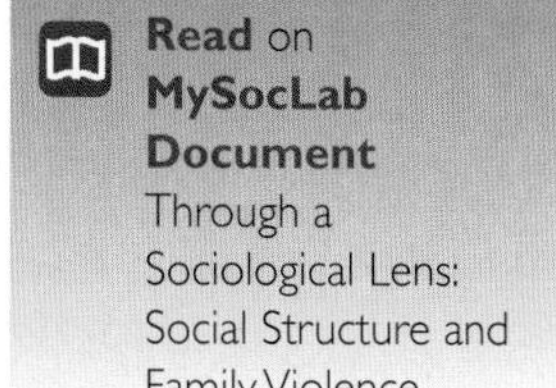

Read on MySocLab
Document
Through a Sociological Lens: Social Structure and Family Violence

Fear of violence, however, is not spread evenly throughout society. Look at Table 5.1 on the next page. The first thing that might strike you is how much more afraid women are than men of becoming victims of violent crime. From this table, you can also see that the elderly are more fearful than the younger, blacks more than whites, and Democrats more than Republicans. Note how fear recedes as income increases—largely because people with higher incomes live in less violent neighborhoods. Some of these neighborhoods are even guarded by gates and guards.

U.S. society has grown much safer over the past 20 years, something we will look at in the next section. Table 5.1 indicates that fears, however, have not dropped to match our reduction in violent crimes.

The Objective Dimension of Violence.

> *We watch our children more often, we tell them we love them, we kiss them goodnight, kiss them before they leave—just knowing that someone who could do this is still out there.*

This is what one parent said after the decomposing body of a little girl was recovered from a drainage ditch in Colorado (Banda 2010). The girl's parents and siblings went through anguish. Her neighborhood was transformed, her friends no longer allowed out of their parents' worried sight. And there is good reason to fear violence in the United States. Look at Figure 5.1 on page 121. From the 1960s to 1991, not only did the amount of violence increase, but so did the **rate of violence**, the number of violent crimes for each 100,000 Americans. If over a 10-year period our population increases 10 percent and rape and murder also increase 10 percent, there would be more rapes and murder but the rate would be the same. The increase in rape and murder would simply have kept pace with the increase in population. People's chances of being raped or murdered would be the same in the two periods of time.

TABLE 5.1 ▸ Are You Afraid to Walk Alone at Night?[1]

	1980		1990		2000		2010[2]	
	Yes	No	Yes	No	Yes	No	Yes	No
SEX								
Male	21%	79%	19%	81%	23%	76%	22%	78%
Female	60%	39%	58%	41%	52%	47%	54%	46%
RACE–ETHNICITY[3]								
White	42%	58%	39%	60%	36%	61%	38%	62%
Black/other	52%	47%	50%	48%	45%	54%	51%	49%
Other							43%	57%
AGE								
18–20 years	45%	54%	43%	57%	40%	58%	39%	61%
21–29 years	41%	59%	33%	65%	41%	58%	39%	61%
30–49 years	39%	60%	38%	62%	36%	63%	36%	64%
50 years and over	47%	52%	48%	51%	41%	58%	43%	57%
EDUCATION								
College	42%	58%	39%	60%	38%	61%	36%	64%
High school graduate	44%	55%	41%	58%	38%	61%	38%	62%
Less than high school	42%	57%	51%	48%	44%	54%	42%	58%
INCOME								
$50,000 and over	NA	NA	NA	NA	28%	71%	23%	77%
$30,000 to $49,999	NA	NA	NA	NA	34%	66%	31%	69%
$20,000 to $29,999	NA	NA	NA	NA	42%	58%	37%	63%
Under $20,000	NA	NA	NA	NA	50%	48%	42%	58%
REGION								
Northeast	47%	53%	40%	59%	37%	62%	38%	62%
Midwest	33%	66%	36%	64%	34%	64%	35%	65%
South	44%	55%	46%	52%	42%	57%	44%	56%
West	52%	48%	41%	58%	42%	57%	42%	58%
POLITICS								
Republican	41%	57%	41%	58%	33%	66%	37%	63%
Democrat	46%	54%	47%	52%	43%	56%	43%	57%
Independent	41%	59%	35%	64%	39%	59%	36%	64%

[1]The question that interviewers asked nationally representative samples of Americans was "Is there any area right around here—that is, within a mile—where you would be afraid to walk alone at night?"

[2]Latest year available.

[3]These two categories were used when this research was first done in the 1960s. For 2010, separate totals were given for black and other.

Sources: Sourcebook of Criminal Justice Statistics 2005:Table 2-37; General Social Survey 2012.

Now look at the years from 1968 to 1980 on Figure 5.1. During those 12 years, the rate of violent crimes *doubled*, soaring from 300 to 600 violent crimes per 100,000 people. In 1980, people's chances of being a victim of violent crime were *twice* what they were in 1968. If the U.S. population had not increased by a single person, there would have been twice as many violent crimes in 1980 as there were in 1968. As you can see,

FIGURE 5.1 ▸ **The Rate of Violence**

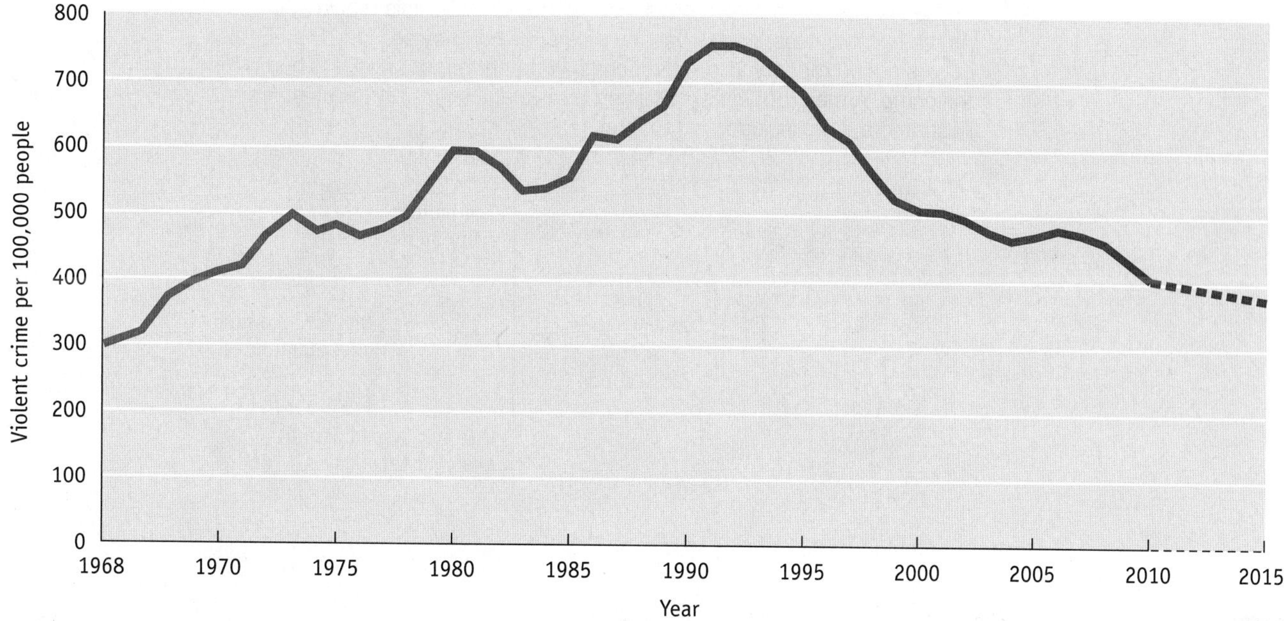

Source: By the author. Based on various editions of *Crime in the United States,* including 1997, 2002, and 2011:Table 1.

the rate then dipped slightly, but again turned sharply upward, reaching its peak in 1991 and 1992.

Table 5.1 also shows the good news. Since 1992, the rate of violent crimes has dropped sharply. Today's rate of murder, rape, robbery, and aggravated assault is *about half* (53 percent) of what it was in 1991–1992.

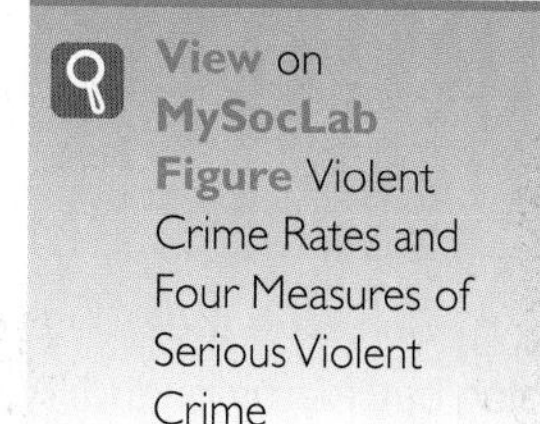

View on MySocLab Figure Violent Crime Rates and Four Measures of Serious Violent Crime

Despite this huge drop in violence, cases like the one I mentioned of the little girl's body being found in a drainage ditch make some people perceive the United States as more dangerous than it used to be. And these people are right. As you can see from Figure 5.1, it all depends on what years you compare. Our streets are much safer today than they were 20 years ago, but they are more dangerous than they were in 1968.

No matter how you interpret these totals, we have a *lot* of violent crime. Look at Figure 5.2 on the next page. Despite our drop in violence, on average, 10 women are raped every hour. This represents about 240 women every day, 1,700 a week, 7,000 a month. Every half minute or so someone attacks someone else (aggravated assault); and every half hour or so an American dies from these attacks (homicide or murder). As you can see, we are not talking about a fistfight here and there, an occasional rape, or isolated incidents of spouses turning on one another.

From your knowledge of U.S. society, you know how significant social location is. When people search for a new home, they take into account the neighborhood and its perceived safety. But few people realize how large a difference social location makes: If you live in Washington, D.C., your chances of getting murdered are 22 times greater than if you live in New Hampshire. African Americans are *six* times more likely than whites to be murdered. In terms of age, those least likely to be murdered are children below age 13 and adults age 60 and over; those most likely to be murdered are men in their 20s (*Statistical Abstract* 2013:Tables 314, 317, 318).

Despite how high it is, the U.S. rate of violence is far from the highest in the world. Look at Figure 5.3 on page 123 to see how the U.S. rate compares with some other countries. From this figure, you can also see how rape and murder tend to run together. Most countries that have a high murder rate also have a high rape rate—and vice versa.

But statistics can be misleading, as we discuss in the Thinking Critically box on page 124.

FIGURE 5.2 ▸ The Clock of Violence

These are U.S. national averages. Crimes do not occur this regularly, of course. As the text indicates, crimes vary by time of day and by season. The FBI also counts armed robbery as a violent crime, whether or not anyone is hurt during the crime. Armed robberies, occurring on average every 1.4 minutes, are not illustrated but are included in the total.

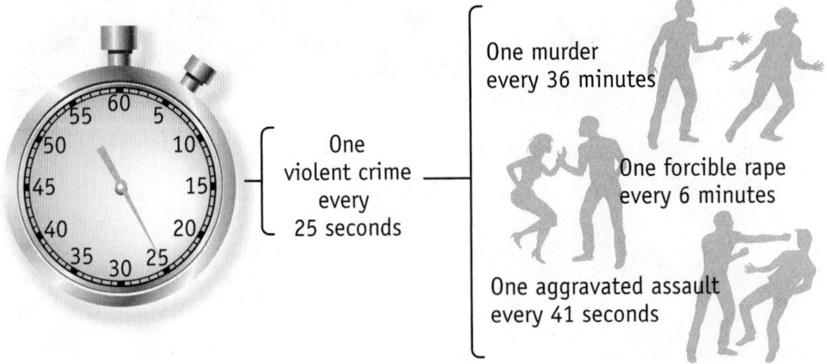

Source: *Crime in the United States* 2012.

Let's look at some of the theories social scientists use to explain violence.

Looking at the Problem Theoretically

Before we analyze violence from a sociological perspective, let's review some contrasting explanations.

Contrasting Approaches to Understanding Violence

5.3 Compare the biological, learning, and sociological explanations of violence.

Biological Explanations. In the 1800s, Cesare Lombroso (1835–1909), an Italian physician, treated thousands of prisoners. He was struck by how different they looked from his regular patients. They had lower foreheads, larger ears, and receding chins. Lombroso (1911) concluded that violent people (and other criminals) are *atavistic*; that is, they are biological throwbacks to an earlier violent, primitive period of humanity.

Anthropologist Konrad Lorenz (1966) also claimed that evolution was the key to explaining violence, but his explanation was quite different. He said that biologically we are not equipped well for killing: We don't have claws, slashing teeth, or great strength. Because of this, we did not develop an inhibitory mechanism that stops violence. When dogs, wolves, and baboons fight, an inhibitory mechanism kicks in when the enemy becomes submissive, and they stop their violence. But we have a powerful intellect, which allowed us to make weapons. The combination of having weapons but not having a mechanism that blocks violence produces terrible bloodshed. In our anger or desire to dominate, we use weapons to destroy one another. As Lionel Tiger and Robin Fox (1971:210) remarked, if baboons carried hand grenades, there would be few baboons left in Africa.

Others have suggested a variety of biological factors to explain human violence—from the shape of the skull (phrenology) to faulty neurotransmitters (George et al. 2006). One theory taken seriously for a time was proposed by anthropologist Earnest Hooton (1939). He concluded that body type is the key to understanding violence: Tall, thin men, he said, tend to be killers, and short, heavy men tend to rape.

Psychologist John Dollard (Dollard et al. 1939/1961), who also stressed that violence is built into our nature, proposed a **frustration–aggression theory of violence**. You know the frustration you feel when you want something but no matter how you try, you can't get it. Dollard conducted a series of experiments on how people whose goals are blocked relieve their frustration by striking out at others. People usually strike out at others in mild ways, such as telling someone off, but sometimes they strike out violently.

FIGURE 5.3 ▸ How Countries Compare in Rape and Murder

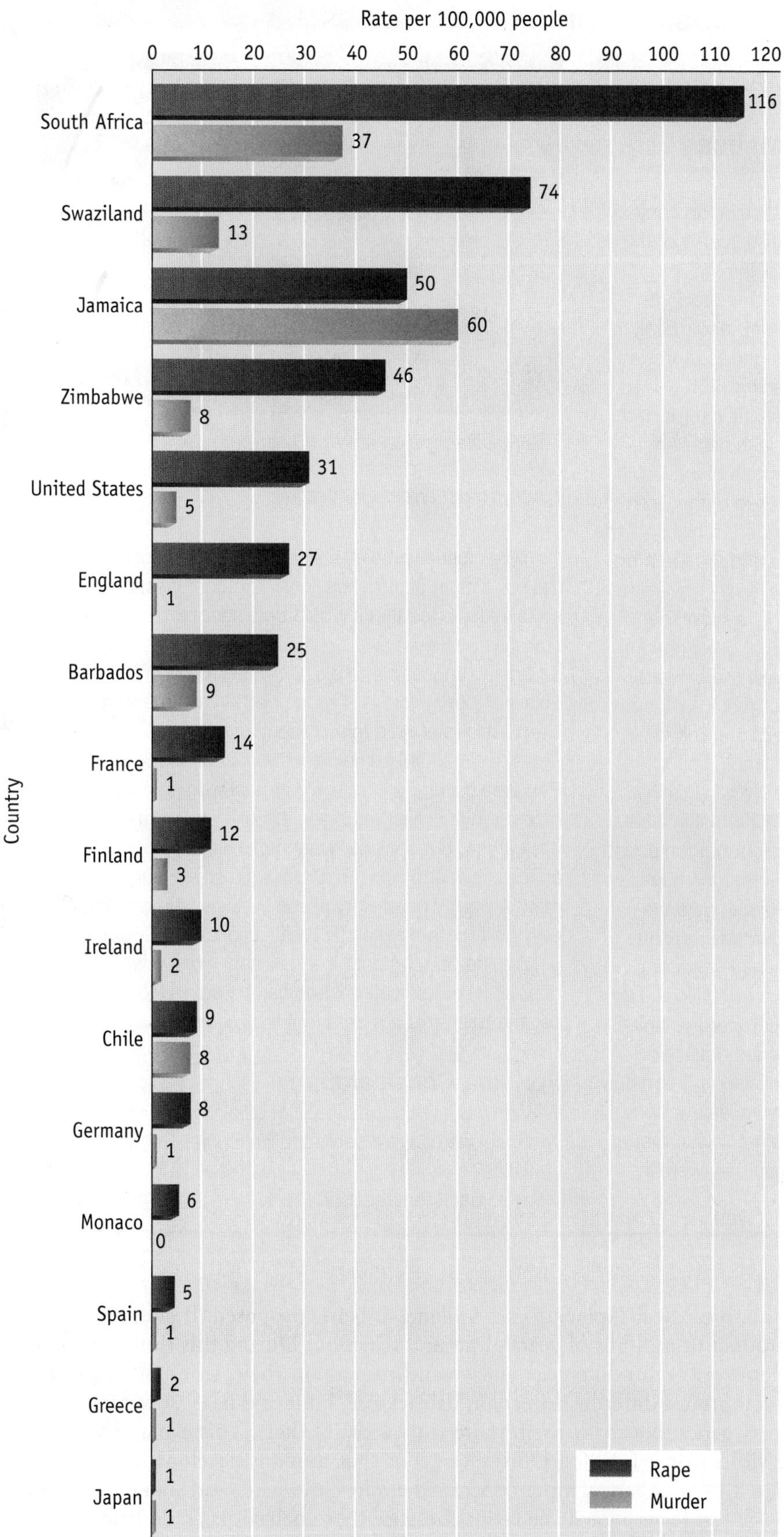

Thinking Critically About Social Problems

Why So Few Pakistani Women Are Raped—Or Why We Have to Be Cautious About Crime Statistics

We must always place crime statistics in the context in which they are produced. Statistics are not things that exist in nature. They are not like apples that you pick from a tree. They are human creations, products of bureaucrats. If the data are gathered freely and openly, statistics can reveal what they are intended to represent. But crime statistics can also be misleading.

To make themselves look better on the international scene, countries have been known to fake data. An outstanding example is the official statistics of the Soviet Union produced by the Central Committee of the Communist Party. Their statistics were intended to highlight the "successes" of their brand of socialism and to hide problems in their economic-political system. Every government would love to produce statistics that make it look better in the eyes of their own people and those of other nations. Rather than blatantly faking data to make the present situation compare favorably with that of years past, some government agencies, including those of the United States, redefine key terms such as "unemployment," "production," "efficiency," and so on.

Governments, then, have a vested interest in what the statistics their agencies produce say about the country and their own performance. Don't think that the numbers in Figure 5.3 on page 123 are exact. Rather, take the totals as an *indication* of how these countries rank on violence. A lot of error gets baked into these statistics. Comparing rape, for example, is notoriously difficult. Not only do some governments keep better records than others, but they also can be using different definitions of rape. Even in the United States, the definition of rape has changed over the years, and even now varies from one state to another. Under the prodding of feminists, more activities today are considered rape than they were in years past.

This Pakistani girl, seated with her parents, was kidnapped on her way home from school and raped by four men. The police did not arrest the men.

We must also be aware of the effects of culture in the production of statistics. In Islamic countries, rapes are so underreported that it would be a sham to include their statistics on Figure 5.3. Consider Pakistan. This country reports an impossible rate of 0.04 per 100,000 people. This is .4 per million, or 4 rapes per 10 million people. Even if this total were to represent accurately all reported rapes, it would still be ridiculously inaccurate. Because of Pakistani culture, only a few Pakistani women report their rapes. Why? For a Westerner, it is difficult to grasp how this can be, but consider what happens if the person she accuses is found not guilty: If she is married, she is automatically guilty of adultery; if she is single, she is automatically guilty of fornication ("Cross National . . ." 2004). And what is the punishment for a Pakistani woman who is guilty of adultery or fornication? She can be stoned to death. To say the least, this is a deterrent to reporting rape.

For Your Consideration

Why do we have to be careful of official statistics? How do you think we can overcome the limitations built into official statistics?

(Go back to page 122.)

Another biological explanation of violence is being proposed. It goes like this: We are the product of millions of years of natural selection. During this time, people who were violent were more likely to survive and to pass on their genes. We carry those genes. Just as groups differ by skin color, hair texture, bone and facial structure, so some groups carry genes that make them more violent than others. This explains why males are more violent than females. During the eons that humans developed, women were more limited by pregnancy, more concerned about child care, and smaller than men. They engaged in fewer violent behaviors because those behaviors could bring harm to themselves or to their children. Women, then, were less likely than men to pass on genes for violence. Geneticists are now trying to identify the specific genes that code for violence (Ferguson and Beaver 2009).

Learning Theories. Learning theories are still being developed (Chan et al. 2011). They can be traced to B. F. Skinner (1948, 1953, 1971) who developed **operant conditioning**. By this term, Skinner meant that we tend to repeat behaviors that are rewarded ("reinforced") and drop behaviors that are not rewarded. The "reward" (or "reinforcement") can be any gain—material items such as candy or food, or symbolic items such as status or even a smile. For a rapist, the reward may be power and sex. For a killer, the reward might be money, revenge, or satisfaction at eliminating an enemy.

To determine if violence is learned through **modeling**, copying another person's behavior, psychologists Albert Bandura and Richard Walters (1963) did some simple experiments that have become classic. They had some children watch an adult hit a Bobo doll (a blow-up clown) and others watch a film of an adult doing this. Other children played in the same setting but did not have the model of violence. Those who saw others hitting the Bobo doll, either in person or on film, tended to do the same thing themselves. Children who had not seen this behavior were less likely to be violent to the doll.

The Sociological Approach. Sociologists do not look for the causes of violence *within* people, whether genes or inhibitory mechanisms. Rather, they focus on matters *outside* people. They sometimes use learning theories, but they are less likely to focus on individuals than on the broader picture. Their basic approach is to understand how the social environment, *social life*, encourages—or discourages—violence. For example, in one society, violence may be channeled into the social roles of warrior, boxer, or football player. Other societies, in contrast, may downplay violence and develop mechanisms to ensure that it rarely occurs.

Explore on **MySocLab** **Activity:** Violence and Altercations with the Police

Let's apply the three sociological perspectives to violence. As we do so, let's try to understand why males are more likely than females to be violent and why violence is higher among members of the working or lower classes.

Symbolic Interactionism

5.4 Explain the symbolic interactionist perspective on violence.

Why do people kill? Consider what a detective on the Dallas police force said back in the 1960s:

> *Murders result from little ol' arguments over nothing at all. . . . Tempers flare. A fight starts, and somebody gets stabbed or shot. I've worked on cases where the principals had been arguing over a 10 cent record on a juke box, or over a dollar gambling debt from a dice game. (Mulvihill et al. 1969:230)*
>
> *More recently, in Philadelphia, a 16-year old boy shot and killed 17-year-old Richard Johnson, who had won a full academic scholarship to a local university. The 16-year old said that Johnson was blocking the door to a convenience store. (Hurdle 2007)*

Symbolic interactionists have developed two theories that help us to understand such violence.

Edwin Sutherland: Differential Association. Sociologist Edwin Sutherland (1947) stressed that people learn criminal behavior by interacting with others. In its simplest form, Sutherland's theory goes like this: People who associate with lawbreakers are more likely to break the law than are people who associate with those who follow the law. Sutherland used the term **differential association** to describe this process.

Let's apply Sutherland's theory to violence:

1. People learn violence from others—not just techniques of violence, but also attitudes, motives, drives, and rationalizations for violence.

2. People who are violent have learned more attitudes (or definitions) that favor violence than they have learned attitudes (or definitions) that favor nonviolence. (Sutherland called this an *excess of definitions*.)
3. The most significant learning (of violence or nonviolence) is that which occurs earliest in life and in interactions that are the most frequent, last the longest, and are the most emotional or meaningful.
4. The mechanisms for learning violence and nonviolence are the same.

Marvin Wolfgang: Subcultures of Violence. Sociologist Marvin Wolfgang developed **subcultural theory**, which is similar to differential association. In a nutshell, this theory says that people who grow up in a subculture that approves of violent behavior have a high chance of becoming violent. Wolfgang wanted to know why the homicide rate is high among lower-class African American males. In a classic study, he (Wolfgang 1958) studied convicted murderers in Philadelphia.

Wolfgang found that the men connected violence with honor and manliness. They viewed insults as a challenge to their manliness or honor, with violence the appropriate response to the insult. Situations that others might perceive as trivial were *not* trivial to them. Anyone who backs down from a confrontation (even if it is about a "little" thing) is seen as less than a real man. He is viewed as a "chicken" or a "girl"—and is ridiculed. With their "rep" at stake, the young men carry weapons both for protection and as a symbol of masculinity. As a result, confrontations that in other groups would be passed over result in homicide.

The reason I am citing classic research from such a long time ago is that its findings apply as vibrantly today as they did when the research was done. Sociologist Victor Rios (2011), who did participant observation of young male African American and Latino gang members in Oakland, California, reports that these same ideas of masculinity continue. They also continue to produce high rates of murder.

Fitting the Theories Together. Differential association and subcultural theory fit together well (Akers and Jensen 2006). Subcultural theory stresses that violence is woven into the life of some groups, and differential association explains how people in these groups learn that violence is an appropriate way to deal with problems.

Can you explain why this photo illustrates differential association? How about subcultural theory?

It is not just the boys and men in these groups who associate violence with "being a man." The girls and women feel the same way. They assume, for example, that "their man" will protect them. He might manage this with threats, but if those aren't enough, he must be ready to fight. If a fight escalates, he might have to use a knife or gun. To do less would lower his image in the eyes of not just other men, but in the view of the women as well.

You can see how the idea that someone should be ready to be violent to protect his image or his friends would lead to violence. As sociologist Elijah Anderson (1990, 2006) documents, for young African American men in the inner city this expectation of being ready to violently confront any slight to one's manliness takes place within a world filled with threats to masculinity. As a defensive measure, so no one will "mess" with them, these men project masculinity by looking tough, as though they are ready to be violent.

Chicano gang members also connect masculinity with the willingness to violently defend honor. Sociologist Ruth Horowitz (1983), who did participant observation of Chicano gangs in Chicago, found that these young men sometimes even seek violence to prove their manliness. In the Spotlight on Social Research box below, Horowitz shares insights that she gained from her research.

Spotlight on Social Research

Studying Violence Among "The Lions"

When she was a graduate student at the University of Chicago, **RUTH HOROWITZ** *(now professor of sociology at New York University) did a participant observation study of young people in a Chicano community in Chicago. Her purpose was not to understand violence, but to understand poverty. She wanted to see how the explanations of poverty that sociologists had developed matched what she observed in "real life." Here is what she wrote for you.*

Two major explanations of poverty are the culture of poverty and the social structure of poverty. According to the *culture of poverty*, poor people have different values than the middle class, and this is why they act as they do. According to the *social structure perspective*, the poor act as they do because, unlike middle-class people, they do not have the same opportunities to attend good schools or to obtain good jobs. Consequently, the poor turn to illegal opportunities, and crime becomes part of their life.

One afternoon, a month after I met the "Lions" gang and shook hands with all of them in the park, several 16-year-old young women introduced themselves. They asked me several questions about myself, and they were able to give me a definition of sociology. They told me about school and their trips around the city. Several of these women went on to college; others became pregnant and married. The life experience of siblings varied, too; some went to school and became white-collar workers, while others ran afoul of the legal system and went to prison.

When I first began my research, the "Lions" were 15 to 17 years old, had guns, and did a lot of fighting. Some had after-school jobs and dressed in tuxedos for *quinceañeras* and weddings. In the streets, these same young men had developed a reputation by being tougher than other gangs. They would even seek opportunities to challenge others. At home and during most parties, in contrast, they were polite and conformed to strict rules of etiquette.

For seven years, I did participant observation with these youths. When I returned after a three-year absence, many of the "Lions" were still hanging out together, but quite a few were working, had married, and had children. A few of the gang members attended college, and others remained in the street. One had been killed in a drug deal gone wrong. A major change was their relationship to violence. Instead of provoking incidents, now they responded only when someone challenged their reputations.

The two models of poverty did apply. Violence had been part of the culture they had learned, and a lack of opportunities did contribute to a sense of being left out. But there was more to it. Actual violence depended on how the "Lions" defined a particular situation. As sociologists phrase this: Violence was situational and constructed interactionally.

In the Mafia, too, the connection between violence and manliness is strong. From this statement by Michael Franzese, a college-educated member of the Mafia, you can glimpse the dynamics that connect manliness, honor, and violence:

> *If somebody were to dishonor my wife or my child, I would view it as something that I had to take into my own hands. I don't see why I have to go to the police. As a man, I would feel that it was an obligation that I had to take care of. And I would have to be prepared in my own mind to kill this guy. This is a basic principle. (Barnes and Shebar 1987)*

In Sum ▸ "Manliness" (or "masculinity") is a powerful symbol that has a dynamic influence on human behavior. It is something to which boys and men aspire. To associate violence with manliness encourages violence. Working-class males incorporate more violence into their views of appropriate male behavior, leading to their higher rates of violence. As a result, year after year, across racial–ethnic lines and in every region of the United States, violence is more prevalent among males than females and among working-class males than males from other social classes. Until the association between masculinity and violence is broken, you can expect these patterns to continue.

Functionalism

5.5 Explain the functionalist perspective on violence.

Emile Durkheim: Asking the Sociological Question. As you might recall, at the beginning of this chapter I said that the sociological question is, *What is it about a society that increases or decreases the likelihood of violence?* This question was first asked by Emile Durkheim, the first university professor to be formally identified as a sociologist. In the 1800s, Durkheim examined murder rates in Paris and suicide rates in several European countries (Durkheim 1897/1951, 1904/1938). He was struck by how consistent these rates were over time. Year after year, the countries that had high rates of violence continued to have high rates, and those with low rates continued to have low rates. Durkheim called this **normal violence**—the violence that a group normally (or usually) has.

Durkheim found this regularity intriguing. Since murder and suicide rates represent the number of deaths by *individuals*—with all their particular passions, frustrations, and other emotions and volatile situations—why don't the rates jump all over the place? To explain this, Durkheim developed the *sociological perspective*: He concluded that society regulates *individual* impulses and desires, resulting in consistent rates of violence.

To appreciate Durkheim's conclusion, consider what life used to be like in farming communities. Children followed in their parents' footsteps and either worked in the village in which they were reared or farmed nearby land. They spent their entire lives in a village where everyone knew one another. Their close bonds and their need of the community to survive helped to restrain individual impulses to lash out violently. Their close relationships (high social integration, as Durkheim called it) and their need to maintain good reputations kept overall rates of violence low.

Now let's add rapid social change. Imagine that the society is industrializing. The villagers move to the city to take jobs where they know few people. Living in the midst of strangers, they face being fired by bosses who care about profits, not workers. They face evictions by landlords who care more about collecting rent than about what happens to a family. Unlike the factors that promote cohesion in a farming community, the city does the opposite. Urban life loosens social bonds, in some instances ripping them apart. Life in the city is more anonymous, and urban dwellers, as sociologists call them, have fewer ties with one another. The norms that applied to village life no longer fit. Durkheim gave the name ***anomie*** to such feelings of being unconnected and uprooted. Under these circumstances, impulses to violence are not as restrained as they are in the village. As a result, the city is a more dangerous place.

Strain Theory: Robert Merton. Another functionalist, Robert Merton (1968), who applied *anomie* to crime in the United States, developed what is called **strain theory**. Success in the form of money or material goods, said Merton, is a **cultural goal**, a goal held out for all Americans. The socialization is highly effective, and almost all Americans learn to want a lot of money and material goods. Society also offers approved (or legitimate) ways to reach success, especially through education, jobs, and career training. Merton called these approved ways **cultural means**. The approved avenues to success, however, are limited. Those who find their legitimate way to success blocked experience what Merton called *strain* (or frustration and anxiety). These people still want success, however, and many turn to illegitimate means to reach it. This is why robbery, theft, and crimes of violence are concentrated among the poor: They have less access to the approved means to achieve success.

Control Theory: Reckless, Gottfredson, and Hirschi. Strain theory does not explain why some people become violent while others do not. We all face obstacles to success, but few of us attack others. To answer this question, sociologist Walter Reckless (1973) developed **control theory**. This theory assumes that all of us have a natural tendency toward violence, and it asks what forms of social control overcome our natural tendencies. Reckless identified *inner* controls (our inner capacity to withstand pressures to commit crime or to be violent) and *outer* controls (groups such as family, friends, and the police that divert us from violence). If our control systems are stronger than the pushes and pulls toward violence, we are not violent. If they are weaker, we are violent.

Sociologists Michael Gottfredson and Travis Hirschi (1990) refined control theory by focusing on the inner controls. They conclude that people who have low self-control get in trouble with the law because they are impulsive, insensitive risk-takers. These traits also make it difficult for them to stay married, to keep a job or friends, to meet long-term commitments, and to be good parents. Low self-control comes from ineffective parenting. The parents did not adequately monitor the child's behavior, did not deal with deviant behaviors when they occurred, or were unfair and inconsistent in their rewards and punishment. These patterns make a child less capable of delaying gratification, less sensitive to the needs of others, and less willing to hold back impulses. One of the consequences is a tendency to violence.

Read on **MySocLab Document** Violent Girls or Relabeled Status Offenders? An Alternative Interpretation of the Data

Conflict Theory

5.6 Explain the conflict perspective on violence.

Violence Is Inherent in Society. As you will recall, the focus of conflict theory is groups competing with one another for limited resources. Conflict can be hidden beneath surface cooperation and even goodwill, but the true nature of human relationships is adversarial, which often results in violence.

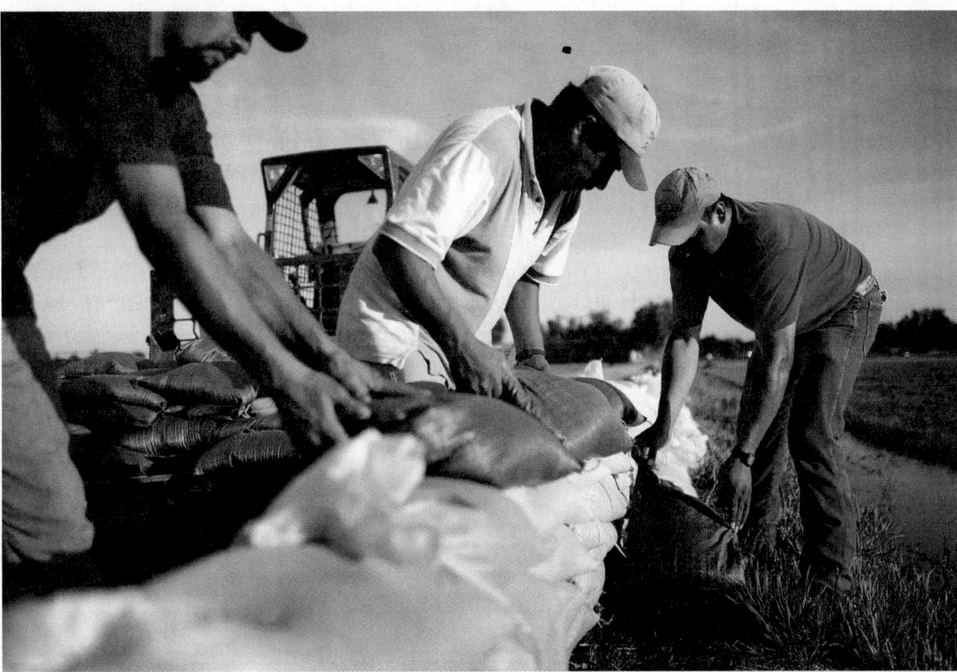

How do conflict theorists relate violence and the economic insecurity of the working class?

Social Class and Violence: The Working Class. ▸ Among the groups that are competing for society's limited resources are the social classes. Marx stressed that there is but one essential division of the social classes: those who own the means of production—the factories, the machines, and capital (investment money)—and those who work for the owners (Marx and Engels 1848/1964, 1906). The workers, who must struggle to put food on the table, pay rent, and buy clothing, are at the mercy of the owners, who make their decisions on the basis of profit, not the workers' welfare. For example, in their search for cheap labor, the owners can close a factory in the United States and open another in China or India.

Working-class men find their economic security especially fragile and experience high frustration. They are paid little, and with unskilled jobs drying up, they face the threat of unemployment. On top of this, they now have to compete with women for the limited jobs. These men commit more violent crimes than do either working-class women or men from higher social classes. And the most deprived—those who are confined to the inner city—have the highest rates of violence as they desperately strike out at one another.

Social Class and Violence: The Capitalist Class. ▸ "This is what is apparent on the surface," say conflict theorists. "Look a little deeper, and you will see that the capitalist class is actually *more* violent than the working class. The wealthy control the police powers of the state, which they use to suppress the underclass. They also control the armed forces, which they send out to protect their investments and keep an oil supply flowing. They care little how many are killed in the process. Unlike the working class, the capitalists don't kill with their own hands, but their toll on human life is much higher. It is the *form* of violence that distinguishes workers from capitalists."

In Sum ▸ Violence is part of all human societies, and true to their calling, sociologists look for *social* causes of violence, factors outside the individual. They want to know why some societies have more violence than others, as well as why some groups in the same society are more violent than others.

Symbolic interactionists stress that each group has its own ideas and expectations about violence. Some groups prefer nonviolent ways of handling disagreements, while others consider violence an appropriate response to many situations. To resolve conflicts, the middle and upper social classes usually turn to the legal system, which transcends personal confrontation. The lower classes, in contrast, are likely to take matters into their own hands—which breeds violence. The groups with which people associate (differential association) have different norms for handling conflict, which increase or decrease people's likelihood of becoming violent.

Functionalists emphasize that conditions that strengthen social bonds reduce violence, and conditions that produce *anomie* increase violence. Violence tends to be higher among groups whose access to culturally approved goals is blocked. Whether an individual will be violent depends on his or her inner and outer controls.

Conflict theorists stress that class exploitation underlies violence. Seldom do members of the working class direct their violence against their oppressors, for the capitalists are able to use the powers of the state to protect their privileged positions. Instead of targeting their oppressors, workers almost always misdirect their violence, aiming it against one another. The capitalists, though, are more violent than the working class, for their wars and destruction of the environment in the pursuit of profits kill far more people.

Now that we've reviewed basic theories of violence, let's turn to research findings on rape and murder.

Research Findings: Rape

5.7 Explain how rape was transformed from a personal problem to a social problem.

The Natural History of Rape as a Social Problem

Believe it or not, but rape was labeled a social problem only during the last third of the last century. This came about because of the persistent efforts of victims, advocates, and feminists. We'll look at how this happened, but first you need to understand two terms.

In this section, we will focus on **forcible rape**—a form of assault where one individual forces another to have any type of sex. Consent is considered absent if the victim is threatened or if the victim's judgment is impaired in some way. Judgment may be considered impaired if a person is disabled, intoxicated, or under age. **Statutory rape** refers to sexual intercourse between an adult and a minor, even if the minor consents.

The Feminist-Conflict View: Transforming Rape from a Personal to a Social Problem. Like the other social problems we discuss in this text, that rape exists does not make rape a social problem. Rape is certainly an objective condition of social life. Rape has been part of society from its beginnings to the present. The Old Testament has accounts of rape from 3,000 years ago and longer. There also are accounts of rape in Greek mythology and in the literature of other ancient peoples.

To gain a fuller background, we need to understand something about the history of gender relations. A woman used to be considered the legal property of her father, property which he passed on to her husband. At that time, rape was a crime against a man's property, either the father's or the husband's. The rapist had "spoiled" (damaged) a man's property (Ullman 2007). Although this patriarchal perspective is no longer part of the Western view, remnants of it do manage to hang on. Some men and women still consider a woman who has been raped as "spoiled goods." In their eyes, the victim of a rape is somehow less than a woman who has not been a victim of this crime.

Until recently, both women and men perceived rape as a personal problem. The woman was often blamed, with the thinking that she, intentionally or unintentionally, had been provocative. Men were seen as being easily aroused sexually, and perhaps the woman had worn revealing clothing or said the wrong things. This view made rape a personal problem, a problem between individuals. Let's see how rape was transformed from a personal to a social problem.

For this, let's go back to the 1960s when Western women were questioning their traditional roles and redefining their place in society. Many were dissatisfied with the roles assigned them, which revolved around husband, home, and children (Friedan 1963; Millett 1970). As women discussed their dissatisfactions during this second wave of feminism, a fundamental change in thinking occurred. More and more women began to think of themselves less as individuals who were facing unique circumstances in life and more as members of a social group that shared the same problems.

Feminists first questioned, then challenged, the idea that rape is an act of passion. They said that the traditional view of rape represents flawed reasoning. It assumes that men's sexual passions are so powerful, almost overwhelming, that men are barely able to keep them in check. The woman did something that excited the man so he lost control and took her by force. This view makes rape the woman's fault, as it was her sexual cues that stimulated the attack.

One of the most poignant statements I have ever read that demolishes this patriarchal view was made by Dorothy Hicks, a physician treating rape victims of all ages in Miami, Florida. She said

> *"What sexual cues? Is an 80-year-old victim or a 4-month-old baby responsible for triggering a man's sex drive?" (Luy 1977)*

As feminists campaigned against rape, they emphasized that power, not sexual arousal, is the root of rape. Rape, they said, is one of the ways that men control women. The fear of rape makes women submissive, helping men to maintain **patriarchy**—men's dominance of women. For example, with the threat of rape looming over them, women are not as free as men to move around society. Women constantly face situations that are similar to an unarmed man going alone at midnight into a crime-ridden area of the city. This new view of rape made rape a form of violence by predators, not an act of passion by sexually stimulated men. It also removed the blame from the victim to the one(s) who committed the rape. Gradually, as this new feminist view took hold, rape was transformed from a personal problem to a social problem.

This feminist view does not suggest that men deliberately use rape to frighten women into submissive positions in society. The practice of power by men is much subtler than this. Both men and women learn "to associate power, dominance, strength, virility, and superiority with masculinity—and submissiveness, passivity, weakness, and inferiority with femininity" (Scully 1990; Scully and Marolla 1985/2007). As boys learn that "masculine" is tied to strength, dominance, and aggression, they assume these characteristics as part of their gender identity. They learn, too, that "real" men don't take "No" for an answer: Real men pursue a goal until they reach it. They also learn that a woman might say "No" when she doesn't really mean it. From pornography, they might even learn that women like to be forced into sexual acts (Reynolds 1976; Finkelhor and Yllo 1985, 1989).

You can see how sharply the feminist view of rape as dominance contrasts with the view of rape as an act of passion. Many states have now incorporated this new view into their legal systems, replacing the legal charge of rape with **criminal sexual assault**. This crime is much broader, including all sexual assaults, completed and attempted, against both males and females.

The Social Patterns of Rape

5.8 Be familiar with the main social patterns of rape.

How Common Is Rape? According to the FBI, 85,000 U.S. women are forcibly raped each year (*Sourcebook of Criminal Justice Statistics* 2012:Table 3-106). This is the official total, the number reported to the police. The actual total is likely 2.5 times higher than this. This means that each year, over 200,000 U.S. women are raped.

You might be wondering why I would say that forcible rape is about 2.5 times higher than the official total. Each month, in what is called *The National Crime Victimization Survey*, researchers interview the members of 10,500 households. They ask about crimes that have happened to them and whether they reported those crimes to the police. On average, about 38 percent of victims report their rapes to the police (Truman and Planty 2012).

Basic Patterns. Here are several patterns that researchers have discovered about rape (*Sourcebook of Criminal Justice Statistics* 2012:Table 3-16; *Statistical Abstract* 2013:Tables 314, 322, 323):

Acquaintanceship: A woman is more likely to be raped by someone she knows than by a stranger. Seven of ten rapes are committed by a relative of the victim or by someone she knows well or at least casually.

Place: A woman is more likely to be raped at or near her home than anywhere else.

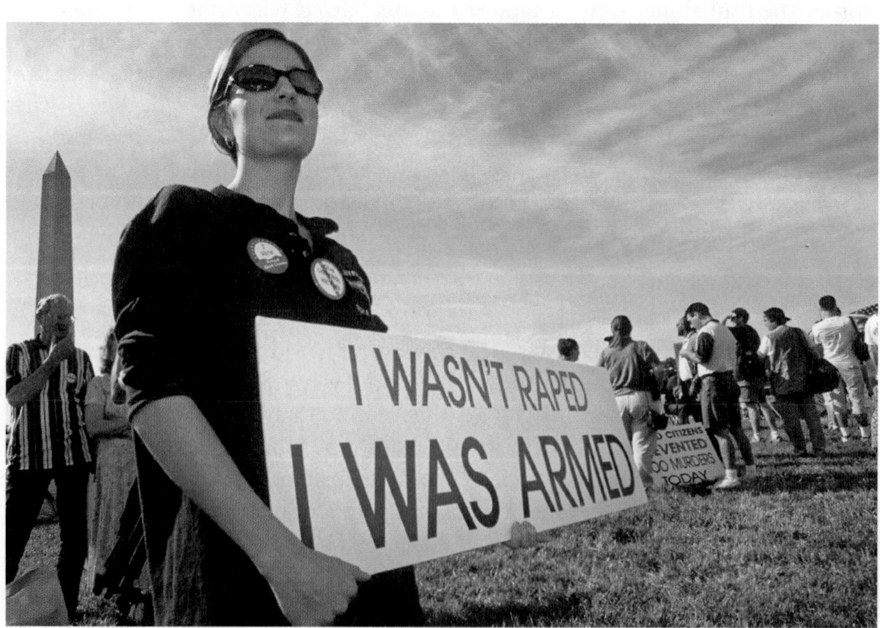

One of the women's reactions to the threat of rape is self-defense classes. Shown here is another reaction, one that goes a step further.

FIGURE 5.4 ▸ Forcible Rape by Month

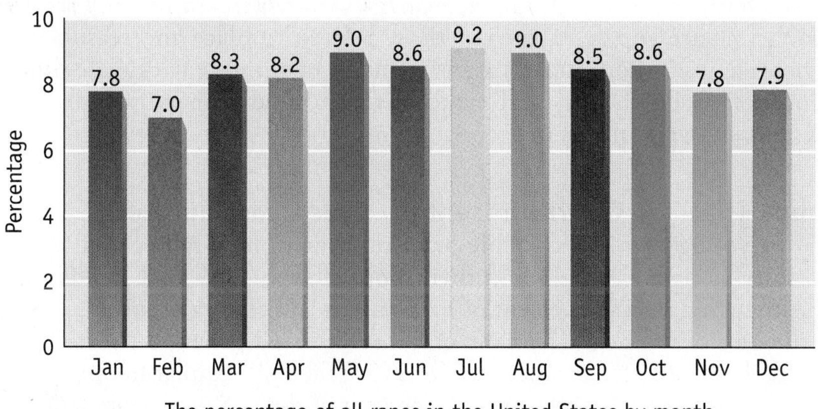

Source: By the author. Based on *FBI Uniform Crime Reports* 2006:Table 2.1.

View on **MySocLab** **Figure** Women Raped or Physically Assaulted in Lifetime by Race/Ethnicity

Season: As Figure 5.4 shows, rapes are more likely to occur in summer than in winter.

Age: The typical victim is between 12 and 34 years old. After 34, rape rates drop sharply.

Income: Poor women are more likely than richer women to be raped. (Women with a household income less than $7,500 are 20 times more likely to be raped than women whose household income is $50,000 or more.)

Region: A woman's chances of being raped are higher in some states than others. Women in Alaska are *six* times more likely to be raped than are women in New Jersey. The Social Map shows which states are the safest and which are the most dangerous.

Weapon: About eight out of ten rapists use no weapon. They depend on surprise, threats, and their physical strength.

Read on **MySocLab** **Document:** Fraternities and Collegiate Rape Culture: Why are Some Fraternities More Dangerous Places for Women?

FIGURE 5.5 ▸ The "Where" of Rape: The Rape Rate per State

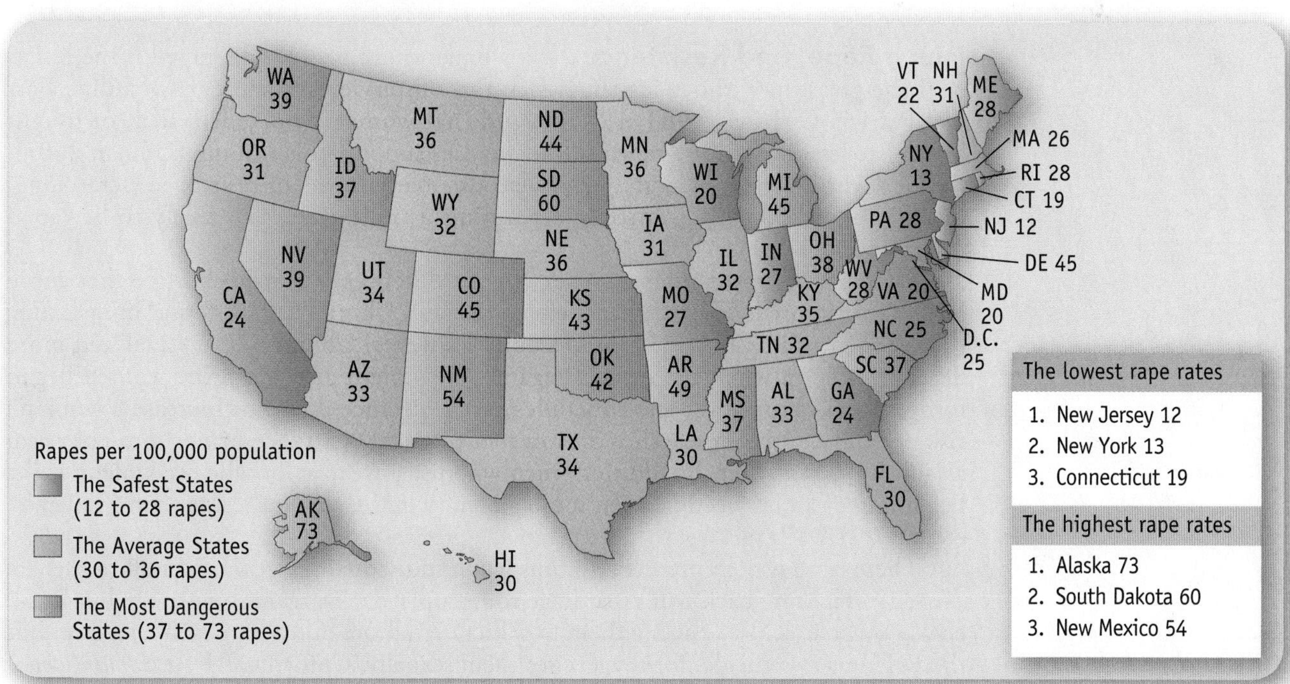

Source: By the author. Based on *Statistical Abstract of the United States* 2012:Table 308.

Because these patterns show up year after year, sociologists conclude that rape is not the act of a few sick men, but, rather, *rape is intimately linked to social factors.* Some of these factors are apparent, such as those related to place and season. For others, we have some indication, such as a greater tie-in of violence with masculinity among men in poverty. The factors that make some states safer or more dangerous than others are not known at present.

TABLE 5.2 ▸ Arrests for Rape, by Age

Age	Percent of the Arrests
10–14	6.0%
15–19	19.2%
20–24	18.8%
25–29	13.6%
30–34	10.8%
35–39	9.7%
40–44	8.0%
45–49	6.5%
50–54	4.2%
55–59	2.2%
60–64	1.3%
65 and over	1.1%

Source: By the author. Based on *Sourcebook of Criminal Justice Statistics* 2011:Table 4.7.2010.

Groups That Are Overrepresented. Rape is committed almost exclusively by young men. From Table 5.2, you can see how rape peaks (based on arrests) at ages 15 to 24 and then drops sharply with each age grouping. Although only 14.7 percent of males in the United States are ages 15 to 24, they account for 38 percent of those arrested for rape (*Sourcebook* 2011:Table 4.7.2010; *Statistical Abstract* 2013:Table 7). Similar findings hold true for race–ethnicity: Only about 13 percent of the U.S. male population is African American, but African American men account for 32 percent of the men who are arrested for rape (*Sourcebook* 2011:Table 4.10.2010; *Statistical Abstract* 2013:Table 6).

Why are African American men overrepresented in rape statistics? For this answer, let's turn to the three sociological theories. The first two focus on social class to explain why lower-class men commit more forcible rapes (or are arrested most often). Following *symbolic interactionism*, we would stress that the lower social classes are more likely to attach violence to the meaning of masculinity. To this, we would add *conflict theory*, that the lower classes are oppressed. As we reviewed earlier, violence is one reaction to oppression. Because African Americans are overrepresented in the lower social classes, they are involved in rape disproportionately. *Functionalism*, specifically *strain theory*, would stress something similar, how African American men are often blocked from legitimate avenues of attaining social status. These frustrations may lead them to turn against those less powerful than themselves. As some have suggested, rape may be a way of establishing power in the face of socially imposed powerlessness (McNeely and Pope 1981).

Injury, Rape, and Resistance. Is a woman more likely to be raped if she resists or if she gives up without a struggle? In their interviews, sociologists Pauline Bart and Patricia O'Brien (1984, 1985) found that women who yelled, fled, or fought back were less likely to be raped. Other studies support this finding (Ullman 2007). Women who resist immediately and who use many forms of resistance (scratching, biting, gouging, kicking, hitting, screaming, running) are less likely to be raped (Ullman 2007).

Women who resist their attackers are less likely to be raped, but are they more likely to be injured? This is what sociologist Sarah Ullman (1998) found in her study of rape victims in Chicago. More recently, however, Ullman (2007) analyzed more detailed data on when the rapists began to be violent and when the women began to fight back. From this, she concludes that resistance does not increase a woman's risk of injury. Other research indicates that physical resistance brings more physical assault by the attacker. In addition, men who use a weapon or who are violent at the beginning of a rape become even more violent when a woman resists them (Balemba et al. 2012).

There is no way to predict anything in an individual situation. Not all rapists are the same. Fighting back will discourage some rapists, even scare some away, but it can enrage other attackers, causing them to inflict even more injury. And some rapists want their victims to struggle, for this excites them sexually. Unfortunately, *a woman who is being attacked doesn't know what kind of rapist she is facing, and she cannot know what the results of her resistance will be.*

5.9 Be familiar with the types of rapists.

At this point, let's look at what kinds of rapists there are.

I have developed the following ten profiles of rapists based on men who have been arrested. Although these profiles illustrate many motivations for rape, I do not know the proportion of rapists within each type or what other types may exist.

The Woman Hater. At some point in his life, the *woman hater* was hurt by a woman who was significant to him. In many cases, this woman was his mother. This hurt inflicted an emotional wound that never healed, leaving a hatred of women. By sexually assaulting women, this man gains a sense of personal power. By degrading his victim and sometimes brutally assaulting her, he retaliates for his festering wound.

The Sadist. Although the *sadist* has no particular negative feelings toward women, he beats his victims because he has learned to receive pleasure from hurting others. By raping women, he combines the pleasure he receives from inflicting pain with the pleasure he receives from sex. Because he enjoys it when his victim begs, pleads, and shows fear, the sadist is likely to increase his sexual excitement by beating or torturing his victim before sexual penetration. He sometimes prolongs his pleasure by continuing to inflict pain on her during and after the rape.

The Generally Violence-Prone. For the *generally violence-prone* man, rape is just *another* act of violence. He sees the world as a violent affair. If he is going to get anything—and this includes sex—he must force it from others. Unlike the previous two types of rapists, his pleasure in rape is rooted in sex, not in violence. He uses only enough violence to make the woman submit. If she resists, he feels that she deserves to be hurt because she is "holding out" on him.

Nicolas Cocaign, a French prisoner convicted of rape, ripped a lung out of his cellmate while he was still alive. He then ate it. Cocaign says he had a bad childhood and his action was a "cry for help." What do you think?

The Revenger. The *revenge rapist* uses rape to get even with someone. His victim may be the person he is angry at, or she may be a substitute for his real target. One man went to collect money that an acquaintance owed him. When he discovered that the man was not home, he said to himself "I'm going to get it one way or another." Then "I grabbed her and started beating the hell out of her. Then I committed the act. I knew what I was doing. I was mad. I could have stopped, but I didn't. I did it to get even with her and her husband" (Scully and Marolla 1985/2007).

The Political. The *political rapist* also chooses his victim as a substitute for his enemy, but, in addition, he uses the rape to make a political statement. In *Soul on Ice* (1968), Eldridge Cleaver recounts how he raped white women to "strike out against the white establishment." Much of the raping by soldiers during war is this type. The soldiers are not motivated by hatred of women, but by hatred of the enemy. Raping "the enemy's women" shows contempt for the enemy and is a badge of their own superiority.

The Walter Mitty. Generally passive and submissive, the *Walter Mitty rapist* has an unrealistic image of masculinity. He uses rape to bridge the gap between the way he perceives how men ought to be and the way he perceives himself. He fantasizes that his victims enjoy being raped—for he is an excellent sex partner. Some carry their fantasy one step further, calling the victim later and trying to make a date with her. The Walter Mitty rapist is unlikely to beat his victim, but he will use as much force as necessary to make her submit.

The Opportunist. Unlike the first six types of rapists, the *opportunist* does not set out to rape. Rather, he takes advantage of an unexpected opportunity, often during a robbery or burglary. For example, one man drove to a local supermarket looking for someone to rob. The first person he found was a pregnant woman. As he threatened her with a knife, the woman, scared out of her wits, blurted out that she would do anything if he didn't hurt her. He said to the interviewer, "I wasn't thinking about sex. But when she said she would do anything not to get hurt, probably because she was pregnant, I thought, 'why not?'" He then forced her to a deserted area where he raped her (Scully and Marolla 2007).

The Date Rapist. Also called an *acquaintance rapist*, the *date rapist* often feels that he deserves sex because he has invested time and money in a date or sexual seduction. For him, the rape is a way of collecting a sexual "payoff" for his investment. Date rapists generally prefer to avoid violence. It is uncommon for date rapists to be reported to the police or to be convicted if they are. Police, prosecutors, judges, and juries tend to think that date rape is not "real" rape, as it does not match their stereotypes. For similar reasons, the victims, too, often feel that it is not the same as rape. A woman may feel guilt, thinking that she contributed to the situation by going with the man or inviting him into her home (Kanin 2003). As the Issues in Social Problems box on the next page shows, contrary to popular belief, date rape consists of much more than a man being more insistent than he should.

The Recreational Rapist. For the *recreational rapist*, rape is an activity to be enjoyed with friends, a thrilling, risky game. As sociologists Diana Scully and Joseph Marolla (1985/2007) discovered in their interviews of rapists in prison, one man may make a date with a victim and then drive her to a predetermined location, where he and his friends rape her. One man said that this practice had become such a part of his group's weekend routine that they had rented a house just for the purpose of recreational rape.

The Husband Rapist. The last type is the *husband rapist*, a man who attacks his own wife. Contrary to common opinion, marital rape is real, not simply a husband who insisted on having sex when his wife didn't want to. After interviewing wives who had become victims of their husbands, sociologists David Finkelhor and Kersti Yllo (1985, 1989) concluded that marital rape can involve violence and sadism every bit as horrible as any we have discussed. Some wives are forced to flee their own homes in terror.

Reactions to Rape

5.10 Summarize the reactions to rape.

Let's look at what happens to rape victims after their attack. We will focus first on personal reactions and then on how the criminal justice system treats rape victims.

The Trauma of Rape. Disbelief and shock are the first reactions reported by rape victims (McIntyre et al. 1979). The event is so frightening and alien that most victims report they could not believe it was actually happening.

The trauma of rape does not end with the physical attack (Feinstein et al. 2011). The woman typically finds her self-concept so wounded and her emotions in such tatters that her whole life is disrupted. Some rape victims deal with their trauma in an *expressive* style, venting their fear, anger, rage, and anxiety by crying and sobbing or by restlessness and tenseness. Others react in a *controlled* style, carefully masking their feelings behind a calm and composed exterior (Burgess and Holmstrom 1974). Investigators often expect an expressive style, and talking with victims who seem calm can confuse them, even make them wonder whether a rape really occurred.

After a rape, life and relationships are no longer the same. Doubt, distrust, and self-blame plague rape victims. Some feel guilty for having been alone in that place at that time. Others feel it was their fault for getting in a compromising situation. If they didn't scream and fight back, that bothers them. They feel that there must have been something—*anything*—that they could have done—or not done—that might have changed the situation. As you can see, such self-doubt is bottomless.

Issues in Social Problems

Date (or Acquaintance) Rape

The public has little understanding of date rape. Some seem to think that it involves a reluctant woman who needs a "push" to go along with what she really wants. Consider these two cases:

> Carol had just turned 18, and it looked as if her dreams had come true. It was only the beginning of her freshman year, and yet she had met Tom, the all-state quarterback. At Wiggins Watering Hole, the college bar, he had walked over to her table and made some crack about the English comp professor. She had laughed, and the two had spent most of the evening talking.
>
> When Tom asked to take her back to the dorm, Carol didn't hesitate. This was the man all the girls wanted to date! At the dorm, he said he would like to talk some more, so she signed him in. Once in the room, he began to kiss her. At first, the kisses felt good. But Tom was not about to stop with kissing. He forced her to the bed and, despite her protests, began to remove her clothing.
>
> With his 240 pounds, and her 117, there wasn't much of a contest. Carol always wondered why she didn't cry out; she was asked this at the trial, at which Tom was found not guilty. This brutal end to her virginity also marked the end of her college career. Unable to shake the depression that followed, Carol left college and moved back with her parents. After a hearing, the university suspended Tom for a few games. Tom then resumed his life as before. He still goes to Wiggins Watering Hole.
>
> * * * * * *
>
> For Letitia, age 27, the evening started out friendly enough. After a cozy dinner at her apartment, her boyfriend suggested that she lie down while he did the dishes. She grabbed this unexpected opportunity. As she lay in bed, though, he walked in with a butcher knife. Her formerly tender lover bound and raped her. When it was over, he fell asleep.

Convictions are difficult to get in date-rape cases. Some prosecutors discourage women from even bringing charges of date rape. A social worker at a rape treatment center summarized the problem well when she said, "Most people are sympathetic when a stranger breaks into your house with a gun and rapes you, but if you say you made a date with the rapist, they always wonder how far you went before you said no."

The "date rape drug"—difficult to stop and difficult to prove that it was used.

What can be done? Campus antirape groups—composed of both women and men—offer one remedy. Lectures and workshops introduce incoming college women to the reality and perils of date rape and to defensive measures they can take. Well-publicized prosecutions can help reduce the risk, and antirape groups can encourage women to press charges and insist that prosecutors file charges. Student groups can also pressure college administrators to react strongly to date rape. As one activist said, "If there were a pattern of assaults on quarterbacks, universities would respond very quickly."

Based on Engelmayer 1983; Seligmann 1984; Taslitz 2005; Macy et al. 2006; Seligman 2008; Bucher and Manasse 2011.

For Your Consideration

Why do you think date rape is so difficult to prosecute? Besides the suggestions made here, what else do you think can be done to reduce date rape?

Compared with women who have not been raped, rape victims are more anxious and depressed and have more thoughts of suicide (Ullman 2007). In addition to having nightmares, many victims become afraid—of being alone, of the dark, of walking on the street, or of doing such ordinary things as shopping and driving. Anything that reminds them of the rape can send them into anxiety and depression—and they never know what will trigger the painful memories. The victim's personal relationships may also deteriorate, for, feeling hurt and less trusting, some women feel less intimate and withdraw emotionally. To complicate matters even further, some husbands and boyfriends wonder what "really" happened, and their suspicions feed this spiral of despair.

Dealing With the Legal System. As a result of the work done by many rape advocates and feminists, police departments have grown more sensitive to rape victims. They have trained women officers to do the interviewing and to collect the evidence needed to pursue a criminal case. Yet, the way the criminal justice system operates continues to add to the victim's suffering, sometimes even placing some of the blame on the victim (Raphael 2008; Eligon 2011).

To conduct their investigation, the police must collect evidence about the attack. This means that they must ask about intimate details. This can embarrass both the victim and the officers. Some officers are insensitive. Others don't believe the attack qualifies as rape if the woman doesn't have bruises and cuts. Some suspect that the victim is using the police to "get even" with a boyfriend. Because some rape charges are bogus, this is a concern (Raphael 2008).

Just when the woman needs compassion the most, when her world has been turned upside down, she can find herself disbelieved, an object of suspicion. One victim gave this account of her experience with the police:

> *They rushed me down to the housing cops who asked me questions like, "Was he your boyfriend?" "Did you know him?" Here I am, hysterical. I'm 12 years old, and I don't know these things even happen to people. Anyway, they took me to the precinct after that, and there about four detectives got me in the room and asked me how long was his penis—like I was supposed to measure it. Actually, they said, "How long was the instrument?" I thought they were referring to the knife—how was I supposed to know? That I could have told them 'cause I was sure enough lookin' at the knife. (Brownmiller 1975:365)*

Even if a woman is fortunate enough to be questioned by sensitive, compassionate police officers who have been trained in rape investigations, this is just the beginning of her experience in the criminal justice system. The victim faces a dilemma: If she fails to press charges, the rapist goes free—and he may well rape again. But if she prosecutes, she must relive her attack, perhaps repeatedly, as she goes over the disturbing details with the prosecuting attorney. Then she must describe everything in a courtroom in front of her rapist, his attorney, a judge, perhaps a jury, journalists, and even the general public. Here, the defense attorney may try to demean her character, for in some states her prior sex life can be examined on the witness stand. Everything she says can and will be challenged. Any fuzziness in her account is an opportunity for the defense attorney to attack her credibility. In the courtroom, the victim can become the accused. As one rape victim said of her experience,

> *I had heard other women say that the trial is the rape. It's no exaggeration. My trial was one of the dirtiest transcripts you could read. Even though I had been warned about the defense attorney, you wouldn't believe the things he asked me to describe. It was very humiliating. I don't understand it. It was like I was the defendant and he was the plaintiff. I wasn't on trial. I don't see where I did anything wrong. I screamed, I struggled. (Brownmiller 1975:36)*

Some call this second victimization the "legal rape" of the victim. Some of it is inevitable. The authorities must first establish that a crime took place. Then at trial the accused has the right to confront the accuser face to face, to question her, and to challenge her testimony. On top of this, remnants of the traditional/patriarchal view of rape remain. If the victim was raped by a stranger who grabbed her as she was walking on the street or who broke into her home, judges and jurors see her as a victim. If the woman was on a date with the man she is accusing of rape, however, or if she knew him, or if he was her boyfriend, some jurors wonder whether the woman changed her mind just before consensual sex and the aroused man just continued with what they both had been intending. In the traditional/patriarchal view, she does not have the right to change her mind.

Other Types of Rape. Although we have concentrated on male–female rape, other types of rape occur. Women also rape. For some, their victims are other women

(Girshick 2004), but there also are occasional reports of women raping men (Bucher et al. 2011). As you can imagine, when a man reports that he was raped by a woman, officials have a difficult time believing that a rape occurred. Men also rape men. The rapist can be a heterosexual or a homosexual (Capers 2011). The rape of men by men occurs frequently in prison. A commission appointed by Congress to study the problem of prison rape reports that each year about 60,000 men are raped in prison ("National Prison Rape . . ." 2009).

TABLE 5.3 ▸ Murder Victims: What Is Their Relationship to the Killer?

Family	24.8%	Other People They Knew 53.1%	
Wife	8.3%	Acquaintances Girlfriend	37.4% 6.8%
Son	3.5%	Friend	5.5%
Daughter	2.7%	Boyfriend	1.8%
Father	1.9%	Neighbor	1.3%
Husband	1.5%	Employer Employee	0.2% 0.1%
Mother	1.5%		
Brother	1.2%	**Strangers**	**22.2%**
Sister	0.3%		
Other Family	3.9%		

Note: These relationships refer to cases in which the relationship between the killer and victim is known. In 44% of killings this relationship is unknown, either because the crime was not solved or the police did not report the relationship.
Source: By the author. Based on *Crime in the United States* 2011:Table 10.

Research Findings: Murder

Americans are fascinated with murder. Every night Americans watch reenactments of beatings, bombings, shootings, slashings, stabbings, drownings, strangulations, poisonings, and other mayhem on television. Beyond this entertainment are the real-life killings and the real-life killers. Like any murder mystery, let's look at the who, what, when, where, and why of murder.

The Social Patterns of Murder

5.11 Summarize the social patterns of murder.

Let's start with some good news that we all welcome and that, as unexpected as it is, has left the experts shaking their heads. The United States is much, much safer than it was 20 years ago. Between 1990 and 2010, the U.S. murder rate plunged, dropping *in half* (49 percent). The murder rate fell from 9.4 killings per 100,000 Americans to 4.8 (*Statistical Abstract of the United States* 2013:Table 312).

Behind those 4.8 murders per 100,000 Americans lie some major social patterns. Let's see what they are.

The "Who" of Murder. Although fears of murder center mostly on strangers, like rape, most murders are committed by someone the victim knew—and often knew well. Look at Table 5.3 on this page, which shows the victims' relationships to their killers. As you can see, strangers account for only 22 percent of U.S. killings. About three of five murder victims are killed by members of their family or by their lovers, friends, neighbors, or other acquaintances. These relationships, which the police can trace, are one of the main reasons that, as Figure 5.6 on this page shows, this crime of violence is the most likely to be solved.

The social class, sex, age, and race–ethnicity of killers are similar to those of rapists. Those in poverty are the most likely to kill. So are younger people.

FIGURE 5.6 ▸ Crimes Cleared by Arrest

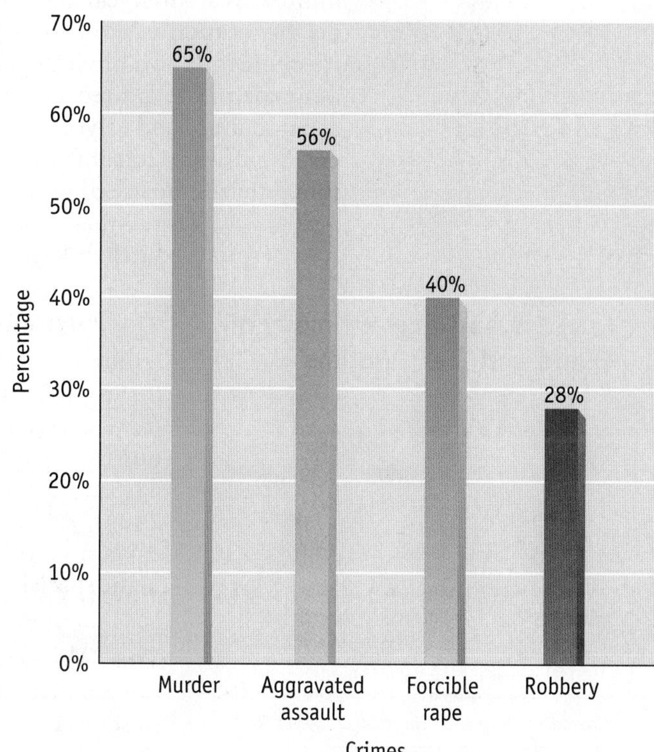

Source: Based on *Crime in the United States* 2011:Table 25.

FIGURE 5.7 ▸ Killers and Their Victims

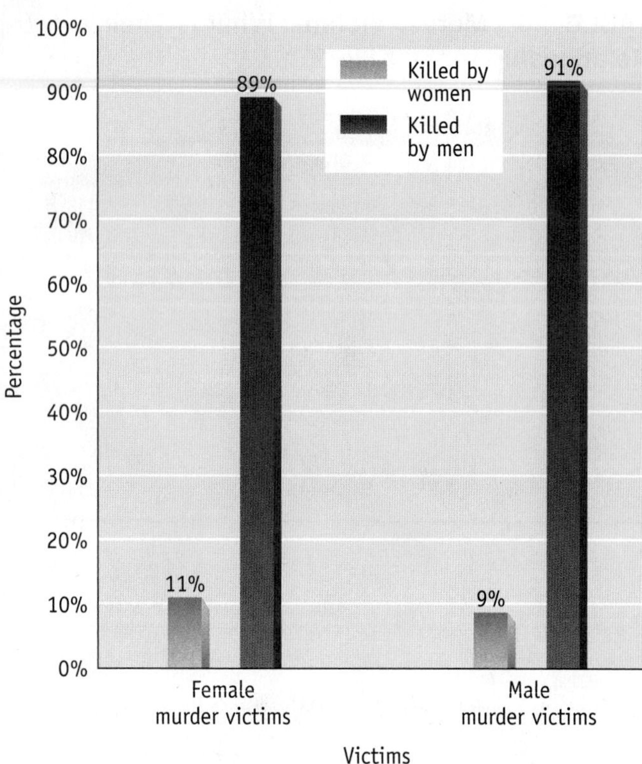

Source: By the author. Based on *Crime in the United States* 2011:Table 6.

Consider this astounding fact: Only 9 to 10 percent of the U.S. population consists of young men ages 17 to 29, but from this group come *57 percent* of the killers (where the age of the killer is known) (*Crime in the United States* 2011:Table 3; *Statistical Abstract* 2013:Table 7).

Figure 5.7 on this page illustrates how much more likely men are to kill than women. Men kill about 90 percent of everyone who is murdered in the United States. Although women make up 51 percent of the U.S. population, they commit only about 10 percent of the murders. As you can see from Table 5.3 on page 139, husbands are five to six times more likely to kill their wives than the reverse. You can also see how much more likely boyfriends are to kill their girlfriends than girlfriends are to kill their boyfriends.

Similar startling differences appear in comparing the murders of African Americans and whites. Although African Americans make up only about 13 percent of the U.S. population, in 48 percent of the cases where the race–ethnicity of the killer is known, the murderer is an African American (*Crime in the United States* 2009:Table 3). From Table 5.4 below, you can see that murder is overwhelmingly *intraracial*—86 percent of white victims are killed by whites, and 92 percent of blacks are killed by blacks.

The "What" of Murder. Although people use a variety of weapons to commit murder, year after year the number one weapon is the gun. The breakdown of murder by weapon is shown on Figure 5.8 on the next page. Guns may be the favorite choice for two obvious reasons: They are highly effective, and they are readily available in the United States. More subtle reasons may be that men identify guns as masculine, and as you saw in Figure 5.7, men are far more likely to be the killers. Significant cultural stereotypes reinforce this image. For example, our culture romanticizes the use of guns among cowboys, hunters, and villains. To settle a quarrel, then, men are much more likely to reach for a gun than, say, a kitchen knife or a bottle of poison.

TABLE 5.4 ▸ Race–Ethnicity of Killers and Their Victims

		Killers	
		White	**Black**
Victims	White	86%	14%
	Black	8%	92%

Note: The source has a small number in category "Other." The number is so small that Latinos must be subsumed in White and Black. The percentages here do not include victims or killers whose race–ethnicity is unknown.
Source: By the author. Based on *Crime in the United States* 2011:Table 6.

The "When" of Murder. Like rape, murder is not evenly distributed across the seasons. And like rape, more murder occurs during the summer months with the least in February (*FBI Uniform Crime Reports* 2005:Table 2.2). Nighttime is more dangerous than daytime, and weekends more dangerous than weekdays. The most dangerous time of the week is Saturday night (McGinty 2006). As sociologist Alex Thio (1978) observed long ago, this may explain why cheap handguns are sometimes referred to as "Saturday night specials."

The "Where" of Murder. From Figure 5.9 on the next page, you can see that, like rape, the murder rate varies tremendously from state to state. People in Louisiana are 11 times more likely to be murdered than are people in New Hampshire. Washington, D.C., is in a class by itself. Its murder rate is 21 times that of New Hampshire.

FIGURE 5.8 ▸ Americans' Choice of Murder Weapons

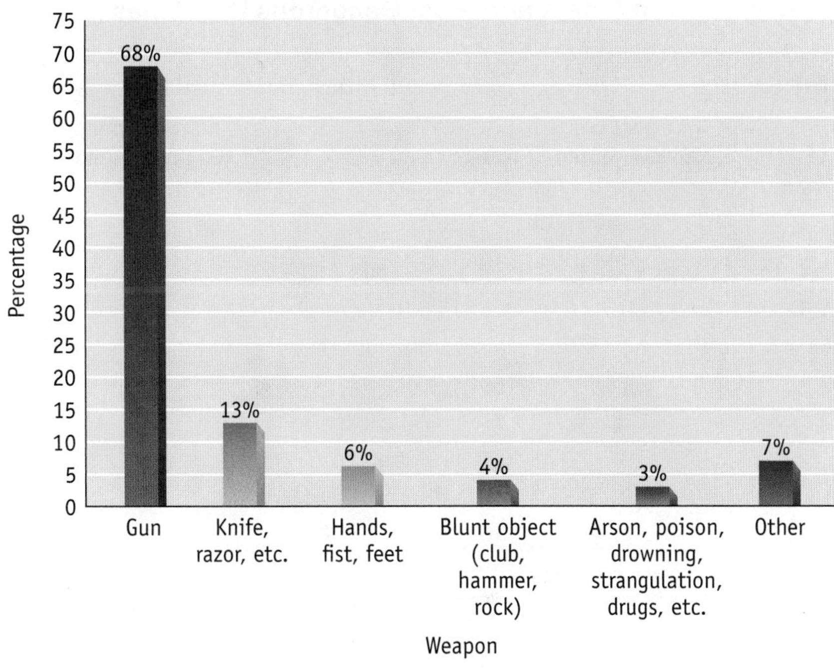

Source: By the author. Based on *Crime in the United States* 2011:Table 11.

Many people think the chances of getting murdered are greater in the city than in the country—and they are right. In large cities, 5 of every 100,000 people are murdered each year. In suburbs, this rate drops to 4, and in rural areas to just 3 (*Crime in the United States* 2011:Table 2). Table 5.5 on the next page, shows how uneven the murder rate is among U.S. cities.

FIGURE 5.9 ▸ The "Where" of Murder: The Murder Rate per State

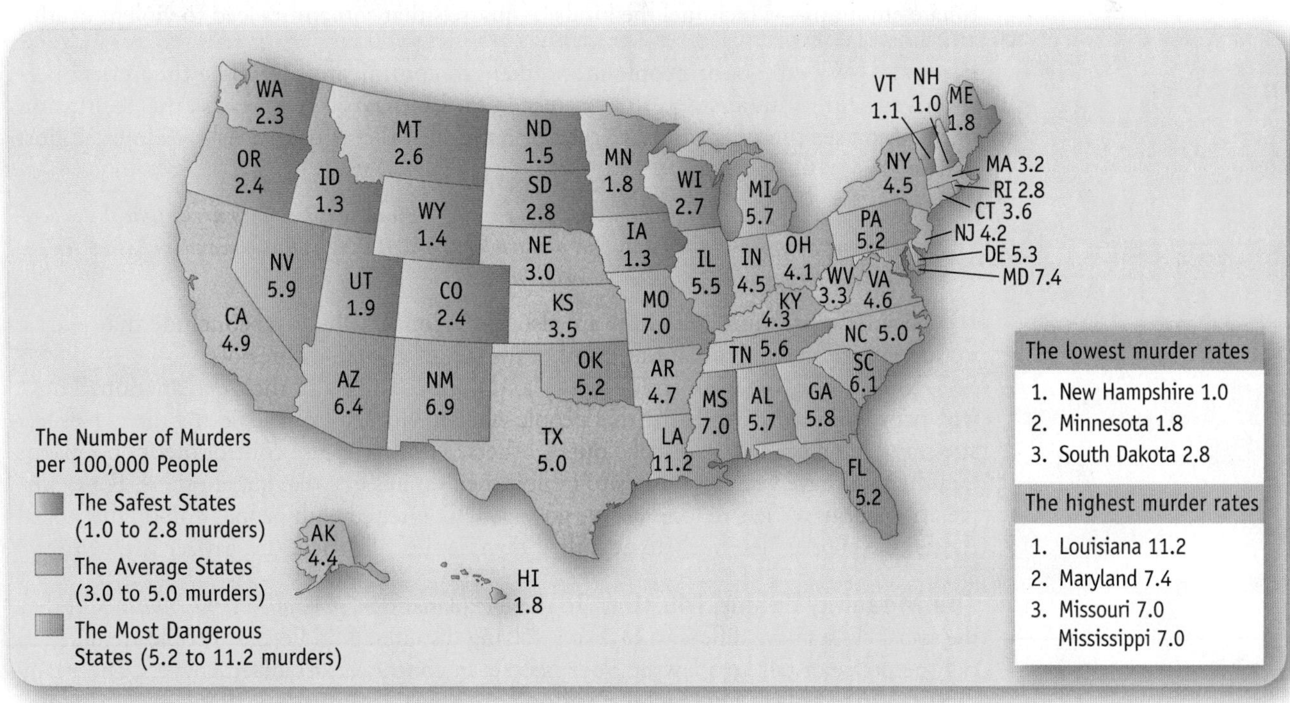

Source: By the author. Based on *Crime in the United States* 2011:Table 5.

TABLE 5.5 ▸ Murder: The Ten Safest and Most Dangerous U.S. Cities

THE SAFEST			THE MOST DANGEROUS		
Rank	City	Murders per 100,000 People	Rank	City	Murders per 100,000 People
1	Plano, TX	1.5	1	New Orleans, LA	52
2	Honolulu, HI	1.5	2	Detroit, MI	40
3	Henderson, NV	1.5	3	St. Louis, MO	40
4	El Paso, TX	1.9	4	Baltimore, MD	37
5	Chandler, AZ	2.0	5	Newark, NJ	29
6	Lincoln, NE	2.0	6	Oakland, CA	26
7	Anaheim, CA	2.7	7	Washington, DC	24
8	Austin, TX	2.9	7	Buffalo, NY	22
9	San Jose, CA	2.9	9	Kansas City, MO	21
10	San Diego, CA	3.1	10	Memphis, TN	20

Note: From data reported by police officials in cities over 250,000 people.
Source: By the author. Based on *Statistical Abstract of the United States* 2012:Table 309.

The "Why" of Murder. Now that we have looked at the "who," "what," "when," and "where" of murder, let's examine the "why." As we examine the reasons behind the social patterns, you will see that they reflect our society.

Explaining the Social Patterns

5.12 Explain the social patterns of murder.

Acquaintanceship. As you saw, most murder victims are killed by someone they know. Indeed, most murders are crimes of passion spurred by heated arguments. Many analysts have pointed out that we are much more likely to argue with people we know than with strangers. It is with people we know that we share our money, property, and intimate emotions—which fuel the kinds of quarrels that sometimes lead to violent death.

View on MySocLab Figure Murder by Relationship

Poverty. Why are poor people more likely to commit murder? The theoretical perspectives help us understand this pattern. *Conflict theorists*, who stress the oppression of the poor, see their high murder rates as a result of their poverty. As sociologist Elliott Currie (1985:160) put it,

> *Brutal conditions breed brutal behavior. To believe otherwise requires us to argue that the experience of being confined to the mean and precarious depths of the American economy has no serious consequences for personal character or social behavior.*

Because most murder victims are also poor, conflict theorists conclude that people in poverty are striking out at one another instead of at their oppressors.

Functionalists use both strain theory and control theory in their explanation. Those who use strain theory emphasize that people who are blocked from achieving their goals feel stress and are more likely to strike out at others. Those who use control theory point out that the poor have weaker controls to inhibit their desires to strike out at others. For example, the poor have "less to lose" if they go to jail. Compared with people from higher social classes, the poor are less likely to own their own homes, and their jobs pay relatively little.

The Meaning Behind Murder. To these explanations, *symbolic interactionists* add that the social classes have different ways of resolving disputes. Middle-class people are likely to call the police or talk to a lawyer. Poor people, in contrast, can't afford lawyers, and many don't trust the police. Those who stand up to others are admired for doing so. As a result, poor people are more likely to settle disagreements directly and personally. Direct confrontations over passionate issues lead to heated words, physical assault, and sometimes death.

To trace the path by which people became involved in killing, Lonnie Athens, a symbolic interactionist, interviewed 58 people serving sentences for murder. He found this general pattern: The killer found something intolerable. A spouse or lover might have refused sex or threatened to leave. Or someone may have said something insulting. The killer interpreted the act as something that called for violence, often because the act threatened the killer's self-image or social standing among friends.

Listen to a woman whom Athens (1980:36–37) interviewed. She said that she was at a party when a stranger accused her of cheating him of $20. The man kept insulting her and laughing at her:

> *Then I told myself, "This man has got to go one way or another; I've just had enough of this (man) messing with me; I'm going to cut his dirty . . . throat." I went into my bedroom, got a $20 bill and my razor. I said to myself . . . "now he's hung himself," and I walked out of the bedroom. I went up to him with a big smile on my face. I held the $20 bill in my hand out in front of me and hid the razor in the other hand. Then I sat on his lap and said, "O.K., you're a fast dude; here's your $20 back." He said, "I'm glad that you are finally admitting it." I looked at him with a smile and said, "Let me seal it with a kiss" . . . and then I bent over like I was going to kiss him and started slicing up his throat.*

Killing as a Manly Act. This last example notwithstanding, why do men kill so much more than women? One reason is that dominance is considered an essential element of masculinity. Among working-class boys and men—and not limited to them—is the view that a "real man" is tough. Their standing in the group may depend on being known as "the kind of guy who can't be pushed around." Not fighting back when insulted is to be a coward, to show a lack of masculinity (Rios 2011).

As we saw earlier (see pages 126–127), among some groups spilling blood brings honor. In the Mafia, to kill is to demonstrate masculinity: Killing is the measure of a man's *capacity as a man.* There, "the more awesome and potent the victim, the more worthy and meritorious the killer" (Arlacchi 1980:113).

Symbolic interactionists stress that while men learn to associate masculinity with acting tough and, when necessary, being violent, women tend to learn less violent ways of handling problems. As a result, *in every society around the world* men kill at a rate several times that of women (Daly and Wilson 1988; Chernoff and Simon 2000). (Biological and evolutionary theorists point to this worldwide pattern of killing as evidence of genetic inheritance. We will continue with a sociological focus on environmental theories.)

Racial–Ethnic Differences. So why do African Americans kill at a higher rate than other racial-ethnic groups? Let's start with symbolic interactionism. It is important to note that almost all murder by African Americans occurs among the very poor. In this subculture, masculinity is highly prized—and the form of masculinity dominant here centers on the willingness to defend oneself aggressively. Functionalists would add that African Americans are socialized to strive for the cultural goal of material success, but discrimination blocks many of them from reaching that goal. This increases their strain, leading to a higher rate of violence, most of which is directed against people nearby.

How about the intraracial pattern of murder that we reviewed? This is primarily due to segregated living and housing patterns. Then what about violence that crosses racial lines? Functionalists stress our society's pattern of money and race–ethnicity. If a robbery (or mugging or burglary) results in a murder across racial lines, it is most likely to involve a poor African American robbing a white, not a poor white robbing an African American. If African Americans possessed more wealth than whites, we would expect this pattern to be reversed.

In *The Declining Significance of Race*, sociologist William Julius Wilson (1978) analyzed the impact of social change on patterns of violence. As African Americans gained more access to education, they took higher-paying jobs and entered the middle class. As they moved out of the ghetto and into more desirable areas of the city and suburbs left behind was an *underclass.* These people are desperately poor and plagued with social problems: poverty, dropping out of school, unemployment, single-parent households, drug addiction, murder, robbery, and rape. As Wilson put it, this group "is increasingly isolated from mainstream patterns and norms of behavior."

Temporal Patterns. The timing of U.S. murder also reflects society. Murders are less frequent during weekdays when people are working and meeting personal and family responsibilities. Murders are higher on weekends when people are more likely to be socializing in public, drinking, and using drugs, with the peak of violence occurring on Saturday night. And because people are more likely to get out of the house and socialize during warm weather, murder is higher during the summer months and lower during winter months.

Geographic Patterns. You also saw how geography plays a role in murder. Since we've had records, now for more than a century, the South's murder rate has been higher than that of the rest of the country. You saw this pattern on the Social Map you looked at on page 141. Because the South's high murder rate persists year after year, some researchers conclude that there is a *southern subculture of violence*. In this subculture, Southerners learn to resolve disagreements in confrontational ways. More violent themes run through southern music, literature, and jokes. Apparently, Southerners are more likely to own guns, to know how to shoot them, and to use guns during quarrels. Sociologists find these explanations suggestive, but not satisfactory (Doerner 1978; Huff-Corzine et al. 1986, 1991; Pridemore and Freilich 2006). We need more research to establish adequate explanations.

Mass Murder and Serial Murder

5.13 Discuss the findings on mass murder and serial murder.

Let's look at two patterns of murder that have gripped the public's attention: mass murder and serial murder.

Mass Murder. **Mass murder** is the killing of four or more people in a single episode (Fox and Levin 2005). By this definition, Amy Bishop in our opening vignette is not a mass murderer because she had three victims, but, unfortunately, there is no problem locating examples. One of the most notorious is Richard Speck, who slaughtered eight nursing students in Chicago one night in 1966. In that same year, Charles Whitman killed 16 people in a sniper attack from a tower at the University of Texas. In 1981, Priscilla Ford deliberately drove her car into a crowd at a Thanksgiving Day parade in Reno, Nevada, killing six. The list goes on: James Huberty shot 21 people at a McDonald's in 1984. In 1991, Julio Gonzalez, unhappy that his girlfriend was breaking up with him, killed 87 people by torching the Happy Land Social Club in the Bronx. In Houston in 2001, Andrea Yates drowned her five small children in the family bathtub while her husband was at work. In 2007, Seung-Hui Cho shot to death 32 students and faculty members at Virginia Tech. In 2012, Adam Lanza shot to death 20 children and 6 adults at an elementary school in Connecticut.

The largest mass murder by a single individual in the United States occurred in 1995 when Timothy McVeigh killed 168 people by blowing up a federal building in Oklahoma City, Oklahoma, McVeigh's stunning number of victims was overshadowed on September 11, 2001, of course, when about 3,000 people lost their lives. This was a different form of mass murder, involving many people who made plans for years, with many people carrying them out. September 11 is better thought of as an act of war.

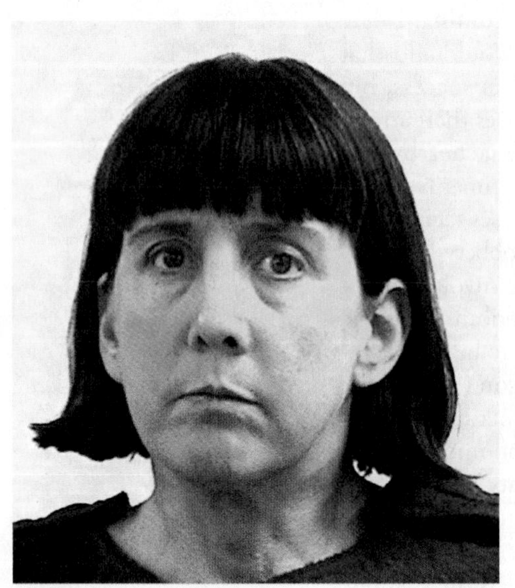
Amy Bishop

Serial Murder. Killing people in three or more separate events is called **serial murder**. The murders may occur over several days, weeks, or even years. The elapsed time between murders distinguishes serial killers from mass murderers. Serial killers are generally less spontaneous and do more planning than mass murderers. But not always, with Timothy McVeigh the prime example.

Some serial killers are motivated by lust and are aroused sexually by killing. The FBI refers to this type of killing as "lust murder." These serial killers like to take souvenirs from their victims. The victims' jewelry, underwear, even body parts remind them of the pleasure the killing gave them (Fox and Levin 2005:44). One of the most bizarre serial killers was

Jeffrey Dahmer of Milwaukee. Dahmer had sex with the dead bodies of the young men he killed, and he fried and ate parts of his victims. In 2009, Anthony Sowell was found to be living with decaying corpses in his home in Cleveland, Ohio. He was charged with killing 11 women. The serial killer with the most victims is Harold Shipman, a quiet, unassuming physician in Manchester, England. From 1977 to 2000, he killed 275 elderly women patients, giving them lethal injections while making house calls. In the Spotlight on Social Research box below, I focus on how a young teenager became a serial killer.

Spotlight on Social Research

Doing Research on a Serial Killer

Dean Corll, age 33, of Houston Texas, raped, tortured, and killed 27 teenaged boys. Two teenagers helped him, Elmer Wayne Henley, 14, and David Brooks, 15. Neither boy had a father living at home, and Corll became a father substitute who molded the boys into killers. Henley and Brooks, who helped Corll pick up young hitchhikers, would sometimes even bring him their own neighbors and high school classmates to rape, torture, and kill.

Elmer Wayne Henley in Corpus Christi, Texas, who was sentenced to six life sentences for his involvement in the kidnapping, torture, rape, and murder of teenaged boys.

The case came to the attention of the police when Henley shot Corll to death.

The reports were shocking: As television crews recorded the event, decaying corpses, one after another, were unearthed from a rented boat storage shed. All the corpses seemed to be teenagers.

My curiosity got the best of me, and I decided to go to Houston. Summer classes were ending in just a few days, and as soon as I taught my last class I took off for a straight-through drive from Illinois. My budget was low (nonexistent, actually), but these were "hippie" times, and it was easy to meet a stranger and find a place to stay for a few nights.

I went to the "morgue," the office where newspapers store their back issues. There I read the reports, from the first revelation of the killings to their current coverage. The accounts included the addresses of victims. On a city map, I marked the home of each local victim, as well as the homes of the killers. As I drove around the neighborhoods, map in hand, at one of the marked homes I saw a man painting his porch. I stopped my car, went over and introduced myself. I asked him if he were the father of a boy who had been killed. Although reluctant to talk about his son's death, he did so. His son had left the house one Saturday to go for a haircut. He never made it home. He told me bitterly that the police had refused to investigate his son's disappearance. They insisted that his son was a runaway.

Elmer Wayne Henley, one of the accused killers, was a neighborhood kid. He lived just down the street.

As I drove by Henley's home, I decided to stop and try to get an interview. As I was knocking on the door, Henley's mother and grandmother came around the side of the house, carrying bags of groceries. I told them who I was and what I wanted. Henley's mother said that she couldn't talk to me, that her attorney had ordered her not to talk to anyone. I explained that I had driven all the way from Illinois to talk to her, and I promised that I would keep whatever she said private until after her son's trial. She agreed to be interviewed, and I went inside her home. While I was talking to her and her mother, three of Henley's friends came over. I was also able to interview them.

To prevent contamination—what one person says in an interview influencing others—I interviewed each person separately. I recorded the interviews in Henley's bedroom, with the door closed. My interviews revealed what since has become common knowledge about serial killers: They successfully lead double lives that catch their friends and family unaware. Henley's mother swore to me that her son was a good boy and that he couldn't possibly be guilty. His high school friends stressed that Elmer couldn't be involved in homosexual rape and murder because he was interested only in girls. For proof of Elmer's innocence, his friends pointed to a pair of girls' panties that were hanging in his bedroom.

Henley and Brooks were tried and found guilty. They had methodically delivered hitchhikers and acquaintances to Corll, and together the three of them had raped, tortured, killed, and buried the boys. Henley and Brooks were sentenced to life terms in Texas prisons, where they remain today.

For Your Consideration

What punishment do you think is appropriate for serial killers. Why?

Almost all serial killers are men, but there are exceptions. Here are three. In the 1980s, Genene Jones, a nurse, killed small children in her care in a hospital and a pediatrics clinic in Kerrville, Texas. In 1988, Dorothea Montalvo Puente killed seven senior citizens so she could keep cashing their Social Security checks. In 2002, Aileen Wuornos was executed for killing five men after she had sex with them.

Have Mass and Serial Murders Become More Common? Many assume that mass and serial murders are more common now than they used to be, but we can't draw this conclusion. In the past, police departments had little communication with one another, and when killings occurred in different jurisdictions the killings were seldom linked. Today's computer programs and more efficient investigative techniques make it easier for the police to recognize that a serial killer is operating in an area.

Social Policy

While I could suggest many policies for dealing with offenders and their victims, the primary concern is the prevention of violence. Let's look at the potential.

Global Concerns: Preventing Violence

5.14 Identify social policies that can reduce or prevent violence.

Here are four social policies that can reduce or prevent violence:

Equality. *First*, researchers have documented that rape is higher in societies in which women are devalued (Lalumiere et al. 2005). The implications for social policy are profound. We can reduce rape by increasing the social value of women. To do this, we need programs in churches and schools, for families, and on television that stress equality.

The Cost of Rape. *Second*, researchers have also documented that rape is lower when the perceived cost of raping is high (Lalumiere et al. 2005). Put more simply, if men think they will be punished, they are less likely to rape. This finding also has profound implications for social policy: To reduce rape, we need social policies that increase the likelihood that rapists will be punished. Of the many possibilities, here is just one. Some men are serial rapists, who commit a large number of rapes. Some rape several times a month until they are caught—which can take years. Long sentences for repeat offenders—with little chance of parole—will prevent many women from being raped. For a related social policy, read the Issues in Social Problems box on the next page.

Read on **MySocLab Document:** Through a Sociological Lens: Social Structure and Family Violence

The Climate of Violence. *Third*, policy makers can support research to determine how our culture creates a climate of violence. Remember the sociological question that was posed at the beginning of this chapter: What in a society increases or decreases the likelihood of violence? As indicated in the first two policies I suggested, we do have some answers to this question. But we need more research to determine what aspects of our culture produce high rates of violence and how they do so. I suggest that researchers

1. Examine cultures with low violence to determine factors that minimize violence
2. Find ways to teach young men to channel their aggression constructively
3. Find ways to increase respect among men and women
4. To the degree that rape and murder are based on economic inequality and blocked goals to opportunities, develop programs that open opportunities for the disadvantaged

Gun Control. As we saw in Figure 5.8 on page 141, most murder victims die from gunshot wounds. Two opposing views on gun control exist, extremes that illustrate why it is difficult to establish social policy for the prevention of violence.

Issues in Social Problems

Rape Kits: Why Wait?

In Los Angeles, the backlog in crime labs is so huge that it takes 8 months for rape kits to be tested.

When a woman reports a rape, the police gather evidence from her body. Part of that evidence consists of swabs taken from wherever the rapist has penetrated her, as well as any residue that is elsewhere on her body and clothing. This evidence is placed in a rape kit and sent to a state laboratory for analysis. DNA evidence from the crime scene is compared with a DNA database. If there is a "hit," a match with DNA records, the police know they are dealing with a serial rapist.

But while a rape kit goes untested, a serial rapist can and will keep raping:

> Catherine was in her forties, living with her young son. She was awakened at midnight by a stranger who raped her, sodomized her, and repeatedly forced her to orally copulate him. When it was over, the police brought her to the Rape Treatment Center. As is the case with all rape victims, her body was a "crime scene". She consented to the collection of evidence.
>
> The detective was told by the crime lab that it would take at least 8 months to analyze Catherine's rape kit. The detective said he knew from the "M.O." in this crime that the rapist was a repeat offender. Eight months was too long to wait. He personally drove the kit to the state lab—where the kit still sat for months. When it was processed, they got a "cold hit." Catherine's rapist was identified. He was in the offender database.
>
> During the months that Catherine's kit sat on a shelf, unopened, the same rapist attacked at least two other victims—one was a child. (Tofte 2009)

The reason for the 8-month wait? Testing rape kits is expensive, costing $1,000 to $1,500 a kit. There are a lot of rapes in this huge metropolitan sprawl of 13 million people, and like other areas of the country, Los Angeles is short on money.

This Texas woman was raped at knifepoint. Twenty-four years later, her rape kit was tested. The DNA identified the rapist.

For Your Consideration

Like the residents of many other states, Californians feel that they are being eaten alive by taxes, and with shortages of money a lot of programs are going unfunded. What would you think about citizens starting a campaign to raise private (nontax) funds to get all the rape kits tested? And it isn't just a California problem. All over the country, untested rape kits collect dust, allowing rapists to remain free (Martindale 2012). How about you beginning a campaign in your state? You could make a difference.

Proponents of gun control argue that because most murders are crimes of passion, emotional outbursts would be less lethal if guns were less accessible. They claim we could reduce the U.S. murder rate by registering all guns and licensing gun owners. They consider gun ownership a custom that has "no redeeming social value."

Opponents of gun control argue that gun ownership is a constitutional right and that Americans need more guns, not less. They argue that if all law-abiding citizens had guns, few rapists and killers would break into homes—and of those who did, many wouldn't survive to do it again. They say that those who argue that guns are the problem are mistaken. They point out that Americans have more guns now than ever before, and the rates of murder and rape have dropped.

Keeping the Issue Alive. The final suggestion follows the feminist/conflict view. If we are going to reduce rape further, we need to keep this issue before the public.

Visitors from other countries, such as this European woman visiting a "gun shop," are often shocked at how many Americans own guns and how easily guns can be purchased.

Only by publicizing the issue of rape was it transformed from a personal to a social problem. We must keep publicizing this problem so our politicians and other officials will spend the resources needed to develop programs to reduce rape. This applies also to murder.

The Future of the Problem

5.15 Discuss the likely future of violence.

Our theoretical perspectives can give us glimpses of the future of the social problem of violence. *Conflict theory* indicates that tensions will always exist between groups that are competing for scarce resources. Short of revolution (which has proven no panacea for any society), the wealthy will retain control, and discrimination will continue. The poor, especially minorities—who suffer the two-edged sword of both poverty and discrimination—will continue to show up disproportionately in crime statistics. The *functionalist* perspective stresses that violence is functional enough to continue: People do get revenge and feel other satisfactions from killing their enemies. Rape does make some men feel dominant and powerful. The *symbolic interactionist* perspective focuses on the twinning of masculinity and violence. Since the combining of these two potent symbols is unlikely to change soon, we can expect violence to continue as men try to live up to cherished cultural images.

It is essential to use the *sociological* perspective to understand both the present and the future of violence. Our high rate of rape and murder *cannot* be laid at the feet of an unusually large number of sociopaths. There are sociopaths, to be sure, but our social patterns of rape and murder are primarily products of our history and our current social structure. Without structural change that reduces social inequality, high rates of violence will remain. Understanding the *social* basis of violence can be the key to bringing change that decreases violence.

MySocLab  Study and Review on MySocLab

Summary and Review

1. Sociologists analyze how *violence* is rooted in society. How a society is organized—its social structure—increases or decreases its amount of violence.
2. Each society has a rate of violence that, without major social change, is fairly constant over time. Sociologists call this a society's *normal violence.*
3. Biologists, anthropologists, and psychologists have theories to account for violence. The sociological response is that whatever predispositions humans have toward violence are encouraged or inhibited by the society in which they live.
4. Symbolic interactionists use two theories to explain violence. The first, *differential association*, stresses that violence is learned in association with other people. The second, *subcultural theory*, emphasizes that some groups are more approving of violence than others. People who grow up or associate with groups that approve of violence are more likely to learn violence.
5. Functionalists stress that some people become disconnected from cultural norms. Durkheim used the term *anomie* to describe this uprooting and estrangement. Anomic individuals are more likely to rape and to kill. Merton's *strain theory* suggests that violence is an alternative path that some people choose when they find the *cultural means* (such as jobs and career training) to reach *cultural goals* (such as financial success) blocked. *Control* (or *containment*) *theory* suggests that the inner and outer controls of rapists and murderers are weaker than their pushes and pulls to commit these acts.
6. Conflict theorists emphasize that the groups that form a society compete for scarce resources. The major division is between those who own the means of production and those who do not. Those at the mercy of the owners have few resources, and they lash out violently—misdirecting their violence onto one another.
7. Feminists challenged the traditional view of rape as a personal problem, a crime of passion. Under their prodding, rape became a social problem; that is, subjective concerns grew, and rape came to be considered a crime of dominance and violence rooted in the structure of relationships between men and women.
8. Rape and murder are not random acts. They reflect society's larger patterns: social class, gender, age, race–ethnicity, timing, location, and acquaintanceship.
9. To prevent violence requires restructuring those aspects of society that foster violence. To determine a rational basis for social policy on these emotionally charged issues, we need research on the social causes of violence.
10. We can reduce rape through social policies that increase the value of females and increase the perceived costs of raping. To keep rape from fading from the public's mind as a social problem and to find workable solutions, we must keep this issue alive.

Key Terms

anomie, 128
control theory, 129
criminal sexual assault, 132
cultural goal, 128
cultural means, 129
differential association, 125
forcible rape, 131
frustration–aggression theory of violence, 122
mass murder, 144
modeling, 125
normal violence, 128
operant conditioning, 125
patriarchy, 131
rate of violence, 119
serial murder, 144
statutory rape, 131
strain theory, 128
subcultural theory, 126
violence, 119

Thinking Critically About Chapter 5

1. What is the *sociological question* of violence? What materials in this chapter indicate that this is the right question to ask?
2. Which four of the profiles of rapists that are discussed on pages 135–136 do you think are the most common? Explain why you think so.
3. As a social policy to reduce rape, the author suggests that we promote programs that increase the social value of females. What programs do you think would work?

6 Crime and Criminal Justice

Listen to Chapter 6 on MySocLab

Learning Objectives. After reading this chapter, you should be able to:

I was recently released from solitary confinement after being held therein for 37 months (months!). A silent system was imposed upon me and to even whisper to the man in the next cell resulted in being beaten by guards, sprayed with chemical mace, blackjacked, stomped and thrown into a strip-cell naked to sleep on a concrete floor without bedding, covering, wash basin or even toilet. The floor served as toilet and bed, and even there the silent system was enforced. . . . I have filed every writ possible against the administrative acts of brutality. The courts have all denied the petitions. Because of my refusal to let the thing die down . . . I am the most hated prisoner in (this) penitentiary, and called a "hard-core incorrigible."

The floor served as toilet and bed.

Maybe I am an incorrigible. . . . I know that thieves must be punished and I don't justify stealing, even though I am a thief myself. But now I don't think I will be a thief when I am released. No, I'm not that rehabilitated. It's just that I no longer think of becoming wealthy by stealing. I now think of killing—killing those who have beaten me and treated me as if I were a dog. I hope and pray for the sake of my own soul and future life of freedom that I am able to overcome the bitterness and hatred which eats daily at my soul.

—A letter from a prisoner in a state prison, as quoted in Zimbardo 1972

The Problem in Sociological Perspective

6.1 Explain what crime is, why crime is relative, and how something becomes a crime.

What Is Crime?

Crime is a fascinating area of human behavior. We may feel almost spellbound as we learn about a crime that is particularly gruesome, or even about a crime that was committed in some unusual way. To understand crime, let's begin by placing it in sociological perspective.

The Essential Nature of Crime: The Law. Before we get into this chapter, we need to answer the question of what crime is. Let's start by looking at what people call "dumb laws."

In Florida, it is illegal to sell alcohol before 1 P.M. on Sunday.

In Arkansas, schoolteachers who cut their hair short cannot get a raise.

In California, animals cannot have sex within 1,500 feet of a church.

The Florida constitution guarantees that pregnant pigs cannot be put in cages.

In New York, women can go topless in public as long as they do not profit from the behavior.

In Texas, you'll break the law if you sell your eye.

More than likely, your state has "dumb laws," and I'm sure that it has laws that make something legal at one time during the day or night but illegal at another time. For example, to sell whiskey, wine, or beer one minute before "closing hour" is legal; to sell them one minute later is a crime.

It might sound strange, but these laws illustrate *the essential nature of crime*. No activity is criminal in and of itself. **Crime** *is the violation of law*. If there is no law, there is no crime. Although we may agree that stealing, kidnapping, and rape are immoral or harmful, only the law can define them as crimes.

The Relativity of Crime. The principle that law defines crime has many implications. One is that *crime is culturally relative*; that is, because laws differ from one society to another, so does crime. Travelers are sometimes shocked when they find that some behavior they take for granted at home is a crime abroad—or that what is illegal at home is taken for granted elsewhere. For example, although eating pork and drinking alcohol are illegal in some Muslim societies, a man there may take several wives as long as he can support them.

The relativity of crime is so great that even within the same society, behavior that is criminal at one time can later be encouraged as a virtue. In China, for example, selling goods to make a profit used to be a crime so serious that it was punishable by death. To teach everyone a lesson, "profiteers" were hung in the public square. When Chinese officials adopted capitalism in the 1990s, however, they decided that letting people make profits would help their economy. The change has been so thorough that now "profiteers," Chinese capitalists, can join the Communist party.

This relativity is so extreme that something that is a crime at one point in time can later be encouraged as a contribution to humanity. One hundred years ago, birth control information and devices could not be sent in the U.S. mail because they were "obscene, lewd, and lascivious." Margaret Sanger, a pioneering feminist, was arrested for breaking this law. Today, most people consider teaching birth control to be a service to an overpopulated world that is running out of natural resources.

Making Something Criminal: A Political Process. Abortion was the social problem featured in Chapter 1. As we reviewed, before 1973 abortion was a crime, and those who performed it were put in prison. After the 1973 *Roe v. Wade* decision by the U.S. Supreme Court, abortion was no longer a crime. If the antiabortion groups succeed in amending the Constitution or if the Supreme Court reverses its 1973 ruling, abortion will again become a crime. As you can see from this example, determining which behavior is criminal is a *political process*. The definition of some act as illegal is the outcome of a struggle among groups that have different interests and viewpoints.

These two principles—that law defines crime and that crime is the outcome of a political process—take us to the significance of power. **Power** may be defined as being able to get what you want despite resistance. What groups in a society have the power to get their views written into law? How do they get authorities to pass laws? Why do some societies punish a behavior while others ignore—or even encourage—the same behavior? Perhaps these questions can be summarized into one: Whose interests do laws protect?

The Scope of the Problem

In considering crime as a social problem, we must also analyze the **criminal justice system**—those agencies that respond to crime: the police, courts, jails, and prisons. On the one hand, crime is a social problem when large numbers of people are upset about it, when they feel that crime threatens their safety, peace, or quality of life. On the other hand, the criminal justice system is a social problem if people are upset about it—perhaps how it fails to prevent crime, fails to rehabilitate offenders, or discriminates against some citizens. In this chapter, we will discuss both crime and the criminal justice system.

6.2 Explain why both crime and the criminal justice system are social problems and why crime is universal.

Crime as a Social Problem

Why Is Crime a Social Problem? As you will recall, to have a social problem we need both objective conditions and subjective concerns. You read in the previous chapter that the **crime rate**—the number of crimes per 100,000 people—has been dropping. You learned that since 1991 our homicide rate has plunged, dropping in half. Yet even with this remarkably lower rate, 13,000 Americans are murdered each year. The rape

Listen on MySocLab
Audio: NPR: Crime Study Challenges Past Assumptions

rate, too, has dropped, yet as you also read in the previous chapter between 85,000 and 200,000 Americans are raped a year. Another 350,000 are robbed, about 700,000 have their cars stolen, and still another 2 million have their homes broken into (*Statistical Abstract* 2013:Table 312).

View on MySocLab **Figure:** Is There More Crime in the United States Than There Was a Year Ago, or Less?

These objective conditions arouse intense subjective concerns. Over and over, people's concerns about crime's potential for their own harm are fed by sensationalized cases in the news or something that happened in their neighborhood or at work. With this heightened awareness of danger, each urban resident knows which areas of the city to avoid. As you saw in Table 5.1 (page 120) of the previous chapter, both men and women have fears about their personal safety. Women, though, have greater fears than men that they might become crime victims, and they are more careful about where they go.

Why Is Crime Universal? Some societies have much lower crime rates than ours, but no society or nation can ever be free of crime. As Emile Durkheim, one of the earliest sociologists, pointed out in 1897, the very nature of crime makes it universal. Each society passes laws against behaviors that it considers a threat to its well-being. (Tribal groups don't "pass written laws." Their rules are part of an oral tradition, with penalties for those who violate them.) Passing a law never eliminates a behavior—it just identifies it as illegal. As Durkheim stressed where there are laws (or rules), there always will be criminals (or rule breakers).

As we consider the social problem of crime, let's first look at the criminal justice system.

Looking at the Problem Theoretically

6.3 Explain how symbols (labels) affected the lives of the Saints and the Roughnecks, their role in police discretion, and why this makes us cautious about crime statistics.

As we saw in Chapter 5, each theoretical perspective provides different insights into the problem of criminal violence. We will now use these perspectives to look at crime and the criminal justice system. Using symbolic interactionism, we will examine the social class bias of police enforcement and again consider why we must view crime statistics with caution. Then, through a functionalist perspective, we will see how crime is an adaptation to a society's core values. Finally, using conflict theory, we will examine why the law comes down hardest on the poor who have stolen little, while it often is lenient toward the wealthy who have stolen much. Let's begin, then, with symbolic interactionism.

Symbolic Interactionism

The Saints and the Roughnecks: Social Class and Labeling. For two years, sociologist William Chambliss (1973/2007) observed two groups of adolescent lawbreakers at "Hanibal High School." He labeled one group the "saints" and the other the "roughnecks."

Chambliss describes the saints as "promising young men, children of good, stable, white, upper-middle-class families, active in school affairs, good pre-college students." He adds that the saints were some of the most delinquent boys in the school. They were "constantly occupied with truancy, drinking, wild driving, petty theft, and vandalism." Yet their teachers and families considered the boys "saints headed for success." Not one saint was ever arrested.

The "roughnecks," Chambliss said, were also white boys of the same age who went to the same high school. These boys, too, were delinquent, although Chambliss estimates that they committed somewhat fewer criminal acts than the saints. Their teachers considered these boys "roughnecks headed for serious trouble," and the police often dealt with them.

Why did the community perceive these boys so differently? Chambliss argues that this was due to *social class*. As symbolic interactionists emphasize, social class affects our perception and behavior. The saints came from respectable, middle-class families, the roughnecks from less respectable, working-class families. These backgrounds led teachers and authorities to expect good behavior from the saints and trouble from the roughnecks. Like the rest of us, the teachers and police saw what they expected to see.

The boys' social class also affected their *visibility*. The saints had automobiles, and they did their drinking and vandalism out of town. Because the roughnecks didn't own cars, they hung around their own street corners, where their rowdy behavior drew the attention of police. This confirmed the ideas that the community had of them.

Social class also equipped the boys with distinct *styles of interaction*. When police or teachers questioned the saints, the boys were apologetic. They showed respect for authority, so important for winning authorities' favor. Their show of respect elicited positive reactions from teachers and police, allowing the boys to escape school and legal problems. Chambliss says that the roughnecks were "almost the polar opposite." When questioned, they were hostile. Even when they tried to put on a veneer of respect, the teachers and police saw through it. The teachers came down hard on the roughnecks, and the police were quick to interrogate and arrest them rather than to warn them.

The saints and the roughnecks illustrate the differential association and subcultural theories introduced in Chapter 5. Although both the saints and the roughnecks were immersed in vandalism and theft, they were reared in different subcultures. The saints learned that college was their birthright; the roughnecks did not. The saints wanted good grades; the roughnecks didn't care. The saints learned middle-class politeness, which showed in their choice of words, tone of voice, and body language; the roughnecks did not. The reactions by authorities to these subcultural or social class "signals" deeply affected the boys' lives.

Chambliss' research illustrates what sociologists call *labeling*, a process that can set people on different paths in life. You can see what different expectations the labels "saint" and "roughneck" carry. They affect people's perceptions and channel behavior in different directions. All but one of the saints went to college. One became a doctor, one a lawyer, one earned a Ph.D., and the others went into management. Two of the roughnecks won athletic scholarships, went to college, and became coaches. One roughneck became a bookie. Two dropped out of high school, were convicted of separate killings, and ended up in prison. No one knows the whereabouts of the other. Although outcomes like these have many "causes," the boys lived up to the labels the community gave them.

Police Discretion. Sociologists Irving Piliavin and Scott Briar (1964) also observed how different styles of interaction affect outcomes with the police. Note in these two events the significance of respect:

> *An 18-year-old white male was accused of statutory rape. The girl's father was prominent in local politics, and he insisted that the police take severe action. During questioning, the youth was polite and cooperative. He addressed the officers as "sir" and answered all questions. He also said that he wanted to marry the girl. The sergeant became sympathetic and decided to try to get the charges against the youth reduced or dropped.*
>
> *A 17-year-old white male was caught having sexual relations with a 15-year-old girl. When he was questioned, he answered with obvious disregard. The officers became irritated and angry. One officer accused the boy of being a "stud," interested only in sex, eating, and sleeping. He added that the young man "probably had knocked up half a dozen girls." The boy just gave back an impassive stare. The officers made out an arrest report and took him to juvenile hall.*

"You look like this sketch of someone who's thinking about committing a crime."

A common perception is that bias in the criminal justice system works only against African Americans and Latinos. Sociological studies, however, indicate that this bias also favors these groups. (See pages 172–173.) Have you had experiences with the police that you know were biased?

Both young men had solid evidence against them. Police even had political pressure to prosecute the 18-year-old. His politeness and cooperation, however, changed the officer's perception. His deference—his respect and regard for police authority—sent a powerful message that put the police on his side. The demeanor of the 17-year-old, in contrast, sent a negative message and elicited negative reactions from the police.

Symbolic interactionists emphasize that the police use stereotypes (labels) as they administer the law. As in the cartoon to the left, the more a suspect matches their idea of "dangerous," "criminal," or even "not belonging in the neighborhood," the more likely they are to arrest that person (Novak and Chamlin 2012). **Police discretion**, deciding whether to arrest someone or to ignore a particular offense, is a routine part of police work, something that officers do daily.

Caution About Crime Statistics. These examples illustrate why sociologists approach crime statistics with caution. As noted in Chapter 2, the "facts" of a social problem are not objective: Social "facts" are produced within a specific social context for a particular purpose. According to official statistics, working-class boys are much more delinquent than middle-class boys. Yet, as we have just seen, social class influences the reactions of authorities, affecting *who shows up in official statistics*.

In Sum ▸ Symbols are an essential part of living in society. As we go through everyday life, we use symbols to interpret what happens to us. Among the symbols that affect our perception and behavior are social class, reputation, and demeanor. Such symbols also affect the perception and behavior of teachers and the police, having far-reaching effects on people's lives.

Functionalism

6.4 Explain how core social values produce crime and how crime is related to the "opportunity structure".

Crime and Society's Core Values. Functionalists consider crime a natural part of society. In fact, crime can reflect a society's core values. As sociologists Richard Cloward and Lloyd Ohlin (1960) pointed out, our society has to fill many positions (dentist, lawyer, teacher, and so on) that require high ability and diligence. To fill them, we must locate and train the most talented people of each generation—whether they are born in wealth or poverty. But there is no way of looking at babies and knowing who the talented and hard-working adults will be. Our society, then, motivates *everyone* to strive for success, provoking an intense competition that allows some of the talented to emerge as victors.

"Regardless of race, sex, or social class, success can be yours" becomes the American mantra. Repeated throughout our schools and media, it motivates the young to compete intensely. By making success a universal goal, our society ensures its survival.

What does "success-can-be-yours" have to do with crime? Almost all of us learn to want success, but the playing field isn't level. As you know so well, some people have many resources to help them become successful, others few. Wanting success but being cut off from the approved means to reach it leads to strain. Look at Table 6.1, which is how sociologist Robert Merton summarized this aspect of *strain theory*.

TABLE 6.1 ▸ Strain Theory: How People Match Their Goals to Their Means

Do They Feel the Strain That Leads to Anomie?	Mode of Adaptation	Cultural Goals	Institutionalized Means
No	Conformity	Accept	Accept
	Deviant Paths:		
Yes	1. Innovation	Accept	Reject
	2. Ritualism	Reject	Accept
	3. Retreatism	Reject	Reject
	4. Rebellion	Reject/Replace	Reject/Replace

The first classification is those who don't feel the strain that leads to *anomie*. These people, the conformists, have access to approved resources, and they strive for success. The others feel strain between society's goals and the approved means to reach them. As you can see from this table, people react to strain in four primary ways:

Innovation: The innovators accept the cultural goals, but they substitute other means of reaching them. An example is someone who pursues wealth through fraud instead of hard work.

Ritualism: The ritualists have given up on achieving success, but they still work in culturally approved ways. An example is a worker who no longer hopes to get ahead, but does just enough to avoid getting fired.

Retreatism: The retreatists reject both the societal goal and the means to achieve it. Some, such as street addicts, retreat into drugs, others into convents.

Rebellion: The rebels are convinced that society is corrupt and reject both societal goals and the means to achieve them. They seek to replace the current social order with a new one.

Innovation is the response that interests us. This is the tie-in of crime and core values that I mentioned. Finding the legitimate means to the cultural goal of success blocked, innovators turn to *illegitimate* means to reach it. As sociologist Albert Cohen (1955) said, much crime is "conformity to the American way."

Social Class and Illegitimate Opportunities. Strain theory helps us understand why the poor commit so many burglaries and robberies. Functionalists stress that society has no problem getting the poor to want material success. Television bombards them with seductive messages. The vivid images of upper-middle-class lives suggest that full-fledged Americans should be able to possess the goods and services portrayed in the commercials and programs. Education is the primary approved means of reaching success, but its doors open only reluctantly to the poor.

To see what I mean by this, you must understand that the schools are middle class, and here contrasting worlds meet head on. In school, the children of the poor confront a bewildering world, one of strict rules and "proper" speech. Their grammar and profanity mark them as different from the children of the middle class. In addition, children in poverty usually attend schools that are inferior to those that educate children from higher social classes (Kozol 1999). These barriers to success create high dropout rates among working-class students, blocking them from many legitimate avenues to financial success.

White-collar criminals generally receive light sentences. Allen Stanford, shown here, is an exception. His $7 billion Ponzi scheme netted him a 110-year prison sentence.

Often, however, a different door opens to the children of the poor, one that Cloward and Ohlin (1960) called **illegitimate opportunity structures**. These are opportunities woven into the texture of life in urban slums: robbery, burglary, drug dealing, prostitution, pimping, gambling, and other income-producing crimes or "hustles." The "hustler," or "player," becomes a model for young people—one of the few in the neighborhood whose material success comes close to the mainstream cultural stereotype.

The middle and upper classes are not free of crime, of course. Functionalists point out that *different* illegitimate opportunities attract them, ones that make *different forms* of crime functional. Instead of pimping, burglary, or mugging, members of the middle and upper classes commit white-collar crime—tax evasion, bribery of public officials, advertising fraud, price fixing, and securities violations. Martha Stewart is a remarkable example. She made over $1 billion the day her company, Martha Stewart Omnimedia, went public on the New York Stock Exchange. Yet, to gain a few thousand dollars, not even chump change for her, Stewart did insider trading (trading stock on the basis of secret information). She was forced to resign her position as head of the company she founded, and she served a few months in a "country club" prison.

Bernard Madoff and Allen Stanford made the list of infamous scoundrels when they were convicted for running worldwide Ponzi schemes (Krauss 2012). Stanford defrauded investors of a staggering $7 billion, but Madoff's $50 billion fraud, the largest in history, dwarfed even this. A **Ponzi scheme** consists of paying "investment profits" to clients, not from the nonexistent profits, but from the money that other clients invest. Madoff and Stanford defrauded wealthy, sophisticated investors, as well as average retired people who were devastated by their losses. Neither received the slap on the wrist usually given to white-collar offenders. Stanford was sentenced to 110 years in prison and Madoff to 150 years. Each man has a life expectancy of only a few years, so the sentences are largely symbolic.

In Sum ▸ Functionalists view property crime as *inherent* in societies that socialize people of all social classes to desire material success when the legitimate means to achieve success are limited. Some who find their means to achieve success blocked turn to illegitimate means. Since there is no ending point of "success," some people, like Stewart, Stanford, and Madoff, who have ample access to legitimate means, turn to illegitimate means so they can achieve even more success.

The cartoonist indicates an essential principle that is highlighted by functionalists—that crime is functional for individuals and society.

Conflict Theory

Sioux Manufacturing in North Dakota made helmets for U.S. troops in Iraq and Afghanistan. They used Kevlar—a fabric that deflects some shrapnel and bullets. The company was accused of using less Kevlar than they were supposed to. This would reduce costs and increase profits—but it would endanger U.S. soldiers, perhaps causing some to die.

Would anyone actually do such a thing? Investigators found that the accusation was true. Employees had even doctored records to show that the company had used the correct amount of Kevlar (Lambert 2008).

6.5 Explain how power and social class are related to social inequality in the legal system.

What was the punishment for a crime this serious? How long did the executives of Sioux Manufacturing spend in prison? Not one spent even a single night in jail. Those who ordered this crime weren't even put on trial. The company paid a fine—and then the government gave it another contract to make more helmets.

Contrast this with poor people who are caught stealing a $5,000 car and sent to prison for years. How can a legal system that proudly boasts "justice for all" be so inconsistent?

Power and Social Class: Inequality in the Legal System. Conflict theorists stress that every society is marked by power and inequality. The most fundamental division of a capitalist society is that between those who own the means of production, called *the ruling class*, and those who sell their labor, called *the working class*.

The working class is made up of three major groups: (1) the upper-level managers and professionals, who hold secure positions that pay well; (2) the stable working-class, white-collar and blue-collar workers whose jobs are less secure and who are paid less, although their jobs are adequate for survival; and (3) the marginal working class, who have little job security and whose labor is in low demand. This group includes most of the unemployed and people who are on welfare. From the marginal working class (also called the "reserve army" of the unemployed) come most burglars, muggers, armed robbers, and car thieves.

Conflict theorists emphasize that the law is quite unlike the ideal we learn in grade school: an institution that administers impartial justice for those accused of crimes. Rather, the ruling class controls the criminal justice system, which uses it to maintain its own privileged position in society. Because of this, the police and courts do not harshly punish the owners of corporations, but, instead, focus their attention on the marginal working class.

Violations by company owners and other members of the ruling class cannot be ignored totally. If their crimes became too flagrant, they could provoke an outcry among the working class and, ultimately, foment revolution. To prevent this, an occasional violation by the powerful is prosecuted—and given huge publicity—as was the case with Stewart, Stanford, and Madoff. Public floggings like this reassure the working class that the criminal justice system applies to all. This helps to create a sense of justice and prevent an uprising.

It is rare, however, for white-collar criminals to appear in court. Most go before a state or federal agency (such as the FTC, the Federal Trade Commission), which has no power to imprison. Headed by people of privilege, the FTC levies fines and orders offenders to stop doing what they were doing. Cases of illegal sales of stocks and bonds, price fixing, restraint of trade, and so on are handled by "gentlemen overseeing gentlemen." In contrast, the property crimes of the working class—burglary, armed robbery, and petty theft—threaten not only the sanctity of private property but also, if allowed to continue, the positions of the powerful. These offenders are channeled into a court system that does have the power to imprison.

In Sum ▸ Conflict theorists regard the criminal justice system not as a system of justice, but as a device used by the powerful to keep themselves in power. This power elite uses law enforcement to control workers, mask injustice, and prevent revolt.

Types of Crime

We'll come back to the criminal justice system, but to better understand crime as a social problem, let's first review research on juvenile delinquency, white-collar crime, professional crime, and organized crime.

Juvenile Delinquency

6.6 Explain how juvenile delinquency developed, the extent of juvenile crime, the delinquent career, neutralization techniques, and how education is related to delinquency.

The Origin of Juvenile Delinquency: A Perceptual Shift. Our twenty-first-century views of child development make it difficult to realize how differently children used to be perceived and treated. Earlier generations did not make the distinctions between children and adults that we do. Historically, children who committed crimes were treated the same as adults. Earlier times were severe. In the 1700s, girls as young as 13 were burned at the stake for their crimes, and 8- and 10-year-old boys were hanged for theirs (Blackstone 1899).

Over the years came a shift in how children were viewed. As part of this cultural transformation, "teenagers" became a separate class of people. Previously, the teen years were just an age, much as ages 30 to 35 are now—there was nothing distinctive about them. As views changed, laws were passed that classified "juveniles" as a separate category in the criminal justice system (Platt 1979). This change in the law produced a new category of crime—**juvenile delinquency**—crime committed by those under age 18.

Watch on **MySocLab Video:** The U.S. Criminal Justice System: Juvenile Corrections

Extent of Juvenile Crime. Some juvenile delinquents commit what are called **status crimes**, behavior that is illegal only because of the individual's age, such as drinking alcohol, running away from home, or violating curfew. For the most part, status crimes are not what bother people about juvenile delinquency. Their primary subjective concerns are the other crimes shown in Figure 6.1.

FIGURE 6.1 ▸ Number of Juveniles[1] Arrested by Type of Offense

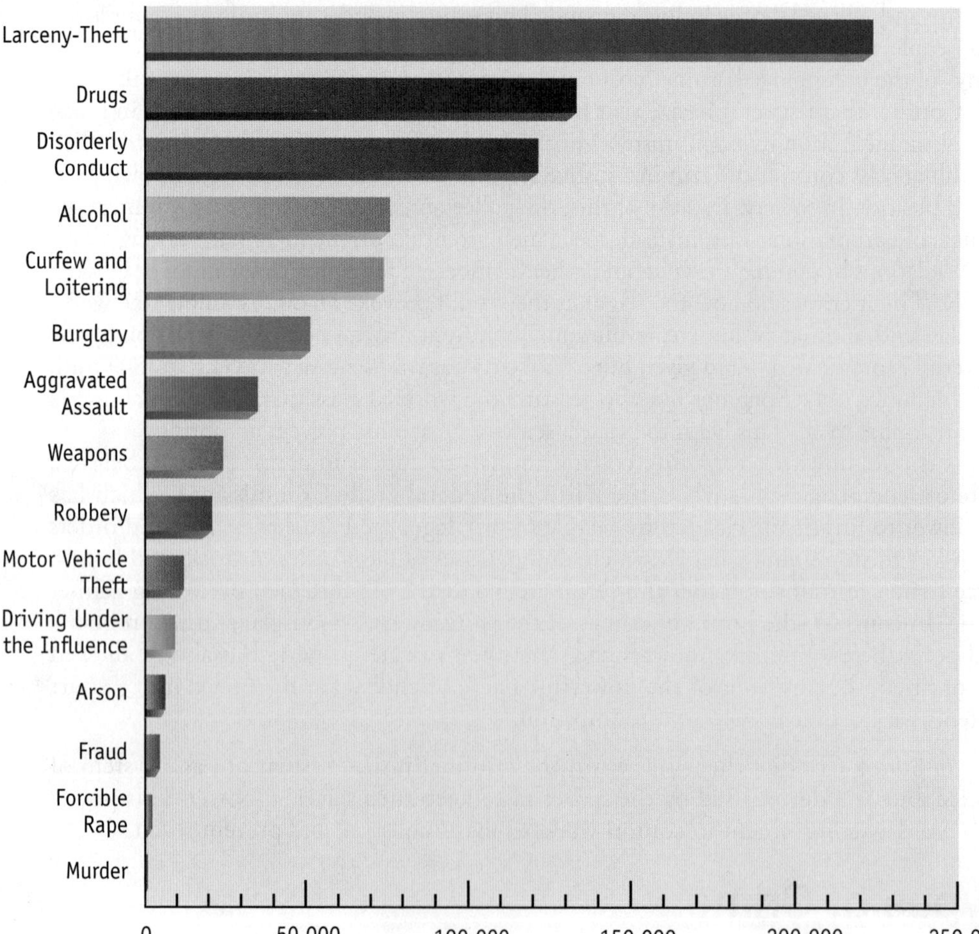

Source: By the author. Based on *Crime in the United States* 2011:Table 41.

[1]Persons under the age 18 arrested in one year.

The "Delinquent Career." When sociologist Howard Snyder (1988) had the opportunity to analyze the court records of 69,000 juvenile delinquents in Phoenix, Arizona, he grabbed it. Poring over these records, he uncovered what he called the "delinquent career," patterns that propel children into continued involvement in crime:

1. After their first arrest, most youths (59 percent) never return to juvenile court.
2. The juveniles most likely to continue delinquent behavior are those arrested a second time before age 16.
3. Juveniles who are charged with a violent crime are likely to have already committed many crimes.
4. The younger that juveniles are when first charged with a violent crime, the greater the likelihood that they will be charged with subsequent violent crimes. (Those charged at age 13 are *twice* as likely to be arrested for a later violent offense as are those first charged at age 16.)
5. The juveniles who are the *most* likely to be rearrested are those whose first charge was burglary, truancy, motor vehicle theft, or robbery.
6. The juveniles who are the *least* likely to be rearrested are those whose first charge was underage drinking, running away, or shoplifting.
7. Girls are less likely to be rearrested than boys.

The rate of women's involvement in both white-collar and street crime is increasing. This woman in prison garb in Philadelphia is charged with murder.

The patterns that Snyder uncovered have been confirmed by other researchers (Forsyth et al. 2011). Since Snyder did his research, two main changes have occurred. You can see these changes on Table 6.2. The first is the extraordinary drop in juvenile crime. Despite there being so many more juveniles now than 30 years ago, the total number of arrests for violent crimes is almost the same, while the arrests for property crimes is less than half of what it used to be. The second change is the much greater involvement of juvenile girls in crime. As you can see, since 1981 the girls' share of arrests for property crimes has doubled. For violent crimes, the girls' increase isn't far behind this.

Neutralizing Deviance. Juvenile delinquents know that their crimes are condemned by society, and yet many manage not to feel guilty about what they do. How they manage this is the focus of the Thinking Critically about Social Problems box on the next page.

Listen on **MySocLab**
Audio: Jim Henslin: Deviance

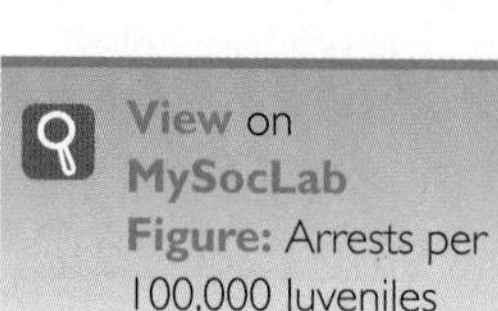

View on **MySocLab**
Figure: Arrests per 100,000 Juveniles Ages 10–17, 1980–2008

TABLE 6.2 ▸ Arrests of Juveniles, by Sex

	Number of Arrests				Percentage of Arrests		
	1981	2000	2010	Change from 1981	1981	2000	2008
Violent Crimes[1]							
Boys	47,415	48,169	43,968	−7%	89%	82%	82%
Girls	5,825	10,686	9,916	+70%	11%	18%	18%
Property Crimes[2]							
Boys	398,924	218,816	170,606	−57%	81%	70%	62%
Girls	95,010	94,888	105,855	+11%	19%	30%	38%

[1]Violent crimes are murder, forcible rape, robbery, and aggravated assault.
[2]Property crimes are burglary, larceny-theft, motor vehicle theft, and arson.
Sources: By the author. Based on *Crime in the United States* 2001:Table 37; *Sourcebook of Criminal Justice Statistics* 1993:Table 35; 2011:Table 4.9. 2010.

Thinking Critically About Social Problems

How to Be "Bad" But Think of Yourself as "Good"

In their classic research on juvenile delinquents, sociologists Gresham Sykes and David Matza (1957) were struck by how little guilt the boys they were studying felt about their crimes. As they listened to the boys, they uncovered what they call **techniques of neutralization**, ways that people deflect social norms. Here is a summary of the five techniques of neutralization that Sykes and Matza found:

1. *Denial of responsibility*. The boys think of themselves as propelled by forces beyond their control. Their unloving parents, bad companions, or bad neighborhoods cause them to break the law. By denying responsibility, they break the link between themselves and their acts. ("I'm just a billiard ball on the pool table of life.")
2. *Denial of injury*. The boys admit that their acts are illegal, but deny that they hurt anyone. They call their vandalism "mischief," "pranks," or "just having a little fun." This breaks the link between them and the consequences of their acts.
3. *Denial of a victim*. If the boys admit that they have done harm, they claim that the injury was not wrong "under the circumstances." The person they hurt was not really a victim. All they did was just "get even" for some wrong. Vandalizing a school, for example, is revenge on unfair teachers; theft is retaliation against gouging storekeepers. Someone they beat up deserved it because he mouthed off to them. With no victims, they transform themselves from wrongdoers into avengers.
4. *Condemnation of the condemners*. Delinquents also take the offensive. They call those who condemn them hypocrites. They accuse the police of being brutal or "on the take." By attacking others, they deflect attention away from their own behavior.

What techniques of neutralization do you think these individuals are using? They are serving on the nation's only chain gang for juveniles, in Maricopa County, Arizona.

5. *Appeal to higher loyalties*. Some delinquents see themselves as caught between two incompatible expectations. The law pulls them one way, loyalty to friends another. The friends win out. If a rival gang hurts a friend, for example, to retaliate is "more moral" than to ignore the injury.

These techniques allow delinquents to neutralize society's norms. Even if delinquents have internalized mainstream values—and not all have—these rationalizations let them commit crimes with a minimum of guilt or shame.

For Your Consideration

Do you see how these techniques of neutralization apply to yourself? We usually precede our neutralizations (rationalizations) with something like, "I couldn't help it because . . ." or "I know I shouldn't have, but I did it because . . ." How have you or people you know used each of these five techniques of neutralization? Which one did you use most recently? Under what circumstances? They do help us sleep at night.

Delinquent Subcultures. Some delinquents have little or no need to neutralize their lawbreaking. They grow up in **delinquent subcultures**, groups in which criminal activities are a normal part of everyday life. In these subcultures, they learn norms that support crime, as well as techniques for committing burglaries, robberies, and so on (Fabio et al. 2011). For an example of such a subculture, see the Thinking Critically box on the next page.

Education and Delinquency. "If we can keep them in school, we can keep them out of trouble. If they drop out, they're lost" is a common sentiment, one that is borne out by sociological research. Those who graduate from high school are less likely to commit crimes (Rosen et al. 1991; Lochner 2004), and almost half (40–46 percent) of those in prisons and jails have not finished high school (*Sourcebook of Criminal Justice Statistics* 2003:Table 6.45). It is costly to educate high school students, but it costs society much more to let them drop out. Based on a study in California, each high school graduate saves the criminal justice

Thinking Critically About Social Problems

Islands in the Street: Urban Gangs in the United States

For more than 10 years, sociologist Martín Sánchez Jankowski (1991) did participant observation of thirty-seven gangs in Boston, Los Angeles, and New York City. The gangs were made up of African Americans, Chicanos, Dominicans, Irish, Jamaicans, and Puerto Ricans. They earned money by gambling, arson, mugging, armed robbery, and selling moonshine, drugs, guns, stolen car parts, and protection. Jankowski ate, slept, and sometimes fought with the gangs, but by mutual agreement he did not participate in drug dealing or in other illegal activities. He was seriously injured twice during the study.

Jankowski's research breaks stereotypes. The motive for joining a gang was not to escape a broken home (there were as many members from intact families as from broken homes), nor was it to seek a substitute family (the same number of boys said they were close to their families as those that said they were not). The reasons were to gain access to money, to maintain anonymity in committing crimes, to get protection, and to have fun (this included access to girls and drugs). The boys also gave a reason that might sound strange to your ears—they wanted to help the community. To understand this, you need to know that in some neighborhoods gangs protect residents from outsiders and spearhead political change (Martinez 2003). There was one more reason: The boys saw the gang as an alternative to the dead-end—and deadening—jobs held by their parents.

Jankowski looked beyond the fierce exterior to get the inside story of gang members. This photo is from Los Encinos, Texas.

Neighborhood residents are ambivalent about gangs. On the one hand, they fear the violence. On the other hand, many adults once belonged to gangs, the gangs often provide better protection than the police, and gang members are the children of people who live in the neighborhood.

Particular gangs will come and go, but gangs will likely always remain part of the city. As functionalists point out, gangs fulfill needs of poor youth who live on the margins of society.

For Your Consideration

What are the needs that youth gangs meet (the functions they fulfill)? Suppose that you have been hired as an urban planner by the City of Los Angeles. How could you arrange to meet the needs that gangs meet in ways that minimize violence and encourage youth to follow mainstream norms?

system about $32,000 and crime victims about $80,000. Over a lifetime, each high school graduate also generates about $500,000 in benefits to the government (Belfield and Levin 2009). This is one case where common sense and sociological research support each other.

White-Collar Crime

> *After flashing photos of executives from Enron and Arthur Andersen on the television monitor, Jon Stewart, the anchor of* The Daily Show, *turned to the camera and shouted, "Why aren't all of you in jail? And not like white-guy jail—jail jail. With people by the weight room going, 'Mmmmm.'" (Leaf 2004)*

6.7 Be familiar with criminogenic cultures, lethal white-collar crime, embezzlement, theft, and the relationship of gender and social class to white-collar crime.

When corporate scandals hit the news, we learn about top executives who have stolen outrageous amounts of money. As with Madoff, Stanford, and Stewart, a handful of white-collar criminals receives stiff sentences for their crimes. But the treatment of white-collar offenders in the criminal justice system generally is easy and their sentences light. Let's explore this.

Criminogenic Subcultures. Back in 1940, sociologist Edwin Sutherland coined the term **white-collar crime** to refer to crimes "committed by people of respectable and high social status in the course of their occupation." He was referring to lawyers who rob people not by guns but by fake documents, executives who authorize products they know have defects that will harm their buyers, and corporations that gain sales by false advertising.

Some executives work within a *criminogenic subculture*, that is, a work environment that encourages and supports the commission of crime. With its high pressure to increase profits and to climb the corporate ladder, in this kind of subculture cutting corners is winked at, even encouraged. If executives are insulated from the consequences of their decisions, which is usually the case, the result can be "ethical numbness," feeling that it is okay to violate the law to gain profits and personal success (Hills 1987).

White-Collar Crimes That Kill. Even old-name, respected corporations participate in white-collar crime—sometimes with devastating results. Lysteria is a deadly disease that food factories must continually guard against. If they let their guard down, they can send poisoned food to the public. In a Sara Lee factory producing Ball Park Franks, the company stopped testing for listeria. Fifteen people who ate Sara Lee's infected hot dogs died. How many executives do you think were sent to prison for life for these murders? None. How about for even 10 or 15 years? Not a chance. Sara Lee pled guilty to two misdemeanors and paid a fine (Mauer 2004).

At first glance, you might think I'm exaggerating—and I wish I were—but even "household name" corporations produce criminogenic subcultures, some so calculatingly brutal that executives plan cold-blooded murder for profit. You might want to read the Thinking Critically box on the next page.

Cold, calculating, homicidal decisions by respected automobile executives—you might think that something like this would never be repeated. Unfortunately, it was—and again by executives of an automobile company. This time it was GM. In 1998, a 13-year-old boy was burned to death when the gas tank of an Oldsmobile Cutlass ruptured. When GM was sued, another smoking memo was discovered. In this one, GM calculated that it would cost only $4.50 per car to fix the problem. GM also figured that the cost of lawsuits would average just $2.40 per car. For an estimated $2.10 savings per car, GM executives decided not to fix the problem (Boot 1998). At their meeting, no one probably shouted, "Let them die!" But that certainly was their decision.

The Pinto and Cutlass cases confirm the perspective of conflict theorists: The powerful can and do manipulate our legal system. They can and do escape punishment for their crimes, including—and lets coin a term, *serial manslaughter*.

To pinpoint what the conflict theorists are really saying, let's reverse matters. What do you think would happen if poor people killed a couple of hundred automobile executives? How about just one or two? In asking these questions, with their obvious answers, we uncover the stunning contrast in the treatment of white-collar crime and street crime in the criminal justice system.

Embezzlement. Back in the 1950s, sociologist Donald Cressey (1953) did a study of embezzlers that became a classic in sociology. He found that embezzlers feel that they have an "unsharable financial problem"—overdue taxes, college expenses, a sick child, or gambling losses. Like juvenile delinquents, embezzlers also neutralize their crime. Many think of their embezzling as a form of borrowing—an unauthorized loan to tide them over during a financial emergency. They intend to pay it back. Some tell themselves that they deserve the money because they are worth more than they are being paid or because their employer has somehow taken advantage of them. As with juvenile delinquents, their techniques of neutralization are usually effective. Although they are stealing from their company, they still consider themselves to be respectable, law-abiding citizens.

Thinking Critically About Social Problems

The Case of the Exploding Pinto

The Pinto was a popular car manufactured by Ford in the 1970s. Following a rear-end crash, three young women in Indiana burned to death when their Pinto burst into flames. The Ford Motor Company was charged with reckless homicide (Strobel 1980; Fisse and Braithwaite 1987). No executives were charged, just Ford itself. It was alleged that Ford knew that in a rear-end collision the Pinto's gas tank could rupture, spew gas, and burn passengers to death (Dowie 1977, 1979). Never mind how a corporation can know anything. The commonsense view is that it is people in the corporation who know things, and they who make criminal decisions. Common sense and the legal system, however, often part ways and walk different paths.

Heart-wrenching evidence that revealed the cold-blooded malice of Ford executives was revealed at the trial. It turned out that installing a cheap piece of plastic could have corrected the problem. The Ford executives faced a difficult decision—whether to pay the $11 per car that it would cost for this little piece of plastic or to sentence drivers and passengers to fiery deaths. Now, this is a difficult choice—at least it was for these executives. Look at the Ford memo below, which was revealed at the trial. The executives compared "Costs," what it would cost the company to install the plastic piece with what it would cost to pay the relatives of those who burned to death. Yes, just that cold blooded.

As you can see, the cost of installing the plastic was higher ($137 million) than what the executives figured Ford would have to pay ($49.5 million) if they allowed people to die. To save $87 million for the company, the executives decided to let 180 people burn to death. Their estimates turned out to be too low: Several hundred people burned to death. Many others were disfigured.

With connections and the right lawyers, some people get away with murder. Ford was acquitted. The company recalled its 1971–1976 Pintos to modify the fuel tank. It also launched a publicity campaign so it could maintain an image of a "good" company. Ford executives claimed that the internal memo was misunderstood. They said that it "related to a proposed federal safety standard and not to the overall design of the Pinto" (Fisse and Braithwaite 1987:253). Despite causing hundreds of deaths, not a single executive was tried in court. In fact, not a single one was even arrested. They remained free, wealthy, and respected in their communities.

For Your Consideration

Do you think that the Ford executives should have been punished by the criminal justice system? Why do you think they weren't? In your answer, apply materials in this chapter and Chapter 5.

Ford's Internal Memo on the Pinto. Benefits and Costs Relating to Fuel Leakage Associated with the Static Rollover Test Portion of FMVSS 208

BENEFITS.

Savings: 180 burn deaths, 180 serious burn injuries, 2,100 burned vehicles.
Unit cost: $200,000 per death, $67,000 per injury, $700 per vehicle.
Total benefit:
180 × ($200,000) + 180 × ($67,000) + 2,100 × ($700) = $49.5 million.

COSTS.

Sales: 11 million cars, 1.5 million light trucks.
Unit cost: $11 per car, $11 per truck.
Total cost: 11,000,000 × ($11) + 1,500,000 × ($11) = $137 million.

Sources: Dowie 1977; Strobel 1980:286.

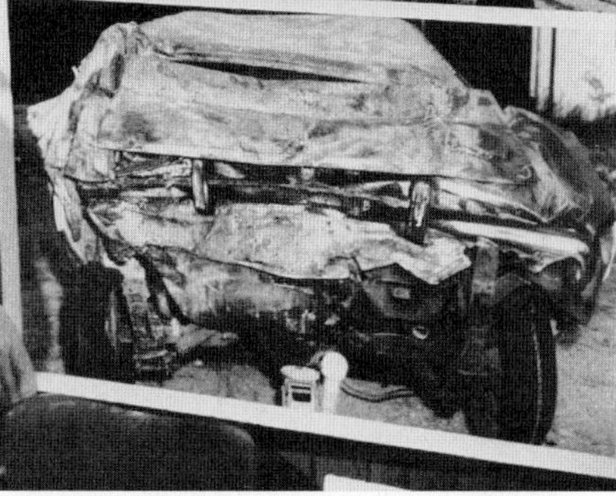

The top photo shows a 1973 Pinto that exploded when tested by Ford. At the bottom is the 1973 Ford Pinto in which three girls died after it was rear-ended.

Not all embezzlers neutralize their crimes (Green 1993). Some even embezzle without trying to justify anything. They just do it because they can (Benson 1985). Researchers have also found that embezzlers have many motives besides financial problems. Some embezzle on an impulse; others embezzle because they are greedy (Nettler 1974). I am sure that there is even "revenge embezzler," who is getting even with the boss, perhaps for some slight the employee feels. There is probably the "daring embezzler," too, who embezzles for the thrill of the act. There probably are also the "upwardly mobile" embezzlers, those who want to "better" themselves and gain a more prominent place in the community. These motives, and whatever others there might be, are yet to be borne out by research.

Employee Theft. When you think of employee theft, you are likely to think of employees stealing things that their company sells or manufactures. The restaurant employee shoving steaks out the back door might come to mind. This type of employee theft is common, but employee theft comes in many forms. Some steal company secrets, such as formulas, manufacturing processes, or even marketing plans. A gray area emerges when an employee goes to work for a competitor and brings knowledge inside his or her head. No documents are stolen, making this crime difficult to prove.

A case that made headlines was the theft of the Bratz dolls. Actually it was just the idea and sketch of the dolls that were stolen. Carter Bryant was a designer working for Mattel, the maker of the iconic Barbie doll. Bryant made some sketches of an idea he had for a new doll. He later went to work for MGA Entertainment, which turned his ideas into the Bratz dolls.

The Bratz were a thundering success—about $3 billion a year—threatening Barbie's dominance of the doll market. After a lot of detective work, Mattel was able to prove that Bryant had drawn his sketches while he was under contract to Mattel. The court ruled that Mattel, not MGA, had the rights to the Bratz dolls. MGA was also ordered to pay $100 million to Mattel (Hyland 2009).

As you can see, white-collar crime is tinged with gray areas. With the Bratz dolls, a judgment call could have gone either way. Perhaps Bryant thought that he had made the sketches on his own time. As sketches, they certainly weren't valuable, just a jumble of lines. The sketches became valuable only when the idea was turned into a successful product. Essentially, this is what an appeals judge decided, for in a later ruling a judge decided that MGA could keep the Bratz (Zimmerman 2010).

Watch on **MySocLab** **Video:** ABC 20/20: Justice and Privilege

Social Class and Crime. White-collar criminals enjoy a privileged position within the criminal justice system. While bank robbers risk their lives for $10,000 and are sentenced to years in prison, corporate executives who manipulate documents worth millions of dollars are at low risk of discovery and practically none of punishment. Because of their social position and ability to manipulate the law, few corporate criminals are punished. Some even get away with murder, as we saw with the Pinto and the Cutlass. Compared with street criminals (Carlson and Chaiken 1987), when arrested, white-collar criminals are

1. More likely to have their cases dismissed by the prosecutor and
2. Less likely to have to put up bail.

If convicted, white-collar criminals are

1. More likely to get probation rather than jail and
2. More likely to get shorter sentences.

It is rare for executives to be convicted for their crimes and, if convicted, unusual for them to serve even a single day in prison. In a study of the 582 largest U.S. corporations, sociologist Marshall Clinard found that criminal charges had been filed against 1,553 executives (Clinard et al. 1979; Clinard 1990). Only 56 of those executives were convicted, giving them better than a 96 percent chance of avoiding conviction if arrested. Of this small number, 40 served no time in prison. The 16 who did serve time averaged just 37 days—about what a poor person would serve for disorderly conduct. Of the 150,000 inmates in our federal prisons, only 1,000 are white-collar criminals (Leaf 2004). In a classic understatement, sociologist Daniel Glaser (1978) said that "criminal law has difficulty dealing with white-collar crime."

Gender in White-Collar Crime. As you saw on Table 6.2 on page 161, girls commit more violent and property crimes than they used to. We find something similar when we turn to white-collar crime, for like men, many women who join the corporate world are enticed by its illegal opportunities. From Table 6.3, you can see that women's share of white-collar crime has increased so much that today as many women as men are being arrested for embezzlement.

As women enter positions of power formerly held by men, they confront the same opportunities to misuse that power. Shown here is Jennifer Carol who was elected Lt. Governor of Florida. She resigned after federal authorities questioned her in a gambling investigation.

Professional Crime

6.8 Know what professional crime is and how professional criminals maintain their secrecy and values.

Crime as Work. People who consider crime to be their occupation are called **professional criminals**. Jewel thieves and counterfeiters—so highly romanticized in movies and novels—are examples of professional criminals. So are fences—those who buy stolen goods for resale. Their activities, although illegal, are a form of work, and they pride themselves on their skills and successes.

In a classic study, Edwin Sutherland (1937) found that professional criminals organize their lives around their "work," much as people who work at legal jobs do. Professional thieves plan their work and may steal almost every day of the year—taking vacations and days off to celebrate birthdays, anniversaries, and holidays. They associate with like-minded people who share their scorn for the "straight world," as well as their values of loyalty and mutual aid. They also teach one another technical skills for committing crimes and ways to avoid detection.

Unlike amateurs, professional criminals are not troubled by their criminality. They have neutralized norms successfully, and to them crime is simply a way to make a living. They see themselves as businesspeople, no different from clerks who sell shoddy merchandise or surgeons who perform unnecessary operations. As you can see from the *Personal Account* box on the next page, they view their activities as just another way of "making it" in U.S. society.

TABLE 6.3 ▸ Arrests for White-Collar Crimes, by Sex

	1981		2000		2010	
	Male	**Female**	**Male**	**Female**	**Male**	**Female**
Embezzlement	70%	30%	50%	50%	50%	50%
Fraud	58%	42%	55%	45%	58%	42%
Forgery and counterfeiting	68%	32%	61%	39%	62%	38%
Stolen property	88%	12%	83%	17%	80%	20%

Note: Not all these acts meet Sutherland's definition of white-collar crime, but from the categories available in the source, these are as close as we can come.

Source: By the author. Based on *FBI Uniform Crime Reports,* various editions, including *Crime in the United States* 2001:Table 42; 2011:Table 42.

Personal Account

Operating a "Chop Shop"

I was teaching an undergraduate course in the sociology of deviance. The usual problem of "What should I write about for my term paper?" came up. When a student told me about the connections he had with a "chop shop," I encouraged him to write his term paper on this topic.

Apparently, each large metropolitan area has at least one "chop shop," a place where stolen cars are "chopped," broken into their various parts. The owner of this "chop shop" in St. Louis, Missouri, kept informed of what parts were in demand. He would then order specific cars to be stolen, paying set prices according to the makes and models he ordered. He and his workers used acetylene torches and other tools to disassemble the cars. They sold the fenders, motors, transmissions, seats, doors, and so on to dealers in used auto parts. The small amount of metal that was left over was hauled away by an older man who sold it for scrap.

Like small business owners across the country, the owner-manager of the "chop shop" carried a great deal of responsibility. He made the business decisions, paid the rent on the shop, and met his weekly payroll. Unlike "straight" employers, however, he paid wages in cash and did not pay taxes. He also had to arrange for a surreptitious supply of oxygen for the acetylene torches. To buy oxygen from regular sources would have aroused suspicion, as he had no legitimate reason for the oxygen.

Like employees of any legitimate business, the workers at the "chop shop" formed a team, with each performing a specialized function. The difference, of course, was that each knew that they were working on stolen cars, a secret knowledge that bound them together. Because their work was risky, with the threat of arrest and prison hanging over their heads, the men needed ways to increase their loyalty, trust, and dependence on one another. In addition to the usual joking and bragging that working class men do at work, they also built a life together outside of work. After work and on weekends they drank at the same tavern, a bar where they could relax, since it was frequented by other professional criminals.

A "chop shop" in Missouri mysteriously burns after the police raided it earlier in the day. The gasoline can in the foreground could have something to do with it.

They also visited one another's homes. By integrating their working and social lives, these men minimized the intrusion of straight values, kept close tabs on one another, and reinforced ideas that the way they made a living was right and desirable.

In their research, sociologists report that professional criminals scorn the values of the straight world, pride themselves on their specialized skills, organize their lives around their work, and depend on in-group loyalty. My student found these traits to be evident among the workers in this "chop shop."

For Your Consideration

A basic principle of sociological research is to cause no harm to your subjects. Even though this was secondary or indirect research, I was careful not to ask my student about his relationship with the owner or workers of the "chop shop." It is likely that one was his relative, or perhaps a neighbor, a friend, or the relative of a friend. He might have even worked there himself. Do you think that sociologists are wrong to take this approach?

Could you ever be a professional criminal? Why or why not?

Organized Crime

6.9 Know what organized crime is and reasons for the Mafia's success.

The professional criminals we just discussed are local and independent. Now let's turn to **organized crime**, an organization of criminals which is part of a larger network, perhaps even national or international in scope.

The Mafia: Origins and Characteristics. The most famous organized crime group, the **Mafia**, originated in Sicily. As *The Godfather* series depicts, the Sicilian government was weak, and local strongmen united to protect their families and communities from bandits. After establishing control over an area, these men functioned as a private government. Like a government, they collected taxes (payments, tribute) in return for protecting their communities from other strongmen (Anderson 1965; Catanzaro 1992; Dimico et al. 2012). As the formal government extended its power from the capital, these men, entrenched in power, maintained their control over areas of Sicily. After the 1860s, they became known as the Mafia.

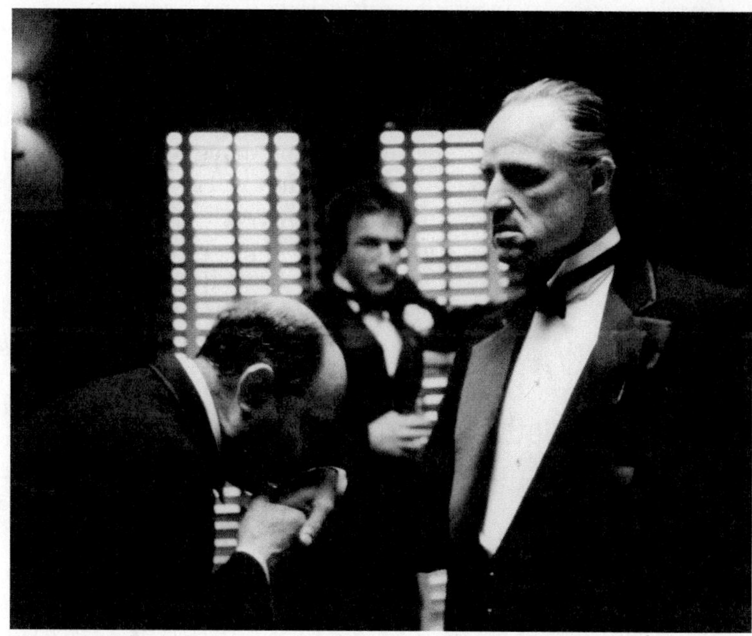

The Godfather, one of the most successful movies of all time, has become the basis for a stereotype of the Sicilian Mafia. As the text explains, there are other mafias as well, and various forms of organized crime.

Unlike the myth, the Sicilians (or Italians) did not introduce organized crime to the United States. Organized crime has gone through several ethnic successions. In New York City, the Irish used to dominate organized crime. They were succeeded by the Jews. Only after that did the Italians take over (Bell 1960). Today, several ethnic groups are involved in organized crime—not just the Sicilians and Italians, but among others also African Americans, Japanese, Puerto Ricans, and Russians (Wagman 1981; Barrett and Gardiner 2011).

In the Sicilian U.S. Mafia, about 5,000 members belong to about 24 "families" of 200 to 700 members each. The families are linked to each other by understandings and "treaties." The leaders of the most powerful families form a "commission" or "combine" to which the weaker families pay deference (Cressey 1969; Riesel 1982a). Members call this structure the Mafia, or **Cosa Nostra** ("our thing").

The Mafia continues to flourish—despite the U.S. government's perpetual "war" against it. A major business is loan-sharking, making private, illegal loans at high rates of interest. In some areas, the group controls the labor unions, the construction trade, and garbage hauling (Penn 1982; Riesel 1982b; Trust 1986). The Mafia also has infiltrated the garment industry of New York City. The gambling industry of Las Vegas was begun by organized crime, and the Mafia still has interests there.

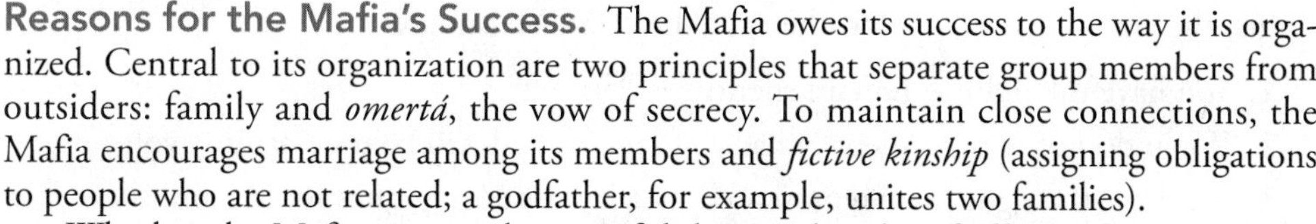

Reasons for the Mafia's Success. The Mafia owes its success to the way it is organized. Central to its organization are two principles that separate group members from outsiders: family and *omertá*, the vow of secrecy. To maintain close connections, the Mafia encourages marriage among its members and *fictive kinship* (assigning obligations to people who are not related; a godfather, for example, unites two families).

Why has the Mafia remained successful despite decades of efforts of the U.S. government to put it out of business? In addition to family ties and *omertá*, here are four more reasons:

1. Organized crime *is* organized. The Mafia has a *bureaucracy* with full-time specialists in different criminal activities.
2. Organized crime offers illegal *services in high demand* (prostitution, gambling, and loan-sharking)—with customers who participate willingly and do not complain to the police.
3. Organized crime wields influence through *political corruption.*
4. Organized crime uses *violence and intimidation* to control victims and its own members (*Organized Crime* 1976).

The Mafia's structure is so effective that from time to time the U.S. ruling class has called on it for help (Simon 1981). During the 1920s and the 1940s, periods of great labor unrest, corporations hired gangsters, especially autoworkers and longshoremen, to break strikes and infiltrate unions. During World War II, U.S. Navy Intelligence asked

Mafia boss Charles "Lucky" Luciano to protect the New York docks from sabotage. Luciano, who was directing Mafia operations from prison, agreed to do so. Luciano also helped get the Sicilian Mafia to support the U.S. invasion of Sicily, likely saving the lives of many U.S. soldiers. As a reward for his help, after the war Luciano was released from prison. Luciano thought he would be given citizenship, but he was deported to Italy.

Just as crime will continue, so will various versions of organized crime. The future of the Mafia, however, is uncertain. In recent years, *omertá* has weakened, and the FBI has infiltrated the organization. With the use of powerful surveillance devices, mobster confessions, and grand jury indictments, even top Mafia bosses have been convicted. One of these bosses, John Gotti, captured the public's attention. Despite his crimes, which included murder, Gotti was romanticized and became a darling of the media. Gotti was convicted and died in prison. His son, also named John, took over the Gambino crime family. When the son was put on trial, he amazed law enforcement by convincing jurors that he had seen the light and left his criminal ways (O'Connor 2010).

The Mafia as a whole appears to be in decline, but it is too soon to sound its death knell. For decades, this group has been adapting to changing circumstances, and it likely will continue to do so for some time.

The Criminal Justice System

6.10 Explain why plea bargaining, bias, recidivism, the death penalty, and the prison experience are part of the criminal justice system as a social problem.

We cannot fully understand crime as a social problem without examining the criminal justice system. To illustrate how this system works let's follow the case of Buddy, Gary, and Clyde.

Plea Bargaining

Following a Case. On a Saturday night, Buddy Hudson, a 19-year-old African American, teamed up with two whites, Gary Carson, 34, and Clyde Johnson, 21, to rob a liquor store. The robbery netted them $2,590. After a week's spending spree—their dreams of drugs and women realized—they tried their luck again. This time, though, their luck ran out. When an alarm went off, they fled, but a patrol car was in the area and they were arrested.

To ensure that the courts could not throw the case out for violating the suspects' rights, the arresting officers read the men the 1966 Miranda warning:

1. You have the right to remain silent.
2. If you do not remain silent, what you say can and will be used against you.
3. You have the right to be represented by a lawyer during questioning and thereafter.
4. If you cannot afford an attorney, the state will provide one at its expense.

The state did provide an attorney. Her advice was to say nothing. She would talk to the prosecuting attorney, who would determine what crimes the suspects would be charged with. After meeting with the state's attorney, she told the men that the evidence against them was solid. They would be charged with armed robbery, resisting arrest, and assault with a deadly weapon. They could go to prison for up to 40 years. She added that she thought she could "cut a deal" and get the charges of assault and resisting arrest dropped in return for a guilty plea to armed robbery. If so, she could get them a 5-to-7 (a minimum of 5 years and a maximum of 7 years in state prison).

The men figured that they could do better if they went to trial. Clyde's mother put up $20,000 to secure her son's release on bond. Unable to raise bond money, Buddy and Gary remained in jail during the 9 months it took for their case to come to trial. (Nine months? See the Issues in Social Problems box on the next page.) Just before the trial, to everyone's surprise, Clyde pled guilty. The judge suspended Clyde's sentence and placed him on probation for 5 years. Buddy and Gary were found guilty of armed robbery. The judge gave Gary a 6-year sentence and Buddy a sentence of 10 to 15 years.

Issues in Social Problems

You Don't Have to Be Poor to Go to Jail—But It Helps

Richard Garrett of Harpersville, Alabama, who is unemployed, couldn't pay his fine for traffic and license violations. He spent 24 months in jail. With interest and collection fees being added, the amount Garrett owes keeps increasing and has reached $10,000.

It isn't a crime to be poor, but poverty doesn't help when you're in trouble with the law. If you can't pay a fine, you go to jail.

"It's the only practical alternative," said Woodrow Wilson, a judge in Bastrop, Louisiana. "Otherwise, some people would never be punished."

In courtrooms across the nation, defendants with ready cash pay and leave. Those without money are ushered from the courtroom to the city jail to pay their debts with days rather than dollars—or to wait until someone bails them out.

In rural areas especially, authorities routinely jail defendants who can't pay fines for minor crimes such as public drunkenness and speeding. They jail the poor even though this violates U.S. Supreme Court rulings. Although legal aid lawyers protest that it is unjust to give better treatment to defendants who have money, indigent defendants keep winding up in jail.

The economic crisis has made things worse. The courts and police are looking for ways to pay for pensions, for police training, even for computers. Many courts are adding "user fees" to those who "use" the courts—that is, to those who are arrested.

Judges and prosecutors claim not to know which defendants are poor. "If they raised the issue, they wouldn't be put in jail," said an Aurora, Colorado, city attorney, "but I don't see that it's the responsibility of the court or the prosecutor to check out their ability to pay fines."

The woman on the right is meeting her public defense attorney for the first time. How do you think her poverty might affect her chances of conviction?

It certainly must be difficult to tell the difference. Are the people sitting in jail for petty offenses poor? Or do they have plenty of money but prefer jail rather than going to their jobs or being home with their families? Really hard to tell.

Some officials have tried, or at least have given the appearance of trying. In Monroe, Louisiana, officials hired a priest to evaluate defendants' finances. They let him go, though, because he sided with the poor too often.

The idea that the courts should be "pay-as-you-go" or that they should produce income to pay for themselves is not part of the American system. To expect this is to pervert justice for the poor.

As Jackie Yeldell, a Bastrop attorney, said, "You can be sure there aren't any wealthy persons in jail."

Based on Schmitt 1982; Bronner 2012; Reynolds and Hall 2012.

For Your Consideration

Do you agree with the judge who said that the only practical alternative is to put poor people in jail, "otherwise, some people would never be punished"? If not, what alternatives can you think of?

When a reporter asked about the differences in sentencing, the judge replied, "I have to show consideration for the defendant who cops a plea. It saves the court the expense of a trial" (Gaylin 1974:188–189). He added that Clyde had a job and that to send him to prison would serve no purpose. Letting him keep his job, however, would increase Clyde's chances of staying out of trouble. When the reporter cautiously said that some people might think that Buddy's longer sentence might have something to do with Buddy being an African American, the judge said, "Race has nothing to do with this case. These are just facts: Gary Carson is older, but he has fewer 'priors' (previous arrests). He doesn't need as stiff a sentence to teach him a lesson. Buddy's 'priors' tell me he's more dangerous."

Explore on **MySocLab**
Activity: The Justice System: Stereotypes of Crime and Justice

Note the principles from this case that illustrate how the criminal justice system can be "more criminal than just" (Newman 1966; Gaylin 1974; Pattis 2005):

1. Some of the poor spend months (even years) behind bars awaiting trial, while those with money use the bond system to buy their release.
2. Defense attorneys encourage plea bargaining, *whether or not the individual is guilty.* In urging his client to accept a jail sentence, one public defender said, "Even if you're innocent, it's a good deal" (Penn 1985).
3. Prosecutors use threats of longer sentences to get guilty pleas. ("Plead guilty to this lesser charge, or I'll charge you with this other crime, which carries a longer sentence.")
4. Judges dislike "unnecessary trials" and impose harsher sentences on those who insist on them.
5. Age, employment, and the number of previous arrests affect sentencing. Even when offenses are the same, those who have better employment histories are given more lenient sentences.
6. The *number of arrests,* not the seriousness of the charges, influences a sentence. Judges often discount the type of charge because they know that plea bargaining changes what people are officially charged with.

Assembly-Line Justice. What is wrong with plea bargaining? We can start with something quite basic: The Sixth Amendment to the Constitution guarantees people accused of a crime the right to be judged by their peers in a "speedy and public" trial. As with Buddy, Gary, and Clyde, in *almost all* cases the trial has been replaced with plea bargains, arrangements worked out behind the scenes (Savitsky 2012). To get people to plead guilty and avoid a trial, prosecutors charge them with more serious crimes and then offer to accept a guilty plea to lesser offenses. As a result, judges and juries hear only *6 percent* of criminal cases (*Sourcebook of Criminal Justice Statistics* 2011:Table 5.46).

What about defense attorneys, provided for free to the poor? Despite their obligation to *defend* their clients, public *defense* attorneys usually suggest to them that they plead guilty (Blumberg 1967; Maynard 1984). As sociologist Abraham Blumberg (1967) noted back in the 1960s, despite their formal job description public defenders develop "implicit understandings" about what their job *really* is: to be team players who produce "assembly-line justice" for the poor. This same process continues.

Can things get worse? With the economic crisis, some public defenders are refusing cases on the basis that they are too overworked. Judges assign them cases anyway (Davey 2010).

Bias in the Criminal Justice System

Read on **MySocLab**
Document: Beyond Crime and Punishment: Prisons and Inequality

Let's discuss racial–ethnic discrimination in the criminal justice system. As you will recall, Buddy, the only African American in the trio, received the most severe sentence. The judge claimed that this was because of Buddy's "priors." What is the answer?

The issue of bias is complicated, and sociologists differ in their conclusions. At first glance, the judicial system certainly seems to discriminate along racial–ethnic lines, especially when it comes to African Americans. Although African Americans make up just 13 percent of the population, they make up 45 percent of U.S. prison inmates (*Sourcebook* 2011:Table 6.34). From Table 6.4, you can see that the percentage of African Americans on death row is more than triple what you would expect from their percentage in the U.S. population. Overall, the criminal justice system has an overwhelming impact on African Americans: On any given day, one of every fourteen black males ages 25 to 34 is in prison—and this does not include the tens of thousands who are in jail (Guerino et al. 2011). Some estimate that one-third of all black males born today will spend time in prison (Mauer 2004).

TABLE 6.4 ▸ Prisoners on Death Row, by Race–Ethnicity

Race–Ethnicity	Number on Death Row	Percentage of Death Row Inmates	Percentage of U.S. Population	More (+) or Less (–) Than What You Would Expect from the Group's Percentage of the U.S. Population[1]
White	1,398	43.4%	65.1%	–33%
African American	1,346	41.8%	12.9%	+324%
Latino	397	12.3%	15.8%	–22%
Asian American	42	1.3%	4.6%	–71%
Native American	36	1.1%	1.0%	+10%
Totals	3,219	100%	100%	

[1]This total is computed by dividing the difference between the group's percentage of the U.S. population and its percentage of death row inmates by its percentage of the U.S. population.

Source: By the author. Based on *Sourcebook of Criminal Justice Statistics* 2012:Table 6.80; *Statistical Abstract of the United States* 2012:Table 11.

These data do *not* let us draw conclusions about bias, however, because they do not account for differences of crime among racial–ethnic groups. We need to compare arrest rates and crime rates. We can do this by comparing arrest rates with what crime victims report about the race–ethnicity of their offenders. When we do this, we end up with mixed results. For some offenses, African Americans are arrested at a higher rate than what the victims report, but for other offenses whites are arrested at a higher rate than what the victims report (*Sourcebook of Criminal Justice Statistics* 2011:Tables 3.29, 4.10).

Granted the racism in U.S. society, it would be counter to reason to assume that there was no bias in the criminal justice system. Here is some of the research that shows this bias. Sociologists Douglas Smith and Christy Visher (1981) trained civilians to ride with the police in Missouri, New York, and Florida. When Smith and Visher analyzed the records of almost 6,000 encounters between police and citizens, they concluded that the police are more likely to arrest African American suspects. Sociologist Gary LaFree (1980) examined the court records of a Midwestern city and found that African Americans who raped white women received more severe sentences than white men who raped white women. In the federal courts, African Americans who commit the same crimes as whites and whose background is similar receive longer sentences (Rhavi and Starr 2012).

Other studies, in contrast, show that bias works in *both* directions, that whites sometimes get more favorable treatment, but at other times minorities do. Here is some of this research. African Americans are given longer prison terms for rape and drugs, but whites receive longer sentences for murder (Butterfield 1999). Latinos are more likely than whites to have their charges dismissed, but if they go to trial they are more likely to be sent to prison (Tinker 1981). Minority suspects are more likely than whites to be released after arrest, but if convicted they are more likely to be given longer sentences (Petersilia 1983). Latinos and whites receive about the same sentences for assault, robbery, burglary, theft, and forgery, but when it comes to drug offenses Latinos are more likely to be sent to prison (Klein et al. 1990). In areas where blacks are a numerical majority, whites are more likely than blacks to be sentenced to prison (Myers and Talarico 1986:246).

At this point, then, we cannot conclude that the courts are biased for or against minorities or for or against whites. The evidence is mixed and not conclusive.

Recidivism

The Revolving Door of America's Prisons.

When inmates are asked "Do you think you could commit the same crime again without getting caught?" about half answer yes. (Zawitz 1998)

If the goal of prisons is to rehabilitate their guests, they are a gross failure. **Recidivism** refers to former prisoners committing more crimes. Look at Figure 6.2, which reports a follow-up study of 272,000 people who were released from prison. You can see that within just 3 years of their release from prison, two out of three prisoners have been arrested, and over half are back in prison. Since this research, the rates have dropped slightly ("State of Recidivism . . ." 2011).

FIGURE 6.2 ▸ Recidivism: What Happens After Prison?

Within a year of release from prison, 44 percent of prisoners were rearrested; within 3 years, 68 percent were rearrested and about half were back in prison.

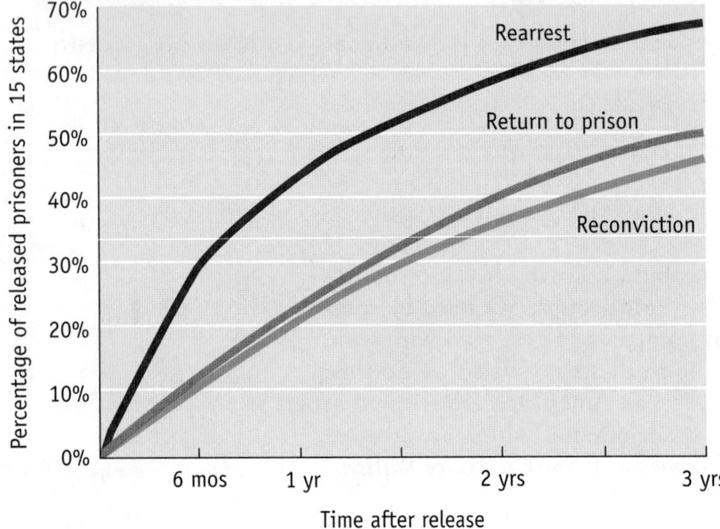

Source: Langan and Levin 2002.

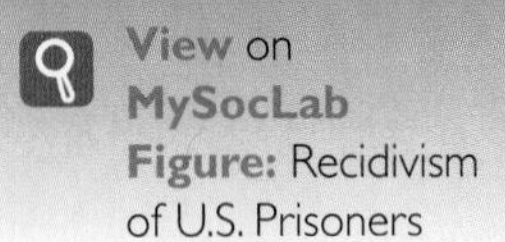

View on MySocLab
Figure: Recidivism of U.S. Prisoners

You might be wondering about the crimes that these former prisoners committed after their release from prison. These statistics, too, are enlightening—and, some would say, frightening. As Table 6.5 on the next page shows, the two-thirds who were rearrested within 3 years of their release were charged with *750,000 new crimes*, an average of 4 each. About 100,000 of these charges were for violent crimes. If we add the number of crimes these individuals were charged with before they were released from prison, we find that the total comes to an astounding 4 million crimes, including 22,000 rapes and 18,000 murders.

Keep in mind that these totals, as high as they are, are less than the actual number of crimes committed. How can we be certain of this? Simply put, few people are caught when they commit their first crime after being released from prison, so, on average, offenders commit more crimes than they are charged with.

The likelihood of recidivism differs by sex, race–ethnicity, and age. Women, whites, and older former prisoners are less likely to get in trouble with the law again (Langan and Levin 2002). Age at release is especially interesting. The older that people are when they come out of prison, the less likely they are to be rearrested and go back to prison. It might be that the older former convicts have learned to stay away from crime. Or it could be that they have learned to avoid getting caught. Or maybe they are just tired.

Researchers have found that, when they are released, *those who have been in prison the most often have the greater their chances of going back to prison.* Grasp the significance of this finding: If prisons were rehabilitating their inmates, the *opposite* of this would happen.

Why Do Our Prisons Fail to Rehabilitate? There are many reasons that our prisons fail to rehabilitate, but here is one: They are socializing agents for criminal behavior. People who have been declared unfit to live in normal society are housed together in prison. One of their favorite topics of conversation over the years is crime. Just as most men boast of their accomplishments to one another, these men boast of theirs—the crimes they've gotten away with and the crimes they'd like to commit. Older, more experienced prisoners also teach younger ones how to commit crimes. It is an irony, of course, that the models for the younger prisoners are criminals who have failed: *All* these mentors have been caught and are serving time in prison.

Here is another reason for our high recidivism: When prisoners are released, they go back to their old environment with no new skills to lead a straight life. Here's how sociologist Gregg Scott (2004) put it:

Over two million men and women are confined to jails and prisons in the U.S. Ninety percent of them eventually return home. After having served a median prison term of 15 months,

TABLE 6.5 ▸ Recidivism: Committing Crime After Prison

Arrest Charge	Number of Arrest Charges in First 3 Years After Prison, of 272,000 Ex-Convicts
All offenses	744,480
Violent Offenses	100,531
Murder[1]	2,871
Kidnapping	2,362
Rape	2,444
Other sexual assault	3,151
Robbery	21,245
Assault	54,604
Other violent	13,854
Property Offenses	208,451
Burglary	40,303
Larceny/theft	79,158
Motor vehicle theft	15,797
Arson	758
Fraud	21,360
Stolen property	21,993
Other property	29,082
Drug Offenses	191,347
Possession	79,435
Trafficking	46,220
Other/unspecified	65,692
Public-Order Offenses	155,751
Weapons	25,647
Probation/parole violations	20,930
Traffic offenses	13,097
Driving under the influence	5,788
Other public-order	90,280
Other Offenses	20,049
Unknown	68,351

[1] Murder includes non-negligent manslaughter and negligent manslaughter.
Source: Sourcebook of Criminal Justice Statistics 2003:Table 6.52.

approximately 1,600 inmates disgorge from state and federal prisons every single day of the week. In the greater Chicago metropolitan area alone roughly 1,500 male ex-convicts return to their neighborhoods each month. They arrive home "wearing an X" on their backs, possessing meager skills of limited portability, and enjoying scanty resources on which to draw in their efforts to "make good," or live a life on the straight and narrow path of desistance. They almost always return to the same disaffected, marginalized neighborhoods in which they resided prior to incarceration but which now offer even fewer legitimate opportunities than before. The majority will stray from the path and wander into a gnarled grove of institutional failure, criminal opportunity, and the uniquely rewarding but ultimately self-defeating whorl of drug dealing and otherwise hustling street gangs.

The Death Penalty

If you bring up the death penalty, or **capital punishment**, in a discussion, you are sure to touch raw nerves. Like attitudes about abortion, opinions are strong. Let's get a little sociological background on the death penalty.

Throughout history, many methods of execution have been used, such as stoning, suffocating, bleeding, firing squads, gas chambers, electrocution, and lethal injection. Shown here is "Black Jack" Ketchum in 1901, who is about to be hanged in Clayton, New Mexico.

Race–Ethnicity. Donald Partington, a lawyer, who was disturbed at what he saw in the courtrooms of Virginia, decided to do some research. He (Partington 1965) examined all executions for rape and attempted rape in that state between 1908 and 1963. Convicted of these crimes were 2,798 men (56 percent white and 44 percent African Americans). Forty-one of these men were executed for rape and thirteen for attempted rape. *All the executed men were African Americans. Not one white man was executed for this crime.*

When judges used to give the death penalty for rape, what really made the difference was the race of the attacker *and* the race of the victim. In their study of rape and capital punishment in Georgia, sociologists Marvin Wolfgang and Marc Reidel (1975) found this: The best predictor of whether a man would be sentenced to death was knowing that the victim was white and the accused black.

In 1972, bias in the death penalty was brought before the Supreme Court. The justices looked at data such as those in the top half of Table 6.6. You can see that at that point 3,859 prisoners had been executed: 54 percent African American and 45 percent white. The Court ruled in *Furman v. Georgia* that capital punishment was being applied unconstitutionally—in a discriminatory fashion. In response to this decision, the states rewrote their laws, and since then 57 percent of those put to death have been white and 34 percent African American.

TABLE 6.6 ▸ Prisoners Executed, by Race–Ethnicity

	WHITE		AFRICAN AMERICAN		NATIVE AMERICAN/ ASIAN AMERICAN		LATINOS		
Year	**Number**	**Percentage**	**Number**	**Percentage**	**Number**	**Percentage**	**Number**	**Percentage**	**Total**
Before the death penalty was abolished									
1930–39	827	50%	816	49%	24	1%			1,667
1940–49	490	38%	781	61%	13	1%			1.284
1950–59	336	47%	376	52%	5	1%			717
1960–69	98	51%	93	49%	0	0%			191
Totals	**1,751**	**45%**	**2,066**	**54%**	**42**	**1%**			**3,859**
Since the death penalty was reinstated									
1970–79	3	100%	0	0%	0	0%	0	0%	3
1980–89	60	51%	48	41%	0	0%	9	8%	117
1990–99	271	58%	163	35%	10	0%	34	7%	478
2000–09	338	57%	200	34%	4	1%	48	8%	590
2010	28	61%	13	28%	0	0%	5	11%	46
Totals	**700**	**57%**	**424**	**34%**	**14**	**1%**	**96**	**8%**	**1,234**

Note: Until the 1970s, the Native American/Asian American category was "Other" and included Latinos. The source says that Latinos have been counted separately since 1977. This is most doubtful, as no Latinos are listed as executed until 1985, and until 2010 the number is disproportionate to the percentage of Latinos in the population. It is likely that until recently most Latinos were counted as whites.

Source: By the author. Based on *Sourcebook of Criminal Justice Statistics* 1998:Table 6.88; 2004:Table 6.86; 2012:Table 6.86.

Gender. The death penalty apparently shows a strong gender bias: Of the 5,093 prisoners who have been executed since 1930, only 44 have been women, a mere 0.9 percent. Since 1976, 1,222 men have been executed, and only 12 women (*Statistical Abstract* 2013:Table 359). At present, only 1.8 percent of prisoners (58 of 3,158) on death row are women (*Sourcebook of Criminal Justice Statistics* 2011:Tables 6.82, 6.83). Do these totals indicate gender bias or real differences in the crimes they committed? We need more research to find out.

View on MySocLab Figure: Women and Men on Death Row

Geography. Geography certainly makes a huge difference in a person's chances of being executed, and there is no doubt about this factor. Look at the Social Map below. You can see that thirty-seven states have the death penalty while thirteen states do not. You can also see how much more willing some states are to execute prisoners than are others. Look at Texas, which holds the record for number of executions. Since executions resumed in 1977, more than one of every three (37 percent) have taken place in Texas. Texas has a large population, though, 26 million people. With its much smaller population of just 3.8 million and its 94 executions since 1977, Oklahoma has executed a higher proportion of its criminals.

The Prison Experience

Let's close this section by looking at a fascinating experiment that can help us understand what goes on behind prison bars.

The Zimbardo Experiment. Philip Zimbardo, a social psychologist, conducted an experiment that has become a classic in the social sciences. Using paid volunteers, Zimbardo (1972/2007) matched twenty-four college students on the basis of their education, race, and parents' social class. He randomly assigned one group as guards and the other as prisoners. Without warning, one night real police cars arrived at the homes of those who had been designated prisoners. They were "arrested," fingerprinted, and taken to the basement of the psychology building at Stanford University, which had been turned into a prison. Both "guards" and "prisoners" were given appropriate uniforms.

Watch on MySocLab Video: The Stanford Prison Experiment

Subject to the arbitrary control of their captors, the prisoners felt a loss of power and personal identity. The guards, in contrast, felt an increase in social power and status.

FIGURE 6.3 ▸ Executions in the United States

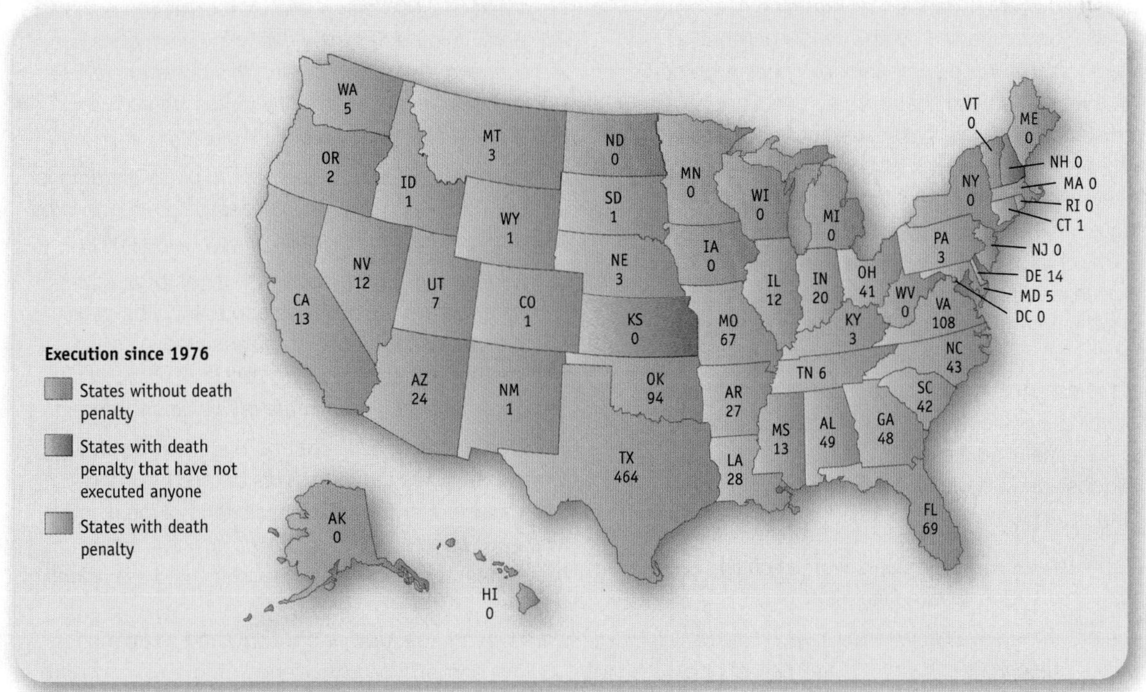

Source: By the author. Based on *Statistical Abstract of the United States* 2013:Table 360.

They also developed strong in-group loyalty. After several days, the guards heard rumors that there was going to be a prison break. They reacted brutally, with about a third treating the prisoners as though they were subhuman. Things started to get out of hand, and after 6 days Zimbardo stopped the experiment.

Zimbardo's experiment illustrates fundamental sociological principles: First, our ideas about the self and other people arise from the way society is structured and the groups to which we belong. Second, from these orientations come the ways we act toward one another. How a prison is organized, then, is more important in determining how guards and prisoners act than are their individual personalities. As guards work in a prison, they come to see themselves as representing morality and the prisoners as enemies who need to be subdued, not people who need to be helped. The guards see their job as maintaining order and upholding authority. If this requires brutality to accomplish, so be it. Being rough is justified. As the guards perform their role within this structure, they eventually come to see prisoners as "animals" who understand nothing but violence.

Zimbardo's experiment was important. It provides insight into what is wrong with our prisons. From it, we can see why prisons, as they are set up, fail to reduce crime. This experiment, though, created a stir in the scientific community. Some fellow social scientists accused Zimbardo of being cruel and irresponsible. With the publicity surrounding this and some other experiments, the federal government developed strict guidelines for research on human subjects. Today, Zimbardo's research couldn't be done, at least in the same way.

If prisons are not the answer, then what is? For an interesting alternative, read the Thinking Critically box on *shaming*.

Thinking Critically About Social Problems

Public Shaming as Social Policy

"Shame on you!"

Do you remember those horrifying words from your childhood? If your childhood was like mine, you do. The words were accompanied by an index finger that pointed directly at me, while another index finger, rubbing on top of it, seemed to send shame in my direction.

With a harsh voice or one that showed disappointment, this gesture was effective. I always felt bad when this happened. I felt even worse when I saw the looks of disappointment or disgust on the faces of my parents or grandparents in response to my childish offense, whatever it may have been.

If you have read Nathaniel Hawthorne's *The Scarlet Letter,* you know about shaming. Hester Prynne, who committed adultery, a serious offense at the time because it struck at the community's moral roots, had to wear a red A on her clothing. For life, wherever she went, she was marked as a shameful adulteress.

This old-fashioned device is coming back. Not the scarlet A, but its equivalent:

An Arizona sheriff makes inmates work in chain gangs, with the men dressed in pink.

A judge ordered thieves to wear sandwich boards that said, "I stole from this store." They had to parade back and forth outside the stores they stole from.

A Texas judge ordered a piano teacher who pled guilty to molesting his young students to give away his prized $12,000 piano and to not play the piano for 20 years. If you don't think this was harsh, consider the shaming that accompanied this punishment: He had to post a sign prominently on the door of his home declaring himself a child molester.

Judges have ordered drunk drivers to put bright orange bumper stickers on their cars that say, "I am a convicted drunk driver. Report any erratic driving to the police."

The Minneapolis police department has organized "shaming details." Prostitutes and their johns must stand handcuffed in front of citizens who let loose with "verbal stones," shouting things like "You're the reason our children aren't safe in this neighborhood!"

Kansas City tried a different approach to prostitution. "John TV" shows the mug shots of men who have been arrested for trying to buy sex and of the women who have been arrested for selling it. Their names, birth dates, and hometowns are displayed prominently.

Do you want to know where convicted sex offenders live? Just go online. Type sex offender and a zip code into your search engine, and they'll pop up on your computer

(continued from previous page)

screen. You can see their photos, names, addresses, dates of birth, description of the offense, convictions, and their current address. Some sites have clickable neighborhood maps on which the offenders' homes pop up. While this information is supposed to be intended to alert citizens to potential danger, it certainly is a powerful shaming device.

Shaming is an old method of punishment, intended to humiliate violators so they conform. This 1910 photo is from China.

Does shaming work? No one knows whether it reduces lawbreaking. But shaming certainly can be powerful. A woman who was convicted of welfare fraud was given the choice of going to jail or wearing a sign in public that said, "I stole food from poor people." She chose jail.

Even if shaming doesn't work, it does satisfy a strong urge to punish, to get even, what sociologists call retribution. In today's eager-to-punish climate, perhaps retribution is purpose enough. And perhaps it does help to restore a moral balance.

(Examples are based on Gerlin 1994; Belluck 1998b; Billeaud 2008; current events.)

For Your Consideration

If you were convicted of shoplifting, would you choose to go to jail for 3 days or to spend three Saturdays from 9 A.M. to 9 P.M. walking back and forth in front of the store you stole from, while holding a large sign that says, "I am a thief. I stole from this store"? Why?

Social Policy

6.11 Discuss retribution, deterrence, rehabilitation, and incapacitation as goals of social policy.

Two Overarching Principles: We can never eliminate these twin social problems of crime and criminal justice, but we can build a more just society. Here are two overarching basic principles to help us do so. For *criminal justice*: We need fair laws whose enforcement is evenhanded throughout society, regardless of people's race–ethnicity, gender, social class, or any other characteristics. For *crime:* Because street crime bothers Americans the most, and street crime is linked to poverty, the *best policy* would be to reduce poverty. Education is an effective way to reduce poverty because, on average, the further that people go in school, the better the jobs they get and the more they earn. In addition, because those who drop out of high school are more likely to end up in prison, programs that help students graduate from high school will help prevent crime, reducing its cost to victims and to society in general.

We will, of course, always have criminals, so we need effective policies for dealing with them. Let's consider the four basic approaches that are being used: retribution, deterrence, rehabilitation, and incapacitation.

Retribution

Paying for the Crime. The basic idea of retribution is to *punish* criminals to demonstrate to others that criminal behavior will not be tolerated. Offenders are thought of as needing to "pay" or "make up" for what they've done. The punishment, then, should fit the crime (Cohen 1940). The *public shaming* that you read about in the box above is an example of retribution. Look at the humiliation that the Chinese women were going through.

Another form of retribution is **restitution**, making offenders compensate their victims for the harm they have done. If people have stolen, for example, they are required to pay the money back. Restitution is practical for property crimes, when the offender can repay the victim. It is less practical for offenders who don't have jobs, although some judges require the unemployed to "work their debt off" in a variety of creative ways. Here are examples of trying to "make the punishment fit the crime":

A Memphis judge invited victims to visit the thief's house and "steal" something back (Stevens 1992).

A Florida judge sentenced a white man who had harassed an interracial couple to work weekends at an African American church.

A Texas judge ordered a deadbeat who had fathered thirteen children to attend Planned Parenthood meetings (Gerlin 1994).

For throwing beer bottles at a car and taunting a woman, a judge in Ohio sentenced two men to walk down the town's main street dressed in women's clothing (Leinwand 2004).

For crimes of violence, retribution might call for unusual measures, such as castration for rapists—acts that courts would declare unconstitutional. A California judge, for example, wanted to withhold AIDS treatment from a man who had raped two teenagers after he was released from prison for a previous rape (Farah 1995). Proponents say that severe crimes merit severe retribution, and for this we should change the Constitution.

Deterrence

Frightening People away from Crime. The purpose of **deterrence** is to make people afraid of punishment so they won't commit crime. This approach views offenders as rational people who weigh the possible consequences of their actions. They will avoid crime if punishment seems likely. Only a few sociologists have taken this "get tough" position. Back in the 1970s, criminologist Ernest van den Haag (1975; van den Haag and Conrad 1983) proposed that we treat juveniles who commit violent crimes the same way we treat adults ("adult crime, adult time"). He also said that we should abolish parole boards and put prisoners to work. With citizens demanding strong action, attempts at deterrence are popular.

Two Principles of Deterrence. Researchers have discovered two significant principles regarding deterrence. First, the longer the interval between a crime and its punishment, the less the deterrence, or fear of the punishment. This underscores the need for speedy trials, already guaranteed by the Constitution, and for swift punishment of the guilty. Second, the more uncertain the penalty, the less deterrence works. To meet this principle, some propose **uniform sentencing**, the same sentence given to everyone convicted of the same crime. The problem, of course, is that crimes are seldom "the same." Each crime involves many circumstances that judges and juries need to consider.

An inmate in a Pennsylvania prison tells teenaged boys what they can expect when they get to prison. "Scared Straight" had unexpected consequences.

Irrationality: Impulse and Taking Chances. Critics of deterrence point out that offenders are not always rational about committing crime. Many act on impulse. Others take such chances that you know they are not weighing the consequences of their actions in the same way most of us would. For example, back in the 1700s in England, pickpockets were hung in public. One might think that this punishment would stop this crime. Instead, when a pickpocket was being hung, other pickpockets worked the crowd. With the crowd's attention riveted on the gallows, the hanging provided easier victims (Hibbert 1963).

"Scared Straight: A Program that Backfired." The mass media once trumpeted a program of deterrence called "Scared Straight." Delinquents were given prison tours, with the expectation that a close-up view of prison would "scare them straight." Leering and shouting obscenities, the inmates said they could hardly wait for the youths to be sent to prison so they could rape them. Those who operated the program reported that it kept 80–90 percent of the youths from further trouble with the law. Follow-up studies by sociologists, however, showed that the program had actually backfired. Criminologist James Finckenauer (1982) matched delinquents on the basis of their sex, race–ethnicity, age, and criminal acts. He then compared those who had been exposed to "Scared Straight" (the experimental group) with delinquents who had not been exposed to it (the control group). Within 6 months, 41 percent of the experimental group were in trouble with the law while only 11 percent of the control group were in trouble.

"Scared Straight" seems like it would work. How could it backfire? Finckenauer suggests that boys were impressed by the macho performance of hypermasculine, in-charge men. (Let your imagination go a little here: You've probably seen photos or TV programs that show the tattoos and muscles and threatening posture that many male convicts display.) The boys want to be powerful men, and this is how they perceived the convicts. Committing a crime after going through the program was one way they could show their peers that the talk hadn't frightened them, that they, too, were macho and couldn't be scared.

The Need of Research. The failure of "Scared Straight" does not mean that programs of deterrence cannot work. It does, however, underline the need for sociological research to find out what does and does not work. We cannot *assume* that a program is successful just because it sounds good, because it appeals to our common sense, or because its operators say that it works. If we are to develop sound social policy, we need solid research to evaluate programs.

Rehabilitation

The goal of **rehabilitation** is to resocialize offenders, to help them stop committing crimes and become conforming citizens (Tyler 2010). Here are some rehabilitation programs (Morash and Anderson 1978):

1. *Probation*: keeping offenders in the community under the supervision of a probation officer
2. *Imprisonment*: confining prisoners with the *goal* of teaching them useful skills or educating them with high school or college courses
3. *Honor farms*: allowing prisoners who have shown good behavior to work and live on a state-owned farm where they remain under supervision
4. *Furloughs*: letting convicts adjust gradually to nonprison life by giving them freedom for a set time, such as weekends toward the end of their sentence
5. *Parole*: releasing prisoners before they serve their full sentence, both as a reward for good behavior and as a threat (holding prison over their heads if they mess up); they report to a supervisor called a parole officer
6. *Halfway houses*: releasing convicts to live in supervised settings outside of prison; they report to parole officers

The public is fed up with failed attempts at rehabilitation (Paparozzi and Demichele 2008).

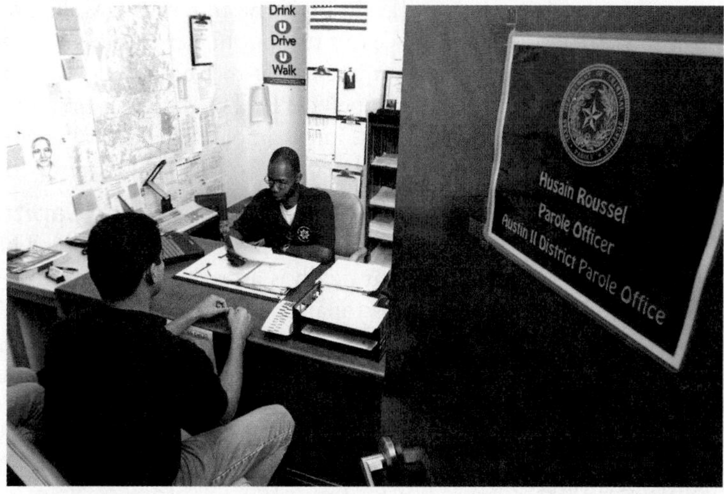

Closely supervising parolees is one attempt to reduce recidivism. This man in Texas is meeting with his parole officer.

Probation is especially scorned as an opportunity for felons to commit more crime. As you saw in Figure 6.2 on page 174 and Table 6.5 on page 175, this perception is accurate. However, the concept of probation is not unsound, just its implementation. To improve the success of probation, it must be limited to convicts with the most promise, who receive follow-up counseling from trained probation officers who have small caseloads. This is expensive, however, and the public is also fed up with spending money on criminals.

Another approach to rehabilitation is **diversion**, diverting offenders *away from* the criminal justice system. Instead of having criminal trials, those accused of minor offenses are dealt with by community organizations or administrative hearings. Diversionary programs have two goals: to avoid stigmatizing offenders and to keep them out of the crime schools that would socialize them into committing more crime.

If rehabilitation programs were successful, almost everyone would favor them. The cost of successful rehabilitation is much less than the price of crime—the cost to victims and the cost of maintaining people in prisons. We need solid data to evaluate programs of rehabilitation, to determine which ones work and the conditions that make them successful.

Incapacitation

With the perception that "nothing works," the public clamors for **incapacitation**, removing offenders from circulation (Loughran et al. 2009). Their view is direct and to the point: Everything else has failed. We can't change people who don't want to change. Get them off the streets so they can't hurt people. Some offenders commit crime after crime ("career criminals"), so let's free ourselves of recidivists.

The usual form of incapacitation is putting people in jail and prison. New technology proves another technique, featured in the Technology and Social Problems box on the next page.

The Debate. Incapacitation has aroused considerable debate among sociologists. Criminologist James Wilson (1975) stated repeatedly that incapacitation is the *only* solution that makes sense. He campaigned for incapacitation, proposing it in books, scholarly journals, and the popular media. Taking the same position, Ernest van den Haag (1975) proposed *added incapacitation*—increasing someone's sentence each time that person is convicted of a crime.

In this debate, most sociologists seem to take the other side, arguing primarily for better programs of rehabilitation. The response of those proposing incapacitation has been that incapacitation works. As evidence, they point to our safer streets and neighborhoods, arguing that the crime rate dropped sharply as we put more offenders in prison. Those who propose rehabilitation argue that the drop came from other factors as well: abortion, a drop in drug use, the reduction of teenage pregnancy, higher employment, less use of heroin and crack (Levitt 2004; Blumstein and Wallman 2006; Joyce 2009). Neither side convinces the other. We can rule out higher employment, for to the surprise of most experts, the crime rate did not increase or rose only slightly when unemployment surged during our economic crisis (Oppel 2011). The debate is on a professional level. On the public level, the drop in the crime rate is ample evidence that incapacitation works—and the public wants more of it.

Let's turn to the most extreme form of incapacitation.

Extreme Incapacitation: Capital Punishment. Proponents of the death penalty argue that it incapacitates totally: The dead don't commit more crimes. They also argue that death is an appropriate punishment for heinous crimes. Opponents reply just as passionately that killing is never justified. They add that capital punishment does not deter others from killing. If capital punishment did deter, then states with the death penalty should have a lower homicide rate than those without it. But they don't. In fact, it is just the opposite. On average, the homicide rate of states with the death penalty is 50 percent higher than that of states without the death penalty (*Crime in the United States* 2011:Table 5). This fact doesn't faze those favoring the death penalty. They reply that this just goes to show that the states that have the death penalty really need it.

Opponents also argue that the death penalty is capricious—jurors deliberate in secret and indulge their prejudices as they recommend death. They add that judges are

Technology and Social Problems

Electronic Monitoring to Reduce Crime

The idea is simple. "It's expensive to keep people in prison, and not everyone who is convicted of a crime should go to prison. Let's use technology to keep tabs on offenders."

The ankle bracelet, simple and effective, is able to transmit an offender's location 24 hours a day. A transmitter is strapped around the offender's ankle, which transmits a signal to a central monitor. If the offender leaves home, it breaks the signal, setting off an alarm at the monitoring station.

The ankle monitor also lowers costs. To keep a juvenile in custody runs about $100 a day, but the cost for home monitoring is just $10 a day. To keep an adult in prison runs about $75 a day, but the cost to use the ankle device is just $12 a day. The costs include equipment and staff.

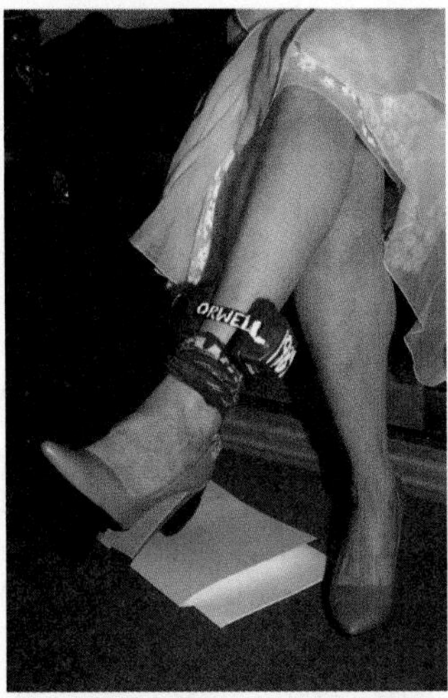

This New York woman was arrested for drunk driving. The monitoring device on her ankle not only lets authorities know where she is, but it also reports her blood alcohol level.

Some jurisdictions follow a pay-as-you go plan. Judges give adult clients a choice—go to jail or pay $12 a day for electronic monitoring. Not eligible are drug dealers, those who committed a violent crime, and those who used guns to commit their crime. In some Florida counties, even those accused of drunk driving have to wear this device and pay its daily cost (author's notes).

The ankle monitor is also suitable for probation and parole. Software can be programmed with an offender's work schedule and location. Probation officers can park outside a workplace to pick up a signal. Failure to show up for work also sets off a signal. Probation officers check to make certain that it isn't a false call, then alert the police.

Hidden within this new technology is another benefit: Because electronic monitoring frees up prison cells, violent offenders can be kept in prison longer.

Another benefit goes to victims of stalking. The software can be programmed to sound an alarm if an offender comes within a specified distance of a victim's home or workplace. Workers at the monitoring station warn the victim, who can leave the area.

Looking to the Future. Future technology will soon make this monitoring tool seem primitive. Signaling devices will be implanted in felons' bodies. The implant will be connected to the Global Positioning System, and satellites will track the precise location of the individual. Software will be programmed with the offender's schedule—times and location of work or rehabilitation classes, routes to and from work. The program will also specify places in the community that are off limits, such as playgrounds and parks for sex offenders. If the individual deviates from the schedule, a computer will notify the police to make an arrest. Perhaps a device will be inserted in an offender's brain that will send pain if the individual deviates from scheduled activities. As technology develops, there could be implants that direct the individual's movements.

Implications. As you probably have been thinking, the capacity to monitor and control people leads to several issues. The first: Can individuals convicted of crime be forced to have implants, or must monitoring devices be limited to those an individual wears? The second is the matter of abuse by authorities. Using such devices on felons can be merely a step toward the goal of monitoring all citizens. With the continuous erosion of our civil rights in the name of protecting us from terrorism and the matching continuous desire of authorities to expand their power, this is a chilling possibility. Implants and the marvels of the Global Positioning System—what more could Big Brother ask to control its citizens?

Based on Campbell 1995; McGarigle 1997; "GPS Creates Global Jail" 1998; Knights 1999; Whitehead 2010.

For Your Consideration

The need to try to keep felons from committing more crimes is obvious. So are the benefits of electronic monitoring. What do you see as the downside, the negative aspects, of electronic monitoring? How would you prevent the abuse indicated in the last paragraph?

irrational—giving mercy to some but not to others. Proponents reply that in their opinion judges and juries are doing a good job under difficult circumstances. Opponents stress that innocent people have been executed: They point to the men released from death row because of DNA testing. Proponents reply that they are happy we have DNA testing, that now we can be even more certain of the guilt of the killers we execute. Each side stands firm, neither convincing the other.

As you can see from Figure 6.4, most Americans favor the death penalty, with men consistently favoring it more than women do. The percentage of men who favor the death penalty is now the lowest it has been since the 1970s, while the percentage of women who favor the death penalty is basically unchanged from that period.

From Figures 6.5 and 6.6 on the next page, you can see how the times have changed. As the states have grown more reluctant to execute prisoners, the number of executions has dropped. The courts, though, have continued to sentence offenders to death, and the number of prisoners on death row has grown.

FIGURE 6.4 ▸ Comparing Men's and Women's Attitudes on the Death Penalty

A nationally representative sample of Americans was asked: "Are you in favor of the death penalty for a person convicted of murder?"

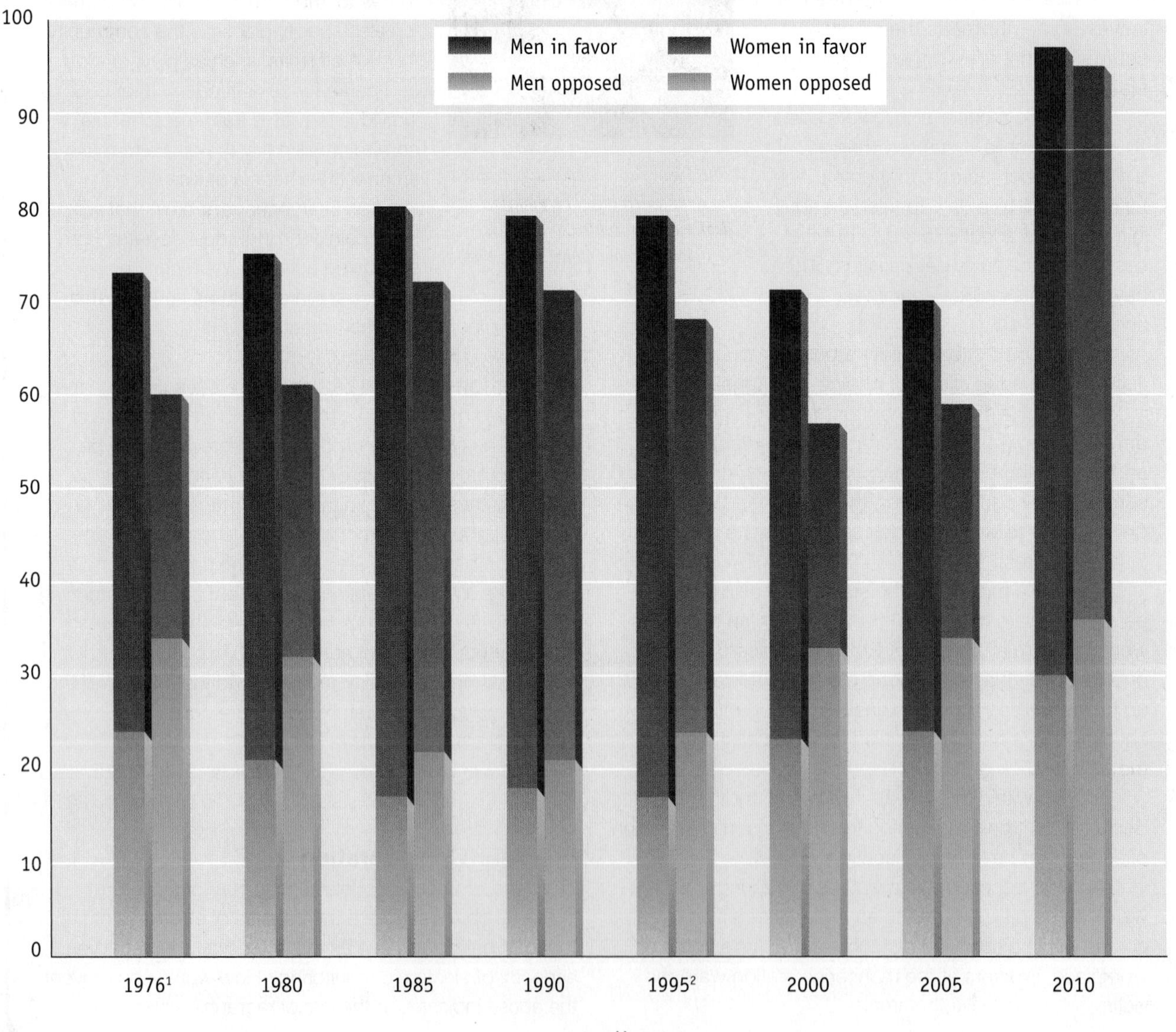

Source: By the author. Based on *Sourcebook of Criminal Justice Statistics* 1994:Table 2.58; 2003:Table 2.50; 2005:Table 2.52; 2010:Table 2.52; 2012:Table 2.52.

[1]1976 was the first year reported in the source.

[2]1995 was not reported, so the average of 1994 and 1996 was used.

FIGURE 6.5 ▸ Executions in the United States

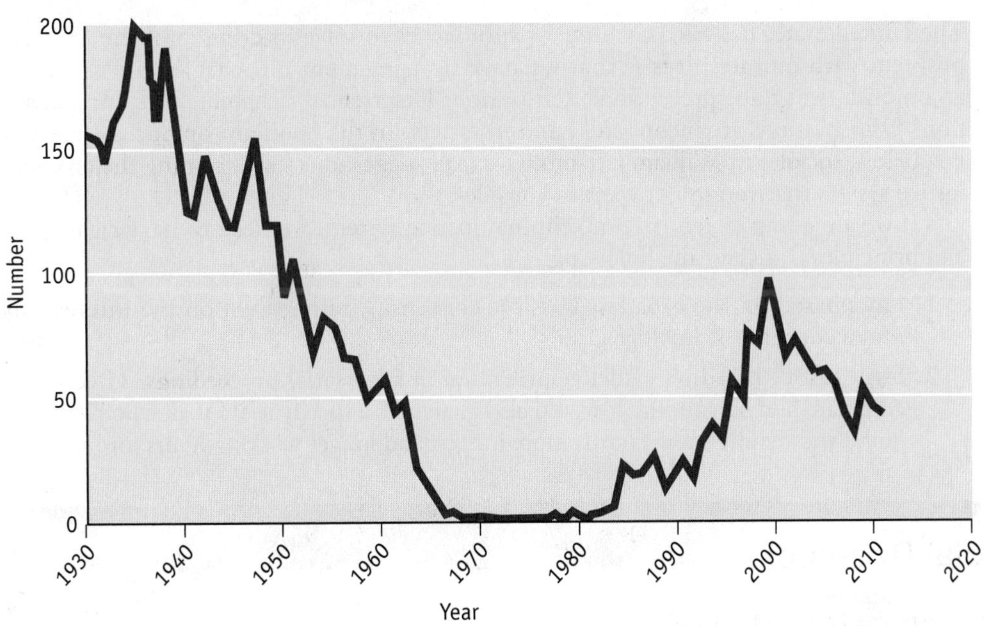

Source: By the author. Based on various editions of *Sourcebook of Criminal Justice Statistics,* including 1998:Table 6.88; 2012:Table 6.85.

FIGURE 6.6 ▸ Persons Under Sentence of Death

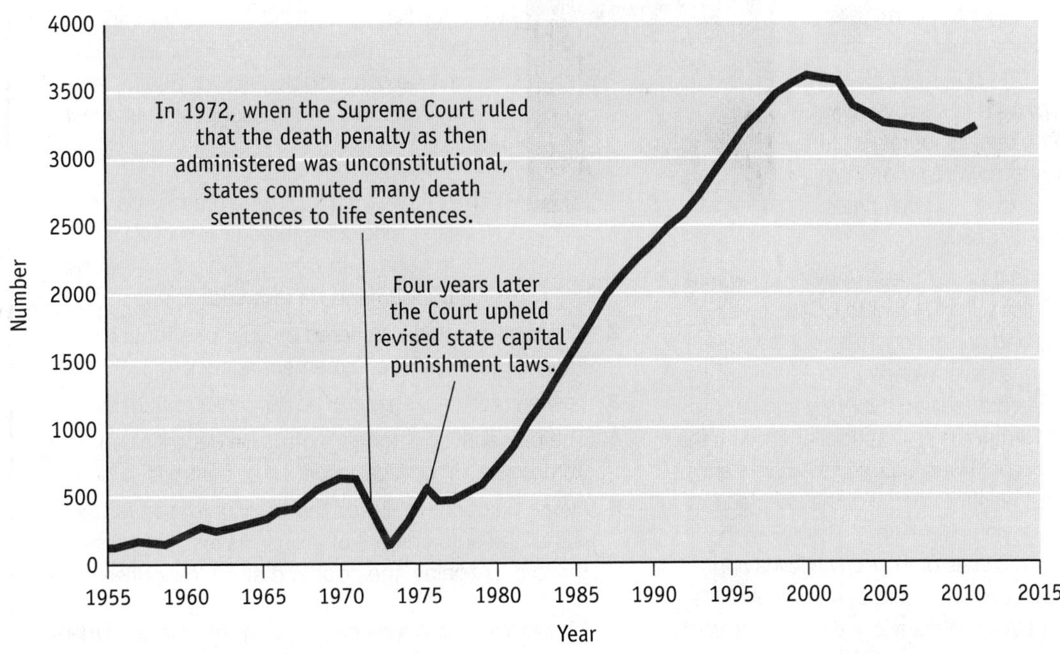

Source: By the author. Based on Greenfield 1991; various editions of *Sourcebook of Criminal Justice Statistics*, including 2012:Table 6.79.

Goals and Principles of Sound Social Policy

The United States has tried a variety of approaches to solve its crime problem. A basic problem with our attempts is that we have no agreement on what we are trying to accomplish. Is it to be prevention? Retribution? Deterrence? Rehabilitation? Incapacitation? Our solutions are inconsistent and in tatters. In the Spotlight on Social Research box below, sociologist William Chambliss makes suggestions for reforming the criminal justice system that you might want to consider.

If we are going to reform our criminal justice system, we need to have clear goals and principles. I suggest the following:

1. Laws based on the broadest possible consensus, rather than on the interests or moral concerns of small groups.
2. Swift justice based on evidence presented in adversarial proceedings. This would eliminate plea bargaining. It would also guarantee a speedy trial for all who plead not guilty and require more courts, more judges, and longer working hours for judges.

Spotlight on Social Research

Doing Research on Criminals

WILLIAM CHAMBLISS, *professor of sociology at George Washington University in Washington, D.C., became interested in criminology during his junior year in high school. That summer, he and a friend hitchhiked from Los Angeles to Walla Walla, Washington, where they worked with convicts picking peas. As Chambliss got to know the men, he was fascinated to discover what the bank robbers, drug dealers, burglars, and thieves were planning to do when they were released from prison—commit more crimes. Here is what he wrote for you.*

After my experiences that summer, I knew that I wanted to be a criminologist. When I went to UCLA, I was exposed to sociology and criminology. There, I developed a passion for both that has never waned.

After college, I was drafted into the Army and sent to Korea where I spent 18 months as a special agent with the Counter Intelligence Corps. I was exposed to an immense amount of crime. But it was the crimes of the state and of the U.S. military that most interested me. They were the most egregious, not the crimes of the petty thieves and burglars or even what today we would call "terrorists." Between the pea fields of Walla Walla and the rice paddies of South Korea, I came to ponder what a short step it is from legitimacy to crime, from interrogation to torture, and from fighting soldiers to shooting and raping civilians.

Over the years, I have done research on organized crime, economic crime, juvenile gangs, and the creation of laws in the United States. I have also studied crime in England, Sweden, Norway, Nigeria, Zambia, and Thailand. Everywhere I have gone, from the slums and drizzling rain of Seattle to the steamy heat of Nigeria, I found the same story: Some of the worst offenders are the least likely to experience the sting of the criminal justice system, while the less powerful fill the courtrooms and the prisons. This bothers me. It just isn't justice.

In one of my books, *Power, Politics and Crime* (Westview 2001), I suggest these social policies:

1. Mandatory minimum sentences be abolished (including three-strikes laws), and, in general, the trend toward more severe punishments be reversed.
2. Crime statistics be gathered by agencies that are independent of law enforcement agencies.
3. Law enforcement agencies be put under civilian control.
4. The prosecuting attorney's office be depoliticized (removed from political influence or control).
5. Drugs be decriminalized. The primary reason for this is that the enforcement of drug laws results in systemic bias against the poor and ethnic minorities.

My journey of discovery in criminology has exposed many shortcomings in the world we live in. It has also given me an opportunity to meet and work with wonderful people, some labeled criminals, others labeled heroes. Although I sometimes wish that "I didn't know now, what I didn't know then," more often I am eternally grateful for the opportunity to explore the world of crime and crime control and to do what I can to help make it more equitable—which is its supposed purpose.

3. More rehabilitation programs, including diversion for most first offenders who did not commit violent crimes. The goal would be to integrate first-time, low-level offenders into the community.
4. "Added incapacitation": Harsh penalties for violent offenders, with the penalty becoming harsher each time a person is convicted of a crime.
5. Task forces to investigate organized crime and white-collar crime. These groups must have the power to subpoena. For a specified time, such as 5 years after they leave a task force, members should not be able to accept employment from the corporations they investigated.
6. Prison reform, including making the position of prison warden a civil service job, training prison guards rigorously and paying them well, giving prisoners the right to continue their education, allowing prisoners to have conjugal visits, and giving *to the nonviolent* the right to visit friends and family on the outside.
7. Unbiased research to determine what prevents crime and changes lawbreakers. In the ideal case, we would compare experimental and control groups. We certainly have the capacity to make such determinations, but we need government officials to approve and fund the research.

The Future of the Problem

Changes in Crime

6.12 Explain the likely future of crime and criminal justice.

Will crime increase or decrease? As you saw in Chapter 5 (Figure 5.1, page 121), the rates of violent crime have been dropping for 20 years. They should be flattening out soon. If the reason has been the huge numbers of people the courts have put behind bars, the rate should continue to drop if the incarceration rate remains high. As indicated, the experts disagree on the cause of the drop in crime, although some of the views are based on ideology, on what an "expert" wants and does not want to see.

If more women take paid jobs, then crimes by women will probably continue to increase. Jobs outside the home expose women to more opportunities for crime, and like men, they are attracted to illegitimate opportunities.

We won't be able to tell whether white-collar crime increases or decreases. With so much white-collar crime going undiscovered and handled informally, we simply have no baseline from which to draw accurate comparisons. If more white-collar crime is handled by the judicial system, it will *appear* to increase, but official statistics could jump, and we still would not know whether this was a real increase.

Organized crime will continue, taking different forms as social conditions change. The old standbys of gambling, loan-sharking, and prostitution will remain standard activities, but we can expect greater involvement in computer crimes such as identity theft. If anti-crime efforts directed against one part of organized crime, such as the Sicilian American Mafia, succeed, that group, much to its distaste, will turn increasingly to legitimate businesses. The Mafia will remain criminal, however, as crime is the heart of its existence.

The Criminal Justice System

The judicial system changes slowly. Firmly entrenched in power, the ruling elite will continue to make certain that the criminal justice system focuses on street crime and mostly overlooks the crimes of the powerful. With profits high, the number of privately owned and operated prisons will increase. Private firms now operate prisons with about 130,000 inmates (Guerino et al. 2011). This change is superficial, merely a switch in who is operating a prison, not change in the prison system.

6.12

Need for Fundamental Change

If we ever get serious about preventing the poor from being recruited to street crime, instead of simply locking them up, we must open the doors to legitimate ways of achieving success. This requires that the poor have access to quality education and training for jobs. If the private sector doesn't create enough jobs for everyone who wants to work, then the government needs to create them. For jobs to be successful for this purpose, they must pay a living wage. Education and good-paying jobs are fundamental to preventing street crime, as people who have high investment in the social system commit fewer such crimes. I don't like ending this chapter on a pessimistic note, but to increase equality and opportunity entails radical change in the social system. I anticipate that the financial costs in providing quality education and jobs training and creation will be resisted bitterly, making it unlikely that this fundamental need will be met.

MySocLab  Study and Review on **MySocLab**

Summary and Review

1. Whether an act is a *crime* depends on the law, which, in turn, depends on *power* relationships in society.
2. Crime is universal, because all societies make rules against acts they consider undesirable. Because laws differ, crime differs from one society to another and in the same society over time.
3. The social problem of crime has two parts: the crimes committed and the criminal justice system. *Crime* is a problem because people are upset about the threat to their lives, property, and well-being. *The criminal justice system* is a problem because people are upset about its failures and want something done about it.
4. Chambliss' study of the "saints" and the "roughnecks" illustrates how social class affects the perception and reactions of authorities, as well as how crime statistics are distorted.
5. Functionalists note that property crimes represent conformity to the goal of success but rejection of the approved means of achieving success. Just as some people have more access to legitimate opportunities, others have more access to *illegitimate opportunities*.
6. Conflict theorists regard the criminal justice system as a tool that the ruling class uses to mask injustice, control workers, and stabilize the social system to keep themselves in power.
7. *Juvenile delinquents* deflect society's norms by using these *neutralization techniques*: denial of responsibility, denial of injury, denial of a victim, condemning the condemners, and an appeal to higher loyalty.
8. *White-collar crime* is extensive but underreported.
9. *Professional criminals* are people who make their living from crime. They scorn the "straight" world, have high in-group loyalty, and take pride in their specialized skills.
10. *Organized crime* is best represented by the Mafia, whose use of violence within a highly developed bureaucracy lies at the heart of its success.
11. The criminal justice system fails to deliver justice because of plea bargaining, a team-player system that subverts public defense attorneys, biases, and prisons that foster hostility and hatred.
12. Because our criminal justice system has no unifying philosophy, our policies of social control are in disarray.
13. To get at the root of the problem of crime and criminal justice requires reform of the criminal justice system and a basic overhaul of our social institutions, especially changes that open more opportunities to the poor.

Key Terms

capital punishment, 175
Cosa Nostra, 169
criminal justice system, 153
deterrence, 181
diversion, 182
illegitimate opportunity structure, 158
incapacitation, 182
juvenile delinquency, 160
Mafia, 168
organized crime, 168
police discretion, 156
Ponzi scheme, 158
power, 153
professional criminals, 167
rehabilitation, 181
restitution, 180
status crimes, 160
uniform sentencing, 180
white-collar crime, 164

Thinking Critically About Chapter 6

1. Which of the three theoretical perspectives (symbolic interactionism, functionalism, or conflict theory) do you think does the best job of explaining the causes of crime? Why?
2. Which of the three perspectives do you think does the best job of explaining why white-collar and street criminals are treated differently? Is your answer to this question different from your answer to Question 1? Explain.
3. Do you think that violent and nonviolent criminals should be punished differently? Why or why not? Consider the case of the criminally negligent manufacturer whose product kills people but who has no contact with the victims versus the street criminal who kills someone during a robbery.
4. Which of the four basic approaches to treating criminals (retribution, deterrence, rehabilitation, and incapacitation) do you think is the most appropriate? Why?

7 Economic Problems: Poverty and Wealth

Listen to Chapter 7 on MySocLab

Learning Objectives. After reading this chapter, you should be able to:

7.1 Summarize the major economic problems facing the United States, the three types of poverty, and the problems with the poverty line. (p. 191)

7.2 Explain how subjective concerns have changed the social problem of poverty over time, structural inequality, the basic distribution of income and wealth in the United States, and the impact of poverty. (p. 194)

7.3 Summarize the different pictures that emerge when you apply symbolic interactionism, functionalism, and conflict theory to the social problem of poverty. (p. 200)

7.4 Summarize research findings on who the poor are, a culture of poverty, who rules the United States, and explanations of global poverty. (p. 204)

7.5 Explain how shifting views have influenced social policy, what progressive taxation is, and what social programs to relieve poverty are being implemented or considered. (p. 215)

7.6 Explain what the likely future of the social problem of poverty is and why. (p. 223)

At age 17, Julie Treadman was facing more than her share of problems. Her boyfriend had deserted her when she told him that she was pregnant. Exhausted and depressed, Julie dropped out of high school. Now five months pregnant, she wondered about her child's future.

When Julie had severe stomach pains, a neighbor called an ambulance, and she was rushed to Lutheran Hospital. When hospital administrators discovered that neither Julie nor her mother had insurance, money, or credit, they refused her admission. Before they could transfer her to a public hospital, however, Julie gave birth to a stillborn baby.

This situation perplexed hospital administrators who didn't want to serve those who wouldn't pay. They ordered the ambulance driver to take Julie—dead baby, umbilical cord, and all—to the public hospital.

Julie gave birth to a stillborn baby.

—Based on an event in St. Louis, Missouri

The Problem in Sociological Perspective

7.1 Summarize the major economic problems facing the United States, the three types of poverty, and the problems with the poverty line.

The United States offers both individual freedoms and the opportunity for education and economic success. These features are so appealing that millions of people immigrate to the United States, both legally or illegally, seeking the chance to climb the social class ladder and attain higher status. For some people, however, such as Julie Treadman in our opening vignette, **social inequality**—the unequal distribution of wealth, income, power, and opportunities—has dire consequences. Julie couldn't pay, and she was denied medical treatment and human dignity. Because this book is about social problems, not social opportunities, our focus in this chapter is on the negative consequences of social inequality.

The United States is made up of many *social classes*. The term **social class** refers to a large group of people who have similar income, education, and job prestige. Picture the various social classes like a ladder, going from the bottom rung, the very poor, to the top rung, the very wealthy. On each rung of the ladder are clustered people who have similar income and education, and whose jobs bring similar prestige. As with Julie Treadman, so it is with all of us: Where you are located on the social class ladder makes a vital difference for what your life is like.

Economic Problems Facing the United States

Because your welfare is tied up with the U.S. economy, this chapter should help you better understand your future. Let's begin by looking at three economic problems facing the United States.

Booms and Busts. The **economy** is the social institution that produces and distributes goods and services. How the economy functions affects us all. At any given time, the U.S. economy is moving through a "boom–bust" cycle. During a "boom," there are plenty of jobs, and the future looks bright and rosy. During a "bust," the jobs dry up, and the future seems dark and gloomy. If you graduate from college during a "boom," you will have your choice of jobs. But if you graduate during a "bust," even though you have worked just as hard as the earlier students and earned the same degree, you will end up struggling to find work—if there is any work to be had.

Stagnant Incomes. Another problem is that people's **real income** (income adjusted for inflation) is now stagnant. After World War II until 1970, the real income of U.S. workers rose steadily. Even after inflation, workers still had more money to spend. Since then, workers' paychecks have grown, but the dollars they contain buy less. Because there are more dollars in their paychecks, workers feel as though they are earning more than they used to, but in constant dollars they make little more than workers did in 1970. Look at Figure 7.1. You will see that it took 40 years for workers to get a real raise of about 76 cents an hour.

What has softened the blow for the average family is that more women have paid jobs. In 1970, 41 percent of wives worked for wages, either full- or part-time. Today, 61 percent of wives do (*Statistical Abstract* 2013:Table 609). Families in which both the husband and wife have paid jobs earn an average of 79 percent more than families in which only the husband works for a paycheck (*Statistical Abstract* 2013:Table 713).

A Debtor Nation. The United States used to have a huge trade surplus, selling more goods to other nations than it bought from them. Now it is the opposite, and we have become the largest debtor nation in the world. We buy goods from other nations at such a frenzied pace that when you calculate what we pay for these items, minus our income from the products we sell, we end up over $500 billion short at the end of each year (*Statistical Abstract* 2013:Table 1315). We also spend vastly more on government services than we collect in taxes. Year after year, these deficits pile up, increasing our **national debt** (the total amount the U.S. government owes). To finance the national debt, which totals about $16 trillion, we pay about $450 billion a year in interest (*Statistical Abstract* 2013:Tables 478, 481). When interest rates rise, so will this national bill. This is money that we cannot use to build schools and colleges, hire teachers, pay for medical services or job programs for the poor, operate Head Start, or pay for any other services to help improve our quality of life.

Before closing this section, let's get an overview of one more economic problem—poverty—perhaps the most visible of all.

FIGURE 7.1 ▸ Average Hourly Earnings, in Current and Constant Dollars

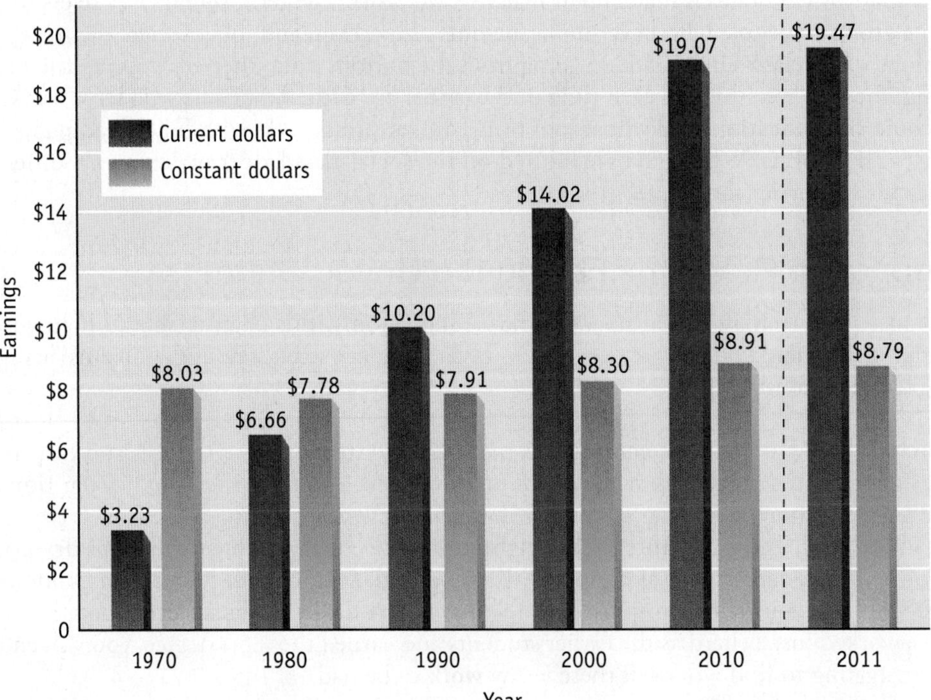

Note: Current dollars are the number of dollars a worker earns. *Constant dollars* means those dollars have been adjusted for inflation, with 1982–1984 as the base.

Source: By the author. Based on *Statistical Abstract of the United States* 1992:Table 650; 1999:Table 698; 2013:Table 656.

The Nature of Poverty

Types of Poverty. You might think that poverty would be easy to define, but its definition is neither simple nor obvious. There are three types of poverty. The first is **biological poverty**, which refers to malnutrition and starvation. It also refers to housing and clothing so inadequate that people suffer from exposure. Our homeless endure biological poverty. So does the young woman on the right in the photo below.

More common is **relative poverty**. This term refers to comparing people's standard of living and concluding that some are worse or better off than others. A lot of relative poverty is not serious—think of those who say they "feel poor" because they can't drive a car as nice as their neighbors do. You've probably experienced relative poverty, if some of your classmates can afford nicer clothing or newer, more powerful laptops than you can. Relative poverty also exists on a global level: What is poverty in the United States would mean very comfortable living in India, where most families have little clothing, little food, and live in just a room or two.

Some nations, such as the United States, also have **official poverty**, an income level that makes someone eligible for welfare benefits. People below this **poverty line** are defined as "poor"; those above this line, even by a dollar, are "not poor." The U.S. poverty guidelines were developed in 1962 by the Social Security Administration (Fisher 1988). At that time, the poor spent about one-third of their income on food, so the poverty line was set by multiplying a low-level food budget by 3. The United States has kept this rough figure, adjusting it annually to match the Consumer Price Index, the official gauge of inflation.

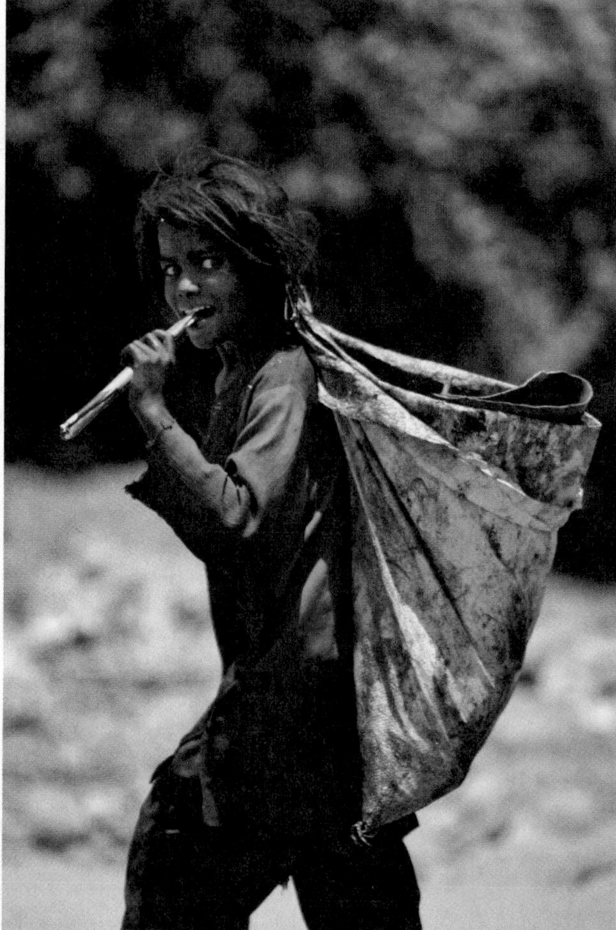

What a world of difference for the rich and the poor around the globe: current life circumstances, hopes for the future, and life orientations. The one is hoping for a new diamond, the other for food. The debutante on the left lives in the United States. The ragpicker on the right lives in India.

Problems with the Poverty Line. Critics say that the poverty line is stuck in a time warp. Sociologist William Julius Wilson (1992) and policy analyst Patricia Ruggles (1990, 1992) point out that food preferences and cooking patterns have changed since the 1960s, but not the government's definition of poverty. They say that poor people actually spend only about 20 percent of their incomes on food, so to determine a poverty line we should multiply their food budget by 5 instead of 3 (Uchitelle 2001). Sociologist Michael Katz (1989) notes another problem with the poverty line: It assumes that everyone cooks all family meals at home and never eats out. Who lives like this, he asks? Others point out that except for Alaska and Hawaii, the poverty line is not adjusted for different costs of living. It costs a bit more to live in Albany, New York, than it does in Albany, Georgia. Finally, the poverty line does not distinguish between urban and rural families. After decades of criticism, the Census Bureau developed alternative ways to measure poverty (Tavernise and Gebeloff 2011), but the official magical line that supposedly separates the "poor" from the "non-poor" has not changed. Using this rock-bottom definition, let's look at "official poverty" in the United States.

The Scope of the Problem

Subjective Concerns and Objective Conditions

7.2 Explain how subjective concerns have changed the social problem of poverty over time, structural inequality, the basic distribution of income and wealth in the United States, and the impact of poverty.

We need to stress again that objective conditions alone—whether defined officially or not—are not enough to make poverty a social problem. Subjective concerns are also essential and, actually, more important. How can subjective concerns be more important than objective conditions, the poverty itself? Consider the extremes: On the one hand, according to our definition of social problems, if poverty is extensive but few people are concerned about it, poverty is *not* a social problem. On the other hand, if poverty is rare but the few cases bother many people and they want to address it, poverty *is* a social problem. This might go against your common sense, so let's look at examples.

Changes in Concerns and Conditions. During the early years of the United States, *most* people were poor. Yet at this time poverty was *not* considered a social problem. Life had always been a struggle for almost everyone in the world, so *poverty was assumed to be a natural part of life.* As industrialization progressed in the nineteenth century, it produced an abundance of jobs and wealth. Poverty declined, but masses of poor people migrated from farms and other countries to U.S. cities. Even though the standard of living increased, this migration made poverty more visible, and leaders began to declare that poverty was a social problem. As immigrants were absorbed into the expanding workforce, however, once again poverty receded from sight.

Then came the Great Depression of the 1930s, when millions of people were thrown out of work. As the ranks of the poor swelled, poverty again grew highly visible. With citizens protesting and organizers leading strikes, government officials declared poverty to be the greatest problem facing the nation. They rushed through legislation that established emergency programs and created millions of jobs. This was followed by World War II, when factories began to operate at full capacity and millions of Americans were sent overseas to fight. With prosperity increasing after the war, poverty continued to recede from sight. Even though the objective condition—millions of people in poverty—remained, subjective concerns eased. Tucked in out-of-the-way rural areas and in urban slums, the poor once again dropped from sight.

Launching the War on Poverty. By making poverty a campaign issue in his 1960 bid for the presidency, President Kennedy tried to arouse concerns about poverty. The result was lukewarm. Then came Michael Harrington's book, *The Other America*, in 1962. Rarely has a single volume of social science transformed people's consciousness as this one. Harrington passionately argued that in the midst of "the affluent society," one-quarter of the nation lived in squalor. The media publicized this book, policy makers read it, and sociologists assigned it to their students.

After succeeding Kennedy, Lyndon Johnson, in his first State of the Union address in January 1964, declared:

> *This administration today, here and now, declares unconditional war on poverty in America. Our chief weapons in a more pinpointed attack will be better schools, and better health, and better homes, and better training, and better job opportunities to help more Americans, especially young Americans escape from squalor and misery and unemployment rolls.* (as quoted in Cancian and Danziger 2009)

The federal government began a raft of programs for the poor: child care, Head Start, legal services, medical services, job training, subsidized housing, and community health centers. The result was dramatic. As you can see from Figure 7.2, in just 10 years the number of Americans below the official poverty line dropped from 22 percent to 13 percent. This reduction made it clear that the problem of poverty can be solved. We simply need effective social policies.

The Situation Today

At the beginning of the twenty-first century, as the war on terrorism and global economic threats drew our attention, subjective concerns about poverty receded. Although the media occasionally highlighted the plight of workers in the steel, textile, or automobile industries, for the most part poverty was relegated to tales of woe featured during Thanksgiving and Christmas fund-raising campaigns. The economic crisis that began to unfold in 2008 brought sporadic outcries about poverty, but the concerns focused on job layoffs and home foreclosures.

Reaching a Plateau. From Figure 7.2, you can see that we have made no progress in reducing poverty since the 1960s and 1970s. During the past 40 years, the percentage of Americans below the poverty line has hovered between 12 and 15 percent. Today it is at that upper range, threatening to burst higher. Although today's percentage of poor

FIGURE 7.2 ▸ Americans below the Poverty Line

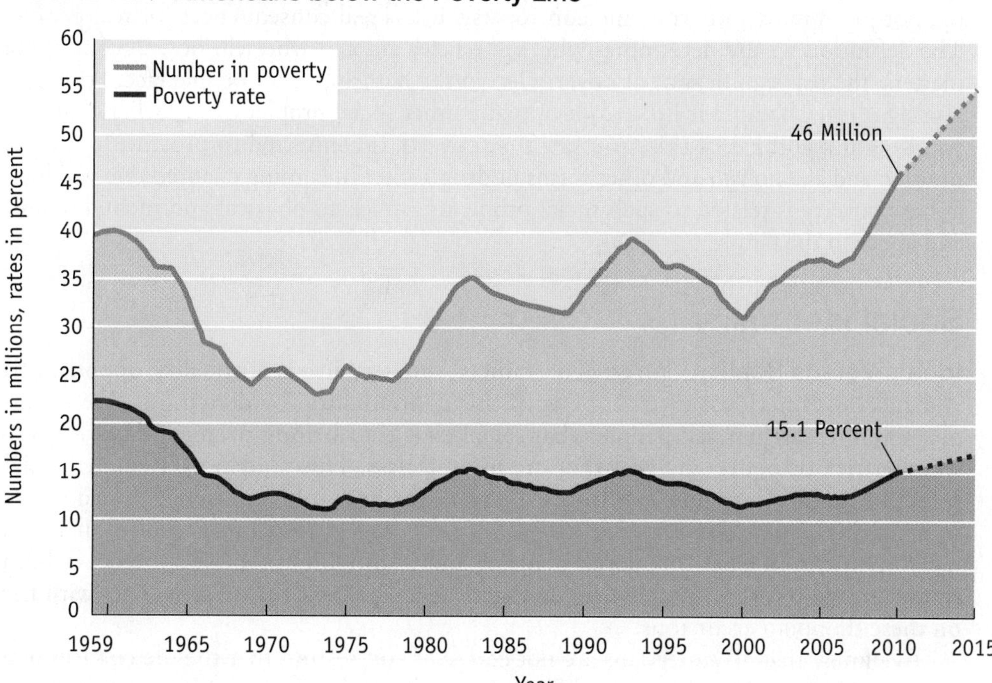

Note: Projections by the author.

Source: By the author. Based on U.S. Census Bureau 2011; *Statistical Abstract of the United States* 2013:Table 721.

is less than it was in the 1950s, with our much larger population more Americans are poor today than before the "war on poverty" began.

Arbitrary and Controversial Numbers. We can reduce or increase the number of "poor" people at will—simply by changing the official definition of poverty. Because the poverty line is a definition chosen by a government agency, we can argue endlessly about whether we have more or less poor people than the government measures. Some say it is higher, that a lot of people who are on the edge of survival aren't counted. Others point out that the government does not count as income many benefits that people receive from antipoverty programs: Medicare, Medicaid, food stamps, and HUD vouchers (government rent subsidies given to poor families). These issues of "more or less" plague the social problem of poverty. What should we count as income? Where should the cutoff for poverty be? Change these and we change the number of people counted as poor.

In the cartoon below you can see how Johnny Hart has insightfully picked up this arbitrary nature of the poverty line.

This cartoon pinpoints the arbitrary nature of the poverty line. This makes me almost think that the creators of the Wizard of Id have been studying sociology.

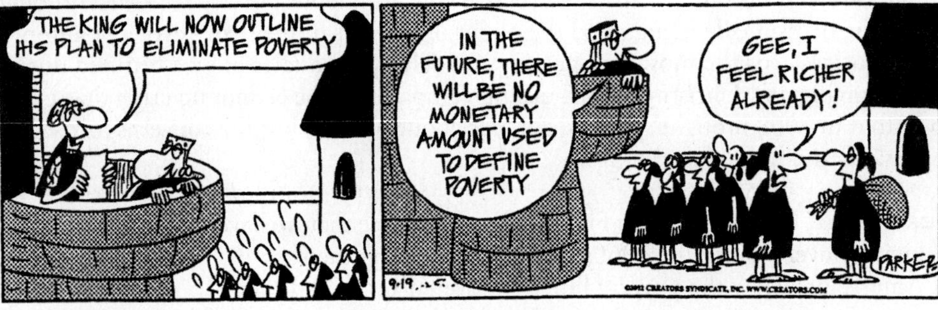

Watch on **MySocLab Video:** Opportunity and Social Class

The Significance of Poverty. Despite the disagreement over numbers, poverty is a fact of life for *millions* of Americans. And where to draw the poverty line is a serious matter, not just a matter of academic controversy. It has real consequences for real people: The definition we use determines who will receive aid and who will not. Beyond these matters, the real significance of poverty lies in the hardships that people face. Poverty is also significant because it is the root of many other social problems. In earlier chapters, you caught a glimpse of this. You saw that poverty is connected to prostitution, rape, murder, and alcoholism and other forms of drug abuse. In coming chapters, we will look at how poverty is related to such social problems as racism, physical and mental illness, and abuse in the family.

Social Inequality

Ideals Versus Reality. Poverty contradicts American ideals of equality, opportunity, and success. Americans often cope with this contradiction by denying it. For example, when researchers ask people what social class they belong to, most Americans—whether rich or poor—say that they are middle class. This tendency fascinates social researchers. Ann Getty (an heir to the Getty oil fortune) told a reporter, "I lead a very ordinary life" (*New York Times* Sept. 7, 1980). *Ordinary?* Her "ordinary life" included not only living in a San Francisco mansion but also flying to Paris to attend fashion shows and shop for clothing by top designers. And she took her personal chef with her on these shopping excursions.

We know that all Americans are not equal, of course, and that the life chances of a waitress' daughter differ immensely from those of a son born to wealthy parents. We all know that the rich and politically connected pass advantages on to their children and the poor and powerless pass disadvantages on to theirs. Because of this, we have social

Poverty is much more than having little money. Poverty means the reduction in life chances.

programs intended to help level the playing field, such as affirmative action, college scholarships, Pell grants, and community colleges.

Structural Inequality. Such programs run up against **structural inequality**, the inequality built into our social institutions. For example, some jobs in our economy pay higher wages and others lower wages, so automatically some people will receive more, others less. Or consider unemployment, another form of structural inequality. If a society has 100 million workers but only 90 million jobs, then 10 million workers will be unemployed, regardless of how hard they look for work. Job training programs cannot solve this structural problem. The solution requires changes in structure—that is, the creation of more jobs. No workable social system has been devised that eliminates structural inequality.

Distribution of Income and Wealth

Inequality of Income. Not surprisingly, structural inequality leads to inequality in **income**, the flow of money people receive from their work and investments. To picture how vast this inequality is, look at Figure 7.3. You can see that the top fifth of the

FIGURE 7.3 ▸ Who Gets What? The Inverted Income Pyramid

How is the income of the United States distributed?

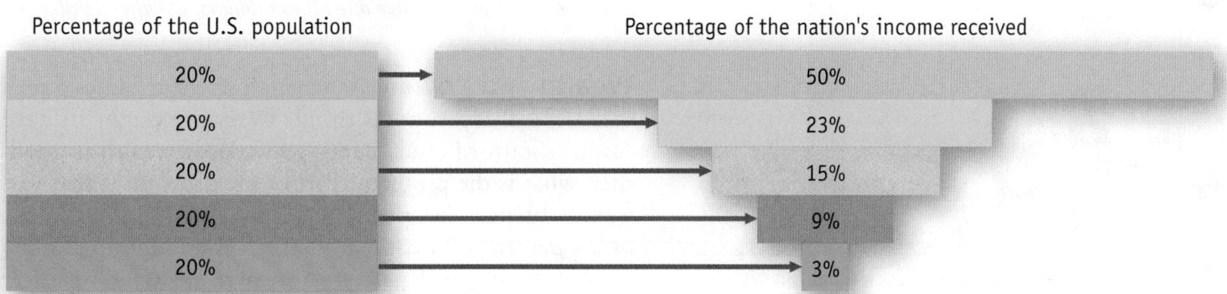

Source: By the author. Based on *Statistical Abstract of the United States* 2013:Table 708.

FIGURE 7.4 ▸ Who Owns What? How the Wealth of the United States Is Distributed

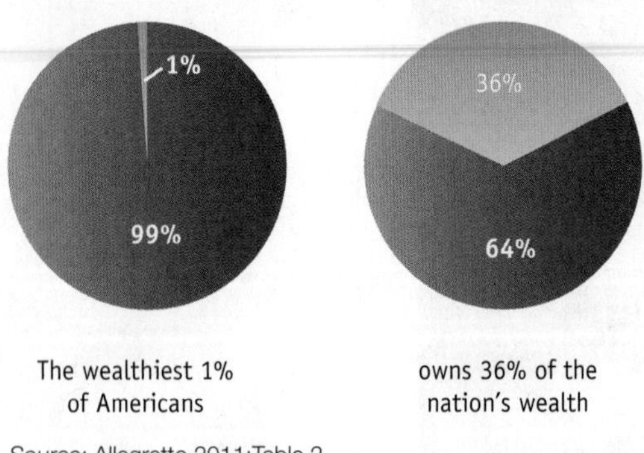

The wealthiest 1% of Americans owns 36% of the nation's wealth

Source: Allegretto 2011:Table 2.

Read on MySocLab Document: Social Class Matters

U.S. population receives *half* of the nation's entire income. The other half is divided among the remaining 80 percent of the population, with the poorest fifth receiving just 3 percent of the nation's income. Despite our numerous antipoverty programs, *income inequality today is greater than it was in the 1940s.*

Inequality of Wealth. Another way to picture financial inequality is to look at the distribution of **wealth**: the property, savings, investments, and economic assets that people own. Americans own about $60 trillion of property, mostly in the form of real estate, corporate stock, mutual funds, and bank accounts (*Statistical Abstract* 2013:Table 734). To give you an idea of how concentrated these assets are among the wealthy, look at Figure 7.4. You can see that more than one-third of the nation's wealth is in the hands of just 1 percent of U.S. families. This 1 percent controls corporate America.

When we look a little more closely at who holds the nation's wealth, a strong racial–ethnic imbalance emerges. Look at Figure 7.5 below which shows the gap in both income and wealth. You can see that the average white person has between six and seven times the wealth of the average minority person. This figure can be misleading, though, if you don't keep Figure 7.4 in mind. The average white person does *not* have $131,000. Wealth is concentrated among just a few, as you saw with Figure 7.4. There are millions of poor white people: What surprises many is that there are *more* poor whites than there are poor African Americans or poor Latinos. We will return to this later.

Worth billions each, the richest people in the United States are Bill Gates and Warren Buffet. The wealth of these two men fluctuates a few billion dollars up and a few billion dollars down as the price of their stocks changes. Warren Buffet is one of the world's most successful stock market investors. Bill Gates dropped out of Harvard to co-found Microsoft Corp., the world's largest software company. Gates and his employees developed MS-DOS, Windows, and Vista, popular computer operating systems. Microsoft gets a licensing fee each time a computer that uses these systems is sold. With the billions of dollars that they have given to the Gates Foundation for global agricultural, educational, and health projects, Gates and Buffet are apparently the most generous men in human history.

FIGURE 7.5 ▸ Income and Wealth (Net Worth) by Race–Ethnicity

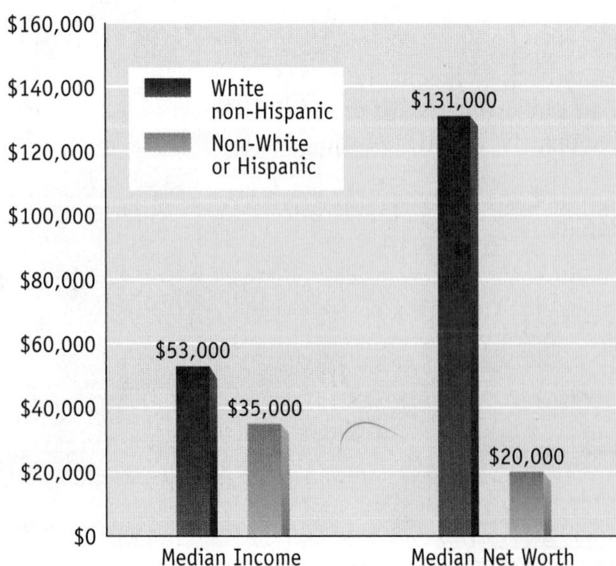

Note: Median income and median net worth 2010.

Source: By the author. Based on Bricker et al. 2012:Tables 1, 4.

Billions of dollars amassed by Gates and Buffet. This number trips easily off the tongue, but how much is a billion dollars? The following illustration may help us grasp the enormity of a billion dollars—*one thousand million dollars:*

> *Suppose you were born on the day Christ was born, that you are still alive today, and that you have been able to save money at the fantastic rate of one cent for every second that you lived—that is, 60 cents for every minute, $36 for every hour, or $864 for every day of your life during these past two thousand years. At that rate, it would take you another thousand years to save one billion dollars. (Shaffer 1986)*

Wealth and Power. As research scientist James Smith said, "Wealth is a good thing. Everyone ought to have some" (Stafford et al. 1986–1987:3). If wealth is good, then what is the problem? Part of the problem is that vast wealth brings vast power. Because owning 10 percent or 20 percent of a company's stock is enough to control the company, the 1 percent of Americans who own over half of all corporate stock wield immense power over the U.S. economy (Beeghley 2008). In their pursuit of even more wealth, these elite can move production to Mexico, India, or China, where labor is cheaper. If they close factories here, throwing thousands of people out of work, this is not their concern. This is just a side consequence of seizing economic opportunities, of following the "hot money." The wealthy make these decisions, not the U.S. workers who lose their jobs in this global game of monopoly. But the U.S. workers must live with the consequences.

The wealthy live in a cocoon of privilege, enjoying beautiful homes in safe neighborhoods, attending the finest schools, and protected from unemployment, injustice in the courts, and an unresponsive political system. To perpetuate their advantages, they have the resources to hire top financial advisors, attorneys, and lobbyists. At the other end of the money spectrum are those who cope with deprivation as part of everyday life. Let's turn our focus on them.

The Impact of Poverty

How does poverty impact people's lives? On the most obvious level, the poor can't afford many movies, and they eat steak less often. But an immense reality of deprivation lies beneath this obvious level. Just as your economic circumstances envelop you, affecting profoundly every aspect of your life, so it is for those who live in poverty. Let's look at some of the consequences of poverty.

Housing and Mortgages.

During the economic crisis when millions of home buyers fell behind on their mortgages, some tried to negotiate lower payments. Here is how one person described his negotiation: "I told her that I probably spend $10 a day on groceries, and she said 'Maybe you can eat less.'" (Morgenson 2008)

View on MySocLab **Figure:** Percentage of Low-Paid Essential Workers Facing Severe Housing Cost Burdens

Most of the poor live in substandard housing. Some rent from landlords who neglect their buildings. The plumbing may not work. The heating system may break down in winter. Roaches and rats may run riot. And, unlike mortgage payments, the monthly rent does not build up equity in a home.

If the poor are able to put together what they need for a down payment, they are hit with higher interest on their loans (Kochhar and Gonzalez-Barrera 2009). Over the lifetime of a loan, these additional higher interest payments can run up to $100,000 (Powell and Roberts 2009). The bottom-line, worst part of this is that the poor are more likely than others to lose their homes.

Some of our "finest," "reputable" banks participated in programs to charge the poor higher interest and extra fees. The bankers saw an opportunity to take advantage of people with less experience in the economic system, and they took it. For discriminating against Latino and African American borrowers, Countrywide Financial was fined $335 million (Savage 2011a).

Education. As you know, public schools are supposed to give all children an equal opportunity to succeed. The poor, however, have a tremendous disadvantage. Property taxes are the main culprit. Because our schools are supported by property taxes, and property in poorer areas produces less tax, the schools that the poor attend have smaller budgets. This translates into outdated textbooks, inexperienced teachers (who can be paid less), and lower test scores. Lower test scores, as you know, affect students' chances of going to college, which, in turn, affects their earnings.

I'm sure that it doesn't come as a surprise to you that the higher a family's income, the greater the likelihood that their children will attend and complete college. If you rank families from the poorest to the richest, at each level of family income

"The poor are getting poorer, but with the rich getting richer it all averages out in the long run."

How we define reality depends to a large extent on where we are located in the social class structure. Poor Americans are not likely to have the view illustrated in this cartoon.

the likelihood increases that their children will go to college (Manski 1992–1993; Reay et al. 2001). This is true regardless of how the child performs on tests. That is, whether children score high or low on tests, those from homes with more money are more likely to go to college (Carnevale and Rose 2003). Similarly, the more money a family has, the more years of schooling their children complete (Conley 2001).

And then there is the *type* of college that children attend. Most poor children who go to college attend community colleges where many take vocational programs. In contrast, most children of the middle class attend state universities. And the children of the wealthy? They go to elite private colleges. Before going to college, many attend private high schools, where classes are small and teachers are well-paid (Persell et al. 1992). The college advisors at these high schools have close ties with admissions officers at elite colleges. Some have networks so efficient that *half* of a private high school's graduating class is admitted to Harvard, Yale, and Princeton (Cookson and Persell 1985/2005).

Jobs. Unlike the career paths open to children of the middle class, the low-paying jobs of the working poor lead to few opportunities. Because their dead-end jobs are often sporadic, with the worker not knowing from day to day if he or she has a job, the incomes of the poor, already low, are erratic. They never know from one week to the next that there will be a paycheck, or how much it will be if there is one. You can see how this makes planning uncertain and life hectic. To the stresses already knitted into their daily lives, job insecurity and unemployment add their own, not just knowing if there will be enough money to buy food and pay the rent but also the need to cope with the bureaucracies of unemployment insurance, welfare, and other social programs.

Criminal Justice. The poor are more likely to be victims of violent crimes and to commit robberies and assaults, crimes for which offenders are punished severely. White-collar crime may be more pervasive and costly to society, but it is less visible and carries milder punishments. As mentioned in the previous chapter, when the poor are arrested, they lack the resources to hire good lawyers to defend themselves. Often, they cannot even post bail, and they remain in jail for months while they await trial. Most prisoners in our jails and prisons are people who were reared in poverty.

In Short: Quality of Life. Wealth and poverty are not just a matter of how much money people have in the bank. Wealth and poverty represent privilege—given or denied. The net result of social inequality is a fundamental difference in people's quality of life. The low-paying jobs of the poor, when they have them, bring no pensions and no medical benefits. The poor live insecurely from paycheck to paycheck, trying to keep one step ahead of having the lights cut off or being evicted. If they get sick, their job may not be there when they return to work. Among the stark consequences: Those living in poverty don't eat as well, their children are more likely to die in infancy, they have more accidents, and they die younger. Like Julie Treadman in our opening vignette, they also have less access to good medical care, which further jeopardizes their well-being.

Looking at the Problem Theoretically

7.3 Summarize the different pictures that emerge when you apply symbolic interactionism, functionalism, and conflict theory to the social problem of poverty.

As you learned in earlier chapters, each theoretical perspective gives a different view of a social problem. Let's look at poverty through our usual three lenses.

Symbolic Interactionism

The Relativity of Poverty.

Andy, Sharon, and their two children live in a small house in a rural area. Andy farms 65 acres and works part-time at a local grocery store. Sharon works part-time as a cook at the Dew Drop Inn. She sews some of the children's clothing. Between their jobs and the farm, they make about $18,000 a year. They grow their own vegetables, buy milk from a neighbor, and fish in a nearby *pond. Integrated into the community and with their basic needs satisfied, they don't think of themselves as poor. Neither do their friends and neighbors.*

Leslie attends a private college. Her parents pay her tuition, fees, books, rent, utilities, insurance, medical bills, transportation, and entertainment. They also give her about $500 a month for "extras." Unlike many of her friends, Leslie has no car, and she complains about how hard it is to get by. Her more affluent friends feel sorry for her.

Between auditions, Keith, a struggling young actor, works as a waiter. He earns about $1,200 a month, which has to cover his rent, food, and all other expenses. To make ends meet, he rooms with three other aspiring actors. "It's difficult to make it," he says, "but one day you'll see my name in lights." Keith sees himself as "struggling"—not poor. Nor do his actor friends think of him as poor.

Maria and her two children live in a housing project. Her rent is subsidized and cheap—$97 a month. Her welfare, Medicaid, and food stamps total $15,287 a year, all tax-free. Her two children attend school during the day, and she takes classes in English at a neighborhood church. Maria considers herself poor, and so do the government and her neighbors.

According to the government standards, all but Leslie are poor, and yet Leslie *feels* poor. Why? This takes us back to relative poverty.

Symbolic interactionists stress that to understand poverty we must focus on what poverty *means* to people. When people evaluate where they are in life, they *compare* themselves with others. In some rural areas, simple marginal living is the norm, and people living in these circumstances don't feel poor. But in Leslie's cosmopolitan circle, people can *feel* deprived if they cannot afford the latest upscale designer clothing from their favorite boutique. The meaning of poverty, then, is *relative*: What poverty is differs from group to group within the same society, as well as from culture to culture and from one era to the next.

How poverty is viewed by the "non-poor" is also significant. If they are seen as good people who are down on their luck, the other social classes will offer "a helping hand" by supporting programs that provide job training and monthly support. If the poor are viewed as "lazy no-goods" who refuse to work—a parasitic drain on society—supportive social policies will receive little backing. Perception and meaning—main elements of symbolic interactionism—are essential for understanding poverty.

Changing Meanings of Poverty. Symbolic interactionists stress that the meaning of poverty changes as social conditions change. Let's take a quick glance at how this happened in the United States.

The way people saw poverty in the early 1700s was remarkably different than how we view it today. At that time, poverty was seen as God's will. The clergy preached that God put the poor on earth to provide an opportunity for the rest of us to show Christian charity (Rothman and Rothman 1972). Poverty was not a social problem, but a personal problem.

At that time, the United States had few cities, and the poor were scattered among hundreds of villages along country roads. As cities grew, so did the concentration of the poor in those cities. By the time of the American Revolution, cities such as Boston, Philadelphia, and New York had set up welfare committees to distinguish between the "deserving" and the "undeserving" poor. The deserving poor were the blind, people with disabilities, and mothers of small children whose husbands had deserted them. The undeserving poor were beggars, peddlers, idlers, drifters, and prostitutes. At this point, the meaning of poverty was changing. Increasingly, poverty was viewed not just as God's will, but also as the result of flawed character.

The development of a social problem was now in process. As the United States industrialized and its cities grew larger, the urban squalor bothered people of good intentions. Reformers launched campaigns to help the poor, and the meaning of poverty continued to change. Poverty came to be seen as the product of corrupt cities. People who had given in to urban temptations—alcohol, crime, and debauchery—were held in the chains of poverty (Rothman and Rothman 1972).

The idea that poverty is God's will is no longer common, but the idea that poverty ought not to exist—and the suspicion that it is due to the character or the behavior of the poor—remains part of our symbolic heritage. We have vacillated between viewing the poor as worthy people who deserve our help and as undeserving people who have brought the ills of poverty down on their own heads.

Functionalism

How Income Inequality Helps Society. In their classic essay, sociologists Kingsley Davis and Wilbert Moore (1945) developed the functionalist perspective on social inequality. Their argument was simple. Some positions in society are more important for society's welfare than others. To attract the highly talented people that these positions require, they must offer high income and prestige. Oil, for example, is vital for the economy, but to learn the technology necessary to find oil takes years of training in geology. To motivate people to postpone gratification and continue studying for years, petroleum geologists, especially geophysicists, must be offered a substantial salary and high respect from others. Anyone can wash dishes, so unskilled workers earn poverty wages at jobs that require little training. Differences in income and prestige, then, that sort people by abilities and drive to succeed, help society function.

How Poverty Is Functional for Society. Functionalists—who tend to see functions in everything—point out that poverty is functional for society. For a summary of how poor people contribute to society's well-being, see the Thinking Critically box on the next page. Functionalists also analyze the dysfunctions of poverty, including alienation and despair, drug abuse, street crime, suicide, and mental illness.

Conflict Theory

Explore on **MySocLab**
Activity: Poverty: Next Door to Greatness: Poverty in Cambridge, MA

The Cause of Social Inequality. Central to conflict theory is the idea that resources are limited and that groups compete for or fight over these resources. In each society, some group has gained control of that society's resources. That group uses those resources to make a better life for itself, to keep itself in power, and to exploit weaker groups. The result is a social class system in which the wealthy pass advantages to their children, while the poor pass disadvantages to theirs.

A General Theory of Social Class. Karl Marx (1818–1883) was the first social analyst to develop a general theory of social class. He argued that social class revolves around a single factor, the *means of production*—the tools, factories, land, and capital used to produce wealth (Marx, 1867/1967; Marx and Engels, 1848/1964). People are either capitalists (*bourgeoisie*), who own the means of production, or they are workers (*proletariat*) who serve the capitalists. The history of a society is the history of conflict between owners and workers, the wealthy and the poor. Because the owners hold the power, they manipulate society's social institutions—legal, political, educational, and religious—to promote their own interests and to control workers.

Marx wrote that the owners' position of power and privilege will not continue forever. The day of reckoning will come when workers shrug off their delusion, **false class consciousness**, the idea that they will start their own business and become wealthy. In its place will arise *class consciousness*, the realization that they are workers no matter what their occupation, whether it be garbage collector or college professor. With their eyes finally opened and with the realization that they all are exploited workers, they will join together and overthrow the capitalists. Seizing the means of production, the workers will use them for the good of all. Poverty will become a distant memory.

Modifications of Conflict Theory. Most sociologists acknowledge that Marx provided valuable insight into relationships between the powerful and the poor, but they find his class division, consisting of just owners and workers, inadequate. According to

Thinking Critically about Social Problems

Why We Need the Poor: How Poverty Helps Society

Most of us think of poverty in negative terms: Poverty is undesirable, and we should get rid of it. Functionalists, in contrast, identify the functions of poverty—that is, the positive consequences that poverty has for society. Consider these twelve functions, most pointed out by sociologist Herbert Gans (1971/2007):

1. *The poor ensure that society's dirty work gets done at low cost.* Many factories, restaurants, farms, and hospitals could not survive in their present state without a poorly paid workforce. If there weren't poor people, who would do society's dirty jobs at low wages?
2. *The poor create jobs for others.* Think of the welfare agencies that serve the poor and—not incidentally—shield the rest of us from them. Most police officers would be without jobs if it weren't for the poor. And what would social workers do for a living?
3. *The poor serve as guinea pigs in medical experiments*. The rest of us benefit from these advances in medicine. How else would we test risky new medicines and surgical techniques?
4. *The poor make the economy more efficient.* They spend their low wages and welfare money on leftover goods such as day-old bread and the many "seconds" that our factories produce. They also buy the clothing, furniture, and cars that the rest of us discard. Where else would these items go if it weren't for the poor?
5. *The poor provide an income for others, even making some wealthy*. Many slum landlords, for example, would have to get jobs if it weren't for the poor. And what would the owners of the many liquor stores in the inner city do without the poor? Or those who offer bail bonds and paycheck loans? And what about the owners of the trailer parks?
6. *The poor provide the frontline soldiers for war.* The youth from poverty can be sacrificed during battle. (German generals used to call them "cannon fodder.") Where else would we get the many people that we need to fill the "grunt" jobs in the armed services—or to test the roads for bombs in such places as Iraq and Afghanistan?
7. *The poor help stabilize our political system.* Most poor people vote for Democrats, so to the degree that this party helps the U.S. political system, the poor contribute to that effort.
8. *The poor provide entertainment*. The lives of the poor are lives of despair—which become the story lines of novels, movies, and television. News programs also attract larger audiences and advertising revenue by featuring the murders, rapes, and other crimes of violence committed by the poor.

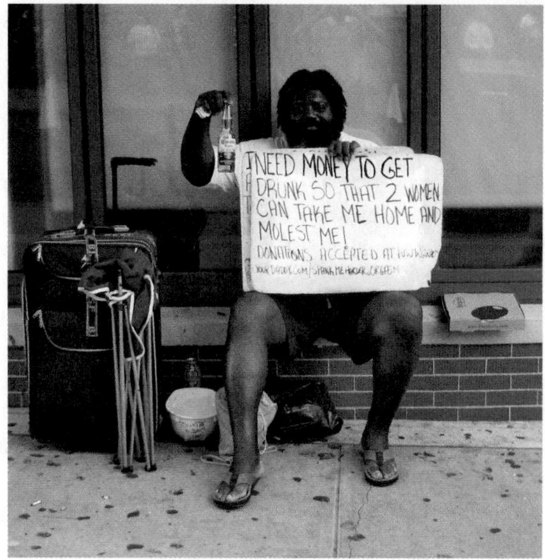

With tough economic times, a lot of people have lost their jobs—and their homes. If this happens, how can you survive? Maybe with a smile and a sense of humor to tap the kindness of strangers. I took this photo outside Boston's Fenway Park.

9. *The poor enrich our music.* They have given us the blues, Negro spirituals, country music (from the Southern poor), rock (the Beatles came from the slums of Liverpool), and hip-hop/rap. Without the devastating experiences of the poor, the rest of us would have fewer tunes to hum.
10. *The poor help motivate us.* That there are "the projects," skid row, homeless shelters, and soup lines keeps the rest of us on our toes. We know that if we don't get an education and work hard—doing whatever our teachers and bosses tell us—we could end up there. The poor have replaced the "bogeyman" of years past.
11. *The poor help our self-concept.* They make us all feel superior. *We* are not like *them.*
12. *The poor provide hope*. The heart-warming accounts of the poor who have "made it," overcoming huge obstacles to achievement, offer motivation for others. If those people could do it, we, too, can overcome our smaller obstacles.

By the time functionalists get through with their analysis, one wonders if society could even exist without the poor.

For Your Consideration

Do you think that we need some people to be poor? What functions of poverty can you think of that are not listed? How can the benefits that the poor provide society be replaced so we will no longer "need" poor people?

Marx, the managers of corporations are workers who serve the capitalists. This may be, but to lump them with factory workers produces a gap so huge that it is difficult to see why they should be included in the same group. We all know how little the managers of corporations, whose decisions can affect tens of thousands of workers around the world, have in common with office and factory workers, whose decisions mainly center around such ordinary things as what kind of breakfast cereal to buy.

Feminist theorists point to another fault with Marx's analysis. They point out that Marx analyzed the exploitation of workers in the paid sector, but he overlooked the unpaid sector, where women perform reproductive and household labor. This is another example, they stress, of men overlooking the contributions of women to the welfare of society. Feminist theorists also point out that Marx ignored key issues of gender, race-ethnicity, and age as areas of exploitation, that they are just as important as those between the owners of production and workers.

In Sum ▸ Conflict theorists stress the relationship between those who have power and those who do not. The problems of the poor are due to their deprived position in a system of stratification, to their relative powerlessness and oppression.

Summary of Theoretical Approaches

Each theoretical lens provides a unique understanding of wealth, poverty, and social inequality. Symbolic interactionists focus on the individual level, making us more sensitive to how social class works in our everyday lives. They explain, for example, why the amount of income that people have (the objective condition) is not the same as how people feel about that amount (subjective views that underlie relative poverty). Functionalists and conflict theorists look at a bigger picture. They examine social structure—in this case, the relationships between the poor and the wealthy, the powerful and the powerless. Where functionalists see inequality as originating from society's need to reward its important positions, conflict theorists stress how the means of production produce inequality.

Research Findings

7.4 Summarize research findings on who the poor are, a culture of poverty, who rules the United States, and explanations of global poverty.

Researchers have looked at poverty in depth. Let's examine the major patterns they have uncovered.

Who are the Poor?

Permanence of Poverty. It may surprise you that most people who fall below the poverty line do not stay there. Most people are poor only for short periods—when they are injured, sick, or during layoffs or slow seasons at work. The total number of poor in the United States remains fairly constant from year to year, but there is much change *within* this total. Each year millions of people rise above the poverty line, but at the same time millions of others fall below it.

Explore on **MySocLab Activity:** Income Inequality in Chicago

State and Region. Where people live makes a huge difference in their chances of being poor. One of the most striking examples is the inner city, where poverty is concentrated. To be born or reared there obviously increases your chances of living in poverty. The rural areas of the country also have higher than average poverty, although certainly not as concentrated as it is in the inner city. Poverty is also higher in some states and even entire regions, as you can see from the Social Map on the next page. The higher rate of poverty in the South that you see on this map has continued for about two centuries.

Race–Ethnicity. As you can see from Figure 7.7, poverty is also related to race–ethnicity: African Americans, Latinos, and Native Americans are *two to three times* as

FIGURE 7.6 ▸ The Geography of U.S. Poverty

What percentage of the population is in poverty?

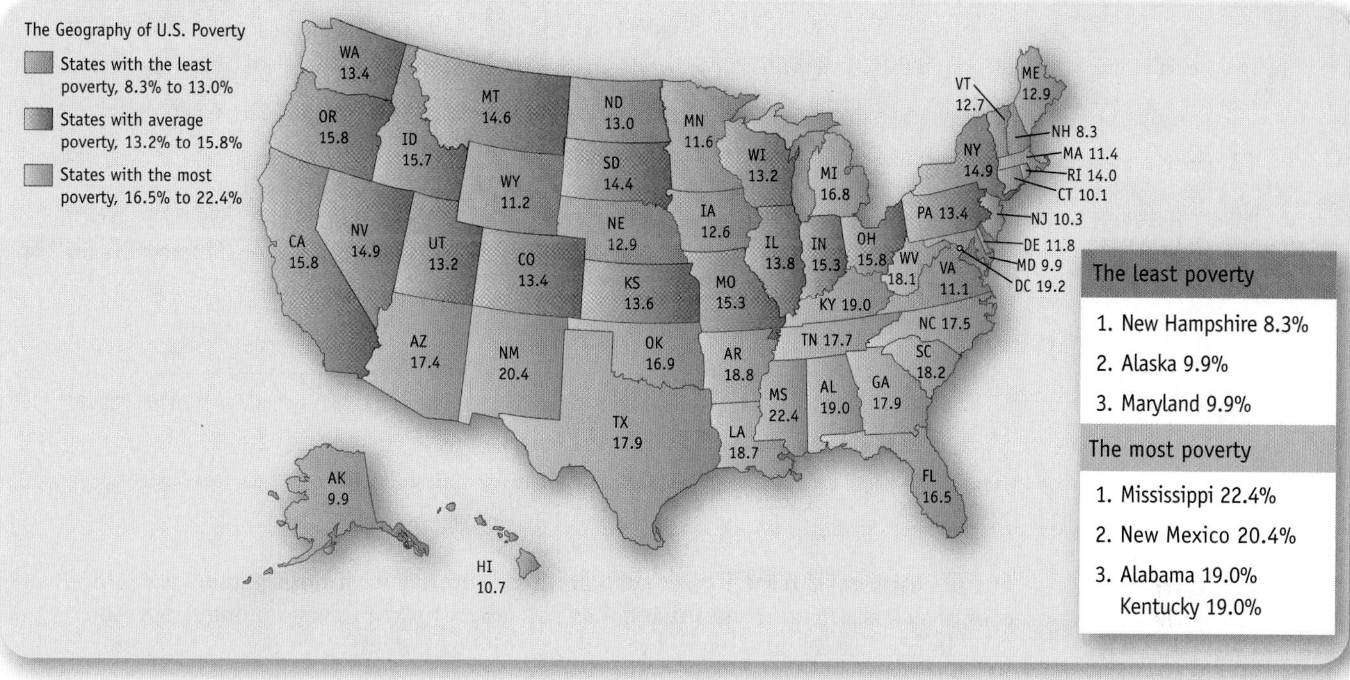

Source: By the author. Based on *Statistical Abstract of the United States* 2013:Table 721.

likely as whites to be poor. If their rates could be reduced to the rate of whites or of Asian Americans, millions of people would no longer live in poverty. They would be spared its many deprivations, so hazardous to the individual and corrosive to society. We should note, however, that progress has been made. As high as these rates are, they are lower than what they were in the 1970s and earlier years. Unfortunately, with our economic crisis, they have been increasing.

Children and the Elderly. Poverty is also related to age. The poverty rate of the elderly is lower than the national average, but the poverty rate of children is higher. As you can see from Figure 7.8 on the next page, the children's rate of poverty is *more than twice as high* as that of the seniors. Note how poverty among the elderly has declined while poverty among children has fluctuated and is now at the upper end of its range.

To get a different view of child poverty, look at Figure 7.9, which shows poverty among children by race–ethnicity. As you can see, poverty is lowest among Asian American children and considerably higher among Latino and African American children. Such extensive poverty in childhood has severe implications for the next generation.

FIGURE 7.7 ▸ Minorities Are More Likely to Be Poor

What percentage of these groups are poor?

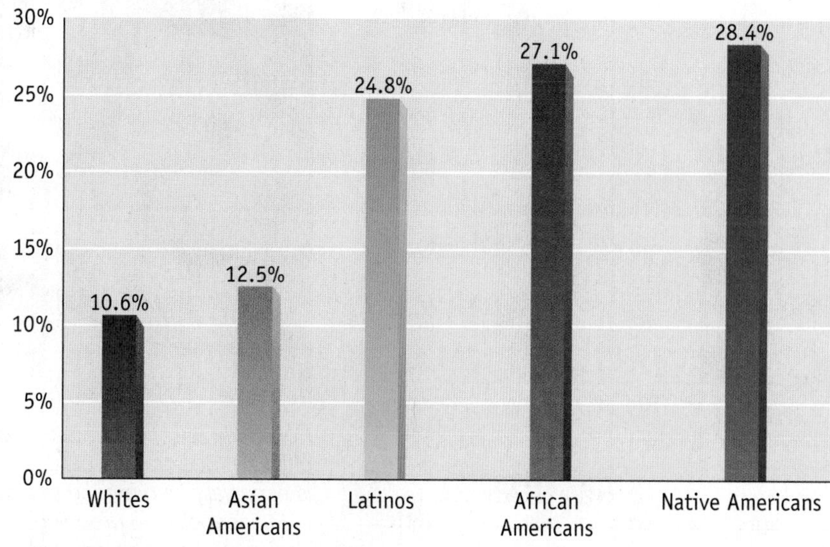

Source: By the author. Based on *Statistical Abstract of the United States* 2013:Table 36.

View on MySocLab **Figure:** Percent of Children Below the Poverty Line for All Children in Families, Children Living with Grandparents, and Children in Single-Mother Households

FIGURE 7.8 ▸ Comparing Poverty of Children and the Elderly

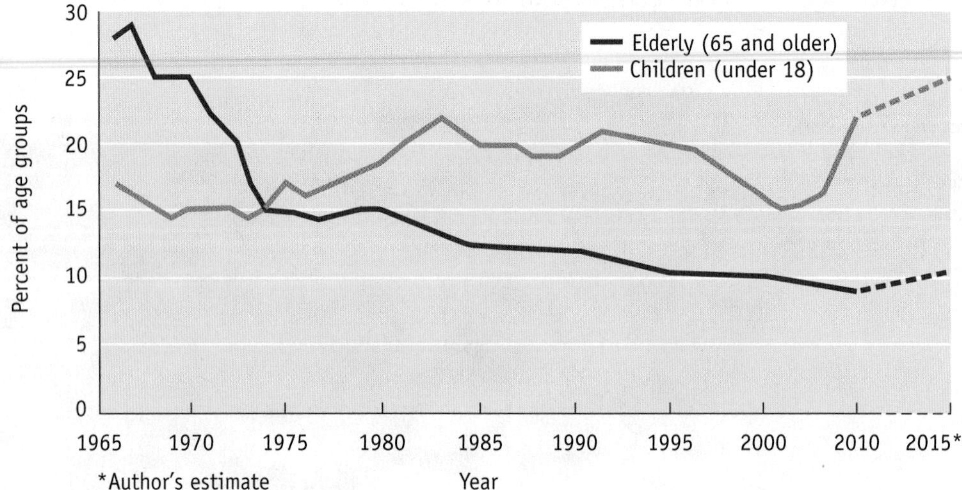

Source: By the author. Based on U.S. Census Bureau 2009; *Statistical Abstract of the United States* 1994:Tables728, 731; 2013:Table 725.

The Feminization of Poverty. Children who live with both parents are seldom poor, which is a major reason that childhood poverty is the lowest among Asian Americans. In contrast, children who live with just one parent are often poor. The reason for this is fairly simple: Two working parents earn more. In addition, as you know, it is usually the mother who heads single-parent families. These women average just *one-third* (33 percent) of what families with two working parents earn (*Statistical Abstract* 2013:Table 713).

Single mothers who bear children at a young age are especially disadvantaged. With their limited skills and ongoing child care responsibilities, how can they compete in the labor market? Women who divorce after being homemakers for years also face distinct disadvantages. Their

FIGURE 7.9 ▸ Child Poverty and Race–Ethnicity

What percentage of children in these groups live in poverty?

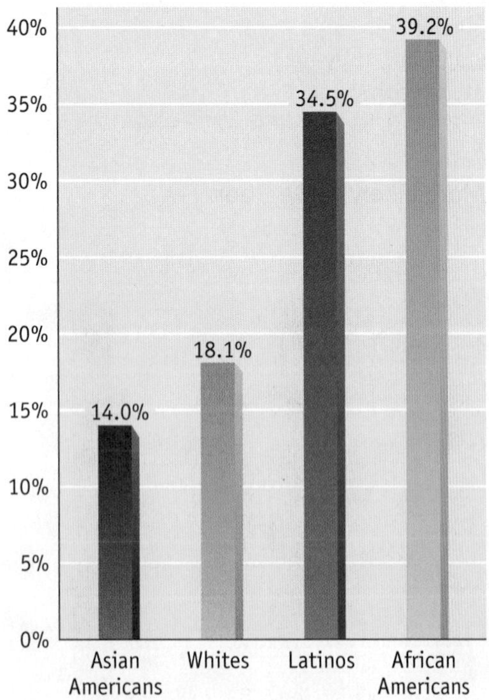

Note: Native Americans are not listed in the source. Their overall poverty rate was about 28.4 percent in 2010. I estimate their child poverty rate to be about 35 percent now.

Source: By the author. Based on *Statistical Abstract of the United States* 2013:Table 724.

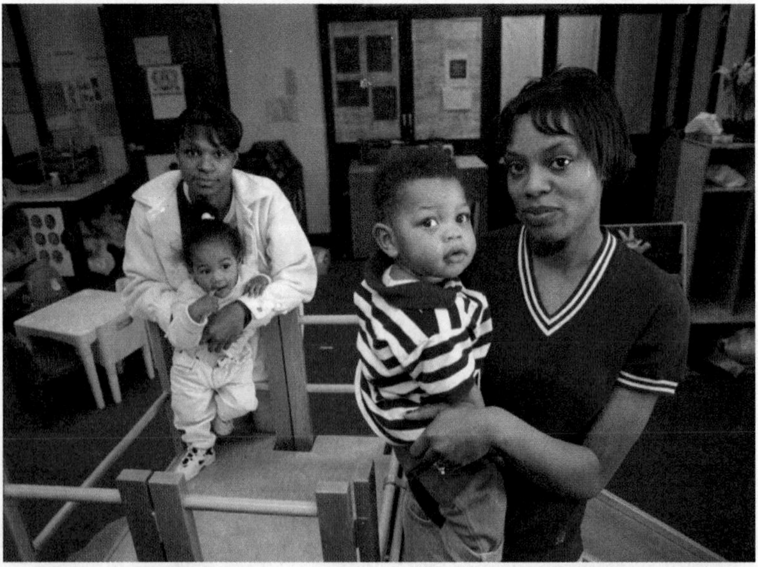

Poverty in the United States has become concentrated among women and children. Sociologists call this pattern the **feminization of poverty**. *Poverty is especially high among teenage mothers. These two high school students in Minneapolis are dropping their children off at day care while they attend classes. The day care helps young women complete high school, increasing their chances of avoiding poverty.*

income usually nosedives after divorce, and with their work skills rusty and no recent employer recommendations, good jobs are rare.

What about child support? As you can see from Figure 7.10, only about two of five single mothers receive all the child support that the courts order the absent fathers to pay. A fourth of the fathers skip out and pay nothing. Add all these factors together, and you can see why women and children are much more likely to be poor.

For a little side venture, and to see how you can avoid poverty and develop a financially secure life, see the Thinking Critically box below.

Minimum Wage Workers. Here is the final pattern of poverty, an obvious one: Most people who work at minimum wage jobs are poor. I am not referring to college students who take such jobs while they are preparing for careers that pay well. Rather, the United States has a large *underclass* made up of people who are locked into minimum wage jobs. They clean motel rooms, wash dishes in restaurants, do the "stoop labor" on farms, and fill the sweatshops of our cities. Some work in small factories or even at home, where they earn a specified amount for each piece of work they complete. For most, poverty will remain their lot in life.

FIGURE 7.10 ▸ Child Support Payments

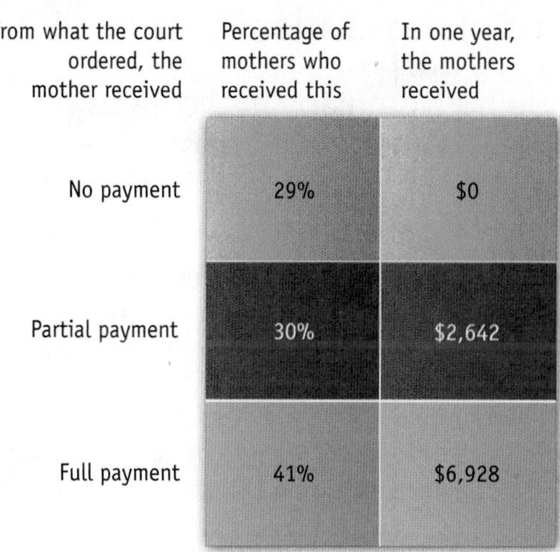

From what the court ordered, the mother received
Percentage of mothers who received this
In one year, the mothers received
No payment
29%
$0
Partial payment
30%
$2,642
Full payment
41%
$6,928

Note: These totals are based on the 51 percent of divorced mothers who had custody of their children and who were supposed to receive payments.

Source: By the author. Based on *Statistical Abstract of the United States* 2013:Table 582.

Blatant Poverty in the Midst of Plenty. How things have changed! Americans used to associate bread lines and soup kitchens with the Great Depression, or perhaps with Charles Dickens' description of nineteenth-century London. Now the homeless are part of every large city across this rich land. Most are tucked out of sight, but the presence of others on our streets and sidewalks reveals the contrast between the American dream and its stark reality. Who are these homeless people, ravaged by hunger and dressed in mismatched layers of out-of-date clothing? How did they get that way? These questions intrigued me, so I set out on a search for answers. I slept with the homeless in their shelters, ate with them there, and interviewed them wherever I could find them. The Thinking Critically box on the next page summarizes some of what I discovered on this sociological adventure.

View on **MySocLab**
Figure: Inflation-Adjusted Value of the Minimum Wage, 1950–2010, in 2010 Dollars

Thinking Critically About Social Problems

How to Avoid Poverty

If you want to avoid poverty, follow these three rules:

1. Finish high school.
2. Get married before you have your first child.
3. Don't have a child until after you reach the age of 20.

This message is being delivered to the black community by African American leaders (Herbert 1998). Hugh Price, president of the National Urban League, and retired General Colin Powell say that 80 percent of African Americans who ignore these principles end up poor, but only 8 percent of those who follow them are poor. Although their statistics may not be exact, the rules are sound—and they apply to all racial–ethnic groups.

Following these three "rules" will certainly help people avoid poverty, but let's look beyond them.

Here are four more "rules" that can help you not only avoid poverty but also develop a more financially secure life:

1. Go to college.
2. Stay married.
3. Avoid the misuse of drugs, including alcohol.
4. Avoid debt, especially on credit cards.

Poverty among people who follow these seven rules is practically nonexistent.

For Your Consideration

What other "rules" would you add to this list? If you or someone else has already broken one or more of the "rules," how can you overcome the consequences and avoid poverty?

Thinking Critically About Social Problems

Being Homeless in the Land of the American Dream

When I met Larry Rice, who runs a shelter for the homeless in St. Louis, Missouri, he said that as a sociologist I should learn firsthand what is happening on our city streets. I was reluctant to leave my comfortable home and office, but Larry baited a hook and lured me onto the streets. He offered to take me to Washington, D.C., where he promised that I would see people sleeping on sidewalk grates within view of the White House. Intrigued at the sight of such a contrast, I agreed to go with him, not knowing that it would change my life.

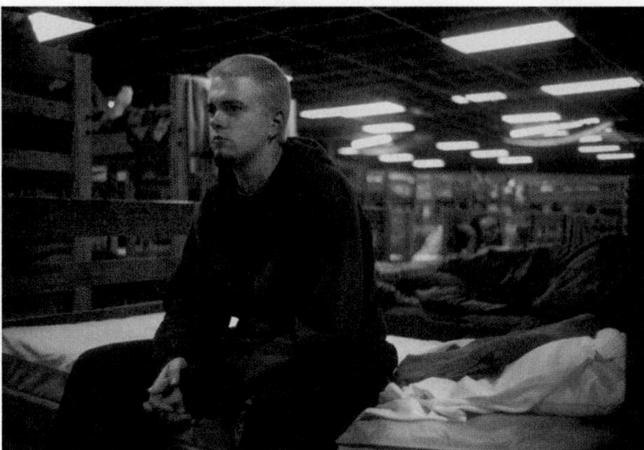

This man in California has a full-time job, but, unable to afford an apartment, he stays at a homeless shelter.

When we arrived in Washington, it was bitter cold. It was December, and I saw what Larry had promised: sorrowful people huddled over the exhaust grates of federal buildings. Not all of the homeless survived the first night I was there. Freddy, who walked on crutches and had become a fixture in Georgetown, froze to death as he sought refuge from the cold in a telephone booth. I vividly recall looking at the telephone booth where Freddy's frozen body was found, still upright, futilely wrapped in a tattered piece of canvas. I went to Freddy's funeral and talked with his friends. To me, Freddy became a person, an individual, not just a faceless, nameless figure shrouded by city shadows.

This experience ignited my sociological curiosity. I felt driven to learn more. I ended up visiting a dozen skid rows in the United States and Canada, sleeping in filthy shelters across North America. I interviewed the homeless in these shelters—and in alleys, on street corners, in parks, and even in dumpsters. I became so troubled by what I experienced that for three months after I returned home, I couldn't get through an entire night without waking up startled by disturbing dreams.

Listen on **MySocLab Audio:** NPR: A Few Small Steps to Homelessness

In this research, I discovered that there are many routes to homelessness. Here are the types of homeless people whom I met:

1. *"Push-outs"*: These people have been pushed out of their homes. Two common types of "push-outs" are teenagers kicked out by their parents and adults evicted by landlords.
2. *Victims of environmental disaster*: This type really surprised me, but they, too, live on our streets. The disasters I came across ranged from fires to dioxin contamination.
3. *The mentally ill*: These people have been discharged from mental hospitals. Although unable to care for themselves, they receive little or no treatment for their problems. Like the teenagers, they are easy victims of the predators who prowl our city streets.
4. *The new poor*: This group consists of unemployed workers whose work skills have become outdated because of technological change.
5. *The technologically unqualified*: Unlike the new poor, these unemployed workers never possessed technological qualifications.
6. *The elderly*: These people have neither savings nor family support; they are old, unemployable, and discarded.
7. *Runaways*: After fleeing intolerable situations, these boys and girls wander our streets.
8. *The demoralized*: After suffering some personal tragedy, these people have given up and retreated into despair. The most common catalyst to their demoralization is divorce.
9. *Alcoholics*: The old-fashioned skid-row wino is still out there.
10. *Ease addicts*: These people actually choose to be homeless. For them, homelessness is a form of "early retirement." They have no responsibilities to others, and they come and go as they want. Some, in their

(continued from previous page)

20s, spend their days playing chess in the parks of San Francisco.

11. *Travel addicts*: These people also choose to be homeless. Addicted to wanderlust, they travel continuously. They even have their own name for themselves: "road dogs."
12. *Excitement addicts*: Among the younger of the homeless, these people enjoy the thrill of danger. They like the excitement that comes from "living on the edge." Being on the streets offers many "edge" opportunities.

As you can see, the homeless are not a single group. Rather, they arrive on our city streets by many "routes." Note how different the "routes" are for the last three types (those who choose homelessness, a minority of the homeless) than for the first nine types, who do not want to be homeless. Because there are many "causes" of homelessness, it should be obvious that there can be no single solution to this social problem. We need multifaceted programs, perhaps based on the various "routes" by which people travel to this dead-end destination.

For Your Consideration

Based on the types of homeless people that I found on our streets, what solutions would you suggest to homelessness? Be practical.

In Sum: Social Structure. The patterns of poverty we have reviewed do not point to laziness, stupidity, or any other personal characteristics as its cause. Instead, they point to *structural features of society*. Poverty follows lines of geography, age, education, gender, race–ethnicity, and marital status. To understand poverty, sociologists examine features of the *social system*: discrimination, marriage and reproductive patterns, education, welfare programs, changes in the economy, and the availability of work. In later chapters, we shall discuss some of these patterns, but for now let's consider an analysis of poverty that has generated considerable controversy in sociology.

Is There a Culture of Poverty?

We boast of vast achievement and of power,
Of human progress knowing no defeat,
Of strange new marvels every day and hour—
And here's the bread line in the wintry street!

Berton Braley, "The Bread Line"

A Culture of Poverty. Why do some people remain poor in the midst of plenty? After years of doing participant observation with poor people and gathering extensive life histories, anthropologist Oscar Lewis (1959, 1966) concluded that people who remain poor year after year have developed a way of life that traps them in poverty. He called this the **culture of poverty**. Perceiving a gulf between themselves and the mainstream, these people feel inferior and insecure. Concluding that they are never going to get out of poverty, they become fatalistic and passive. They develop low aspirations and think about the present, not the future. Some become self-destructive, as illustrated by their high rates of alcoholism, physical violence, and family abuse. Their lives become marked by broken marriages, desertion, single-parent households, and self-defeating despair. Their way of life, this *culture of poverty* as Lewis called it, makes it almost impossible for them to break out of poverty.

Sociologists do not like the concept of a culture of poverty because it appears to blame poor people for their poverty. As I just stressed, sociologists look instead at *structural* causes of poverty. Herbert Gans, introduced in the earlier section on the functions of poverty, has also written extensively on this topic. He expresses his dislike of this concept in the Spotlight on Social Research box on the next page.

Spotlight on Social Research

Demonizing the Poor

HERBERT GANS, *professor of sociology at Columbia University, is a past president of the American Sociological Association. He has written extensively on urban poverty and antipoverty policy. Here is what he wrote for you.*

Ever since the 1950s, sociologists have led poverty researchers in studying America's victimized and demonized poor—although they have not done nearly enough research on their victimizers and demonizers.

Perhaps because I am a refugee from Nazi Germany and came to the United States dirt-poor, a significant part of my teaching and research has been about poverty and antipoverty policy. I have been concerned with the victimized and demonized, as well as the agencies and institutions that victimize and demonize the poor. In the early 1960s, I wrote *The Urban Villagers,* a book about a low-income neighborhood in Boston that was demonized as a slum and about its residents who were victimized when their neighborhood was torn down.

Later in the 1960s, I wrote a good deal about poverty and antipoverty policy—what is today called public sociology. Along with other sociologists, I analyzed and criticized the "culture of poverty" arguments, which suggested that the poor practice a culture that helps to keep them poor and prevents their escaping from poverty. We argued that blaming the victims for their victimization diverted attention away from what really keeps them poor: the shortage of secure and decent-paying jobs, the failures of the welfare program, and racism. Although their victimization resulted in depression and pathology, it was not a culture of poverty.

I returned to antipoverty research in the late 1980s, when a new version of, and a new term for, the culture of poverty argument appeared. This time, the poor were demonized as an "underclass," an alleged stratum that existed under respectable society. This underclass was accused of such moral shortcomings as not wanting to work, turning to welfare or street crime instead, being promiscuous, and avoiding marriage.

My interest in victimizers and demonizers made me wonder who invented and spread the new blaming term. In 1995, I wrote *The War Against the Poor,* which identified its inventors. The book also described how journalists, social scientists, and political conservatives combined to use and popularize the term.

Since the late 1990s, when welfare reform and a boom in low-wage jobs enabled more poor people to work, their demonization has declined—at least for the moment. However, if enough working poor lose their jobs to a weak economy, they surely will be demonized again—with the same old arguments, but perhaps with another new term. Then sociologists must show once more that blaming the victims only makes it harder for the poor to escape from poverty.

Testing the Concept. The culture of poverty is an interesting concept, but is it true? To find out, economist Patricia Ruggles examined national statistics of poverty and found that, contrary to popular belief, few poor adults pass poverty on to the next generation: *Most children of the poor do not grow up to be poor.* Only 1 of 5 people who are poor as children are still poor as adults (Corcoran et al. 1985; Sawhill 1988; Ruggles 1989, 1990). But in support of Lewis' culture of poverty, Ruggles also found that 1 percent of the U.S. population remains poor year in and year out. They were poor 20 years ago, they are poor today, and they will be poor tomorrow. This group shares three primary characteristics: Most are African American, are unemployed, and live in female-headed households.

From Ruggles' research, it seems fair to conclude that a few people do adopt a culture of poverty. They learn behaviors that keep them poor, and they pass this way of life on to their children. Because most people who are poor today will not be poor in just a few years, however, we can conclude that only a few people adopt a culture of poverty. Almost all do not.

We have been focusing on the poor and powerless. Now let's turn to the other extreme of social class.

Who Rules the United States?

Who Has The Power? Conflict theorists stress that to understand social life we must understand who controls society's scarce resources. Like wealth, power is a scarce resource: Some people have much of it, while others have little or none. Max Weber, an early sociologist, defined **power** as the ability to get your way despite resistance (Weber 1921/1964). The possession of power is especially significant because it determines who gets the lion's share of the other resources in society. Let's ask, then, who makes the major decisions in the United States?

The Power Elite. Sociologist C. Wright Mills (1959a) argued that a **power elite** rules the United States. He said that a small group made up of the top military, political, and business leaders makes decisions that direct the country—and shakes the world. Figure 7.11 illustrates Mills' view of the power elite.

Mills stressed that the power elite is not a formal group. It meets neither in secret nor in public. In fact, some members may not even think they belong to it. But, structurally, it exists. The power elite consists of top leaders whose interests have merged. As people move from one top position to another, the power elite gains cohesion. White House aides join powerful law firms. A law partner joins the president's cabinet or is appointed secretary of the treasury. The head of the treasury becomes the CEO of a leading bank or corporation. An air force colonel retires and then takes over the sales division of Boeing or General Dynamics.

FIGURE 7.11 ▸ **How Is Power Distributed in the United States? The Model Proposed by C. Wright Mills**

Source: Based on Mills 1959a.

Because the Power Elite does not meet as a group, it cannot be photographed. The Forbes are part of this group. Shown here are Malcolm Forbes and his three brothers at the Forbes Building. Their collection of nine Faberge Easter eggs that used to belong to the czars of Russia sold at auction for $100 million.

Read on **MySocLab Document:** C. Wright Mills, The Power Elitve

Because these people share interests and experiences in business and politics, they think alike on major issues. In addition, they come from similar backgrounds, and they share similar values. Most are WASPs, White Anglo-Saxon Protestants, who attended exclusive prep schools and Ivy League colleges. Many belong to the same private clubs and vacation at the same exclusive resorts. These people, then, are united by shared backgrounds, contacts, ideologies, values, and interests (Domhoff 1974, 1990, 2009).

Mills said that the three groups that make up the power elite—the top political, military, and corporate leaders—are not equal in power. To identify who was dominant, Mills did not point to the president, however, or even to the generals and admirals, but, rather, to the heads of corporations. Because all three segments of the power elite view capitalism as essential to the welfare of the country, national policy centers on business interests. Making decisions that promote U.S. business works to the mutual benefit of all three groups.

Sociologist William Domhoff (1990, 2009) prefers to use the term "ruling class" instead of power elite. He studied the 1 percent of Americans who belong to the super-rich. These people are so wealthy that *they are worth more than 90 percent of the rest of the nation* (Beeghley 2008). This 1 percent controls the nation's top corporations and foundations, even the boards that oversee our major universities. They also own the nation's major newspapers, magazines, and television stations. Members of this powerful group attempt, quite successfully, to shape the consciousness of the nation. It is no accident, says Domhoff, that from this group come most of the president's cabinet and top ambassadors.

Conflict theorists stress that we should not think of the power elite or ruling class as a group that meets and makes specific decisions. Rather, with their interlocking economic and political interests, their behavior stems not from a grand conspiracy to control the country but from mutual interest in solving the problems that face big business (Useem 1984). Able to ensure that the country adopts the social policies that it deems desirable—from interest rates to sending troops abroad—this powerful group sets the economic and political agenda under which the rest of the country lives (Domhoff 1990, 2009).

Explore on **MySocLab** **Activity:** Collars and Colors in America

The Pluralist View. Not all sociologists agree that a power elite is pulling the strings behind the scenes. The **pluralists** present a contrasting view. Pluralists argue that many **interest groups**—people united by their mutual interests in some matter—are competing for social, economic, and political power. *No single group is in control.* As unions, industries, professional associations, and the like compete with one another, consensus is reached, or at least tradeoffs are agreed on, that allow decisions to be made and society to function.

Sociologist David Riesman (1951) and his colleagues, who developed this *pluralist view of power*, put it this way: Power is dispersed because the country's many groups are divided by essential differences. This makes united policy or action impossible (Kornhauser 1961; Marger 1987; Beeghley 2008). Mills replied that members of the power elite settle important differences among themselves.

Continuing Research on the Controversy. The controversy between the pluralists and the sociologists who support the view of the power elite is long-standing and unresolved. In 1961, sociologist Robert Dahl published a study on power in New Haven, Connecticut, the home of Yale University. He found little overlap between the social elites of the university and the town and little influence by either of them on the city's policies. Dahl's research became classic in support of the pluralistic view of power in the United States.

Conflict theorists remained unconvinced. William Domhoff (1978b) reanalyzed Dahl's data. Unlike Dahl, Domhoff found that Yale University, New Haven's businesses, and its other social institutions were interlocked extensively. His conclusion was that a power elite of corporate heads, bankers, social leaders, and politicians shapes New Haven's economy. He also documented how this local power elite is connected to national elites. Domhoff suggests that each major city in the United States has such a power center and that lines run from these cities to the national power structure.

Economists did research that has intriguing implications. Examining the relationships among 72 U.S. companies that deal with low-level radioactive waste, they found extensive connections among the companies' directors. These companies are so bound together, the researchers concluded, that they form a power bloc (Hayden et al. 2002). It is possible, and perhaps likely, that each type of industry (insurance, airlines, banking, and so on) in the United States has its own similar interlocking power structure. We need more research to find out.

Other sociologists have found similar interconnections among the boards of directors of major corporations (Moore 1979; Useem 1979). They conclude that there is an interlocking power elite. Yet, because researchers are unable to study how decisions are made (for example, policy on the Middle East), their research does not demonstrate that U.S. elites form a cohesive ruling group.

The Culture of Wealth. Although the question of a cohesive ruling group must remain open until we have more evidence, this brings us to another significant question: Does the culture of the elite—its institutions, customs, values, worldviews, family ties, and connections—allow the rich and powerful to perpetuate their privileges? In other words, is there a **culture of wealth** that keeps people from falling down the social class ladder, just as some claim that a culture of poverty makes it difficult for poor people to climb even a single rung of that ladder? Of course, there is. The elite of any city, region, or nation—indeed of any group—tend to develop common sentiments and share similar values and goals. The sociological problem is not to determine whether this occurs but to discover how it operates. That a culture of wealth exists, however, does not mean that the elite work together to rule the country. This is a different matter entirely.

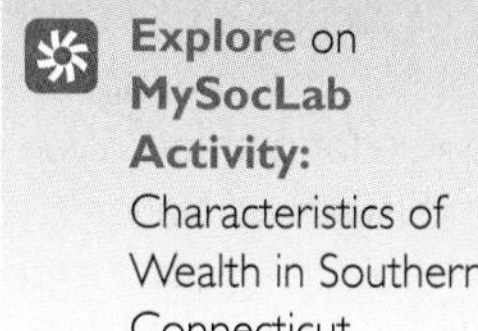

Explore on
MySocLab
Activity:
Characteristics of
Wealth in Southern
Connecticut

It is precisely here that many sociologists see danger—that the concentration of wealth and power violates the democratic processes on which our country is premised. Interlocking interests by wealthy people in powerful positions can result in a few non-elected individuals wielding immense control over the country.

Can? Those who support the power elite view say that this is the way the country *is* run. This, for example, is why the Obama administration bailed out the big banks with billions of taxpayers' dollars (or, more accurately, why the politicians indebted the children of future generations for the sake of Wall Street).

Inequality and Global Poverty

Global Stratification. Just as the United States is stratified into different social classes, so the globe is stratified into rich and poor nations. The Most Industrialized Nations, which are wealthy, have **residual poverty**, or pockets of poverty. Most of the Least Industrialized Nations, in contrast, have **mass poverty**: In some, *most* citizens live on less than $1,000 a year. These people are malnourished, chronically ill, and die young. The Global Glimpse box on the next page reports on the abysmal conditions faced by some children in nations that experience mass poverty.

One intriguing issue arises: Why do some nations remain poor year after year? Let's try to find the answer.

Economic Colonialism. Some analysts think that exploitation is the answer. The powerful nations used to practice *political colonialism.* To obtain raw materials, they invaded and conquered weaker nations. They would post a military force in these nations, and their "business representatives" would extract the resources they wanted. These weaker, formerly serf nations now have political freedom. Today's dominant nations, instead of invading weaker nations, exploit them by a process called **economic colonialism**. The Most Industrialized Nations buy raw materials from the poor nations and sell them manufactured products. With the Most Industrialized Nations dominating the global markets, the poor nations sell their food and natural resources—from

A Global Glimpse

Killing Kids for Fun and Profit

What is childhood like in the Least Industrialized Nations? As in the United States, the answer depends on who your parents are. If your parents are rich, childhood can be pleasant. If you are born into poverty but live where there is plenty to eat, life can still be good—although you will lack books, television, and education. But you probably won't miss them. If you live in a slum, however, life can be horrible, worse than in the slums of the Most Industrialized Nations. Let's take a glimpse of the slums (*favelas*) of Brazil.

Alcoholism, drug abuse, child abuse, wife beating, a lot of crime, and not having enough food—you can take these for granted. Even in the inner cities of the Most Industrialized Nations, you would expect these things.

You might not expect this, though: Poverty is so deep that children and adults swarm over garbage dumps to find enough decaying food to keep them alive. Sociologist Martha Huggins (1993) reports that the owners of these dumps hire armed guards to keep the poor out—so they can sell the garbage for pig food. And here's something else you might not expect: Death squads murder some of these children. Some associations of shop owners even put assassins on retainer and auction victims off to the lowest bidder! The going rate is half a month's salary—figured at the low Brazilian minimum wage. Some of the hired killers are policemen.

Life is cheap in the Least Industrialized Nations—but death squads for children? To understand how this could possibly be, we need to note that Brazil has a fragile political structure and a long history of violence. With high poverty and a small middle class, the potential of mob violence and revolution always lurk in the background. The "dangerous classes," as they are known, are ominous, a threat to the status quo. Groups of homeless children, who have no jobs or prospects of getting work, roam the streets.

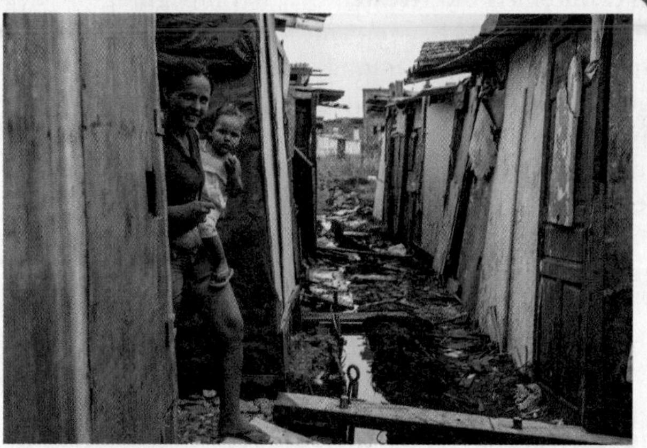

Life in the slums isn't healthy for anyone. You can see the open sewage trench in this Brazilian favela. *Beyond this negative aspect of living here are the death squads discussed in this box.*

To survive, these children scramble in and out of traffic to wash the windshields of cars that are stopped at red lights. They shine shoes, beg, steal, and sell their bodies.

The street children annoy the "respectable" classes, who see them as trouble. When they get older, what kind of productive adults will they be? Just more criminals. Sometimes the children break into stores. They hurt business, for customers feel intimidated when they see poorly dressed adolescents clustered in front of a store. Some children even sell items in competition with the stores. Without social institutions to care for these children, one solution is to kill them. As Huggins notes, murder sends a clear message to the children, especially if it is accompanied by torture—gouging out the eyes, ripping open the chest, cutting off the genitals, raping the girls, and burning the victim's body.

For Your Consideration

Can the Most Industrialized Nations do anything about this situation? Or is it none of our business? Is it, though unfortunate, an internal affair for the Brazilians to handle?

bananas and coffee to copper and manganese—at prices that barely allow them to keep up with their expanding populations. Few actually do keep up, and each year they fall deeper in debt to the Most Industrialized Nations. As a result, these nations are unable to accumulate the capital they need to develop their own industries. Year after year, they remain poor.

Political pressure—accompanied by the veiled and not-so-veiled threat of military intervention—is often the force that maintains economic colonialism. Consider the oil-rich nations of the Middle East. What do you think would happen if one of these nations were to try to break the yoke of economic colonialism? What if one of these nations were to gain control over its own resources—or even become dominant in this region? It could then control the flow of oil to the West, set high oil prices, and lead the Most Industrialized Nations by the nose. Do you think that the Most Industrialized Nations would allow this? The answer should be obvious. When Iraq made an attempt to dominate this region, the United States and its allies invaded, supposedly on behalf of Kuwait, but those who look at history through the lens of economic colonialism see it differently. The Gulf Wars, both the first and second ones, were a response to threats to the West's economic colonialism of the Middle East.

If another country in this region tries to become independently dominant, we can expect another violent reprisal of some sort. As I write this, Iran seems to be filling this role.

National Power Elites. You might have noticed that in the example I gave of economic colonialism, the oil-rich nations are not poor. In each of these nations, though, the wealth is hoarded by a national power elite. This takes us to our second answer as to why some nations remain poor. In these nations, a *national elite* uses the nation's resources as though they were its personal possession—which is how the elite does think of them. The elite's first goal is to keep itself in power, and it uses these resources for this purpose. The West is happy, for example, when the oil-rich nations exchange their oil wealth for sophisticated jet fighters and other weapons. It is not the West's concern how a national power elite uses these weapons. Its members can exploit their citizens to their hearts' content—as long as the oil keeps flowing.

The national power elites also have the goal of using the nation's wealth for their own pleasure, to enjoy a luxurious lifestyle, and to build prestige for themselves both within their country and among their neighbors. The power elite lives a sophisticated, upper-class lifestyle in the capital city, with vacation homes at the seashore or in neighboring countries. Its members send their children to elite universities, to Oxford, the Sorbonne, and Harvard. The national power elite operates businesses that are guaranteed success because they are protected from competition and given lush government contracts. To make investments in these countries, the multinational corporations pay bribes, politely called "offset fees" or "subsidies," which go to these elites.

A Culture of Poverty. Some suggest a third explanation for why poverty continues in the Least Industrialized Nations—they suffer from a culture of poverty. John Kenneth Galbraith (1979), who reported on his experiences as U.S. Ambassador to India, said that India has a culture of fatalistic resignation, reinforced by religion. He pointed out that most of the world's poor make a living off the land. With barely enough to live on, these poor farmers are reluctant to experiment with different crops or ways of farming: Something new might fail, which would lead to hunger or death. Their religion also teaches them to accept their lot in life as God's will and to look for rewards in the afterlife. Galbraith emphasized that poor countries do not lack resources. Most have many natural resources—most much greater than resource-starved Japan. Their weak position in world markets, however, combined with their fatalistic culture, makes it unlikely that they will rise from poverty.

In Sum ▸ Which explanation is the right one? As you read an explanation, you probably felt inclined to agree with it, only to read another and think that it might be right. Professional analysts, too, find no agreement on these explanations, although they tend to choose one and argue it as the truth. The fairest conclusion seems to be that all three hold some degree of truth, that together they give a fuller explanation than any does separately. Also, each is lacking. None, for example, would explain the current rise of China on the world stage of power.

Social Policy

7.5 Explain how shifting views have influenced social policy, what progressive taxation is, and what social programs to relieve poverty are being implemented or considered.

Changing Views and Changing Social Policy

How people view the causes of social problems influences the social policies they favor. As you saw, when poverty was thought to be God's will, the proper response was thought to be a personal religious duty to shelter, feed, and clothe the poor. As people's views change, so do their ideas regarding which social policies are appropriate.

Early United States. During the time of the American Revolution, poor people were viewed as wayward and lazy. Boston opened a "workhouse" where the poor had to work until they showed that they had acquired self-discipline and an appreciation of hard work. Philadelphia Quakers built almshouses that took in poor women and children. These social policies marked a departure from providing relief on an individual basis. The government was beginning to provide institutionalized care of the poor (Nash 1979).

In the 1830s, people believed that the squalor of cities caused poverty, so the logical solution was to take the poor away from the city's corrupting influence. Life in the country would restore poor people's basic sense of decency and order (Rothman 1971). This attempt failed when institutions in the country filled up and budgets were cut. The institutions became human warehouses of the worst sort.

It is difficult to remove ourselves from the views that dominate us at our own historical moment, but let's try to appreciate the attitudes of the time. Consider this statement from Henry Ward Beecher, who was the most prominent clergyman of his day:

> *It is said that a dollar a day is not enough for a wife and five or six children. No, not if the man smokes and drinks beer. . . . But is not a dollar a day enough to buy bread with? Water costs nothing, and a man who cannot live on bread and water is not fit to live. A family may live on good bread and water in the morning, water and bread at midday, and good water and bread at night. (quoted in Thayer 1997)*

A dollar went a lot farther in those days, to be sure, and people did pump water freely from backyard wells. But to live on only bread and water—and for that to be considered right?

The Great Depression. Then came the 1930s, when the United States was thrown into the Great Depression. As businesses closed and unemployment skyrocketed, so did poverty. Many people who previously worked hard and supported their families did not have enough food to eat. Their economic security jerked from beneath them, people who had once occupied the middle class lined up with the "old poor" in breadlines. At his 1937 inaugural address, President Franklin D. Roosevelt said, "Millions of families are trying to live on incomes so meager that the pall of family disaster hangs over them day by day. . . . I see one-third of a nation ill-housed, ill-clad, and ill-nourished" (quoted in Fisher 1988).

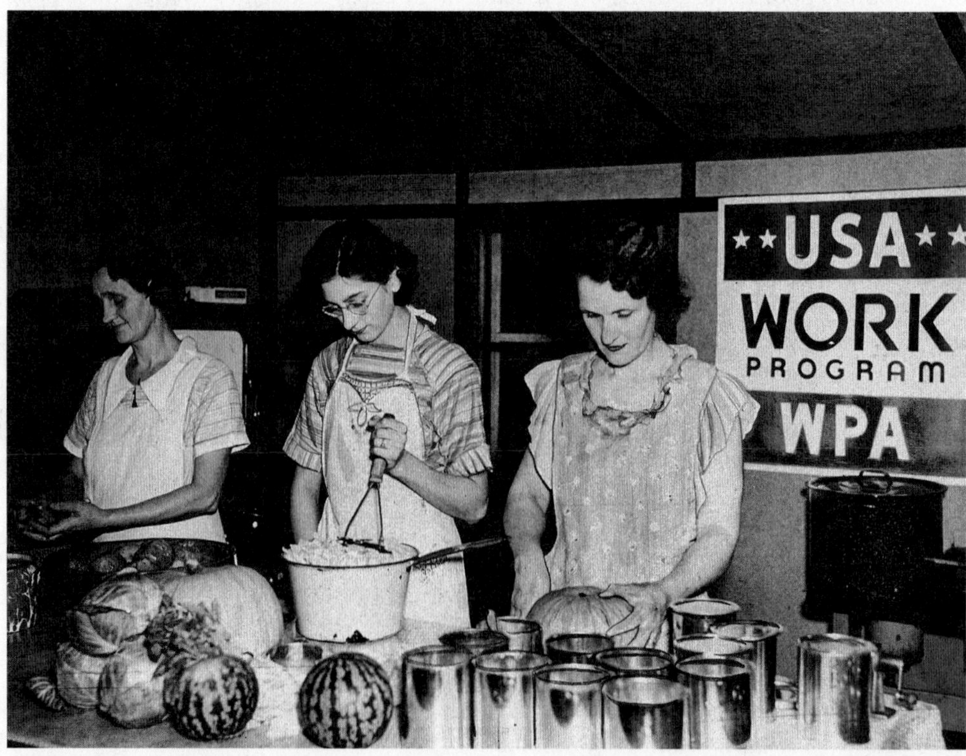

To help those suffering during the Great Depression of the 1930s, the federal government began the Works Progress Administration (WPA). Participants followed the traditional gender roles of the time, with men doing construction and women using homemaking skills.

As masses of people became poor, once again the nation's perspective changed. No longer was poverty viewed as the result of God's will, flawed character, or the corruption of the city. Rather, poverty came to be seen as the result of institutional (economic) failure—the lack of jobs. To match this shift in view, the Roosevelt administration created job programs to build parks and public facilities across the nation. They also established basic welfare to help families survive until the husband-father could get a job.

World War II. During World War II, when the economy picked up, poverty declined sharply. As jobs became available and men went back to work—and, during World War II, women also—poverty didn't disappear. It was, however, less visible. As described earlier in this chapter, new programs came in when poverty was "rediscovered" in the 1960s. Some programs provided education and training so the poor could get jobs. Other programs were based on the assumption that some of the poor, such as single mothers, children, and the elderly, needed to be subsidized.

The Basic Difference—Cause as Inside or Outside of People. As you can see, views have shifted between attributing poverty to forces within the individual (laziness, stupidity, corruption) and to forces outside the individual (God, the evil city, the economy). These contrasting assumptions bring with them different ideas of which social policies are appropriate. To assume that the causes of poverty lie *within* people leads to such policies as teaching self-discipline and sterilization. To assume that the causes of poverty lie *outside* the individual leads to such policies as education, social reform, job training, and stimulating the economy. Our cycles of social reform still reflect this duality of internal and external forces.

Although different generations define poverty differently, in each era these two core questions remain: What is the cause of poverty and what should we do about it?

Let's look at today's social policies.

Progressive Taxation

To reduce social inequality, the United States has a policy of **progressive taxation**. This means that tax rates progress (increase) as income progresses (increases). It is important to understand that it is not just the amount of taxes that are paid, but the rate itself that increases: The higher the income, the higher the tax rate. You can see this progression on Table 7.1 on the next page. As Americans earn more, they not only pay more dollars in taxes, but they also pay a larger percentage of their income in taxes. Despite the many criticisms leveled against our tax system, as you can see, the richest 237,000 Americans, those who make a million dollars or more a year, pay more taxes than the entire 87 million people in the first six categories. But is this enough? This, of course, is another issue, one based on ideas of values and fairness.

To help the poor, we have a social policy called the Per Child Tax Credit, commonly called a *negative income tax*. Parents whose income falls below a specified amount get a tax credit of $1,000 per child. If their income is low enough, they not only pay no tax, but they also get a check from the government when they file their tax form (Internal Revenue Service 2013).

There is no question that progressive taxation raises huge sums. (Try adding the totals shown on Table 7.1.) The question is what the politicians do with these immense amounts. Some of the additional money raised by taxing wealthier people at higher rates is redistributed to the poor through welfare, Medicaid, housing subsidies, child care, job training, and food stamps, but some of it is used to build submarines, missiles, and bridges that go nowhere. Perhaps a reasonable social policy would be to build a system to hold politicians accountable for how they spend our tax money. I don't want to be too critical, but if they can spend billions of dollars to bail out Wall Street bankers who made investing mistakes, why can't they do a better job of financing public assistance programs, such as those we will now discuss?

TABLE 7.1 ▸ Income Taxes Paid by Americans

Adjusted Gross Income	Number of Returns	Tax Paid as a Percentage of Adjusted Gross Income	Approximate Tax Paid by Each Individual	Total Tax Paid
$1,000–$4,999	8,648,000	4	$146	$1,000,000,000
$5,000–$10,999	14,659,000	3	$225	$3,000,000,000
$11,000–$18,999	18,389,000	3	$384	$7,000,000,000
$19,000–$29,999	20,841,000	5	$1,129	$24,000,000,000
$30,000–$39,999	14,372,000	6	$2,101	$30,000,000,000
$40,000–$49,999	10,796,000	7	$3,031	$33,000,000,000
$50,000–$74,999	18,695,000	8	$4,740	$89,000,000,000
$75,000–$99,999	11,464,000	8	$7,326	$84,000,000,000
$100,000–$199,999	13,522,000	12	$15,873	$215,000,000,000
$200,000–$499,999	3,195,000	20	$55,475	$178,000,000,000
$500,000–$999,999	493,000	24	$164,233	$81,000,000,000
$1,000,000 or more	237,000	24	$753,994	$179,000,000,000

Source: By the author. Based on *Statistical Abstract of the United States* 2013:Table 496.

Public Assistance Programs

We can divide public assistance programs into the following four types.

Social Insurance. This type of program, which includes unemployment compensation and Social Security, is designed to help people help themselves. Money is deducted from workers' paychecks, and workers are able to draw on this pool when they need it. Few oppose helping workers who are laid off when an entire industry, such as steel or automobiles, is hit by recession.

Teaching Job Skills. The second type of program is intended to help the poor become self-supporting so that they no longer need social welfare. Most of these programs, such as the Job Corps, center on teaching job skills. Some also teach personal grooming, punctuality, and politeness so that prospective workers can meet employer expectations.

Welfare. A third type of program is *welfare*—giving money, food, housing, and medical care to people who have a low enough income to qualify for them. The distinction between deserving and undeserving is replaced by a humanitarian notion that people in need should be helped regardless of who is responsible for their problems. Some of these programs such as Temporary Assistance for Needy Families (TANF), food stamps, and public housing generate controversy because people think they encourage laziness and single women to bear children. Many also think that people who receive this help could work if they wanted to. This stereotyping of the poor has consequences for their lives, the topic of the Thinking Critically box on the next page.

Workfare. A fourth type of program is *workfare*. Critics claim that welfare reduces people's incentive to work. They say, "Why will people work if they can get money, housing, and food free?" As U.S. welfare rolls swelled to 14 million people in the early 1990s, criticisms grew louder and shriller. The media ran stories about "welfare queens" who collected welfare checks and drove "welfare Cadillacs." "Welfare queen" refers to a woman who is thought to be ripping off the welfare system. She could work, but collects welfare instead, perhaps several checks under different names, often while men support her at home. This term is used to demean single mothers, especially African American women who need assistance.

Thinking Critically About Social Problems

Welfare: How to Ravage the Self-Concept

This was written by Christine Hoffman as an assignment in my introductory course in sociology. I am grateful for her permission to use it in this form.

My husband left me shortly after I was diagnosed with multiple sclerosis. At the time, I had five children. My oldest child was 14, and my youngest was 7. My physician, believing I would be seriously disabled, helped get me on Social Security disability. The process took several months, and so it became necessary for me to go on public aid and food stamps.

By the time I needed to depend on my family in the face of a crisis, there weren't any resources left to draw on. My father had passed away, and my mother was retired, living on a modest income based on Social Security and my father's pension. Isn't it funny how there is no social stigma attached to Social Security benefits for the elderly? People look at this money as an entitlement—"We worked for it." But people who have to depend on public aid for existence are looked at like vermin and accused of being lazy.

I can tell you from my own experience that a great deal of the lethargy that comes from long periods on welfare is due primarily to the attitudes of the people you have to come into contact with in these programs. I've been through the gamut: from rude, surly caseworkers at Public Aid, to patronizing nurses at the WIC [Women, Infants, and Children] clinic ("You have *how* many children?"), to the accusing tone of the food pantry workers when you have to go begging for a handout before the 30-day time span has expired. After a while your dignity is gone, and you start to believe that you really are the disgusting human trash they all make you out to be.

This woman is waiting in a county welfare office in Sacramento, California. She is fearful that with the state's budget deficit the food stamps for her daughter will be cut.

For Your Consideration

If you think that the self-concept is important, why should the poor have any less right to a good self-concept than people who aren't poor? Why should poor people have to endure the experiences that Christine describes? How can we improve the welfare delivery system?

As criticism mounted, the federal government passed the 1996 *Personal Responsibility and Work Opportunity Reconciliation Act.* This law requires states to place a lifetime cap on welfare assistance and compels welfare recipients to look for work and take available jobs. It makes 5 years the maximum length of time that someone can collect welfare. In some states, it is less. Unmarried teen parents must attend school and live at home or in some other adult-supervised setting.

Workfare was met with severe criticism ("It's a way of throwing the poor into the streets"), but national welfare rolls plummeted by 60 percent (Haskins 2006). Unfortunately, many people who no longer are on welfare have no jobs. Perhaps there are a few who don't want to work, but most of these people can't work because of bad health, lack of transportation, lack of child care, or addiction to alcohol or other drugs (Goodman 2010). Many of those who do have jobs earn so little that they remain in poverty. On the bright side, however, about two of five who have left welfare for workfare are no longer in poverty.

Since the economic crisis that began in 2008, the economy has hemorrhaged millions of jobs. We don't have complete studies yet, but with the lifetime limitations on welfare assistance, one in five low-income single mothers now has no earnings and no cash government assistance (Loprest and Nichols 2011). In both our cities and suburbs, you can see people picking through garbage.

It seems reasonable that the goal should not be to just cut people off welfare, but to increase their ability to compete in the job market. This takes us back to teaching job skills, so vital for avoiding welfare in the first place.

Feminized Poverty and Child Support

As we reviewed earlier, poverty is largely feminized; that is, women with children make up most of the poor. As feminist theorists point out, this imbalance exists because women do not receive equal pay. On this broader level, social policies that lead to flexible work schedules and higher pay for women will help. So will improvements in women's job training for career advancement. At the same time, social policies that promote better child care facilities and child care assistance will also help.

It also seems reasonable that absent fathers, whether or not they were married to their children's mothers, should support the children they fathered, rather than letting these children become the government's responsibility. The courts can award child care support that better reflects the father's earnings. The courts can also do a better job of making sure that fathers pay the child support that they order them to pay. Recall from Figure 7.10 on page 207 that most mothers do not receive their full awards—and that one-fourth receive nothing from the fathers of their children. Some fathers, of course, are unemployed and can pay little or nothing. In those instances, it seems reasonable for the state to support those children to lift them out of poverty and to prepare them for a productive future.

Private Agencies and Faith-Based Programs

When we think of aid for the poor, we generally think of the government. The United States also has thousands of private agencies and volunteer organizations that work to help the poor. Because these groups work mainly with the desperate poor, tucked in out-of-the-way urban centers and rural areas, few Americans see them in action. The Salvation Army, for example, runs soup kitchens and homeless shelters, as do other religious groups. The Salvation Army's efforts on behalf of the poor include alcohol counseling and job training.

Until the past few years, the federal government did not fund religious charities on the basis that doing so would violate the principle of separation of church and state. Religious charities are now allowed to compete for federal funds. Without weighing in on the issue of whether the government should fund religious charities, I will point out that without the efforts of religious groups the social problem of poverty would be much worse than it is. Their long history of charity hospitals and other programs for the poor is outstanding. The quality of faith-based groups, however, varies widely. When I slept and ate in the homeless shelters, I found that some have a personal, encouraging touch. Others, however, show a disgusting disrespect for the homeless people they are supposedly helping. All programs—private, government, or faith-based—must be monitored carefully.

The Purpose of Helping the Poor

What is the purpose of helping the poor? For faith-based organizations, the purpose is connected with their ideas of what God wants them to do. For private groups, the purpose is simply humanitarian: "It's good to help people." Conflict sociologists suggest that when the government offers welfare, the underlying motive is quite different. Let's look at this view.

Regulating the Poor. Conflict sociologists Frances Piven and Richard Cloward (1971, 1982, 1989, 1997) argue that because of its "booms" and "busts," capitalism needs a flexible supply of low-skilled, low-paid temporary workers. These people can be put to work when the economy expands and discarded when the economy slows. Welfare is a tool to maintain this pool of temporary workers. It keeps the temporary labor supply from starving during slowdowns so they are available during the next business expansion. To support this assertion, Piven and Cloward point to the changing rules of welfare: In times of high unemployment, when political disorder looms, welfare rules soften. This quiets the impoverished, keeping them from rioting, so they can receive their weekly check. When temporary workers are needed during "boom" times, the welfare rules are tightened. In short, conclude these theorists, the purpose of welfare is to control the unemployed, to maintain social order, and to provide capitalists a pool of cheap labor.

Following Piven and Cloward's analysis, it is no coincidence that the *Personal Responsibility and Work Opportunity Reconciliation Act* was passed during the longest "boom" in U.S. history. When more workers were needed, the federal government required states to force the unemployed into the labor market by tightening their rules for welfare eligibility. Some states even fingerprinted applicants for welfare and sent investigators to their homes. During this time, the states began to emphasize job training instead of welfare. New York City even changed the name of its locations from "welfare centers" to "job centers."

Read on **MySocLab**
Document: The End of Welfare As We Know It: An Overview of the PRWORA

Jobs and Child Care

A direct way to deal with poverty is to provide jobs. The federal government lifted millions out of poverty during the Great Depression by providing jobs building bridges, roads, parks, and public buildings. Programs that create jobs stimulate the economy, for the workers spend the money they earn. This, in turn, produces even more jobs. People who approve of job creation disagree violently, however, about how those jobs should be created. Some argue that it is the government's responsibility to create jobs, while others insist that this is the role of private business.

This debate may never be resolved. Rather than becoming embroiled in it, let's highlight two principles. First, regardless of the path we use to get there, what is important is that jobs be available. Second, to be effective in fighting poverty, the jobs should provide a wage that lifts people out of poverty or be a stepping-stone to jobs that do so. Dead-end jobs that keep people in poverty do not meet this goal. Additionally, jobs are often in the suburbs, where they are inaccessible to inner-city poor. To overcome this limitation, we need to provide transportation for the poor. Finally, because much poverty clusters around women and children, we need quality child care facilities.

Education Accounts

Education is an effective way of reducing poverty. The more education people get, the less likely they are to be poor or unemployed. To spur education, we can offer *education accounts*. The government can establish a credit of, say, \$50,000 or \$75,000 for *every citizen* at age 18 who graduates from high school (Haveman and Scholz 1994–1995; Oliver and Shapiro 1995). Students would choose from approved colleges and technical and vocational schools. This money (which would be adjusted annually for inflation) could be spent only for direct educational costs, such as tuition, books, and living expenses. To continue to qualify for the funds, students would have to make specified progress in their program. An attractive aspect of this proposal is that ultimately it would cost little or nothing: Not only would this program reduce welfare, but it would also increase people's earning power *for their entire lives.* The additional taxes from these larger earnings would make up for the costs of the education accounts.

Upward social mobility through education removes poverty, but as you can see from the Issues in Social Problems box on the next page, it does create personal conflicts.

Issues in Social Problems

A Foot in Each World: Upward Mobility on the Social Class Ladder

I want to begin on a personal note. I was born in poverty. My mother went to the eleventh grade, my father only to the seventh. Education was my way out, opening a new world for me and leading to the writing of this textbook. I was touched when I read sociologist David Croteau's account of his change in social class. Like me, Croteau was born into a blue-collar family and was the first in his family to attend college. He describes his experience of upward mobility as only someone who has gone through it could. What he says matches what I experienced so well that I want to share his account with you.

If this coal miner in Illinois were your father and you go to college, can you see how your worlds would become separated?

After brief periods as a logger and a shipworker, my father worked in a paper mill. . . . My mother, after stints as a domestic and factory worker, toiled at home raising four children. . . .

That paper mill played a central role in my life, not only because my father and other family members worked there, but because it served as a source of motivation for me. As long as I can remember, I was determined not to work in the mill. . . .

Neither of my parents had attended high school, let alone college, so I was left rudderless in choosing schools. The two part-time guidance counselors at my regional high school of more than seven hundred students were not helpful. One had suggested to me that perhaps, despite my excellent grades, welding would be more "practical" for someone with my "background." After applying to an eclectic collection of schools, I made the only logical choice: the one that offered me the most scholarship money. It was an elite private college in the Boston area.

From the very first day, my college education brought with it a new awareness of how different cultures could be. I have a vivid memory of the awkwardness and discomfort on my parents' faces when they met my assigned roommate and his obviously wealthy parents (both doctors) in the totally alien environment of a college dorm. (I was not feeling any better.) Cultures rarely confront each other so poignantly.

I shared my parents' discomfort as I learned lessons that would make it increasingly difficult for me to return to my working-class community. In both my formal and informal education, I was immersed in middle-class culture. Employment expectations ("careers," not jobs), food ("ethnic," not meat and potatoes), dress (natural fibers, not synthetic), music (folk and progressive/alternative rock, not heavy metal), entertainment and leisure (something other than television and hockey) were all different from what I was accustomed to.

Perhaps the most striking difference I encountered was the sense of entitlement shared by other students. For most of my middle-class peers, college seemed to be little more than a nuisance and an unexceptional part of their lives. Often choreographed by their parents, college was an expected step towards a large world of broad opportunities. But for me school always seemed a luxury, and I had a strange sense that one day I would be told some terrible administrative error had been made and I would be sent packing back home to serve my time in the mill where I *really* belonged. . . .

But as I was learning to better analyze and understand the world in which I lived, I was drifting away from the world from which I had come. My education had equipped me with middle-class skills and had introduced me to middle-class values, attitudes, and ways of thinking . . . but I still had strong attachments to my roots and to my working-class family and friends. I had a foot in each world but was completely comfortable in neither of them. Having been socialized into two different classes, I was constantly aware—sometimes painfully so—of the differences between these cultures. . . .

Such a confrontation of cultures is fertile ground for sociological analysis. That is what my training has taught me. My lived experience of this class divide has, for me, made more than an academic question.

Source: Croteau 1995:xxiv–xxviii.

For Your Consideration

How does your college experience compare with Croteau's account? How does your social location make it similar or different?

Giving the Poor More Money

For our final social policy, let's consider a radical proposal. Why not eliminate poverty by giving poor people enough money so they are no longer poor? This is such an obvious solution. But what would happen if we did this?

The Income Maintenance Experiments. As some social scientists were considering this obvious solution, they wondered what poor people would do with the money. To find out, they developed the *income maintenance experiments*, and they convinced the federal government to go along with their plan. In the 1970s, thousands of poor people were given weekly checks. Would they spend it on liquor? Would they work less? How would the free money affect relations between husbands and wives?

Random samples of poor people in Denver, Seattle, and New Jersey were given different amounts of money (West and Steiger 1980; Moffitt 2004). Both urban and rural people were selected. If they went to work, only part of the money they received was cut. This was to help avoid the **welfare wall**—the disincentive to work that comes when the amount that people earn from working is not much more than what they get on welfare. The families were guaranteed this money for either 3 or 5 years—no matter how they spent the money—so they could change their living habits without worrying that the program might end suddenly.

What were the results? Some people did work less. The reduction in work averaged 9 percent for husbands, 23 percent for wives, and 15 percent for female heads of households (West and Steiger 1980). The people who quit working were glad to get away from unpleasant jobs that paid poorly. Most people, however, continued to work as much as before.

Compared with control groups, the people in this program spent more on durable goods (cars, refrigerators, TVs) than they did on nondurable goods (food, entertainment) (Pozdena and Johnson 1979). In households headed by women, most of the new spending went for better housing. With the security that came from a regular income over several years, they saved less and went into debt more—just like many families who are not poor.

With so many negative attitudes about the poor, this program was never put into practice. We can speculate about what the results would be today if the government adopted this program, but with our mushrooming deficits such an approach to poverty would have zero chance of being adopted.

The Future of the Problem

7.6 Explain what the likely future of the social problem of poverty is and why.

Poverty begs for a solution. The homeless, the rural poor, and those trapped in the inner cities can't be wished away. But no solution comes without a high price tag.

Some say, "Let's spend whatever it costs, because it's right. We can worry about the bill later. Besides," they add, "if we can afford all those weapons for the military or the billions to bail out bankers, we can afford programs to help the poor." Others, in contrast, argue that it is not right to saddle future generations with our spending. Their position is, "If we can't pay for programs now, we can't afford them."

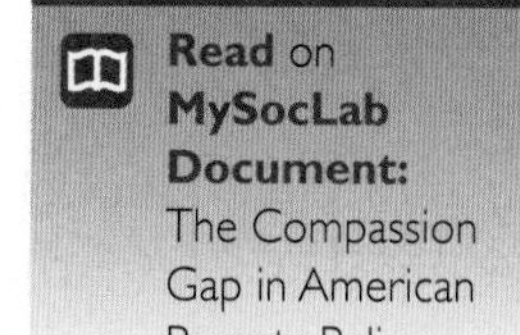

Read on MySocLab
Document:
The Compassion Gap in American Poverty Policy

Most Americans seem to find themselves somewhere between these arguments—claiming it is not right to have homeless people huddled over heating grates or children's futures blocked or their lives cut short because of their parents' poverty, but not knowing what to do about the situation. With the politicians and the public not seeing any clear solutions, with views continuing of the "deserving" and the "undeserving," and with the poor remaining disorganized and having little political clout, I anticipate that we will continue with our present piecemeal programs. From time to time, there will be the illusion of progress. And quite discouragingly, the structural dimension of this social problem will be mostly lost from sight and the poor will continue to be blamed for their poverty.

MySocLab ✓ Study and Review on MySocLab

Summary and Review

1. There are several types of *poverty. Biological poverty* refers to starvation and malnutrition. *Relative poverty* is the feeling of being poor in comparison with others, although one may be well off objectively. *Official poverty* refers to falling below arbitrary standards set by the government. Poverty follows lines of age, gender, geography, and race–ethnicity.
2. Symbolic interactionists examine how the meaning of *income* (for example, whether people see themselves as being rich or poor) differs from its objective measures. Functionalists emphasize that *social inequality* is a way of allocating talented people to society's more demanding tasks and less talented people to its less demanding tasks. They point out that although poverty may be dysfunctional for individuals, it is functional for society. Conflict theorists stress that those who win the struggle for society's limited resources oppress those who lose.

   Conflict theorists also stress that a *power elite* of top politicians and corporate and military leaders makes society's big decisions. *Pluralists* disagree. They view society as made up of many *interest groups* that compete with one another in a marketplace of power and ideas.
3. Why do some people remain in poverty year after year? Some suggest that the reason is a *culture of poverty*, self-defeating behaviors that parents pass on to their children. Most sociologists, in contrast, view what is called the culture of poverty not as the cause of poverty but, rather, as the result of poverty. Why do some countries remain in poverty year after year? Some suggest that this is because they have a national culture of poverty. Others look to *economic colonialism* and exploitation by national elites.
4. Policies for dealing with poverty have been as diverse as the beliefs about its causes. In the 1700s, poverty was considered God's will, and it was a person's religious duty to help the poor. Personal moral failure has also been considered to be a cause of poverty. During the Great Depression, the poor were considered victims of economic conditions and were helped on a massive scale. Welfare programs cause bitter debate. Rules have been tightened to make fewer people eligible for welfare and to "encourage" the poor to take jobs. Where conservatives think that individuals should take more personal responsibility, liberals view government action as more appropriate.
5. The future is not likely to bring an end to poverty but, rather, a continuvation of our piecemeal welfare programs. It is likely that Americans will continue to be divided on the matter of the "deserving" and "undeserving" poor and to what extent they should be helped.

Key Terms

Thinking Critically About Chapter 7

1. What is your reaction to Herbert Gans' observations on how poverty helps society? Do you think Gans is serious? (See the Thinking Critically box on page 203. Also consider his presentation on page 210.)
2. Review the different rates of poverty by age, geography, and race–ethnicity. (See Figures 7.6, 7.7, 7.8, and 7.9 on pages 205–206.) Now explain them. To do so sociologically, you might want to begin by asking, "Why don't all groups have the same rate of poverty?"
3. A central debate in sociology has been whether the power elite or the pluralist view is correct. Which do you think is right? Why?
4. What do you think can be done to solve the social problem of poverty?

8 Racial–Ethnic Relations

Listen to Chapter 8 on MySocLab

Learning Objectives. After reading this chapter, you should be able to:

8.1 Distinguish between minority and dominant groups, know the origin and goals of minority groups and the policies of dominant groups, and explain why race is a social category. **(p. 227)**

8.2 Explain why the melting pot failed to melt and what makes racial–ethnic relations a social problem; summarize basic information on institutional and unintended discrimination. **(p. 231)**

8.3 Discuss the perspectives that emerge when you apply symbolic interactionism, functionalism, and conflict theory to racial–ethnic relations. **(p. 239)**

8.4 Be familiar with why Latino is an umbrella term, the issues of unauthorized immigrants and the use of Spanish, the relative economic well-being of Latinos, and their political divisions and potential. **(p. 246)**

8.5 Be familiar with the civil rights history of African Americans, their relative economic well-being, and the controversy over race versus social class. **(p. 249)**

8.6 Be familiar with why Asian American is an umbrella term, the history of discrimination against Asian Americans, their relative economic well-being, and their political situation. **(p. 252)**

8.7 Be familiar with why Native American is an umbrella term, their relations with settlers, the significance of disease, justifying labels, education and culture conflict, casinos, and self-determination. **(p. 255)**

8.8 Summarize social policy regarding cultural pluralism, preventing discrimination, and the dilemma of affirmative action. **(p. 258)**

8.9 Discuss the likely future of racial–ethnic relations. **(p. 260)**

The six or seven high school boys in Medford, New York, who hung out together liked to go "beaner hopping"—their term for hunting Latinos. They would drive around town, looking for someone they could harass and beat up. ("Beaner" refers to beans, a staple in the Hispanic diet.)

It wasn't an everyday activity—just something they did about once a week, the boys said.

On this Saturday, they began early. Seeing one man in his driveway, they stopped their SUV and shot him several times with a BB gun. That night, they came across two men walking near the train station. Surrounding the men, they called them "Mexicans" and "illegals." They accused them of taking money from Americans.

One of the men ran. A few boys chased after him. The other man, Marcelo Lucero, fought back. Taking off his belt, Lucero hit one of his taunters, Jeffrey Conroy, in the face. Enraged, Conroy pulled out a knife and stabbed Lucero in the chest. Lucero died a few minutes later.

Was this a hate crime? It certainly seemed like it, but when details emerged, the situation grew murky. One of the defendants has a black father and a Puerto Rican mother. His lawyer claimed that because of this, he cannot possibly be guilty of a hate crime against a Latino. Interesting position.

Then there is the swastika on Conroy's leg, usually an indicator of hate. On the other hand, Conroy's girlfriend is from Bolivia, so perhaps it wasn't a hate crime.

Conroy's Bolivian girlfriend defended Conroy. She said, "I dated him for about four years. He never said anything anti-Hispanic to me. He didn't care what you were. They're saying that he's a supremacist. It's not true. He's a very loving person."

Certainly another interesting position.

When it came to selecting a jury, the situation grew even murkier.

Hundreds of potential jurors were questioned to find a dozen people who said they could be fair. Many said they had negative feelings about the illegal immigrants in their town, and they asked to be excused from jury duty.

"They're saying that he's a supremacist. It's not true. He's a very loving person."

Then there were those who said they didn't think they could be fair because they were married to someone of Mexican descent, or they worked with Mexicans and liked them.

Hate crime? Maybe. Or maybe just guys who got a kick out of beating up people, and they found the illegal immigrants easy victims. Many are afraid of going to the police.

The jury found Conroy guilty, and the judge sentenced him to 25 years in prison.

Based on Buckley 2008; Fernandez 2010a, 2010b, 2010c.

The Problem in Sociological Perspective

Prejudice, discrimination, and racial–ethnic violence are an unfortunate fact of life in the United States. Hostilities and tensions among groups surface on the street, at schools, and with occasional media-captivating events like those profiled in our opening vignette.

To better understand this social problem, let's start by looking at the bigger picture.

8.1 Distinguish between minority and dominant groups, know the origin and goals of minority groups and the policies of dominant groups, and explain why race is a social category.

Minority and Dominant Groups

Prejudice and Discrimination Worldwide. Prejudice and discrimination exist around the world. In Northern Ireland, Protestants and Roman Catholics discriminate against one another (McDonald 2012). In Israel, wealthier Jews, primarily of European descent, discriminate against poorer Jews of Asian and African backgrounds. In Japan, the Japanese discriminate against just about anyone who isn't Japanese, especially the Koreans and Ainu who live there (Spivak 1980; Fields 1986; "Law Enacted . . ." 1997). In Europe, Muslim immigrants are singled out for harassment and violence (Donadio 2008). In Egypt, Muslims discriminate against Christians (Hendawi and Michael 2012). And to move beyond any specific group, we can note that in every society, men discriminate against women.

Prejudice and discrimination are often confused. **Prejudice** is an attitude—a prejudging of some sort. The prejudging is usually negative, but it can be positive. **Discrimination**, in contrast, is an action. It refers to treating someone or some group unfairly. Unfair treatment is often based on appearance—age, race–ethnicity, sex, height, weight, disability, clothing, and the like. People also discriminate against others on the basis of their income, education, sexual orientation, and religious or political beliefs.

Minority Does Not Mean Smaller. People who are discriminated against because they belong to a particular group are called a **minority group**. As sociologist Louis Wirth (1945) defined them, these are people who are singled out for unequal treatment on the basis of their physical or cultural characteristics *and* who regard themselves as objects of collective discrimination. Discrimination denies a minority's full participation in society.

Minority in this sense does not necessarily mean *numerical* minority. In South Africa, the descendants of Dutch settlers used to be in political control of the country. They discriminated against the much larger population of blacks in housing, jobs, and education. In colonial India, a handful of British discriminated against 350 million Indians. Although there are more women than men, in every society men discriminate against

"Minority" does not necessarily mean smaller. Less than 100,000 British troops ruled India's 350 million people at its independence in 1947.

women. Accordingly, we refer to those who discriminate as the **dominant group**. This group, which has more power, privileges, and higher social status, can be either larger or smaller in number than the minority group.

The Origin of Minority Groups. Minority groups come into existence either through political expansion or migration. Some groups become minorities when a government expands its political boundaries. As a Latino whose family has lived in New Mexico for generations said, "We didn't move across the border—the border moved across us." A second way that minority groups originate is through migration—when people who have different physical characteristics or customs move to a new country. The migration can be involuntary, as with Africans who were forcibly brought to the United States, or voluntary, as with Turks who chose to move to Germany for work.

View on MySocLab Figure: The Distribution of Dominant and Minority Groups

Minorities come into existence, then, when people who have different customs, languages, values, or physical characteristics come under control of the same political system. There, some groups who share physical and cultural traits discriminate against those who have different traits. The losers in this power struggle are forced into minority-group status, while the winners enjoy the higher status and greater privileges that dominance brings.

Characteristics of Minority Groups. Anthropologists Charles Wagley and Marvin Harris (1958) noted that minority groups share five characteristics:

1. *Ascribed status:* Membership comes through birth.
2. *Prejudice:* The dominant group holds the minority's physical or cultural traits in low esteem.
3. *Discrimination:* The dominant group treats members of the minority group unequally.
4. *Endogamy:* Minority members tend to marry within their group.
5. *Common identity:* Minority members identify with one another because of their shared physical or cultural traits—and the disadvantages these traits bring.

To sense a common identity is powerful. Because members of minority groups possess similar cultural or physical traits, tend to marry within their own group, and experience discrimination at the hands of a dominant group, a feeling of common identity often unites them. This identity (a sense of "we" versus "them") is sometimes so strong that members of a minority group feel that they share a common destiny.

Goals of Minority Groups. Minority groups differ on what they want to accomplish in regard to the dominant group. Wirth (1945) identified four objectives:

1. **Assimilation:** Wanting to be treated as individuals, not as members of a separate group, members of the minority group adopt the culture of the dominant group and are absorbed into the larger society.
2. **Pluralism:** The minority wants to live peacefully with the dominant group, yet maintain the differences that set it apart and are important to its identity.
3. **Secession:** Wanting cultural and political independence, the minority seeks to separate itself and form a separate nation.
4. **Militancy:** Convinced of its own superiority, the minority wants to reverse the status and dominate the society.

Policies of Dominant Groups. Dominant groups also differ in their objectives regarding minority groups. Figure 8.1 on the next page outlines six policies of dominant

FIGURE 8.1 ▸ Policies of Dominant Groups Toward Minority Groups

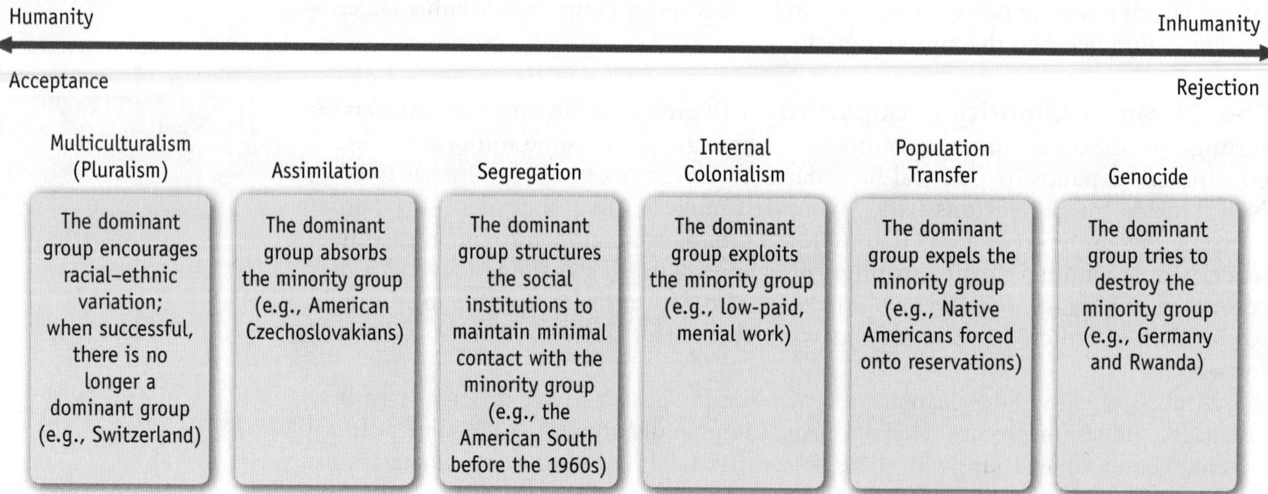

Source: By the author. Based on Simpson and Yinger 1972; Henslin 2010.

groups identified by sociologists George Simpson and J. Milton Yinger. As we review these policies, you can see how they can help or hinder minorities.

1. **Pluralism**. *Pluralism* (multiculturalism) exists when a dominant group permits or even encourages cultural differences. The "hands-off" policy toward immigrant associations and foreign-language newspapers in the United States is an example. In Switzerland, the French, Italian, German, and Romish Swiss, who live peacefully together in a political and economic unit, have retained their separate languages and other customs. None of these groups is considered a minority.
2. **Assimilation**. *Assimilation* is an attempt to eliminate the minority by absorbing it into the mainstream culture. In *forced assimilation*, the dominant group bans the minority's religion, language, and other distinctive customs. In the former Soviet Union, the Russians treated Armenians this way. *Permissible assimilation*, in contrast, lets the minority adopt the dominant customs at its own pace. In the United States, we expect that cultural minorities will gradually give up their distinctive customs, such as unique clothing and language, and adopt the customs of the dominant culture.
3. **Segregation**. *Segregation* is an attempt by the dominant group to keep a minority "in its place"—that is, subservient, exploitable, and "off by itself." In South Africa between 1948 and 1990, the small number of whites who controlled the nation established **apartheid** (ah-'pär-tāte), a system of rules that segregated blacks and whites in almost all spheres of life. In the face of international sanctions that threatened the nation's economy, the whites dismantled apartheid.
4. **Internal colonialism**. *Colonialism* refers to a more powerful nation making a colony of a weaker nation so it can exploit its resources; *internal colonialism* refers to a dominant group exploiting a minority group's labor.
5. **Population transfer**. In *direct population transfer*, the dominant group transfers the minority to a specified area or forces it to leave the country. In the 1400s, for example, King Ferdinand and Queen Isabella (who financed Columbus' voyage to North America) drove the Jews and Moors out of Spain. *Indirect population transfer* occurs when the dominant group makes life so miserable for a minority that its members "choose" to leave. Facing the bitter conditions of czarist Russia, for example, millions of Jews made this "choice."
6. **Genocide**. Hatred, fear, or greed can motivate the dominant group to turn to a policy of extermination, or *genocide*. The most infamous example is the Holocaust. Between 1933 and 1945, the Nazis slaughtered about 6 million Jews, hundreds

of thousands of Slavs, a quarter of a million Gypsies, and unknown numbers of homosexuals, communists, people with disabilities, and the mentally ill—all people whom Hitler considered too "impure" to be part of his mythical Aryan race.

Race and Ethnicity

Ideas of Racial Superiority. Hitler was convinced that **race**—the inherited physical characteristics that identify a group of people—made some groups superior and others inferior. In his mind, tall, fair-skinned, mostly blond-haired people called the Aryans formed a "super race." This race, he said, was responsible for the cultural achievements of Europe. The Aryans had a destiny—to establish a higher culture, a new world order. To fulfill this destiny, the Aryans had to avoid "racial mixing," the "contamination" that comes from breeding with "inferior races." To preserve Aryan biology and culture, the "inferior races" needed to be isolated or destroyed. Some "lower races" could remain to perform tasks too lowly for Aryans to perform.

Although most people today find Hitler's ideas bizarre, in the 1930s both the public and the scientific community took views like this seriously. Many biologists and anthropologists in Europe and the United States believed that sharp lines divided the "races" and that some were inherently superior to others. It is not surprising that these scientists always concluded that Caucasians were the superior "race," for they themselves were Caucasian.

A related development of the time was *eugenics*—attempts to improve humans through selective breeding. Underlying eugenics was the assumption of racial superiority. The idea of eugenics was so popular during Hitler's time that it was approved by scientists, educators, health specialists, religious leaders, and prominent politicians of the Western nations, including the United States.

The idea of racial superiority, which justifies one group's rule over another, is certainly less popular today, but it does persist. Almost everyone assumes that "race" really exists, identifies with some "racial" group, and classifies other people into different "racial" groups. Some think that their "race" is superior to others.

Race as an Arbitrary Social Category. People have such a mixture of physical characteristics—skin color, hair texture, nose and head shapes, height, eye color, and so on—that there is no pure race. Instead, biologists have found that human characteristics flow endlessly into one another, a melding that makes any attempt to draw sharp distinctions arbitrary. Even the large groupings of humans that can be classified by blood type and gene frequencies contain tremendous variation. From the Thinking Critically box on the next page, you can see how arbitrary racial classifications are.

Clarifying Terms. Wanting to avoid a term as imprecise as *race*, many sociologists, as I will do in this chapter, use the term *racial–ethnic group*. The term *ethnic* is derived from the Greek word *ethnos*, meaning "people" or "nation." A **racial–ethnic group** refers to people who identify with one another on the basis of their ancestry and cultural heritage. Their sense of belonging may center on unique physical characteristics, foods, dress, names, language, music, and religion. As we just reviewed, collective discrimination and intermarriage may also generate a common identity.

The Scope of the Problem

8.2 Explain why the melting pot failed to melt and what makes racial–ethnic relations a social problem; summarize basic information on institutional and unintended discrimination.

The many racial–ethnic groups that make up the United States have distinct histories, customs, and identities. The largest groups are listed in Figure 8.2 on page 233. We'll come back to this figure several times.

Immigrants and the Melting Pot

The Melting Pot: Invitations and Walls. Throughout U.S. history, immigrants have confronted **Anglo-conformity;** that is, they were expected to speak English and

Thinking Critically About Social Problems

Can a Plane Ride Change Your Race?

According to common sense, the title of this box is nonsense—our racial classifications represent biological differences. Yet contrary to "common sense," sociologists stress that what we call races are *social* classifications, not biological categories.

Sociologists point out that *our "race" depends more on the society in which we live than on our biological characteristics*. For example, the racial categories that are common in the United States are merely one of *numerous* ways by which people around the world classify physical appearances. Although groups around the world use different categories, each group assumes that its categories are natural, merely a logical response to visible physical differences.

What "race" are this Brazilian mother and child? Is the mother's "race" different from her daughter's "race"? The text explains why "race" is such an unreliable concept that a person's "race" changes even with geography.

To better understand this essential sociological point—that race is more social than it is biological—consider this: In the United States, children who are born to the same parents are all of the same race. I am sure that you are thinking, "What could be more natural?" This is the common view of Americans. But in Brazil, children who are born to the same parents can be of different races—if their appearances differ. "What could be more natural?" assume Brazilians.

Consider how Americans usually classify a child who is born to a "black" mother and a "white" father. Why do they usually say that the child is "black"? Wouldn't it be equally logical to classify the child as "white"? Similarly, if a child's grandmother is "black" but all her other ancestors are "white," the child is often considered "black." Yet she has much more "white ancestry" than "black ancestry." Why, then, is she considered "black"? Certainly not because of biology. Rather, such thinking is a legacy of slavery. Before the Civil War, numerous children were born whose fathers were white slave masters and whose mothers were black slaves. In an attempt to preserve the "purity" of their "race," whites classified anyone with even a "drop of black blood" as "not white."

Race is so social—and fluid—that even a plane ride can change a person's race. In the city of Salvador in Brazil, people classify one another by the color of their skin and eyes, the breadth of their nose and lips, and the color and curliness of their hair. They use at least seven terms for what we call white and black. Consider again a U.S. child who has one "white" and one "black" parent. Although she is "black" in the United States, if she flies to Brazil, she will belong to one of their several "whiter" categories (Fish 1995).

On the flight just mentioned, did the girl's "race" actually change? Our common sense revolts at this, I know, but it actually did. We want to argue that because her biological characteristics remain unchanged, her race remains unchanged. This is because we think of race as biological, when *race is actually a label we use to describe perceived biological characteristics.* Simply put, the race we "are" depends on *where* we are—on who is doing the classifying.

"Racial" classifications are fluid, not fixed. Even now, you can see changes occurring in the United States. Our new terms "multiracial" and "two or more races" indicate changing ideas about race.

Who knows? Fifty years from now, we might have entirely different "racial" classifications. Many hope that we would have none by then, but given our history this is unlikely.

For Your Consideration

How would you explain to someone the sociological point that race is more a social classification than a biological one? Can you come up with any arguments to refute this sociological view? How do you think our racial–ethnic classifications will change in the future?

  **Read** on **MySocLab Document:** Beyond the Melting Pot Reconsidered

adopt other Anglo-Saxon ways of life. The nation's Founders intended to produce a modified version of England. Many thought that the evolving society would become a **melting pot**—that it would "melt" European immigrants into a new cultural and biological blend. As sociologist Milton Gordon (1964) put it, "The stocks and folkways of Europe [would be], figuratively speaking, indiscriminately mixed in the political pot of

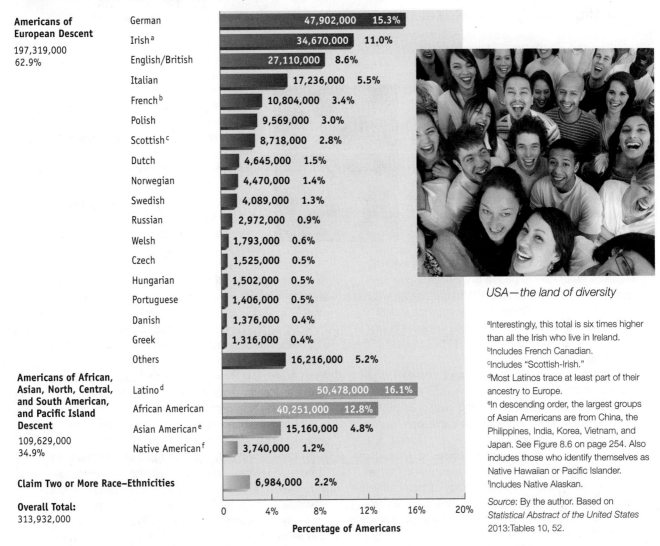

FIGURE 8.2 ▸ U.S. Racial–Ethnic Groups

Group	Ancestry	Number	Percentage
Americans of European Descent 197,319,000 62.9%	German	47,902,000	15.3%
	Irish[a]	34,670,000	11.0%
	English/British	27,110,000	8.6%
	Italian	17,236,000	5.5%
	French[b]	10,804,000	3.4%
	Polish	9,569,000	3.0%
	Scottish[c]	8,718,000	2.8%
	Dutch	4,645,000	1.5%
	Norwegian	4,470,000	1.4%
	Swedish	4,089,000	1.3%
	Russian	2,972,000	0.9%
	Welsh	1,793,000	0.6%
	Czech	1,525,000	0.5%
	Hungarian	1,502,000	0.5%
	Portuguese	1,406,000	0.5%
	Danish	1,376,000	0.4%
	Greek	1,316,000	0.4%
	Others	16,216,000	5.2%
Americans of African, Asian, North, Central, and South American, and Pacific Island Descent 109,629,000 34.9%	Latino[d]	50,478,000	16.1%
	African American	40,251,000	12.8%
	Asian American[e]	15,160,000	4.8%
	Native American[f]	3,740,000	1.2%
Claim Two or More Race–Ethnicities		6,984,000	2.2%
Overall Total: 313,932,000			

Percentage of Americans (axis: 0, 4%, 8%, 12%, 16%, 20%)

USA—the land of diversity

[a]Interestingly, this total is six times higher than all the Irish who live in Ireland.
[b]Includes French Canadian.
[c]Includes "Scottish-Irish."
[d]Most Latinos trace at least part of their ancestry to Europe.
[e]In descending order, the largest groups of Asian Americans are from China, the Philippines, India, Korea, Vietnam, and Japan. See Figure 8.6 on page 254. Also includes those who identify themselves as Native Hawaiian or Pacific Islander.
[f]Includes Native Alaskan.

Source: By the author. Based on *Statistical Abstract of the United States* 2013:Tables 10, 52.

the emerging nation and melted together by the fires of American influence and interaction into a distinctly new type."

For most European immigrants, the melting pot became a reality. Most lost their specific ethnic identities and merged into mainstream culture. They might have some vague ethnic identity—"I'm three-quarters German and one-quarter mixed Italian and Greek, with some English thrown in"—but they tend to think of themselves as "just American." For some groups, however, their cultural and ethnic identities remain strong, especially recent immigrants from Mexico, Cuba, Haiti, Vietnam, Laos, India, and Islamic countries. And some who want to get "melted" have found that their appearance evokes stereotypes that make such melting elusive. This is the topic of the Spotlight on Social Research box on the next page.

Some people were not invited to join the melting pot. Americans of Western European background set up walls to prevent nonwhites from becoming part of this new "biological mix." To protect themselves from "racial impurity," they passed laws that put blacks and whites in separate schools and made it illegal for blacks and whites to marry.

Stereotypes. Each group of immigrants that entered the United States confronted prejudice based on **stereotypes**—generalizations of what people are like. Some of these stereotypes were highly negative. The English immigrants, for example, despised the

Spotlight on Social Research

Being a "Foreign" American

***NAZLI KIBRIA**, professor of sociology at Boston University, did research on second-generation Chinese and Korean Americans. She explored their experience of being identified by others as "Asian." In this essay, she reports on how "racial identities" serve as markers (or signals) in everyday social encounters. These "markers" are based on how people perceive the physical characteristics of others. This is what she wrote for you.*

I use the term "second-generation Chinese and Korean Americans" to refer to people of Chinese and Korean ancestry who were born and/or from a young age reared in the United States. Based on their encounters with people of non-Asian origin, I explored the ways in which they experience the identity marker of "Asian race" in their daily lives.

In their everyday social encounters, non-Asian Americans often assume that Chinese and Korean Americans are "foreigners." With the perception of "Asian" often comes an image of an unassimilable alien—a presence that is fundamentally and unalterably outside of, if not diametrically opposite to, what "American" is. Many of my informants said that they frequently were asked, "Where are you from?" While this question may be intended as an inquiry about one's regional origin in the United States (e.g., "Are you from Southern California?"), when asked of Asian Americans it is often meant as a question about nationality and ethnic origins. In fact, informants told me that if they answered the question in local terms (such as, "I'm from Boston"), the person often followed up with something like, "Yes, but where are you really from?"

My informants had several ways of responding to these queries. In some situations, they interpreted the question as innocuous or even positive, as an effort on the part of the questioner to avoid making generalizations about Asian Americans and to establish the individual's specific ethnic identity. At other times, in contrast, my informants interpreted the question as an assumption that everyone of Asian origin is a foreigner and not American.

Among the strategies that my informants used to neutralize or at least to deflect the assumption of their foreignness were dis-identifiers. To remove an identity of "foreignness" and provide an identity of "American," they used symbols, such as language, dress, demeanor, and even the people with whom they were seen or associated. Language was one of their main dis-identifiers. During an encounter with strangers, they would deflect their presumed foreignness by speaking fluent and unaccented English. The need to use dis-identifiers produced an awareness among my informants that for Asian Americans, the achievement and acceptance of an American identity requires vigilance and work.

Ascribing "foreignness" to second-generation Chinese and Korean Americans not only casts doubt upon their identity as Americans, but also signals authentic ethnicity. That is, the dominant society assumes that second-generation Chinese and Korean Americans have ties to a community and culture that is either located or rooted outside the U.S. mainstream. These ties are assumed to be strong and genuine, rather than contrived or fake. My informants were especially aware of this assumption of ethnic authenticity when a non-Asian American would ask them to interpret Asian, Korean, or Chinese cultural practices or in some other way to display their ethnic cultural knowledge.

For Your Consideration

What is your race–ethnicity? How has this identity been an influence in your life? How have others reacted to it?

Irish immigrants, viewing them as dirty, lazy, untrustworthy drunkards. As you know, negative stereotypes have not disappeared. From the jokes you have heard, and perhaps told, you know how these stereotypes paint others in, shall we say, unflattering terms. The Thinking Critically box on the next page explores an extreme, people who manipulate stereotypes to breed hatred.

What is the Problem?

Like poverty, prejudice and discrimination are not necessarily social problems. They can simply be facts of life. To have a social problem, we must have both objective conditions and subjective concerns. People must be upset about the objective conditions and

Thinking Critically About Social Problems

What Should We Do About Hate Speech?

The Internet has become a marvelous source of information. This tool allows social researchers to pack an entire library, and more, in their luggage and take it with them around the world. As I write this in Latvia, I am able to keep up with political, economic, and social events by reading a couple of daily newspapers from the States. I am also able to type a few words into a search engine and bring up research articles on almost any topic. I still marvel as I use this tool, both at the information it makes available and the freedom it offers to do research around the world.

The Internet is also a remarkable source of misinformation. Anyone can put up a Web site or blog and fill it with lies or distortions of truth. They can give vent to anger, seek revenge for perceived wrongs, and spew hatred.

These negative communications are upsetting. Consider these statements:

> Civil Rights come out of the barrel of a gun, and we mean to give the niggers and Jews all the civil rights they can handle. . . . Our security team will see that no live targets escape from the range. Any who refuse to run or can't for any reason will be fed to the dogs. The dogs appreciate a good feed as much as we do.
>
> —An invitation to a summer conference held by the Aryan Nations at Hayden Lake, Idaho. (quoted in Murphy 1999)

> Who's pimping the world? The hairy hands of the Zionist. . . . The so-called Jew claims that there were six million in Nazi Germany. I am here today to tell you that there is absolutely no . . . evidence to substantiate, to prove that six million so-called Jews lost their lives in Nazi Germany. . . . Don't let no hooked-nose, bagel-eating, lox-eating, perpetrating-a-fraud so-called Jew who just crawled out of the ghettoes of Europe just a few days ago. . . .
>
> —Statements of Khalid Abdul Muhammad (quoted in Herbert 1988)

Should hate speech be a protected right?

Hatred knows no racial–ethnic boundaries; the first statement was made by a white, the second by an African American.

Should we ban such statements from the Internet and other forms of the mass media? Should we punish their authors as lawbreakers? Or should we allow statements like these to be circulated as part of free speech, regardless of their inflammatory rhetoric, the twisting of fact, or the hatred they spew?

Canada has banned hate speech, and Germany makes it a crime to display Nazi symbols or to deny that the Holocaust took place (Waldron 2012). Ernst Zundel, a German immigrant to Canada, ran afoul of these laws. He was arrested and deported to Germany, where he was tried on the charge of saying that the Holocaust did not happen. Zundel was found guilty and served 5 years in prison. When he was released from prison, supporters shouted "Bravo!" and gave him flowers (Frey 2010).

For Your Consideration

Many recoil at the possibility of censoring ideas. They take the position that all censorship poses a threat to our freedoms. As much as we dislike hatred, its censorship is an attack on free speech. That people can be put in prison for expressing ideas, as with Zundel in Germany, sends a chill up the spine of the advocates of free speech. They point out that next time it might be *your* ideas that are banned because some politicians decide that they don't like them. On the other side of this argument are those who say that hatred is powerful and can lead to violence. They point out that Hitler began with ideas. Passing laws against hate speech and punishing those who express those ideas, they say, is reasonable.

What do you think?

TABLE 8.1 ▸ Indicators of Relative Economic Well-Being

	Family Income		Families In Poverty	
	Median Family Income	Compared to Whites	Percentage Below Poverty	Compared to Whites
Whites	$67,900		10.6%	
Asian Americans	$76,700	13% higher	12.5%	18% higher
Latinos	$41,100	39% lower	24.8%	233% higher
African Americans	$39,900	41% lower	27.1%	256% higher
Native Americans	$39,700	42% lower	28.4%	268% higher

Note: These totals are for families, which have less poverty than "persons," the unit of the tables in Chapter 7.
Source: By the author. Based on *Statistical Abstract of the United States* 2013:Table 36.

want to do something about them. When it comes to prejudice and discrimination, we do have both objective conditions and subjective concerns—and in abundance. Many people are upset that some groups are deprived of the rights to which citizenship entitles them—the equality guaranteed by the Constitution of "life, liberty, and the pursuit of happiness." As we analyze the social problem of racial–ethnic relations, we shall focus on discrimination that violates equality.

Watch on **MySocLab Video:** Racial Stereotypes and Discrimination

Effects of Discrimination. We can measure discrimination and determine how many people are denied some particular benefit of society, but too often we end up focusing on numbers and miss how discrimination affects its victims. Look at Table 8.1. You can see that African Americans, Latinos, and Native Americans earn about 40 percent less than that of whites. You can see, too, that their poverty is about two and a half times that of whites. These are cold numbers, but underlying them are real people whose lives are affected adversely. We reviewed some of the implications of poverty in the previous chapter. At issue is not whether people can afford a boat, a new car, or some exotic vacation, but whether they can afford nourishing food and education or find the money to fix a broken-down car.

Poverty also translates into life and death. Look at Table 8.2. Compared with white babies, African American babies are *more than twice* as likely to die before they reach their first birthday. You can see that the chances of African American women dying during childbirth are also *more than twice* as high as that of white women. Now look at life expectancy. On average, African American women die about 3 years younger than white women and African American men die 5 years younger than white men. The primary reason is simple: With higher incomes, people can afford safer neighborhoods, better nutrition, housing, and medical care. The result is a longer life.

TABLE 8.2 ▸ Health and Race–Ethnicity

	Infant Deaths[1]	Maternal Deaths[1]	Life Expectancy	
			Male	Female
Whites	5.5	10.0	75.9	80.8
African Americans	12.7	26.5	70.9	77.4

[1]The death rates given here are the number per 1,000. Infant deaths refer to the number of infants under 1-year-old who die in a year per 1,000 live births. The source does not provide data for other racial–ethnic groups.
Source: By the author. Based on *Statistical Abstract of the United States* 2013: Tables 110, 118.

Institutional Discrimination in the Past. To understand discrimination, we need to move beyond thinking in terms of **individual discrimination**, one person treating another badly on the basis of race–ethnicity. Although this certainly creates problems, it is an individual matter and does not qualify as a social problem.

Sociologists encourage us to move beyond individual situations and to think in broader terms. They point to **institutional discrimination**, inequality built into the social system that oppresses whole groups. For example, for generations whites denied

African Americans the right to vote, join labor unions, work at higher-paying, more prestigious jobs, attend good schools, or receive care at decent hospitals.

The National Association of Real Estate Boards (NAR) provides an infamous example. Not only did the NAR once practice institutional discrimination as a routine matter, but it even defended racial discrimination as a *moral* act. Here is a statement from its 1924 code of ethics:

> *A Realtor should never be instrumental in introducing into a neighborhood . . . members of any race or nationality, or individuals whose presence will clearly be detrimental to property values in that neighborhood. (Newman et al. 1978:149)*

Did the federal government take realtors to court over this blatant discrimination? On the contrary, the government backed the institutional discrimination. If developers of subdivisions wanted to obtain a loan from the Federal Housing Authority (FHA), *they had to exclude nonwhites* (Valocchi 1994; Oliver and Shapiro 1995). Even after World War II, the FHA denied loans to anyone who would "unsettle a neighborhood." Again, the discrimination was considered a *moral* act, done to protect people's property. No one was hiding this. The FHA manual was explicit: "If a neighborhood is to retain stability, it is necessary that properties shall continue to be occupied by the same social and racial classes" (Duster 1988:288).

How times have changed. And with them, so have federal agencies and the NAR. In 1950, under pressure, the NAR deleted the reference to race or nationality. The NAR kept resisting the change, though, and didn't take a position to support fair housing until 1972.

Institutional Discrimination Today. Has institutional discrimination disappeared, fading into a distant, unpleasant memory? Many aspects of institutional discrimination, such as the discrimination practiced by the NAR, strike the contemporary ear as strange, but this aspect of social life remains alive and well (Beeman et al. 2010). Look at Figure 8.3, which illustrates mortgage loans, another aspect of housing. You can see that *minorities are still more likely to be turned down for a loan—whether their incomes are below or above the median income of their community.*

View on **MySocLab**
Figure: Cloaked Discrimination in Apartment Rentals

FIGURE 8.3 ▸ Buying a House: Institutional Discrimination and Predatory Lending

This figure, based on a national sample, illustrates *institutional discrimination*. Rejecting the loan applications of minorities and gouging them with higher interest rates are a nationwide practice, not the acts of a rogue banker here or there. Because the discrimination is part of the banking system, it is also called *systemic discrimination*.

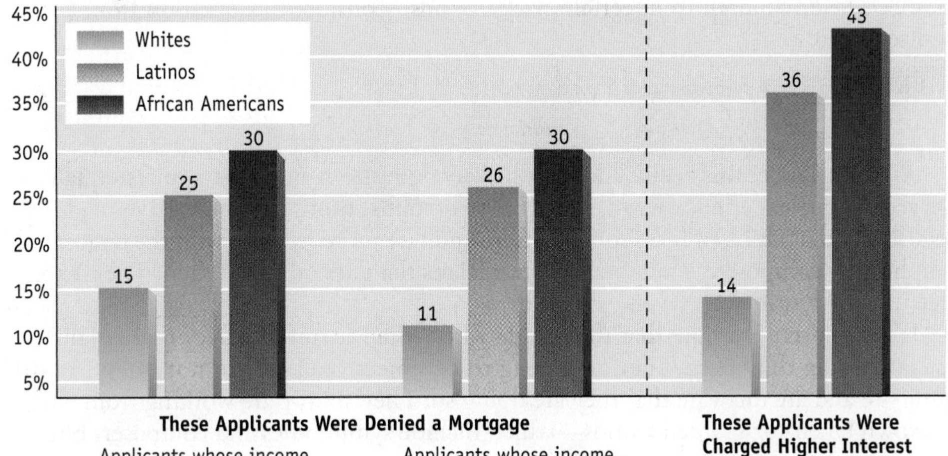

Source: By the author. Based on Thomas 1991.

Beyond this harsh finding lies another just as devastating. In the credit crisis that caused so many to lose their homes, African Americans and Latinos were hit harder than whites. The last set of bars on Figure 8.3 shows a major reason for this: *Banks purposely targeted minorities to charge higher interest rates.* This was not just a banker or two or three or a dozen that did this. Like the NAR neighborhood discrimination, this discrimination was intended. It was institutional, built into the structure of banking.

Unintended Institutional Discrimination. Here is a fascinating aspect of institutional discrimination: *It can occur even when those who are doing the discriminating are unaware of it.* Let's look at IQ testing as an example.

Imagine that you are in the fifth grade and your class is going to be given an IQ test. For "politically correct" reasons, the test is no longer called an IQ test. It has been renamed The Achievement Predictor (TAP). Your teacher tells you and your classmates to do your best because the test results are going to affect your future. This is rather vague, but it makes you feel a little nervous. You intend to do your best anyway. You don't want anyone to think you're mentally challenged.

The booklets are passed out face down. You fill out the blanks on the back, carefully printing the date, your name, class, school, and teacher. At your teacher's command, for this is a timed test, you turn the booklet over, open it, and eagerly read the first question. You can hardly believe your eyes when you read:

1. *If you throw the dice and "7" is showing on the top, what is facing down?*

___seven ___snake eyes ___box cars ___little Joes ___eleven

This question confuses you. You haven't the slightest idea of what the correct answer might be. When you play Monopoly, you never look under the dice.

Since your teacher said that it is better to guess than to leave an answer blank, you put a check mark on something. Then you go to the second question, which only increases your confusion and frustration. Here is what you read:

2. *Which word is out of place here?*

___splib ___blood ___gray ___spook ___black

Again, you have no idea of what choice is correct, so you put a check on anything. The questions that follow are just like these first two. You continue to add check marks, for the most part, meaninglessly. As this seemingly endless nonsense continues, somewhere in the process you give up. No longer do you read the questions thoroughly, for it doesn't seem to affect which blank you check.

It is obvious that you performed poorly on this test. It should also be obvious why—you were being tested on things far removed from your background of experiences. Some questions favor children from certain backgrounds. Consider this question from a standardized IQ test:

A symphony is to a composer as a book is to a(n) _______:

___paper ___sculptor ___musician ___author ___man

At first glance, this seems like an objective question, one that applies equally to everyone. Your experience with Little Joes and splibs, though, should have made you more aware that children from some backgrounds are more familiar with the concepts of symphonies, composers, sculptors, and musicians than are other children. Their experience tilts the test in their favor.

It is important to note that the people who write the questions for these evaluative tests are doing their best. They are trying to be objective. They do not intend to discriminate and are unaware that they are doing so. They simply are working from within their own taken-for-granted worlds—which include symphonies and composers but not Little Joes and splibs.

The questions that "you" tried to answer were suggested by Adrian Dove (n.d.), a social worker in Watts (East Los Angeles). These questions are slanted toward a specific nonwhite, lower-class experience. With these *particular* cultural biases, can you see why children from some social backgrounds will perform better than others?

Unintended institutional discrimination also shows up in the practice of medicine. Researchers have found that physicians are more likely to recommend knee replacements for their white patients than for either their Latino or African American patients (Skinner et al. 2003). White patients are also more likely than African American patients to receive coronary bypass surgery (Smedley et al. 2003). Why should this be? Actually, no one yet knows. The nature of the discrimination here is confusing, because even African American physicians are more likely to give preventive care to white patients (Stolberg 2001). Discovering how race–ethnicity becomes part of medical decision making will be a fascinating area of future research. Perhaps you will become one of the researchers who will explore this area of social life.

In short, institutional discrimination is built into our social system. It operates throughout society—with those involved often unaware of what they are doing.

Looking at the Problem Theoretically

Although usually much less open and direct than the events in our opening vignette, prejudice and discrimination are a part of many relations between racial–ethnic groups in the United States. Let's look at how sociologists use theory to better understand them.

8.3 Discuss the perspectives that emerge when you apply symbolic interactionism, functionalism, and conflict theory to racial–ethnic relations.

Symbolic Interactionism: Labels

> *"What's in a name?" asked Juliet. "That which we call a rose, by any other name would smell as sweet."*

What Juliet said is true of roses, but in human relations words are not meaningless. The labels we learn both color the way we see the world and influence our behavior.

Socialization and Prejudice. No one is born prejudiced, with stereotypes, or wanting to discriminate. We are not born with even a single value or belief. But each of us is born into a particular family and racial–ethnic group. There we learn values, beliefs, and ways to perceive the world. There we also learn how to label members of other groups. We might learn prejudice and discrimination as a routine part of everyday life. Or we might learn that prejudice and discrimination are wrong.

Labels and Selective Perception. As we grow up, we learn stereotypes, ways of classifying entire groups of people—men, women, the elderly, racial–ethnic groups, people with disabilities, even people who are good at math, music, or sports. Learning to classify people—to "place them in boxes"—is a normal, necessary, and inevitable part of our socialization, our learning the ways of our society. These labels or stereotypes become lenses through which we view people. They create **selective perception**, leading us to see certain things while blinding us to others.

Many racial–ethnic labels are emotionally laden. The term "nigger," for example, is so loaded with negative emotions that most won't say the word, using the phrase "the N word" instead. There is nothing neutral about "cracker," "dago," "kraut," "limey," "mick," "spic," "wetback," or the many other labels that people use to refer to members of racial–ethnic groups. The emotional impact of such words overpowers us, blocking perception of positive characteristics (Allport 1954). As Simpson and Yinger (1972) put it, we fit new experiences into old categories by selecting those cues that harmonize with our prejudgment or stereotype.

Labels and Morality. Dehumanizing labels are so powerful that they can help people commit acts that otherwise would challenge their moral sense. For example, by labeling Native Americans as "savages," the U.S. cavalry and settlers perceived them as something less than human. This made it easier to destroy tribe after tribe (Garbarino 1976). In South Africa, the Dutch settlers labeled the native Hottentots as jungle animals, a label that salved their consciences as they wiped out these people. In Tasmania, the labels the

British settlers used were so effective that the settlers even hunted the local population for sport and dog food. In Brazil today, much as in U.S. history, miners, ranchers, and loggers are wiping out Indian tribes as they seize their lands (Linden 1991; "Guardian of Brazil Indians . . ." 1997).

Negative terms and stereotypes, then, are dangerous. They create selective perception, justify discrimination, and in extreme instances even facilitate mass murder. Groups that build an identity around hatred pose a special threat. In the *Spotlight on Social Research* box on the next page, Raphael Ezekiel discusses his research on such groups.

In Sum ▸ Symbolic interactionists examine how labels (terms, classifications, symbols, or stereotypes) affect how we look at life and how we act. They analyze how we learn labels, how we use labels to classify one another, how our classifications create selective perception and sort people out for different kinds of life experiences, and how labels are used to justify discrimination and violence.

Functionalism: Costs and Benefits

Why does racial–ethnic discrimination persist in the United States—and in other parts of the world? As you may recall, functionalists argue that the benefits of a social pattern (some characteristic of society) must be greater than its costs, or else that pattern will disappear. The benefits (functions) of discrimination, then, must outweigh its costs (dysfunctions). How can this be?

Functions and Dysfunctions of Discrimination. The discrimination woven into U.S. history benefited the dominant group. Whites gained free farm land, forests, lakes, and gold by killing Native Americans or transferring them to reservations. They benefited from owning slaves, acquiring cheap labor and selling the slaves' labor as masons, carpenters, or factory workers. Slave labor allowed many owners to live a "genteel" life of leisure or to pursue art, education, science, and other "refinements."

Slavery and the invasion of the West also had dysfunctions at that time: deaths, broken families, rapes of female slaves, and shortened lives. They also left a legacy of dysfunction: racial–ethnic tensions, hostilities, hatreds, and fears. It would appear that such high costs of discrimination would lead to its elimination. But because racial–ethnic discrimination remains a fact of life in the United States, functionalists search for its benefits, or functions. Just as discrimination was functional for the dominant group in the past, today's dominant group benefits from it as well. Let's look at two functions of discrimination, dirty work and ethnocentrism.

Getting Dirty Work Done. **Racial–ethnic stratification**, the unequal distribution of a society's resources based on race–ethnicity, helps get society's **dirty work** done. Sociologist Herbert Gans (2007) defines dirty work as society's "physically dirty or dangerous, temporary, dead-end and underpaid, undignified and menial jobs." Sociologist Emile Durkheim (1893/1964) stressed that society needs a **division of labor**, people performing different or specialized tasks. Dirty work, such as collecting garbage, is one of those tasks, a necessary but rather disagreeable one.

One way to get the dirty work done is to pay high wages to compensate for the unpleasant, degrading nature of the work. Obviously, we have not chosen this road. Another is to force people to do such jobs for low wages. No one forces people to collect garbage by waving whips over their heads. Stratification accomplishes this and is quite functional. People who find the doors to higher-paying, more prestigious jobs closed to them take the dirty jobs. This makes sure these jobs get done and get done cheaply.

Racial–Ethnic Succession in Dirty Work. When a racial–ethnic group climbs the social class ladder, it leaves the dirty work behind. Because the dirty work still has to be done, other groups take over those tasks. For example, many African Americans have moved into the middle class, and unauthorized immigrants are doing much of the work they used to do. Those who have entered the United States illegally have little control

Spotlight on Social Research

Studying Neo-Nazis and Klans

RAFAEL EZEKIEL, *a senior researcher with the Harvard School of Public Health, says that his interest in racism was stimulated by the contradictions he experienced as a child growing up with liberal, northern, Jewish parents in a deeply racist East Texas town. Here is what he wrote for you.*

Dear students,

Jim Henslin asked me to write about my fieldwork. I got stuck, so I decided to interview myself.

Interviewer: What did you do, Professor?

Rafe: I spent three years hanging out with a neo-Nazi group in Detroit. After that, I interviewed national leaders from neo-Nazi groups and from Klans. I also went to their national and regional meetings. My book, *The Racist Mind,* comes from that work.

Interviewer: Did they know you were a Jew?

Rafe: I made sure they knew I was a Jew and opposed to racism. Good interviewing is interplay between you and your respondent—kind of a dance. That requires trust; trust requires openness and honesty.

Interviewer: But, then, why did they talk with you?

Rafe: Because I told them the truth—that I believe every person creates a life that makes sense to him or her, and my professional work is to go onto the turf of people whose lives seem unusual to most folk and let these people tell me, in their own words, the sense their lives make to them. That made sense to them.

Interviewer: Did you find anything out?

Rafe: Yeah. The leaders and members are real different. The leaders are men—this is essentially a male movement—force, macho, blood, all that. The leaders are not motivated primarily by hate or by racism. They are motivated primarily by hunger for power: Power is the goal; racism is the tool. To move a crowd by what they say. To scare a community by saying that they're coming. To fill the media with scare stories. A whole lot of this is theater—they provide the stimulus; we provide the fantasies.

There are always suckers whom you can recruit by talking racism. If you line up 100 white Americans, ranked by how much they fear and dislike African Americans, the big leaders wouldn't be at the head of the line—they'd be about 30 places back.

Interviewer: And the ordinary members?

Rafe: That's a whole different story. This is not a movement built on hate. It's a movement built on fear. When you talk with a member, talk honestly about his life—his, again—the emotion you sense under the surface is fear. The kids in the Detroit group felt, deep down, that their own lives might be snuffed out at any moment, like a candle in the wind.

Interviewer: Do you have any hints on how to do good fieldwork?

Rafe: Yeah. First, check yourself out—why are you doing this? What does it mean to you? Second, be real—with them, with yourself. Third, field notes. When you finish your interview and start home, roll the interview around in your mind. Don't analyze, just let it play in your mind. Like remembering a dream. Don't talk to anyone—no phoning—don't listen to the radio—just keep the interview rolling around. Go straight home and start writing. Write first pure emotion—primary process stuff—associations, feelings. What's going on inside you after this interview? What does it remind you of? Then write your secondary process stuff—what went on and what you think it means. Then, in terms of your project, where does this take you? Do you need more questions? Respondents? Finally, ask yourself: "So what?" What difference does it make to the world what you think you are understanding? As you write that, you will be writing much of your book.

For Your Consideration

Would you have thought that it would have ever been possible for a Jew to study the Klan and other hate groups? How did Ezekiel manage to do this? He is dispassionate in this analysis, but in his book he reveals some of the fear he felt during his research. Could you ever do such research?

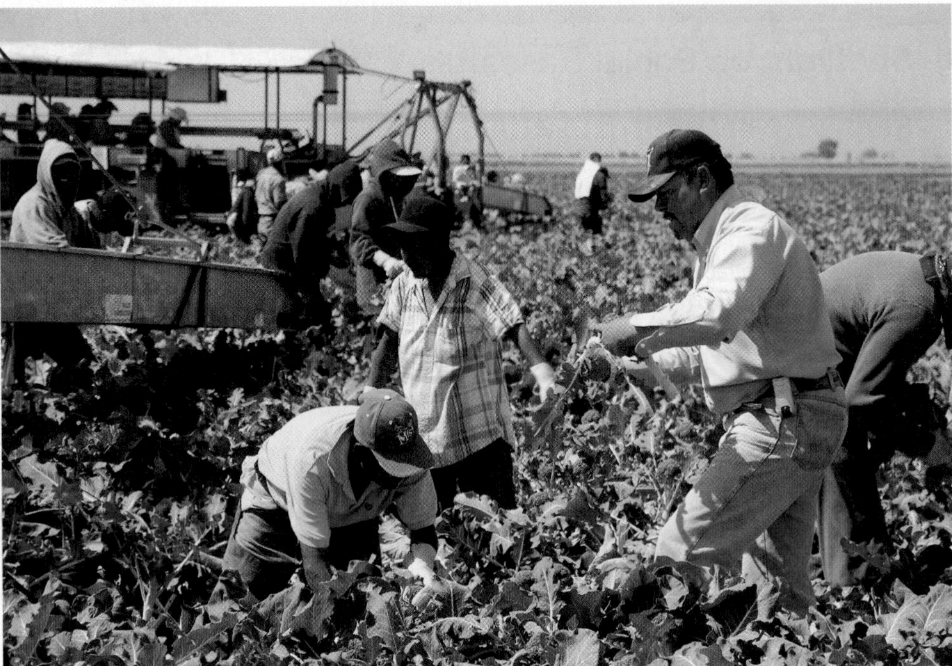

Watch on MySocLab Video: Latino Laborers

For a society to function, it must make sure that its "dirty work" is done. The text discusses the racial–ethnic succession in this process.

over their working conditions. They take jobs that practically no one else will do, often working long hours in crowded, dirty, sometimes dangerous conditions. And they work cheaply, for many employers can avoid paying unemployment compensation, Social Security, hospitalization, overtime pay, or vacations.

Apart from what one could say about the injustice of this situation, it is functional. The dirty work gets done, and *most* Americans benefit: They eat the produce that the unauthorized immigrants pick and wear the clothing they make. The immigrants also benefit: They earn far more than they would in their home country. Their families, left behind in desperate conditions, also benefit as these workers in the United States send them part of their earnings. Even the government of Mexico benefits, for this vast migration siphons off millions of its more ambitious and dissatisfied citizens—those who otherwise might form a restless mass, eventually directing their energies toward overthrowing an oppressive Mexican elite.

Ethnocentrism. Another function of racial–ethnic inequality is **ethnocentrism**, a type of prejudice that can be summarized as "My group's ways are right, and your group's ways are wrong." Ethnocentrism helps the dominant group justify its higher social position and greater share of society's resources. Members of the group don't have to question why they get more than others or feel guilty about it, for aren't they superior? They can simply look around and see that their group is performing not the dirty work like those other people, but the more responsible, respectable, prestigious, and high-paying jobs.

Racial–ethnic stratification also produces ethnocentrism among members of minority groups. Their visible differences and the discrimination they face because of their distinctiveness create cohesion, a sense of identity with one another. Seeing that other groups have "made it" nourishes the hope that they, too, will succeed. The ethnocentrism is quite functional: It encourages minority groups to work hard, minimizes rebellion, and makes them willing to put up with demeaning circumstances in the hope of a better future.

Destruction of Human Potential. Prejudice and discrimination also have severe dysfunctions. They interfere with people's well-being—from a diminished sense of self to inadequate nourishment and early death. As they lower children's self-esteem, they discourage high goals and decrease the capacity to succeed in school and work. Confronting discrimination, many minority children drop out of school and waste their potential in low-level jobs or street crime. Society is the ultimate loser in this destruction of human potential: It is denied the contributions that these youngsters could have made. And if a group becomes too alienated, it can riot, demanding change while venting anger and hatred in the destruction of property and lives. Under the right conditions, discrimination can also lead to revolution, whose end can be quite dysfunctional for those currently in power.

In Sum ▸ Functionalists are often misunderstood: To identify social benefits that come from negative behaviors, such as discrimination, can be viewed as justifying that behavior. Functionalists do not defend discrimination. Rather, by uncovering the functions that underlie discrimination, they give us a better understanding of why this behavior continues. Stressing both the functions and dysfunctions of racial–ethnic stratification, they reveal some of the less visible consequences of institutional arrangements.

Conflict Theory: The Labor Market

> *What had seemed a personal hatred of me, an inexplicable refusal of southern whites to confront their own emotions, and a stubborn willingness of blacks to acquiesce, became the inevitable consequence of a ruthless system which kept itself alive and well by encouraging spite, competition, and the oppression of one group by another. Profit was the word: the cold and constant motive for the behavior, the contempt and despair I had seen. (Davis 1974)*

With these words, Angela Davis, an African American Marxist, recounted her understanding of U.S. racial–ethnic relations. What did she mean?

Pitting Worker Against Worker. According to Marxist conflict theory, the dominant group pits racial–ethnic groups against one another in order to exploit workers and increase profit. Here is how the process works:

The United States has a **capitalist economy;** that is, our economic system is based on investing capital with the goal of making a profit. Profit is the result of selling items for more than they cost to produce. In conflict theory, this is called extracting the **surplus value of labor**. For example, if each item that a factory produces costs the owners of the factory $1 for materials; $1 for rent, utilities, and transportation; $1 for advertising, insurance, and the cost of borrowing money; and $1 for a worker to run a machine, the total cost of the item is $4. If the owners sell the item for $5, they make $1 profit. Conflict theorists claim that the profit represents a surplus value resulting from the labor used to produce the item. That is, the item increased in value *because* the worker added his or her labor to the item.

The Split-Labor Market. Lower wages increase profit. To keep wages low, capitalists use a **split-labor market;** that is, they weaken the bargaining power of workers by splitting them along racial–ethnic lines (Reich 1972, 1981; Alimahomed-Wilson 2012). Workers who are fearful and distrustful of one another are unable to unite and demand higher wages and more benefits.

To maintain a split-labor market, the unemployed are a valuable tool. If everyone who wants to work has a job, workers can threaten to quit unless they receive higher pay and better working conditions. But workers without jobs provide a pool of needy workers that owners can dip into when they need them—to expand production or to break a strike. When the economy contracts or when the strike is settled, these workers—called a **reserve labor force**—can be laid off to rejoin the unemployed, with no unsettling effects on society. Minority workers are ideal for the reserve labor force as the dominant group of white workers seldom objects to what happens to unemployed members of minority groups (Willhelm 1980).

Consequences of a Split-Labor Market. The consequences of splitting labor along racial–ethnic lines are devastating. It encourages minorities and whites to view one another as enemies, able to gain an advantage only at the expense of the other. Whites can come to think of themselves as moral, hardworking taxpayers and view competing minority members as lazy people who swell welfare rolls, supported by taxes that whites pay. The minority, in turn, can come to view themselves as pathetic victims unable to get ahead because of ruthless, untrustworthy, hate-mongering whites.

As you can see, to divide workers in these ways produces a chasm of disunity and distrust. Instead of identifying with one another as workers, members of each group oppose one another as competitors. The division and opposition prevent whites and minorities from realizing that "the other" is an essential part of their own class interests. Blinded, they do not see that each is a victim of a common enemy, the wealthy, who, to line their own pockets, use racial–ethnic divisions to oppress both.

Riots and other violence that result from racial–ethnic division put pressure on the power elite. Feeling threatened, they often try to defuse the situation by offering concessions. They give a little here and there, whatever seems necessary, to quiet the low-paid workers and the unemployed. They might increase welfare benefits, allow token representation on committees, or offer government aid to reconstruct inner cities. These acts are not intended to improve the lives of the disadvantaged. Their purpose is to defuse the situation and protect the privileged positions of the powerful.

In Sum ▸ Conflict theorists stress that racial–ethnic antagonisms divide the working class and strengthen the position of the powerful. The split-labor market pits one racial–ethnic group against another, preventing the solidarity that would allow workers to challenge control of the United States by those who own the means of production. From the conflict perspective, racial–ethnic discrimination will end only when white and minority workers come to see that they both are oppressed and understand that they have the same oppressor. Then they can unite to create a new social order, one in which they will receive the full value of their labor in a society characterized by racial–ethnic harmony.

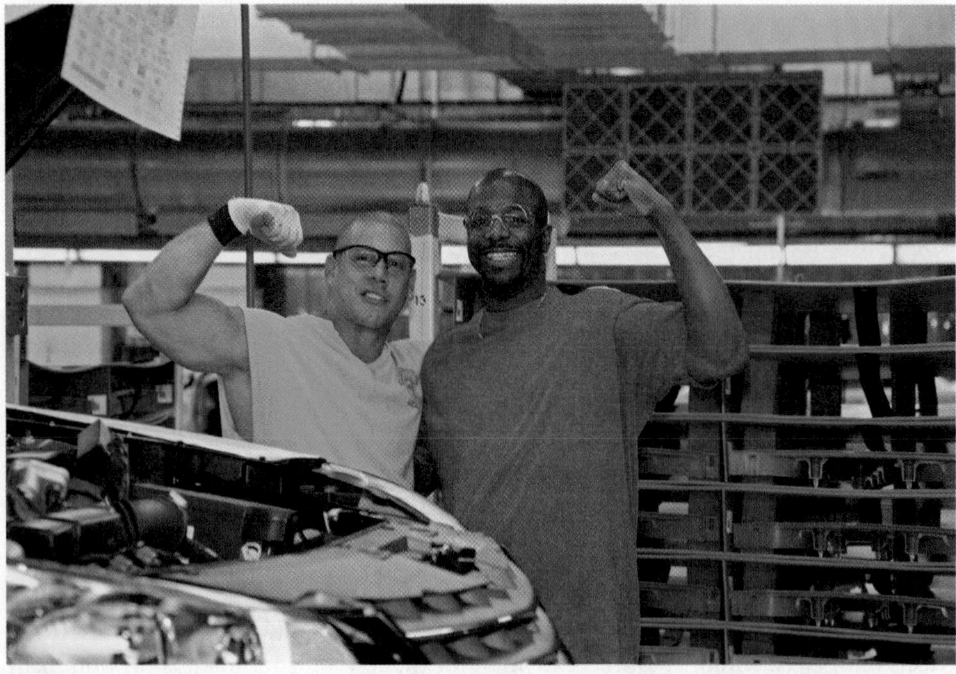

Power can come from unity. The split-labor market is used to weaken worker solidarity by exploiting racial–ethnic, gender, and age divisions.

Summary of the Theoretical Perspectives

None of the theoretical perspectives has an exclusive claim to truth. Rather, each focuses on selective aspects of racial–ethnic relations. Symbolic interactionists alert us to the powerful role of labels in defining human relations, how they are lenses through which we view ourselves and others. If those labels provide demeaning, negative views of others, they help people discriminate with a clear conscience. Functionalists turn our attention not only to the costs of discrimination, but also to its benefits—its role in the division of labor and the consequences of the ethnocentrism it produces. Conflict theorists stress how prejudice and discrimination destroy worker solidarity, enabling owners to hold down wages and increase profits. Each theoretical lens, then, produces a unique understanding of racial–ethnic relations. Combined, these perspectives provide greater understanding of discrimination than does any one of them alone.

Research Findings

As you saw on Figure 8.2 on page 233, whites make up 63 percent of the U.S. population and minorities 35 percent. About 2 percent of Americans claim two or more races. Because minority groups tend to cluster in regions, these groups are far from distributed evenly across the nation. The Social Map on this page shows this clustering. The extreme distributions are found in Maine and Vermont, where whites outnumber minorities 19 to 1, and Hawaii, where minorities outnumber whites 3 to 1.

In this section, we have the opportunity to answer significant questions: What problems do minority groups in the United States face? How do the groups differ from one another? How are relationships between groups changing? What strategies are minority groups using to bring about social change? To answer these questions, we shall present an overview of the four largest minority groups in the United States, from largest to smallest: Latinos, African Americans, Asian Americans, and Native Americans.

FIGURE 8.4 ▸ The Distribution of Dominant and Minority Groups in the United States

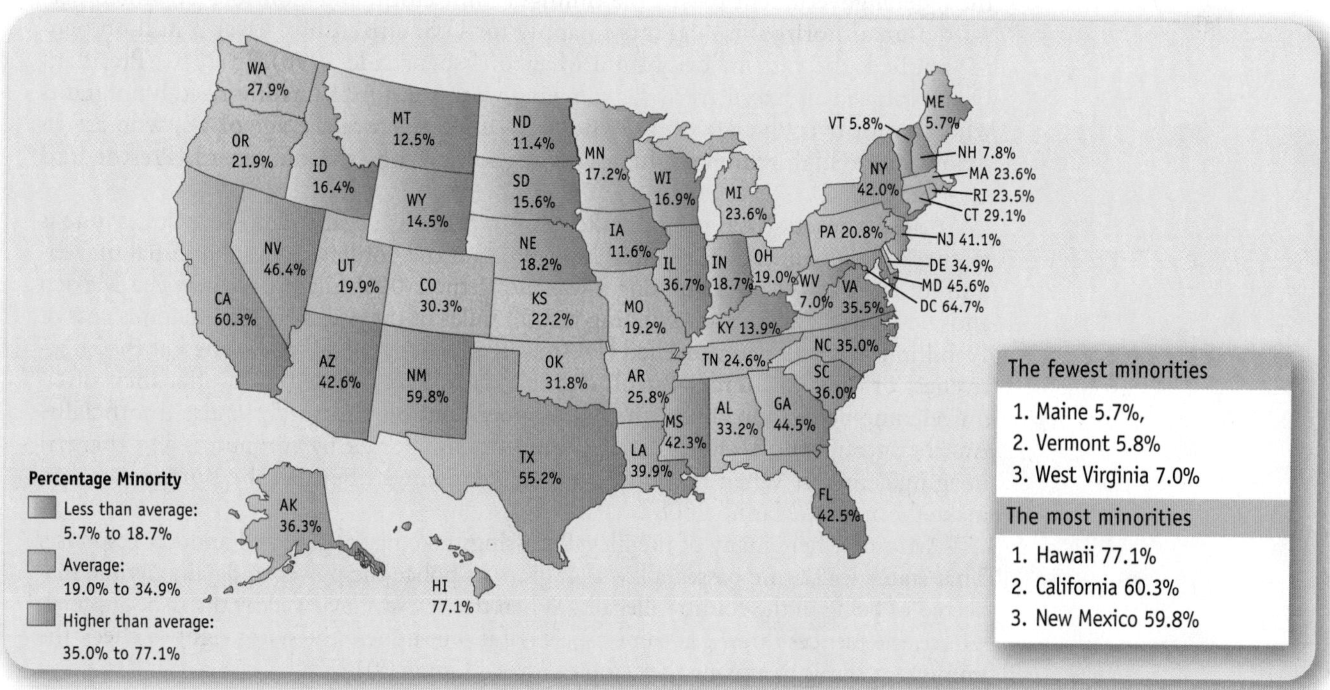

Source: By the author. Based on *Statistical Abstract of the United States* 2013:Table 18.

Latinos (Hispanics)

8.4 Be familiar with why Latino is an umbrella term, the issues of unauthorized immigrants and the use of Spanish, the relative economic well-being of Latinos, and their political divisions and potential.

Umbrella Term. *Latino* is an umbrella term, a single label that refers to people from many cultures. This term is an attempt to incorporate diverse people into the same "group," people who trace their origins to the Spanish-speaking countries of Latin America. Together, Latinos form the largest ethnic group in the United States. Few Latinos, however, consider themselves a single ethnic group. Instead, they think of themselves as Americans of Mexican origin (*Mexicanos* or *Chicanos*), Americans of Cuban origin (*Cubanos*), Americans from Puerto Rico (*Puertoricanos*), and so on. Nor do most identify readily with the umbrella term *Hispanic*, which they also consider to be an artificial grouping of peoples.

It is important, then, to remember that *Latino* and *Hispanic* lump people from many cultures into a single category. It is also important to stress that *Latino* and *Hispanic* do not refer to race, but to ethnic groups. Latinos may identify themselves as African American, white, or Native American. Some even refer to themselves as *Afro Latino.*

Country of Origin. The label Latino applies to 32 to 35 million people from Mexico, 7 million from Central and South America, 4 to 5 million people from Puerto Rico, and 2 million from Cuba (*Statistical Abstract* 2013:Table 37). Although most Latinos of Mexican origin live in the Southwest, most Latinos from Puerto Rico live in New York City, and those from Cuba live primarily in Florida.

Unauthorized Immigrants. Officially tallied at 49 million, the number of Latinos in the United States is considerably higher than this. Although most Latinos are U.S. citizens, about 9 million have entered the country illegally (7 million from Mexico and 2 million from Central and South America) (*Statistical Abstract* 2013:Table 45). Although the economic crisis has shrunk the number of unauthorized immigrants (Jordan 2012), each year about 500,000 people are returned to Mexico or Central and South America (*Statistical Abstract* 2013:Table 541). Some come to the United States for temporary work and then return home. Most do not.

This massive illegal entry into the United States has aroused intense public concern. One reaction has been to open paths to citizenship or work permits. In 1986, the federal government passed the Immigration Reform and Control Act, which permitted unauthorized immigrants to apply for U.S. citizenship. Over 3 million people applied, the vast majority from Mexico (Espenshade 1990). In 2012, President Obama signed an Executive Order allowing work permits to unauthorized immigrants who are not over the age of 30, who arrived here before the age of 16, who are in school or are high school graduates, and who have no criminal record (Preston and Cushman 2012).

Another reaction has been to take steps to prevent illegal entry. The primary one is to check documents at entry points and to patrol the borders. A more unusual prevention measure was to start building a wall along the 2,000 mile border between Mexico and the United States. After building just 53 miles of the wall at the horrendous cost of $1 billion, the wall was cancelled (Preston 2011). With many dissatisfied at the effectiveness of the U.S. Border Patrol, citizen groups have jumped in to offer their often unwelcome help. One group, the Minutemen, patrols the border, quite unofficially. Another group, the Techno Patriots, monitors the border by computers and thermal imaging cameras. When they confirm illegal crossings, they call the Border Patrol to make the arrests (Marino 2008).

Arizona, where many of the illegal crossings take place, gave still another response. That state's legislature passed a law that gives its police the power to detain anyone suspected of being in the country illegally. When the law was reviewed by the U.S. Supreme Court, the justices threw out some aspects of it, but upheld the state's right to check the immigrant status of anyone they stop or arrest (Liptak 2012).

To gain insight into why this vast subterranean migration exists, see the Issues in Social Problems box.

Issues in Social Problems

The Illegal Travel Guide

Manuel was a drinking buddy of Jose's, a man I had met when I was living in Colima, Mexico. At 45, Manuel was friendly, outgoing, and enterprising.

Manuel, who had lived in the United States for 7 years, spoke fluent English. Preferring to live in his home town in Colima, where he palled around with his childhood friends, Manuel always seemed to have money and free time.

When Manuel invited me to go with him on a business trip, I accepted. I never could figure out how Manuel made a living or how he could afford a car, a luxury that none of his friends had. As we traveled from one remote village to another, Manuel would sell used clothing that he had heaped in the back of his older-model Ford station wagon.

At one stop, Manuel took me into a dirt-floored, thatched-roof hut. While chickens ran in and out, Manuel whispered to a slender man of about 23. The poverty was overwhelming. Juan, as his name turned out to be, had a partial grade school education. He also had a wife, four hungry children under the age of 5, and two pigs—his main food supply. Although eager to work, Juan had no job, for there was simply no work available in this remote village.

Manuel explained that he was not only selling clothing but was also lining up migrants to the United States. For a fee, he would take a man to the border and introduce him to a "wolf," who would help him make a night crossing into the promised land.

When I saw the hope in Juan's face, I knew nothing would stop him. He was borrowing every cent he could from every friend and relative so he could scrape the money together. Although he risked losing everything if apprehended, Juan would make the trip, for wealth beckoned on the other side. He knew people who had been there and spoke glowingly of its opportunities. Manuel, of course, stoked the fires of hope.

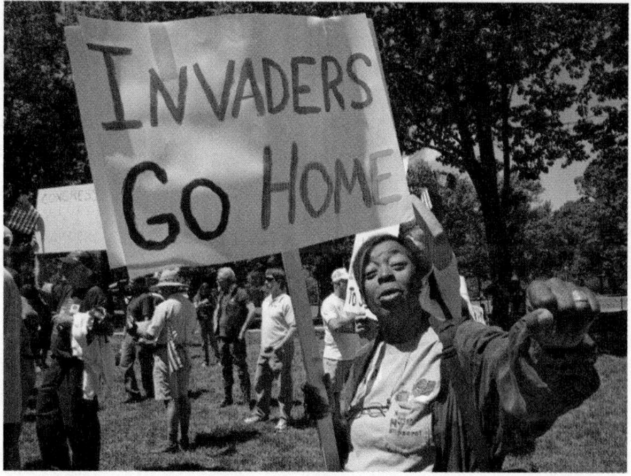

The migration of millions of undocumented people across the southern U.S. border has aroused intense concern. This protester is a member of the Minuteman Project.

Amidst the children playing on the dirt floor with chickens pecking about them was a man who loved his family. In order to make the desperate bid for a better life, he would suffer an enforced absence, as well as the uncertainties of a foreign land whose customs he did not know.

Juan opened his billfold, took something out, and slowly handed it to me. I felt tears as I saw the tenderness with which he handled this piece of paper. It was his passport to the land of opportunity: a Social Security card made out in his name, sent by a friend who had already made the trip and who was waiting for Juan on the other side of the border.

Only the United States could fulfill his dream.

For Your Consideration

Do you think that this vast stream of immigrants illegally crossing the Mexican–U.S. border is destined to continue until its root causes are addressed? What do you think is the best way to deal with this issue? Why?

Residence. With this vast migration, millions more Latinos live in the United States than Canadians (35 million) live in Canada. As Figure 8.5 shows, seven of every ten Latinos live in just six states—California, Texas, Florida, New York, Illinois, and Arizona. With its prominent Latino presence, Miami has been called "the capital of South America."

Spanish. The factor that clearly distinguishes Latinos from other U.S. minorities is the Spanish language. Although not all Latinos speak Spanish, most do. About 37 million Latinos speak Spanish at home (*Statistical Abstract* 2013:Table 53). Many cannot speak English or can do so only with difficulty. Being fluent only in Spanish in a society where English is spoken almost exclusively remains an obstacle.

FIGURE 8.5 ▸ Where U.S. Latinos Live

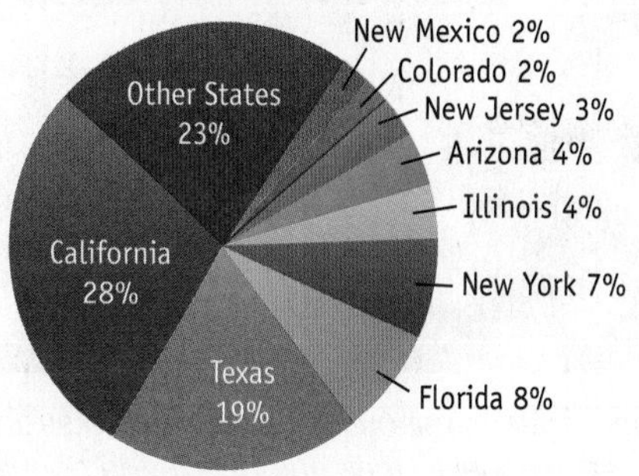

Source: By the author. Based on *Statistical Abstract of the United States* 2013:Table 18.

Despite the 1848 Treaty of Hidalgo, which guarantees Mexicans the right to maintain their culture, from 1855 until 1968 California banned teaching in Spanish in school. In a 1974 decision (*Lau v. Nichols*), the U.S. Supreme Court ruled that using only English to teach Spanish-speaking students violated their civil rights. This decision paved the way for bilingual instruction for Spanish-speaking children (Vidal 1977; Lopez 1980).

The growing use of Spanish has stoked controversy (Fund 2007). Senator S. I. Hayakawa of Hawaii initiated an "English-only" movement in 1981. The constitutional amendment he proposed never got off the ground, but thirty states have passed laws that declare English their official language (Newman et al. 2012).

Economic Well-Being. Latinos fare poorly on indicators of economic well-being (see Table 8.1 on page 236). Their family income averages only three-fifths that of whites, and they are more than twice as likely as whites to be poor. In addition, their unemployment rate is half again as high as that of whites, and only one in eight is a college graduate. At *every* level of education, from a high school diploma on, whites earn more (*Statistical Abstract* 2013:Tables 36, 237, 639). In response to their position in U.S. society, some Latinos have begun a movement that rejects assimilation and emphasizes the maintenance of Latino culture. Others work toward faster assimilation.

Politics. Latinos hold only a fraction of elected positions. Because of their huge numbers, we might expect about 16 of the 100 U.S. senators to be Latino. How many are there? *Two*. In addition, Latinos hold only 7 percent of the seats in the U.S. House of Representatives (*Statistical Abstract* 2013:Table 421). Yet, compared with the past, even these small totals represent substantial gains. On the positive side, several Latinos have been elected as state governors, including the first Latina to become a governor (Susana Martinez of New Mexico in 2010).

In recent years, minorities have gained a stronger political presence, but not nearly equal to their numbers in the population. Shown here is Susana Martinez, the governor of New Mexico. She is the first Latina to be elected as a state governor.

It is likely that Latinos soon will play a larger role in U.S. politics, perhaps one day even beyond their overall numbers. This is because the six states in which they are concentrated hold one-third of the 538 electoral votes: California (55), Texas (38), New York (29), Florida (29), Illinois (20), and Arizona (11). Latinos have received presidential appointments to major federal positions, such as Secretary of the Interior, Secretary of Transportation, and Secretary of Housing and Urban Development.

Divisions based on country of origin hold back the potential political power of Latinos. These distinctions nourish disunity and create political disagreements. As I mentioned, Latinos do not think of themselves as a single people, and national origin is highly significant. People from Puerto Rico, for example, feel little sense of unity with people from Mexico. It is similarly the case with those from Venezuela, Colombia, or El Salvador. It used to be the same with Europeans who emigrated from Germany and Sweden or from England and France. With time, however, the importance of identifying with the European country of origin was lost, and they came to think of themselves as Americans. Perhaps this will happen to Latinos as well.

Social class divisions also obstruct unity among Latinos. In some cases, even when they come from the same country, the differences in their backgrounds are severe. Most of the half million Cubans who fled their homeland after Fidel Castro came to power in 1959 were well-educated, financially comfortable professionals or businesspeople. In contrast, the 100,000 "boat people" who arrived 20 years later were mainly lower-class refugees to whom the earlier arrivals would hardly have spoken in Cuba. The earlier arrivals have prospered in Florida and control many businesses and financial institutions: There continues to be a vast gulf between them and the more recent immigrants.

African Americans

It was 1955, in Montgomery, Alabama. As specified by law, whites took the front seats of the bus, and blacks went to the back. As the bus filled up, blacks had to give up their seats to whites.

When Rosa Parks, a 42-year-old African American woman and secretary of the Montgomery NAACP, was told that she would have to stand so that white folks could sit, she refused (Bray 1995). She stubbornly sat there while the bus driver fumed and whites felt insulted. Her arrest touched off mass demonstrations, led 50,000 blacks to boycott the city's buses for a year, and thrust an otherwise unknown preacher into a historic role.

Reverend Martin Luther King, Jr., who had majored in sociology at Morehouse College in Atlanta, Georgia, took control. He organized car pools and preached nonviolence. Incensed at this radical organizer and at the stirrings in the normally compliant black community, segregationists also put their beliefs into practice—by bombing the homes of blacks and dynamiting a church.

8.5 Be familiar with the civil rights history of African Americans, their relative economic well-being, and the controversy over race versus social class.

Civil Disobedience and American Apartheid. In 1943, the U.S. Supreme Court ruled that African Americans had the legal right to attend public schools with whites. Before this, they had to go to "colored" schools. In 1944, the Court ruled that African Americans could vote in southern primaries. Change was slow, and during the 1950s, the South was still practicing a form of apartheid. African Americans, then called Negroes, were not allowed to stay at hotels or to eat in restaurants that whites patronized. They had to use separate toilets, water fountains, and swimming pools. Some states had miscegenation laws prohibiting marriage between Negroes and whites, laws that weren't struck down until 1967 (O'Hare 1992).

To break institutional barriers that supported "American apartheid" Martin Luther King, Jr., led African Americans in **civil disobedience**, deliberately but peacefully disobeying laws considered unjust. Inspired by the writings of Henry David Thoreau and the success of Mahatma Gandhi, King (1958) based his strategy on these principles:

Watch on
MySocLab
Video: Martin Luther King Speech 1963

1. Actively resist evil, but nonviolently
2. Don't try to defeat or humiliate opponents, but try instead to win their friendship and understanding
3. Attack the forces of evil rather than the people who are doing the evil
4. Be willing to accept suffering without retaliating
5. Refuse to hate the opponent
6. Act with the conviction that the universe is on the side of justice

King found no overnight success, but he and his followers persisted. Gradually, more barriers came down. In 1964 Congress passed the Civil Rights Act, making it illegal to discriminate in hotels, theaters, and other public places. Then, in 1965, the Voting Rights Act banned literacy tests that whites had used to keep African Americans from voting.

Urban Revolts. Encouraged by these gains, African Americans experienced **rising expectations;** that is, they expected better conditions to follow right away. The lives of poor African Americans, however, changed little, if at all. Frustrations built, finally exploding in Watts in 1965, when residents of this central Los Angeles ghetto took to the streets in an "urban revolt." The violence, which occurred despite the protests of

Dr. King, precipitated a white backlash that threatened the multiracial coalition that King had spearheaded. Congress refused to enact civil rights legislation in both 1967 and 1968. When King was assassinated on April 4, 1968, ghettos across the nation erupted in fiery violence. Under threat of the destruction of the nation's cities, Congress reluctantly passed the sweeping Civil Rights Act of 1968.

From Militancy to Moderacy. After King's death, black militants rushed in to fill the void in leadership. Like King, they emphasized black unity and black pride, but, unlike King, some of them proclaimed that violence was the way to gain equality. Flashed across the nation's television screens were images of the Black Panthers, brandishing rifles and parading in military-style uniforms. The talk of revolution by black militants stirred fear and hostility among whites, and the authorities turned violently on the most outspoken leaders. In a nighttime raid in 1969, the FBI and the Chicago police assassinated Fred Hampton, the head of the Chicago Black Panthers. They shot him while he was sleeping in his bed (Haas 2009).

With photos of the bloodied bodies circulating in the mass media, the black leadership fragmented. Some argued for secession from the United States, others for total integration. They disagreed over whether violent confrontation or peaceful protest was the way to go. In the end, those who made the case for integration and political action won. As more moderate approaches replaced militancy, even the Black Panthers changed their tactics. Instead of challenging white authority and confronting police, they switched to community organizing, providing breakfasts for schoolchildren, and running for political office. Lacking a charismatic leader to replace King, the momentum that had propelled the struggle for equality faded.

Continued Gains. Change has been gradual, but over time the change has been profound. Today's race relations are vastly different from those that Rosa Parks confronted when she refused to move to the back of the bus. African Americans have made remarkable gains in politics, education, and jobs. At 10 percent, the number

In the 1960s, the Black Panthers sowed fear among law enforcement officers and politicians, launching a retaliation that resulted in the assassination of leaders of this group. This photo was taken on the statehouse steps of Olympia, Washington, in 1969.

of African Americans in the U.S. House of Representatives is *two to three times* what it was a generation ago (*Statistical Abstract* 1989:Table 423; 2013:Table 421). As college enrollments increased, the middle class expanded, and today 54 percent of all African American families make more than $35,000 a year. Two in five earn more than $50,000 a year. One in eight has an income over $100,000 a year (*Statistical Abstract* 2013:Table 710).

Watch on
MySocLab
Video: Economics of the African–American Family

African Americans have also become prominent in politics. Jesse Jackson (another sociology major) competed for the Democratic presidential nomination in 1984 and 1988. In 1989, L. Douglas Wilder was elected governor of Virginia, and in 2006 Deval Patrick became governor of Massachusetts. These accomplishments, of course, pale in comparison to the election of Barack Obama as president of the United States in 2008 and his reelection in 2012.

Current Losses. Despite these remarkable gains, African Americans continue to lag behind in politics, economics, and education. From their percentage of the U.S. population, we might expect about twelve African American senators. How many are there? *Zero*. There have only been six in U.S. history. As Table 8.1 on page 236 shows, the income of African Americans is 41 percent lower than that of whites, and their poverty is much higher. From Table 8.3 on page 254, you can see how they compare in college education. That two of five African American families have incomes over $50,000 is only part of the story. The other part is that almost one of every five families makes less than $15,000 a year.

Race or Social Class? A Sociological Debate. The upward mobility of millions of African Americans into the middle class has created two worlds of African American experience—one educated and affluent, the other uneducated and poor. This division of African Americans into "haves" and "have-nots" has fueled a sociological controversy (Landry and Marsh 2011). Sociologist William Julius Wilson (1978, 2000, 2007) argues that social class has become more important than race in determining the life chances of African Americans. Before civil rights legislation, he says, the African American experience was dominated by race. Throughout the United States, African Americans were excluded from avenues of economic advancement: good schools and good jobs. When civil rights laws opened new opportunities, African Americans seized them. Just as legislation began to open doors to African Americans, however, manufacturing jobs dried up, and many blue-collar jobs were moved to the suburbs. As better-educated African Americans obtained white-collar jobs, they moved out of the inner city. Left behind were those with poor education and few skills.

Wilson stresses how significant these two worlds of African American experience are. The group that is stuck in the inner city lives in poverty, attends poor schools, and faces dead-end jobs or welfare. This group is filled with hopelessness and despair, combined with apathy or hostility. In contrast, those who have moved up the social class ladder live in comfortable homes in secure neighborhoods. Their jobs provide decent incomes, and they send their children to good schools. With middle-class experiences shaping their views on life, their aspirations and values have little in common with those of African Americans who remain poor. According to Wilson, then, social class—not race—is the more significant factor in the lives of African Americans.

Some sociologists reply that this analysis overlooks the discrimination that continues to underlie the African American experience. They note that African Americans who do the same work as whites average less pay (Willie 1991; Herring 2002) and even receive fewer tips (Lynn et al. 2008). Others document how young black males experience daily indignities and are objects of suspicion and police brutality (Rios 2011). These, they argue, point to racial discrimination, not to social class.

What is the answer to this debate? Wilson would reply that it is not an either-or question. My book is titled *The **Declining** Significance of Race*, he would say, not ***The Absence** of Race*. Certainly racism is still alive, he would add, but today social class is

Barack Obama, taking the oath of office, after being re-elected as president of the United States. Obama's wife and two daughters look on as the U.S. Supreme Court Chief Justice administers the oath.

more central to the African American experience than is racial discrimination. For years, he has been stressing the need to provide jobs for the poor in the inner city—for work provides an anchor to a responsible life (Wilson 1996, 2007, 2009).

Asian Americans

8.6 Be familiar with why Asian American is an umbrella term, the history of discrimination against Asian Americans, their relative economic well-being, and their political situation.

It was a quiet Sunday morning, December 7, 1941, a day destined to live in infamy, as President Roosevelt was later to say.

At dawn, waves of Japanese bombers began an attack on Pearl Harbor, the United States' major naval station in the Pacific Ocean. At Oahu, Hawaii, the Japanese pilots found the U.S. Pacific Fleet anchored in shallow waters, unprepared for battle. The Americans were sitting ducks.

In response, the United States declared war on Japan, entering World War II and leaving no American untouched. Some left home to battle overseas; others left their farms to work in factories that supported the war effort. All lived with the rationing of food, gasoline, sugar, coffee, and other essentials.

Relocation Camps. This event had an especially disruptive effect on Americans of Japanese descent. Just as waves of planes flew over Pearl Harbor, so waves of suspicion and hostility rolled over the 110,000 Japanese Americans who called the United States "home." Overnight, Japanese Americans became the most detested racial–ethnic group in the country (Daniels 1975). Many Americans feared that Japan would invade the United States and that Japanese Americans would sabotage military installations on the West Coast. Although not a single Japanese American had committed even one act of sabotage, on February 1, 1942, President Franklin Roosevelt signed Executive Order 9066, authorizing the removal of people considered threats to military areas. All people on the West Coast who were *one-eighth* Japanese or more were jailed in detention centers called relocation camps. These people were charged with no crime; they were neither indicted nor given a trial. Having one Japanese great-grandmother or great-grandfather was sufficient reason to be put in prison.

Intercontinental Railroad, Discrimination and Segregation. This was not the first time that Asian Americans encountered discrimination. For years, Americans of

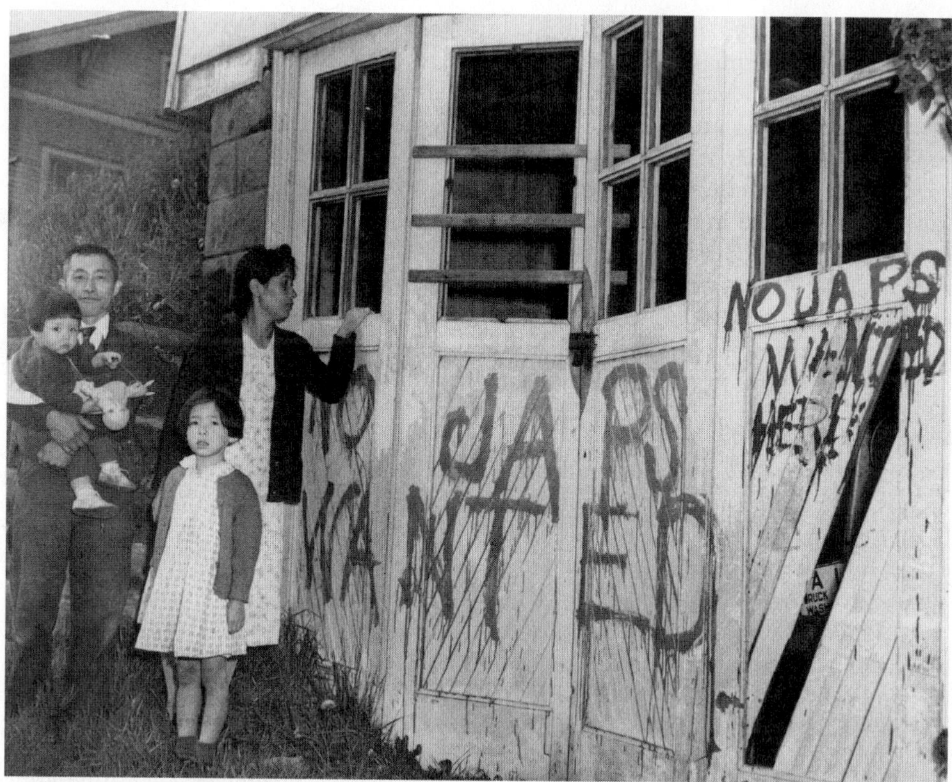

In 1942, Japanese Americans were considered a threat to the security of the United States. They were taken from their homes and locked up in detention camps patrolled by armed guards. After their release at war's end, some returned home to scenes like this.

European background had discriminated against Americans of Asian ancestry because of their differences in appearance and lifestyle. In the 1800s, the United States government promoted an intercontinental railroad to unite the east and west coasts. Short on labor, those building the railroad turned to China. Their ads and agents brought about 200,000 Chinese workers to the United States. Although 90 percent of the workers for the Central Pacific Railroad were Chinese, when the famous golden spike was driven at Promontory, Utah, in 1869 to mark the joining of the Union Pacific and the Central Pacific railroads, white workers prevented the Chinese from being in the photo of this historic event (Schaefer 2012). After the railroad was finished, many Chinese settled in the West. To intimidate their new competition, white workers formed mobs and vigilante groups.

As fears of "alien genes and germs" grew, legislators passed anti-Chinese laws (Schrieke 1936). In 1850, the California legislature passed the Foreign Miner's Act, levying a special tax on Chinese (and Latinos) of $20 a month. At this time, the average Chinese person made a dollar a day. The California Supreme Court ruled that Chinese could not testify against whites in court (Carlson and Colburn 1972). In 1882 Congress passed the Chinese Exclusion Act, suspending all Chinese immigration for 10 years. Four years later, the Statue of Liberty was dedicated. The tired, the poor, and the huddled masses it was to welcome obviously did not include the Chinese.

In the face of such severe discrimination, Chinese immigrants formed segregated communities known as "Chinatowns." Three stages were involved in their development (Yuan 1963). In the first, *involuntary segregation*, Chinese immigrants lived in separate areas because whites refused to let them live near them. Then came *voluntary segregation:* They chose to remain in the segregated community because that was where their friends and relatives lived. There they were able to help one another, avoid language barriers, and follow their customs and traditional religions. The final stage, now in process, is *gradual assimilation:* As Chinese Americans become acculturated, they move out of Chinatown and into mainstream culture.

Spillover Bigotry. The relocation camps of World War II were not the first discrimination that immigrants from Japan experienced. When they first began to immigrate, they met spillover bigotry that had been directed against the Chinese. They also confronted discriminatory laws. Even the U.S. Constitution was used against them. Although only whites could be citizens under the original Constitution, it was amended in the 1860s to include African Americans (Amott and Matthaei 1991). Because Asians had not been named in the amendments, the U.S. Supreme Court ruled that they were prohibited from becoming citizens (Schaefer 2004). This ruling provided an opportunity for California politicians. In 1913, they passed the Alien Land Act, prohibiting anyone who was ineligible for citizenship from owning land. (Most Native Americans were not granted citizenship in their own land until 1924; the Chinese gained citizenship in 1943; for those born in Japan, the exclusion remained until 1952.)

Explore on **MySocLab**
Activity: The Asian Population of the United States: The Diversity of Cultures

Another Umbrella Term. The 14 million Asian Americans living in the United States are diverse. As you can see from Figure 8.6, they come from many different nations. As a result, Asian Americans are divided by many cultural heritages, including different languages and religions. *With no unifying culture or "race," why should people of so many backgrounds be lumped together and assigned a single label?* Think about it. What culture or race–ethnicity do Samoans and Vietnamese have in common? Or Laotians and Pakistanis? Or people from Guam and those from China? Those from Japan and those from India? Yet all these groups—and more—are lumped together and called Asian Americans. As a result, any "average" that is computed for Asian Americans conceals a lot of differences. Let's look at some of these averages.

FIGURE 8.6 ▸ Countries of Origin of Asian Americans

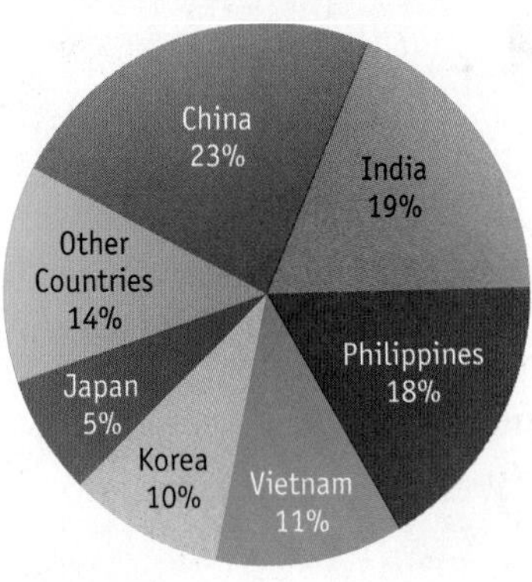

Reasons for Financial Success. The high average income of Asian Americans can be traced to three major factors: family life, educational achievement, and assimilation into mainstream culture. Of all ethnic groups, including whites, Asian American children are the most likely to grow up with two parents and the least likely to be born to single mothers (*Statistical Abstract* 2013:Tables 69, 89). Common in these families is a stress on self-discipline, thrift, and hard work (Suzuki 1985; Bell 1991). This early socialization provides strong impetus for the other two factors.

The second factor is their unprecedented rate of college graduation. As you can see from Table 8.3, 50 percent of Asian Americans complete college. To realize how

TABLE 8.3 ▸ Race–Ethnicity and Education

	Education Completed				Doctorates		
Racial–Ethnic Group	Less Than High School	High School	Some College	College (BA or Higher)	Number Awarded	Percentage of all U.S. Doctorates[1]	Percentage of U.S. Population
Whites	9.3%	29.3%	21.9%	31.4%	39,648	74.3%	62.9%
Latinos	37.8%	26.5%	17.2%	13.0%	2,540	5.8%	16.1%
Country or Area of Origin							
Cuba	NA[2]	NA	NA	26.2%	NA	NA	0.6%
Puerto Rico	NA	NA	NA	17.5%	NA	NA	1.4%
Central and South America	NA	NA	NA	18.9%	NA	NA	2.2%
Mexico	NA	NA	NA	10.6%	NA	NA	10.4%
African Americans	18.1%	31.7%	24.9%	17.9%	4,434	7.4%	12.8%
Asian Americans	14.6%	16.0%	13.1%	49.9%	3,875	11.8%	4.8%
Native Americans	22.7%	30.7%	25.6%	13.4%	332	0.7%	1.2%

[1]Percentage after the doctorates awarded to nonresidents have been deducted from the total.
[2]Not Available
Source: By the author. Based on *Statistical Abstract of the United States* 2013:Tables 36, 37, 300, and Figure 8.2 of this text.

stunning this is, compare this rate with that of the other groups shown on this table. This educational achievement, in turn, opens doors to economic success.

The most striking indication of the third factor, assimilation, is a high rate of intermarriage. Of all racial–ethnic groups, Asian Americans are the most likely to marry someone of a different racial–ethnic group (Wang 2012). Of Asian Americans who graduate from college, about 40 percent of the men and 60 percent of the women marry a non-Asian American (Qian and Lichter 2007). The intermarriage of Japanese Americans is so extensive that two of every three of their children have one parent who is not of Japanese descent (Schaefer 2012). Chinese Americans are close behind (Alba and Nee 2003).

Politics. Asian Americans are becoming more prominent in politics. With about half of its citizens being Asian American, Hawaii has elected Asian American governors and sent several Asian American senators to Washington, including the one now serving there (Lee 1998; *Statistical Abstract* 2013:Table 421). The first Asian American governor outside of Hawaii was Gary Locke, who served from 1997 to 2005 as governor of Washington, a state in which Asian Americans make up less than 6 percent of the population. In 2008, Bobby Jindal became the first Indian American governor when he was elected governor of Louisiana, a state in which Asian Americans make up less than 2 percent of the population.

Native Americans

> *"I don't go so far as to think that the only good Indians are dead Indians, but I believe nine out of ten are—and I shouldn't inquire too closely in the case of the tenth. The most vicious cowboy has more moral principle than the average Indian.*
>
> —Teddy Roosevelt, 1886 (President of the United States 1901–1909)

8.7 Be familiar with why Native American is an umbrella term, their relations with settlers, the significance of disease, justifying labels, education and culture conflict, casinos, and self-determination.

Another Umbrella Term. When Columbus arrived on the shores of the "New World," Native Americans numbered about 10 million (Schaefer 2012). They were not a single group of people living in separate tribes. They spoke over 700 languages, and their variety of cultures ranged from nomadic hunters and gatherers to farmers who lived in wooden houses. Each group had its own norms and values—and the usual ethnocentric pride in its own culture.

Four hundred years later, when Teddy Roosevelt, who spoke the words above, became president of the United States, because of disease and warfare the number of Native Americans had plunged to just 250,000. Today, there are 4 million Native Americans, divided among more than 500 tribes. Native Americans, who today speak 169 different languages, do not think of themselves as a single people who fit neatly within a single label (Siebens and Julian 2011).

Conflict. At first, relations between the European settlers and Native Americans were peaceful. Some American (and Canadian) authorities even encouraged marriage between whites and Native Americans. In 1784, Patrick Henry introduced a bill in the Virginia House of Delegates offering tax relief, free education, and cash bonuses to whites and Indians who intermarried (Kaplan 1990). As more Europeans arrived, they began a relentless push westward. Native Americans stood in the way of expansion, and Europeans adopted a policy of *genocide*. As part of this policy (which they called "pacification"), the U.S. Cavalry slaughtered tens of thousands of Native Americans. When the cavalry butchered the huge herds of buffalo on which the Great Plains Indians depended, many thousands more died from malnutrition and disease. Because Native Americans had no immunity to European diseases, more of them died from smallpox, measles, and the flu than from battle wounds (Kitano 1974; Dobyns 1983; Schaefer 2012).

In reading accounts from this period, I was struck by the barbarity of government agents. One of the most grisly acts was the distribution of blankets contaminated with smallpox. The blankets were given as a peace offering. Another was the Trail of Tears, the result of a government change in policy from genocide to population transfer.

The Trail of Tears was a forced march from the Carolinas and Georgia to "reservations" in Oklahoma, a journey of 1,000 miles. Fifteen thousand Cherokees were forced to make this midwinter march in light clothing. Falling from exhaustion, 4,000 people, mostly elderly and children, were left to die.

Treaties. Recognizing each tribe as a separate nation, the U.S. government signed separate treaties with the tribes. These treaties granted each tribe specified lands forever. The treaties were broken when white settlers demanded more Indian land and natural resources. In 1874, for instance, when gold was discovered in South Dakota's Black Hills, whites flooded the reservation lands. The cavalry supported the settlers, resulting in the well-known defeat of "General" (actually, Lt. Colonel) Custer at Little Big Horn in 1876 (Churchill and Vander Wall 1990). The symbolic end to Native American resistance may have been the 1890 massacre at Wounded Knee, South Dakota, where the U.S. Cavalry killed 300 (out of 350) Native American men, women, and children (Kitano 1974; Olson et al. 1997). After the massacre, the soldiers threw the bodies into a mass grave (DiSilvestro 2006).

Justifying Labels. As noted earlier, people use stereotypes and labels to justify inhumane acts. So it was with the U.S. Indian policy. The Europeans who populated the Americas viewed Native Americans as stupid, lying, thieving, murdering, pagan "savages" (Simpson and Yinger 1972). Killing dangerous savages was viewed as a way to make the world a safer place for intelligent, civilized people. After a war, the victors, not the losers, write the history books. The whites' choice of terms as they wrote theirs is fascinating. They called themselves "pioneers" and "settlers," not "invaders." They labeled their military successes "victories," but they gave the term "massacres" to the military victories of the Native Americans. They didn't call their seizure of Native American lands "invasion" or "theft," but, rather, "settling the land." And the Native Americans' defense of their homelands against overwhelming numbers? Not "courageous," but "treacherous" (Josephy 1970).

Education and Culture Conflict. After the federal government moved the Native Americans to reservations, the Bureau of Indian Affairs (BIA), an agency of the federal government that was assigned the responsibility of overseeing Native Americans, opened schools in an attempt to "civilize" the Indians—that is, to replace the Native American cultures with that of the European Americans. The BIA took thousands of Native American children from their parents and forced them to attend off-reservation boarding schools. The effects still linger, and even today many Native Americans mistrust the intentions of white authorities (McCarty 2009).

Anthropologists Murray and Rosalie Wax (1964, 1965, 1967, 1971) found a huge cultural gap between the home and school lives of Native American children. The parents taught their children to be independent, but at school they were rewarded for being dependent on their teachers. Native American parents taught their children not to embarrass their peers, but their teachers expected them to correct one another in the classroom. Because the school system is based on the values of the dominant group and undermines Native American culture, many parents are alienated from their children's schools and refuse to visit them. The teachers, stung by the rejection of their good intentions, avoid the homes of their students.

Dead center in this conflict between schools and the reservation are the children. Torn between home and school, they generally choose their family and tribe. Lacking motivation to do well in school, they tend to drop out. As the Waxes expressed it, the deck is so stacked against Native American children that they are, in effect, pushed out of school. That they continue to drop out of high school at a high rate and graduate from college at a low rate (see Table 8.3 on page 254) indicates that such contrasting orientations continue.

Well-Being. Table 8.1 on page 236 shows how Native Americans rank on indicators of economic well-being. You can see how much lower their incomes are than those of whites and that their rate of poverty is higher than that of all groups. In addition, and not shown on this table, the life expectancy of Native Americans is less than that of the nation as a whole: One in four Native Americans dies before the age of 25, compared with the national average of one in seven. Their suicide rate is higher than that of any other racial–ethnic group, and their rate of alcoholism runs perhaps five times that of the national average (Snipp and Sorkin 1986; O'Hare 1992; Centers for Disease Control 2009a; Crosby et al. 2011). It seems fair to conclude that it is common for Native Americans to find life in the dominant white society far from satisfying.

Current Struggles. Native Americans are sometimes called the invisible minority. With one-third of Native Americans living on reservations, most in just four states—Oklahoma, California, Arizona, and New Mexico—most Americans are hardly aware of their presence (Schaefer 2012). In addition, for the past 100 years or so, seldom have Native Americans made headlines by disrupting the dominant culture. Today's conflicts center on Native Americans trying to enforce their treaties with the United States. Minor legal skirmishes have centered on maintaining traditional fishing and hunting rights. Major legal battles are being fought over the waters of the Arkansas, Colorado, San Juan, and Rio Grande rivers—which were guaranteed by treaty. Native Americans have also sued to reclaim millions of acres of land from New England to the Southwest. Originally Congress guaranteed these lands to Native American tribes "in perpetuity"—an unlimited time, generation after generation.

The federal government's primary legal strategy is to prevent cases being heard by making perpetual motions for postponement. In some instances, legal cases are never heard. Those who originally filed the motion die; others lose interest as proceedings drag on for years, sometimes for generations. Some tribes, however, have won legal battles. Blue Lake, in New Mexico, a heavily forested area sacred to the Taos Pueblo tribe, has been returned to the tribe. Alaskan Native Americans, primarily the Inuits and Aleuts, were awarded a cash settlement of nearly $1 billion and legal title to 40 million acres.

The vast majority of these legal claims remain undecided in court, putting "clouds" on many titles of ownership to real estate. In the state of New York, clouded titles have

Wearing traditional clothing and teaching customs to children are ways by which parents and tribal leaders are trying to reclaim an authentic Native American identity, not easy to do in a society dominated by the descendants of the people who defeated their ancestors.

made it difficult for some people to sell their land even though they have owned it for 200 years (Olson 2002). Some whites have hit upon a legal strategy that goes straight to the jugular: They are trying to strip Native Americans of their legal status as separate nations. This would remove their immunity from lawsuits. So far, such attempts have failed (Anderson and Moller 1998).

The Casinos. It is the casinos, though, that have attracted the most attention. In 1988, Congress passed a law that allows Native Americans to operate gambling establishments on reservations. Now over 200 tribes operate casinos. *They bring in $26 billion a year, more than all the casinos in Las Vegas* (Pratt 2011; *Statistical Abstract* 2013: Table 1273). The Oneida tribe of New York, which has only 1,000 members, runs a casino that nets $232,000 a year for each man, woman, and child (Peterson 2003). This amount pales in comparison with that of the Mashantucket Pequot tribe of Connecticut. With 800 members, this tribe brings in about $2 million *a day* just from its slot machines (Allen 2008; Gannon 2008). Incredibly, one tribe has only *one* member: She has her own casino (Bartlett and Steele 2002). Native Americans who are wealthy are an exception, of course, as is evident from Table 8.1 on page 236.

Self-Determination. Native Americans had no overarching term for the many tribes that inhabited North and South America. The term *Indian* was given to them by Columbus, who mistakenly thought that he had landed in India. The name stuck, and many Native Americans still use it to refer to themselves (Shively 1999). Whites also invented the term *Native American.* Thinking of the 500 culturally distinct tribes as "one people," then, is a European American way of thought and labeling. The tribes see themselves as many nations, many peoples, and they insist on the right to self-determination—to remain unassimilated in the dominant culture and to run their own affairs as separate peoples.

That there are these many separate identities has served the dominant whites well, for they have not had to face a united Native America. Perhaps, then, the most significant change is the development of **pan-Indianism**. Emphasizing common elements that run through their many separate cultures, some Native Americans are trying to build a united identity and work toward the welfare of all Native Americans. If effective, national Native American organizations will develop. United, these groups could place greater pressure on the courts to hear Native American lawsuits. They could also develop self-help measures centering on Native American values. Pan-Indianism, however, is a controversial topic among Native Americans. Some reject it in favor of ethnic diversity, identifying with their own tribe, and preferring to stress the many Native American histories, languages, and even musical styles (Rolo, n.d.).

Social Policy

8.8 Summarize social policy regarding cultural pluralism, preventing discrimination, and the dilemma of affirmative action.

A unified society certainly is desirable, especially in contrast to a broken, fragmented one, with hostile groups working at cross-currents. We have more than adequate experience, however, to know that it is futile to try to force everyone into the same mold. And which mold would it be anyway? Accordingly, it seems reasonable for social policy to center on the twin goals of encouraging cultural pluralism and preventing discrimination. Let's see what social policies might help us reach these goals.

Encouraging Cultural Pluralism

Explore on **MySocLab** **Activity:** Diversity within American Society

Appreciating Diversity. *Cultural integrity* is essential if we are to promote the first goal, that of encouraging cultural pluralism. Cultural integrity refers to accepting and appreciating diverse backgrounds. Here are steps that can bring this about:

1. Establishing national, state, and local "cultural centers" that feature a group's heritage

2. Holding "ethnic appreciation days" in public schools, featuring ethnic customs, dress, dances, history, and food
3. Teaching history (and any courses with an historical emphasis) in ways that recognize the contributions of the many groups that make up the United States
4. Teaching foreign languages from grade school through high school—starting early enough that all students learn to converse in one foreign language

The first two suggestions are easy to implement and go a long way toward encouraging appreciation of cultural diversity and pride in one's own heritage. Because our schools are so segregated, we need cultural exchanges among public and private schools. For this proposal to be effective, the approach must be honest. Students will see through dishonest attempts to appreciate multiculturalism or to "stretch" some group's contributions to the mainstream culture. Technical advances in teaching foreign languages can make the fourth proposal a reality. As today's trade, travel, and communications expand, learning other languages could benefit the nation as a whole.

Pride in One's Heritage and Participation in the Mainstream Culture. The emphasis of cultural pluralism on pride in one's own racial–ethnic heritage does not mean a retreat into a racial–ethnic culture. Although children of minority groups should be encouraged to take pride in their rich heritage, if they are to participate in the mainstream culture, then like the children of the dominant group, they, too, need to become proficient at English and other basic skills. The school system is uniquely equipped to teach them these skills. Anyone who does not learn to speak English or who fails to get a good education is at a severe disadvantage in competing for jobs, especially for positions that pay well and offer advancement.

Preventing Discrimination

Using the Legal System. To prevent discrimination, the legal system is a powerful tool. It can be used to ensure that minorities are not discriminated against in jobs, housing, education, or any other area of social life. The Civil Rights Act of 1964, which forbids discrimination by race, color, creed, national origin, and sex, must be enforced. This law applies to unions, employment agencies, and, as amended in 1972, to any business with 15 or more employees. This law prohibits discrimination in voting, public accommodations, federally supported programs, and federally supported institutions such as colleges and hospitals. Preventing discrimination also requires funding the Equal Employment Opportunity Commission (EEOC)—the organization that is empowered to investigate complaints of discrimination and to recommend action to the Department of Justice.

The Dilemma of Affirmative Action

The *Bakke* Case. The Civil Rights Act of 1964 posed a dilemma: How do we make up for past discrimination without creating new discrimination? In the *Bakke* case (1973), Allan Bakke argued that the rejection of his application to the medical school of the University of California at Davis was an act of discrimination. The school had admitted minorities who had scored lower than he had on the entrance exam and who had lower grade point averages than his. Bakke argued that had he been a member of a minority group, he would have been admitted (Sindler 1978). In other words, the university was racist—it had discriminated against him because he was white. The U.S. Supreme Court agreed, ruling that the Davis medical school had to admit Bakke because it had used illegal quotas.

Cloudy Guidance. Following the *Bakke* case, the U.S. Supreme Court issued rulings that confused everyone: Colleges cannot use quotas to determine whom they admit—but they can use race as a factor to create a diverse student body (Walsh 1996). In its 1989 *City of Richmond* decision, the Court ruled that state and local governments "must almost always avoid racial quotas" in awarding construction contracts. "Almost always" left everyone scratching their heads. No one knew where and when or in what ways preferential treatment was or was not constitutional.

Proposition 209. With the U.S. Supreme Court's cloudy guidance, this national debate continued. Few were fond of affirmative action, but no one saw alternatives to erase the consequences of past discrimination. Then during the 1990s, the tide turned against affirmative action, with a series of rulings by circuit courts and the U.S. Supreme Court. Perhaps the most significant development was *Proposition 209*, a 1996 amendment to the California state constitution that banned race and gender preferences in hiring and college admissions. Despite appeals by a coalition of civil rights groups, the U.S. Supreme Court upheld the California law.

The University of Michigan Case. In 2003, the *University of Michigan* case came before the Supreme Court. White applicants who had been denied admission to the university claimed that they had been discriminated against because the admissions committees had given extra points to applicants from underrepresented minority groups. Again, the Court's ruling was ambiguous. The Court ruled that universities can give minorities an edge in admissions, but they cannot use a point system to do so. Race can be a "plus factor," but in the Court's words, there must be "a meaningful individualized review of applicants."

Officials found this ruling murky. To remove ambiguity, voters in California, Michigan, and Nebraska added amendments to their state constitutions that make it illegal for public institutions to consider race or sex in hiring, in awarding contracts, or in college admissions (Espenshade and Radford 2009; Perez-Pena 2012).

The New Haven Firefighters Case. To decide which firefighters should be promoted, the city of New Haven, Connecticut, gave the candidates a test. When African Americans scored poorly on the tests and all the promotions would have gone to whites and one Latino, the city decided to ignore the test results. The whites and Latino sued, and the case came before the Supreme Court, which ruled in their favor. The Court concluded that although the city's goal of diversity was fine, by ignoring the test results the city was adopting an illegal quota system (Liptak 2009).

Absent constitutional amendments or voter referenda that ban considerations of race, cities and states that want to use race–ethnicity in hiring or promotion and in college admissions have no firm guidelines to follow. As more cases come before the Supreme Court, the rulings will depend not solely on the Constitution, which is open to contradictory interpretations, but, rather, largely on the political makeup of the Court—on who retires and what justices holding what political views replace them.

The Future of the Problem

Progress

8.9 Discuss the likely future of racial–ethnic relations.

Most Americans today reject the discrimination that was taken for granted in earlier times or—strange to our ears—that was even assumed to be morally correct. Over the years, progress has been slow, even inconsistent, but the result has been expanding opportunities for minority groups. Huge gaps remain, however, between our ideals of equality and the reality of racial–ethnic relations as we experience them today.

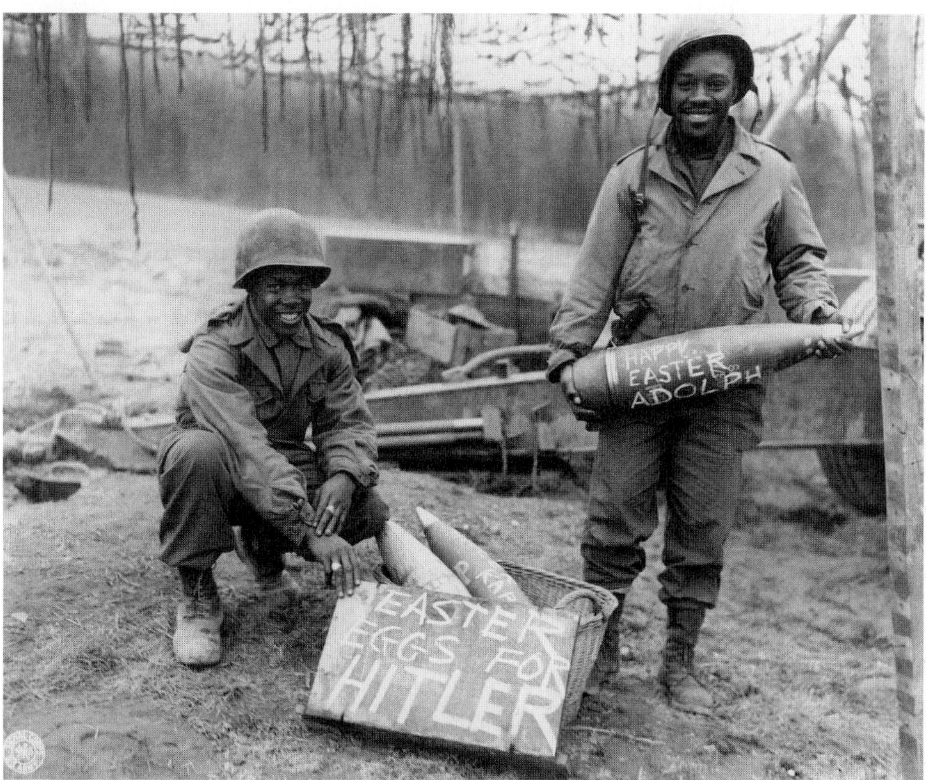

In World War II, segregation extended into the armed forces, with African Americans fighting in what were called "All Negro" units. This photo was taken December 16, 1944, on the Western front, as U.S. troops were advancing on the German army.

World War II was especially significant for improving racial–ethnic relations. Prior to this war, the U.S. government supported racist policies. Segregation ("American apartheid") was assumed to be moral and forever an essential part of the U.S. landscape. The war brought severe dislocations that dispelled these assumptions. As war industries expanded in the North, jobs opened up and hundreds of thousands of African Americans migrated from the South to the North looking for work. Although they fought in all-black units at this time, several hundred thousand African American soldiers, dislodged from the segregation back home, were thrust into cultural experiences that changed their views on racial–ethnic relations. Exposed to new ways of life in Europe, they returned home with visions of positive change. After the war, the federal government, grudgingly accepting the change from segregation to integration, broke down many of the institutional barriers that had been set up against minorities. In light of this history, we can expect the future to bring fewer barriers and greater equality.

An Ongoing Struggle

Racial–ethnic relations are haunted by barriers to equality, and it will require concerted effort to remove them. Affirmative action was designed to overcome these barriers, but, as you know, it has come under heavy attack. By their very nature, court rulings are victories for one side but defeat for the other. Although some court cases represent incompatible philosophical positions, inconsistent and vague court rulings solve nothing. They only breed confusion. With a continuing need to remedy inequalities, the proper role of affirmative action in a multicultural society is likely to remain center stage for quite some time.

 **Explore** on **MySocLab**
Activity: Race and Ethnicity: Improvement is Better than Assistance? Race, Spending, and Patterns of Inequality

Jobs are likely to be the major focus in the continuing struggle for equality. Because access to jobs and careers determines much of our quality of life, we are likely to see continued efforts to reduce structural barriers and increase education. Increasingly, workers must be prepared to compete in a world that demands more technical expertise. What occurs in education, then, is of vital importance for the future of racial–ethnic relations.

Disparities in Education

Read on **MySocLab Document:** Racial Stratification and Education in the United States: Why Inequality Persists

For most Americans, education holds the key to the future—and it is no different for racial–ethnic minorities. Those who receive the better education get the better jobs and enjoy more satisfying lifestyles. Any group that receives less schooling than the national average faces disadvantages in our technological society.

Granted this principle, then, let's see what Table 8.3 on page 254 might indicate about the future. I already mentioned the outstanding rate of college graduation of Asian Americans, how it exceeds that of other groups by far. Their rate is almost four times higher than that of Latinos and Native Americans, almost three times that of African Americans, and 60 percent higher than that of whites. They also earn doctorate degrees at two and a half times their percentage of the population. You can see how this high achievement brightens the future for Asian Americans, opening doors to professions and managerial positions. This table also indicates that with their educational achievement whites will do quite well, but that the future is less bright for the other groups, especially for Latinos and Native Americans. They are much less prepared to compete in our growing technical society.

To fall behind in education is to fall behind on almost all indicators of well-being. If you go back to Table 8.1 on page 236, you can see how closely each group's relative position in income and poverty matches its attainment in education. It isn't difficult to figure out why, since you know that education opens doors of opportunity, and the lack of education closes them. To develop policies that produce greater educational achievement, I suggest the funding of a "think tank" composed of top educators from our many racial–ethnic groups. Their purpose will not be to produce more research on how education works, as we have plenty of that, but to propose testable policies to increase the educational attainment of the groups that are underachieving in education.

An Underclass

As a nation, do we have sufficient desire to raise the educational achievement of African Americans, Latinos, and Native Americans? A disturbing possibility is that we have a permanent **underclass** (Wilson 1978, 1987, 2009). That is, society may already have thrown up its collective hands and consigned to the poverty-plagued, crime-ridden inner city an underclass that will endure. This alienated group has little education, lives primarily in single-parent families, and has high rates of births to single mothers, drug abuse, violent crime, and death by murder. Such self-defeating behaviors keep people from succeeding in mainstream society. Indeed, they even keep them separated from mainstream society.

Unless we develop effective social policy to reach this underclass, the tragic cycle will continue. Many of the children born in these conditions will be fated to repeat their parents' despair. A primary structural factor that makes this sorry possibility likely is that most jobs are located in the suburbs. Those who live in the inner city lack the means of transportation to reach those jobs and the finances to move closer to them.

These conditions carry severe implications for society as a whole. When large groups of people remain isolated from mainstream society, receive a meager education, can't get jobs, and are denied proper police protection, some precipitating incident can ignite the powder keg of hostilities, resulting in an explosion of collective violence. With little being done about the problems of inner cities, we can expect turmoil. At some point, riots are likely, and although it has become a distant memory, we may see a repeat of the 1992 riots in Los Angeles.

Militancy

Militants, whether from a minority group or the dominant group, are an unpredictable factor in racial–ethnic relations. Although racial–ethnic pride is laudable—as discussed in the social policy section, such pride should be encouraged—some people mistake pride in one's own group as hatred of and the need to demean other groups. Groups that preach hatred will continue to appear, their leaders trying to create divisions by building on hostilities and negative stereotypes. Occasional outbursts by hate groups, though dramatic, will pose no serious threat to those working toward a future of equality.

The American Dilemma

In 1944, Gunnar Myrdal (1898–1987), a sociologist from Sweden, wrote *An American Dilemma*. Myrdal said that the United States was caught between two major forces: prejudice and discrimination and the "American creed" of equality as expressed in religion and the Declaration of Independence. Myrdal was confident that Americans would resolve racial tensions by following the higher values of the "American creed." Myrdal was right, and conditions are remarkably better today than they were back then. The dilemma that Myrdal identified, however, remains.

Valleys of hatred and despair follow peaks of good will and high hopes. We have seen this in the past, and the future will bring more of the same. Although as individuals we have little power or influence, our actions, collectively, are significant. Ultimately, these actions give shape to racial–ethnic relations. None of us can overcome structural barriers alone, yet, together, we can dismantle them. I do not mean to sound Pollyannaish, but through our collective efforts we can help to create a more positive future.

MySocLab  Study and Review on **MySocLab**

Summary and Review

1. *Discrimination* occurs worldwide, as *racial–ethnic groups* living in the same society struggle for dominance. The various groups tend to perceive one another through *stereotypes.*
2. *Minority groups* share five characteristics: unequal treatment, distinctive traits, solidarity, membership by birth, and marriage within their own group. Minority groups have four objectives: *pluralism, assimilation, secession*, and *militancy*. Six policies of dominant groups are *multiculturalism* (*pluralism*), *assimilation, segregation, internal colonialism, population transfer,* and *genocide.*
3. Although the idea of *race* is significant in human behavior, biologically speaking, no human group represents a "pure race."
4. Discrimination affects quality of life and can be a life-and-death matter, affecting mortality rates.
5. *Individual discrimination* consists of overt acts by individuals. *Institutional discrimination* is discrimination that is built into the social system.
6. Symbolic interactionists focus on how symbols of race–ethnicity divide people and influence their behavior, particularly how they affect perception, sort people into different life experiences, and justify discrimination and violence. Functionalists analyze functions of discrimination, such as fostering *ethnocentrism* and ensuring that society's *dirty work* gets done. They also analyze its dysfunctions, such as destroying human potential. Marxist conflict theorists stress that racial–ethnic divisions among workers help capitalists control workers and increase their profits.
7. Native Americans, Latinos, and African Americans have less education, higher unemployment, lower incomes, and higher rates of poverty than whites and

Asian Americans. The pressures that these groups have placed on white-controlled social institutions have forced social change. Underlying the high social and economic gains of Asian Americans are assimilation and family values that stress hard work, thrift, and education.

8. Major cleavages along social class lines divide U.S. racial–ethnic groups. Some sociologists argue that social class has become more significant than race–ethnicity in determining an individual's life chances.

9. Social policies should encourage cultural pluralism and prevent discrimination. Groups that attain the most education have the brightest future. The major struggle is over jobs. Dilemmas concerning affirmative action continue.

10. With the creation of an *underclass*, we can expect urban riots. In no foreseeable future will *prejudice* and discrimination be eliminated. A storm cloud on the horizon is the resurgence of groups that preach division and hatred.

Key Terms

Anglo-conformity, 231
apartheid, 230
capitalist economy, 243
civil disobedience, 249
dirty work, 240
discrimination, 228
division of labor, 240
dominant group, 229
ethnocentrism, 242
individual discrimination, 236
institutional discrimination, 236
melting pot, 232
minority group, 228
pan-Indianism, 258
prejudice, 228
race, 231
racial–ethnic group, 231
reserve labor force, 243
riots, 244
rising expectations, 249
selective perception, 239
split-labor market, 243
stereotypes, 233
surplus value of labor, 243
underclass, 262

Thinking Critically About Chapter 8

1. On page 229 is a list of five characteristics that minority groups share. Pick any minority group in the United States and give examples of how these five characteristics apply to that group.
2. On page 229 is a list of four objectives or goals of minority groups. Explain how each objective applies to African Americans, to Asian Americans, to Latinos, and to Native Americans. Do these groups emphasize these objectives in the same way? If not, why do you think there are differences?
3. Which of the six policies of dominant groups that Simpson and Yinger identify (p. 230) do you think that whites are directing toward African Americans? Toward Native Americans? Toward Latinos? Toward Asian Americans?
4. What is your opinion about the laws against hate speech? Do you think that these laws should be eliminated or that they should be strengthened and enforced? Explain.
5. Which of the three sociological perspectives (symbolic interactionism, functionalism, or conflict theory) do you think best explains why prejudice and discrimination exist in the United States? Explain.

9 Inequalities of Gender and Sexual Orientation

Listen to Chapter 9 on **MySocLab**

Learning Objectives. After reading this chapter, you should be able to:

9.1 Explain why sociologists consider women to be a minority group and how gender discrimination became a social problem. **(p. 266)**

9.2 Discuss whether male dominance is universal, the sexual stratification of work, and major areas of gender discrimination. **(p. 267)**

9.3 Use the symbolic interactionist perspective to explain socialization into gender. **(p. 269)**

9.4 Discuss the two functionalist theories of the origin of gender discrimination. **(p. 270)**

9.5 Review the conflict/feminist account of women's struggle for equality in the United States. **(p. 271)**

9.6 Be able to discuss differences between the sexes, discrimination in everyday life and in education, the portrayal of the sexes in the mass media, gender relations in politics, the gender pay gap, and sexual harassment. **(p. 275)**

9.7 Contrast homosexual behavior and homosexuality, explain changing attitudes toward homosexuals and the conflict view of homosexuality, and discuss research on homosexuality. **(p. 295)**

9.8 Apply the feminist/conflict and symbolic interactionist perspectives to gendered violence. **(p. 304)**

9.9 Compare middle-of-the-road social policies with those appropriate to the radical and conservative extremists. **(p. 305)**

9.10 Discuss the likely future of gender discrimination. **(p. 306)**

Some relatives cursed the mother. Others consoled the father.

Just a minute earlier, these people had been keeping vigil outside the delivery room of a Delhi hospital. The woman's husband had been telling jokes and laughing with the men. None of the men had mentioned what everyone knew might happen. The women had been knitting and recalling their own deliveries. They, too, didn't bring up the taboo topic, although all had been thinking about it.

Strangling baby girls at birth might be a thing of the past.

What had changed this scene? The nurse had brought the bad news—the newborn is a girl.

This scene is familiar in India. The birth of a son is seen as a gift from God; the birth of a daughter, at best, a disappointment.

An Indian girl stands little chance of earning money for her family. In Hindu society, almost all women are expected to remain at home with their family. Jobs for women, especially uneducated women, are few—and most Indian women are uneducated.

The parents of an Indian girl also have to pay dowry money when the girl marries.

To avoid having girl babies, many Indian women use ultrasound. Doctors take portable ultrasound equipment to India's villages. If the fetus is female, many women have an abortion. Common? Indian women have given birth to millions fewer girl babies than boy babies.

Female infanticide also persists, especially in India's tens of thousands of tradition-locked villages. Authorities seldom document specific instances. They usually consider this a family matter.

"Strangling baby girls at birth might be a thing of the past," says sociologist Promilla Kapur, who specializes in research on Indian women. "However, what used to be done in a fairly crude manner is still often achieved indirectly."

—Based on Page 2007; Wonacottt 2007; Mohanty 2012.

The Problem in Sociological Perspective

9.1 Explain why sociologists consider women to be a minority group and how gender discrimination became a social problem.

You can see how important the sex of a child is in India. Parents living in poverty feel despair at the birth of a girl. "It's like watering someone else's plant," they say. They must feed and clothe her, but she can contribute practically nothing to the family income. Then she marries, and they have to pay a dowry. But the birth of a boy? The parents rejoice at this. A boy will grow into a man who can help sustain them in their old age.

Women as a Minority Group

Although the Indian situation is extreme, *sex is the major sorting device in every society in the world.* In our own society, as we'll examine in this chapter, men are paid more for the same work, and, despite changes, they continue to dominate politics and public life. Even though females make up 50.8 percent of the U.S. population (*Statistical Abstract* 2013:Table 7), sociologists consider women a minority group because of their position relative to men, the dominant group.

The Development of Gender Discrimination as a Social Problem

Sociologists have not always referred to women as a minority group. They attached this label only gradually, as they began to note parallels between the social positions of women and men and those of African Americans and whites. In 1944, Swedish sociologist Gunnar Myrdal mentioned these parallels in *An American Dilemma.* He noted that in the seventeenth century the legal status of black slaves was derived from the legal status of women and children, whose lives were controlled by male heads of households. In 1951 an American sociologist, Helen Hacker, was the first to apply the term *minority* to women. She documented the discrimination against women at that time, how they were "barred from certain activities or, if admitted, . . . treated unequally."

Just as the perception of sociologists was changing, so was that of women, who began to challenge the traditional relations between the sexes. Many came to see themselves not as *individuals* who had less status than men, but as a *group* of people who were discriminated against. During the 1960s and 1970s, women publicized their grievances at being second-class citizens dominated by men. Subjective concerns grew, and large numbers of women in the United States and around the world demanded that discrimination against women be addressed. Recalling our definition of social problems, you can see that this new evaluation of the relative positions of women and men transformed what had been only an objective condition of society into a social problem. Sociologists then began to investigate **sexism**, the belief that one sex is innately superior to the other and the discrimination that results from this belief.

Watch on **MySocLab Video:** Michael Kimmel: How Gender Became "Visible" to Sociologists

Many objective conditions of this problem have changed since the 1960s and 1970s, a period of unrest and agitation. We'll analyze our current situation, but first let's look at some broad findings about sexism.

The Scope of the Problem

Is Male Dominance Universal?

9.2 Discuss whether male dominance is universal, the sexual stratification of work, and major areas of gender discrimination.

When did sexism begin? Some social scientists, such as anthropologist Marvin Harris (1977:46), claim that men's domination of society "has been in continuous existence throughout virtually the entire globe from the earliest times to the present." After reviewing the evidence, historian and feminist Gerda Lerner (1986:31) agreed, saying that "there is not a single society known where women-as-a-group have decision-making power over men (as a group)." She also concluded that the earliest societies had the least amount of gender discrimination. In those societies, women contributed about 60 percent of the group's total food.

Conclusions of universal domination by men make some social analysts apprehensive: If people think that men have always dominated every society around the world, some will conclude that this behavior is innate. They might then use this conclusion to justify men's domination of women today. This could be the primary reason that not all sociologists accept the conclusion of the universality of male dominance (Epstein 1989, 2010).

Watch on **MySocLab Video:** Gender and Inequality

Don't women presidents, prime ministers, and monarchs disprove the universal domination of society by men? Sociologists point out that these are *individual* women in positions of power, not women-as-a-group in control of a society. Even those societies led by a woman are dominated by men, for men hold almost all key positions in politics. Rwanda comes closest to political equality between the sexes: 56 percent of its lower house and 39 percent of its upper house are women. With women making up 50 percent of its single house, Andorra ranks next. These are remarkable exceptions, for the average of all of the world's countries is about 18 percent. Seven countries, including Saudi Arabia, have no women in their house or senate (Inter-Parliamentary Union 2012).

The Sexual Stratification of Work

Every society stratifies its members by sex; that is, they single out males and females for different activities. Around the world, for example, most work is **sex-typed**, associated with one sex or the other. As a result, many thought that anatomy required men and women to be assigned particular work.

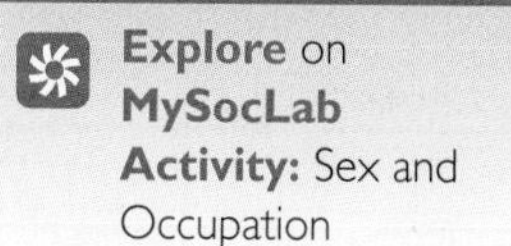

Explore on **MySocLab Activity:** Sex and Occupation

In 1937, anthropologist George Murdock blew this gender myth out of the water. He illustrated beyond doubt what we take for granted today, that biology does not

When men do an activity that is usually assigned to women, the prestige of the activity increases.

determine occupational destiny. In his review of the reports that anthropologists had made on 324 societies, Murdock found that what is considered "male" or "female" work differs from one society to another. For example, in some societies the care of cattle is women's work; in others, it is men's work. Three types of labor were almost always defined as men's work—making weapons, pursuing sea mammals, and hunting. Four types of work were usually assigned to women—making clothing, cooking, carrying water, and grinding grain. No specific work was universally assigned to women, but one was to men—metalworking.

That one society assigns a certain kind of work to men while another assigns it to women—how is this relevant to a discussion of sexism? Social scientists have discovered a startling principle: *When work is assigned to men, it is considered important and given greater prestige* (Linton 1936; Rosaldo 1974; Reskin and Bielby 2005). If taking care of cattle is men's work, then cattle care is thought to be important and carries high prestige. If taking care of cattle is women's work, however, it is considered less important and carries less prestige. To cite an example closer to home, when delivering babies was "women's work," the responsibility of midwives, this job was given low prestige. But when men took over delivering babies (despite opposition from women), its prestige shot up (Ehrenreich and English 1973). *It is the sex that is associated with the work that provides its prestige, not the work itself.*

Major Areas of Discrimination

Sexism pervades every society of the world, touching almost every aspect of our social life. In her classic 1951 article, Helen Hacker listed the following types of discrimination against U.S. women at that time:

1. *Political and legal.* Women were often barred from jury duty and public office.
2. *Education.* Professional schools, such as architecture and medicine, applied quotas for women.
3. *Economic.* Women were usually relegated to work that fell under the supervision of men, for which they received unequal pay, promotion, and responsibility.
4. *Social.* Women were permitted less freedom of movement, fewer deviations in dress, speech, and manners, and a narrower range of personality expression.

Hacker also described how women's three major roles—sister/daughter, wife, and mother—fit this pattern of discrimination. She said that a sister does more housework than her brother, a wife is expected to subordinate her interests to those of her husband, and a mother bears the stigma for an illegitimate child.

Sex discrimination in the United States has changed so drastically that Hacker seems to be describing another society. In a sociological sense, she is. Women are no longer barred from jury duty and public office, nor do they face quotas in professional schools. You probably noticed that on a couple of significant levels, though, Hacker's analysis remains remarkably current. Women still struggle against unequal treatment in jobs, politics, and other areas of social life.

Looking at the Problem Theoretically

Why are societies sexist? Let's use our theoretical lenses to see what contrasting perspectives emerge.

Symbolic Interactionism

Basic Terms. We must distinguish between two terms. When we consider how males and females differ, we usually think first of **sex**, the different *biological* equipment of males and females. Then we might think about **gender**, how we express our "maleness" or "femaleness." Symbolic interactionists stress that sex is biological, and gender is learned, or social.

9.3 Use the symbolic interactionist perspective to explain socialization into gender.

Watch on **MySocLab**
Video: Gender Socialization

Socialization into Gender Roles. Symbolic interactionists study how we are socialized into **gender roles**, the attitudes and behaviors expected of boys and men because they are male and girls and women because they are female. The process begins *before* birth. While the wife is pregnant, the couple imagines their future child's participation in gendered (sex-typed) activities. A father may see himself teaching his son how to play baseball or hockey. In her mind's eye, a mother may see herself tying a little pink bow on her daughter's hair—and thinking how cute she will look.

When the child is born, the parents announce its sex to the world. Through cards, telephone calls, blogs, and e-mail, they proclaim "It's a girl!" or "It's a boy!" Even local newspapers report this momentous event. And momentous it is, for *in every society of the world this announcement launches babies into their single most significant life-shaping circumstance.* Sex is a **master trait**, cutting across all other identities in life. Whatever else we may be, we are always male or female.

Cast onto the stage of life with a gender role to play, we spend much of our childhood and young adult life learning how to manage this assignment. Throughout the world, parents are the first of many "significant others" to teach children their gender roles. In U.S. society, parents begin by dressing boy babies in blue and girl babies in pink, colors imbued with gender expectations. Parents coach their children about gender throughout childhood ("Boys don't do that!"… "Girls don't do that!"). Through their words and especially their actions, parents also teach their children about what they should be like as husband or wife.

These initial directions lay our basic foundation of gender. As we go through life, we continue to build on this foundation, refining our gender roles as we perform before different audiences. As sociologists say, we "do gender" all of our lives.

Interpreting Classic Research. Let's look at classic research done by psychologists Susan Goldberg and Michael Lewis (1960), who observed how mothers teach gender roles without being aware that they are doing so.

> *Goldberg and Lewis recruited mothers of 6-month-olds to come into their laboratory so they could observe the development of their children. Unobtrusively, they studied how the mothers interacted with their babies. They found that the mothers kept their girls closer to them than their sons. By the time the children were 13 months old, the girls were more reluctant than the boys to leave their mothers. During play, they remained closer to their mothers and returned to them sooner and more often than the boys did.*
>
> *Goldberg and Lewis followed up their initial observations with an interesting experiment. They surrounded each mother with colorful toys and placed her child on the other side of a small barrier. The girls were more likely to cry and motion for help, while the boys were more likely to try to climb over or go around the barrier.*

"Sex brought us together, but gender drove us apart."

The distinctions between sex and gender that sociologists have drawn are becoming part of public consciousness.

Gender roles are flexible, varying from culture to culture. As some entertainers such as Adam Lambert bend gender, the outer edges of gender acceptability are challenged and changed.

The researchers' conclusion? The mothers produced the different behaviors of the little girls and little boys. Without knowing it, the mothers had rewarded their daughters for passive and dependent behavior, while rewarding their sons for aggressive and independent behavior. But are these the right conclusions? Were these differences brought about by the mother's behavior, as the researchers concluded? Or were the researchers observing genetic differences that had begun to appear at the age of 13 months? In short, had the mothers created those different behaviors, or were they merely responding to differences inherent in their children? As a sociologist, I prefer the environmental explanation, but we don't yet have enough evidence to draw a firm conclusion.

The Dominant Symbolic Interactionist Position. Most symbolic interactionists assume that gender differences like those that Goldberg and Lewis observed are learned. They emphasize how socialization produces the behaviors. It starts with stereotypes of the sexes. Since males are labeled aggressive and dominant, boys tend to fulfill those expectations by being aggressive and dominant—and they are given approval for doing so. Since females are considered more passive and submissive, girls receive approval for fulfilling those expectations. Not everyone follows gender scripts, but most do.

In Sum ▸ Symbolic interactionists highlight how society uses the labels *male* and *female* to sort its members into separate groups, a process that starts within the family and is reinforced by other social institutions. As a result, males and females acquire different expectations of themselves and of one another, with males and females learning that certain activities—and even feelings—are appropriate for their gender. This socialization process is so effective that we all learn to evaluate ourselves on the basis of how well we "do gender."

Functionalism

9.4 Discuss the two functionalist theories of the origin of gender discrimination.

If male dominance is universal, or even nearly universal, how did it come about? Although the origins of sexism are lost in history, functionalists have developed two theories to account for it. The first is social—the necessity to survive warfare. The second is biological—based on human reproduction.

Rewards for Warriors. The first theory was proposed by anthropologist Marvin Harris (1977). His controversial explanation goes like this: In preliterate times, humans lived in small groups. Because these groups fought with one another, to survive each group had to recruit people who would fight in hand-to-hand combat. People feared injury and death, of course, so the recruiting wasn't easy. To coax people into bravery, groups developed rewards and punishments. Because an average woman is only 85 percent the size of an average man and has only two-thirds his strength, men became the warriors. And females? They became the men's reward for risking their lives. The women were used for sexual pleasure and labor. Some groups allowed only men who had previously faced an enemy to marry. Even today, in some tribal groups such as the Barabaig of Tanzania, women are rewards for men who show bravery (Aposporos 2004).

The consequences were severe. To make the system work, men were trained from birth for combat, while women were trained from birth to be submissive to men. Men assigned the "drudge work" to women—weeding, seed grinding, fetching water and firewood, cooking, even carrying household possessions during moves. Because men preferred to avoid these onerous tasks—and could do so if they had one or more wives—offering women as a reward to men who risked their lives in combat worked.

Reproduction. The second theory for the universality of gender stratification, based on human reproduction, also goes back to early human history (Lerner 1986; Hope and Stover 1987; Friedl 1990). Since early people did not live long, for the group to survive women had to give birth to many children. Carrying a child for 9 months, giving birth, and nursing babies limited women's activities. With a child in their wombs or at their breasts and one on their hips or on their backs, women were encumbered physically. As a result, women everywhere took on tasks associated with home and child care, while men took over hunting large animals and other tasks that required longer absence from the base camp (Huber 1990).

Again, the consequences were severe: This division of labor brought power and prestige to men. They made and controlled the weapons used for hunting and warfare. They would return triumphantly to camp with their kill, providing meat for the group. Outside the camp, they made contact with other tribes and accumulated possessions in trade. Sometimes they would return with prisoners taken in raids. In contrast, the taken-for-granted activities of child care and cooking gave women nothing to boast about. But those who risked their lives in hunting and warfare, now that was another story. The men's weapons, their items of trade, and the knowledge they gained from their contacts with other groups became sources of power and prestige.

In Sum ▸ Whether gender stratification resulted from warfare and bravery or childbirth and child care, each theory leads to the same result—a **patriarchal society**, one in which men rule over women. To justify their dominance, men developed ideas that linked manhood with superiority. To avoid "contamination" by females, now deemed inferior, men shrouded some of their activities in secrecy and established rules and rituals that excluded women. Today's male dominance is a perpetuation of these patterns laid down in early history.

Although tribal societies developed into larger groups and hand-to-hand combat and hunting dangerous animals ceased to be routine, men, enjoying their privileges and power, held onto them. Reluctant to abandon their privileged position of dominance, men still use cultural devices to control women. For an example, see the Global Glimpse box on the next page.

Conflict/Feminist Theory

To apply conflict theory to sexism, let's begin with these four principles:

9.5 Review the conflict/feminist account of women's struggle for equality in the United States.

Four Principles of Power.

1. Power yields privilege. In every society, the powerful enjoy the best resources available.
2. The privileged lifestyles of those in power encourage them to feel that they are superior beings.
3. To support their feelings of superiority, the powerful clothe themselves with ideologies that justify their position.
4. To maintain their position in society, the powerful use the social institutions. As a group, men are no exception to these principles. They, too, cling to their positions, cultivate images of female inferiority to justify their greater privilege, and use economic and legal weapons against women. As Helen Hacker (1951) put it,

In the wake of the Industrial Revolution, as women acquired industrial, business, and professional skills, they increasingly sought employment in competition with men. Men were quick to perceive them as a rival group and made use of economic, legal, and ideological weapons to eliminate or reduce

A Global Glimpse

Female Circumcision

> *"Lie down there," the excisor suddenly said to me [when I was 12], pointing to a mat on the ground. No sooner had I laid down than I felt my frail, thin legs grasped by heavy hands and pulled wide apart. . . . Two women on each side of me pinned me to the ground . . . I underwent the ablation of the labia minor and then of the clitoris. The operation seemed to go on forever. I was in the throes of agony, torn apart both physically and psychologically. It was the rule that girls of my age did not weep in this situation. I broke the rule. I cried and screamed with pain . . .!*
>
> *Afterwards they forced me, not only to walk back to join the other girls who had already been excised, but to dance with them. I was doing my best, but then I fainted. . . . It was a month before I was completely healed. When I was better, everyone mocked me, as I hadn't been brave, they said. (Walker and Parmar 1993:107–108)*

Worldwide, between 100 million and 140 million females have been circumcised, mostly in Muslim Africa and in some parts of Malaysia and Indonesia (World Health Organization 2012). Figure 9.1 on the next page shows both the estimated percentages of women who have been circumcised in 15 countries and the percentage of women in those countries who want circumcision to continue.

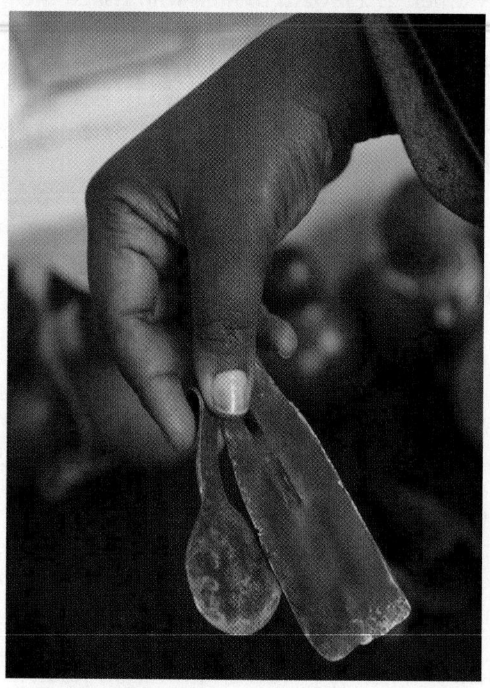

These tools were used to perform female circumcision in Tanzania.

FIGURE 9.1 ▸ Women Who Have Been Circumcised and Women Who Want Female Circumcision to Continue

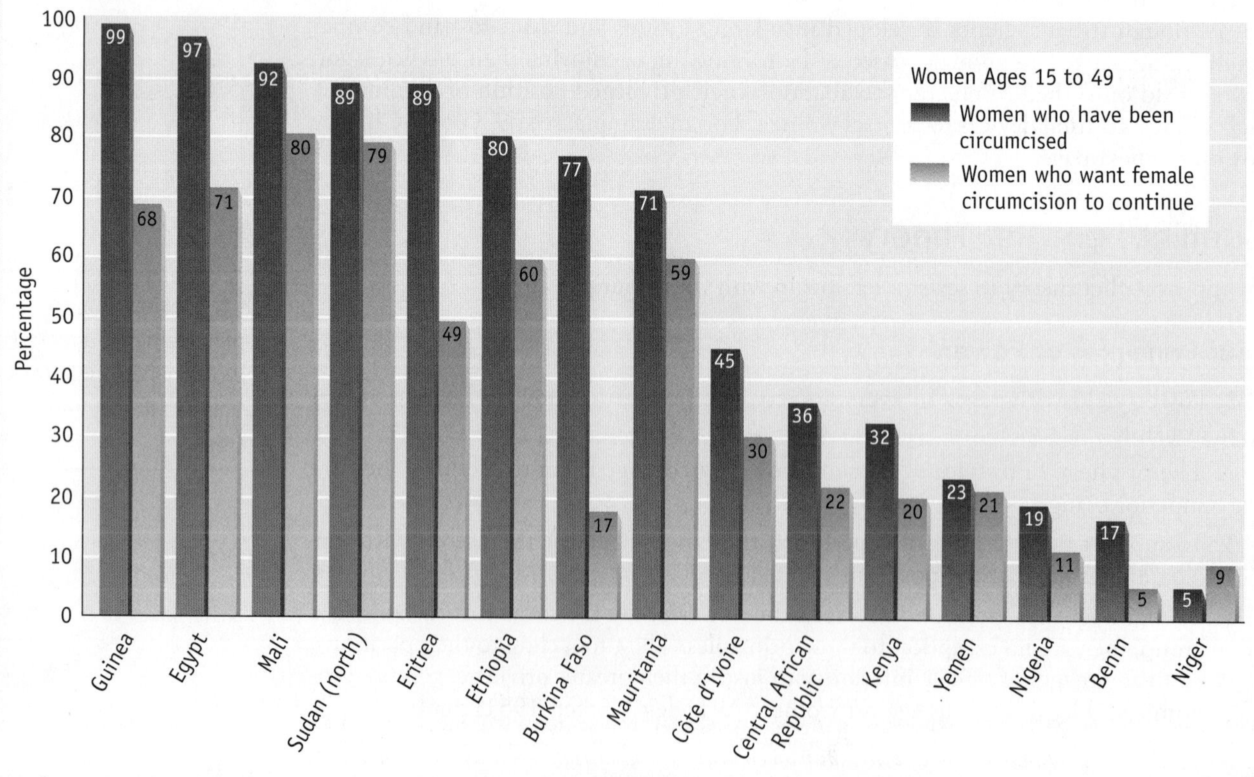

Source: UNICEF 2005:Figure 18.

(continued from previous page)

In some cultures, the surgery occurs 7 to 10 days after birth, but in others it is not performed until girls reach adolescence. Among most groups, it takes place between the ages of 4 and 8. Because the surgery is usually done without anesthesia, the pain is so excruciating that adults hold the girl down. In urban areas, physicians sometimes perform the operation; in rural areas, neighborhood women usually do it.

In some cultures, only the girl's clitoris is cut off; in others, more is removed. In Sudan, the Nubia cut away most of the girl's genitalia, then sew together the remaining outer edges. They bind the girl's legs from her ankles to her waist for several weeks while scar tissue closes up the vagina. They leave a small opening the diameter of a pencil for the passage of urine and menstrual fluids. When a woman marries, the opening is cut wider to permit sexual intercourse. Before a woman gives birth, the opening is enlarged further. After birth, the vagina is again sutured shut; this cycle of deinfibulation and reinfibulation begins anew with each birth.

What are the reasons for circumcising girls? Some groups believe that it reduces female sexual desire, making it more likely that a woman will be a virgin at marriage and, afterward, remain faithful to her husband. Others think that women can't bear children if they aren't circumcised.

The surgery has strong support among many women. Some mothers and grandmothers even insist that the custom continue. Their concern is that their daughters marry well, and in some of these societies uncircumcised women are considered impure and are not allowed to marry.

Feminists respond that female circumcision is a form of ritual torture to control female sexuality. They point out that men dominate the societies that practice it.

Change is on its way: A social movement to ban female circumcision has developed, and the World Health Organization has declared that female circumcision is a human rights issue. Uganda and a dozen other African countries have banned the circumcision of females. In most countries, though, these laws go unenforced. In Egypt, which prohibited female circumcision in 1996, almost all girls continue to be circumcised (Leopold 2012).

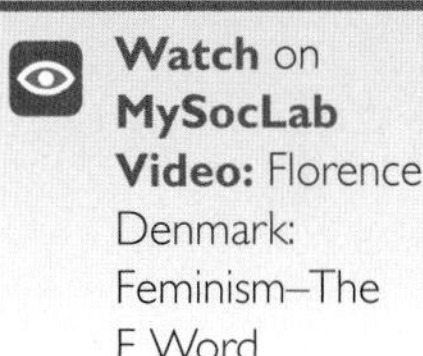
Watch on **MySocLab Video:** Florence Denmark: Feminism–The F Word

Change is rapid in Senegal, which is becoming a model for how to bring about the end of female circumcision. Accompanied by education programs, the elders of a village agree to stop the practice. They celebrate the change with a ceremony attended by government dignitaries. With much intermarriage among villages, a chain reaction is occurring as villages agree to stop female circumcision (Dugger 2011).

For Your Consideration

Do you think that the members of one culture have the right to judge the customs of another culture as inferior or wrong and to then try to get rid of it? If so, under what circumstances? What makes us right and them wrong?

Let's go further. There is agitation against the circumcision of boys. Already, one court in Germany has ruled that the circumcision of boys "amounts to bodily harm even if the parents consent to the circumcision" ("German Court . . ." 2012). Do you think the same principle should apply to both female and male circumcision? Why or why not?

their competition. They excluded women from the trade unions, made contracts with employers to prevent their hiring women, passed laws restricting the employment of married women, caricatured the working woman, and carried on ceaseless propaganda to return women to the home or keep them there.

As mentioned, many feminists use conflict theory in their analyses of the relationship between women and men. Among the issues they highlight is discrimination in the workplace. The "quiet revolution"—women leaving the home for paid work—brought resistance from men, as Hacker says, but it also equipped many women for economic and emotional independence. In the 1960s and 1970s, feminists thought that more women working in the paid labor force was the recipe for ending sexism in society. But the discrimination at work continued. Even today, women still face lower wages, lower prestige, and sexual harassment. We'll get into some of these issues in a moment.

The Struggle for Equality. Now that we live in the midst of much greater gender equality, it is easy to lose sight of the bitter struggle by which women gained their rights. In the 1800s, almost every woman was under the legal control of a man, either her father or husband. Women could not vote, testify in court, make legal contracts, hold property in their own name, or even spend their own wages (which by law belonged to the husband). To secure these rights, women had to confront men and the social institutions that men dominated. Men first denied women the right to speak in public, spat upon some who did, slapped their faces, tripped them, pelted them with burning cigar stubs, and hurled obscenities at them. Despite the opposition, leaders of the women's movement persisted. They chained themselves to the iron grillwork of public buildings and went on talking while the police sawed them loose. When arrested, these women would go on hunger strikes in jail.

In 1916, feminists—then called **suffragists**—formed the National Woman's Party. Their main goal was to attain the right to vote. In January 1917, they began to picket outside the White House. After the women had protested for 6 months, authorities grew tired of "the nonsense" and arrested them. The women refused to pay their fines, and judges sent hundreds of suffragists to prison, including two leaders, Lucy Burns and Alice Paul. Their treatment in jail illustrates how seriously these women had threatened male privilege:

> *The guards from the male prison fell upon us. I saw Miss Lincoln, a slight young girl, thrown to the floor. Mrs. Nolan, a delicate old lady of seventy-three, was mastered by two men. . . . Whittaker (the Superintendent) in the center of the room directed the whole attack, inciting the guards to every brutality. Two men brought in Dorothy Day, twisting her arms above her head. Suddenly they lifted her and brought her body down twice over the back of an iron bench. . . . The bed broke Mrs. Nolan's fall, but Mrs. Cosu hit the wall. They had been there a few minutes when Mrs. Lewis, all doubled over like a sack of flour, was thrown in. Her head struck the iron bed and she fell to the floor senseless. As for Lucy Burns, they handcuffed her wrists and fastened the handcuffs over her head to the cell door. (Cowley 1969:13)*

Today it is difficult to imagine women in the United States being treated this way for trying to gain rights that men already possess. Despite the opposition, the early suffragists were persistent and outspoken. Using bold tactics, they forced a historical shift in the balance of power.

Discrimination against women continues today, but it is more subtle: hidden quotas, sexist jokes, and the assumption that men should occupy the most responsible

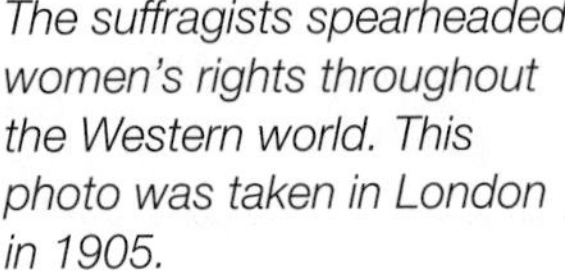

The suffragists spearheaded women's rights throughout the Western world. This photo was taken in London in 1905.

positions. The term **glass ceiling** describes this conceptual blockage that keeps women from achieving the higher positions in the workplace.

The struggle against discrimination is not over. Women continue to press for a greater share of society's power and privileges. They pressure lawmakers, compete for jobs, and fight obstacles that inhibit advancement at work.

In Sum ▸ From the conflict-feminist perspective, the historical relationship of men and women can be written in terms of women's struggle against men's dominance. Men have controlled society's resources, and with them, women-as-a-group. Social equality comes about by forcing those in power to yield—for those in power do not willingly share their control of society's institutions.

We will examine today's ongoing struggle, but first let's pause to consider again the question of natural differences between the sexes.

Research Findings

Are There Natural Differences Between the Sexes?

9.6 Be able to discuss differences between the sexes, discrimination in everyday life and in education, the portrayal of the sexes in the mass media, gender relations in politics, the gender pay gap, and sexual harassment.

Apart from obvious physical differences between men and women, what natural differences exist between the sexes? Is one sex innately more intelligent? more aggressive? dominant? protective? nurturing? tender? loving? passive? These questions are intriguing, but how do you separate culture from biology? To try to do this, researchers use four approaches.

Studies of Children. The *first* explanation focuses on childhood. If girls and boys show consistent differences at early ages, biology may be the cause. And researchers have found two areas of consistent difference: Girls do better with words, and boys do better with numbers. Girls talk earlier than boys and form sentences at an earlier age (Zosuls and Ruble 2009). They also read earlier and do better in grammar and spelling. In contrast, when it comes to math, boys outperform girls. This holds true if we compare their overall scores or just the scores of those who have taken specific courses: general math, algebra, geometry, or calculus (*Digest of Education Statistics* 2012:Table 143).

Look at Figure 9.2 on the next page, which shows the results of the SAT tests since they were first given in 1967. You can see how consistent the gender difference in math is: It holds year after year. Although girls have a verbal edge during their younger ages, you can see from this figure that by the time they take the SAT tests this edge has disappeared.

Does biology explain these differences? Some researchers think so. For 15 years, psychologist and feminist Camilla Benbow searched for an environmental explanation. Gradually, she ruled out all possibilities and concluded—reluctantly, she stressed—that these results are due to "a basic biological difference between the sexes in brain functions" (Goleman 1987). Other social scientists point to cultural factors. To explain young girls' higher verbal performance, they stress three social causes: (1) girls identify more with their mothers (who are more verbal), (2) both mothers and fathers hold and speak to their daughters more than to their sons, and (3) little girls' games are more linguistic than boys' games (Bardwick 1971).

From the verbal scores shown on Figure 9.2, it is easy to see the environment at work: Girls used to outperform boys on the SAT verbal scores, but for the past 40 years boys have done better. It is more difficult to see the environment as the explanation for the gender difference in math, but some researchers point out that in many nations the math scores of girls are improving (Hyde and Mertz 2009). This is not happening in the United States. Over a period of 40 years, from 1972 to 2011, the average score of boys in mathematics improved 5 points, that of girls 6 points, an inconsequential difference (National Center for Education Statistics 2011). If at some point the girls catch up or outperform the boys, we can be certain that the social environment holds the explanation. Currently, we are groping for explanations.

FIGURE 9.2 ▸ The SAT Tests: Comparing the Scores of Boys and Girls

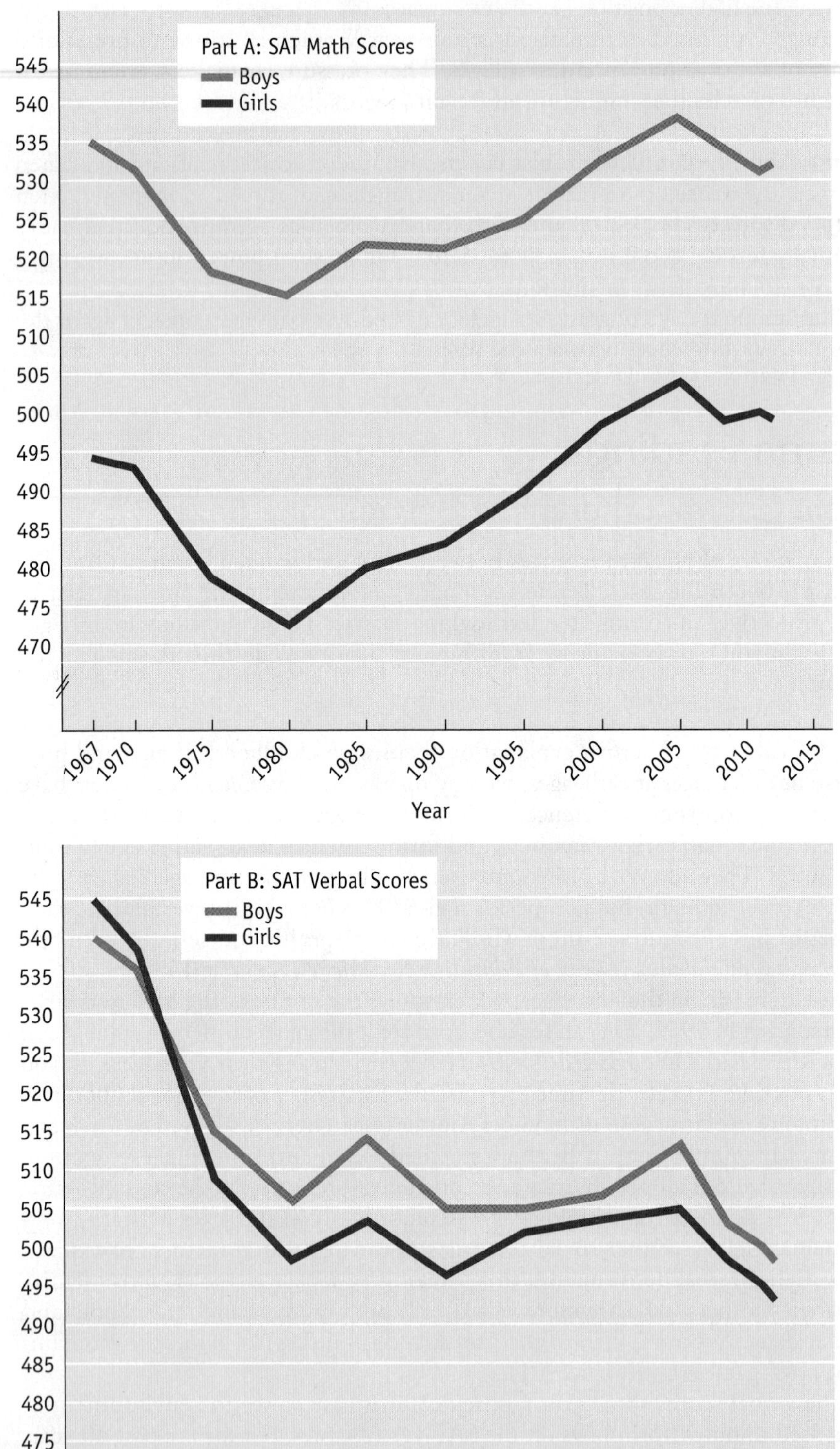

Source: By the author. Based on College Board 2012.

Aggression is another area in which boys and girls show differences. At all ages, boys are more aggressive than girls. Boys also receive more pleasure from hurting things and from seeing "bad people" killed on television (Benenson et al. 2008). But does this mean that males are *innately* more "aggressive" than females? Perhaps. Aggression could be wired into boys' brains. Even if this is the case, parents also subtly (or not so subtly) encourage their sons to be strong and tough. You've likely heard parents say to their sons, "stick up for your rights," "show you're not a sissy," or "don't let anyone push you around." At the same time, many parents express displeasure when their daughters fight, but show approval over their daughters' "cute" behavior, daintiness, and compliance. Not all parents are like this, of course, and some teach their daughters to fight back, even to be the aggressor.

It is likely that *both* environmental and biological influences are at work. A neuroscientist put it this way: There are slight differences between girl and boy babies' brains, but parents magnify them by reinforcing behaviors that match their gender stereotypes (Eliot 2010).

Cross-Cultural Studies. Researchers have also compared men and women cross-culturally. A few sociologists argue that patriarchy is the consequence of men responding to their biological predispositions to master the environment (Goldberg 2011). Almost all sociologists, though, take the position that socialization shapes women and men into comparatively dominant and submissive roles (Epstein 2011).

Are men more competitive by nature than women, and women more nurturing than men? From what you generally see, it's easy to conclude that this is the way the world is. But here's a little experiment that you might find interesting. A team of economists (Gneezy et al. 2009) chose two contrasting societies, the Maasai in Tanzania and the Khasi in India. The Maasai are *patriarchal.* The men think of their wives as their property, and they care more for their cattle than they do for their wives. The Khasi are *matrilineal.* They trace their lineage through the women in the family. The women own the property and pass it on to their daughters. They also earn more than their husbands do.

> *To do their experiment, the researchers paid Maasai and Khasi men and women to throw a tennis ball into a bucket. Each had 10 tries. The men and women could choose to be paid a set amount for each successful throw. Or they could choose to be paid three times that amount for each successful throw, but only if they played against an opponent and beat that person. They could not see the opponent, who remained in another room.*
>
> *The results? The Maasai men chose to compete about twice as often as did the Maasai women. In contrast, the Khasi women were more likely to choose the competitive form of payment.*

Obviously, this one experiment with a few people from a few villages is not sufficient to draw firm conclusions, but it does suggest that competition is a learned form of gender behavior. In Maasai society, the men are in control. It is they who compete with one another. The Maasai men were twice as likely as the Maasai women to choose the competitive situation. But in Khasi society, the women are the more competitive, and the Khasi women were more likely than the Khasi men to choose the competitive situation. Again, this is only suggestive. We need a lot more research, and creative experiments far beyond throwing tennis balls.

Studies of Animals. Another attempt to resolve nature versus nurture arguments is doing research on animals. Research on aggression in monkeys is fascinating, as differences show up early and consistently: "Within a month after birth, male rhesus monkeys are wrestling, pushing, biting, and tugging, while female monkeys are beginning to act shy, turning their heads away when challenged to a fight by young males" (Bardwick 1971:91).

> *The males quickly surpass the females in the rate of achieving independence from their mothers (helped by the way the mothers punish them more, pay less attention to them, and hold and carry them less). The males had higher general activity levels, did more biting, pushing, shoving, yanking, grabbing, and jerking. They also did more thumbsucking and more manipulation of their genitals.*

We must always be cautious when drawing conclusions about humans from animal research, of course. To understate the matter, humans are not monkeys. Aggression, however, is related to the level of **testosterone**—a hormone produced by the testicles that stimulates primary and secondary sex traits in men (Bardwick 1971; Eisenegger et al. 2011), a factor that we shall now consider.

The Study of Vietnam Veterans. The fourth approach is also intriguing. The U.S. government collected data on testosterone levels among Vietnam veterans. To be certain the study was representative, the researchers chose a random sample of 4,462 men. Until this time, research on testosterone and human behavior was based on small samples. With this government study, sociologists gained access to a large random sample.

Researchers found that when the veterans with high levels of testosterone were younger, they were more likely to get in trouble with parents, teachers, and the law. As adults, they were more likely to use hard drugs, get into fights, end up in low-status jobs, and have more sexual partners. They were also less likely to marry. Those who did marry were more likely to have affairs, hit their wives, and, not surprising, to get divorced (Dabbs and Morris 1990; Booth and Dabbs 1993).

Can we conclude that the more aggressive behavior of these men was based in biology? At first glance, it looks like this, but there is much more to it. Not all men who have high testosterone levels got into trouble with the law or mistreated their wives. The main difference—and sociologists are pleased with this—was *social class*: High-testosterone men from lower social classes are more likely to be involved in antisocial behaviors than are high-testosterone men from higher social classes (Dabbs and Morris 1990). This indicates that *social* factors (socialization, life situations, self-definitions) are a significant part of the explanation for these men's behavior. The task before us is to uncover the rest of the puzzle—how social factors work in combination with biological factors.

More Research on Humans. Research on the effects of testosterone in humans continues. The results are intriguing. Not only do higher levels of testosterone lead to higher dominance, but the reverse is also true: Dominance behavior, such as winning a game, also produces higher levels of testosterone. This has made it difficult to determine which causes

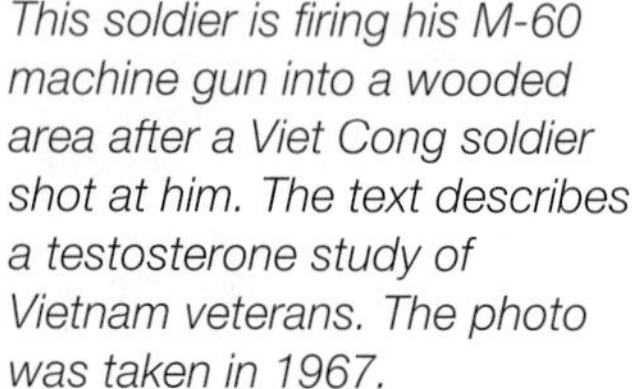

This soldier is firing his M-60 machine gun into a wooded area after a Viet Cong soldier shot at him. The text describes a testosterone study of Vietnam veterans. The photo was taken in 1967.

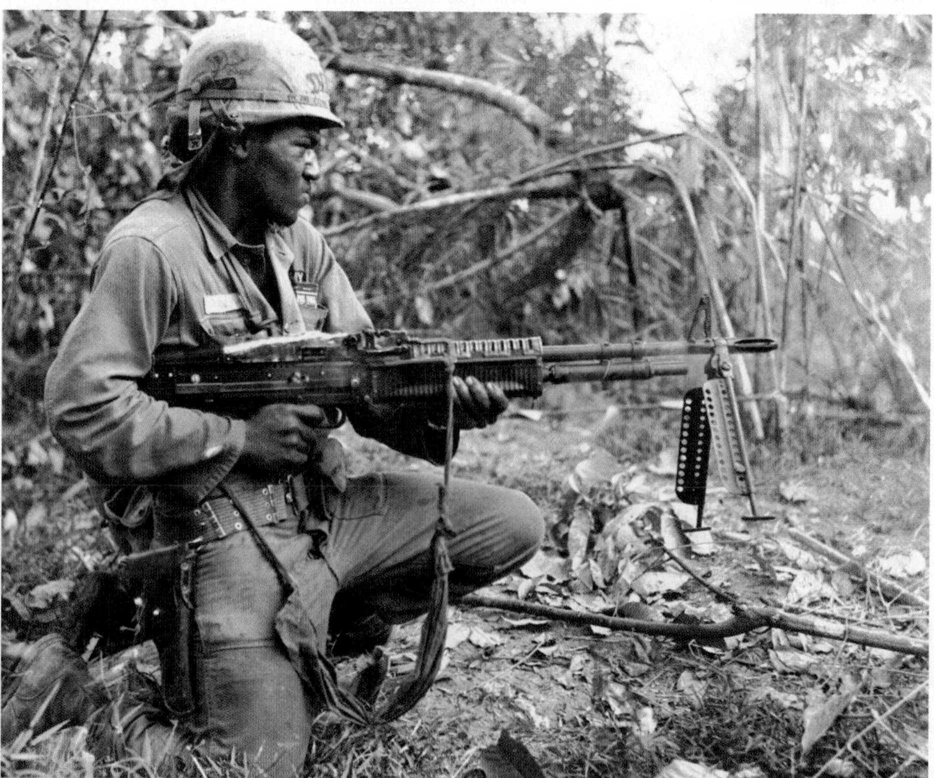

which. Controlled studies in which cause can be determined help. When researchers administer single doses of testosterone, dominance behavior increases. This is true of *both* males and females. They seek higher status and show less concern for the feelings of others (Eisenegger et al. 2011). Researchers are investigating how the testosterone changes people's behaviors, which they think might be through a triggering of other hormones.

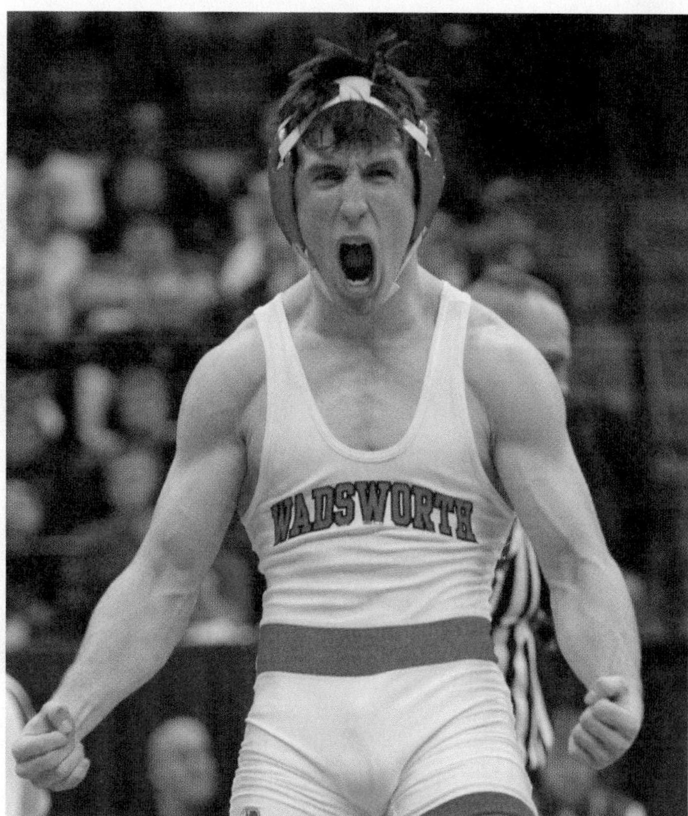

Among the intriguing findings from the research on hormones is that dominance behavior increases testosterone.

Reconciling the Findings. From current evidence, we can conclude that *if* biology provides males and females different temperaments or any type of behavioral predisposition, culture can magnify or override those differences. Each culture lays out gender guidelines for its men and women, and boys and girls are socialized to do gender according to those particular guidelines. We usually are unaware of how the environment shapes children to become different types of men and women, often assuming that the differences we see are evidence of "natural" or "genetic" differences between the sexes. In the years to come, unraveling the influences of socialization and biology should prove to be an exciting—and controversial—area of sociological research.

Avoiding Ideology. At this point, we have no final answer to the question of nature or nurture. Some researchers are convinced that differences in aggression, nurturing, and so on are innate; others are equally convinced that they are learned. Like other areas of science, we must examine data with an open mind, not try to make evidence fit either biology or culture because we prefer one or the other explanation. Unfortunately, research on differences between men and women has become emotionally charged, and findings that either favor or disfavor biology or culture are often interpreted through an ideological lens. They are seen as support for one's position, or a threat to it. This, of course, is not science. Data, not ideology, will one day answer the nature versus nurture question once and for all. (And it is likely that it will not be an either-or answer.)

In the meantime, almost all of us can agree on this principle: Whatever differences men and women might have in their behavior or orientations—no matter whether those differences are rooted in biology or culture or both—none provides a legitimate reason for discrimination. As sociologist Janet Chafetz (1990:30) said, there is no reason for "different" to become translated into "unequal."

Let's examine inequality between the sexes, with a focus on U.S. society.

Everyday Life

In everyday life, women find that many men have low regard for their interests, attitudes, and contributions. This negative, sometimes demeaning, attitude flows from the dominant view that pervades society: Masculinity represents strength, while femininity is perceived as weakness. With this orientation to life built into our culture, we learn it at an early age. As a result, most of it lies below our awareness. Let's try to make it more visible.

We can gain clues to how femininity is devalued by looking at gender in the military and sports. Let's go back to World War II when a team of researchers headed by sociologist Samuel Stouffer studied the motivation of combat soldiers. Out of this research came a sociological classic, *The American Soldier*. Stouffer and his colleagues (Stouffer et al. 1949:132) reported that officers hurled feminine terms at soldiers who underperformed:

As women accomplish more in areas traditionally dominated by men, it is likely that the definition of femininity will change and the devaluation of femininity decrease. Shown here is Jasmine Bailey, Illinois-Chicago guard.

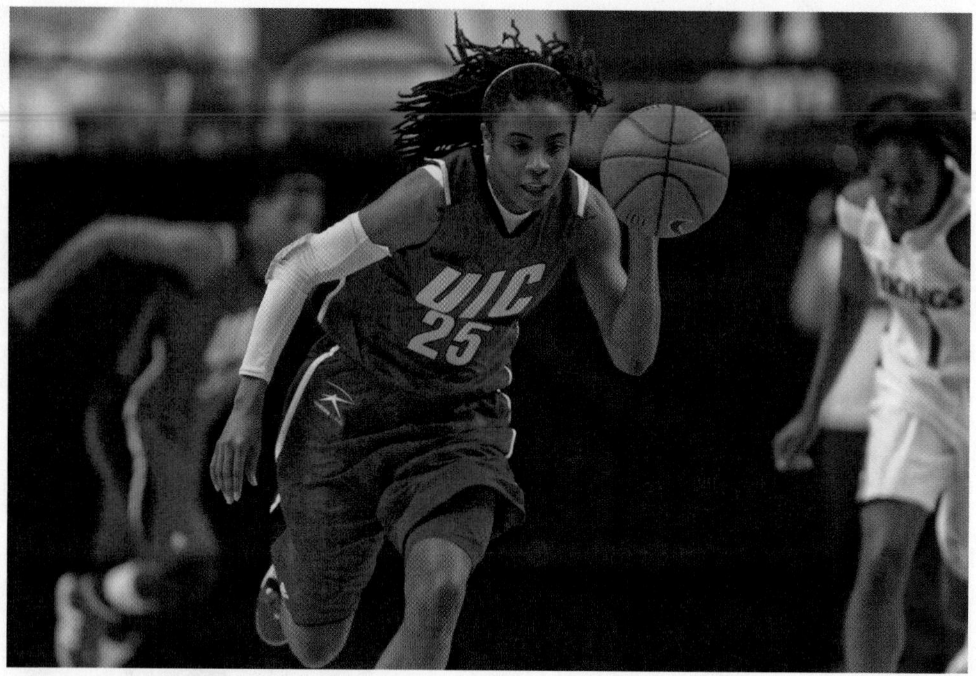

"Whatsa matter, bud—got lace on your drawers?" During the Vietnam War, military officers also used accusations of femininity to motivate soldiers. Drill sergeants would mock their troops by saying, "Can't hack it, little girls?" (Eisenhart 1975). Not just World War II and Vietnam. This same practice continues. In the Marines, sergeants shame male recruits by comparing their performance to a woman's (Gilham 1989). If a male soldier shows hesitation during maneuvers, others mock him, calling him a "girl" (Miller 2007).

We can see this same behavior in sports. Watching basketball, sociologists Jean Stockard and Miriam Johnson (1980) heard boys shout to others who missed the basket, "You play like a woman!" Anthropologist Douglas Foley, who studied high school football in Texas, heard ex-football players tell boys who had a bad game that they were "wearing skirts" (Foley 1990/2006). Describing more of the same, sociologist Donna Eder (1995) reported that junior-high boys call one another "girl" if they don't hit hard enough during a football game. You've probably heard this yourself.

Most people dismiss such remarks as insignificant: "That's just people talking." Stockard and Johnson point out, however, that this is more than "just talk." Such comments reveal a disparaging attitude toward women's abilities and accomplishments, an attitude that women face as part of their everyday lives. They make this telling point: "There is no comparable phenomenon among women, for young girls do not insult each other by calling each other 'man.'"

Although we are seeing changes in male–female relationships, the devaluation of women continues to be a background feature of social life. Why is this important? As sociologist Carol Whitehurst (1977) pointed out, this devaluation of things feminine underlies all other forms of oppression.

Education

Discrimination in the Past. To gain a better understanding of today's situation in education, let's take a glimpse into the past. About a century ago, leading educators claimed that women's wombs dominated their mental life. Dr. Edward Clarke, for example, a member of Harvard University's medical faculty, warned women that studying was dangerous for them:

> *A girl upon whom Nature, for a limited period and for a definite purpose, imposes so great a physiological task, will not have as much power left for the tasks of school, as the boy of whom Nature requires less at the corresponding epoch. (quoted in Andersen 1988:35)*

Medical students at Women's Medical College in Philadelphia, Pennsylvania, about 1900. This was one of the first colleges to allow women to dissect bodies. Previously, with dissection thought inappropriate for women, they learned anatomy and physiology from skeletons.

To preserve their fragile health, Clarke added that young women should study only one-third as much as men. And during menstruation, they shouldn't study at all.

Views like Clarke's certainly put women at an educational disadvantage. Women who followed his warning and studied less than men would obviously do worse overall. This, in turn, would confirm the stereotype that women's brains weren't as capable as men's—and that their proper place was in the home.

Discrimination in Other Countries. It has been a long time since American women faced discrimination in education, but in some countries it is still severe. On Table 9.1, you can see where women have the lowest literacy rates compared to men. Nineteen of these twenty-three countries are located in Africa and four in Asia.

Men Falling Behind. What a vital contrast between the literacy rates shown in Table 9.1 and the situation of women in the United States. In U.S. colleges, there are almost *3 million more women* than men. Women earn 57 percent of all bachelor's degrees (*Statistical Abstract* 2013:Tables 279, 299). With such totals, it might seem that gender equality has been achieved. Perhaps we've even developed a new form of gender inequality and, as discussed in the Thinking Critically box on the next page, we need affirmative action for men.

TABLE 9.1 ▸ Countries Where the Literacy Rate of Women Is Less Than 75% of That of the Men

Percentage	Country
29%	Afghanistan
31%	Chad
37%	Niger
42%	Guinea
46%	Ethiopia
51%	Mali
52%	Central African Republic
53%	Yemen
53%	Benin
56%	Togo
58%	Mozambique
59%	Burkina Faso
61%	Senegal
62%	Nepal
63%	Morocco
63%	Cote d'Ivoire
63%	Bhutan
65%	Angola
67%	Democratic Republic of the Congo
71%	India
72%	Guinea-Bissau
73%	Sudan
73%	Egypt

Source: By the author. Based on UNICEF 2010:Table 8.

Thinking Critically About Social Problems

Affirmative Action for Men?

The idea that we might need affirmative action *for men* was first proposed by psychologist Judith Kleinfeld (2002a). Many laughed when they heard this suggestion. After all, men still dominate societies around the world, as they have for millennia. As we have discussed in this chapter, as men exercised their dominance they suppressed and harmed women. To think that men would ever need affirmative action does seem humorous at best. Certainly nothing to be taken seriously.

Instead of making a knee-jerk reaction, though, let's pause, step back, and try to see whether the idea has any merit. Consider the statistics we just reviewed. Although there are approximately as many men as women (women slightly outnumber men), there are almost three million more women than men in college. Not only do they earn more bachelor's degrees than men do, but they also earn *60 percent* of all master's degrees (*Statistical Abstract* 2013:Table 299). Not only have women caught up with men in these areas, but they have also surpassed them, an accomplishment both impressive and laudable.

This gender gap in favor of women applies to all racial–ethnic groups. In all of them, more women than men are attending college and earning more bachelor's and master's degrees. This is not a temporary situation, like lead cars changing place at the Indy 500. The national statistics that the government publishes each year are consistent. For decades, women have been steadily adding to their proportion of college student enrollment and the degrees they earn.

Why have the men fallen behind? With college enrollment open equally to both men and women, why don't enrollment and degrees match the relative proportions of women and men in the population (51 percent and 49 percent)? Although no one yet knows the answers—and there are a lot of suggestions being thrown about—some have begun to consider this gender gap a problem in need of a solution. In a first, Clark University in Massachusetts has begun a support program for men to help them adjust to their minority status (Gibbs 2008). I assume that other colleges will follow, as these totals have serious implications for the future of society—just as they did when fewer women were enrolled in college.

Do you think we need affirmative action for men in college?

For Your Consideration

Do you think that women's and men's current college enrollments and degree totals represent anything other than an interesting historical change? Why do you think that men have fallen behind? Do you think we should start affirmative action and special remedial and motivational courses for men? Why or why not? Behind the scenes, so as not to get anyone upset, some colleges have begun to reject more qualified women to get closer to a male–female balance (Kingsbury 2007). What do you think about this?

Gender Tracking. But let's look beneath the surface of this historical change. Underlying college attendance and the degrees is *gender tracking;* that is, college degrees tend to follow gender, which reinforces male–female distinctions. Here are two extremes: Men earn 94 percent of the associate degrees in the "masculine" field of construction trades, while women are awarded 95 percent of the associate degrees in the "feminine" field of "family and consumer sciences" (*Statistical Abstract* 2013:Table 302). Because gender socialization gives men and women different orientations to life, they enter college with gender-linked aspirations. Socialization—not some presumed innate characteristic—channels men and women into different educational paths.

A Man's World. When they enter college, most students face "a man's world." Not only are most of their professors men, but they also study mostly male authors in their literature courses, discuss the thinking of men in their philosophy courses, and read almost exclusively about famous men in their history courses. Little is known about how this affects the orientations of female and male students, but it certainly has to be significant. Men who have taken courses in gender studies taught by women have told me how upsetting it is to be immersed in "women's world of thought." Women's immersion in what we can call the "men's world of thought" starts early and is taken for granted. Its impact, though less perceptible, is just as severe.

Completing the Doctorate. Although women now outnumber men in college and earn 57 percent of the bachelor's degrees, as well as 60 percent of the master's degrees, something happens on the way to the doctorate. Look at Table 9.2, which gives us a snapshot of doctoral programs in the sciences. Note how aspirations (enrollment) and achievements (doctorates earned) are sex linked. In five of these doctoral programs, men outnumber women, and in three, women outnumber men. In all but engineering, however, women are less likely to complete the doctorate.

I am not suggesting that graduate faculties purposely discriminate against women. Perhaps what I mentioned earlier about most faculty being men and most of the researchers, theorists, and writers being studied also being men has something to do with it. Perhaps. Apparently, though, the core reason is simpler: Women are more likely to get sidetracked by marriage and family responsibilities. These responsibilities also have serious consequences for women in the world of work, as you will see shortly.

A Developing Social Problem? I would like to conclude this section by referring back to an earlier point, the decrease in men's college enrollments. That almost 3 million more women than men are enrolled in college, and that they earn 57 percent of the bachelor's degrees and 60 percent of the master's degrees, indicates that we have undergone a dramatic shift in education. Following the basic model of social problems that I have stressed throughout this text, at this point these statistics reflect only objective conditions. To have a social problem, we must have widespread social concerns. If enough people become upset about the smaller enrollment of men in college and their lesser educational achievements, a social problem will emerge—this time with men as the objects of discrimination. If this happens, do you think that we will see affirmative action, special scholarships, remedial help, and retention programs—for men?

The Mass Media

The mass media help to shape gender roles by portraying certain behaviors as "right" for boys and other behaviors as "right" for girls. These messages influence

TABLE 9.2 ▸ Doctorates in Science, by Sex

	Students Enrolled		Doctorates Conferred		Completion Ratio[1] Higher (+) or Lower (–) than Expected	
Field	**Women**	**Men**	**Women**	**Men**	**Women**	**Men**
Engineering	23%	77%	23%	77%	–0	+0
Psychology	75%	25%	70%	30%	–7	+20
Agriculture	49%	51%	45%	55%	–8	+8
Biological sciences	57%	43%	52%	48%	–9	+12
Physical sciences	33%	67%	30%	70%	–9	+4
Social sciences	53%	47%	48%	52%	–9	+11
Computer sciences	24%	76%	21%	79%	–13	+4
Mathematics	34%	66%	29%	71%	–15	+8

[1]The formula for the completion ratio is X minus Y divided by Y times 100, where X is the doctorates conferred and Y is the proportion enrolled in a program.

Source: By the author. Based on *Statistical Abstract of the United States* 2013:Tables 821, 825.

our ideas about "proper" sexual relationships and body images. To gain insight into how this occurs, let's look first at children's books, then at television, music, and advertising.

Children's Books. When you were a child, picture books were probably part of your young life. It is likely that your parents read them to you, pausing to show you the pictures, with your little hands tracing elements of the illustrations. These books provide entertainment, but they do much more than this. The pictures and stories give children a view of the cultural world that they are about to enter. From the characters in the stories—the illustrations and the "action"—children learn what behavior and attitudes are considered appropriate for the sexes.

When sociologists examined children's picture books in the 1970s, almost all the books featured boys and men. Even most animals were males! Girls were usually portrayed as passive and doll-like, while the boys were more active and adventurous. The girls helped their brothers and fathers, while the boys did things requiring independence and self-confidence (Weitzman et al. 1972). Rarely was a girl the story's main character. Feminists protested these stereotypes. Some even formed their own publishing company to counteract them.

So where are we today? Somewhere farther down the road to equality, but still quite a distance from this destination. The top-selling children's books have more female characters than they used to, but there are still about half again as many male as female characters. The girls are more likely to be portrayed indoors and the boys outdoors (Hamilton et al. 2006; McCabe et al. 2011). Even in coloring books, males continue to be shown as more active than females (Fitzpatrick and McPherson 2010). And most of the animals continue to be males.

As lopsided as things remain, there have been changes. Not only are there more female characters today, but the females are also portrayed as doing things that only males did in older books. Males, in contrast, are not often portrayed as doing things that females do. Males, for example, are seldom depicted as caring for the children or doing grocery shopping, and they are rarely seen doing housework (Gooden and Gooden 2001; Adams et al. 2011). As gender roles continue to change, I am sure that these depictions will, too.

Television and Movies. If you've watched youngsters while they are watching children's videos or television, you've probably noticed how engrossed they are. They can hardly lift their eyes from "the action" when you try to get their attention. What are children learning through these powerful media that transmit ideas through words and moving images? To find out, researchers counted characters on children's television and analyzed what they were doing. They always reported that the male characters vastly outnumbered the female characters. And today? More of the same. Male characters still outnumber female characters—and vastly so, by two to one (Baker and Raney 2007; Smith and Cook 2008).

But within these numbers lies fundamental change. In children's cartoons, females used to be portrayed as less intelligent, less brave, and more dependent and emotional. The female superheroes in children's cartoons today are still portrayed as more emotional, but they are now shown to be just as intelligent, brave, and powerful as the male superheroes. They are even portrayed as aggressive as the males (Baker and Raney 2007). Then there is *Katniss Everdeen*, whose athletic, archery, and fighting skills are nothing short of amazing. We have a long way to go, but the journey has begun.

Movies and adult television continue the pattern of featuring more male than female characters. On television, males are about twice as likely to be prime-time characters (Glascock 2001; "Fall Colors" 2004). An analysis of the movies nominated as best pictures for the Academy Awards shows the same: Men are about twice as likely as women to have speaking parts (Smith et al. 2012). Men are also depicted as retaining their sex appeal longer than women, as well as attracting younger partners.

Today's mass media are portraying women in stereotype-breaking roles, such as Katniss Everdeen in The Hunger Games.

Body image is another key part of doing gender, and television is effective in teaching us what we "should" look like. Sociologists have found that most female characters are below average in weight. Viewers not only learn that thinness is desirable, but they also see a "distorted and unrealistic picture of women's bodies" compared with what most women actually look like (Fouts and Burggraf 1999; Smith and Cook 2008). Sociologist Lori Fowler (2008) reports that these images make such an impact that some mothers give breast implants to their daughters as high school graduation gifts—even when they are aware that the silicone can lead to health problems.

Music. There are so many kinds (genres) of music that it is difficult to summarize sexism and sex roles in music, but here are a few observations. In many songs for teens and preteens, boys learn to dominate male–female relationships. Lyrics instruct girls to be sexy, passive, and dependent—and to control boys by manipulating their sexual impulses. In music videos, females often are background ornaments for dominant male singers (Ward et al 2005). Some rap groups glorify male sexual aggression and revel in humiliating women. In country–western music, one theme is aggressive and dominant men and passive and dependent women. These dominant men do have a tender side, however. They cry into their beers after their cheating woman has left them. But, never mind, some honky-tonk woman is waiting to revel in her newly found, dominant man.

Advertising

You are aware that you see a lot of advertising—in magazines, on buses, on television every few minutes, and even on sports uniforms. But you might be surprised at the extent to which the media bombard you with pitches for their products. If you are average, you are exposed to a blistering 200,000 commercials a year (Kacen 2011).

Commercials do much more than simply sell products. They also portray women and men and how they do so influences our perception of the sexes. Back in the 1970s, women were primarily depicted as "housekeepers, mothers, and menial workers." Since that time, fewer women are shown as menial workers, but advertising continues to reinforce stereotypical gender roles. Commercials aimed at children are more likely to show girls as cooperative and boys as aggressive. They are also more likely to show girls at home and boys outdoors (Larson 2001). Women are shown as making most purchases, and often as supportive counterparts to men (Ganahl et al. 2003).

Feminists have protested exposing the female body to sell products. Obviously, Paris Hilton's body has nothing to do with Carl's Jr. hamburgers. What is your position on this? Why?

Even when women are depicted as professionals, they are often shown as weaker employees who just can't get along without a man's assistance (Lindner 2004).

And I'm sure you've noticed this one: The use of the female body—especially exposed breasts and close-ups of the female rear to sell products. For decades, feminists have objected to how advertisers sexualize the female body as an attention-getting device to promote whatever they are selling. To show their displeasure, some feminists spray painted billboards, turning them into pro-woman messages (Rakow 1992). One of their more humorous and attention-getting examples was repainting a billboard that featured a woman reclining on a car so it said "When I'm not lying on cars, I'm a brain surgeon."

With the tens of thousands of commercials that are thrown at us, the portrayal of stereotypes can be a powerful influence in how we see the world. A change in the message can also be powerful. The attempt by feminists to reduce the exploitation of the female body in selling products, however, has changed nothing. Those barely clothed female bodies are still used to sell new cars—whether scantily clad young women are lying on them, standing by them, or even driving them. The same forms are used to sell hamburgers and cruises. One major change has taken place, though—the male body is exposed more. No longer do we see just rippling chests and biceps, but we also have a focus on the male crotch. I suppose that this is a growing equality of sorts.

Peer Groups. The mass media influence our views of the self and the world, and our peer groups turn into their enforcing agent. They select aspects of the gender messages, ruthlessly forcing their interpretation of how those ideas and images should be expressed. To read more on this topic, see the Spotlight on Social Research box on the next page.

In Sum ▸ The mass media—children's books, television, music, and advertising—influence our views of the self and the world. These images shape our expectations of the way we "ought" to be—how we should act and even feel. Although we aren't aware that it is occurring, we tend to view one another and ourselves through the images that are presented to us as "normal" and "right." The portrayal of boys and men as dominant continues, but there has been significant change. Most remarkable is the new portrayal of girls not only as more active and dominant but also as aggressive, even fierce.

The images of the sexes that we learn as children channel our behavior along expected avenues. These images continue to influence us as we "do gender" as adults. Let's turn to how this works out in politics.

The World of Politics

The Current Situation. Politics gives us another way to see the relative positions of men and women. One of the best historical indicators is this: Since 1789, nearly 1,900 men have served in the U.S. Senate, but only 42 women have served. Similarly, only 31 women have held the office of governor, and none has ever held the office of president. Not until 1992 was the first African American woman (Carol Moseley-Braun) elected to the Senate. None has been elected since. The first Asian American female senator, Mazie Hirono, was elected in Hawaii in 2012. As of yet, no Latina has been elected to the Senate (Baumann 2006; Manning and Shogan 2012).

Spotlight on Social Research

Sitting In on Adolescent Conversations

DONNA EDER, *professor of sociology at Indiana University, did research on gender dynamics and adolescent bullying and gossip in middle school. She explored the ways that common activities like teasing, insulting, and gossiping often reinforce gender roles and social status. In this essay, she discusses why girls become more insecure during middle school years and how adolescents try to build up their own self-esteem by making fun of social isolates. Here is what she wrote for you.*

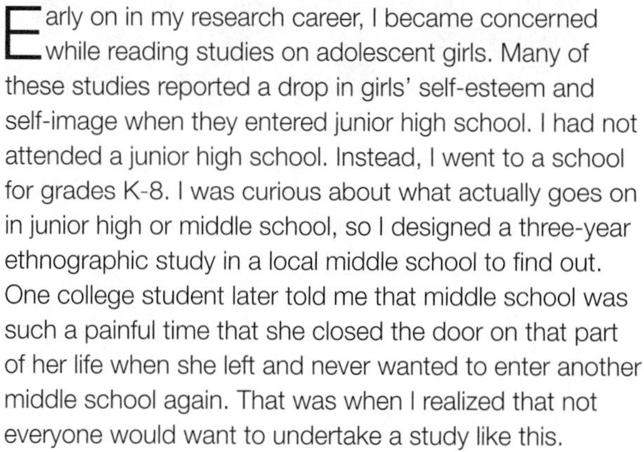

Early on in my research career, I became concerned while reading studies on adolescent girls. Many of these studies reported a drop in girls' self-esteem and self-image when they entered junior high school. I had not attended a junior high school. Instead, I went to a school for grades K-8. I was curious about what actually goes on in junior high or middle school, so I designed a three-year ethnographic study in a local middle school to find out. One college student later told me that middle school was such a painful time that she closed the door on that part of her life when she left and never wanted to enter another middle school again. That was when I realized that not everyone would want to undertake a study like this.

I hired both female and male assistants to observe lunchtime interaction along with me as I wanted to study both girls and boys from different social class backgrounds. We also attended after-school sports events and cheerleading practices. All of us took field notes after we left the setting and tape recorded lunch time conversations.

Some of the things we observed were painful to watch. Through our recordings of gossip and ridicule, we learned a lot about what might make girls so insecure. For one thing, much of the gossip involved negative comments on other girls' appearance as well as their "stuck up" behavior. When we looked closely at the nature of the gossip, we found something interesting. The only time that anyone disagreed with someone's negative evaluation was if they did so early on, right after the remark was made. Once even one other person agreed with it, no one seemed willing to challenge the "group" view. So in order to participate in the gossip, you pretty much needed to join in with the negative comments or else be sure to speak up quickly.

This is one way we saw how "meaning is constructed in the interaction"—an important concept of symbolic interactionism. When we studied teasing, we also saw the power of a response to shape the meaning of an exchange. One day during volley ball practice, a girl said that another girl was showing off her new bra through her white tee-shirt. The girl responded by saying, "If I want to show off my bra I'll do it like this," lifting her shirt up. By responding playfully, she disarmed the insulter, and her teammates all joined in on the laughter.

In this large middle school, status hierarchies were based on appearance, social class, and intelligence. Since the girls had little control over most of these attributes, one way they tried to become more popular was by making friends with popular students. Of course, the popular girls (cheerleaders and those considered to be more attractive) could not befriend everyone who wanted to be their friend. This led to a cycle of popularity in which once well-liked girls became disliked and viewed as snobs for not returning others' offers of friendship.

Those at the bottom of the status rankings were isolates, eating lunch by themselves or with other low status students. As isolates, they were frequent targets of ridicule from students trying to build themselves up by putting others down. Both boys and girls picked on the isolates, most of whom lacked the skills to turn the exchanges into playful ones.

After finishing this study, I wanted to do something constructive about the problems that we had witnessed at this middle school. I formed an after-school club which we brought to many elementary schools as part of an undergraduate service-learning experience. We called it KACTIS—Kids Against Cruel Treatment in Schools. Through KACTIS, we taught children the power of their response to ridicule, using role playing to show them how they could turn a potentially serious comment into a joking one. In one skit, the children decided that if a bully tried to keep them from using the water fountain, they would just collapse to the floor as if they were dying of thirst. When they acted this out, the bully got annoyed and walked away. After the skit, a second grader happily reported to me that they had learned how to trick the bully.

We also taught children to be more direct in their feedback to others rather than rely on gossip. In addition, we showed them how they could intervene on behalf of another child who was being bullied or ridiculed. I hope that some of these skills proved useful to these elementary students when they entered middle school. Meanwhile, my college students who provided the service-learning also learned a lot about conflict resolution, showing that we are never too old to learn new strategies to help us get through the problems we face in everyday life.

Hillary Rodham Clinton illustrates the greater prominence of women in U.S. politics. She is now being groomed for a run at the presidency in 2016. Clinton is showcased here with foreign ministers of the Gulf oil producing countries.

We are undergoing fundamental change in politics. In 2007, Nancy Pelosi was elected Speaker of the House of Representatives, the first woman to hold this position. Seventy-two of the 435 House members are women, still a great underrepresentation, but one of the highest totals ever. In the executive branch, three women have served as U.S. secretary of state. Two women have run as vice-presidential nominees of major parties, Geraldine Ferraro as a Democrat and Sarah Palin as a Republican. In 2008, Hillary Clinton was the first woman to win a presidential primary and only narrowly lost the Democratic Party nomination to Barack Obama.

Despite the changes that mark greater equality between the sexes, men continue to dominate politics. From Figure 9.3, you can see how vastly underrepresented women

FIGURE 9.3 ▸ Who Controls U.S. Politics?

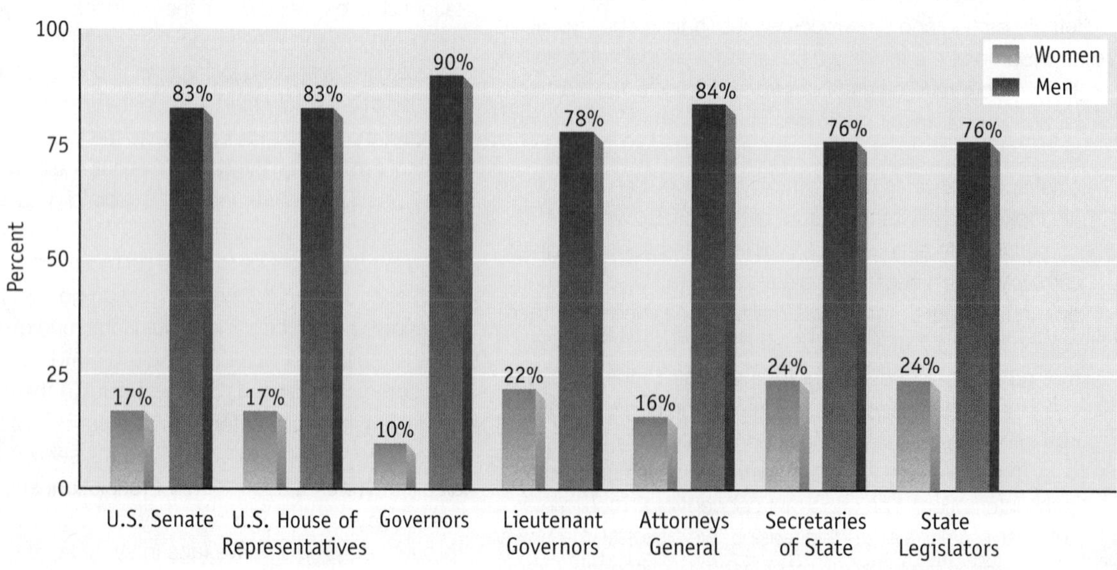

Source: By the author. Based on Center for American Women and Politics 2012, 2013.

FIGURE 9.4 ▸ Women in State Legislatures

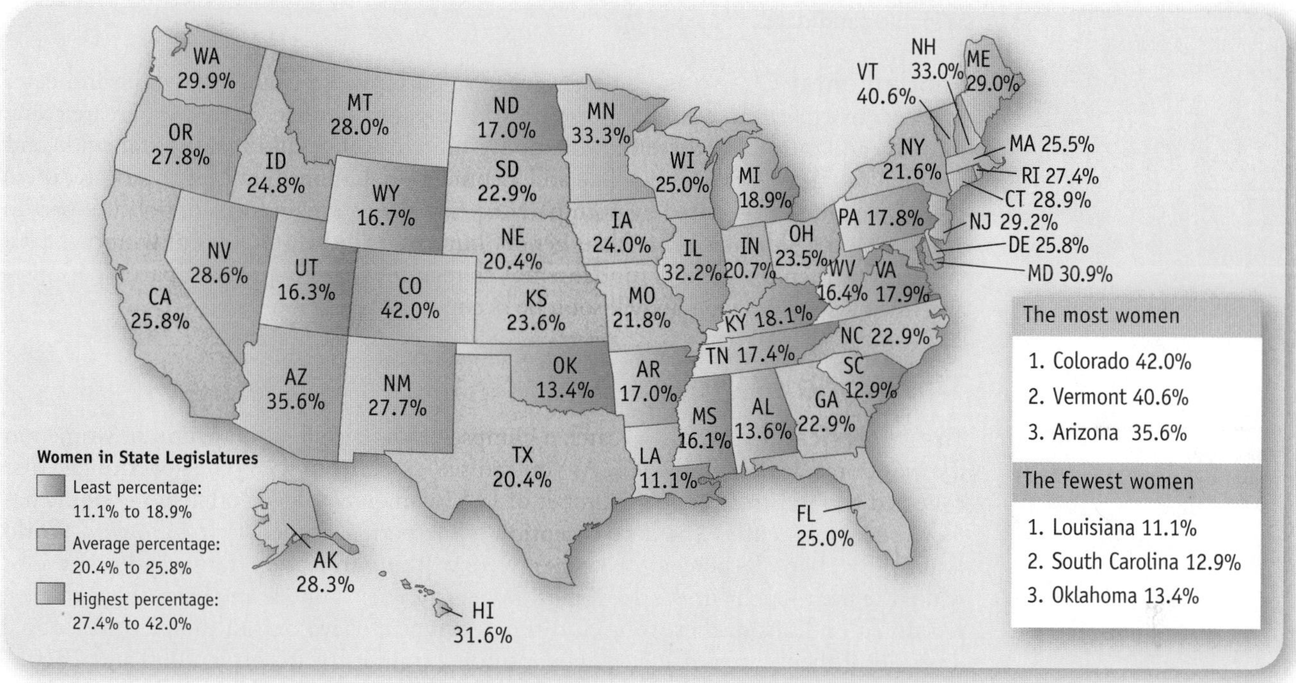

Source: By the author. Based on National Council of State Legislatures 2013.

are in political decision making. The principle is this: *The higher the office, the fewer the women who hold the office.*

For a rough indicator of how political power is distributed between men and women on the state level, look at the Social Map above. You can see that in no state legislature do women equal the number of men. There is wide variation in the political power of women, from 11 percent of legislators in Louisiana to 42 percent in Colorado. As you can see, women hold the highest percentage of state offices in the West.

Why Don't Women Dominate Politics? Between *7 and 8 million* more women than men are of voting age (*Statistical Abstract* 2013:Table 407). With their overwhelming numbers, women could take political control of the nation. Why don't they?

The Syllogism of Masculinity ▸ The answer appears to be socialization. As we have seen, social institutions continue to socialize men into positions of authority and women into accepting this authority. This leads to the following reasoning:

Dominance is masculine.
Politics is a form of dominance.
Therefore, politics is masculine.

The perception of politics as unfeminine puts severe restraints on women's recruitment, participation, and performance in politics.

The Power of Sex Roles ▸ Other explanations for the continued dominance of politics by men center on the relative positions of men and women in other areas of society. First, women have been underrepresented in law and business, the careers from which most politicians come. Most women also find the irregular hours that it takes to run for elective office incompatible with home life. For men, this conflict is not as severe, as their typical work schedules are more likely to take them away from home. Women are also less likely to have a supportive spouse who will play an unassuming background role while providing child care, encouragement, and voter appeal. Finally, until recently men have been reluctant to bring women into decision-making roles or to regard them as viable candidates.

Fundamental Changes. These restrictive patterns are changing, which indicates that we can expect more women to seek and win political office. More women are going into law and business, where they are doing more traveling and making statewide and national contacts. Although women still assume more responsibility for child care, these tasks are increasingly shared by both parents. And today a main focus of political parties as they select candidates is not their gender but, instead, their chances of winning. This generation, then, is seeing a fundamental change in women's political participation—and it is likely that a woman will soon be occupying the Oval Office.

The World of Work

Watch on **MySocLab** **Video:** Women in the Workplace

The Historical Pattern. To catch a glimpse of the overall participation of women in the workforce, look at Table 9.3. As you can see, since 1890 when the government first collected this information, the number of U.S. women employed outside the home has increased consistently. The lone exception is the period immediately following World War II. By 1945, 38 percent of women were working in factory, farm, and office jobs while the men fought in World War II. When the men came home from the war, they reclaimed millions of these jobs, and the percentage of women in the paid workforce dropped. It then started rising again, continuing until it leveled off in 2000 and 2010.

The percentage of those ages 16 and older who are in the labor force at least part-time is referred to as the **labor force participation rate**. About 1980, for the first time in U.S. history, half of all American working-age women were employed outside the home at least part-time. Today, nearly half of all U.S. workers are women. The Social Map on the next page shows how the percentage of women working for wages differs by state. The rate ranges from 48 percent in West Virginia to 68 percent in North Dakota.

TABLE 9.3 ▸ Women in the Civilian Labor Force

Year	Number of Female Workers	As a Percentage of All Workers	As a Percentage of Working-Age Women
1890	4,000,000	17%	18%
1900	5,000,000	18%	20%
1920	8,000,000	20%	23%
1930	10,000,000	22%	24%
1940	14,000,000	25%	29%
1945	19,000,000	36%	38%
1950	18,000,000	30%	34%
1960	23,000,000	33%	36%
1970	32,000,000	37%	41%
1980	46,000,000	43%	52%
1990	57,000,000	45%	58%
2000	66,000,000	46%	60%
2010	72,000,000	47%	59%
2020[1]	77,000,000	47%	57%

Note: Pre-1940 totals include women 14 and over; totals for 1940 and after are for women 16 and over.

[1]Estimate by the U.S. Dept. of Labor.

Sources: By the author. Based on *1969 Handbook on Women Workers* 1969:10; *Manpower Report to the President* 1971:203, 205; Mills and Palumbo 1980:6, 45; U.S. Bureau of the Census, various years; *Statistical Abstract of the United States* 2003:Table 588; 2013:Table 597.

FIGURE 9.5 ▸ How Likely Are Women to Work for Wages?

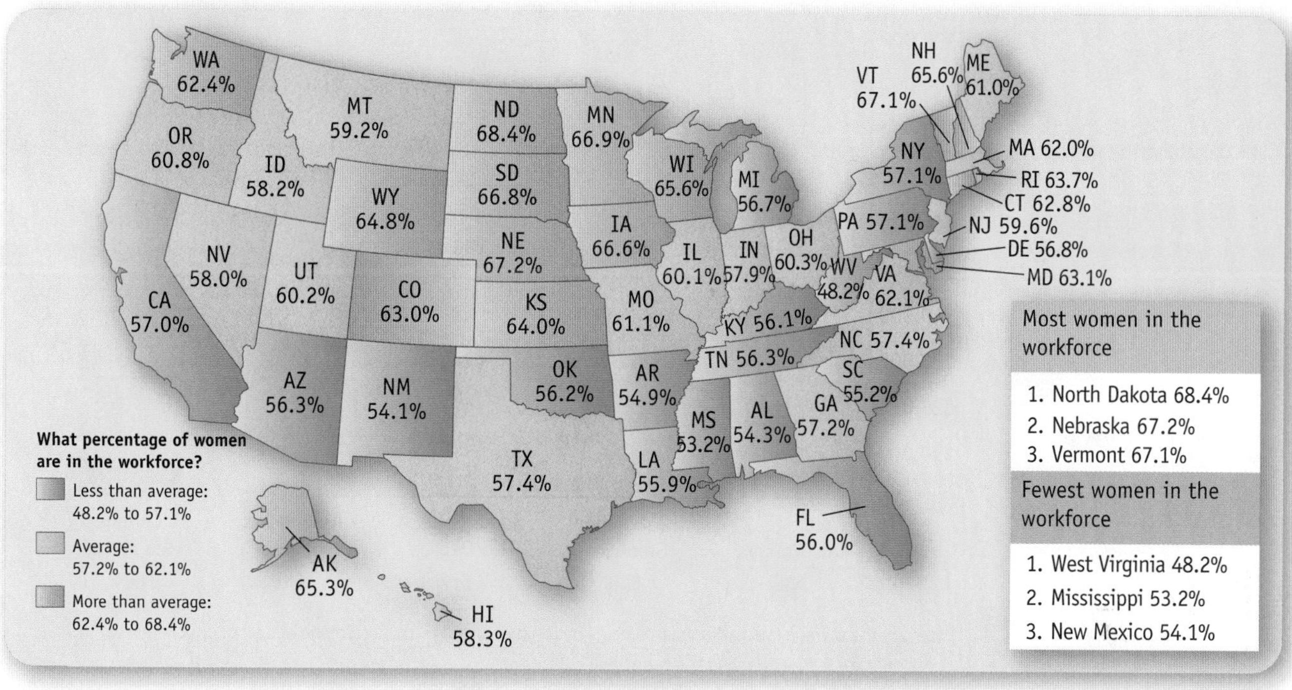

Source: By the author. Based on *Statistical Abstract of the United States* 2012:Table 594.

From these changes, you might think that work has become a level playing field for men and women. The world of work, though, is no exception to the general pattern of discrimination against women. Women come up against "old boys' networks"—social contacts that keep jobs, promotions, and opportunities circulating among men. To overcome this exclusion, some women professionals have developed "new girls' networks." They pass opportunities among one another, purposefully excluding men in order to help the careers of women.

The Gender Pay Gap. To pinpoint discrimination, we need more than anecdotes about some particular woman who is paid less than some man for the same work. What we need are hard numbers that apply across the nation. Figure 9.6 on the next page provides this. You can see that even though they have the same amount of education, the average man earns considerably more than the average woman. You can also see that this is true at all levels of education, whether the workers have completed only high school or are college graduates. *At all ages and at all levels of education, the average woman is paid less than the average man.* This gender gap also shows up in all occupations. There isn't a single occupation in which the average woman earns more than the average man.

This pay gap certainly will affect your future—to the advantage of the male readers of this text and to the disadvantage of the female readers. Keep in mind that Figure 9.6 does not illustrate some select type of jobs. It shows the national results of *all* jobs in the United States—and only full-time, year-round workers. The women average only 72 percent of what the men make. Until 1980, women's earnings were just 60 percent of men's, which means that today's 72 percent is an improvement!

We are not talking about the difference between a hamburger and a steak sandwich. These differences translate into a huge amount of money. If you assume that a man and a woman work full-time from the age of 25 until retiring at age 65, you have 40 years of earnings. Multiply the average annual earnings shown in Figure 9.6 by 40, and you will see what an astounding total the gender gap produces in favor of men: *Between the ages of 25 and 65, the average man who graduates from college will earn over a million dollars ($1,225,000) more than the average woman who graduates from college.*

FIGURE 9.6 ▸ The Cash Penalty for Being Female (or the Cash Reward for Being Male)[1]

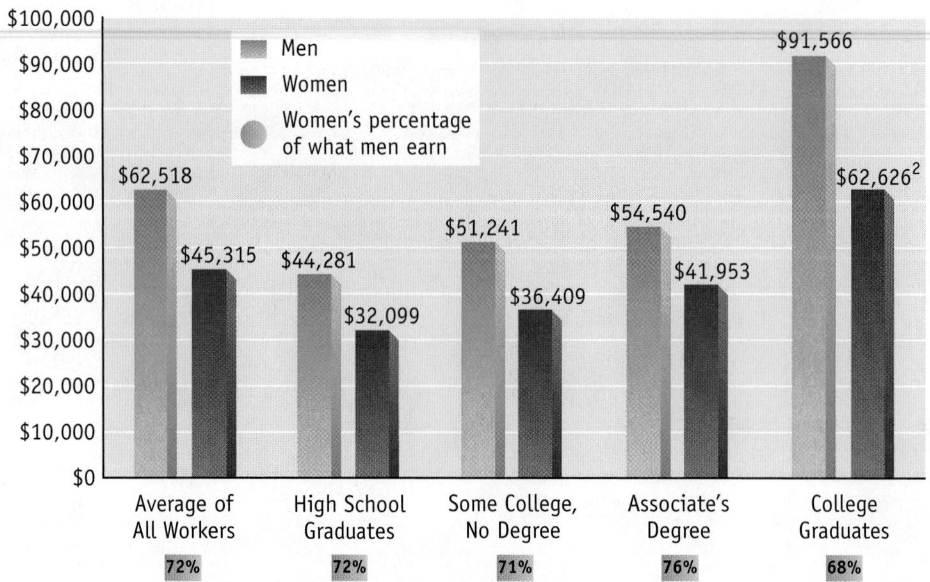

[1]These are the average (median) annual earnings of full-time workers. The percentage at the bottom of each bar indicates the women's average percentage of the men's income.

[2]Bachelor's and all higher degrees, including professional degrees.

Source; By the author. Based on *Statistical Abstract of the United States* 2013:Table 717.

Reasons for the Gender Pay Gap. Why do we have a pay gap between women and men? Recall that there is gender tracking in education: Women and men tend to take different majors in college. Perhaps, as a result, women end up in jobs that pay less. Another possibility is that women professionals, such as physicians, work fewer hours than do men in the same profession (Jagsi et al. 2012). Researchers have found that both of these factors are important and that they account for about half the pay gap.

Researchers have also found something else. Studying men and women who received MBAs from the University of Chicago, they found that at hiring, the women were paid 12 percent less than the men (Bertrand et al. 2009). They report that the men also had slightly higher grades and took more courses in finance. This initial gender gap grew, and after 9 years it had jumped to 38 percent. (These are highly paid workers, and by this time the men were making $150,000 a year more than the women.) As the researchers explored further, they found that the women had more career interruptions, primarily because of children, and that they worked 24 percent fewer hours, again because of children. The answer, then, appears to be a combination of gender discrimination and what sociologists call the *child penalty*—the missed opportunities because of giving birth and taking care of children.

In Sum ▸ We need more research on the reasons for the gender pay gap, especially the penalty for career interruptions and working fewer hours. Since the pay gap is so common, however, cutting across all occupations and all levels of education, it seems fair to conclude that employers place a higher value on men and pay them more. The sociological task is to probe the pay gap further, detail exactly how it works, and suggest how educators and policy makers can use these findings to bring about greater equality.

Sexual Harassment

Another form of discrimination is **sexual harassment**—unwanted sexual advances made by a person in power. These solicitations often are tied to promotions or demotions in the workplace. When a supervisor makes a sexual advance, the worker, who has less power, is at a considerable disadvantage in warding it off. The most vulnerable victims are those who lack job alternatives.

A Personal Problem: Just Individuals. The traditional view of sexual harassment makes it a *personal* problem, a matter of individual sexual attraction. A man gets interested in a woman and makes an advance; the woman accepts, rejects, or says "maybe." Perhaps her body language even "signals" that she *wants* to be approached sexually. There are always sexual attractions between men and women; some just happen to take place at work. From this traditional view, these are individual events and do not qualify as part of a *social* problem.

Explore on **MySocLab Activity:** Power Dynamics in the Workforce: the Case of Sexual Harassment

A Social Problem: Feminists and Relative Power. In 1979, Catharine MacKinnon, an attorney and professor, wrote a book on sexual harassment that changed our thinking. Rejecting the traditional view, MacKinnon argued that sexual harassment is a *structural* matter; that is, it is built into the work setting. She noted that two conditions of work encourage sexual harassment. The first is that most women occupy an inferior status in boss–worker relations. The second is an emphasis on women as sex objects. Women are sometimes hired because of their sexual attributes, a background condition that usually is hidden under the requirement that the newly hired be young, "attractive" women who will make a "good appearance" to the public. In short, sexual harassment sometimes begins with hiring procedures that judge women on their bodies, not their job qualifications.

Although MacKinnon's analysis is accepted widely now, it was controversial at the time. Until 1976, sexual harassment was literally unspeakable—because it had no name. The traditional view dominated, and women considered unwanted sexual advances as something that happened to them as individuals. They did not draw a connection between those advances and their lower position at work. As feminists raised awareness of the *group* nature of these objective conditions, women gradually concluded that the sexual advances by men in more powerful positions at work were part of a general problem. As subjective concerns grew—more women coming to the same conclusion, being upset about it, and demanding that something be done—sexual harassment as a *social* problem was born.

Sexual Harassment as an Evolving Term. As MacKinnon pointed out, sexual harassment can be just a single encounter at work or consist of a series of incidents. At times, sexual relations are even made a condition for being hired, retained, or promoted. There are various forms of sexual harassment, as MacKinnon (1979:29) noted:

> *Sexual harassment takes both verbal and physical forms. . . . Verbal sexual harassment can include anything from passing but persistent comments on a woman's body or body parts to the experience of an eighteen-year-old file clerk whose boss regularly called her in to his office "to tell me the intimate details of his marriage and to ask what I thought about different sexual positions." Pornography is sometimes used. Physical forms range from repeated collisions that leave the impression of "accident" to outright rape. One woman reported unmistakable sexual molestation which fell between these extremes: "My boss . . . runs his hand up my leg or blouse. He hugs me to him and then tells me he is 'just naturally affectionate.'"*

The Equal Employment Opportunity Commission (EEOC) broadened the definition of sexual harassment to include all unwelcome verbal or physical conduct of a sexual nature that affects an individual's employment, interferes with an individual's work performance, or creates an intimidating, hostile, or offensive work environment. The offender does not have to be a boss, nor does the victim have to be a female. The intimidating, hostile, or offensive behavior can be from fellow workers or agents of the employer ("Facts About . . ." 2006). The definition has also been broadened to include unwanted sexual behavior from fellow students.

You can see that some of the key terms in this definition are broad and subject to interpretation. One person can find some behavior intimidating, hostile, or offensive, while another person can view that same act quite differently. The legal concept has become so fuzzy that a woman whose boss did *not* ask her for sexual favors—while he asked all the other women—was ruled a victim of sexual harassment (Hayes 1991). In addition, as discussed in the Spotlight on Social Research box below, what passes for acceptable behavior in one work setting can be taken as sexual harassment in another.

Difficult Choices. A worker who is sexually harassed by a boss has limited options. Objecting, submitting, or ignoring the act are all risky (MacKinnon 1979:52). Let's say that the victim is a woman. If she objects, she may be hounded until she quits or is fired. If she submits, the man may tire of her. If she ignores it, she can get drawn into a cat-and-mouse game with few exits: He may tire of the game and turn to someone else, or he may fire her so he can hire a more willing victim.

Spotlight on Social Research

Sexual Harassment at Two Magazines

KIRSTEN DELLINGER, *associate professor of sociology at the University of Mississippi, says that her interest in gender and sexuality in organizations emerged from her own early work experiences. As she worked with autistic adults in one setting and children in another, she wondered why most workers were women and why they earned little and received little respect. From these initial observations, she turned her attention to how work is organized and the role of gender and sexuality in the work setting. Here is what she wrote for you.*

I have been intrigued by the research that explores how organizations are "gendered" and "sexualized." One of the themes in this literature is how workplace policies create and maintain ideologies about masculinity and femininity. Another is how workers construct their gender identities through their everyday interactions. What is acceptable or not differs from one work setting to another. Take the example of sexual harassment.

Have you ever heard people say that sexual harassment is impossible to solve in the workplace because "it all depends on what an individual finds offensive"? Sally finds the joke about women's bodies funny, but Julie doesn't. Harry likes to tell stories about homosexuals, but Frank cringes when he hears them. Julie and Frank keep their mouths shut, because they hold lower positions at work. Much survey research on sexual harassment emphasizes this individualistic level. Researchers ask people if, in their opinion, certain behaviors (such as patting someone's butt) are sexual harassment or not.

Instead of taking this individualistic perspective, in my research I examine how the *social context* influences how people define sexual harassment. The research that I did with Christine Williams underlines the symbolic interactionist perspective that whether a behavior is sexual harassment or not depends on the definitions that people apply to it. And those definitions, as we found out, depend more on the social context than on individualistic perspectives.

We studied workers at two magazines who were doing the same jobs: editors, accountants, and administrative assistants. The magazines were quite different: a heterosexual men's pornographic magazine and a feminist magazine. Workers at the men's magazine, *Gentleman's Sophisticate*, worked in a "locker room" culture. Sexual joking was common, even about the magazine itself. At the same time, these workers had strict norms against discussing highly personal aspects of their own lives. Sexual harassment was defined as a violation of personal boundaries, not by how sexual a conversation was. In contrast, workers at the feminist magazine, *Womyn*, worked in something that was closer to what you find in an all-women's dorm: They expected one another to share personal aspects about their sexual lives. They wanted to analyze them through a feminist framework. These women defined sexual harassment as an abuse of power. Editors talked about being careful with the power that they had over interns, most of whom were college students. Workers at *Gentleman's Sophisticate* and at *Womyn* were using different workplace norms to define and to deal with sexual harassment.

For Your Consideration

How do you define sexual harassment? Do you think your definition would change if you worked two years at each of these magazines?

Or she can file a claim of sexual harassment—and run the risk of frustration, embarrassment, and retaliation at work. Victims have taken these risks, however, and they have gradually transformed the workplace. The landmark decision came in 1998. Three hundred women who worked at the Illinois plant of Mitsubishi Motors claimed that the company tolerated a hostile work environment. Some claimed fellow workers had groped them; others said their bosses threatened to fire them if they didn't agree to have sex. The women were awarded $34 million, an average of $113,000 each. The size of the award caught employers' attention nationwide, making them aware that tolerating sexual harassment can hurt the bottom line and bring the wrath of stockholders and upper management.

Racial–Ethnic Lines. When sexual harassment crosses racial–ethnic lines, victims are put at a special disadvantage. If they protest, they can be accused of being insensitive to cultural differences—perhaps they misunderstood what "normal" gender interaction is in another racial–ethnic group. Or they can be perceived as prejudiced—offended by the sexual offer because it was made by someone of a different race–ethnicity. The implication is that they would have welcomed the suggestion had it been made by someone of their own race–ethnicity.

Not Just a Woman's Problem. Sexual harassment used to be perceived as exclusively a woman's problem. But no longer. Men also find themselves victims, and men now file one of every six legal claims (Mattioli 2010). One man claimed that his chief financial officer—a woman—made sexual advances "almost daily." Another objected that his supervisor told him that she had dreamed about him naked. Men who make claims of sexual harassment often receive little sympathy. Some men don't understand why a man would take offense at sexual advances from a woman, even if she is his boss (Carton 1994; Mattioli 2010). They would be happy for a woman, boss or not, to "hit" on them. "Why not have some fun at work?" is their response. I anticipate that norms will change to catch up with women's growing power in the workplace.

In 1998, the Supreme Court broadened sexual harassment laws to include people of the same sex, and the law now covers the harassment of homosexuals by heterosexuals and of heterosexuals by homosexuals. As a sign of changing times, both heterosexual and homosexual men are filing claims against both heterosexual and homosexual bosses.

We now turn to discussing homosexuality.

Homosexuality

How many people identify themselves as homosexual? With changing norms, how much opposition is there to homosexuality today? To gain a broader context for understanding homosexuality, let's begin by looking at same-sex sexual relations in global perspective.

9.7 Contrast homosexual behavior and homosexuality, explain changing attitudes toward homosexuals and the conflict view of homosexuality, and discuss research on homosexuality.

Background: Getting the Larger Picture

Homosexual Behavior Versus Homosexuality. Attitudes toward **homosexual behavior**—sexual acts between people of the same sex—vary widely around the world. To many Americans, the customs of the Sambia and the Keraki of New Guinea are startling. The Sambia believe that boys will remain small and weak if they do not swallow a man's semen. To ensure that the boys develop into strong men, Sambian boys have oral sex with men of the tribe. The homosexual behavior of the Keraki occurs during their puberty rites, which are kept secret from females. At this time, older boys and the unmarried men have anal intercourse with the younger boys. Until these boys marry (a woman), at the puberty rites, they, too, have anal intercourse with the younger boys (Ford and Beach 1972). For both the Sambia and the Keraki, homosexual behaviors are considered a rite of passage to "masculinization." Both Sambian and Keraki boys go on to live heterosexual lives; they marry women and become fathers (Gilmore 1990). Note

Homosexuals continue to struggle for legal equality, with marriage the "hot-button" issue. They have adopted the rainbow flag as a symbol of unity.

that the Keraki and Sambian puberty rites are examples of *homosexual behavior*. They do not involve a homosexual identity.

In contrast to homosexual behavior is **homosexuality**—a sexual orientation involving an attraction to or preference for people of one's own sex. In no society is homosexuality the dominant norm. From a functionalist viewpoint, the primary reason for this is the family's role in human societies. To perpetuate the human group, adults are expected to become parents, and all societies build the family around some form of mother, father, and children. General homosexuality would upset this biologically based arrangement.

In the Thinking Critically box on the next page, we examine developments in biology that might eventually become a major influence in how people view homosexuality.

View on MySocLab **Figure:** Attitudes toward Homosexual Relations, 1973–2010

Attitudes in the United States. In recent years, Americans have grown more accepting of those who identify themselves as homosexual. But strong negative attitudes remain. The term **homophobia** was first used in an academic publication by psychologist Kenneth Smith (1971) and popularized by psychologist George Weinberg (1972). The meaning of the term has changed since then. It originally referred to fear of homosexuals, but its general meaning today is dislike or intolerance of homosexuals. The term **homophobe** is used to refer to a person who has such attitudes.

To get an overview of American attitudes toward homosexuals, look at Table 9.4 on page 298. What might strike you are the divisions that show up here. Most Americans (64 percent) think that homosexual relations between consenting adults should be legal, but a sizable number, one of three, think that homosexual relations—even between consenting adults—should be illegal. Because this research is from a well-chosen national sample, it allows us to generalize to the U.S. population. You can see that attitudes toward homosexual behavior follow social paths—the same that we've seen before: age, income, education, geography, and politics. The opinions expressed by blacks and whites on this topic are closer than on any other subject I have ever seen.

Legal Changes. The social institutions of U.S. society presume the norm of **heterosexuality**, a sexual orientation involving an attraction to or preference for people of the opposite sex. Some researchers refer to the presumption of heterosexuality in social life as *compulsive heterosexuality* (Sartore and Cunningham 2009). Until 1960, *all states* had laws that made even private, consensual sexual acts between adults of the same sex illegal.

Thinking Critically About Social Problems

Can Animals Be Gay? Same-Sex Sexual Behavior among Animals

Life is never as simple as it sometimes seems or as we would like it to be. Whether in everyday life or in science, something always comes along to complicate our neat classifications.

Two sexes? This is quite evident to everyone. But I recall when I was working as an orderly at Barnes Hospital in St. Louis, Missouri, the nurses saying that a hermaphrodite had been admitted as a patient. Following the curiosity that has driven me all my life, I took the opportunity to talk to the individual. While I was in his room, he asked me if I wanted to see both his sex organs. I did. I say "he" because this is how the individual self-identified, even though he had both a penis and a vagina.

A female pair at a Lysan albatross colony in Kaena Point, Hawaii.

Only heterosexual relations being part of the natural order? Many think this is self-evident, too. But not so fast. Over the years, biologists have observed same-sex sexual behavior among animals. Some bighorn rams, for example, mount one another. Some fruit flies do the same thing. And some female monkeys mount other female monkeys in the manner that male monkeys mount female monkeys.

If you've ever been around young male dogs, you might have noticed something similar: a young male dog attempting to mount another male dog, meeting resistance and giving up. Those same male dogs are so "horny," if that term applies, that they will mount (people call it "humping") a human leg. And the dogs don't care if it's the leg of a male or a female. This is always highly embarrassing to the dog's owner—and to the owner of the leg.

Same-sex sexual behavior among animals has perplexed biologists, who evaluate life from a Darwinian perspective. Same-sex sexual behavior should have died out because it would be nonreproductive for a species. Genes for this behavior, if they existed, should have been washed out of the species' gene pool.

Because same-sex sexual behavior in animals didn't make sense, biologists usually reported the observations as a sort of footnote to research. No one took them seriously.

Until now, that is.

Biologists are now studying this behavior. In Hawaii, Lindsay Young, who is studying the Laysan albatross, was confused when she saw two eggs in a single nest. Each female bird can lay only one egg a year, yet some nests held two eggs. With the nests too small for two eggs, one egg is discarded, and the two birds take turns sitting on the remaining egg. On a hunch, Young took blood samples of the birds in the nests that had held two eggs. It turned out that these pairs were always female. As Young expanded the testing, she found that about a third (31 percent) of all the pairs in this albatross colony are female.

The females in these pairs apparently get pregnant by inviting males to have sex with them. They then go back to their female partner, with whom, by the way, they never have sex. Each lays an egg, and one is discarded.

Homosexual behavior in animals? The biologists don't say this. They say that to use the term *homosexual* is anthropomorphic; that is, it attributes human characteristics to animals. (We tend to be anthropomorphic: The season changes and you stand in front of a mirror looking at yourself in your new swimsuit. Your dog is watching you, you'd swear, with a quizzical look on his face, thinking about how different you look in your swimsuit.) As the biologists report the behaviors they observe, they stress that we cannot draw conclusions about human sexual behavior from observations of animal sexual behavior.

You can be sure, though, that a lot of people will draw these conclusions. What the biologists have observed can be used by both those who favor and those who disfavor homosexuality. The one side will say, "Since some animals have sex with other animals of the same sex, homosexuality is inborn." Actually, the biologists don't claim that the same-sex sexual behaviors they observe are genetic. They point out that they might be an adaptation to the environment.

And those who disfavor homosexuality will say, "Just because a behavior exists among animals does not mean that it is desirable for humans." They will point out that the researchers of the albatross colony in Hawaii have also observed male albatrosses pinning female albatrosses to the ground and raping them. They have even observed gang rape, where the male birds seriously injured the female bird.

Based on Mooallem 2010.

For Your Consideration

You can see that doing research on same-sex sexual behavior among animals is a fascinating development in biology. You can also see that it can fuel the arguments of both those who favor and those who disfavor homosexuality. How do you think this new research should apply to understanding human sexual behavior?

TABLE 9.4 ▸ Attitudes toward the Legality of Homosexual Relations

Question: "Do you think gay or lesbian relations between consenting adults should or should not be legal?"

	Should Be Legal	**Should Not Be Legal**	**No Opinion/ Refused**
National	64%	32%	4%
Sex			
Male	62%	34%	4%
Female	65%	31%	4%
Race–Ethnicity[1]			
Black	67%	31%	2%
White	66%	30%	5%
Age			
18–29 years	81%	17%	1%
30–49 years	63%	34%	3%
50–64 years	64%	31%	5%
65 years and older	43%	49%	8%
Education			
High school or less	57%	39%	3%
Some college	69%	26%	5%
College graduate	64%	32%	4%
College postgraduate	73%	23%	5%
Income			
Under $20,000	49%	47%	5%
$20,000–$29,999	60%	39%	1%
$30,000–$49,999	61%	34%	6%
$50,000–$74,999	75%	23%	2%
$75,000 and over	73%	22%	5%
Region			
South	59%	37%	4%
Midwest	62%	31%	7%
West	71%	25%	3%
East	65%	32%	3%
Politics			
Republican	41%	52%	6%
Independent	73%	23%	4%
Democrat	75%	23%	2%

[1]Only these two groups are listed in the source.

Source: Sourcebook of Criminal Justice Statistics 2011:Table 2.99.

In 2003, Texas and eleven other states still had these laws on their books, but in that year the U.S. Supreme Court in *Lawrence et al. v. Texas* struck the laws down (Liptak 2005).

Watch on **MySocLab Video:** Michael Bailey: Being Gay in the U.S

Over the years, homosexuals have been the victims of violent acts because of their sexual orientation, but until 1990 there was no way of tracking the extent of their victimization. In that year, Congress passed the *Hate Crime Statistics Act*, and the FBI began to collect data on **hate crimes**. These are crimes such as assault or vandalism that are motivated by dislike or hatred of the victim's race, religion, ethnicity, sexual orientation, disability, or national origin. Each year, about 1,500 homosexuals are the victims of hate crimes. This compares to twenty-one heterosexuals who are victimized by homosexuals

(*Statistical Abstract* 2013:Table 328). Since not all victims file reports and not all police agencies report these data to the FBI, the actual numbers are higher.

Homosexuals face considerably less discrimination today than a decade or two ago. Supported by the American Civil Liberties Union, gay liberation groups have campaigned to repeal oppressive laws. The Civil Service Commission used to deny federal employment to homosexuals, but no longer. The *Employment Equality (Sexual Orientation) Regulations* of 2003 ban sexual discrimination in the workplace, and no longer do corporations like AT&T, GM, Ford, and IBM discriminate against homosexuals in hiring or promotion procedures.

The change has been gradual, but dramatic. An outstanding example is the Defense Department which used to discharge any soldier who was discovered to be homosexual. Then came a transitional period. For 18 years, from 1993 to 2011, the military followed a "Don't Ask, Don't Tell" policy, which meant that soldiers could serve in the military as long as they kept their homosexuality a secret. They now can be both open about their sexual orientation and serve in the military (Whitlock 2011).

In order to better understand homosexual–heterosexual relations, let's use the lens of conflict theory.

Homosexuality Viewed Theoretically: Applying Conflict Theory

Homosexuals have found politics a useful tool to forge social change and overcome discrimination. *Coming out of the closet*—publicly asserting a homosexual identity—they marched in public demonstrations and campaigned for legal reform. Beginning with local campaigns in San Francisco and New York to demand equality and basic human rights, homosexuals expanded their campaigns and made an impact on national politics. As a result, politicians now study homosexual voting patterns in an effort to win votes.

Over the past couple of decades, homosexual rights have become a prominent social issue. The promotion of the acceptance of homosexuality as an alternative lifestyle has generated intense opposition, especially from those heterosexuals who view homosexuality as immoral. Because some of the opposition is rooted in deeply held religious beliefs, as is the controversy over abortion, the demand for acceptance will continue to be resisted. Gradually, however, attitudes and legislation are changing.

Beginning in 2001, several countries, including the Netherlands, Belgium, Canada, Spain, Norway, South Africa, and Sweden, began to recognize same-sex marriage. In the United States, in contrast, same-sex marriage became the flashpoint for opposing positions. From Table 9.5, you can see how Americans split on this issue. Women are considerably more likely

TABLE 9.5 ▸ Attitudes Toward the Legality of Same-Sex Marriage

Question: "Do you favor or oppose allowing gay and lesbian couples to marry legally?"

	Favor	Oppose	Don't Know
Overall Sex	47%	44%	9%
Men	43%	47%	9%
Women	51%	40%	8%
Race–Ethnicity			
Latino	50%	39%	11%
White	48%	44%	8%
African American	39%	51%	10%
Age			
18–29	64%	30%	6%
30–49	50%	42%	8%
50–64	42%	48%	10%
65+	31%	56%	12%
Education			
College graduate	59%	34%	7%
Some college	49%	42%	9%
High School or less	39%	52%	9%
Region			
West	52%	39%	9%
Northeast	59%	33%	8%
Midwest	48%	43%	9%
South	39%	52%	9%
Family Income			
Less than $30,000	45%	46%	9%
$30,000 to $49,999	44%	48%	8%
$50,000 to $74,999	51%	43%	7%
$75,000 to $99,999	54%	38%	8%
$100,000 and over	58%	35%	7%

Source: Pew Research 2012.

The issue of same-sex marriage has ignited controversy across the United States.

to favor same-sex marriage, as are the younger and more educated. You can also see large gaps by race–ethnicity and region.

Several states, including Connecticut, Massachusetts, and Vermont, granted homosexuals the right to marry. California's response illustrates the polarizing nature of this issue. After its supreme court approved same-sex marriage, California voters passed *Proposition 8*, an amendment to the state constitution that limits marriage to a man and a woman. As I write this, the constitutionality of *Proposition 8* is being considered by the U.S. Supreme Court. Its decision could be limited to California, or it could be sweeping and apply to the 50 states. One possible outcome is that all laws that prohibit same-sex marriages will be declared unconstitutional.

Some states hit upon a compromise. Instead of legalizing same-sex marriages, they offer civil unions or domestic partnerships. Homosexuals were pleased to have some legal recognition of their partnerships, but they pointed out that civil unions aren't the same as marriage. Legal rights, such as making medical decisions for a partner in a coma, are recognized only in the states that offer civil unions. Fearing that civil unions might expand into legal marriage or that their state's supreme court might rule same-sex marriage constitutional, voters in 26 states passed constitutional amendments limiting marriage to one man and one woman. Congress passed a similar law, *The Defense of Marriage Act of 1996*, denying federal benefits to married people of the same sex ("Same-Sex Marriage . . ." 2010). The overarching final decision is not in, but the contradictions beg to be resolved.

What homosexuals want is full legal rights in all areas, including legal marriage in all states and marriage that is recognized by the federal government. Having tasted partial victory, they are not about to stop their struggle until they attain not just the right to marry but equal rights in housing and employment, including the right to work in all occupations, including grade-school teaching, with open homosexual identities. As you can see, with opposing sides holding down firm lines, the controversy will not end soon.

Research on Homosexuality

Let's review three major studies on homosexuality and then research on homosexual behavior in prison.

The Kinsey Research. Alfred Kinsey and his associates included homosexual behavior in their 1948 path-breaking study, *Sexual Behavior in the Human Male*. To understand the Kinsey findings, keep in mind the distinction between homosexual behavior and homosexuality. Based on case histories of about 5,300 males, Kinsey found that 37 percent of men in the United States had at least one sexual experience with a same-sex partner that resulted in orgasm. Such experiences, however, did not translate into homosexuality. As Kinsey pointed out, most of these homosexual behaviors were a form of experimentation, and almost all of these males went on to live heterosexual lives. Kinsey concluded that about 4 percent of American males are exclusively homosexual.

Kinsey's findings unleashed a storm of criticism. The primary problem was that Kinsey's sample was biased, and there was no scientific way to generalize from his findings. Kinsey had recruited some subjects from prisons and reform schools, men who obviously did not represent the general population. He also interviewed only lower-class white males (Himmelhoch and Fava 1955). Researchers no longer trust Kinsey's findings, although an occasional uninformed writer will quote Kinsey as though what he found had something to do with people other than those in his sample.

The Laumann Research. In contrast, a team of researchers headed by sociologist Edward Laumann (1994) has done reliable research on sexual behavior in the United States. Because Laumann interviewed a representative sample of the U.S. population, we can generalize his findings to the entire U.S. population. As you can see from Figure 9.7, Laumann found that during the preceding 5 years, 2.2 percent of women and 4.1 percent of men in the United States had sex with a same-sex partner. When the time period is extended to include all the years of their lives, these totals increase to 3.8 percent for women and 7.1 percent for men. This is a far cry from Kinsey's 37 percent for men.

As Figure 9.7 also shows, 1.4 percent of U.S. women and 2.8 percent of U.S. men identify themselves as homosexuals. These percentages are almost identical to those who reported that they had sex with a same-sex partner during the preceding year (1.3 percent of women and 2.7 percent of men). These figures may be slightly high, as the Laumann researchers included bisexuals in the homosexual data.

In the Spotlight on Social Research on page 53, Laumann explains why he did his research and the opposition he experienced.

As you might recall from Chapter 2, sociologists do quantitative and qualitative research. Laumann did quantitative research, using a sampling technique so good that it allows us to generalize his findings to the broader U.S. population. Sociologists who do qualitative research, in contrast, focus on the smaller picture, helping us understand people's perspectives and motivations. As we learn how people construct their worlds, we have a better understanding of how and why they make their decisions. Let's turn to qualitative research.

The Humphreys Research. To collect data on homosexual behavior, sociologist Laud Humphreys, then a graduate student in sociology, devised an ingenious but widely criticized research method. Humphreys knew that some men have impersonal sex in public restrooms, meeting places they call "tearooms." He began hanging around

FIGURE 9.7 ▸ Homosexual Identity and Having Sex with Someone of the Same Sex

Percentage of Americans	Male	Female
Identifies self as either a homosexual or a bisexual	2.8	1.4
Had sex with someone of the same sex during the past year	2.7	1.3
Had sex with someone of the same sex during the past 5 years	4.1	2.2
Had sex with someone of the same sex at any time since puberty*	7.1	3.8

*Note: Another form of this question yielded 4.3 percent for women and 9.1 percent for men.

Source: Laumann et al. 1994:293–296.

these restrooms, taking the role of "watch queen," the one who warns participants when strangers approach the restroom. Humphreys (1970/1975) recorded how the men used a system of gestures to initiate sex at the urinal and then moved to a toilet stall for fellatio (oral sex). The sex was quick and anonymous, usually occurring without the exchange of a single word.

Humphreys also noticed that many of the men he observed having tearoom sex wore wedding rings, and he wanted to know why these married men engaged in homosexual acts. He decided to interview them, but he knew that they would run from a researcher. The men parked nearby, and Humphreys wrote down their license plate numbers. Using a contact in the police department, he traced their home addresses. With the cooperation of his professors, who were conducting a health survey, he had these men added to their sample. Humphreys then interviewed the men in their homes, supposedly for the purpose of the medical research, but really to get background information on the tearoom participants. For this deception, Humphreys found himself criticized severely by both sociologists and the public. He also came close to having his Ph.D. revoked.

Humphreys learned that 38 percent of the tearoom participants he observed were married men who identified themselves as heterosexuals. In the interviews, the men reported that their wives often refused to have sex. Humphreys concluded that unlike an affair with a woman, having quick, anonymous sex in a tearoom did not threaten the men's emotional attachment to their wives or present a threat to their families. Tearoom sex was like stopping at a convenience store on the way home from work, except that this stop was for free oral sex. In essence, the tearoom functioned as a free house of prostitution, a place where the men could obtain quick oral sex with no emotional entanglement. Sociologists Jay Corzine and Richard Kirby (1977) discovered similar homosexual behavior at truck stops: Heterosexual truckers have sex with homosexuals who search out partners at highway rest areas.

This research underscores the distinction that sociologists make between *homosexual behavior* and *homosexuality*. Homosexual behavior characterized the married men who visited the tea rooms for quick sex, while homosexuality was the orientation of the men in the tea rooms who gave the sex.

Homosexual Behavior in Prison. In certain places, such as prisons and boarding schools, **situational homosexual behavior** is common. This term refers to homosexual acts of people who, if members of the opposite sex were available, would choose to have sex with them. To better understand situational homosexual behavior, let's look at a study of inmates in the state prison at Soledad, California.

The text distinguishes between homosexuality and situational homosexual behavior. Can you explain why the "queen" in prison does not engage in situational homosexual behavior?

Sociologist George Kirkham (1971) found that the prisoners identified themselves and one another as "queens," "punks," and "wolves." The men used the label "queens" to refer to inmates who prefer male sexual partners. The queens do not engage in situational homosexual behavior, for, in prison or out, they prefer male partners. Kirkham found that to attract fellow prisoners, the queens exaggerate aspects of female sexuality. They adopt feminine nicknames ("Peaches," "Dee-Dee"), tear the back pockets off of tight prison denims to make them more form-fitting, use cosmetics made from medical and food supplies, and wear jewelry produced in hobby shops. The queens lets their hair grow as long as the guards will allow and show an exaggerated "swish" as they walk.

When the heterosexual men first enter the prison, they have no interest in the queens. As months pass, however, and as the femininity of the queens evoke their memory and longing for women, some heterosexual men have sex with them. Some even enter into long-term relationships with queens, establishing relationships that resemble a marriage, with the expectation of sexual fidelity. These relationships are brittle, though, for most queens are promiscuous. Some queens are also forced into prostitution by prison pimps.

A second sexual identity the prisoners use is "punk." A punk has low social status, ranking just above the "rat," or squealer. There are two types of punks: "canteen punks" who exchange sex for candy, cigarettes, or personal favors, and "pressure punks" who give sex to other men because of beatings or the threat of violence. Punks are despised by other prisoners because they sacrifice their manhood, either to obtain goods and services or out of fear and weakness.

How do prisoners become pressure punks? Some are beaten and gang-raped and then forced into this status for the rest of their prison term. Others are tricked into it. Some new inmates, unacquainted with prison ways, are victims of rigged gambling games. Others accept cigarettes or money from experienced inmates. If they can't pay the debt when the other inmates demand it, they are told they can give sex as payment. At this point, the individual has only two choices—to submit or fight. A man who submits is marked as a punk from then on and forced to continue to provide sex for the rest of his prison term.

In some prisons, gangs "claim" any man who is identified as homosexual. They gang rape him and turn him into a sex slave for his entire prison term. They also "rent" him out or "sell" him if they want to. In some prisons, gangs divide up the men they identify as homosexuals. If one gang has a sex slave and another does not, when the next person they identify as a homosexual is admitted to the prison, the gang without a sex slave claims that individual (Liptak 2004).

The third sexual identity is the "wolf." Although the wolf has sex with punks, he does not lose his status as a "man." In order to remain a "man" and still engage in sex with other men, he presents an image of exaggerated masculinity or toughness. Because force and rape match the machismo image that prisoners hold, the violence that surrounds the wolf's sexual acts allow him to be viewed as masculine. The wolf must also keep his sexual acts emotionless and impersonal. Some wolves "own" punks and prostitute them for cigarettes, drugs, or other favors.

Situational homosexual behavior, whether in prison or in tearooms, helps us understand how some heterosexuals participate in homosexual acts and yet maintain a heterosexual identity.

The Emergence of Prison Rape as a Social Problem. It took decades of agitation by concerned former prisoners and officials for prison rape to emerge as a social problem. Preventing the subjective concerns that were needed to change prison rape from an objective condition to a social problem was the common feeling that men in prison were "bad" people who deserved whatever punishment they received. After public hearings, in 2003 the federal *Prison Rape Elimination Act* was passed. The transformation of prison rape into a social problem is not yet complete, however. Evidence of this is that jokes about prison rape remain common, even on popular TV programs. To see what I mean, suppose that those same comedians were to joke about men raping women. The outcry would be deafening. In contrast, jokes about prison rape remain a topic of humor met with laughter.

Sexual Orientation as a Social Problem

Watch on **MySocLab** **Video:** Sexual Orientation

As I have stressed throughout this text, for a social problem to exist, we need both objective conditions and subjective concerns. There must be a large number of people who are upset by some objective conditions and agitate to change them. Following this definition, when homosexuals quietly accepted the objective conditions that made them second-class citizens, we had personal problems. There was no social problem even though there were many objective conditions—the vast discrimination—from being rejected for home ownership to being dishonorably discharged from the military, from being fired at work to being bullied at school. When large numbers of homosexuals came out of the closet and began to protest these objective conditions, however, we had the subjective concerns necessary for a social problem.

Just as you saw that this analysis applies to prison rape, so it applies to people whose sexual orientation differs from the majority. It is not just gays and lesbians who now openly object to their status in society and who no longer quietly accept the discrimination. Among others also protesting and demanding change are **transgender persons** (those whose internal gender identity does not match the gender role that society has assigned them based on their sex organs) and **bisexuals** (those who are sexually attracted to both men and women). The concepts of objective conditions and social concerns, then, can be valuable tools for your understanding of the changes that are occurring in society. If you observe events closely, you will be able to see social problems emerging.

Violence Against Women

9.8 Apply the feminist/conflict and symbolic interactionist perspectives to gendered violence.

As our final topic, let's look at gendered violence.

Gendered Violence: Rape, Murder, and Abuse in the Family

Read on **MySocLab Document:** Is Violence Against Women About Women or About Violence?

Fears of rape and murder surround girls and women in this society. They are aware that they can be attacked while on a routine errand or on the way to school. We have already discussed rape and murder in Chapter 5, and there is no need to go beyond that chapter's materials. We need to stress one of the main points of that chapter, though: Women tend to be the victims, men the rapists and killers.

In the family, too, females are also disproportionately the victims of abuse, whether incest or battering by a spouse. These are topics we will review in Chapter 11, so it is sufficient to just mention them in this context. Earlier in this chapter (pages 272–273), we discussed female circumcision as a form of violence against women.

Another form of violence, one alien to Western culture, is "honor killing." In some societies, such as Pakistan, Jordan, and Kurdistan, a woman who is thought to have brought disgrace to her family is killed by a male relative—usually a brother or her husband, but sometimes her father or uncle. What threat to the family's honor can be so severe that the men kill a daughter, wife, or sister? The usual reason is sex outside of marriage. Even a woman who has been raped is in danger of becoming the victim of an honor killing (Falkenberg 2008; Yardley 2010). Killing the girl or woman removes the "stain" she has brought to the family and restores its honor in the community. Sharing this view, the police in these countries generally ignore honor killings, viewing them as private family matters.

Applying the Feminist/Conflict Perspective

To explain why girls and women are so often the victims of violence at the hands of men, some sociologists use conflict or feminist theory. They stress that we need to view violence against women as a form of power and control. Some men use violence to maintain their dominance, control, or authority over their wives and children. Violence is a way of keeping these less powerful family members "in line."

Applying Symbolic Interactionism

Sociologists also use symbolic interactionism to understand gendered violence. Strength and virility are held out as goals for boys to achieve. Both boys and girls are surrounded by men in positions of power. As they see men dominate society, they learn to associate power, dominance, strength, virility, and superiority with masculinity (Scully 1990). Weakness becomes equated with femininity, dominance and power with masculinity. As boys and men come to judge themselves in these terms, violence becomes one way to express dominance and power.

The models of violence that surround boys also encourage them to be violent. Of the many examples that we could select, let's highlight video games, whose themes are often sexist, violent, and sexually explicit. In many of these games, the goal is to hunt down and kill enemies. In some games, those to be hunted down and killed are robots and monsters, in others men, and in still others barely clad young women. Although the form may change over time, symbols of violence continue to be a constant feature of the male world.

Social Policy

9.9 Compare middle-of-the-road social policies with those appropriate to the radical and conservative extremists.

As we have seen with other social problems, social policy can be effective in reducing inequality. Let's turn to an overview of social policy as it applies to inequalities of gender and sexual orientation.

As you know, people want social policies that match their assumptions of what is right, or of how things in life should be. But in our large, diverse society, people come from many backgrounds. Holding vastly contrasting views, they prefer vastly contrasting social policies. Any proposal for social policy that I make, then, will land in the midst of controversy. No matter what the proposal is, it will violate someone's views of what is right or wrong, desirable or undesirable. As we consider social policy for reducing sex discrimination, we will examine a wide spectrum of views. You will see what I mean as we look at the *radical extremists* and *conservative extremists*, terms I have developed from the views of individuals, groups, and organizations that stand on opposing sides of issues that center on gender and sexual orientation.

The Radical Extremists

Discrimination is so rooted in society, say the *radical extremists*, that the only way to get rid of it is to restructure society. As sociologist Jessie Bernard (1971) stressed, it is not enough to demand equal pay, to break the glass ceiling, or to reduce gender hostilities. These are only surface manifestations of the social roots of sexism. What we need, Bernard claimed, are social policies that eradicate these roots.

Because the roots of sexism reach back into childhood socialization, to succeed we would need to remove distinctions between boys and girls. Girls and boys would have to be socialized in the same way. They would have to be treated equally in the family and throughout their education, from preschool to graduate school. This would include gym, sports, and sexual orientation. Husbands and wives would have to share housework equally, and both parents would have to compete equally in the world of work. Ultimately, men and women would hold all positions in our social institutions equally (Bernard 1971).

Such extreme social policies are not plausible in our society—unless we have a dictator to enforce them. These goals are not likely to ever be achieved.

The Conservative Extremists

The social policies preferred by the *conservative extremists* are remarkably different. They believe that gender distinctions of boys and girls and men and women are not only natural, but also that they ought to be encouraged. They argue that a woman's natural and proper role is that of a homemaking wife and mother. A man's natural and proper role is that of a breadwinning husband and father. Social policy should support these basic gender distinctions. They should encourage girls to become full-time wives and mothers and boys to be the protectors and primary source of financial support of their wives and children. For example, children's picture books and school texts should present women and men in these traditional roles. Tax breaks should go to full-time homemakers, and job preference should be given to men who are supporting dependents.

Again, absent a dictator, these social policies are not plausible in our diverse society. These goals, too, are not likely to ever be achieved.

Middle-of-the-Road Policies

Innumerable positions fall between these two extremes. It is likely that some of the more middle-of-the-road policies reflect your views and the causes you support: policies that promote the end of the gender pay gap, the right for both mother and father to take extended leaves from work when a child is born or sick, protection of sexual minorities from discrimination, tough enforcement of child support awards, and, at home, more child care by fathers and more equitable distribution of housework.

The Future of the Problem

9.10 Discuss the likely future of gender discrimination.

Although gender discrimination is likely to remain a fact of life, historical trends point toward growing equality between women and men of all sexual orientations. The future will bring more attempts to break stereotypes, to eliminate the gender gap in pay, and to gain for people of any gender orientation greater access to leadership and authority, whether in business and politics or any other area of social life. The change is likely to be gradual, but as time passes also likely to be significant.

Homosexuality and the Future

At the center of controversy over social policy about homosexuality lie two primary issues. The first is the political struggle by homosexuals to be allowed legal marriage. This issue is likely to be decided by the U.S. Supreme Court, perhaps shortly after this book goes to press. Although it will appear to be decided according to the U.S. Constitution, the deciding factor will not be the Constitution, but, rather, the political orientations and personal biases of the justices who make up the Court.

The second issue centers on homosexuals serving as role models—for them to be openly homosexual and to occupy positions that mold the orientations of youth, such as public school teachers and scout leaders. Like legal marriage, this issue also provokes high disagreement between those who favor homosexual rights and those who disapprove of homosexuality. The vast middle ground is likely to be occupied by those who believe that homosexuality should be discouraged but that discrimination of homosexuals is wrong. Although tensions run high, granted current trends it is likely that this issue will be decided in favor of greater freedom of social participation by people with homosexual orientations.

The World of Work: "At Work" and at Home

The most significant social trend that will affect gender relations is the employment of women. As women continue to gain in education and as more women join the paid workforce, power relationships between women and men at work will continue to shift toward greater equality. We will see remarkable changes in this area. This includes the world of politics—and a soon-to-be female president.

Listen on MySocLab Audio: NPR: Women's Pay Disparity a Growing Campaign Issue

Equal pay will remain an issue. Reaching this goal certainly will not happen overnight, but it is likely that we will gradually inch toward it. We can expect women to make greater use of the Equal Pay Act of 1963 (forbidding discrimination in salaries), Title VII of the Civil Rights Act of 1964 (forbidding discrimination on the basis of sex), and the Fourteenth Amendment (forbidding a state to "deny any person within its jurisdiction the equal protection of the laws"). Such legal pressures will not eliminate the problem, but they will continue to undermine the remaining sexist structure of work.

As more women earn paychecks and as the size of those paychecks increases, relations between husbands and wives will continue to shift. Wives who work outside the home make more family decisions than wives who work only at home, and the future will bring more family power to women. We will also see husbands take on greater responsibilities for housework and children.

This takes us to a thorny question, that of what equality of housework and child care means. We will never have equality in the sense of husbands and wives working an equal number of hours per week at each task. Such a rigid view of equality does not match the way people live their lives. All tasks involve personal preferences and practical matters, which individual wives and husbands will decide for themselves. Ultimately, what one couple determines to be equality, another couple will see as inequality. This issue will always remain. The trend is toward greater participation by wives and husbands in areas that have traditionally been seen as the proper area of one sex or another. This trend will continue.

Changing Gender Stereotypes and Orientations

The increasing numbers of women in the workforce are already changing gender stereotypes, a change that will continue. Children who see both mother and father bringing home paychecks take it for granted that a man is not the exclusive breadwinner and that a woman is more than a housewife or homemaker. They grow up with a mother who more fully participates in family decisions, and not infrequently is the primary decision maker. As gendered roles that push us into activities dictated by our culture bend, stereotypes will break, and we will see fundamental change in both self-perception and in gender relationships.

One consequence of changing gender roles will be that both men and women will be freed to do activities compatible with their preferences as *individuals*—not because an activity matches a stereotype that they must live up to. As activities become more gender-neutral, men and women will develop a new consciousness of who they are and of their potential in life. This will free men to play more supportive roles and "get more in touch with their feelings," while it will free women to take more leadership roles and become more assertive. As sociologist Janet Giele (1978) said, the ultimate possibility for the future is a new concept of the human personality. We must await the unfolding of the future to reveal what such "greater wholeness" of men and women looks like, but it is on the way.

Watch on **MySocLab** **Video:** Changing Gender Roles at Home

MySocLab  Study and Review on **MySocLab**

Summary and Review

1. Although there are more females than males in the world, around the globe men discriminate against women. Consequently, sociologists refer to men as a dominant group and women as a minority group.
2. Every society *sex-types* occupations; that is, in each society some work is considered suitable for men and other work appropriate for women. There is no inherent biological connection between work and its assignment to women or men, for "women's work" of one society may be "men's work" in another. In all societies, "men's work" is given greater prestige than "women's work."
3. Symbolic interactionists examine *gender* (masculinity and femininity), looking at how each society socializes the sexes into its ideas of what men and women ought to be like. Socialization includes learning *sexism*, the belief that one *sex* is innately superior to the other and the discriminatory practices that result from this belief.
4. Functionalists theorize that sexual discrimination is based on the need of early human groups to engage in hand-to-hand combat. Men had the physical advantage but needed to be motivated to become warriors. Women, offered as inducements for men

to fight, were assigned the drudge work of society. A second functionalist explanation is that because women were encumbered physically through childbearing and nursing, men became dominant as they took control of warfare and trade.

5. Conflict theorists emphasize that the rights that U.S. women enjoy came out of a power struggle with men. The confrontations between the sexes in the late 1800s and early 1900s have been replaced by legal pressure and economic and educational competition.
6. With the difficulty of separating nature and nurture, we do not know the extent of natural differences between the sexes. Both genetics and socialization can explain females' earlier proficiency in verbal skills and males' greater aggressiveness and abilities at mathematics.
7. Women confront discrimination in most areas of life, including a belittling attitude from men. Although women outnumber men as voters, men dominate politics; women tend to see politics as incompatible with femininity and motherhood.
8. A gender gap in pay exists at all educational levels. Over a lifetime, the cost to the average woman who graduates from college is over $1 million. *Sexual harassment* at work affects primarily women, but both heterosexual and homosexual men are also victims.
9. In applying conflict theory to *homosexuality*, we see that fundamental tensions exist between homosexuals and heterosexuals and that their adjustment to one another is uneasy.
10. Social policies to deal with inequalities of gender and sexual orientation are controversial because they represent contrasting and incompatible ideas of what is right.
11. In the future, even larger numbers of women will be employed outside the home. This will continue to change power relationships at home and at work and break down traditional stereotypes. The direction of the future is toward greater equality between the sexes, but the emergent outcome of personality and preferences remains to be seen.

Key Terms

bisexuals, 304
female infanticide, 266
gender, 269
gender roles, 269
glass ceiling, 275
hate crimes, 298
heterosexuality, 296
homophobe, 296
homophobia, 296
homosexual behavior, 295
homosexuality, 296
labor force participation rate, 290
master trait, 269
patriarchal society, 271
sex-typed, 267
sex, 269
sexism, 267
sexual harassment, 292
situational homosexual behavior, 302
suffragists, 274
testosterone, 278
transgender persons, 278

Thinking Critically About Chapter 9

1. List three examples of sexism in the United States. In what ways do you think that your list would be different if you had written it 10 years ago? In what ways do you think it would be different if you were to write it 10 years from now?
2. Which of the three theoretical perspectives (symbolic interactionism, functionalism, or conflict theory) do you think best explains gender discrimination in the United States? Why?
3. What are the main changes that you see occurring in gender roles? Why do you think we are experiencing these changes?

10 Medical Care: Physical and Mental Illness

Listen to Chapter 10 on **MySocLab**

Learning Objectives. After reading this chapter, you should be able to:

10.1 Explain what is *social* about illness. Include lifestyle, iatrogenesis, changing ideas, and the environment. **(p. 310)**

10.2 Explain why the social organization of medicine is part of a social problem. **(p. 313)**

10.3 Summarize some of the aspects of physical illness that make it a social problem. **(p. 317)**

10.4 Summarize some of the aspects of mental illness that make it a social problem. **(p. 321)**

10.5 Discuss the perspectives that emerge when you apply symbolic interactionism, functionalism, and conflict theory to health, illness, and the practice of medicine. **(p. 323)**

10.6 Summarize changes in health problems and infectious diseases, the relationship of the environment and disease, and social inequalities in physical and mental illness. **(p. 328)**

10.7 Summarize social policy regarding medical care. **(p. 336)**

10.8 Discuss the likely future of medical care as a social problem. **(p. 343)**

To prepare for the birth of their first child, Kathie Persall and her husband, Hank, read books and articles about childbirth and took childbirth classes together. At 5 o'clock one morning, as Kathie woke from a fitful sleep, the protective "bag of waters" that surrounded her fetus broke.

By 10:00 A.M., Kathie was on the maternity ward, hooked up to an electronic fetal monitor and an intravenous feeding tube. She was informed of the hospital's rule that to prevent infection, delivery must take place within 24 hours after the waters break. At 11:00 A.M., the resident physician (not her own doctor) said that they would speed up Kathie's labor by using Pitocin, a powerful drug.

The nurse wiggled the bottle, and a large dose of Pitocin sped through Kathie's veins. Kathie writhed in pain as a massive contraction took over her body.

Kathie's sister, Carol, knew that inducing labor could lead to cesarean section. She urged Hank to get Kathie off Pitocin, but Kathie and Hank felt that they couldn't tell the doctor what to do. By evening, the doctor decided that Kathie's cervix wasn't dilating rapidly enough and he increased the Pitocin. A nurse, thinking that the flow of Pitocin looked blocked, wiggled the bottle. A large dose sped through Kathie's veins. Kathie writhed in pain as a massive contraction took over her body. The fetal monitor set off an alarm, indicating that the baby's heartbeat had dropped from 160 to 40 beats per minute. The doctor rushed in, cut off the Pitocin, and gave Kathie another drug to stop the contraction. He told Kathie and Hank that a cesarean might be necessary. Hank, who had been trying to comfort Kathie, protested. The doctor told them that they needed to sign a consent form, that they could face an emergency at any time. On the form, Hank and Kathie read a long list of things that could go wrong. They didn't want to sign the form, but how could they resist? Kathie was in pain and exhausted.

At midnight, the doctor told Kathie that a cesarean was necessary because she had dilated only 5 centimeters in 13 hours of labor. At 1:10 A.M., Kathie went into surgery. When the baby was born, Kathie was vomiting so severely from the anesthetic that she could not even look at her new son. It took Kathie 7 weeks to recover physically from the cesarean surgery. She was left with a disfiguring scar, but this was nothing compared with her anger at the doctors, the hospital, and the medical procedures that had created the need for surgery, denying her and her husband the kind of delivery they had looked forward to.

Earlier we focused on the twin problems of crime and the criminal justice system. As we consider medical care in this chapter, we again need to focus on twin problems, in this case, illness and the medical care system. Our focus will be on how *social* factors affect health.

The Problem in Sociological Perspective: The Social Nature of Health and Illness

10.1 Explain what is *social* about illness. Include lifestyle, iatrogenesis, changing ideas, and the environment.

Not Just Biology

Most of us think of illness in biological terms, but there are significant social components as well. In the extreme, what it means to be sick can differ from one culture to another. In a large, pluralistic society like ours, "sickness" and "health" can even differ from one group to another. This may seem strange—isn't a fever always a sign of illness? Not always. While some take a low-grade fever as a sign of illness, others dismiss it as "just a little temperature."

For insight on how culture can determine "sickness" and "health," see the photo to the right.

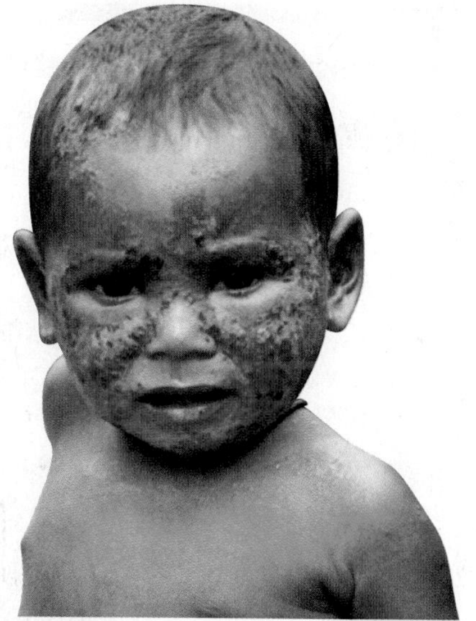

We define health and illness according to our culture. If almost everyone in a village had this skin disease, the villagers might consider it normal—and those without it the unhealthy ones. I photographed this infant in a jungle village in Orissa, India, so remote that it could be reached only by following a foot path.

Industrialization and Lifestyle. The social nature of health and illness becomes apparent when we consider industrialization and lifestyle. When the United States changed from a farming nation to one where people worked in factories and offices, heart disease became the number one killer. The reason? As industrialization brought higher incomes, people changed their lifestyle. They ate richer foods and weren't as physically active, which led to more heart attacks. As you know, the pursuit of pleasure is also often a cause of disease. Consider some consequences of unprotected sex—gonorrhea, herpes, syphilis, chlamydia, HIV, and ugly genital warts. Then, too, there are the many diseases that come from smoking, drinking, and doing drugs. The social causes of illness and disease, then, take us far beyond biology.

Iatrogenesis

> *I remember a doctor who presented a mistake so reckless and uncaring that I wanted to stand up and throttle him. I didn't have to. One of my colleagues doled out a much more appropriate punishment: He pulled a newspaper out of his pocket, and began reading the obituary of the recently-deceased patient. She was somebody's mother, she was somebody's daughter (Gupta 2012).*

This statement was made by a doctor who was upset about **iatrogenesis**, medical errors that harm patients. You saw a minor example in our opening vignette. When the nurse jiggled Kathie's bottle of Pitocin, the baby's heartbeat plummeted, and Kathie and the baby needed emergency care.

You might think that iatrogenesis would be rare. It is not. It is stunningly common—and in *many* instances fatal. Each year, about 100,000 Americans die needlessly at the hands of doctors and nurses (Gupta 2012). One in ten surgical patients dies from preventable medical errors (HealthGrades 2011). *If the number of Americans killed by medical errors were an official classification of death, it would rank as the 5th leading cause of death* (*Statistical Abstract* 2013:Table 124). In the Thinking Critically box on the next page, we examine medical incompetence, another aspect of iatrogenesis.

Changing Ideas About Health and Illness

Physicians' involvement in pregnancy also highlights the *social* nature of health and illness. Physicians have defined a natural process (pregnancy and birth) as a medical problem, one that requires fetal monitors, powerful drugs, and medical supervision. As in our opening vignette, many doctors define a woman as "ill" if she does not deliver a baby within 24 hours after her water breaks. This is an arbitrary definition of "illness." It has been imposed on a natural process in which some women deliver a baby an hour after their water breaks, but others not for 48 hours or longer.

That the meaning of "symptoms" can change is another indication of the social nature of "disease." Coal mining provides an excellent example. Longtime miners used to complain to doctors that they were short of breath and that they were coughing up blood. The doctors said that these weren't signs of a disease. They were things that "just happened" to coal workers. To get their definition accepted, the miners had to fight the medical profession. They did succeed, and the miners' struggle to get their disease recognized led to a new understanding of how the environment can cause illness (Smith 1987).

The "new" disease, coal workers' pneumoconiosis (CWP), turned out to be preventable. After safety measures were put into effect, this disease among coal miners dropped in half (Centers for Disease Control and Prevention 2008a).

Thinking Critically about Social Problems

How Incompetent Can a Doctor Be?

When ultrasound showed that one of the twins had defects, the woman asked her doctor to abort it. He removed the healthy fetus.

Another woman went into the hospital with a problem with her lungs. Her surgeon did a hysterectomy.

Tests showed that a man had a cancerous kidney. The surgeon removed the healthy one.

A man was supposed to have a circumcision. The surgeon removed both of his testicles.

Someone hung the scan backwards. The surgeon operated on the wrong side of the patent's brain.

And then there's the Oops! moment: In the midst of surgery, the doctor realized that he was removing the wrong leg. But it was too late. He had to complete the amputation.

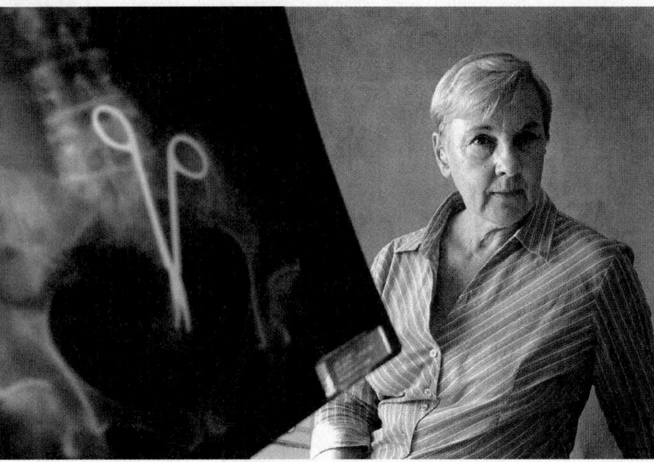

This woman complained of severe abdominal pain after her surgery. She was told that it was normal to feel such pain. After complaining for 18 months, the doctor took this X-ray.

No, I'm not making these up. These are actual cases (Steinhauer and Fessenden 2001; Seiden and Barach 2006; Childs 2007; Puzic 2010; Gupta 2012). There is also the woman who had the wrong foot amputated, the man who . . . In fact, some physicians operate on the wrong patient altogether. There are about 4,000 wrong-patient, wrong-side, or wrong-procedure surgeries a year in the United States (Senders and Kanzki 2008).

To prevent these mistakes, maybe surgeons should put a mark on the patient's body where the incision is to be made. Using indelible ink, both patient and doctor could sign their names at that spot. Before the surgeon makes an incision, he or she can check the signatures.

If this suggestion sounds ridiculous, you should know that I'm not being sarcastic. Mistakes are so flagrant that some hospitals actually do have the doctor and patient sign the coming surgical area on the patient's body.

I once had such confidence in the medical profession (the tough entrance requirements for medical school, the years of study, the supervision, and evaluations) that I didn't think there were incompetent doctors. Some weren't as good as others, to be sure, but not incompetent. Then on a postdoctoral fellowship I studied suicide in Missouri. As I pored over the coroner's records, I was awestruck when I saw a doctor's decision that a person who had been shot several times might have committed suicide. Later, I read about a father in Warren, Ohio, who was convinced that his 20-year-old daughter, who was found dead in a field, had not committed suicide. For 17 years, this man kept the case alive. As he doggedly pursued the issue, it eventually became apparent that the coroner had missed "obvious" clues—like "suspicious marks" on her neck. The woman's former boyfriend was charged with strangling her.

When this case became public, the sheriff investigated the coroner. Over the years, the coroner had made these strange decisions:

- Suicide—the man had been run over with a bulldozer and shot
- Suicide—an inmate was found hanged on his knees with toilet paper stuffed in his mouth
- Death by carbon monoxide from a lawn mower—the lawn mower didn't work
- Death by carbon monoxide—no carbon monoxide was found in the person's blood

This coroner had served as president of the Ohio State Medical Association three years before his exposure.

Makes you wonder, doesn't it?

Based on "Father's Persistence Pays Off" 1995; Steinhauer 2001; Steinhauer and Fessenden 2001; Associated Press 2010; Gupta 2012.

For Your Consideration

What system would you suggest to discover and remove incompetent medical students and practicing physicians?

Environment and Disease on a Global Level

Medical researchers continue to investigate how the environment affects disease. They look at how human activities reshape the environment, which, in turn, has profound effects on the diseases that humans experience. We explore this topic in the Global Glimpse box on the next page.

In Sum ▸ We usually think of illness and disease as biological matters. Biology is certainly involved, but what is considered health and illness is also a *social* matter. At one point in time, a physical condition such as pregnancy can be considered as a natural event, and at another time it can be considered a medical matter. What we consider to be the causes of health problems also goes beyond biology. Just as doctors once viewed "black lung problems" as "weakness" on the part of some coal miners, they now define this condition as a disease stemming from the miners' environment.

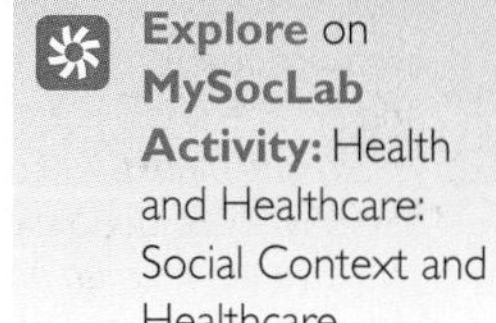

Explore on **MySocLab**
Activity: Health and Healthcare: Social Context and Healthcare

The Problem in Sociological Perspective: The Social Organization of Medicine

When we look at issues of health as social problems, we look not only at illness and disease but also at the *system* of health care. To make this clearer, let's consider medical costs, cesarean births, and the quality of medical care.

10.2 Explain why the social organization of medicine is part of a social problem.

An Explosion in Medical Costs

As most of us know, it can be expensive to visit a doctor, but it wasn't always this way. To see how little it used to cost to have a baby, look at this on page. The 1962 bill of $113.85 included a 3-day stay in the hospital for the mother, her anesthetic, lab fees, medicine, dressings, delivery room, nursery, her son's circumcision, and even his bracelet. Today, an uncomplicated vaginal delivery with a 3-day stay in the hospital runs about $8,287: $5,868 for the hospital, $785 for the anesthesiologist, and $1,634 for the attending physician (Health Blue Book 2012). A circumcision will cost an additional $300, almost triple the entire 1962 cost (Rabin 2011).

Figure 10.2 on page 315 provides another illustration of how medical costs have soared. In 1960, the nation's medical bill ran $28 billion. By 2012, the cost had exploded to $3 trillion, more than *100 times higher.* During this time, the cost of other goods increased eight times. If medical costs had increased at the same rate as average inflation and considering that the population had also increased by 75 percent, the nation's annual medical bill would run about $400 billion, just *one-seventh to one-eighth* of what it is now.

Why did the nation's medical bill explode? There are three primary reasons: First, there are more elderly people in our population. (The standard of living increased during this time, and people now live longer. Overall, the elderly need considerably more medical treatment than the younger.) A second reason is that we have a lot of new technology, which is expensive. The third reason is that we approach medical care as a commodity to be sold for profit. Let's look at this third reason.

FIGURE 10.1 ▸ **Hospital Bill for Childbirth, 1962**

Source: From the author's files. The individual wishes to remain anonymous, so the name has been redacted. Historical note: The bill says Mr. because at this time the husband was responsible for the payment.

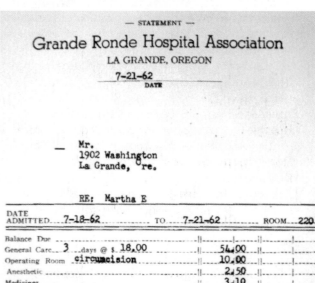

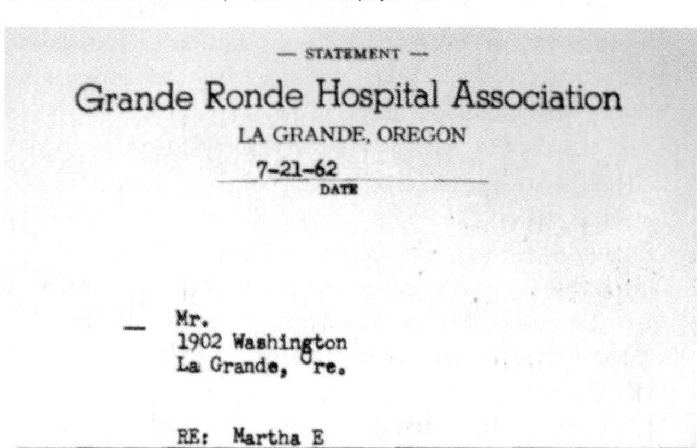

— STATEMENT —

Grande Ronde Hospital Association
LA GRANDE, OREGON

7-21-62
DATE

Mr.
1902 Washington
La Grande, Ore.

RE: Martha E

DATE ADMITTED 7-18-62 TO 7-21-62 ROOM 220

Balance Due	
General Care 3 days @ $ 18.00	54.00
Operating Room circumcision	10.00
Anesthetic	2.50
Medicines	3.10
Surgical Dressings	2.25
Delivery Room	20.00
Laboratory	3.00
X-Ray	
Oxygen	
Treatments	
Special Drugs	
Nursery	18.00
Bracelet	1.00
total	113.85

Accounts not paid when due are subject to interest charge.

A Global Glimpse

Solving Medical Mysteries: Cholera, Bats, and Ticks

Back in the 1800s, fear stalked the city of London. An outbreak of deadly cholera had hit the city. There was no cure, and no one knew where this silent killer would strike next. Londoners, healthy one day, were dead a day or two later. The disease hit men and women, the elderly and young. The public and authorities were alarmed, and London physicians were left perplexed. Nothing made sense.

John Snow, a physician, came up with a new idea. Taking a city map, he marked where each victim had lived. He saw that the marks were clustered around certain city wells. Snow speculated that some wells were contaminated and that if they were shut down, the epidemic could be halted. To find out, he removed the pump handle from one well in an area where 500 people had died in just the previous 10 days (Cooper 2002; Lloyd 2006). The cholera was stopped in its tracks, defeated not by medicine but by medical investigation.

Researchers are studying the relationship of disease and the environment. How does clearing the forests lead to humans getting diseases from bats?

You can see how tracking the *social* causes of disease can be significant for human health and why it is an essential aspect of medicine. Medical mysteries like the cholera epidemic of London reappear. For example, asthma has doubled among preschoolers in the United States. Also, many U.S. campers come down with Lyme disease, but a few years back they didn't. Surprising changes in disease also occur in other parts of the world. Malaysia has experienced the Nipah virus and an increase in malaria.

Let's look at these health problems and see how researchers are tracing their changing patterns to changes in the environment. Let's start with the Nipah virus.

In the 1990s, Malaysians cleared a lot of forests. At the same time, there were extensive forest fires in nearby Sumatra. In these forests lived the fruit bats, which carry the Nipah virus. With much of their natural habitat destroyed, the bats migrated. In their search for food, they moved closer to where humans lived, some even settling in backyard fruit trees. The Nipah virus also migrated—from the fruit bats to pigs and then to people.

Clearing the forests also brought an unexpected increase in malaria. The clearing left countless holes where the trees had been. When it rains, these holes filled with water, turning the holes into breeding grounds for malaria-carrying mosquitoes. The millions of plastic bags that people discard around the world are doing the same thing. Crumpled, they, too, collect water, becoming breeding sites for mosquitoes and contributing to an increase in malaria.

But why has asthma more than doubled among U.S. preschool children? It can't be because of clearing forests or discarding plastic bags. Researchers aren't positive yet, but they are narrowing the cause. The major suspect turns out to be diesel exhaust, emissions that both trigger asthma and magnify its problems (National Resources Defense Council 2002; Wargo et al. 2006).

And the increase in Lyme disease? Researchers are pointing to global warming. There are more ticks because the warmer earth provides a more hospitable environment. With more ticks, more humans are bitten, leading to an increase in Lyme disease. As global warming continues, the ticks that carry Lyme disease will migrate northward from the United States into Canada. Soon Canadian campers will also be at risk (Gatewood et al. 2009).

Medical researchers are trying to tease out more connections between human activities and disease. In Chapter 13, which focuses on the environment, I will be stressing that "everything is connected to everything else." The relationship between human activities, the environment, and disease is an example of this principle.

For Your Consideration

Have you ever had an illness that was related to the environment? Aren't all illnesses related to the environment in some way? So what's new about the information in this box?

FIGURE 10.2 ▸ **The Nation's Medical Bill: Soaring Costs**

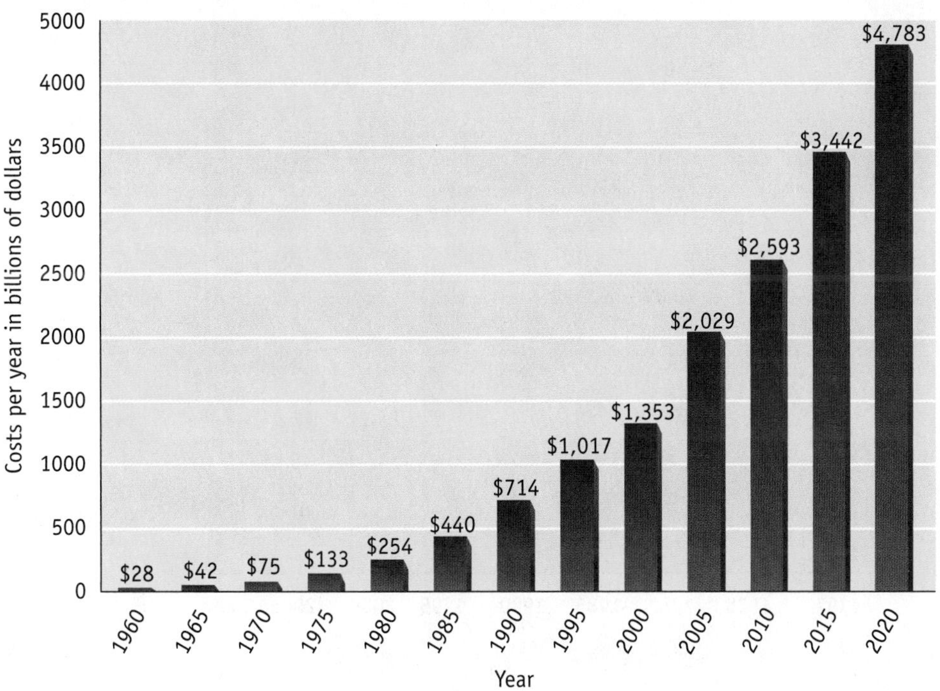

Note: The 2011 source projects costs to year 2019. I added the additional year's projection.

Source: By the author. Based on *Statistical Abstract of the United States* 2011:Table 130; 2013:Table 137.

Medicine for Profit: A Two-Tier System of Medical Care

Medicine for profit is also known as a *fee-for-service medical system*. Under this system, physicians are like mechanics and plumbers: They collect a fee for each service they perform. And like mechanics and plumbers, the more services they sell, the more money they make. In a fee-for-service system, health care is a commodity to be sold, not a citizen's right.

Our fee-for-service system has led to a **two-tier system of medical care:** one for those who can afford good insurance, and another for those who cannot. Because our society treats health care as a commodity to be sold to the highest bidder, our medical care ranges from the finest in the world at major universities to that provided by an underground network of unlicensed, foreign-trained physicians who can barely understand their patients.

Medicine for Profit: Cesarean Delivery

Kathie, in our opening vignette, had an expensive **cesarean section** (C-section), her baby delivered through abdominal surgery. Although a mistake by a nurse triggered events that made her surgery necessary, the extra profits that come from cesarean deliveries motivate many doctors to prefer this method of delivering babies. As shown in Figure 10.3 on the next page, in 1970 about one of nineteen babies was delivered by cesarean section; now the total is one of every three (33 percent).

Why the Increase in Cesarean Births? Do you think that women in the United States are becoming less healthy, so that more of them need this surgery?

I'm sure you know the answer—that today's women aren't less healthy than women in the past. Actually today's women are healthier. How do we know? The best single indicator of health is longevity, how long people live. And women are living longer today. If it isn't women's health, then the answer must have something to do with the medical system. This is apparent when we find that some hospitals have much higher

FIGURE 10.3 ▶ The Increase in Cesarean Births

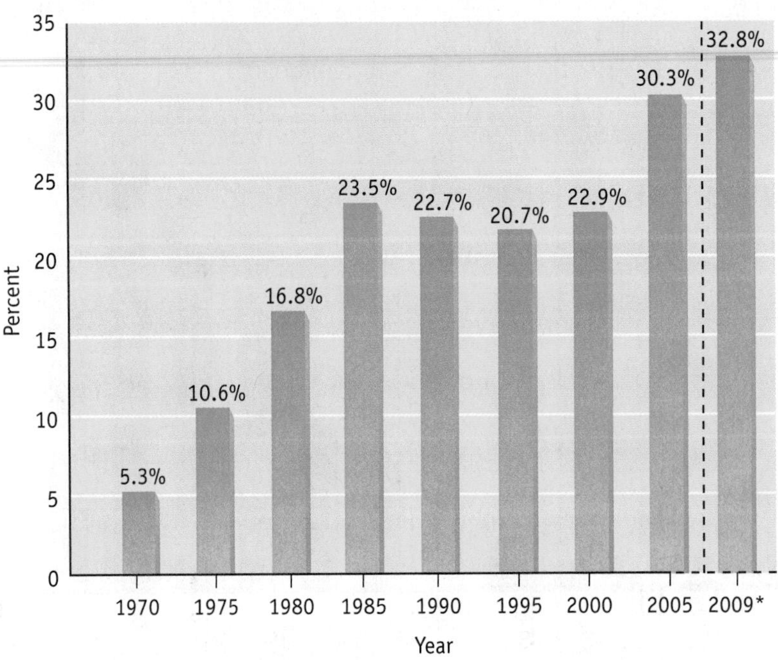

*Latest year available

Sources: By the author. Based on *Statistical Abstract of the United States* 1990:Tables 88, 89; 2013:Table 90.

rates of cesarean delivery than other hospitals. It is the same with states; some have lower rates, others higher rates (Menacker and Hamilton 2010; Martin et al. 2011).

Why have C-sections become common even though this type of delivery carries greater health risks for the mother: bleeding, blood clots, sterility, and death (Baldo 2008; Kuklina et al. 2009)? Compared with women who give birth vaginally, women who have cesarean births also have to stay in the hospital longer, and they are more likely to be rehospitalized after childbirth. Their new babies are also more likely to have breathing problems and to require intensive care (Menacker and Hamilton 2010; Rabin 2012). Finally, and many find this shocking: *Most cesarean deliveries are medically unnecessary*. Then why are one-third of U.S. births by C-section?

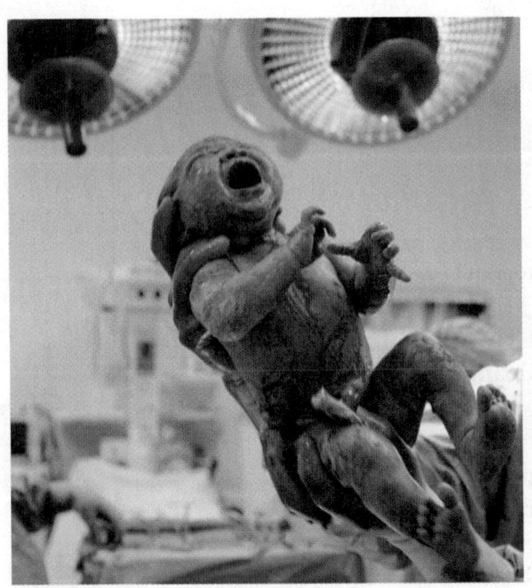

This baby has just been born by C-section. The text discusses the reasons that this medical procedure has become common.

Profit: The major reason for the increase in Cesarean births seems to be more income for obstetricians—doctors who specialize in childbirth. Being able to charge much more for cesarean births motivates them to recommend this surgery. Obstetricians' income has increased so much that, with the exception of other surgeons and anesthesiologists, it is higher than that of all other medical specialties (Bureau of Labor Statistics 2012).

Convenience: Another reason for this increase is that cesarean births *allow doctors to take control* of the delivery process. Instead of having to come into the delivery room at 3 A.M.—something no one likes to do—the doctor can decide when the baby will be born. *Both* convenience and higher profits motivate doctors to do more C-sections. Now that births are scheduled around the physician's preference, more births occur on Tuesday than on any other day of the week (Martin et al. 2011:Table 1-3).

Technology: Another reason is modern technology. Almost all U.S. women who give birth do so in a hospital, and almost all of these women are attached to a fetal monitor during their labor. The monitor sets off an alarm when the fetus is in distress, but many of these signals are false (Signore et al. 2009). With no standard way of interpreting the distress signals and doctors wanting to take the safest route, the use of fetal monitors increases the number of cesarean deliveries (American College . . . 2009).

Preference: Finally, some women ask their doctors for a C-section because they fear the labor pains that come with vaginal childbirth or because they, too, want to control the time of delivery. It is difficult for doctors to refuse such requests—especially since a C-section means both convenience and profit (Nilstun et al. 2008).

A Feminist Controversy. Cesarean births have become not only a social issue, but also cause for controversy among feminists. The central issue is the relative power of women (Beckett 2005; Davis-Floyd 2007). Some feminists say that cesarean delivery takes the power over childbirth away from women and puts it in the hands of doctors. Kathie, in our opening vignette, would agree. Others, in contrast, take the view that cesarean delivery can empower women. They point out that it isn't always the physician who decides that a woman will have a cesarean delivery: As just mentioned, some women tell their doctors how and when they want to deliver their children.

The Scope of the Problem

To better understand the scope of medical problems, let's look first at physical illness as a social problem, then at issues regarding mental illness.

10.3 Summarize some of the aspects of physical illness that make it a social problem.

Physical Illness as a Social Problem

Life Expectancy. One way that social researchers evaluate the general health of a society is to analyze life expectancy. In the United States, life expectancy has been rising for over a century. In 1900, the average person died before seeing the age of 50. In contrast, the average boy born today can expect to live to age 76, the average girl to age 81 (*Statistical Abstract* 2013:Table 109). These are national averages, and group averages *never* apply to individuals. Your particular life expectancy is not 76 or 81 or any other group average.

As with so many other conditions in society, life expectancy is related to income and education: Those who have higher incomes and education live longer. Life expectancy is also related to race–ethnicity: Whites live an average of 4 years longer than African Americans (*Statistical Abstract* 2013:Table 107); Asian Americans live the longest, while Native Americans have the shortest lives. If we could improve social conditions so that everyone has the same educational and environmental conditions as the wealthy, we would save five to eight lives for every one that is saved by advances in medicine (Woolf et al. 2010). Sociology contains a lot of practical lessons, as you've probably noticed by

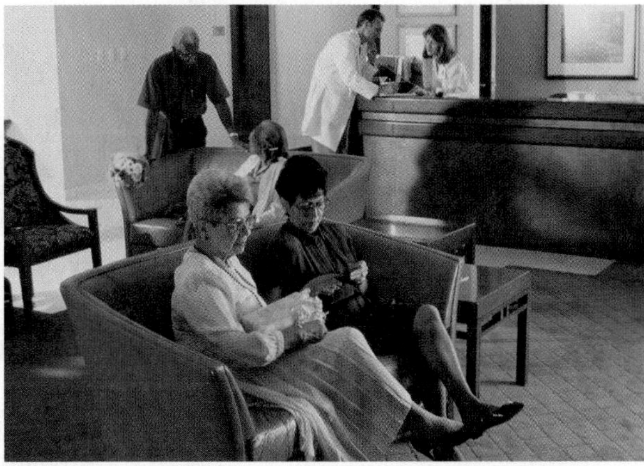

To illustrate our two-tier medical system, I chose two photos of patients waiting for the doctor. I'm sure you have no problem telling which is which.

now. The practical lesson from this is that if your goal is to save lives, you might want to go into public health instead of medicine.

Infant Mortality. One reason that life expectancy has increased is that infant mortality has declined. The **infant mortality rate** (the number of babies who die before their first birthday, per 1,000 live births) is another way to measure a group's well-being: It reflects the quality of nutrition, the health of mothers and babies, and the quality of health care. In 1960, the U.S. infant mortality rate was 26 deaths per 1,000 births. Now it is just a fourth of that, 6.6 per 1,000 births (*Statistical Abstract* 1990:Table 110; 2013:Table 119). On the Social Map on this page, you can see how infant deaths are distributed among the states. In general, the states with the highest rates of infant mortality cluster in the Southeast, and those with the lowest rate in the West. Here again we see *social* influences on health, illness, and even the death of babies.

Although our infant mortality rate has dropped, many still find it a cause for concern. To see why, look at Figure 10.5 on the next page, where you can see that the U.S. rate is higher than that of several other nations. The cold numbers on this table translate into avoidable deaths. If our rate were the same as Japan's, *most* of the 28,000 infants that die in the United States each year would live (*Statistical Abstract* 2013:Table 81).

Why is the infant mortality rate higher in the United States than in the other nations shown on Figure 10.5? The primary reason is the huge pockets of poverty in the United States. As you saw in Chapter 7, poverty is especially high among African Americans, Latinos, and Native Americans. Their higher rates of infant mortality reflect this poverty and increase the overall U.S. rate. To put the matter in the simplest terms: To live on the edge of survival is not good for pregnant women. They get sick more often, experience more stress, have more emotional problems, don't eat as healthful foods, and receive less prenatal care.

FIGURE 10.4 ▸ The Geography of Death: Infant Mortality Rates

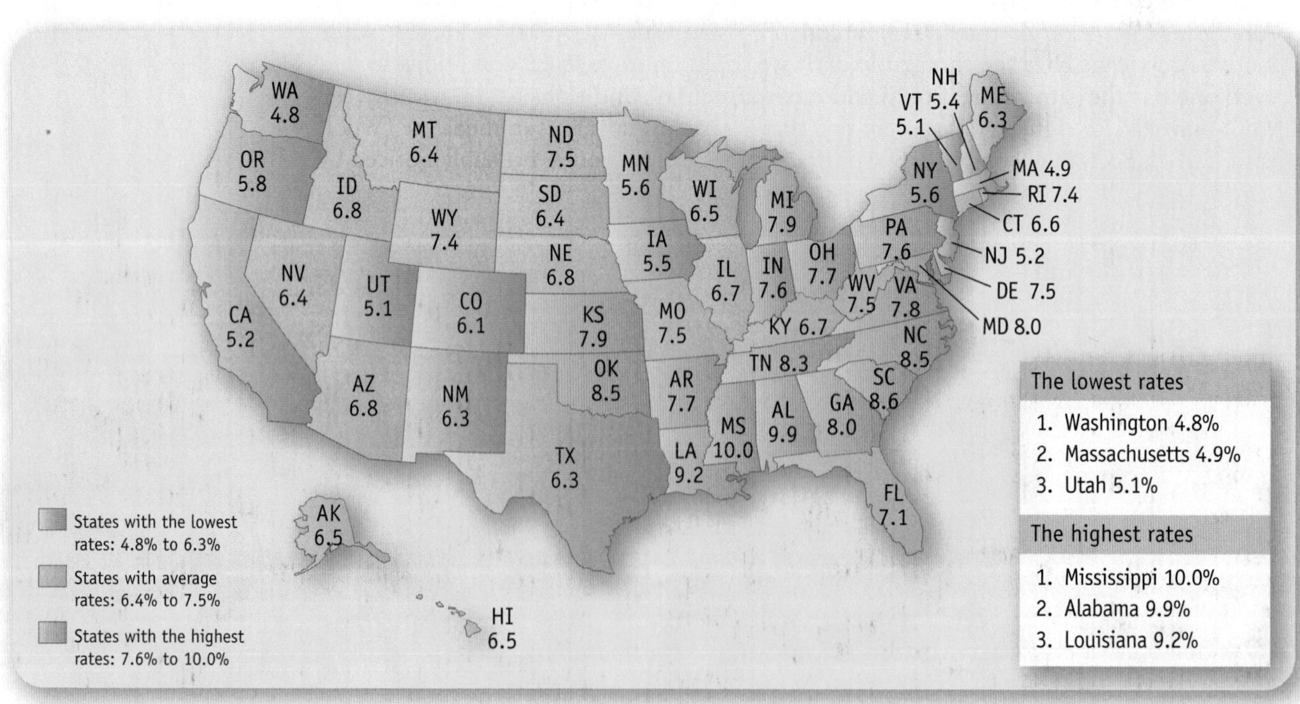

Source: By the author. Based on *Statistical Abstract of the United States* 2012:Table 116.

FIGURE 10.5 ▸ **Infant Mortality Rates**

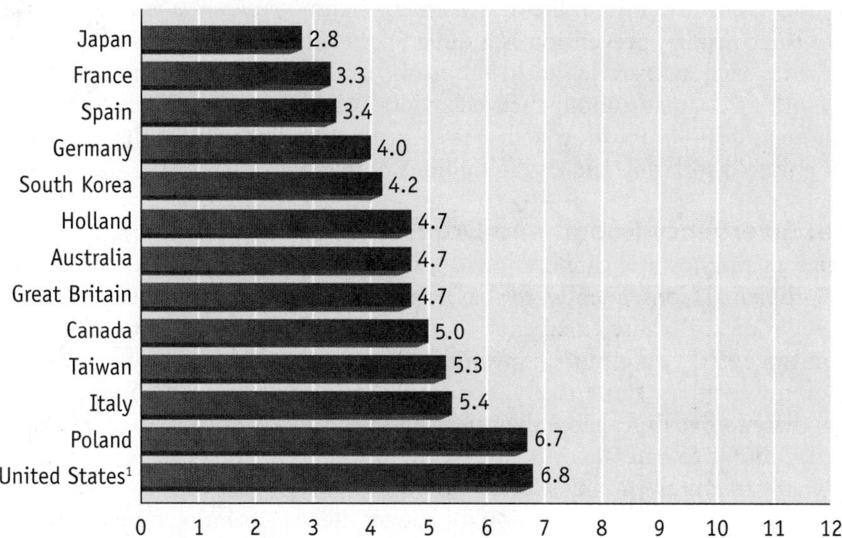

Note: These are the countries listed in the source whose rates of infant mortality are less than that of the United States. Infant mortality is defined as the babies who die before their first birthday per 1,000 live births. For some unknown reason, seven countries that were listed in earlier editions of the source as having lower rates of infant mortality than the United States have been dropped from the current source. These countries are Belgium, Cuba, Czech Republic, Greece, Portugal, Sweden, and Switzerland. It is likely that they are still lower.

[1]The U.S. total is taken from the more detailed listing on Table 116 of the source.

Source: By the author. Based on *Statistical Abstract of the United States* 2012:Tables 116, 1339.

Lifestyle. Although poverty is important, lifestyle may be even more significant. Sociologist Ruben Rumbaut and geographer John Weeks (1994) found that despite higher rates of poverty, Vietnamese and Cambodian refugees in California had lower rates of infant mortality than U.S.-born California women who were better off financially.

This puzzled the researchers who expected that the higher poverty would lead to higher infant mortality rates. As they explored this puzzle, they found the answer not in biology but in *social* conditions: The U.S.-born women had gained more weight during pregnancy, were more likely to have abused drugs, and had "surgically scarred uteruses" from abortions. The immigrant women lived a more conservative lifestyle.

It is difficult to overstate the importance of lifestyle in determining health and illness, for *lifestyle is the major cause of illness and death.* To mention the most obvious: Overeating and lack of exercise lead to heart attacks and strokes, smoking causes cancer, and the abuse of alcohol harms essential body organs. These are all part of the *social* nature of physical illness.

Sexually transmitted diseases (STDs) also illustrate how lifestyle is related to health. To again state the obvious: Singles who practice abstinence run zero risk of STDs. So do couples who never had sex before they marry, and then remain sexually faithful after marriage. All others are at risk, a risk that rises with the number of sexual partners and the amount of unprotected sex. Although people with more sexual partners and unprotected sex have a greater chance of acquiring an STD, it's possible to contract gonorrhea, syphilis, and even HIV with just the first sexual encounter.

Heroic and Preventive Medicine. At the core of the social problem of medical care lies this contradiction: We live in an age of *chronic* illnesses (lingering and ongoing medical problems), while our medical services are geared for *acute* illnesses (those that have a sudden onset, a sharp rise, and a short duration). Our approach to cancer, heart disease, and other chronic disorders is heroic, hospital-based, and expensive. Intervening after a disease is advanced requires highly trained specialists, technical equipment, and expensive drugs. Patients who have serious illnesses want the best care, and the medical world has taught us that "the best" means complex, technical, and expensive.

Unlike *heroic medicine*—the attention-getting situations you see in movies and on television of doctors intervening in life–death emergencies—*preventive medicine* is not dramatic. On the contrary, prevention is a quiet sort of thing. It consists of routine, everyday activities such as exercise, healthful eating, and avoiding smoking and other drug abuse. Nothing dramatic about such behaviors. Yet it is not heroic medicine but public health measures—promoting such health-generating behaviors—that hold the key to limiting untold suffering and saving millions of lives.

Quick Care: Emergency Rooms and Drugstores. The emphasis in U.S. medicine on specialists and hospital care has led to a shortage of primary care doctors who treat routine problems. Consequently, for basic medical care, many patients go to hospital emergency rooms. Because emergency rooms stay open day and night and do not require appointments, they are more convenient than visiting a doctor's office. Emergency services, however, are more costly. Treating a splinter or fever in an emergency room can run three to five times more than treating it in a doctor's office. In an effort to limit emergency rooms to emergency medical care, insurance companies now refuse to pay for routine treatment given in emergency rooms.

Drugstores have entered the competition for patient dollars, operating over 1,000 "in-store clinics." In these clinics, a nurse or physician's assistant examines people with "smaller" problems—from the sniffles and ear infections to pinkeye and bronchitis (Landro 2012). The average cost of treatment is just one-fifth of what emergency rooms charge.

Uneven Distribution of Doctors. Another problem with the medical delivery system is an uneven distribution of doctors. Some areas have an abundance of physicians, while other regions have few doctors. It is difficult for small towns, which offer few cultural attractions, to attract doctors, while large cities near major hospitals have them in abundance. The states reflect this same unevenness. As you can see on the Social Map below, the highest rate of doctors is in the Northeast. Massachusetts has two and a half times more doctors per 100,000 people than Idaho.

FIGURE 10.6 ▸ **Where the Doctors Are**

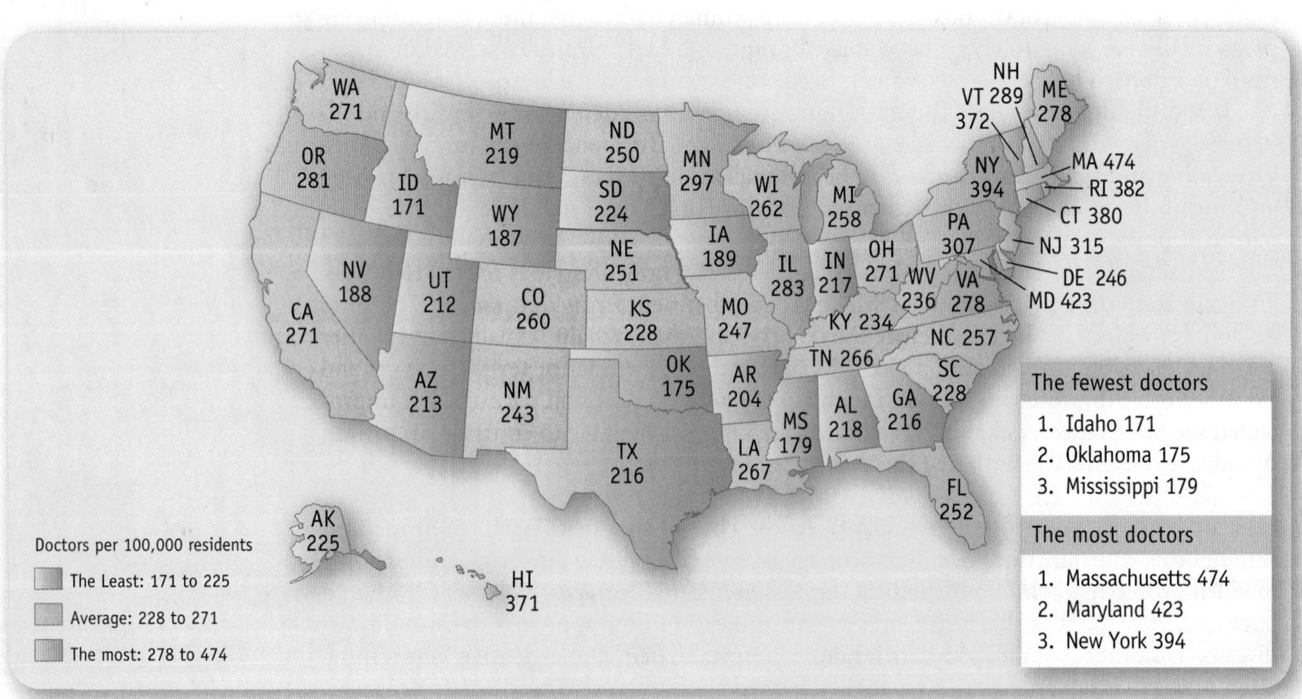

Source: By the author. Based on *Statistical Abstract of the United States* 2012:Table 165.

Mental Illness as a Social Problem

10.4 Summarize some of the aspects of mental illness that make it a social problem.

Measuring Mental Illness. Some experts argue that mental illness has increased because people today experience more stress while their social support systems (family, friends, and community) have become weaker. This sounds good and could be true, but, frankly, it is just as possible that there is less mental illness today than in past years. Such then-and-now totals are impossible to compare because we don't know how much mental illness there is today, much less how much mental illness there used to be. Any totals you read are just fuzzy speculation. Experts don't even agree on how to define various forms of mental illness—and the definitions they use keep changing. We can dispense, then, with the notion that mental illness is more common today, for there is no way of knowing one way or the other.

The Social Nature of Mental Illness. What exactly is mental illness? This question lands us in the midst of controversy. Some psychiatrists see mental illness behind each shadow, while others deny that mental illness exists (Szasz 1961; Manderscheid et al. 2010). Whatever mental illness is—if it exists, that is—it has a strong social basis. That is, people who experience more stress are more likely to also experience what are known as mental problems.

Mental problems are assumed to be the primary reason for suicide, although the matter is not this simple. In the Issues in Social Problems box on the next page, you can see how suicide is related to social conditions and also how suicide changed from a personal problem to a social problem and then back again to a personal problem.

A Two-Tier System of Mental Health Delivery. Just as problems of physical illness have two parts—the illnesses and the medical delivery system—so do problems of mental illness. Let's see how the medical delivery system is part of this problem. Here is something I observed when I did research on the homeless:

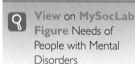

View on MySocLab Figure Needs of People with Mental Disorders

I watched as an elderly nude man, looking confused, struggled to put on his clothing. With his bare hands, the man had ripped the wires out of the homeless shelter's electrical box and then, with the police in pursuit, had run from one darkened room to another.

I asked the officers where they were going to take the man, and they replied, "To Malcolm Bliss" (the state mental hospital). When I commented, "I guess he'll be there for quite a while," an officer replied, "Probably for just a day or two. We picked him up last week when he was crawling under cars at a traffic light—and they let him out after two days."

The police explained that only people who are a danger to others or themselves are admitted as long-term psychiatric patients. Visualizing this old man crawling under cars in traffic and risking electrocution by ripping out electrical wires with his bare hands, I marveled at the definition of "danger" that the psychiatrists must be using. Here in front of me, the two-tiered medical system was stripped of its coverings. A middle-class or wealthy person would have received different treatment. Of course, such a person would not have been in a shelter for the homeless in the first place.

The reason why so many mentally ill homeless wander our city streets today goes back to the 1970s when state psychiatric hospitals discharged tens of thousands of mentally ill patients. The idea behind **deinstitutionalization**, as these discharges were called, was that these people could lead more normal lives in the community than they could in mental hospitals. The plan was to support them with medication and community health services. Few of the planned community centers were ever funded, however, and most patients were simply abandoned on the streets to fend for themselves. A few were institutionalized again when no one could tolerate their presence, but most were left to wander the streets homeless, no matter how bizarre their behavior.

It may be difficult to imagine medical and governmental authorities simply abandoning disoriented mentally ill patients on the streets, but they did precisely this. The cruel way that deinstitutionalization was carried out across the United States is illustrated by

Issues in Social Problems

Suicide: The Making and Unmaking of a Social Problem

Deliberately drawing a razor blade across one's wrist, putting a gun in one's mouth and pulling the trigger, or taking poison—these chill the imagination. More than 100 years ago, sociologist Emile Durkheim (1897/1951) documented how suicide is more than an individual act, how it is related to social conditions. When Durkheim analyzed the suicide rates of different countries, he noticed that year after year each country's rate remained about the same. Look at Figure 10.7. From one year to the next, these rates show little change. Ten years from now Hungary and Japan will have higher suicide rates than the United States has, and Greece and Mexico will have lower rates. Suicide rates are so regular that you can expect about 32,000 to 34,000 Americans to kill themselves this year, and next year, and the year after that (*Statistical Abstract* 2010:Table 114; 2013:Table 121).

From Figure 10.7, you can see that in each country men are more likely than women to kill themselves. In the United States, for every woman who kills herself, four men do the same. This ratio holds true year after year. Yet year after year women attempt suicide more often than men. This is interpreted as meaning that women's suicide attempts are more likely to be "cries for help," but men are more likely to mean it. This is true, but there is also the matter of gender in the choice of method: Women are more likely to take pills, men to use guns. Pills allow more time for discovery before death and life-saving intervention, while a bullet does not.

I spent a (depressing) year studying suicide. As I reviewed the coroner's records, I was impressed by the role of gender in suicide. Before taking pills, women tended to "pretty" themselves with makeup and to smooth the bed cover. You could see that they had in mind an image of how they would look when they were discovered. And comfort in death: One woman turned on the gas and then rested her head on a pillow in the oven. Not all women commit suicide like this, of course. Some do blow their brains out, but this is more likely to be a man's way of death.

Suicide illustrates the making and unmaking of a social problem. In the 1960s, our suicide rates—just as they are now—were somewhere in the middle of those of the industrialized nations. But at that time, mental health professionals began to publicize the idea that suicide was a national problem. The objective conditions hadn't changed; that is, there was no increase in suicide, but subjective concerns grew as mental health professionals and government officials used the mass media to arouse the public. The idea of swift intervention when people contemplate or attempt suicide was appealing, and across the nation the National Institute of Mental Health began to finance suicide prevention centers to conquer what had become a social problem.

The suicide prevention centers failed to reduce the suicide rate, subjective concerns decreased, as did funding, and most centers closed their doors. From time to time, subjective concerns grow, such as after the suicide

FIGURE 10.7 ▸ Suicide: Comparing Countries

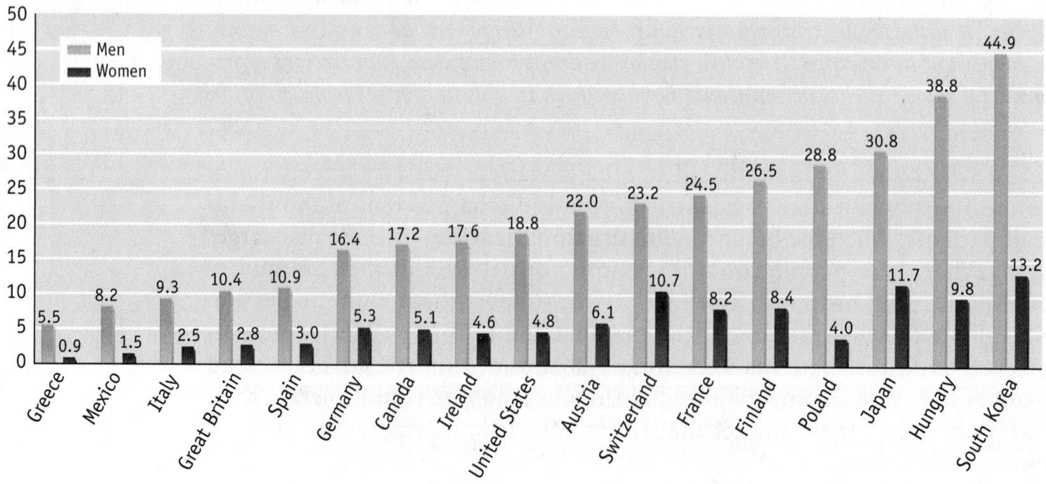

Note: Rate per 100,000 people. Years vary, with most data from 2010.

Sources: Organization for Economic Cooperation and Development 2012:Figure 1.7.1.

(continued from previous page)

of a famous person or a series of suicides in some high school. But subjective concerns have dropped to such an extent that suicide is again a personal problem, not a social problem. Note that during this social construction of a social problem the objective condition, the rate of suicide, did not change.

For Your Consideration

Can you explain why objective conditions are not sufficient to have a social problem? Why did suicide change from a personal problem to a social problem? Why has it changed back to a personal problem? Can you think of other examples of this process?

this event in Texas: Patients from the state psychiatric hospital were loaded in a van and driven to Houston where they were dumped at the Greyhound bus station on skid row (Karlen and Burgower 1985). In 2013, it was revealed that Nevada had improved on this lesson in saving money. Nevada was sending its discharged poor mental patients on one-way bus rides to 47 states (Winter 2013).

Looking at the Problem Theoretically

Let's look at how our theoretical perspectives apply to health, illness, and the practice of medicine.

10.5 Discuss the perspectives that emerge when you apply symbolic interactionism, functionalism, and conflict theory to health, illness, and the practice of medicine.

Symbolic Interactionism

As we have reviewed, symbolic interactionists focus on how people determine meaning and how those meanings influence their behavior. Let's look at how determining meaning applies to health and illness.

The Meaning of Symptoms. If we feel something unusual, we try to figure out what our feelings mean. We wonder what symbol or label we should apply. Are these "out-of-the-ordinary feelings" symptoms of an illness? Do they mean that we should go to bed? Call a doctor? Or just carry on with everyday life? To determine what our feelings mean, we use definitions (or labels) that our culture provides.

Because social classes and subcultures equip their members with distinctive ways of viewing life, people from different backgrounds interpret their experiences differently.

The homeless are the castoffs of postindustrial society. Unwanted and unneeded, they are left to wander the city streets and countryside. Only grudgingly are their needs attended to. This photo was taken in San Francisco.

Back pain is an example. People from the lower classes are likely to regard back pain as part of life. "This is what happens to people when they get older." People from the middle classes, in contrast, are more likely to view back pain as a health problem that needs to be treated by a doctor. It is the same with cold or flu symptoms. For many people, these feelings indicate a need to go to a doctor and "get a shot." To those who follow alternative medicine, these same symptoms indicate a need to drink more water or to take vitamin C or other antioxidants. In short, we use cultural and subcultural symbols to determine what our symptoms mean.

The Significance of Definitions. Just as social classes and subcultural groups perceive illness differently, so groups compete to get their views of health accepted. This, in turn, changes the way we view health, illness, and medicine. For example, the American Psychiatric Association (APA) used to list homosexuality as a mental illness, and it approved therapists to treat it. Using **conversion therapy** (sometimes called reorientation or reparative therapy), psychiatrists would attempt to change a person's sexual orientation. Homosexuals objected to being defined as mentally ill and having their sexual orientation treated as an illness. After lobbying and putting pressure on the APA, in 1973 the APA dropped homosexuality as a form of mental illness. Conversion therapy has fallen into disfavor. A few therapists still practice it, though not without controversy (Saletan 2012).

Just as medicine and psychiatry can decide that some behavior is no longer an illness, so they can declare that other behaviors are illnesses. What had been called drunkenness, for example, was relabeled as the disease of alcoholism. As we reviewed in Chapter 4, through a similar process, unruly and inattentive children have been reclassified as children suffering from attention-deficit disorder.

The labels that we apply to health and illness have a direct impact on how we see the world. If we define alcohol abuse as a disease, we perceive an alcohol abuser as sick; if we define the abuse as drunkenness, we might think of the person as sinful or morally weak. Different views also lead to contrasting ideas of what is thought to be appropriate social policy: If we consider alcohol abuse to be a disease, we might think that sympathy and medical help are appropriate responses; if we define alcohol abuse as a moral failing, we might think that shaming or punishment is more appropriate. In short, our social groups provide different labels (symbols or definitions) for us to apply to human behavior. When we apply a label, it becomes a lens through which we view objective conditions and determine appropriate responses.

Conflicting Referral Networks. As symbolic interactionists study how meaning is determined in the practice of medicine, they analyze interactions between doctors and patients. In classic research, Eliot Freidson (1961) examined how patients and doctors use different frames of reference. Patients use a **lay referral network**—family, friends, neighbors, and co-workers with whom they talk about their medical problems. This network helps people decide which doctor to see—or even whether to see a doctor at all. In this lay referral network, how people perceive a physician's personality, knowledge, and ability to sympathize with patients is important. So is their perception of the doctor's confidence. Doctors who show uncertainty create fear, while those who appear confident instill trust. Patients also want to be sure they get a shot or a prescription, not just advice to go on a diet or to get more rest. The advice might be the more appropriate response to the patient's problem, but the patient expects something "more professional" from the physician. This translates into "medicine" that only a doctor can give.

The physician's frame of reference, in contrast, is a **professional referral network**—made up of other physicians and medical professionals. In this network, the meaning of "doctoring" is different, for their training in medical schools has emphasized organs, symptoms, and diseases apart from the person. Sympathy for the patient is less important than determining why some organ is malfunctioning and prescribing appropriate treatment (Conrad 1995).

You can see, then, how the different referral networks of patients and physicians produce contradictory meanings. Because the expectations of patients and doctors are so different, their worlds can collide. Let's look at such a collision of expectations.

Depersonalization.

> *Mary Duffy was lying in bed still groggy on the morning after her breast surgery, when a group of white-coated strangers filed into her hospital room. Without a word, one of them, a man, leaned over, pulled back her blanket, and stripped her nightgown from her shoulders. He began to talk about carcinomas to the half-dozen medical students who had encircled her bed, staring at her naked body with detached curiosity. Abruptly, the doctor said to her, "Have you passed gas yet?" (Carey 2005)*

It's difficult to imagine that doctors would treat a patient as an object to the extent that this surgeon did. But as you can see, some do. Sociologist call such behavior **depersonalization**—treating a person as an inanimate object.

Depersonalization happens routinely in medical settings. It is as though medical personnel think that people who check into a hospital have also checked their personality, feelings, and personal needs into their medical folder. Sociologists who have studied depersonalization in public clinics note how the poor have to wait for hours, aren't looked directly in the eyes when spoken to, and are addressed as numbers rather than by name. If they aren't able to see a doctor that day, it's just one of those things. After all, what do poor people have to do that's important, anyway?

© A.BACALL
"Of course I'm listening to your expression of spiritual suffering. Don't you see me making eye contact, striking an open posture, leaning towards you and nodding empathetically?"

Physicians are often criticized for bad communications with patients. Can we really expect them to empathize with patients when they see one sick person after another all day long?

Patients who are depersonalized feel a gap between themselves and their doctors, and they have a greater tendency to sue their doctors. The threat of malpractice suits, in turn, produces **defensive medicine**; that is, doctors order lab tests and consultations that the patient may not need in order to leave a "paper trail" to show they did everything reasonable. Preparing for possible lawsuits adds billions to the nation's medical bill.

Functionalism

Let's apply our second theoretical perspective to medical care.

Who Benefits? Functionalists assume that customs or social institutions persist because they fulfill social needs. This perspective raises interesting questions: Whose needs are met by a health care system that is hospital-based and oriented toward acute illnesses? What are the benefits of depersonalizing patients or of making childbirth a rigorous medical procedure?

Fee-for-Service Means Profits. Let's start with the obvious: It is difficult for doctors to make money from people who are healthy. Sick people mean patients for doctors, and patients mean money for treating them. On top of this, patients who get well quickly bring less profit. But a high-profit-producing hospital-based system oriented toward acute illness—now that's a dream come true. Everyone—medical suppliers, hospitals, and drug companies—makes money from patients who are given intensive care. Each year, about 36 million patients–one of every eight or nine Americans–are admitted to a hospital and stay an average of 5 days (*Statistical Abstract* 2013:Tables 6, 181). The average daily cost is shown in Figure 10.8 on the next page. The shorter bars on this figure represent what a day's stay in the hospital would cost if medical costs had risen at the same rate as inflation. Like the bill for delivering a baby on page 313, this figure illustrates the skyrocketing costs of medical care better than words can say.

View on MySocLab Figure Spending on Healthcare, Selected Countries

FIGURE 10.8 ▸ How Much Does It Cost to Stay in the Hospital? One Day's Cost Compared to Inflation

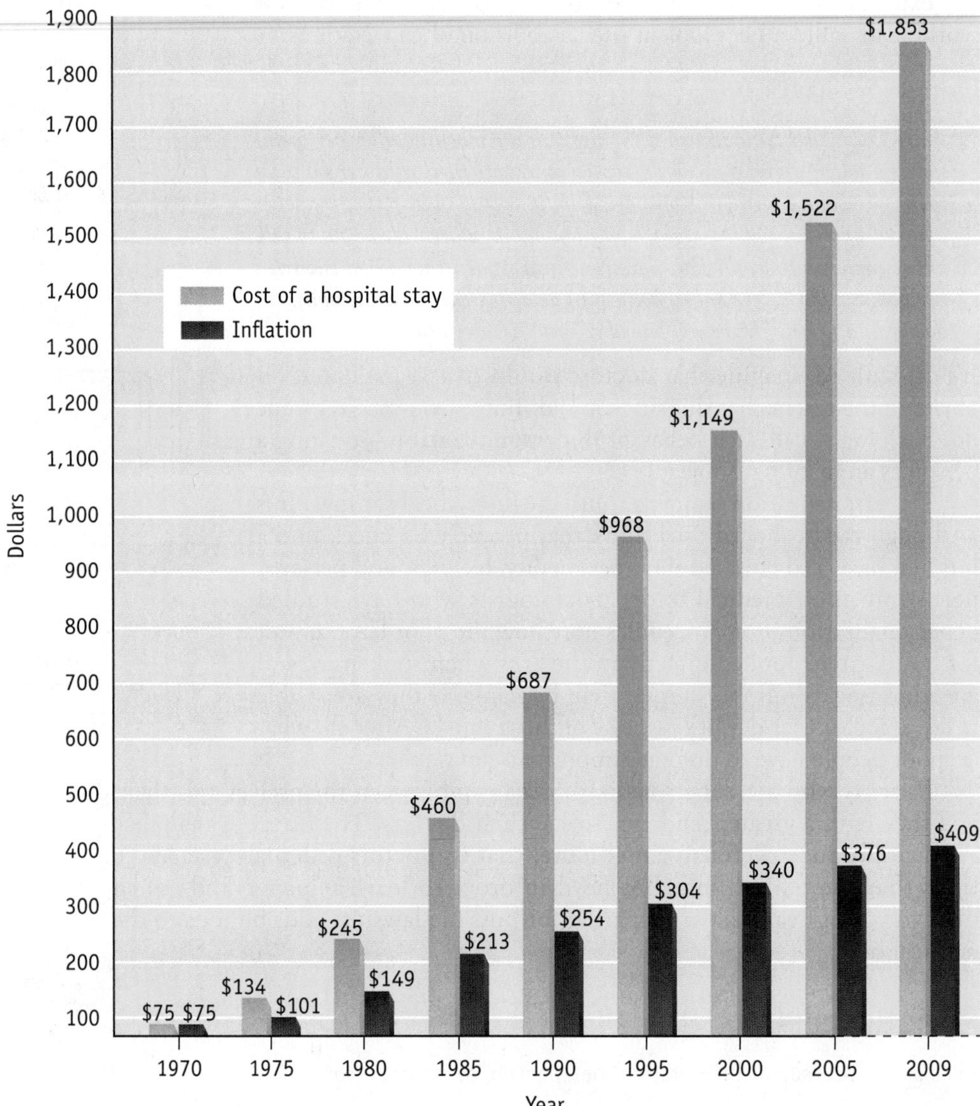

Source: By the author. Based on *Statistical Abstract of the United States* 1998:Table 137; 2013:Table 176.

Despite feeble denials from the medical profession, profits, not health care, are the engine that drives the U.S. health care system. Our fee-for-service system means that the more services doctors sell and the higher price they charge for each one, the more they earn. One result is unnecessary surgery, such as *most* cesarean sections. Another example is hysterectomies, which we will review in the next section on the conflict perspective.

Physicians, nurses, and investors in the U.S. health care industry, then, benefit from our fee-for-service system. But they aren't the only ones. Patients also benefit, for this system lets them shop around. They can choose which doctor to see and what services to purchase. That this system is functional for patients is indicated by our rising life expectancy and decreasing infant mortality rates.

A Self-Correcting System. I have mentioned problems with our fee-for-service system, but functionalists reply that the system is self-correcting. For example, although the medical system is oriented to acute illnesses, after environmental health problems were recognized as serious, the government passed antipollution laws and formed the Environmental Protection Agency (EPA). Medical schools also responded, adding training programs in environmental medicine. Similarly, expensive insurance has led to the development of managed care (discussed later) and outpatient surgery. In short, functionalists view our fee-for-service health care as a system that responds to shifting needs of the nation.

The Global Level. Functionalists also analyze functions and dysfunctions of medicine on a global level. An excellent example is the exporting of Western medicine to the Least Industrialized Nations. The vaccines and medicines sent to these nations were functional because they reduced death rates on a global scale. But they were also dysfunctional because they set the conditions for the global population explosion that worries so many. We will discuss this topic in Chapter 12.

Conflict/Feminist Theory

As we turn to the conflict perspective, you will not be surprised to learn that conflict sociologists disagree with the functionalist view. In fact, they argue the opposite—that the U.S. medical system is *not* self-correcting. Conflict sociologists view patterns of illness and health care in the United States as the outcome of clashes between interest groups. One of their main arguments is that the poor are sicker than others because they have lost the struggle for high-quality education, food, housing, jobs, and medical care.

Medicaid. What about Medicaid, which benefits the poor? Conflict sociologists point out that this program developed out of conflict. In the 1960s, resentment about how shabbily the poor were treated in the medical system had grown so vocal that politicians were forced to take action. To reduce the pressure and satisfy the public, Congress proposed Medicaid for the poor. However, the physicians' union, the American Medical Association (AMA), thought that Medicaid would be a first step to socialized medicine. Fearing that Medicaid was an attack on its profitable fee-for-service system, the AMA spent millions of dollars lobbying to prevent Congress from approving Medicaid. Caught between the public's demand for change and the intense lobbying of the AMA, Congress designed Medicaid to satisfy both—more medical coverage for the poor but retaining the doctor's profitable fee-for-service system.

Colliding Interests of Doctors and Patients. Conflict theorists also have a different view of the doctor–patient relationship. Those adhering to the Marxist perspective emphasize that doctors and patients form two classes—those who control medicine and those who receive treatment. As the dominant class, physicians try to control the doctor–patient relationship. As you probably know, it is not unusual for doctors to say a few words to patients—often using difficult-to-understand professional terms—and then send the patients on their way. This, say conflict theorists, is no accident. By not explaining their procedures and diagnoses in down-to-earth terms, physicians try to keep the oppressed class of patients ignorant and dependent (Waitzkin and Waterman 1974). As conflict sociologists put it: In a capitalist system of production for profit, the alienation of patient and physician is like that of owner and worker, inevitable when the interests of the one (making a profit from the illness) oppose those of the other (getting well at the least expense).

Women's Reproductive Organs. Sociologists who have done participant observation of doctors report a bias *against* women's reproductive organs. Sociologist Sue Fisher (1986), for example, was surprised to hear surgeons recommend total hysterectomy (the removal of both the uterus and the ovaries) even when no cancer was present. She found that male doctors refer to the uterus and ovaries as "potentially disease-producing" organs—useless and unnecessary after childbearing age. Some surgeons routinely recommend this profitable operation for every woman who has finished bearing children. Although each year a half million American women have hysterectomies, *most* are unnecessary (Cohen et al. 2011; *Statistical Abstract* 2013:Table 174). It is no wonder that feminist conflict sociologists refer to hysterectomies as a "war on the womb" (Fisher 1986).

What money-making organs the uterus and ovaries become when they are defined as "potentially disease-producing." The more surgery, the more profits. But women aren't exactly pleased at having these organs cut out of their bodies, so surgeons have to drum up business by "selling" hysterectomies. Here is what one resident physician said to sociologist Diana Scully (1994):

You have to look for your surgical procedures; you have to go after patients. Because no one is crazy enough to come and say, "Hey, here I am. I want you to operate on me." You have to sometimes convince the patient that she is really sick—if she is, of course [laughs], and that she is better off with a surgical procedure.

Some surgeons try to scare women into "buying" the operation. Look at this horrendous example:

When Mrs. J., a 47-year-old schoolteacher, was told in a routine examination that she had a "uterine fibroid" and needed a hysterectomy (removal of her uterus), the only thing she could think of was "tumor." She asked the doctor if it was cancerous, and he frightened her more by saying, "Sometimes when we go in, we find them to be cancerous." Fearing cancer of the uterus, she consulted two other physicians and learned that the fibroid was small, common in middle-aged women, and soon likely to shrink on its own as she went into menopause. (Larned 1977:195–196)

Imagine this woman picturing herself lying in a casket, her tearful family inconsolable after the loss of their wife and mother. Why do you think that the surgeon did not tell her the rest of the truth—that fibroids are not likely to turn into cancer and that several nonsurgical treatments are available?

In Sum ▸ From a conflict/feminist perspective, the medical system is an industry whose goals are profit and power. To reach these goals, its practitioners exploit sick people (Reynolds 1973). Conflict theorists argue that their perspective best explains why medical care for the rich is better than that for the poor: Profits, not health care, are the goal of the U.S. medical system. Physicians are businesspeople, patients are customers, and health care is the commodity for sale. The government pays an increasing proportion of the nation's health care bill because it perpetuates and underwrites the interests of capitalist industries—including medicine. Conflict theorists argue that health care should be a right of *all* citizens and that people's illnesses and diseases should not be exploited for profit.

Research Findings

10.6 Summarize changes in health problems and infectious diseases, the relationship of the environment and disease, and social inequalities in physical and mental illness.

Sociologists do a lot of research on health problems and the medical system. In keeping with the theme of this book, our focus will be on social inequalities of health and health care. First, we will discuss physical health problems: age, race, and social class; our two-tier system of medicine; and how health insurance creates inequalities. We will then discuss social inequalities in mental illness.

Historical Changes in Health Problems

The Top Ten Killers. On Figure 10.9, you can compare today's ten leading causes of death with those of 1900. The changes indicated by this figure make the *social* nature of death evident. As you can see, only six of today's ten leading causes of death are the same as back then.

To see the *social* basis of even the cause of death, note that in 1900 "senility" was the ninth leading cause of death. This seems to have been a catch-all category for "old age," which we don't consider a cause of death today. When the elderly didn't die from diarrhea, pneumonia, or something recognizable, doctors at that time said they died from "senility." It is likely that this category included what we call Alzheimer's disease today.

FIGURE 10.9 ▸ **The 10 Leading Causes of Death in the United States**

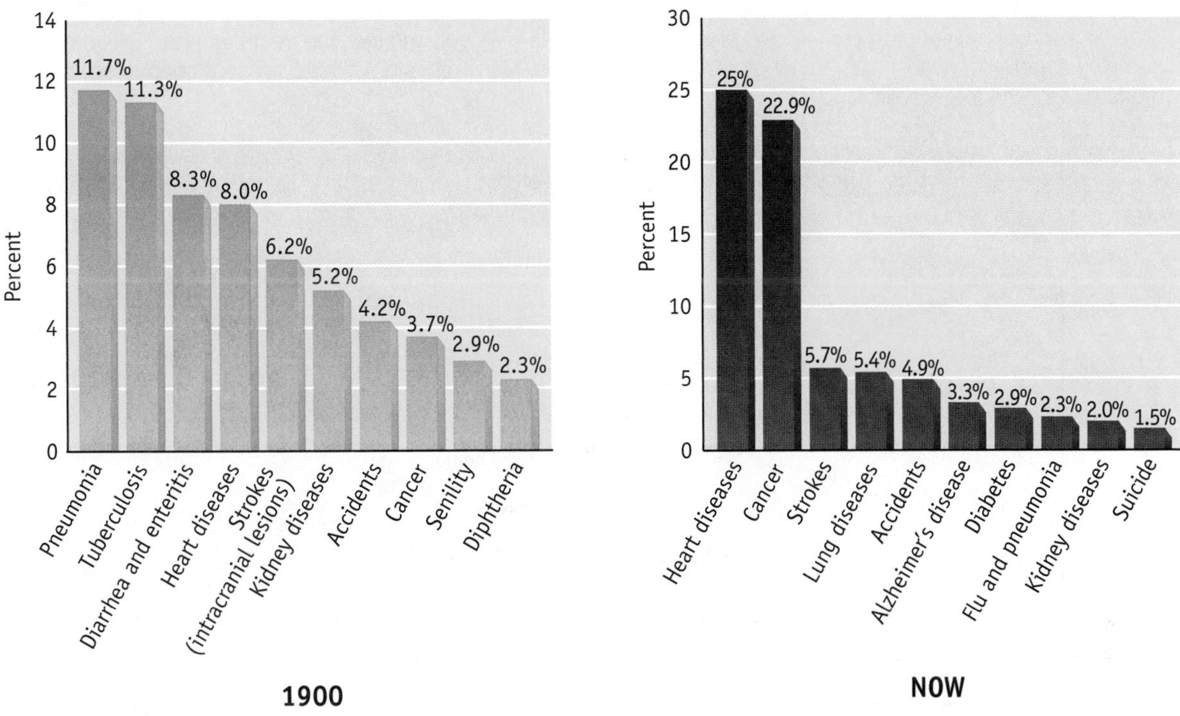

Sources: By the author. Centers for Disease Control and Prevention 2009 (for year 1900); *Statistical Abstract* 2013:Table 125.

To emphasize even further the *social* nature of death, note how causes of death are related to lifestyle. In 1900, lifestyle factors like smoking cigarettes and the intake of high amounts of sugar weren't common, and lung diseases and diabetes didn't make the top ten list. With broad changes in lifestyle came changes in leading causes of death.

Infectious Diseases

A Decline in Infectious Diseases. From Figure 10.9, you can see how deadly infectious diseases used to be. In 1900, pneumonia was the number one killer, with tuberculosis (TB) close behind. As you can see, even diarrhea was often fatal. Every family feared polio, whooping cough, German measles, smallpox, and diphtheria. Then, during the first half of the 20th century, these diseases receded. As death rates dropped, life expectancy gradually rose, going from 47 years to about 80. What happened?

The usual answer is that modern medicine wiped out these diseases. I don't want to detract from the many accomplishments of modern medicine, for most of us know someone who would not be alive if it weren't for coronary byass surgery or some organ transplant. And prescription drugs and vaccinations have been significant in preventing, treating, and curing some diseases, such as syphilis, bacterial pneumonia, and hypertension.

But most infectious killers of the 19th century were declining *before* antibiotics, immunizations, or specific drugs were developed (McKeown 1980). Although medical myth has it that new drugs and vaccinations conquered TB in the 1950s, you can see from Figure 10.10 that TB had been declining since the 1800s. If modern medicine didn't conquer this infectious disease so feared by earlier generations, what did? *The answer is that cleaner public water supplies and better living conditions improved overall health.* Deaths from these infectious killers declined as people's immune systems grew stronger, as they became healthier from cleaner water, better food, and better housing.

FIGURE 10.10 ▸ The "Conquest" of Tuberculosis

Tuberculosis used to be one of the greatest killers. Many people believe that modern medicine "conquered" TB with the discovery of streptomycin in 1947 and a vaccine in 1954. As you can see, the death rate for TB had been declining steadily for almost 100 years before these discoveries. Many other infectious diseases "conquered" by modern medicine follow a similar pattern.

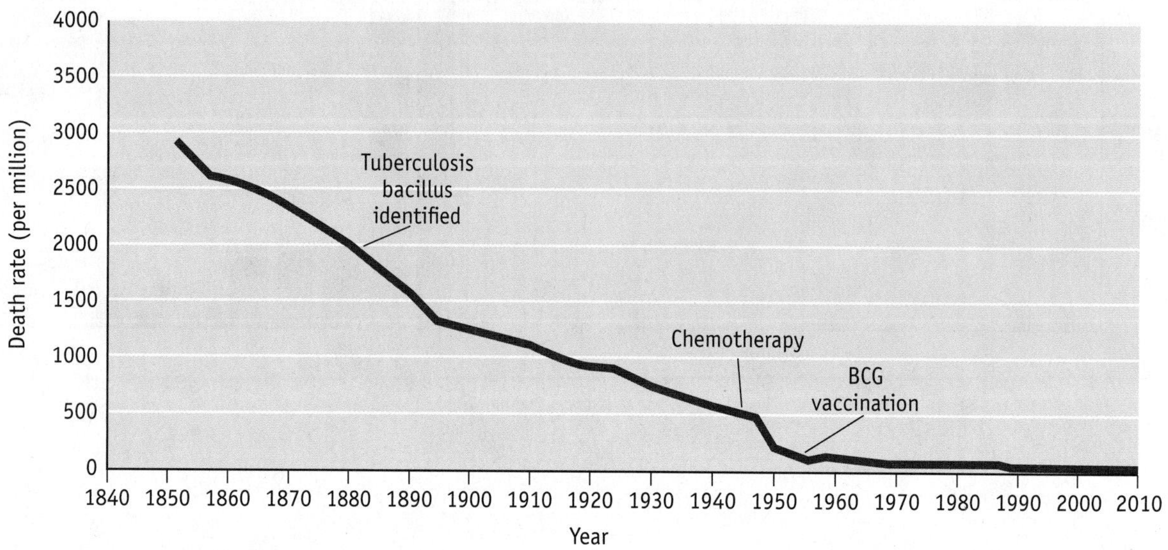

Source: McKeown 1980; *Statistical Abstract of the United States* 2013:Table 188.

The Resurgence of Infectious Diseases

It started with a cough, an autumn hack that refused to go away.

Then came the fevers. They bathed and chilled the skinny frame of Oswaldo Juarez, a 19-year-old Peruvian visiting the United States to study English. His lungs clattered, his chest tightened and he ached with every gasp. During a wheezing fit at 4 A.M., Juarez felt a warm knot rise from his throat. He ran to the bathroom sink and spewed a mouthful of blood.

"I'm dying," he told himself, "because when you cough blood, it's something really bad."

Oswaldo Juarez had been infected with extremely drug-resistant TB (XXDR), the first case in the United States (Mason and Mendoza 2009). Since then, a handful of XXDR cases have shown up ("TB in the United States" 2012).

Infectious diseases have a way of fighting back. They go underground and develop new strains that are resistant to drugs and vaccines. This may be happening with all the infectious diseases that we thought our drugs had either cured or brought under control (Rohani and Drake 2011). The implications are severe on both a personal level, your own health, and on a global level. Let's look at some aspects of this threat to our health in the Technology and Social Problems box on the next page.

Health officials so fear an outbreak of drug-resistant TB that they now arrest patients who refuse treatment and lock them in guarded hospital rooms until their treatment is complete (Hench 2006; Wholsen 2012). The most feared infectious disease today, however, is HIV/AIDS. Let's look at how this disease is related to behavior and the environment.

How Disease Is Related to Behavior and Environment: HIV/AIDS and Other STDs

Background. HIV/AIDS is an excellent example of the relationship among behavior, environment, and disease. When this disease first came to the public's attention, almost all victims were men who had sex with men. Other victims were intravenous drug users and hemophiliacs who were exposed to the disease through contaminated blood. Then drug-using prostitutes who shared needles spread the disease to heterosexual men. Today, the disease affects people from all walks of life, and women account for more than one-quarter of all new HIV cases.

Technology and Social Problems

Superbugs in the Global Village

Simon Sparrow, a 17-month-old toddler, was just learning to feed himself. His family was startled out of sleep one early morning when Simon let out a primal scream. They rushed Simon to the hospital, where he was diagnosed with a virus and asthma and sent home. Fifteen hours later, he was dead. (Chase 2006)

What killed Simon? It was a new strain of staph infection. This germ can penetrate bones and lungs, leaving abscesses that require surgery. Simon died so quickly that he was spared this suffering.

This new form of staph (*community-associated methicillin-resistant Staphylococcus aureus,* which, fortunately has a shortened name—CA-MRSA) is blamed for 18,000 deaths a year in the United States (Tanner 2010). Health authorities are alarmed. CA-MRSA and the other drug-resistant bacteria are appearing at various spots around the world. Their fear is that someone, somewhere, will come down with a germ that is resistant to every antibiotic—and that with global travel, in just a matter of days the new strain will spread throughout the global village.

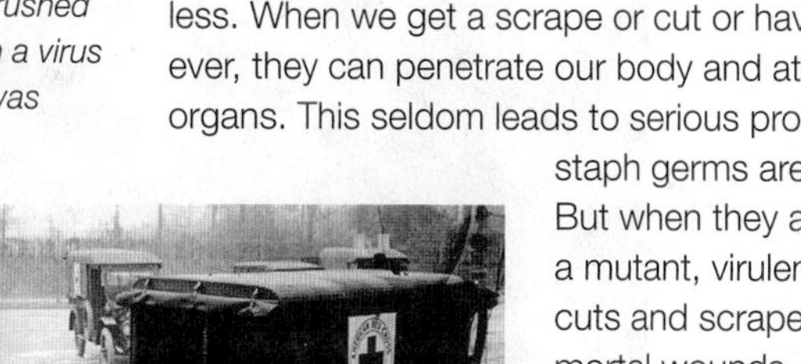

American Red Cross in operation during the Spanish flu epidemic of 1918–1920. The flu killed 25 million people worldwide.

Following the discovery of penicillin in the 1940s came a series of effective microbe killers. By the 1970s, more than 100 antibiotics sat on pharmacy shelves. The war against microbes had been won, or so the medical industry thought. Researchers relaxed and stopped developing new antibiotics. Some promising new drugs, already in development, were canceled as superfluous (Chase 2006).

But something serious was happening behind the scenes. When hit with antibiotics, the weaker germs die off. The stronger ones, though, can mutate and survive. This is especially likely to happen when people stop taking a drug because they feel better, instead of completing their full course of medical treatment. The more that antibiotics are used and misused, the more that drug-resistant bugs develop (Mason and Mendoza 2009).

Staph germs are all around us. We all carry staph germs on our skin and in our nose. There they are harmless. When we get a scrape or cut or have surgery, however, they can penetrate our body and attack our internal organs. This seldom leads to serious problems, as most staph germs are relatively mild. But when they are replaced by a mutant, virulent strain, simple cuts and scrapes can become mortal wounds. A patient who goes to the hospital for a sore throat or routine surgery can be carried out in a coffin.

The threat that these mutant strains pose is serious, and pharmaceutical firms are searching for the next generation of antibiotics to fight the next generation of microbes. Let's suppose that we win this close race and develop new antibiotics in time to prevent a global epidemic. Will we then repeat this process—overprescribing, not completing the course of treatments—with the microbes again mutating and developing resistance to the new drugs?

Granted the past, I am certain this will happen. We have a medical establishment eager for profits and the tendency of patients to quit taking medicine when they feel better, but before their invasive microbes are destroyed totally. A sage once said that those who do not learn from history are doomed to repeat it. I would add that although we study history, and even know its lessons, in some instances we stubbornly set ourselves on a course destined to repeat it. This, I fear, is one such case.

For Your Consideration

It is easy to stop taking medication when you feel better. It's like, "I'm cured. Why take those last six pills in that bottle?" Do you know anyone who has not completed an entire course of treatment prescribed by a physician? Have you? Do you realize the global health implications of doing this?

Orphans in Rundu, Namibia, whose parents died from AIDS are lined up at a feeding station, which they depend on for survival.

A Global Epidemic. HIV/AIDS is a global epidemic. About 3 million people are infected each year, and about 2 million people die from AIDS each year. The global death toll numbers about 30 million. Hit the hardest is sub-Saharan Africa, which has about 22 million of the world's 33 million HIV/AIDS cases (*Statistical Abstract* 2012:Table 1341). HIV/AIDS is so common in this region that it has become the area's leading cause of death. The main reasons for the prevalence of HIV/AIDS in sub-Saharan Africa are a lack of sex education, unprotected sex, and prostitution.

Children are also victims. Born to AIDS-infected mothers, many come into this world with this disease. In Swaziland, HIV/AIDS is so common that two of every five babies are born HIV-infected. Others get the disease from their mother's milk. Part of the devastation of AIDS is the orphans it leaves behind. Worldwide, 17 million children have been orphaned because of AIDS, most of them in sub-Saharan Africa (AVERT 2008; UNAIDS 2010).

FIGURE 10.11 ▸ Adults Living with HIV/AIDS

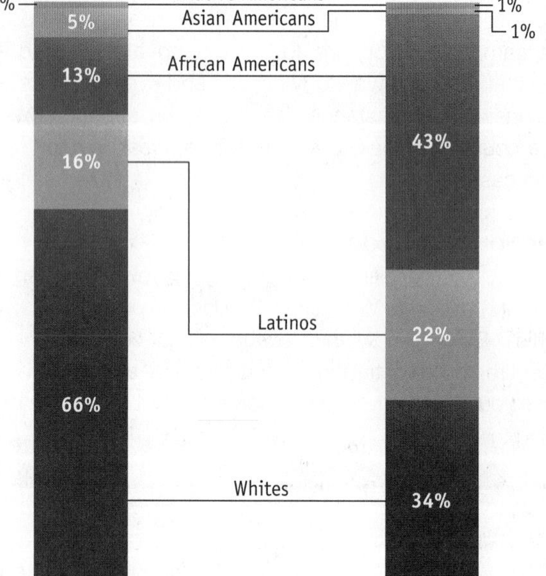

Source: By the author. Based in *Statistical Abstract of the United States* 2012:Tables 10, 187.

HIV/AIDS in the United States. Antiretroviral drugs (ARVs) can slow HIV infection, preventing full-blown AIDS from appearing for up to 20 years. When the ARVs were first developed, they were expensive, costing $10,000–$15,000 per patient per year. With today's generic versions, the cost to treat a patient for a year has dropped to just $335 (Venkatesh et al. 2012). Although these drugs can hold back the symptoms of AIDS, they do *not* prevent people from infecting others with HIV. In the United States, the combination of antiretroviral drugs and education about unprotected sex has held this disease in check. The number of annual new HIV/AIDS cases has dropped from 80,000 in 1992 to 48,000 now. The number of annual deaths from AIDS has dropped by two-thirds, from 50,000 in 1995 to 17,000 now (*Statistical Abstract* 1998: Table 144; Centers for Disease Control and Prevention 2010, 2012).

Figure 10.11 shows how HIV/AIDS is related to race–ethnicity. The reason that racial–ethnic groups have different rates of this disease is not genetic. No group is more or less susceptible to HIV/AIDS because of biological factors. The reasons are social: multiple sex partners, unprotected sex, and drug users sharing needles.

Ominous Changes. The HIV virus mutates rapidly, and medical researchers fear that the drugs being used to fight HIV/AIDS today might be only a temporary fix. Some individuals have contracted strains of HIV that are resistant to protease inhibitors, one kind of antiretroviral drug (Reuman et al. 2010). If drug-resistant strains become widespread, the epidemic will surge again. Several new drugs, however, hold the promise of picking up where these drugs leave off.

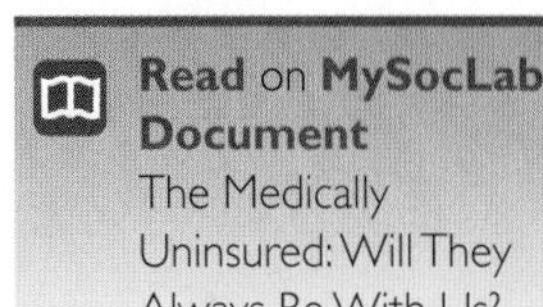

Watch on
MySocLab Video:
ABC Primetime: AIDS in Black America

HIV is not the only sexually transmitted disease (STD), of course, and for all STDs *social* factors or behavior are important. You might be interested in following up this line of thought in the Thinking Critically box below.

Social Inequalities in Physical Illness

Poverty and Health. From your reading of earlier chapters, you should not be surprised to learn that economic factors largely determine who will be healthy and who will be sick. Poor children, for example, are more likely to be undernourished or to lack a balanced diet. As a result, they are more vulnerable to disease. *In general, the poorer people are, the sicker they are.* Even their death rates are higher.

Read on **MySocLab Document**
The Medically Uninsured: Will They Always Be With Us?

Thinking Critically About Social Problems

"I Didn't Have Sexual Relations with That Woman!" What Is Sex, and So What?

In one of the many public dramas of Bill Clinton's life, this one at a White House press conference televised to the nation, the president said, "I did not have sexual relations with that woman!"

Many people believed him, and many did not. Almost all were disgusted, though, with the presidency degenerating to this point. But not as disgusted as they were when the transcripts of Clinton's trials were published. And titillated, too, as they read accounts about oral-genital contact between Clinton and a White House intern, Monica Lewinsky.

"I didn't have sex with that woman," said Clinton to the nation. Considering the steamy revelations of his "whatever-it-was" relationship with Monica Lewinsky, well, you decide.

Was Clinton lying? At first blush, it seems so. There is no doubt that he was covering up, but was he lying? As Clinton emphasized with his famous "It depends on what 'is' is" statement about his relationship with Lewinsky, it all depends on definitions. Just what do you mean by a particular word?

The symbolic interactionists are thrilled, of course, for what they do for a living—and for their pleasure—is studying the meaning of people's communications.

It now looks as if Clinton may simply have been ahead of his time. Only 20 percent of today's college students consider oral-genital relations to be having sex.

What is significant about this?

Unprotected sex can lead to sexually transmitted diseases (STDs). Now everyone knows this, but those who don't think that oral-genital contact is sex might think they can't get STDs from it.

And how wrong they would be! On the list of what someone can get from unprotected (no condom) oral-genital contact is a bunch of things that no one wants: herpes, syphilis, gonorrhea, human papillomavirus, hepatitis A, and HIV. They can also get little critters called intestinal parasites.

Based on Hans et al. 2010.

For Your Consideration

Do you think that oral-genital contact is having sex? Why or why not? Why do you think the definition of what it means to have sex is changing?

This takes us to the heart of the matter—social inequality—the essential factor that underlies our patterns of disease and death (Dow et al. 2010). Let's look at social class.

Occupational Health Hazards.

On September 12, Jimmy Willis, a former subway conductor, rushed to Ground Zero to volunteer alongside thousands of workers who had been sent by the city government. For about 10 days, they helped clear out a towering 6-story mass of rubble known as "the Pile." They carved a path "5 feet at a time" through a morass of concrete and bodies, with little or no respiratory protection. Since then, breathing problems and asthma have dogged these workers. (Chen 2007; Kim 2012)

After the collapse of the World Trade Center on September 11, 2001, volunteers and city workers were exposed to severe environmental contamination at Ground Zero. During these initial recovery efforts, most of the volunteers and employees wore inadequate protection, or none at all.

Although this was an unusual event, it illustrates this principle: Health problems that are a result of employment hit the working class harder. The executive at headquarters is less likely than the worker at the manufacturing plant to be exposed to toxic chemicals—the carbon monoxide, mercury, and uranium that destroy the kidneys, and the heavy metals that invade the nervous system. It is the same for factory noise. It is the working-class ear that is likely to be damaged, not that of the executive.

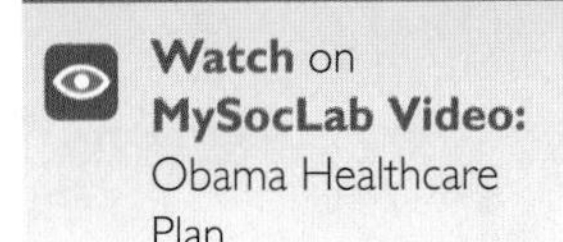

Reducing Inequalities: Health Care Reform. In 2010, after rancorous debate that extended over a year, Congress passed the Patient Protection and Affordable Care Act. The intention of this law is to reduce the inequalities in health care by requiring all U.S. citizens and legal residents to have medical insurance. Those who cannot afford health insurance will be provided it by raising taxes on those who have higher incomes ("Focus on Health . . ." 2010). The law withstood challenges and was upheld by the U.S. Supreme Court (Kliff 2012).

Read on MySocLab Document Health Care Reform–A Woman's Issue

Only as the years pass will we see what impact this law has on inequalities in health care. We can be certain that the law will *not* eliminate the inequalities. These are built into our social structure. People with higher incomes will always be able to afford higher-quality medical care. And, as with the example cited of Ground Zero, unless there is fundamental change—which there will not be—the poor will continue to be exposed to more harmful conditions at work. The poor will also continue to eat less healthy food, exercise less, and have a higher rate of obesity. The end result is that they will continue to suffer from more health problems and to die at a younger age.

FIGURE 10.12 ▸ Social Class and Mental Problems

Results of the Srole study of mental health problems among adults. Number 1 is the wealthiest, number 6 the poorest.

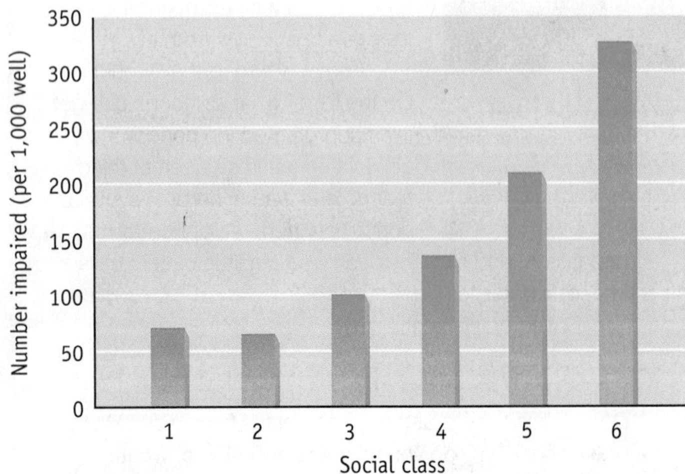

Source: Srole 1978.

Social Class and Mental Illness

Background. Do some social classes have more emotional problems than others? Sociologists have answered this intriguing question time and again. Since 1939, they have found that people's emotional well-being gets worse the lower they are on the social class ladder. Those in the lower social classes are more likely to be depressed, anxious, nervous, and phobic (fearful). Numerous studies have confirmed this finding (Faris and Dunham 1939; Srole et al. 1978; Lundberg 1991; Sareen et al. 2011).

As I mentioned, the term *mental illness* is vague. To overcome this problem, sociologist Leo Srole and his colleagues at Columbia University defined their own set of symptoms and then interviewed a representative sample of New Yorkers. The results of this classic study, the Midtown Manhattan Project, are shown in Figure 10.12.

Like researchers both before and after them, they found that the poor have considerably more emotional problems.

Why do the poor suffer more mental disorders than people in other classes? Let's compare two competing explanations.

The Drift Hypothesis. The first, the *drift hypothesis*, is based on the idea that people with emotional difficulties tend to be less successful in life. People from higher-income families who have mental problems tend to drift downward, landing in the lower classes (Fox 1990). One result is that those mental disorders thought to have a genetic base, such as schizophrenia and depression, have become concentrated among the poor. Even if these genetic predispositions once were distributed evenly among the social classes, the drift downward has redistributed them. Another result is that the poor have a larger percentage of mentally disturbed parents. Their children are more likely to learn pathological ways of coping with the world, making them less able to deal with the challenges of education and career. They, too, are more likely to end up living in poverty.

You can see how this explanation takes us to the nature–nurture controversy we reviewed in the preceding chapter. There we saw how difficult it is to separate genetic influences from the effects of socialization. The many attempts to unravel this thorny problem regarding mental illness have also satisfied no one. The answer may be on the horizon. With the decoding of the human genome system, researchers have begun to match specific genes with mental illnesses (Smoller 2013).

The Environmental Hypothesis. The second explanation, the *environmental hypothesis*, is the one that sociologists prefer. To see how this works, let's rephrase the basic finding that the lower classes have more mental illnesses this way: People in the lower social classes tend to be sadder, more anxious, and more fearful, while those in the higher social classes tend to be happier, less anxious, and less fearful. Sociologists regard these differences in emotions (or "feeling states") as the product of different environments. In short, they see social class as producing "mental health" and "mental illness."

Can social class really do this? Consider how social class sorts people into different kinds of lives. Because of social class, some people enjoy job security, solid finances, and good physical health, medical care, and marriages. Not only do these people have greater security at the present, but they also have greater hopes for the future. They realistically plan and look forward to larger houses, new cars, exotic vacations, college degrees for their children, and a relaxing, enjoyable retirement. You can see how this type of life can produce better mental health. Compare this with the stress-filled lives of people who live in poverty. Their jobs don't offer security. With low wages, they live from paycheck to paycheck. Unpaid bills pile up. They have high rates of divorce, alcoholism, violence, worse physical health, and less access to good medical care. The contrasting conditions of social class, then, either support people's mental well-being or deal severe blows to it.

Social Class Differences in Mental Health Care. To better understand how mental health care is related to social inequality, let's consider types of therapy. In **individual psychotherapy**, a therapist listens and tries to guide the patient toward a resolution of emotional problems. One type of psychotherapy is **psychoanalysis**, which Sigmund Freud pioneered as a way to uncover the subconscious motives, fantasies, and fears that shape people's behavior. The patient meets an analyst several times a week and talks about whatever comes to mind, while the analyst listens for hidden patterns, particularly those that reveal unresolved conflicts from childhood. More common is **short-term directive therapy**, in which a counselor focuses on current situations to help clients understand their problems. In **group therapy**, several patients, with the guidance of a therapist, help each other cope with their problems.

Another treatment is **drug therapy**, the use of tranquilizers, antidepressants, and antipsychotic drugs to relieve people's problems and help them cope with life. As discussed in Chapters 2 and 4, some of these drugs have serious side effects. Drug therapy is often criticized as treating symptoms without offering a cure.

Quick counseling between commercials is probably no less effective than most forms of talk therapy. Shown here is media figure Dr. Drew Pinsky, who, like "Dr. Phil," has perfected the "look of empathy." See the cartoon on page 325.

For some illnesses, especially depression, doctors treat some patients with **electroconvulsive therapy (ECT)** (also called electroshock therapy). They attach wires to either side of a patient's skull and send low-voltage electric shocks through the brain. Memory loss is a possible (and permanent) side effect.

The type of therapy that troubled people receive does not depend on what kind of problems they have, but on their ability to pay. People who have money and good insurance are more likely to be guided through their problems with **talk therapy**—psychotherapy, group therapy, and so on. "Talk" therapy is expensive, and few poor or uninsured people receive it. The poor are usually given drug therapy, sometimes derisively called **pharmaceutical straitjackets**—drugs that make patients drowsy, lethargic, and easier to handle.

Although the patterns of treatment differ by social class, we don't know that this represents inequality. Despite the many years that these therapies have been used, *we do not know which therapies work.* Costly psychoanalysis could be less (or more) effective than drug therapy. It is even possible that no therapy is more effective than all of these. Since we don't know which therapies are more (or less) effective, we don't know whether the poor are receiving worse—or better—treatment for their emotional problems. We need rigorous studies to evaluate the effectiveness of the various ways of treating mental problems.

In Sum ▸ Sociologists consider social inequality to be a root cause of mental problems. Social inequality is also related to the medical treatment people receive for their physical and mental problems. Health reform is intended to address some of these inequalities in medical care. We won't know the results of these changes in the medical delivery system for years. Let's turn now to other social policy.

Social Policy

10.7 Summarize social policy regarding medical care.

Let's review some of the major social policies that have been put into practice to improve the quality of medical care and to reduce its cost.

Prepaid Medical Care

Watch on **MySocLab Video:** Managed Care

To reduce the cost of providing health care for their workers, some employers buy **prepaid or managed care**. The best-known type is the **health maintenance organization (HMO)**. A business pays a set fee to a medical corporation (the HMO), which covers all the health needs of the company's employees. If an employee's health care costs less than the fee, the HMO makes money; if it costs more, the HMO loses money. Because the HMO receives no more than this fee, its directors are motivated to reduce costs. Doctors are paid salaries, but they can receive bonuses if they reduce patient costs.

The Positive Side: Healthier Lifestyles. Because doctors make more money when patients stay well, they are motivated to treat medical problems before they become serious and more expensive. They encourage preventive care, such as immunizations, well-baby checkups, mammograms, and physicals (Ilminen 2006). They urge patients to adopt a lifestyle that improves health: better diet, exercise, rest, and avoiding the abuse of drugs, including alcohol. This lifestyle reduces medical tests, surgery, and hospital admissions. HMO doctors also lower costs by keeping the length of hospital stays to the bare minimum. The reduction in costs can be dramatic, as HMO patients have less surgery and fewer hospitalizations than fee-for-service patients (Cuffel et al. 1999; Basu 2007).

The Negative Side: Profits and a Conflict of Interest. As you read this description of HMOs, you may have perceived the built-in conflict of interest. Should it be profits or patient care? An unintended consequence of reducing costs by cutting down on tests and hospitalization is that HMO doctors withhold some *necessary* treatments, tests, and hospitalizations. For example, a woman I know was sent home from the hospital even though she was still bleeding from her surgery. If she had remained longer, she would have used up more than her "share" of allotted costs and eaten into the HMO's profits. This would not have happened to a fee-for-service patient who could afford to pay for the health care. On the contrary, doctors would advise such a patient *not* to leave the hospital until the bleeding stopped.

One reason that many physicians oppose HMOs is because they have to get permission to give certain treatments (Mathews 2012). Some administrators of HMOs, whose job is to produce profits, end up dictating to doctors what treatment they can give their patients. ("You can do that if you want to, but we won't pay for it.") Some HMOs even determine the number of patients the doctors must see each day. One HMO insisted that its physicians see eight patients an hour, limiting them to 7½ minutes per visit. This did not leave the doctors enough time for completing paperwork, analyzing lab results, and, of course, calling HMO officials to get approval for treatment (Greenhouse 1999).

Read on **MySocLab**
Document
Healing in a Hurry: Hospitals in the Managed-Care Age

As you can imagine, limiting medical treatment in order to increase profits can lead to severe problems. Here is just one:

A doctor noticed a lump in one of her own breasts. When she called the radiology department of the hospital where she worked to schedule a mammogram, she was told that she would have to wait 6 months. The hospital's HMO allowed one mammogram every 2 years, and she had had a mammogram 18 months earlier. She had to appeal to the HMO's board of directors, who agreed to let her be an exception to the rule. She had breast cancer (Gibbs and Bower 2006).

Being Paid to Stay Healthy

Another attempt to reduce costs is to give workers a rebate for staying healthy—or at least for staying away from doctors. In return for accepting a high annual insurance deductible, employees who spend less than the deductible are paid the difference between it and their insurance claims. If the deductible is, say, $1,500, workers who claim only $100 for medical treatment collect $1,400, a nice bonus. Where this program has been tried, employee health costs go down. As one employee said, "Now I feel I have an investment in my own health."

Physician Extenders

Yet another strategy for controlling costs is the use of *physician extenders*, people who have been trained to assist doctors in caring for patients. The two primary types are *physician assistants* and *nurse practitioners*, who work under the supervision of physicians. Half to three-fourths of all the problems that are dealt with in a typical doctor's office are aches, sniffles, and other trivial matters. It makes financial sense to delegate routine and time-consuming medical care to lower-paid physician extenders. Physician assistants and nurse practitioners also manage routine tasks like giving school physicals and educating patients who have chronic disorders.

An in-house rivalry has developed. Physician assistants and nurse practitioners don't like doctors breathing down their necks, and they want more independence in treating patients. Their efforts to attain greater autonomy are resisted by doctors, of course, who feel their turf is being invaded (Aston and Foubister 1998). In general, the attitude of the medical profession is, "If they want to do more, they can go to medical school."

Physician assistants and nurse practitioners keep pushing the issue. They have gained more autonomy, and they now run the in-store clinics mentioned earlier, and in some states they can prescribe basic medications for simple matters (Villegas 2010). The battle is heating up. Nurses are earning "doctor of nursing" degrees and calling themselves "doctors." The physicians are responding by trying to get state legislators to limit the title of doctor only to themselves (Harris 2011).

Training Physicians

Let's start with a startling statistic. Medical schools graduate about 16,000 physicians a year, the same today as 25 years ago when there were 70 million fewer Americans (*Statistical Abstract* 2013:Tables 2, 304). This total alone should give you insight into why some areas have the doctor shortage we discussed—and how limiting the number of new physicians drives up medical costs.

Although the number of graduates has stayed the same, as you can see from Figure 10.13, a fundamental change has occurred in the gender makeup of those graduates. This change in gender is not likely to have any significant effect on how medicine is practiced. The medical delivery system is in place, with depersonalization and the profit motive built into it, which is likely to make gender irrelevant. Female doctors are as likely as male doctors to be generous or greedy, patient or profit-oriented, and to favor heroic medicine or preventive medicine.

Here is a simple, direct, and far-reaching proposal for social policy: To reduce the costs of health care, overcome the doctor shortage, and provide more care for the poor, let's train more physicians. The government could finance new medical schools. The schools could be tuition-free, and the students could be paid a monthly salary. In return, for each year the graduates were supported in medical school, they would spend one year in areas where there is a doctor shortage. These new physicians would not be given final certification until they completed their years of public service. During those years, the government would pay for their medical malpractice insurance and pay them a salary equal to what the average American earns. The United States already has the National Health Service Corps, which offers support for students in medical school, but this would be a much more extensive program.

A social policy to increase competition among doctors would be met with shrill protest from the American Medical Association. The AMA stifles competition by limiting the number of medical graduates. If medical schools graduated enough new physicians to produce strong competition among doctors, the cost of medical care would drop, threatening the power of this medical monopoly.

FIGURE 10.13 ▸ **M.D. Degrees, by Sex**

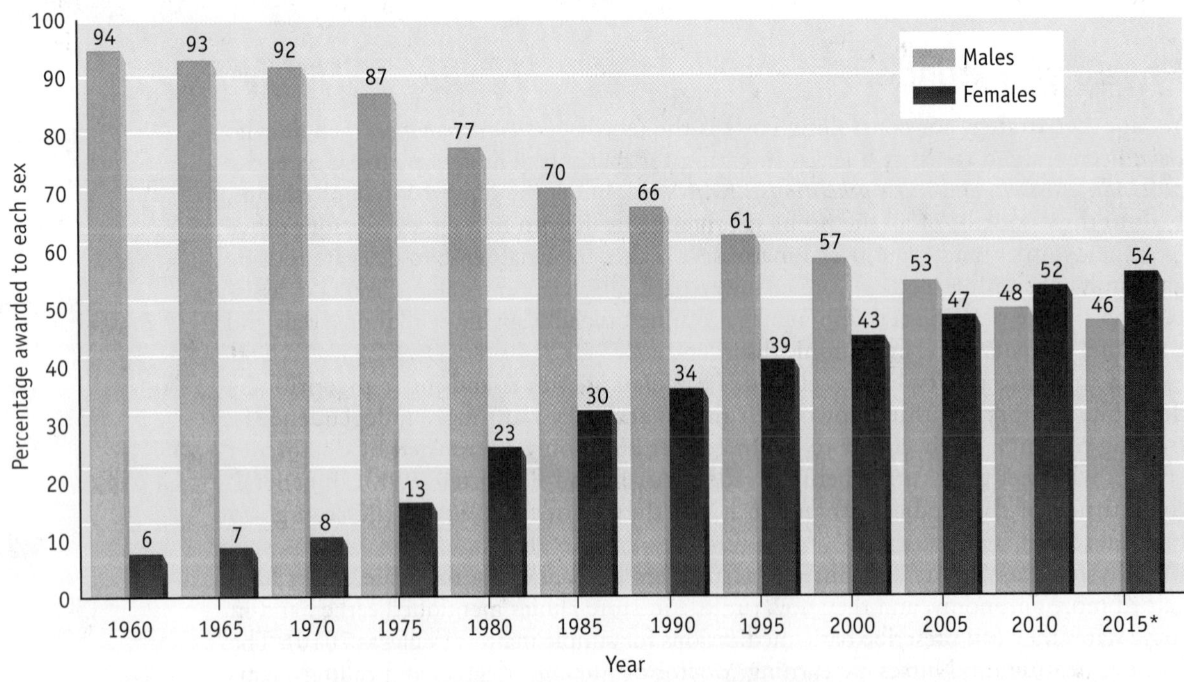

*Author's estimate

Sources: Statistical Abstract of the United States 1994:Table 295; 2013:Table 304.

Home Health Care

On Figure 10.8 (page 326), you saw how expensive hospitalization is. To help reduce this cost, when possible doctors are substituting **home health care** (also called **domiciliary care**), treatment given in a patient's home. Most elderly patients prefer home health care, not only because it is less expensive but also because they find it more humane to be treated at home than in an unfamiliar and often depersonalized nursing home or hospital.

We can extend this concept by establishing group homes and apartments for the mentally disturbed and the chronically ill who have difficulty living in the community on their own. There, we can provide them home health care. Such programs would be costly, of course, and granted our ongoing, huge budget deficits, we can ill afford them. You can also anticipate the objection that we would be spending more money on the "unworthy."

Preventive Medicine

Prevention—taking steps that preserve health or avoid illness and disease—can be highly effective. The most preventable cause of premature death is smoking. Each year, *a half million* (492,000) Americans die from nicotine in its various forms (Centers for Disease Control and Prevention 2011). When we add deaths from high blood pressure and obesity, we find that *half* of all deaths in the United States are premature and postponable (Danaei et al. 2009). Let's look at how we can improve health and avoid premature deaths.

Three Types of Preventive Medicine. There are three types of prevention. **Primary prevention** keeps a disease from occurring in the first place. Examples are improving nutrition and giving childhood vaccinations. **Secondary prevention** refers to detecting a disease before it comes to the attention of a physician. An example is self-examination for breast cancer. **Tertiary prevention** refers to preventing further damage from a disease that has been detected. This is often the same as regular medical care. Examples are maintaining a diabetic on insulin and controlling an infection so that it doesn't lead to death.

Food and Health. Primary prevention has a huge payoff for improving health. Proper nutrition, exercise, rest, and avoiding tobacco and the abuse of alcohol and other drugs strengthen the immune system and help people avoid many diseases. Many cancers can

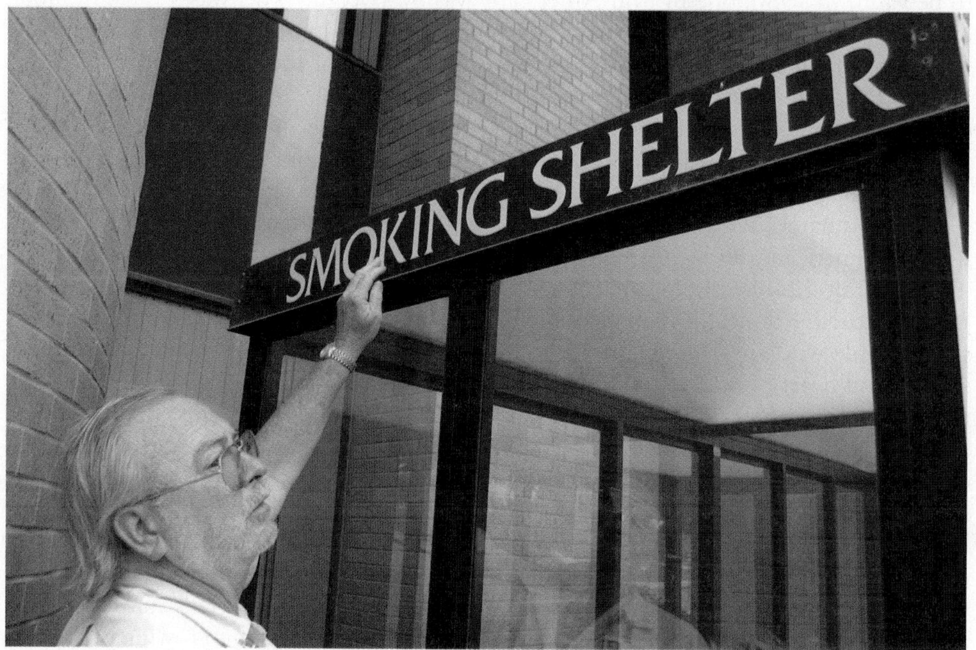

The anti-smoking movement has become so dominant that some smokers say they feel isolated and rejected, shoved off into little areas and treated like deviants.

be prevented by a diet rich in beta-carotene, raw fruits, vegetables, and nuts. Supplements of natural vitamin C and E also reduce the risk of cancer. So do wheat bran, canola oil, soy milk, cantaloupe, avocados, olive oil, red wine, and leafy green vegetables—cabbage, broccoli, brussels sprouts, and spinach (Biello 2006; Kushi et al. 2012).

Studies of the effects of milk on health are mixed. Some research indicates that milk can reduce cancer (Cho et al. 2004; Nielsen et al. 2011), but other research indicates that milk might increase the risk of cancer (Mayne et al. 1995; Shaw 2007). If milk does increase the risk of cancer, this could be due not to the milk but to its contaminants—pesticides, herbicides, and bovine growth hormones. The growth hormones that are fed to cows may pave the way for cancer by inhibiting the body's natural cancer fighters (Epstein 1999). Some accuse Monsanto, a global corporate giant that produces bovine growth hormones, of caring more about profits than people's health. To this, conflict theorists would reply, "Big surprise!"

Immunizations. Immunizing children is effective primary prevention. Not only do immunizations save lives but also they save vast amounts of money that otherwise would be spent on medical treatment. Yet about 10 percent of U.S. children have not been immunized against measles, mumps, diphtheria, hepatitis, and polio (*Statistical Abstract* 2013:Table 196). This is the average. The total is higher in rural and poor areas.

Preventing Drug Abuse. Although not usually thought of as preventive medicine, no program would be complete unless it also included preventing drug abuse. From what we learned in Chapter 4, to reduce drug abuse is to prevent many health problems. Drug abuse prevention programs that are directed against smoking and alcohol abuse could prevent the untimely deaths of hundreds of thousands of people *each year.* Drug abuse programs, then, are another way to improve the nation's health.

Eating Ourselves to Death. Something disturbing is happening in the United States, and it does not bode well for health. Let me share these two events with you:

While waiting for a space shot at Cape Canaveral, Florida, I struck up a conversation with a British couple in their 20s. I asked about their impression of the United States. Hesitantly, they said that they had never seen so many fat people in their lives.

When a friend from Spain arrived, he asked me why there were so many fat Americans.

Are these valid perceptions or ethnocentric observations of foreigners? They seem to be valid. In 1980, one of four Americans was overweight. This was a huge number of people. But since then this already-large percentage has jumped to three of every five (62 percent) Americans ages 18 to 44. And nearly three of four (72 percent) of those ages 45 to 64 are overweight (*Statistical Abstract* 1998:Table 242; 2013:Table 213). In short, Americans eat too much and don't get enough exercise.

Some will say, "So what?" What "fat" is comes from some arbitrary idea of how much people should weigh. And maybe this idea came from a skinny person.

Unfortunately, we are talking about a great deal more than arbitrary ideas. About 215,000 Americans die each year from the extra pounds they carry (Danaei et al. 2009). This is about *12 times* the number of Americans who dies from AIDS. Obesity is also more destructive to health than alcohol abuse. Why so many deaths? Among other reasons, people who are overweight are more likely to suffer from diabetes and to have strokes and heart attacks (Kumanyika 2005; Franks et al. 2010). And compared with thinner people, when the obese come down with these health problems, they are more likely to die from them (Calle et al. 2003; Franks 2010).

This unprecedented increase in the weight of Americans flies in the face of what we know about preventing health problems. Why is this occurring? The cause is not biological, but social. With the onslaught of advertising, the average American drinks about *50 gallons* of soft drinks a year (*Statistical Abstract* 2013:Table 220). Add this to the cultural taste for fattening, sweetened, processed foods, and the pounds pile on. Within this cultural setting and because fattening, sugary foods taste good, it is difficult to halt this growing problem.

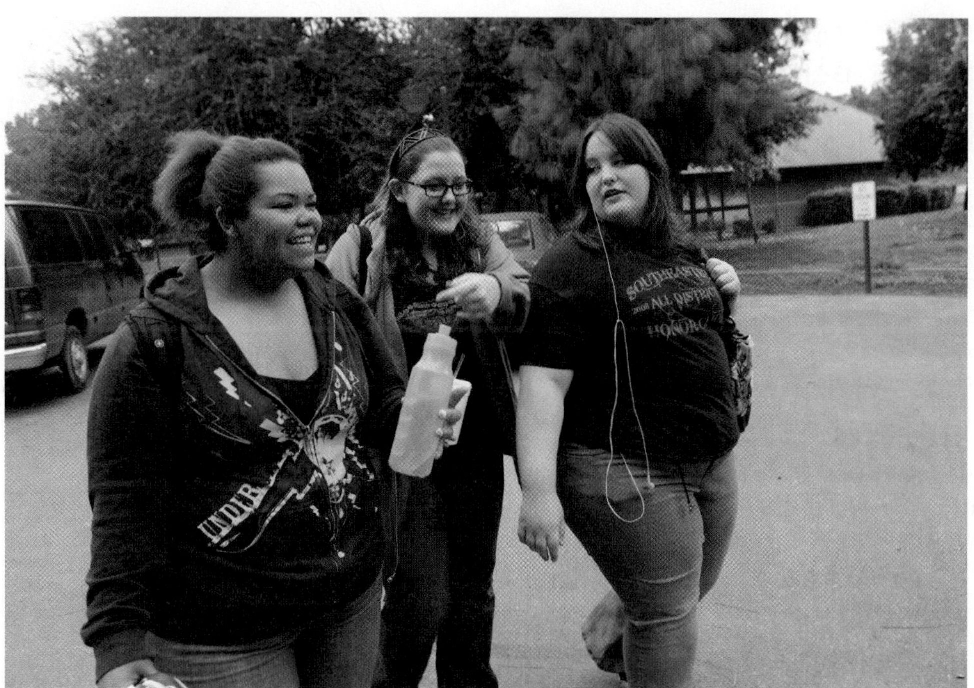

One attempt to solve the growing problem of obesity is education. These three friends are enrolled in a high school in Reedley, California, that helps students lose weight as they learn their academic subjects.

It is also significant to note that the primary emphasis in our culture is not prevention. The primary cultural orientation is to visit a doctor when health problems arise, not to avoid health problems through healthier foods and lifestyles.

The Problem with Preventive Medicine. The problem with preventive medicine is that it isn't appealing—it doesn't taste good like all those sugary foods. It violates our desire to eat sweets and swill soft drinks and alcohol. And it goes against the pleasure we receive from being lazy couch potatoes. But these things are killing us. If we want health, we have to work at it. This means eating healthful foods, getting the sleep we need, and forcing ourselves to do the exercises that our bodies rebel against but that they require for good health.

If the medical profession were to give preventive medicine the same priority it gives heroic medicine and the treatment of acute conditions, the nation's health would improve. But preventive medicine doesn't show immediate results, and taking a pill is a lot easier than losing weight and exercising. Preventive medicine is also less appealing to medical professionals who have been trained for open-heart surgery, screaming ambulances, and rushing about in emergency rooms—or at least prescribing pills. Not incidentally, it is difficult for physicians to make money by preventing illness.

To see how lifestyle can affect people's health on a national basis, read the *Spotlight on Social Research* box on the next page.

Humanizing Health Care

Jeanne Kennedy, the chief patient representative at Stanford Hospital in Palo Alto, California, broke her knee cap rushing to a meeting. A member of her staff wheeled her to the employee health department, where a nurse practitioner she had worked with for years began to arrange for her care. But the nurse spoke to the woman pushing the wheelchair and ignored Mrs. Kennedy.

"It was crazy," she said, "Here I was in my own hospital, hurt but perfectly capable, and she's being very professional, but she's talking over my head as if I were a child. And we worked together. She knew me!" (Carey 2005)

Patients hate being depersonalized, but how can you overcome it? Even when medical students have a strong desire to treat patients as people, the pressures of their training,

Spotlight on Social Research

Solving a Medical Mystery

WILLIAM COCKERHAM, *professor of sociology at the University of Alabama at Birmingham, studies international aspects of health. He has done research on health and lifestyles in Russia and Eastern Europe, and he is doing similar research in Japan. Here is what he wrote for you.*

In the mid-1990s, I attended a medical sociology conference in Vienna. Sociologists from the former socialist countries in Eastern Europe reported that their countries were in the midst of a health crisis. They said that men were dying prematurely and that the life expectancy for women had either declined or stagnated. What was striking about their presentations and in the discussions that followed was that no one could explain why this was occurring. That in peacetime an entire group of industrialized societies was experiencing a prolonged deterioration in the health of the population was unexpected.

The lack of an explanation for this crisis presented an intriguing research question. The killer turned out to be an increase in heart disease that had begun in the mid-1960s. A review of the evidence showed that infectious diseases, environmental pollution, and poor medical care were not enough to cause this surge in mortality. A clue that other social factors were important was the fact that the rise in death rates was not universal. Heart disease differed by gender, age, urban–rural locale, education, and region. Those most affected were middle-aged, urban men who did manual work.

We now knew the "what" and the "who," but not the "why." To discover the "why," I traveled to Russia and Eastern Europe. There, I collected data from clinics, hospitals, and ministries of health. I also interviewed public health experts, physicians, and sociologists. In addition, I observed how the people lived.

I uncovered three reasons for the increase in premature deaths. The first was policy failures: the failure to address the increase in heart disease and to adopt measures to lower smoking and drinking. The second seemed to be stress, which had increased with the collapse of communism: Workers had lost jobs and state benefits, such as housing and food subsidies. In addition, inflation had made their money worth less, driving down the value of their pensions and salaries. The third—and the primary reason—turned out to be unhealthy lifestyles. Heavy drinking and smoking and lack of exercise characterized the people who died prematurely from heart disease. To say "heavy" drinking is an understatement: Adult Russian males, who comprise 25 percent of the population, drink 90 percent of the alcohol consumed in a country that averages 14 gallons per person annually.

I did not have enough data, however, to determine conclusively that stress—which has a well-established connection to heart disease—was especially important. A grant from the European Union provided funds to survey 18,000 people in eight countries of the former Soviet Union. This survey showed that women actually are more stressed than men. While stress undoubtedly makes the women's lives less pleasant and has consequences for their health, it is not killing enough of them prematurely to come close to the mortality rates of the men. As bad as the situation may be for the women, the key to explaining the health crisis ultimately lies in the men's behavior.

accompanied by the faculty's stress on organs, disease, and dysfunctions, change the students' attitude about patients. Listen to this medical student:

> *Somebody will say, "Listen to Mrs. Jones's heart. It's just a little thing flubbing on the table." And you forget about the rest of her . . . and it helps in learning in the sense that you can go in to a patient, put your stethoscope on the heart, listen to it, and walk out. . . . The advantage is that you can go in a short time and see a patient, get the important things out of the patient, and leave. (Haas and Shaffir 1993:437)*

Ultimately, medical training needs to stress the *inherent worth* of patients—that each individual is valuable and deserves personal attention. Achieving this is certainly an uphill battle, because depersonalization has become almost instinctive to medical personnel. The best social policy, it seems, is the same as the one I proposed to overcome the doctor shortage. If we train enough doctors, we will produce strong competition for patients. Of necessity, doctors will have to treat patients as people. Those who don't will have fewer patients—and less profit.

In Sum ▸ The aim of these policies is to reduce the cost of medical care, improve health by preventing disease, and humanize the treatment of patients. These simple, direct policies offer inexpensive alternatives to highly technological and costly medical care. But as we discuss in the little box below, for one problem there is an even simpler solution.

The Future of the Problem

To try to catch a glimpse of the future, let's look at trends in medical technology and in changing the direction of medicine.

10.8 Discuss the likely future of medical care as a social problem.

Technological Advances

New Technology. Both doctors and patients like new technology. They both derive satisfaction from technology that improves the diagnoses and treatment of medical problems. In the coming years, we can expect doctors to continue to adopt new medical technology and patients to expect their doctors and hospitals to have whatever technology is new. Within this context, the manufacturers of medical equipment will continue to develop and market cutting-edge technologies. You can expect, then, that medical costs will continue to escalate.

Issues in Social Problems

Doctors, Please Wash Your Hands!

Do you recall the statement I made at the beginning of this chapter, that each year about 100,000 Americans die needlessly at the hands of doctors and nurses? Many of these deaths are so easily preventable that it is infuriating to anyone who knows anything about them.

Let's look at one type, deaths from catheterization. This term refers to inserting a little tube in a vein to deliver drugs or other liquids. This allows a nurse to make quick, easy connections to a tube that is attached to a bag of fluids. About 40,000 patients each year were getting blood stream infections from the catheters. About 5,000 to 10,000 of the patients died from the infections.

After new procedures were followed, the infections and deaths were cut almost in half.

What new procedures could have such dramatic results? Here are the main ones:

1. The doctors wash their hands.
2. The area where the needle is inserted is sterilized.

And there is a third. Nurses are given a check list and—breaking with tradition—the nurse is authorized to tell the doctor that he or she must wash and must follow the checklist and to report the doctor if he or she does not do so (Mathews 2012).

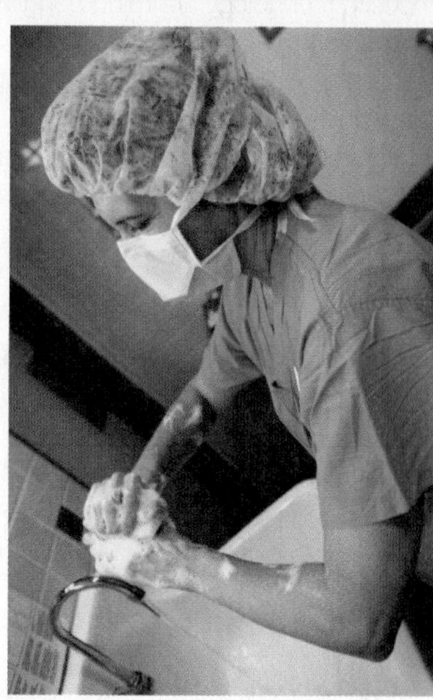

It's a chore for doctors and nurses to wash their hands before visiting each patient. When they don't, they spread disease. Fresh latex gloves for each patient visit are one solution.

For Your Consideration

What is your reaction to this? To me, this is incredible, and I can hardly stop gritting my teeth at a medical profession that still kills patients out of sloth. The ignorance ended long ago when it was proven—to the amazements of physicians—that there are little things called germs and that women were dying in childbirth because the doctors were transmitting diseases with their dirty hands. Reluctantly, the doctors began to wash their hands. Evidently, they have to keep learning this lesson—and evidently patients have to keep dying until they really learn it.

Ethical Dilemmas. Out of these technological advances have arisen ethical problems that plague medical professionals and laypeople alike. If people can be kept alive artificially, must doctors keep them alive? Does "brain dead" really mean "dead"? If so, should physicians be allowed to "harvest body parts" from people who (only because of machines) are still breathing? Should medical researchers be allowed to test dangerous drugs on these people, because, after all, they are "really" dead?

In the Technology and Social Problems box below, we consider how technological advances hold the potential for improving our lives and create further ethical dilemmas.

The Internet. The Internet has helped some patients regain control over their medical care. People who have rare diseases, for example, can participate in online discussion groups. Although people don't meet personally, they share their experiences and knowledge with one another. Some doctors are surprised—and dismayed—when their patients know more than they do about a new treatment or some new research. Not only

Technology and Social Problems

"Need a New Body Part? Grab Your Printer"

The advances in technology are mind boggling. Some are so astounding that it is difficult to grasp that what is being developed is even possible. Let's explore one of these leap-frogging changes.

3-D printers are fascinating. Like the replicator of *Star Trek*, the technology allows us to print entire items. By laying down fine layers of whatever substance an item is made of, we can reproduce exact replicas of the item. This can be an item as simple as a cup or as complicated as a motorcycle. And you can drink from the replicated cup or ride the motorcycle, whose parts work.

We have just begun to explore the implications of this fascinating achievement in technology. How will we apply it beyond making car parts on demand?

How about making human parts? I'm talking about printing real, genuine body parts such as working blood vessels, real veins and arteries that transport blood through the body. And maybe we can print working livers and kidneys so good that we can transplant them into real people.

This isn't just some futurist's dream. 3-D bioprinters that can replicate body tissues and organs are now being developed. Their laser-guided nozzles extrude "bio-inks" of human cells onto a mold. After about 24 hours, the mold is removed, with a bioreactor keeping the tissue alive. As the tissue stitches itself together, it becomes the particular organ it was intended to be (Hotz 2012).

No 3-D-printed kidneys or hearts yet, but they appear to be on the way. One of the problems to be overcome is developing a capillary system to feed the developing tissue. But if you look carefully at the gleams in the bioengineers' eyes, you will see the reflection of patients' X-rays and CT scans transformed into digital diagrams for printed body parts.

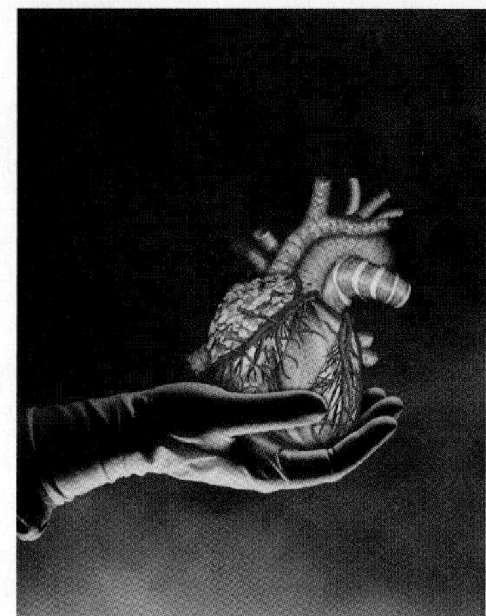

Technology is transforming medicine. In the future, we might be able to grow new body parts, replacing those that wear out.

What a potential future. Absolutely mind boggling.

For Your Consideration

When the time comes that we can actually print replacement body parts—and this is likely to occur soon—do you think that we will be able to continually replace our worn-out parts so we can live indefinitely, or at least for a couple of hundred years or so? And if Mary Leticia, a star athlete, decides to enhance her running by printing a new knee, one that improves her performance, should she be allowed to compete with people who are left with their old joints?

Then there is the matter of social equality. If a rich woman needs a new body part, because she can pay for it should she be given precedence over a poor woman? How about a prisoner convicted of rape and murder? Should he be given the same consideration as your sociology instructor?

do physicians feel threatened because they no longer are the sole possessors of esoteric knowledge on rare diseases or even the treatment of common disorders, but they also fear that patients can be picking up misinformation on the Internet. Sharing information online can also contaminate medical experiments. Some patients are able to determine whether they are receiving an experimental drug or a *placebo*, a substance that is designed to look like a medicine but that has no medical value (Bulkeley 1995).

Redirecting Medicine

The Carlson Predictions. In the 1970s, Rick Carlson (1975) predicted that a more complex and stressful society was on its way. He said that we would have a large aging population with incurable degenerative diseases and more illnesses resulting from lifestyle and environmental deterioration. Carlson held out little hope that our medical system would stress preventive medicine or work on overcoming environmental and lifestyle causes of illness. He concluded that poverty would not be cured and that the poor would continue to have more illnesses than the affluent. He was mostly right. Slowly—as in how an iceberg turns—however, the medical profession is changing. We'll come back to this.

The Potential. Carlson argued that we can change our health care system and meet the health care issues facing the nation. An effective system, he said, would *encourage people to demand better health rather than more medicine*. This requires an awareness of the factors that influence health, from those under the individual's control to environmental factors under the community's control.

To make this potential a reality, our educational system can stress preventive and environmental medicine. From kindergarten through college, programs can feature the prevention of medical problems: food safety, occupational safety, nutrition, and exercise. At all grade levels, too, students can be required to get exercise through rigorous physical education. To reduce stress, which is related to many illnesses, we can design more relaxing work environments in offices and schools, build parks and extensive hiking and bike paths in our communities, and reduce noise pollution.

The potential for improving the general health of our population is high. With the growing awareness of how social factors underlie health and illness, the demand for preventing health problems will grow. Resistance will continue from the medical establishment, but I expect that gradually medical tradition and culture will change. The future is likely to see both heroic intervention and preventive medicine existing alongside one another.

Study and Review on MySocLab

Summary and Review

1. What people consider to be health and illness depends on culture and social class. Physical and mental health problems are based on both biological and social factors.
2. Industrialization has brought better health, but with it has come an increase in cancer, heart disease, drug addiction, and other chronic illnesses caused by lifestyle, aging, and environmental pollution. HIV/AIDS illustrates the relationship among behavior, environment, and disease. Physical and emotional problems are more common among the poor. To explain the relationship between social class and mental illness, sociologists prefer environmental explanations rather than genetic ones.
3. The U.S. medical system is centered on specialized, hospital-based, and heroic intervention.

A fee-for-service system increases medical costs. Preventive medicine redirects the emphasis to people's lifestyles and environment.

4. Social inequalities plague physical and mental health care. In our fee-for-service system, health care is not a right but a commodity sold to the highest bidder. The United States has a *two-tier system of medical care*—public clinics and poorer treatment for the poor and private clinics and better treatment for the more affluent. Despite health reform and universal insurance, the poor and affluent will not receive the same medical treatment.
5. Two policies designed to control medical costs are to pay patients to stay healthy and to pay doctors to reduce unnecessary medical care. *HMOs* are a form of *managed care* that provides a fixed amount of money to a medical corporation to attend to the health needs of a group of people. Medical services and tests come directly off the corporate bottom line, leading to a conflict of interest in treating patients. On the positive side, it costs the HMO less if they catch problems early and if they practice preventive medicine.
6. The medical profession is experiencing a tension among its traditional focus on heroic intervention in acute problems, the need to treat chronic problems, and the emerging focus on preventing medical problems by changing lifestyles. Within this tension, there is likely to develop increased emphasis on preventive medicine—better health habits, a cleaner environment, and education designed to teach people how to take care of themselves and to manage their illnesses.

Key Terms

cesarean section, 315
conversion therapy, 324
defensive medicine, 325
deinstitutionalization, 321
depersonalization, 325
domiciliary care, 339
drug therapy, 335
electroconvulsive therapy (ECT), 336
group therapy, 335
health maintenance organization (HMO), 336
home health care, 339
iatrogenesis, 311
individual psychotherapy, 335
infant mortality rate, 318
lay referral network, 324
pharmaceutical straitjackets, 336
prepaid or managed care, 336
primary prevention, 339
professional referral network, 324
psychoanalysis, 335
secondary prevention, 339
short-term directive therapy, 335
talk therapy, 336
tertiary prevention, 339
two-tier system of medical care, 315

Thinking Critically About Chapter 10

1. What do you think the government's role should be in medical care? Why?
2. Why do you think women live longer than men?
3. Which of the theoretical perspectives (symbolic interactionism, functionalism, or conflict theory) do you think best explains health care problems in the United States? Why do you think so?

11 The Changing Family

Listen to Chapter 11 on MySocLab

Learning Objectives. After reading this chapter, you should be able to:

11.1 Summarize how the Industrial Revolution changed the family. **(p. 348)**

11.2 Understand how divorce, one-parent families, violence, and runaway children are part of the problem. **(p. 351)**

11.3 Discuss the perspectives that emerge when you apply symbolic interactionism, functionalism, and conflict theory to why divorce is common. **(p. 358)**

11.4 Summarize research findings on postponing marriage, couples without children, family violence, sexual abuse, the elderly, and the death of the family. **(p. 366)**

11.5 Explain the controversy over professional intrusion in the family and the dilemma of family policy. **(p. 380)**

11.6 Discuss the trends and social changes that are likely to affect family relationships. **(p. 381)**

Nancy and Antoine were pleased. Their 4-year-old daughter, Janelle, had been accepted at Rainbow Gardens Preschool in Manhattan Beach, California, a prosperous suburb of Los Angeles. The preschool came highly recommended by their close friends, whose son was attending the school. With Nancy's promotion and Antoine's new job, schedules had become more difficult, and Rainbow Gardens was able to handle their need for flexible hours.

She had begun to have nightmares.

At first, Janelle loved preschool. She would happily leave whichever parent drove her to school for the pleasures of her little friends and the gentle care of loving teachers. Then, gradually, almost imperceptibly, a change came over her. At first, Janelle became reluctant to leave her parents. Then she began to whimper in the mornings when they were getting her ready for school. And lately she had begun to have nightmares. She was waking up crying and screaming several times a week, something she had never done before. They took Janelle to a counselor. She said it was nothing to worry about, that all kids go through things like this from time to time. This was just a "developmental adjustment" and a "separation anxiety." Their daughter would be just fine in a little while.

When allegations of sexual abuse of 3-, 4-, and 5-year-olds at Rainbow Gardens made headlines, parents around the nation were devastated. The unthinkable had become real. "Was it happening at our preschool, too? Could it be happening with our child?" they wondered. But for Nancy and Antoine, it was more than a nagging question. Overnight, Janelle's nightmares, her crying, and her bed-wetting took on new meaning. Those gentle teachers, so affectionate with the children, child molesters? Janelle undressed, photographed, forced to commit sexual acts with adults, and threatened with the death of her puppy if she told?

Nancy and Antoine don't know. It is either this or simply a "developmental adjustment," maybe just a normal "separation anxiety." Now it is Nancy's and Antoine's turn for nightmares.

The Problem in Sociological Perspective

Watch on **MySocLab Video:** Day Care

Nightmare at Rainbow Gardens could be the title of a horror movie, a real-life one for some parents. During the 1980s, rumors spread that day care centers were filled with child molesters. A kind of hysteria swept the country, with preschool teachers suspect. Some teachers were tried and convicted, sometimes on flimsy evidence (Rabinowitz 2004). A Massachusetts man served 18 years in prison before his pleas of innocence were finally acknowledged. Although the headlines of that time were based on hysteria, some children are abused at day school, a frightening prospect for parents. Why aren't the children at home with their families? Why are 5 million U.S. children entrusted to the care of strangers in day care (*Statistical Abstract* 2013:Table 589)?

Day care is part of a sea change that has swept our society, engulfing families and forcing them to adjust. As we review problems facing families in this chapter, we'll stress this theme: the impact of social change.

Effects of the Industrial Revolution on the Family

11.1 Summarize how the industrial revolution changed the family.

Let's begin by looking at the Industrial Revolution, the most significant event to affect the family. Before industrialization, economic survival was perilous. It was common for families to live on the edge of disaster. There were no factories, offices, or public schools, and both parents and children worked at home together. When industrialization moved production to factories, the consequences for family life were so extensive that they continue to influence us today. Here are some of the consequences.

Men Left Home. Men left home to work in factories. This created a divide between the husband-father and the other family members. During workday hours—which were long, about 12 to 14 hours a day—the husband-father was at work in the factory, while the wife and children were working at home. No longer did the family members share activities during working hours. Separated from the household, the husband-father's orientation to life changed.

When millions of men left home to fight overseas during World War II, women took over their civilian jobs. This photo was taken in 1943 at Lockheed Aircraft in Burbank, California.

Children Became an Economic Liability. Industrialization transformed children from an economic asset into an economic liability. When production was farm-based, children contributed to their family's survival—they fed chickens, milked cows, and worked in the fields. After industrialization, children no longer helped produce food, but they still consumed it.

Formal Education. Industrialization brought a need for more formal education and opened opportunities to acquire it. As children spent more years in school, they became dependent on their parents for a longer time. Their prolonged education and longer dependency made them even more expensive.

A Lower Birthrate. The discovery of vulcanized rubber during the 1840s made large-scale production of the condom possible. With further refinements in design and manufacture in the 1920s, the condom allowed couples to limit births (Douvan 1980; Laslett 1980). The birth control pill that came in the 1970s allowed couples even more control over pregnancy. On Figure 11.1 below, you can see how the U.S. birthrate plunged.

FIGURE 11.1 ▸ U.S. Birthrate, 1890–2050

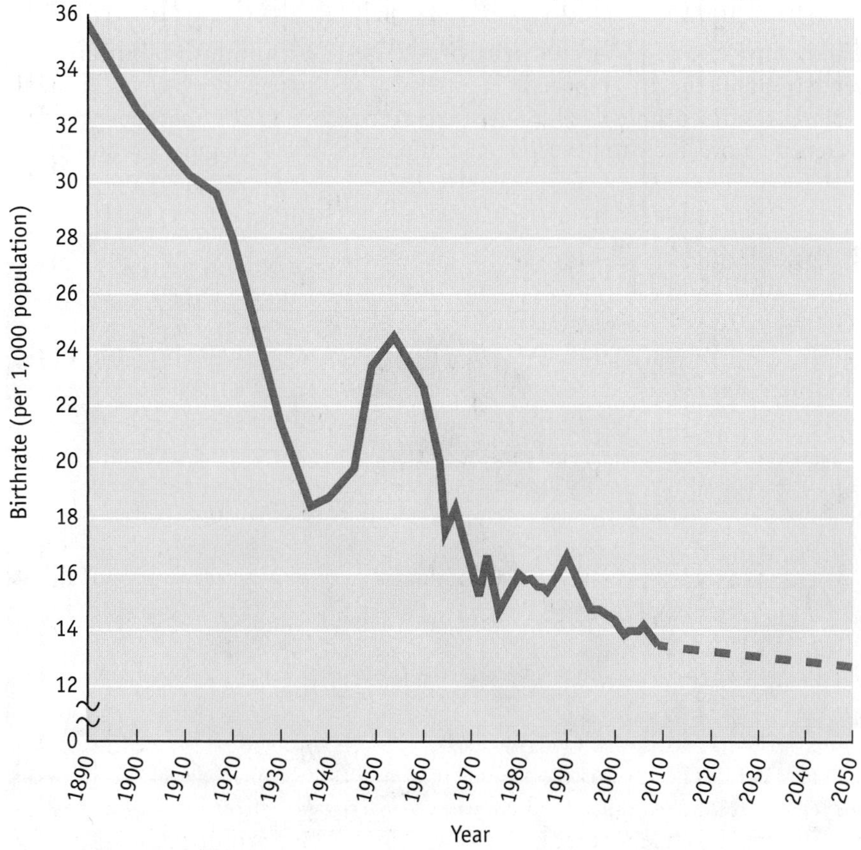

Note: The projection is the author's estimate.

Source: By the author. Based on *Statistical Abstract of the United States,* various editions; 2001:Table 4; 2013:Table 81.

From Rural to Urban. Industrialization also changed where people lived. In the 1800s, almost everyone lived on farms. As production moved to city factories, workers moved to where the work was. Housing in the city was more expensive, another reason for couples to have fewer children.

Loss of Functions. Families used to be responsible for producing their own food and clothing, educating their children, and providing their own medical care. As industrialization spread, other institutions began to take over these functions. Factories produced food and clothing, schools educated the children, and health care systems took over the care of illness. Losing these functions weakened families.

Watch on **MySocLab Video:** Women's Changing Family Role

Changes in Women's Roles. Industrialization also changed women's roles. The farm wife used to be responsible for basic food production (milk, butter, eggs, vegetables), preparation (baking and cooking), and storage (canning). She also made, washed, ironed, and mended the family's clothing; cleaned the house; and took care of the children, the sick, and the elderly. As her functions were reduced, the wife/mother increasingly became an "emotional provider"; that is, she spent more time lavishing attention upon her breadwinner husband and on her diminishing number of children.

Greater Equality. Industrialization also brought greater equality to husbands and wives. As men's and women's roles changed, so did ideas about how their relationship "ought to be." This change was gradual and did not happen without struggle. Men were reluctant to give up their more privileged positions. The struggle over equality (authority and decision making) is still a primary source of tension in today's marriages.

More Divorce. Before industrialization, divorce was rare. But with the changes just outlined, especially the reduced functions of the family and the lower birthrate, marriages became fragile.

Longer Lives and More Intergenerational Ties. With industrialization came improvements in public health, especially a purer water supply and advances in medicine. With better health, people lived longer than ever before. One consequence is that today's children are more likely to have living grandparents, and even great-grandparents.

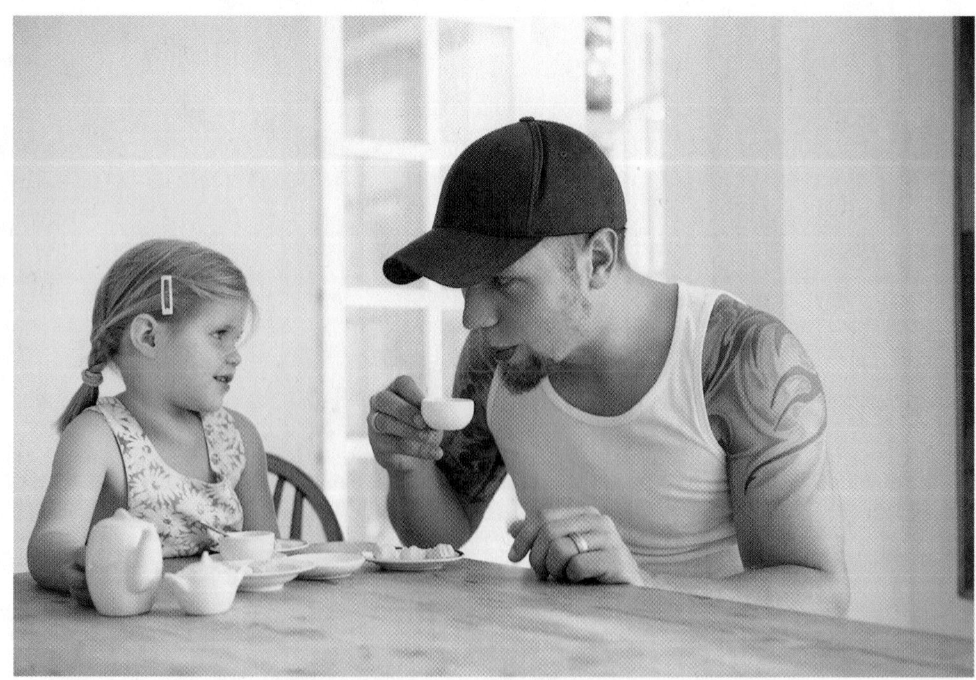

The family is always adjusting to changes that are taking place in society. As ideas of masculinity change, for example, behaviors that once were not acceptable for men come to be thought of as normal. After those changes become standard, a current generation may have difficulty understanding why such behaviors ever threatened men's sense of "masculinity."

This is new in world history. Many grandparents who live nearby provide in-home day care while the children's mothers are at work. In an age of telecommunication, grandparents who live far from their grandchildren are still able to participate in their lives.

The "Quiet Revolution." One of the fundamental changes in family life was a transformation of women's roles—women leaving home to enter the paid workforce. As office work expanded, employers hired more and more women. Then during World War II, millions of women took over the factory jobs the men left when they went off to war. This process continued, with the 1980s marking the first time in history that half of married women worked for wages at least part-time outside the home. Today 60 percent do (*Statistical Abstract* 2013:Table 607). Because women working at paid jobs outside the home bring extensive change to family relationships, it is sometimes called the *quiet revolution*.

In Sum ▸ For the family to provide for the well-being of its members, it must adjust to the changes that occur in society. In some ways, the family is always in transition. Just as the family adapted to the Industrial Revolution, so today it is coping with the post-industrialization of society.

Read on **MySocLab Document** The Way We Weren't: The Myth and Reality of the 'Traditional' Family

The Scope of the Problem

11.2 Understand how divorce, one-parent families, violence, and runaway children are part of the problem.

A lot of people are bothered by what is happening to today's families. Our current social changes are powerful, and many families are having a hard time. Some even think that the family is disintegrating. As always, we want to move beyond subjective concerns and examine objective conditions. What indications, if any, might suggest that the family is in trouble?

Divorce

When you say "family problems," divorce is one of the first things that people think of. On Figure 11.2 below, you can trace the changes in divorce since 1890. From something rare, divorce has become so common that it has disrupted the family life of millions of Americans. Another way to look at the trend in divorce is to compare the number of Americans who are getting married with the number who are getting divorced. As Figure 11.3 on the next page shows, for every two couples getting married, another couple is ending its marriage. Note this is *not* the same as saying one out of every two marriages ends in divorce. The divorces are coming from marriages of earlier years.

FIGURE 11.2 ▸ How Many Millions of Americans Are Divorced?

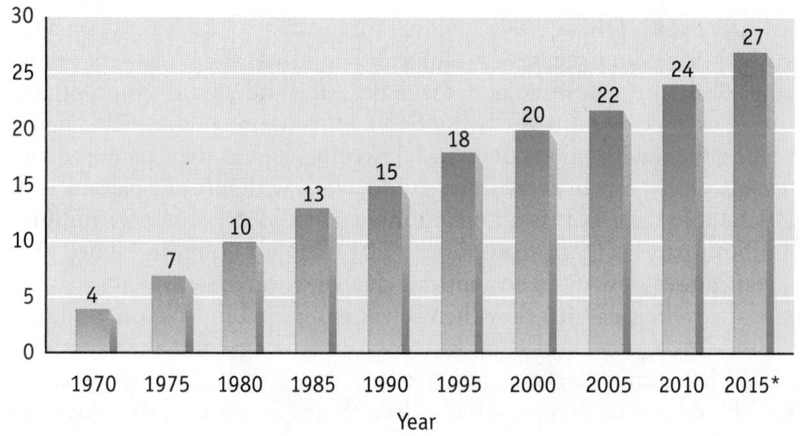

*Author's estimate.

Source: By the author. Based on *Statistical Abstract of the United States* 1989:Table 50; 2013:Table 56.

FIGURE 11.3 ▸ American Marriage, American Divorce

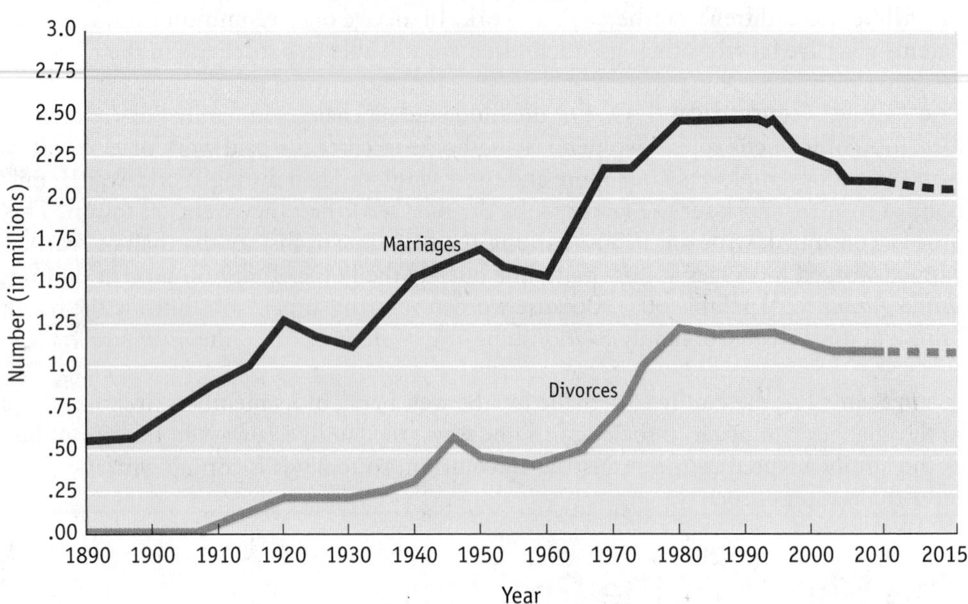

Note: Broken lines indicate the author's estimates.

Source: By the author. Based on *Statistical Abstract of the United States,* various editions and 2013:Tables 82, 135.

Explore on **MySocLab Activity:** The Marital Status of Americans

Is Divorce a Sign of Weakness, or Maybe of Strength? This might surprise you, but it's possible to interpret divorce statistics as a sign that marriages are improving and families are becoming stronger. Here's the thinking: No longer willing to put up with miserable marriages, men and women end them. They then look for new partners, and most end up with more satisfying marriages. In fact, they keep divorcing and looking until they find a relationship that satisfies them enough to at least stay together.

Whether or not this interpretation is correct, if you look closely at Figure 11.3 you will see something positive about our divorce rate. After rising for about 80 years, the divorce rate peaked in 1980 and then held steady for about 15 years. After this, it started dropping and since then has been holding at the lower levels. As you can see, marriage has followed this same path. The ratio of approximately one divorce for every two marriages has also held steady. This is a national ratio, which does not hold for the individual states. From the Social Map on the next page, you can see how the divorce rate of some states is much higher or lower than others. In the extreme, Nevada's divorce rate is triple that of Massachusetts.

Watch on **MySocLab Video:** Divorce and Adolescence

The Children of Divorce. Divorce also involves things that we can't measure with numbers—the crushed hopes and dreams of adults and children; the bitterness, anger, and lifelong scarring. And on the positive side, for many relief and an indication of new beginnings. Each year, divorce disrupts the lives of about 1 million children (Fagan and Churchill 2012), filling them with uncertainty and unsettling fears as their parents break up. Divorce is so extensive that one of every three children lives with just one parent (U.S. Census Bureau 2012:Table C3). This is a huge number of children, about 25 million, who don't live with both parents (*Statistical Abstract* 2013:Table 11). From Figure 11.5 on the next page, you can see how these percentages change with race–ethnicity.

The children of quarreling parents find themselves embroiled in turmoil, a murky world filled with no clear answers. If their parents remain together, they live in a troubled family. If their parents divorce, they live in a new situation of uncertainty. Researchers debate the effects of divorce on children: Some claim that divorce scars children for life, while others say they are better off removed from unhealthy relationships. Divorce has no single effect on children, so both are probably true. Some are hurt, and some are helped.

FIGURE 11.4 ▸ Divorce and Geography

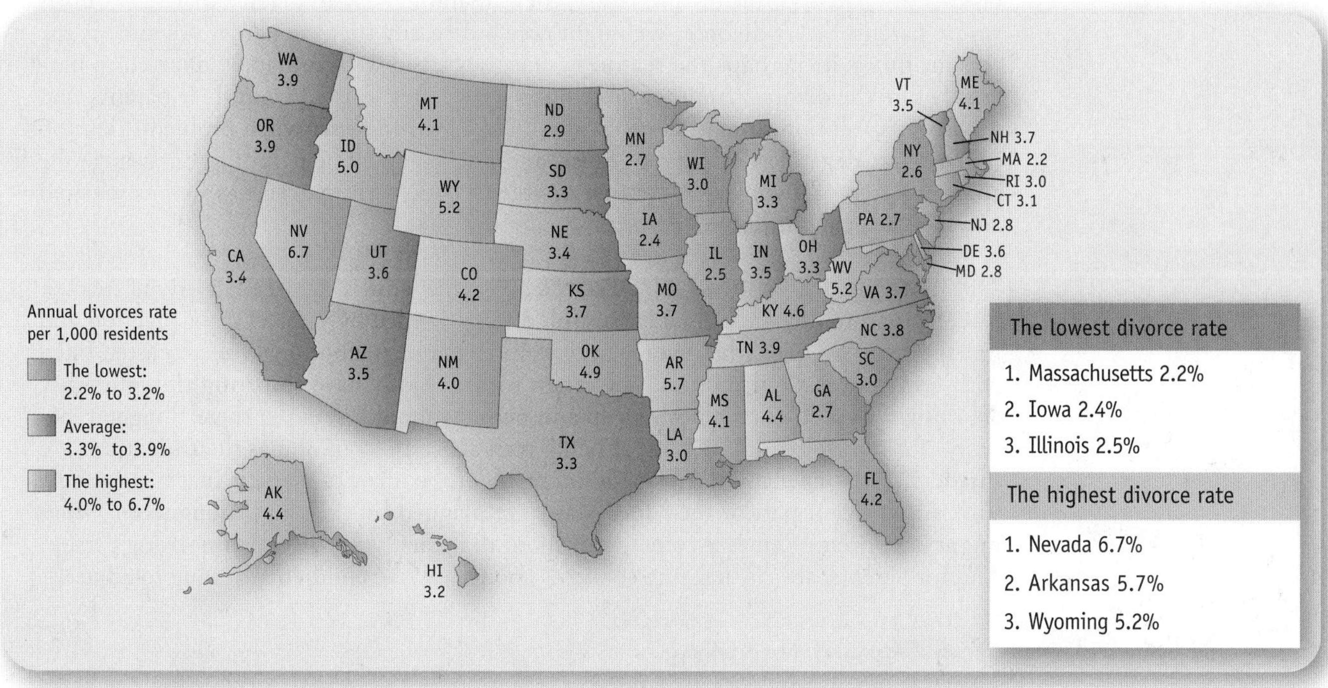

Note: Data for California, Georgia, Hawaii, Indiana, Louisiana, and Minnesota are the least accurate. Based on earlier editions in the source, they have been decreased by the average decrease in U.S. divorce.

Source: By the author. Based on *Statistical Abstract of the United States* 1990:Table 133; 2012:Table 133.

FIGURE 11.5 ▸ Where Do U.S. Children Live?

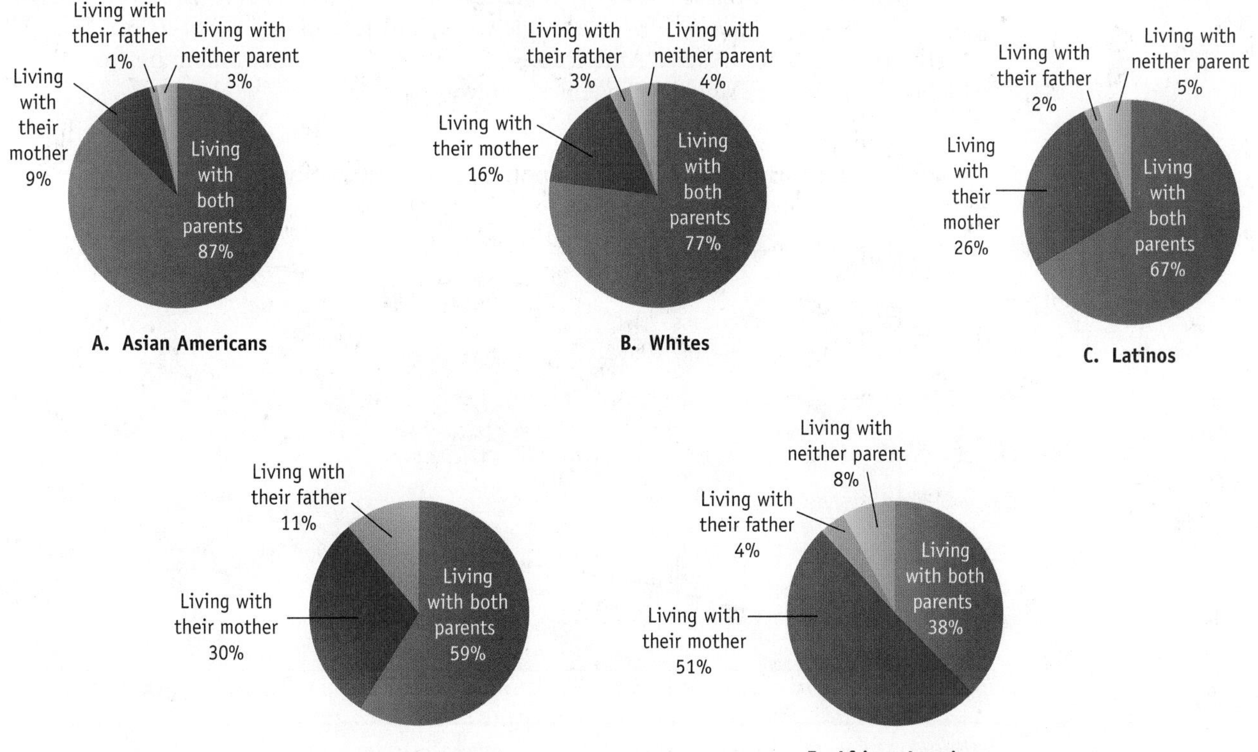

Sources: By the author. For Native Americans, Kreider and Elliott 2009:Table 1. For other groups, U.S. Census Bureau 2012:Table C3; *Statistical Abstract of the United States* 2013:Table 69.

But one result of divorce is *the divorce cycle* (Wolfinger 2005). When the children of divorced parents grow up and marry, they are more likely to divorce than are couples whose parents didn't divorce. We might conclude easily that the parent's divorce is the reason. But is it? Perhaps the reason is that they lived with unhappy, quarreling parents before the divorce. Another possibility is that they learned from their parents that divorce is a solution to marital problems—and they run faster when problems develop in marriage. Regardless of the root cause, and they could all be part of it, on average the adult children of divorced parents are unable to cope with marriage as well as married adults whose parents did not divorce.

The Nagging Dilemma of Divorce. For few adults divorce is a trivial matter. The decision to divorce is usually painful, often preceded by years of dissatisfaction and unhappiness. Couples who divorce find themselves on an emotional roller-coaster, filled with fears and anxiety about an uncertain future. Many have recurring thoughts that they might be able to patch things up and perhaps should "hang in there" longer, especially "for the children." Feelings of being torn apart are common as their identities are shredded. No longer can they depend on many of the identity markers that had become such a significant part of their life. Many are plagued by guilt and thoughts of "what might have been." Remorse comes, too, about the years "wasted" with the wrong person. And for parents, always, nagging concerns about how the children are going to adjust.

One-Parent Families

Births to Unmarried Women. Figure 11.6 shows how births to single women have increased over the years. The total number of babies born to unmarried women is huge, about 1.7 million a year. Of all babies born in the United States, two of every five (41 percent) are now born to single mothers (*Statistical Abstract* 2013:Table 89). This is 50 percent higher than it was in 1990.

As you have seen throughout this text, social problems often follow lines of race–ethnicity. This pattern also shows up in matters of the family. From Figure 11.6, you can see how the proportion of births to single women differs among racial–ethnic groups. Births to unmarried Native American and African American women are four times higher than births to single Asian American women.

FIGURE 11.6 ▸ Births to Single Women by Race–Ethnicity

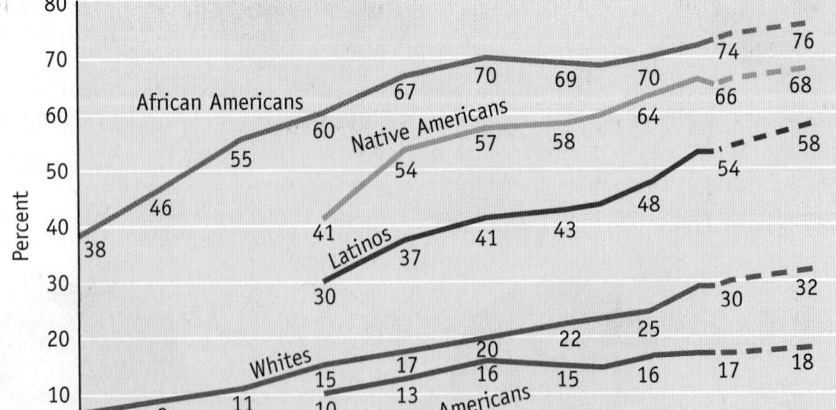

Note: In 2000, the source began to list non-Hispanic blacks and non-Hispanic whites. I adjusted the 1995 total for whites accordingly. (The source total for blacks was unchanged.) Broken lines indicate the author's estimates.

Source: By the author. Based on *Statistical Abstract of the United States* 1992:Table 87; 1998:Table 100; 2013:Table 89.

Having Just One Parent. Divorce and births to single women can be looked at as individual matters, of course, and they are. When multiplied by millions, though, their consequences reverberate throughout society. The numbers are staggering. With our high rates of divorce and births to single women, *17 million* children live without fathers at home. Nearly *3 million* live without their mothers. Another *3 million* live with neither parent (*Statistical Abstract* 2013:Table 69). As always, overall statistics conceal significant variations. The Social Map below shows how the states compare in the percentage of families that are headed by single parents. You can see how single parenting is concentrated in the South.

The primary problem is that children of single and divorced parents are denied benefits that children in two-parent families take for granted. Among other significant factors, this means that these children are much more likely to have to grapple with poverty and all the problems that it brings.

Impact on Children ▸ Being reared by only one parent has a significant impact on children. One of the most remarkable is that these children are more likely to drop out of school and get in trouble with the law. This applies to every region of the country and to every racial–ethnic group. There just are no exceptions. There is no group in which children reared by both parents are more likely to drop out of school or to get in trouble with the law.

It is much more difficult for a single mother or father to be an effective parent than it is for a mother and father who are working together to rear their children. The two have more time to help with homework and even to play with the children. They also are able to discuss the children's problems, decide on courses of action, and back each other up when it comes to dealing with rebellious teenagers. What a disadvantage single parents have. Because of work demands, most are less involved in the lives of their children. The extra pressures also lead to inconsistent discipline and more arguments with their children (McLanahan 1996).

Read on MySocLab Document
Life Without Father: What Happens to the Children?

Absence of the Father ▸ Not having their father as a role model is significant for children. Millions of boys and girls must learn the male role from their mothers, their mother's boyfriends, and from television and the streets. They often end up with grossly

FIGURE 11.7 ▸ Families Headed by Single Parents

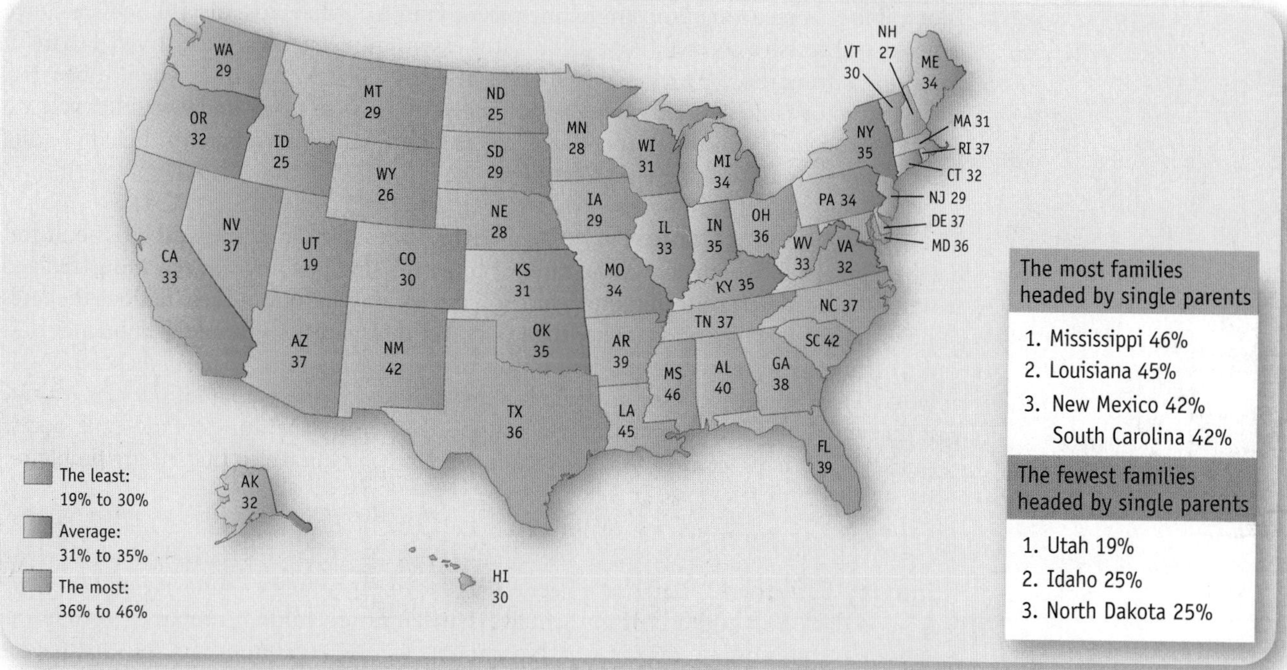

Source: By the author. Based on "Kids Count Data Sheet" 2012.

inadequate role models. Some are fortunate in being able to learn positive masculinity from highly involved grandparents and uncles.

Absence of the father is related to some of the social problems we reviewed in earlier chapters. For example, the higher a group's rate of single-mother families, the more violent crimes that group has. This statistic says nothing about the individual child, of course. Although children from mother-headed homes are more likely to drop out of school and get in trouble with the law, any particular child may grow up to become an artist, an astronaut, or (and what can you expect of this author!) a sociologist. But *on average* the absence of a father leads to less education and more violent crime.

As much as we might like it to be otherwise, by herself the average mother does not do the same job of rearing children that a mother and father do together. Sociologist Travis Hirschi (Pope 1988:117–118) says that, all else being equal, one parent is probably sufficient. The problem, he says, is that rarely is all else equal:

> *The single parent (usually a woman) must devote a good deal to support and maintenance activities that are at least to some extent shared in the two-parent family. Further, she must do so in the absence of psychological or social support. As a result, she is less able to devote time to monitoring and punishment, and is more likely to be involved in negative, abusive contacts with her children.*

The impact of the father is so powerful that even fathers who do not live with the mother and children can make a difference. If a nonresident father is involved in his children's everyday lives, the children are more likely to stay in school and stay out of trouble with the law. Unfortunately, involved nonresident fathers are the exception: *Most* fathers who don't live with their children are not involved in their children's lives (Hawkins et al. 2007; Cheadle et al. 2010).

Trying to Be Two Parents ▸ One-parent families are not limited to fatherless families, of course. As I mentioned, close to 3 million children are being reared by their fathers. This presents tremendous obstacles that are not easily overcome. Some are mirror images of the mother-headed family, especially the problem of a single father teaching womanhood to his daughter, a task that in a two-parent family falls primarily on the mother. Whether man or woman, the single parent must try to be both mother and father. If not impossible, this certainly is a formidable responsibility.

Discipline ▸ A recurring problem in one-parent families is **defective discipline**—excessive leniency or excessive control (Pope 1988). It is easy to understand why. I survived (barely) parenting during those precarious teen years. It is difficult to determine when to be strict and when to be lenient—and no matter which you choose to never know whether you are right or wrong. To find the proper balance is not easy for any two parents, but more difficult for one parent to achieve than for two.

The Cross-Cultural Context ▸ Let's go beyond these findings and add cross-cultural data. Figure 11.8, which shows the rates of births to single women in ten industrialized nations, might stretch your thinking a bit. You can see that in four of these nations the rates of births to single women are higher than ours. Yet their rates of juvenile delinquency and violent crime are lower than ours. This means that something other than single parenting is at work. That "something else" is the culture within which one-parent families live. I suggest that the significant factors are family support systems, subcultures of violence, access to guns, and perhaps views of life. We sociologists have *not* unraveled this thorny problem.

Other Problems

Runaway Children. Because no central agency keeps track of runaway children, we lack good data. You might hear in the news that 1 million children run away from home each year, but this number is not real. No one knows the actual number. This one is simply made up to gain the public's attention. We do know that each year the police arrest about 60,000 children for running away from home (*Sourcebook of Criminal Justice Statistics* 2009:Table 4.6). At a minimum, we can assume that these runaway children are not fleeing happy homes. Many are trying to escape intolerable situations—incest, beatings, and other debilitating family conditions.

The streets are tough, and survival is precarious. Some runaways or "**push-outs**"—children who have been shoved out by parents who no longer want them—fall into the hands of predators, making their already bruised, fragile lives even more desperate. Some **pedophiles** (adults who are sexually attracted to children) and pimps search bus stations for victims, looking for children who appear lonely, confused, and vulnerable. When children tire of sleeping in doorways, the alternative to hunger is to beg, steal, or turn to the only thing they have—their bodies. Many runaways get involved in prostitution and pornography when they have no money and no place to go.

How times change! In the 1890s, this was standard child discipline, even the use of a special paddling board. Fathers also used their belts and switches (little branches cut from trees).

Family Violence. Another indication of family problems is violence. Police and welfare workers know the scene all too well: the battered child, wife, husband, parent, or even grandparent. About 70,000 people are arrested each year for "offenses against family and children" (*Sourcebook of Criminal Justice Statistics* 2012:Table 4.6).

FIGURE 11.8 ▸ Births to Single Women* in Ten Most Industrialized Nations

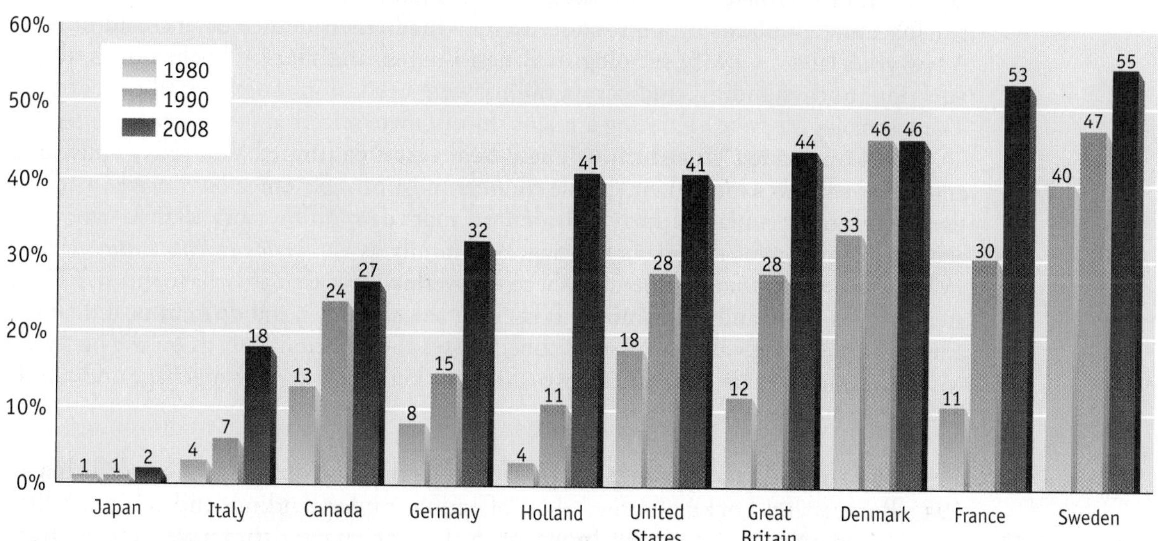

*As a percentage of all births. For some countries, the latest year available is 2007.

Source: By the author. Based on *Statistical Abstract of the United States* 2013:Table 1351.

Sociologists Suzanne Steinmetz and Murray Straus (1974; Straus 1992) point out that it would be hard to find a group in the United States in which violence is more of an everyday occurrence than in the family. As with other crimes, the data reflect only reported crimes, so the actual number is higher.

Listen on MySocLab Audio: NPR: Military Combats High Divorce Rate

In Sum ▸ Violence, divorce, runaway children, and so on indicate severe problems in the American family. They do *not* indicate, however, that the family is disintegrating. Although the contemporary family is in trouble, as a social institution it will endure. Humans have found no satisfactory substitute for the family, and millions of people report that marriage and family meet their needs for intimacy and sense of identity and belonging. The focus of this book, however, is on *social problems*, so I am not extolling the satisfactions and even joys some find in marriage and family life.

At this point, let's see what different pictures emerge when we turn our theoretical lenses on divorce, to see why it is so common.

Looking at the Problem Theoretically: Why Is Divorce Common?

11.3 Discuss the perspectives that emerge when you apply symbolic interactionism, functionalism, and conflict theory to why divorce is common.

For most of us, the family is our major support system. Our family nourishes and protects us when we are young. It gives us security and love and shapes our personality. Sociologists call the family that rears us our **family of orientation** because it introduces us to the world and teaches us ways to cope with life. As a result, most people around the world try to establish stability, identity, and intimacy through marriage. A married couple having its first child forms what is called a **family of procreation**.

With the high value placed on marriage and family and the many benefits they offer, why is divorce common? Let's use our theoretical perspectives to better understand how divorce is related to changes in society. As always, each perspective is a lens that yields a unique interpretation, but, as you will see, these perspectives dovetail neatly with one another.

Symbolic Interactionism: Changing Symbols

To explain why our divorce rate is so high, symbolic interactionists examine what people *expect* out of marriage. In 1933, sociologist William Ogburn noted that people were placing more emphasis on personality as they made their choice of husband or wife. A few years later, in 1945, sociologists Ernest Burgess and Harvey Locke observed that affection, understanding, and compatibility were becoming more central to marriage. These sociologists were observing a major shift in mate selection.

An "Overloaded" Institution. These trends have continued, and today's husbands and wives tend to expect their spouse to meet most of their emotional needs. Because these expectations place a heavy burden on marriage, often more than it can manage, sociologists refer to today's marriage and family as an *overloaded institution* (Lasch 1977). One reason that families have become overloaded is that they have shrunk. There are fewer children, and few families today have the children's grandparent or unmarried aunt or uncle living with them. This concentrates the emotional needs on the husband, wife, and, increasingly, just one or two children. Let's look at how marriage and family have become "overloaded."

The Love Symbol: Immersed in Unrealistic Expectations. Recall that in 1945 Burgess and Locke observed that "affection, understanding, and compatibility" were becoming more important in marriage. These characteristics have changed from "becoming important" to being considered an essential part of a "healthy" marriage. They have been bound symbolically into what we call "love," idealized in phrases like "Love conquers all" and "Find your true love." Love is now so central in our expectations that it has become *the* reason that people marry. Our "natural" response has become "Why else would you marry?"

Our cultural expectation of "finding your one true love" who will bring you "true happiness" sets us up for disappointment. We come to expect that marriage will give us some sort of emotional high. Marriage simply cannot deliver this. When disappointments arise in marriage, as they inevitably do, and usually fairly soon after the "I dos" are said, spouses tend to blame one another. Each believes that the other has somehow failed the relationship. Their engulfment in the *idea* of love—what love is supposed to do for them—blinds them to the reality of day-to-day married life. Our culture promotes an impossibility: that marriage, ideally a lifelong relationship, should be based on a temporary emotional state.

For a highly contrasting view of love and its role in mate selection, see the Global Glimpse box on the next page.

Changing Ideas About Children. Ideas about children have also undergone a deep shift, so much so that some customs of earlier generations can seem strange to us. Some analysts say that because people in medieval society viewed children as miniature adults, there was no sharp separation between the worlds of adults and children (Aries 1962). At the age of 7, boys began to work as apprentices, learning an occupation, while girls remained home, learning homemaking duties associated with marriage.

These customs don't make sense to us. We consider age 7 to be a tender phase of early childhood, not a time for apprenticeship. In short, children have undergone a cultural transformation from miniature adults into impressionable, vulnerable, and innocent beings. As ideas of children have changed, so have ideas of parenting. These new expectations have placed even more stress on marriage.

Changing Expectations of Parenting. It might surprise you, but until about 1940 U.S. children "became adults" when they graduated from the eighth grade. For most, this was the end of their formal schooling, and they went to work. Because we now expect children to be dependent *much* longer, and think of 14- and 15-year-olds as children, not as young adults, we expect parents to continue to nurture them for many more years. We have even developed new ideas of "good" parenting, notions unheard of during earlier generations, such as expecting parents to help their children achieve "self-actualization" so they can "reach their full potential." Our newly expanded tasks of child rearing, accompanied by the greater emotional ties between parents and children that we have come to expect, have thrust the family into even greater "emotional overload" (Lasch 1977).

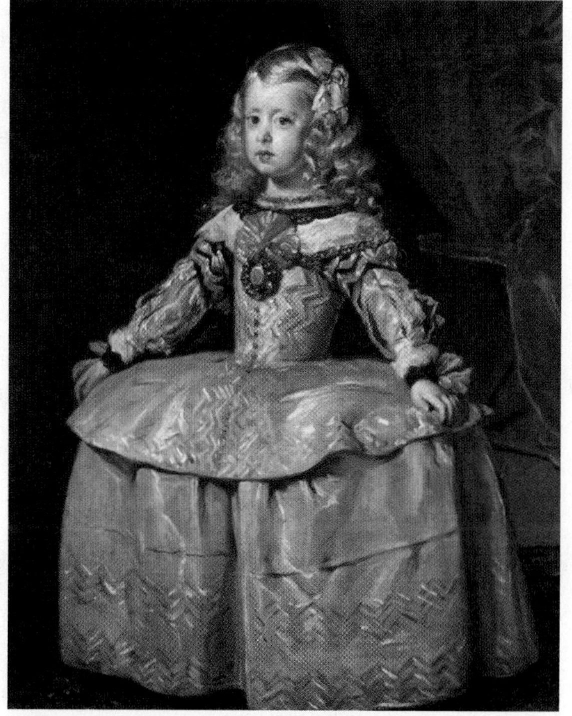

Childhood varies from culture to culture and changes with time. The little girl in this 1656 painting by Diego Rodriguez de Velázquez is Infanta Margarita Teresa. Because the paintings of the 1600s and 1700s show children dressed as adults, some conclude that Europeans at this time saw children as miniature adults.

Changing Marital Roles. Just as you would expect, as parenting roles shift, so do marital roles. It used to be assumed as "natural" that the husband would be the **breadwinner**, that his earnings would be the primary source of support for the family. It was also assumed that the wife would be the **homemaker**, that she would stay home, take care of the house and children, and attend to the personal needs of her husband. If each did these things well, they were considered a good husband and father, wife and mother. Traditional roles—whatever their faults—provided clear-cut guidelines for newlyweds. After a couple married, each knew what to expect of the other.

Today, the roles of husband and wife are not defined clearly, and newlyweds are expected to work out their own marital reality. Although this gives them a great deal of flexibility, it

A Global Glimpse

Arranged Marriage in India: Probing Beneath the Surface

The idea that parents should choose their child's husband or wife shocks Western sensibilities. Arranged marriage seems to violate our basic ideas of the rights of individuals to forge their own path in life. And it does just that. In fact, this is what is wrong with the Western system, say the Indians. Young people don't have the experience to make such life-significant decisions. They need to depend on their elders, who have more experience. Their parents know them well, have their best interests at heart, and can make a much better choice of mate than they can.

At a wedding ceremony in Maharashtra, India, the couple gets their first intimate look at one another.

Such thinking is foreign to us, of course. It is almost the polar opposite of what we expect and see as the right way to do things. The distinction gets even more complicated when we learn that Indians' ideas of love are also different from ours. We expect love to occur before marriage, and to base marriage on love. Indians expect to base marriage on wise parental decisions, and then love will develop after marriage.

We each—the Westerner and the Indian—shake our heads in wonderment at the strange customs of the other. Each wonders how life could possibly work out the way the other does things.

But each system works. So perhaps we can learn from one another. Let me share with you what I learned from the experience of an Indian friend. As I saw an arranged marriage unfold, I realized that there is much more to this process than met my Western eye.

> My friend, Atal, began to look for a husband for his daughter, Bhanumati. From my Western perspective, this was a strange approach to marriage, but as I observed the process my perspective changed. I saw that this was a burden for Atal. It was a part of his marital role, and everyone—his wife, daughter, and son—was looking to him expectantly. They had full confidence that he would do right, a confidence that placed a heavy burden on his shoulders.
>
> Bhanumati is a pretty young woman, age 23, intelligent, with an engaging personality. She is also educated, with a master's degree in English. Despite her education, Bhanumati would never question this process of mate selection. Nor will her brother when it comes time to arrange his marriage. This is the traditional way of mate selection in India, the way that makes sense to the people who live there.
>
> I saw Atal's disappointment as he tried to fulfill his duty of arranging a good marriage for his daughter. He made several overtures to families of eligible sons, only to be rejected. My friend is a poor man, and he was unable to afford the dowry that these parents demanded. Atal's problem was unexpectedly solved when a young American visitor "fell in love" with Bhanumati. This man, an engineer with a good job, would make a good husband. Everyone—Atal, his wife, and his daughter—approved of the match. The man, of course, had to follow the Indian custom of seeing his future bride only in the presence of her parents or brother.

Behind the scenes of arranged marriages, as you can sense, there is much more than the father's decision. The responsibility is laid on him, but to fulfill it and keep a good family life, he must have his family's agreement. Without it, the system fails.

My friend is a good man, a gentle and considerate husband and father. Tradition laid this responsibility on him, and he fulfilled it well. You can see that other men might have used this power to benefit themselves and not their child. You can also see how this duty is an example of the *patriarchy* we reviewed in Chapter 9, of how power is vested in men.

As strange as it seems to us, the Indian view of love works. With the marriage arranged, Bhanumati is freed to develop feelings of love for her husband-to-be. From marriage, the Indians say, comes love. We, of course, say that marriage comes from love. Americans and Indians confuse one another, but perhaps sharing this experience will help you to understand a different way of life.

For Your Consideration

Why do you think that educated Indians still go along with the custom of arranged marriages? What advantages and disadvantages do you see in their system of mate selection? In the U.S. system of mate selection?

also produces tension and conflict. A couple's ideas may not mesh. Who is supposed to do what housework? How should they divide child-rearing responsibilities? How much should they save? How much should they spend? On what? Wives are asking to what extent they should be career-oriented, while husbands wonder how much more they should focus on the home. When guidelines for any role, including marriage and parenting, are unclear, frustration and discontent are inevitable. How do you fulfill a marital role if you can't agree on what that role is?

In Sum ▸ What marriage means to people has changed. The idea that love brings unlimited emotional satisfaction has become a source of shattered dreams. Our new ideas about children, parenting, and being a husband or wife also place tremendous pressure on spouses. This pressure and the tensions it brings create an "emotional overload" that becomes a push toward divorce.

Perception of Alternatives. While these historical changes in the expectations of marriage were occurring, more women began to work outside the home. This, too, changed people's ideas about marriage. As wives earned paychecks of their own, they began to perceive alternatives to living in unhappy marriages. As symbolic interactionists stress, the *perception of alternatives* is an essential first step to making divorce possible.

Changing Ideas About Divorce. It is difficult for us to grasp how seriously divorce was once taken. Divorce used to represent failure, irresponsibility, even immorality. Divorced people were social outcasts. Suspected of immoral behavior, they no longer were welcome as dinner guests. As divorce became more common, however, its meaning was transformed—from a symbol of failure to a "new start." Divorce no longer suggested shame and immorality, but, rather, opportunity and self-actualization. This symbolic leap added one more push toward divorce. When divorce carries a stigma, it is held in check, but to view divorce as a sign of personal change and development sets the stage for ending marriages. The thinking becomes "Maybe this is no longer right for me, if it ever was, and it is time to move on." Couples even tell others, "We just outgrew one another."

Divorce is common among Americans, but far from new with them. This 1789 French painting shows a judge making decisions in a divorce—and the impatience of the new partners.

Legal Changes. You might be surprised, too, at how difficult it once was to get a divorce. One spouse was required to prove severe abuse or adultery. In New York, where adultery was the only grounds for divorce, witnesses had to testify under oath at a trial that one spouse had committed adultery. As the stigma attached to divorce shrank, laws against divorce relaxed. Today, in most states "incompatibility," which simply means that two people aren't getting along, has become adequate grounds for divorce. In many states, couples can work out their own "no-fault" divorce, and judges simply sign the paperwork. In Florida, the couple can sign papers in a lawyer's office, and they don't even have to appear in court. Such legal changes have further reduced the stigma attached to divorce, which, in turn, has contributed to the high divorce rate.

Are These Changes Good or Bad? Symbolic interactionists take the position that nothing is good or bad in and of itself. They view "goodness" and "badness" as value judgments that are imposed on people's behavior. Depending on its assumptions, one group is alarmed at increases in divorce and changes in marital roles, new views on parenting, and so on. Another group looks at these same changes and feels pleased that the family is evolving. Symbolic interactionists do not take a stand that either is correct or better, for symbolic interactionism has no framework for making value judgments.

In Sum ▸ To explain why the divorce rate has increased, symbolic interactionists analyze how symbols—ideas, meanings, and expectations—associated with marriage and family life have changed. They stress that symbols both reflect and create reality. That is, symbols not only represent people's ideas but also influence people's ideas and behaviors.

Functionalism: Declining Functions

When functionalists analyze social change, they look at how change in one part of society affects its other parts. Earlier in this chapter, we examined the impact of industrialization and urbanization on marriage and family. You will recall that the birthrate fell as children became more costly. This is an example of how change in one part of the system (work) brought about change in another (family). Let's look now at how functionalists explain our high rate of divorce.

For background, we should note that functionalists have identified seven key functions of the family. They point out that around the world the family provides

1. economic production
2. socialization of children
3. care of the sick and injured
4. care of the aged
5. recreation
6. sexual control of family members
7. reproduction.

Let's see what effects the Industrial Revolution and urbanization had on these seven traditional functions of the family—and how a reduction of these functions are related to divorce.

Economic Production. Before industrialization, the members of a family worked together as an economic team. Survival was precarious. Even getting enough food and adequate clothing was a problem. To survive, the members of a family—like it or not—were forced to cooperate. *When industrialization moved production from home to factory, it disrupted this team.* No longer working as a unit, the husband-father was separated from the daily activities of the family and the wife-mother from the production of income. The older children, who went to work for wages, grew less dependent on their family.

Socialization of Children. While economic production was changing, the state and federal governments were growing larger, more centralized, and more powerful. One consequence was that the government began to take over some of the family's functions, which weakened family relationships. For example, when lawmakers passed mandatory education laws, it became illegal for parents not to send their children to school. They faced fines and jail if they did not put their children in the government's care. In this way, the government took over much of the responsibility for socializing children.

Listen on **MySocLab Audio:** NPR: Raising Children, Caring for Parents

Care of the Sick and Aged. Care of the sick and aged followed a similar course. Before industrialization, medicine was a family matter. There were few trained physicians, and family members cared for their sick at home. As medical schools developed, along with hospitals and drugs, medicine came under government control. Gradually medical care shifted from the family to medical specialists. It was similarly the case with care of the aged. As the central government expanded and its agencies multiplied, care of the aged, too, became a government obligation.

Recreation. As industrialization progressed, the country became more affluent and the family's disposable income increased. Businesses sprang up to compete for that income. Before the Industrial Age, entertainment and "fun" had consisted primarily of home-based activities—card games, parlor and barn dances, sleigh rides, and so on. As family-centered activities gave way to paid events, the family lost much of its recreational function.

Control of Sexuality. The family traditionally controlled the sexual behavior of its members. Only sexual relations in marriage were viewed as legitimate. Sexual relations outside marriage—even between engaged couples—were considered immoral. Although this was only an ideal, and marriage never enjoyed a monopoly on sexual relations, the **sexual revolution** opened many alternatives to marital sex. The changed standards of sexual behavior weakened the family's control over the sexuality of its members.

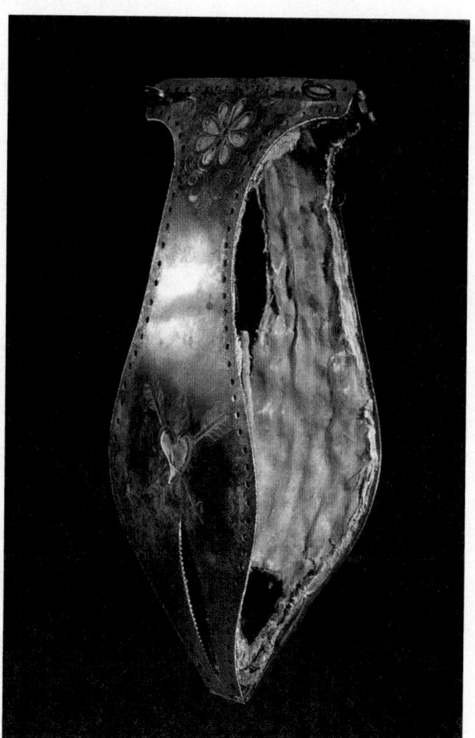

Seldom is the control of sexuality as direct and forceful as the chastity belt of the 1500s. A husband who was about to go on a long journey locked a chastity belt on his wife to make sure she would be loyal to him while he was away.

Reproduction. Even reproduction has increasingly moved outside the traditional family unit of husband and wife. As we reviewed earlier, two of five births in the United States are to single women. If the increase continues at its current rate, within 15 years half of all births will be to unmarried women. Other significant changes have altered the face of reproduction. It is especially significant that married women can get abortions without informing their husbands and that teens can obtain birth control without parental consent.

Can reproduction move even farther away from the family? Some envision a future in which men or women, single or married, homosexual or heterosexual, put in orders for the kind of children they want. They will specify the child's sex, race–ethnicity, height, hair color, eye color, body type, even intelligence, personality traits, and ability in music, art, poetry, and sports (Bagne 1992). Sociologist Judith Lorber (1980:527) suggested that our future might even include "professional breeders":

> *A system of completely professional breeders and child rearers could be conducted with the best of modern technology—fertility drugs for multiple births, sperm banks, embryo transfers, and uterine implants. . . . Professional breeders could be paid top salaries, like today's athletes, for the 15–20 years of their prime childbearing time. Those who were impregnated could live in well-run dormitories, with excellent physical care, food, and entertainment.*

In Sum ▸ Functionalists stress that the loss of functions has weakened the family unit. The fewer functions that family members have in common, the fewer are their "ties that bind." As family bonds have weakened, the family has become more fragile, with divorce the inevitable consequence of eroded functions.

Conflict and Feminist Theory: Shifting Power Relations

Conflict and feminist theorists point us in a different direction. They stress that marriage and family roles reflect the basic social inequality that runs throughout society. In general, men dominate and exploit women, and marriage and family life is simply one of the means by which they do this.

Male Domination of Marriage and Family. Historically, women have served men as wife, sister, and mother. The wife was expected to prepare her husband's food, to take care of his clothing, and to satisfy his sexual and emotional needs. The woman's life was expected to revolve around her home, including the care of the children. This backstage work is called **reproductive labor**—the work that a wife performs behind the scenes that allows her breadwinner husband to flourish in his more public life.

Traditionally, fathers have controlled all the members of the family. As in India today and as discussed in the Global Glimpse box on page 360, deciding who a daughter or son would marry was a father's right. To forge alliances, kings would arrange for their daughters to marry the sons of other kings. Members of the nobility would do the same, arranging for their children to marry "suitably," which meant that the marriage would provide an advantage for the father's lineage. Over time, fathers in the West gradually lost this right. While arranged marriages are no longer part of our current marital customs, the traditional wedding ceremony reflects this lost right. As the mother sits passively to the side, the father walks his daughter down the aisle and "gives" her to her husband. This is but a pale reflection of the power that men have wielded historically, but it is a reflection nonetheless.

More dangerous is the power of physical discipline often granted to men. Both custom and the law once allowed men to discipline not only their children, but also their wives. Not too far in our own past, a husband could spank his wife—if she "needed" it. Beating a wife was considered permissible if she became rebellious or had an affair. In some areas—such as Pakistan—husbands are still permitted to beat their wives as a form of discipline. In Chapter 9, we reviewed "honor killings," the ultimate sanction that men can give women for violating the rules by which they control them.

The 1950s marked a watershed era in U.S. middle-class families. With the husband's income adequate to support a family comfortably, the wife was expected to focus on the home. This historical period is bathed in images that characterized only a minority of families, images that form a mythical lens through which we view that "ideal" period of family life.

Marriage as an Arena for an Ongoing Historical Struggle. Industrialization brought major change to husband–wife relationships. As more and more women took paid jobs, their experiences at work changed their views of the world. Increasingly, wives came to resent arrangements that women at earlier periods had taken for granted. Housework and child care (or as sociologists put it, the division of labor at home) became a pivotal source of conflict. Women started chafing—and complaining—that it was unfair for them to work at jobs outside the home and to shoulder almost all the housework and child care. From Figure 11.9 on the next page, you can see that the wives' dissatisfaction was not with the total hours that husbands spent

FIGURE 11.9 ▸ In Two-Paycheck Marriages, How Do Husbands and Wives Divide Up Family Responsibilities?

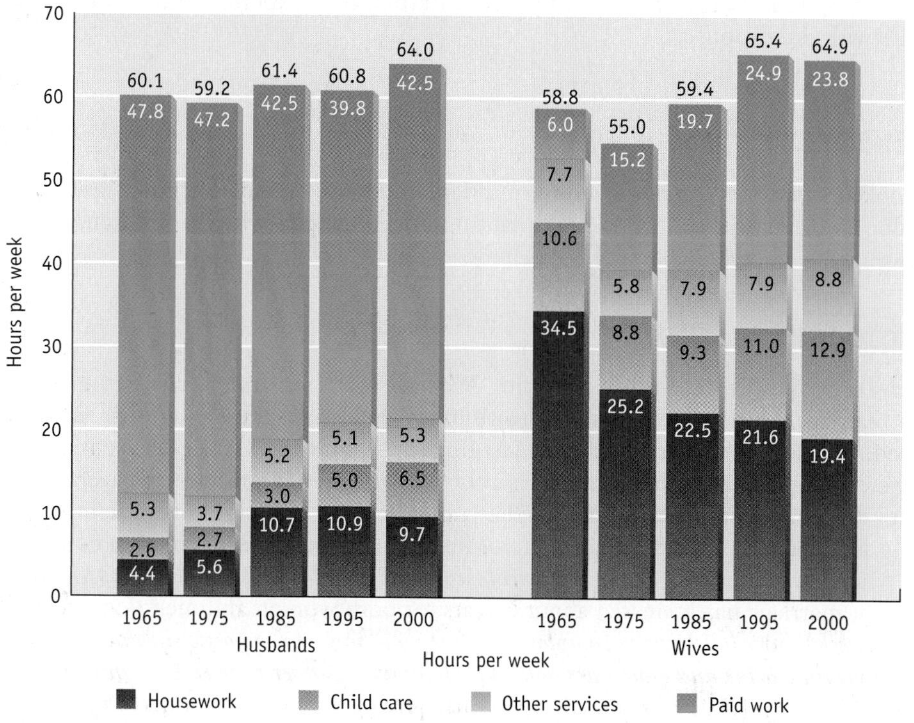

Note: Housework hours are from Table 5.1 of the source, child care from Table 4.1, and work hours and total hours from Table 3.4. Other services is derived by subtracting the hours for housework, child care, and paid work from the total hours.
Source: By the author. Based on Bianchi et al. 2006.

on family responsibilities. In some years, husbands spent more hours per week than their wives did. The wives' complaint was that the husbands weren't picking up a fair share of the housework and child care. The husbands resented this accusation, pointing out how many more hours they were putting in at work.

As you can see from Figure 11.9, over time the division of family labor gradually changed in the direction that the wives wanted. In 1965, husbands in two-paycheck marriages put in 7.0 hours a week on housework and child care. By 2000, at 16.2 hours a week, their total had more than doubled. It is still considerably less than what their wives put in on these tasks, but the husbands' work hours, although reduced, remain much higher. Today's husbands and wives continue to put in about the same total hours per week, but with a closer balance of tasks than they used to have.

As I have stressed, families always adjust to changes in society. The economic crisis of 2008 was no exception. When unemployment hit men harder, partially because of the severe drop in male-dominated construction, women picked up the slack. *More* wives went to work during the Great Recession. Husbands, in turn, took on more child care and housework (Berik and Kongar 2011). If we had the identical data and could add a more recent year to Figure 11.9, the direction would be the same, toward greater equality.

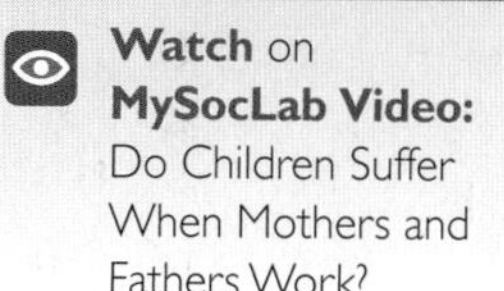

Watch on
MySocLab Video:
Do Children Suffer When Mothers and Fathers Work?

In Sum ▸ At the root of many marital problems lies the struggle of husbands and wives to achieve a satisfying balance of work, child care, and housework. Compared with the past, today's wives are considerably less dependent on their husbands for financial security. With greater independence, wives are less willing to put up with relationships that they don't find fulfilling. Conflict and feminist theorists view the high divorce rate not as a sign that the family has become weaker but, rather, that women have made headway in their millennia-old struggle with men, that they are gaining equality in marriage (Zinn and Eitzen 1990).

Husbands and wives view their conflict through a different lens. They don't see their marital problems as part of grand, flowing tides of history. Changes in historical relationships are not part of their perspective. Rather, they experience direct, personal troubles with their spouse.

Research Findings

11.4 Summarize research findings on postponing marriage, couples without children, family violence, sexual abuse, the elderly, and the death of the family.

Let's look at some of the major trends in marriage and family today. They are significant: marrying at a later age, cohabitation, remaining single, couples with no children, family violence, sexual abuse, and care of the elderly.

Postponing Marriage

The U-Turn in Age at First Marriage. We have had a remarkable change in the age at first marriage. During each decade from 1890 to 1950, the average age at first marriage dropped. By 1955, the typical bride had just turned 20. Having just left her teens, brides then were younger than at any other time in U.S. history. Ten years later, the average age of first-time American grooms was 22, the youngest since the U.S. government began keeping such records. These younger ages for first marriage held steady for about 10 years or so, when they turned upward (*Statistical Abstract* 1971:Table 79). With this U-Turn, age at first marriage has increased about 6 years for both women and men (Copen et al. 2012). *The U-Turn has been so complete that we now have the opposite situation: Today's average first-time bride and groom are now older than at any other time in U.S. history.*

From Figure 11.10, you can see one consequence of postponing marriage—how common it now is to be single during the late 20s. You take this for granted, of course, since this is what you see going on around you. But look at how it used to be. A few

FIGURE 11.10 ▸ The Growing Number of Singles

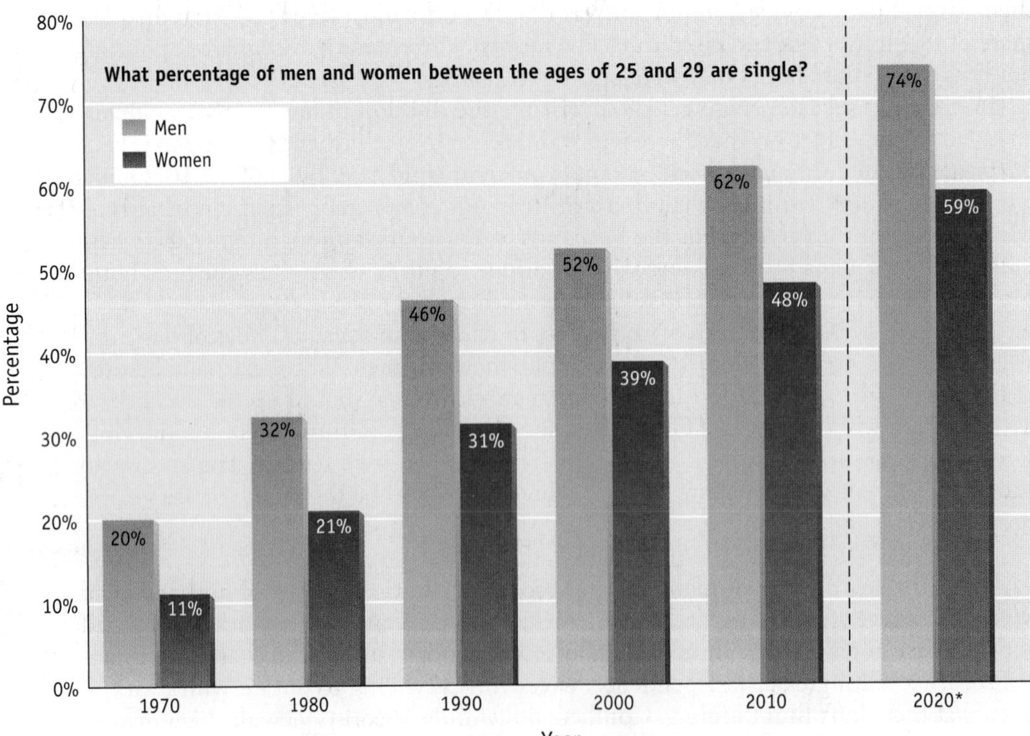

*Author's estimate

Source: By the author. Based on *Statistical Abstract of the United States* 2013:Table 57 and earlier years.

decades ago, *most men and women between the ages of 25 and 29 were married. Now most are single.* As you can see from this figure, the percentage of single women between the ages of 25 and 29 is more than *four* times higher today than it was in 1970. During this same time, the number of single men of this age has tripled.

Why have we had this extensive change? Read on.

Cohabitation. To explain this change, sociologists point to data like those shown in Figure 11.11. Look at the sharp increase in **cohabitation**, living together in a sexual relationship outside of marriage. Sociologists estimate that if cohabitation had not increased like this, so many more people would have married that we would have little change in the average age at first marriage (Copen et al. 2012).

Most couples don't cohabit because they are opposed to marriage. Rather, they are opposed to marriage at this particular time in their lives. They are attracted to one another and want a relationship that is more uniting and fulfilling than just "going together" or "hooking up." But many fear that their relationship isn't strong enough to handle the commitments and responsibilities of marriage. Some hope that a strong commitment will develop, and they will marry later. Others know that their relationship is temporary, and cohabiting is just a time between relationships.

Financial concerns are another reason that some couples cohabit. Some people do not want to commingle assets, and cohabitation makes it easier for them to keep separate bank accounts and spending patterns. With marriage considered a declaration of financial independence from parents, cohabitation allows many young adults, especially college students, to keep getting support from their parents. Some of the widowed cohabit so they won't lose the pension or Social Security earned by their deceased spouse. Similarly, marriage would destroy the alimony of some divorced women, but cohabitation keeps it safe.

FIGURE 11.11 ▸ Cohabitation in the United States

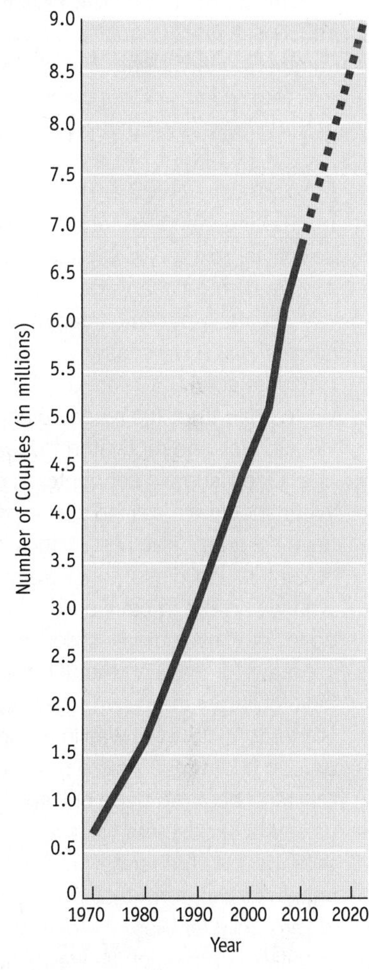

Note: The broken line is the author's estimate.
Source: By the author. Based on U.S. Bureau of the Census 2007 and *Statistical Abstract of the United States* 1995:Table 60; 2013:Table 63.

Remaining Single. Women who remain single into their 30s encounter stigma (Ganong and Sharp 2010). Family and friends wonder why the woman "hasn't been able to find a husband." They might question whether she is really straight, make snide remarks that she might have some huge hidden flaw, or say she is being too picky. Feelings of being an outsider are especially strong at weddings as well as at social events where most participants are couples.

Few people view single life as a permanent alternative to marriage, but some do. As sociologist Peter Stein (1992) found, those who plan on remaining single all their lives still feel a strong need for intimacy, sharing, and community. To attain these satisfactions, which marriage and family offer, the permanent singles cultivate a network of people who feel the same as they do about marriage. The friendships they develop satisfy their needs for intimacy.

Couples Without Children

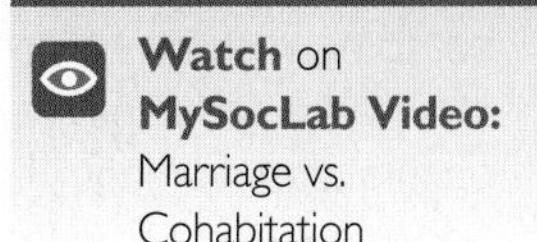

The Problem with Terms. What term should we use to refer to married couples without children? *Childless* is the usual term, but some couples resent it. From the discussion in the Spotlight on Social Research box on the next page, you will see why I avoided the term *childless* in the heading above.

International Comparisons. The percentage of wives who do not bear a child varies widely around the world. At 28 percent, Germany ranks the highest, while at 7 percent Portugal ranks the lowest. We don't have totals for non-Western nations. In the United States, about one of five (19 percent) wives does not give birth (Basten 2009). This rate has increased so rapidly that U.S. couples without children are now *twice* as common as they were 20 years ago.

11.4

Spotlight on Social Research

Choosing Not to Have Children

CYNTHIA SHINABARGER REED *is professor of psychology and sociology at Tarrant County College.* **ROBERT E. REED** *is adjunct instructor of sociology at Tarrant County College. This husband and wife team does research on couples without children. Here is what they wrote for you.*

People who choose not to have children have received little attention from social scientists. Textbooks on sociology of the family usually include no more than a paragraph or two on this topic.

We each became interested in researching individuals who have chosen not to have children while in graduate school. We are a child-free couple and when we learned that little research had been done on people like us, we were motivated to learn more about the child-free. One issue we encountered has to do with **labeling**: What should we call individuals who have chosen not to have children? Traditionally they have been referred to as "voluntarily childless" to differentiate them from people who would like to have children but have been unable to conceive ("involuntarily childless"). This term has been criticized for implying that people who choose not to have children are missing something important. Later, the term "child-free" was introduced, a term which many argued had a much more positive connotation. However, this term has also been criticized for implying that individuals who choose not to have children are free of something bad, as the terms "fat-free" and "cholesterol-free" imply. Another term that has recently been introduced is zero-child families. We perceive this term as having a negative connotation as well. This controversy led us to wonder what other people who have chosen not to have children would prefer to be called. In a recent study of men who have chosen not to have children, we found that the respondents preferred the label "child-free."

Although some couples, like us, make the decision not to have children prior to marriage, for the majority of child-free couples the decision is a gradual one that occurs after marriage. The process begins with a postponement of children for a definite period of time. The couple wants to wait until both finish school or become established in their careers. This is followed by an indefinite postponement. The couple decides "it just isn't the right time." Later, when the couple realizes that time for having children is running out, they begin to discuss the advantages and disadvantages of having children. This is followed by the acceptance of the choice to remain child-free.

People make the decision to be child-free for a variety of reasons. We have found most of these have to do with lifestyle issues. Many of the individuals we have interviewed stated they wanted more free time in order to focus on their marriage relationships and their careers. Many also mentioned the economic benefits of remaining child-free.

The United States is a pronatalist society, and people who choose not to have children are often stereotyped negatively. They are often perceived as materialistic, individualistic, career oriented, selfish, immature, child-haters, lazy, insensitive, lonely, and unhappy. Our interviews with child-free individuals have revealed that some have encountered negative reactions from family, friends, and co-workers regarding their decision. Many were asked why they made this choice, implying that there must be a reason for making such an unpopular choice. Couples who have children are not typically questioned about their decision since it is consistent with society's norms. Some of the people we interviewed stated that others reacted to their decision by looking at them as if they were crazy or by simply ignoring the decision and continuing to ask them when they were going to have children.

Our research with child-free individuals indicates that most of the stereotypes are not correct. While child-free women are typically very well educated and career-oriented, both child-free women and men usually indicate that they like children but do not want to be with children 24/7. While a few of the people we interviewed said that at some point they had reconsidered their decision, all reported being happy with their choice and satisfied with their lifestyle.

Choosing Not to Have Children. Some couples agree before marriage not to have children, while others plan to have children but never do. Sociologist Jean Veevers (1973, 1980) found that women who don't make the decision before marriage go through four stages: First, they postpone getting pregnant while they work toward a specific goal, such as graduating from college or buying a house. Then they shift their postponement to a vague future, a "sometime," such as when they feel financially independent. This vague future never seems to arrive. During the third stage, they decide that not having children isn't so bad, that they *might* want to remain this way. When they reach the fourth stage, they view their marriage without children as a permanent rather than a temporary state.

Veevers' study is a classic in this field, but the research was based on only 52 wives. More recent research shows additional pathways to not having children. Some couples choose to remain without children, then decide to have children, only to find out that they cannot have them. Other couples waver throughout their marriage between wanting and not wanting children. For some wives, not having children challenges their ideas of femininity (Basten 2009).

The situation is even more complicated than this.

I have friends in Spain who chose not to have children. Now in her late 40s, the wife has decided that her biological clock is ticking too fast, and she wants to get pregnant. Her husband, however, has no desire to have a child, and he feels that his wife is violating their agreement. Tensions have risen in their already tense relationship. She has become resentful that he doesn't see things the way she does, and he is resentful that she has had such an abrupt change of mind. She is considering making a purchase at a sperm bank, whether he agrees or not.

The Mythical Child. Many couples without children feel stigmatized. Friends and relatives put pressure on them to bear children. Veevers found that these pressures peak during the couples' third and fourth years of marriage, then gradually decrease. The couples in Veevers' sample often talked about a "mythical child"—the one they would adopt "one day." Few couples contacted an adoption agency, however, and of those who did, none followed up with their initial contact. Talking about a "mythical child" helped the couples adjust by making it seem that not having a child was temporary, assuring one another that they would have a child in the future. It also affirmed to themselves and others that they liked children. Even after the wives became too old to give birth, they still talked about the mythical child. At this point, the mythical child symbolized that they might adopt a child one day.

Happiness and Old Age. Researchers have found that couples who choose not to have children tend to have higher incomes and to be more educated, less religious, and less traditional in their gender roles. They also are happier than couples who have children—probably because they have more leisure, fewer bills to pay, and more money to spend on discretionary items like travel and entertainment.

"What about when they are old?" you might ask. "Not having those intergenerational ties probably catches up with them, and at that point they pay a high cost for their choice not to have children." Researchers have investigated this, too. They have found that in old age couples without children are just as happy as those who have children. It turns out that their expanded social ties with nonrelatives provide a satisfying support system (Bures et al. 2009).

Family Violence

When the frail, 70-year-old woman refused to hand over her money, the middle-aged man pushed her to the floor. She sprawled there, stunned and helpless, while he screamed insults. The woman became even more upset when the police arrived. She told them that she didn't want her attacker to be arrested.

This was not the first time—nor would it be the last—that her son would attack her.

Read on
MySocLab
Document
Through a
Sociological Lens:
Social Structure and
Family Violence

Extent of Violence. Sociologists Murray Straus, Susan Steinmetz, and Richard Gelles studied this cruel irony—that the family, the group we most often look to for intimacy and love, is often characterized by violence. To determine the amount and types of family violence, these researchers interviewed nationally representative samples. The participants in this research were asked to report slapping, pushing, kicking, biting, and use of weapons (Straus et al. 1980; Straus and Gelles 1988; Straus 1992).

The most violent family members are the children. During the year preceding the interviews, two-thirds of the children had attacked a brother or sister. Most had shoved or thrown things, but one-third had kicked or bitten a sibling. In rare instances, the attack involved a knife or gun. Straus suggests that these totals are severe underestimates.

The FBI reports violent crime rates per 100,000 people, but sociologists found family violence to be so common that they report it in rates per 100 people. Each year, 16 of every 100 husbands and wives physically attack one another. This is one spouse out of every six. No other violent crime even comes close to this rate.

Because most couples (84 percent) were not violent during the past year and most violence is mild (such as slapping), some dismiss these figures with a "so what" attitude. To this, Straus and Gelles (1988)reply (paraphrased):

> *Let's suppose we are talking about a university. Would anyone say that there wasn't much of a problem because, after all, 84 percent of the faculty didn't slap a student last year? Or would anyone argue that this isn't significant because, after all, most of the 16 percent of faculty members who were violent only slapped students, rather than punching or beating them?*

Watch on **MySocLab Video:** Different Types of Partner Violence

Experiencing Intimate Partner Violence. As you've seen so far in this book, sociologists do research on all kinds of topics. Sometimes they become interested in a particular social problem because of their personal experience with it. This is how it was for sociologist Kathleen Ferraro. In the Spotlight on Social Research box on the next page, she shares her experiences with **intimate partner violence**—physical, emotional, and sexual abuse within a relationship.

Equality Between the Sexes? This may surprise you, but women are as likely as men to attack their intimate partner (Gelles 1980; Lussier et al. 2009; Straus 2012). It is a different matter, however, when it comes to the *effects* of violence. Then sexual equality vanishes. As Straus points out, even though she may cast the first coffeepot, he usually casts the last and most damaging blow. Because most men are bigger and stronger, women are at a disadvantage in this literal battle of the sexes: After violence between intimate partners, more women than men need medical attention. When the worst happens, and one kills another, six times out of seven the woman is the victim (*FBI Uniform Crime Reports* 2010:Table 10). Like other crimes, violence between intimate partners has dropped in recent years (Catalano 2010).

Social Class and Violence. Although violence occurs in all social classes, it follows well-worn "social channels." Spouses in some social classes are much more likely to be abusers—or victims—than others. The highest rates of violence (Gelles 1980) are found among

- low-income families
- blue-collar workers
- families in which the husband is unemployed
- families with above-average numbers of children
- people with less education
- individuals who have no religious affiliation
- people under 30.

Why are blue-collar spouses, especially husbands, more violent than white-collar spouses? Researchers suggest that one of the reasons is that blue-collar husbands experience more stress than their white-collar counterparts. Even if blue-collar husbands do experience more stress, this does not explain why that stress gets translated into violence toward their wives. Nor does it explain why *most* blue-collar husbands, no matter how high their stress, do *not* attack their wives. We certainly need more research on family violence. Perhaps you will be the researcher who does such an enlightening study. We do need it.

Spotlight on Social Research

Intimate Partner Violence

KATHLEEN FERRARO, *professor of sociology at Northern Arizona University, wanted to be a sociologist from the time she was 12. She never imagined, though, that her research would focus on "intimate partner violence," because she never knew that this existed. Here is what she wrote for you.*

I found out about "intimate partner violence" at age 23 when I married my first husband. He went to high school with me and came from a well-respected family. He was a naturalist and a bird-watcher, did not drink or use drugs, and showed no violent tendencies. After we exchanged vows, however, he changed almost immediately, displaying the "power and control" tactics that have become so well known today. He monitored my movements, eating, clothing, friends, money, makeup, and language. If I challenged his commands, he slapped or kicked me or pushed me down.

I left him on these occasions, staying with other graduate students at Arizona State University, but I had no way to understand what was happening. My husband always convinced me to return. He stalked and threatened to kill me, even in front of police officers, but my faculty mentor, Albert J. Mayer, and my friends hid me until my father-in-law came to take my husband back to our hometown on the other side of the country. I obtained a single-party, no-fault divorce and never saw him again.

These events took place in 1974 and 1975, before the battered women's movement transformed public understanding of "domestic violence." In a graduate class on social deviance, Erdwin Pfuhl required us to write a paper on a form of deviance with which we had personal experience. I could not think of anything. While I waited outside his office to ask for help, another woman struck up a conversation with me, and I learned that her boyfriend abused her. That was the moment that I began to think sociologically about my own experience. I discovered that there was a battered women's shelter in my city, and I began to volunteer there and to interview staff members. This was the beginning of the battered women's movement and the beginning of a lifetime of research, teaching, and activism for me. I joined with a group of people to establish another shelter, and that is where I conducted the interviews and ethnographic work for my dissertation, *Battered Women and the Shelter Movement,* and for the *Social Problems* article, "How Women Experience Battering: The Process of Victimization."

The women taught me how difficult it is to make sense of the violence and emotional abuse that come from a person they love and believe loves them. The rationalizations the women used to understand what was happening to them were similar to those used by people who commit crimes, the "techniques of neutralization" described by Gresham Sykes and David Matza. For women at the shelter, these techniques included denial of victimization, denial of the victimizer, denial of injury, denial of options, appeal to higher loyalties, and the salvation ethic. Because of fear, lack of resources, and institutional failure to respond to battering, the women found escape from violent relationships to be difficult and precarious. Leaving an abuser does not necessarily end the violence—women are often at most risk during the time they are leaving the abuser.

Alcohol and Violence. From what you know about drinking, I'm sure it won't surprise you to learn that sociologists have found that the more alcohol that people consume, the more likely they are to attack one another. Sociologists Glenda Kantor and Murray Straus (1987) found these extremes: Couples who do not drink have the lowest rates of violence, while alcoholics have the highest rates.

The Social Heredity of Violence. Straus, Gelles, and Steinmetz also discovered what they call the *social heredity of violence*—children learn from their parents that violence is a way to solve problems. After the children who grow up in violent homes marry, they apply this family lesson to their own marriage. As Figure 11.12 shows, the more violence that children experience during their teen years, the more likely they are

FIGURE 11.12 ▸ How Marital Violence Is Related to the Family Violence That Teenagers Experience

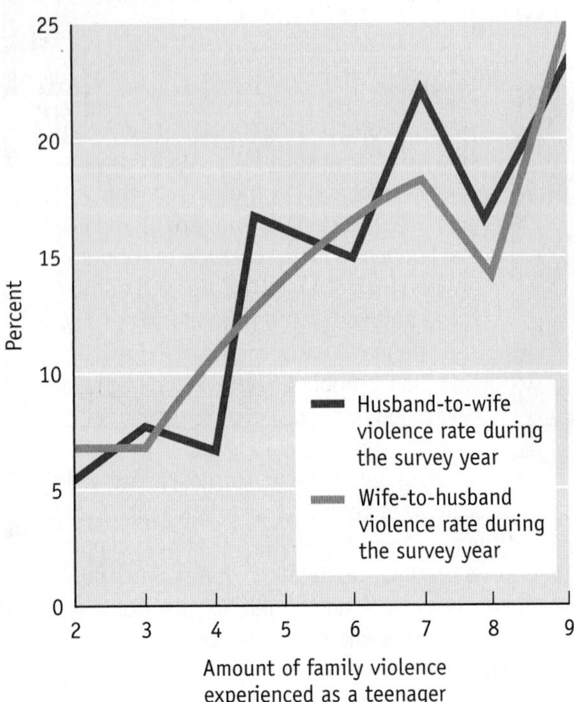

Source: Straus et al.1980:112.

to be violent in their own marriage. Here is how the researchers (Straus et al. 1980:113) explain Figure 11.12:

> *Those with scores of zero are the people whose parents did not hit them and did not hit each other. At the other extreme are people with scores of 9. They are the people whose parents frequently hit them when they were teenagers and whose parents were frequently violent with each other.*

The researchers point out that the social heredity of violence is so powerful that

> *When one member of a couple had experienced the double whammy of being hit as a child and observing his or her parents hitting each other, there was a one in three chance that at least one act of violence had occurred during the year of the study!*

Why Doesn't She Just Leave? Some wives remain with husbands who abuse them. Why? This question has intrigued members of the public and sociologists alike. Researchers have studied many samples of women, and they have found remarkably consistent answers. Findings from one of these studies are featured in the Issues in Social Problems box on the next page.

Spouse Abuse as a Defense for Homicide. Some wives, of course, leave their husbands after the first attack and never return. Others remain in the relationship, only to murder their partners after enduring years of abuse. Being an abused wife has been used as a defense for killing husbands. Although this defense elicits sympathy from the jury and likely mitigates punishment, it seldom is successful. But sometimes it is. Listen to Cindy Hudo, a 21-year-old mother of two in Charleston, South Carolina, who was charged with the murder of her husband, Buba. Here is what she said:

> *I start in the car and I get down the road and I see Buba walking, and he's real mad. I just look at him. So, I pull over, you know, and I'm trying, you know—"I didn't know to pick you up. You know, I'm sorry." And he didn't even say nothing to me. He just started hitting on me. And that's all I wanted to do, was just get home, because I was just self-conscious. I don't want nobody to see him hitting me, because I didn't want him to look bad. I had to go to work in a half-hour, because I was working a double-shift. And he told me I had forty minutes to get all my furniture out of the house and get my clothes and be out or he was going to throw them out.*
>
> *And I was sitting there, because I could talk him down. You know, because I didn't want to leave him. I just talked to him. I said, "Buba, I don't want to leave." I said, "This is my house." And then he told me . . . (unclear) my kids. And I said, "No, you're not taking my kids from me. That's too much." And so I said, "Just let me leave. Just let me take the kids. And, you know I'll go, and you know, I won't keep the kids from you or nothing like that." And he said, "I'm going to take them and you're getting out."*
>
> *[Buba then loaded a shotgun, pointed it at Cindy, and said] "The only way you're going to get out of this is if you kill me and I'll—I'll kill you." [Buba then gave the shotgun to Cindy and] just turned around and walked right down the hall, because he knew I wouldn't do nothing. And I just sat there a minute. And I don't know what happened. I just, you know, I went to the bedroom and I seen him laying there and I just shot him. He moved. I shot him again because I thought he was going to get up again. . . .*
>
> *I loved him too much. And I just wanted to help him. (20/20, October 18, 1979)*

No one knows if the killing occurred the way Cindy recounted it. Did Buba give the loaded shotgun to Cindy? Or did she load it herself while Buba was sleeping and

Issues in Social Problems

"Why Doesn't She Just Leave?" The Dilemma of Abused Women

"Why would she ever put up with violence?" is a question on everyone's mind. From the outside, it looks so easy. Just pack up and leave. "I know I wouldn't put up with anything like that."

Yet this is not what typically happens. Women tend to stay with their men after they are abused. Some stay only a short while, to be sure, but others remain in abusive situations for years. Why?

Sociologist Ann Goetting (2001) asked this question, too. To get the answer, she interviewed women who had made the break. Goetting wanted to find out what set these women apart. How were they able to leave, when so many can't seem to? She found that

1. These women had a positive self-concept.
   Simply put, they believed that they deserved better.
2. They broke with traditional values.
   They did not believe that a wife had to stay with her husband no matter what.
3. They found adequate finances.
   For some this was easy, but to accumulate enough money to move out, some of the women saved for years, putting away just a little each week.
4. They had supportive family and friends.
   A support network served as a source of encouragement to help them rescue themselves.

If you take the opposite of these four characteristics, you have the answer to why some women put up with abuse: They don't think they deserve anything better; they believe it is their duty to stay no matter what; they don't think they can make it financially; and they lack a supportive network. These four factors are not of equal importance. For some women, the lack of finances is the most significant, while for others it can be a low self-concept. For all women, the support network—or the lack of one—plays a significant role.

A survivor of extreme domestic violence shares her experience of being nearly burned to death by her ex-husband.

For Your Consideration

On the basis of these findings, what would you say to a woman whose husband or partner is abusing her? How do you think women's shelters fit into this explanation? What other parts of this puzzle can you think of—such as the role of love? Would you give a different answer to a *man* whose wife or partner is abusing him?

then creep up on him and shoot him in cold blood? Despite these nagging questions, and although Cindy had shot and killed her husband, who at the time was unarmed and unresisting, a jury acquitted Cindy on the basis that she was a battered wife.

No matter how understandable the desire to kill may be under conditions of abuse and brutality, this defense raises questions about justifying murder.

Sexual Abuse: Marital Rape

Extent and Timing of Marital Rape. How common is marital rape? Although this area of human behavior is shrouded in secrecy, sociologists have made it a topic of their research (Black et al. 2011). When David Finkelhor and Kersti Yllo (1985, 1989) interviewed 330 women in Boston, 10 percent reported that their husbands had used physical force to compel them to have sex. Another sociologist, Diana Russell (1980), estimated that 12 percent of married women have been raped by their husbands. These totals are only estimates, but if either is anywhere near accurate they represent a lot of women. With 58 million married women in the United States, even the lower estimate would translate into the astounding total of close to 6 million women who have been raped by their husbands (*Statistical Abstract* 2013:Table 61).

Marital rape is most likely to occur during a separation or when a marriage is breaking up. In rare instances, however, husbands rape their wives throughout marriage. Finkelhor and Yllo found that one woman had endured marital rape for 24 years. Her marriage ended only when her husband divorced her!

Types of Marital Rape. From interviews with fifty women whose husbands had raped them, Finkelhor and Yllo found three types of marital rape:

1. *Nonbattering rape.* In about 40 percent of the cases, the husband raped his wife without intending to harm her. The attack was usually preceded by a conflict over sex, such as the husband feeling insulted when his wife refused to have sex.
2. *Battering rape.* In about 48 percent of the cases, the husband intentionally hurt his wife during the rape. He was retaliating for some supposed wrongdoing on his wife's part.
3. *Perverted rape.* In these instances, about 6 percent, the husband seemed to be sexually aroused by the violence. These husbands forced their wives to submit to unusual sexual acts.

Effects of Marital Rape. How did the rapes affect the wives? The short-term effects were anger, accompanied by grief, despair, shame, and feelings of "dirtiness." The most common long-term effect was the woman's inability to trust intimate relationships or to function sexually.

Why Do Some Women Put Up with Marital Rape? Although most women quickly leave a marriage after being raped by their husbands, some remain. Why? The answers are similar to those you read in the box on page 373. Most of these women are afraid to leave. They fear that they don't have the skills to make it on their own or they lack support networks. Some are afraid that their children will suffer or that their husband will retaliate. With low self-esteem and little support, they feel they cannot survive without their husbands.

Sexual Abuse: Incest

In Australia, 61-year-old John Deaves and 39-year-old Jenny Deaves went on television. They talked about their love for one another and about their new baby.

The audience reacted with disgust. What bothered them wasn't the difference in their ages. They were upset that John is Jenny's father. (Childs 2008)

Sociologists have investigated **incest**—forbidden sexual relations between relatives, such as brothers and sisters or parents and children. Like that of John and Jenny Deaves, revelations of incest are met with repugnance. The prohibition of incest is one of the few issues on which almost all Americans strongly agree. Some analysts suggest that avoidance of incest is hard-wired into our brains (Childs 2008). Around the world, incest is almost always viewed as abhorrent, sinful, or unnatural.

With the huge variation in human behavior around the world, there are even exceptions to this almost universal repugnance to incest. These exceptions include brother–sister marriages among the Incas of Peru, the Egyptian pharaohs, and the common people of Egypt under Roman rule (Leavitt 2013). In East Africa, Thonga lion hunters are allowed to have sex with their daughters on the night before a big hunt (La Barre 1954; Beals and Hoijer 1965).

Extent of Incest. With its generally strong condemnation, one might think incest is rare, but is it? Sociologist Diana Russell (1986), who interviewed 930 women in San Francisco, found that before these women turned age 18, 16 percent had been victims of incest. Her operational definition of incest, however, was so broad that it included not only sexual relations with relatives but also unwanted kisses. In only 5 of 100 cases were the police informed. Although this research does not match common assumptions about what incest is, it indicates that incest is likely more common than the numbers that are officially reported. Again, we need more research.

Brother–sister sexual relations are the most common form of incest. This brother and sister in Germany made the news when it was revealed that they had four children together. He was put in prison, she was placed in social services, and the children were put in foster care.

Who Are the Offenders? Incest can occur between any family members, but sex between children seems to be the most common form. An analysis of 13,000 cases of sibling incest showed that most incest occurs between brothers and sisters, with the sex initiated by a brother who is five years older than his sister (Krienert and Walsh 2011). In one-fourth of the cases, though, the victim is a younger brother, and in 13 percent of the cases it is the sister who is the offender. Most offenders are between the ages of 13 and 15, and most victims are age 12 or younger. In most cases, the parents treat the incest as a family matter to be dealt with privately.

Effects on Victims. As you can imagine, incest can create enormous burdens for its victims (Bartoi and Kinder 1998; Lewin 1998). Here is what Susan Forward, a psychotherapist who was herself a victim of incest, says:

> *I understand incest not only as a psychotherapist but as a victim. When I was fifteen my father's playful seductiveness turned into highly sexualized fondling. This is a difficult admission for me to make, but even more painful is the fact that I enjoyed my father's attentions.*
>
> *I felt enormously guilty about my participation in the incest, as if I had been responsible. I know now I was not. It was my father's responsibility as an adult and as a parent to prevent sexual contact between us, but I didn't understand that at the time.*
>
> *I also felt guilty about competing with my mother—who was only thirty-three and very attractive.*
>
> *I was flattered by my father's attraction to me, and his caresses felt good, but after several months my guilt became too great. I somehow found the courage to tell him to stop, and he did. The psychological damage, however, had already been done.*
>
> *As my guilt feelings accumulated, my self-image deteriorated. I felt like a "bad girl." I began to punish myself unconsciously, most prominently by marrying an unloving man instead of pursuing the acting career I had dreamed of since I was five. Later, when my children were in school, I finally got a job on a television series. Good jobs followed and success was within my grasp. But my guilt still fought me on a [sub]conscious level, telling me that I didn't deserve success. So I allowed myself—[sub]consciously, of course, to become overweight and matronly at twenty-eight. My acting career stagnated. My marriage was a mess. I was desperately unhappy. Yet I had absolutely no idea that there was any connection between what my father had done to me and the problems in my life. (Forward and Buck 1978:1)*

The Pro-Incest Lobby. A small group of people claim that incest is not a problem. The problem, they say, is the *attitude* toward incest. The **Pedophile Liberation Army (PLA)** argues that if people changed their attitudes about adults having sex with children, then incest would no longer be an issue. This pro-incest lobby claims that there should be no law against incest because sexual attraction toward children is healthy. People who adopt this view also argue that prohibiting incest ruins affectionate relationships and the sexual love that can forge strong bonds between children and adults (De Mott 1980).

If the PLA ever were to succeed in removing what has been called the "last taboo," the change could be devastating. Despite loosened sexual norms, however, the chances of incest becoming an approved behavior range from remote to impossible.

Old Age and Widowhood

Problems of Adjustment. Most Americans today survive to old age. As we reviewed in Chapter 2, old age brings many problems of adjustment, especially deteriorating health, the death of loved ones, and the knowledge of one's own impending death. When the elderly retire from productive roles, their sense of social worth can be challenged. They may even face attitudes that they have become parasites—that they are draining the health care system or robbing younger workers by bankrupting the Social Security system.

From Extended to Nuclear. Several generations ago, Americans lived in **extended families**; that is, other relatives, perhaps grandparents or aunts and uncles, lived with the parents and their children. During this agrarian period, the aged, who owned land, could maintain positions of authority, gradually relinquishing control while easing younger family members into responsible roles. Although we cannot be sure, the transition to old age may have been smoother and perhaps less painful than it is today. Even though they may have been living in a productive extended family, however, their adjustment to deteriorating health, the death of loved ones, and the knowledge that they, too, would soon die could not have been easy.

The Myth of Family Abandonment. The **nuclear family**, consisting of parents and children, has become our dominant family form. Compared with the larger extended family, the nuclear family is smaller, making it easier for its members to become isolated. The media sometimes paint a grim picture of isolated elderly, abandoned and embittered, living out their last remorseful years stowed away in some apartment crammed full of old newspapers and memorabilia from the past.

A team of sociologists who studied the residents of Muncie, Indiana, found that, contrary to this picture, the elderly maintain close contact with their adult children (Caplow et al. 1982). As you can see in Figure 11.13, 63 percent of Americans ages 65 to 74 are still living with their spouse. Only one of four or five lives alone. Even among those who are age 75 and over, 46 percent live with their spouses and just under two of five live alone.

FIGURE 11.13 ▸ Living Arrangements of the Elderly

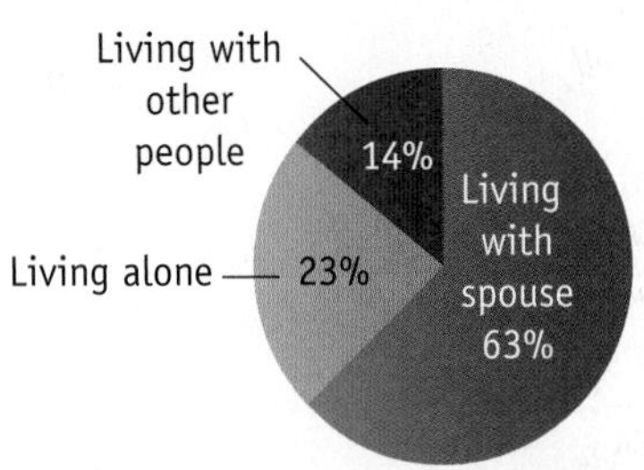

People ages 65 to 74

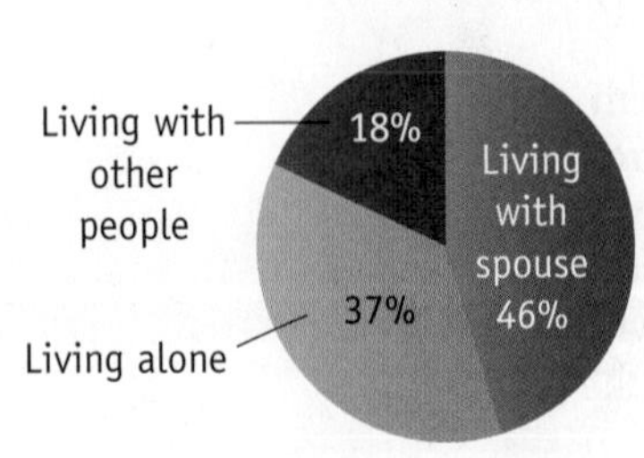

People ages 75 and over

Source: By the author. Based on *Statistical Abstract of the United States* 2013:Table 58.

"Intimacy at a Distance" ▸ Sociologist Elaine Brody (1978) says that in the United States both the elderly and the young *prefer* to live apart. The elderly prefer to live near, but not with, their children—a situation described as "intimacy at a distance." Sociologist Suzanne Steinmetz (1988) reports that parents and their adult children who live together tend to "get on one another's nerves." The elderly appear to be expressing their own independence and respecting the privacy of their children when they want to live near, but not with, their children. Far from abandoning their aged parents, children remain key figures in their support system (Bengtson et al. 1990).

The Institutionalized Elderly. The 3 percent of the aged who live in nursing homes are *not* typical of older people (*Statistical Abstract* 2013:Tables 9, 198). Three of four are age 75 or older. Almost all (80 percent) are widowed or divorced, or have never married, leaving them without family to care for them. Most of these elderly are in such poor health that they need help to bathe, dress, and eat (Harrington et al. 2011).

Nursing home residents who need constant care confirm stereotypes about the elderly. They certainly are not a healthy group, but remember that nursing home residents do *not* represent elderly people in general. On the contrary, *most* elderly Americans enjoy good health and the company of their family and friends.

Adjusting to Widowhood. Even for people who enjoy good health and family relationships in their older years, death comes eventually. When death ends a marriage, the impact is so severe that the surviving spouse tends to die earlier than expected (Shor et al. 2012). These earlier-than-expected deaths, observed around the world, are called the *widowhood effect.* Facing life without the partner who had become such an essential part of life is traumatic. In the midst of disrupted family relationships and the loss of social roles, the widowed face five

"Money can't buy happiness" is an old saying. But it is not true. Money does buy happiness. Compared with poor people, wealthier people are more satisfied with life—and more optimistic about the future. Their health is better, they live longer, and even their marriages last longer.

main problems: loneliness, anxiety, depression, financial strain, and more physical health problems (Hiltz 1989; Holden et al. 2010; Shor et al. 2012).

Widows and widowers who have more adequate incomes make a better adjustment to the death of their spouse (Holden et al. 2010). The reason seems to be that having an adequate income produces less stress. Back in the 1970s, sociologist Robert Atchley (1975) studied retired schoolteachers and retired employees of a telephone company whose wife or husband had died. He found that those who were more active in organizations, had more contact with friends, and had adequate money made a better adjustment.

The End of Marriage and the Traditional Family?

Have we come to the end of marriage and the traditional family? Let's review some of the changes in marriage and family with this question in mind.

Marriage Is Weakening. Some seem to think that marriage is coming to an end. As we discussed earlier, our divorce rate is high, cohabitation has skyrocketed, and people are postponing marriage. If cohabitation continues to increase as it has, eventually most people will live together, not marry. As you can see from Table 11.1, with women having fewer children the size of the average family has become smaller. It's difficult to see how smaller equals stronger. On top of this, 41 percent of U.S. children are born to unmarried women. As more and more couples cohabit and as more and more unmarried women bear children, perhaps marriage will become a quaint custom reserved for a few traditionalists.

Marriage Continues Strong. But there is another side to today's marriage and family. Cohabitation has not replaced marriage. It has become a step on the way to marriage, and most people who marry today have lived with their new spouse prior to their marriage. Although people are taking longer to say "I do," millions are still making these vows. Look at Figure 11.14. You can see that by the time women reach their early thirties, about three out of four are married. It takes men a little longer, but

TABLE 11.1 ▸ Average Size of the U.S. Family (Persons per family)

1960	1970	1980	1990	2000	2010
3.67	3.62	3.29	3.17	3.17	3.16

Source: By the author. Based on *Statistical Abstract of the United States* 1991:Table 61; 2013:Table 59.

FIGURE 11.14 ▶ The Percentage of Americans Who Have Never Married

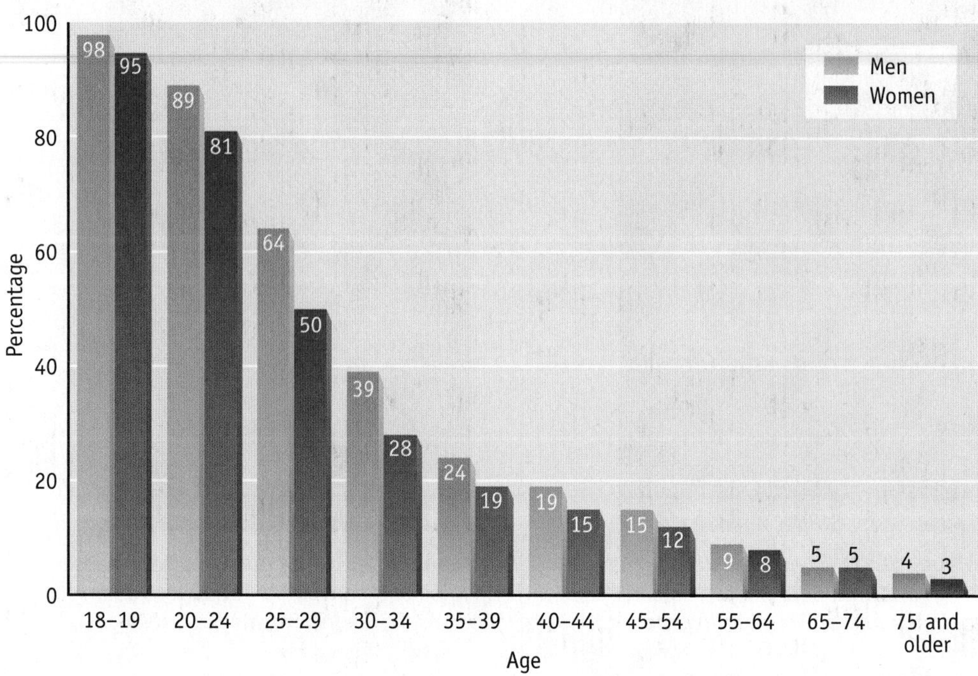

Source: By the author. Based on *Statistical Abstract of the United States* 2013:Table 57.

they soon hit this same total. By old age, about 96 percent of Americans have married. Records are somewhat uncertain, but this could be the *highest* percentage of marriage in our history.

The Middletown Research ▶ Sociological research from Muncie, Indiana, indicates that American family life is not disintegrating; it is actually improving. Muncie, Indiana, is one of the most thoroughly researched cities in the United States. In the 1920s and 1930s, sociologists Robert and Helen Lynd (1929, 1937) analyzed family life in this middle-American city, which they called "Middletown." In the 1980s, other sociologists went back to Muncie to find out whether the family had declined during those 50 years. To see whether it had, they compared current rates of suicide, mental illness, and domestic violence with the rates from the 1920s and 1930s. To their surprise, Theodore Caplow and his fellow researchers (Caplow et al. 1982) found that these problems were *less* frequent in Middletown than they had been two generations earlier.

And instead of alienation, the researchers found community. Most parents and their grown children keep in close touch. The nuclear families are not isolated units, as some stereotypes paint them. Rather, the nuclear families are embedded in larger kin and friendship networks, which are vital for people's well-being. These networks help people meet their emotional needs, especially their need to feel connected to others. They also meet people's physical needs, with relatives and friends helping one another when they are sick or in financial need.

Perhaps these researchers' most surprising finding was that marriage had become more vibrant. Marriage in the 1920s was shallower. Then husbands and wives lived more separate lives and didn't talk as much with one another. With male and female roles now less segregated, husbands and wives talk things over more—and they are *more satisfied* with marriage. After reviewing their data, these researchers conclude: "for most of their members most of the time, Middletown's composite families provide a safe and comfortable niche in a hazardous world." *The idea that the family has declined is a "sociological myth."*

Changes and Challenges. Despite such a positive assessment from the Middletown research, U.S. families face severe problems. You've read about some of them in this chapter. Look at Figure 11.15 on the next page. One of the most striking aspects

FIGURE 11.15 ▸ What Are Americans' Living Arrangements?

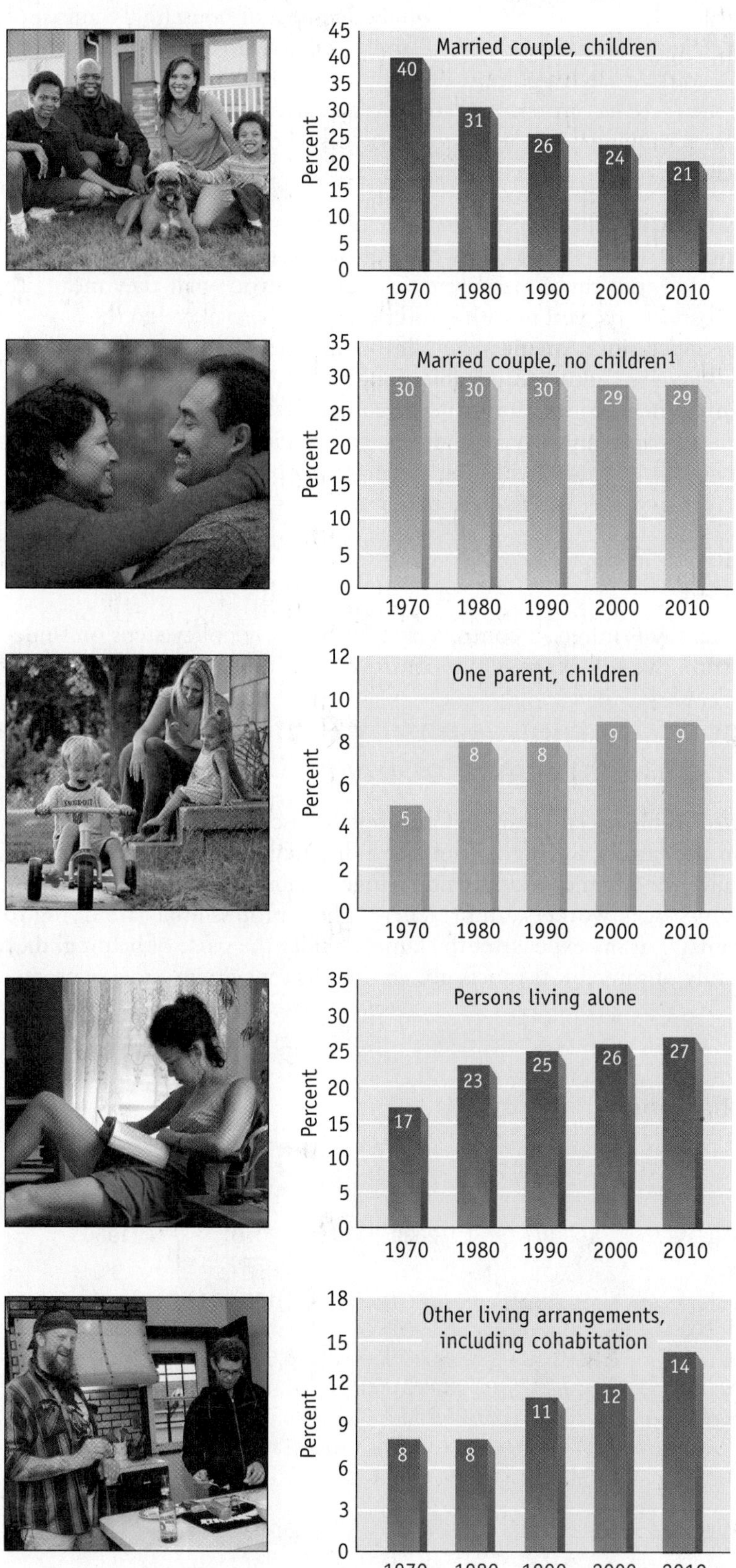

[1]"Married couple, no children" includes childless or child-free couples, but most of these couples are "empty nesters": Their children have grown and left home.

Source: By the author. Based on *Statistical Abstract of the United States* 2000:Table 60; 2013:Table 59.

of this figure is the decline of married couples with children at home. In the past 40 or 50 years, the number has dropped in half. Today only one-fifth of households consist of married couples with children. Our stereotypes of "family" will have to catch up with reality.

From Table 11.2, you can catch a glimpse of other ways that U.S. families are changing. As you can see, the three largest changes are increases in cohabitation, living alone, and children living with only one parent. At the very least, none of these indicate that marriage is strengthening.

Explore on **MySocLab Activity:** Family Diversity: Who Takes Care of Whom?

What Do These Changes Mean? As symbolic interactionists stress, you can measure objective conditions such as the rate of divorce or the number of children who are living with one parent, but those measurements don't tell you what they mean. To understand objective conditions, you must interpret them. How shall we do this?

Let's try for a fair conclusion: American families are experiencing severe disruptions. We can see this from runaways, divorce, cohabitation, births to single women, and violence. At the same time, some areas of family life have improved over the years, especially relationships between husbands and wives. And, finally, Americans retain high hope for healthy, satisfying marriage and family life. Although young people are postponing the age at which they first marry, they continue to marry at a high rate.

Social Policy

11.5 Explain the controversy over professional intrusion in the family and the dilemma of family policy.

Social policy for the family is mired in controversy because every policy steps on someone's toes. In this section, we will examine this controversy.

The Lasch Accusation: Intrusions by Professionals and the Coming Therapeutic Society

In *Haven in a Heartless World*, social historian Christopher Lasch (1977) said that people are trying to find in the family a refuge of love and decency in a cruel and heartless world. The family, however, often cannot provide refuge because it has been besieged by professionals—doctors, social workers, and teachers. These professionals are trying to enlarge their own domains at the expense of the family. Under the guise of helping, they have stripped the family of some of its functions, eroding its capacity to provide protective intimacy.

TABLE 11.2 ▸ How U.S. Families Are Changing

	1980	1990	2000	2010	Change Since 1980
Marriages	2,390,000	2,440,000	2,330,000	2,250,000	–5.9%
Divorces	1,190,000	1,180,000	1,180,000	1,160,000	–2.5%
Married couples	52,300,000	56,300,000	56,500,000	58,410,000	+11.7%
Unmarried couples	1,590,000	2,860,000	4,900,000	6,500,000	+409%
People living alone	18,300,000	23,000,000	28,725,000	31,400,000	+72%
Married couples with children at home	24,960,000	24,540,000	25,250,000	24,575,000	–1.5%
Children living with both parents	48,650,000	46,500,000	49,760,000	51,850,000	+6.5%
Children living with one parent	12,500,000	15,840,000	19,160,000	19,800,000	+58%
Average size of household	2.76	2.63	2.62	2.59	–6.2%
Married women who are employed	24,980,000	30,970,000	35,150,000	36,740,000	+47%
Births to single women	665,700	1,165,000	1,347,000	1,727,000	+263%

Note: Marriages, divorces, and births to single women are events that occurred in the given year. The other items are not events, but total counts.

Source: By the author. Based on *Statistical Abstract of the United States* 1989:Table 58; 1992:Tables 49, 52, 56, 69, 73, 82, 89, 127, 619; 2012: Tables 59, 61, 62, 69, 85, 132, 133, 597.

How could Lasch come to such a conclusion? Consider the professionals who claim to be experts in sex. These sexperts write books and magazine articles about what sexual relations between husband and wife "ought" to be like. Hundreds of "Dr. Phils" and "Phil wannabes" appear as self-styled experts on radio and television and in magazines, where they proclaim their expertise. This makes husbands and wives feel less capable of working out their own sexual problems, for only "sexual experts" have the "real" answers. Or consider the professionals who stake claim to child rearing. They profess to know the best ways to rear children, sometimes even *the* correct way to do so. This makes parents worry that, as mere laypeople, they might be damaging their children through well-intended but clumsy, improper parenting. Parents are encouraged to look to "professionals," who now intrude into the traditionally private areas of family life.

In short, Lasch says, we are on a road that leads to a *therapeutic society*, one in which "experts" claim that all problems—including those in the family—are their domain. The "concern" expressed by "experts" about the plight of the family, publicized on television and radio, in magazines and books, only masks what is really happening: These outside agents are trying to take away the parent's authority and place the family under their control. On top of this, as Lasch emphasizes, there is no evidence that these so-called experts benefit the family. They are simply marketing their services and products in order to establish self-serving mini-empires.

As you would expect, professionals have reacted bitterly to this attack on their skills, accomplishments, and motives. They deny that they have self-serving motives or that they intrude into family life, undermine its authority, and cause families to have less "self-sufficiency" (Joffe 1978). On the contrary, the "professionals" say that their goal is to empower the family so it can handle the problems of life. The troubled family needs them, they insist.

The Dilemma of Family Policy: Taking Sides

Lasch's claims expose how any social policy addressing family needs will likely find itself on one side or the other of issues that divide well-meaning people who have the best interests of families at heart. For example, consider what seems to be a neutral matter, making financial aid available to troubled families. One might assume that such a policy would only help families. Another side, however, may view providing financial aid as an attack on family self-sufficiency. They might see it as discouraging families from looking out for themselves—making them further dependent on outside sources, perhaps on the coming therapeutic society.

Almost all policy falls on one side or the other of this explosive issue. In the Thinking Critically box on the next page, we consider a more controversial matter.

The Future of the Problem

Social Change

11.6 Discuss the trends and social changes that are likely to affect family relationships.

Social change is the hallmark of the United States. Seemingly overnight, familiar landmarks are torn down and replaced by a strip mall or by another of an endless series of fast-food outlets. Computers recognize your speech, type your message, and check your grammar; devices connected to the Global Positioning System announce your location, guide you through traffic in a strange city, and provide an ongoing trail for authorities to follow. On the Internet, type something in English and it can be translated instantly (if not 100 percent accurately) into any major language before being transmitted to someone in a distant part of the world. Soon you'll be able to have one telephone number that will stay with you for life and will be valid throughout the world. Change is so rapid and extensive that parents and children live in different worlds—so much so that some grown children who are visiting their parents after an absence of months or even years find that after the first hour or two they have little left to talk about.

Thinking Critically About Social Problems

"You Want Birth Control, Little Girl?"

Fiona is 14 years old. Her parents told her that she cannot have sex because premarital sex is a sin. Fiona is afraid that if she does not have sex with her boyfriend, he will date more cooperative girls. She also is madly in love with her boyfriend and wants to please him. She is sure he is the "right one" and that the two of them will have a marvelous life together.

Fiona went to a family planning clinic and explained her problem. The counselors encouraged her to assert herself against her domineering, old-fashioned parents. They assured her that she could come to them for a free and confidential abortion if she became pregnant. They also offered her a Norplant.

Should 14-year-old girls be given birth control?

Who is right in this example? As symbolic interactionists stress, our understanding of what "right" is depends on our values. Sociologist Carole Joffe (1978), who originated this example for discussion purposes, put it this way: From one perspective, the decision of a teenager to seek out contraception is a step forward in gaining her independence. But from another perspective, giving contraceptives to a young teenager does not represent a step toward independence but, rather, an intrusion into family privacy.

And what if we change the age in this example just a bit? How about two years up, or two years down? Assume that Fiona is 12 years old or that she is 16 years old. Your opinion about ages 12, 14, and 16, where do they come from? Do you see how these ages and what is appropriate for them represent your personal values? And do you see where your values come from? How, then, can one group force its values on another group?

This is the essence of the dilemma. As symbolic interactionists stress, we come from different corners of life, and in those corners we learn perspectives, views of the world. We can't help but view the world from the perspectives we learn.

For Your Consideration

What is your opinion about a family planning clinic giving birth control to a minor over the objection of her family? To a 12-year-old girl? To a 14-year-old? To a 16-year-old? How do you think such a dilemma should be resolved?

Future Shock

The speed, extent, and intensity of today's social change overpower us. Alvin Toffler (1971) coined the term *future shock* to refer to this dizzying barrage of change to which we have no leisure or opportunity to adjust. **Future shock** is the vertigo, the confusion, the disorientation that we experience when our familiar worlds are jerked out from under us.

Future shock has hit the U.S. family. But this isn't new. The family has already faced industrialization and urbanization, events that transformed almost all human relationships. Now computers are changing work, education, recreation, news, entertainment—and family relationships. Parents and children text and e-mail one another from office, school, and home, giving brief updates on changing plans.

Because the family is continuing to adapt to changing social conditions, its future is unclear, but let's venture into these uncharted waters.

Anticipating the Future

The romantic notions of love and marriage are established firmly in our culture. The idea of love is so firmly embedded in our cultural psyche that it will continue to be the "proper" basis for marriage. I expect that age at first marriage will continue upward a while longer, then stabilize. Cohabitation will do the same, continuing to increase for about another decade and then leveling off. More married women will work for pay outside the home, eventually reaching a plateau at about 70 percent. Marriage will become even more oriented around companionship. This orientation, coupled with more wives working outside the home, will be a stimulus for husbands and wives to develop more equal relationships. Women's incomes will increase relative to those of men, which will be another push for greater equality. With couples marrying at older ages after attaining higher levels of education, the divorce rate will decline. Even so, marriage will remain fragile, and the United States will continue to have one of the highest divorce rates in the world. Whether you interpret such changes as good, bad, or indifferent depends, of course, on your values.

The Ideological Struggle

Finally, it seems obvious, and quite significant, that competing groups will continue to try to influence family values and family policy. With their incompatible views of what is right and of what the good life is, these groups will continue to battle one another. This struggle, which might seem theoretical or abstract, is destined to influence your family life.

Although the outcome is uncertain, the future certainly looks exciting.

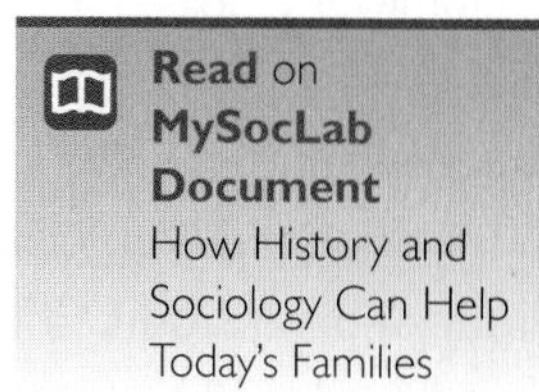

Read on MySocLab Document
How History and Sociology Can Help Today's Families

MySocLab  Study and Review on MySocLab

Summary and Review

1. The family is always adjusting to social change. One of the most significant effects of the Industrial Revolution was the removal of economic production from the household.
2. Whether change within the family is perceived as a social problem or merely as a form of adaptation depends on people's values. Indicators that many see as evidence of a social problem are divorce, runaway children, births to single women, one-parent families, and violence and sexual abuse in the family.
3. In analyzing why the U.S. divorce rate is high, symbolic interactionists stress the changing expectations of marriage; functionalists, the declining functions of the family; and conflict theorists, the struggle for equality in marriage.
4. The average age at first marriage declined from 1890 to about 1955, then began to increase about 1970. Today, the average age at first marriage is perhaps the highest in our history. The primary reason is *cohabitation*. As many people postpone marriage, a growing proportion of the young remain single.
5. The reasons married couples do not have children are infertility, a decision to not have children, and the postponement of children until not having them becomes inevitable.
6. Physical violence between family members is common. Although wives initiate about as much violence as husbands, they are injured more often. People reared in violent homes are more likely to be violent to their own spouses and children. Incest and marital rape seem to be more frequent than commonly supposed.
7. Most adult children and their parents keep in close touch. The elderly prefer "intimacy at a distance," living near their children, but not with them. Those who are better off financially adjust better to the death of a spouse.
8. Contrary to stereotypes, the "Middletown" studies indicate that husbands and wives are more satisfied with married life than they were 50 years ago.
9. Social policy on the family is controversial because it pits individual rights against the intervention of

"experts." Some accuse "family professionals" of trying to expand their domain at the expense of the family.

10. The future is likely to bring increases in cohabitation, later age at first marriage, more wives working outside the home, and greater marital equality. Groups that are concerned about the family differ in their ideas about the way the family "should" be. It remains to be seen which groups with their clashing ideas will be most influential in determining social policy.

Key Terms

breadwinner, 359
cohabitation, 367
defective discipline, 356
extended families, 376
family of orientation, 358
family of procreation, 358
future shock, 382
homemaker, 359
incest, 374
intimate partner violence, 370
labeling, 368
nuclear family, 376
Pedophile Liberation Army (PLA), 375
pedophiles, 357
pushouts, 357
reproductive labor, 364
sexual revolution, 363

Thinking Critically About Chapter 11

1. What do you consider to be the three greatest benefits and the three greatest downsides of the changes in the U.S. families? Do you think that these changes are bringing more negatives or positives? Explain.
2. Which perspective (symbolic interactionism, functionalism, or conflict theory) do you think does the best job of explaining the changes that are taking place in U.S. families? Explain.
3. Rank the seven traditional functions of the family (p. 362) according to how important you think they are today. Explain your rankings.
4. With the huge increase in cohabitation, the growing number of singles, the high divorce rate, the number of runaways, and the extent of abuse in families, how can the author not conclude that marriage is doomed? Explain.

12 Urbanization and Population

Listen to the Chapter 12 on MySocLab

Learning Objectives. After reading this chapter, you should be able to:

12.1 Discuss the evolution of cities and describe the significance of urbanization. **(p. 386)**

12.2 Explain what is *urban* about urban problems. **(p. 388)**

12.3 Discuss the perspectives that emerge when you apply symbolic interactionism, functionalism, and conflict theory to urban problems. **(p. 390)**

12.4 Summarize research findings on urban alienation and community, urban dwellers, urban violence, and transitions in power and resources. **(p. 393)**

12.5 Summarize social policy that can build community in the city. **(p. 399)**

12.6 Discuss the likely future of urban problems. **(p. 404)**

12.7 Contrast the explanations for Europe's surge in population and the views of the pessimists and the optimists. **(p. 405)**

12.8 Describe how the New Malthusians and the Anti-Malthusians view world population growth and food supply. **(p. 408)**

12.9 Discuss the perspectives that emerge when you apply symbolic interactionism, functionalism, and conflict theory to world population. **(p. 411)**

12.10 Summarize how the New Malthusians and the Anti-Malthusians interpret research findings on population change. **(p. 417)**

12.11 Compare the social policy implications of the New Malthusians and the Anti-Malthusians. **(p. 419)**

12.12 Compare the two futures as seen by the New Malthusians and the Anti-Malthusians. **(p. 421)**

Kellie Moiser was a 17-year-old high school student who worked part-time at the corner ice cream store. From childhood, she had dreamed of becoming a model. Kellie's mother encouraged her dream, hoping that it would be a way out of poverty.

But Kellie never got the chance.

And a little blood didn't bother him.

Michael Hagan, 23, also lived in her area of south-central Los Angeles. He liked Olde English "800" Malt Liquor, especially when he smoked PCP.

He also liked guns.

And a little blood didn't bother him, either.

One Monday evening, Hagan was on a binge with other members of his gang, when they decided to go after a rival gang. They piled into an old Buick and sped toward enemy turf. There they spotted four teenagers, two boys and two girls.

The teenagers were not gang members. They were just kids who had gone out for ice cream. When they saw the gun, they ran. Kellie didn't run fast enough. Hagan methodically pumped fifteen slugs into her, six into her back.

The police didn't have much to go on, witnesses clammed up, and detectives had other priorities.

Kellie's mother didn't have much to go on either, but she set out to find her daughter's killer. Out of a fury born of grief, she stormed the streets in search of the killers. She even barged into local drug houses. The word got around, and a sympathetic inmate in the county jail sent her a letter telling her the name of the shooter.

Kellie's mother shook her head in disbelief when she found out who had killed her daughter. She said, "I knew these gang members when they were just babies. Now look at them. They've turned into killers."

Hagan, the shooter, says, "Jail ain't bad. To me, life ain't much better on the streets than in jail. I can live here. No problem."

"The gang is your family," Hagan explains. "If you're a Crip, I fight for you, no matter what the odds. If you're the enemy, it's do or die."

Hagan adds, "If I had a son, I'd give him a choice: Either he can go to school and be a goody-goody, or he can hit the streets."

—Based on Hull 1987

In this chapter, we will look at both urban problems and problems of world population growth. Let's consider urban problems first.

Urbanization: The Problem in Sociological Perspective

12.1 Discuss the evolution of cities and describe the significance of urbanization.

Hagan is part of an urban nightmare—muggings on unsafe streets, drive-by shootings, senseless killings. As we look at the history of cities, we want to ask how cities can influence violent behavior.

The Evolution of Cities

Perhaps as early as 7,000 years ago, people built small cities with massive defensive walls, such as biblically famous Jericho (Homblin 1973). Cities on a larger scale appeared about 3500 B.C., around the time that writing was invented (Chandler and Fox 1974; Hawley 1981). The earliest cities emerged in several parts of the world—in Asia (Iran, Iraq, India, China), West Africa (Egypt), Europe, and Central and South America (Fischer 1976; Flanagan 1990).

About 5,500 years ago, Norway was home to one of the first cities of Europe. The city, which had been buried under sand, was not discovered until 2010 (Goll 2010). In the Americas, the first city was Caral, in what is now Peru (Fountain 2001). It was also discovered recently, covered by jungle growth.

Why did cities develop? The key is agriculture. Only when a society produces a surplus of food can people stop farming and gather in cities to pursue other occupations. We can even define a **city** as a large number of people who live in one place and do not produce their own food. As agricultural techniques became more efficient, they spurred urban development.

During the fourth millennium B.C., the plow was invented: As this invention spread, it brought an agricultural surplus that stimulated the development of towns and cities around the world. Although an improvement over the digging stick, early plows were primitive, and for the next 5,000 years there was only enough food surplus to allow a small minority of the world's population to live in urban areas.

Then came the Industrial Revolution of the 1700s and 1800s. It sparked an urban revolution around the world, one we are still experiencing today. The Industrial Revolution stimulated not only the invention of mechanical means of farming, which brought food in abundance, but also mechanical means of transportation and communication. These inventions allowed people, resources, and products to be moved efficiently—factors upon which modern cities depend.

From Rural to Urban

Cities, then, are not new to the world scene. But **urbanization**—the movement of masses of people to cities, which then have a growing influence on society—is quite recent. In 1800 only 3 percent of the world's population lived in cities (Hauser and Schnore 1965), but by 2008, for the first time in history, more people lived in cities than in rural areas. Urbanization is highest in the industrialized world, where 75 percent of people live in cities. This drops to 28 percent for the Least Industrialized Nations. Globally, 51 percent of the world's people live in cities (Haub and Kaneda 2012). As you can see from the Social Map, urbanization in the United States also differs considerably from state to state.

FIGURE 12.1 ▸ How Urban Is Your State? The Rural–Urban Makeup of the United States

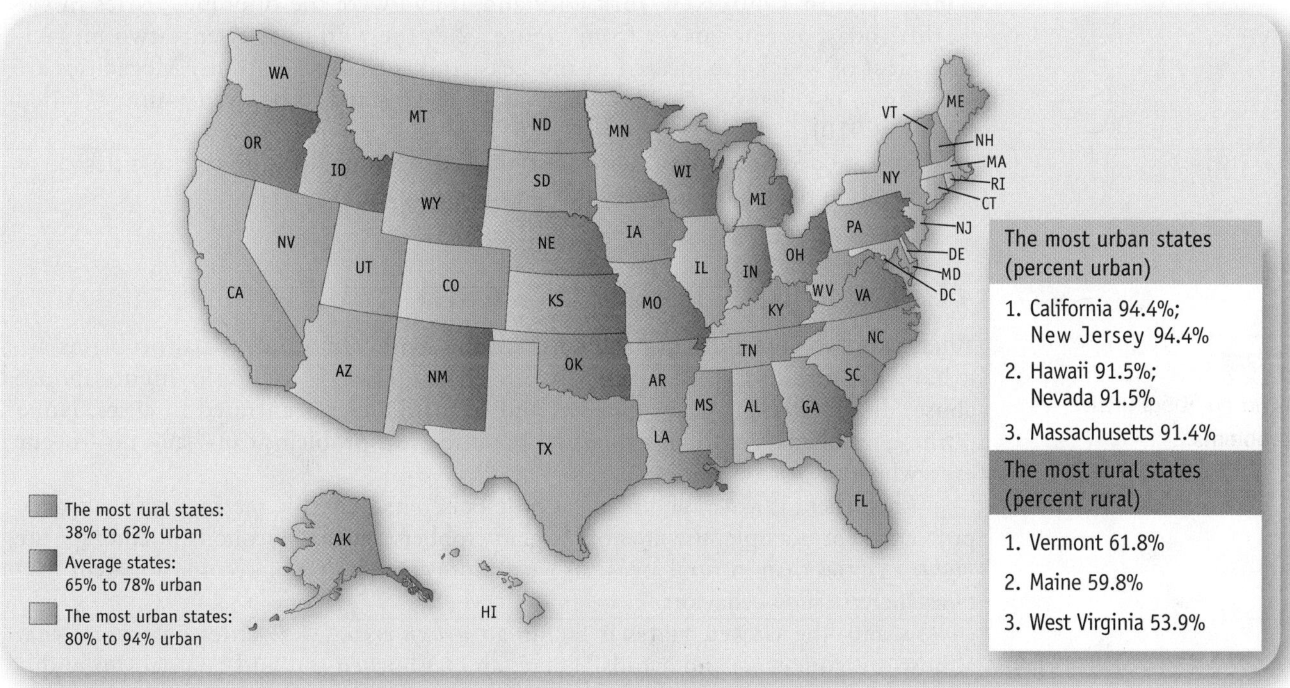

Source: By the author. Based on *Statistical Abstract of the United States* 2013:Table 29.

FIGURE 12.2 ▸ The World's 22 Megacities

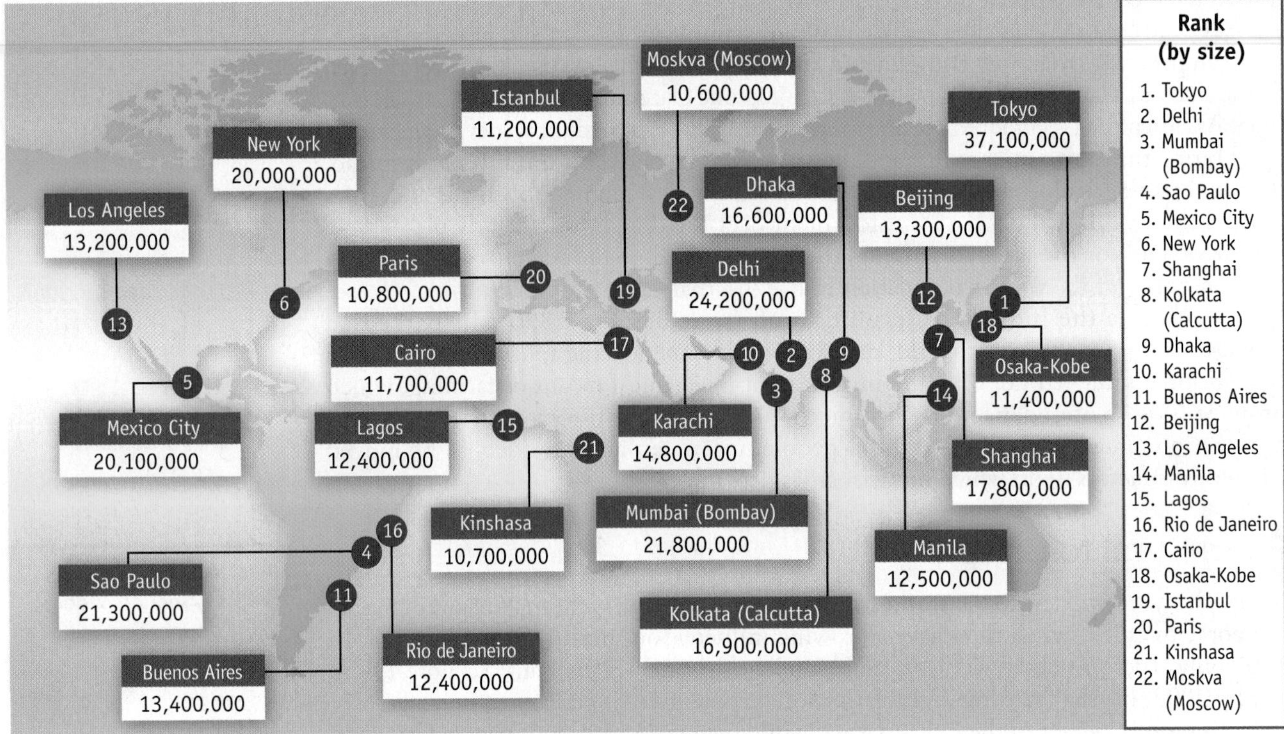

Note: Includes contiguous cities. Los Angeles, for example, includes Long Beach, and New York includes Newark.
Source: By the author. Based on United Nations 2009b:Table 3.

People expect a lot from cities—good jobs, good housing, educational opportunities, entertainment, a variety of restaurants, easy shopping, and an all-around more convenient life than they find on the farm and in villages. With their many attractions, cities are growing larger. When a city's population hits 10 million, it is called a **megacity**. In 1950, New York City and Tokyo were the only megacities in the world. Today, as you can see from Figure 12.2, the world has twenty-two megacities, most of which are located in the Least Industrialized Nations. Megacities are growing so fast that by the year 2025 there are expected to be twenty-nine (United Nations 2010).

Why are people in the Least Industrialized Nations flocking to the cities? Let's explore this in the Global Glimpse box on the next page.

The Scope of the Problem

12.2 Explain what is *urban* about urban problems.

What is urban about urban problems? In one sense, almost all social problems are urban. Because most Americans live in cities, poverty, unemployment, spouse abuse, drug addiction, rape, murder, and so forth are concentrated in cities. None of these problems are urban by nature, because these problems can—and do—occur everywhere.

What, then, is *urban* about social problems? First, city life *increases* rates of social problems. For example, the *rates* of burglary, robbery, suicide, alcoholism, and rape are *higher* in cities than in rural areas. As we explore city life, it will become apparent why cities increase such behaviors.

Second, the United States is facing an *urban crisis.* U.S. cities have areas that almost everyone fears and avoids. There, amidst burned-out and boarded-up buildings, addicts and the unemployed slouch on apartment steps. Drug dealers openly

A Global Glimpse

Why City Slums Are Better Than Living in the Country

At the bottom of a ravine near Mexico City is a bunch of shacks. Some of the parents have 14 children. "We used to live up there," Señora Gonzalez gestured toward the mountain, "in those caves. Our only hope was one day to have a place to live. And now we do." She smiled with pride at the jerry-built shacks . . . each one had a collection of flowers planted in tin cans. "One day, we hope to extend the water pipes and drainage—perhaps even pave. . . ."

And what was the name of her community? Señora Gonzalez beamed. "Esperanza!" (McDowell 1984:172)

Nairobi, Kenya

Esperanza means hope in Spanish. What started as a trickle has become a torrent. In 1930, only one Latin American city had over a million people—now fifty do! The world's cities are growing by a million people each week (Moreno et al. 2012). The rural poor are flocking to the cities at such a rate that, as you saw in Figure 12.2 on page 388, the Least Industrialized Nations now contain *most* of the world's largest cities.

The migrants establish illegal squatter settlements outside the city. There they build shacks from scrap boards, cardboard, and bits of corrugated metal. Even flattened tin cans are scavenged for building material. The squatters enjoy no city facilities, public transportation, water, sewers, or garbage pickup. After thousands of squatters have settled an area, the city reluctantly acknowledges their right to live there and adds bus service and minimal water lines. Hundreds of people use a single spigot. About *5 million* of Mexico City's residents live in such squalid conditions, with hundreds of thousands more pouring in each year.

Why this rush to live in the city under such miserable conditions? On the one hand are the "push" factors that come from the breakdown of traditional rural life. More children are surviving because of a safer water supply and modern medicine. As rural populations multiply, the parents no longer have enough land to divide among their children. With neither land nor jobs, there is hunger and despair. On the other hand are the "pull" factors that draw people to the cities—jobs, schools, housing, and even a more stimulating life.

How will these nations adjust to this vast migration? Authorities in Brazil, Guatemala, and other countries have sent in the police and even the army to evict the settlers. After a violent dispersal, the settlers return—and others stream in. The roads, water and sewer lines, electricity, schools, and public facilities must be built. But these poor countries don't have the resources to build them. As wrenching as the adjustment will be, these countries must—and somehow will—make the transition. They have no choice.

For Your Consideration

What solutions do you see to the vast migration to the cities of the Least Industrialized Nations?

work "their" street corners, a lucrative turf that they defend by violence. Gang members prowl filthy streets, mugging and killing. Those who enter these areas do so at their peril—and this includes those who live there. During economic downturns, some cities lay off teachers and shorten the school year because they cannot meet payroll. They slash budgets for the public library and garbage collection. Some even reduce police and fire protection.

U.S. cities are in such bad shape across the nation that the middle class has rushed to the suburbs. Their flight has abandoned the inner city to the poor, further impoverishing it. The term **urban crisis** refers to this cluster of interrelated urban problems. Later in the chapter, we will use sociological theory to consider solutions to the urban crisis.

Listen on **MySocLab Audio:** NPR: Stay or Go?: Shrinking Cities Raise Questions

Looking at the Problem Theoretically

12.3 Discuss the perspectives that emerge when you apply symbolic interactionism, functionalism, and conflict theory to urban problems.

As usual, our three theoretical perspectives yield contrasting insights. We will apply symbolic interactionism to the inner city, looking at the social organization of the "slum." Functionalist theory will make visible the zones of activity that develop as a city expands. Finally, using the conflict perspective, we will see how power and social class are related to urban problems.

Symbolic Interactionism

Middle-class Americans fear the inner city and avoid it—unable to understand why anyone would live "like that." These are outsiders' views.

Gaining an Insider's View. As you will recall, symbolic interactionists try to see how life looks to the people who live it. They try to discover the meanings that people attach to their experiences, how they view their situation, and how they cope with their problems. When this approach to research is applied to urban life, it sometimes is called the **Chicago School of Sociology**. This term is used because in the 1920s and 1930s sociologists at the University of Chicago used participant observation to produce what became classic studies of urban life. In 1923, Nels Anderson wrote *The Hobo,* followed in 1927 by Frederic Thrasher's *The Gang*. In 1929, in *The Gold Coast and the Slum,* Harvey Zorbaugh contrasted the rich and the poor in Chicago. Then in 1932, Paul Cressey published *Taxi-Dance Hall,* his research on women who were paid "a dime a dance" to dance with men. Making the city their sociological laboratory, these sociologists focused mostly on the lives of the poor.

Whyte's Classic Study. In this tradition, sociologist William Foote Whyte lived as a participant observer in an inner city for 3 years. In *Street Corner Society* (1943, 1995), the classic book recounting his experiences, Whyte explains that what may seem disorganized to outsiders is, in fact, a tightly knit way of life. By participating in the residents' lives—hanging around the street corner with "the boys," going to dances, bowling, playing baseball—Whyte found that the young men separated themselves into two main groups: "*the college boys,*" who were upward bound, and "*the corner boys,*" who remained in their old neighborhood. Each group had its own statuses, its own norms, and its own ways of controlling its members.

Anderson's Studies. As a graduate student at the University of Chicago, Elijah Anderson continued this type of research in another Chicago slum. Doing participant observation at Jelly's, a bar and liquor store in an African American area, Anderson (1978) uncovered intricate boundaries that unite and separate people from one another. From what might seem like a shapeless group—"just a bunch of people"—Anderson found separate clusters of people, each with its own norms, values, and ideas of life. Here are the three main groups that he found at Jelly's:

> *The regulars*. These men see and present themselves as hard-working. They follow mainstream values, are proud of their involvement in families, and have aspirations of getting ahead. Their values can be summed up with the single word *decency*—working regularly and treating other people right.
>
> *The wineheads*. These men neither value work, nor do they work regularly. Their main concern is getting enough money to buy wine. They beg from others and have low status.
>
> *The hoodlums*. These men pride themselves on "being tough" and having access to easy money. They are involved in petty theft, stickups, burglaries, and fencing stolen property. The other men at Jelly's do not trust them, nor do they trust one another.

A Mosaic of Social Worlds. Symbolic interactionists are fascinated with the contrasts of the city—its many groups with their distinctive ways of life. They study how people within each area of the city stake out territory, establish social boundaries, and work out a sense of identity and belonging. They remind us that when we look at a run-down area, we need to see beyond the decaying buildings. Like people everywhere, people in the inner city develop social networks and interact on the basis of background assumptions.

Symbolic interactionists also remind us that the poor do not experience urban problems in the abstract. For example, the poor do not experience the *concept* of urban decay. Rather, they deal with cutbacks in city services; buses that run late or not at all; factories that move to Mexico or China and wipe out their jobs overnight—and killers like Hagan who stalk their neighborhoods.

Functionalism

A Classic Model of the City. Sociologists at the University of Chicago also did urban research that reflects the functionalist perspective. Look at Figure 12.3, which is taken from one of these classic studies, research by Ernest Burgess on the growth of cities. You can see that Burgess identified five urban zones, each with distinct functions. He visualized the city as expanding outward from its center, the central business district (Zone I). The city's slums are in Zone II, which encircles the downtown area. To escape the slums, skilled and thrifty workers move outward, to Zone III. The better apartment buildings, residential hotels, single-family dwellings, and gated communities where the

FIGURE 12.3 ▸ Burgess' Concentric Zones: Illustrating the Growth of the City

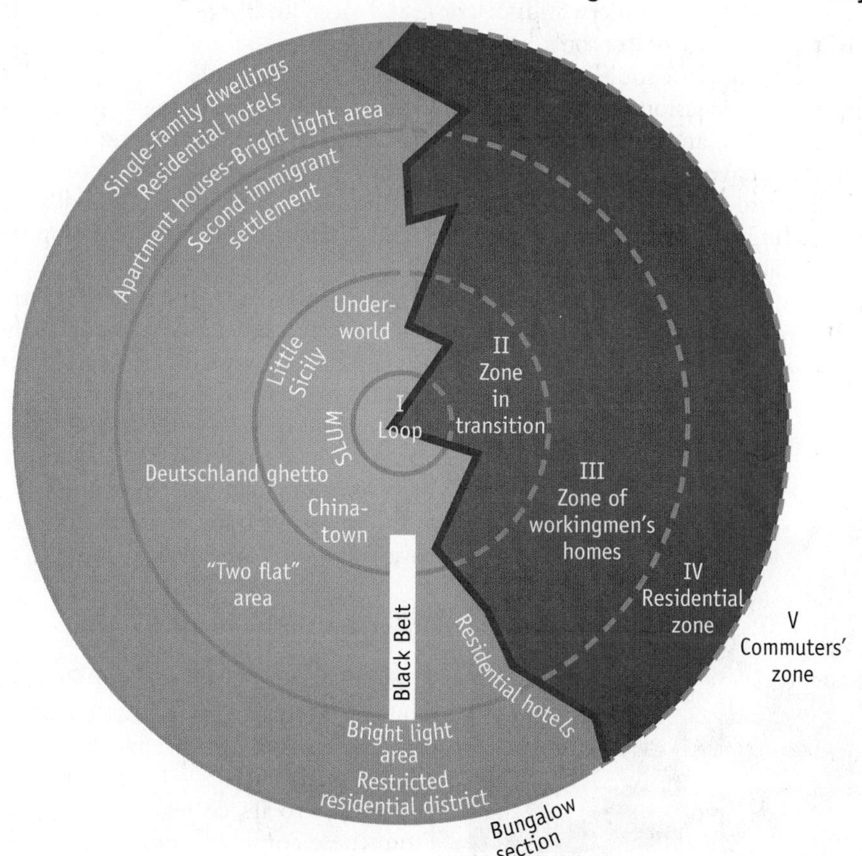

Note: This is Burgess' depiction of how concentric zones flow from the central business district as a city expands. The left side shows the city of Chicago in 1925. The jagged vertical line represents the shore of Lake Michigan.

Source: From Ernest W. Burgess, "The Growth of the City: An Introduction to a Research Project" in *The City,* Robert E. Park, Ernest W. Burgess, and Roderick D. McKenzie, eds. Chicago: University of Chicago Press, 1925. (Pages 47–62 in the 1967 edition). Reprinted with the permission of the University of Chicago Press.

View on MySocLab Figure: How Cities Develop: Models of Urban Growth wealthy live are located in Zone IV. Still farther out, beyond the city limits, is Zone V, a commuter zone of suburbs and satellite cities.

Burgess said that his **concentric zone theory** explained the "tendencies of any town or city to expand radially from its central business district." He noted, however, that no "city fits perfectly this ideal scheme." Because of physical obstructions, such as lakes or mountains, some cities don't follow this model. Burgess also noted that businesses deviate from this model when they locate in outlying zones.

Explore on **MySocLab**
Activity: Urban Profile: Philadelphia

Mobility in the City. The classic model of urban growth shown in Figure 12.3 helps us understand urban problems. Burgess stressed that city dwellers are always on the move. In addition to commuting for work, school, shopping, and recreation, they move into better zones when they can afford to. This creates an **invasion–succession cycle** in which one group moves into an area already occupied by people who have different characteristics. The invasion creates antagonisms between the groups: The one resents displacement; the other feels unwelcome. Today, however, people move not only outward, away from a city's center, but also toward it. We will come back to this recent change in urban patterns.

The Zone in Transition. Burgess also noted that the areas that are the most mobile have the most severe social problems: These areas lack a sense of community and suffer from *anomie*, or alienation. As Burgess put it, high mobility leads to juvenile delinquency, gangs, crime, poverty, the breakup of families, and—in a term seldom used today—promiscuity. Mobility and its accompanying problems are concentrated in Zone II, which Burgess called a *zone in transition.* He said that here we find the city's "poverty, degradation, and disease," the "underworlds of crime and vice." In Burgess' colorful phrase, this zone is "the purgatory of lost souls."

This zone of "lost souls" also attracts another group, people who Burgess said are "obsessed with the vision of a new and better world." He was referring to social workers, preachers, artists, and political radicals. Since Burgess' time, something else has happened: Some have looked beyond the appearance of the area and perceived "financial value." In a process called *urban renewal,* they have torn down the old and built new office buildings, financial centers, stadiums, and luxury hotels. This redevelopment of the area attracts people *toward* the city center.

Although Burgess' concentric zone model has many critics (Alihan 1938; Harris and Ullman 1945; La Gory et al. 1980), our purpose here is to note how his model highlights the city's *zones of functional specialties.* All cities have areas dominated by a specific type of business or activity—clusters of warehouses, auto dealerships, boutiques, or fast-food restaurants. Cities also have zones that, if I can phrase it like this, "specialize" in urban problems—red-light districts and areas of poverty, gangs, and violent crime.

Social problems are clustered in the Zone in Transition, such as this area in Holyoke, Massachusetts.

Conflict Theory

Class Conflict and Urban Problems. Conflict theorists argue that class conflict underlies urban problems. The wealthy control a city's affairs—from its newspapers and banks to its colleges and businesses. From these command posts, they make the decisions that run the city. These decisions always center on keeping their power and privileges intact.

To illustrate how the business elite influence government policy to their own advantage without regard for the consequences to inner-city residents, sociologist Manuel Castells (1977, 1983, 1989) points to something you wouldn't expect—the development of interstate highways.

In the late 1800s and early 1900s, business leaders built multistory buildings to house their factories. The development of assembly lines made these buildings obsolete. Instead of the efficiencies of assembly lines, they were stuck with moving raw materials and manufactured goods from one floor to another. They needed single-story factories. The interstate highways and city expressways, built at taxpayer expense, made it profitable to relocate production to the suburbs. With the suburb's lower land prices and often lower taxes as well, the factory owners were able to build single-story factories and adopt the more efficient assembly-line techniques.

Moving factories and offices to the suburbs led to the city's decline. The flight of payroll—the jobs and spending by management and workers—ravished the city's tax base. It crippled the city's ability to maintain services and help the many poor who were left behind. As the poor became concentrated in the inner city—with its few jobs and bad schools coupled with despair and hopelessness—the city became increasingly desperate and dangerous. In effect, corporate leaders abandoned the city, which they no longer needed, leaving the poor to fend for themselves.

Today, the city remains the repository of the poor and powerless. Adjacent to the resurrected areas we just discussed live the huddled masses—the destitute of an affluent society. The poor are bypassed—some say oppressed—by leaders who pursue their own personal, political, and economic interests. Because the capacity of the underclass to riot poses a threat to the powerful and privileged, the police keep a sharp eye on the urban poor, controlling their areas with an iron fist. Legions of social workers are also dispatched into their midst, not from altruism, say conflict theorists, but to keep the poor quiet in order to preserve the status quo.

Research Findings

12.4 Summarize research findings on urban alienation and community, urban dwellers, urban violence, and transitions in power and resources.

As we examine research findings, let's first consider alienation and community in the city and then look in depth at the decline of the inner city, urban violence, and the changes that are affecting cities in the United States.

The city is a mosaic of people and experiences. People of vastly different backgrounds are usually spatially separated, living in different areas of the city. The homeless man and these women who enjoy a more privileged lifestyle are an obvious exception.

Alienation in the City

In a classic essay, sociologist Louis Wirth (1938) noted that urban dwellers live anonymous lives marked by segmented and superficial encounters. This type of relationship, he said, undermines kinship and neighborhood, the traditional bases of social control and feelings of solidarity. This encourages urbanites to grow aloof and indifferent to other people's problems. In short, the price of the personal freedom that the city offers is alienation. Seldom, however, does alienation get to this point:

In crowded traffic on a bridge going into Detroit, Deletha Word bumped the car ahead of her. The damage was minor, but the driver, Martell Welch, jumped out. Cursing, he pulled Deletha from her car, pushed her onto the hood, and began beating her. Martell's friends got out to watch. One of them held Deletha down while Martell took a car jack and smashed Deletha's car. Scared for her life, Deletha broke away, fleeing to the bridge's railing. Martell and his friends taunted her, shouting, "Jump, bitch, jump!" Deletha plunged to her death (Stokes and Zeman 1995). Welch was convicted of second-degree murder and sentenced to 16 to 40 years in prison.

This certainly is not an ordinary situation, although anyone who lives in a large city knows that even a minor traffic accident can explode into road rage. And you never know who that stranger in the mall—or even next door—really is. The most common reason for the city's impersonality and self-interest is not fear of danger, however, but the impossibility of dealing with crowds as individuals. People need to find focus within the many stimuli that come buzzing in from the bustle of the city, and ignoring others is part of this self-interested focus (Berman et al. 2008).

Community in the City

I don't want to give the impression that the city is inevitably alienating. Far from it. Here is another aspect of the attack on Deletha Word. After Deletha went over the railing, two men jumped in after her, risking their own lives in futile attempts to save her.

Many people find community in the city. Sociologist Herbert Gans, a symbolic interactionist who did participant observation in the West End of Boston, was so impressed with the area's sense of community that he titled his classic book *The Urban Villagers* (1962). Here is how Gans described his introduction to the area and his changed perspective:

After a few weeks of living in the West End, my observations—and my perceptions of the area—changed drastically. The search for an apartment quickly indicated that the individual units were usually in much better condition than the outside or the hallways of the buildings. Subsequently, in wandering through the West End, and in using it as a resident, I developed a kind of selective perception, in which my eye focused only on those parts of the area that were actually being used by people. Vacant buildings and boarded-up stores were no longer so visible, and the totally deserted alleys or streets were outside the set of paths normally traversed, either by myself or by the West Enders. The dirt and spilled-over garbage remained, but, since they were concentrated in street gutters and empty lots, they were not really harmful to anyone and thus were not as noticeable as during my initial observations.

Since much of the area's life took place on the street, faces became familiar very quickly. I met my neighbors on the stairs and in front of my building. And, once a shopping pattern developed, I saw the same storekeepers frequently, as well as the area "characters" who wandered through the streets everyday on a fairly regular route and schedule. In short, the exotic quality of the stores and the residents also wore off as I became used to seeing them.

Gans had found a *community* within what appeared to outsiders to be a rough, crime-infested area of the city. The people living there, in contrast, identified with the area and with one another. Its residents enjoyed networks of friends and acquaintances.

Despite the area's substandard buildings, most West Enders had chosen to live here. *To them, this was a low-rent district, not a slum.*

Most West Enders had low-paying, insecure jobs. Other residents were elderly, living on small pensions. Unlike the middle class, these people didn't care about their "address." The area's inconveniences were something they put up with in exchange for low rent. In general, they were content with their neighborhood.

Who Lives in the City?

Whether people find alienation or community in the city depends on whom you are talking about. As with almost everything in life, social class is especially significant. The city's wealthier residents enjoy greater security, which reduces alienation and increases satisfaction with city life (Santos 2009).

Explore on **MySocLab**
Activity: Where Do Americans Live

There also are different types of urban dwellers, each with distinctive experiences. As we review the five types that Gans (1962, 1968, 1991) identified, try to see where you fit.

The Cosmopolites. These are the intellectuals, professionals, artists, and entertainers who have been attracted to the city. They value its conveniences and cultural benefits.

The Singles. Usually in their early 20s to early 30s, the singles have settled in the city temporarily. For them, urban life is a stage in their life course. Businesses and services, such as singles bars and apartment complexes, cater to their needs and desires. After they marry, many move to the suburbs.

The Ethnic Villagers. Feeling a sense of identity, working-class members of the same ethnic group band together. They form tightly knit neighborhoods that resemble villages and small towns. Family- and peer-oriented, they try to isolate themselves from the dangers and problems of urban life.

The Deprived. Destitute, emotionally disturbed, and with little income, education, or work skills, the deprived live in neighborhoods that are more like urban jungles than urban villages. Some of the deprived stalk those jungles in search of prey. Neither predator nor prey has much hope for anything better in life—for themselves or for their children.

Some people find community in the city through their associations: work, shopping, school, church, and, as in the photo on the left, from neighborhood events. For others, as for the man in the photo on the right, the city is a collection of nameless faces.

The Trapped. These people don't live in the area by choice, either. Some were trapped when another group "invaded" their neighborhood and they could not afford to move. Others found themselves trapped in a downward spiral. They started life in a higher social class, but they drifted downward because of personal problems—mental or physical illness or addiction to alcohol or other drugs. There also are the elderly who are trapped by poverty and not wanted elsewhere. Like the deprived, the trapped suffer from high rates of assault, mugging, and rape.

Explore on **MySocLab Activity:** Fifty Years in Brooklyn

In Sum ▸ Within the city's rich mosaic of social diversity, not all urban dwellers experience the city in the same way. Each group has its own lifestyle, and each has distinct experiences. Some people welcome the city's cultural diversity and mix with several groups. Others find community by retreating into the security of ethnic enclaves. Still others feel trapped and deprived. To them, the city is an urban jungle, a nightmare of threats to their health and safety.

Urban Violence: Youth Gangs

We have already discussed violence in Chapters 5 and 6. Now we'll look at violence in the context of urban problems, focusing first on violence by youth gangs.

Listen on **MySocLab Audio:** NPR: Professor Turns "Gang Leader for a Day"

The Neighborhood. As you know, the neighborhood you grow up in has a fundamental influence on your orientation to life. In some neighborhoods, you know that violence is going to happen. Even if you can't predict exactly when or where, there are going to be muggings and rapes, and from time to time someone is going to be knifed or shot. The presence of armed police and wailing sirens is a taken-for-granted background expectation of "the way life is." From Ruth Horowitz's research on the Lions in Chapter 5 (page 127), you saw that in some neighborhoods gang members use violence to prove themselves. By being willing to risk injury to defend themselves against insults and to protect the members of their gang, these young men receive valued recognition as worthy people. Joining one gang is also a way to protect themselves from other gangs (Melde et al. 2009)! You can see that living in a neighborhood where violence is woven into the fabric of everyday life leads to a way of perceiving the world that differs radically from the way the middle class views life.

Two Classic Studies: Cohen and Miller. Sociologists have studied gangs for almost a century (Thrasher 1927). Of their many studies, let's look at two classics, those by Cohen and Miller.

Sociologist Albert Cohen (1955) found two keys to understanding gangs: the desire of boys to have a valued identity and a clash between middle-class and lower-class values. The schools are located in an area of poverty, but they are run by middle-class teachers and administrators. They use middle-class standards to judge the boys' speech, behavior, and performance on tests. Confronted with these contrary values, the boys feel that they don't fit in and that their teachers look down on them. In a defensive reaction, they form a gang of like-minded boys. Their rejection of middle-class standards is so thorough that doing well in school becomes equated with girls and sissies.

Sociologist Walter Miller (1958) also studied why lower-class boys find gangs so appealing. He, too, found the key in identity. The gangs have six main values: trouble, excitement, toughness, smartness, autonomy, and fate. The better that boys demonstrate these values, the higher their status. Making trouble not only provides excitement, but it also allows the boys to show that they are tough, smart, and autonomous (independent). The boys also think of their lives as controlled by fate: If they get hurt or killed, this is because their number came up. In short, these lower-class boys reject the world of middle-class values that rejects them, crushing their spirits by marking them as failures. The gang's alternative world of values offers the boys an opportunity to achieve a sense of self-worth through the positive recognition of their peers.

Supergangs. For the most part, the gangs in these classic studies were groups of adolescents who did nothing worse than get high, skip school, write graffiti, steal from parked cars, get into a fight now and then, and vandalize property. I say "nothing worse" because today's **supergangs**, such as the Crips and Bloods and the many like them, not only steal and deal drugs but as with Hagan in our opening vignette, they also kill. The findings of Cohen and Miller, however, still apply. The El Rukins/Black P. Stone Nation, the Gangster Disciples, the Vice Lords, the Latin Kings, as well as the more infamous Crips and Bloods, follow the same pattern. They are based on the boys' rejection of middle-class norms—which throw failure into their faces and seem irrelevant to their lives—replacing these norms with standards that allow the boys to achieve positive recognition and a sense of self-worth. The form of gangs might change over time, but the basic principles on which they operate and by which they attract lower-class boys remain the same.

Global Aspects of Gangs. There are local gangs in every urban area around the globe. What is different is the growing global connection of some urban gangs. Today there are Hells Angels in Germany and Latino gangs (its members exiled from the United States) in Honduras. The MS-13 in Los Angeles has expanded to El Salvador, and gangs tied to Chinese Triads are found in Los Angeles; Russian gangs operate in Chicago; the Crips are in Holland; and Mexican gangs have moved into San Diego (Hagedorn 2005).

You have seen how and why gangs attract lower-class youth. It is the same on the global level. Around the world, gangs attract the disenfranchised, the neglected, those who are left out of the legitimate political process. This takes us to a significant element that goes far beyond what we have reviewed so far: On the global level, gangs provide an alternative political structure. They give power to those who are bypassed by political systems. In some instances, the power of the gang is so great that the established political powers must take them into account when they develop social policy (Hagedorn 2005).

Girl Gangs. Many lower-class girls also find the middle-class values of the school oppressive, and for them, too, the contrarian values of gangs beckon. Some girls reject

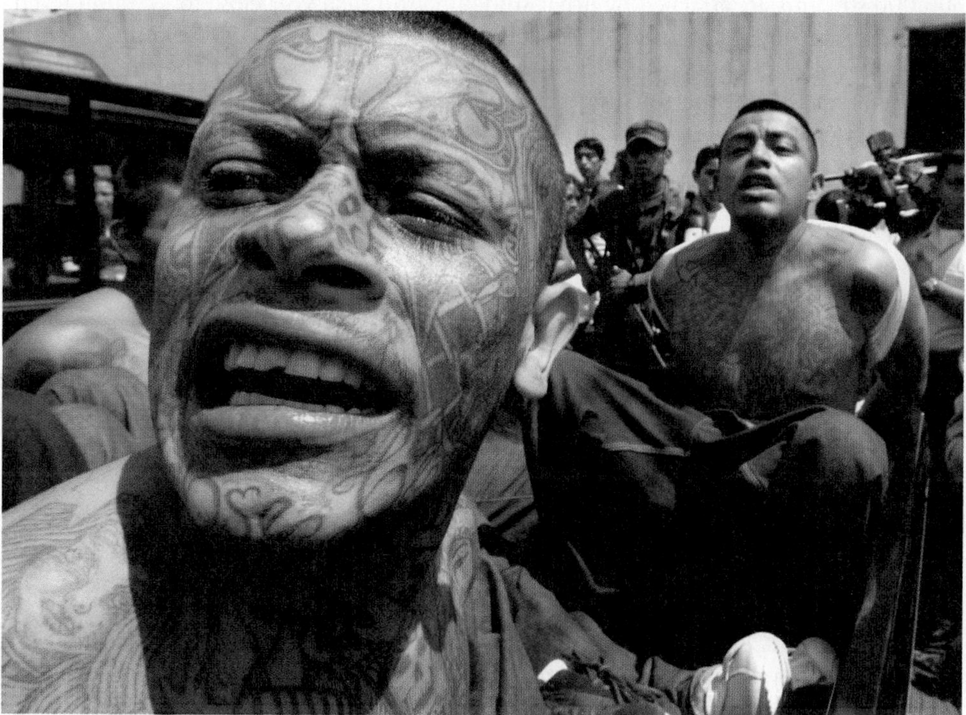

Gang members deported from the United States have formed violent gangs in El Salvador, Honduras, and Guatemala. Two of them, the Mara 18 and the Mara Salvatrucha, have been at war. Just before this photo was taken, seventeen died in a battle between these gangs in this juvenile prison in Guatemala City.

the "soft feminism" of the middle class, replacing it with toughness and aggression—characteristics that work better in their life situation. Within this framework, however, no matter their tough demeanor, they are expected to be submissive to the boys (Vigil 2002). Here is one indication of how dominant the boys in these groups are: When girls are initiated into the gang, the boys can require them to have sex with one or several of the male gang members. For the most part, girls play supportive roles in the boys' gangs, such as by hiding weapons and drugs and providing alibis and sex. With some exceptions, girl gangs are auxiliaries of boy gangs (Vigil 2002).

Urban Violence: Schools

With events like the slaughter of kindergarten children in Sandy Hook, Connecticut, seared in our mind—images of terrified little children cowering before a sociopath—some states require lockdown, or "Code Blue," drills: Each classroom is equipped with a phone. The classroom's doors and windows are locked. Its shades are drawn. The students are trained to remain absolutely silent. Like an armed intruder, a school official wanders the halls, listening for the slightest sound that would indicate that someone is in the classroom (Kelley 2008; Altimari and Lender 2013).

South Dakota has gone beyond this and has made it legal for teachers to carry guns (Elgion 2013).

What an incredible change in U.S. schools. School officials have feared for years that "it could happen in my school." The shooting deaths of 20 kindergarten students at their Sandy Hook elementary school in Connecticut have confirmed their fears. Just what school is safe? And from what unknown psycho? Will teachers and school principals all over the country have to carry guns to defend students?

It isn't only students and strangers who go on killing sprees in schools. Even a college instructor can turn out to be a killer. Recall Amy Bishop who was featured in our opening vignette in Chapter 5. We can hope that this event will always remain a unique case.

School violence takes many forms other than shootings, of course. Each year, about 300,000 students are attacked by other students. And each year close to 100,000 teachers are attacked by their students (Lunenburg 2010). In some high schools and even middle schools, rapes and assaults go unreported. Guilt stops some teachers from reporting assaults; they feel that the assault would not have occurred if they had somehow done a better job in the classroom. Other teachers find it easier to ignore an attack, because assault cases can require several appearances in court. Still others don't report attacks because they fear reprisal from students.

The bottom line is that most interactions, whether at school or elsewhere, are based on trust. No one knows when or where someone will violate that trust, and we cannot live our lives in fear. The challenge is to identify the psychopaths before they hurt others and to get them the help they need—without the rest of us having to give up our freedoms. This is a precarious balance between our needs for security and our needs for freedom of movement, association, and the expression of political opinion. We can expect many heated debates on this issue.

Urban Transitions: Changes in Power

In addition to violence, U.S. cities face extensive change. Let's consider changes in power and regional restratification.

Minority Leadership. A major change in U.S. cities is the transition of power from whites to African Americans and Latinos. In 1964, there were only 70 elected African American officials at all levels of U.S. government. Today there are over 9,000. Latinos have also increased their total, from a handful to 6,000 (Eisinger 1980; *Statistical Abstract* 2013:Table 429).

If a city is to be well-governed, its major groups must cooperate with one another. If whites were to withdraw their cooperation from an elected minority mayor, winning control of the formal apparatus of government would be a hollow victory. To see what happened after African Americans were elected as mayors of Detroit and Atlanta, sociologist Peter Eisinger (1980) interviewed the business, political, and social leaders of these cities. Instead of engaging in confrontational politics, the white elite had chosen to cooperate and build coalitions. This does not mean that rivalries between racial–ethnic groups will end, of course, just that politicians know when to cut deals.

Regional Restratification. A change that is having a deep impact on U.S. cities is **regional restratification**, a shift in a region's population, wealth, and power. Look at Table 12.1 below. From this list, you can see that five of the ten fastest-growing U.S. cities are in the West, and five are in the South. Of the ten declining U.S. cities, six are in the Northeast, two in the South, and two in the Midwest. New Orleans, a special case, has not yet recovered from Hurricane Katrina. The population of the Northeast and the Midwest is not shrinking, but it is growing at a much slower pace than that of the West and South.

It is easy to miss the deep significance of this population shift. A growing population brings with it greater wealth and political power. The tax base of the West and South is growing, and these areas are gaining representatives in Congress. The result is that these regions are gaining in wealth and power to cope with their urban problems. Other areas are losing resources, although their problems are not declining. This is a remarkable regional shift. In only one other period of U.S. history—the Civil War—has the balance of power among the states undergone such rapid and extensive change.

Let's look at the potential for improving the quality of life in U.S. cities.

Social Policy

12.5 Summarize social policy that can build community in the city.

Many despair that the crises facing our cities cannot be solved. The federal and state governments have tried many programs, but some say they have simply shuffled money from one faddish urban program to another. No one says they have a lot to show for all the spending. Some even insist that government programs have made the problems worse. Shortly before she died, Jane Jacobs (2004), an influential urban expert, warned that things were getting so bad that a dark age threatens to engulf our civilization. She indicated, however, that there was still hope.

With our many resources, we can make that hope a reality. We have the capacity to make our cities inviting places to live, places that add to our quality of life. The question, of course, is, Do we have the will to do this? Let's look at some of the possibilities.

TABLE 12.1 ▸ The Shrinking and Fastest-Growing Cities

The Shrinking Cities			The Fastest-Growing Cities		
1.	−11.3%	New Orleans, LA	1.	+41.8%	Las Vegas, NV
2.	−6.2%	Youngstown, OH	2.	+41.8%	Raleigh, NC
3.	−3.5%	Detroit, MI	3.	+40.3%	Cape Coral–Ft. Myers, FL
4.	−3.3%	Cleveland, OH	4.	+39.8%	Provo, UT
5.	−3.1%	Pittsburgh, PA	5.	+39.7%	Greeley, CO
6.	−3.0%	Buffalo–Niagara Falls, NY	6.	+37.3%	Austin, TX
7.	−2.4%	Flint, MI	7.	+37.0%	Myrtle Beach, SC
8.	−1.7%	Charleston, WV	8.	+36.1%	McAllen, TX
9.	−1.2%	Toledo, OH	9.	+33.5%	Fayetteville, AR
10.	−0.8%	Dayton, OH	10.	+32.8%	Port St. Lucie, FL

Note: Population change from 2000 to 2010, the latest years available.
Source: By the author. Based on *Statistical Abstract of the United States* 2012:Table 20.

Read on **MySocLab Document** Life and Death in the City: Neighborhoods in Context

The Goal: Establishing Community

Read on MySocLab Document Death of a Neighborhood

At times, urban problems seem so deep and severe that we can feel despair about ever finding solutions. That urban problems are human problems—the products of mistakes, of bad social policy and ill-conceived decisions—means that they can be solved.

To bring about effective change, we first need to know what goal we want to reach. As sociologists remind us, the goal should be to create a sense of community (Karp et al. 1991), the essence of quality of life. To reach this goal, we must preserve and develop neighborhoods that people enjoy. Apart from avoiding "urban renewal" programs that destroy neighborhoods and social relationships, what programs to develop community seem reasonable? Of the many possible programs that can halt decline and revitalize urban areas, let's look at two: empowerment zones and educating the poor.

Empowerment Zones

To have community, people need jobs. To get employers to move back into an area, **empowerment zones** (also known as *enterprise zones*) have been tried by most states. Empowerment zones are based on these principles:

1. Businesses that locate in a designated zone—an economically depressed area with high unemployment—receive tax breaks and wage credits for each full-time, qualified employee they hire.
2. If businesses already in the empowerment zone improve their facilities, they receive credits on their property tax.
3. Businesses that locate in the empowerment zone, or that remain there, are eligible for low-interest loans.

The purposes of empowerment zones are to generate employment and stimulate economic growth. It is difficult to meet these goals, though, when the jobs transferred there are low-paying, which they usually are. An additional obstacle is that businesses often shy away from empowerment zones because the costs of additional security can outweigh the benefits gained from locating there. Another problem is of a different kind: Enticing businesses to move into the zone can contribute to blight in the areas they leave behind.

Evaluating the results of empowerment zones is difficult. The basic problem facing researchers is this: If you measure employment, earnings, or poverty in an empowerment zone, how do you know what they would have been if the area had not been designated an empowerment zone? Overall, the results have been disappointing: Researchers have concluded that empowerment zones have had little impact on those who live in the area (Ferguson 2001).

But the potential is huge. In the Thinking Critically box on the next page, let's look at an outstanding exception to this evaluation of "little impact."

Educating the Poor

You are personally familiar with the promise of education, how it can make a significant difference in people's lives. One of those differences, as you know, is to qualify people for better jobs. Schools can transform lives, but are our schools capable of handling today's urban poor?

Here is what sociologist Herbert Gans said back in the 1960s:

> *The public-school system has never learned how to teach poor children, mainly because it has not needed to do so. In the past, those who could not or would not learn what the schools taught dropped out quietly and went to work. Today, such children drop out less quietly, and they cannot find work. Consequently, the schools have to learn how to hold them, not only when they drop out physically, but long before, in the early elementary grades, when they begin to drop out in spirit (Gans 1968:292).*

Thinking Critically About Social Problems

Reclaiming Harlem: A Twist in the Invasion–Succession Cycle

The story is well known. The inner city is filled with crack, crime, and corruption. It stinks from foul, festering filth strewn on the streets and piled up around burned-out buildings. Only those who have no choice live in these desolate, despairing areas where predators stalk their prey. Dange lurks around every corner.

What is not so well known is that affluent African Americans are reclaiming some of these areas.

Howard Sanders was living the American Dream. After earning a degree from Harvard Business School, he took a position with a Manhattan investment firm. He lived in an exclusive apartment on Central Park West, but he missed Harlem, where he had grown up. He moved back, along with his wife and daughter.

The "world famous" Apollo Theater survived the decline of Harlem and is now part of its rejuvenation.

African American lawyers, doctors, professors, and bankers are doing the same.

What's the attraction? The first is nostalgia, a cultural yearning for Harlem past, the time of legend and folklore. It was here that black writers and artists lived in the 1920s, here that the blues and jazz attracted young and accomplished musicians.

The second reason is that Harlem offered housing values. Some homes, built In the 1800s, boasted five bedrooms and 6,000 square feet. They sold for a song, even with Honduran mahogany. Some brownstones were in good condition, although others were only shells and had to be rebuilt from the inside out.

What happened was the rebuilding of a community. Some people who had "made" it wanted to be role models. They wanted children in the community to see them going to and returning from work.

When the middle class moved out of Harlem and the area was taken over by drug dealers, prostitutes, and gangs, the amenities moved out, too. When the young professionals moved back in, the amenities returned. There were no coffee shops, restaurants, jazz clubs, florists, copy centers, dentist and optometrist offices, or art galleries—the types of things urbanites take for granted. Now there are.

The police have also helped to change the character of Harlem. No longer do they just rush in, sirens wailing and guns drawn, to confront emergencies and shootouts. Instead, the police have become a normal part of this urban scene. Not only did they shut down the open-air drug markets, but they also began enforcing laws against urinating on the streets, something they used to ignore as too trivial to matter for "that area." The greater safety of the area has attracted even more of the middle class. And with them, the expectations of a middle-class way of life.

The change is so extensive that former president Clinton chose to locate his office here, and Magic Johnson opened a Starbucks and a multiplex.

Another side of the story has emerged—tension between the people who were already living in Harlem and the newcomers. Social class is often the source of the irritation. Each class has its own ways, and the classes often grate on each other's nerves. The old-timers like loud music, for example, while the newcomers prefer a more sedate lifestyle. Then there is the old power establishment. They feel slighted if the newcomers don't ask their blessing before they open a business. On their part, the new business owners feel they don't need to get those old people's permission to open anything.

There is another issue as well. Remember those large houses that sold for a song? No longer. Vacant lots now bring a million dollars. Rents have shot upward, and tenants' associations protest, their moans mostly muffled and unheard.

And the poor? The same as has happened in other gentrified areas. Most are pushed out, block by block, forced into adjoining rundown streets.

The in-fighting of this emerging drama mostly involves African Americans. The issue is not race, but social class. The "invasion–succession cycle," as sociologists call it, is continuing, but this time with a twist—an "invasion" back in.

Sources: Based on Leland 2003; Hyra 2006; Williams 2008; Haughney 2009; Barnard 2012.

For Your Consideration

Would you be willing to move into an area of high crime in order to get a good housing bargain? How do you think the current residents of an area being gentrified can be protected from rising rents and allowed to continue to live in the area? Should they be?

It is dispiriting to read Gans' comment from the middle of the last century and to know that little has changed. How pitifully frustrating that you can make the same statement today, and still be accurate. It is also despairing to know that the implications of educational failure are greater today. Unlike the past, few unskilled jobs are available, and today's school dropouts live with less hope—and with a greater tendency to lash out violently.

So what can we do? Let's look at the principles that can help transform the education of the poor.

Principles for Success. To start with, we need concerned teachers. The problem is not that we lack them. We have highly principled and well-intentioned teachers and administrators in abundance. These people want to make a difference in the lives of the children entrusted to their care (Gerstl-Pepin 2006). Educators, however, seldom measure their effectiveness or analyze how they can improve the ways they teach the poor. If asked how to improve education, their usual answer is "More money." Administrators become enamored with fancifully named, currently faddish, and unproved educational programs. If not this, then more money for some public monument to their own position—that is, new buildings and facilities. And as an educator, I say this with despair.

New buildings do look good, and they give the impression that something solid is being accomplished. But it is not new buildings that make good schools—at least, not any more than old buildings do. The key to effective teaching is not the building, but, rather, nourishing the students' desire to learn. Few poor children lack the desire to learn when they begin school. As they stay in school, however, it is common for their eyes to gloss over and for them to view schools as irrelevant to their lives and future. As sociologists Herbert Gans pointed out back in 1968, to do a better job of educating the poor, we need

1. motivated teachers
2. new teaching methods
3. smaller classes
4. innovative curricula that build on the aspirations of inner-city youth
5. a more decentralized and less bureaucratized school system
6. work-study programs
7. scholarships to encourage adult dropouts to return to school.

I want to add that these are the minimum that we need to educate the poor and help turn our cities around. We also need cooperative learning, child care facilities, and positive reinforcement. More controversial, but quite defensible, is a renewed emphasis on basic learning in grade school (such as memorizing the multiplication tables); a deemphasis on "feelings of self-worth" as an educational goal, replacing it with academic subjects; and a strong trades program that leads to good-paying apprenticeships. This seems to run against mainstream assumptions, but why assume that every high school student should go to college?

To see the potential that education has for making a success of our cities, read the Thinking Critically box on the next page.

In Sum ▸ If we have learned anything from the recent past, it is that *replacing buildings does not cure urban ills.* How do more attractive housing and schools eliminate poverty and unemployment, whose consequences reverberate throughout society? They lie at the root of many of the problems we have discussed here and in earlier chapters, from violent crime to dysfunctional families. As sociologist William Julius Wilson (1987) stressed, to solve poverty and unemployment we need a revitalized economy that offers people jobs. Perhaps the simplest summary is this: Greater access to jobs, education, and justice will reduce urban problems, but these problems will persist to the same degree that these inequalities persist.

Thinking Critically About Social Problems

Educating for Success: Reestablishing Community in the Learning Process

Education is in crisis. Children are being promoted from one grade to another whether they learn or not. Some students graduate from high school not knowing how to do simple math, unable to read even help wanted ads. Many don't know how to prepare a résumé and have no idea how to prepare for a job interview. Budgets are cut, programs trimmed, teachers burned out, and students unmotivated.

"Sow the wind and reap the whirlwind," said Hosea, an Old Testament prophet. And sowing a future of illiterate adults, of poverty and unemployment, welfare dependency, crime, and despair will bring a whirlwind of shattered community. Our nation will be severed in two, those who have and those who don't. We will always have inequalities, but if the divisions grow extensive enough, and those in the disprivileged part feel hopeless, our inequalities can destroy society.

Community involvement can produce quality education, such as at this charter school in Bronx, New York, started by a grass roots organization.

Can education make a difference in this sorry picture? How about for the most impoverished of society, the children of the inner city? To find out, a team from Yale worked with the staff and parents in two grade schools in New Haven, Connecticut. The schools were in low-income neighborhoods. They were 99 percent African American and plagued by the usual inner-city problems. Student achievement, which had been the lowest in the city, soared to the third and fourth highest. As measured on standardized tests, the students' achievement levels jumped to 9 months *above* their grade level in one school, and 12 months ahead in the other. Attendance and behavior also improved dramatically.

How were such outstanding achievements accomplished? First, the team made a radical assumption, that the problem was not "poor students"—which is what most people assume—but, rather, the educational system. This is radical because it puts the responsibility on the shoulders of the staff. It makes teachers and administrators responsible for meeting the needs that the children's background created. Second, the staff fostered a feeling of common cause. Leadership was transferred from a central office to the grass roots—to those who worked in the schools and rubbed shoulders with the students. In their new leadership position, these people not only discussed the problems they were encountering, but they also were able to make decisions. And they did this as a unit, a team. Third, parents, staff, and students interacted frequently. This allowed students to identify with adults who valued and encouraged learning, reflecting a solid educational principle that learning is based on modeling and imitation. Fourth, a sense of community was engendered as trust, mutual respect, and a common cause developed among not just teachers and administrators, but also parents and students.

Using this same assumption—that inadequate teaching, not inadequate students, is the reason that poor children do poorly in school—Jaime Escalante motivated his students in an East Los Angeles inner-city school to perform so well on national calculus tests that officials thought the students must have cheated. Students in poverty can do well—if schools teach well.

Based on Comer 1986; Escalante and Dirmann 1990; Hilliard 1991; Levine 2004; Jacob and Ludwig 2009.

For Your Consideration

How would you apply these principles to change a troubled school in your area? What other principles from this text would you use?

The Future of the Problem

12.6 Discuss the likely future of urban problems.

Current trends are firmly established and are likely to persist. I foresee, then, the following.

Higher Costs and Lower Income

Our cities are caught in a bind. On the one hand, the demand for services is increasing, while on the other hand, the economic crisis has reduced the sales and property taxes that the cities need to pay for these services. In addition, to finance many programs our cities depend on money from the state and federal governments—which are broke and cutting back. Caught in this financial squeeze, some cities have laid off teachers and shortened the school year. They have also cut back on street cleaning, recreation programs, and activities for children and the elderly. Some cities have cut back especially hard in their poor areas, because those cutbacks upset middle-class voters the least.

The Homeless

The homeless will continue to live on our city streets. Their presence will create an outcry—not over their misery but over their visibility. In response to this pressure, city officials will use the police to disperse the homeless to less visible areas. This will make the city's historical, artsy, and sports areas more appealing to tourism and business, but it will do nothing to solve the problem of homelessness or poverty.

Gentrification

Commuting long distances to work is expensive and time-consuming, and, with inflation, is likely to grow more costly. These factors will increase **gentrification**, the process in which more affluent people move into an area and rehabilitate its buildings. The attractions of the city that we discussed earlier coupled with low-priced houses in deteriorated areas will also draw more of the middle class back to the city. Although their neighborhood grows more attractive, the poor resent the invasion of people with more money. As property values increase, so do taxes and rents, forcing many of the poorer residents to move out to try find lower rent.

The usual pattern of gentrification is for better-off whites to move into an area of the city, displacing minority poor. As you saw in the box on Harlem on page 401, this isn't always the case. Even when it is, though, sociologists have found that it isn't only the whites who benefit. Gentrification also draws middle-class minorities to the neighborhood and improves their incomes (McKinnish et al. 2008).

Principles for Shaping the Future

What our cities will look like in the future depends both on trends yet to appear and on the social policies we adopt now. The following three principles can provide a solid foundation for shaping that future:

1. As a cultural center of work and play, the city offers vast potential for satisfying people's needs, even providing a basic structure for human happiness.
2. The city is a social creation, and so are its negative features. As such, they can be overcome.
3. To design a future that overcomes urban problems, social policies should incorporate basic human needs—social, psychological, physical, and spiritual. As stressed in this chapter, the shorthand word for this is *community*.

These three principles can help us forge a future that enhances the quality of life, maximizes human potential, and creates urban areas that satisfy the human need for belonging.

Population: The Problem in Sociological Perspective

We have already discussed a major change in population, the historical development of cities and their current spectacular growth. Before we examine other population trends, we should define **demography**—the study of the size, composition, growth, and distribution of human populations. This definition makes demography sound like a pretty dry subject, but this area of sociology takes us to events so significant that they are reshaping global relations. As you will see, these events have a direct affect on *your* future. But as with cities, to get to the present we first need to step through the door of history.

12.7 Contrast the explanations for Europe's surge in population and the views of the pessimists and the optimists.

A Population Mystery

Watch on MySocLab Video: Demography: The Study of Population

The Mystery: A Population Explosion. For most of history, the world's population increased at a snail's pace. When Jesus was born 2,000 years ago, the population of the *entire world* was only about the same as that of the United States today. By 1750, Europe had 140 million inhabitants. Then came a sudden, unexpected surge in population: In just 50 years, Europe's population jumped by 48 million. Fifty years later, in 1850, it had increased by another 68 million, reaching a total of 256 million. What caused this population explosion?

Two Explanations: Public Health or the Potato? Demographers have come up with two rather different explanations to explain this population surge. G. T. Griffith (1926) argued that Europe's increase was due to improved public health. He said that better medical knowledge, hospitals, housing, water, and sanitation lowered the **death rate**, the number of deaths per 1,000 people. As fewer children died and more people lived longer, the population jumped.

Griffith's explanation is widely accepted, and makes good sense, but some demographers suggest an entirely different reason. Thomas McKeown (1977) claimed that the population of Europe remained low until 1750 because Europeans practiced **infanticide**, killing infants shortly after birth. Then came the potato, he said, and Europe's population surged!

I know this explanation sounds a little strange, so let's probe it a little. Griffith said that the Europeans practiced infanticide to keep their population in line with their available food. Without infanticide, they would have outstripped their food supply, leading to mass starvation. Then in the 1500s, the Spaniards, who conquered South America, discovered the potato, which was cultivated in the Andean highlands. They brought this unfamiliar food back with them, and gradually the Europeans adopted it. By 1800, the potato had become the main food of the poor in northern and central Europe. As this "miracle" plant expanded the food supply, the Europeans stopped practicing infanticide, and their population almost doubled in 100 years.

Did the potato have such an impact on history? Demographers still debate the cause of Europe's population explosion, but whatever the specifics are, you can see that changes in human behavior—from the adoption of new medical and sanitation practices to simple changes in diet—can have far-reaching effects on a population. This takes us into the heart of demography—and an ongoing controversy.

Demographers in Debate

Thomas Malthus, the Gloomy Prophet. Back in 1798, Thomas Malthus, an English economist, also analyzed Europe's surge in population. As he did so, he grew alarmed, viewing this change as a sign of coming doom. He then wrote an influential book, *An Essay on the Principle of Population.* In it, Malthus argued that populations grow geometrically, that is, from 2 to 4 to 8 to 16 and so forth, but the food supply increases only arithmetically, that is, from 1 to 2 to 3 to 4 and so on. His book's central message was this warning: If births go unchecked, the population of the world will outstrip its food supply.

The Pessimists: The New Malthusians. Malthus set of an alarm that you can still hear today, and his conclusions are still debated. One group—let's call them the *New Malthusians*—argues that Malthus was right. Today's situation is as grim, if not grimmer, than Malthus imagined. The world's population has gone unchecked, and just as Malthus warned us, it has exploded.

World population is following an **exponential growth curve**, meaning that growth doubles during equal intervals of time. The implications of exponential growth are startling. To illustrate them, sociologist William Faunce (1981:84) told this parable:

> *A poor man saved a rich man's life. Very grateful, the rich man offered a reward. The poor man replied that he would like his reward to be spread out over a four-week period, with each day's amount being twice what he received on the preceding day. He also said he would be happy to receive only one penny on the first day. The rich man immediately handed over the penny and congratulated himself on how cheaply he had gotten by.*
>
> *At the end of the first week, the rich man checked to see how much he owed and was pleased to find that the total was only $1.27. By the end of the second week, he owed only $163.83. On the twenty-first day, however, the rich man was surprised to find that the total had grown to $20,971.51. When the twenty-eighth day arrived, the rich man was shocked to discover that he owed $1,342,177.28 for that day alone and that the total reward had jumped to $2,684,354.56!*

This acceleration is precisely what alarms the New Malthusians. They claim that we have now entered the "fourth week" of an exponential growth curve. Look at Figure 12.4 to see why they think the day of reckoning is just around the corner. It took from the beginning of time to 1800 for the world's population to reach its first billion. It then took only 130 years (1930) to add a second billion. Like a bullet train, the process accelerated, and just 30 years later (1960) the world's population hit 3 billion. The time it took to reach the fourth billion was cut in half, to only 15 years (1975). Then just 12 years later (in 1987) the total reached 5 billion, in another 12 years it hit 6 billion (in 1999), and in yet another 12 years it hit 7 billion (in 2011).

To get another view of what alarms the New Malthusians, look at Figure 12.5. On average, every minute of every day, 160 babies are born. At sunset, the world has 231,000 more people than it did the day before. In one year, this increase totals 84 million people. In just 4 years, the world adds more people than the entire population of the United States. *In just the next 12 years the world's population will increase as much as it did during the first 1,800 years after the birth of Jesus.*

These totals terrify the New Malthusians. In the year 2050, the population of just India and China will be as large as the entire world population was in 1960 (Haub and

FIGURE 12.4 ▸ World Population Growth Over 2,000 Years

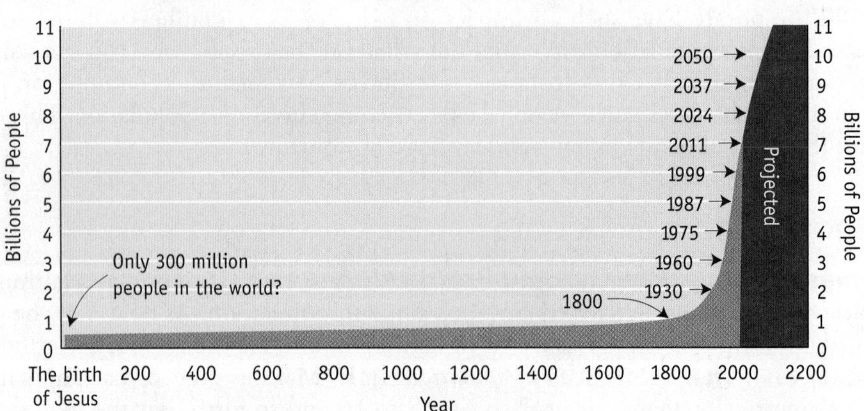

Source: Modified from Piotrow 1973, with projections based on Haub and Kaneda 2012.

FIGURE 12.5 ▸ How Fast Is the World's Population Growing?

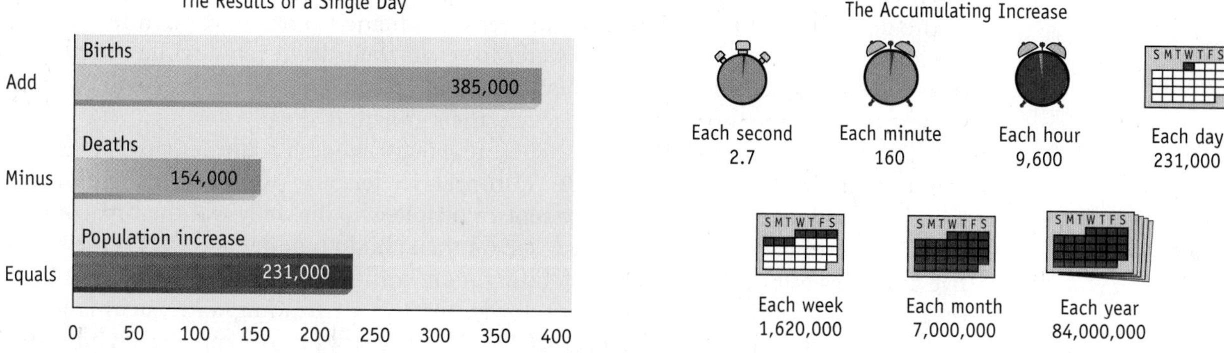

Source: By the author. Totals rounded. Based on Haub and Kaneda 2012.

Kaneda 2012). "We are headed for a showdown between population and food," the New Malthusians warn us. "We will run out of food if we don't curtail population growth. Soon you will see more televised images of pitiful, starving children."

The Optimists: The Anti-Malthusians. All of this seems obvious, and no one wants to live shoulder-to-shoulder and fight for scraps. How, then, can anyone argue with the New Malthusians?

An optimistic group of demographers, whom we can call the *Anti-Malthusians,* paint a far different picture. They believe that Europe's **demographic transition** provides a more accurate glimpse of the future. This transition is diagrammed in Figure 12.6 below. During most of its history, Europe was in Stage 1. Its population remained about the same from year to year, with its high death rates offsetting its high birthrates. Then came Stage 2, the population explosion that so upset Malthus. Europe's population surged because birthrates remained high while death rates dropped. Finally, Europe made the transition to Stage 3: The population stabilized as people brought their birthrates into line with their lower death rates.

FIGURE 12.6 ▸ The Demographic Transition

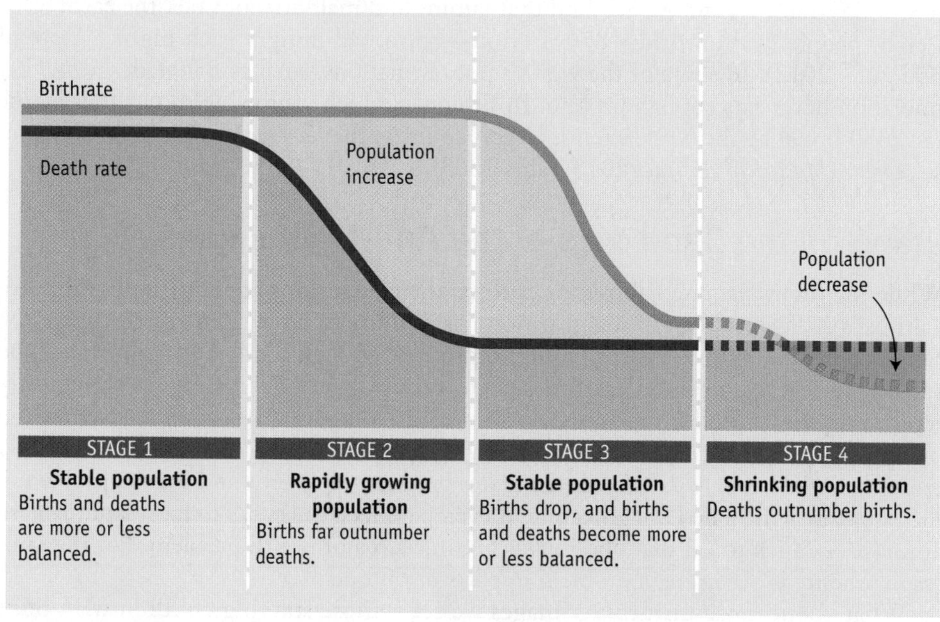

Note: The standard demographic transition is depicted by Stages 1–3. Stage 4 has been suggested by some Anti-Malthusians.

This, say the Anti-Malthusians, will also happen in the Least Industrialized Nations. Their current surge in population growth simply indicates that they have reached Stage 2 of the demographic transition. Hybrid seeds, medicine from the Most Industrialized Nations, and purer public drinking water have cut their death rates, while their birthrates have remained high. When they move into Stage 3, as surely they will, we will wonder what all the fuss was about. In fact, their growth is already slowing.

The demographic transition was so successful that European countries, now in Stage 4, worry about *not having enough babies*. European leaders fear **population shrinkage**, a failure to produce enough children to replace people who die. Italy was the first country in the world to have more people over age 65 than children under age 15. Of the forty-five countries of Europe, fourteen are filling more coffins than cradles, shrinking a little each year. Twenty-six are growing very slowly, and five are treading water, neither growing nor shrinking (Haub and Kaneda 2012). You might want to jump ahead and take a peek at the global map on page 415.

Anti-Malthusians predict that this same demographic transition will occur in the poorer nations of the world. Today's rapid growth should not be a cause for concern—it merely indicates that these countries have reached the second stage of the demographic transition. Already their growth rate has slowed. Look again at Figure 12.4 on page 406. It took the world's population 12 years to go from 4 to 5 billion, and then another 12 years to go from 5 to 6 billion. If population growth had kept accelerating as it had been doing, adding this last billion people would have taken less than 12 years. Instead, population growth is tapering off, the precise slowing that we would expect as these nations enter the third stage of the demographic transition.

Demography is one of those significant factors that works quietly behind the scenes to affect our lives in ways that are mostly invisible to us. To catch a glimpse of some of these quiet influences—which can become explosive—see the *Spotlight on Social Research* box on the next page.

The Scope of the Problem

Sitting on the Shoulders of the New Malthusians

12.8 Describe how the New Malthusians and the Anti-Malthusians view world population growth and food supply.

At its current rate of growth, the world's population will double in about 58 years. Can the world support twice its present population? To answer this question, we can ask how the world is doing right now. We find that famine and malnutrition stalk the earth. One in eight people in the world—870 million—go to bed hungry each night ("State of Food . . . " 2012). In some of the world's poorest nations, such as Bangladesh, *half* the population never eats enough protein. In Ethiopia, which is growing so fast that by the year 2050 it will be the world's tenth largest country, the *average* income is $400 for an entire year (*Statistical Abstract* 2013:Table 1363).

Sitting on the Shoulders of the Anti-Malthusians

"While the totals just cited above are correct, the conclusions are not," reply the Anti-Malthusians. The problem of malnutrition has nothing to do with the earth having too many people, nor with the earth failing to produce enough food. The amount of food available for every person on earth has been *increasing*, not decreasing. Every country records how much food it produces. As Figure 12.7 on page 410 shows, *despite the billions of people who have been added to the earth's population, more food is available for each person now than in the past.* The United States produces so much food that its problem is where to store it all. The U.S. government even pays its farmers *not* to farm land. Americans have so much to eat that obesity has become a major health problem. For the same reason, obesity is becoming a problem in parts of Europe.

What about those disturbing images we see—those starving children with bony arms, protruding stomachs, and flies crawling over their faces? How can anyone deny that there is a food shortage? The Anti-Malthusians reply that the starving people in

Spotlight on Social Research

Where the People Are

JACK GOLDSTONE *is a sociologist and professor of public policy at George Mason University. He does research on democracy, economic development, social movements, and regime change. He connects all of these to changes in population. Here is what he wrote for you.*

Like most people, I never thought much about population. Countries grow over time, of course, and I always assumed that was a good thing. People had one, two, or three children, they grew up and had children, and so society continued from one generation to the next. I didn't think there was much else to it.

There were worries in the 1960s that global population growth was going too far too fast. Paul Ehrlich and others revived the concerns of Thomas Malthus—a nineteenth-century English parson that you read about in this text—that population growth was going to crowd the planet and use up all our food, land, and water. It was true that population growth reached alarming levels in the late 1900s, as world population surged to five, then six billion people. Yet despite that growth, the global economy grew and food production more than kept up. More and more people in India and China were lifted out of poverty. The rate of population growth slowed down. And the air and water got cleaner in Los Angeles, Tokyo, and New York.

While these events reassured most people, I noticed something odd about this picture. Growth was not slowing down evenly around the world. Instead, the Most Industrialized Nations were experiencing a drastic decline in the number of children, to less than two children per woman, even as life expectancy increased. The result was that these rich countries had more and more older people relative to the number of younger workers. Meanwhile, in many of the Least Industrialized Nations, especially in Africa, the Middle East, and central Asia, population growth was continuing at very high rates. In these countries, women continued to bear large numbers of children, and more and more of them were surviving to have children themselves. Africa, which in 1950 had far fewer people than Europe, was on its way to having as many people as China and India *combined*. More importantly, the world was dividing into two different groups of countries—rich countries that were getting older and had shrinking or stagnant populations, and poorer countries that were very young (some with half their population under 15!) and growing very fast.

What will happen in this unbalanced world? As we saw with the Arab Revolts of 2011, the Least Industrialized Nations that don't satisfy the demands of their surging young populations for jobs are likely to see youth movements and regime change. Then there are the middle-income countries—like Brazil, Turkey, Mexico, and India—that have lowered their population growth rate to a moderate level, but that are still providing solid growth in the labor force of young workers. In these countries, we can expect to see strong economic growth in the years ahead.

In a class by themselves are the Most Industrialized Nations that face shrinking numbers of young workers combined with rising numbers of retirees who need pensions and vast amounts of expensive health care. Major worries of these nations are budget deficits, sluggish economies, and a reduced ability to fund both social and military spending.

This imbalance of population growth is driving a vast global migration. To find jobs, young people and families are moving from poor countries with fast-growing populations to the richer countries with slow-growing populations. In countries like the United States, Canada, and Australia, the recent immigrants are contributing to changes in domestic politics. The minorities are becoming important groups of voters, and they are demanding change.

As you can see, population *does* matter. It is not just some abstract concept. Our current unevenness in global population growth is changing what is happening within countries and between countries. A whole new field of *political demography* is emerging. The focus in this emerging area of study is on how population changes can reshape politics. These days, I find myself explaining these patterns to government officials, who are worried about spending and security; to business executives, who are concerned about where their future workers and markets will be found; and to seniors and youth organizations, who are trying to figure out their place in this fast-changing world. I consider myself fortunate to be able to teach others how national and global processes of population change can help us understand some of the major events that are taking place in our world, and in some instances upsetting the political order.

FIGURE 12.7 ▸ **How Much Food Does the World Produce per Person?**

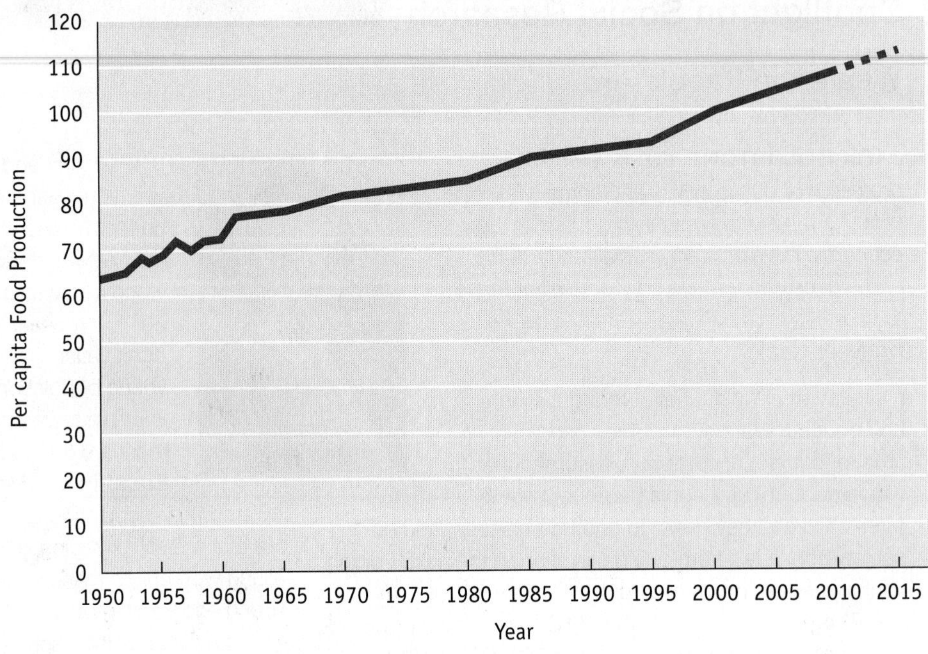

Note: Projections from 2010 are by the author.

Sources: Simon 1981:58; *Statistical Abstract of the United States* 1988:Table 1411; 1998:Tables 1380, 1381, 1382, 1383; 2010:Tables 1335, 1337, 1338, 1339; recomputed to 1948–52 base.

those photos certainly aren't getting enough food. The reason for this, though, is not that the earth is failing to produce enough food for them. The problem is that the abundance of food is not distributed adequately. If we were to redistribute a mere 5 percent of the grain grown in the Most Industrialized Nations, we could prevent *all* the malnutrition and starvation in the entire world (Conti 1980).

How about the perception that Africa is overcrowded, that it has so many people that it is outstripping its food supply? Everyone knows this. This might surprise you, but contrary to common belief, the starvation in Africa that upsets the world does *not* occur because there are too many people. The cause is drought and civil war. Africa has 23 percent of the earth's land, but only 15 percent of the earth's population (Haub and Kaneda 2012). Civil wars in Africa disrupt food production and block humanitarian aid from reaching its suffering people.

The source of starvation is not that the earth has too many people or that it does not produce enough food. This horror is caused by a combination of agricultural inefficiency, political corruption, maldistribution of the earth's abundance, and war—not too little food.

In Sum ▸ Looking at the same evidence, the New Malthusians and Anti-Malthusians arrive at different conclusions. Much like the pessimists who look at the water in a glass and conclude that the glass is half empty, the New Malthusians conclude that population growth is out of control and we are about to run out of food. Like the optimists who consider the same glass of water half full, the Anti-Malthusians conclude that our era enjoys the greatest abundance that the world has ever known—and this abundance is growing. The scope of the population problem depends on perception—whether one sees the glass as half empty or half full.

No one can settle this argument for you. You will have to read the evidence and make up your own mind. As you do, remember the symbolic interactionist principle that *facts never interpret themselves*: To interpret anything, we place it within a framework that gives it meaning. As we consider issues of population and food in the coming pages, we will return to this basic principle from time to time. For now, let's apply the sociological theories.

War, not too many people, is a major cause of malnutrition and starvation in Africa. These people in the Democratic Republic of Congo are fleeing the fighting between rebels and government troops.

Looking at the Problem Theoretically

As usual, our theoretical lenses provide contrasting perspectives. We will use symbolic interactionism to better understand why the population of the Least Industrialized Nations is growing so fast. Functionalism will illuminate the relationship between modern medicine and the twin problems of population and food. Finally, conflict theory yields a controversial analysis of food, profits, and international relations. Together, these perspectives help us understand the social problem of population and food.

12.9 Discuss the perspectives that emerge when you apply symbolic interactionism, functionalism, and conflict theory to world population.

Symbolic Interactionism

Why Do the Poor Have So Many Children? Let's start with something that doesn't seem to make sense. Look at Figure 12.8 on the next page. You can see that the population of the Least Industrialized Nations is growing so fast that it looks like someone marching up a steep hill. In contrast, the population of the Most Industrialized Nations looks as if it is standing still. Why is *almost* all the increase in the world's population coming from the Least Industrialized Nations?

Doesn't it seem obvious that if you were poor and faced hunger and disease, starvation and death, that you would want to have few children? Could it be that the adults in the Least Industrialized Nations don't know how to prevent pregnancy? The question is worth asking, but this is not the case. Cheap and effective birth control techniques are available, but many of the poor won't use them because they *want* large families (Burns 1994).

To see why, let's use symbolic interactionism.

Seeing the World as They See It. By **taking the role of the other**—that is, seeing things from another person's perspective—we can make sense of people's experiences. Let me share with you something that happened when I was living in a remote area of Mexico:

> *The image still haunts me. There stood Celia, age 30, her distended stomach visible proof that her thirteenth child was on its way. Her oldest was only 14 years old! A mere boy by our standards, he had already gone as far in school as he ever would. Each morning, he joined the men to work in the fields. Each evening around twilight, I saw him return home, exhausted from hard labor in the subtropical sun.*

FIGURE 12.8 ▸ Where Is the World's Population Growth Taking Place?

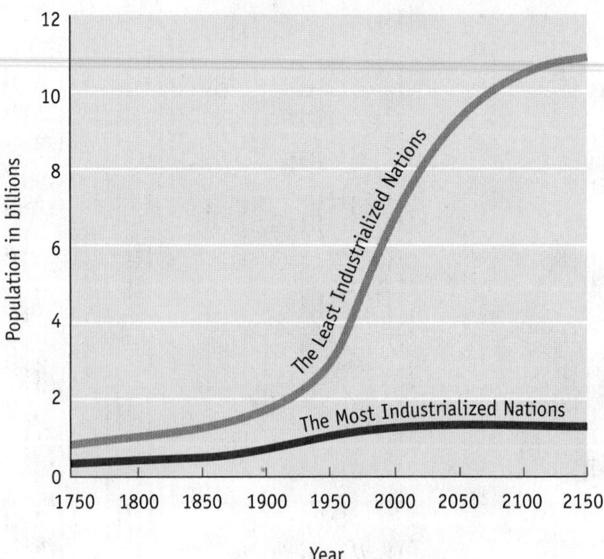

Sources: "The World of the Child 6 Billion" 2000; Haub and Kaneda 2012.

Celia and Angel's home reflected the family's poverty. A thatched hut consisting of only a single room served as home for all fourteen members of the family. At night, the parents and younger children crowded into a double bed, while the eldest boy slept in a hammock. As in many homes in the village, the other children slept on mats spread on the dirt floor—despite the crawling scorpions.

The home was meagerly furnished. It had only a gas stove, a table, and a cabinet where Celia stored her few cooking utensils and clay dishes. There were no closets; clothes hung on pegs in the walls. There also were no chairs, not even one. I was used to the poverty in the village, but this really startled me. The family was too poor to afford even a single chair.

Celia beamed as she told me how much she looked forward to the birth of her next child. Could she really mean it? It was hard to imagine that any woman would want to be in her situation.

Celia meant every word. She was as full of delighted anticipation as she had been with her first child—and with all the others in between. To understand the desires of billions of poor people like Celia and Angel, we must move beyond our own culture and understand life from their perspective. In the Least Industrialized Nations, people's identities center on their children. Motherhood is the most exalted status a woman can achieve. Through childbearing, a woman fulfills her destiny and finds personal worth. The more children she bears, the more she fulfills this purpose. Similarly, the more children that a man fathers, the more he proves his manhood. It is especially sons that he desires, for through them, his name lives on.

Most of these people live in small communities where they share values and identify with one another. In this *Gemeinschaft* community of like-minded people, pregnancy is viewed as a sign of God's favor. As people produce more children, the community grants them higher status. The barren woman, not the woman with a dozen children, is to be pitied.

For these people, children are also *economic assets*—not the costly responsibilities they are in an urbanized world. How can this possibly be? The poor in the Least Industrialized Nations have no social security, no medical insurance, and no unemployment benefits. Most live on less than $2 a day (Haub and Kaneda 2012). This motivates them to have *more* children, for *the children are their social security*. When parents become too old to work, their adult children take care of them. The more children they have, the firmer their security is.

It is also useful to know that children in the Least Industrialized Nations start to contribute financially to the family long before the parents are old. Look at Figure 12.9. This, too, should help you take the role of the other to understand why the surge in the world's population is coming from the Least Industrialized Nations.

FIGURE 12.9 ▸ Why the Poor Need Children

Children are an economic asset in the Least Industrialized Nations. Based on a survey in Indonesia, this figure shows that boys and girls can be net income earners for their families by the age of 9 or 10.

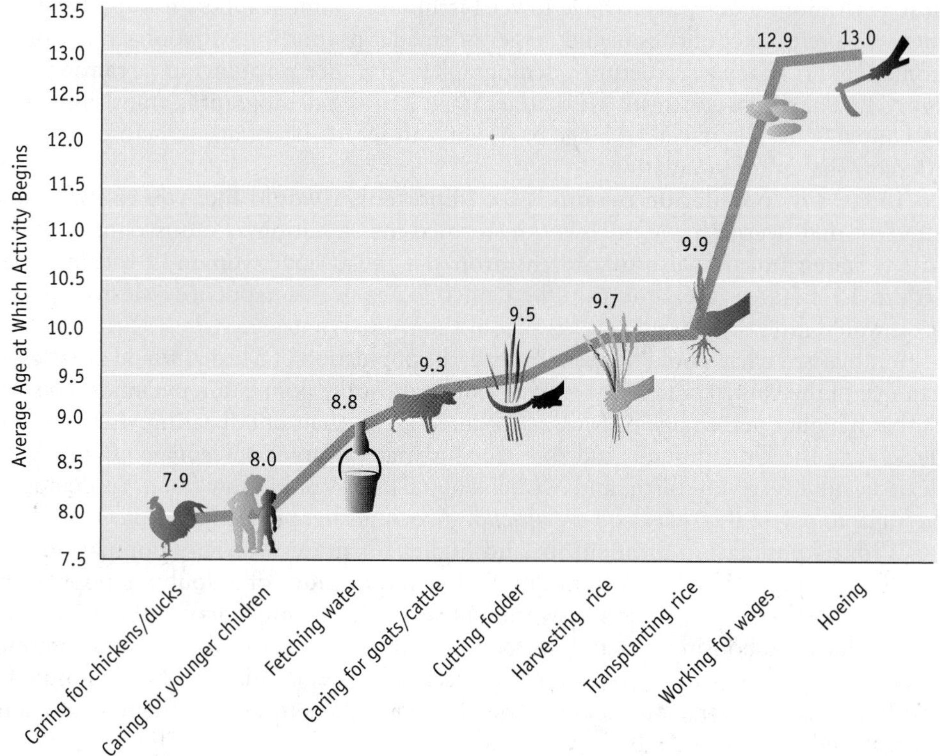

Source: U.N. Fund for Population Activities.

In Sum ▸ People's ideas of the "right" number of children reflect their life situation. To impose our ideas onto people in other cultures is to overlook their experiences and perspectives. To understand the behavior of any group, we must see things as they see them.

Functionalism

As we apply the functionalist perspective, keep in mind that functionalists want to determine *objectively* the functions or dysfunctions of behaviors and events, without judging those consequences as good or bad.

Catastrophes Are Functional. As we saw with poverty, rape, murder, drug addiction, and racial–ethnic discrimination, functionalists identify functions even in deviant, illegal, or abhorrent events. With regard to the world's population growth, functionalists stress that even war, natural disasters, disease, and famine are functional. Historically, these mass killers held the world's population in check, ensuring that humans did not outstrip their food supply.

Modern Medicine and Public Health: Latent Dysfunctions. Throughout history, the balance between population and food has been precarious. Ordinarily, high death rates have canceled out high birthrates, and populations have remained stable. Exporting modern medicine to the Least Industrialized Nations, however, upset this balance. Along with better nutrition and sanitation, Western drugs brought under control those nations' major killers—smallpox, diphtheria, typhoid, measles, and other infectious diseases. As a result, the death rates in these nations plunged, but their birthrates were untouched. Not only did millions of people who otherwise would have died survive, but they also reproduced. This has taken the Least Industrialized Nations into the second stage of demographic transition (see Figure 12.6 on page 407).

View on **MySocLab**
Figure: (a) Crude Birth Rates and Crude Death Rates, (b) Infant Mortality Rates, and (c) Life Expectancy around the World, 2010

Population Pyramids. Countries in the second stage of the demographic transition have a lot of young people, while those in the third and fourth stages have a lot of older people. Obviously, countries with more young people have higher birthrates, and those with more older people have lower birthrates. Demographers use the term *age structure* to refer to countries having larger or smaller proportions of younger and older people. To illustrate age structures, demographers produce **population pyramids**, like Figure 12.10, which contrasts Mexico, in Stage 2 of the demographic transition, with the United States, in advanced Stage 3. As you can see, different age structures produce different "shapes" of populations.

To see why population pyramids are important, I would like you to imagine a miracle—that overnight, Mexico is transformed into a nation as industrialized as the United States. Imagine also that births drop and the average woman in Mexico gives birth to 2.1 children, the same as in the United States. If this happened, Mexico's population would grow at the same rate as that of the United States, right?

But this isn't what would happen. Instead, the population of Mexico would grow faster than that of the United States. To see why, look again at the population pyramids. You can see that a higher percentage of Mexican women are in their childbearing years. Even if Mexico and the United States had the same birthrate, a larger percentage of women in Mexico would be giving birth, and Mexico's population would grow faster. As demographers like to phrase this, Mexico's *age structure* gives it greater *population momentum.*

With its population momentum and higher birthrate, Mexico's population will double in 44 years (Haub and Kent 2009). The implications of a doubling population are mind-boggling. *Just to stay even*, within 44 years Mexico must double the number of available jobs and housing facilities; its food production; its transportation and communication facilities; its water, gas, sewer, and electrical systems; and its schools, hospitals, civic buildings, theaters, stores, and parks. If Mexico fails to double them, its already meager standard of living will drop even further.

FIGURE 12.10 ▸ **Population Pyramids of Mexico and the United States**

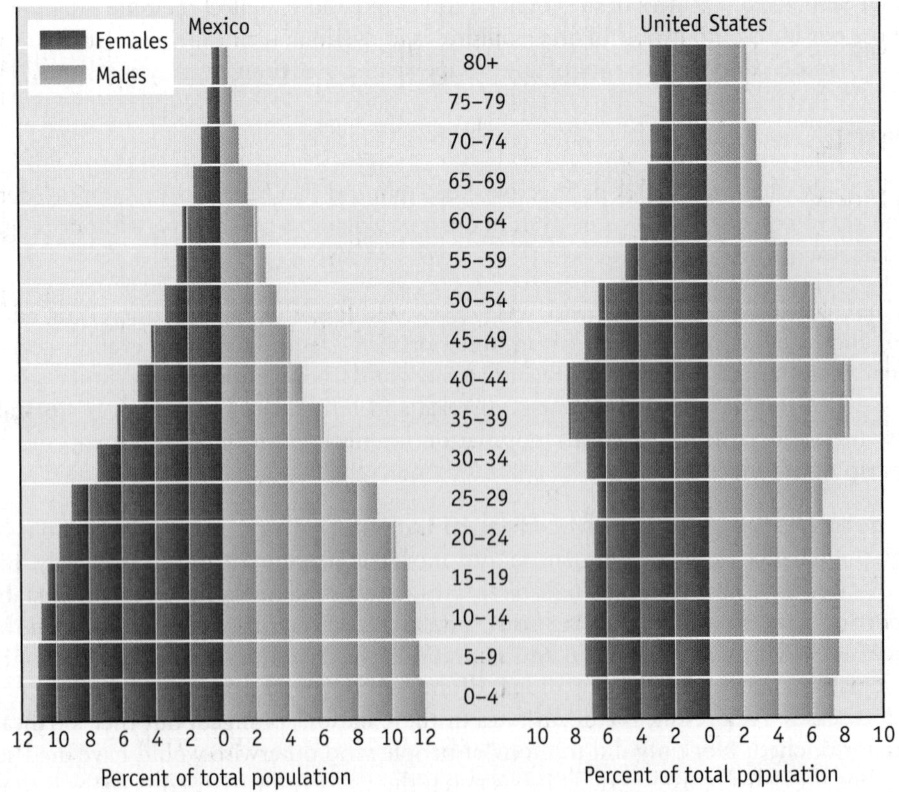

Source: By the author. Computed from the U.S. Bureau of the Census 2006b:Table 94.

As you can see from Figure 12.11, the doubling time of the world's nations is quite uneven.

In Sum ▶ Functionalists analyze how exporting Western medicine and public sanitation into the Least Industrialized Nations caused a surge in their population. Their rapid population growth outstripped their food supply, resulting in malnutrition, mass starvation, and political unrest. Because these negative consequences were not anticipated or intended, sociologists call them **latent dysfunctions**.

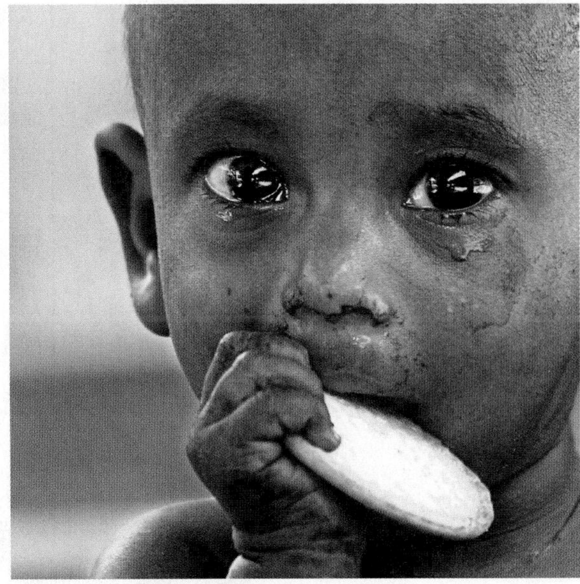

The text explains the reasons for hunger and malnourishment. This photo was taken in Bangladesh.

Conflict Theory

When we look at problems of population growth and food from the conflict perspective, we get an entirely different view.

Profits, Biofuel, and Food Politics. We are so used to hearing about the food aid the West gives the poorer nations that this might surprise you—the Least Industrialized Nations also contribute to the diet of the rich nations. For example, each year the United States imports $100 billion in food, much of it from the Least Industrialized Nations (*Statistical Abstract* 2013:Table 862). As social critic Michael Harrington (1977) pointed out long ago, the major profits from this food go not to the poor countries that produce it, but to corporations in the Most Industrialized Nations that process and distribute it.

FIGURE 12.11 ▶ **How Long Will It Take for Population to Double?**

1–49 years
50–99 years
100 years or longer
Countries with shrinking populations

China 140 years
North America 117 years
Europe 700 years
Asia (except China) 58 years
Africa 29 years
Central America 41 years
South America 54 years
Australia 100 years

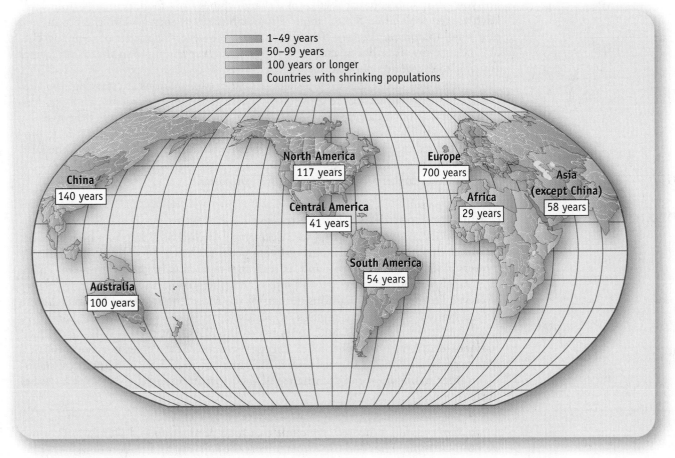

Source: By the author. Based on Haub and Kent 2009.

Is this the future of the world, as the New Malthusians fear? This photo was taken in Dalian, Liaoning, China.

As conflict theorists stress, for these corporations food is a money-making enterprise, not a means of solving world hunger. As you know, about 10 percent of the gasoline you pump into your car is ethanol. Ethanol comes from food, primarily from corn. Each year in the United States, about 5 *billion* bushels of corn go into the production of ethanol (*Statistical Abstract* 2013:Table 870). Whatever the merits of reducing U.S. dependence on oil imports, each gallon of ethanol represents food that is no longer available to the world's population.

I mentioned earlier that even though people in some nations are starving, the U.S. government pays farmers *not* to grow crops. These government payments are large, running about $12 billion a year (*Statistical Abstract* 2013:Table 854). Conflict theorists say that the reason for these payments is **food politics**—paying farmers to limit food production creates an artificial shortage that drives up grain prices. This caters to the farm vote by keeping grain prices high. The reason for food politics, stress conflict theorists, is profit, with no concern for what is right, just, or moral.

Population Control. To wrap up this section, let's revisit the implications of a population doubling, which can lead to a declining standard of living. Conflict theorists point out that a declining standard of living poses the threat of political instability—protests, riots, even revolution—and, in response, repression by the government. Political instability in one country can spill into others, threatening an entire region's balance of power. Fearing such disruptions, leaders of the Most Industrialized Nations use the United Nations to direct a campaign of worldwide birth control. With one hand they give agricultural aid, IUDs, and condoms to the masses in the Least Industrialized Nations—while, with the other hand, they sell weapons to the elites in these countries. Both actions, say conflict theorists, serve the same purpose: promoting political stability in order to maintain the dominance of the Most Industrialized Nations in global stratification.

In Sum ▸ Conflict theorists conclude that food production and population control are political tools. The food crisis that affects the starving and undernourished is the result of food politics, not Malthusian inevitabilities.

Research Findings

As we review research findings on population and food, let's continue to compare the positions of the New Malthusians and the Anti-Malthusians.

12.10 Summarize how the New Malthusians and the Anti-Malthusians interpret research findings on population change.

The New Malthusians

Tsunamis and Population Growth. As you know, an earthquake on the ocean floor can cause a huge wave, sometimes 30, 40, or 50 feet high. These waves, called tsunamis, are so powerful that they can roll for hundreds and even thousands of miles before they reach land. The worst tsunami in recorded history occurred in 2004. It hit Indonesia with such force that it killed 233,000 people. At the time, Indonesia had an annual growth rate of 1.6 percent, its *rate of natural increase,* as demographers call it. With a population of 220 million, Indonesia was growing by 3,300,000 people each year, 9,041 people each day (Haub 2004). It took Indonesia only *26 days* to replace the 233,000 people it lost to the tsunami.

This kind of growth, say the New Malthusians, is like a tsunami—a destructive wave that threatens to overwhelm us and destroy our future.

Less Food for More People. As there are more and more people in the world, there will be less and less food for each person. The world's fishing grounds are being destroyed by pollution and overfishing. At our current rate of harvesting fish, the world's fishing stocks will *collapse* in the year 2048 (Worm et al. 2006). Land unsuitable for cultivation has already been pushed into production, and we are running into a global water shortage as extensive irrigation depletes the world's aquifers (Patrick 2012). As the wells run dry, food production will drop.

The Elusive Goal of Zero Population Growth. Let's suppose that the world somehow manages to achieve **zero population growth**—that is, adults having only enough children to replace themselves. On average, each woman would bear 2.1 children, the extra 0.1 child making up for those who die before reproducing. It seems obvious that the world's population problem would then disappear, right? Wrong. *The population momentum that we discussed earlier would keep the world's population growing for 50 to 70 years before it leveled off.*

Consider Africa as an example. *Forty-one percent* of Africans are not yet age 15 (Haub and Kaneda 2012). This means that more Africans will enter the reproductive ages each year than will leave them. If Africa attained zero population growth, its growth *rate* would fall for 50 or 70 years, but its population would continue to increase during this time before it finally leveled off.

And, add the New Malthusians, Africa isn't even close to zero population growth. The average African woman gives birth to almost five (4.7) children, not two (Haub and Kaneda 2012). In the news, you hear about the many deaths from HIV/AIDS, and in some places even starvation, but despite these conditions Africa has the fastest-growing population of any of the world's continents.

The Anti-Malthusians

Larger Populations Are Good. The view of the Anti-Malthusians is almost the polar opposite. They claim that more people are *good* for the world, that larger populations lead to *higher* standards of living (Simon 1977, 1982, 1991). Larger populations force countries to use their land more efficiently, which increases productivity. They also create larger markets. This promotes more efficient manufacturing, lowering production costs and making more goods available. With larger populations, many social investments become profitable, especially railroads, highways, irrigation systems, and ports. These investments, which don't pay off in sparse populations, spur productivity and increase a country's capacity to deliver that productivity to its people. Finally, a growing world population means that more geniuses will be born. They will contribute to everyone's welfare.

Food Production Is Outpacing Population Growth. The Anti-Malthusians stress that the world's food production is *outpacing* the world's population growth. (Recall Figure 12.7 on page 410.) Although the world's population has "exploded," there is now *more* food for each person in the entire world than there was 50 or even 100 or 200 years ago. When it comes to fishing grounds, the Anti-Malthusians argue that the world's fish harvest has not fallen. Instead, the world's fish harvest is 45 percent *higher* now than it was in 1990 (*Statistical Abstract* 2012:Table 1375). If the world's population increase is dramatic—and it is—then the world's food increase is even more dramatic.

Has the Population Explosion Peaked?

The Anti-Malthusians. The Anti-Malthusians point out that the world's rate of population growth is slowing. Between 1965 and 1975, the world's population grew an average of 2 percent each year. During the 1980s, the growth rate dropped to 1.7 percent. Now it has dropped to 1.2 percent (*Statistical Abstract* 1991:Table 1434; Haub and Kaneda 2012).This huge reduction in the world's population growth—40 percent—is evidence that the world is following the demographic transition. I think you'll enjoy the Global Glimpse box, which gives insight into this process.

A Global Glimpse

"I'd Like to Have Twenty Children"

In 1976, an anthropologist who was making a documentary in an African village in Kenya asked a 26-year-old mother of two how many children she wanted. The woman looked at her bulging stomach, giggled, and said, "I'd like to have 20 children."

The documentary then went into a freeze frame, with a subtitle stating that the woman had given birth to twins.

This image haunted John Tierney, a *New York Times* reporter. "What is wrong with her?" he wondered. "What would become of her family?" Ten years later, Tierney went to Kenya to follow up on the story. He found the woman, Fanisi Kalusa, living in the same hut, the twins healthy. She was now 36, with seven children, aged 4 to 16.

When Tierney asked about her wanting 20 children, Fanisi laughed, and said, "I've rejected that idea because there is not enough food to meet the demand."

Most African men dislike birth control, but her husband had agreed to limit their family size. He had his mother put a curse on his wife to make her barren—a standard practice in the area.

Fanisi went along with the curse—but without telling her husband, she visited a clinic for a free IUD.

Initially, she wanted 20 children who would be available when she needed help on the farm and support in old age. But now, children have become expensive in Kenya. For each child, parents must pay $10 a year in tuition, a burden many poor cannot afford. In addition, many children are moving to the city, breaking close family bonds and threatening the custom of adult children providing support for their aged parents.

How do these eleven children in Namibia, who all live in this little house with their parents, fit into the demographic transition?

Fanisi told her 16-year-old daughter to have only six children. Fanisi's daughter told Tierney that she thought four would be about right.

Based on Tierney 1986;Haub and Kent 2009.

For Your Consideration

What do you think? Will Africa successfully move to the next stage in the demographic transition? Anti-Malthusians point to Fanisi Kalusa as evidence that they will. But the New Malthusians worry that Kenya is growing at 2.7 percent each year—more than four times as fast as the United States.

The New Malthusians. Advocates of zero population growth don't quarrel with these numbers, but they say that they don't mean what the Anti-Malthusians think they do. These totals indicate only that the *rate* of population growth has slowed. The world's population growth hasn't even leveled off. It is still exploding.

Social Policy

12.11 Compare the social policy implications of the New Malthusians and the Anti-Malthusians.

In trying to determine rational social policy, the New and Anti-Malthusians disagree on almost everything, except for the need to increase world food production. Rather than taking sides, let's consider the radically different implications of their views for social policy.

Policy Implications of the Anti-Malthusians

Encouraging Population Growth and Technological Development. If larger populations are good for the world, then it follows that social policy ought to encourage larger families. To implement the Anti-Malthusian position, we could take the following steps:

1. Reduce the age of consent to have sex to match the age at which girls are biologically able to reproduce. This would get more young women pregnant.
2. Encourage teenagers to experiment sexually.
3. Offer incentives for women to bear many children—lower taxes, paid maternity leave, subsidized housing and food, and free nannies, child care, and medical care. Women can earn cash bonuses for having children, with larger bonuses for each successive child.
4. Discourage the education of women, because the less education women have, the more children they bear.
5. Make abortion and birth control illegal.
6. Export Western medicine and public health techniques to the Least Industrialized Nations. This will reduce deaths so there will be more people to reproduce.
7. Encourage science, technology, industry, and agriculture. Developments in these areas can help improve the standard of living of huge populations.

Policy Implications of the New Malthusians

Malthus' Machiavellian Proposal. In *An Essay on the Principle of Population* (1798/1926), Thomas Malthus made these radical suggestions for limiting population:

> *We should . . . encourage . . . destruction. . . . Instead of recommending cleanliness to the poor, we should encourage contrary habits. In our towns we should make the streets narrower, crowd more people into the houses, and court the return of the plague. In the country, we should build villages near stagnant pools, and particularly encourage settlements in all marshy and unwholesome situations. . . . But above all, we should reprobate [reject] specific remedies for ravaging diseases.*

You can see that such policies to increase filth and spread disease follow logically from the New Malthusian position. Such policies, of course, have been rejected as not being humane. But let's continue on Malthus' path to see what other social policies might follow from this position.

More Generally Unacceptable Policies. If we were to implement Malthus' recommendations, some rather severe social policies would be called for. Among them would be these:

1. Encourage infanticide.
2. Refuse to send food to areas of famine and starvation.

3. Withdraw modern medicine from the Least Industrialized Nations, including vaccines, antibiotics, and medicines for HIV/AIDS.
4. Raise the age of sexual consent and the age at which people are allowed to marry.
5. Require a license to have children.
6. Require abortions for women who become pregnant without a license.
7. Encourage homosexual unions, since they don't produce children.
8. Sterilize enough baby girls to assure zero population growth.
9. Sterilize each woman after she gives birth to her first child.
10. Establish a national system of free abortions on demand to any woman of any age for any reason.

I know that these positions sound extreme, perhaps even ludicrous, but some New Malthusians take even more extreme positions. Environmentalist Pentti Linkola suggested that we annihilate most of the human race (Milbank 1994). He compared humanity to a sinking ship with 100 passengers and a lifeboat that can hold only 10. He said, "We need to end aid to the Third World, stop giving asylum to refugees—and a war would be good, too." To let us know that he is serious, he added, "If there were a button I could press that meant millions of people would die, I would gladly sacrifice myself."

Achieving Zero Population Growth. There are also less radical, more generally acceptable, social policy implications of the New Malthusians. One of their common goals is to achieve zero population growth. What motivates most people to have fewer children is not some abstract notion of a world population problem but the attitudes, beliefs, and values they learn. Let's consider what social policies might encourage such views.

1. Encourage women to go to college and to graduate school. Again, the more education that women attain, the fewer children they bear.
2. Encourage women to want careers. Women with careers have fewer children.
3. Distribute free or low-cost birth control devices to everyone, including teenagers.
4. Teach zero population growth to schoolchildren, warning them about the coming tsunami of uncontrolled population growth.

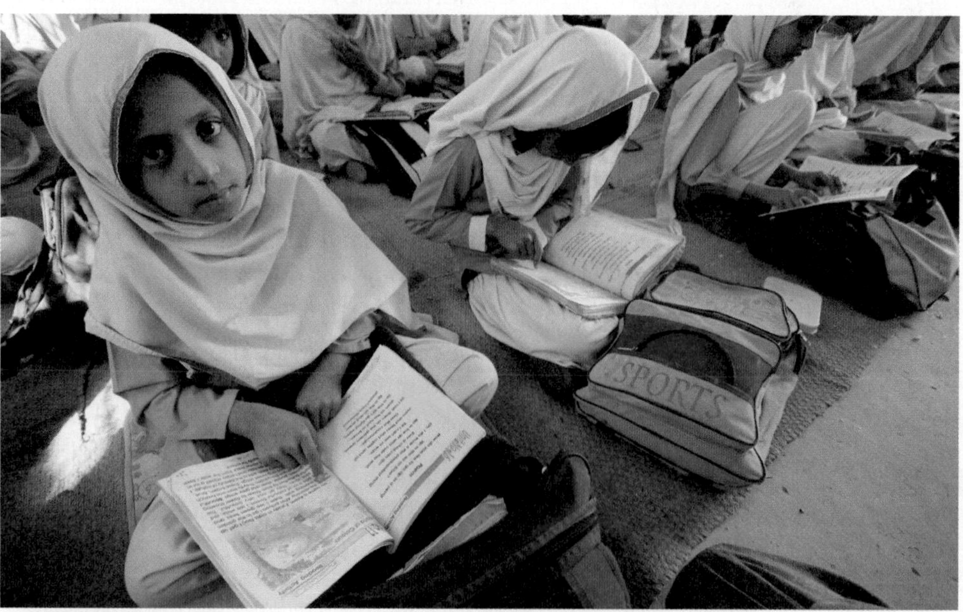

Why is more education for girls a social policy suggestion of the New Malthusians? This photo was taken in Pakistan.

5. Pay women to be sterilized. The payment can be small. Fifty dollars goes a long way in the Least Industrialized Nations, where many annual incomes are less than $1,000. Each $50 or $100 invested now will save huge amounts in the years to come.
6. Make international aid dependent on a country reforming its agriculture.

This last item, though it might seem cold and brutal, was tried successfully when India experienced mass starvation during the mid–twentieth century. Instead of just shipping supplies of food, which would have made India dependent on the West, the United States made each shipment depend on progress in meeting monthly agricultural goals. Today, not only does India feed itself, but it is a net exporter of food (Bajaj 2012). These countries have the capacity to be food independent. China broke up its communal farms and, using profit-oriented incentives, now produces more food than it needs for its incredible 1.3 billion people (Critchfield 1986; Agriculture and Agri-Food. . ." 2010).

The Future of the Problem

Not surprisingly, the New and Anti-Malthusians also disagree sharply on their perception of the future. Let's look at how they see things.

12.12 Compare the two futures as seen by the New Malthusians and the Anti-Malthusians.

The New Malthusians: The Pessimistic View

Underlying the New Malthusians' view of the future is this hard fact: Many of the world's natural resources such as petroleum and minerals are finite, as are the growing capacity of our land and the carrying capacity of our oceans. Our present population growth, economic development, and use of these resources are a quick path to their exhaustion. We are heading toward a gray and dismal future. Here is what the New Malthusians foresee.

High Food Prices and Starvation. Populations will outstrip their food production. In the face of higher demand and lower supply, the price of food will increase. This will place a tremendous burden on the Least Industrialized Nations. Already poor, and burdened by debt to the Most Industrialized Nations, they cannot afford to import much food. With 48 percent of the world's people living on less than $2 a day (Haub and Kent 2009), the coming starvation will be severe.

More Famines and Refugees. As food shortages get worse and starvation spreads, the world will face a flood of economic refugees. Neither the Least Industrialized Nations nor the Most Industrialized Nations will accept these hundreds of thousands of poor, uneducated, culturally foreign people who seek refuge and the opportunity for a more promising, abundant life. To take them in would heighten social tensions in their lands. Hundreds of thousands, if not millions, of dislocated people will live for decades in "temporary" refugee camps.

Riots, Revolutions, and Repression. As masses of people flock to the cities of the Least Industrialized in search of work and a better life, they will be met with rising food prices and food shortages. The people's response will be food riots and revolution. The national implication: To maintain social order, governments— encouraged by their elites, who want to maintain their privileges—will become more repressive. The international implication: Because political and civil disorder can upset the global balance of power that the Most Industrialized Nations try to maintain, the more powerful and wealthy nations will either encourage such repression or "look the other way" when it occurs.

In Sum: A Bleak Future for the World. If we paint a picture of the future of the world, we would have to use the color gray for desperate. Famine, malnutrition, and starvation, now striking at just a spot or two on the globe, are ready to stalk victims around the world. Pollution and other environmental destruction will also grow widespread as a bloated number of people try to carve out a meager living from the earth's fragile surface. As the Least Industrialized Nations struggle for food and other resources, they will be torn apart by riots and civil wars. War will also break out as nation fights nation for control of resources.

The Anti-Malthusians: The Optimistic View

"You are using the wrong color to paint our future," say the Anti-Malthusians. "We need bright colors to match our coming bright future," they say as they scoff at the conclusions of the New Malthusians.

Let's see why they take this position.

Population Shrinkage. If you want to peer into the future, they stress, review Figure 12.6 on page 407. Many nations have entered the fourth stage of the demographic transition, and their populations have begun to shrink. The world's other nations will also enter this fourth stage. Despite their current rapid population growth, they, too, will fill more coffins than cradles. As this process continues, the population of the world will begin to *shrink*. Future concerns will be the opposite of today's, shifting from what we can do about population growth to what we can do about population shrinkage.

Technology and Abundance. Our future will bring even greater abundance to the world's people. As education and knowledge increase, the world's nations will take better care of their natural systems (fishing grounds, forests, and grasslands). These are renewable resources, and, carefully managed, they will produce all that the world, even a growing one, will ever need.

In our emerging **biotech society**, bioengineering will produce pest-resistant plants that produce their own fertilizers. From gene splicing will come cereals that replace nitrogen in the soil, allowing farmers to bypass expensive petroleum-based fertilizers. We will produce low-fat cows and chickens that lay several eggs a day.

If this sounds unrealistic, note that biotech agriculture already exists. We have not just cloned animals, but we have also produced **designer animals**, gene-spliced farm animals that produce more meat and milk. We have corn that makes its own insecticide (Kilman 2006), goats that produce spider silk, and animals that produce medicine (Kristoff 2002;Osborne 2002). We have created the first human-made organism (Hotz 2010), another science-fiction accomplishment that heralds a future of infinite possibilities and abundance.

Which Will It Be?

Will the earth be filled with so many people that there is not enough food for them all? Or are the Anti-Malthusians right, and the world's nations will manage their resources, feed and clothe themselves, and provide an even higher standard of living for everyone? Could population shrinkage even replace the world's population explosion?

With such drastically contrasting viewpoints by experts who look at the same evidence, we cannot side with one group or the other. We can only await the future as it unfolds. Coming generations are going to wonder why we didn't see what is so obvious to them, but hindsight is so perfect—and frustrating for those of us who must look into the future from the present. We can only anticipate what is to come based on the evidence we have at the moment. Instead of either of the extreme futures that the New Malthusians and the Anti Malthusians foresee, another possibility is that we will end up with something in between.

MySocLab ✓ Study and Review on MySocLab

Summary and Review

1. The world is in the midst of an urban explosion. In 1900, about 13 percent of the world's population lived in cities. Today about 51 percent do. The U.S. total is closing in on 80 percent.
2. Symbolic interactionists emphasize that rundown areas of the city that appear disorganized and threatening to outsiders may be viable communities to those who live there. It takes an insider's frame of reference to understand these worlds.
3. According to functionalists, specialized zones develop as a city grows. Each zone meets certain needs of a city's residents, and people with distinctive characteristics live in each. Antagonisms result from the *invasion–succession cycle,* as one group displaces another. Urban problems are generally concentrated in the area adjacent to the central business district.
4. According to the conflict perspective, business leaders caused the decline of the inner city by influencing politicians to build new highways. This subsidized the relocation of their businesses to the suburbs and the shipping of their products. Suburban development came at the city's expense, removing jobs, reducing its tax base, and spurring flight of the middle class.
5. Violence from youth gangs and in our schools remains a problem.
6. The transition of urban power from whites to racial–ethnic minorities has gone smoothly. The *regional restratification* of the United States, a shift in population to the West and South, is leaving the cities of the North and East with fewer resources to deal with their urban problems.
7. *Demographers* study the size, composition, growth, and distribution of human populations. They disagree as to why Europe's population surged after 1750. Some cite improved public health, others a change in diet.
8. In 1798, Thomas Malthus predicted that the world's population would outstrip its food supply. His prediction is still controversial. The New Malthusians fear that the population of the world is entering the latter stages of an *exponential growth curve,* with most growth in the nations least able to afford it. They favor an immediate cutback in population. The Anti-Malthusians claim that the world is producing more than enough food; the problem is disrupted food production and distribution.
9. By applying symbolic interactionism, we can see why the birthrate is higher in the Least Industrialized Nations. There, children, who are viewed as a blessing from God, give the parents status in the present, and provide security for the future.
10. By applying functionalism, we can see that exporting medicine and public health techniques from the Most Industrialized Nations was a *latent dysfunction* for the Least Industrialized Nations. It upset the balance between their birthrates and death rates.
11. Conflict theorists stress that the hunger some nations experience is due to *food politics,* which intensify problems in the Least Industrialized Nations.
12. Demographers who take a New Malthusian position stress that the world will outstrip its food supply if we fail to reduce world population growth. Even if we attain zero population growth, because of *population momentum* it would take 50 to 70 years for the world's population to stabilize.
13. Demographers who take an Anti-Malthusian position argue that the earth can support many more people. Food production is outpacing population growth, and a growing population is a spur to greater productivity.
14. The New Malthusians recommend social policies that will curb population growth. The Anti-Malthusians advocate policies that encourage (or do not discourage) population growth. Both sides agree that we should stimulate agricultural development.
15. The New and Anti-Malthusians envision contrasting futures. The New Malthusians anticipate widespread hunger and starvation in the Least Industrialized Nations, which will lead to political repression. The Anti-Malthusians stress that the world's nations hold the potential for meeting human needs, that one day the world will face the problem of population shrinkage.

Key Terms

biotech society, 422
Chicago School of Sociology, 390
city, 387
concentric zone theory, 392
death rate, 405
demographic transition, 407
demography, 405
designer animals, 422
empowerment zones, 400
exponential growth curve, 406
food politics, 416
gentrification, 404
infanticide, 405
invasion–succession cycle, 392
latent dysfunctions, 415
megacity, 388
population pyramids, 414
population shrinkage, 408
regional restratification, 399
supergangs, 397
urban crisis, 389
urbanization, 387
zero population growth, 417

Thinking Critically About Chapter 12

1. Which do you think does the best job of explaining urban problems—the symbolic interactionist, functionalist, or conflict perspective? Why?
2. Do you think the New Malthusians or the Anti-Malthusians are right in their views of population and food? Why?
3. Which perspective (symbolic interactionism, functionalism, or conflict theory) do you think best explains the world's problems of population and food? Explain.

13 The Environmental Crisis

Listen to Chapter 13 on MySocLab

Learning Objectives. After reading this chapter, you should be able to:

13.1 Summarize environmental catastrophes of the past and describe the tragedy of the commons. **(p. 426)**

13.2 Explain what "everything is connected to everything else" means and how this lies at the root of environmental problems. **(p. 428)**

13.3 Discuss the perspectives that emerge when you apply symbolic interactionism, functionalism, and conflict theory to environmental problems. **(p. 429)**

13.4 Be able to summarize issues regarding pollution: air, global warming, land, water, chemical, nuclear, and food. **(p. 433)**

13.5 Compare how the pessimistic and optimistic environmentalists interpret research findings. **(p. 447)**

13.6 Know how frameworks of interpretation lead to different social policies. Summarize potential social policies to cope with environmental problems. **(p. 454)**

13.7 Discuss the likely future of environmental problems. **(p. 460)**

A great record. Seven years without a serious accident. British Petroleum (BP) officials decided that the captain and crew deserved recognition for their achievement in safety. Despite storms and other dangers in the Gulf of Mexico, the crew had drilled through 13,000 feet of rock—and this in deep water, 5,000 feet below the surface. A marvelous technological accomplishment.

The BP officials climbed out of the helicopter and scrambled aboard the *Deepwater Horizon*, a three-story-tall, intricate piece of machinery. The rig housed all the equipment needed to drill in deep water and to provide relative comfort for the 126 people who called it their temporary home.

An explosion blew doors off hinges, a fire melted steel equipment, and flames shot 250 feet into the night air.

After giving the ritual congratulations for the rig's commendable safety record, the executives would fly back to headquarters and relax in the more upscale surroundings that befit their status. The captain of the *Deepwater Horizon* would then direct the transfer of the oil rig to another site, where the crew would do more routine drilling, adding another well for a mechanized world increasingly hungry for energy.

But, first, there were a few details to take care of. One was to seal the pipe so no oil would escape. Protecting the environment and all that. A routine matter, something the experts did all the time. Then disconnect the rig and take off to the new assignment.

And, of course, bask in the warmth of the well-deserved commendation for safety.

Unfortunately, a little mishap stepped in to frustrate these plans.

An explosion blew doors off hinges, a fire melted steel equipment, and flames shot 250 feet into the night air. Some workers were crushed by flying objects. Others panicked and jumped off the drilling platform into the frigid waters 75 feet below. In addition to the many injured, eleven men died.

In the midst of the frenzy and confusion, while the dazed men in command were trying to figure out what to do, a 23-year-old realized that no one had sent a distress signal. She grabbed the radio and sent out a call over the frequency monitored by the Coast Guard. "Mayday! Mayday! This is *Deepwater Horizon.* We have an uncontrollable fire!"

On hearing her words, the Captain shouted, "I didn't authorize you to do that!"

"I'm sorry," she replied.

For months, the world watched as millions of barrels of oil gushed out of the broken pipe on the ocean floor, another in a long series of human-caused environmental disasters.

—Based on Blackmon et al. 2010.

The Problem in Sociological Perspective

13.1 Summarize environmental catastrophes of the past and describe the tragedy of the commons.

To better understand today's environmental problems, let's start with the distant past.

Environmental Destruction in the Past: The Myth of the Noble Savage

The Myth. In early history, so the story goes, humans lived in harmony with their environment. They considered themselves one with the water, earth, sky, animals, and plants. Unlike people today, who destroy their environment for shortsighted gains, people used the earth's resources wisely. Their presence did not disrupt the earth's natural systems. An old woman of the Wintu tribe explained:

> *The white people never cared for land or deer or bear. When we Indians kill meat, we eat it all up. When we dig roots, we make little holes. . . . We shake down acorns and pine nuts. We don't chop down trees. We only use dead wood. But the white people plow up the ground, pull up the trees, kill everything. . . . How can the spirit of the earth like the white man? . . . Everywhere the white man has touched it, it is sore. (Lee 1959:163)*

The problem is that this account of the past isn't true. Sociologist William Burch (1971) called the image of earlier people living in harmony with nature a myth. He says that the social sciences should stop perpetuating romanticized views of the past and set the matter straight.

Okay. Let's try. Let's peer into the past. When we do, we see humans extinguishing animals and destroying civilizations.

The Extinction of Animals. Carnivorous kangaroos, giant lizards, and horned turtles the size of automobiles used to roam Australia. These animals became extinct when humans set fire to trees and shrubs to keep warm or to clear the land (Hotz 1999). In North America, the early inhabitants burned forests to help them hunt and to control mosquitoes. Their fires and hunts wiped out three-fourths of the animals weighing more than 100 pounds (Lutz 1959; Martin 1967; Hotz 1999). Early humans may have extinguished more species of large animals than humans have in all the years since they invented writing.

Earlier destruction of the environment appears to have been so extensive that it even brought down entire civilizations. Environmentalists point out three examples.

The Mesopotamians. In the lush river basin of the Tigris and Euphrates, in what is now Iraq, the Mesopotamians developed a culture marked by achievements in architecture, mathematics, and science. Although scholars argue about the reason for the collapse of this civilization, one of the most persuasive explanations involves its extensive irrigation system. Providing abundant food, irrigation allowed Mesopotamian civilization to flourish. The irrigation system did not have drainage, however, and as irrigation water evaporated, it left salty water behind (McAnany and Yoffee 2009). Over the centuries, as this water seeped into the earth, the underground water table rose, making the land too salty for crops. Eventually, agriculture collapsed and, with it, the Mesopotamian civilization.

The Maya. In what today is Guatemala and Yucatán, another civilization met a similar fate. The Maya developed their culture over 17 centuries, reaching their peak in agriculture, architecture, and science about 900 A.D. Then, within decades, 90 percent of the Maya disappeared, their population dropping from 5 million to fewer than half a million. The cause may have been environmental destruction. Samples from lake beds indicate heavy soil erosion. As the population increased, the Maya cleared the land of trees. Topsoil washed from the denuded land, and with it went the agricultural productivity on which their civilization depended (Fernandez et al. 2005).

The Anasazi. In what is now Arizona and New Mexico, the Anasazi built roads, an irrigation system, and pueblos of stone and masonry (Budiansky 1987). Some pueblos were four or five stories high. One had 800 rooms. As their population grew, the Anasazi cut down so many trees in the canyons that they had to travel 50 miles or more to gather wood for fuel. With the forest stripped beyond its ability to replenish itself, the civilization collapsed.

The Tragedy of the Commons

Far from being thoughtful caretakers of their environment, earlier humans were like us. They destroyed limited resources thoughtlessly. Because today's civilizations are larger, however, our capacity for destruction is greater.

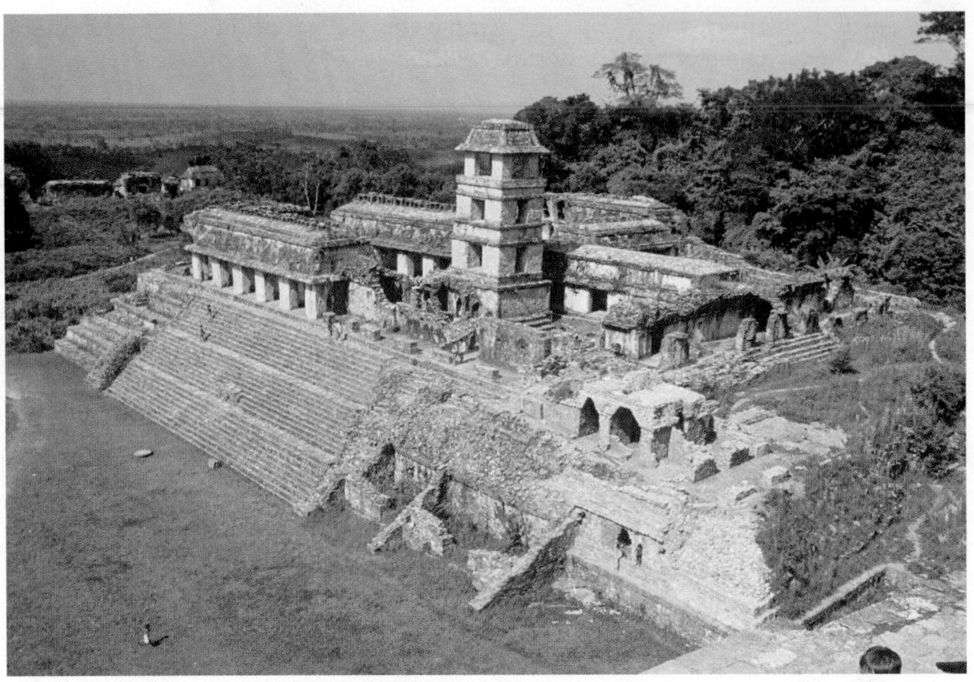
As with people today, earlier humans modified and also destroyed the natural environment. This photo of Palenque in Mexico is a remnant of the Maya civilization.

Central to understanding how humans can be so thoughtless is this principle: Self-interest often works against the logic of environmental preservation. Biologist Garrett Hardin (1968) told this parable called *the tragedy of the commons.*

> *Let us picture a pasture open to everyone. The number of cattle exactly matches the amount of available grass. Each herdsman, however, will seek to maximize his own gain. He thinks to himself: "If I add a cow to my herd, I will receive all the proceeds from the sale of this additional animal. The little overgrazing that this extra animal causes will be shared by all the other herdsmen."*
>
> *This herdsman adds another animal to his herd. This works, so he eventually adds another . . . and another. And, for the same reason, the other herdsmen who share the commons do the same. Each is part of a system that rewards individuals for increasing the size of their herds. And therein lays the tragedy of the commons. The pasture is limited, and additional stress eventually causes it—and the civilization that depends on it—to fail. As each pursues his or her own interest, all rush to their collective ruin.*

In Sum ▸ An irony of human life is that—just as in our opening vignette about the *Deepwater Horizon*—our efforts to improve life sometimes destroy the very environment on which life depends. Environmental destruction is not new; it is woven throughout human history.

The Scope of the Problem

13.2 Explain what "everything is connected to everything else" means and how this lies at the root of environmental problems.

You can see how humans of the past also harmed their environments, sometimes to such an extent that their civilizations collapsed. Will we do the same? For the first time in world history, our earth must meet the needs of more and more billions of people who demand an ever-increasing standard of living. Satisfying this incessant demand depends on our new technology, which, like the *Deepwater Horizon*, can fail us. Now that we have magnified our capacity for harm, the destruction of our environment is a frightening possibility.

Let's look at the scope of the problem today.

"Everything Is Connected to Everything Else"

When I first heard the words "Everything is connected to everything else," they caught me by surprise. As I contemplated this statement, I began to think about the world in a different way. Let's explore some of the implications of these words.

Seeing Connections. This simple statement, "Everything is connected to everything else," holds the key to understanding environmental problems. Let me begin by sharing a little story.

> *My grandfather lived on a remote farm in northern Minnesota, way up on the Canadian border. Yet in this remote spot his actions had global consequences. He used to spray his fields with DDT, the practice at the time. The excess DDT, a virulent pesticide, ran from the fields into a creek. The creek ran into a local river. From that little river, the DDT flowed into larger rivers, and then into one that led to the Mississippi River. In this, the major watershed of the United States, the DDT my grandfather had used joined thousands of chemicals from tens of thousands of farms and businesses. Flowing into New Orleans, these chemicals were responsible for the area's higher than average rates of cancer. From there, these chemicals flowed into the Atlantic, entering a food chain that ended up on people's dinner plates around the world.*

This is a homely little story, but I think it makes the point well. We tend to focus on our immediate world, the little things that affect us on an everyday level—our job or school, our families and friends, a local basketball game or picnic in the park. It is imperative that we raise our eyes and see interconnections. We need to become aware of how we are part of a global, interdependent system. Or, more simply put, how "everything is connected to everything else."

Threatening the Planet. Essential to our environmental problems are the population explosion we discussed in the previous chapter and the industrialization emphasized throughout this text, each accompanied by a relentless and global drive for higher living standards. If in this process we deplete our natural resources, as some past civilizations have, our civilization, too, will collapse. This is a fear of some *ecologists*, scientists who study **ecology**—the relationship between living things and their environment.

Of the many human actions that are upsetting our planet's precarious balance, a primary threat to humanity's welfare is **pollution**, the accumulation in the air, water, and land of substances harmful to living things. As we just saw, pollution goes far back in history, but in recent years it has intensified beyond anything the earth has ever seen. The world's industrial giants, which long have spewed their wastes onto our earth as though it were a sewer and not the heritage we are leaving coming generations, have been joined in this furious onslaught by China and India. Are we leaving a legacy of death for the future generations that will walk the earth's fragile surface? Let's see what the problem is and whether we can avoid this lethal legacy.

Looking at the Problem Theoretically

How did the environment become a social problem? We will use symbolic interactionism to trace this process. Then through functionalism, we will focus on the interdependence of people and their environment. Finally, we'll use the lens of conflict theory to examine the clashing interests of environmentalists and those who pollute.

13.3 Discuss the perspectives that emerge when you apply symbolic interactionism, functionalism, and conflict theory to environmental problems.

Symbolic Interactionism

How did the environment become a social problem? The dangers seem so obvious that you might wonder why I'm even asking such a question. Just thinking of the *Deepwater Horizon* catastrophe can bring chills up the spine. Environmental decay is all around us, from the wells that used to yield pure water, now closed because of benzene poisons, to pregnant women having to limit how much fish they eat because of mercury contamination.

But it was not always this way. Just two or three generations ago, people rarely thought of the environment as a problem. How, then, did this social problem emerge?

Objective Conditions But Little Subjective Concern. As we saw in Chapter 1, for a social problem to exist it isn't enough to have harmful objective conditions. We must also have subjective concerns. In the 1800s, hundreds of coal-fired steel plants in the United States created extensive and highly visible pollution. Coal dust seeped into houses, and people coughed up black grime. But people considered this a local matter, not part of a social problem. Grit on the streets, blackened skies, and hacking coughs were thought to be just unfortunate costs of economic survival.

Even the disappearance of animal species didn't produce a social problem. The passenger pigeon, during its mass annual migration, used to darken the skies for days. Its extinction in 1914 was seen as unfortunate—an interesting bit of history, perhaps—but not tragic. The near extinction of the bison was welcomed by many European Americans as a way to defeat the Indians.

From the way we look at the world today, such events strike a strange note. They make us wonder about the way people used to think. If pollution and extinction did not bring the widespread concerns that are part of the way we look at life, how, then, did they develop? This is just what sociologists Clay Schoenfeld, Robert Meier, and Robert Griffin (1979) decided to find out. Let's see what they discovered.

The Conservation Movement. Looking through the historical records, these sociologists found that the environment had already become an issue in the late 1800s. At that time, Theodore Roosevelt, president of the United States from 1901 to 1909, spearheaded a conservation movement. An avid hunter, Roosevelt had become concerned that the wildlife he liked to kill was disappearing from our wilderness areas (Gale 1972; Morrison et al. 1972). In one of the ironies of history, Roosevelt, who liked killing animals so much that he would roam Africa in search of elephants, tigers, and lions, supported legislation to establish our system of national parks, setting aside millions of acres for public use.

Teddy Roosevelt, president of the United States from 1901 to 1909, kneels proudly by a jaguar he shot in Brazil in 1913. The text explains how a concern for "conserving" wilderness areas to prevent hunters from running out of moving targets evolved into today's environmental movement.

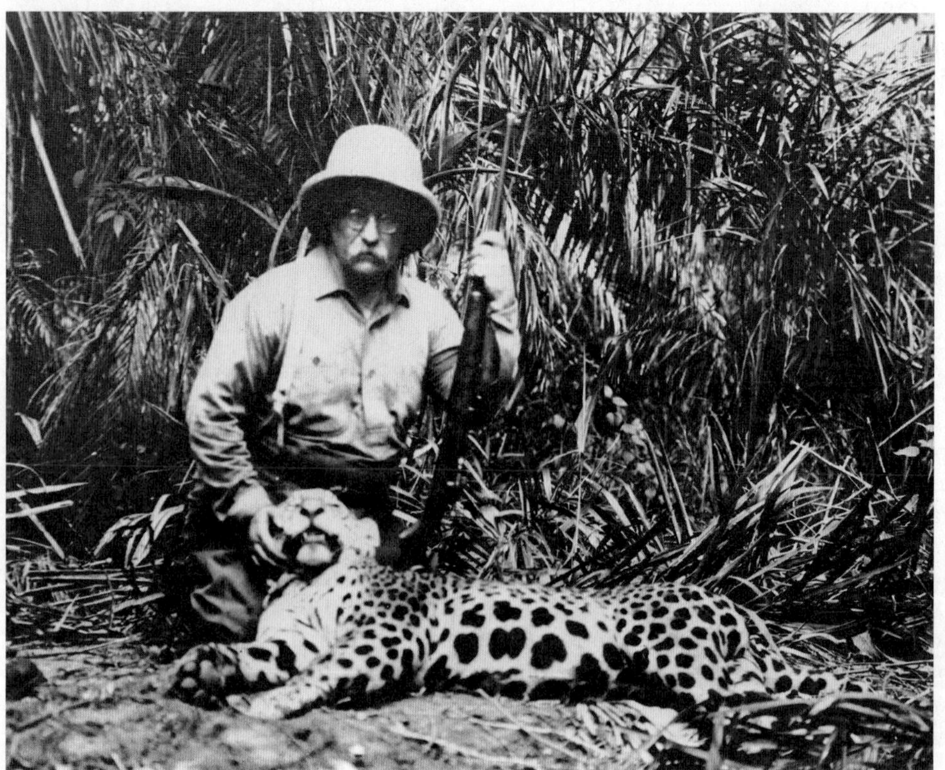

From Conservation to Environment. Obviously, conserving wilderness areas to make certain that hunters do not run out of moving targets is vastly different from concerns about the quality of our land, air, and water. How, then, did "conservation" change to "environmental concern"? Schoenfeld, Meier, and Griffin found five stages in this transition, beginning with professionals and ending with an aroused public:

1. *Professionals* were the first to become concerned about the environment. Geographers, especially, became troubled by our rampant use of natural resources. In 1959, they began to write journal articles about environmental problems and to present papers at their conventions.
2. *Interest groups* then began to form around specific issues.
3. *Government agencies,* aroused by the activities of the interest groups, began to issue environmental reports.
4. Then the *news media* discovered the issue. Like everyone else, it was difficult for reporters to understand that people, resources, and technology are all part of a single, larger system. They tended to see things in terms of unrelated, flashy news stories, such as a train wreck that spilled contaminants. As reporters began to understand the basic environmental principle—that "everything is connected to everything else"—they grew capable of connecting events and communicating these connections to the public.
5. *The public* was aroused by the stories in the mass media. In 1962, Rachel Carson published *The Silent Spring,* about the dangers of pesticides. This blockbuster alerted Americans to environmental hazards, but it focused on a single issue and didn't lead the public or the news media to explore the interconnections among environmental events. Then, in 1969 an oil well erupted off the coast of California, and the public was outraged when the oil blackened Santa Barbara's beautiful beaches (Davies and Davies 1975). Later that same year came the single most effective environmental message of the century—the first view of Earth from the moon. This stunning glimpse of the planet from the outside helped make the public aware that we all live on a fragile, finite "spaceship"—and that for our survival we had better take good care of it.

In Sum ▶ Symbolic interactionists focus on the symbols that we use to communicate our experiences in life, how our symbols create and maintain our ideas of reality. Our views of the environment changed radically as professionals, reporters, and the general public began to see individual events as interconnected parts of a global problem. This new perception transformed ideas of ourselves, our relationship with other living things, and even what we consider to be our place in the universe.

This change in how we symbolize ourselves and our world is still in process: We still have a difficult time connecting our individual actions with a distant future.

Functionalism

The Essence of Functionalism: Interconnections. The idea that everything is connected to everything else is becoming part of our intuitive understanding of the world. We all are aware that though we are individuals, we are part of a larger group. We also know that the small groups to which we belong are parts of a larger society and that our nation is part of a global network. Slowly, we are coming to grasp that we all are part of a global social system, that what each of us does—whether an individual, group, or nation—affects the others.

This picture of humanity forming a global network is a functional analysis. Each unit is part of a larger structure, with the activities of one part having functional or dysfunctional consequences for the other parts. The more technical term for this interconnected system in the environment is **ecosystem**—all life on the planet is interconnected in finely balanced cycles that take place on the thin layer of the earth's surface.

Poachers kill elephants so they can harvest their tusks and sell the ivory on the black market. The tusk carried by the park ranger in Tanzania was just confiscated from poachers.

The Ecosystem. Both biologists and sociologists who work on environmental problems stress how our survival depends on the earth's *ecosystem*, on delicately balanced connections among air, water, and soil. Oxygen in the air we breathe depends on plant life. Water, to be pure, depends on plants and microorganisms in our lakes and streams. The soil depends on biological processes if it is to produce food and fuel. Anything that disrupts this finely tuned, interconnected system threatens the balanced cycles on which our existence depends. And the major offender in disrupting the ecosystem? Humans—primarily through industrialization.

Functions and Dysfunctions of Industrialization. We humans are so intelligent and highly adaptable that we have expanded into every habitable region of the globe. The variety of cultures we developed has allowed us to adapt to mountains and plains, to deserts and oceans, even to steamy jungles and bitterly cold ice-bound regions. Our intelligence has allowed us to dominate the earth. In this process, we have domesticated plants and animals and harnessed the energy of animals and rivers, the sun and the wind.

It was our invention of the steam engine that allowed us to harness energy on a scale unknown in history. As we saw in Chapter 11, the Industrial Revolution that followed created countless new jobs and great wealth. Because of this revolution, the average person in the industrialized world enjoys a standard of living previously attained only by the wealthy. However, in our frenetic drive to produce material wealth, we thoughtlessly discarded our toxic industrial wastes in almost every corner of the earth. Perhaps the greatest irony in history is that we are repeating the folly of earlier peoples, with our pursuit of a better life damaging the environment that allows us life in the first place.

In Sum ▸ Functionalists focus on how the parts of a social system are interconnected. As with earlier civilizations such as the Mesopotamian, the Maya, and the Anasazi, our economic and political systems depend on a fragile ecosystem. The failure of our ecosystem would mean the collapse of our society. Although we still have problems conceptualizing this, we have begun to think of ourselves as part of a complex, living machine called the environment.

Conflict Theory

Have you ever heard any group defend dirty water or filthy air? Of course not. Yet there are opposing sides on environmental issues. While some view us as being on the verge of catastrophe and stress that we need immediate and stringent regulation, others view laws to protect the environment as arbitrary and irrational controls over private actions. Let's look at this conflict.

On One Side: Environmental Groups. On one side are the groups organized to fight what they view as environmental threats. These environmental action groups consist of such organizations as the Izaak Walton League, Greenpeace, the National Wildlife Federation, the Sierra Club, Americans for Safe Food, and Earth First! Here's how the Izaak Walton League expresses this position:

> *There is no justification for water pollution. The people of the United States are entitled to wholesome surface and groundwater, usable for all human needs (Izaak Walton League 2000:11). [We need to] toughen drinking water standards to protect people against cancer-causing chemicals and deadly microorganisms (Izaak Walton League 2009:17).*

Environmental action groups have become a powerful political force. With chapters across the nation, these groups maintain lobbyists in Washington and state capitals, they promote legislation aggressively, and they hire lawyers to fight environmental cases in the courts.

On the Other Side: Polluters. The industrial polluters face a dilemma. No one would tolerate them saying that they favor pollution. Yet pollution controls are expensive and add nothing to the value of their products. Manufacturers in the Most Industrialized Nations must compete with businesses in the Least Industrialized Nations that enjoy a double-edged advantage: Their labor costs are low and their governments don't require them to install costly pollution controls in the manufacturing process.

To remain competitive, U.S. manufacturers lobby in Washington and the state capitals to try to keep pollution laws from being passed or, if passed, to make sure their enforcement is without teeth. You probably know how strongly the automobile industry has opposed legal standards that require higher mileage. Their position is reported regularly in the news. Some of this is just public posturing, with the real decisions made behind stage. Consider this historical example of how the automobile industry used its political connections so they could continue to pollute:

> *In 1951, when it was discovered that automobiles were the major cause of smog in Los Angeles, the suggestion was made to develop electric cars. The auto industry formed a committee to study this proposal. The White House stacked the committee with representatives from the auto and oil industries. Their "surprising" conclusion: a recommendation against even doing research on electric vehicles. (Davies and Davies 1975)*

Sometimes industry's political clout is truly amazing. As the Thinking Critically box on the next page illustrates, the industrial giants have even been able to get laws passed that make pollution profitable.

In Sum ▶ As conflict theorists examine environmental problems, they focus on colliding interests. The conflict is between the environmental activists who want to eliminate what they see as dangers to public welfare and the groups that see profits more important than pollution. Over and over, those who campaign to develop a healthier society run head on into groups that see the cure as worse than the problem.

Research Findings: Pollution

13.4 Be able to summarize issues regarding pollution: air, global warming, land, water, chemical, nuclear, and food.

How badly has our environment been hurt? Let's examine the pollution of our air, land, water, and food supply and look at energy and resources. We also want to consider whether the environmental crisis has been exaggerated.

Let's begin with air pollution.

Thinking Critically about Social Problems

How to Get Paid to Pollute: Corporate Welfare and Big Welfare Bucks

Welfare is a highly controversial topic in the United States. It arouses criticism among the wealthy and the middle class, who view welfare recipients as parasites. But have you heard about *corporate welfare?*

Corporate welfare describes handouts given to corporations. A state will reduce a company's taxes if it will remain within the state. A state may even offer land or buildings at a bargain price to a business because it is going to hire workers.

Corporate welfare even goes to companies that are known polluters. Borden Chemicals in Louisiana has buried hazardous wastes without a permit and released clouds of chemicals so thick that the police have had to shut down the highway that runs near the plant. Borden even contaminated the groundwater beneath its plant, threatening the aquifer that provides drinking water for residents of Louisiana and Texas.

Borden's pollution has cost the company dearly: $3.6 million in fines, $3 million to clean up the groundwater, and $400,000 for local emergency response units. That's a hefty $7 million. But when we take into account corporate welfare, the company didn't make out so badly. Its $15 million in reduced and canceled property taxes brought Borden a net gain of $8 million (Bartlett and Steele 1998). And that's not counting the savings the company racked up by not having to properly dispose of its toxic wastes in the first place.

Louisiana, which offers an incentive to help start-up companies, defines "start-up" somewhat strangely. Although Exxon Corporation (now Exxon Mobil, the largest corporation in the United States) opened for business about 125 years ago, Louisiana canceled $213 million in property taxes under its start-up program. Another little "start-up" was Shell Oil Company, which had $140 million slashed from its taxes (Bartlett and Steele 1998). You might be familiar with some of the other "start-ups": International Paper, Dow Chemical, Union Carbide, Boise Cascade, Georgia Pacific, and Procter & Gamble.

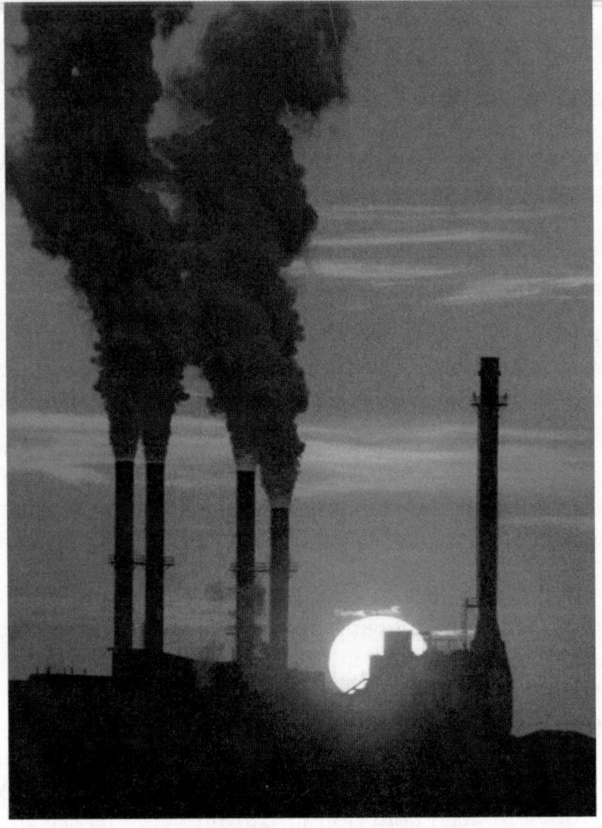

You might want to think about this photo the next time you use sugar. This sugar factory in Florida is thought to pollute the everglades.

For Your Consideration

Apply the functionalist, symbolic interactionist, and conflict perspectives to corporate welfare. Which do you think provides the best explanation of corporate welfare? Why?

Air Pollution

Air Pollution Can Kill.

A "killer smog," a mixture of smoke and fog, settled over Donora, Pennsylvania, during the last five days of October 1948. Of the 12,300 people who lived in this steel mill town, about half (5,910) became sick. Another 1,440 were "severely affected." Seventeen died.

Front-page news stories compared Donora to the Meuse Valley in Belgium, where 60 people died in 1930. Both were heavily industrialized, and both had ***thermal inversions****, a layer of cold air sealing in a lower layer of warm air. Thermal inversions trap harmful smoke, exhaust, and particles.*

The residents' reactions sound hauntingly familiar. The local doctor described the deaths as murder, but the superintendent of the steel factory said, "I can't conceive how our plant has anything to do with the condition. There has been no change in the process since 1915." The workers, who saw dense smoke and fog as part of their way of life, said, "That smoke coming out of those stacks is putting bread and butter on our tables." And the public? Most just shrugged their shoulders and went about their business. (Bowen 1972)

Four years later, a smog settled on London, *killing 4,000 people* in just 5 days (Thorsheim 2004). People grew fearful, not knowing what was happening. Gradually, facts emerged about **air pollution**, poisons in the air that accumulate in the body. Besides causing eye, nose, and throat irritations, air pollution can cause bronchitis, emphysema, and lung cancer. As we have seen, it can even bring sudden death.

Causes of Air Pollution. Other than by-products from burning coal, which, as you've seen, can be severe, what causes air pollution? Let's find out.

Fossil Fuels ▸ The main cause of air pollution is the burning of **fossil fuels**—substances that are derived from living things. Besides coal, examples include wood, petroleum, and natural gas. As power plants and factories burn fossil fuels to produce electricity and manufacture the goods we consume, pollutants pour into the air. The worst polluter, however, is the internal combustion engine. The exhausts of cars, trucks, and buses emit poisons—sulfur dioxide, nitrogen oxide, hydrocarbons, and carbon monoxide. Vehicles also leave behind **carcinogens** (cancer-causing substances) from the asbestos in their brake linings.

Watch on
MySocLab Video:
PBS: Planet Forward-
Fossil Fuels and Beyond

Pollution is almost always unintended. On occasion, however, pollution is the result of a deliberate, spiteful act. The most dramatic example occurred in 1991 after U.S.-led forces defeated the Iraqi army in Kuwait. During their retreat, the Iraqi military ignited 600 oil wells, storage tanks, and refineries. The soot from the fires circled the globe (Naj 1992).

Waste Incineration ▸ A second major source of air pollution is burning waste. The burning of plastics is especially damaging to our health because it creates PCBs (polychlorinated biphenyls), a potent toxin. Plastics are not **biodegradable**; that is, they do not disintegrate after being exposed to normal bacteria. Even steel rusts, but plastics endure almost indefinitely. Burning is one way to get rid of them.

Fluorocarbon Gases ▸ A third source of air pollution is fluorocarbon gases. These gases are thought to damage the **ozone shield**, the layer in the earth's upper stratosphere that screens out much of the sun's ultraviolet rays. High-intensity ultraviolet rays harm most life forms. In humans, they cause skin cancer and cataracts; in plants, they reduce growth and cause genetic mutations. When the dangers of fluorocarbon gases were realized, their use in aerosol cans, refrigerators, and air conditioners was reduced or eliminated. Scientists expect that the ozone layer will repair itself, but it will take another 60 years (U.S. Environmental Protection Agency 2008).

Changes in Air Pollution. For several decades, environmentalists have protested, laws have been passed and enforced, and pollution control devices have been added to manufacturing processes. Has this made any difference in the air that you and I breathe? Look at Figure 13.1 on the next page. As you can see, we have made huge strides in cleaning up the air. Emissions of sulfur dioxide and volatile organic compounds have been cut sharply. The most stunning change is the amount of lead in our air, now less than 1 percent of what it was in 1970. The primary reason for the reduction of lead is lead-free gasoline. (Gasoline used to contain lead as an anti-knock additive.) Despite these sharp improvements, we still have a long way to go. About 124 million Americans live in counties that don't meet air quality standards (EPA 2012).

Global Warming: Scientific Controversy

Basic Background. Carbon dioxide and water vapor form an invisible blanket around the globe that allows sunlight to enter, but traps heat. Without this global blanket, temperatures would plummet, and the earth would be unable to support life. If the

FIGURE 13.1 ▸ U.S. Air Quality

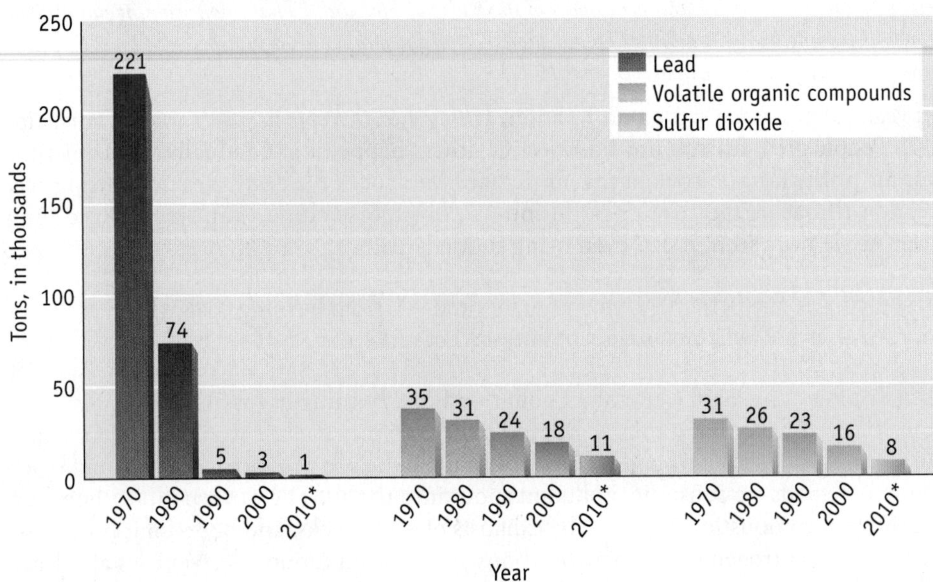

*Latest year available.

Source: By the author. Based on *Statistical Abstract of the United States* earlier years and 2010:Tables 360, 361; 2013:Tables 379, 380; Environmental Protection Agency 2012a.

blanket grows too thick, however, in what is called the **greenhouse effect**, it will trap too much heat and bring devastating consequences for our environment.

Explore on **MySocLab Activity:** NPR: Climate Connections

Most climate scientists, *climatologists*, agree that the cause of global warming is an increase in carbon dioxide because of human activity, and that the consequences will be severe. We burn more fossil fuels than humans did in the past, releasing more carbon dioxide into the air. In effect, the carbon dioxide smudges the atmospheric window through which our earth's daily heat escapes to outer space. Environmentalists refer to the earth's higher temperatures as **global warming**.

As the earth warms, the glaciers are starting to melt. Here is just one:

The world's largest tropical glacier is in Peru. This 7.5-mile-long mountain glacier, 18,600 feet above sea level, often gets snow but never rain. The Quelcayya, as it is called, is shrinking by about 100 feet a year. As the ice receded, researchers discovered a moss-like plant that had been frozen in the glacier. Carbon dating showed the plant to be over 5,000 years old. The last time this plant wasn't covered with snow and ice, the Egyptians were busy inventing hieroglyphics. (Regaldo 2004)

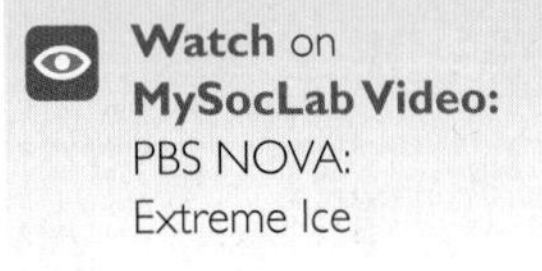

Watch on **MySocLab Video:** PBS NOVA: Extreme Ice

The Warnings. With the earth warming and the glaciers melting, climatologists have issued grave warnings. They say that if we don't reduce the output of carbon dioxide, the world will face such severe consequences as these (Brown 2001; Parmesan and Yohe 2003; National Academy of Sciences 2010):

1. The climate boundaries will shift about 400 miles north, resulting in a longer growing season in the United States, Canada, and Russia.
2. Summers will be hotter, and there will be more forest fires, droughts, floods, and outbreaks of diseases—malaria, dengue fever, cholera.
3. Many species of plants and animals will become extinct.
4. Problems in the Least Industrialized Nations will be worse, as they have fewer resources to meet the crisis.
5. We will have more tornados and hurricanes.
6. As the polar ice caps melt, the oceans will rise several feet, eroding the world's shorelines. This will obliterate some island nations. One of these nations, Kiribati,

Likely consequences of global warming are described in the text. One is a rise of the oceans because of the melting of glaciers, such as this one in Norway.

is making plans to move its population of 106,000 to Fiji, which is 1,500 miles away (Perry 2012). The ministry of tourism of another, the Maldives, suggested that their national slogan should be "Come see us while we're still here." (Dickey and Rogers 2002)

The Scientific Skeptics. Another group of climatologists reply, "Not so fast. We need to be more cautious in drawing conclusions." This group used to argue that temperatures fluctuate too much to conclude that we are experiencing global warming, but most have given up this argument. Most of these skeptics now agree that global warming is real, but they point out that we do not know that its cause is human activity (Borenstein 2011). Their most compelling argument is that throughout history the earth has warmed and cooled, with no consistent correlation with carbon dioxide. During the earth's ice age, the atmosphere had an even higher concentration of carbon dioxide than it does today. We are experiencing another of the earth's natural warm/cold cycles. The causes could be changes in sun cycles or sea currents or in the cosmic rays that hit the earth (Broad 2006a).

Some of these scientific skeptics agree that the current warming is partially due to the Industrial Revolution, but this is not a cause for alarm. A former president of the National Academy of Sciences said that the increased carbon dioxide will increase plant growth and be "a wonderful and unexpected gift from the industrial revolution" (Stevens 1998). A group of scientists that takes this view concurs, saying, "A warmer world will be a safer and healthier world for humans and wildlife alike" (Idso and Singer 2010).

Healthy Debate. Do you recall the pessimists and the optimists we discussed in the previous chapter, whose views of the world's population and food are almost polar opposites? We have something similar here, but with different groups of pessimistic and optimistic scientists. Here, too, each is looking at the same evidence and drawing different conclusions. Lines between these groups have hardened, and, quite unscientifically, they have thrown nasty names back and forth. The group that says global warming comes from human activity has accused the other of being charlatans for industry, while the group that points to natural cycles has accused the other of faking data.

Beyond the rhetoric of the hardened views, we can expect that out of this controversy the facts will become apparent. In this open debate, climatologists will come to the right conclusions regarding global warming, its cause, its negative and positive consequences, and what actions will be appropriate.

FIGURE 13.2 ▸ Ounces of Solid Waste Each American Generates Each Day

These totals are based on the solid wastes from residential and commercial trash collections. The totals do not include mining, agricultural, and industrial processing, demolition and construction wastes, sewage sludge, or junked autos and obsolete equipment.

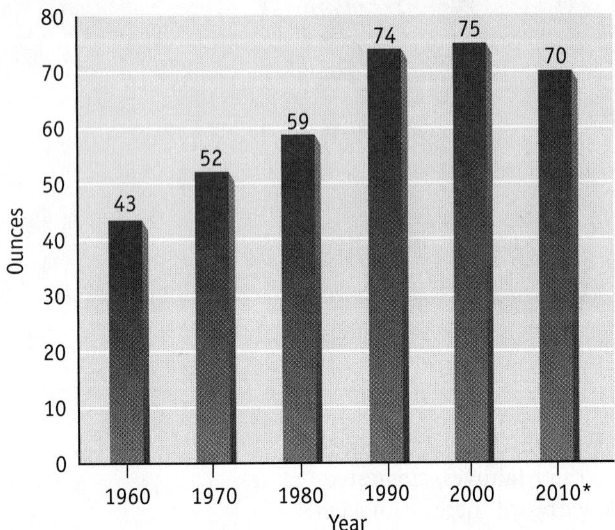

*Latest year available.

Source: By the author. Based on *Statistical Abstract of the United States* 1994:Table 370; 2013:Table 384.

Land Pollution

It was such a beautiful day that Tamara and Bill decided to skip their social problems class and have a picnic on the beach. As they walked hand in hand, they found that they had to step around sewage that had washed ashore the night before. Their stomachs turned when they saw blood samples and contaminated needles that must have come from a hospital. All they could think of was AIDS.

They decided to leave—and didn't eat their lunch.

Garbage. If you look at Figure 13.2, you will see how much garbage each American produces each day. At 4.4 pounds per person per day, we produce about *500 billion pounds* of garbage each year. About a pound and a half of each person's average daily waste is recovered (paper, glass, metals, plastics, rubber, wood), but each day the average American sends between two and three pounds of solid waste to landfills (*Statistical Abstract* 2013:Table 384). From this figure, you can see something positive, that we are now producing less garbage than 20 years ago.

Humans have always had the problem of what to do with their wastes. They usually just dumped them nearby. We can identify many Stone Age villages by the mounds of oyster and mussel shells their inhabitants left behind. Our cities used to dump their waste into a pit, light it, and forget it. But with today's awareness of how burning garbage pollutes the air and adds to global warming, this is no longer allowed. Cities must now use garbage incinerators—fancifully called *resource recovery plants*—that are approved by the Environmental Protection Agency (EPA). With federal regulations requiring utilities to buy power generated by these garbage-burning plants, they partially pay for themselves.

Some towns still bury their wastes in gullies and swampy areas, but chemicals from the garbage are seeping into the groundwater. With safe landfills filling up, some eastern states tried to ship their problem to the Midwest. When these states refused to accept the garbage, the case went to the Supreme Court, which ruled that the states could not refuse the shipments. This decision opened landfills across the Midwest to the hard-pressed, more populated eastern states (Bailey 1992). As a consequence, some Midwestern states have become the "garbage cans" of other states.

Strip Mining. Another problem of land pollution is **strip mining**, which occurs where coal lies so close to the surface that it can be retrieved by stripping away the soil. Strip mining, which has scarred more than 5 million acres of U.S. land, not only makes the land ugly but also poisons it. When the land is stripped bare of its forest and plant life, salt leeches from the coal. Although current federal regulations require mining companies to return land to its original condition, many believe that doing so is impossible. Today the western areas of the United States and huge areas in Canada are vulnerable, for vast amounts of shale and coal lie just beneath the surface.

Water Pollution

Drinking Water. Many people are concerned—and rightly so, it turns out—about the quality of their drinking water. Let's see if we can zero in and pinpoint the problem. Of the *60,000 chemicals* used in the United States, some of which cause cancer, how many are regulated by the EPA to make certain that our drinking water is safe? You might find this hard to believe, but the answer is 91 (Wall 2010).

I used to live in a town located on the banks of the Mississippi River. Although thousands of upstream industries discharge their wastes into this river, my town retrieved its drinking water from it. To "purify" this filthy river water, the water company filtered out the larger objects (condoms and worms and the like) and then added more chemicals to the rest. Hundreds of other towns along the Mississippi do the same. Water treated in this way meets the standards set by the EPA. The drinking water of one of ten Americans doesn't meet even these woeful health standards (Duskin 2003).

Acid Rain.

> *A silent spring fell over parts of the western Adirondacks. Brook trout vanished from Big Moose Lake—along with crayfish and frogs, loons, kingfishers, and most of the swallows. Pollutants from Midwest factories left more than 300 lakes devoid of fish (Blumenthal 1981; Ehrlich and Ehrlich 1981; Stevens 1996).*

How do factory emissions in the Midwest destroy lakes in Canada and the northeastern states? The story starts with a problem that power plants in the Midwest tried to solve. When these plants burn coal and oil to produce electricity, they produce a lot of smoke. To protect their communities, the utility companies built more than 175 smokestacks 500 feet tall or higher. This solved the problem—or so it seemed. Sent high into the air, the pollutants from these "megastacks" don't land in the local communities. They remain aloft, far out of sight, for days, even weeks. The smoke's "chemical soup" contains sulfur dioxide and nitrogen oxide, which moisture in the air turns into sulfuric and nitric acid. Spilling across the Canadian border, this "airborne sewer" falls to the earth as **acid rain**.

Acid rain is not new, although its industrial cause is. Tests on ice samples from glaciers show heavy concentrations of acids 350 years ago. This was before industrialization, so this acid rain probably came from volcanic activity and organic decomposition (LaBastille 1979; Lynch 1980). Our intensified use of fossil fuels, however, has transformed acid rain into a global social problem. Today, acid rain damages crops and forests around the world, as well as such world-famous landmarks as the Colosseum in Rome, the Taj Mahal in India, and the Lincoln Memorial in Washington. Acid rain also produces chemical reactions that release toxic metals into the public water supply, causing about 1,000 deaths a year (EPA 2009).

In Figure 13.1 on page 436, you saw how sulfur dioxide emissions have been cut. Although this has reduced acid rain, the problem continues. Some lakes are regaining the chemical balance that will support plants and animals, but for reasons yet unknown, some of the lakes are not recovering (EPA 2009).

The Great Lakes. The Great Lakes of the United States form the largest surface freshwater system on Earth (EPA 2012b). This giant network of waterways—Huron, Ontario, Michigan, Erie, and Superior—contains *1 of every 5 gallons of the entire world's surface freshwater.* The pollution comes when toxic chemicals used or produced by industry enter the Great Lakes. Then, as the EPA (2012b) puts it:

> *Small bottom-dwellers ingest the toxins as they feed in the mud. As larger animals eat these smaller animals, the toxins move up the food chain, with their concentrations getting higher, often thousands of times higher. Fish at the top of the food chain, such as lake trout and salmon, can be unsafe to eat in some areas because of the heavy concentrations of toxic substances in their tissues.*

Disturbed by this pollution, environmentalists pressured Congress, which mandated that the EPA clean up these lakes. The concentration of heavy metals has been reduced somewhat, but the problem is so huge that it may take generations to solve (EPA 2012b).

When toxic chemicals in the Great Lakes were brought to the public's attention, an additional problem surfaced. Foreign species, some of which had hitchhiked across the world, had entered the lakes from the ballast of boats. In the Great Lakes, these species no longer face the forces that keep them in check in their natural habitat. Without this, they multiply, threatening the native species. Zebra mussels, for example, have destroyed almost all native clams (EPA 2012b). Following pressure from environmentalists, the Environmental Protection Agency is working on this problem, too. Among their efforts is building an electric barrier to prevent invasive species from entering the Great Lakes.

Oil Spills. Long gone are the days when you could insert a pipe in the ground in Texas and watch oil come gushing out. Those oil gushers have been replaced with high-tech geophysical exploration for oil in remote recesses on our planet. One of these remote spots is the deep ocean floor, bringing the consequences recounted in this chapter's opening vignette. Through miscalculations, the *Deepwater Horizon* spewed about 200 million gallons into the Gulf of Mexico.

Oil must also be transported from where it is pumped to where it can be refined into products such as gasoline, diesel, and lubricants. Accidents also happen during its transportation. Until 1989, the worst oil spill occurred when the *Exxon Valdez*, a 1,000-foot-long supertanker, ran aground. When this supertanker ruptured, it leaked 11 million gallons of crude oil into the pristine waters of Alaska's Prince William Sound, fouling 1,300 miles of untouched coastline (Wells and McCoy 1989; Rosen 1999). Less dramatic, but thunderous in its consequences, is oil lost from pipelines. In 1994, a pipeline in Siberia burst, dumping *300 million gallons* onto the tundra and into rivers (Rosett 1994; Garelik 1996). This spillage goes down as the worst in human history, a record that we hope will never be broken.

Chemical Pollution

Explore on **MySocLab** **Activity:** Toxic Town

Hundreds of families unwittingly purchased homes next to a chemical waste dump that had been covered over with clay. A grade school was built there, too. Over the years, deadly poisons seeped into the yards, homes, and the school playground. Common among the residents were urinary tract infections, swollen joints, headaches, and fragile bones. So were miscarriages, stillbirths, and kidney, lung, and bladder cancers. There were also the strange births. One girl was born deaf, with a cleft palate, and two rows of teeth. Another child was born with one kidney, and yet another with three ears (Brown n.d.; Shribman 1989; James 2008).

This was *Love Canal*, a little community in the state of New York. The homes had been built next to a dump site where Hooker Chemical Company had buried 44 million pounds of waste. The home buyers didn't know about the chemical waste. They learned of it only after the health problems—and the strange births—led to an investigation.

A house in Love Canal.

In the 1970s, the federal government ordered all pregnant women and children under age 2 to move out of Love Canal (Brody 1976; Brown n.d.). As health problems continued, in 1980 the government relocated 710 families and then bulldozed their homes (Shribman 1989). The parent company of Hooker Chemical paid restitution of $129 million. Health problems—especially cancer at an early age—continue to plague the children who were born at Love Canal (James 2008).

Not a single barrel of the 20,000 tons of chemical wastes has been moved out of Love Canal. A fence has been built around it, though.

Producing Chemicals. The production of chemicals is essential to the world's welfare. Without them, we would not be able to feed our billions of people or enjoy the technological marvels that we take for granted, from our automobiles to televisions and computers. The production of these chemicals, though essential, poses dangers that we seldom think about. In our Global Glimpse box below, let's turn our attention to this for a moment.

Disposing of Chemical Wastes. What is the right way to get rid of chemical wastes? U.S. industries dispose of about 4 billion pounds of toxic wastes each year (*Statistical Abstract* 2013:Table 388). Companies used to simply burn their wastes or

A Global Glimpse

The Roulette Wheel of Environmental Disaster

While a scattering of people waited for early-morning trains in Bhopal, India, a maintenance worker at the nearby Union Carbide plant heard rumbling in a storage tank. Then came the sound of cracking concrete. The tank held methyl isocyanate (MIC), a chemical used in making pesticides. A white gas began seeping from the tank, then spread through the region on the northwesterly wind.

At the Vijoy Hotel near the railroad station, sociologist Swapan Saha woke up with a terrible pain in his chest. "It was like breathing fire," he said. Wrapping a damp towel around his nose and mouth, Saha went outside to investigate. Scores of victims lay dead on the platform at the train station. "I thought at first there must have been a gigantic railway accident," he recalled. Then he noticed a pall of white smoke on the ground, and an acrid smell in the air. People were retching, vomiting, and defecating uncontrollably. Dogs, cows, and water buffaloes also lay on the ground, twitching in death agonies. Saha staggered back to the hotel. Half blind by now, he sat down to write a farewell letter to his wife.

Saha survived. More than 2,500 others did not. (Whitaker 1984; Spaeth 1989)

A woman shows a photo taken of her before she was blinded by Union Carbide's toxic chemicals at Bhopal.

Not all the deaths occurred immediately. The leak contaminated the area's groundwater, claiming more lives over the following years. The Indian government estimates that this accident caused 5,000 to 22,000 deaths (Hertsgaard 2004; Bhattacharya 2012). Twenty-six years later, in 2010, Indian courts convicted eight Union Carbide officials of negligent homicide. They were each sentenced to two years in prison—even though one of the individuals had already died (Magnier and Rana 2010). Two years later, U.S. courts ruled that Union Carbide was not responsible for cleaning up the toxic mess. That was the responsibility of its Indian subsidiary. (Bhattacharya 2012)

Although this event took place in India, an accident like this could happen anywhere that chemicals are manufactured. As an expert on workplace safety put it, "It's like a giant roulette wheel. This time the marble came to a stop in a little place in India. But the next time it could be the United States" (Whitaker 1984).

For Your Consideration

Do you think that a similar accident could happen in the United States? Why or why not? What steps do you think we should take to prevent such an accident?

pour them into the rivers and oceans, polluting our air and water. Today, they still do, but under the watchful eye of the Environmental Protection Agency. Some wastes are burned in approved containers, while others are injected into the Earth. Others are still buried with an "out-of-sight-out-of-mind" mentality, blindly shoved into dumps. As you saw with Love Canal, this certainly doesn't get rid of the problem. The containers buried in the dumps—now fancifully called landfills—slowly disintegrate, allowing lethal chemical wastes to rise to the surface or to leach into rivers and groundwater.

The EPA doesn't allow all chemicals to be buried. Some must go through expensive processes to render them harmless. This has created opportunities for organized crime (Brown n.d.). Legal disposal of a tankful of chemical waste might cost $40,000, but criminals will dispose of it for half that amount. Their disposal methods haven't exactly been approved by the EPA. They drive an 8,000-gallon tank truck full of liquid waste to a wooded area and dump it in 8 minutes flat. The industrial company that produced the waste (a legitimate business) feigns ignorance. On 21 acres of marshland on Staten Island, men "well known to law enforcement agents" deposited 700,000 gallons of waste oil in barrels. In North Carolina, one "midnight dumper" simply opened the spigots on a tankload of PCBs and then drove until the tank was empty.

Hazardous Waste Sites: The National Priority List. With thousands of toxic dump sites, chemical wastes are a ticking time bomb. You can check to see how your state ranks on the Social Map below. This map shows the *worst* of the many hazardous waste sites in the United States, those so hazardous they have been placed on a national priority cleanup list. These sites pose such a risk to people's health that they need *immediate* attention. The sites shown on this map will be cleaned up *when* and *if* Congress appropriates money to do so. Since these sites remain untouched year after year, some surrounded by fences to keep people out, it is obvious that the priorities of Congress do not lie here.

FIGURE 13.3 ▸ Hazardous Waste Sites on the National Priority List

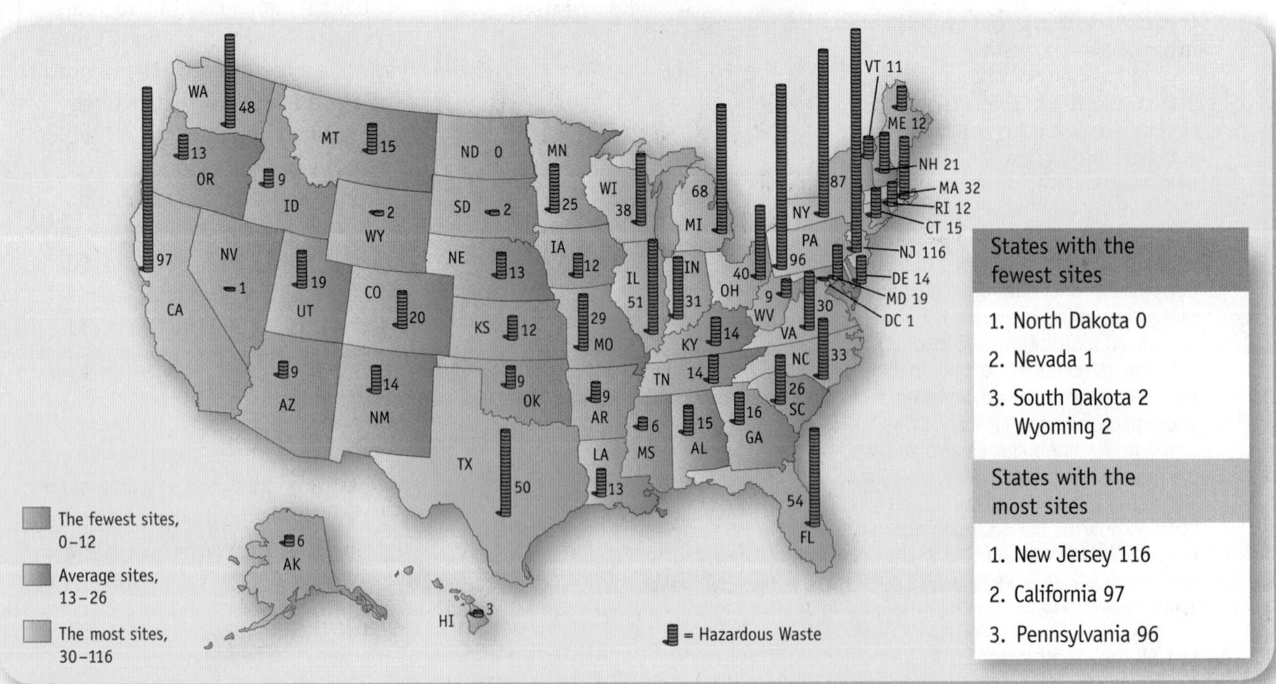

Source: By the author. Based on *Statistical Abstract of the United States* 2013:Table 391.

Nuclear Pollution

The World's First Nuclear Waste Disaster: Kyshtym. Russia's Ural River Valley is a remote place, and it was here that the Soviet government decided to develop its first atomic bomb. In Kyshtym, the Soviets built a nuclear reactor to obtain plutonium. Accounts vary as to how they disposed of the millions of gallons of nuclear waste produced by this reactor. Some say they bored holes into the ground and poured the liquid wastes into them (Solomon and Rather 1980). Others report that they piled the waste onto a dry lake bed (Clines 1998). Perhaps they did both. Either way, a chemical reaction took place. In 1957, the waste exploded, sending radioactive dust high into the air.

The radioactive fallout from the explosion devastated the area. Maps before the explosion show thirty villages and towns around Kyshtym. On maps printed after 1958, those communities are nowhere to be seen. Thousands of people had to be evacuated permanently from a 1,000-square-kilometer area.

The Puny Nuclear Reactor Accident: Three Mile Island. In comparison, the worst nuclear accident in the United States was puny. In 1979 at Three Mile Island, Pennsylvania, a reactor leaked, people panicked, and 100,000 residents fled (Rabinovitz 1998). The news was alarming, but the contamination was minimal, and people moved back to their homes. Despite the fright it caused, this minor loss of coolant seems to have exposed people to less radiation than they get at the dentist's office (Williams 1980).

The World's Worst Nuclear Reactor Disaster: Chernobyl. Then we have the other extreme, this one, like Kyshtym, also in the former USSR. This is what happened at Chernobyl, in the Ukraine:

> *Meltdown. The word froze in the mouth of the operating engineer. An explosion had blown a 1,000-ton steel cover off a nuclear reactor, obliterating the containment structure.*
>
> *It was too late to flee: No one can outrun deadly radiation. For 10 days, the world watched the drama, the fire raging and radioactive materials spewing into the air.*
>
> *Chernobyl's cloud of radioactive gases migrated slowly around the world. In 2 weeks, its airborne waste was detected in the United States and Tokyo (Flavin 1987). Canadians were advised not to drink rainwater, and farmers in Great Britain were ordered not to grow certain crops because of the radioactive fallout (Dufay n.d.).*

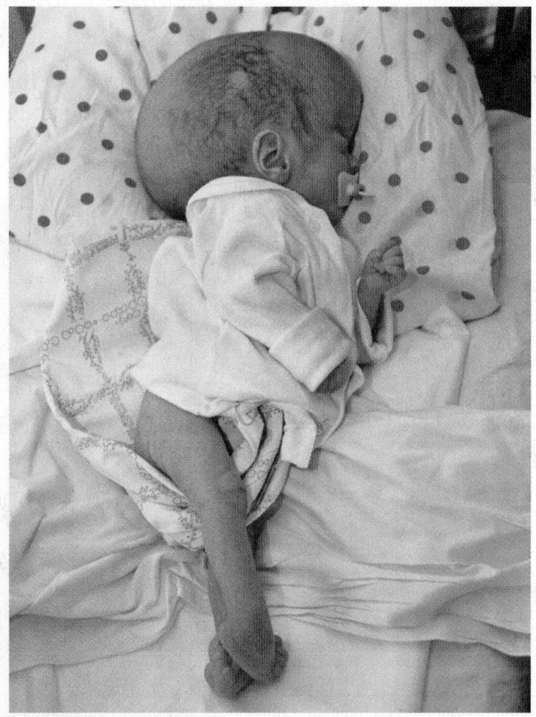

One of the victims of the nuclear accident at Chernobyl. Because of the birth defects, the parents gave the child to an orphanage.

Over 300,000 people were evacuated. International medical teams rushed to the scene, and despite emergency transplants of bone marrow and fetal liver cells, 31 people died during the first months. About 12,000 square miles of farm- and forestlands were so contaminated that they may be useless for two generations or longer. Some people, even though they are aware of the risk, have moved back into the contaminated areas (Dufay n.d.). "This is our home," they say. "Where else can we live?" Some farmers are again growing crops and raising livestock in areas contaminated by the Chernobyl disaster. On a personal note, when I was in Latvia, I was warned not to eat strawberries because they had been grown in areas contaminated by the Chernobyl disaster. I saw others buy the strawberries, however.

When United Nations researchers did a 20-year follow-up study of Chernobyl, they found that the health effects were much milder than expected. The levels of leukemia—one of the main fears—turned out to be within the normal range. About 4,000 cases of thyroid cancer were found, primarily among adults who had been children at the time; they had consumed milk from cows that had eaten radiation-contaminated grass. This disease, though, is treatable and has resulted in only a few deaths

("Stakeholders and Radiological . . ." 2006). This is encouraging news, and we await future studies to see if they confirm these initial findings.

The Fukushima Nuclear Disaster. Then nuclear disaster struck again. Not in Russia, but in Japan in 2011. An earthquake damaged a nuclear reactor at Fukushima. While the damage was being brought under control, a tsunami hit Japan's coast, knocking out the plant's capacity to cool the reactor. This was followed by an explosion that released radiation. As I write this, many of Japan's fishing boats sit idle because so many ocean fish are filled with poisons (Tabuchi 2012). As might be expected, the Japanese government keeps minimizing the extent of the harm to people's health. In place of self-serving pronouncements, we eventually should have objective research and learn the extent of the damage.

Food Pollution

After a visit to Orlando, Florida, I drove to my home in the Florida panhandle. The night I arrived home, I came down with a fever. I decided to "tough it out" so I could continue to write, confident that the fever would subside. After three days, however, the fever persisted. In intense pain and on the verge of delirium. I gave up, drove to the nearest hospital, and went to the emergency room.

I soon found myself attached to IV bags, my body pierced with needles. Tests showed that I was infected with Escherichia coli (E. coli), which can be fatal. After a week in the hospital and being presented with a humongous medical bill, I was able to go home.

What had happened? The best guess is that some restaurant worker in Orlando who handled my food hadn't washed his or her hands after defecating. *E. coli* is a bacterium that lives in our digestive system, where it plays a beneficial role. But it becomes dangerous when our food or water is contaminated with feces. *E. coli* is only one of the many disease-causing substances in our food.

Let's look at more problems of **food pollution**. There are three types: (1) like *E. coli*, disease-causing germs in our food, (2) harmful chemicals added to our food, and (3) genetically modified food. Let's look at all three.

Diseases in our Food.

Chickens ▸ If you have the stomach for it, consider how chickens are processed (Ingersoll 1990). Slaughter lines run so fast that inspectors have two seconds to scrutinize each chicken carcass, inside and out, for signs of disease and feces. "After a while, it gets to be a blur," inspectors say.

A "chicken factory" in Washington. Each cage provides the floor space of a piece of paper. Authorities closed this one up when they found about 1,000 dead chickens among the 1,500 live ones.

Food processing is supposed to reduce food contamination, but the way we process chickens can increase it. In one plant, 57 percent of chickens arrived contaminated with disease-causing bacteria. This is horrible to contemplate, but listen to this: 76 percent left the plant infected. During processing, contaminants are passed from carcass to carcass. The two primary culprits of this bird-to-bird contamination are automatic disemboweling knives and vats of chilled water in which the chickens are dipped before going into the freezer. Says a microbiologist, *"Even if you chlorinate the chilled water, it's still like soaking birds in a toilet."* To this, industry officials reply reassuringly, "It may spread bacteria from bird to bird, but it also dilutes the overall effect" ("Of Birds and Bacteria" 2003).

Why doesn't the U.S. poultry industry switch from chilled water to blasting the chickens with cold air, as they do in Europe? I personally find the reason horrible. Federal regulations allow each chicken carcass to soak up to 8 percent of its weight in water. This allows the chicken industry to sell hundreds of thousands of gallons of disease-ridden water at poultry prices.

Scientists at *Consumer Reports* did research on the problem. They bought chickens at supermarkets in twenty-five cities nationwide ("Of Birds and Bacteria" 2003). These included major brands, supermarket brands, and chickens sold at health food stores. *Half* of the chickens were contaminated with *Salmonella* or *Campylobacter*, bacteria that can make people sick. They repeated the study in 2010, buying chickens at over 100 stores (Consumer Reports 2010). The results this time? The situation was even worse: *Two-thirds* of the chickens had *Salmonella* or *Campylobacter.*

If *Salmonella* and *Campylobacter* are so common, you might be wondering whether they are really harmful. The answer is clear: Over three million Americans get sick from diseases in chickens and other foods each year. Of these, 25,000 end up in the hospital, and 500 die (Consumer Reports 2010).

To avoid getting sick from the filthy chickens sold in our stores, researchers suggest that you pick the chickens lowest in the supermarket freezer (where it is colder), separate raw chicken from other foods, not let any foods touch the area where you prepare the chicken, and cook the chicken thoroughly. They say not to forget to wash your hands thoroughly. You need to remove all chicken juices—the blood and the filthy water (recall that "chill water" that the U.S. Department of Agriculture allows the chickens to absorb).

If someone ever says to you, "I'm so hungry I could die for a chicken," you can reply, "Yes, you could."

Not Just Chicken ▸ Other foods are also so contaminated that they kill. And because of inadequate testing, you never know what food it will be. Here are some cases: Twenty people died after they ate hot dogs produced by a subsidiary of Sara Lee. The hot dogs were contaminated with *Listeria monocytogenes*. Forty people died after eating Jalisco brand soft cheese—also contaminated with listeria (Burros 1999). Odwalla produced apple juice that was infected with *E. coli*—14 children developed a life-threatening disease that ravages kidneys. A 16-month-old girl died (Belluck 1998a). In 2009, 600 people became ill from products made from peanuts from the Peanut Corp. of America. Nine were carried from the hospital in coffins. In 2010, over half a billion eggs were recalled from grocery stores after 1,500 people were infected with *Salmonella* (Neuman 2010).

Chemical Additives. Let's turn to the second type of food pollution, chemicals added to our food to lengthen its shelf life, enhance its appearance, or alter its taste.

Food Flavorings and Colorings ▸ Food companies sprinkle our food with over 2,000 chemical compounds. The "cherry" flavor in soft drinks, pies, and shakes, for example, is made of 13 chemicals.

How safe are these chemicals? The agency responsible for overseeing the safety of food is the Food and Drug Administration (FDA). The FDA sometimes seems less interested in the health of the public than in protecting business from inconveniences. A startling example occurred in the 1970s, when Red Dye No. 2 was the most common food coloring in the United States. When researchers reported that rats and mice fed

Red Dye No. 2 developed cancer, it took 5 years for the FDA to ban this dye—and only after public interest groups flooded Congress and the agency with petitions.

Many find little comfort in knowing that Red Dye Nos. 3, 8, 9, 19, 37, and 40 replaced Red Dye No. 2 to color food. Some of these dyes damage DNA and cause cancer in animals (Brooks 1985, 1987; Tsuda 2001). Red Dye No. 40 has been banned by some European countries—yet it remains approved by the FDA to make our food look more appealing (Perry 2010).

Food Preservatives ▸ Sulfites are used to keep food from discoloring. They are spread over raw fruits and vegetables, especially at salad bars, to keep them "looking fresh." Sulfites are also added to beer, wine, and bakery goods, sprinkled over shrimp and fish, mixed with dairy and grain products, and added to fruit juices and frozen potatoes.

The sulfites make some people sick, especially those who suffer from asthma. A few even die from allergic reactions. After years of complaints—and no regulation—the FDA finally took action. The agency didn't ban sulfites, however, but said that companies have to put a warning label on their products (Dingell 1985; Ingersoll 1988; Food and Drug Administration 1994; Magee et al. 2005). This is like putting a warning sign on a little fence around a chemical dump.

Synergism and Cumulative Effects ▸ A problem with food additives is that they are *synergistic*—that is, they interact with one another. An additive that is not hazardous by itself can become dangerous when combined with another additive. For example, the nitrites that give hot dogs, ham, and bacon their inviting red color appear to be safe in and of themselves. In the presence of amines, however, nitrites become nitrosamines—potent carcinogens. Every organ in every species of animal ever exposed to nitrosamines developed cancer. Amines are commonly added to beer, wine, cereals, tea, fish, cigarettes, streptomycin, Librium, and Contac cold medicine. Synergism makes hot dogs and beer an unhealthy combination, the same with a ham sandwich and a cup of tea. Look at Figure 13.4 for another illustration of polluted food.

Many chemical additives are harmless in small amounts. But some build up in our bodies. When they reach a certain level, they begin to destroy tissues and organs. The level at which destruction begins varies from person to person.

Profits Ahead of Health. Food production is the largest industry in the United States. Sales in our 90,000 grocery stores total about $600 billion a year (*Statistical Abstract* 2013:Table 1061).

FIGURE 13.4 ▸ Bon Appétit?

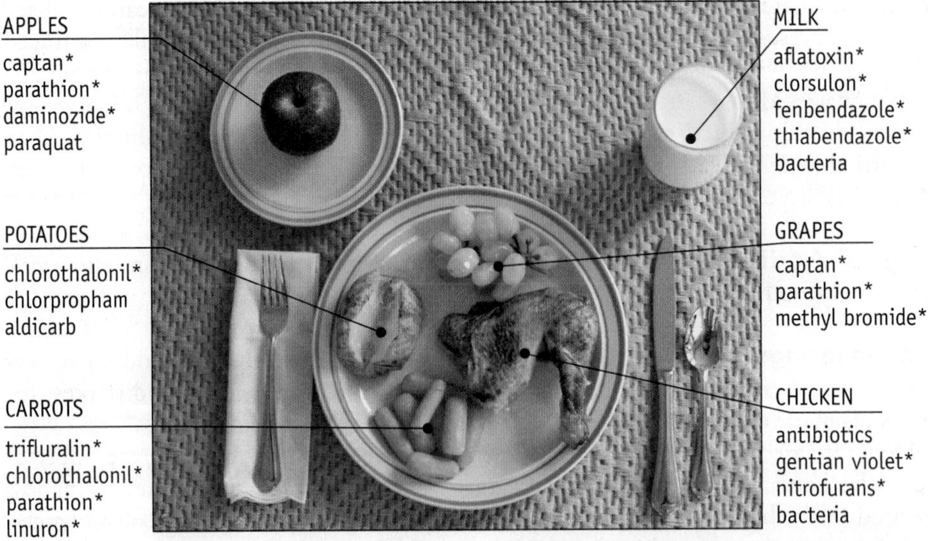

These contaminants are often but not always in the items pictured above.
*Known or suspected carcinogen.

The food industry adulterates our food with harmful chemicals not because it is necessary but because it is profitable. The chemicals slow spoilage and increase sales by making food appeal to the public's conditioned taste and sight. Certainly the food chain is long—that is, getting food from grower to consumer is a lengthy process—and the food industry must use effective ways to preserve food. We have many ways to do this that don't harm people's health: pickling, smoking, salting, canning, freezing, drying, freeze-drying, and vacuum packing. When the food industry chooses to preserve food in ways that harm health, we can say that those who control the food industry put profits ahead of health.

Some of our food is polluted before it is processed. Animals are given antibiotics to keep them from getting sick and growth hormones to cause them to grow faster. Farmers spray pesticides on fruits and vegetables to prevent insect damage. When we eat these fruits and vegetables or animals or their products, such as milk and cheese, some of these substances end up in our bodies. Some accumulate there until they reach a tipping point or are set off by some catalyst and trigger cancer.

Genetically Modified Foods (GMOs). It doesn't take an expert to figure out that pollution can harm us, that we should avoid diseases in our foods, and that at least some chemicals added to foods are harmful. However, when it comes to **genetically modified foods**—foods derived from plants or animals in which genetic materials have been transferred from one species to another, or in which genes have been manipulated in a way that does not occur in nature—we land in the midst of controversy. Not only are governments and businesses, with their competing economic interests, quarreling with one another, but so are scientists. They simply cannot agree whether genetically modified foods are harmful or not.

Listen on **MySocLab Audio:** NPR: Genetically Modified Crops

Even placing the topic of genetically modified foods in this section of the book is controversial. It might imply that modifying foods genetically is a form of food pollution. But locating this topic here is not intended to communicate such a message, only to stress that some scientists take this position.

The issue is simply this. Modifying foods genetically is new. This technology has the potential to increase the world's food supply, but its consequences are unknown. U.S. companies have spearheaded the development of genetically modified foods, and they stand to reap huge profits if the new strains are accepted around the world. European agricultural interests, which fear competition, spearhead opposition. They are joined by environmentalists who fear both unknown health consequences of these foods and the harm they might bring to the environment if they replace natural varieties.

The controversy continues (Moskin 2012). Depending on the outcome of scientific studies, American and European agricultural interests stand to gain or to lose hundreds of millions of dollars a year (Umberger 2005). The United States and European Union don't order scientists to produce studies proving their position, but scientists on both sides of the Atlantic know that the European Union wants to prove that genetically modified foods are harmful, and the United States and Canada to show that they are not harmful. Although research is being conducted within this highly charged political context, science—not economics or politics—will win. No matter who produces a study, the other side will examine it rigorously. Subjected to objective techniques of replication (repetition) and measurement, these studies will ultimately demonstrate that one or the other economic–political side is correct. Of course, each side could be partially correct—that is, some genetically modified foods could prove to be harmful, and others safe. We will have to await the data to know the outcome of this controversy.

Research Findings: Conflicting Interpretations

13.5 Compare how the pessimistic and optimistic environmentalists interpret research findings.

Almost everything we have reviewed about the environment reflects negative findings and opinions. Before turning to a surprising contrasting view, let's continue on this negative path a while longer as we consider energy and resources.

The Pessimistic Environmentalists

One group of experts argues that we are facing energy and resource shortages so vast that they will shatter the foundations of civilization. These **pessimistic environmentalists** can't understand why most of us are so shortsighted that we become concerned only when the price of gasoline goes up. We miss the bigger picture—that for its existence, our civilization depends on substances whose supplies are limited.

Oil. The pessimistic environmentalists almost pull out their hair at the way most of us think about oil and other resources. They can't understand why we aren't alarmed about what is so obvious. No matter how ample the supply of oil might be at the present, oil reserves are not infinite. At some point, we will reach the end of being able to pump oil from the ground. As we get close to this, the price of oil will shoot sky high. And when we do run out of oil, just like those of the Mesopotamian, Maya, and Anasazi, our civilization will collapse. Running out of oil, they stress, is not a matter of *if,* only of *when.*

And depletion does not apply only to oil. We have the same problem with the minerals on which our way of life depends.

Minerals. The pessimistic environmentalists also foresee a bleak outlook for essential minerals, substances such as chromium, cobalt, copper, molybdenum, and vanadium. Industry depends on minerals. Without them, we would have neither cars nor computers. Economies around the world are expanding ferociously. The Most Industrialized Nations depend on an economic expansion of 2 or 3 percent a year in order to keep people employed and their standard of living increasing. At the same time, India, China, and other nations have joined the industrialized nations in this furious, competitive demand for the earth's limited and irreplaceable resources. Soon we will run out of these essential minerals. Substitute materials may buy us time, but we are reaching limits that will stop the expansion of the world's economies and bring our civilizations to a screeching halt.

FIGURE 13.5 ▸ The Ogallala Aquifer

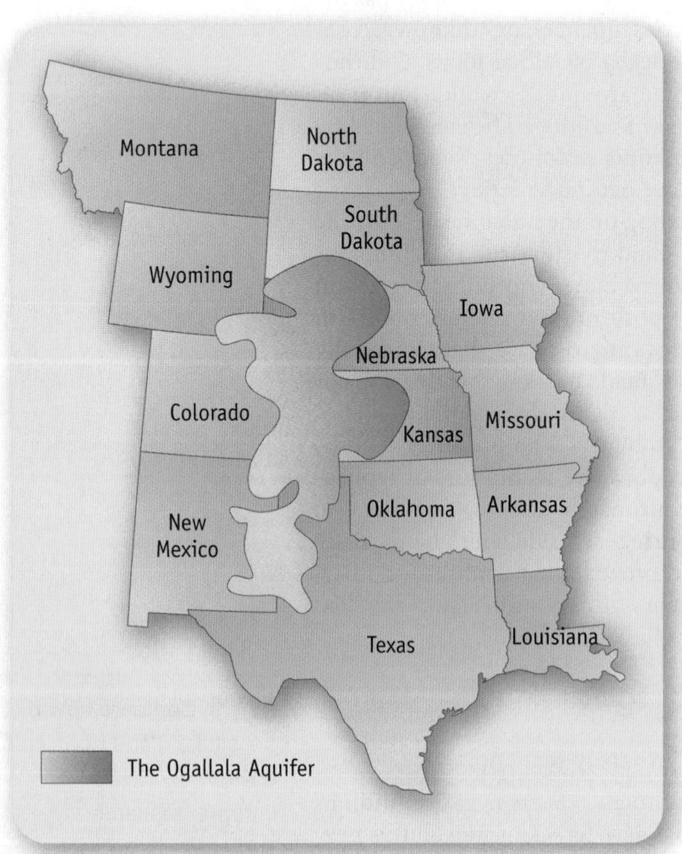

The Water Shortage. Then there is the issue of fresh water. We turn on the faucet, and before our eyes is an endless supply of running water. We can take showers as long as we want, or we can fill our bathtubs. We can flush the toilet as often as we want. Those who have swimming pools fill them with water. So what is the problem?

Gradually, we are learning a bitter lesson. Of all the water on earth, 97 percent is salt water. A little over 2 percent is frozen in glacial ice. This leaves about 1 percent for all agricultural, industrial, and personal uses. Contrary to appearance, we are entering a water crisis. Communities have begun to quarrel about who has a right to the water in the Great Lakes. California and Arizona argue about who has the right to the water of the Colorado River. States are going to court, suing each other over water rights.

To illustrate the coming crisis, consider the Ogallala aquifer. As shown in Figure 13.5, this huge aquifer runs from South Dakota to Texas. It waters the nation's breadbasket, where farmers grow one-fifth of the entire U.S. agricultural crop (Little 2009). In this same area, ranchers raise nearly half the nation's cattle. Yet we are depleting this underground water (Thier 2010). Some say that desert is the natural condition of much of this area, now in pasture and farmlands (Stevens 1996). Perhaps, then, its primary tourist attraction is destined to be giant sand dunes. Frank Popper, the head of the Department of Urban Studies at Rutgers University, predicts that one day hardly anyone will live in this region. He says that we should replant the native prairie grasses, reintroduce the buffalo, and turn off the lights (Farney 1989).

Water is far more than just a U.S. problem. Water shortage is global, with nations disputing who has the right to the water in the rivers that mark their borders or that flow from one nation into another. As industry expands around the world to meet the needs of growing populations, the need—and demands—for water will increase. The coming confrontations over water may become so severe that nations will go to war over water rights.

Do you think the water shortage will ever become so severe that people will resort to drinking water from the toilet? I'm sure you nodded your head negatively, but don't be so sure. Read the Thinking Critically box below.

In Sum ▸ That our resources are finite and we are depleting them is obvious: There is only so much oil and natural gas, only so many mineral deposits and fresh water. When we run out of them, as we will, our factories will grow silent, our cars will sit in the driveway, and our homes will grow cold.

The Optimistic Environmentalists

There is another side to this matter, one that is seldom heard. Some experts, whom I call the **optimistic environmentalists**, say that alarmist doomsayers have captured the attention of the media. With their dire predictions and woeful exaggerations, they paint

Thinking Critically about Social Problems

From the Toilet to the Tap: Overcoming the Yuck Factor

Would you drink water from someone's toilet?

This is a serious question. The water shortage is becoming so severe that some people are doing exactly this.

Okay, they aren't like dogs that slurp water from the toilet. And they don't scoop it up in a glass. But they do drink it. After the toilet water (and the shower water and the dirty dish water) goes down the drain, it ends up at a central station where the toilet paper and other "solids" are diverted and the rest is strained through holes smaller than bacteria. Then the water goes through reverse osmosis, which removes most molecules that are not water. Finally the water is exposed to ultraviolet light. The result, say the experts, is the equivalent of distilled water.

You probably wouldn't want to scoop water out of this toilet and drink it, but if it goes through a purification process first?

"Maybe so, and you can drink it if you want to, but not me," is the reaction of many.

But a lot of people are drinking this water. In Orange County, California (the home of Disney Land), 70 million gallons of such water (called "treated effluent") are returned to the aquifer each day. In Singapore, about 15 percent of the water is treated effluent. On space missions, the astronauts drink their own recycled urine.

"From the toilet to the tap" seems to be the wave of the future.

"That's not accurate," reply the experts again. "Get it straight. It's from toilet to treatment to tap. And we call it potable reuse."

"I don't care what you call it. I wouldn't even want my cat to drink it," said one woman.

"I'll stick with bottled spring water," said one man.

"If science says it's clean, then it's fine," is another response, growing more common as people get used to the idea, the "yuck factor" receding.

Based on Barringer 2012; National Research Council 2008, 2012.

For Your Consideration

What is your reaction to treated effluent? Would you drink it? How about to treated toilet water? It does seem to make a difference what you call it, doesn't it?

a bleak picture of the future. Isolated incidents, although tragic, make sensational headlines, but they don't give us the larger picture. If we take a more realistic, dispassionate view, they say, we will see that our situation is a lot more pleasant than the pessimists make it appear. Let's look at their arguments.

Resources Are Not Getting Scarcer. Seeming to fly in the face of logic and reality, economist Julian Simon insisted that raw materials are *not* getting scarcer. He said that when something that people want grows scarce, its price increases. To see whether raw materials are becoming scarcer, we can look at their price. The long-term trend is lower prices, which means *less scarcity.* Here is how Simon put it (Simon 1980:11):

> *The cost trends of almost every natural resource—whether measured in labor time required to produce the resource, or even in the price relative to other consumer goods—have been downward over the course of recorded history. An hour's work in the United States has brought increasingly more of copper, wheat, and oil from 1800 to the present. . . . These trends imply that the raw materials have been getting increasingly available and less scarce.*

This view so infuriated the pessimistic environmentalists that it led to one of history's famous bets. This fascinating bet is recounted in the Thinking Critically box below.

Thinking Critically about Social Problems

Put Your Money Where Your Mouth Is: The Simon–Ehrlich Bet

To say that Professors Julian Simon and Paul Ehrlich didn't like each other would be an understatement. *Detest* would be more appropriate. Simon was an economist who taught at the University of Maryland. Ehrlich, a demographer and biologist, taught at Stanford.

Ordinarily, their paths would not have crossed. They lived a continent apart, and they worked in different fields.

Paul Ehrlich

Julian L. Simon

But then life changed for both of them.

Ehrlich came out swinging. In 1968, he wrote a book that scared millions of people and fueled the environmental movement. He said that the world's population was growing so fast that food would soon be scarce. Prices were going to soar, and life expectancy would drop. His book, with the pop title, *The Population Bomb,* sold 3 million copies. The book scared the American public, aroused an environmentalist movement, and made Ehrlich rich. From obscurity in the classroom, he was vaulted to prominence as a guest on talk shows.

Fame and fortune. A prestigious job at Stanford. Unless he started to sexually harass his students or come to class drunk, how could that be spoiled?

Then along came Simon. Simon started grumbling in public, muttering that Ehrlich's book was a piece of, well, you know what—rotten catfish. Simon even claimed that the truth was the opposite of Ehrlich's headline-grabbing screams about a dire future. Larger populations, asserted Simon, would mean more abundance, not less. Prices would drop, not increase. Life expectancy would increase, not drop.

Simon and Ehrlich began to call each other names. They wrote nasty comments about one another in academic journals. Scholars, who usually write dispassionate articles for one another, were amused at the unusual display of passion and vitriol.

Ehrlich still had the public on his side. He kept repeating his doomsday predictions. He was a founder of Earth Day, and at its first gathering in 1970 he spoke to a crowd of 200,000.

(continued from previous page)

Simon was there, too, telling his side of the story. He had an audience of sixteen.

Simon didn't like this, but there wasn't much he could do about the public latching on to Ehrlich's ideas, not his.

Then Simon made an intriguing proposal. Without mentioning Ehrlich by name, he challenged any pessimistic environmentalist to a bet (Toth 1998). The opponent could select *any* commodity, and Simon would bet that its price would drop. "After all," he said, "contrary to common sense, resources are growing more plentiful, and they will drop in price."

"Put your money where your mouth is if you don't agree," Simon challenged, none too gently.

This was too much for Ehrlich—who knew that he was the target of the challenge. In October 1980, he accepted the bet. Then he did a little boasting of his own. He said, "I'll accept Simon's astonishing offer before other greedy people jump in" (Tierney 1990).

The bet was on. If the prices of chrome, copper, nickel, tin, and tungsten were higher in 10 years, Ehrlich would win; if they were lower, Simon would win. To be sure there could be no misunderstandings, the two wrote their bet down, signed a contract, and publicized it widely.

During the ensuing years, the two kept goading one another—and the world's population kept growing. During the next ten years, it soared by more than 800 million people, the greatest increase in history.

Ten years later to the day, the two checked prices.

Ehrlich was chagrined. The price of all five metals had dropped. He quietly sent Simon a check. He enclosed no letter.

Simon gloated publicly. "Now you know who's right," he said. "And if you think this was just a fluke, let's do it again, Ehrlich. And this time, let's put up some real money. How about $20,000?"

Ehrlich refused, saying that the matter was of minor importance.

Simon laughed and continued to poke fun at Ehrlich. Then students started to do the same, calling Ehrlich the nuttiest professor at Stanford.

The two never reconciled.

Julian Simon died at age 65 in 1990. Paul Ehrlich stayed on at Stanford, where he still teaches. These days he focuses more on butterflies, his research specialty. But he does give interviews, and his message is the same ("To Avoid Disaster. . ." 2012).

For Your Consideration

Do you think Simon's winning the bet with Ehrlich was a fluke? With natural resources finite (a limited amount), why aren't their prices (in terms of hours worked or inflation-adjusted dollars) increasing instead of declining?

To illustrate how the prices of raw materials have been falling relative to wages, Simon used copper as an example. As Figure 13.6 illustrates, over the past century it has taken less and less time to earn enough to buy a pound of copper.

FIGURE 13.6 ▸ The Price of Copper Relative to Wages

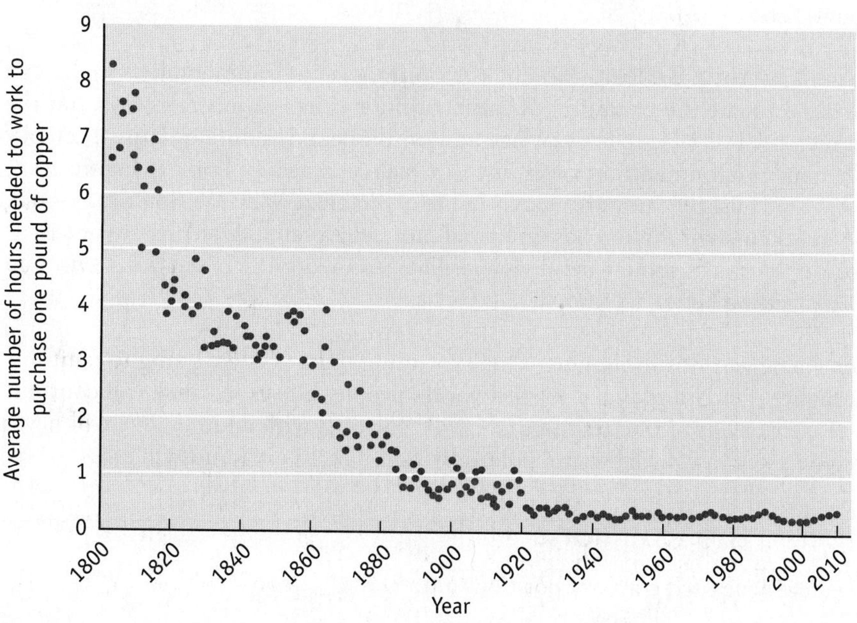

Sources: Historical Statistics of the United States 1976; *Statistical Abstract of the United States* 2010:Tables 629, 872.

Energy. And energy? Here too, Simon stressed that to get the answer we need to look at long-term prices. The historical prices of electricity and coal, for example, have moved downward, indicating a stable and even increasing supply of these forms of energy. Be sure to look at long-term trends, Simon stressed. Short-term prices, like what you pay at the gas station from week to week, give a distorted picture. Prices jump around week by week and year by year for any number of reasons, such as civil wars and hurricanes that disrupt supply.

The Technological Fix. The optimistic environmentalists claim that improved technology will solve whatever threats we face. If we should ever exhaust a particular resource, our technology will produce a substitute. New technologies will replace older technologies. In fact, technology is rushing so headlong into the future that it sometimes produces new materials before the old ones are even threatened. Fiber-optic cable, for example, is rapidly replacing copper wire for the transmission of sound and images. Just a few years ago, the optimists point out, the pessimists were saying that we would run out of copper. Take another look at Figure 13.6.

It is the same for pollution. We have had predictions of disaster in the past, the optimists argue, and our technology has always seen us through. The present is no exception. To get their point across, some use a bit of humor. In 1900, the pollution problem was manure. At that time, the main means of transportation was the horse, and ugly, festering mounds of manure would pile up on city streets. When motorized vehicles replaced horses, the manure problem disappeared. The present is no different, and we will develop technology to counter threats to our environment.

Pessimistic Environmentalists Cause Disease. The optimistic environmentalists also point out that we must be cautious about the solutions of pessimistic environmentalists, that they can do more harm than good. Edward Teller (1980), the man most responsible for the hydrogen bomb, said that environmental regulations cause disease. What did he mean by such a strange statement? DDT was banned, he said, when environmentalists objected that its use harmed the environment. Then mosquitoes multiplied, and in one country alone, Sri Lanka, 2 million people came down with malaria. To combat this disease, DDT had to be brought back. Teller added, "I challenge anybody to show me a case where lack of environmental protection has made two million people as seriously sick as the disease caused by the environmentalists."

Things Are Getting Better. Finally, the optimistic environmentalists make this point: We can evaluate the condition of the environment in a number of ways, but the single best measure is life expectancy. When an environment deteriorates, life expectancy drops. When an environment improves, life expectancy increases. Look at Figure 13.7, which shows the consistent upward march in life expectancy. Why are Americans living longer? Because our environment has improved, not deteriorated. Don't let anyone twist reality in order to match some woeful view of life. Stop worrying about what *might* go wrong. Life is getting better, so enjoy it.

In Sum ▸ The world is improving. Our expanding industries are going to continue to bring a higher standard of living for the world's people. Life expectancy will continue to climb. If we run out of one resource, we will replace it with another. We will never run out of energy, and we will control pollution. Social life is on an upswing.

Reconciling the Positions

How do we reconcile such contrary positions among the "experts"?

FIGURE 13.7 ▸ Life Expectancy in the United States, by Year of Birth

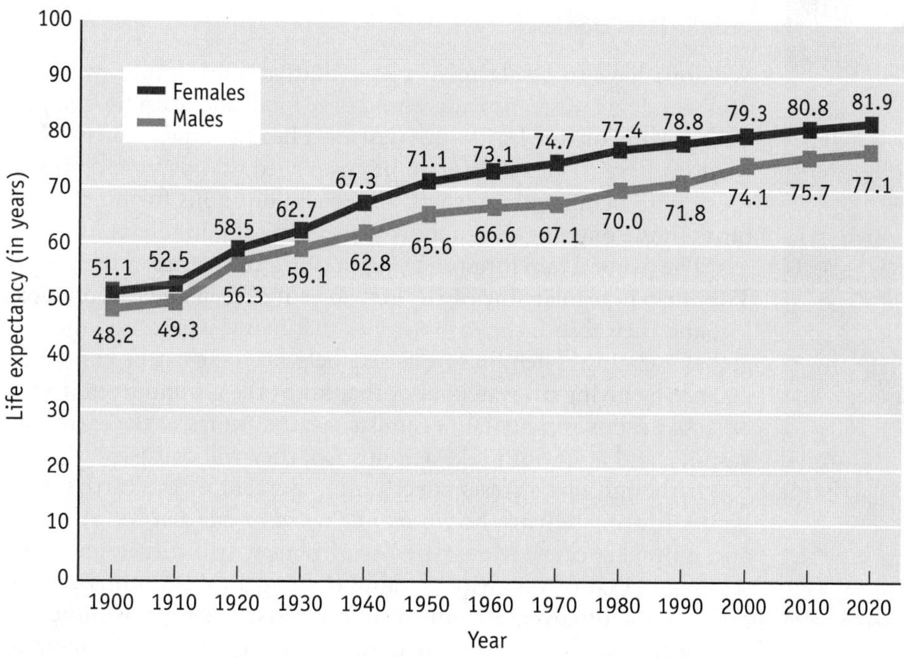

Sources: By the author. Based on *Historical Statistics of the United States* 1976:Table B 116, 117; *Statistical Abstract of the United States* 1989:Table 106; 2013:Table 108.

Frameworks of Interpretation. As stressed in Chapter 2, objective conditions—or the things that we call social facts—do not come with built-in meanings. We have to interpret them. All of us, as the symbolic interactionists stress, fit "facts" into some framework. The framework that we choose influences our conclusions. This basic principle applies to "experts" and "nonexperts" alike.

Consider how this principle works when it comes to the environment—whether pollution, energy, or resources: If we assume that the environment is deteriorating and our resources are becoming scarce or even disappearing, we interpret data one way. In contrast, if we assume that resources are abundant and either will not shrink or will be replaced by substitutes, we make far different interpretations. The framework within which we interpret objective conditions makes the difference in how we interpret "facts."

Science at Work ▸ Does this mean that we are left only with opinions, and opposing ones at that? Perhaps for the moment, but not indefinitely. As pointed out earlier about the controversies over global warming and genetically modified food, science is at work and objective studies will win out. Barring political interference, as opposing sides present their evidence, air their views, and try to disprove the other, the best data will become apparent. As scientists produce more data on the environmental crisis, the exaggerations of each side will become apparent. Eventually, we will know which position has the better data on pollution, energy, and resources.

Implications of the Frameworks ▸ Meanwhile, we must draw our own conclusions—which affect how we perceive the problem and the solutions we favor. On an individual level, our conclusions influence our choices about energy use and lifestyles. On the political level, the conclusions have far greater implications: The well-being of billions of people depends on them—including future generations. Everyone will benefit if this debate and its related research are allowed to continue unencumbered by politics, so that social policies can be based not on biases and ideology but on sound data and logic.

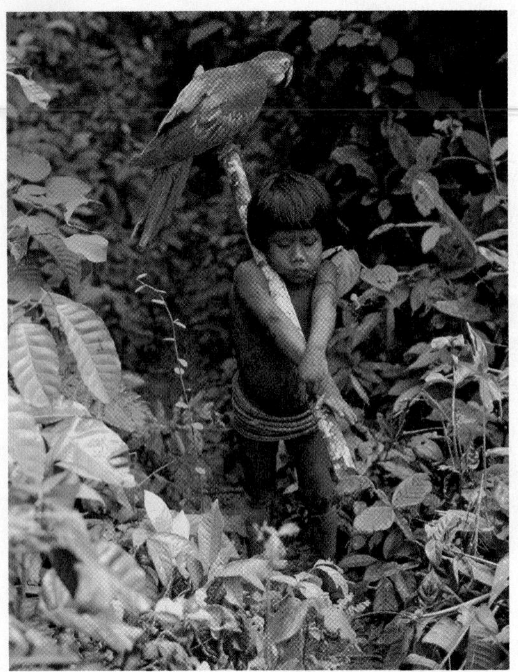

Not many hunting and gathering groups remain on earth, but some still live in the rain forests of South America. This boy, carrying a macaw, is a member of the Urueu-Wau-Wau tribe.

Resource Destruction: The Tropical Rain Forests

We don't have to be alarmists to see that, at a minimum, we must deal with toxic waste, provide wholesome food, and learn how to preserve, create, or—at least—not destroy a healthy environment. And we don't have to be alarmists to be concerned that plant and animal species are being extinguished. Especially ominous for humanity's future is the ongoing destruction of the tropical rain forests.

The tropical rain forests have been called the "lungs of the earth." They help to regulate the earth's exchange of oxygen and carbon dioxide, and they absorb the carbon gases that many experts say underlie global warming. The rain forests also help keep the earth's climate in balance by giving off water vapor that keeps the ground from drying out. As the environmental pessimists say, the "lungs of the earth" are gasping, and if we don't take action soon, they will collapse.

Although rain forests cover only 7 percent of the earth's total land surface, they are home to *one-third to one-half* of all plant and animal species. Many species of plants, still unstudied, possess medicinal or nutritional value (Cheng 1995; Simons 2005). Some of the discoveries from the rain forests have been astounding: A flower from Madagascar is used in the treatment of leukemia, and a frog in Peru produces a painkiller more powerful, but less addictive, than morphine (Wolfensohn and Fuller 1998). A chemical from a rain forest plant in Panama is thought to be effective in treating malaria (Roach 2003).

Even knowing that the rain forests are essential for humanity's welfare, people keep clearing them. In the process, they extinguish thousands of plant and animal species (Durning 1990; Wolfensohn and Fuller 1998; "The Price of Success" 2004). As biologists remind us, a species lost is a species gone forever. We are exchanging our future for some lumber, farms, and pastures.

Social Policy

13.6 Know how frameworks of interpretation lead to different social policies. Summarize potential social policies to cope with environmental problems.

Before we examine specific social policies, let's first consider how these contrasting frameworks of interpretation lead to vastly different social policies.

Oppositional Viewpoints and Overarching Solutions

From these contrasting frameworks flow three approaches to social policy. As you will see, each also implies a different type of society.

The Steady-State Society. As we have seen, the pessimistic environmentalists argue that it is folly to expect the world's economies and standards of living to increase endlessly. Based on their position that pollution is endangering the world and resources are diminishing, they have come up with an overarching solution called the **steady-state society**. By this term, they mean that we must stabilize industrial output at the level it is now. If we do this, we will slow the rate at which we pollute the environment and use up resources. This slowdown will give us time to solve problems of pollution and to develop alternative resources before the shortages develop that will destroy our civilization. To reach a steady-state society will require painful adjustments. It means that we will have to curb our growing appetite for the material goods that support our current lifestyles.

The Scaled-Back Society. A more pessimistic group of environmentalists argues that it is not enough to develop a steady-state society. The pace at which we are polluting our environment and using our resources is far beyond anything the earth can sustain. We must develop a **scaled-back society**. That is, we must reduce our industrial output and our standard of living. Only after we cut back to some optimal level—one that experts will determine—can we move to a steady-state society. This will require not "adjustments" but, rather, sacrifice as we lower our material standards. Scaling back is essential for the survival of earth. All of us, except the poorest, must learn to get by with less. Some who take this position add that once we have scaled back our expectations and have learned to live simpler, less-materialistic lifestyles, we will find life more satisfying.

The Expanding Society. Optimistic environmentalists scoff at the arguments of the pessimists. Not only can we solve the current environmental crisis, they say, but we can also enjoy even higher standards of living. We can bring pollution under control through international agreements and develop alternative substances for any resources that are running short. As we do this, we can increase our industrial output and create a world of even greater material abundance. It is foolish to even consider a steady-state or scaled-back society. Either of these societies would deny billions of people a better life.

Regardless of whether we agree—partially, reluctantly, or wholeheartedly—with the pessimistic or optimistic environmentalists, it seems reasonable to take the position that we need social policies regarding pollution and energy. Let's consider possible policies.

Explore on **MySocLab**
Activity: Problems of Place: The Southern Californian Sprawl

Pollution

Preventing the Misuse of Toxic Chemicals. A pressing problem is the misuse of toxic chemicals. Let's see what can be done.

International Controls ▸ As the Global Glimpse box on the next page highlights, banning the use of a toxic chemical in the United States doesn't prevent its use elsewhere. As a result, that chemical eventually shows up on our dinner plates by way of a food chain that stretches to us from the Least Industrialized Nations. To protect the people in these nations, hazardous chemicals need to be labeled in the language of the country to which they are shipped, with their proper use and dangers clearly stated in plain words. To protect people everywhere, no company or its subsidiaries should be allowed to manufacture chemicals whose use is banned in the company's home country. The United States can call a summit to establish international controls.

Holding Industry Accountable ▸ To prevent misuse, industry must be held accountable. Congress passed the *Community Right to Know Act of 1986*. It requires that each year companies submit to a state agency and to local fire departments a list of the hazardous chemicals they use or manufacture. Some states have passed their own right-to-know laws, requiring businesses to inform their employees of the hazardous chemicals they will be exposed to at work.

Some environmentalists say that this is not enough. They want a comprehensive policy for toxic chemicals. In this "cradle-to-grave" approach, all toxic chemicals would have to be approved for sale and use, registered as they enter the marketplace, and monitored throughout their lifetime. The public would have access to information on chemical releases, and the worst polluters would be publicized (Friends of the Earth 2004).

Preventing Food Pollution. A second pressing problem is food pollution. There is no compelling reason to allow diseases to be transmitted in food. With the available alternative forms of food processing and preservation, there also is no compelling reason to add dangerous chemicals to make our food look or taste better or to lengthen its shelf life. At a minimum, no chemical should be added to our food until it is proven safe for human consumption.

State-of-the-art testing can detect banned chemicals in our food, whether imported or domestic. We can shut down U.S. companies that violate chemical restrictions

A Global Glimpse

The Circle of Poison

In U.S. ports from Gulfport, Mississippi, to Oakland, California, you can watch forklifts loading 55-gallon drums onto the decks of vessels bound for Central and South America.

What's in the drums? Heptachlor, chlordane, BHC, and other chemicals on their way to the plantations of Latin America. Because these pesticides are linked to cancer and sterility, they are banned or severely restricted in the United States. U.S. companies, however, can manufacture them here and market them in the industrializing countries. There, most workers who handle these chemicals cannot read. They have no idea what the warnings on the labels say. Yet these chemicals will contaminate them, their family, and their food and water.

Pesticides that are banned here don't disappear—they come back to haunt us. The fruit grown in these countries appears on our kitchen tables—along with the poisons used to protect them from insects. BHC comes back in your coffee. DDT, applied to cotton in El Salvador, shows up in beef carcasses imported through Miami. Nearly half of the green coffee beans we import are contaminated with pesticides, potential carcinogens. And the situation worsens, for the free trade zones that stimulate the globalization of capitalism increase the importation of these products.

These farm workers in Brazil are protesting the use of pesticides that have caused the deaths of their fellow workers.

Based on a newsletter from Frances Moore Lappe, founder of Food First; Ingersoll 1990; Allen 1991; "U.S. Pesticide Exports" 1994.

For Your Consideration

How can you avoid the chemicals that are banned here but arrive in imported food? Do you think U.S. corporations should be allowed to manufacture and export to other countries chemicals that are banned in the United States? Explain.

and ban food imports from countries where this occurs. To be effective, the legal penalties need to be directed against the *managers and directors* of companies that violate such laws.

Industrial Wastes. A third area of concern is proper disposal of the unwanted by-products of industrialization.

Detoxifying Wastes ▸ We already know how to detoxify most industrial wastes. We probably could learn to detoxify the rest. Recycling waste products is especially promising because it turns noxious wastes into safe and usable products. To develop better technology to recycle and detoxify wastes, we could establish a superfund to finance cooperative research by scientists.

Hazardous Waste Sites ▸ As you saw from Figure 13.3 on page 442, across the nation are thousands of hazardous waste sites that pose a danger to people's health. Congress has established a superfund to clean up these sites and has spent $20 billion to begin the process. Some estimate that the bill for this cleanup will run as high as $500 billion. No one knows, of course, but if this estimate is correct that's $1,600 for every person in the United States. The basic choice is to either fund the cleanup or build higher fences around the sites and let the wastes continue to leach into our groundwater. The choice seems to be a large bill or slow poison.

Nuclear Wastes: The Problem with No Solution ▸ Because they stay lethal for thousands of years, leftover plutonium and other nuclear wastes have perplexed the experts. While scientists have tried to figure out how to store something that is beyond human experience, *100 million* pounds of radioactive waste have accumulated. These tons of nuclear waste are stored in *temporary* containers (Bezdek 2009; Morse 2012). The waste's new home was supposed to be in Yucca Mountain near Las Vegas, Nevada. At a huge expense, storage chambers were carved from an ancient salt bed, nearly half a mile below ground. Geologists said this salt deposit has been stable for 250 million years (Brooke 1999).

This sounds like an ideal solution, but critics pointed out a deadly flaw in the plan: No one knows if the containers for the waste—stainless steel lined with lead—will last a thousand years, much less ten thousand years. This flaw bothered Nevada officials, who sued to stop the radioactive waste from coming into their state. Las Vegas officials jumped into the fray, saying that they would use armed force to stop the trucks and railroad cars carrying the waste through their city on the way to Yucca Mountain. Facing this standoff, the U.S. government backed off. Federal officials first postponed delivery until the year 2017 and then declared that the Yucca Mountain facility wasn't really right in the first place (Tetreault 2006; Bezdek 2009; Wald 2010).

Even the Yucca Mountain storage—if it were used—would be only a partial solution. While the arguments and standoffs have gone on, nuclear power plants have continued to produce so much waste that even Yucca Mountain can't hold it all (Bezdek 2009). The arguments are so old that some of the nuclear facilities that produced the waste have even been retired and demolished. All that is left are the temporary storage facilities that hold their waste (Wald 2010). The situation would be humorous, if it weren't so serious.

The arguments and standoffs continue—while the wastes, now 70,000 tons, continue to accumulate—with no one having a solution (Johnson 2013).

The Greenhouse Effect. What can we do to solve the greenhouse effect? An immediate step would be to plant vast numbers of trees around the world, for they thrive on carbon dioxide. To the extent that carbon dioxide is a danger to the world, nations can reduce the amounts they produce. In 1997, the Most Industrialized Nations agreed in Kyoto, Japan, to reduce the amount of carbon dioxide they produce. This agreement has proven not only controversial but also difficult to implement. Fearful of the cost of compliance, Canada and the United States withdrew from the Kyoto Protocol (Struck 2006). Eventually the dust from the controversy that swirls around the greenhouse effect and global warming will settle down. Better facts will emerge, and logical agreements will be reached. We will have to await the specifics as they emerge.

Listen on
MySocLab Audio:
NPR: Amazon
Rainforest Update

The Rain Forests. We must also develop social policies to prevent the destruction of the world's rain forests. I propose two policies: (1) Make it illegal to import timber that comes from rain forests. This will require an international agreement; the ban won't work if only a nation here and there passes such laws. (2) Industrialized nations can *purchase the rights to not develop the rain forests.* This policy would preserve millions of acres and thousands of plant and animal species for future generations. The rights would extend indefinitely and be overseen by an international watchdog agency.

No social policy is simple, of course, and policies concerning the rain forests bring their own complications. Brazil, for example, which has extensive rain forests, knows that the United States prospered by cutting down most of its forests for farmland. Brazilian officials find it ironic that the United States wants them to preserve Brazil's forests for the benefit of Americans (Goering 1998; Zibechi 2005).

An Overarching Solution. An overarching policy is to produce less of what harms the environment. We can change our production techniques and equipment, redesign our products, and do more in-process recycling (Doran 2006). We have the capacity to take these steps, but to take them we must be convinced that our fragile environment is being harmed and that it is worth the effort and costs to change our ways. To return to one of the main points I made earlier: Whether or not we have this perspective depends on the framework of interpretation that we choose.

Energy

Technology and Energy: Energy Abundance from Fracturing. Technology is sometimes thought of as the silver bullet that will save the day. Somehow, we will develop new technology that solves our problems.

And for energy, this could be the case. With new technology, we can now drill slant-wise, instead of just horizontally, which allows us to tap reservoirs of oil that previously were inaccessible. But the most astounding new technology is *fracturing ("fracking")*, using pressurized liquids to break shale rocks, giving us access to their hidden pools of natural gas. The result is nothing short of amazing. So much natural gas is being tapped in the United States that its price has plummeted. Companies are building vast pipelines to transport the gas, and building terminals to export it to Japan and other countries that don't have these reserves. We now are producing so much natural gas that we might become not only energy self-sufficient (instead of a net importer of oil) but also a net exporter of energy.

Is there another side to this positive development? Of course. And the pessimists step right up to the plate. The liquids used to break up the shale are going to seep into the aquifers and pollute our drinking water. Breaking the shale disturbs natural rock formations and can cause earthquakes. And in the process of removing and transporting the natural gas a lot of methane escapes. The methane is even worse for global warming than carbon dioxide (Zeller 2011).

Again, instead of coming down on one side or the other, we will have to let the scientific studies provide the evidence. But aside from new deposits of natural gas and petroleum, only two types of solutions for energy exist: alternative forms of energy and energy conservation. Let's look at these.

Alternative Forms of Energy. What forms of energy can be alternatives to our heavy dependence on natural gas and petroleum?

Coal ▸ We have enough coal in the United States to satisfy our energy needs for centuries. We can transform coal into liquids and gases—and we can do so at a price that is competitive with petroleum (Wu 2006). We would have to ensure that such processes do not contribute to pollution.

Synthetic Fuels ▸ **Synthetic fuels** (called **synfuels**) can be developed from garbage, sawdust, and other waste. The decay of organic substances such as sewage and straw produces methane and methanol, gases that motors can burn efficiently. Synfuels offer the potential to solve two problems at once: the disposal of our organic garbage and the production of alternative fuels. We may be able to plant fields of common milkweed, turning them into "petroleum farms" as factories extract **hydrocarbons**—the backbone of motor fuels, lubricants, turpentine, and rubber—from those plants.

Other Alternative Fuels ▸ Hydrogen, too, holds great potential. As a basic component of air and water, hydrogen is available in limitless amounts. Other alternative sources of energy include the wind, ocean tides, **geothermal energy** (heat from beneath the earth's crust), and **nuclear fusion** (combining atoms, as opposed to nuclear fission, which splits atoms). Especially promising is harnessing the sun. Solar power is infinite, and technologies such as the photovoltaic cell, which changes sunlight into electricity, can trap it.

Successful social policy to develop alternative fuels is going to be costly, but the potential payoff for the country and the world is huge. So are the potential profits for companies that succeed in this effort.

Energy Conservation. A simple solution is to conserve energy. Conservation involves everything from insulating homes, businesses, and factories to working four 10-hour shifts a week instead of five 8-hour shifts. This change in working patterns would cut commuting expenses by 20 percent and allow factories to fire up their boilers less often. The potential savings from conservation are dramatic, but it does involve changing patterns of behavior that are rooted firmly in culture, hardly an easy matter.

Our Homes ▸ In reaction to the growing price of energy, we have made our homes more energy efficient (*Statistical Abstract* 2010:Table 894). But we still have a long way to go. The "*Lo-Cal house*," developed at the University of Illinois, can cut fuel bills by about two-thirds. These savings stem from the design of the house, without help from solar panels. About 85 percent of the total window area in the house faces south, the house is heavily insulated, and its roof overhangs by 30 inches, letting sunshine in during the winter but excluding it during the summer.

Quite promising is *net zero housing*, houses that produce as much energy as they use. They do this through trapping solar and wind power (Carlton 2009). A home design that comes close to this uses a *solar envelope*. This house is built within a second set of walls that provide a "skin" to trap and distribute the sun's heat. Even in northern climates, a furnace is needed on only the cloudiest days of winter. Its ingenious design also cools the house in the summer by drawing in cool air from a chamber under the house.

Our Cars ▸ We have also greatly increased the energy efficiency of our cars. The average car today gets 74 percent better mileage than cars did 40 years ago, from 13.5 miles per gallon to 23.5 miles per gallon (*Statistical Abstract* 2013:Table 1108). We have a long way to go, and the potential is intriguing. The main innovation has been the hybrid car, which uses both electricity and gasoline to propel it. Hybrid cars burn about 25 percent less gasoline than regular cars, but there are much greater possibilities. Soon, hydrogen fuel-cell vehicles will go 300 miles on a single tank of compressed hydrogen (Tollefson 2010). Propelling cars by burning hydrogen can also reduce global warming, because water, instead of carbon dioxide, flows out of the vehicle's exhaust.

Explore on **MySocLab Activity:** Riding a Bicycle to Work

Cogeneration ▸ Another form of conservation is **cogeneration**, producing electricity as part of normal operations, such as generating electricity from the heat and steam that industrial boilers produce. This is not a new idea. In 1900, cogenerators produced more than half of the nation's electricity. Now they produce only about 3 percent. To encourage cogeneration, federal law requires that utility companies purchase a firm's excess production at the utility's standard costs. The advantage for utility companies is that they can add to their capacity to provide electricity without having to invest in building new power plants (Devine 2004).

***In Sum* ▸** If the pessimistic environmentalists are correct, we soon will see the end of some of the resources on which our civilization depends. If we haven't implemented the right social policies before this happens, the coming shortages will force us to do so. If the optimists are right, we won't have to make difficult choices. Market forces will point us in the right direction. If we run short of something, the pursuit of profits will lead people to develop new technology and alternative sources. Those convinced of this view tell us, "Just don't interfere with the market forces, and the balance will occur naturally."

Moral Issues in a Global Age

In addition to the fundamentally differing perspectives presented by the pessimists and optimists, determining social policy touches on philosophical and moral issues.

The Dilemma of Global Solutions. Because the environmental crisis is global, its solution requires global social policy. Some organization—whether the United Nations or the World Trade Organization or another international body—will need to take the lead in solving environmental problems by proposing international laws that benefit all nations. Because such laws will conflict with the individual sovereignty of nations, some nations are likely to reject this type of legislation as violating their national interest. This brings us face-to-face with philosophical, moral issues.

Consider these questions. Do nations have a fundamental right to use resources—whether from their own land or those they import—in any way they wish? Do they even have a fundamental right to pollute, if they choose to do so? If not, then do nations possess some fundamental right to impose their view of pollution and resources on others? If so, what is the basis of that right? Is it some "greater good" for the world's benefit? If so, who decides what that "greater good" is and how it should be enforced? Assumptions of a "greater good," as conflict theorists remind us, can be excuses for the Most Industrialized Nations to bully the Least Industrialized Nations. If there is such a right, it certainly isn't likely that the weaker nations would be able to impose their ideas of pollution and resource depletion on the more powerful nations.

The Future of the Problem

13.7 Discuss the likely future of environmental problems.

If we take a l-o-n-g view, many of these problems will take care of themselves. Our groundwater, for example, will rid itself of most pollutants eventually. The problem is that the self-cleansing process takes significant time—about 1,400 years for the groundwater to cycle through the aquifers (Bogo 2001).

So let's try to get a glimpse of a more immediate future, considering what is likely to take place during the coming decades. Let's first examine energy conservation and pollution. After this, we'll again look through the eyes of the pessimists and optimists.

To glimpse the potential of technology in solving our problems, you can read about the BioStove in the Technology and Social Problems box below.

Technology and Social Problems

The BioStove: The Technological Fix

As science has advanced, we have come to depend more and more on its developments. Applied correctly, the technology that arises from science holds abundant promise for the well-being of humanity.

How do we meet the needs of a world population that is growing by a billion people every dozen years? We know that this growth cannot continue forever, or eventually we will all have to sleep standing up. I exaggerate somewhat to make the point, but global population growth is persisting without letup. Perhaps the optimists are right and after stage 3 of the demographic transition we will face the problem of a shrinking world population.

We will see. In the meantime, how do we meet the needs of our vast, growing population? Technology's promise is bright, and the BioStove is one of the latest developments that the ingenuity of humans has come up with.

About three billion people, almost half the world's population, use wood as their cooking fuel. Many of their stoves are smoky affairs, and the deaths from smoke inhalation are estimated to be higher than the deaths from malaria. Alexander Drummond and Jonathan Cedar set out to solve this problem. They created a thermonuclear chip which uses wasted heat to produce electricity. The electricity powers a fan which reduces the smoke by 94 percent. In addition, the stove cuts fuel consumption by half (Sprung 2012).

The BioStove being used in India.

There's more. The stove has a little USB port. The electricity the stove produces can charge electronic devices, cell phones and the like.

For Your Consideration

Do you think that technology will solve the problems that we call the environmental crisis? Why or why not?

Energy

As we strive for higher standards of living, we increase our demands for energy. On Table 11.1 on page 377, you saw how the size of the average household has shrunk. Yet during this time the average size of a new home has risen by two-thirds—from 1,500 square feet to about 2,500. We also furnish our homes with more energy-eating appliances. In 1970, 34 percent of new homes had central air-conditioning; now 88 percent do (*Statistical Abstract* 1989:Tables 58, 1231; 2013:Tables 984, 1001). We might complain about the price of gasoline, but the higher cost hasn't reduced our driving. We drive our cars more miles a year than we did 30 years ago (*Statistical Abstract* 2013:Table 1107).

The demands for more energy are growing throughout the world, especially in India and China, which together hold a third of the world's population. Not only are they industrializing at a fast pace, which places tremendous demands on energy, but also millions of their people are joining the middle class. In their new status, with their many cars and household appliances, they use much more energy. Unless we sink into a lasting global depression, this expansion of their industrial base and the extensive upper social mobility will continue. As we and the rest of the industrialized world continue our wasteful ways, it is likely that energy shortages will occur and prices increase. We likely will develop more technology to harness alternative forms of energy, making these sources of energy widely available at low prices. International oil companies will invest in alternative forms of energy, turning them into profitable enterprises.

Pollution

The picture of pollution is less positive. We have no overarching plans for chemical and nuclear pollution that would ensure the long-range health of our population.

If bringing pollution under control required only technology, we could assume a future with cleaner air, water, and land. But politics is always involved. Likely we will never see a national policy that focuses on making our environment as free of pollution as possible. Outrage over some catastrophe—as with *Deepwater Horizon*—will produce specific changes from time to time, but when the crisis is over, the media's attention will turn elsewhere and not much outrage will remain.

The Greens. Environmentalists in Europe have formed political parties. The Green Party, as the one in Germany is called, holds seats in the national parliament and in several of Germany's states. It bargains those seats for power in coalition governments. The United States, too, has a Green Party, but it is so weak that it has a difficult time mustering enough support to even get on the ballot, much less to win elections. This could change. Some unexpected event could etch the environment into national consciousness, making it a top political issue. In the meantime, as Robert Gottlieb discusses in the *Spotlight on Social Research* box on the next page, environmentalists have begun to apply their perspective to urban life.

A Lack of Unity. The future of pollution depends on a fragile balance of power among groups whose interests sometimes coalesce and sometimes conflict. At this point, there is no coalescence, nor is there a strong environmental alliance under a green banner. Certainly people are concerned about the world they will leave for their children, but environmentalists, often local in orientation or fragmented by multiple visions and political strategies, lack a unifying voice. Even so, opposing groups can overcome differences in order to make the environment a top priority, as illustrated by Christians and Jews joining forces under the banner "Creation Care." Their message: "We are called to be stewards, not exploiters, of the earth" (Watanabe 1998). Though the potential is present, the voice is weak.

Environmental Injustice. A special concern of sociologists is how unequal power has led to **environmental injustice**—pollution doing the most harm to minorities and the poor (Lerner 2010). Polluting industries locate where land is cheaper—and, as is no surprise to you, the wealthy don't build their homes on cheap land. As a result,

Spotlight on Social Research

The Marriage of Community and Environment

ROBERT GOTTLIEB, *professor of urban environmental policy at Occidental College, has found that something new is happening in the environmental movement. He calls it a marriage of community and environment. Living in Los Angeles and writing and teaching about the urban environment make this "marriage" particularly compelling for him. Here is what he wrote for you.*

When I first arrived in Los Angeles in 1969, the city, with its sprawling landscapes of subdivisions and freeways, had a reputation as the "anti-environment." I never focused on the fact that Los Angeles had a river until the 1980s, when one of my students brought to my attention the growing advocacy around the revitalization of the asphalt-and-concrete-encased Los Angeles River. Since then, I've been able to document the creation in Los Angeles of a new kind of community-based environmentalism: where urban rivers and streams and other green spaces and community places in the city are re-envisioned.

This marriage of community and environment has made an impact on environmental groups. Open space has long referred to places outside urban areas or at the urban edge where there is little or no development. Earlier battles for open space sought to *preserve* environmental assets, such as habitat, wildlife, and other forms of biodiversity. Their focus was not on built environments where there is little or no existing green space, where density is high, where the land is contaminated, and where the acquisition of land for parks or recreation seems only a distant possibility.

That's changing. Environmental advocates have begun to redefine the issue of open space as the need to re-envision *community spaces* and to reclaim rather than simply preserve such places. Many environmentalists now embrace community gardens, farmers markets in low-income communities, re-landscaping projects, and recreational opportunities in densely populated areas. I had the opportunity to direct an educational program on the Los Angeles River—the very symbol of both the anti-environment and efforts to re-envision the river as a community and environmental asset.

If you define the marriage of community and environment as an effort to re-envision—or reconstruct or reclaim—these kinds of community and environmental assets, then a different kind of environmental agenda begins to emerge. This agenda would focus on a neighborhood's transportation needs, on access to and quality of food, on health concerns like asthma, and on schools as re-landscaped, livable places rather than fortress-like, asphalt jungles. In this marriage, the greening agenda becomes a justice agenda. It leads us to understand that nature belongs in the city as well as outside it.

low-income communities, often inhabited by minorities, are more likely to be exposed to pollution. In the struggle for environmental justice, sociologists have studied, formed, and joined groups that fight to stop polluting plants and block the construction of new ones. This struggle for justice is likely to continue.

The Environmental Pessimists and Optimists

Finally, let's look at the future through the eyes of the two groups who see practically nothing alike.

The Picture Painted by the Pessimists. Pessimists paint a gloomy future, of course. Pollution will continue with only superficial improvements here and there, and the depletion of resources will accelerate. The countdown has already begun, and "RDP Day" (Resource-Depletion and Pollution Day) is on its way. This is the day when we will have depleted our vital resources and pollution will be so extensive that we won't be able to fix it. With its industrial base undermined, modern society will disintegrate, bringing tragedy to all. Desperate, people will flee. But to where? Even the countryside will be too polluted to support anything but a minimum of life.

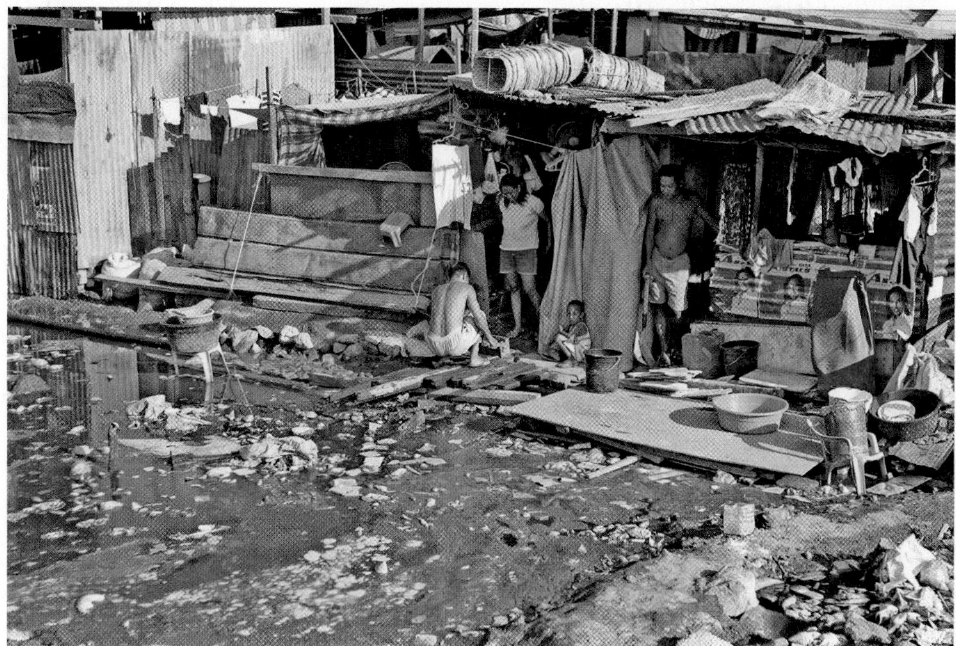

Is this the future of humanity? The picture painted by the environmental pessimists looks something like this photo taken in Manila, Philippines. What can we do to avoid it?

Can such a gloomy future be averted? Yes, reply the pessimists, but only if we develop a steady-state or, better, a scaled-back society. To level off our energy consumption or reduce it severely, we need to cut back on our material gadgets and quit striving for more material possessions. We have built our society on the assumption that resources are inexhaustible, so our withdrawal pains will be enormous. But once we recover from the shock of being forced into a drastically different lifestyle, we may find that a simpler way of life is rewarding: Feeling less compulsion to own things, life will slow down and we can enjoy social relationships more.

The Picture Painted by the Optimists. And what does the future look like to the environmental optimists? Our present path is fine, they say. We already have more resources than we need for the foreseeable future. Scientists will continue to make breakthroughs, putting even more energy at our disposal. The development of hydrogen fuel cell technology holds the potential for giving us energy in unlimited quantities. From this source alone, we might meet all the world's energy needs now and in the future (Bishop and Wells 1989; Stevens 1989; Low 2008).

Neither is pollution a fearsome problem. Scientists are discovering enzymes, microbes, and molecules that eat pollutants and clean up contaminated groundwater (Wall 2010). They have discovered a bacterium that has adapted to fifteen times the dose of radiation it takes to kill humans. This bacterium, and others yet to be discovered or developed, will break our nuclear wastes into relatively harmless components (Fialka 2004).

The principle is this: Pollution will be solved to the extent that people demand a cleaner environment and are willing to pay for prevention and cleanup. Because people are demanding it, the environment is already getting cleaner—and it will continue to improve. Consequently, the future promises a healthier environment, an even higher standard of living, and a continued increase in our life expectancy.

Who Is Right? What *is* the future of the environmental crisis? Is humanity at a crossroads, as the pessimists insist, with our current course dooming us to destruction? Or are the optimists right, with our current course leading us to a delightful future? Could the future turn out to be even gloomier than the environmental pessimists imagine, with nuclear war, the worst pollution of all, destroying our ecosystem—and humanity?

We who are the audience—and either the beneficiaries or the victims—of this unfolding drama will have to await its outcome.

MySocLab ✓ Study and Review on MySocLab

Summary and Review

1. The destruction of the environment, which began millennia ago, may have destroyed ancient civilizations. Industrialization has intensified this process.
2. The nations of the world share a common *ecosystem*, which makes the environmental crisis a global matter: Even individual acts of *pollution* can have international consequences.
3. Symbolic interactionists have studied how the environment became a social problem, how objective conditions were translated into subjective concerns. Concerns about the environment began with professionals, were picked up by interest groups and government agencies, and then by the press, which aroused the public.
4. Functionalists stress that all life on earth is interdependent. ("Everything is connected to everything else.") We all are part of a huge, complex living machine called the earth. Industrialization has dysfunctional consequences for the *ecosystem*.
5. Conflict theorists stress the conflict between environmentalists, who battle to reduce environmental threat, and industrial leaders, who fight for the right to pollute while earning a profit.
6. Some measures of air and water pollution show improvement, but the results are mixed, and pollution continues. The *greenhouse effect* could cause a global climate change that would bring far-ranging consequences for humanity.
7. *Strip mining* and the disposal of solid wastes despoil the land. Industrial wastes threaten our drinking water and many of our lakes and rivers. *Acid* and *mercury rain* imperil animal and plant life.
8. Chemical pollutants pervade our environment. Leaching from landfills is extensive. Nuclear pollution is ominous, as illustrated by the Kyshtym, Chernobyl, and Fukushima disasters. Food additives are a form of pollution. Genetic modification of foods might be another form.
9. Alarmed at the environmental crisis, pessimists advocate a *steady-state society*—one based on zero economic growth—or a *scaled-back society*, based on deliberately shrinking the economy. Optimists, convinced that we can continue industrial growth and use technology to solve environmental problems, advocate an expanded economy. Regardless of who is right, pollution is a global problem that requires international social policies.
10. The environmental pessimists and optimists paint contrasting pictures of the future. We don't yet know who is right, but with our coal reserves and other alternative forms of energy, accompanied by developing technology, our energy future looks positive. The outlook for pollution, however, is less positive. The environmental movement is fragmented, but it has the potential to become a powerful global force.

Key Terms

Thinking Critically About Chapter 13

1. Which of the theoretical perspectives (symbolic interactionism, functionalism, or conflict theory) do you think does the best job of explaining the environmental crisis? Why?
2. How far do you think the government should go to reduce pollution? Should the executives who run polluting corporations be jailed? Should the government shut down polluters? What else could or should the government do?
3. Some scientists argue that problems of pollution and the scarcity of resources are best solved by free enterprise. They believe that the market is better equipped than governments to solve these problems. What do you think of their position?
4. Do you think that the U.S. government has the power or authority to demand a steady-state society? Do you think it is advisable? Why or why not?

14 War, Terrorism, and the Balance of Power

Listen to Chapter 14 on MySocLab

Learning Objectives. After reading this chapter, you should be able to:

14.1 Explain why war is common and know the essential conditions of war and the fuels of war. **(p. 467)**

14.2 Describe how extensive war has been and currently is. **(p. 471)**

14.3 Discuss the perspectives that emerge when you apply symbolic interactionism, functionalism, and conflict theory to war. **(p. 473)**

14.4 Summarize what reduces war, the costs of war, dehumanization, the military–industrial complex, accidental war, and biological, chemical, and cyber warfare. **(p. 478)**

14.5 Discuss terrorism: revolutionary, repressive, state-sponsored, and criminal, as well as weapons of mass destruction. **(p. 491)**

14.6 Summarize social policies regarding terrorism, the MAD way to peace, policies that can bring peace, and how self-preservation figures in the survival of humanity. **(p. 498)**

14.7 Discuss the likely future of war and terrorism. **(p. 502)**

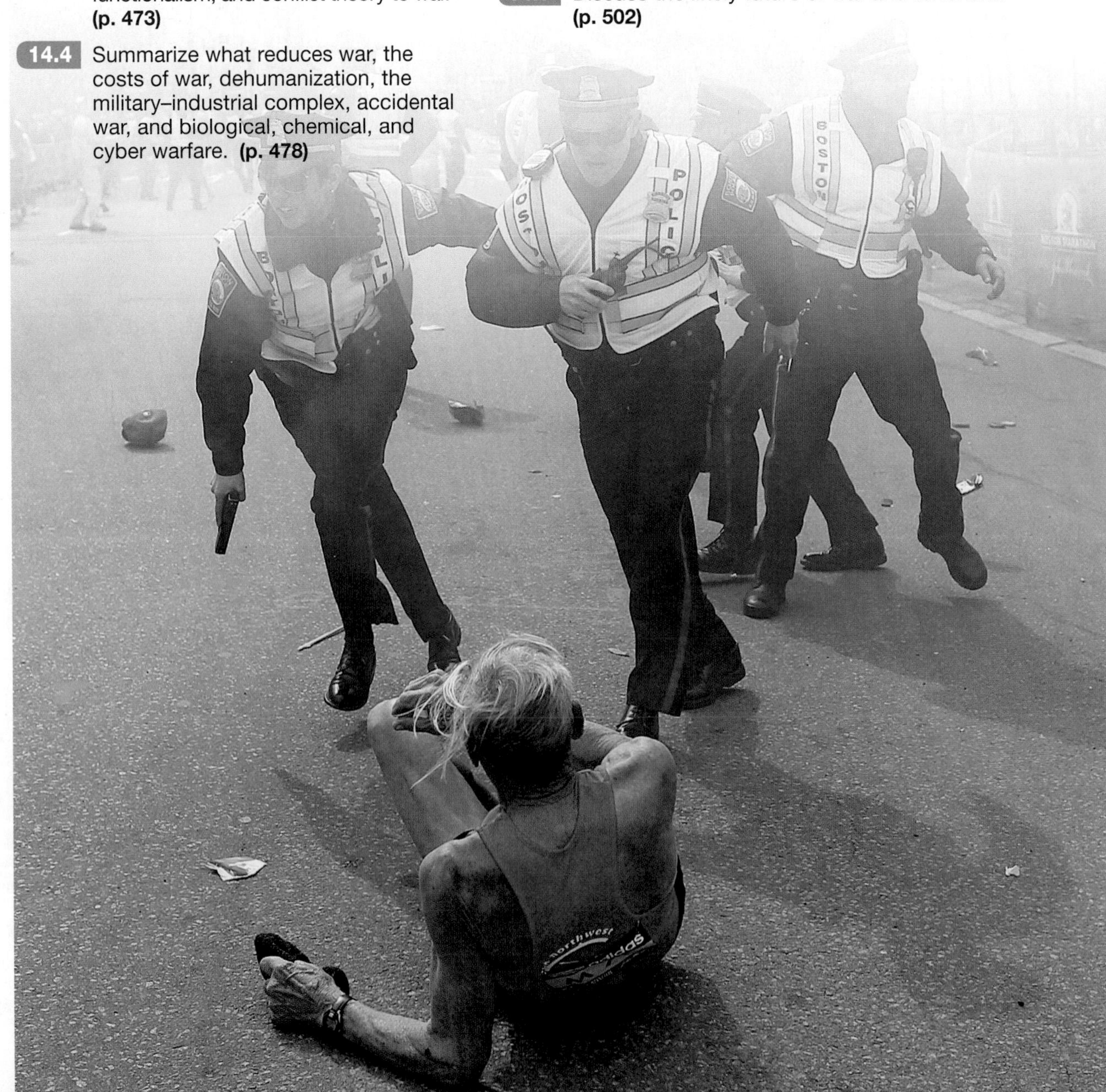

September 11, 2001, has been seared into the national consciousness. That day, which began like so many before it—a bright dawn, shining sun, and people going about their everyday lives—was destined to change the United States. No longer would our assumptions about life be the same.

When the commercial jets that had been transformed into lethal missiles struck the Twin Towers and the Pentagon, the United States was shaken to its roots. At dawn, these two global symbols, one of capitalism and the other of global military power, had stood tall and proud. A few hours later, one had been destroyed, the other crippled.

Americans shook their heads in confusion. Who could have done this? And why? As confusion turned to anger, the face of the enemy was beamed throughout the media to the United States and the world. The nation's response was swift and violent. U.S. Special Forces, accompanied by missiles directed from remote locations, attacked al-Qaeda in Afghanistan.

The United States declared war on terrorism—as it steeled itself against more attacks from an enemy hidden in their midst. Where would this unseen enemy strike next? The White House? A nuclear plant? Even the local mall or some sports event?

The United States was shaken to its roots

9/11 brought back unpleasant memories of the surprise attack at Pearl Harbor in 1941, which led to the United States declaring war on Japan. And as in 1941, Americans feared that sleeper cells in the United States were ready to attack—at any time, from almost anywhere. This time, though, there were no uniformed soldiers, no front lines, and no country to defeat. No one was safe in a battleground that faded into a murky back stage in which enemy and friend looked alike.

How will we even know when this war is over? After all, will there ever be an end to enemies and terrorist threats against the United States?

In this chapter, we examine the causes and consequences of war and terrorism, even the possibility that violence might end our civilization. We also look at 9/11 in a different light in order to try to understand why it happened. Compared with all other social problems that we have analyzed in the previous chapters, this one has the greatest potential of turning your life upside down.

The Problem in Sociological Perspective

After the attack at Pearl Harbor in 1941, the United States entered World War II. Although avowed enemies, the Soviet Union (a union of communist countries) and the United States (a capitalist country) became uneasy allies, fighting on the same side. From the end of that war in 1945 until the end of the 1980s, the Soviet Union and the West were caught up in an **arms race**. Each furiously developed and produced new weapons, threatening one another and trying to outmatch the other's power of destruction. During these decades, called the **Cold War**, the West and the Soviet Union built arsenals of nuclear weapons that had (and still have) the capacity to destroy the world many times over. As you can see from the Thinking Critically box on the next page, each side's distrust and fears of the other led to ironic twists of events.

14.1 Explain why war is common and know the essential conditions of war and the fuels of war.

Thinking Critically About Social Problems

Personalizing the Cold War: Economic–Political Systems in Conflict

Fear of nuclear attack was rampant in the 1950s and 1960s. Teachers taught their children to hide under desks, while others built bomb shelters in their back yards. The school photo is from 1952 in New Jersey, the bomb shelter from 1961 in California.

The Cold War. Capitalist and socialist (or communist) economies seem to be almost mirror images of each other. Capitalists believe that socialism is immoral because it denies people the freedom of choice. People can't even decide where they will live and work and go to school—others make those decisions for them. For their part, socialists believe that their economic system is good and that capitalism is immoral. They are convinced that an economy based on making profits is unfair, that it causes the poor to suffer. Each side believed its position so strongly that during a period called the Cold War, they faced off, snarling, threatening, and brandishing their weapons. Their face-off was called a *cold* war because neither side unleashed its weapons, turning it hot. During this time, though, emotions did run hot, as each viewed the other as a mortal enemy that deserved to be exterminated.

As tensions escalated, each side lived in constant fear of nuclear attack by the other. In the 1950s, Americans were so fearful of a Soviet attack that many built bomb shelters in their homes. On the states bordering Canada, schoolchildren were posted on top of school buildings, instructed to look for Russian planes sneaking over the border with nuclear bombs. The children, even those in grade school, were given plane silhouettes to help them determine if a plane was American or Soviet. They were posted next to a telephone connected to some central command. U.S. schools also held bomb drills. Children were instructed to hide under their desks in case the evil Russians dropped an atomic bomb. (Don't even try to imagine what good hiding under a desk would do. Fear gripped the country, and Americans were in a state of near panic.)

The Soviet Union and its satellite nations were gripped by the same fear. Students there were taught that the evil Americans might drop nuclear bombs at any time. Because the Americans might also use biological weapons (called "invasive bacteria" at that time), the students were issued gas masks. Contests were held to see which students could put the gas masks on the fastest. High school students were also taught how to assemble and load Kalashnikov rifles—just as effective in coping with a nuclear attack as hiding under desks.

I know that these events sound strange, some humorous, others perhaps even macabre. But they give you a picture of what the times were like, how people—not just Americans, but Russians, as well—thought that the Cold War might turn hot at any moment. The evil enemy (the other) stood ready to pounce and destroy.

Cool Drafts Left Over from the Cold War. Those frigid days are over—and we hope, forever. The nukes are supposedly no longer aimed at Moscow and Washington. These former mortal enemies now trade with one another. Their citizens visit one another's countries. They continue to disagree, but their squabbles are mostly about who is taking some supposed unfair trade advantage of the other. But—and keep this in mind—national economic interests, which can run high and hot, often underlie war. Today's more relaxed relations and minor squabbles could be but an interlude between another outbreak of hostilities.

If you think I am exaggerating, consider this. In 2007, the United States announced plans to build missile sites in Poland and Czechoslovakia, on Russia's border, supposedly to guard against missiles launched by some "rogue nation." U.S. officials knew this announcement would provoke a strong response from Russia. (Imagine if Russia announced plans to build a missile base in Mexico or Canada.) Russian authorities said that if the United States put its missiles in these places Russia would launch nuclear bombs. The United States replied defiantly that it was going ahead with its plans. The

(continued from previous page)

United States quietly pulled back, however, and did not build these missile sites.

The tensions continue. The United States is developing PGS, Prompt Global Strike, by which it can quickly strike targets anywhere on earth with conventional weapons (Woolf 2012). Russia has issued a warning, saying that it won't know whether the U.S. missiles are loaded with conventional or nuclear weapons. For its security, said the Russians, in the event of a launch Russia would have to assume the worst. Once again, our existence would depend on accurate interpretations.

An occasional, almost bizarre event, also reminds us that hostilities continue to underlie relations between the United States and Russia. In 2012, Putin, miffed at the United States, had the Russian parliament pass a law that forbids Americans from adopting Russian children. Such mild symbolic acts certainly are preferable to flaunting a nuclear arsenal that can destroy humanity itself.

For Your Consideration

Russia and the United States have not become buddies. Tensions still exist between them. What do you think it would take for these tensions to break out into war?

Based on sources cited plus the author's notes, news events, and interviews in Latvia.

When the Soviet Union adopted capitalism in the 1980s, the Cold War came to an end. The nuclear weapons that these nations developed, however, did not end. These weapons remain, still so powerful that in an instant they are able to reduce major cities to rubble and transform world powers into barren deserts. If we could put into a single event all the catastrophes that the world has ever experienced throughout its history, it would pale in comparison with nuclear war.

Why Is War Common?

That war today could wipe out humanity is new, but war itself is not. Human groups have always fought each other. Why do they do so?

An Instinct to Fight? Because war has been common throughout history, some analysts suggest that humans have an instinct for aggression. Anthropologist Konrad Lorenz (1966) said that our instinct for aggression used to be functional. It ensured that the fittest survived. It also forced humans to colonize the entire world as they fled from one another's innate aggression. In today's society, however, as Lorenz put it, this instinct has become a "hereditary evil" left from our primitive past.

The Sociological Answer: Societies Channel Aggression. To find the answer to why war exists, sociologists do not look *within* people. Whether humans have an instinct for aggression is not the point. People will always disagree about something, so conflicts always arise among people who live near one another. *What is significant are the norms that groups establish to deal with their inevitable conflicts.*

To illustrate this principle, let's look at two extremes. The first is a society that nourishes aggression. As you read about the Yanomamö in the Global Glimpse box on the next page, you will see why they represent this extreme. The other extreme is represented by the Eskimos of East Greenland. Instead of fighting, their norms require that hostile individuals *sing* to one another! Actually, they sing about their grievances, and their song duels go like this:

> *The singing style is highly conventionalized. The successful singer uses the traditional patterns of composition which he attempts to deliver with such finesse as to delight the audience to enthusiastic applause. He who is most heartily applauded is "winner." . . . One of the advantages of the song duel carried on at length is that it gives the public time to come to a consensus about who is correct or who should admit guilt in the dispute. . . . Gradually more people are laughing a little harder at one of the duelist's verses than at the other's, until it becomes apparent where the sympathy of the community lies, and then opinion quickly becomes unanimous and the loser retires. (Fromm 1973)*

A Global Glimpse

Nourishing Aggression: The Yanomamö

The Yanomamö men of the Amazon rain forest often attack neighboring villages, killing the men and kidnapping the women. Villagers also fight with one another. Fights often begin over sex: infidelity, seductions, or failure to give a promised girl in marriage. Sometimes the men challenge one another to a duel. One man stands, muscles tensed, feet firmly planted, while the other hits him as hard as he can once in the chest. Then the other man gets his turn. This continues until one man can no longer return the blow. Sometimes men take turns pounding one another over the head with a long wooden club. At other times, they even use axes and machetes—and neglect to await their turn. When relatives are drawn in, fights turn into brawls. These games can trigger feuds between Yanomamö villages. When someone is killed, relatives seek revenge. Feuds are self-feeding, for each killing requires retaliation.

As discussed in this box, the Yanomamö are a violent people. Shown here is a Yanomamö man in a non-violent activity. Ebene, a hallucinogenic drug, is being blown into his nose.

Why do the men fight like this? Anthropologist Napoleon Chagnon, who lived with the Yanomamö and analyzed their relationships, concluded that the basic reason is *social status.* Because violence is considered to be the mark of a true man, a reputation for violence gives a Yanomamö man high status. Almost everyone everywhere wants more status, to be looked up to by others, and the Yanomamö have developed a system that integrates violence and status.

There is also another factor, one that is less apparent: Success at violence gives men more access to women. Chagnon found that the men in this northern Venezuelan jungle who have killed at least one other person have more wives and children than those who have never killed. An especially successful warrior may have six wives. The higher status that comes with killing makes a man an attractive candidate for marriages—which are arranged by the men.

"How primitive they are!" we might say, smugly acknowledging our higher technology and education. But as Chagnon points out, the Yanomamö are not that different from us. Although we don't reward our war heroes with additional wives, we do award them medals, seats in the U.S. Senate, and sometimes even the presidency. As Chagnon points out and as presidential campaigns illustrate, the military record of candidates is important in U.S. politics.

Are we any different, then, from the Yanomamö—aside from being more indirect in the ways we reward "war behaviors"?

Based on Allman 1988; Chagnon 1988.

For Your Consideration

In what ways do we encourage (reward) and discourage human aggression? In what ways do we channel human aggression into socially acceptable forms? What prevents us from breaking down into little groups that are at war with one another?

Other groups channel aggression into rituals involving violence. It is common for the Tiwi of northern Australia to settle differences through spear-throwing duels.

> *When a dispute is between an accuser and a defendant, which is commonly the case, the accuser ritually hurls the spears from a prescribed distance, while the defendant dodges them. The public can applaud the speed, force, and accuracy of the accuser as he hurls his spears, or they can applaud the adroitness with which the defendant dodges them. After a time, unanimity is achieved as the approval for one or the other's skill gradually becomes overwhelming. When the defendant realizes that the community is finally considering him guilty, he is supposed to fail to dodge a spear and allow himself to be wounded in some fleshy part of his body. Conversely, the accuser simply stops throwing the spears when he becomes aware that public opinion is going against him. (Fromm 1973)*

In Sum ▸ Social scientists have found that war is not universal. War is one option that some groups choose for settling disagreements, but not all societies offer this option (Fry et al. 2009). The Mission Indians of North America, the Arunta of Australia, the

Andaman Islanders of the South Pacific, and the Eskimos of the Arctic, for example, have established ways to handle quarrels, but they do not have organized battles that pit one tribe against another. These groups don't even have a word for war (Lesser 1968). To understand war, then, sociologists look for *social* causes—conditions in society that encourage or discourage aggression and that shape aggression into organized combat between groups.

Let's look at the social conditions that encourage groups to choose war to handle their disagreements.

Why Do Some Groups Choose War?

War—an organized form of aggression that involves armed conflict between politically distinct groups—is often part of national policy. Why do some groups choose war to handle disputes when less drastic solutions are available?

Three Essential Conditions of War. Sociologist Nicholas Timasheff (1965) became intrigued by this question. After studying armed conflicts, he identified three essential conditions of war. The *first* is a cultural tradition for war. Because war has become part of a people's thinking, they view war as a way to resolve conflict with another nation. The *second* is an antagonistic situation in which groups confront incompatible objectives. Each, for example, might want the same land or resources. A cultural tradition for war and an antagonistic situation are essential, but they are not enough. They provide the fuel, but there also has to be a spark to ignite it. This *third* condition moves the nations from thinking about war to actually engaging in it.

Seven "Sparks" That Set Off War. To identify the sparks that ignite a war, Timasheff studied wars throughout history. He found seven sparks that ignite antagonistic situations, causing them to flame into war. They include the opportunity to

1. Get revenge (settle "old scores" from previous conflicts)
2. Dictate one's will to a weaker nation
3. Protect or enhance prestige (to protect the nation's "honor")
4. Unite rival groups within one's country
5. Protect or exalt the nation's leaders
6. Satisfy the national aspirations of ethnic groups (to bring "our people" who are living in another country into our borders)
7. Convert others to religious and ideological beliefs.

The Scope of the Problem

You can't watch a day's news reports without hearing about a war being fought somewhere in the world. And the United States regularly sends its troops to other countries. Have countries always fought this much?

14.2 Describe how extensive war has been and currently is.

War in the History of the West

To find out how common war has been in history, sociologist Pitirim Sorokin (1937) went all the way back to 500 B.C. He identified 967 wars in Europe from then to 1925 A.D., an average of one war every 2 to 3 years. Counting the years in which a country was at war, Germany spent the least amount of time in war (28 percent) and Spain the most (67 percent). Since William the Conqueror took power in 1066, England had been at war for 56 of each 100 years. During the previous 1,000 years, Russia had only one peaceful quarter century.

Read on MySocLab Document: Blowback: U.S. Actions Abroad Have Repeatedly Led to Unintended, Indefensible Consequences

And the United States? It turns out that we are one of the most aggressive nations in the world. From 1850 to 1980, we sent troops to other parts of the world more than 150 times (Kohn 1988). That's more than once a year. We continue this tradition of warfare today. At our current rate, it won't be long before the total reaches 200. Today we are "at war" with no one; that is, Congress has not declared an official war. Despite this, we have "intervened" (as U.S. politicians like to call it) in this order: El Salvador, Honduras, Libya, Grenada, Panama, Afghanistan, Iraq, Somalia, Haiti, Bosnia, Sudan, Kosovo—and then back again to Afghanistan and Iraq. As I write this, the media are reporting that the need to bomb nuclear sites in Iran and North Korea is growing urgent. The targets of our "military interventions" differ throughout time, but not our perception of endless enemies and our readiness to attack them.

Measuring War in Terms of Deaths

View on MySocLab Figure: Deaths of Americans in Eleven U.S. Wars

War may be hell, as General William T. Sherman said, but some wars are more hellish than others. Consider the following. Since 1829, there have been approximately

- 80 wars in which 3,000 to 30,000 people died
- 42 wars in which 30,000 to 300,000 people died
- 12 wars in which 300,000 to 3,000,000 people died
- 2 wars (World Wars I and II) in which 3,000,000 to 31,000,000 people died (Richardson 1960; updated to 2013).

If your brother or sister dies in a war, of course, it matters little that there were 3,000 or 3 million other victims of that war. On a personal level, we measure things by how they affect us.

Our Growing Capacity to Kill. To understand war, we need to recognize how greatly industrialization has increased our capacity to kill. Consider bombs. When Germany and England were at each other's throats during World War I, fewer than 3 of every 100,000 people in these countries died from bombs. During the next 20 years, scientists "advanced" this new instrument of human destruction as well as the aircraft to deliver it, and during World War II bombs killed about 300 of every 100,000 English and Germans (Hart 1957). Scientists have continued to "advance" our killing technology, and if nations were to unleash nuclear weapons against one another today, the deaths of past wars would pale in comparison. Some of our "advanced" weapons have the capacity to destroy every living thing on earth.

The Slaughter Continues. Many have hoped that war would become a relic of our primitive past. With higher levels of education, the thinking went, we humans would finally achieve a more advanced state. From our peaceful ways of resolving political conflict, we could look back smugly and reflect on how people used to slaughter one another.

Listen on MyHistoryLab Audio: NPR: The Long War In Afghanistan

As we all know, this description doesn't even come close to matching reality. Two generations ago, the United States fought in Vietnam for 7 years—with a loss of 58,000 Americans and 1 million Vietnamese (Hirschman et al. 1995). The death toll of the Soviet Union's 9-year war in Afghanistan ran about 1 million Afghans and perhaps 20,000 Soviet soldiers (Armitage 1989). Iran and Iraq fought an 8-year war at a cost of 400,000 lives. About 4,500 U.S. and other coalition soldiers died in Iraq, while estimates of Iraqi deaths run over a half million (Tavernise and McNeil 2006; O'Hanlon and Livingston 2010). At the time of this writing, Afghanistan, the longest war in U.S. history, is winding down.

In Sum ▸ War, then, as Sorokin sadly concluded in the 1930s, remains common. Sorokin added that his era was one of the bloodiest periods in the history of Western civilization—and perhaps in the history of humanity. Our era continues on this bloody path. Even after generations pass, some groups claim the right to hate eternally—and to pass this bitter heritage to their children. The Israelis and Palestinians, as reported in our nightly news, each claim rightful vengeance for atrocities of the past. So do Pakistanis and Indians, Kyrgyz and Uzbeks, Georgians and Russians, and on and on. The soldiers of China, India, Israel, Russia, and the United States stand armed and ready to battle. Suicide bombers continue to fuel enmities, launching armies around the globe. Drones silently patrol the skies, operators far away, safely ensconced in hidden quarters, giving the command to launch missiles on the unsuspecting.

Looking at the Problem Theoretically

Let's use sociological theory to better understand the social problem of war.

14.3 Discuss the perspectives that emerge when you apply symbolic interactionism, functionalism, and conflict theory to war.

Symbolic Interactionism

As you know from previous chapters, symbolic interactionists emphasize how significant *perceptions* are in human behavior. You know this from your own experience, of course, for your own behavior depends on how you perceive a situation. But did you know that the fate of the world has also depended on people's perceptions? Let's see how this can be.

Perceptions and the Arms Race. As I mentioned, during the Cold War the United States and the Soviet Union viewed each other as mortal enemies. Fearing one another, each interpreted the actions of the other as evil. If one side were to underestimate the enemy, it could prove fatal. To be on the safe side, each magnified the destructive capacity of the other. Because neither had valid data, each had to *guess* what the other intended. Both used their guesses to choose what seemed to be the most practical response.

This guessing game led to an ironic self-fulfilling prophecy. When one superpower thought that the other might build a certain weapon, it rushed to build that weapon itself. Sometimes the other nation had no intention of building the weapon, but when that nation learned that the other was doing so, it felt no choice but to also build it. What were intended as countermeasures were twisted into aggressive actions. Each stimulated the other nation to build weapons it had no intention to build and could not afford.

This almost sounds like science fiction, but listen to how Robert McNamara explained it. As the U.S. Secretary of Defense, McNamara was an insider who saw this insidious process at work (Kurth 1974):

> *In 1961 when I became Secretary of Defense, the Soviet Union possessed a very small operational arsenal of intercontinental missiles. However, they did possess the technological and industrial capacity to enlarge that arsenal very substantially over the succeeding several years. We had no evidence that the Soviets did plan, in fact, fully to use that capability. But, as I have pointed out, a strategic planner must be conservative in his calculations; that is, he must prepare for the worst plausible case and not be content to hope and prepare merely for the most probable.*
>
> *Since we could not be certain of Soviet intentions, since we could not be sure that they would not undertake a massive buildup, we had to insure against such an eventuality by undertaking ourselves a major buildup of the Minuteman and Polaris forces. . . . But the blunt fact remains that if we had more accurate information about planned Soviet strategic forces, we simply would not have needed to build as large a nuclear arsenal as we have today.*

This buildup of **intercontinental ballistic missiles (ICBMs)** illustrates a primary principle of symbolic interactionism—that meanings are central to human behavior. Because U.S. officials assumed that the Soviets were preparing for war, we built ICBMs so we could retaliate if we had to. This signaled to the Soviets that the United States was preparing to attack, and they also needed to build ICBMs. The nuclear arms race was based on interpretations of what each nation thought the other would do.

This example illustrates how *symbols are so powerful that they can take on a life of their own.* Although McNamara's initial perception of Soviet intentions might have been wrong, our buildup of missiles became proof to the Soviets that they needed to build more missiles. When the Soviets did so, this became proof to us that our interpretation was right. To keep ahead, we then needed to build even more powerful weapons. *Perceptions, not facts, usually guide human behavior.*

Perceptions and the "First Strike." This *principle of perceptions* is significant in all of human life. We like to think that we act on facts in our everyday lives, but we really act on our perceptions of "facts," on how we "think" things are. This basic principle of life takes on ominous significance when two nations are considering war. As long as these nations perceive war as a no-win situation, they will try to avoid it, even though they despise and fear one another.

But what if one nation thinks that the other will eventually attack and that striking first will destroy the other's capacity to attack? As you might guess, that nation may strike first. This was a dilemma during the Cold War. Generals of the U.S. Air Force even argued a *first-strike policy,* that we should attack Russia if it meant that we could win the war (Kurth 1974). Apparently, Soviet generals made the same argument. You can see how tense and dangerous things were at that time. In this situation, each felt the need to signal to the other that a strike against it would be foolish. Both the Soviet Union and the United States would let information slip about new weapons and defense systems like "Star Wars." It is scary to think that our lives—and those of the world—depended upon each side correctly interpreting the signals of the other!

Unfortunately, the past still clings to us. Both Russia and the United States still stubbornly hold onto the right of first-strike (Kozin 2013).

In Sum ▸ Symbolic interactionists stress that we choose courses of action based on how we perceive events. When we apply this principle to war, we see that nations often lack facts about what an enemy is doing. In this void, they make decisions based on their perceptions of current and potential acts of the adversary. In the Cold War, this principle of perceptions led to an arms race between Russia and the United States so severe that these countries developed weapons that could destroy humanity.

The functions of the form of hostility, conquest, and killing called war are discussed in the text. This painting is of one of the numerous sea battles between the European powers in the 1500s.

Functionalism

The functionalist perspective provides another picture of war. Let's look at war's functions and dysfunctions.

The Functions of War. In 1939, the world was in turmoil. Hitler's tanks and *Luftwaffe* (air force) were rampaging through Europe. Japan had invaded China and was threatening the South Pacific. With the United States on the brink of entering the war, sociologist Robert Park (1941) decided to analyze the social functions of war. Here are the functions that he and others identified.

Extension of Territory ▸ Park found that the world's countries had been born in war. The nations that existed in 1939—like those of today—had come into being because one group extended its political boundaries and conquered other groups. Today's United States, for example, would not exist if it hadn't been for the Indian wars and the wars with France, Great Britain, Spain, and Mexico. A major function of war, said Park, is the *extension of territory*, an enlargement of a group's political boundaries.

Economic Gain ▸ A second function of war is *economic gain*: access to treasure, markets, and raw materials such as oil (Pruitt and Snyder 1969). War also increases payrolls, production, and profits. World War II put millions of unemployed people to work and helped lift the United States out of the Great Depression. Even the threat of war can bring economic gain. As sociologist C. Wright Mills (1958) noted back in the 1950s, spending for "war readiness" benefits big business.

Social Integration ▸ A third function of war is *social integration.* If groups within a country are in conflict, they often put aside their differences and cooperate to repel their "mutual enemy" (Coser 1956; Timasheff 1965; Hoffman 2006). After the war, the groups are likely to return to their unfinished conflicts. Afghanistan, for example, is fragmented into groups separated by religious, class, tribal, and clan loyalties that reach back for centuries. When the Soviets invaded Afghanistan in 1979, these groups worked together to repel their common enemy. As soon as they defeated the Soviets, which took 9 years, they renewed their divisions and turned on one another. That the U.S. military fought in Afghanistan and Iraq united some enemies in the Arab world. When the United States leaves this region, these enemies, as before, will again turn on one another.

Social Change ▸ Sociologist Georg Simmel (1904) identified *social change* as a fourth function of war. The development of science and technology is one of those changes. Five centuries ago, for example, Leonardo da Vinci designed war machines for his patron. Since then, war has prompted aerodynamic designs, the harnessing of nuclear energy, and satellites. We even owe our interstate highways to war. When General Eisenhower arrived in Germany after its defeat in World War II, he was impressed by its *autobahns.* When he became president of the United States, Eisenhower decided that we needed highways like these so we could move soldiers, weapons, and supplies rapidly across the country in case the Soviets attacked. The Internet, too, came out of war; it was developed by the U.S. military as an alternative form of communication.

War also stimulates developments in surgery: Soldiers need to be patched up quickly so they can be sent back to battle. Currently under development is *long-distance surgery*: Using computers and robots, a surgeon in the United States can operate on a wounded soldier who is in some remote region of the world.

Other Functions ▸ Another function of war is *ideological*—advancing a political or religious system over an opposing one. Between the 11th and 14th centuries, European Crusaders traveled to the Holy Land to fight Islam. Today, al-Qaeda and its supporters violently advocate their ideological agenda. *Vengeance* or *punishment* is another function of war (Pruitt and Snyder 1969). Like people, nations can accumulate hurts and slights, and, under the right circumstances, use war to "get even." *Military security* is another function of war. That is, a nation does not desire an asset in and of itself, but attacks to prevent an enemy from using that asset against it. This is why Israel bombed Iraq's nuclear plants in 1981 and Syria in 2013, and why Iran may become a target. Another function of war is to *increase the credibility* of a nation's threats or guarantees. By going to war, other nations will see that a nation must be taken seriously, that it means what it says.

Multiple Functions ▸ No war serves a single function. A war can involve territory, revenge, ideology, and military security. When a conflict gets drawn out, the functions can even change. The Crusades began in 1095 when Pope Urban II urged Roman Catholics to go to war and reclaim the Holy Land. Ideological purposes may have dominated at first, but the Crusades also provided treasure and territory. Nine Crusades and 200 years later, all the functions of war had been incorporated in this single, sporadic war. If the "war against terrorism" goes on for decades, as seems likely, it, too, will end up serving all functions of war.

Functions for the Victors ▸ War is usually functional for the victors. Rome, for example, conquered most of the known world, subjugating one region after another to Roman power and exploiting their resources. To the acclaim of citizens and Caesar alike, generals would return triumphantly to Rome, marching in formation down the main avenue and into the main square, laden with treasure and slaves. The treasure enriched the government and its elite. Some of the slaves brought to Rome after the fall of Greece were educated Greeks, who served as tutors for the elite's children. In the latter part of the empire, slaves provided entertainment, their deaths in the Colosseum yielding pleasure for Rome's jaded citizens.

Functions for the Losers ▸ Although war is dysfunctional for losers, especially in terms of deaths, property destroyed, territories lost, and humiliation, losers can also benefit from war. One of the most remarkable examples occurred after World War II. After Japan's humiliating defeat, the county embraced Western technology. This change not only increased their standard of living and life expectancy, but also placed them in a world leadership position that they had failed to win through war. No social change is without its dysfunctions, however, and Japan's, too, has come at a price: the disruption of its traditional way of life.

Functions for Individuals ▸ War also has functions for soldiers and leaders. Soldiers often report that battle presents them with the challenge to "see what I'm made of." Officers who organize battles derive satisfaction from outmaneuvering the enemy, gaining advantage through surprise attacks, and being acclaimed the victor. War also serves as an avenue of social mobility. New officer positions are created, and individuals are promoted. The prestige of winning can also bring political prominence. George Washington, Andrew Jackson, Ulysses S. Grant, and Dwight D. Eisenhower, generals of the army, were awarded the presidency of the United States. Colin Powell went from general to national security advisor. From there, he became U.S. Secretary of State, one of the most powerful positions in the world.

Dysfunctions of War ▸ In stark contrast to the functions we reviewed are war's dysfunctions. Defeat, of course, is war's most well-known dysfunction, as are the destruction of cities, the loss of territory, and the deaths of soldiers and citizens. We can also number the fatherless and motherless children among war's dysfunctions, as well as the bitterness that can span generations. Even military victory can bring dysfunctions.

What dysfunctions of war can you identify in this photo from Somalia?

The victor can grow dependent on the exploitation of subjugated peoples. When that control ends, as inevitably it does, the economic pain is severe. For decades, Great Britain suffered withdrawal pains after it lost many of its colonies as a result of the fervor for independence ushered in by World War II. With the breakup of the Soviet empire, forged by war, Russia experienced this same dysfunction.

In Sum ▸ The many functions of war include the extension of territory, economic gain, social integration of rival groups, and social change. Among the dysfunctions of war are deaths, destruction of property, and loss of territory. There can also be dysfunctions for the victors of war and functions for the losers of war.

Conflict Theory

Three Reasons Nations Go to War. Let's try to understand better why nations go to war. Here are three reasons stressed by conflict theorists.

Resources ▸ Back in the 1300s, Ibn Khaldun of Tunis stressed that as groups struggle to survive, they compete for scarce resources. Inevitably, they come into conflict with one another, and war is one way they resolve their conflict.

Building on this explanation, conflict theorists have developed what they see as the central force in human history, the struggle for control over resources. In each society, some group gains control. This group, which conflict theorists call the **bourgeoisie**, uses society's resources to keep itself in power and to exploit the less powerful. As the bourgeoisie expands its power beyond its borders, it comes into conflict with the bourgeoisie of another country. Their quarrel over resources often leads to war. Those who hold power don't do the fighting, of course. Instead, they send young men (and sometimes young women) to battle for them. Most of these soldiers come from poor workers, the **proletariat**. The German generals used the term "cannon fodder" to refer to the young men among the poor who died in such outrageous numbers in their wars.

Expansion of Markets ▸ The second explanation focuses on the expansion of markets. In 1902, John Hobson, an economist, noted that as capitalism grows, it develops surplus capital. Business leaders want to invest this capital, so they look for ways to expand their markets. They then persuade the government to go to war and take over other lands. The result is **imperialism**, the pursuit of profits and markets by war and threat of war.

A Military Machine ▸ Another economist, Joseph Schumpeter, proposed a third explanation. He said (1919/1955) that the political elite build a strong military machine because it brings them power and prestige. Because the military machine was built to be used—sitting around idle was not its purpose—its very existence encourages war.

Because the military machine is so relevant for our situation today, let's look at it in more detail.

The Military Machine, the Power Elite, and the Globalization of Capitalism. Conflict theorists note that after World War I the United States dismantled its military, and U.S. war industries returned to their peacetime pursuits (Barber 1972). World War II, however, marked a turning point in U.S. history. When this war was over, the United States did not dismantle its war machine, as it had previously (Eisenhower 1961/1972). Instead, facing the Cold War, the United States, the Soviet Union, Great Britain, and France kept their military machines. Today, the United States military has *one and a half million* personnel on active duty and another million or so in reserve (*Statistical Abstract* 2013:Tables 519, 521).

Even when its archenemy turned away from communism to transform itself into a capitalist ally, the West did not disarm and join Russia in a new world of peace. On the contrary, the West continued to arm millions of its people and to develop new weapons, some even designed to turn space into a new venue of warfare. As Russia reestablishes its economy, it is regaining some of its lost political leverage. To propel itself as a prestigious power on the world stage, it is rebuilding its military machine. China, too, has been building its military forces. Backed by its two million soldiers and its first aircraft carrier, China has begun to flex its muscle by claiming sovereignty over disputed islands in the East China Sea ("The Dragon's New Teeth" 2012).

To understand why huge military forces have become a fact of life today, conflict theorists stress that we should look at the top levels of power. There we see the *power elite*—the top leaders of the military, business, and politics. As sociologist C. Wright Mills stressed, the interests of these groups have merged, with each benefiting from a strong military. Generals always support a powerful military, of course: This is their reason for being, and greater power bolsters their position.

This isn't new, but to this picture we need to add global capitalism. Business has increasingly expanded around the globe, and business leaders want a powerful military to protect their worldwide investments. That same military can protect them at home, putting down riots by upset citizens, or even suppressing a revolution. Politicians are sensitive to what the business elite wants because they depend on them to stay in office. To finance the military machine so desired by generals and business leaders, politicians invoke the terms *national security* and *homeland security*. Who can be against the protection of the nation?

In Sum ▸ Conflict theorists stress that the interests of nations collide as they compete with one another for resources and markets. The power elite of each nation uses its military to advance its interests. The United States uses its military machine to advance capitalism around the globe. U.S. armed forces join with those of Great Britain, France, Canada, and Australia to make the world safe for capitalism. The result, says Mills (1958:2), is that "war is no longer an interruption of peace; in our time; peace itself has become an uneasy interlude between wars. . . ."

Research Findings: War

14.4 Summarize what reduces war, the costs of war, dehumanization, the military–industrial complex, accidental war, and biological, chemical, and cyber warfare.

With war so prevalent—and today's weapons so powerful that they jeopardize even the existence of humanity—let's identify factors that reduce the likelihood of war. After this, we will examine the costs of war, both economic and human. Finally, we'll look at the power of the military–industrial complex in our lives, the possibility of accidental nuclear war, and biological and chemical warfare. To get an idea of the variety of research that sociologists do on war, see the Spotlight on Social Research box on the next page.

What Reduces War?

To see what reduces war, Quincy Wright (1942), a professor of international law, studied war throughout history. His findings, combined with those of physicist-mathematician Lewis Richardson (1960), are not encouraging. Here is what they found (Nettler 1976):

1. *Type of religion* does *not* reduce warfare. A nation in which Christianity is dominant does not go to war less than a nation in which Islam is dominant.
2. *Type of government* does *not* reduce warfare. Democracies and republics are neither more nor less peaceful than dictatorships and monarchies.
3. *Prosperity* does *not* reduce warfare. Prosperous nations are neither more nor less peaceful than poor nations. Nor do periods of prosperity reduce fighting.
4. *A shared religion* does *not* reduce warfare between nations.
5. *A common language* does *not* reduce warfare.
6. *More education* does *not* reduce warfare. Education does not create an "enlightened" preference for peace; countries with high education are as likely to go to war as those with low education.
7. *Being "neighbors"* does *not* reduce warfare. Rather, the *opposite* is true: Shared boundaries stimulate fights over territory. The more boundaries that countries share, the more wars they fight with one another.

Spotlight on Social Research

Adventures in Military Sociology

MORTEN ENDER, *professor at the United States Military Academy at West Point, does research on war, peace, and the military. In this essay, he discusses how he became interested in doing research on the military and his research experiences in Iraq. Here is what he wrote for you.*

Although an American, I spent many years living in West Germany during the Cold War. I often reflected on the impact that World War II had on the German people as well as on the Americans living there. Both world wars had a profound impact on my own family. After WWI, my maternal great-grandparents were forced to move to the hinterland of Germany and a more meager lifestyle. U.S. bombers destroyed my paternal great-grandfather's printing plant during WWII, and a generation later, my mother married an American soldier stationed in Germany. I came to the United States for the first time on a U.S. troop ship. My family's many moves during my formative years and the stories I heard of war sparked my interest in social change, especially radical and intense change, at the individual level.

When I began studying the military, I tried to develop knowledge in areas that had received little sociological attention, such as death and dying in a military context and military children. We learned that when a member of the military dies, the response is highly bureaucratic and task-focused, yet the notification and casualty officers keep the best interests of the survivors in mind. We also discovered that military children, who often live outside the country of their passport because of their parents' careers, have much in common with children of foreign service workers, missionaries, and those in international business.

I also had the opportunity to travel to Iraq and apply my sociological research skills to studying the Iraqi people. In a dangerous and compelling research environment, my research team helped assess the attitudes and opinions of Iraqis about their major social institutions—economics, politics, criminal justice, the family, education, the military, and medical care. We also studied Iraqi adolescents—their self-esteem and how they perceived their personal safety.

Because I was "embedded" with U.S. soldiers in Iraq, I was able to interview them, as well as observe their day-to-day activities on and off the Forward Operating Base. Some of the topics I explored were boredom, issues with families and spouses back in the States and Germany, and how they went about their jobs. One of the most notable findings is the decentralized nature of U.S. soldiering in Iraq. Previous wars were characterized by a hierarchical military situation; in Iraq, small groups of soldiers down to the level of 22-year-old platoon leaders make profound leadership decisions. For example, one might be responsible for training an entire police force for a neighborhood, or another might interact with the local leadership in a community, working with local mayors. This decentralized soldiering offers the opportunity to be creative and exercise autonomy. I asked soldiers an open-ended question on a survey about whether they use any creativity. A typical response was

> Every day! This place was not what we expected and therefore we have had to adapt on many occasions. One example is up-armoring of vehicles. Soldiers are very adaptive and creative and come up with very good ideas that other units are now using. Scheduling is another example. We are short many soldiers and have had to develop shift work that fits the number of people we have.

I also studied the soldiers' morale, cohesion, preparation, leadership, and attitudes toward the mission. In many of these areas I found evidence contrary to common expectations. For example, morale is high among soldiers in Iraq—in some cases higher than when they are at home. Further, many soldiers told me they enjoyed the mission in Iraq. They liked being a part of something larger than themselves. I found the soldiers to be very focused and committed to their jobs—the small-scale, daily missions. One day, at one of the larger post-exchanges (PXs)—which is affectionately called Wal-Mart because it has everything—I struck up a conversation with a 23-year-old Army reserve specialist from Woodstock, New York. He owned a small business back home, and his brother and wife were managing it for him. He was headed home for his once-a-year two-week R&R (rest and relaxation), but with great misgivings. His job in Iraq involved responsibility for training two 44- and 47-year-old Iraqi police officers. He appeared genuinely worried that although his "guys" had received the proper socialization into the policing role, without his structure and discipline, although for only a short while, they would fall back into bad habits, possibly putting themselves and others at risk. I asked why he didn't stay, and he said his sergeant was making him take some time off.

These findings are disheartening. It seems only common sense that democracy, prosperity, increased education, and a shared religion and language would reduce war. They don't. Experts can make up fancy terms like "conflict resolution," but despite all efforts to reduce war, the world's nations are *not* becoming more peaceful. And today's wars have become more lethal, killing more people than ever before in history. As sociologist Gwynne Nettler (1976) ruefully observed, the Nobel Peace Prize is typically awarded to a citizen of a nation that has recently been at war. Perhaps, he said, the prize is awarded on the basis of need, rather than as a recognition of achievement.

Money Spent on War

The Cold Numbers. The nations of the world spend about $1.5 trillion a year arming themselves (CIA 2010; Perlo-Freeman 2010). This number that trips so easily off the tongue comes to about $225 a year for every man, woman, and child on the entire planet.

Look at Table 14.1. You can see that the United States outspends its nearest competitor by about five times. As a percentage of its gross national product, however, you can see that Saudi Arabia spends more on its military. You might be surprised to see that India, where most people live in poverty, appears on this list of top spenders. India, like China, is so split by factions that its wealthy elite can hold the country together only by the power of its military.

Figure 14.1 on the next page shows how the United States has been increasing its military spending. The higher spending reflects the wars in Afghanistan and Iraq, as well as the cost of keeping over 200,000 troops on bases around the world—the only nation to do this (*Statistical Abstract* 2013:Table 525).

Listen on MySocLab Audio: NPR: Spending on Contracts in Iraq Nears $100B

What Is a Billion? As you probably have noticed from news reports, politicians throw the number billion around casually as they spend the nation's money. It is difficult, if not impossible, to wrap our minds around what one billion is, so how can we understand the $700 billion that the United States spends each year on what it euphemistically calls national defense? Consider this:

> *Let's suppose that you want to circle the earth with dollar bills. Each dollar bill is about 6 inches long. Laid end to end, it would take about 263 million bills to encircle the earth at the equator. The dollar bills of today's $700 billion "defense" budget would go around the earth 2,660 times.*

A more realistic picture of what the United States spends on war would include the costs of running the Central Intelligence Agency, the National Aeronautics and Space Administration, the Agency for International Development, and the Department of Homeland Security. Some argue it should also include the amounts spent on the Overseas Private Investment Corporation, the International Monetary Fund, and the World Bank (Greenberger 1994). If we include these costs, we would have to keep on wrapping those bills around the equator.

Another way to view the dollar costs of the military is to look at what the United States has spent to wage its wars. You can see a summary of these costs on Table 14.2. These huge amounts do not include its "little interventions" in places such as Bosnia and Kosovo.

TABLE 14.1 ▸ What Countries Spend the Most on Their Military?

Rank	Country	Amount (in billions)	% GNP
1	United States	$711	4.5%
2	China	$143	1.7%
3	Russia	$72	2.9%
4	United Kingdom	$63	2.8%
5	France	$62	2.6%
6	Japan	$59	1.3%
7	India	$49	1.1%
8	Saudi Arabia	$48	6.5%
9	Germany	$47	1.5%
10	Brazil	$35	1.4%

Sources: By the author. Based on CIA 2010; SIPRI 2012; *Statistical Abstract of the United States* 2013:Table 1420.

Lost Alternative Purchases. Let's try one more way to see what our many wars cost us. What other items could we buy with the same money? These are old totals, but I can't find anyone who has updated them. The general idea, however, remains. For what we pay for

1. one aircraft carrier, we could build 12,000 high schools
2. one naval weapons plant, we could build twenty-six 160-bed hospitals
3. one jet bomber, we could provide school lunches for 1 million children a year
4. one prototype bomber, we could pay the annual salaries of 250,000 teachers (de Silva 1980).

Money goes a lot further in the Least Industrialized Nations. There, the price of one tank would buy 1,000 classrooms. Many people dream of a more peaceful world in which military dollars are redirected toward education, medicine, and the enlightenment of nations. We do not live in such a world—and from all indications, we may never live in one.

Our armed forces employ 1.1 million soldiers and 700,000 civilians. Add the 1.1 million men and women in the reserves and National Guard, and the total comes to about 3 million people (*Statistical Abstract* 2013:Tables 516, 522, 523). For the cost of employing these 3 million men and women to fight or to be ready for war, we could pay 3 million people to work for the public good. We have 200,000 soldiers stationed in foreign countries. Think of how many tens of thousands of people we could send to poorer countries to build schools and hospitals, and reduce suffering. You probably can think of other uses for the large amounts of money we spend on the military.

But What Choice Is There? You might be thinking, "Yes, that's a nice thought, but it isn't practical. Without a military, an enemy would crush us." This dilemma is real. The United States does face it, just as other nations do. Although the military is costly both in money spent and benefits forgone, not spending this money would leave us vulnerable to attack. In light of the world's history, an assumption of danger is well founded, and we need a strong military. Only if all nations were to become pacifists and all dangers of attack cease would military preparedness become unnecessary.

The size of the armed forces, the amount of money we spend on the military, and the purposes for which the soldiers are used, however, are different matters entirely. It certainly is worth asking why the United States is the only nation to post troops in 130 countries around the world (Nekoomaram 2009). Just what interests are we protecting?

Deaths from War

During the 1700s, wars were fought according to aristocratic ideals. Small professional armies waged short, limited campaigns. In battle, the soldiers, wearing brightly colored uniforms, marched in formation. Accompanied them were flying flags and teenaged boys

FIGURE 14.1 ▸ U.S. Military Expenditures Since 1990

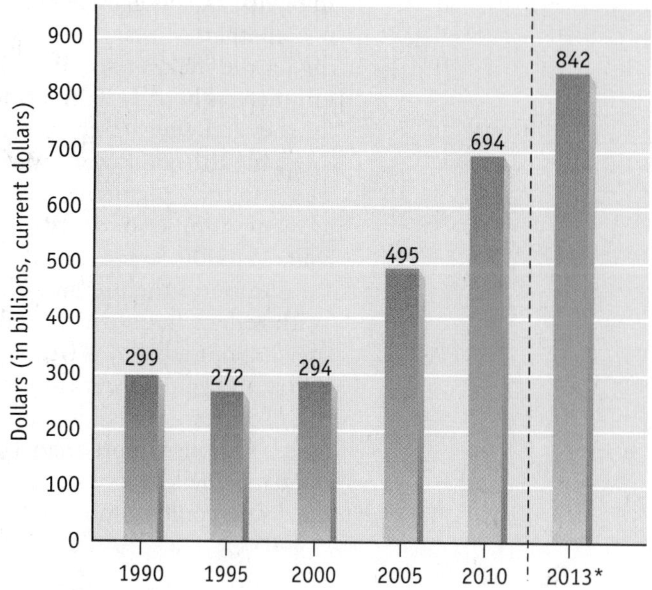

*Estimated.

Source: By the author. Based on *Statistical Abstract of the United States* 2013:Table 511.

TABLE 14.2 ▸ What Has the United States Spent on Its Wars?

War of 1812	$630,000,000
Mexican War	$1,155,000,000
American Revolution	$2,100,000,000
Spanish–American War	$6,300,000,000
Civil War	$48,300,000,000
Gulf War	$152,000,000,000
Korean War	$273,000,000,000
World War I	$390,000,000,000
Afghanistan	$444,000,000,000
Vietnam War	$580,000,000,000
Iraq War	$815,000,000,000
World War II	$3150,000,000,000
Total	$5,863,000,000,000

Note: The costs listed in *Statistical Abstract* are in 1967 dollars. To account for inflation, these amounts were increased by 355 percent and the costs of service-connected benefits were added. Where a range was listed, the mean was used. The costs do *not* include interest payments on war loans, nor are they reduced by the financial benefits to the United States, such as the acquisition of territory, as with California and Texas in the Mexican War. The costs for Afghanistan and Iraq are in current dollars, not adjusted for inflation.

These are rough estimates, not actual costs. The costs of the many "military interventions" such as in Grenada, Panama, Somalia, and Haiti are not listed in the source.

Sources: By the author. Based on *Statistical Abstract of the United States* 1993:Table 553, a table dropped after 1993. The cost for the Gulf War is from Conahan 1991, adjusted for inflation. The costs for Afghanistan and Iraq are in current dollars from Belasco 2009, 2011, totals that keep increasing.

playing drums, flutes, and other musical instruments. War at this time was considered to be like a chess game, with generals from aristocratic backgrounds matching wits with one another. Military officers, viewing war as a test of bravery, looked forward to fighting on the "field of honor." Townspeople viewed military encounters as a form of entertainment. The rich would ride to the battlefield in carriages, taking with them picnic lunches and wine, all the better to enjoy the "entertainment."

This attitude toward war persisted even until the time of our Civil War, when the rich also took picnic lunches with them to watch battles (Burns 1990). But with the growing number of deaths, attitudes changed. During the 4 brutal years of the Civil War, 620,000 Americans died, more than in all our other wars combined, from the Revolution to the present. No longer is there a "field of honor," if ever there was one. With today's mass armies and the capacity to deliver wholesale death, with industries spewing out advanced weapons, and with civilians no longer spared, an image of pageantry and games is far from reality.

Most fearful of all, today's weapons are so destructive that they threaten human existence. Although more than 100 million people have died in war since 1700, by today's standards the killing was rather inefficient (Gartner 1988). If we had another world war, the deaths could number in the hundreds of millions—if anyone were left to count them.

Dehumanization in War

Watch on
MySocLab Video:
Survey of US Troopson

Although we often calculate the cost of war in terms of money and deaths, war involves many other costs. Especially significant is war's toll on morality. War tends to break down norms that regulate human behavior. When soldiers are exposed to brutality and killing, they learn to *dehumanize* their opponents. That is, they come to see them as objects, not people. To dehumanize people removes the obligation to treat them as human beings.

Characteristics of Dehumanization. Social scientists have identified four key characteristics of **dehumanization** (Bernard et al. 1971):

1. *Increased emotional distance from others.* The individual stops identifying with others, seeing them as lacking basic human qualities. They become not people, but an object called "the enemy."
2. *An emphasis on following orders.* Orders and regulations become all-important. Those who do the "dirty work" don't question their orders, even if they involve atrocities. A person will say, "I don't like it, but it's necessary" or "We all have to die some day."
3. *Inability to resist pressures.* Fears of losing one's job or the respect of one's peers and supervisors or of having one's integrity and loyalty questioned become more important than morality.
4. *Diminished personal responsibility.* People come to see themselves as a small cog in a large machine. They are not responsible, because they have no choice. They are simply obeying orders. The superiors know best, for they have the information to judge what is right and wrong. The individual reasons "Who am I to question this?"

When dehumanization occurs, consciences become so numbed that people can dissociate killing—even torture—from their "normal self." Torture and killing become "dirty work" that has to be done. Those who do this "dirty work" think of themselves as duty-bound to obey orders, not to question them. The "higher-ups" who make the decisions are responsible, not the simple soldier who follows orders.

Dehumanization in Prolonged Conflicts. Sociologist Tamotsu Shibutani (1970) pointed out that dehumanization is especially common in prolonged conflicts. Long wars come to be viewed as a struggle between good and evil. People who don't want to torture or kill conclude that the survival of good (democracy, freedom, the nation, our way of life) hangs in the balance. This requires that they suspend moral standards. War, then, exalts treachery, brutality, and killing—and we give medals to honor behavior that we would otherwise condemn.

Dehumanization by the Nazis and Japanese. To participate in such acts, soldiers try to neutralize the morality they learned as children. During World War II, ordinary Germans—not Nazi ideologues—staffed concentration camps. They viewed the Jewish inmates as a blight on society. Surgeons who had been educated at top universities, whose profession called for them to be highly sensitive to people's needs, viewed the inmates as lesser humans than themselves. Methodically and dispassionately, they mutilated Jewish inmates just to study the results. Some doctors immersed Jews in vats of freezing water, considering their deaths insignificant because the results of the experiments might save the lives of German pilots shot down over the North Atlantic (Gellhorn 1959). The photos on this page are part of the research that these medical personnel produced.

The horrors of the Nazis were so extreme that no one could match them. Or so it might seem. Then we learn what the Japanese did. During World War II, they beheaded U.S. prisoners of war. Others they buried alive (Chang 1997). They also tortured prisoners and performed medical experiments on them (Daws 1994). In one experiment, Japanese doctors pumped U.S. prisoners full of horse blood. In another, they injected them with typhus, typhoid, smallpox, and other diseases. In one test, they lined up 10 prisoners of war "behind a protective screen with their naked buttocks exposed to see what damage would result when a bomb was detonated" (Leighty 1981). In China, the Japanese experimented with germ warfare, killing perhaps hundreds of thousands of Chinese using anthrax, typhoid, and plague (Harris 1994).

To them, those they killed were no longer real people. They had been transformed mentally into a "subhuman enemy."

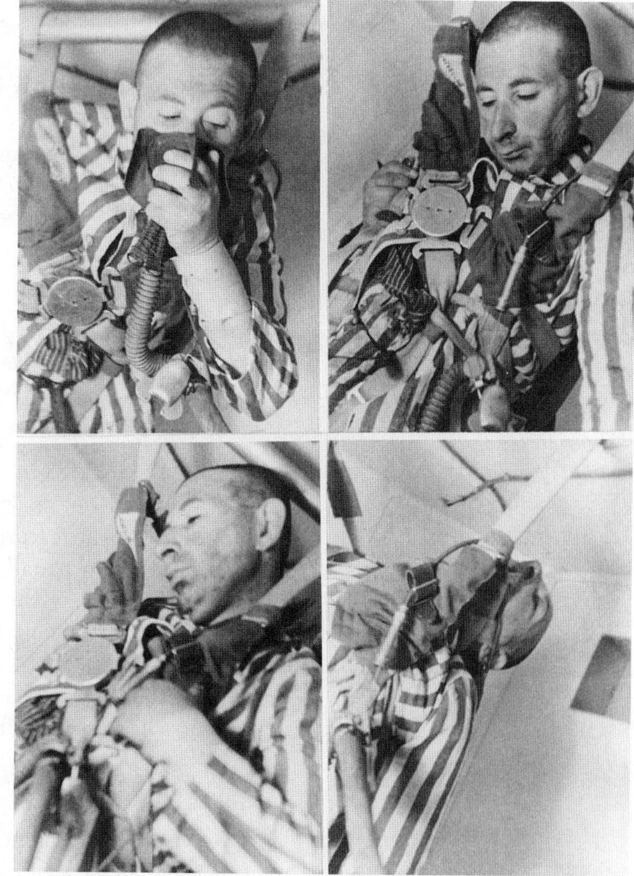

The extent to which dehumanization can alienate us from ordinary human feelings is incredible. To measure the effects of compression and decompression, German doctors placed this inmate of a concentration camp in a pressure chamber. As the doctors manipulated the air pressure, they observed and photographed the man's death.

Dehumanization by the U.S. Military. The Germans and Japanese carried dehumanization to horrifying limits, but they were not unique. U.S. soldiers in Vietnam also dehumanized their opponents. To U.S. soldiers, the Vietnamese became less than human—they were transformed into "gooks," "dinks," and "slants." Some soldiers became so effective at dehumanization that they shot mothers fleeing with their babies, the act dissociated from the self. Others found dehumanization more difficult, but it was better not to question the morality of the act. It was better to think of what they did as part of the larger scheme of things, such as saving people from communism—or as rightful retaliation for fellow soldiers who had been killed: "I don't like doing this, but this is war."

Something similar is happening today. When U.S. (and coalition) forces bomb military targets, civilians are often killed. The military does not refer to them as "murdered children, mothers, and fathers." They don't even call them "dead people" or "dead civilians." Instead, the military has developed a term that removes people entirely. To refer to the unintentional deaths of civilians during combat operations, the military uses the term *collateral damage*. Talk about symbolizing people out of existence!

Children often bear the scars of war. These children are fleeing flaming napalm that was intended to root out Viet Cong. The photo was taken in 1972 in Trang Bang, Vietnam.

When Dehumanization Fails. Although techniques of neutralization can protect the self, they are not foolproof. And when they fail, they can lead to crippling guilt. Tim, for example, was a Marine interrogator in Vietnam. Beating prisoners to gain information was part of his job. When beating did not work, he used electric shock by attaching "two wires of a field telephone to the earlobe, the cheek, the temple, or sometimes the balls or the crotch" (Smith 1980:27). One day while Tim was interrogating a 16-year-old girl, he began to think:

> *Why are we killing all these people? These aren't soldiers. I'm beating on this girl—and it all hit me. I'm beating up this girl, what for? Who am I? . . . It was as if for the first time I was looking at myself. Here's this guy, slapping, beating on this girl—for what? . . . For the first time I was looking at this person, a detainee, as a real human being, not as a source of information.*

You can see how dehumanization failed Tim. And this change in perspective—from "source of information" to "person"—had a direct effect on his job. As he said, "I wasn't a very good interrogator from that time on. I lost all motivation."

Dehumanization usually holds up well while at war, with soldiers surrounded by army buddies who view the enemy in the same way. Upon returning home, however, former soldiers are resocialized into more standard norms—which tends to break down the definitions that worked for them during war. As this occurs, many former soldiers become disturbed by the harm they did during the war. Before putting a bullet in his head, here is what a soldier from California wrote in his suicide note:

> *I can't sleep anymore. When I was in Vietnam, we came across a North Vietnamese soldier with a man, a woman, and a 3- or 4-year-old girl. We had to shoot them all. I can't get the little girl's face out of my mind. I hope that God will forgive me. I hope the people in this country who made millions of dollars off the men, women, and children that died in that war can sleep at night (I can't, and I didn't make a cent). (Smith 1980:15)*

The norms of dehumanization also failed some of the Japanese soldiers who had participated in the atrocities of World War II. After keeping quiet for 50 years, some of them publicly confessed their mass rapes and killings (Chang 1997). This offended other former Japanese soldiers, who denounced the confessions.

Let's turn from what has been a symbolic interactionist analysis of war to the conflict perspective and examine how organizations profit from warfare.

The Military–Industrial Complex

The Military as an Economic Force. The military has become a powerful force in the U.S. economy. Many of the billions of dollars listed on Tables 14.1 and 14.2 on pages 480 and 481 go to the companies that produce **armaments**—guidance systems, bombs, missiles, tanks, planes, guns, ships, submarines, and other weapons. There is no end to the need for more military weapons. Like cell phones and computers, they quickly become obsolete and need to be replaced with more sophisticated models.

Read on **MySocLab**
Document:
Military Partisanship

The billions of dollars spent on military contracts and by military employees also make the military a powerhouse in the U.S. economy. Table 14.3 shows the 10 states that receive the most income from military contracts. As you can see, each of these states receives several billion dollars. The many military employees in these states support their local economies. Military spending likely has the greatest impact on the state of Virginia. This state of 8 million people has over $18 billion in military contracts. Its many defense (war) workers bring in several more billions a year.

Table 14.3 can help you understand why it is difficult to reduce military spending. When—rarely, but occasionally—the military decides that a base is no longer needed, unions and businesses send lobbyists to Washington to fight to keep it. That the military no longer needs or wants the base pales in comparison with the state's need to keep the money flowing into it's economy. In this case, the slogan NIMBY (Not In My Back Yard) has changed to KIMBY (Keep It In My Back Yard).

The interests of the military and defense industries have become so intertwined that the two have become known as the **military–industrial complex**. The word incestuous comes to mind to describe their symbiotic relationship. Here is what happens: The defense industry hires top-ranking military officers when they retire. Their job is to sell military products (planes, guns, armored vehicles, etc.). Who do they contact to make the sale? Officers in the military who are in charge of purchases, of course. Some of these officers are old friends, while others are friends of friends. Even if they don't know the individuals, their cooperation is built in as these officers are eyeing high-paying jobs in the defense industry when they retire from the military.

And round and round the circle goes.

The relationship with Congress is also cozy. When the military–industrial complex asks for billions of dollars to develop new weapons and to maintain the armed forces,

TABLE 14.3 ▸ Where Defense Dollars Go: The Top 10 States

Rank	State	Payroll for Military Contracts	Military Employees	Civilian Employees
1	Texas	$20,000,000,000	132,000	48,000
2	Virginia	$18,000,000,000	63,000	25,000
3	California	$15,000,000,000	118,000	61,000
4	Georgia	$12,000,000,000	74,000	37,000
5	North Carolina	$11,000,000,000	116,000	21,000
6	Florida	$9,000,000,000	43,000	28,000
7	Washington	$8,000,000,000	46,000	28,000
8	Maryland	$6,000,000,000	29,000	35,000
9	Alabama	$5,000,000,000	12,000	25,000
10	Hawaii	$4,000,000,000	41,000	18,000

Source: By the author. Based on *Statistical Abstract of the United States* 2013:Tables 514 and 516.

Congress listens. How difficult it is to resist the siren call for more military spending. The military parades a constant stream of enemies before Congress, each of which, of course, requires more planes, ammunition, and so forth. Not only is it patriotic to support the military, but military spending also means that senators and representatives can channel contracts into their home districts. This makes them popular at home and increases their chance of being reelected, apparently their primary purpose in life.

The Business of Death. To focus on the profits for corporations, the spending in local economies, and congressional elections can take our eyes off a fundamental characteristic of the military and the industries that support it: They represent death. Their existence depends on killing.

And the military–industrial complex is efficient at its business of death. During the arms race, the West and the Soviet Union gave some of their top scientists the assignment of increasing the destructive power of weapons. The capacity for inflicting death grew so sharply that in 1970 a critic noted that *if a bomb the size of the one dropped on Hiroshima had exploded every single day from the birth of Christ until that year, the total force of those bombs would be less than the destructive capacity of the United States* (Melman 1970).

To the destructive capacity of the United States, we can add the nuclear weapons of Russia, France, Great Britain, and other countries shown on the Social Map on the next two pages. It is almost impossible to grasp the destructive capacity that these nations possess. Consider this: The explosive energy of nuclear weapons is measured in megatons. If you had 1 million tons of TNT, you would have one **megaton**. The United States has over 3,000 megatons of explosive power. Let's assume that the total of the other nuclear nations combined equals only that of the United States. Now think of a freight train filled with gunpowder stretching from the earth to the moon. That wouldn't even come close to the destructive power these nations have stored up. You would have to make it *eight* times longer, 2 million miles long (Cf., *Nucleus* 1981).

Poets have written elegantly about the folly of humanity, but perhaps this image of a train filled with gunpowder that is eight times longer than a trip to the moon is more vivid.

A Glimmer of Hope. In the midst of this nuclear folly lies a glimmer of hope. Since the Cold War ended, Russia and the United States have negotiated a series of agreements to reduce their nuclear stockpiles. The latest one, called New START (New Strategic Arms Reduction Treaty), shrinks each country's nuclear arsenal from 2,200 nuclear warheads to 1,500 warheads (Baker and Bilefsky 2010). Top U.S. military commanders are saying that this number is still more than we need and have asked for a reduction to 900 warheads (Shanker 2012). Perhaps one day we can have the pleasure of **nuclear disarmament**, getting rid of all nuclear weapons.

While the reduction of nuclear weapons makes the world safer, we need to note that Russia and the United States are merely *reducing excess capacity:* Each nation can still destroy the other many times over—and still take the rest of the world along with it.

The Possibility of Accidental War

Nuclear proliferation, more and more nations possessing nuclear weapons, increases the risk that nuclear weapons will end up in the hands of a group that wants to bend nations to their will. The technology—how to design, engineer, and build nuclear weapons—has even been put on the market. The "father of the Pakistani bomb," Abdul Qadeer Khan, who headed Pakistan's nuclear program, sold blueprints and parts for making nuclear bombs to Iran and North Korea (Rubin 2004). A major fear of the West is that al-Qaeda will get its hands on nuclear weapons.

The threat of nuclear war comes from many directions: conflict between major powers, dictators of small nations, and terrorists from no nations. Is it possible, too, that nuclear missiles could be unleashed accidentally? Let's consider this chilling thought.

FIGURE 14.2 ▸ The Nuclear Club: Members, Former Members, and Aspiring Members

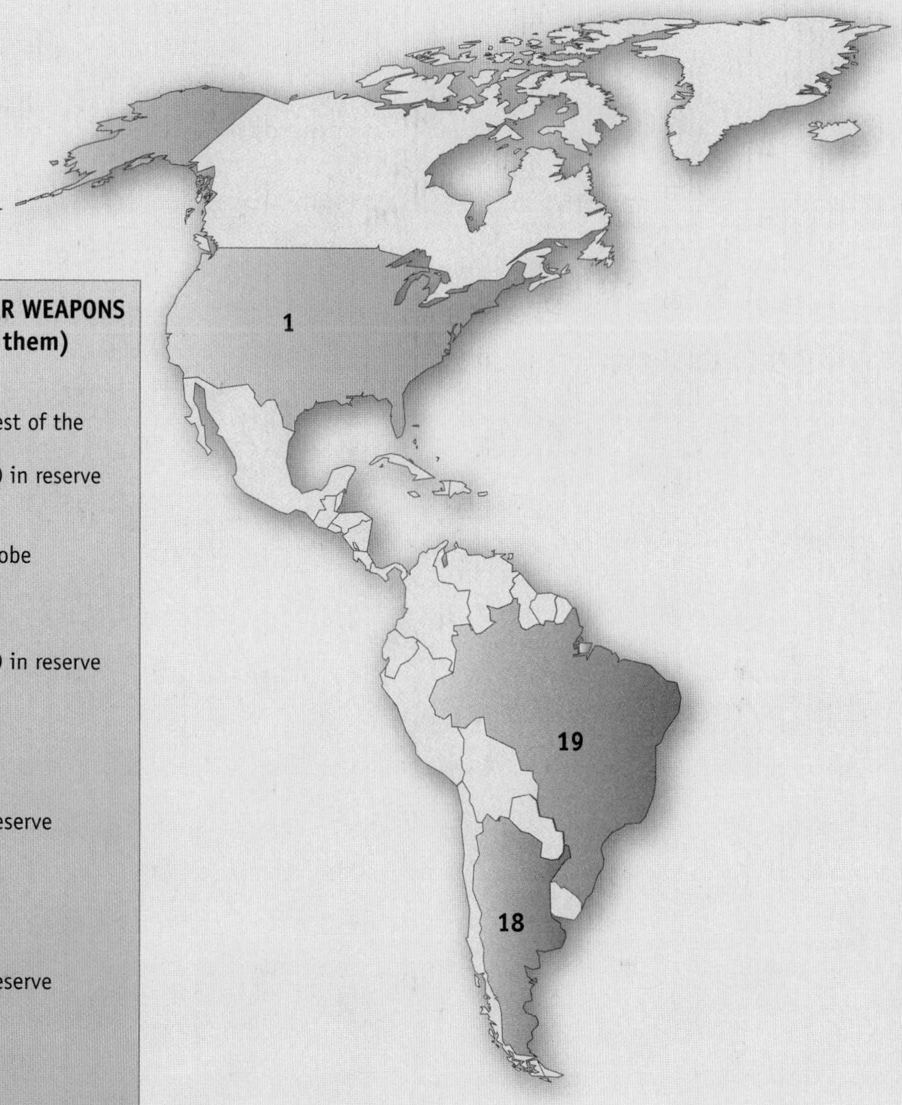

COUNTRIES THAT HAVE NUCLEAR WEAPONS (and the year they developed them)

1. 1945, United States
Tests: Over 1,030; more than the rest of the world combined.
Warheads: 2,150 on missiles, 5,850 in reserve
Has missiles on submarines
Range: 8,100 miles
Is able to reach any spot on the globe

2. 1949, Russia
Tests: 715
Warheads: 1,800 on missiles, 8,200 in reserve
Has missiles on submarines
Range: 6,800 miles

3. 1960, France
Tests: 210
Warheads: 290 on missiles, 10 in reserve
Has missiles on submarines
Range: 3,300 miles

4. 1952, Great Britain
Tests: 45
Warheads: 160 on missiles, 65 in reserve
Has missiles on submarines
Range: 7,500 miles

5. 1964, China
Tests: 45
Warheads: 240
Has missiles on submarines
Range: 6,800 miles

6. 1967, Israel
Tests: Unknown
Warheads: 80
Range: 1,200 miles

7. 1974, India
Tests: 6
Warheads: 100
Range: 1,550 miles

8. 1998, Pakistan
Tests: 6
Warheads: 100
Range: 1,000 miles

9. 2006, North Korea
Tests: 2
Warheads: About 10
Range: 1,000 miles

COUNTRIES THAT ARE DEVELOPING NUCLEAR WEAPONS

10. Iran
Tests: None yet
Warheads: None yet
Range: 1,200 miles
As of this writing in 2013, is enriching uranium and under U.N. sanctions

Note: Many items are estimates from specialists and should be taken as approximate.

Sources: Various, including Crail 2010; "Nuclear Weapons . . ." 2010; Kile 2012; SIPRI 2012.

FIGURE 14.2 ▸ *Continued*

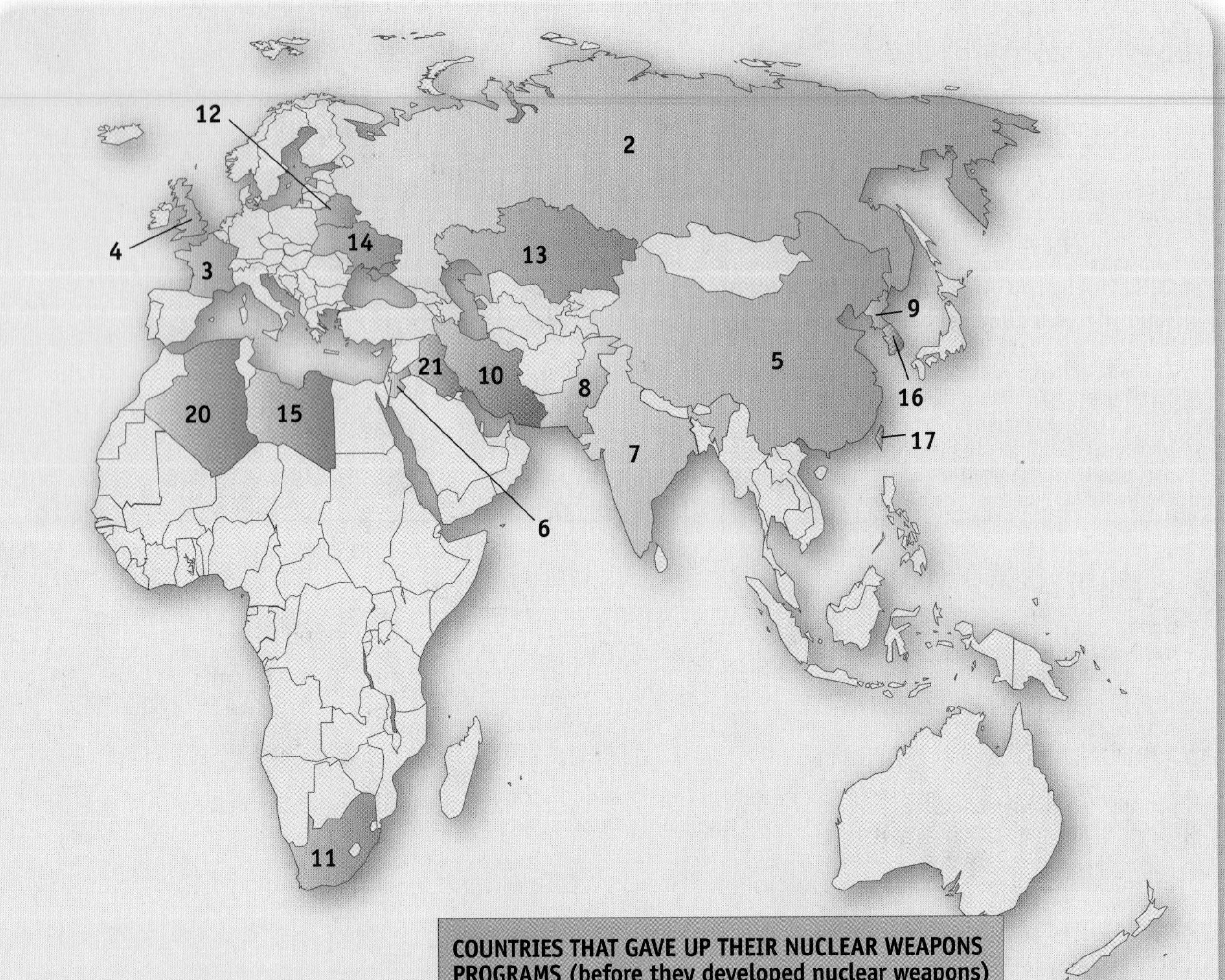

COUNTRIES THAT HAVE GIVEN UP NUCLEAR WEAPONS

11. 1991, South Africa
Dismantled its nuclear arsenal and signed the Nuclear Non-Proliferation Treaty

12. 1991, Belarus
Returned to Russia the nuclear weapons left on its soil when the Soviet Union broke up in 1991

13. 1991, Kazakhstan
Returned to Russia the nuclear weapons left on its soil when the Soviet Union broke up in 1991

14. 1991, Ukraine
Returned to Russia the nuclear weapons left on its soil when the Soviet Union broke up in 1991

COUNTRIES THAT GAVE UP THEIR NUCLEAR WEAPONS PROGRAMS (before they developed nuclear weapons)

15. 1975 and 2003, Libya
In 1975, signed the Nuclear Non-Proliferation Treaty but violated it by continuing its nuclear program. Gave up its program in 2003.

16. 1975, South Korea
Gave up its program and signed the Nuclear Non-Proliferation Treaty.

17. 1978 and 1988, Taiwan
In 1978, gave up its program. Began again, and in 1988 again discontinued it.

18. 1990, Argentina
Stopped its program and signed a nuclear weapons-free zone agreement in South America

19. 1990, Brazil
Stopped its program and in 1998 signed a nuclear weapons-free zone agreement in South America

20. 1991, Algeria
Dismantled its program and signed the Nuclear Non-Proliferation Treaty

21. 1991, Iraq
Program stopped with U.S.-led invasion (Gulf War)

Computer Failure. Although few people know it, we have come close to unintended launchings of nuclear missiles. Here is an actual event:

Back in 1980, a military computer reported that Russia had fired missiles at the United States. The United States immediately went to red alert. U.S. bombers plotted courses toward pre-selected targets in the Soviet Union, and we prepared our missiles for launching. The countdown toward nuclear devastation had begun. (U.S. News & World Report, June 24, 1980)

Russia had *not* launched missiles. A computer had malfunctioned. Fortunately, the error was caught in time. If it hadn't, you wouldn't be reading this book.

Human Error. The obliteration of humanity could also come from simple human error. Here's another real-life event:

On October 28, 1962, the North American Defense Command was informed that Cuba had launched a nuclear missile, and it was about to hit Tampa, Florida. The U.S. began a countdown for its retaliatory strike. Then someone noticed that there had been no explosion in Tampa. (Sagan 1994)

It turned out that a radar operator had accidentally inserted into the system a test tape that simulated an attack from Cuba. If the United States had launched immediately, instead of waiting a few moments, Cuba would have been destroyed. The Soviet Union, Cuba's ally at the time, might have responded with an attack of its own.

Nuclear Accidents. It can make your hair stand on end—since the unintended detonation of a nuclear weapon could signal the end of human civilization—but here are some real-life nuclear accidents. These were reported by Rear Admiral Gene LaRocque, U.S. Navy (retired):

The George Washington, *a missile submarine, ran into a Japanese ship and sank it.*
The Scorpion *and the* Thresher, *two nuclear attack submarines, sank in the ocean.*
When a mechanic dropped a wrench in a missile silo in Arkansas, a missile was launched.
Several nuclear weapons have fallen out of planes, through open bomb bays. (Keyes n.d.)

From a symbolic interactionist point of view, though, this is my favorite:

A nuclear weapon fell from a plane into a swamp in the Carolinas. The Air Force was unable to find it! So what did they do about such an outrageous situation? The solution they hit upon was Orwellian. The Defense Department bought the land, put a fence around it and called it a "nuclear safety area." (Keyes n.d.)

Fortunately for us, in none of these incidents did a nuclear weapon detonate. We have no assurance that similar accidents will not happen again or that, if they occur, that the weapons will not explode. The military is well aware of the possibility of accidental nuclear war, which is one reason they want to reduce the number of nuclear missiles (Shanker 2012).

Nuclear Sabotage. The U.S. government has repeatedly assured us—and the world—that a missile cannot be launched without proper authorization. Any talk to the contrary, they say, is alarmist. Is it?

The year was 1962. President Kennedy had backed down in the Bay of Pigs invasion of Cuba, and the Soviet military thought that he would back down from them as well. Khrushchev, the premier of the Soviet Union, decided to ship missiles to Cuba. The CIA reported that the missiles would be capable of destroying the Pentagon, New York City, and other U.S. cities. Kennedy warned Khrushchev to order the ships back and set up a blockade to intercept them. The world waited tensely, television reporting the location of the ships as they neared the blockade.

Behind the scenes, though, something was taking place that the world did not know about:

At the height of the Cuban crisis, officers at Malmstrom Air Force Base in Montana, who also doubted the resolve of President Kennedy to give the order to bomb the Soviets, did what was supposedly impossible: They manipulated their Minutemen missiles so they could launch them on their own.

After the crisis, the Air Force investigated how officers at Malmstrom had given themselves the ability to launch missiles—and kept it secret. (Sagan 1994)

Nature. Even natural events can set off an accidental war.

In 1983, the Soviets set up a new surveillance system to monitor nuclear weapons in North Dakota. The sun lined up in such a way that it fooled the system into reporting that the United States had launched five missiles at the Soviet Union.

If the Russian military officers in charge of giving the order to launch missiles in case of an attack by the United States had been informed, you probably would not be here today. Fortunately for us and the world, the Russian officer in charge of the system had an incredibly cool head. He refused to report the launch to his superiors. He said, "When people start a war, they don't start it with only five missiles" (Lewis 2004).

The Significance of Symbolic Interaction. These hair-raising events demonstrate the significance of symbolic interaction. To understand an event, we must interpret it. If the Russian in charge of the surveillance system had not interpreted the event correctly, the world might have been plunged into nuclear war. And if a missile were launched accidentally, perhaps even destroying a city, as could happen with a computer malfunction or an unauthorized launch, military and political leaders would have to answer this question: Is this an accident, an unauthorized attack by a madman, or an authorized attack?

Fortunately, the United States and Russia have agreed to notify the other if either spots a missile—and to help each other track and destroy it (Greenberger 1992). Although their intention is to protect one another against missile attacks by a third nation, their cooperation also helps to prevent accidental nuclear war.

Biological and Chemical Warfare

One of the strangest quirks of human thinking is this—to kill with bullets or bombs is considered normal, but to kill with gas is deemed abnormal. During World War I, the French and Germans shocked the world by using poison gas. After that war, in 1925, the major powers met in Geneva, where they signed an agreement banning the use of poison gases in warfare. In 1972, they agreed not to use biological weapons either (Seib 1981). In 1989, 145 nations met to try to put an end to chemical weapons (Revzin 1989). They failed.

Biological and Chemical Agents in War. Only a few nations have ever used biological and chemical agents as weapons. In World War I, France and Germany used mustard gas on each other. In World War II, as I already mentioned, Japan used biological weapons against the Chinese. Other instances of chemical warfare include Iran and Iraq using mustard gas against one another in the 1980s. The Soviets have been accused of using chemicals against their enemies in Afghanistan, but they deny the accusations (Douglass 1998). In 2013, the government of Syria reportedly used chemical weapons in its civil war. For using poison gas to quell an uprising by the Kurds, Saddam Hussein was sentenced to death. Photos of his victims helped support the U.S. decision to invade Iraq.

In the 1960s and 1970s, the United States dropped 20 million gallons of **Agent Orange**—a chemical defoliant—on Vietnam (Ives 2012). Agent Orange was not intended as a weapon to kill people, but as a way of destroying crops and clearing terrain. Spraying stopped when Vietnamese women gave birth to deformed babies, such as the young man shown in the photo on the next page. After the war, thousands of Vietnam veterans claimed that Agent Orange had damaged their health. In 1989, each soldier who had sued the government was awarded about $12,000. The military finally acknowledged the problem, and its budget now includes $13 billion to treat health problems caused by Agent Orange ("Senate Passes . . ." 2010). In addition, the United States is cleaning the contamination from one of its former bases in Vietnam (Ives 2012).

The Treaty with a Giant Flaw. The military's logic is sometimes difficult to follow. The Pentagon once attempted to convince Congress that the United States could use chemical weapons to bring about peace. If the United States developed more powerful chemical weapons, they argued, the Soviets would agree to "a complete and verifiable ban on the development, production, and stockpiling of chemical weapons" because this more powerful weapon would be "dangling over their heads" (*Wall Street Journal,* February 9, 1982).

Even without that particular weapon, the United States, Russia, and most nations of the world have signed a Chemical Weapons Convention. They have agreed not to produce, stockpile, or use chemical weapons. The nations that have chemical weapons are destroying them. The flaw? Biological weapons are not covered by this treaty.

Continued Research and Production. The end of the Cold War did not mark the end of the development of biological weapons. Russia even announced that it had genetically engineered an anthrax microbe that attacks blood cells, making vaccines useless (Broad and Miller 1998). Supposedly, Russia has also armed its ICBM warheads with plague, anthrax, and smallpox (Douglass 1998). If so, we may assume that the United States has done the same. Even if Russia and the United States end their race toward biological destruction, this would not mean that other nations, also pursuing these same goals, would cease their efforts.

With the world's stockpiles of lethal biological agents, combined with a spreading knowledge of how to develop and deploy them, we live with the possibility that terrorists will get their hands on these weapons. Let's consider this possibility.

The human costs of war far outnumber the soldiers who are killed and maimed. Shown here is a victim of Agent Orange, a defoliant used by U.S. troops in Vietnam to clear the forests to disrupt the movement of troops and supplies from the north. Birth defects, especially the absence of vital organs (brains, eyes, kidneys, and so on), were a major factor in terminating the massive use of chemical defoliants during this war.

Cyber Warfare

Like other parts of social life, warfare adapts to changing technology. The most powerful recent technological change centers on computers, which are changing the face of war. In the Thinking Critically box on the next page, we will look at just one of these changes, giving us a glimpse of what is to come.

Research Findings: Terrorism

14.5 Discuss terrorism: revolutionary, repressive, state-sponsored, and criminal, as well as weapons of mass destruction.

How times change. When I wrote this section for the first edition of this book, terrorism was only a theoretical topic. There had been no terrorist attacks on U.S. soil, although they were taking place elsewhere. The potential that I discussed back then seemed, at the time, so remote from everyday life.

Then came 9/11, which made terrorism a part of our daily life. Although we don't live in fear, anyone who flies sees Homeland Security at work. The fear of U.S. officials that terrorists would strike again, hitting some soft spot, such as a nuclear plant or a major sports event, became a reality when homemade bombs exploded at the Boston Marathon.

Let's take a closer look at **terrorism**, using the means of war—intimidation, coercion, and violence—to achieve objectives (Boston et al. 1977). We can divide terrorism into several types: revolutionary, repressive, state-sponsored, criminal, and using weapons of mass destruction.

Thinking Critically About Social Problems

Cyber War and Cyber Defense

Iran's nuclear enrichment program had progressed quite well. But as five thousand centrifuges were whirring away, Iranian scientists stared in disbelief. Although their computers reported that everything was fine, the centrifuges suddenly sped up and slowed down, ripping their delicate parts into shreds.

Iran had been hit by the *Stuxnet worm*, a malware that the United States and Israel had surreptitiously entered into Iran's computer codes. Iran's goal of producing material for a nuclear bomb had been set back by months or perhaps by years (Sanger 2012).

Every country in conflict with another looks for an edge. The computer's marvelous strength—its capacity to store and retrieve information and to execute commands—can be turned into a weakness, an Achilles heel that can bring down the powerful.

To turn strength into weakness brings both delight and fear to generals around the world. Their delight comes from the mouthwatering anticipation that they might use this capacity against their enemies. Their fear? That their enemies might use this capacity against them.

Cyber weapons offer intriguing potential for warfare. With malware, missiles that have been ordered airborne to strike enemy targets will sit in their silos like wounded birds taking refuge in their nests. If an enemy were to disrupt vital communications, they could transform our computer screens into windows of darkness. Or military files might be filled with false information fed by the enemy. If military leaders couldn't communicate with their troops, they would be left open to easy attack. This fear pervades the military—on both sides, wherever those fluid sides line up today.

This is not some far-off future. As the Iranians discovered, cyber war has begun. The United States, too, is a victim, with thousands of attacks launched against its military computers. The attackers? Just round up the usual suspect, China (Mozur 2013). The purpose of the attacks seems to be to find the chinks in the armor, the spots where malicious computer code can be installed unawares—like *Stuxnet*—to be unleashed at some designated moment. The targets extend beyond the military: a nation's electrical grid, its banking system, stock exchange, oil and gas pipelines, air traffic control system, and Internet and cell phone communications.

The United States is spending billions of dollars in preparation for cyber war. The U.S. Air Force runs an *Office for Cyberspace Operations*, while the Navy operates an aptly named *Center for Information Dominance*. An overarching group, the *U.S. Cyber Command*, has the assignment to integrate the cyber warfare capacities of the military with those of the National Security Agency (Barnes 2012).

The games have begun. The outcome, unfortunately, might not resemble a game.

For Your Consideration

Do you think that the United States should use cyber warfare to probe the weaknesses of potential enemies? Do you think it should insert malicious codes in Russia's and China's military and central civilian computers—just in case it needs to unleash them during some future conflict? If the target discovered the implanted codes, what do you think the consequences might be?

Revolutionary Terrorism

In this first type, **revolutionary terrorism**, terrorists try to overthrow a government. Revolutionary terrorists don't appear out of nowhere, as though they spontaneously sprang into existence in a social vacuum. Let's consider the background factors and goals of revolutionary terrorists.

Background Factors. Walter Laqueur (1977), a political scientist, found these background factors to be common among revolutionary terrorists:

1. A segregated, ethnic, cultural, or religious minority
2. Perceptions of being deprived or oppressed
3. Higher-than-average unemployment or inflation
4. External encouragement (often from an ethnic, cultural, or religious counterpart living elsewhere)

5. A historical "them" (a group the minority blames for its condition)
6. Frustrated elites who provide leadership and justify ideological violence

Political Theater and the Goals of Revolutionary Terrorism. A group that chooses revolutionary terrorism usually has tried to change its situation by going through the official channels. Finding authorities unresponsive to their grievances, the group attempts to

1. publicize the group and its grievances
2. demonstrate the government's vulnerability, and
3. force political and social change.

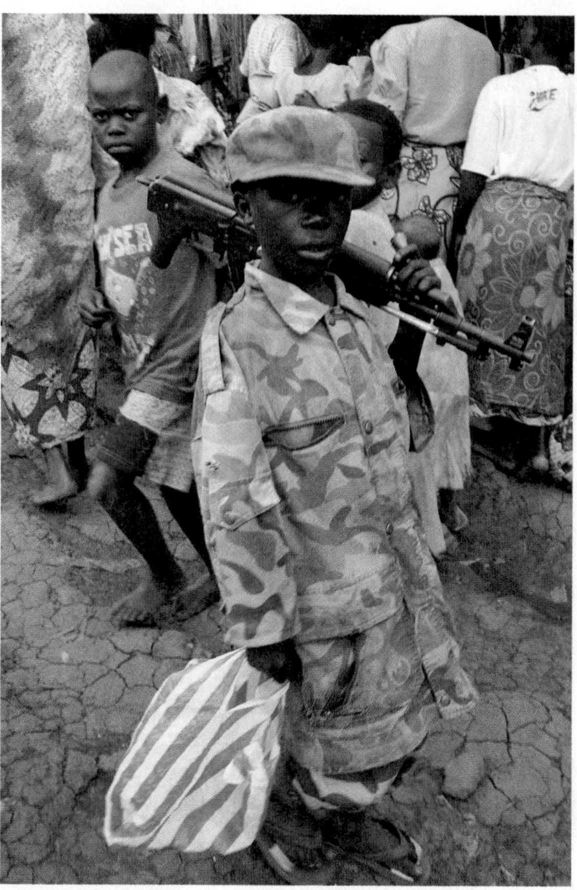

A boy with a toy? No, a soldier with a real rifle shopping in the Democratic Republic of Congo.

Because terrorists seek publicity for their "cause" and choose targets that will give them media attention, terrorism is sometimes called **political theater**. As political scientist Brian Jenkins (1987) put it, "Terrorists want a lot of people watching, not a lot of people dead." He said this before 9/11, however, and I would add that "a lot of people dead" gets the publicity that terrorists seek.

September 11 was the kind of drama that served al-Qaeda's goals well. Their two targets were not random choices. On the contrary, they were symbols of what al-Qaeda wants to destroy. The World Trade Center symbolized U.S. dominance of global capitalism, while the Pentagon represents the U.S. military. The timing—a busy Tuesday workday morning—meant that a huge audience could gather immediately. The act was more effective than even the terrorists could imagine, of course, for they did not anticipate the collapse of the Twin Towers. Yet they did collapse and, in even more dramatic fashion, took with them over 300 firefighters. The message could not have been clearer, nor a worldwide audience summoned as quickly.

As the United States has continued to fight al-Qaeda in Afghanistan and Pakistan, this group's threat within the United States has receded. Those who study al-Qaeda, however, recall that Suleiman Abu Ghaith, a spokesman for the group, said that al-Qaeda's goal is to kill 4 million Americans (Simon 2004). Al-Qaeda is consumed by such hatred of the United States that we can expect attacks whenever the group finds the means to pull them off. As the bombings at the Boston Marathon demonstrated, those "means" include disaffected youth already in the United States. The Global Glimpse box on the next page explores this issue in more detail.

Watch on **MySocLab Video:** NYC Terrorist Plot

A Sense of Morality. To terrorist groups like al-Qaeda, acts of bloodshed are seen as righteous acts. Using the neutralization techniques discussed in Chapter 6 (page 162), terrorists appeal to a higher morality in justifying their actions. It does not matter to them that almost everyone else in the world views their actions as evil—al-Qaeda's leaders are convinced of their moral superiority. As they see it, their "cause" justifies mass killing of civilians, for these deaths can usher in their apocalyptic vision of Islamic rule.

It is this conviction of a righteous cause that makes revolutionary terrorists such formidable opponents. Some revolutionaries become so dedicated to "the cause" that they give up everything, even their lives. Listen to Karari Njama, of Mau Mau, a militant group whose goal was to liberate Kenya from British rule:

> *No one can serve two masters. In order to become a strong faithful warrior who would persevere to the last minute, one had to renounce all worldly wealth, including his family. . . . In fact, I had said to my wife . . . not to expect any sort of help from me for at least ten years' time. I had instructed her to take care of herself and our beloved daughter. I had trained myself to think of the fight, and the*

A Global Glimpse

Why They Hate Us: Al-Qaeda and Lost Power and Glory

How can we make sense of 9/11? Why is al-Qaeda dead set on destroying the United States? To understand this, we have to go back in history and sketch a broad background:

1. In earlier centuries, the Arabs were powerful. They had developed an advanced civilization and were world leaders in agriculture, architecture, astronomy, mathematics, medicine, and metallurgy. Their empire extended into Europe. The terraced fields the Arabs developed are still a distinctive feature of southern Spain.
2. In the late 1400s, Queen Isabella and King Ferdinand married, uniting two provinces of what is now Spain. They turned their united armies against their neighbors, including the Arabs, who ruled vast parts of this region.
3. In addition to motives of gaining territory and treasure, this was a religious war. The goal was to drive out all non–Roman Catholics from the Iberian peninsula (Spain). The pope blessed the armies, wanting the infidels out of Europe. The Jews, who were not a political force, were given three choices: to convert to Christianity, to leave the area, or to die by the sword.
4. After a series of battles, with heavy losses on both sides, the Roman Catholic armies defeated the Islamic armies. The Arabs retreated back to Africa, although they continued to control other parts of Europe for another hundred years. As their political and economic power declined, so did their leadership in academics and the arts.
5. As their political and military power grew, the Europeans conquered peoples around the globe. Part of this global push for dominance included the British and the French conquering Arab lands. That dominance became especially valuable when vast pools of oil were discovered there. The British needed uninterrupted supplies of oil for their factories and homes—and for the warships with which they patrolled a globe on which "the sun never set on the British flag."
6. In the 1920s, to maintain their rule and to settle squabbles among the Arabs, who at that time were loose confederations of tribes and clans, the British divided the Arab lands into countries. Drawing arbitrary lines on maps, they declared that those lines marked one country from another. They also set up Arab rulers in these new countries.
7. As England's power weakened, the British began to lose control over Arab lands. Wanting to protect the supply of oil coming to the West, the United States stepped in. It supported cooperative Arab leaders, keeping them submissive by giving them military aid in return for oil. At times, the Americans even set up puppets to head a country, as with the Shah of Iran, who was deposed by revolutionaries in 1979.

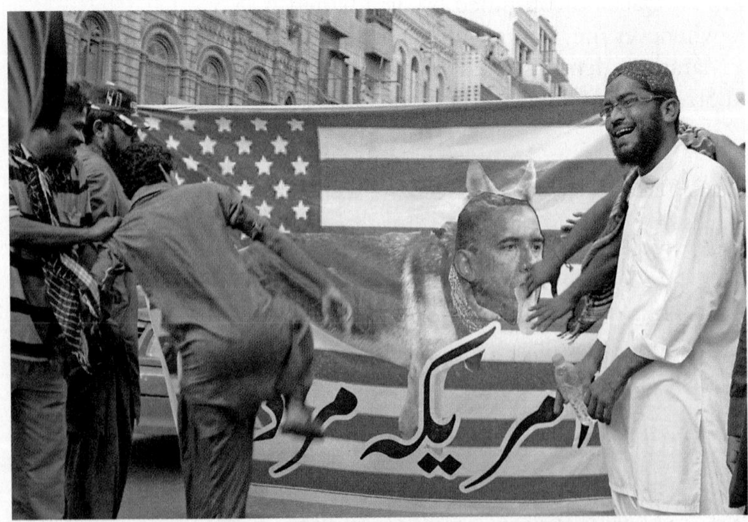

Why are there such violent feelings against the United States, when most Americans feel they are trying to help? This photo was taken in Karachi, Pakistan.

Having sketched this brief historical outline, let's move to the present. Using symbolic interactionism, we will try to understand why al-Qaeda and similar groups hate the West.

8. Many Arabs long for their golden past—the time when their lands were marked by grandeur and wealth, by power and prestige. Those longings stand in sharp contrast to today's shame—domination by the West and, despite vast oil wealth, most Arabs living in poverty.
9. A militant movement needs an inspirational ideology to spur people to action. When personal sacrifice is required, the cause must be greater than the individual. Islam serves this purpose. What stunning images are

(continued from previous page)

conjured up when al-Qaeda refers to the West as the *Great Infidel* polluting a holy land, the *Evil One* plundering resources and holding people captive through their puppet leaders, and the *Great Satan* arming Israel, the Arab archenemy!

10. Destroying the power of the Great Infidel, then, becomes an act of service to Allah. Losing one's life in this service becomes a holy sacrifice. The loss of individual life is nothing in comparison with this noble cause.
11. The Great Infidel's vast military power—soldiers, planes, ships, missiles, and bombs—makes traditional warfare fruitless. Suicide attacks, in contrast, are effective because they can target vulnerable spots, and the enemy can't predict the target or when it will be hit. To attack the enemy on its own soil is not only daring and prestigious, but it also sows fear. This requires long-range planning, coordination, patience, and people so dedicated that they will give their lives to the holy cause.
12. The goal of suicide attacks is not for David to destroy Goliath but, rather, to strike fear, create outrage, and generate publicity. If the Great Infidel can be provoked to send invading armies into sacred lands, so much the better. The more Arabs that Americans kill, the easier it is to inflame passions and recruit others to join the movement for independence.
13. The ultimate goal is pan-Arab unity, which surpasses the artificial boundaries that Western powers drew on blank maps. It will not be Iraqis, Syrians, Saudi Arabians, or any such group, but Arabs (and Persians), united by a shared vision of the glory and rightness of Islam, who will defeat the West.
14. The West will not easily give up its control over Arab oil, so the struggle will last for decades.

For Your Consideration

Why is this symbolic interactionist analysis so different from what you usually hear from your politicians or what you read or see in the mass media? What insights do you think it provides to help you to understand the terrorism directed against the United States? Where do you think this analysis misses the mark? Why?

African Government; and nothing of the country's progress before independence. I had learned to forget all pleasures and imagination of the past. I confined my thoughts (to) the fight only—the end of which would open my thoughts to the normal world. (Schreiber 1978:32)

Repressive Terrorism

A second type of terrorism is **repressive terrorism**, that waged by a government against its own citizens. Let's look at several examples.

Argentina

Diana worked among the poor in Buenos Aires. One midnight, soldiers broke down her door, rushed in, and knocked her to the floor. They blindfolded her and beat her. They then threw her into a car and drove to a building with an underground chamber. For six straight hours, they threatened, tortured, and interrogated her about church leaders, the Vatican Council, and the Jews.

Beaten beyond all tears, she suddenly blurted, "Good God, aren't you Christians?"

Abrupt silence followed. One of the soldiers grabbed her hand and pressed her fingers to a metal cross on his chest. Afterward, they seemed to give up on her. "I'm convinced that small incident saved my life," she says. "The man apparently wanted to be recognized as a person rather than a torturer. He couldn't have that recognition without making me a person, too, rather than an object to be disposed of."

Diana was later taken back to her apartment and held there for two days by four officers who took turns raping her. The police then released her. (Cornell, 1981)

Brutality and killing are typical of repressive terrorism: In this case, the generals who headed the military dictatorship of Argentina feared that their government might collapse and fall into the hands of revolutionaries. Between 1976 and 1983, they arrested tens of thousands of people like Diana. They tortured and executed thousands, even dropping some captives alive from airplanes into the ocean.

Cambodia. Pol Pot, the dictator of Cambodia who directed the Khmer Rouge, launched perhaps the most horrific repressive terrorism that any government has ever inflicted on its people. For almost 4 years, from April 1975 to January 1979, Cambodia was Pol Pot's private slaughterhouse. On an average day, the Khmer Rouge killed 1,500 Cambodians. In just 45 months, the government slaughtered about 2 million people (Wain 1981). Most had their heads bashed in, but many were beaten to death with rubber hoses and bamboo sticks.

The Khmer Rouge targeted *all* intellectuals, for they represented an elite, and the Pol Pot government was attempting to develop a classless society (Miles 1980). Being able to speak a foreign language was enough to merit execution. In one area of Cambodia, members of the Khmer Rouge could count only to 10. Anyone who could count higher was an "intellectual." To ferret them out, the Khmer Rouge would have someone count other people—and execute those who counted to 20, instead of counting two groups of 10. Only 50 of Cambodia's 800 doctors survived.

My visit to the Tuol Sleng prison in Phnom Penh, the capital of Cambodia, where prisoners were tortured, is still vivid in my mind.

> *The buildings are maintained as a museum so the people won't forget. I could see the metal cots on which the prisoners had been chained, torture devices used to break the men, women, and children before they were executed. Emblazoned on my mind is a cabinet of skulls—the larger ones of adults and the smaller ones of children—each cracked where someone struck them to death. There is also a huge vat that once had a wooden bar above it. The vat was filled with water, and the victims, hung upside down, were lowered slowly head first into the water. They could be immersed as many times as the torturers wanted, until they finally were forced to drink their death.*

During its bloody rule of Cambodia from 1975 to 1979, Pol Pot's Khmer Rouge murdered between 1 and 2 million people. To save ammunition, they used hammers and axe handles to break the skulls. From the skull that this girl in Phnom Penh, Cambodia, is playing with, you can see the victim's death blow.

Russia. Repressive terrorism is a way to silence criticism and suppress ideas. Soviet officials were sensitive to criticism of any sort, and they even persecuted poets and artists who dared to express "incorrect" political thought. They also felt threatened by religion, with party leaders referring to the Church as "the enemy within" (Ra'anan et al. 1986). Authorities felt so threatened by alternative views that they beat to death Christians who dared to witness to Christ (Wurmbrand 1970). Andrei Sakharov (1977), a dissenter, recounted the persecution of Baptists, the True Orthodox church, Pentecostals, and Uniates:

> *It is a common practice of the Russian government to take children away from parents who are evangelical; that is, they believe that Jesus of Nazareth is God incarnate or the Savior who should be placed ahead of the State. Pastors of underground churches are regularly arrested, beaten, tortured, and killed.*

This changed abruptly when Russian officials switched to capitalism and allowed competing religions in the country.

State-Sponsored Terrorism

In the third type, **state-sponsored terrorism**, a government finances, trains, and arms terrorists. Colonel Muammar Gadhafi of Libya viewed terrorism as a legitimate extension of the state. He bankrolled terrorists and provided training camps for them. He also brought down a passenger plane over Lockerbie, Scotland, killing all 259 people aboard the plane (Polti 2012). After the U.S. Air Force tried to kill him by bombing his palace, Gadhafi became more clandestine in his support of terrorism. Later, after years of economic sanctions that worsened conditions in his country, Gadhafi renounced his support of terrorism and invited international inspectors to verify that he had dismantled his efforts to produce nuclear weapons.

The West continued to resent Gadhafi, however, and bankrolled rebels who overthrew his regime and killed him.

Criminal Terrorism

Some criminals use terrorism to attain their objectives. A well-known example of **criminal terrorism** involves the Russian mafias. The plural is needed as there are many organized Russian crime groups. To maintain their sources of wealth, these gangsters intimidate and kill anyone who opposes them. They terrorize both the public and government officials into submission. As the executions of reporters, prosecutors, judges, and other government officials in Russia attest, death awaits those who dare to investigate or prosecute this organization.

Here are some personal observations of people who appear to be members of one of the Russian mafias.

> *When I was in Riga, the capital of Latvia, some of the scenes were like the stereotypes portrayed in movies. People reported to be part of the Russian mafias, attended by bodyguards, buzzed around the city in new shiny black cars, paying little attention to the speed limit and parking where they wanted. When I was looking for an apartment, one owner, burly bodyguards at his side, boasted of two special features he had installed in the apartment—the bomb proof floor and the bullet proof door.*
>
> *The Russian mafias appear confident that they are untouchable. While sitting at an outside beach restaurant run by Russians in Jurmala, Latvia, I surreptitiously watched eight muscular men, whose appearance was that of the bodyguards seen around town. As one man became animated in his conversation, my wife quietly translated for me. As the others listened raptly, he proudly boasted of how he had brandished a gun and the amount of money involved in a deal that took only 45 minutes.*

Narcoterrorism. Another form of criminal terrorism, **narcoterrorism**, centers on drugs. Some narcoterrorists, such as those in Colombia, have a political agenda, and drug dealing is a way to finance their goal of revolution. These international drug dealers even assassinated justices of the Colombian supreme court, terrorizing the government until it abandoned its extradition treaty with the United States. Mehemet Ali Agca sold drugs to finance his attempted assassination of Pope John Paul II (Oakley 1985; Ehrenfeld 1990). For other narcoterrorists, money is the objective, and terrorism is simply a way to protect and extend their drug operations. This is what is currently happening in Mexico, as recounted in Chapter 4, page 111.

Weapons of Mass Destruction (WMDS)

Let's consider the possibility that terrorists will use nuclear and biological weapons.

Nuclear Terrorism. Because plutonium is often used in the manufacture of nuclear weapons, you would think it would be guarded carefully—right? Listen to this. About 5,000 pounds of plutonium is missing from U.S. nuclear facilities. A former security agent reported that protective measures at the Rocky Flats weapons factory near Denver were so lax that it was "like having a window in a bank vault" (Hosenball 1999). When asked about the missing plutonium, officials took a cavalier attitude. "What's to worry?" they said. The plutonium "probably got stuck in pipes and manufacturing tools." (2½ tons!) The solution? Simple. The officials suspended the troublemaker who reported that the plutonium was missing.

After the collapse of the Soviet Union, some nuclear materials were said to be secured only by a chain-link fence and a night watchman (Bunn and Wier 2004). Whether it really was this bad or not, I don't know, but one worker at a nuclear plant simply hid nuclear material in his protective gloves when he walked out the gate (Zaitseva and Hand 2003). At another site, officials didn't know how to keep terrorists out. Then they hit upon a solution: They poured six feet of concrete over plutonium-contaminated earth (Barry 2011). On the brighter side, much of the nuclear material that Russia produced has been destroyed (Bunn and Wier 2004). Despite this progress, uranium smuggled from Russia continues to be intercepted (Butler 2010).

Because of the horrendous destruction from nuclear attack, at some point terrorists could hold a government captive. They don't need missiles if they can smuggle "dirty bombs" or other nuclear weapons into a country. Few of the tens of thousands of containers arriving each day at U.S. ports are searched. What would U.S. officials do if terrorists threatened to detonate a nuclear weapon in the heart of New York City or Los Angeles?

Biological Terrorism. Perhaps an even greater threat is **biological terrorism**, the use of diseases such as anthrax, smallpox, or the plague as a *bioweapon*. The knowledge of how to grow these biological agents is spreading. Especially fear-provoking is that, unlike conventional and nuclear weapons, bioweapons can be transported in tiny containers. This reality of biological terrorism was driven home to Americans in 2001, when envelopes containing anthrax were sent through the U.S. mails. In its largest investigation ever, the FBI concluded that Bruce Ivins, a microbiologist who had worked with anthrax at the Army's biodefense laboratory at Fort Detrick, Maryland, was the anthrax killer. Ivins committed suicide before he could be charged with a crime (Shane 2010a).

You can explore biological terrorism further in the Technology and Social Problems box on the next page.

Social Policy

14.6 Summarize social policies regarding terrorism, the MAD way to peace, policies that can bring peace, and how self-preservation figures in the survival of humanity.

Let's examine social policies that attempt to address two major problems we have reviewed in this chapter, political terrorism and nuclear war.

Terrorism

The Overarching Principle. The key principle in dealing with terrorists is "Don't give in to their demands, for this encourages more terrorism." This principle poses a dilemma—not meeting demands can bring immediate costs: property damage, injuries, and deaths. Giving in to terrorists encourages terrorists—because their tactic worked.

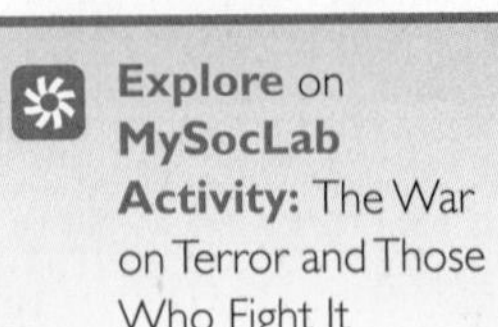

Explore on MySocLab
Activity: The War on Terror and Those Who Fight It

Ten Basic Policies. Anti-terrorism experts suggest the following as effective social policies (Bremer 1988; Ehrenfeld 1990; FBI 1998; "National Strategy . . ." 2006):

1. Promise anything during negotiations. Promises made under threat are not valid.
2. Make no distinction between terrorists and their state sponsors. Even though they hide behind the scenes, states that sponsor terrorists are not neutral and should not be treated as neutrals. This principle allows both retaliatory and preemptive acts.
3. Use economic and political sanctions to break the connection between terrorists and the states that provide them weapons, financing, safe houses, training areas, and identity documents in return for terrorism done on their behalf.
4. Treat terrorists as war criminals. Track them, arrest them, and punish them. Bomb them, if this is what it takes.
5. Discourage media coverage because publicity is a goal of terrorists. Make it illegal for the media to pay terrorists for interviews.

Listen on **MySocLab Audio:** NPR: Interrogation and National Security

Technology and Social Problems

Our Future: Biological Terrorism in the Twenty-First Century

Picture a Russian biohacker who designs a deadly form of the common flu virus and sells it on the Internet. The terrorist group that buys the design sends it to a lab tech in Pakistan, who uses tools that are widely available to make the required modifications. The product is then shipped by mail to men and women in London or Rome who infect themselves. They board airplanes headed to destinations around the world, infecting fellow passengers and people in crowded terminals. The infection spreads quickly, going global in days—long before anyone detects it. (Robb 2007)

With a death toll in the millions, scenarios like this haunt U.S. officials. Few safeguards exist to protect against such an attack. There would be no warning, no attempt to hold the United States hostage in order to extort billions of dollars. The motive would be revenge for humiliations suffered at the hands of the United States. The goal would be not profit or fear, but the annihilation of the United States itself.

How seriously officials are taking the bioterrorist threat is indicated by the money Congress appropriates to the Department of Homeland Security. This agency's budget is $68 billion. Another $6 billion is being spent for Project BioShield (*Statistical Abstract* 2013:Table 535). Project BioShield is designed not only to provide medical countermeasures against bioweapons but also against chemical, radiological, and nuclear weapons ("Project BioShield" 2010). Officials have stockpiled vaccines around the country and trained emergency medical teams in major cities. Military personnel at Central Command, those sent to South Korea and those assigned to "biodefense missions," are vaccinated against anthrax (Norris 2009).

If a biological attack occurs, U.S. officials have a plan. It is not to evacuate populations, but to try to prevent the disease from spreading by blocking roads and stopping people at gunpoint from fleeing cities. Plans also include a military takeover of state and local governments to fight the chaos that would result from a biological attack (Miller and Broad 1999). For at least a while after a biological attack, the Pentagon would take direct control over the United States.

As in this scene in Connecticut, to prepare for what many fear will come, Homeland Security is holding mock terrorist drills in major cities across the nation.

An ancient Chinese proverb states "May you live in exciting times." This simple saying is actually a curse, the hope that an enemy's life will be chaotic. We live in exciting times. Let's hope that the curse with which we live—weapons of mass destruction, hatreds engendered by foreign domination, and retaliatory action by terrorists—does not result in our destruction.

For Your Consideration

What steps do you think the government should take to counter the threat of bioweapons? Would you be willing to give up the freedoms you currently have, to be assured that you were safe from weapons of mass destruction?

6. Establish international extradition and prosecution agreements: Terrorists need to know that if they are caught anywhere, they will be extradited and put on trial.
7. Develop an international organization to coordinate worldwide intelligence and advise nations. It would also direct international teams to respond to specific events—such as freeing hostages or locating evidence to identify sponsors of terrorists.
8. Offer large rewards for information leading to the capture or death of terrorists. Just as in the old west, rewards can be paid on a "dead-or-alive" basis. With rewards of $50,000, $1 million, or $5 million, terrorists will never know whether associates can be trusted. Informants should be guaranteed safe passage and offered new identities.

9. Cut the funding of terrorist organizations so they don't have money for travel, weapons, and training.
10. Infiltrate terrorist organizations.

Many specific actions flow from these ten policies. Let's consider two.

Preemptive Strikes. As an example of a preemptive strike, the Iraq War represents the second of the ten policies. Because Saddam Hussein supposedly possessed weapons of mass destruction and was intending to use them against the West, the United States (with troops from a few other nations) made a preemptive strike. He did not have WMDs. Some doubt that U.S. officials are so incompetent as not to know that Hussein did not have these weapons. Others say that they are this incompetent. Either way of reasoning makes the basis for invading Iraq suspect.

Targeted Killings. When the CIA determines that someone is responsible for a terrorist attack, that person can be put on a "hit list" and marked for assassination (Becker and Savage 2012; Savage 2012). A favorite way to carry out targeted killings is to track the person with a drone—an unmanned plane. When the individual is spotted, a missile is fired. If the individual's family is also killed, it is marked up to the "collateral damage" we discussed earlier.

Targeted killings are also a policy of Russia's FSB and Israel's Mossad. Instead of drones and missiles, their more usual methods are old-fashioned shootings. They sometimes are rather creative, though, and use poisoned umbrellas and nuclear isotopes. Is there a difference?

Nuclear Threats as a Path to Peace

A MAD Way to Peace. The primary policy that the United States and the former Soviet Union pursued during the Cold War was **mutual assured destruction (MAD)**. The two countries used threats and the fear of mutual destruction to prevent the other from striking first. Each was afraid to use its nuclear arsenal, because even out of the ashes missiles would be launched that would destroy the other. Because neither country would survive, there was no benefit in attacking the other.

The path to peace, then, has been a MAD one. Each superpower stockpiled weapons of mass destruction—nuclear, chemical, and biological—and signaled to the other that it was willing to unleash those weapons. The resulting balance of power—or terror—kept these two superpowers from attacking each other. Sociologist Nicholas Timasheff (1965:291) explained how it worked:

> *Each party may consider that it has a fair chance to win, but each party also knows that the cost of victory would be prohibitive; physical destruction of 90–95 percent of the total population, almost complete destruction of industrial equipment, transformation of almost the total territory into an uninhabitable area because of radiation, contamination of air, water, plants and animals and other natural resources. Under these circumstances, victory can be worse than the most crucial defeat before this atomic age. Each of the parties to the possible conflict has full reason to refrain from attack.*

A New Precarious Balance of Power. Canada, France, Germany, Italy, Japan, Russia, the United Kingdom, and the United States work together in an organization called G8. G8 is working out a new balance of power—sometimes called the **New World Order**. The balance, however, is precarious. Of its many sources of disequilibrium, one is the proliferation of nuclear weapons. Poor nations may not be able to sit at G8's bargaining table, but if they join the nuclear club, G8 will listen to them. India and Pakistan, historical enemies that quarrel over boundaries that separate the two nations, each have nuclear bombs. India has developed a missile system that can be fired from mobile launchers. Not only can India's missiles hit targets in Pakistan, but they can also reach Beijing and Shanghai (Norris and Kristensen 2005). Each additional country that gains nuclear weapons increases the threat to this current balance of power. G8 is especially fearful of nuclear weapons in the hands of North Korea and Iran.

Even local conflicts can upset this precarious balance of power. Local conflicts pose the threat of heating up and bringing in other nations, destabilizing an entire region. Such fears led to the quick action that **NATO (North Atlantic Treaty Organization)** took against Serbia. Bombs speak louder than words, as Slobodan Milošević, the president of Serbia, discovered. Serving to restrain G8, though, are the two million soldiers that North Korea can unleash on South Korea and uncertainty regarding China's reaction if G8 bombs nuclear sites in North Korea.

Potential Policies for Peace

Social policies that encourage peace include disarmament, interlocking networks of mutual interests, and international law. Let's look at each.

Disarmament. Although we all want a safer world, not everyone agrees with disarmament. The primary argument against disarmament is that only a strong military and the will to use it can make a nation secure. If we have adequate safeguards to protect ourselves from attack (an endless argument about what adequate means), eliminating biological, nuclear, and chemical weapons certainly can help make the world safer. As we discussed, slight progress has been made in reducing the number of nuclear weapons, but what G8 calls "rogue nations" (read: nations that G8 doesn't trust, currently Iran and North Korea) are developing their own nuclear weapons and the missiles to deliver them. By the time you read this, G8 (or Israel with G8's approval) might have exercised the doctrine of *first strike*, eliminating this threat.

I need to stress that the danger of WMDs is growing, not decreasing. Bioweapons are especially fearsome, not only because of their capacity to inflict mass death but also because the knowledge of how to produce them is spreading.

Interlocking Networks. The key to peace, say some, is to develop interlocking networks of mutual interest. They argue that the more a nation depends on another for its own well-being, the less likely it is to destroy that nation. If true, the surprising route that leads to such interdependence could be global capitalism, which links the world's nations to one another in a **global economy**. As nations become more interwoven, their affairs become more interdependent. To develop further interlocking interests, then, we should encourage trade among the world's nations. To stimulate peace, we can also encourage communication, travel, and cultural and scientific exchanges.

International Law. International law is essential for world peace. If each nation is a law unto itself and feels free to wage war when its goals are frustrated, we can never achieve peace. Most nations, however, are unwilling to yield sovereignty to an international organization. We are far from having effective international law, as evidenced by NATO's bombing of Kosovo. Despite the "good" reason for the bombing—the prevention of ethnic slaughter—NATO placed itself above international law by attacking without the approval of the United Nations. Later, Russia did the same when it attacked Georgia. The United States also refuses to submit to the **International Criminal Court**, as U.S. officials fear that they could be charged with war crimes (Sewall and Kaysen 2000). This fear is not groundless, for "one group's freedom fighter is another group's terrorist."

Survival as a Mutual Benefit

In the end, perhaps what will prevent the annihilation of humanity will be the desire for self-preservation. Leaders don't want themselves, their families, or their country destroyed. Unfortunately, as we know with suicide bombers, some individuals will gladly sacrifice themselves in order to destroy archenemies. If terrorist groups get their hands on WMDs, they won't lack for volunteers to put them to use. And you can never be certain what any leader of a country might do in bleak and bitter moments. Albert Speer (1970), one of Hitler's close associates, noted that when Hitler realized that the war was lost, he wanted to destroy his own country.

In Sum ▸ The best social policies would be those that remove weapons of mass destruction from humanity. I foresee no social policy, though, that will eliminate these weapons, whether nuclear, biological, or chemical. The knowledge of how to produce weapons of mass destruction has proliferated, and the best we can hope for are social policies that limit and prevent their use.

The Future of the Problem

Arms Sales, War, and Terrorism

14.7 Discuss the likely future of war and terrorism.

A Personal Note: Each time I prepare a new edition of this book, I am appalled at the data I review for this section on arms sales. To better understand the cold numbers that follow—billions here and billions there—think about what those numbers mean. In the mass media, you occasionally see men in Africa, Asia, and South America carrying powerful automatic weapons. Where do these weapons come from? Behind this vast global killing machine are people who make fortunes selling the weapons of death. This has to be the most immoral of all enterprises on earth (next to trafficking in women and children for sex).

As you read this section, then, think about the blood that these totals represent—the women who are brutally raped as they cower powerlessly before men who carry the guns sold by arms merchants for their unconscionable profit, the children who are slaughtered or who live without parents, and the men who die trying to defend their families.

These aren't just numbers. You are looking at the twisted face of death.

TABLE 14.4 ▸ Buying and Selling the Weapons of Death: The Global Arms Trade

The Top 10 Sellers

Rank	Supplier	Dollars of Sales 2008–2011
1	United States	$54,000,000,000
2	Russia	$28,000,000,000
3	Germany	$11,000,000,000
4	Great Britain	$11,000,000,000
5	China	$8,000,000,000
6	Israel	$7,000,000,000
7	France	$7,000,000,000
8	Sweden	$6,000,000,000
9	Italy	$5,000,000,000
10	Canada	$4,000,000,000

The Top 10 Buyers

Rank	Recipient	Dollars of Purchases 2008–20011
1	Saudi Arabia	$10,000,000,000
2	India	$10,000,000,000
3	Pakistan	$7,000,000,000
4	Algeria	$5,000,000,000
5	Egypt	$5,000,000,000
6	South Korea	$4,000,000,000
7	Israel	$4,000,000,000
8	Venezuela	$4,000,000,000
9	China	$4,000,000,000
10	Iraq	$3,000,000,000

Note: The Most Industrialized Nations also buy weapons, but those totals are not given in the source. Even the United States purchases weapons from Great Britain and other countries. The totals are rounded to the nearest billion. If two nations have the same total when rounding, I kept their rank order.

Source: By the author. Based on Grimmett and Kerr 2012:Tables 23, 38.

War and Terrorism Fueled by Profits. One of the easiest predictions to make in this book is that wars will continue to be fueled by the merchants of death. Look at Table 14.4. The factories in these top-selling nations produce far more weapons than their militaries can possibly use—and the owners are hungry for profits. As you can see, in this race to sell death the United States far outpaces its nearest competitor. The second part of Table 14.4 shows the profitable outlet these producers of weapons have found for their excess capacity. Many weapons end up in private hands, where men use them to extort money, food, and sex, holding entire villages and regions in captivity. With those who make the profits not caring about the destruction of human life, this merchandising in death will continue.

Why Poor Nations Spend So Much on Weapons. Look again at the bottom part of Table 14.4. You can see the huge amounts that the Least Industrialized Nations spend on the

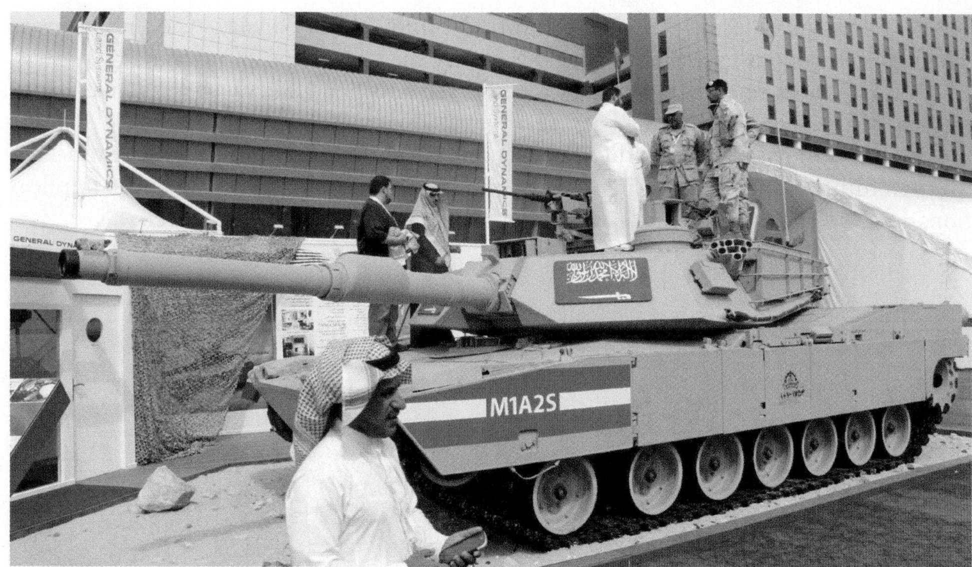

Want to buy a tank? Missles? War planes? You can—if you are a member of some country's elite that the United States wants to keep in power. This photo of a U.S. MIA25 SEP Abrams battle tank for sale was taken in Abu Dhabi, the United Arab Emirates.

weapons of war. Most of the citizens of India, Pakistan, Algeria, and Egypt live in poverty. These nations need the money they spend on weapons to feed, house, and educate their people. The potential of aggression by neighboring countries requires a military, to be sure, but there is another reason: The power elites of the nations shown in this part of the table are insecure. The weapons they buy keep them in power. They need a strong military to protect themselves from both uprisings of their own people and attacks from the rival power elites of neighboring nations. This self-feeding fear perpetuates the endless need to update their supply of powerful arms.

Terrorism

Terrorism will continue to make the news. Here are likely possibilities.

Revolutionary Terrorism. Some revolutionary terrorists are motivated by bitter hatred. Others simply want political change. It seems almost inevitable that as time goes on, revolutionary terrorists, such as those who bombed the Pentagon and the World Trade Center in New York City, will acquire more sophisticated weapons. That we will one day face weapons of mass destruction—nuclear, chemical, and biological—is also likely. With advances in genetic engineering, the potential of biological weapons grows ever more ominous.

Repressive Terrorism. Repressive terrorism will continue, particularly in China, Central and South America, Africa, and the Middle East. Demands for more democratic government will be met with heavy-handed repression, in some cases so extreme that the people will be cowering in fear of their own government. Political repression, in turn, may stimulate resistance—and the bloody struggles will continue.

State-Sponsored Terrorism. It is likely that state-sponsored terrorism will decrease. We won't see fewer heads of state who would like to sponsor terrorists and send them against their enemies. Rather, investigative techniques have become more powerful, enabling state-sponsored sources to be more easily tracked and destroyed. This is a powerful deterrent.

Russia. After seven decades of persecution in Russia, people gained freedom of speech, press, politics, education, religion, and the arts. Increased trade and cultural exchanges with the West reduced suspicions and hostilities on both sides. Russia's membership in

NATO allows us to visualize a kinder future. Nothing about Russia is certain, however. The nation's arduous experiment with democracy may prove too threatening to its leaders. If hard-liners return to power, we could see another Cold War, with arsenals of nuclear weapons hanging in the balance.

I expect that we will muddle through our current and future threats. A muddle-through future, while not exciting to contemplate, is certainly preferable to the implications of some of the problems of war and terrorism sketched in this chapter.

It is likely that one of the challenges of the "muddle-through" society will be preventing, and in some instances adjusting to, terroristic attacks, such as the bombings at the Boston Marathon in 2013.

MySocLab  Study and Review on MySocLab

Summary and Review

1. The three essential conditions of war are a cultural tradition for war, an antagonistic situation, and a "spark" that sets off the war. Wars have occurred throughout history, but today's wars are much more destructive.
2. Symbolic interactionists analyze how symbols (perceptions) underlie war. During the Cold War, the West and the Soviets saw each other as mortal enemies. Each felt obliged to arm itself, setting off a nuclear arms race. Nuclear weapons symbolize a country's capacity to destroy an enemy.
3. Functionalists identify these functions of war: the extension of political boundaries, social integration, economic gain, social change, ideology, vengeance, military security, and credibility. The dysfunctions of war are defeat, dependence, and destruction.
4. Conflict theorists identify four causes of war: competition for resources, a conflict of interests, a surplus of capital, and the dominance of a military machine.
5. Humans are no more peaceful today than in earlier times. The following do *not* diminish the chances

of war: the type of government, the group's religion, prosperity, a common language or religion, shared political boundaries, or level of education.

6. Modern weapons are expensive and come at the cost of alternative expenditures. A major cost of war is *dehumanization.*

7. Both business and the military gain from producing, selling, and using weapons. The *military–industrial complex* is a powerful force in promoting war.

8. One of the more serious threats facing humanity is weapons of mass destruction: biological, chemical, and nuclear. Unless effective international controls are put into place, these weapons will proliferate, one day leading to vast destruction.

9. *Political terrorism*—that is, the use of war to achieve political objectives—is of three types: *revolutionary terrorism,* waged by groups (or in rare cases, individuals) against the state; *repressive terrorism,* waged by the state against its own people; and *state-sponsored terrorism,* waged by one state against another. *Criminal terrorism* cuts across these types.

10. Disarmament, international law, and growing interlocking interests among the nations of the world could increase the chances for peace.

11. The future holds more terrorism and war. All-out nuclear war is unlikely because it means mutual destruction. Revolutionary terrorism will continue. This, in turn, will stimulate repressive terrorism. Al-Qaeda and its supporters are likely to remain agents of terrorism. The Cold War could erupt again if hard-liners return to power in Russia.

Key Terms

Agent Orange, 490
armaments, 485
arms race, 467
biological terrorism, 498
bourgeoisie, 477
Cold War, 467
criminal terrorism, 497
dehumanization, 482
global economy, 501
imperialism, 477
intercontinental ballistic missiles (ICBMs), 473
International Criminal Court, 501
megaton, 486
military–industrial complex, 485
mutual assured destruction (MAD), 500
narcoterrorism, 497
NATO (North Atlantic Treaty Organization), 501
New World Order, 500
nuclear disarmament, 486
nuclear proliferation, 486
political theater, 493
proletariat, 477
repressive terrorism, 495
revolutionary terrorism, 492
state-sponsored terrorism, 496
terrorism, 491
war, 471

Thinking Critically About Chapter 14

1. Sociologist Nicholas Timasheff identified three essential conditions of war and seven "sparks" that can ignite these conditions into war (page 471). Analyze a war that the United States has participated in. In this war, what were the essential conditions and the sparks?

2. The functions of war are summarized on pages 474–477. Apply these functions to the war on terrorism. How about the dysfunctions?

3. Do you think that the United States has the right to intervene in another country to protect our economic or political interests? Under what conditions is intervention justified? Explain.

4. Do you think that other countries have the right to intervene in the United States to protect their economic or political interests? Under what conditions is intervention justified? Explain.

Glossary

A

acid rain Rain with heavy concentrations of sulfuric and nitric acids; a result of air pollution.

addiction Dependence on a substance to make it through the day.

ageism Discrimination against people on the basis of their age; this concept is not limited to older people.

Agent Orange A chemical defoliant used in Vietnam that caused birth defects and other negative effects on health.

air pollution Air that is harmful to breathe because of burning fossil fuels and other human activities—as well as of natural events, like volcanic eruptions. Effects include eye, nose, and throat irritations; bronchitis, emphysema, and lung cancer.

alcoholic A person with severe alcohol-related problems.

Anglo-conformity Requiring or expecting everyone in the United States to adopt the dominant culture, the customs inherited from English settlers.

anomie The feeling of being estranged, uprooted, unanchored, normless—not knowing what rules to apply to the situations one faces.

antiretroviral drugs (ARVs) Medications that can slow down and even reverse the progression of HIV infection; can delay the onset of AIDS by 20 years or more.

apartheid As practiced in South Africa, the enforced segregation of people on the basis of their perceived race or ethnicity.

armaments Bombs, missiles, tanks, planes, guns, ships, submarines, and other weapons.

arms race The attempt by nations to outmatch one another's war capabilities; usually refers to the buildup of weapons during the Cold War standoff between the Soviet Union and the West.

ascribed status A position held as a result of one's birth.

assimilation The absorption of a minority group or individual into the mainstream culture.

attention-deficit hyperactivity disorder (ADHD) A condition, as defined by the medical community, that causes children not to pay attention and to disrupt classroom activities. Also known as hyperactivity, attention-deficit disorder, and hyperkinesis. The social problems associated with it include possible overmedication of children and medicalization of everyday problems.

B

binge drinking Consuming on a single occasion five or more drinks by men or four or more drinks by women.

biodegradable Capable of disintegrating in outdoor weather, when exposed to microorganisms.

biological poverty Material deprivation so severe that it affects one's health (biological functioning).

biological terrorism Use of an agent that causes disease—anthrax, smallpox, or the plague, for instance—as a weapon.

biotech society A future society in which bioengineering (the manipulation of genetic materials) to produce food and other materials is central to that society.

bisexuals People who are sexually attracted to both men and women.

black market The production, exchange, and sale of goods or services not reported to government officials.

bourgeoisie Marx's term for society's power elite, which uses society's resources to keep itself in power and to exploit the less powerful; also called capitalists.

breadwinner A worker whose earnings are the primary source of support for a family.

C

capital punishment The death penalty.

capitalism An economic system that is based on the private ownership of property. An economic system characterized by the private ownership of the means of production, market competition, and the pursuit of profit. See *socialism.*

capitalist Owner of the means of production (land, factories, tools) who controls the labor of workers.

capitalist economy An economic system based on investing capital with the goal of making a profit.

carcinogen A cancer-causing substance.

case study A type of research design that focuses on a single case. The case or subject of the study can be an individual, an event, or an organization, such as a church, hospital, or abortion clinic.

causation Relationship in which one thing (variable) produces an effect on something else (another variable).

cesarean section (C-section) A form of surgery in which a baby is delivered through an incision made in the mother's abdomen and uterus.

Chicago school of sociology Refers to research that stresses participant observation, symbolic interactionism, and seeing things from an insider's point of view, as practiced by the Department of Sociology at the University of Chicago in the 1920s.

city Place of residence for a large number of people who live there permanently; city residents do not produce their own food.

civil disobedience Deliberate but peaceful refusal to obey laws that are considered unjust.

cogeneration Production of electricity as a by-product of a business's ordinary operations.

cohabitation Living together in a sexual relationship outside marriage.

Cold War A period of hostilities after World War II between the former Soviet Union and nations of the West.

collateral damage Euphemism for unintended casualties and destruction inflicted on civilians in the course of military operations.

combat stress reaction ("shell shock") The emotional and physical reactions soldiers experience because of the trauma of combat.

common sense The ideas common to a society or to some group within a society that people use to make sense out of their experiences.

community A place that people identify with and where people identify with one another.

concentric zone theory A theory developed by Ernest Burgess suggesting that as cities expand outward from their center they develop areas, or zones, that have specialized functions. The area closest to the central business district—the zone in transition—has the most severe urban problems.

conflict theory A sociological theory that views society as a system in competition and conflict. Each group in society attempts to further its own interests, even at the expense of others. Those who gain power exploit people and resources for their own benefit. Social problems stem from exploitation and resistance to exploitation.

control group The group in an experiment that is not exposed to an experience (or independent variable).

control theory A sociological theory that focuses on two control systems—inner controls and outer controls—which work against our tendencies to deviate.

conversion therapy A form of psychotherapy aimed at changing gay, lesbian, and bisexual people's sexual orientations to heterosexual, or at eliminating or diminishing same-sex desires and behaviors.

corporate welfare Handouts given to corporations, usually in the form of tax breaks; may also be reductions in rent or bargain-priced real estate.

correlation Two or more things occurring together.

Cosa Nostra The term by which East Coast mobsters refer to the Mafia. See *Mafia.*

craving An intense desire for something, often alcohol or another drug.

crime Any act prohibited by law.

crime rate The number of crimes per some unit of population, most commonly the number of crimes per 100,000 people.

criminal justice system The agencies that respond to crime, including the police, courts, jails, and prisons.

criminal sexual assault Also called rape; includes sexual assaults, completed and attempted, aggravated and non-aggravated, against both males and females.

criminal terrorism Using terrorism to achieve criminal objectives.

cultural feminism A branch of feminism which argues that biology leads to behavioral differences between men and women and that women and men should celebrate these differences. Cultural feminists claim that women are inherently kinder and gentler.

cultural goal A goal held out as legitimate for the members of a society.

cultural means The approved ways of reaching cultural goals.

culture of poverty Characteristics of the poor—such as dropping out of school, family violence, and alcoholism—that trap the poor in poverty.

culture of wealth Characteristics of the wealthy—such as social connections and educational achievement—that help keep them from falling down the social-class ladder.

D

death rate The number of deaths per 1,000 people per year.

defective discipline Excessive leniency or excessive control in rearing children.

defensive medicine Medical procedures performed by physicians to protect themselves in case they are sued for malpractice.

dehumanization Process of viewing and treating people as objects not deserving the treatment ordinarily accorded humans.

deinstitutionalization The release of institutionalized people, especially psychiatric patients, from an institution for placement and care in the community.

dehumanize Viewing and treating people as objects not deserveng the treatment ordinarily accorded humans.

delinquent subculture A group whose members are oriented toward illegal acts.

demographic transition A four-stage process of population growth. The first is high birthrates and high death rates. The second is high birthrates and low death rates. The third is low birthrates and low death rates. The fourth is birthrates so low that a population shrinks.

demography The study of the size, composition, growth, and distribution of human populations.

dependency ratio In terms of Social Security, the number of workers compared with the number of recipients.

depersonalization People being treated as inanimate objects; often found in medical settings.

designer animals Gene-spliced farm animals.

deterrence Preventing an act by producing fear; often refers to crime or war.

differential association A symbolic interactionist theory which stresses that people learn values and behavior by associating with people who have those values or practice the behavior. The theory assumes that people learn crime and violence in the same way that people learn to follow laws or to be cooperative.

dirty work The tasks in society that are considered undesirable and low-level.

discrimination Singling people out for unfair treatment.

diversion A response to crime that diverts offenders away from the criminal justice system, keeping them out of the courts and jails.

division of labor People performing different sets of specialized tasks.

documents Written records; in its extended sense, refers to moving images, such as videos and movies.

domiciliary care (home health care) Health care provided in the patient's home.

dominant group The group that has more power, privilege, and prestige and that discriminates against minority groups.

drug abuse Use of drugs in such a way that they harm people's health, impair their physical or mental functioning, or interfere with their social life.

drug A substance that people take to produce a change in their thinking, consciousness, emotions, bodily functions, or behavior.

drug addiction Dependence on the consumption of a drug to make it through the day. Also known as drug dependence.

drug therapy The use of drugs such as tranquilizers and antidepressants to treat emotional problems.

dual labor market A pool of workers consisting of those who are regularly employed and better-paid and those who are temporary and low-paid.

dysfunction A part of a social system that is not performing its intended function adequately.

E

ecofeminism A branch of feminism which stresses that patriarchy is bad not only for women but also for the environment and that women must take the lead in preserving the environment.

ecology The study of the relationship between living things and their environment.

economic colonialism One nation dominating another nation economically in order to exploit that nation's people and resources.

economy A system of producing and distributing goods and services.

ecosystem The interconnection of life on the planet's outer surface; a fragile web made up of organisms and their environment.

electroconvulsive therapy (ECT) A treatment for emotional problems in which a low-voltage electric current (a shock) is sent through the brain. Also known as electroshock therapy.

endogamy The practice of marrying within one's group; can refer to a village, culture, or racial-ethnic group.

environmental injustice The poor and minorities being harmed by polluting industries (and other forms of pollution, such as dumping) because the factories and activities are located in their neighborhoods.

ethnocentrism The view that my group's ways are right and your group's ways are wrong.

euthanasia Killing someone out of a sense of mercy or compassion; also called mercy killing.

experiment A research design that divides a group into an *experimental group* (those who are exposed to some experience) and a *control group* (those who are not exposed to the experience). Measurements are taken before and after to determine the effects of the experience.

experimental group The group in an experiment that is exposed to an experience (or independent variable).

exponential growth curve When growth doubles during approximately equal intervals, the acceleration that appears in the later stages of that growth.

extended family A family in which relatives, such as the "older generation" or unmarried aunts and uncles, live with the parents and their children.

F

false class consciousness Acceptance of the view of the dominant class and failing to recognize that one is being exploited.

family of orientation The family into which people are born and from which they receive their basic orientations to life.

family of procreation The family that is formed by marriage and that generally results in procreation, or the birth of children.

female infanticide Killing baby girls.

feminist theory A sociological perspective that focuses on the power relationships between men and women; comes in several varieties, usually with the aim to transform society as well as to study it.

feminization of poverty poverty being concentrated among women.

fetal alcohol syndrome A cluster of congenital problems caused by the alcohol consumption of the newborn's mother when she was pregnant.

fetal narcotic syndrome A cluster of congenital problems caused by the narcotic use of the newborn's mother when she was pregnant.

field study (or *field work* or *participant observation*) A method of gathering information through direct observation of some setting.

food chain The arrangement of organisms according to food sources; each organism on the chain is a food source for the organism above it.

food politics Controlling food production in order to control food prices: Paying farmers to leave their land fallow creates an artificial shortage that drives up grain prices.

food pollution (also called food contamination) The transmission of disease during food processing or the addition of chemicals to food to help process it, lengthen its shelf life, or enhance its appearance or taste.

forcible rape Forced sexual relations. See *statutory rape.*

fossil fuels Substances (such as wood, coal, petroleum, and natural gas) used as fuels that are derived from living things.

frustration–aggression theory of violence A psychological theory which stresses that the likelihood of aggression increases when a goal is blocked.

function The contribution of a part to its system; or people's actions that contribute to the equilibrium of a social system.

functionalism (also called *functional analysis, functional theory,* and *the functional perspective*) A sociological theory that focuses on how a system consists of interconnected parts, each part contributing in some way to the equilibrium or stability of the system. The contribution of each part is called its *function.* Functionalists view a social problem as a *dysfunction,* the failure of some part of the system to function correctly.

future shock The confusion or disorientation that accompanies rapid social change.

G

gender How we express our "maleness" or "femaleness." Refers to socialization or culture. Commonly called femininity or masculinity. See also *sex.*

gender roles The behaviors and attitudes expected of people because they are males or females.

generalize To apply the findings learned in one setting, group, or sample to other settings or groups.

generalized other The people or groups that people take into account as they consider or evaluate a course of action. ("What would people think?")

genetically modified foods (GMF) Foods coming from a plant or animal whose genes have been modified in a way that does not occur in nature.

genocide The systematic killing of a people, usually racial–ethnic minorities.

genomics The study of genes and how they relate to health and illness.

gentrification More affluent people moving into an area and displacing poorer people and renovating the homes they lived in.

geothermal energy Heat from beneath the earth's surface.

glass ceiling An invisible social barrier that keeps women from rising to levels of authority within an organization.

global economy The economic interdependence of the nations of the world.

global warming An increase in the earth's temperature because of the *greenhouse effect.*

green party A political party whose central issue is environmental concerns.

greenhouse effect The concentration of gases in the atmosphere that forms a blanket around the earth, allowing sunlight to enter freely but slowing the release of heat.

group therapy A treatment for emotional problems in which members of the group talk about their problems and help one another cope with them.

H

hate crime Crime such as assault or vandalism that is motivated by dislike or hatred of the victim's race-ethnicity, religion, sexual orientation, disability, or national origin.

health maintenance organization (HMO) An organization that has contracted to take care of the medical needs of a group for a set price for a year.

heterosexuality The sexual preference for people of the opposite sex.

home health care Organized health services for people who are living at home with chronic or disabling diseases.

homemaker The partner in a marriage, traditionally the woman, who stays home, takes care of the house and children, and attends to the personal needs of the other partner; now extended to cohabiting relationships.

homophobe Technically, someone who fears homosexuals, but more commonly, someone who dislikes homosexuals.

homophobia Fear, dislike, or intolerance of homosexuals.

homosexual behavior Sexual relations between people of the same sex, regardless of their sexual preference.

homosexuality The sexual preference for people of one's own sex.

hydrocarbons Materials whose essential elements are hydrogen and carbon, the backbone of motor fuels and lubricants.

I

iatrogenesis Unintentionally causing an illnesses or other health problem as a result of medical care; illnesses acquired in a hospital are iatrogenic.

illegitimate opportunity structure The opportunity built into someone's social world to learn and participate in illegal activities.

imperialism The expansion of a country and the dominance of subjugated peoples.

incapacitation A response to crime that focuses on removing offenders from circulation.

incest Sexual relations between relatives, such as brothers and sisters or parents and their children.

incompatibility In terms of marriage and family, differences between a husband and wife that make it difficult for them to get along well.

income The flow of money people receive from their work and investments.

individual discrimination Discrimination by one person against another.

individual psychotherapy Treatment for emotional problems in which a therapist listens and tries to guide the client toward a resolution of his or her problems.

infant mortality rate The number of babies who die before one year of age, per 1,000 live births.

infanticide Killing infants shortly after birth, sometimes as a form of population control, and often directed against girls.

intercontinental ballistic missiles (ICBMs) Long-range nuclear weapons.

institutional discrimination Discrimination built into the social system that oppresses whole groups.

interest groups Groups organized around some specific interest (from the dairy industry to animal rights).

internal colonialism Exploitation by a dominant group of a minority group, where both live in the same country.

International Criminal Court (ICC) Court established in 2002 to investigate and prosecute genocide, crimes against humanity, and war crimes.

interview A method of gathering information in which the researcher asks questions. In a *structured* interview, the researcher asks preset questions; in an *unstructured* interview, people talk about their experiences, with the researcher making certain that specific areas are covered.

intimate partner violence Abuse within an intimate relationship; can be physical, sexual, or psychological.

invasion–succession cycle One group moving into an area that is inhabited by a group that has different characteristics. Moving in represents the invasion; dominating the area, the succession.

J

juvenile delinquency The legal term for the law-breaking behavior of children and adolescents.

L

labeling Stereotyping, or putting a tag on people, and treating them accordingly.

labor force participation rate The proportion of the population 16 years and older that is in the labor force.

latent dysfunction The unintended consequence of people's actions that disrupts the equilibrium or stability of a social system or the adjustment of its parts.

latent function The unintended consequence of people's actions that contributes to the equilibrium or stability of a social system or the functioning of its parts.

lay referral network Friends, relatives, and acquaintances from whom sick people get their ideas about health and illness and suggestions about who to see to treat their illnesses. See also *professional referral network*.

liberal feminism A branch of feminism which stresses that oppression exists because of the way men and women are socialized.

long-distance surgery A surgeon in one location being able, with the aid of computers and robots, to operate on a patient who is in another location, even in a remote region of the world.

looking-glass self Refers to our self-images being dependent on what we think others think of us. We see ourselves, in other words, as a reflection in the eyes of others; hence the term *looking-glass* self.

M

Mafia An organized crime group. The Sicilian-American version is bureaucratized with specialized personnel and departmentalization.

managed care (prepaid care) Programs initiated by health insurance companies to keep health care costs down, often through financial incentives; medical decisions are often made not by patient and physician but by an insurance company employee. An HMO is one example.

manifest function The consequences of people's actions that are *intended* to contribute to the adaptation, adjustment, or equilibrium of a social system or its parts.

masochists People who receive sexual gratification from experiencing pain.

mass murder The killing of four or more people at one time in one location.

mass poverty Poverty so widespread in some location that most people are poor.

master trait A trait, such as age, disability, or sex, considered so important that it overrides an individual's other characteristics.

medicalization of human problems Making the problems of daily life a matter of sickness to be handled by the medical profession.

megacity An urban area of over 10 million people.

megaton The explosive power of 1 million tons of TNT.

melting pot The expectation that the European immigrants to the United States would "melt" or blend together—that is, interact, intermarry, and form a new cultural and biological blend.

methadone maintenance A program for heroin addicts in which the narcotic methadone is substituted for the narcotic heroin.

method (research method or **research design)** Way of doing research.

militancy Seeking to dominate, sometimes with the threat of violence if demands are not met.

military–industrial complex The merged interests of the military, business, and politicians to produce armaments.

minority group A group of people who, on the basis of physical or cultural characteristics, are singled out for unequal treatment and who regard themselves as objects of discrimination.

modeling Copying another's behavior.

moral entrepreneur A crusading reformer who wages battle to enforce his or her ideas of morality.

mutual assured destruction (MAD) The precarious balance of power between two nations that exists because neither country would survive a war, removing the benefit of attacking the other.

N

narcoterrorism Terrorism that revolves around drugs. Some narcoterrorists use drug dealing to finance their political goals.

national debt The total amount that a nation owes; its total annual deficits minus its total annual surpluses.

national security The condition of the nation, in terms of threats from the outside and the inside.

NATO (North Atlantic Treaty Organization) A political and military alliance originally among twelve nations of the North Atlantic; now includes 28 nations.

New World Order Refers to the new balance of power being attempted by the G-8 nations.

normal violence The amount of violence that a group usually has.

nuclear disarmament The process by which nations remove nuclear weapons from their arsenals.

nuclear family A family that consists of a husband, wife, and their children.

nuclear fusion Process of combining atoms, as opposed to nuclear fission, which is the splitting of atoms.

nuclear proliferation The spread of nuclear weapons to more and more nations.

nuclear terrorism Use of nuclear weapons, or the threat to use them, as a way to gain objectives.

O

objective condition A condition of society that can be measured. One of the two essential characteristics of a social problem. See *subjective concern.*

observation A means of gathering information whereby the researcher directly observes what is occurring in a setting. In the *overt* form, people know they are being studied; in the *covert* form, they do not.

official poverty The level of income that a government recognizes as constituting poverty.

operant conditioning Principle holding that if some behavior is rewarded ("reinforced"), it will occur again.

optimistic environmentalists Environmentalists who believe that conditions are much better than the gloomy picture painted by the pessimistic environmentalists.

organized crime Organizations whose goal is to profit from criminal activities.

ozone shield A layer of the earth's upper stratosphere that screens out much of the sun's ultraviolet rays.

P

pan-Indianism A movement that goes beyond tribal identity to work for the welfare of all Native Americans.

participant observation (or *field study*) A method of gathering information through direct observation of some setting.

patriarchal society A social system in which the father is the head of the family and men have authority over women and children.

patriarchy Rule by men as a group over women as a group.

Pedophile Liberation Army (PLA) A group which argues that if people changed their attitudes about adults having sex with children, incest would no longer be an issue.

pedophiles Adults who are sexually attracted to children.

personal trouble An individual's own experience of a social problem.

pessimistic environmentalists Environmentalists who argue that we are facing energy and resource shortages so vast and pollution so great that they will shatter the foundations of the industrialized world.

pharmaceutical straitjacket Refers to drugs given in mental hospitals that make patients drowsy, lethargic, and easier to handle.

plea bargaining Pleading guilty to a lesser crime in exchange for a reduced sentence.

pluralists analysts who view power in society as balanced among many competing groups.

police discretion The decisions that the police make about whether to overlook or to enforce a law.

political process A power struggle between groups based on their competing interests or ideologies.

political theater A name sometimes given to terroristic acts because terrorists seek to use dramatic means to publicize their "cause."

political terrorism The use of war to achieve political objectives.

pollution The presence of substances that interfere with socially desired uses of air, water, land, or food.

Ponzi scheme The payment of "investment profits" to clients, not from profits, but from the money that other clients invest.

population In research, refers to the group that one wishes to study.

population pyramid A graphic representation of a population, showing the number in age levels by sex.

population shrinkage The shrinking of a country's population because its birthrate and immigration are too low to replace the people who die or emigrate.

population transfer A minority relocating within a society or leaving the society altogether. In *direct transfer,* the minority is moved forcibly; in *indirect transfer,* the dominant group makes life so miserable for the members of a minority group that they "choose" to leave.

pornography Writings, pictures, or objects that are intended to arouse sexual interest and are considered offensive or filthy.

poverty line The official measure of poverty; based on three times a low-cost food budget.

power The capacity to get your way even in the face of opposition.

power elite A small group of wealthy, powerful people who make the major economic and political decisions of a group or country.

prejudice An attitude whereby one prejudges others, usually negatively.

primary prevention Measures that keep a disease from occurring, such as vaccinations. See also *secondary prevention, tertiary prevention.*

professional criminal A person who earns a living from crime.

professional referral network The health care professionals that physicians and nurses use to evaluate their medical activities. See also *lay referral network.*

progressive taxation Refers to tax rates progressing (increasing) as income progresses (increases).

proletariat Marx's term for the workers, whose labor is exploited by the capitalists.

prostitution The renting of one's body for sexual purposes.

psychoanalysis A treatment for emotional problems created by Sigmund Freud; the goal is to uncover subconscious motives, fantasies, and fears by having patients speak about whatever comes to mind.

psychological dependence The craving for a drug even though there no longer is a physical dependence on that drug.

pushouts Children who have been kicked out of the family home by parents who no longer want them.

Q

questionnaire Written questions used to gather information in research.

R

race A group of people whose inherited physical characteristics distinguish it from others; a problematic term because it usually is used in a way that has no scientific basis; race is a social construct.

racial–ethnic group A group of people who identify with one another on the basis of their ancestry and cultural heritage. Also called an ethnic group.

racial–ethnic stratification Society or another group divided along racial–ethnic lines; the unequal distribution of resources on the basis of race–ethnicity.

radical feminism A branch of feminism that advocates eliminating patriarchy to free men and women from rigid gender roles.

random sample A sample that gives everyone in the group being studied an equal chance of being included in the research.

rate of violence The number of violent acts per some unit of population, usually per 100,000 people.

real income Income that is adjusted for inflation.

recidivism Former prisoners committing more crimes.

reference group A group whose standards people refer to when they evaluate themselves.

regional restratification A shift in the population and relative wealth and power of the regions that make up a country. The current shift in the United States is toward the sunbelt.

rehabilitation A response to crime that is designed to resocialize or reform offenders, so that they can become law-abiding citizens.

relative poverty Deprivation as measured by the standards of one's society and culture. On a personal level, people think of themselves as poor or not poor on the basis of their reference groups.

repressive terrorism Terrorism directed by a government against its own citizens.

reproductive labor Labor performed by wives at home that supports the breadwinner husband.

research method (or **research design**) The methods that sociologists use to study social life. For social problems, these are *case studies, experiments, field studies,* and *surveys.*

reserve labor force The unemployed, who can be put to work during periods of labor strife or economic expansion and laid off when these conditions change. Also called *reserve labor army.*

residual poverty Pockets of poverty in an otherwise affluent society.

resource recovery plants Garbage-burning plants that generate power; utilities are required by the federal government to buy the power, which means that the plants partially pay for themselves.

restitution A form of retribution by which offenders compensate their victims.

retribution A response to crime based on restoring the moral balance upset by a criminal act. Making thieves repay what they stole is an example.

revolutionary terrorism Terrorism used in an attempt to bring about change in the political structure.

riot Violent crowd behavior aimed against people and property.

rising expectations The belief that better conditions will come soon. Rising expectations develop when institutional barriers begin to fall; if conditions do not change soon, frustration builds, sometimes resulting in group violence.

role ambivalence Feeling both positive and negative about one's role.

RU486 (Mifeprex) An oral drug, used both as "a morning-after pill" (emergency contraceptive) to prevent attachment of a fertilized ovum to the uterine wall and as an abortion agent to terminate pregnancy in women up to the 7th week of pregnancy.

S

sadists People who receive sexual gratification by inflicting pain on others. See *masochists.*

sample A relatively small number of people who are intended to represent the larger group from which they are selected.

scaled-back society Reduction of industrial output and standard of living to some designated level.

secession A minority withdrawing from a society to establish its own nation.

secondary prevention Early detection and precautions that keep a disease from getting worse.

segregation Confining a group or an activity to specified geographical areas.

selective perception Seeing certain things, while being blind to others.

serial murder Killing several victims in three or more separate events.

sex The physical identity of a person as male or female. Refers to biology. See also *gender.*

sex tourism Travel to another country for sexual purposes.

sex-typing Associating something with one sex or the other. "Men's work" and "women's work" are examples of the sex-typing of occupations.

sexism The belief that one sex is innately superior to the other and the discrimination that supports such a belief.

sexual harassment Unwelcome sexual advances, requests for sexual favors, and other verbal or physical conduct of a sexual nature; usually connected to school or one's job.

sexual revolution Drastic relaxation in standards of sexual behavior, starting in the 1960s.

short-term directive therapy A treatment for emotional problems in which a therapist actively tries to solve the client's problems.

situational homosexual behavior Homosexual behavior by someone who has a heterosexual identity; often occurs in same-sex settings such as prisons or boarding schools.

social class Broad grouping of people in a society based on their income, education, and occupational prestige.

social construction of reality The way people make sense of life by giving meaning to their experiences.

social inequality The unequal distribution of wealth, income, power, and other opportunities.

social location An individual's position within society or its groups.

social problem Some aspect of society (an objective condition) that large numbers of people are concerned about and would like changed (subjective concerns).

socialism An economic system characterized by the public ownership of the means of production, central planning, and the distribution of goods without a profit motive. See *capitalism.*

socialist feminism A branch of feminism that stresses the direct link between capitalism and the oppression of women.

sociological imagination (or **sociological perspective**) A framework of thought that looks at the broad social context that shapes people's experiences. This perspective helps people transcend personal experiences and emotions in order to see the larger picture that affects their situation.

sociological perspective Another term for *sociological imagination.*

sociology The systematic and objective study of the groups that make up society; includes the relationships of those groups to one another and interaction within the groups.

solar envelope A second set of walls around a house that provide a "skin" to trap and distribute the sun's heat.

split-labor market Workers who are split along lines of age, race–ethnicity, or gender; those in charge try to take advantage of this split to keep wages low by sowing distrust.

state-sponsored terrorism A country supporting terrorism against another nation.

statutory rape Consensual sexual relations in which one person is under the legal age of consent. See *forcible rape.*

status crime Behavior that is illegal only because of the individual's age, such as drinking alcohol, running away from home, or violating curfew.

steady-state society A society in which the economy does not grow or shrink.

stereotype A generalization of what people are like.

strain theory A functionalist theory that stresses how people adapt when their access to the cultural means to reach cultural goals is blocked.

strip mining Mining coal that lies so close to the surface that it can be retrieved by stripping away the soil.

structural inequality Inequality that is built into social institutions.

structure The interrelations between the parts or subunits of society or some other social system.

structured interviews Interviews that use closed-ended questions.

subcultural theory A symbolic interactionist theory that stresses how a group's orientations—its norms, attitudes, values, beliefs, and behaviors—influence people.

subjective concern The concern or distress that people feel about some aspect of society. One of the two essential characteristics of a social problem. See *objective condition.*

suffragists Advocates in the 19th and early 20th centuries for more rights for women, especially the right to vote.

supergang A large, violent, criminal gang; many have affiliates in other cities and even in other countries.

surplus value of labor If an item sells for more than what it cost to produce, the profit (or surplus value) is said to result from the value of the labor that went into producing the item.

survey Research using questionnaires or interviews that focuses on a sample of people from a target population. The sample is intended to represent the larger group from which it is selected.

symbiosis A mutually beneficial relationship.

symbolic interactionism A sociological theory that focuses on the meanings that objects and events have for people, and how people develop and use symbols to communicate with one another. Social problems are not objective conditions but, rather, the conditions that people have decided to call social problems.

symbol An item of social life to which we give meaning and that we then use to communicate with one another. Symbols include signs, gestures, words, and even our posture and appearance.

synfuels Alternative fuels developed from garbage, sawdust, and other waste.

T

taking the role of the other Putting oneself in someone else's shoes to try to see things as that person sees them.

talk therapy Treatments of emotional problems that are based on "talking" (psychotherapy, group therapy, etc.).

techniques of neutralization Ways that people justify their norm-breaking activities, making their behaviors more acceptable to themselves and others.

temple prostitution Prostitution that takes place in a temple, as a type of worship.

terrorism Using the means of war to create fear in order to try to achieve objectives.

tertiary prevention Medical care of an existing disease aimed at preventing further damage.

testosterone A male hormone produced by the testes that stimulates the development of male sexual characteristics.

theory An explanation of how two or more concepts, such as age and suicide, are related to one another.

thermal inversion A layer of cold air sealing in a lower layer of warm air.

total war No-holds-barred warfare.

transgender persons People whose personal gender identity does not match the gender role that society has assigned them based on their sex organs.

two-tier system of medical care A medical delivery system in which the poor receive one type of medical care and the affluent another.

U

underclass Alienated people who live primarily in the inner cities; they have little education and high rates of unemployment, female-headed families, welfare dependency, violent crimes, drug abuse, and births to single women.

uniform sentencing Imposing the same sentence on everyone who is convicted of the same crime.

unstructured interviews Interviews that use open-ended questions.

urban crisis The interrelated problems of cities, including their governance, financing, poverty, violence, crime, and deterioration of services.

urbanization The process whereby cities grow.

V

value A belief about whether something is good or bad, desirable or undesirable.

victimless crime An illegal act to which the participants consent.

violence The use of physical force to injure people or to destroy their property.

W

war Violent armed conflict between countries.

wealth Savings, property, investments, income, and other economic assets.

welfare wall The disincentive to work when the income from working is not much more than the income from welfare.

white-collar crime Crimes committed by executives and others in the corporate world as part of their job; for instance, knowingly producing dangerous vehicles, altering drug test data, and creating false advertising.

withdrawal The distress that people feel when they don't take a drug to which they are addicted.

Z

zero population growth A population that is neither growing nor shrinking because women bear only enough children to replace those who die.

References

All new references are printed in blue.

"49 Bodies Found on Mexico Roadway." Associated Press, May 14, 2012.

Achenbaum, W. Andrew. *Old Age in the New Land: The American Experience Since 1970.* Baltimore: Johns Hopkins University Press, 1978.

Ackerman, John P., Tracy Riggins, and Maureen M. Black. "A Review of the Effects of Prenatal Cocaine Exposure Among School-Aged Children." *Pediatrics, 125,* 3, February 2010:554.

Adams, David. "Top Senator Denies Sex Tourism Claim as FBI Raids Donor's Offices." Reuters, January 30, 2013.

Adams, Matthew, Carl Walker, and Paul O'Connell. "Invisible or Involved Fathers? A Content Analysis of Parenting in Young Children's Picturebooks." *Sex Roles, 65,* 3–4, 2011:259–270.

Agriculture and Agri-Food Canada. "Inside Japan: Processed Food Trade." *Market Indicator Report,* March 2010.

Akers, Ronald L., and Gary F. Jensen. "Empirical Status of Social Learning Theory: Past, Present, and Future." In *Taking Stock: The Status of Criminological Theory, 15,* Frances T. Cullen, John Paul Wright, and Kristie R. Blevins, eds. New Brunswick, NJ: Transaction, 2006:37–76.

Alba, Richard, and Victor Nee. *Remaking the American Mainstream: Assimilation and Contemporary Immigration.* Cambridge, Mass.: Harvard University Press, 2003.

Alihan, Milla A. *Social Ecology.* New York: Columbia University Press, 1938.

Alimahomed-Wilson, Jake. "Black Longshoremen and the Fight for Equality in an 'Anti-Racist' Union." *Race and Class, 53,* 4, 2012:39–53.

Allegretto, Sylvia A "The State of Working America's Wealth." Economic Policy Institute, Briefing Paper #202, March 23, 2011.

Allen, Charlotte Low. "Anti-Abortion Movement's Anti-Establishment Face." *Wall Street Journal,* December 8, 1988:A14.

Allen, H. "In Shadow of Troubled Year, Mashantuckets to Choose Two Tribal Councilors." *New London Day,* October 31, 2008.

Allman, William F., "A Laboratory of Human Conflict." *U.S. News & World Report,* April 11, 1988:57–58.

Allport, Gordon. *The Nature of Prejudice.* Reading, Mass.: Addison-Wesley, 1954.

Altimari, Dave, and Jon Lender. "Sandy Hook Shooter Adam Lanza Wore Earplugs." *Hartford Currant,* January 6, 2013.

American College of Obstetricians and Gynecologists: Women's Health Care Physicians. "Intrapartum Fetal Heart Rate Monitoring: Nomenclature, Interpretation, and General Management Principles." *ACOG Practice Bulletin, 114,* 1, July 2009:192–202.

Amott, Teresa, and Julie Matthaei. *Race, Gender, and Work: A Multicultural Economic History of Women in the United States.* Boston: South End, 1991.

Andersen, Margaret L. *Thinking About Women: Sociological Perspectives on Sex and Gender.* New York: Macmillan, 1988.

Anderson, D. Mark, and Daniel I. Rees. "Medical Marijuana Laws, Traffic Fatalities, and Alcohol Consumption." Bonn, Germany: IZA Discussion Paper No. 6112, November 2011.

Anderson, Elijah. "Streetwise." In *Society: Readings to Accompany Sociology: A Down-to-Earth Approach, Core Concepts,* James M. Henslin, ed. Boston: Allyn & Bacon, 2006:54–63.

Anderson, Elijah. *A Place on the Corner.* Chicago: University of Chicago Press, 1978.

Anderson, Elijah. *Streetwise: Race, Class, and Change in an Urban Community.* Chicago: University of Chicago Press, 1990.

Anderson, Jack, and Jan Moller. "Gorton Under Republican Fire for Indian Wars." January 1998.

Anderson, Robert T. "From Mafia to Cosa Nostra." *American Journal of Sociology, 71,* November 1965:302–310.

Anslinger, Harry J., and Courtney Ryley Cooper. "Marijuana: Assassin of Youth." *American Magazine,* July 1937.

Aposporos, Demetra. "Hunting for Glory with the Barabaig of Tanzania." *National Geographic,* July 2004.

Aries, Philippe. *Centuries of Childhood: A Social History of Family Life.* Robert Baldick, trans. New York: Vintage, 1962.

Arlacchi, P. *Mafia, Peasants and Great Estates: Society in Traditional Calabria.* Cambridge: Cambridge University Press, 1980.

Armitage, Richard L. "Red Army Retreat Doesn't Signal End of U.S. Obligation." *Wall Street Journal,* February 7, 1989:A20.

Ashley, Richard. *Cocaine: Its History, Uses, and Effects.* New York: St. Martin's, 1975.

Aston, G., and V. Foubister. "MD and Physician Extender Turf War." *The American Medical News, 41,* 1998:27, 9–10.

Athens, Lonnie H. *Violent Criminal Acts and Actors: A Symbolic Interactionist Study.* Boston: Routledge, 1980.

AVERT. *AIDS Orphans.* 2008. Online. http://www.avert.org/aidsorphans.htm

Bagne, Paul. "High-Tech Breeding." In *Marriage and Family in a Changing Society,* 4th ed., James M. Henslin, ed. New York: Free Press, 1992:226–234.

Bailey, Jeff. "Economics of Trash Shift as Cities Learn Dumps Aren't So Full." *Wall Street Journal,* June 2, 1992:A1, A7.

Bajaj, Vikas. "As Grain Piles Up, India's Poor Still Go Hungry." *New York Times,* June 7, 2012.

Baker, Kaysee, and Arthur A. Raney. " 'Equally Super' Gender-Role Stereotyping of Superheroes in Children's Animated Programs." *Mass Communication and Society, 10,* 1, 2007:25–41.

Baker, Peter, and Dan Bilefsky. "Russia and U.S. Sign Nuclear Arms Reduction Pact." *New York Times,* April 8, 2010.

Baldo, M. H. "Caesarean Section in Countries of the Eastern Mediterranean Region." *La Revue de Santé de la Méditerranée orientale, 14,* 2:2008.

Balemba, Samantha, Eric Beauregard, and Tom Mieczkowsi. "To Resist or Not to Resist? The Effect of Context and Crime Characteristics on Sex Offenders' Reaction to Victim Resistance." *Crime and Delinquency, XX(X),* May 2012:1–24.

Banda, P. Solomon. "Man, 18, Had Sex with Girl Later Found Dead." Associated Press, May 21, 2010.

Bandura, Albert, and Richard H. Walters. *Social Learning and Personality Development.* New York: Holt, 1963.

Barber, James Allen, Jr. "The Military-Industrial Complex." In *The Military and American Society: Essays and Readings,* Stephen E. Ambrose and James A. Barber, Jr., eds. New York: Free Press, 1972.

Bardwick, Judith M. *Psychology of Women: A Study of Bio-Cultural Conflicts.* New York: Harper & Row, 1971.

Barkley, R. A. *Attention-Deficit Hyperactivity Disorder: A Handbook for Diagnosis and Treatment,* 3rd ed. New York: Guilford, 2006.

Barnard, Anne. "Mormon Church's Plan for Land Upset Harlem." *New York Times,* January 9, 2012.

Barnes, Edward, and William Shebar. "Quitting the Mafia." *Life,* December 1987:108–112.

Barnes, Julian E. "Pentagon Digs in on Cyberwar Front." Wall Street Journal, July 6, 2012.

Baron, Larry. "Immoral, Inviolate or Inconclusive?" *Society,* July/August 1987:6–12.

Barrett, Devlin, and Sean Gardiner. "Structure Keeps Mafia Atop Crime Heap." *Wall Street Journal,* January 29, 2011.

Barringer, Felicity. "As 'Yuck Factor' Subsides, Treated Wastewater Flows from Taps." *New York Times,* February 9, 2012.

Barron, J. "Medical Examiner Rules Ledger's Death Accidental." *New York Times,* February 7, 2008.

"Barry Bonds Prosecutor: No Jail Time 'Almost Laughable.'" *L.A. Now,* December 16, 2011.

Barry, Ellen. "Old Soviet Nuclear Site in Asia Has Unlikely Sentinel: The U.S." *New York Times,* May 21, 2011.

Bart, Pauline B., and Patricia H. O'Brien. "How the Women Stopped Their Rapes." *Signs, 10,* 1984.

Bart, Pauline B., and Patricia H. O'Brien. *Stopping Rape: Successful Survival Strategies.* New York: Pergamon, 1985.

Bartlett, Donald L., and James B. Steele. "Wheel of Misfortune." *Time,* December 16, 2002:44–58.

Bassett, Laura. "Virginia Board of Health Passes Strictest Abortion Clinic Regulations in the Nation" *Huffington Post,* September 15, 2011.

Basten, Stuart. "Voluntary Childlessness and Being Childfree." University of Oxford. The Future of Human Reproduction: Working Paper #5. June 2009.

Basu, Jayasree. "Do HMOs Reduce Preventable Hospitalizations for Medicare Beneficiaries?" *Medical Care Research and Review, 64,* 5, October 2007:544–567.

Baumann, Mary. U.S. Senate Historical Office. Personal communication, September 14, 2006.

Beck, Melinda. "Raising the Chance of Some Cancers with Two Drinks a Day." *Wall Street Journal,* November 1, 2011.

Becker, Howard S. "Editor's Introduction." In *Social Problems: A Modern Approach.* Howard S. Becker, ed. New York: Wiley, 1966:1–31.

Becker, Howard S. "History, Culture, and Subjective Experience: An Exploration of the Social Bases of Drug Induced Experiences." *Journal of Health and Social Behavior, 7,* June 1967:163–176.

Becker, Jo, and Scott Shane. "Secret 'Kill List' Proves a Test of Obama's Principles and Will." *New York Times,* May 29, 2012.

Beckett, Katherine. "Choosing Cesarean: Feminism and the Politics of Childbirth in the United States." *Feminist Theory, 6,* 3, 2005:251–275.

Beddoe, Christine, C., Michael Hall, and Chris Ryan. *The Incidence of Sexual Exploitation of Children in Tourism.* Madrid: World Tourism Organization, 2001.

Beech, Hannah. "Unhappy Returns." *Time,* July 26–August 2, 2004.

Beeghley, Leonard. *The Structure of Social Stratification in the United States,* 5th ed. Boston: Allyn & Bacon, 2008.

Beeman, Angie, Davita Silfen Glasberg, and Colleen Casey. "Whiteness as Property: Predatory Lending and the Reproduction of Racialized Inequality." *Critical Sociology, 37,* 1, 2010:27–45.

Belasco, Amy. "The Cost of Iraq, Afghanistan, and Other Global War on Terror Operations Since 9/11." Washington: Congressional Research Service, March 29, 2011.

Belfield, Clive R., and Henry M. Levin. "High School Dropouts and the Economic Losses from Juvenile Delinquency." California Dropout Research Project Report #16, September 2009.

Bell, Daniel. *The End of Ideology.* New York: Free Press, 1960.

Bell, David A. "An American Success Story: The Triumph of Asian-Americans." In *Sociological Footprints: Introductory Readings in Sociology,* 5th ed., Leonard Cargan and Jeanne H. Ballantine, eds. Belmont, Calif.: Wadsworth, 1991:308–316.

Belluck, Pam. "First-Ever Criminal Conviction Levied in Food Poisoning Case." *New York Times,* July 24, 1998a.

Belluck, Pam. "Forget Prisons: Americans Cry Out for the Pillory." *New York Times,* October 4, 1998b.

Benenson, Joyce F., Hassina P. Carder, and Sarah J. Geib-Cole. "The Development of Boys' Preferential Pleasure in Physical Aggression." *Aggressive Behavior, 34,* 2008:154–166.

Bengtson, Vern L., Carolyn Rosenthal, and Linda Burton. "Families and Aging: Diversity and Heterogeneity." In *Handbook of Aging and the Social Sciences,* 3rd ed., Robert H. Binstock and Linda K. George, eds. San Diego: Academic Press, 1990:263–287.

Benson, Michael L. "Denying the Guilty Mind: Accounting for Involvement in White-Collar Crime." *Criminology, 23,* November 1985:585–607.

Berger, Peter. L. *Invitation to Sociology.* New York: Doubleday, 1963.

Berik, Gunseli, and Ebru Kongar. "Time Use of Mothers and Fathers in Hard Times and Better Times: The U.S. Business Cycle of 2003–2010." Levy Economics Institute: Working Paper No. 696, November 2011.

Berkey, C. S., W. C. Willet, A. L. Frazier, B. Rosner, R. M. Tamimi, H. R. H. Rockett, and G. A. Colditz. "Prospective Study of Adolescent Alcohol Consumption and Risk of Benign Breast Disease in Young Women. *Pediatrics,* May 2010:2009–2347.

Berman, Marc G., John Jonides, and Stephen Kaplan. "The Cognitive Benefits of Interacting with Nature." *Psychological Science, 19,* 12, 2008:1207–1212.

Bernard, Viola W., Perry Ottenberg, and Fritz Redl. "Dehumanization: A Composite Psychological Defense in Relation to Modern War." In *The Triple Revolution Emerging: Social Problems in Depth,* Robert Perucci and Marc Pilisuk, eds. Boston: Little, Brown, 1971:17–34.

Bernstein, Elizabeth. "The Meaning of the Purchase: Desire, Demand, and the Commerce of Sex." *Ethnography, 2,* 3, 2001:389–420.

Bertrand, Marianne, Claudia Goldin, and Lawrence F. Katz. "Dynamics of the Gender Gap for Young Professionals in the Corporate and Financial Sectors." National Bureau of Economic Research Working Paper Number 14681, September 2009.

Bhattacharya, Prasenjit. "Union Carbide Not Liable in Bhopal Gas Cleanup, says US Court." *Hydrocarbon Processing Magazine,* July 2, 2012.

Biello, David. "Vegetable Compounds Combat Cancer." *Scientific American Online,* April 5, 2006.

Billeaud, Jacques. "Arizona Sheriff Defends Illegal-Immigrant Sweeps." *Seattle Times,* April 26, 2008.

Black, M. C., K. C. Basile, M. J. Breiding, et al. *The National Intimate Partner and Sexual Violence Survey.* Atlanta, GA.: National Center for Injury Prevention and Control, 2011.

Blackmon, Douglas A., Vanessa O'Connell, Alexandra Berzon, and Ana Campoy. "There Was Nobody in Charge." *Wall Street Journal,* May 27, 2010.

Blackstone, Sir William. *Commentaries on the Laws of England,* 4th ed., Thomas M. Cooley, ed. Chicago: Callaghan and Co., 1899.

Blum, Richard H., Eva Blum, and E. Garfield. *Drug Education: Results and Recommendations.* Lexington, Mass.: Heath, 1976.

Blumberg, Abraham S. "The Practice of Law as Confidence Game: Organizational Cooptation of a Profession." *Law and Social Review, 1,* 1967:15–39.

Blumemthal, Ralph. "Polluted Midwest Rain Is Killing New York Lakes." *Alton Telegraph,* June 8, 1981.

Blumstein, Alfred, and Joel Wallman, eds. *The Crime Drop in America,* 2nd ed. New York: Cambridge University Press, 2006.

Boden, Paul. "Restricting Pornography—The Slippery Slope to Censorship." *Urban Times,* May 31, 2012.

Bone, James. "Prostitute Behind Spitzer Sex Scandal Revealed." *The Times,* March 13, 2008.

Boot, Max. "Your Money or Your Life? That Depends." *Wall Street Journal,* March 4, 1998:A18.

Borenstein, Seth. "Richard Muller, Global Warming Skeptic, Now Agrees Climate Change Is Real." *New York Times,* October 30, 2011.

Boston, Guy D., Kevin O'Brien, and Joanne Palumbo, *Terrorism: A Selected Bibliography,* 2nd ed. Washington, D. C.: National Institute of Law Enforcement and Criminal Justice, March 1977.

Bowen, Crosswell. "Donora, Pennsylvania." In *Society and Environment: The Coming Collision,* Rex R. Campbell and Jerry L. Wade, eds. Boston: Allyn and Bacon, 1972:163–168.

Brannigan, Augustine. "Is Obscenity Criminogenic?" *Society,* July/August 1987:12–19.

Bray, Chad, and Rob Barry. "Long Jail Terms on Rise." *Wall Street Journal,* October 13, 2011.

Bray, Rosemary L. "Rosa Parks: A Legendary Moment, a Lifetime of Activism. *Ms., 6,* 3, November-December 1995:45–47.

Brecher, Edward M., and the Editors of Consumer Reports. *Licit and Illicit Drugs.* Boston: Little, Brown, 1972.

Bremer, L. Paul III. "Terrorism: Myths and Reality." *Department of State Bulletin,* May 1988:63.

Brewer, Devon D., John J. Potterat, Sharon B. Garrett, Stephen Q. Muth, John M. Roberts, Danuta Kasprzyk, Daniel E. Montano, and William W. Darrow. "Prostitution and the Sex Discrepancy in Reported Number of Sex Partners." *Proceedings of the National Academy of Sciences, 97,* 22, October 24, 2000:12385–12388.

Bricker, Jesse, Arthur B. Kennickell, Kevin B. Moore, and John Sabelhaus. "Changes in U.S. Family Finances from 2007 to 2010: Evidence from the Survey of Consumer Finances." *Federal Reserve Bulletin, 98,* 2, June 2012.

Broad, William J. "In Ancient Fossils, Seeds of a New Debate on Warming." *New York Times,* November 7, 2006a.

Broad, William J. "U.S. Web Site Is Said to Reveal a Nuclear Primer." *New York Times,* November 3, 2006b.

Broad, William J., and Judith Miller. "Rocky Start for U.S. Plan to Stockpile Vaccines to Fight Germ Warfare." *New York Times,* August 7, 1998.

Brody, Elaine M. "The Aging of the Family." *Annals of the American Academy of Political and Social Science, 438,* July 1978:13–27.

Brody, Jane E. "1,100 Tested in Michigan for Effects of Toxin That Poisoned Food in '73." *New York Times,* November 5, 1976.

"Broken Promise to Our Children: The 1998 State Tobacco Settlement 11 Years Later." American Lung Association, December 9, 2009.

Bronner, Ethan. "Poor Land in Jail as Companies Add Huge Fees for Probation." *New York Times,* July 2, 2012.

Brooks, Jack. *FDA Continues to Permit the Illegal Marketing of Carcinogenic Additives.* Twenty-fifth Report of the Committee on Government Operations. Washington, D.C.: U.S. Government Printing Office, 1987.

Brooks, Jack. *HHS' Failure to Enforce the Food, Drug, and Cosmetic Act: The Case of Cancer-Causing Color Additives.* Eleventh Report of the Committee on Government Operations. Washington, D.C.: U.S. Government Printing Office, 1985.

Brown, Donald A. "The Ethical Dimensions of Global Environmental Issues." *Daedalus, 130,* 4, Fall 2001:59–69.

Brown, Janet Welsh. Environmental Defense Fund Letter. New York, n.d.

Brownmiller, Susan. *Against Our Will: Men, Women, and Rape.* New York: Simon & Schuster, 1975.

Bucher, Jacob, and Michelle Manasse. "When Screams Are Not Released. A Study of Communication and Consent in Acquaintance Rape Situations." *Women and Criminal Justice, 21,* 3, 2011:123–140.

Buckley, Cara. "Teenagers' Violent 'Sport' Led to Killing on Long Island, Officials Say." *New York Times,* November 21, 2008.

Budiansky, Stephen A. "The Trees Fell—And So Did the People." *U.S. News & World Report,* February 9, 1987:75.

Buff, Stephen A. "Lois Lee Takes Back Children from the Night." *ASA Footnotes, 15,* 5, May, 1987:1, 2.

Bulkeley, William M. "Untested Treatments, Cures Find Stronghold on On-Line Services." *Wall Street Journal,* February 27, 1995:A1, A7.

Bunn, Matthew, and Anthony Wier. "Preventing a Nuclear 9/11." *Washington Post,* September 12, 2004.

Burch, William R., Jr. *Daydreams and Nightmares: A Sociological Essay on the American Environment.* New York: Harper & Row, 1971.

Bureau of Labor Statistics. "Physicians and Surgeons." *Occupational Outlook Handbook.* U.S. Department of Labor, 2012.

Bures, Regina M., Tanya Koropeckyj-Cox, and Michael Loree. "Childlessness, Parenthood, and Depressive Symptoms Among Middle-Aged and Older Adults." *Journal of Family Issues, 30,* 5, May 2009:670–687.

Burgess, Ann Wolbert, and Lynda Lytle Holmstrom. "Rape Trauma Syndrome." *American Journal of Psychiatry, 131,* 1974:981–986.

Burgess, Ernest W. "The Growth of the City: An Introduction to a Research Project." In *The City,* Robert E. Park, Ernest W. Burgess, and Roderick D. McKenzie, eds. Chicago: University of Chicago Press, 1925 (pages 47–62 in the 1967 edition).

Burgess, Ernest W., and Harvey J. Locke. *The Family: From Institution to Companionship.* New York: American Book, 1945.

Burns, John F. "Bangladesh, Still Poor, Cuts Birth Rate Sharply." *New York Times,* September 13, 1994:A10.

Burns, Kenneth Lauren. "The Civil War: A Film by Ken Burns." Public Broadcasting Service, 1990.

Burros, Marian. "Experts Worry About the Return of a Deadly Germ in Cold Cuts." *New York Times,* March 14, 1999.

Burroughs, William. "Excerpts from 'Deposition: Testimony Concerning a Sickness.'" In *Drugs in American Life,* Morrow Wilson and Suzanne Wilson, eds. New York: Wilson, 1975:133–158.

Butler, Desmond. "Georgia Confirms Highly Enriched Uranium Seizure." Associated Press, April 21, 2010.

Butterfield, Fox. "Prison Population Increases as Release of Inmates Slows." *New York Times,* January 11, 1999.

Cahoun, L., Cox, L., & Chitale, R. "Celebrity Addictions: Painkillers and Hollywood." ABC News Medical Unit, February 22, 2008.

Calle, Eugenia E., Carmen Rodriguez, Kimberly Walker-Thurmond, and Michael J. Thun. "Overweight, Obesity, and Mortality from Cancer in a Prospectively Studied Cohort of U.S. Adults." *New England Journal of Medicine, 348,* 17, April 24, 2003.

Campbell, Duncan. "Electronic Tagging May be Used for Prisoners Released on Parole." *Guardian,* August 12, 1995.

Campo-Flores, Arian. "A Crackdown on Call Girls." *Newsweek,* September 2, 2002.

Cancian, Maria, and Sheldon Danziger. "Changing Poverty and Changing Antipoverty Policies." Institute for Research on Poverty, Discussion Paper no. 1364-09. April 2009.

Capers, Bennett. "Real Rape Too." *California Law Review, 99,* 2011:1259–1308.

Caplow, Theodore, et al. *Middletown Families: Fifty Years of Change and Continuity.* Minneapolis: University of Minnesota Press, 1982.

Carey, Benedict. "In the Hospital, a Degrading Shift from Person to Patient." *New York Times,* August 16, 2005.

Carlson, Rick J. *The End of Medicine.* New York: Wiley, 1975.

Carlton, Jeff. "Dallas Police Aim to Help, Not Jail Prostitutes." Associated Press, January 5, 2010.

Carlton, Jim. "Builders Zero In on New Goal of Energy-Neutral Housing." *Wall Street Journal,* December 23, 2009.

Carnevale, Anthony P., and Stephen J. Rose. "Socioeconomic Status, Race/Ethnicity, and Selective College Admissions." New York: The Century Foundation, March 2003.

Carnevale, Mary Lu. "New Jolt for Nynex: Bawdy 'Conventions' of Buyers, Suppliers." *Wall Street Journal,* July 12, 1990:A1, A6.

Carpenter, Rhiannon, Adelle Fishlock, Ann Mulroy, Beth Oxley, Kate Russell, Claire Salter, Nicole Williams, and Catherine Heffernan. "After 'Unit 1421': An Exploratory Study Into Female Students' Attitudes and Behaviors Towards Binge Drinking at Leeds University." *Journal of Public Health, 30,* 1, 2008:8–13.

Carroll, C. R. *Drugs in Modern Society,* 5th ed. New York: McGraw-Hill, 2000.

Carton, Barbara. "At Jenny Craig, Men Are Ones Who Claim Sex Discrimination." *Wall Street Journal,* November 29, 1994:A1, A7.

Castaneda, Carlos. *A Separate Reality: Further Conversations with Don Juan.* New York: Simon & Schuster, 1971.

Castaneda, Carlos. *Tales of Power.* New York: Simon & Schuster, 1974.

Castaneda, Carlos. *The Teachings of Don Juan: A Yaqui Way of Knowledge.* New York: Ballantine, 1968.

Castells, M. (1983) *The City and the Grass Roots.* Berkeley: Univerisyt of California Press.

Castells, M. (1989) *The Informational City.* Oxford, England:Blackwell.

Castells, M. (1997) *The Urban Question: A Marxist Approach* (Alan Sheridan, Trans.) Cambridge, MA: MIT Press.

Castells, Manuel. *The City and the Grass Roots.* Berkeley: University of California Press, 1983.

Castells, Manuel. *The Informational City.* Oxford, England: Blackwell, 1989.

Castells, Manuel. *The Urban Question: A Marxist Approach.* Alan Sheridan, trans. Cambridge, Mass.: MIT Press, 1977.

Catalano, Shannan. "Intimate Partner Violence in the United States." National Crime Victimization Survey, 2010.

Catanzaro, Raimondo. *Men of Respect: A Social History of the Mafia.* New York: Free Press, 1992.

Cates, Jim A., and Jeffrey Markley. "Demographic, Clinical, and Personality Variables Associated with Male Prostitution By Choice." *Adolescence, 27,* 107, Fall 1992:695–706.

Cave, Damien. "Mexico Updates Death Toll in Drug War to 47,515, But Critics Dispute the Data." *New York Times,* January 11, 2012.

Centers for Disease Control and Prevention. (2006c) *Leading causes of death 1990–1998.*

Center for American Women and Politics. "Women in Elective Office 2012." June 2012.

Centers for Disease Control and Prevention. "AIDS Surveillance—Trends (1985–2010)." Hyattsville, Maryland: Department of Health and Human Services, 2012.

Centers for Disease Control and Prevention. "Alcohol and Pregnancy." Hyattsville, Maryland: Department of Health and Human Services, 2013c.

Centers for Disease Control and Prevention. "Alcohol and Public Health: Frequently Asked Questions." Hyattsville, Maryland: Department of Health and Human Services, 2013b.

Centers for Disease Control and Prevention. *Deaths, Percent of Total Deaths, and Death Rates for the Leading Causes of Death: United States and Each State, 2003.* 2006a.

Centers for Disease Control and Prevention. *HIV/AIDS Surveillance Report, 16, 2005.*

Centers for Disease Control and Prevention. *HIV/AIDS Surveillance Report, 19,* 2009c.

Centers for Disease Control and Prevention. *HIV Surveillance Report: Diagnoses of HIV infection and AIDS in the United States and Dependent Areas, 2009.* Hyattsville, Maryland: Department of Health and Human Services, 2010.

Centers for Disease Control and Prevention. *Leading Causes of Death, 1900–1998.* 2006b.

Centers for Disease Control and Prevention. *National Nursing Home Survey,* 2008b.

Centers for Disease Control and Prevention. "National Suicide Statistics at a Glance." September 30, 2009a.

Centers for Disease Control and Prevention. "State-Specific Smoking-Attributable Mortality and Years of Potential Life Lost—United States, 2000–2004." *Morbidity and Mortality Weekly Report, 58,* 2, January 23, 2009b:29–33.

Centers for Disease Control and Prevention. "Tobacco Related Mortality." Hyattsville, Maryland: Department of Health and Human Services, 2011.

Centers for Disease Control and Prevention. "Tobacco-Related Mortality," Hyattsville, Maryland: Department of Health and Human Services, 2013a.

Chafetz, Janet Saltzman. *Gender Equity: An Integrated Theory of Stability and Change.* Newbury Park, Calif.: Sage, 1990.

Chamblss, William J. *Power, Politics, and Crime.* Boulder, Co.: Westview Press, 2001.

Chambliss, William J. "The Saints and the Roughnecks." In *Down to Earth Sociology: Introductory Readings,* 15th ed., James M. Henslin, ed. New York: Free Press, 2014. (Originally published in *Society, 11,* 1, 1973:24–31)

Chan, Heng Choon, Kathleen M. Heide, and Eric Beauregard. "What Propels Sexual Murderers: A Proposed Integrated Theory of Social Learning and Routine Activities Theories." *International Journal of Offender Therapy and Comparative Criminology, 55,* 2, 2011:228–250.

Chandler, Tertius, and Gerald Fox. *3000 Years of Urban Growth.* NewYork: Academic Press, 1974.

Chang, Iris. *The Rape of Nanking: The Forgotten Holocaust of World War II.* New York: Basic Books, 1997.

Chase, Marilyn. "Defying Treatment, a New, Virulent Bug Sparks Health Fears." *Wall Street Journal,* January 20, 2006.

Cheadle, Jacob, Paul R. Amato, and Valerie King. "Patterns of Nonresident Father Involvement." *Demography, 47,* 2010:205–226.

Chen, M. "Ground Zero: The Most Dangerous Workplace." *The New Standard,* 2007.

Cheng, V. "328 Useful Drugs Are Said to Lie Hidden in Tropical Forests." *New York Times,* June 27, 1995:C4.

Chernoff, Nina W., and Rita J. Simon. "Women and Crime the World Over." *Gender Issues, 18,* 3, Summer 2000:5–20.

Childs, Dan. "Medical Errors, Past and Present." ABC News, November 27, 2007.

Chiplock, Megan. "Marijuana Chemical May Slow Multiple Sclerosis." Temple University News Service, May 12, 2009.

Cho, Eunyoung, et al. "Dairy Foods, Calcium, and Colorectal Cancer: A Pooled Analysis of 10 Cohort Studies." *Journal of the National Cancer Institute, 96,* 13, July 7, 2004:1015–1022.

Churchill, Ward, and Jim Vander Wall. *Agents of Repression: The FBI's Secret Wars Against the Black Panther Party and the American Indian Movement.* Boston: South End Press, 1990.

CIA (Central Intelligence Agency). *CIA World Factbook,* published annually.

Clayton, R. R., A Catterello, and B. M. Johnstone. "The Effectiveness of Drug Abuse Resistance Education (Project DARE): 5-Year Follow-Up Results." *Preventive Medicine, 25,* 1996:307–318.

Cleaver, Eldridge. *Soul on Ice.* New York: McGraw-Hill, 1968.

Clinard, Marshall B. *Corporate Corruption: The Abuse of Power.* New York: Praeger, 1990.

Clinard, Marshall B., Peter C. Yeager, Jeanne Brisette, David Petrashek, and Elizabeth harries. *Illegal Corporate Behavior.* Washington, D.C.: U.S. Department of Justice, 1979.

Clines, Francis X. "Soviets Now Admit '57 Nuclear Blast." *New York Times,* June 18, 1998.

Cloward, Richard A., and Lloyd E. Ohlin. *Delinquency and Opportunity: A Theory of Delinquent Gangs.* New York: Free Press, 1960.

Code, Lorraine, ed. *Encyclopedia of Feminist Theories.* London: Routledge, 2000.

Cohen, Albert K. *Delinquent Boys: The Culture of the Gang.* New York: Free Press, 1955.

Cohen, Morris R. "Moral Aspects of the Criminal Law." *Yale Law Journal, 49,* April 1940:1009–1026.

Cohen, Susan M., H. K. Linenberger, L. E. Wehry, and H. K. Welz. "Recovery after Hysterectomy: A Year-Long Look." *Obstetrics and Gynaecology, 2,* 3, 2011: WMC001761.

Cokkinides, Priti Bandi, Catherine McMahon, Ahmedin Jemal, Thomas Glynn, and Elizabeth Ward. "Tobacco Control in the United States: Recent Progress and Opportunities." *CA: A Cancer Journal for Clinicians, 59,* May 2010:352–365.

College Board. "SAT: Total Group Profile, 2012 College-Bound Seniors." September 24, 2012.

Conley, Dalton. "Capital for College: Parental Assets and Postsecondary Schooling." *Sociology of Education, 74,* 1, January 2001:59–68.

Consumer Reports. "Unsafe Chicken." *Consumer Reports,* January 2010.

Conti, Massimo. "The Famine Controversy." *World Press Review, 27,* January 1980:56.

Cookson, Peter W., Jr., and Caroline Hodges Persell. "Preparing for Power: Cultural Capital and Elite Boarding Schools." In *Life in Society: Readings to Accompany Sociology: A Down-to-Earth Approach,* 7th ed., James M. Henslin, ed. Boston: Allyn & Bacon 2005:175–185. (Originally published in *Preparing for Power,* by Peter W. Cookson and Caroline H. Persell, 1985.)

Cooper, P. F. "Historical Aspects of Wastewater Treatment." In *Decentralized Sanitation and Reuse: Concepts, Systems and Implementation,* P. Lens. G. Zeeman, and G. Lettinga, eds. London:IWA, 2002:11–38.

Copen, Casey E., Kimberly Daniels, Jonathan Vespa, and William D. Mosher. "First Marriages in the United States: Data from the 2006–2010 National Survey of Family Growth." *National Health Statistics Reports, 49,* March 22, 2012.

Corcoran, Mary, Greg J. Duncan, Gerald Gurin, and Patricia Gurin. "Myth and Reality: The Causes and Persistence of Poverty." *Journal of Policy Analysis and Management, 4,* 4, 1985:516–536.

Cordoba, Jose de. "Mexico Nabs Gulf Cartel Boss." *Wall Street Journal,* September 14, 2012.

Corless, Inge B., Teri Lindgren, William Holzemer, et al. "Marijuana Effectiveness as an HIV Self-Care Strategy." *Clinical Nursing Research,18,* 2, May 2009:172–193.

Cornell, George W. "Modern Persecutions Mirror Those of Jesus." Associated Press, April 13, 1981.

Courtesy of The Gray Panthers.

Corzine, Jay, and Richard Kirby. "Cruising the Truckers: Sexual Encounters in a Highway Rest Area." *Urban Life, 6,* July 1977:171–192.

Coser, Lewis A. *Masters of Sociological Thought: Ideas in Historical and Social Context.* New York: Harcourt, 1977.

Coser, Lewis A. *The Functions of Social Conflict.* New York: Free Press, 1956.

Cowley, Joyce. (1969). *Pioneers of Women's Liberation.* New York: Merit.

Cressey, Donald R. *Other People's Money.* New York: Free Press, 1953.

Cressey, Donald R. *Theft of the Nation: The Structure and Operations of Organized Crime in America.* New York: Harper & Row, 1969.

Crime in the United States, Washington, D.C.: U.S. Department of Justice, Federal Bureau of Investigation. 2009 and earlier years.

Critchfield, Richard. "China's Agricultural Success Story." *Wall Street Journal,* January 13, 1986:25.

Crosby, Alex E., LaVonne Ortega, and Mark R. Stevens. "Suicide: United Sates, 1999–2007." *Morbidity and Mortality Weekly Report, 60,* 1, Supplements, January 4, 2011:56–59.

"Cross National Comparison of Rape Rates: Problems and Issues." Working Paper #18. Statistical Commission and UN Economic Commission for Europe, October 28, 2004.

Croteau, David. *Politics and the Class Divide: Working People and the Middle-Class Left.* Philadelphia: Temple University Press, 1995.

Crum, Travis. "Meth Lab Growth Hurting Hotels, Motels." *Charlestown Gazette,* May 27, 2012.

Cuffel, B., W. Goldman, and H. Schlesinger. "Does Managing Behavioral Health Care Services Increase the Cost of Providing Medical Care? *Journal of Behavioral Health Services and Research 26,* 4, 1999:372–380.

Currie, Elliott. *Confronting Crime: An American Challenge.* New York: Pantheon, 1985.

Dabbs, James M., Jr., and Robin Morris. "Testosterone, Social Class, and Antisocial Behavior in a Sample of 4,462 Men." *Psychological Science, 1,* 3, May 1990: 209–211.

Dahl, Robert A. *Who Governs?* New Haven, Conn.: Yale University Press, 1961.

Daling Janet R., David R. Doody, Xiaofei Sun, et al. "Association of Marijuana Use and the Incidence of Testicular Germ Cell Tumors," *Cancer,* March 15, 2009:1215–1223.

Daly, Martin, and Margo Wilson. *Homicide.* New York: Aldine de Gruyter, 1988.

Danaei, Goodarz, Eric L. Ding, Dariush Mazaffarian, et al. "The Preventable Causes of Death in the United States: Comparative Risk Assessment of Dietary, Lifestyle, and Metabolic Risk Factors." *PLoS Medicine, 6,* 4, April 28, 2009.

Daniels, Roger. *The Decision to Relocate the Japanese Americans.* Philadelphia: Lippincott, 1975.

Dash, Leon. "When Children Want Children." *Society, 27,* 5, July–August 1990:17–19.

Davey, Monica. "Budget Woes Hit Defense Lawyers for the Indigent." *New York Times,* September 9, 2010.

Davies, J. Clarence III, and Barbara S. Davies. *The Politics of Pollution,* 2nd ed. Indianapolis, Ind.: Bobbs-Merrill, 1975.

Davis-Floyd, Robbie E. "Giving Birth the American Way." In *Down to Earth Sociology: Introductory Readings,* 14th ed., James M. Henslin, ed. New York: The Free Press 2007:432–445.

Davis, Angela. *Angela Davis: An Autobiography.* New York: Random House, 1974.

Davis, Kingsley. "Sexual Behavior." In *Contemporary Social Problems,* 2nd ed., Robert Merton and Robert Nisbet, eds. New York: Harcourt, 1966.

Davis, Kingsley, and Wilbert E. Moore. "Some Principles of Stratification." *American Sociological Review, 10,* 1945:242–249.

Davis, Nanette J. "Prostitution: Identity, Career, and Legal-Economic Enterprise." In *The Sociology of Sex: An Introductory Reader,* James M. Henslin and Edward Sagarin, eds. New York: Schocken, 1978:297–322.

Daws, Gavin. *Prisoners of the Japanese: POWs of World War II in the Pacific.* New York: Morrow, 1994.

de Silva, Rex. 1980. "Developing the Third World." *World Press Review,* May 1980:48.

Denes, Magda. *In Necessity and Sorrow: Life and Death in an Abortion Hospital.* New York: Basic Books, 1976.

DeRios, Marlene Dobkin, and David E. Smith. "Drug Use and Abuse in Cross-Cultural Perspective." *Human Organization, 36,* 1977:14–21.

Dewan, Shaila, and Katie Zezima."Twists Multiply in Alabama Shooting Case." *New York Times,* February 14, 2010.

Dewan, Shaila, Stephanie Saul, and Katie Zezima. "For Professor, Fury Just Beneath the Surface." *New York Times,* February 20, 2010.

Diamond, Milton. "Pornography, Public Acceptance and Sex Related Crime: A Review." *International Journal of Law and Psychiatry, 32,* 2009:304–314.

Dickey, Christopher, and Adam Rogers. "Smoke and Mirrors." *Newsweek,* February 25, 2002.

Dickson, Donald T. "Bureaucracy and Morality: An Organizational Perspective on a Moral Crusade." *Social Problems, 16,* Fall 1968:143–156.

Digest of Education Statistics, National Center for Education Statistics, 2012.

Dimico, Arcangelo, Alessia Isopi, and Ola Olsson. "Origins of the Sicilian Mafia: The Market for Lemons." Gothenburg, Sweden: University of Gothenburg, Working Papers in Economics, No 532, May 2012.

Dingell, John D. *Sulfites: Hearing Before the Subcommittee on Oversight and Investigations of the Committee on Energy and Commerce, House of Representatives.* Washington, D.C.: U.S. Government Printing Office, March 27, 1985.

DiSilvestro, Roger I. *In the Shadow of Wounded Knee: The Untold Final Chapter of the Indian Wars.* New York: Walker and Co., 2006.

Dobyns, Henry F. *Their Numbers Became Thinned: Native American Population Dynamics in Eastern North America.* Knoxville: University of Tennessee Press, 1983.

Dodd, Mike. "McGwire Quietly Makes Big Impact as Hitting Coach." *USA Today,* October 20, 2011.

Doerner, William G. "The Index of Southernness Revisited: The Influence of Wherefrom upon Whodunnit." *Criminology, 16,* May 1978:47–56.

Dollard, John, Neal E. Miller, Leonard W. Doob, O. H. Mowrer, and Robert R. Sears. *Frustration and Aggression.* New Haven, Conn.: Yale University Press, 1961. (Originally published 1939)

Domhoff, G. William. *The Bohemian Grove and Other Retreats: A Study in Ruling-Class Cohesiveness.* New York: Harper & Row, 1974.

Domhoff, G. William. *The Power Elite and the State: How Policy Is Made in America.* New York: Aldine de Gruyter, 1990.

Domhoff, G. William. *The Powers That Be.* New York: Random House, 1978a.

Domhoff, G. William. *Who Really Rules?* New Brunswick, N.J.: Transaction, 1978b.

Domhoff, G. William. *Who Rules America: Power and Politics,* 6th ed. New York: McGraw-Hill, 2009.

Donadio, Rachel. "Italy's Attacks on Migrants Fuel Debate on Racism." *New York Times,* October 12, 2008.

Douglass, Joseph D. "A Biological Weapons Threat Worse Than Saddam." *Wall Street Journal,* March 10, 1998:A22.

Douvan, Elizabeth. "Is the American Family Obsolete?" University of California, University Extension, Courses by Newspaper, San Diego, 1980.

Dove, Adrian. "Soul Folk 'Chitling' Test or the Dove Counterbalance Intelligence Test." Mimeo, n.d.

Dow, William H., Robert F. Schoeni, Nancy E. Adler, and Judith Stewart. "Evaluating the Evidence Base: Policies and Inter ventions to Address Socioeconomic Status Gradients in Health." *Annals of the New York Academy of Sciences, 1186,* 2010:240–251.

Dowie, Mark. 1979. "The Corporate Crime of the Century." *Mother Jones, 4,* November 1979:23–25, 37.

Dowie, Mark. "Pinto Madness." *Mother Jones, 2,* September–October 1977:18–32.

Downing, Alexandra, and Veronika Khvorostuhna. "Women Are on Top: How Feminist porn is Changing a Male-dominated Industry." *Canadian University Press,* February 25, 2012.

Drug Enforcement Administration. *Opium Poppy Cultivation and Heroin Processing in Southeast Asia.* Washington, DC: U.S. Department of Justice, 2001.

Dubar, Helen. "American Discovers Child Pornography." In *Human Sexuality 80/81,* James R. Barbour, ed. Guilford, Conn.: Dushkin, 1980.

Dufay, Joanne. "Ten Years After Chernobyl: A Witness to the Devastation." Greenpeace online, n.d.

Dugger, Celia W. "Senegal Curbs a Bloody Rite for Girls and Women." *New York Times,* October 15, 2011.

Dumas, Daisy. "'I Know They Aren't Going to Call. I Don't Want Them to Call": How Women Who Want No-strings-attached Sex Are Fuelling Boom in Gigolo Services." *Mail Online,* February 17, 2012.

Durkheim, Emile. *The Division of Labor in Society,* George Simpson, trans. New York: Free Press, 1964. (Originally published 1893)

Durkheim, Emile. *The Rules of Sociological Method,* Sir George E. G. Catlin, ed. New York: Macmillan, 1938. (Originally published 1904; 8th ed. 1950)

Durkheim, Emile. *Suicide,* John A. Spaulding and George Simpson, trans. New York: Free Press, 1951. (Originally published 1897)

Durning, Alan. "Cradles of Life." In *Social Problems 90/91,* Leroy W. Barnes, ed. Guilford, Conn.: Dushkin, 1990:231–241.

Duskin, Edgar W. "Environment Continues to Get Better." *Southwest Farm Press,* August 7, 2003.

Duster, Troy. "From Structural Analysis to Public Policy." *Contemporary Sociology, 17,* 3, May 1988:287–290.

Duster, Troy. *The Legalization of Morality: Law, Drugs, and Moral Judgment.* New York: Free Press, 1970.

Eberstadt, Nick. *The Poverty of Communism.* New Brunswick, N.J.: Transaction, 1988.

Eckholm, Erik. "Anti-Abortion Groups Are Split on Legal Tactics." *New York Times,* December 4, 2011.

Eder, Donna. *School Talk: Gender and Adolescent Culture.* New Brunswick, N.J.: Rutgers University Press, 1995.

"Effects of Alcohol on a Fetus." U.S. Department of Health and Human Services: Substance Abuse and Mental Health Services Administration, 2007.

Ehrenfeld, Rachel. *Narcoterrorism.* New York: Basic Books, 1990.

Ehrenreich, Barbara, and Deirdre English. *Witches, Midwives, and Nurses: A History of Women Healers.* Old Westbury, N.Y.: Feminist Press, 1973.

Ehrlich, Paul R., and Anne H. Ehrlich. *Extinction: The Causes and Consequences of the Disappearance of Species.* New York: Random House, 1981.

Eisenegger, Christoph, Johannes Haushofer, and Ernst Fehr. "The Role of Testosterone in Social Interaction." *Trends in Cognitive Sciences, 15,* 6, June 2011:263–271.

Eisenhart, R. Wayne. "You Can't Hack It, Little Girl: A Discussion of the Covert Psychological Agenda of Modern Combat Training." *Journal of Social Issues, 31,* Fall 1975:13–23.

Eisenhower, Dwight D. "From 'Farewell Address to the Nation,' January 17, 1961." In *The Military and American Society: Essays and Readings,* Stephen E. Ambrose and James A. Barber, Jr., eds. New York: Free Press, 1972:61–63.

Eisinger, Peter K. *The Politics of Displacement: Racial and Ethnic Transition in Three American Cities.* Campbell Calif.: Academic Press, 1980.

Elgion, John. "A State Backs Guns in Class for Teachers." *New York Times,* March 8, 2013.

Eligon, John. "Privacy Disappears at a Trial about Rape." New York Times, May 8, 2011.

Eliot, Lise. *Pink Brain, Blue Brain: How Small Differences Grow Into Troublesome Gaps—And What We Can Do About It.* Oneworld Publications, 2010.

Ellemers, Naomi, and Jolanda Jetten. "The Many Ways to Be Marginal in a Group." *Personality and Social Psychology Review, 17,* 1, 2013:3–21.

Ellis, Havelock. "Mescal: A New Artificial Paradise." *Annual Report of the Smithsonian Institution, 52,* 1897:547–548.

Ellis, Havelock. "Mescal: A Study of a Divine Plant." *Popular Science Monthly, 61,* 1902:52–71.

Eng, James. "Texas Begins Enforcing Strict Anti-Abortion Sonogram Law." *MSNBC News,* February 8, 2012.

Engelmayer, Paul A. "Violence by Students, from Rape to Racism, Raises College Worries." *Wall Street Journal,* November 21, 1983:1, 18.

Environmental Protection Agency. "Air Quality Trends." Online, 2012a.

Environmental Protection Agency. "The Great Lakes." Online, 2012b.

EPA (United States Environmental Protection Agency). "Acid Rain and Related Programs: 2008 Highlights." U.S. Environmental Protection Agency, Office of Air Quality Planning and Standards, 2009.

Epstein, Cynthia Fuchs. "The Nature-Nurture Controversy: Biology Versus Culture: Culture Is the Answer." In James M. Henslin, *Essentials of Sociology: A Down-to-Earth Approach,* 9th ed. Boston: Allyn and Bacon, 2011.

Epstein, Cynthia Fuchs. Letter to the author, January 26, 1989.

Epstein, Cynthia. "Similarity and Difference: The Sociology of Gender Distinction." In *Handbook of the Sociology of Gender,* Janet Saltzman Chafetz, ed. New York: Kluwer Academic/Plenum Publishers, 1999.

Espenshade, Thomas J. "A Short History of U.S. Policy toward Illegal Immigration." *Population Today,* February 1990:6–9.

Espenshade, Thomas J., an Alexandria Walton Radford. *No Longer Separate, Not Yet Equal: Race and Class in Elite College Admission and Campus Life.* Princeton, N.J.: Princeton University Press, 2009.

Fabio, Anthony, Tu Li-Chuan, Rolf Loeber, and Jacqueline Cohen. "Neighborhood Socioeconomic Disadvantage and the Shape of the Age-Crime Curve." *American Journal of Public Health, 101, S1,* 2011:S325-S331.

"Facts About Sexual Harassment." U.S. Equal Employment Opportunity Commission, Online, 2006.

Fagan, Patrick F., and Aaron Churchill. "The Effects of Divorce on Children." Washington, D.C.: Marriage and Religion Research Institute, January 2012.

"Fall Colors: 2003–04 Prime Time Diversity Report." Oakland, Calif.: Children Now, 2004.

Farah, Judy. "Crime and Creative Punishment." *Wall Street Journal,* March 15, 1995:A15.

Faris, R. E. L., and W. W. Dunham. *Mental Disorders in Urban Areas.* Chicago: University of Chicago Press, 1939.

Farley, Melissa, Nicole Matthews, Sarah Deer, et al. *Garden of Truth: The Prostitution and Trafficking of Native Women in Minnesota.* Saint Paul, Minnesota: William Mitchell College of Law, October 27, 2011.

"Father's Persistence Pays Off." Associated Press. February 12, 1995.

Faupel, Charles E., and Carl B. Klockars. "Drugs-Crime Connections: Elaborations from the Life Histories of Hard-Core Addicts." *Social Problems, 34,* 1, February 1987:54–68.

FBI Uniform Crime Reports. Washington, D.C.: U.S. Government Printing Office, annual.

Feinstein, Brian A., Kathryn L Humphreys, Michelle J. Bovin, Brian P. Marx, and Patricia A. Resick. "Victim-Offender Relationship Status Moderates the Relationship of Peritraumatic Emotional Responses, Active Resistance, and Posttraumatic Stress Symptomatology in Female Rape Survivors." *Psychological Trauma: Theory, Research, Practice, and Policy, 3,* 2, 2011:192–200.

Feng, Zhanlian, Mary L. Fennell, Denise A. Tyler, Melissa Clark, and Vincent Mor. "Growth of Racial and Ethnic Minorities in U.S. Nursing Homes by Demographics and Possible Disparities in Options." *Health Affairs, 30,* 7, 2011:1358–1365.

Ferguson, Christopher J., and Kevin M. Beaver. "Natural Born Killers: The Genetic Origin of Extreme Violence." *Aggression and Violent Behavior, 14,* 2009:286–294.

Ferguson, Ronald E. "Community Revitalization, Jobs, and the Well-Being of the Inner-City Poor." In *Understanding Poverty,* Sheldon H. Danziger and Robert H. Haveman, eds. New York: Russell Sage, 2001:417–443.

Fergusson, David M., L. John Horwood, and Annette L. Beutrais. "Cannabis and Educational Attainment." *Addiction,* 2003:1681–1692.

Fernandez, Fabian G., Kristofer D. Johnson, Richard E. Terry, Sheldon Nelson, and David Webster. "Soil Resources of the Ancient Maya at Piedras Negras, Guatemala." *American Journal of the Soil Science Society, 696,* October 27, 2005:2020–2032.

Fernandez, Manny. "In Jury Selection for Hate Crime, a Struggle to Find Tolerance." *New York Times,* March 8, 2010a.

Fernandez, Manny. "Layers of Contradiction in L.I. Hate-Crime Trial." *New York Times,* March 26, 2010b.

Fernandez, Manny. "L.I. Man Gets 25-Year Term in Killing of Immigrant." *New York Times,* May 26, 2010c.

"Fetal Alcohol Spectrum Disorder Among Native Americans." U.S. Department of Health and Human Services: Substance Abuse and Mental Health Services Administration, 2007.

Fialka, John J. "Pentagon Outlines Plans to Use Troops to Join Border 'War' Against Drugs." *Wall Street Journal,* February 23, 1988:A10.

Fialka, John J. "Position Available: Indestructible Bugs To Eat Nuclear Waste." *Wall Street Journal,* November 16, 2004:A1.

Fields, George. "Racism Is Accepted Practice in Japan." *Wall Street Journal,* November 10, 1986:19.

Finckenauer, James O. *Scared Straight and the Panacea Phenomenon.* Englewood Cliffs, N.J.: Prentice Hall, 1982.

Finkelhor, David, and Kersti Yllo. *License to Rape: Sexual Abuse of Wives.* New York: Holt, 1985.

Finkelhor, David, and Kersti Yllo. "Marital Rape: The Myth versus the Reality." In *Marriage and Family in a Changing Society,* James M. Henslin, ed. New York: Free Press, 1989:382–391.

Firestone, Shulamith. *The Dialectic of Sex: The Case for Feminist Revolution.* New York: Morrow, 1970.

"First Death Sentence Under New Drug Law." *New York Times,* May 15, 1991:A24.

Fischer, Claude S. *The Urban Experience.* New York: Harcourt, 1976.

Fischer, CLAUDE. S. (1976). *The urban experience.* New York: Harcourt.

Fish, Jefferson M. "Mixed Blood." *Psychology Today, 28,* 6, November-December 1995:55–58, 60, 61, 76, 80.

Fisher, Gordon M. "Setting American Standards of Poverty: A Look Back." *Focus, 19,* 2, Spring 1988:47–52.

Fisher, Sue. *In the Patient's Best Interest: Women and the Politics of Medical Decisions.* New Brunswick, N.J.: Rutgers University Press, 1986.

Fisse, B., & Braithwaite, J. (1987). The impact of publicity on corporate offenders: Ford Motor Company and the Pinto papers. In M. D. Ermann & R. J. Lundman (Eds.), *Corporate and governmental deviance: Problems of organizational behavior in contemporary society* (3rd ed.; 244–262). New York: Oxford University Press.

Fitzpatrick, Maureen J. and Barbara J. McPherson. "Coloring Within the Lines: Gender Stereotypes in Contemporary Coloring Books." *Sex Roles, 62,* 2010:127–137.

Flanagan, William G. *Urban Sociology: Images and Structure.* Boston: Allyn and Bacon, 1990.

Flavin, Christopher. "Reassessing Nuclear Power." In *State of the World,* Lester R. Brown, ed. New York: Norton, 1987:57–80.

"Focus on Health Reform: Summary of New Health Reform Law." The Henry J. Kaiser Family Foundation, April 8, 2010.

Foley, Douglas E. "The Great American Football Ritual." In *Society: Readings to Accompany Core Concepts,* James M. Henslin, ed. Boston: Allyn & Bacon, 2006:64–76. (Originally published 1990)

Foley, Meraiah. "Australia to Test Web Filter to Block Banned Content." *New York Times,* December 14, 2008.

Food and Drug Administration. "Food Allergies—Rare But Risky." *FDA Consumer,* May 1994.

Ford, Clellan S., and Frank A. Beach. *Patterns of Sexual Behavior.* New York: Harper Colophon, 1972.

Forero, Juan. "Bolivia's Knot: No to Cocaine, But Yes to Coca." *New York Times,* February 12, 2006.

Forliti, Amy. "New Legal Issue: Payment for Child Porn Victims." Associated Press, February 8, 2010.

"Former FBI Agent Arrested on Child Porn Charges." *The Indy Channel,* May 14, 2012.

Forsyth, Craig J., Gary Asmus, York A, Forsyth, Billy R. Stokes, and Mike Mayne. "Child Delinquents: Examining the Market for Criminal Futures." *Delinquent Behavior, 32,* 5, 2011:441–450.

Fountain, Henry. "Archaeological Site in Peru Is Called Oldest City in America." *New York Times,* April 27, 2001.

Fouts, Gregory, and Kimberley Burggraf. "Television Situation Comedies: Female Body Images and Verbal Reinforcements." *Sex Roles: A Journal of Research,* March 1999.

Fowler, L. *Breast Implants for Graduation? Parent and Adolescent Narratives*. Dissertation, University of North Texas, 2008.

Fox, James Alan, and Jack Levin. *Extreme Killing: Understanding Serial and Mass Murder*. Thousand Oaks, Calif.: Sage, 2005.

Fox, John W. "Social Class, Mental Illness, and Social Mobility: The Social Selection-Drift Hypothesis for Serious Mental Illness." *Journal of Health and Social Behavior, 31,* 4, December 1990:344–353.

Franks, Paul W., Robert L. Hanson, William, C. Knowler, et al. "Childhood Obesity, Other Cardiovascular Risk Factors, and Premature Death." *New England Journal of Medicine, 362*, 6, February 11, 2010.

Freed, Anne O. "How Japanese Families Cope with Fragile Elderly." In *Perspectives in Social Gerontology,* Robert B. Enright, Jr., ed. Boston: Allyn & Bacon, 1994:76–86.

Freund, Matthew, Nancy Lee, and Terri Leonard. *Journal of Sex Research, 28,* 4, November 1991: 579–591.

Frey, George. "Ernst Zundel Released from German Prison." Associated Press, March 1, 2010.

Friedan, Betty. *The Feminine Mystique.* New York: Norton, 1963.

Friedl, Ernestine. "Society and Sex Roles." In *Conformity and Conflict: Readings in Cultural Anthropology.* James P. Spradley and David W. McCurdy, eds. Glenview Ill.: Scott, Foresman, 1990: 229–238.

Friess, Steve. "Betting on the Studs." *Newsweek,* December 12, 2005.

Fromm, Erich. *The Anatomy of Human Destructiveness.* New York: Holt, 1973.

Fry, Douglas P., Bruce D. Bonta, and Karoline Baszarkiewicz. "Learning from Extant Cultures of Peace." In Joseph de Rivera, ed. *Handbook on Building Cultures of Peace*. PLACE: Springer Sciences, 2009:11–26.

Fund, John. "English-Only Showdown." *Wall Street Journal,* November 28, 2007.

Galbraith, John Kenneth. *The Nature of Mass Poverty.* Cambridge, Mass.: Harvard University Press, 1979.

Gale, Richard P. "From Sit-In to Hike-In: A Comparison of the Civil Rights and Environmental Movements." In *Social Behavior, Natural Resources, and the Environment,* William R. Burch, Jr., Neil H. Cheek, Jr., and Lee Taylor, eds. New York: Harper & Row, 1972:280–305.

Galliher, John R., and Allyn Walker. "The Puzzle of the Social Origins of the Marihuana Tax Act of 1937." *Social Problems, 24,* February 1977:367–376.

Ganahl, Dennis J., Thomas J. Prinsen, and Sara Baker Netzley. "A Content Analysis of Prime Time Commercials: A Contextual Framework of Gender Representation." *Sex Roles, 49,* 9/10, November 2003: 545–551.

Gannon, M. "Casino slot profits plunge in September." *Norwich Bulletin, October 16, 2008.* Retrieved from http://www.norwichbulletin.com

Ganong, Larry, and Elizabeth Sharp. "I'm a Loser, I'm Not Married, Let's Just All Look at Me." *Journal of Family Issues*, June 2010.

Gans, Herbert J. "The Uses of Poverty: The Poor Pay All." In *Down to Earth Sociology: Introductory Readings,* 15th ed., James M. Henslin, ed. New York: Free Press, 2014. (Originally published in *Social Policy,* July/August 1971:20–24)

Gans, Herbert J. "The Way We'll Live Soon." *Washington Post,* September 1, 1991:BW3.

Gans, Herbert J. *People and Plans: Essays on Urban Problems and Solutions.* New York: Basic Books, 1968.

Gans, Herbert J. *The Urban Villagers.* New York: Free Press, 1962.

Garbarino, Merwin S. *American Indian Heritage.* Boston: Little, Brown, 1976.

Garelik, Glenn. "Russia's Legacy of Death." *National Wildlife,* June–July 1996.

Garrison, Chad "Drug Companies Fight Missouri Effort to Make Sudafed a Prescription Drug." *Riverfront Times*, February 2, 2010.

Gartner, Michael. "A Dream of Peace, the Reality of Never-Ending Wars." *Wall Street Journal,* December 22, 1988:A13.

Gatewood, Anne G., Kelly A.Liebman, Gwenael Vourc'h, et al. "Climate and Tick Seasonality Are Predictors of *Borrelia burgdorferi* Genotype Distribution." *Applied and Environmental Microbiology, 75*, 8, April 2009:2476–2483.

Gay, Jill. "The 'Patriotic' Prostitute." *The Progressive,* February 1985:34–36.

Gaylin, Willard. *Partial Justice: A Study of Bias in Sentencing.* New York: Knopf, 1974.

Gelles, Richard I. "The Myth of Battered Husbands and New Facts About Family Violence." In *Social Problems 80–81,* Robert L. David, ed. Guilford, Conn.: Dushkin, 1980.

Gellhorn, Martha. *The Face of War.* New York: Simon & Schuster, 1959.

Gemme, Robert. "Prostitution: A Legal, Criminological, and Sexological Perspective." *Canadian Journal of Human Sexuality, 2,* 4, Winter 1993: 227–237.

General Social Survey. Chicago: National Opinion Research Center, 2008; dataset from the Survey Documentation and Analysis archive at the University of California, Berkeley.

General Social Survey: National Opinion Research Center. GSS 1972–2010 cumulative data file, February 2012. Documentation and Analysis archive at the University of California.

George, David T., Monte J. Phillips, Linda Doty, John C. Umhau, and Robert R. Rawlings. "A Model Linking Biology, Behavior, and Psychiatric Diagnoses in Perpetrators of Domestic Violence." *Medical Hypotheses,* 2006.

Gerlin, Andrea. "Quirky Sentences Make Bad Guys Squirm." *Wall Street Journal,* August 4, 1994:B1, B2.

"German Court Rules Religious Circumcision an Assault on Boys." Associated Press, June 26, 2012.

Gerstl-Pepin, Cynthia I. "The Paradox of Poverty Narratives: Educators Struggling with Children Left Behind." *Educational Policy, 20,* 1, March 2006:143–162.

Gibbs, Nancy. "Affirmative Action for Boys." *Time,* April 3, 2008.

Gibbs, Nancy, and Amanda Bower. "Q: What Scares Doctors? A: Being the Patient." *Time,* May 1, 2006.

Giddens, Anthony. "Georg Simmel." In *The Founding Fathers of Social Science,* Timothy Raison, ed. Baltimore: Penguin, 1969:165–173.

Gilham, Steven A. "The Marines Build Men: Resocialization in Recruit Training." In *The Sociological Outlook: A Text with Readings,* 2nd ed., Reid Luhman, ed. San Diego, Calif.: Collegiate Press, 1989: 232–244.

Gilmore, David G. *Manhood in the Making: Cultural Concepts of Masculinity.* New Haven, Conn.: Yale University Press, 1990.

Girshick, L. B. *Woman-to-Woman Sexual Violence*. Boston: Northeastern University Press, 2004.

Glascock, Jack. "Gender Roles on Prime-Time Network Television: Demographics and Behaviors." *Journal of Broadcasting and Electronics Media, 45,* Fall 2001:656–669.

Glaser, Daniel. *Crime in Our Changing Society.* New York: Holt, 1978.

Gneezy, Uri, Kenneth L. Leonard, and John A. List. "Gender Differ ences in Competition: Evidence from a Matrilineal and a Patriarchal Society." *Econometrica, 77,* 5, September 2009:1637–1664.

Goldberg, S., and Lewis, Michael. (1969, March) Play Behavior in the Year-old Infant: Early Sex Differences. *Child Development,* 40, 21–31.

Goldberg, Steven. "The Nature–Nurture Controversy: Biology Versus Culture: Biology Is the Answer." In James M. Henslin, *Essentials of Sociology: A Down-to-Earth Approach,* 9th ed. Boston: Allyn and Bacon, 2011.

Goleman, Daniel. "Girls and Math: Is Biology Really Destiny?" *New York Times,* August 2, 1987:42–44, 46.

Goll, Sven. "Archaeologists Find Mini-Pompeii." *Views and News from Norway,* October 1, 2010.

Goode, Erich. *Drugs in American Society,* 3rd ed. New York: Knopf, 1989.

Gooden, Angela M., and Mark A. Gooden. "Gender Representation in Notable Children's Picture Books: 1995–1999." *Sex Roles, 45,* 1/2, July 2001: 89–101.

Goodman, Peter S. "Cuts to Child Care Subsidy Thwart More Job Seekers." *New York Times,* May 23, 2010.

Gordon, Milton. *Assimilation in American Life.* New York: Oxford University Press, 1964.

Gorman, Dennis M., and J. Charles Huber, Jr. "The Social Construction of 'Evidence-Based' Drug Prevention Programs: A Reanalysis of Data From the Drug Abuse Resistance (DARE) Program." *Evaluation Review, 33,* 4, 2009:396–414.

Gottfredson, Michael, and Travis Hirschi. *A General Theory of Crime.* Stanford, Calif.: Stanford University Press, 1990.

"GPS Creates Global Jail." Online, April 8, 1998.

Grant, Igor, J. Hampton Atkinson, Andrew Mattison, and Thomas J. Coates. "Report to the Legislature and Governor of the State of California Presenting Findings Pursuant to SB847 Which Created the CMCR and Provided State Funding." Center for Medicinal Cannabis Research, University of California San Diego Health Sciences, February 11, 2010.

Green, Gary S. "White-Collar Crime and the Study of Embezzlement." *Annals of the American Academy of Political and Social Sciences, 525,* January 1993:95–106.

Greenberger, Robert S. "U.S., Russia Agree to Faster Timetable for Destruction of Nuclear Arsenals." *Wall Street Journal,* September 29, 1994:A22.

Greenberger, Robert S. "U.S., Russia Will Explore Joint System for Early Warning of Missile Attacks." *Wall Street Journal,* February 19,1992:A7.

Greenfield, L. A. Capital Punishment 1990. *Bureau of Justice Statistics Bulletin,* September 1991.

Greenhouse, Steven. "Doctors, Under Pressure from H.M.O.'s, Are Ready Union Recruits." *New York Times,* February 4, 1999.

Griffith, G. T. *Population Problems of the Age of Malthus.* Cambridge: Cambridge University Press, 1926.

Grimmett. Richard F., and Paul K. Kerr. "Conventional Arms Transfers to Developing Nations 2004–2011.' Washington, D.C.: Congressional Research Service, August 24, 2012.

"Guardian of Brazil Indians Faces Many Foes." Reuters online, June 10, 1997.

Guerino, Paul, Paige M. Harrison, and William J. Sabol. "Prisoners in 2010." Bureau of Justice Statistics, December 2011.

Gupta, Sanjay. "Dr. Sanjay Gupta on Combating Medical Errors." CBS News, March 11, 2012.

Gusfield, Joseph R. *Symbolic Crusade: Status Politics and the American Temperance Movement.* Urbana: University of Illinois Press, 1963.

Haas, Jack, and William Shaffir. "The Cloak of Competence." In *Down-to-Earth Sociology: Introductory Readings,* 7th ed., James M. Henslin, ed. New York: Free Press, 1993.

Haas, Jeffrey. *The Assassination of Fred Hampton by the FBI and the Chicago Police: Forty Years Later.* Chicago: Lawrence Hill Books, 2009.

Hacker, Helen Mayer. "Women as a Minority Group." *Social Forces, 30,* October 1951:60–69.

Hagedorn, John M. "The Global Impact of Gangs." *Journal of Contemporary Criminal Justice, 21,* 2, May 2005:153–169.

Hale, Beth. "Briton Jailed for Four Years in Dubai after Customs Find Cannabis Weighing Less Than a Grain of Sugar Under His Shoe." *Daily Mail,* February 8, 2008.

Hall, Susan. *Gentleman of Leisure: A Year in the Life of a Pimp.* New York: New American Library, 1972.

Hall, Wayne, and Louise Degenhardt. "Adverse Health Effects of Non-Medical Cannabis Use." *Lancet, 374,* October 17, 2009.

Hamdan, Ashraf H. "Neonatal Abstinence Syndrome." *Emedicine Pediatrics,* March 3, 2010:1–25.

Hamilton, Mykol C., David Anderson, Michelle Broaddus, and Kate Young. "Gender Stereotyping and Under-representation of Female Characters in 200 Popular Children's Picture Books: A Twenty-first Century Update." *Sex Roles, 55,* 2006:757–765.

Hans, Jason D., Martie Gillen, and Katrina Akande. "Sex Redefined: The Reclassification of Oral-Genital Contact." *Perspectives on Sexual and Reproductive Health,* June 2010.

Hanson, David J. *Preventing Alcohol Abuse: Alcohol, Culture, and Control.* Westport, Conn.: Praeger, 1995.

Hardin, Garrett. "The Tragedy of the Commons." *Science, 162,* December 1968:1243–1248.

Harrington, Charlene, Helen Carrillo, et al. *Nursing Home Facilities, Staffing, Residents and Facility Deficiencies, 2005 Through 2010.* San Francisco, Calif.: University of California, October 2011.

Harrington, Michael. *The Vast Majority: A Journey to the World's Poor.* New York: Simon & Schuster, 1977.

Harris, Chauncy, and Edward Ullman. "The Nature of Cities." *Annals of the American Academy of Political and Social Science, 242,* November 1945: 7–17.

Harris, Diana K., and Michael L. Benson. *Maltreatment of Patients in Nursing Homes: There Is No Safe Place.* New York: Haworth Pastoral Press, 2006.

Harris, Gardiner. "Panel Advises Disclosure of Drugs' Psychotic Effects." *New York Times,* March 23, 2006.

Harris, Gardiner. "When the Nurse Wants to Be Called 'Doctor.'" *New York Times,* October 1, 2011.

Harris, Marvin. "Why Men Dominate Women." *New York Times Magazine,* November 13, 1977:46, 115, 117, 123.

Harris, Sheldon H. *Factories of Death.* New York: Routledge, 1994.

Hart, C. W. M., and Arnold R. Pilling. *The Tiwi of North Australia,* Fieldwork Edition. New York: Holt, Rinehart and Winston, 1979.

Hart, Carl L., and Charles Ksir. *Drugs, Society, and Human Behavior,* 14th ed. New York: McGraw-Hill, 2011

Haub, Carl, and Diana Cornelius. "World Population Data Sheet." Washington, D.C.: Population Reference Bureau, 2004.

Haub, Carl, and Toshiko Kaneda. "World Population Data Sheet." Washington, D.C.: Population Reference Bureau, 2012.

Hauser, Philip, and Leo Schnore, eds. *The Study of Urbanization.* New York: Wiley, 1965.

Haveman, Robert H., and John Karl Scholz. "The Clinton Welfare Reform Plan: Will It End Poverty as We Know It?" *Focus, 16,* 2, Winter 1994–95:1–11.

Hawkins, D. N., Amato, P. R., King, V. "Nonresident Father Involvement and Adolescent Well-Being: Father Effects or Child Effects?" *American Sociological Review, 72,* 6, 2007: 990–1010.

Hawley, Amos H. *Urban Society: An Ecological Approach.* New York: Wiley, 1981.

Hayden, F. Gregory, Kellee R. Wood, and Asuman Kaya. "The Use of Power Blocs of Integrated Corporate Directorships to Articulate a Power Structure: Case Study and Research Recommendations." *Journal of Economic Issues, 36,* 3, September 2002:671–706.

Hayes, Arthur S. "How the Courts Define Harassment." *Wall Street Journal,* October 11, 1991:B1, B3.

Healthcare Blue Book, online August 6, 2012. http://www.healthcarebluebook.com/page_Results.aspx?id=153&dataset=hosp

HealthGrades. "Eighth Annual Patient Safety in American Hospitals Study." March 2011.

"Hello Kitty Robot Receptionist Debuts in Japan." Reuters, January 26, 2006.

Helmer, J. *Drugs and Minority Oppression.* New York: Seabury, 1975.

Hench, David. "Jail Sends TB Patient to Hospital in Boston." *Portland Press Herald,* September 28, 2006.

Hendawi, Hamza, and Maggie Michael. "Pope Shenouda III Funeral: Egypt's Copts Mourn Their 'Protector.'" *Guardian,* March 20, 2012.

Hendren, John. "3 Nursing Home Patients Killed by 'Chemical Restraints.'" *ABC World News online.* January 5, 2010.

Henriques, Fernando. *Prostitution and Society.* New York: Grove, 1966.

Henslin, James M. *Essentials of Sociology: A Down-to-Earth Approach,* 10th ed. Boston: Allyn and Bacon, 2013.

Henslin, James M. *Sociology: A Down-to-Earth Approach,* 10th ed. Boston: Allyn and Bacon, 2010.

Herbert, Bob. "Don't Flunk the Future." *New York Times,* August 13, 1998.

Herbert, Bob. "The Hate Virus." *New York Times,* August 10, 1988.

Heron, Melonie. "Deaths: Leading Causes for 2008." *National Vital Statistics Reports, 60,* 6, June 6, 2012.

Herring, Cedric. "Is Job Discrimination Dead?" *Contexts*, Summer 2002:13–18.

Heyl, Barbara Sherman. *The Madam as Entrepreneur: Career Management in House Prostitution.* New Brunswick, N.J.: Transaction, 1979.

Hibbert, Christopher. *The Roots of Evil: A Social History of Crime and Punishment.* New York: Minerva, 1963.

Hilliard, Asa, III. "Do We Have the Will to Educate All Children?" *Educational Leadership, 49,* September 1991:31–36.

Hills, Stuart L., ed. *Corporate Violence: Injury and Death for Profit.* Totowa, N.J.: Rowman & Littlefield, 1987.

Himes, Christine L. "Elderly Americans." *Population Bulletin, 56,* 1, December 2001:1–40.

Hirschi, Travis. *Causes of Delinquency.* Berkeley: University of California Press, 1969.

Hirschman, Charles, Samuel Preston, and Vu Manh Loi. "Vietnamese Casualties During the American War: A New Estimate." *Population and Development Review, 21,* 4 December 1995:783–812.

Hodgson, James F. *Games Pimps Play: Pimps, Players and Wives-In-Law.* Toronto: Canadian Scholars' Press, 1997.

Hoffman, Albert. "Psychotomimetic Agents." In *Drugs Affecting the Central Nervous System* (vol. 2). New York: Marcel Dekker, 1968.

Hoffman, Stanley. "The Foreign Policy the U.S. Needs." *New York Review of Books, 53,* 13, August 10, 2006.

Holbrook, Troy Lisa, Michael R. Galarneau, Judy L. Dye, Kimberly Quinn, and Amber L. Dougherty. "Morphine Use after Combat Injury in Iraq and Post-Traumatic Stress Disorder." *New England Journal of Medicine, 362,* 2, January 14, 2010.

Holm, Erik, and Ulrike Dauer. "Insurer Hired Prostitutes." *Wall Street Journal,* May 19, 2011.

Holman, Richard L. "World Wire." *Wall Street Journal,* July 28, 1994:A10.

Holtzman, Abraham. *The Townsend Movement: A Political Study.* New York: Bookman, 1963.

Homblin, Dora Jane. *The First Cities.* Boston: Little, Brown, Time-Life Books, 1973.

Hooton, Earnest A. *Crime and the Man.* Cambridge, Mass.: Harvard University Press, 1939.

Hope, Christine A., and Ronald G. Stover. "Gender Status, Monotheism, and Social Complexity." *Social Forces, 65,* 1987:1132–1138.

Hornblower, M. "Prostitution: The Skin Trade." *Time,* June 21, 1993:45–51.

Horowitz, Ruth. *Honor and the American Dream: Culture and Identity in a Chicano Community.* New Brunswick, N.J.: Rutgers University Press, 1983.

"Horror as Nine Bodies Found Hanged from Bridge and 14 Heads Decapitated and Dumped Along U.S. Border in Mexico." Associated Press, May 4, 2012.

Hosenball, Mark. "A Plutonium Mystery." *Newsweek,* May 3, 1999:62–64.

Hotz, Robert Lee. "Early Humans' Fire Use Linked to Extinctions." *Los Angeles Times*, January 8, 1999.

Hotz, Robert Lee. "Printing Evolves: An Inkjet for Living Tissue." *Wall Street Journal,* September 18, 2012.

Hotz, Robert Lee. "Scientists Create Synthetic Organism." *Wall Street Journal,* May 21, 2010.

Howell, Karen K., Mary Ellen Lynch, Kathleen A. Platzman, G. Harold Smith, and Claire D. Coles. "Prenatal Alcohol Exposure and Ability, Academic Achievement, and School Functioning in Adolescence: A Longitudinal Follow-Up." *Journal of Pediatric Psychology, 31,* 1, 2006:116–126.

Huber, Joan. "Micro-Macro Links in Gender Stratification." *American Sociological Review, 55,* February 1990:1–10.

Hudson, Robert B. "The 'Graying' of the Federal Budget and Its Consequences for Old-Age Policy." *The Gerontologist, 18,* October 1978:428–440.

Huff, Aimee Dinnin. "Buying the Girlfriend Experience: A Exploration of the Consumption Experiences of Male Customers of Escorts." *Research in Consumer Behavior, 13,* 2011:111–126.

Huff-Corzine, Lin, Jay Corzine, and David C. Moore. "Deadly Connections: Culture, Poverty, and the Direction of Lethal Violence." *Social Forces, 69,* 3, March 1991:715–732.

Huff-Corzine, Lin, Jay Corzine, and David C. Moore. "Southern Exposure: Deciphering the South's Influence on Homicide Rates." *Social Forces, 64,* 1986:906–924.

Hull, Jon D. "Life and Death with the Gangs." *Time,* August 24, 1987:21–22.

Humphreys, Laud. *Tearoom Trade.* Chicago: Aldine, 1970. (Expanded version, Chicago: Aldine-Atherton, 1975.)

Hurdle, John. "Philadelphia Struggles to Quell an Epidemic of Gun Violence." *New York Times,* April 16, 2007.

Huxley, Aldous. *The Doors of Perception.* New York: Harper & Row, 1954.

Hyde, Janet S., and Janet E. Mertz. "Gender, Culture, and Mathematics Performance." *Proceedings of the National Academy of Sciences of the United States of America, 106,* 22, June 2, 2009:8801–8807.

Hyland, Alexa. "Mattel Fears MGA Is Trying to Keep the Bratz; Court Documents Reveal War Over Judgment Against Rival." *Los Angeles Business Journa*l, March 16, 2009.

Idso, Craig, and S. Fred Singer. "Climate Change Reconsidered: 2009 Report of the Nongovernmental International Panel on Climate Change." Chicago, IL.: The Heartland Institute, June 2, 2009.

Ilminen, Gary R. "New Strategies Ramping Up Quality in Wisconsin Medicaid Managed Care." *Home Health Care Management & Practice, 18,* 3, April 2006:235–238.

Inciardi, James A. *The War on Drugs: Heroin, Cocaine, Crime, and Public Policy.* Mountain View, Calif.: Mayfield, 1986.

Ingersoll, Bruce. "Faster Slaughter Lines Are Contaminating Much U.S. Poultry." *Wall Street Journal,* November 16, 1990:A1, A6.

Ingersoll, Bruce. "FDA Is Proposing Limits on Sulfites in Range of Foods." *Wall Street Journal,* December 20, 1988:C21.

Inter-Parliamentary Union. "Women in National Parliaments." May 31, 2012.

Internal Revenue Service. "10 Facts about the Child Tax Credit." 2013.

Isbell, Harris. "Historical Development of Attitudes Toward Opiate Addiction in the United States." In *Man and Civilization: Conflict, and Creativity,* Seymour M. Farber and Roger H. L. Wilson, eds. New York: McGraw-Hill, 1969:154–170.

Ives, Mike. "Agent Orange Vietnam Cleanup Started by U.S." Associated Press, August 9, 2012.

Izaak Walton League of America. "Conservation Policies," 2000.

Jacob, Brian A., and Jens Ludwig. "Improving Educational Outcomes for Poor Children." Focus, 26, 2, Fall 2009:56–61.

Jacobs, Jane. *Dark Age Ahead.* New York: Random House, 2004.

Jaffe, Jerome H. "Drug Addiction and Drug Abuse." In *The Pharmacological Basis of Therapeutics,* Louis S. Goodman and Alfred Gilmann, eds. New York: Macmillan, 1965:285–311.

Jagsi, Reshma, Kent A Griffith, Abigail Stewart, Dana Sambuco, Rochelle DeCastro, and Peter A. Ubel. "Gender Differences in the Salaries of Physician Researchers." *Journal of the American Medical Association*, 307, 22, June 13, 2012:2410–2417.

James, Jennifer, and J. Meyerding. "Early Sexual Experiences in Prostitution." *Archives of Sexual Behavior, 7,* 1977:31–42.

James, Susan Donaldson. "Love Canal's Lethal Legacy Persists." ABC News, August 11, 2008.

Jekielek, Susan M. "Parental Conflict, Marital Disruption and Children's Emotional Well-Being." *Social Forces, 76,* 3, March 1998:905–935.

Jenkins, Brian Michael. "The Future Course of Terrorism." *The Futurist,* July-August 1987:8.

Jensen, Peter S., L. Eugene Arnold, James M. Swanson, et al. "3-Year Follow-up of the NIMH MTA Study." *Journal of the American Academy of Child and Adolescent Psychiatry, 46,* 8, August 2007.

Jha, Prabhat. "Avoidable Global Cancer Deaths and Total Deaths from Smoking." *Nature Review, 9,* September 2009:655–664.

Jha, Prabhat, Maya A. Kesler, Rajesh Kumar, et al. "Trends in Selective Abortions of Girls in India: Analysis of Nationally Representative Birth Histories from 1990 to 2005 and Census Data from 1991 to 2011." *The Lancet, 377,* June 4, 2011:1921–1928.

Johnson, Bruce D., Paul J. Goldstein, Edward Preble, James Schmeidler, Douglas S. Lipton, Barry Spunt, and Thomas Miller. *Taking Care of Business: The Economics of Crime by Heroin Abusers.* Lexington, Mass.: Lexington Books, 1985.

Johnson, Keith. "How Should We Deal With Nuclear Waste?" *Wall Street Journal,* April 15, 2013.

Johnston, Lloyd D., Patrick M. O'Malley, Jerald G. Bachman, and John E. Schulenberg. *Monitoring the Future: National Survey Results on Drug Use, 1975–2011. Volume I, Secondary School Students.* Ann Arbor: Institute for Social Research, the University of Michigan, 2012.

Johnston, Lloyd D., Patrick M. O'Malley, Jerald G. Bachman, and John E. Schulenberg. *Monitoring the Future: National Survey Results on Drug Use, 1975–2011. Volume II, College Students and Adults Ages19–50.* Ann Arbor: Institute for Social Research, the University of Michigan, 2011.

Jordan, Miriam. "Asians Top Immigration Class." *Wall Street Journal,* June 19, 2012.

Josephy, Alvin M., Jr. "Indians in History." *Atlantic Monthly,* June 1970:67–72.

Joyce, Theodore J. "Abortion and Crime: A Review." Cambridge, MA: NBER working paper 15098, 2009.

Julien, Robert M. *A Primer of Drug Action.* New York: Worth Publishers, 2001.

Juncosa, Barbara. "Is 100 the New 80?: Centenarians Studied to Find the Secret of Longevity." *Scientific American,* October 28, 2008.

Kacen, Jacqueline J. "Advertising Effectiveness." New York: *Wiley International Encyclopedia of Marketing,* 2011.

Kalayjian, Tro. "Investment Opportunities in Women's Health." *Seeking Alpha* (online), June 4, 2010.

Kalb, Claudia. "Drugged-Out Toddlers." *Newsweek,* March 6, 2000.

Kanin, Eugene J. "Date Rapists: Differential Sexual Socialization and Relative Deprivation." In *Violence and Society: A Reader,* Matthew Silberman, ed. Upper Saddle River, N.J.: Prentice Hall, 2003: 207–225.

Kantor, Glenda Kaufman, and Murray A. Straus. "The 'Drunken Bum' Theory of Wife Beating." *Social Problems, 34,* 3, June 1987:213–230.

Kaplan, Sidney. "Historical Efforts to Encourage White-Indian Intermarriage in the United States and Canada." *International Social Science Review, 65,* 3, Summer,1990: 126–132.

Karlen, Neal, and Barbara Burgower. "Dumping the Mentally Ill." *Newsweek,* 105, January 7, 1985:17.

Karmen, Andrew. "The Narcotics Problem: Views from the Left." In *Is America Possible? Social Problems from Conservative, Liberal, and Socialist Perspectives,* 2nd ed., Henry Etzkowitz, ed. St. Paul, Minn.: West, 1980:171–180.

Karp, David A., Gregory P. Stone, and William C. Yoels. *Being Urban: A Sociology of City Life,* 2nd ed. New York: Praeger, 1991.

Katz, Michael B. *The Undeserving Poor: From the War on Poverty to the War on Welfare.* New York: Pantheon, 1989.

Kelley, Tina. "In an Era of School Shootings, a New Drill." *New York Times*, March 25, 2008.

Kelly, Erin, Shane Darke, and Joanne Ross. "A Review of Drug Use and Driving Epidemiology, Impairment, Risk Factors ad Risk Perceptions." *Drug and Alcohol Review, 23,* 2004:319–344.

Kemper, Peter, Harriet L. Komisar, and Lisa Alexcih. "Long-Term Care over an Uncertain Future: What Can Current Retirees Expect?" *Inquiry, 42,* 4, 2006:335–350.

Kepner, Tyler. "McGwire Admits That He Used Steroids." *New York Times*, January 12, 2010.

Keyes, Ken, Jr. *The Hundredth Monkey.* St. Mary, Ky.: Vision Books, n.d.

Kile, Shannon N. "World Nuclear Forces." *SIPRI Yearbook 2012.* Oxford: Oxford University Press, 2012:307–350.

Kilman, Scott. "Seed Firms Bolster Crops Using Traits of Distant Relatives." *Wall Street Journal,* October 31, 2006.

Kim, Hyun, Robin Herbert, Philip Landrigan, et al. "Increased Rates of Asthma among World Trade Center Disaster Responders." *American Journal of Industrial Medicine, 55,* 2012:44–53.

King, Martin Luther, Jr. *Stride Toward Freedom: The Montgomery Story.* New York: Harper, 1958.

Kingsbury, Alex, "Many Colleges Reject Women at Higher Rates Than for Men." *U. S. News & World Report,* June 27, 2007.

Kinsey, Alfred C., Wardell B. Pomeroy, Clyde E. Mantin, and Paul H. Gebhard. *Sexual Behavior in the Human Female.* New York: Saunders, 1953.

Kirkham, George L. "Homosexuality in Prison." In *Studies in the Sociology of Sex,* James M. Henslin, ed. New York: Appleton, 1971:325–349.

Kirkpatrick, Melanie. "On the Abortion Barricades." *Wall Street Journal,* April 23, 1992:A14.

Kishkovsky, Sophia. "Russians Adopt U.S. Tactics in Opposing Abortion." *New York Times,* June 9, 2011.

Kitano, Harry H. L. *Race Relations.* Englewood Cliffs N.J.: Prentice Hall, 1974.

Kleiman, Mark A. R., Jonathan P. Caulkins, and Angela Hawken. "Rethinking the War on Drugs." *Wall Street Journal,* April 22, 2012.

Klein, Stephen, Joan Petersilia, and Susan Turner. "Race and Imprisonment Decisions in California." *Science, 247,* 4944, February 16, 1990:812–816.

Kleinfeld, Judith S. "Gender and Myth: Data about Student Performance. In *Through the Eyes of Social Science,* 6th ed., Frank Zulke and Jacqueline P. Kirley, eds. Prospect Heights, IL.: Waveland Press, 2002a:380–393.

Kleinman, Paul H., Eric D. Wish, Shreey Deren, Gregory Rainone, and Ellen Morehouse. "Daily Marijuana Use and Problem Behaviors Among Adolescents." *International Journal of the Addictions, 22,* 12, 1987.

Kliff, Sarah. "The Supreme Court Upholds the Health Care Reform Law." *Washington Post,* June 28, 2012.

Knights, Roger. "Electronic Tagging in Practice." *Teleconnect,* January 22, 1999.

Kochhar, Rakesh, and Ana Gonzalez-Barrera. "Through Boom and Bust: Minorities, Immigrants and Homeownership." Washington, D.C.: Pew Hispanic Center, May 12, 2009.

Kohn, Alfie. "Make Love, Not War." *Psychology Today,* June 1988:35–38.

Kornhauser, William. "'Power Elite' or 'Veto Groups'?" In *Culture and Social Character,* Seymour Martin Lipset and Leo Lowenthal, eds. Glencoe, Ill.: Free Press, 1961:252–267.

Kozin, Vladimir. "U.S.-NATO Missile System: First-Strike Potential Aimed at Russia." Global Research, March 2, 2013.

Kozol, Jonathan. "Savage Inequalities."in *Down-to-Earth Sociology: Introductory Readings,* 10th ed., James M. Henslin, ed. New York: Free Press, 1999: 343–351.

Krauss, Clifford. "Stanford Sentenced to 110-Year Term in $7 Billion Ponzi Case." *New York Times,* June 14, 2012.

Kravets, David. "U.S. Manga Obscenity Conviction Roils Comics World." *Wired,* May 28, 2009.

Kreider, Rose M., and Diana B. Elliott. "America's Families and Living Arrangements, 2007." *Current Population Reports,* September 2009.

Krienert, Jessie L., and Jeffrey A. Walsh. "Characteristics and Perceptions of Child Sexual Abuse." *Journal of Child Sexual Abuse 20,* 2011:353–372.

Kristoff, Nicholas D. "Interview with a Humanoid." *New York Times,* July 23, 2002.

Kruk, Joanna, and Hassan Y. Aboul-Enein. "Environmental Exposure, and Other Risk Factors in Breast Cancer." *Current Cancer Therapy Reviews, 2,* 1, February 2006:3–21.

Kuklina, Elena V., Susan F. Meikle, Dinise J. Jamieson, et al. "Severe Obstetric Morbidity in the United States." *Obstetrics and Gynecology, 113,* 2, February 2009:293–299.

Kumanyika, Shiriki. "Obesity, Health Disparities, and Prevention Paradigms: Hard Questions and Hard Choices." *Preventing Chronic Disease, 2,* 4, October 2005.

Kurth, James R. "American Military Policy and Advanced Weapons." In *Social Problems and Public Policy: Inequality and Justice,* Lee Rainwater, ed. Chicago: Aldine, 1974:336–352.

Kurtz, S., Inciardi, J., Surratt, H., and Cottler, L. "Prescription Drug Abuse Among Ecstasy Users in Miami." *Journal of Addictive Diseases, 24,* 4, 2005:1–16.

Kushi, Lawrence H., Colleen Doyle, Marji McCullough, et al. "Physical Activity for Cancer Prevention: Reducing the Risk of Cancer with Healthy Food Choices and Physical Activity." *CA, A Cancer Journal for Clinicians, 62,* 2012:30–67.

Kusum. "The Use of Pre-Natal Diagnostic Techniques for Sex Selection: The Indian Scene." *Bioethics, 7,* 2–3, April 1993:149–165.

Kutchinsky, Berl. "The Effects of Easy Availability of Pornography on the Incidence of Sex Crimes in Copenhagen: The Danish Experience." *Journal of Social Issues, 29,* 1973:163–181.

La Gory, Mark, Russell Ward, and Thomas Juravich. "The Age Segregation Process." *Urban Affairs Quarterly, 16,* 1980:59–80.

LaBastille, Anne. "The Deadly Toll of Acid Rain: All of Nature Is Suffering." *Science Digest, 86,* October 1979:61–66.

Lacayo, Richard. "Crusading Against the Pro-Choice Movement." *Time,* October 21, 1991.

LaFree, Gary D. "The Effect of Sexual Stratification by Race on Official Reactions to Rape." *American Sociological Review, 45,* October 1980:842–854.

Lalumiere, Martin L., Grant T. Harris, Vernon L. Quinsey, and Marnie E. Rice. *The Causes of Rape: Understanding Individual Differences in Male Propensity for Sexual Aggression.* Washington, D.C.: American Psychological Association, 2005.

Lambert, Bruce. "Manufacturer in $2 Million Accord With U.S. on Deficient Kevlar in Military Helmets." *Wall Street Journal,* February 6, 2008.

Lamberti, Rob. "Ontario Child-porn Raids Net 55 Arrests." *Toronto Sun,* February 2, 2012.

Landes, David S. *The Wealth and Poverty of Nations: Why Some Are Rich and Some So Poor.* New York: W.W. Norton, 1998.

Landro, Laura. "The Pharmacist Is In and Nudging You to Take Your Pills." *Wall Street Journal,* June 26, 2012.

Landry, Bart, and Kris Marsh. "The Evolution of the New Black Middle Class." Annual Review of Sociology, 37, 2011:373–394.

Langan, Patrick A., and David J. Levin. "Recidivism of Prisoners Released in 1994." Bureau of Justice, Special Report. June 2002.

Laqueur, Walter. *Terrorism.* Boston: Little, Brown, 1977.

Larned, Deborah. "The Epidemic in Unnecessary Hysterectomies." In *Seizing Our Bodies: The Politics of Women's Health,* Claudia Dreyfus, ed. New York: Random House, 1977.

Larson, Mary Strom. "Interactions, Activities and Gender in Children's Television Commercials: A Content Analysis." *Journal of Broadcasting and Electronic Media, 45,* Winter 2001:41–51.

"Las tabacaleras cortejan a las mujeres jovenes." Associated Press, AOL Noticias, May 27, 2010.

Lasch, Christopher. *Haven in a Heartless World: The Family Besieged.* New York: Basic Books, 1977.

Laslett, Barbara. "Family, Social Change Can Often Spell Trouble." University of California, University Extension, Course by Newspaper, San Diego, 1980.

Laumann, Edward O., John H. Gagnon, Robert T. Michael, and Stuart Michaels. *The Social Organization of Sexuality: Sexual Practices in the United States.* Chicago: University of Chicago Press, 1994.

Leaf, Clifton. "Enough Is Enough." In *Sociology,* 33rd ed., Kurt Finsterbusch, ed. New York: McGraw-Hill/Dushkin, 2004:52–59.

Leavitt, Gregory C. "Tyler versus Westermarck: Explaining the Incest Taboo." *Sociology Mind, 13,* 1, 2013:45–51.

Lee, Dorothy. *Freedom and Culture.* Englewood Cliffs, N.J.: Prentice Hall, 1959.

Lee, Sharon M. "Asian Americans: Diverse and Growing." *Population Bulletin, 53,* 2, June 1998:1–39.

Lee, Soo Yeun, Seung Min Oh, and Kyu Hyuck Chung. "Estrogenic Effects of Marijuana Smoke Condensate and Cannabinoid Compounds." *Toxicology and Applied Pharmacology* 2006:214,270–278.

Lee-Gonyea, Jenifer A., Tammy Castle, and Nathan E. Gomyea. "Laid to Order: Male Escorts Advertising on the Internet." *Deviant Behavior, 30,* 2009:321–348.

Leighty, Keith E. "Germ Testing by Japanese Killed POWs." Associated Press, October 31, 1981.

Leinwand, Donna. "Judges Write Creative Sentences." *USA Today,* February 24, 2004.

Lender, Mark Edward, and James Kirby Martin. *Drinking in America: A History.* New York: Free Press, 1982.

Leopold, Evelyn. "Female Circumcision—90 Percent of Childbearing Women in Egypt?" *Huffington Post,* January 9, 2012.

Lerner, Gerda. *The Creation of Patriarchy.* New York: Oxford University Press, 1986.

Lerner, Robert, Althea K. Nagai, and Stanley Rothman. "Abortion and Social Change in America." *Society, 2,* 27, January–February 1990:8–15.

Lerner, Steve. *Sacrifice Zones: The Front Lines of Toxic Chemical Exposure in the United States.* Cambridge, Mass.: MIT Press, 2010.

Lesser, Alexander. "War and the State." In *War: The Anthropology of Armed Conflict and Aggression,* Morton Fried, Marvin Harris, and Robert Murphy, eds. Garden City, N.Y.: Natural History, 1968.

Leuchtag, Alice. "Human Rights, Sex Trafficking, and Prostitution." In *Social Problems,* 32nd ed., Kurt Pinsterbusch, ed. New York: McGraw-Hill/Dushkin, 2004:88–93.

Levine, Art. "Drug Education Gets an F." *U.S. News & World Report,* October 13, 1986:63–64.

Levinson, Daniel R. "Overmedication of Nursing Home Patients Troubling." Washington, D.C.: Report by Office of Inspector General, U.S. Department of Health and Human Services, May 9, 2011.

Lewis, Jeffrey. "What If Space Were Weaponized? Possible Conse quences for Crisis Scenarios." Washington, D.C.: Center for Defense Information, July 2004.

Lewis, Karen J. "Abortion: Judicial Control." Washington, D.C.: Congressional Research Service, American Law Division. Mimeo. September 13, 1988.

Lewis, Oscar. "The Culture of Poverty." *Scientific American,* 115, October 1966:19–25.

Lewis, Oscar. *Five Families.* New York: Basic Books, 1959.

Lewis, Peter W., and Kenneth D. Peoples. *The Supreme Court and the Criminal Process: Cases and Comments.* Philadelphia: Saunders, 1978.

Light, Donald W. "The Overlooked Epidemic in Harmful Side Effects from Prescription Drugs." *The SSSP Newsletter, 42,* 3, Fall 2011.

Linden, Eugene. "Lost Tribes, Lost Knowledge." *Time,* September 23, 1991:46, 48, 50, 52, 54, 56.

Lindner, Katharina. "Images of Women in General Interest and Fashion Magazine Advertisements from 1955 to 2002." *Sex Roles, 51,* 7/8, October 2004:409–421.

Linton, Ralph. *The Study of Man.* New York: Appleton, 1936.

Liptak, Adam. "Blocking Parts of Arizona Law, Justices Allow Its Centerpiece." *New York Times,* June 25, 2012.

Liptak, Adam. "Ex-Inmate's Suit Offers View into Sexual Slavery in Prisons." *New York Times,* October 16, 2004.

Liptak, Adam. "Kansas Law on Gay Sex by Teenagers Overturned." *New York Times,* October 22, 2005.

Liptak, Adam. "Supreme Court Finds Bias Against White Firefighters." *New York Times,* June 30, 2009.

Little, Jane Braxton. "The Ogallala Aquifer: Saving a Vital U.S. Water Source." *National Geographic,* March 2009.

Little, Peter D., and Michael M. Horowitz (eds.). *Lands at Risk in the Third World: Local-Level Perspectives.* Boulder, Colo.: Westview, 1987.

Livingston, K. "Ritalin: Miracle Drug or Cop-Out?" *The Public Interest.* April 15, 1997.

Lochner, Lance. "Education, Work, and Crime: A Human Capital Approach." *International Economic Review 45,* 3, August 2004:811–843.

Locy, Toni, and Joan Biskupic. "Anti-Porn Filters in Libraries Upheld." *USA Today,* June 23, 2003.

Lombroso, Cesare. *Crime: Its Causes and Remedies,* H. P. Horton, trans. Boston: Little, Brown, 1911.

Loprest, Pamela, and Austin Nichols. "Characteristics of Low-Income Single Mothers Disconnected from Work and Public Assistance." Low-Income Working Families Fact Sheet. Washington, D.C.: The Urban Institute, 2011.

Lorber, Judith. "Beyond Equality of the Sexes: The Question of Children." In *Marriage and Family in a Changing Society,* James M. Henslin, ed. New York: Free Press, 1980:522–533.

Lorenz, Konrad. *On Aggression.* New York: Harcourt, 1966.

Loughran, Thomas A., Edward P. Mulvey, Carol A. Schubert, et al. "Estimating a Dose-Response Relationship Between Length of Stay and Future Recidivism in Serious Juvenile Offenders." *Criminology, 47*, July 2009:699–740.

Lucas, Ann M. "The Work of Sex Work: Elite Prostitutes' Vocational Orientations and Experiences." *Deviant Behavior, 26*, 2005:513–546.

Luckenbill, David F. "Deviant Career Mobility: The Case of Male Prostitutes." *Social Problems 33*, 4, April 1986: 283–296.

Luker, Kristen. *Taking Chances: Abortion and the Decision Not to Contracept.* Berkeley: University of California Press, 1975.

Lundberg, Ollie. "Causal Explanations for Class Inequality in Health: An Empirical Analysis." *Social Science and Medicine, 32*, 4, 1991:385–393.

Lunenburg, Fred C. "School Violence in America's Schools." *Focus on Colleges, Universities, and Schools, 4*, 1, 2010:1–6.

Lussier, Patrick, David P. Farrington, and Terrie E. Moffitt. "Is the Antisocial Child Father of the Abusive Man? A 40-Year Prospective Longitudinal Study on the Developmental Antecedents of Intimate Partner Violence." *Criminology, 47*, 3, 2009:741–779.

Lutz, Harold J. *Aboriginal Man and White Man as Historical Causes of Fires in the Boreal Forest, with Particular Reference to Alaska.* New Haven, Conn.: Yale University School of Forestry. No. 65, 1959 [as referenced in Burch 1971].

Luy, Mary Lynn M. "Rape: Not a Sex Act—A Violent Crime, An Interview with Dr. Dorothy J. Hicks." *Modern Medicine.* February 15, 1977:36–41.

Lynd, Robert S., and Helen M Lynd. *Middletown in Transition.* New York: Harcourt, 1937.

Lynn, Michael, Michael Sturman, Christie Ganley, Elizabeth Adams, Mathew Douglas, and Jessica McNeil. "Consumer Racial Discrimination in Tipping: A Replication and Extension." *Journal of Applied Social Psychology, 38*, 4, 2008:1045–1060.

Macartney, Suzanne. "Child Poverty in the United States 2009 and 2010: Selected Race Groups and Hispanic Origin." U.S. Census Bureau, Community Survey Briefs, November 2011.

Mackellar, Landis, and David Horlacher. "Population Ageing in Japan: A Brief Survey." *The European Journal of Social Sciences, 13*, 4, December 2000.

MacKinnon, Catharine A. *Sexual Harassment of Working Women: A Case of Sex Discrimination.* New Haven, Conn.: Yale University Press, 1979.

Macy, Rebecca J., Paula S. Nurius, and Jeanette Norris. "Responding in Their Best Interests: Contextualizing Women's Coping With Acquaintance Sexual Aggression." *Violence Against Women, 12*, 5, May 2006:478–500.

Magee, Elizabeth A., Laurie M. Edmond, Shiona M. Tasker, San Choon Kong, Richard Curno, and John H. Cummings. "Associations Between Diet and Disease Activity in Ulcerative Colitis." *Nutrition Journal, 4*, 7, February 10, 2005.

Malamuth, Neil M., Gert Martin Hald, and Mary Koss. "Pornography, Individual Differences in Risk an d Men's Acceptance of Violence Against Women in a Representative Sample." Sex Roles, 66, 2012:427–439.

Malamuth, Neil M., Tamara Addison, and Mary Koss. "Pornography and Sexual Aggression: Are There Reliable Effects and Can We Understand Them? *Annual Review of Sex Research, 11*, 2000:26–91.

Malthus, Thomas Robert. *First Essay on Population.* London: Macmillan, 1926. (Originally published 1798)

Manderscheid, Ronald W., Carol D. Ryff, Elsie J. Freeman, Lela R. McKnight, Satvinder Dhingra, and Tara W. Strine. "Evolving Definitions of Mental Illness and Wellness." *Preventing Chronic Disease: Public Health Research, Practice, and Policy. 7*, 1, January 2010.

Manning, Jennifer E., and Colleen J. Shogan. "Women in the United States Congress: 1917–2012. Washington, D.C.: Congressional Research Service, January 27, 2012.

Manpower Report to the President. Washington, D.C.: U.S. Department of Labor, Manpower Administration, April 1971.

Manski, Charles F. "Income and Higher Education." *Focus, 14*, 3, Winter 1992–93:14–19.

Marger, Martin N. *Elites and Masses: An Introduction to Political Sociology,* 2nd ed. Belmont, Calif.: Wadsworth, 1987.

Marino, David. "Border Watch Group 'Techno Patriots' Still Growing." KVDA News 4, Tucson, Arizona, February 14, 2008.

Marino, David. "Border Watch Group 'Techno Patriots' Still Growing." Tucson, Arizona: KVOA News 4, February 14, 2008.

Markman, Joe. "Rescued Child Prostitutes Not Receiving Help" *Los Angeles Times*, December 8, 2009.

Martin, Joyce A., Brady E. Hamilton, Stephanie J. Ventura, et al. "Births: Final Data for 2009." *National Vital Statistics Reports. 60*, 1, November 3, 2011.

Martin, Paul Schultz. "Prehistoric Overkill." In *Pleistocene Extinctions: The Search for a Cause,* Paul Schultz Martin and H. E. Wright, Jr., eds. New Haven, Conn.: Yale University Press, 1967.

Martindale, Mike. "Thousands of Rape Kits Remain Untested." *Detroit News,* May 15, 2012.

Martinez, Juan Francisco Esteva. "Urban Street Activists: Gang and Community Efforts to Bring Peace and Justice to Los Angeles Neighborhoods." In *Gangs and Society: Alternative Perspectives,* Louis Kontos, David Brotherton, and Luis Barrios, eds. New York: Columbia University Press, 2003: 95–115.

Marx, Karl. *Das Kapital.* New York: International, 1967. (Originally published 1867–1895)

Marx, Karl, and Friedrich Engels. *Capital: A Critique of Political Economy,* E. Aveling, trans. Chicago: Charles Kerr, 1906.

Marx, Karl, and Friedrich Engels. *The Communist Manifesto,* S. Moore, trans. New York: Washington Square, 1964. (Originally published 1848)

Mascio, B. *The Daughters and Sons of Elder Care,* 2007. Online. http://www.seniorsapprove.com/daughter.html

Mason, Margie, and Martha Mendoza. "First Case of Highly Drug-Resistant TB Found in U.S." Associated Press, December 27, 2009.

Mathews, Anna Wilde. "Program Cuts Rate of Deadly Catheter Infections." *Wall Street Journal,* September 10, 2012.

Mathews, Anna Wilde. "Remember Managed Care? It's Quietly Coming Back." *Wall Street Journal,* August 2, 2012.

Mattioli, Dana. "More Men Make Harassment Claims." *Wall Street Journal,* March 23, 2010.

Mauer, Marc. "Race, Class, and the Development of Criminal Justice Policy." *Review of Policy Research, 21*, 1, 2004:79–92.

Maynard, Douglas W. *Inside Plea Bargaining: The Language of Negotiation.* New York: Plenum, 1984.

Mayne, Susan Taylor, Dwight T. Janerich, Peter Greenwald, Sherry Chorost, Cathy Tucci, Muhammad B. Zaman, Myron R. Melamed, Maureen Kiely, and Martin F. McKneally. "Dietary Beta Carotene and Lung Cancer Risk in U.S. Nonsmokers."

Journal of the National Cancer Institute, 86, 1, January 5, 1995:33–38.

McAnany, Patricia A., and Norman Yoffee, eds. *Questioning Collapse: Human Resilience, Ecological Vulnerability, and the Aftermath of Empire.* Cambridge: Cambridge University Press, 2009.

McCabe, Janice, Emily Fairchild, Liz Grauerholz, Bernice A. Pescosolido, and Daniel Tope. "Gender in Twentieth-Century Children's Books: Patterns of Disparity in Titles and Central Characters." *Gender and Society, 25,* 2, April 2011:197–226.

McCarty, Teresa L. "The Impact of High-Stakes Accountability Policies on Native American Learners: Evidence from Research." *Teaching Education, 20,* 1, 2009:7–29.

McDonald, Henry. "Sinn Fein Minister Found Guilty of Discrimination." *Guardian,* June 20, 2012.

McGarigle, Bill. "Satellite Tracking for House Arrest." *Geo Info,* May 1997.

McGinty, Jo Craven. "New York Killers, and Those Killed, by Numbers." *New York Times,* April 28, 2006.

McIntyre, Jennie, Thelma Myint, and Lynn Curtis. "Sexual Assault Outcomes: Completed and Attempted Rapes." Paper presented at the annual meeting of the American Sociological Association. Boston, 1979.

McKeown, Thomas. *The Modern Rise of Population.* New York: Academic Press, 1977.

McKeown, Thomas. *The Role of Medicine: Dream, Mirage, or Nemesis?* Princeton, N.J.: Princeton University Press, 1980.

McKinley, James C., Jr. "Mexico: Grisly Message from Drug Gang." *New York Times,* October 30, 2006a.

McKinley, James C., Jr., "With Beheadings and Attacks, Drug Gangs Terrorize Mexico." *New York Times,* October 26, 2006b.

McKinley, James C., Jr., and Marc Lacey. "Mexico's Drug War Brings New Brutality." *New York Times,* October 25, 2006.

McKinnish, Terra, Randall Walsh, and Kirk White. "Who Gentrifies Low-Income Neighborhoods?" National Bureau of Economic Research, Working Paper 14036, May 2008.

McLanahan, S. "Child Support Enforcement and Child Well-Being: Greater Security or Greater Conflict?" *Child Support and Child Well-Being.* Washington: Urban Institute Press, 1996:239–56

McLemore, S. Dale. *Racial and Ethnic Relations in America.* Boston: Allyn and Bacon, 1994.

McManus, Michael J. "Introduction." In Final Report of the Attorney General's Commission on Pornography. Nashville, Tenn.: Rutledge Hill, 1986: ix–l.

McNeely, R. L., and Carl E. Pope. "Socioeconomic and Racial Issues in the Measurement of Criminal Involvement." In *Race, Crime, and Criminal Justice,* R. L. McNeely and Carl E. Pope, eds. Beverly Hills, Calif.: Sage, 1981:31–47.

Meese Commission. *Final Report of the Attorney General's Commission on Pornography.* Washington, D.C.: U.S. Department of Justice, 1986.

Melde, Chris, Terrance J. Taylor, and Finn-Aage Esbensen. "'I Got Your Back': An Examination of the Protective Function of Gang Membership in Adolescence." *Criminology, 47,* 2, 2009: 565–594.

Melloan, George. "Europe Struggles with the Burdens of Old Age." *Wall Street Journal,* December 12, 1994:A15.

Melman, Seymour. *Pentagon Capitalism.* New York: McGraw-Hill, 1970.

Melody, G. F. "Chronic Pelvic Congestion in Prostitutes." *Medical Aspects of Human Sexuality, 3,* November 1969:103–104.

Menacker, Fay, and Brady E. Hamilton. "Recent Trends in Cesarean Delivery in the United States." *NCHS Data Brief, 35,* March 2010.

Merton, Robert K. *Social Theory and Social Structure,* enlarged ed. New York: Free Press, 1968.

"Mexican Drug Gang Beheads Another Blogger and Dumps Body and Severed Head in Street with Bloody Warning Note." *Daily Mail,* November 10, 2011.

Meyer, H. *Old English Coffee Houses.* Emmaus, Pa.: Rodale, 1954.

Michelman, Kate. As quoted in "NARAL," pamphlet published by the National Abortion Rights Action League, 1988:1.

Milbank, Dana. "In His Solitude, A Finnish Thinker Posits Cataclysms." *Wall Street Journal,* May 20, 1994:A1, A8.

Miller, Judith, and William J. Broad. "Clinton Describes Terrorism Threat for 21st Century." *New York Times,* January 22, 1999.

Miller, Michael W. "Quality Stuff: Firm Is Peddling Cocaine, and Deals Are Legit." *Wall Street Journal,* October 27, 1994:A1, A8.

Miller, Walter B. "Lower-Class Culture as a Generating Milieu of Gang Delinquency." *Journal of Social Issues, 14,* 1958:5–19.

Millett, Kate. *Sexual Politics.* Garden City, N.Y.: Doubleday, 1970.

Millett, Kate. *The Prostitution Papers: A Candid Dialogue.* New York: Avon, 1973.

Millman, Joel. "State Rings in Pot Law." *Wall Street Journal,* December 7, 2012.

Mills, C. Wright. *The Causes of World War Three.* New York: Simon & Schuster, 1958.

Mills, C. Wright. *The Sociological Imagination.* New York: Oxford University Press, 1959b.

Mills, Karen M., and Thomas J. Palumbo. *A Statistical Portrait of Women in the United States: 1978.* Washington, D.C.: U.S. Government Printing Office, 1980.

Milner, Christina, and Richard Milner. *Black Players.* Boston: Little Brown, 1972.

Moffett, Matt, and Eduardo Kaplan. "Uruguay Considers Selling Marijuana." *Wall Street Journal,* June 21, 20012.

Moffitt, Robert A. "The Idea of a Negative Income Tax: Past, Present, and Future." *Focus, 23,* 2, Summer 2004.

Mohanty, Ranjani Iyer. "Trash Bin Babies: India's Female Infanticide Crisis." *The Atlantic,* May 25, 2012.

Monto, Martin A. "Female Prostitution, Customers, and Violence." *Violence Against Women, 10,* 2, February 2004: 160–188.

Mooallem, Jon. "Can Animals Be Gay? *New York Times,* March 29, 2010.

Moore, Brent A., Erik M. Augustson, Richard P. Moser, and Alan J. Budney. "Respiratory Effects of Marijuana and Tobacco Use in a U.S. Sample." *Journal of General Internal Medicine, 20,* 2004:33–37.

Moore, Gwen. "The Structure of a National Elite Network." *American Sociological Review, 44,* October 1979:673–691.

Moore, Solomon. "Justice Dept. Seeks Equity in Sentences for Cocaine." *New York Times,* April 29, 2009.

Morash, Merry A., and Etta A. Anderson. "Liberal Thinking on Rehabilitation: A Work-Able Solution to Crime." *Social Problems, 25,* June 1978:556–563.

Moreno, Eduardo Lopez, Oyebanji Oyeyinka, and Gora Mboup. *State of the World's Cities 2010/2011: Bridging the Urban Divide.* London: UN Habitat, 2012.

Morgan, Patricia A. "The Legislation of Drug Law: Economic Crisis and Social Control." *Journal of Drug Issues, 8,* Winter 1978:54–62.

Morgenson, G. "Silence of the Lenders: Is Anyone Listening?" *New York Times,* July 13, 2008.

Mori, Kathryn, and Carolyn Scearce. "Robot Nation: Robots an the Declining Japanese Population." *ProQuest*, September 2010.
Morse, Andrew. Waste-Plant Dispute Builds." *Wall Street Journal*, September 10, 2012.
Moskin, Julia. "Modified Crops Tap a Wellspring of Protest." *New York Times*, February 8, 2012.
Mozur, Paul. "China Alleges Cyberattacks Originated in U.S." *Wall Street Journal*, March 1, 2013.
Mulvihill, Donald J., Melvin M. Tumin, and Lynn A. Curtis. *Crimes of Violence: A Staff Report to the National Commission on the Causes and Prevention of Violence.* Washington, D.C.: U.S. Government Printing Office, 1969.
Murphy, Kim. "Last Stand of an Aging Aryan." *Los Angeles Times*, January 10, 1999.
Myers, Martha A., and Susette M. Talarico. "The Social Contexts of Racial Discrimination in Sentencing." *Social Problems, 33*, 3, February 1986:236–251.
Myrdal, Gunnar. *An American Dilemma.* New York: Harper, 1944.
Naj, Amal Kumar. "Kuwait Oil-Well Fires Did Little Damage to the Global Environment, Study Says." *Wall Street Journal*, May 15, 1992:B5.
Nash, Gary B. *The Urban Crucible.* Cambridge, Mass.: Harvard University Press, 1979.
National Academy of Sciences. "America's Climate Choices." 2010.
National Center for Education Statistics. *Digest of Education Statistics*, 2011:Table 143.
National Council of State Legislatures. "Women in State Legislatures: 2013 Legislative Session," January 18, 2013.
National Prison Rape Elimination Commission Report. Washington, D.C.: June 2009.
National Research Council. *Committee on Sustainable Underground Storage of Recoverable Water.* Washington, D.C.: The National Academies Press, 2008.
National Research Council. *Water Reuse: Potential for Expanding the Nation's Water Supply Through Reuse of Municipal Wastewater.* Washington, D.C.: The National Academies Press, 2012.
"National Strategy for Combatting Terrorism." Washington, D.C.: The White House, September 2006.
National Women's Political Caucus. "News & Opinions: 1998 Election Results." November 5, 1998.
Nekoomaram, Ladan. "U.S. Military Presence in Foreign Countries Exceeds Rest of World." *American Observer, 15*, 15, November 10, 2009.
Nettler, Gwynn. "Embezzlement Without Problems." *British Journal of Criminology, 14*, January 1974:70–77.
Nettler, Gwynn. *Social Concerns.* New York: McGraw-Hill, 1976.
Neuman, William. "Egg Farms Violated Safety Rules." *New York Times*, August 30, 2010.
Newman, Benjamin J., Todd K. Hartman, and Charles S. Taber. "Foreign Language Exposure, Cultural Threat, and Opposition to Immigration." *Political Psychology, 33*, 5, 2012:635–657.
Newman, Donald J. *Conviction: The Determination of Guilt or Innocence Without Trial.* Boston: Little, Brown, 1966.
Newman, Dorothy K., Nancy J. Amidei, Barbara L. Cater, Dawn Day, William J. Kruvant, and Jack S. Russell. *Protest, Politics, and Prosperity: Black Americans and White Institutions, 1940–1975.* New York: Pantheon, 1978.
Newsday. *The Heroin Trail.* New York. Holt, Rinehart, & Winston, 1974.
Nielsen, Tina S., Galam Khan, Jennifer Davis, et al. "Prepubertal Exposure to Cow's Milk Reduces Susceptibility Carcinogen-Induces Mammary Tumorigenesis in Rats." *International Journal of Cancer, 128*, 2011:12–20.
Nilstun, Tore, Marwan Habiba, Goran Lingman, et al. "Cesarean Delivery on Maternal Request: Can the Ethical Problem Be Solved by the Principlist Approach?" *BMC Medical Ethics, 9*, 11, June 17, 2008:1–8.
Nishio, Harry Kaneharu. "Japan's Welfare Vision: Dealing with a Rapidly Increasing Elderly Population." In *The Graying of the World: Who Will Care for the Frail Elderly?* New York: Haworth, 1994:233–260.
Norris, Jimmy. "Anthrax Shots Reduced." *Stars and Stripes*, March 6, 2009.
Norris, Robert S., and Hans M. Kristensen. "India's Nuclear Forces, 2005." *Bulletin of the Atomic Scientists, 61*, 5, September/October 2005:73–75.
Norton, Michael I., and Samuel R. Sommers. "Whites See Racism as a Zero-Sum Game That They Are Now Losing." *Perspectives on Psychological Sciences*, 6, 2011:215–218.
Novak, Kenneth J., and Mitchell B. Chamlin. "Racial Threat, Suspicion, and Police Behavior: The Impact of Race and Place in Traffic Enforcement." Crime and Delinquency, 58, 2, 2012:275–300.
"Nuclear Weapons: Who Has What at a Glance." Arms Control Association, July 2010.
Nucleus: A Report to Union of Concerned Scientists Sponsors, 3, Spring–Summer 1981.
O'Connell, Pamela Licalzi. "Web Erotica Aims for New Female Customers." *New York Times*, August 13, 1998.
O'Connor, Anahad. "Government Ends Case Against Gotti." *New York Times*, January 14, 2010.
O'Hanlon, Michael E. and Ian Livingston. "Iraq Index: Tracking Variables of Reconstruction & Security in Post-Saddam Iraq." Brookings, May 25, 2010.
O'Hare, William P. "America's Minorities: The Demographics of Diversity." *Population Bulletin, 47*, 4, December 1992:1–47.
Oakley, Robert B. "Combating International Terrorism." *Department of State Bulletin*, June 1985:73–78.
OECD. "Health at a Glance 2009: OECD Indicators," 2009.
"Of Birds and Bacteria." *Consumer Reports*, January 2003.
Oliver, Melvin L., and Thomas M. Shapiro. *Black Wealth/White Wealth: A New Perspective on Racial Inequality.* New York: Routledge, 1995.
Olson, James S., Mark Baxter, Jason M. Tetzloff, and Darren Pierson. *Encyclopedia of American Indian Civil Rights.* Westport, Conn.: Greenwood Press, 1997.
Olson, Walter K. "Give It Back to the Indians?" *City Journal*, Autumn 2002.
Onishi, Norimitsu, "Cities Balk as Federal Law on Marijuana Is Enforced." *New York Times*, June 30, 2012.
Oppel, Richard A. "Steady Decline in Major Crimes Baffles Experts." *New York Times*, May 23 2011.
Organization for Economic Cooperation and Development. Statistical Extracts Online, 2012.
Organized Crime: Report of the Task Force on Organized Crime. Washington, D.C.: National Advisory Committee on Criminal Justice Standards and Goals, 1976.
Osborne, Lawrence. "Got Silk?" *New York Times Magazine*, June 15, 2002.
Otten, Alan L. "People Patterns." *Wall Street Journal*, January 27, 1995:B1.

Park, Robert E. "The Social Function of War." *American Journal of Sociology, 46,* January 1941:551–570.

Parmesan, Camille, and Gary Yohe. "A Globally Coherent Fingerprint of Climate Change Impacts Across Natural Systems." *Nature,* January 2003:37–42.

Partington, Donald H. "The Incidence of the Death Penalty for Rape in Virginia." *Washington and Lee Law Review, 22,* 1965:43–75.

Patrick, Stewart M. "The Coming Global Water Crisis." *The Atlantic,* May 9, 2012.

Pattis, Norm. "A Plea on Plea Bargains: Don't Tie Hands of Justice." *Connecticut Law Tribune,* October 17, 2005.

Paul, Pamela. *Pornified: How Pornography Is Transforming Our Lives, Our Relationships, and Our Families.* New York: Henry Holt, 2005.

Peele, Stanton. "The Addiction Experience." In *Social Problems: A Critical Thinking Approach,* Paul J. Baker and Louis E. Anderson, eds. Belmont, Calif.: Wadsworth, 1987:210–218.

Penn, Stanley. "How Public Defenders Deal with the Pressure of the Crowded Courts." *Wall Street Journal,* July 5, 1985:1, 22.

Penn, Stanley. "Organized Crime Finds Rich Pickings in Rise of Union Health Plans." *Wall Street Journal,* October 5, 1982:1, 26.

Perez-Pena, Richard. "To Enroll More Minority Students, Colleges Work Around the Courts." *New York Times,* April 1, 2012.

Perl, Raphael F. "Taliban and the Drug Trade." CRS Report for Congress, October 5, 2001.

Perlo-Freeman, Sam, Olawale Ismail, and Carina Solmirano. "Military Expenditure." *SIPRI Yearbook.* Oxford: Oxford University Press, 2010:179–258.

Perry, Nick. "Kiribati Global Warming Fears: Entire Nation May Move to Fiji." Huffington Post, March 9, 2012.

Perry, Susan. "Food-dye Warning Labels Are Now Required in Europe; Will the FDA Do the Same?" MinnPost.com, July 29, 2010.

Persell, Caroline Hodges, Sophia Catsambis, and Peter W. Cookson, Jr. "Family Background, School Type, and College Attendance: A Conjoint System of Cultural Capital Transmission." *Journal of Research on Adolescence, 2,* 1, 1992:1–23.

Pestka, Elizabeth L. "Genetic Counseling for Mental Health Disorders." *Journal of the American Psychiatric Nurses Association, 11,* 6, 2006:338–343.

Petersilia, Joan. *Racial Disparities in the Criminal Justice System.* Santa Monica, Calif.: Rand, June 1983.

Peterson, Iver. "1993 Deal for Indian Casino Is Called a Model to Avoid." *New York Times,* June 30, 2003.

Pew Research Center for the People and the Press. "Gay Marriage Gains More Acceptance." October 6, 2010.

Pew Research Center for the People and the Press. "Two-Thirds of Democrats Now Support Gay Marriage." July 31, 2012.

Pierson, Ransdell. "Lilly Profit Beats Forecast; Focus on New Drug Data." Reuters, April 25, 2012.

Piliavin, Irving, and Scott Briar. "Police Encounters with Juveniles." *American Journal of Sociology, 70,* September 1964:206–214.

Pillemer, Karl, and David W. Moore. "Abuse of Patients in Nursing Homes: Findings from a Survey of Staff." *The Gerontologist, 29,* 3, 1989:314–320.

Pilot, Jessica. "Secrets of a Hipster Hooker." *Radar,* September 2008.

Piotrow, Phylis Tilson. *World Population Crisis: The United States' Response.* New York: Praeger, 1973.

Pittman, David J. "The Male House of Prostitution." *Transaction, 8,* March–April 1971:21–27.

Piven, Frances Fox, and Richard A. Cloward. *The Breaking of the American Social Compact.* New York: New Press, 1997.

Piven, Frances Fox, and Richard A. Cloward. *The New Class War: Reagan's Attack on the Welfare State and Its Consequences.* New York: Pantheon, 1982.

Piven, Frances Fox, and Richard A. Cloward. *Regulating the Poor.* New York: Vintage, 1971.

Piven, Frances Fox, and Richard A. Cloward. *Why Americans Don't Vote.* New York: Random House, 1989.

Platt, Anthony M. *The Child Savers.* Chicago: University of Chicago Press, 1979.

Polti, Daniel. "Death of a Terrorist." *New York Times,* May 22, 2012.

Pope, Carl E. "The Family, Delinquency, and Crime." In *Mental Illness, Delinquency, Addictions, and Neglect,* Elam W. Nunnally, Catherine S. Chilmam, and Fred M. Cox, eds. Newbury Park, Calif.: Sage, 1988:108–127.

Potterat, John J., Donald E. Woodhouse, John B. Muth, and Stephen Q. Muth. "Estimating the Prevalence and Career Longevity of Prostitute Women." *Journal of Sex Research, 27,* 2, May 1990:233–243.

Powell, Michael, and Janet Roberts. "Minorities Hit Hardest by Foreclosures in New York." *New York Times,* May 15, 2009.

Powers, Ashley. "Male Prostitution Is Nevada's Newest Legal Profession." *Los Angeles Times,* January 6, 2010.

Pozdena, Randall J., and Terry R. Johnson. *Income Maintenance and Asset Demand.* Menlo Park, Calif.: SRI International, March, 1979.

Pratt, Timothy. "Nevada's Gambling Revenue Rises after Two Year Slump." Reuters, February 10, 2011.

"Prenatal Substance Exposure: Factsheet." Berkeley, Calif.: National Abandoned Infants Assistance Resource Center, April 2008.

Preston, Julia, and John H. Cushman, Jr. "Obama to Permit Young Migrants to Remain in U.S." *New York Times,* June 16, 2012.

Preston, Julia. "Homeland Security Cancels 'Virtual Fence' after Billion Is Spent." *New York Times,* January 14, 2011.

Pridemore, William Alex, and Joshua D. Freilich. "A Test of Recent Subcultural Explanations of White Violence in the United States." *Journal of Criminal Justice, 34,* 2006:1–16.

"Project BioShield." U.S Department of Health and Human Services. Online, June 2010.

Pruitt, A.D., and Peter Grant. "Tribal Casino Rules Revisited." *Wall Street Journal,* September 21, 2009.

Prus, Robert, and Styllianoss Irini. Hookers, *Rounders, and Desk Clerks: The Social Organization of the Hotel Community.* Salem, Wis.: Sheffield, 1988.

Pulliam, Susan, and Chad Bray. "Rajaratnam Slapped With 11-Year Prison Term for Orchestrating Insider Scheme." *Wall Street Journal,* October 14, 2011.

Puzic, Sonja. "Windsor Dr. Barbara Heartwell's Surgical Privileges at Hotel-Dieu Grace Hospital Reinstated." *Windsor-Star,* March 12, 2010.

Qian, Zhenchao, and Daniel T. Lichter. "Social Boundaries and Marital Assimilation: Interpreting Trends in Racial and Ethnic Intermarriage." *American Sociological Review, 72,* February 2007: 68–94.

Rabin, Roni Caryn. "C-Sections Pose Respiratory Risks for Some Small Preemies." *New York Times,* February 9, 2012.

Rabin, Roni Caryn. "Circumcise or Don't? Quandary for Parents." *New York Times,* August 22, 2011.

Rabinovitz, J. (1998, July 7). "Three Mile Island: Cleaned Up, and for Sale." *New York Times,* July 7, 1998. Retrieved from http://www.nytimes.com

Rabinowitz, Dorothy. *No Crueler Tyrannies: Accusation, False Witness, and Other Terrors of Our Times.* New York: Simon & Schuster, 2004.

Radnofsky, Louise. "Catholics Sue Over Health Mandate." *Wall Street Journal,* May 23, 2012.

Rakow, Lana F. "'Don't Hate Me Because I'm Beautiful': Feminist Resistance to Advertising's Irresistible Meanings." *Southern Communication Journal, 57,* 2, Winter 1992:132–142.

Raphael, Jody. "Book Review: Until Proven Innocent: Political Correctness and the Shameful Injustices of the Duke Lacrosse Rape Case." *Violence Against Women, 14,* 3, March 2008:370–375.

Ray, Oakley S. *Drugs, Society, and Human Behavior,* 8th ed. New York: McGraw-Hill, 1998.

Ray, Oakley, and Charles J. Ksir. *Drugs, Society, and Human Behavior,* 10th ed. New York: McGraw-Hill, 2004.

Reasons, Charles E., ed. *The Criminologist: Crime and the Criminal.* Pacific Palisades, Calif.: Goodyear, 1974.

Reay, Diane, Jacqueline Davies, Miriam David, and Stephen J. Ball. "Choice of Degrees or Degrees of Choice? Class, 'Race,' and the Higher Education Choice Process." *Sociology, 35,* 4, November 2001: 855–876.

Reckless, Walter C. *The Crime Problem,* 5th ed. New York: Appleton, 1973.

Regaldo, Antonio. "When a Plant Emerges From Melting Glacier, Is It Global Warming?" *Wall Street Journal,* October 22, 2004:B1.

Regushevskaya, Elena. *Abortions and Sexually Transmitted Infections Among Women in St. Petersburg in the Early 2000s: Comparison by Population Based Surveys in Estonia and Finland.* Dissertation, University of Tampere, Finland, 2009.

Rehm, Jurgen, Gerhard Gmel, Christopher T. Sempos, and Maurizio Trevisan. "Alcohol-Related Morbidity and Mortality." *Alcohol Research and Health, 27,* 1, 2003:39–51.

Reichert, Loren D., and James H. Frey. "The Organization of Bell Desk Prostitution." *Sociology and Social Research, 69,* 4, July 1985:516–526.

Reiss, Albert J. "The Sociological Integration of Queers and Peers." *Social Problems, 9,* Fall 1961:102–120.

Reskin, Barbara, and Denise D. Bielby. "A Sociological Perspective on Gender and Career Outcomes." *Journal of Economic Perspectives, 19,* 1, Winter 2005:71–86.

Reuman, E. C., S. Y. Rhee, and R. W. Shafer. "Constrained Patterns of Covariation and Clustering of HIV-1 Non-nucleoside Reverse Transcriptase Inhibitor Resistance Mutations." *Journal of Antimicrobial Chemotherapy,* May 12, 2010.

Revzin, Philip. "U.S. Claims Progress at Global Meeting Discussing Ban on Chemical Weapons." *Wall Street Journal,* January 9, 1989:A3.

Reynolds, Carl, and Jeff Hall. "Courts Are Not Revenue Centers." Conference of State Court Administrators, 2011–2012 Policy Paper, 2012.

Reynolds, Janice. "Rape as Social Control." In *Social Problems in American Society,* 2nd ed., James M. Henslin and Larry T. Reynolds, eds. Boston: Holbrook, 1976:79–86.

Reynolds, Janice. "The Medical Institution: The Death and Disease-producing Appendage." In *American Society: A Critical Analysis,* Larry T. Reynolds and James M. Henslin, eds. New York: McKay, 1973:198–224.

Rhavi, M. Marit, and Sonja B. Starr. "Racial Disparity in Federal Criminal Charging and Its Sentencing Consequences." University of Michigan Law and Economics, Empirical Legal Studies Center Paper, January 15, 2012.

Richardson, Lewis F. *Statistics of Deadly Quarrels.* Chicago: Quadrangle, 1960.

Richey, Warren. "Supreme Court Refuses to Resolve Confusion over Child Pornography Law." *Christian Science Monitor,* November 28, 2011.

Riesel, Victor. "Crackdown on Mobsters." Syndicated column, January 16, 1982a.

Riesel, Victor. "Racketeers Infest New Jersey Construction Trade." Syndicated column, January 25, 1982b.

Riesman, David, Nathan Glazer, and Reuel Denney. *The Lonely Crowd: A Study of the Changing American Character.* New Haven, Conn.: Yale University Press, 1951.

Riley, K. Jack. "Crack, Powder Cocaine, and Heroin. Drug Purchase and Use Patterns in Six U.S. Cities." National Institute of Justice, online, December 12, 1998.

Rios, Victor M. *Punished: Policing the Lives of Black and Latino Boys.* New York: New York University Press, 2011.

Risen, James, and David Johnston. "Bush Has Widened Authority of C.I.A. to Kill Terrorists." *New York Times,* December 15, 2002.

Roach, John. "Rain Forest Plan Blends Drug Research, Conservation." *National Geographic News,* October 7, 2003.

Roberts, Sam. "U.S. Births Hint at Bias for Boys in Some Asians." *New York Times,* June 14, 2009.

Rockwell, Don. "Social Problems: Alcohol and Marijuana." *Journal of Psychedelic Drugs, 5,* Fall 1972:49–55.

Roe, Kathleen M. "Private Troubles and Public Issues: Providing Abortion Amid Competing Definitions." *Social Science and Medicine, 29,* 10, 1989:1191–1198.

Roffman, Roger, and Roger S. Stephens, eds. *Cannabis Dependence: Its Nature, Consequences, and Treatment.* Cambridge: Cambridge University Press, 2006.

Rohani, Pejman, and John M. Drake. "The Decline and Resurgence of Pertussis in the U.S." *Epidemics, 3,* 2011:183–188.

Rolo, Mark Anthony. "Marked Media." *The Circle.* Online, n.d.

Rosaldo, Michelle Zimbalist. "Women, Culture, and Society: A Theoretical Overview." In *Women, Culture, and Society,* Michelle Zimbalist Rosaldo and Louise Lamphere, eds. Stanford, Calif.: Stanford University Press, 1974.

Rose-Jacobs, Ruth, Deborah Waber, Marjorie Beeghly, et al. "Intrauterine Cocaine Exposure and Executive Functioning in Middle Childhood." *Neurotoxicology and Teratology, 31,* 2009:159–168.

Rosen, Lawrence, Leonard Savitz, Michael Lalli, and Stanley Turner. "Early Delinquency, High School Graduation, and Adult Criminality." *Sociological Viewpoints, 7,* Fall 1991:37–60.

Rosen, Yereth. "Exxon Valdez Oil Spill of 1989 Crippled Sound, Alaskans Say." Reuters, March 14, 1999.

Rosenthal, Norman E. "Helping 'Children of the Night'—Transcending a Different Type of PTSD." *Fox News,* January 27, 2012.

Rosett, Claudia. "Big Oil-Pipeline Spill in Russia May Be a Sign of Things to Come." *Wall Street Journal,* October 27, 1994:A14.

Rothman, David J. *The Discovery of the Asylum.* Boston: Little, Brown, 1971.

Rothman, David J., and Sheila M. Rothman. *On Their Own.* Reading, Mass.: Addison-Wesley, 1972.

Rovner, Julie. "'Partial-Birth Abortion': Separating Fact from Spin." National Public Radio Online, February 21, 2006.

Rubin, Trudy. "Nuclear 'Supermarket' Another Concern for U.S." *Philadelphia Inquirer,* February 8, 2004.

Ruethling, Gretchen. "27 Charged in International Online Pornography Ring." *New York Times,* March 16, 2006.

Ruggles, Patricia. *Drawing the Line: Alternative Poverty Measures and Their Implication for Public Policy.* Washington, D.C.: Urban Institute, 1990.

Ruggles, Patricia. "Measuring Poverty." *Focus, 14,* 1, Spring 1992:1–5.

Ruggles, Patricia. *Short and Long Term Poverty in the United States: Measuring the American "Underclass."* Washington, D.C.: Urban Institute, June 1989.

Rumbaut, Ruben G., and John R. Weeks. "Unraveling a Public Health Enigma: Why Do Immigrants Experience Superior Perinatal Health Outcomes?" Paper presented at the annual meeting of the American Public Health Association, 1994.

Russell, Diana E. H. "Rape in Marriage: A Case Against Legalized Crime." Paper presented at the annual meeting of the American Society of Criminology, 1980.

Ryan, Andrea Kay. "The Lasting Effects of Marijuana Use on Educational Attainment in Midlife." *Substance Use and Misuse, 45,* 2010:554–597.

Sagan, Scott D. "The Perils of Proliferation: Organization Theory, Deterrence Theory, and the Spread of Nuclear Weapons." *International Security, 18,* 4, Spring 1994: 66–107.

Sakharov, Andrei. "Text of Sakharov Letter to Carter on Human Rights." *New York Times,* January 29, 1977.

Saletan, William. "Fifty Shades of Gay." *Slate,* May 22, 2012.

"Same-Sex Marriage, Civil Unions, and Domestic Partnerships." *New York Times*, April 1, 2010.

Sanger, Daid E. John Markoff, and Thorn Shanker. "*U. S. Plans Attack and Defense in Cyberspace Warfare.*" *New York Times,* April 27, 2009.

Santos, Fernanda. "Are New Yorkers Satisfied? That Depends." *New York Times*, March 7, 2009.

Sareen, Jitender, Tracie O. Afifi, Katherine A. McMillan, and Gordon J. G. Asmundson. "Relationship between Household Income and Mental Disorders." *Archives of General Psychiatry, 68,* 4, 2011:419–427.

Sartore, Melanie L., and George B. Cunningham. "Gender, Sexual Prejudice and Sport Participation: Implications for Sexual Minorities." *Sex Roles, 60,* 2009:100–113.

Saulny, Susan. "With Cars as eth Labs, Evidence Litters Roads." *New York Times,* April 14, 2010.

Savage, Charlie. "Countrywide Will Settle a Bias Suit." *New York Times,* December 21, 2011a.

Savage, Charlie. "Secret Memo Made Legal Case to Kill a Citizen." *New York Times,* October 8, 2011.

Savage, Charlie. "U.S. Law May Allow Killings, Holder Says." *New York Times,* March 5, 2012.

Savitsky, Douglas. "Is Plea Bargaining a Rational Choice? Plea Bargaining as an Engine of Racial Stratification and Overcrowding in the United States Prison System." *Rationality and Society, 24,* 2, 2012:131–167.

Sawhill, Isabel V. "Poverty in the U.S.: Why Is It So Persistent?" *Journal of Economic Literature, 26,* 3, September 1988: 1073–1119.

Schaefer, Richard T. *Racial and Ethnic Groups,* 9th ed. Upper Saddle River, N.J.: Prentice Hall, 2004.

Schaefer, Richard T. *Racial and Ethnic Groups* 13th ed.. Boston: Pearson Education, 2012.

Schmidt, Gunter, and Volkmar Sigusch. "Sex Differences in Response to Psychosexual Stimulation by Films and Slides." *Journal of Sex Research, 6,* November, 268–283.

Schmidt, Michael S., and Thom Shanker. "To Smuggle More Drugs, Traffickers Go Under the Sea." *New York Times,* September 9, 2012.

Schmitt, Richard B. "Some Towns Jail Indigents Illegally and Get Free Labor." *Wall Street Journal,* February 2, 1982:1, 16.

Schoenfeld, A. Clay, Robert F. Meier, and Robert J. Griffin. "Constructing a Social Problem: The Press and the Environment." *Social Problems, 27,* October 1979:38–61.

Schottland, Charles I. *The Social Security Plan in the U.S.* New York: Appleton, 1963.

Schreiber, Jan. *The Ultimate Weapon: Terrorists and the World Order.* New York: Morrow, 1978.

Schrieke, Bertram J. *Alien Americans.* New York: Viking, 1936.

Schumpeter, Joseph A. *The Sociology of Imperialism.* New York: Meridian, 1955. (Originally published 1919)

Schwartz, John. "Child Pornography, and an Issue of Restitution." *New York Times*, February 2, 2010.

Schwarz, Alan. "Risky Rise of the Good-Grade Pill." *New York Times,* June 9, 2012.

Scott, G. (2004). "'It's a sucker's outfit': How Urban Gangs Enable and Impede the Reintegration of Ex-convicts." *Ethnography, 51,* 1, 2004:107–140.

Scully, D., and Marolla, J. "Riding the Bull at Gilley's": Convicted Rapists Describe the Rewards of Rape. In *Down-to-Earth Sociology: Introductory Readings,* 15th ed., James M. Henslin, ed. New York: Free Press, 2014. (Originally published in *Social Problems, 32,* 3, 1985:251–263)

Scully, Diana. "Negotiating to Do Surgery." In *Dominant Issues in Medical Sociology,* 3rd ed. Howard D. Schwartz, ed. New York: McGraw-Hill, 1994:146–152.

Scully, Diana. *Understanding Sexual Violence: A Study of Convicted Rapists.* Boston: Unwin Hyman, 1990.

Seib, Gerald F. "U.S. Aides Say Toxins on a Cambodian Leaf Hint at Chemical War." *Wall Street Journal,* September 15, 1981:22.

Seiden, Samuel C., and Paul Barach. "Wrong-Side/Wrong-Site, Wrong Procedure, and Wrong-Patient Adverse Events." *Archives of Surgery, 141,* 2006:931–939.

Seligman, L. "Anti-Rape Group Reaches Out to Fraternities." *The Daily Pennsylvanian,* 2008. Online.

Seligmann, Jean. "The Date Who Rapes." *Newsweek,* April 9, 1984:91–92.

"Senate Passes Military Spending Bill." UPI, May 28, 2010.

Senders, John W., and Regine Kanzki. "The Egocentric Surgeon or the Roots of Wrong Side Surgery." *Quality and Safety in Health Care 17,* 2008:396–400.

Sewall, Sarah B., and Carl Kaysen, eds. *The United States and the International Criminal Court: National Security and International Law.* Lanham, Md.: Rowman and Littlefield, 2000.

Sewell, R. Andrew, James Poling, and Mehmet Sofuoghu. "The Effect of Cannabis Compared with Alcohol on Driving." *American Journal on Addictions, 18,* 2009:185–193.

Shaffer, Harry G. "$1,000,000,000,000." *Republic,* May 1986:24.

Shafir, Gershon, and Yoav Peled. "Citizenship and Stratification in an Ethnic Democracy." *Ethnic and Racial Studies, 21,* 3, May 1998:408–427.

Shane, Scott. "F.B.I., Laying Out Evidence, Closes Anthrax Case." *New York Times,* February 19, 2010a.

Shanker, Thom. "Former Commander of U.S. Nuclear Forces Calls for Large Cut in Warheads." *New York Times,* May 15, 2012

Shaw, Jonathan. "Modern Milk." *Harvard Magazine,* May-June 2007.

Shaw, Sue. "Wretched of the Earth." *New Statesman, 20,* March 1987:19–20.

Shibutani, Tamotsu. "On the Personification of Adversaries." In *Human Nature and Collective Behavior,* Tamotsu Shibutani, ed. Englewood Cliffs, N.J.: Prentice Hall, 1970:223–233.

Shively, JoEllen. "Cowboys and Indians." In *Down-to-Earth Sociology: Introductory Readings,* 10th ed., James M. Henslin, ed. New York: Free Press, 1999:104–116.

Shor, Eran, David J. Roelfs, Misty Currell, et al. "Widowhood and Mortality: A Meta-Analysis and Meta-Regression." *Demography, 49,* 2012:575–606.

Shorter, Edward. "Why Psychiatry Needs Therapy." *Wall Street Journal,* February 27, 2010.

Shribman, David. "Even After 10 Years, Victims of Love Canal Can't Quite Escape It." *Wall Street Journal,* March 9, 1989:A1, A8.

Siebens, Julie, and Tiffany Julian. "Native North American Languages Spoken at Home in the United States and Puerto Rico: 2006–2010." Washington, D.C.: U.S. Census Bureau, December 2011.

Signore, Caroline, Roger K. Freeman, and Catherine Y. Spong. "Antenatal Testing: A Reevaluation" *Obstetrics and Gynecology, 113,* 3, March 2009:687–701.

Silverman, Deidre. "Sexual Harassment: The Working Women's Dilemma." *Building Feminist Theory: Essays from Quest.* New York: Longman, 1981:84–93.

Simmel, Georg. "The Sociology of Conflict." *American Journal of Sociology, 9,* January 1904:490–525; March 1904:672–689; and May 1904:798–811.

Simon, Julian L. "Global Confusion, 1980: A Hard Look at the Global 2000 Report." *Public Interest, 62,* Winter 1980:3–20.

Simon, Julian L. *The Ultimate Resource.* Princeton, N.J.: Princeton University Press, 1981.

Simon, Steven. "The New Terrorism: Securing the Nation Against a Messianic Foe." In *Sociology,* 33rd ed., Kurt Finsterbusch, ed., New York: McGraw-Hill/Dushkin, 2004:215–220.

Simons, Marlise. "Social Change and Amazon Indians." In *Life in Society: Readings to Accompany Sociology: A Down-to-Earth Approach,* 7th ed. James M. Henslin, ed. Boston: Allyn & Bacon, 2005:158–165.

Simpson, George Eaton, and J. Milton Yinger. *Racial and Cultural Minorities: An Analysis of Prejudice and Discrimination,* 4th ed. New York: Harper & Row, 1972.

Sindler, Allan P. *Bakke, De Funis, and Minority Admissions: The Quest for Equal Opportunity.* New York: Longman, 1978.

Skinner, B. F. *Beyond Freedom and Dignity.* New York: Knopf, 1971.

Skinner, B. F. *Science and Human Behavior.* New York: Macmillan, 1953.

Skinner, B. F. *Walden Two.* New York: Macmillan, 1948.

Skinner, Jonathan, James N. Weinstein, Scott M. Sporer, and John E. Wennberg. "Racial, Ethnic, and Geographic Disparities in Rates of Knee Arthroplasty Among Medicare Patients." *New England Journal of Medicine, 349,* 14, October 2, 2003: 1350–1359.

Smedley, Brian D., Adrienne Y. Stith, and Alan R. Nelson, eds. *Unequal Treatment: Confronting Racial and Ethnic Disparities in Health Care.* Washington, D.C.: The National Academies Press, 2003.

Smith, Barbara Ellen. *Digging Our Own Graves: Coal Miners and the Struggle over Black Lung Disease.* Philadelphia: Temple University Press, 1987.

Smith, Clark. "Oral History as 'Therapy': Combatants' Accounts of Vietnam War." In *Strangers at Home: Vietnam Veterans Since the War,* Charles R. Figley and Seymore Leventman (eds.). New York: Praeger, 1980:9–34.

Smith, Douglas A., and Christy A. Visher. "Street-Level Justice: Situational Determinants of Police Arrest Decisions." *Social Problems, 29,* December 1981:167–177.

Smith, Kenneth. "Homophobia: A Tentative Personality Profile." *Psychological Reports, 29,* 3, 1971:1091–1094.

Smith, Kristen F., and Vern L. Bengtson. "Positive Consequences of Institutionalization: Solidarity Between Elderly Parents and Their Middle-Aged Children." *The Gerontologist, 19,* October 1979:438–447.

Smith, Stacy L, and Crystal Allene Cook. "Gender Stereotypes: An Analysis of Popular Films and TV." Conference, The Geena Davis Institute on Gender in Media, 2008:12–23.

Smith, Stacy L, Marc Choueiti, and Stephanie Gall. "Asymmetrical Academy Awards 2: Another Look at Gender in Best Picture Nominated Films from 1977 to 2010." Los Angeles Calif.: Annenberg School of for Communication and Journalism, 2012.

Smoller, Jordan. "Identification of Risk Loci with Shared Effects on Five Major Psychiatric Disorders: A Genome-Wide Analysis." The Lancet. April 20, 2013:1371–1379.

Snipp, C. Matthew, and Alan L. Sorkin, "American Indian Housing: An Overview of Conditions and Public Policy." In *Race, Ethnicity, and Minority Housing in the United States,* Jamshid A. Momeni, ed. New York: Greenwood, 1986:147–175.

Snow, Ronald W., and Orville R. Cunningham. "Age, Machismo, and the Drinking Locations of Drunken Drivers: A Research Note." *Deviant Behavior, 6,* 1985:57–66.

Snyder, Howard. *Court Careers of Juvenile Offenders.* Washington, D.C.: Office of Juvenile Justice and Delinquency Prevention, 1988.

Soens, Darren. "Child Porn Sweep Nets Multiple Arrests." *WPRI News,* April 12, 2012.

Solomon, Deborah. "Shift in Federal Bench Spurs Governors, Legislators to Battle Roe." *Wall Street Journal,* March 9, 2006.

Solomon, Jeanne, and Dan Rather. "The Kyshtym Disaster." A segment of *60 Minutes,* November 9, 1980 (Jean Solomon, producer, and Dan Rather, interviewer).

Sorokin, Pitrim A. *Social and Cultural Dynamics,* 4 vols. New York: American Book, 1937, 1941.

Sourcebook of Criminal Justice Statistics. Washington, D.C.: U.S. Government Printing Office, annual.

Sourcebook of Criminal Justice Statistics. Washington, D.C.: U.S. Government Printing Office, published annually.

Specter, Michael. "TB Carriers See Clash of Liberty and Health." *New York Times,* October 14, 1992:A1, A20.

Speer, Albert. *Inside the Third Reich,* Richard and Clara Winston, trans. New York: Avon, 1970.

Spillman, Brenda. "Financial Preparedness for Long-Term Care Needs in Old Age." *Consumer Knowledge and Financial Decisions,* 2012:239–253.

Spivak, Jonathan. "Israel's Discrimination Problem." *Wall Street Journal,* December 3, 1980:28.

Sprung, Shlomo. "Two Americans Invented a Stove that Could Help Billions of People." *Business Insider, August 22,* 2012.

Spunt, Barry. "The Current New York City Heroin Scene." *Substance Use and Misuse, 38,* 10, 2003:1539–1549.

Srole, Leo, et al. *Mental Health in the Metropolis: The Midtown Manhattan Study.* New York: New York University Press, 1978.

Sroufe, L. Alan. "Ritalin Gone Wrong." *New York Times,* January 28, 2012.

Stafford, Linda, Sonya R. Kennedy, JoAnne E. Lehman, and Gail Arnold. "Wealth in America." *ISR Newsletter,* Winter 1986–87.

"Stakeholders and Radiological Protection: Lessons from Chernobyl 20 Years After." Committee on Radiation Protection and Public Health. Nuclear Energy Agency, 2006.

"State of Food Insecurity in the World 2005." Food and Agriculture Organization of the United Nations, 2005.

"State of Food Insecurity in the World 2012." Food and Agriculture Organization of the United Nations, 2012.

"State of Recidivism: The Revolving Door of America's Prisons." Washington, D.C.: PEW Center on the States, 2011.

Statistical Abstract of the United States. Washington, D.C.: U.S. Bureau of the Census, annual.

Statistical Abstract of the United States. Washington, D.C.: U.S. Government Printing Office. Published annually for 131 years until 2012 when the U.S. government was too broke to continue its publication. The 2013 edition was published by Bernan Press in Lanham, Maryland.

Statistical Handbook of Japan. Tokyo: The Statistics Bureau, Ministry of Internal Affairs and Communications of Japan, 2009.

Stein, Peter J. "The Diverse World of Single Adults." In *Marriage and Family in a Changing Society,* 4th ed., James M. Henslin, ed. New York: Free Press, 1992:93–103.

Steinhauer, Jennifer, and Ford Fessenden. "Medical Retreads: Doctors Punished by State But Prized at the Hospitals." *New York Times,* March 27, 2001.

Steinhauer, Jennifer. "For Women in Medicine, a Road to Compromise, Not Perks." *New York Times,* March 1, 1999b.

Steinhauer, Jennifer. "So, the Tumor Is on the Left, Right?" *New York Times,* April 1, 2001.

Steinhoff, Patricia G., and Milton Diamond. *Abortion Politics: The Hawaii Experience.* Honolulu: University press of Hawaii, 1977.

Steinmetz, Suzanne K. *Duty Bound: Elder Abuse and Family Care.* Newbury Park, Calif.: Sage, 1988.

Steinmetz, Suzanne K., and Murray A. Straus (eds.). *Violence in the Family.* New York: Dodd Mead, 1974.

Stevens, Amy. "Sensible Victims Will Be Hoping Their Burglar Drives Up in a Rolls." *Wall Street Journal,* April 8, 1992:B1.

Stevens, William K. "Great Plains or Great Desert?" *New York Times,* May 28, 1996.

Stevens, William K. "Science Academy Disputes Attack on Global Warming." *New York Times,* April 22, 1998.

Stockard, Jean, and Miriam M. Johnson. *Sex Roles: Sex Inequality and Sex Role Development.* Englewood Cliffs, N.J.: Prentice Hall, 1980.

Stokes, M., and D. Zeman. Detroit: "Is Apathy to Blame for a Brutal Death?" *Newsweek,* September 4, 1995.

Stolberg, Sheryl Gay. "Blacks Found on Short End of Heart Attack Procedure." *New York Times,* May 10, 2001.

Stouffer, Samuel A., Arthur A. Lumsdaine, Marion Harper Lumsdaine, Robin M. Williams, Jr., M. Brewster Smith, Irving L. Janis, Shirley A. Star, and Leonard S. Cottrell, Jr. *The American Soldier: Combat and Its Aftermath,* vol. 2. New York: Wiley, 1949.

Straus, Murray A. "Blaming the Messenger for the Bad News about Partner Violence by Women: The Methodological, Theoretical, and Value Basis of the Purported Invalidity of the Conflict Tactic Scales." *Behavioral Sciences and the Law,* 2012.

Straus, Murray A. "Explaining Family Violence." *Marriage and Family in a Changing Society,* 4th ed., James M. Henslin, ed. New York: Free Press, 1992:344–356.

Straus, Murray A., and Richard J. Gelles. "Violence in American Families: How Much Is There and Why Does It Occur?" In *Troubled Relationships,* Elam W. Nunnally, Catherine S. Chilman, and Fred M. Cox, eds. Newbury Park, Calif.: Sage, 1988:141–162.

Straus, Murray A., Richard J. Gelles, and Suzanne K. Steinmetz. *Behind Closed Doors: Violence in the American Family.* New York: Anchor/Doubleday, 1980.

Strobel, Lee. *Reckless Homicide: Ford's Pinto Trial.* South Bend, Ind.: And Books, 1980.

Strohschein, Lisa A. "Parental Divorce and Child Mental Health Trajectories." *Journal of Marriage and Family, 67,* 2005:1286–1300.

Sutherland, Edwin H. "The White Collar Criminal." *American Sociological Review, 5,* 1940:1–12.

Sutherland, Edwin H. *The Professional Thief.* Chicago: University of Chicago Press, 1937.

Sutherland, Edwin H. *White Collar Crime.* New York: Dryden, 1949.

Suzuki, Bob H. "Asian-American Families." In *Marriage and Family in a Changing Society,* 2nd ed., James M. Henslin, ed. New York: Free Press, 1985:104–119.

Sweet, Laurel J., Jessica Van Sack, Jessica Fargen, and Ira Kantor. "'Oddball' Portrait of Amy Bishop Emerges." *Boston Herald,* February 15, 2010.

Sykes, Gresham M., and David Matza. "Techniques of Neutralization: A Theory of Delinquency." *American Sociological Review, 22,* December 1957:664–670.

Szasz, Thomas. *Ceremonial Chemistry: The Ritual Persecution of Drugs, Addicts, and Pushers.* Garden City, N.Y.: Anchor, 1975.

Szasz, Thomas. *The Myth of Mental Illness.* Harper & Row, 1961.

Tabuchi, Hiroko. "Fish Off Japan's Coast Said to Contain Elevated Levels of Cesium." *New York Times,* October 25, 2012.

Tanner, Lindsey. "Dramatic Surge Seen in Kids Hospitalized with MRSA." Associated Press, May 16, 2010.

Tarm, Michael. "Former DEA Heads: Nullify Washington, Colorado Laws." *Huffington Post,* March 5, 2013.

Taslitz, Andrew E. "Willfully Blinded: On Date Rape and Self-Deception." *Harvard Journal of Law & Gender,* 2005:381–446

Tavernise, Sabrina, and Donald G. McNeil, Jr. "Iraqi Dead May Total 600,000, Study Says." *New York Times,* October 10, 2006.

Tavernise, Sabrina, and Robert Gebeloff. "New Way to Tally Poor Recasts View of Poverty." *New York Times,* November 7, 2011.

"TB in the United States, A Snapshot: 2011." *CDC Fact Sheet,* Center for Disease Control, March 2012.

Teller, Edward. "The Energy Crisis: No Contingency Plan." San Diego, Calif.: World Research, 1980.

Tetreault, Steve. "Judge Dismisses Suit, But State is Happy." *Las Vegas Review-Journal,* September 28, 2006.

Thavorncharoensap, Montarat, Yot Teerawattananon, Jomkwan Yothasamut, Chanida Lertpitakpong, and Usa Chaikledkaew. "The Economic Impact of Alcohol Consumption: A Systematic Review." *Substance Abuse Treatment, Prevention, and Policy,* November 2009.

Thayer, Frederick C. "The Holy War on Surplus Americans: Soviet Dogma, Old-time Religion and Classical Economics." *Social Policy, 28,* 1, Fall 1997:8–18.

"The Dragon's New Teeth." *The Economist,* April 7, 2012.

The Twelve Steps are reprinted with permission of Alcoholics Anonymous World Services, Inc. ("AAWS") Permission to reprint the Twelve Steps does not mean that AAWS has reviewed or approved the contents of this publication, or that AAWS necessarily agrees with the views expressed herein. A.A. is a program of recovery from alcoholism only - use of the Twelve Steps in connection with programs and activities which are patterned after A.A., but which address other problems, or in any other non-A.A. context, does not imply otherwise.

"The Price of Success." *Economist, 371,* 8371, April 17, 2004.

Thier, Dave. "Time, Water Running Out for America's Biggest Aquifer." AOL News, April 21, 2010.

Thio, Alex. *Deviant Behavior. Boston: Houghton Mifflin, 1978.*

Thorsheim, Peter. "Interpreting the London Fog Disaster of 1952." In *Smoke and Mirrors: The Politics and Culture of Air Pollution,* E. Malanie DuPuis, ed. New York: New York University Press, 2004:154–169.

Thrasher, Frederic M. *The Gang.* Chicago: University of Chicago Press, 1927.

Tiger, Lionel, and Robin Fox. *The Imperial Animal.* New York: Holt, 1971.

Timasheff, Nicholas S. *War and Revolution.* Joseph F. Scheuer, ed. New York: Sheed & Ward, 1965.

Tinker, John N. "Ethnic Bias in California Courts: A Case Study of Chicano and Anglo Felony Defendants." Paper presented at the annual meeting of the Society for the Study of Social Problems," 1981.

"To Avoid Disaster, Limit Population and Consumption." *Living on Earth,* June 8, 2012.

Tofte, Sarah. "Testing Justice: The Rape Kit Backlog in Los Angeles City and County." Human Rights Watch, March 2009.

Trebach, Arnold S. *The Great Drug War: And Radical Proposals That Could Make America Safe Again.* New York: Macmillan, 1987.

Truman, Jennifer L., and Michael Planty. "Criminal Victimization, 2011." Washington, D.C.: U.S. Department of Justice, Bureau of Justice Statistics, October 2012:1–19.

Trust, Cathy. "Presidential Panel Says 4 Major Unions Have Connections to Organized Crime." *Wall Street Journal,* January 15, 1986:48.

Tsatsou, Panayiota. "Gender and Sexuality in the Internet Era." In *The Handbook of Gender, Sex, and Media,* Karen Ross, ed. New York: John Wiley, 2012:516–534.

Tsuda, S., M. Murakami, N. Matsusaka, K. Kano, K. Taniguchi, Y. F. Sasaki. "DNA Damage Induced by Red Food Dyes Orally Administered to Pregnant and Male Mice." *Toxicological Sciences, 61,* 1, May 2001:92–99.

Turner, Jonathan H. *The Structure of Sociological Theory.* Homewood, Ill.: Dorsey, 1978.

Tyler, Tom R. "Legitimacy in Corrections: Policy Implications." *American Society of Criminology, 9,* 1, 2010:127–134.

U. S. Census Bureau. *Current Population Survey, Annual Social and Economic Supplement,* 2009.

U.S. Census Bureau. *Current Population Survey, Annual Social and Economic Supplement, 2011.*

U.S. Bureau of Labor Statistics. "Occupational Employment Statistics, May 2009 National Industry-Specific Occupational Employment and Wage Estimates." May 2010.

U.S. Census Bureau. "America's Families and Living Arrangements 2011. 2012.

U.S. Department of the Treasury. "Fact Sheet: History of the U.S. Tax System." March 2010.

U.S. Environmental Protection Agency. *Protecting the stratospheric ozone layer,* 2008. Online.

Uchitelle, Louis. "How to Define Poverty? Let Us Count the Ways." *New York Times,* May 28, 2001.

Ullman, Sarah E. "A 10-Year Update of 'Review and Critique of Empirical Studies of Rape Avoidance.'" *Criminal Justice and Behavior, 34,* 2007:411–429.

Ullman, Sarah E. "Does Offender Violence Escalate When Rape Victims Fight Back?" *Journal of Interpersonal Violence, 13,* 2, April 1998:179–192.

Umberger, Alison. "The Transatlantic Dispute over Genetically Modified Organisms" Culture, Politics and Economics." *International Affairs Review, 14,* 1, Spring 2005.

UNAIDS. "Report on the Global AIDS Epidemic," 2010.

UNAIDS. *AIDS Epidemic Update. World Health Organization,* 2009.

UNICEF. "Female Genital Mutilation/Cutting: A Statistical Exploration." New York: United Nations, November 2005.

UNICEF. *State of the World's Children 2009.* UNICEF Media Centre, New York, 2010.

Useem, Michael. "The Social Organization of the American Business Elite." *American Sociological Review, 44,* August 1979:553–572.

Useem, Michael. *The Inner Circle: Large Corporations and the Rise of Business Political Activity in the U.S. and U.K.* New York: Oxford University Press, 1984.

Valocchi, Steve. "The Racial Basis of Capitalism and the State, and the Impact of the New Deal on African Americans." *Social Problems, 41,* 3, August 1994:347–362.

van den Haag, Ernest, and John P. Conrad. *The Death Penalty: A Debate.* New York: Plenum, 1983.

van den Haag, Ernest. *Punishing Criminals: Concerning a Very Old and Painful Question.* New York: Basic Books, 1975.

Veevers, Jean E. "Voluntarily Childless Wives." *Sociology and Social Research, 57,* April 1973:356–366.

Veevers, Jean E. *Childless by Choice.* Toronto: Butterworths, 1980.

Velleman, Richard. "Influences on How Children and Young People Learn About and Behave Towards Alcohol." Joseph Rowntree Foundation, November 2009.

Venkatesh, Kartik K., Kenneth H. Mayer, and Charles C. J. Carpenter. "Low-Cost Generic Drugs under the President's Emergency Plan for AIDS Relief Drove Down Treatment Cost; More Are Needed." *Health Affairs, 31,* 7, July 2012:1429–1438.

Vidal, David. "Bilingual Education Is Thriving but Criticized." *New York Times,* January 30, 1977.

Vigil, James Diego. *A Rainbow of Gangs: Street Cultures in the Mega-City.* Austin: University of Texas Press, 2002.

Villegas, Andrew. "Doctor Shortage Fuels Nurse's Push for Expanded Role." *Kaiser Health News,* February 22, 2010.

Wagley, Charles, and Marvin Harris. *Minorities in the New World.* New York: Columbia University Press, 1958.

Wagman, Robert. "Is Japanese Mafia Threat to U.S.?" Syndicated column, November 27, 1981.

Wain, Barry. "Cambodia: What Remains of the Killing Ground." *Wall Street Journal,* January 29, 1981: 24.

Waitzkin, Howard, and Barbara Waterman. *The Exploitation of Illness in Capitalist Society.* New York: Bobbs-Merrill, 1974.

Wald, Matthew L. "Court Forces a Rethinking of Nuclear Fuel Storage." *New York Times,* June 8, 2012.

Waldron, Jeremy. *The Harm in Hate Speech.* Cambridge, Mass.: Harvard University Press, 2012.

Walker, Alice, and Pratibha Parmar. *Warrior Marks: Female Genital Mutilation and the Sexual Binding of Women.* New York: Harcourt Brace, 1993.

Wall, Mike. "INL Research Probes Microbes' Potential to Clean Up Groundwater." Idaho National Laboratory, 2010.

Walsh, Edward, and Amy Goldstein. "Supreme Court Upholds Two Key Abortion Rights." *Washington Post,* June 29, 2000.

Walsh, Mark. "Supreme Court Refuses to Weigh Race-Based College Admissions." Education Week on the WEB, July 1, 1996.

Wang, Haibin, Sudhansu K. Dey, and Mauro Maccarrone. "Jekyll and Hyde: Two Faces of Cannabinoid Signaling in Male and Female Fertility." *Endocrine Reviews* 27, 5, 2006:427–448.

Wang, Wendy. "The Rise of Intermarriage: Rates, Characteristics Vary by Race and Gender." Washington, D.C.: PEW Research Center, February 16, 2012.

Ward, L. Monique, Edwina Hansbrough, and Eboni Walker. "Contributions of Music Video Exposure to Black Adolescents' Gender and Sexual Schemas." *Journal of Adolescent Research, 20,* 2, March 2005:143–166.

Wargo, John, Linda Wargo, and Nancy Alderman. "The Harmful Effects of Vehicle Exhaust: A Case for Policy Change." New Haven, Conn.: Environment and Human Health, 2006.

Wax, Murray L. *Indian Americans: Unity and Diversity.* Englewood Cliffs, N.J.: Prentice Hall, 1971.

Wax, Murray L., and Rosalie H. Wax. "Cultural Deprivation as an Educational Ideology." *Journal of American Indian Education, 3,* January 15–18, 1964.

Wax, Murray L., and Rosalie H. Wax. "Indian Education for What?" *Midcontinent American Studies Journal, 6,* Fall 1965:164–170.

Wax, Rosalie H. "The Warrior Dropouts." *Trans-Action, 4,* May 1967:40–46.

Weber, M. *Theory of Social and Economic Organization.* London: Free Press, 1964. (Originally published 1921)

Wechsler, Henry, and Toben F. Nelson. "What We Have Learned From the Harvard School of Public Health College Alcohol Study: Focusing Attention on College Student Alcohol Consumption and the Environmental Conditions That Promote It." *Journal of Studies on Alcohol and Drugs, 69,* 4, 2008:481–490.

Weinberg, George. *Society and the Healthy Homosexual.* New York: Doubleday, 1972.

Weiss, C., E. Murphy-Graham, and A. G. Gandhi. "The Fairy Godmother and Her Warts: Making the Dream of Evidence-Based Policy Come True." *American Journal of Evaluation, 29,* 2008:29–47.

Weitzer, Ronald. "Prostitution: Facts and Fictions." *Contexts, 6,* 4, Fall 2007:28–33.

Weitzer, Ronald. "Sociology of Sex Work." *Annual Review of Sociology, 35,* 2009:213–234.

Wells, Ken, and Charles McCoy. "Exxon Says Fast Containment of Oil Spill in Alaska Could Have Caused Explosion." *Wall Street Journal,* April 5, 1989:A3.

West, Richard W., and Gary Steiger. *The Effects of the Seattle and Denver Income Management Experiments on Alternative Measures of Labor Supply.* Menlo Park, Calif.: SRI International Research Memorandum, 72, May 1980.

Westreich, Laurence M. "Anabolic Androgenic Steroid Use Pharmacology, Prevalence, and Psychiatric Aspects Check Points." *Psychiatric Times, 25,* 1, January 1, 2008.

Wheeler, Madeline. "Gender-Selective Abortion in India Is on the Rise." *Christian Science Monitor,* October 14, 2009.

Whitaker, Mark. "'It Was Like Breathing Fire . . .'" *Newsweek,* December 17, 1984:26–32.

White, Helene Raskin. "Marijuana Use and Delinquency: A Test of the 'Independent Cause' Hypothesis." *Journal of Drug Issues, 21,* 2, Spring 1991:231–256.

Whitehead, Tom. "Warning of New Era of Surveillance State." *The Telegraph,* November 12, 2010.

Whitehurst, Carol A. *Women in America: The Oppressed Majority.* Santa Monica, Calif.: Goodyear, 1977.

Whitlock, Craig. "Military Certifies Repeal of 'Don't Ask' Policy." *Washington Post,* July 22, 2011.

Wholsen, Marcus. "Tuberculosis in California: Health Officials Testing 35 Babies for TB Exposure." Huffington Post, May 23, 2012.

Whyte, William Foote. "Street Corner Society." In *Down to Earth Sociology: Introductory Readings,* 8th ed., James M. Henslin, ed. New York: Free Press, 1995:59–67.

Whyte, William Foote. *Street Corner Society.* Chicago: University of Chicago Press, 1943.

Williams, Robert C. "Three Mile Island as History." *Washington University Magazine, 50,* October 1980:56, 58–59, 61–63.

Williamson, Celia, and Terry Cluse-Tolar. "Pimp-Controlled Prostitution." *Violence Against Women, 8,* 9, September 2002:1074–1092.

Willie, Charles Vert. "Caste, Class, and Family Life Experiences." *Research in Race and Ethnic Relations, 6,* 1991:65–84.

Wilson, James Q. "Lock 'Em Up and Other Thoughts on Crime." *New York Times Magazine,* March 9, 1975:11, 44–48.

Wilson, William Julius. "Jobless Poverty: A New Form of Social Dislocation in the Inner-City Ghetto." In *The Inequality Reader: Contemporary and Foundational Readings in Race, Class and Gender,* David B. Grusky and Szonja Szelenyi, eds. Boulder: Westview Press, 2007:142–152.

Wilson, William Julius. *More Than Just Race: Being Black and Poor in the Inner City.* New York: W.W. Norton, 2009.

Wilson, William Julius. *The Bridge over the Racial Divide: Rising Inequality and Coalition Politics.* Berkeley: University of California Press, 2000.

Wilson, William Julius. Scholar in Residence Lecture at Southern Illinois University, Edwardsville, June 14, 1992.

Wilson, William Julius. *The Declining Significance of Race: Blacks and Changing American Institutions.* Chicago: University of Chicago Press, 1978.

Wilson, William Julius. *The Truly Disadvantaged: The Inner City, the Underclass, and Public Policy.* Chicago: University of Chicago Press, 1987.

Wilson, William Julius. *When Work Disappears: The World of the New Urban Poor.* Chicago: University of Chicago Press, 1996.

Wingfield, Nick, and Justin Scheck. "Push for Looser Pot Laws Gains Momentum." *Wall Street Journal,* January 16, 2010.

Winick, Charles. "Physician Narcotic Addicts." *Social Problems, 9,* Fall 1961:174–186.

Wirth, Louis. "The Problem of Minority Groups." In *The Science of Man in the World Crisis,* Ralph Linton, ed. New York: Columbia University Press, 1945.

Wirth, Louis. "Urbanism as a Way of Life." *American Journal of Sociology, 44,* July 1938:1–24.

Wolfensohn, James D., and Kathryn S. Fuller. "Making Common Cause: Seeing the Forest for the Trees." *International Herald Tribune,* May 27, 1998:11.

Wolfgang, Marvin E. *Patterns in Criminal Homicide.* Philadelphia: University of Pennsylvania Press, 1958.

Wolfgang, Marvin, E., and Marc Reidel. "Rape, Race, and the Death Penalty." *American Journal of Orthopsychiatry, 45,* July 1975:658–668.

Wolfinger, Nicholas H. *Understanding the Divorce Cycle: The Children of Divorce in Their Own Marriages.* New York: University of Cambridge Press 2005.

Wonacott, Peter. "India's Skewed Sex Ratio Puts GE Sales in Spotlight." *Wall Street Journal,* April 18, 2007.

Woolf, Amy. "Conventional Prompt Global Strike and Long-Range Ballistic Missiles: Background and Issues." Washington: Congressional Research Service, July 6, 2012.

Woolf, Steven H, Resa M. Jones, Robert E. Johnson, et al. "Avertable Deaths Associated with Household Income in Virginia." *American Journal of Public Health, 100,*4, April 2010:750–755.

World Health Organization. "Female Genital Mutilation: Fact Sheet Number 241." United Nations, February 2012.

World Population Profile. Washington, D.C.: Bureau of the Census, U.S. Department of Commerce, various years.

Worm, Boris, et al. "Impacts of Biodiversity Loss on Ocean Ecosystem Services. *Science, 314,* 5800, November 3, 2006:787–790.

Wren, Christopher S. "Methadone Use Emerged in City Where It Is Now Challenged." *New York Times,* October 3, 1998.

Wright, Quincy. *A Study of War,* 2 vols. Chicago: University of Chicago Press, 1942.

Wurmbrand, Richard. Torturado Por Cristo: La Iglesia Martir de Hoy. Cuernavaca, Mexico: 1970.

Yablonsky, Judy. "Survey Finds World Trend Toward More Liberal Abortion Laws." Associated Press, May 20, 1981.

Yardley, Jim. "In India, Castes, Honor and Killings Intertwine." *New York Times,* July 9, 2010.

Yeoman, Ian, and Michelle Mars. "Robots, Men and Sex Tourism." *Science Direct, 4,* May 2012.

Yuan, D. Y. "Voluntary Segregation: A Study of New York Chinatown." *Phylon, 24,* Fall 1963:255–265.

Zaitseva, Lyudmila, and Kevin Hand. "Nuclear Smuggling Chains: Suppliers, Intermediaries, and End-Users." *American Behavioral Scientist, 46,* 6, February 2003:822–844.

Zawitz, Marianne W., ed. *Report to the Nation on Crime and Justice,* 2nd ed. Washington, D.C.: U.S. Department of Justice, Bureau of Justice Statistics, July 1988.

Zeller, Tom, Jr., "Studies Say Natural Gas Has Its Own Environmental Problems." *New York Times,* April 11, 2011.

Zernike, Kate. "Hospitals Say Meth Cases Are Rising, and Hurt Care." *New York Times,* January 18, 2006.

Zhang, Ming, Billy R. Martin, Martin W. Adler, et al. "Modulation of Cannabinoid Receptor Activation as a Neurprotective Strategy for EAE and Stroke." *Journal of Neuroimmune Pharmacology*, 4, 2009:249–259.

Zhang, Zhenmei, Lawrence B. Schiamberg, James Oehmke, et al. "Neglect of Older Adults in Michigan Nursing Homes." *Journal of Elder Abuse and Neglect, 23,* 2011:58–74.

Zimbardo, Philip G. "The Pathology of Imprisonment." *Society, 9,* 6, April 1972:4–8.

Zimbardo, Philip G. "The Pathology of Imprisonment." In *Down to Earth Sociology: Introductory Readings,* 15th ed., James M. Henslin, ed. New York: Free Press, 2014. (Originally published in *Society, 9,* 6, 1972:4–8)

Zimmerman, Ann. "As Shoplifters Use High-Tech Scams, Retail Losses Rise." *Wall Street Journal,* October 25, 2006.

Zinn, Maxine Baca, and D. Stanley Eitzen. *Diversity in Families,* 2nd ed. New York: HarperCollins, 1990.

Zosuls, Kristina M., and Diane N. Ruble. "The Acquisition of Gender Labels in Infancy: Implications for Sex-Typed Play." *Developmental Psychology, 45,* 3, May 2009:688–701.

Chapter 1: p. 1: Brendan Smialowski/AFP/Getty Images; p. 6: Divyakant Solanki/epa/Corbis; p. 8: John Watney/Photo Researchers, Inc.; p. 19: Kris Timken/Getty Images; p. 21: © Robert Weber/The New Yorker Collection/www.cartoonbank.com; p. 22: James M. Henslin

Chapter 2: p. 25: Ariel Skelley/Getty Images; p. 28, left: Alamy; p. 28, right: Bellurget Jean Louis/Getty Images; p. 30: Dina Rudick/The Boston Globe via Getty Images; p. 35: Bettmann/Corbis; p. 39: Patrick Landmann/Getty Images; p. 40: Courtesy of Phyllis Moen; p. 43: Bill Greene/The Boston Globe/Getty Images; p. 46, left: James M. Henslin; p. 46, right: James M. Henslin; p. 47: Li-Hua Lan/Syracuse Newspapers/The Image Works; p. 48, bottom: © David Bacon/The Image Works; p. 48, top: Jeff Malet/Newscom

Chapter 3: p. 51: Rudy Sulgan/Corbis; p. 53: Courtesy of Edward O. Laumann; p. 54: Sotheby"s/akg-images/Newscom; p. 55, bottom: James M. Henslin; p. 55, top: Alamy; p. 56: Pascal Deloche/GODONG/Newscom; p. 59: Getty Images; p. 60: John Powell/Topfoto/The Image Works; p. 64: Sean Sprague/The Images Works; p. 65: Newscom; p. 66: Newscom; p. 67: Newscom; p. 69: Mike Derer/AP Images; p. 73: Charles Gatewood/The Image Works; p. 75: Anoek de Groot/AFP/Getty Images/Newscom; p. 76: LM Otero/AP Images; p. 77: Maxppp/Landov

Chapter 4: p. 79: David Kadlubowski/Corbis; p. 81: Alamy; p. 83, left: New York Daily News/Getty Images; p. 83, right: AP Images; p. 86: Sean Sprague/The Image Works; p. 87, left: Joel Ryan/AP Images; p. 87, right: Landov; p. 89: Robert Buakty/AP Images; p. 90: Courtesy of James A. Inciardi; p. 94: Bob Daemmrich/The Image Works; 97: George A. Hiriliman Productions, Inc./20th Century Fox/Photofest; p. 99: Newscom; p. 100: Mark Horn/Getty Images; p. 101: Rick Wilking/Reuters /Landov; p. 102: AP Images; p. 105: Faces of Meth/Multnomah County Sheriff's Office; p. 107: Alamy; p. 110: Landov; p. 111: AP Images

Chapter 5: p. 117: The Image Works; p. 124: NAEEM UL HAQ/Newscom; p. 126: Alamy; p. 127: Courtesy of Ruth Horowitz; p. 129: Joe Raedle/Getty Images; p. 131: Jim West/The Image Works; p. 132: Jim West/The Image Works; p. 135: BEAUFILS/SIPA/Newscom; p. 137: Chris Rout/Alamy; p. 144: Amy Bishop/AP Images; p. 145: Ted Powers/AP Images; p. 147: AP Images; p. 148: James M. Henslin

Chapter 6: p. 151: Andrew Kelly/Reuters/Landov; p. 156: © David Sipress/The New Yorker Collection/www.cartoonbank.com; p. 158, bottom: By permission of John L. Hart FLP and Creators Syndicate, Inc.; p. 158, top: Steve Campbell/Reuters/Landov; p. 161: Danny Drake/AP Images; p. 162: Jack Kurtz/Corbis; p. 163: Bob Daemmrich/The Image Works; p. 165: AP Images; p. 167: J Pat Carter/AP Images; p. 168: Jeff Stead, The Examiner/AP Images; p. 169: Courtesy Everett Collection; p. 171: Andrew Lichtenstein/The Image Works; p. 176: Bettmann/Corbis; p. 179: ullstein bild/The Image Works; p. 180: Mark Ludak/The Image Works; p. 181: Bob Daemmrich/The Image Work; p. 183: Richard Corkery/NY Daily News Archive/Getty Images; p. 186: Courtesy of William Chambliss

Chapter 7: p. 190: Peter Turnley/Corbis; p. 193, left: Bob Daemmrich/The Image Works; p. 193, right: Channi Anand/AP Images; p. 196: By permission of John L. Hart FLP and Creators Syndicate, Inc.; p. 197: Alison Wright/Corbis; p. 199: Joseph Mirachi/The New Yorker Collection/www.cartoonbank.com; p. 203: James M. Henslin; p. 206: Dawn Vlillella/AP Images; p. 208: Bob Sacha/Corbis; p. 210: Courtesy of Warna Oosterbann, Photo provided by Herbert Gans; p. 211: David LEFRANC/Getty Images; p. 214: Getty Images; p. 216: AP Images; p. 219: Rich Pedroncelli/AP Images; p. 222: Seth Perlman/AP Images

Chapter 8: p. 226: Kevin Dietsch/Newscom; p. 228: Hulton-Deutsch Collection/Corbis; p. 232: Edvard March/Corbis; p. 233: Getty Images; p. 234: Boston University © 2007, Photo provided by Nazli Kibria; p. 235: Jim West/Alamy; p. 241: Courtesy of Rafael Ezekiel; p. 242: Jacob Lopez/AP Images; p. 244: Jim West/The Image Works; p. 247: Jim West/Alamy; p. 248: Alamy; p. 250: Washington State Archives; p. 252: LARRY DOWNING/Getty Images; p. 253: AP Images; p. 257: Dan Barba/Newscom; p. 261: The Image Works

Chapter 9: p. 265: Ali Jarekji/REUTERS/Landov; p. 268: Deborah Jaffe/Corbis; p. 269: Barbara Smaller/The New Yorker Collection/www.cartoonbank.com; p. 270: Landov; p. 272: Sala Lewis/PA Photos/Landov; p. 274: Manchester Daily Express/Getty Images; p. 278: Bettmann/Corbis; p. 279: John Kuntz/The Plain Dealer/Landov; p. 280: Alamy; p. 281: Bettmann/Corbis; p. 282: James Marshall/The Image Works; p. 285: Image Works; p. 286: Jeff Vespa/Getty Images p. 287: Donna Eder; p. 288: Landov; p. 294: Courtesy of Kirsten Dellinger; p. 296: Jim West/Alamy; p. 297: Dr. Lindsay Young/Pacific Rim Conservation; p. 300: Alamy; p. 302: Shepard Sherbell/Corbis

Chapter 10: p. 309: Reena Rose Sibayan/The Jersey Journal/Landov; p. 311: James M. Henslin; p. 312: Grant Turner/Newscom; p. 313: James M. Henslin; p. 314: John Earnshaw/Alamy; p. 316: Darron R. Silva/Getty Images; p. 317, left: Todd Bigelow/Alamy; p. 317, right: Steven Peters/Getty Images; p. 323: Brant Ward/Corbis; p. 325: © Aaron Bacall Reproduction rights obtainable from www.CartoonStock.com; p. 331: AKG Images/The Image Works; p. 332: Sean Sprague/The Image Works; p. 333: Joyce Naltchayan/Getty Images; p. 336: Paul Buck/Corbis; p. 339: AP Images; p. 341: Justin Sullivan/Getty Images; p. 342: Courtesy of Dr. Cockerham; p. 343: Alvis Upitis/Getty Images; p. 344: Michel Tcherevkoff/Getty Images

Chapter 11: p. 347: Elizabeth Crew/The Image Works; p. 349: Landov; p. 350: Heide Benser/Corbis; p. 357: Landov; p. 359: Francis G. Mayer/Corbis; p. 360: Dinodia/The Image Works; p. 361: Getty Images; p. 363: SSPL/The Image Works; p. 364: Armstrong G Robert/Alamy; p. 368, left: Cynthia Shinabarger Reed; p. 368, right: Robert E. Reed; p. 371: Courtesy of Kathleen Ferraro; p. 373: Syracuse Newspapers/M Gabel/the Image Works; p. 375: Leipzig/Corbis; p. 377, left: Alamy; p. 377, right: Alamy; p. 379, bottom: Chicago

Tribune/MCT /Landov; p. 379, bottom middle: David M. Grossman/The Image Works; p. 379, middle: Kansas City Star/MCT /Landov; p. 379, top: Shutterstock; p. 379, top middle: Don Hammond/Design Pics/Newscom; p. 382: Corbis

Chapter 12: p. 385: Dinodia/The Image Works; p. 389: Sean Sprague/The Image Works; p. 392: Denis Jr. Tangney/Getty Images; p. 393: Ulrich Baumgarten/Getty Images; p. 395, left: Newscom; p. 395, right: Ed Kashi/Corbis; p. 397: Orlando Sierra/AFP/Getty Images/Newscom; p. 401: Peter Bennett/Alamy; p. 403: Arlene Gottfried/The Image Works; p. 409: Jack A. Goldstone; p. 411: DAI KUROKAWA/Newscom; p. 415: Shafiqul Islam Shafiq/DrikNEWS/Majority World/The Image Works; p. 416: Wang Xizeng/ChinaFotoPress/c40/ZUMA Press/Newscom; p. 418: Karin Retief/Trace Images/The Image Works; p. 420: Iqbal Hussian/Xinhua /Landov

Chapter 13: p. 425: Alamy; p. 428: H. Wilhelmy/DPA/Landov LLC; p. 430: Bettmann/Corbis; p. 432, left: John Giustina/Getty Images; p. 432, right: Tom Stoddart Archive/Getty Images; p. 434: Luis Alvarez/Associated Press; p. 437: Hans Strand/Barcroft Media/Landov; p. 440: Galen Rowell/Corbis; p. 441: Raj Patidar/Landov; p. 443: Johann Haas/Landov; p. 444: AP Images; p. 446: James M. Henslin; p. 449: Newscom; p. 450, left: Gerardo Ceballos/Paul R. Ehrlich; p. 450, right: Transaction Publishers; p. 454: Loren McIntyre/Newscom; p. 456: Celso Junior/Landov; p. 460: BioLiteStove; p. 462: Robert Gottlieb; p. 463: Zoriah/The Image Works

Chapter 14: p. 466: Getty Images; p. 468, left: AP Images; p. 468, right: Corbis; p. 470: Arnold Newman/Getty Images; p. 474: Corbis; p. 476: Feisal Omar/REUTERS/Landov; p. 479: Morton Ender; p. 483: Bettmann/Corbis; p. 484: Nick Ut/AP Images; p. 491: Les Stone/Corbis; p. 493: Simon Maina/Newscom; p. 494: Ilyas Dean/The Image Works; p. 496: Newscom; p. 499: DON EMMERT/AFP/Getty Images; p. 503: An Jiang/Xinhua/Landov; p. 504: John Tlumacki/The Boston Globe/Getty Images

Name Index

C

D

E

F

G

H

I

J

K

L

M

S

T

U

V

W

Y

Z

E

G

N

O

P

Q

R

S

T

U

V

W

Y

Z